Thomas Hardy

AN
ANNOTATED
BIBLIOGRAPHY
OF WRITINGS
ABOUT HIM

COMPILED AND EDITED BY

HELMUT E. GERBER

AND

W. EUGENE DAVIS

NORTHERN ILLINOIS UNIVERSITY PRESS
DE KALB, ILLINOIS

Helmut E. Gerber is Professor of English at Arizona State University at Tempe, Arizona

W. Eugene Davis is Assistant Professor of English at Purdue University at Lafayette, Indiana

Library of Congress Cataloging in Publication Data
Gerber, Helmut E   1920–
    Thomas Hardy: an annotated bibliography of writings about him.
    (An Annotated secondary bibliography series on English literature in transition, 1880–1920)
    1.   Hardy, Thomas, 1840–1928—Bibliography.
I.   Davis, W. Eugene, 1934–   joint author.
II.   Title.   III.   Series
Z8386.5.G47   016.823′8   72–7514
ISBN 0–87580–039–4

c C

7|4242

Preface

Following the principles established in the first two volumes of the A. S. B. Series, we have again tried to compile a bibliography as broadly representative of the writings on Thomas Hardy as possible. The 3,153 entries, dated between 1871 and 1969, include abstracts of writings in eleven languages and publications of all kinds: reviews, general appreciations, bibliographies, biographies, critical books, documented articles, chapters in books, scattered references in books and articles, Ph.D. dissertations, letters to the editors of major newspapers and journals, introductions to editions of Hardy's works, and explications in anthologies and "case books." We have included some trivia, but we have attempted definitive coverage of clearly important writings on Hardy. We have tried to supply fairly long abstracts of material not readily accessible and of major foreign language items.

As always in such a large-scale undertaking, we have necessarily fallen short of our ideal. We hope that users of this bibliography will call to our attention significant items we have failed to include. We plan to compensate for such omissions in the present volume in a supplement, as soon as such a volume is feasible. We have often been hampered by inaccuracies in indexes, catalogues, and bibliographies on which we drew for our compilation. We have again encountered some of the problems that plague all researchers: missing or mutilated materials and inaccessible titles. Our greatest problem remains the inadequacy of resources for dealing with some foreign language areas.

Insofar as inclusions and exclusions are concerned, we have followed much the same principles as in the two preceding volumes in this series. We generally do not include reviews of secondary works, for in most instances the abstracter has provided a comment on the secondary work or its value is revealed in the abstract; however, we have provided abstracts of some reviews of the second Mrs. Hardy's "biographies," for it is certain that

Hardy dictated and certainly oversaw the material that went into these volumes. We have again excluded undergraduate honors theses and M.A. theses. We have listed Ph.D. dissertations without abstracts but with references to Dissertation Abstracts or similar series, when applicable. We have verified dissertation titles in such reference works as DA and Lawrence F. McNamee's Dissertations in English and American Literature (1968) and its Supplement (1969). We have provided abstracts of foreign language dissertations whenever possible, since these were often printed. Once more we regret the omission of many Slavic and Oriental language items, especially many in Japanese, but these either did not come to our attention, were unavailable in the libraries to which we had access, or could not be abstracted for lack of a sufficient number of abstracters expert in the relevant languages. We have probably omitted many items published in 1968 and 1969 because they were not yet listed in standard annual bibliographies or the journals were being bound or for other reasons were not accessible in time to be included.

Our principles for the form of entries and abstracts are essentially the same as in the earlier volumes. We have made every effort to place entries under date of first publication and provide data on reprintings and later revisions or translations. We have avoided listings under different dates of essentially the same items. In the abstracts, we have tried to represent the original author's voice as honestly and accurately as abstracts, paraphrases, selected quotations, and human nature allow. Abstracters' critical comments and various kinds of cross-references appear in square brackets at the ends of abstracts. To give this book maximum usefulness for a variety of research purposes, we have provided five different indexes.

We regard this volume on Hardy as a beginning; we hope to continue filling in the gaps and supplementing this project. If we have significantly reduced the drab chore of locating and sorting out the rapidly increasing quantity of writings on Hardy, and if we have provided a reference work that will reduce the perpetuation of inanities and the repetition of what has been written too often, we shall have attained our primary goals.

ACKNOWLEDGMENTS

Any cooperative project of the magnitude of the volumes in the A. S. B. Series necessarily involves many people. This is particularly true of volumes which require five to ten years of research to complete. The compilation of secondary materials for the present volume was begun long before there was the slightest hope for a series such as is now a reality. Especially during the past eight years, the co-editors have had the help of many selfless and dedicated people, colleagues in the broadest sense: graduate students, work-study students, typists, and literally more than a hundred librarians. We have also been fortunate in having the warm cooperation of our several department chairman: Professor Barriss Mills, Russell Cosper, and Jacob Adler, Purdue University; Charles Hagelman, Northern Illinois University, and Wilfred Ferrell, Arizona State University.

We owe most to the patience and hard work of the contributors (listed opposite the title page). While the editors are responsible for the large bulk of abstracts and assume full responsibility for the final form of all abstracts, we could not have produced a volume nearly so thorough as this one without the help of our major contributors. They have given unstintingly of their time and energy, in most instances while teaching full time and while engaged on research of their own.

In addition, we are indebted to many individuals for volunteering their special talents when we needed them: Takako Takenaka (Purdue University) and Kensuke Morimatsu (Tokyo) for abstracts from Japanese, Joseph Laurenti (Illinois State University) for help with some Italian items, Doris R. Asmundsson (Queensborough Community College) for help with items in Scandanavian languages, Gunnil Sjörberg (University of Pennsylvania) for help with an abstract of a Swedish article, and many more who often sat informally at our elbows or looked helpfully over our shoulders. Others who came to our relief at critical times also warrant our thanks for their help: Bernard Anderson (Swarthmore College), Philip Armato (Northern Illinois University), Merlin Cheney (Weber State College), Robert Felgar (Virginia Wesleyan College), Robert Hammarberg (Purdue University), Alma Kadragic (Lehman College, CUNY), Robert Magliola (Purdue University), Earl Wilcox (Winthrop College).

Some of us have had the benefit of much help along the way from a host of graduate assistants: Thomas Cardoza, Ronald Fortune, Elizabeth Frick, and Cynthia Walker, and work-study assistant Ella Lampkin—all of Purdue University; Charles O'Malley, Judith Risily, Dona Ruby, and Kristina Valaitis (now at Arizona State University)—all while at Northern Illinois University. Warranting the special gratitude of H. E. Gerber for graciously and energetically having allowed themselves to be tumbled into this project in its most chaotic stage are Barbara Blakey, Bernard Quint, and Mary Ellen Quint—all of Arizona State University. They have abstracted, filed, alphabetized, proofed typescripts, and somehow managed to keep H. E. Gerber in reasonably good humor during the seemingly endless preparation and checking of four of the indexes. Without their help, this volume would have suffered much in thoroughness and accuracy.

Some of our major contributors also wish to acknowledge the able assistance of students: William Halloran thanks Lawrence F. Schuetz and Edward Bednar, both of the University of Wisconsin at Milwaukee; William Morgan thanks Stanley LeGore, Sandra Leman, and Michael Breen, all of Illinois State University; and Robert Schweik acknowledges the help of Robert Neuman, SUNY at Fredonia.

We all share an equal indebtedness to the many libraries which responded patiently to our inquiries and to the interlibrary loan departments whose staffs sought out scarce titles for us, often on the basis of very inadequate or even totally incorrect bibliographical data. Among these libraries and their staffs we single out a few for providing especially helpful service: Arizona State University Library; Bowling Green State University Library; British Museum; Colby College Library, where the late Carl J. Weber built a superb Hardy collection; Dorset County Library; Dorset County Museum; Duke University Library; Karl Albert Ludwig Library of the University of Freiburg; University of Illinois Library (Urbana and Chicago Circle campuses); Illinois State University Library, especially Sharon Hartzel of the Interlibrary Loan Section; Indiana University Library; Kansas University Library; Marquette University Library; University of Maryland (Baltimore County) Library, especially Virginia Loouis and Marjorie Davis of the Interlibrary Loan Section; Bibliothèque Universitaire Montpellier; Northern Illinois University Library; University of Pennsylvania Library; Purdue University Libraries; and the Toledo Public Library. Although our list could be extended by another hundred names, we shall allow the libraries named above to serve as emblems of the cooperation we have had from all the libraries whose facilities have served us.

Those few of us who have occasionally had some reduction in our teaching loads are grateful to our sympathetic colleagues and department chairmen for their support. We wish especially to express our thanks for research grants which helped defray costs of travel, photographic reproductions, supplies, and the like—the University of Kansas for a University Research Fund Grant to Peter Casagrande, Northern Illinois University for a Council of Academic Deans Research Grant to H. E. Gerber, the Research Board of the Graduate College of the University of Illinois for a grant to Dale Kramer, and Winthrop College for a Winthrop Research Grant to Jack Weaver.

For typing and proofreading W. E. Davis commends Janet Reed and Shirley M. Davis, and H. E. Gerber commends Jeanine Brundage, Robin Gillespie, and Nicholas Fratt.

All modern Hardy researchers are indebted to the seminal work of Richard L. Purdy, Carl J. Weber, and J. O. Bailey. While their work will be supplemented and modified in details, it is unlikely to be superseded.

Finally, we both take pleasure in expressing our gratitude to Professor J. O. Bailey, University of North Carolina, for sharing with us, during a three-day visit, his detailed knowledge of secondary materials. Even to the last day of proofreading, his recently published THE POETRY OF THOMAS HARDY: A HANDBOOK AND A COMMENTARY (1970) has been an indispensable aid.

HELMUT E. GERBER
W. EUGENE DAVIS

Contents

NOTE ON ENTRY STYLE

Titles of Hardy's books appear in italic type; titles of his stories, in roman capitals and lower case with quotation marks. Titles of books by other authors, collections of stories and letters edited by other writers, and names of periodicals and newspapers appear in capitals and small capitals. The translations appearing in parentheses are confined to meanings of the phrases; however, it should be noted that the titles of translations are seldom literal ones.

Thomas Hardy

AN ANNOTATED BIBLIOGRAPHY
OF WRITINGS ABOUT HIM

A Checklist

OF THE WORKS OF THOMAS HARDY
CITED IN THIS BIBLIOGRAPHY

I. FICTION

A. SEPARATE WORKS

The Poor Man and the Lady. [Never published]

Desperate Remedies. Lond, 1871; NY, 1874.

Under the Greenwood Tree. Lond, 1872; NY, 1873.

A Pair of Blue Eyes. Lond, 1873; NY, 1873.

Far From the Madding Crowd. Lond, 1874; NY, 1874.

The Hand of Ethelberta. Lond, 1876; NY, 1876.

The Return of the Native. Lond, 1878; NY, 1878.

The Trumpet-Major. Lond, 1880; NY, 1880.

A Laodicean. Lond, 1881; NY, 1881.

Two on a Tower. Lond, 1882; NY, 1882.

The Mayor of Casterbridge. Lond, 1886; NY, 1886.

The Woodlanders. Lond, 1887; NY, 1887.

Wessex Tales. Lond, 1888; NY, 1888. Contents: "The Three Strangers,"
"The Withered Arm," "Fellow-Townsmen," "Interlopers at the
Knap," "The Distracted Preacher."

Tess of the d'Urbervilles. Lond, 1891; NY, 1892.

A Group of Noble Dames. Lond, 1891; NY, 1891. Contents: "The First
Countess of Wessex," "Barbara of the House of Grebe," "The March-
ioness of Stonehenge," "Lady Mottisfont," "The Lady Icenway,"
"Squire Petrick's Lady," "Anna, Lady Baxby," "The Lady Penelope,"
"The Duchess of Hamptonshire," "The Honourable Laura."

Life's Little Ironies. Lond, 1894; NY, 1894. Contents: "The Son's Veto,"
"For Conscience' Sake," "A Tragedy of Two Ambitions," "On the
Western Circuit," "To Please His Wife," "The Melancholy Hussar of

the German Legion," "The Fiddler of Reels," "A Tradition of Eighteen Hundred and Four," "A Few Crusted Characters."

Jude the Obscure. Lond, [1895]; NY, [1895].

The Well-Beloved. Lond, 1897; NY, 1897.

A Changed Man and Other Tales. Lond, 1913; NY, 1913. Contents: "A Changed Man," "The Waiting Supper," "Alicia's Diary," "The Grave by the Handpost," "Enter a Dragoon," "A Tryst at an Ancient Earthwork," "What the Shepherd Saw," "A Committee-Man of 'The Terror,' " "Master John Horseleigh, Knight," "The Duke's Reappearance," "A Mere Interlude," "The Romantic Adventures of a Milkmaid."

An Indiscretion in the Life of an Heiress. Lond, 1934; Baltimore, 1935. [H's adaptation of the main plot of *The Poor Man and the Lady*.]

B. Collected Editions

The Wessex Novels. Lond, 1895–1896. 16 vols Contents:

Volume I—*Tess of the d'Urbervilles.*
Volume II—*Far From the Madding Crowd.*
Volume III—*The Mayor of Casterbridge.*
Volume IV—*A Pair of Blue Eyes.*
Volume V—*Two on a Tower.*
Volume VI—*The Return of the Native.*
Volume VII—*The Woodlanders.*
Volume VIII—*Jude the Obscure.*
Volume IX—*The Trumpet-Major.*
Volume X—*The Hand of Ethelberta.*
Volume XI—*A Laodicean.*
Volume XII—*Desperate Remedies.*
Volume XIII—*Wessex Tales.*
Volume XIV—*Life's Little Ironies.*
Volume XV—*A Group of Noble Dames.*
Volume XVI—*Under the Greenwood Tree.*

The Short Stories of Thomas Hardy. Lond, 1928.

Also see Wessex Edition.

II. POEMS

A. Separate Volumes

Wessex Poems. Lond, 1898; NY, 1899.

Poems of the Past and the Present. Lond, [1901]; NY, 1901.

Time's Laughingstocks. Lond, 1909.
Satires of Circumstance, Lyrics and Reveries. Lond, 1914.
Moments of Vision. Lond, 1917.
Late Lyrics and Earlier. Lond, 1922.
Human Shows, Far Phantasies, Songs, and Trifles. Lond, 1925; NY, 1925.
Winter Words. Lond, 1928; NY, 1928.

B. COLLECTED EDITIONS

Selected Poems. Lond, 1916.
Collected Poems. Lond, 1919.
Chosen Poems. Lond, 1927.
Selected Poems, ed by G. M. Young. Lond, 1940.
Also see Wessex Edition.

III. PLAYS

A. SEPARATE WORKS

Dramatic adaptations of Hardy's short stories and novels by Hardy or by others are noted in the Index of Primary Titles under the entry for the relevant novel or story.
The Dynasts, Part First. Lond, [1904]; NY, 1904.
The Dynasts, Part Second. Lond, [1906]; NY, 1905.
The Dynasts, Part Third. Lond, 1908; NY, 1908.
The Play of 'Saint George.' Lond, 1921.
The Famous Tragedy of the Queen of Cornwall. Lond, 1923; NY, 1923.

B. COLLECTED EDITIONS

The Dynasts [complete]. Lond, 1910.
Also see Wessex Edition.

IV. AUTOBIOGRAPHY, ESSAYS, LETTERS, EDITED WORKS

Select Poems of William Barnes. Chosen and ed, with a preface and glossorial notes by Thomas Hardy. Lond, 1908.
The Early Life of Thomas Hardy: 1840–1891, compiled . . . by Florence Emily Hardy. Lond, 1928; NY, 1928.
The Later Years of Thomas Hardy: 1892–1928, by Florence Emily Hardy. Lond, 1930; NY, 1930.

Life and Art, ed by Ernest Brennecke, Jr. NY, 1925. ["Essays, Notes and Letters collected for the first time."]

Thomas Hardy's Notebooks, and Some Letters from Julia Augusta Martin, ed by Evelyn Hardy. Lond, 1955.

'Dearest Emmie' Thomas Hardy's Letters to His First Wife, ed by Carl J. Weber. London, 1963.

The Architectural Notebooks of Thomas Hardy, ed by C. J. P. Beatty. Dorchester, Dorset, 1966.

Thomas Hardy's Personal Writings, ed by Harold Orel. Kansas, 1966.

V. COLLECTED EDITIONS

Wessex Edition. Lond, 1912–1931; NY, 1915–1931. 24 vols Contents:

The Wessex Novels

I. Novels of Character and Environment

Volume I—*Tess of the d'Urbervilles.*
Volume II—*Far From the Madding Crowd.*
Volume III—*Jude the Obscure.*
Volume IV—*The Return of the Native.*
Volume V—*The Mayor of Casterbridge.*
Volume VI—*The Woodlanders.*
Volume VII—*Under the Greenwood Tree.*
Volume VIII—*Life's Little Ironies.*
Volume IX—*Wessex Tales.*

II. Romances and Fantasies

Volume X—*A Pair of Blue Eyes.*
Volume XI—*The Trumpet-Major.*
Volume XII—*Two on a Tower.*
Volume XIII—*The Well-Beloved.*
Volume XIV—*A Group of Noble Dames.*

III. Novels of Ingenuity

Volume XV—*Desperate Remedies.*
Volume XVI—*The Hand of Ethelberta.*
Volume XVII—*A Laodicean.*

IV. Mixed Novels

Vol. XVIII—*A Changed Man.*

Verse

Volume I—*Wessex Poems, Poems of the Past and the Present.*
Volume II—*The Dynasts, Parts First and Second.*

Volume III—*The Dynasts, Part Third, Time's Laughingstocks.*
Volume IV—*Satires of Circumstance, Moments of Vision.*
Volume V—*Late Lyrics and Earlier, The Famous Tragedy of the Queen of Cornwall.*
Volume VI—*Human Shows, Winter Words.*

Introduction

The ninety-nine years (1871–1969) of published responses to the writings of Thomas Hardy covered by this bibliography may be broken into four periods to suggest something about the correlation between Hardy's literary life and his "press" and to facilitate discussion of a few important trends in those responses. In the first period, 1871–1896, Hardy established himself with critics and general readers as an important novelist, but recurring storms of controversy made his life difficult at times. During the second, 1897–1928, Hardy the poet and dramatist lost some of this "celebrity," but by the time of his death in 1928 he had gained a measure of national respect tendered to few English authors of the last one hundred years. The third period, 1929–1939, was a time of falling reputation for Hardy. In the fourth, 1940–1969, beginning with a centenary celebration curtailed by the incipient World War, the rediscovery of much that had been undervalued and the reassessment of Hardy the man and artist proceeded without pause.

Hardy was a self-made novelist. He surely learned much from reading George Eliot's novels, as several reviewers of *Far From the Madding Crowd* observed, and those of other contemporaries like Anthony Trollope, and he was certainly influenced by the advice and suggestions of editors and readers. George Meredith's warning to the callow author of *The Poor Man and the Lady* not to "nail his colours to the mast" so blatantly in a first book is only one well-remembered example among many. Even so, as a novelist Hardy made his own way. In terms of characterization (his use of philosophical rustics and his love of pretty, wild, changeable heroines), setting (his creation of the timeless Wessex milieu), and plot (his predilection for the grotesque and for involved, coincidental plots), the "Hardy Novel" came to have a clearly defined shape, one that Hardy gradually evolved out of his own inner awareness of what best suited his artistic aims and his background.

A graph representing Hardy's popular success in the first period begins at zero at the time of the publication of *Desperate Remedies* and climbs slowly during *Under the Greenwood Tree* and *A Pair of Blue Eyes*. After

Far From the Madding Crowd the climb becomes much sharper; it levels out for *The Hand of Ethelberta* but becomes greater after *The Return of the Native*. Again a plateau occurs for *The Trumpet-Major, A Laodicean,* and *Two on a Tower;* a sharper rise commences for *The Mayor of Caster-bridge* and *The Woodlanders*; and the graph ends with an almost vertical rise at the time of *Tess of the d'Urbervilles* and *Jude the Obscure*. Thus by the mid-1890s, the man who had confessed to editor Leslie Stephen in the 1870s a desire merely to be regarded "a good hand at a serial" had succeeded brilliantly. But not without paying a high price. Hardy aroused such hostility and misunderstanding in certain segments of the English reading public that after *The Well-Beloved* he chose to write no more novels. Essentially this choice resulted from the breakdown of Hardy's "Victorian Compromise" with his readers.

In his early career, Hardy was as safe a novelist as Mrs. Grundy could wish. But as he developed, he became increasingly interested in what he called, in a preface to *Jude*, "the fret and fever, derision and disaster, that may press in the wake of the strongest passion known to humanity," in more mundane words, the problems of sex and marriage. Though this desire to study a sensitive portion of the anatomy of Victorian society was incompatible with his aim to be a successful serialist, Hardy managed, for a time, an uneasy marriage between them by wearing two hats: novelist and serialist. As Mary Ellen Chase's book THOMAS HARDY FROM SERIAL TO NOVEL documents, Hardy deliberately euphemized the stronger language, characters, and happenings in several of his novels so that they could appear in the pages of Victorian periodicals. The book versions were of course more outspoken, but not until *Woodlanders* did Hardy's frankness arouse much comment. The compromise finally broke down completely with *Tess* and *Jude*. *Tess* had been declined by two magazine editors before its acceptance—in a much bowdlerized form—by the GRAPHIC. Perhaps Hardy foresaw similar difficulties with the serial version of *Jude*. He sought unsuccessfully to cancel his agreement with HARPER'S MAGAZINE to supply a serial, and so had to dismember that novel as he had *Tess*. The compromise also failed when Hardy published restored versions of both works in book form. The story of how these two masterworks were greeted by the critics is best read in the reviews themselves (many are reprinted in THOMAS HARDY AND HIS READERS: A SELECTION OF CONTEMPORARY REVIEWS, ed by Laurence Lerner and John Holmstrom); suffice it to say that after the allegorical *The Well-Beloved,* Hardy published no more fiction.

Secondary material on Hardy in this first period consists almost entirely of reviews of his novels, varied by an occasional article by someone who had visited Hardy at Max Gate—a kind of article more in evidence after 1896. The reviews are by and large favorable: Hardy's first reviewers in England and America perceived that despite one's misgivings about Hardy's too-philosophical peasants, his clumsy use of coincidence, or his use of forced diction, one had to admit Hardy was no common novel-writer. The ambivalence of Andrew Lang (26) about *Madding Crowd,* and a reviewer (48) about *Native* are typical: both grant Hardy vision and power, but both are annoyed by glaring flaws. From reviews of his first novel to his last, this ambivalence about Hardy's achievement is a dominant note of contemporary reception.

The reviewers did grant, however, a certain progression or at least a shift of emphasis as Hardy's career developed. The works most often singled out as turning points are *Native, Woodlanders,* and of course *Tess.* As the reviewers interpreted this progression, Hardy wrote less spontaneously, more often now to illustrate or defend a definite position or thesis than to tell a good story (see 49); he more and more insistently affronted his readers' moral sense (114 and 194); and his vision of man and his hopes for happiness or success in life grew ever darker. For all that, more critics pronounced *Tess* Hardy's masterpiece than any of his earlier, more appealing novels. There were, naturally, few full-dress studies of Hardy or his works in these years, but Lionel Johnson's sensitive THE ART OF THOMAS HARDY retains for us more than mere historical importance.

The neat dichotomy suggested by the titles of Hardy's disguised autobiography, THE EARLY LIFE OF THOMAS HARDY, 1840–1891 and THE LATER YEARS OF THOMAS HARDY, 1892–1928 should not be taken too seriously, especially in light of the tremendous quantity of *belles lettres* (almost entirely verse and drama) Hardy wrote in his "later years." Moreover, much of this later work gives us glimpses of a man passionately alive, seeing and experiencing life with unusual clarity—as in "I Look Into My Glass," in which a persona with "wasting skin" experiences "throbbings of noontide" in his "fragile frame at eve." The three decades covered by this second phase of Hardy secondary material were indisputably years of advancing age and cares—most notably the death of Emma Lavinia, his first wife, in 1912 and the outbreak of World War I. While such sorrows as these cannot have been recompensed, Hardy's life must have been, in the main, tranquil. He was certainly well-off financially; he enjoyed the fortress-like security of Max Gate for work and meditation, and he must have taken satisfaction in the spread of interest in and respect for his work.

Moreover, what Hardy chose to publish in these years was of prime importance in maintaining the equilibrium of his personal and artistic lives. As noted earlier, having grown tired of being verbally "shot at" for expressing himself frankly in fiction, Hardy became publicly what he had privately been all along—a poet. He took this decision seriously indeed. His eight volumes of verse constitute an incredible record of energy and creativity for a man who was nearly sixty before the first appeared. And the composition of Hardy's *magnum opus* in this genre, *The Dynasts* ("An Epic-Drama of the War with Napoleon, in Three Parts, Nineteen Acts, and One Hundred and Thirty Scenes"), spread over many years.

Hardy's decision to turn to poetry as a vehicle for his ideas seemingly rested on his conviction—expressed in a diary entry for 17 Oct 1896—that he, "a harmless agnostic," could more fully express in verse those ideas which "run counter to the inert crystallized opinion . . . which the vast body of men have vested interests in supporting." His later experience as a published poet proved him right. As a poet he was never as roughly handled by critics and common readers as he had been for publishing novels. But neither was he as widely read, nor as influential. But here, a paradox: Hardy, the writer who turned from novels to poems to escape the strictures of certain hostile segments of society, gained ever-widening fame during his career as poet, *largely on account of his novels.*

In the last decade of his life Hardy added no peaks to the range of his achievements, but he did diversify the landscape with his first published plays, *The Play of St. George* and *The Famous Tragedy of the Queen of Cornwall,* and he oversaw the first collected edition of his short stories. By the late 1920s he had become a literary institution. Hardy's Wessex had become a vast garden whose center was Max Gate, inhabited by a small, unassuming, aged man who seemed universally revered and was mentioned several times as a deserving candidate for the newly established Nobel Prize. When he died, writers for the press, like the figure "Time" in W. H. Auden's poem "In Memory of W. B. Yeats," forgave the passionate poet and novelist whose views had so infuriated them. They pardoned Hardy "for writing well."

Hardy's imposing achievements as a novelist proved to be a burden to the contemporary appreciation and assessment of both his shorter poems and *The Dynasts*. F.Y.E. (370) called the poems in Hardy's first two collections "in great part, translated prose." Similarly, a reviewer of *Poems of the Past and the Present* (390) observed that "poetry is not his proper medium. He does not move easily in it." The critics were struck and often impressed by the personality of Hardy's verse, the "tang" which made it unique. Typical of many reviewers, Lionel Johnson (340) and Annie Macdonell (346) shared a glimpse of the uncompromising toughness, the hard clarity of Hardy's vision in *Wessex Poems*. The critics found much to complain about in Hardy's verse: his odd coinages and resurrections of long-dead words, his unmusical ear, the somberness of his vision. But few critics of Hardy's poetry cared to bite with the fatal intent of an anonymous reviewer (353) who called *Wessex Poems* "a curious and slipshod volume," the bulk of which Hardy should have burned. Like the shorter poems, *The Dynasts* was often read at first as the work of a displaced novelist. The simple rustics were regarded as finer character studies than the great men (435, 448); as a drama it was found wanting in action (440) and credibility (448). But like his shorter poems, it came in time to be seen for what it was—the massive result of years of careful study and meditation about one of man's cataclysms. Max Beerbohm (433) was among those first readers of the epic-drama who called it "a noble achievement."

As noted earlier, Hardy's steadily-growing renown in these years was largely due to the spread of interest in his novels; John Cunliffe in ENGLISH LITERATURE DURING THE LAST HALF CENTURY, for example, noted a general neglect of Hardy's poems and felt the preference for his novels was justified. Critics continued to disagree about which of Hardy's novels were the most artistic, but Hardy's major novels were generally agreed to include *Madding Crowd, Native, Mayor, Woodlanders, Tess,* and *Jude.* Critics began applauding Hardy's talent for artistically structuring his narratives (459), for speaking out against injustices (759), for the austere morality of *Tess* and *Jude* (586), and even, by his emphasis on the power of fate and life's uncertainties (457), for helping mankind rid themselves of a "swelled head."

Among the books which reflect and, at the time, intensified this interest in Hardy's novels, a popular edition of *Mayor,* with an introduction by J. F. A. Pyre, is the first of a long series of Hardy novels edited, with an introduction (perhaps with notes and appendices), which publishers— mostly American—issued to make Hardy's novels more accessible to a new generation. In the last decade of Hardy's life appeared a few works still of major importance. Joseph Warren Beach in THE TECHNIQUE OF THOMAS HARDY stressed the division of Hardy's novels into successes and failures, the former determined largely by the closeness of Hardy's adherence to a dramatic ideal. Mary Ellen Chase, THOMAS HARDY FROM SERIAL TO NOVEL, revealed the bowdlerizations Hardy made in three novels for serial readers. "Thomas Hardy's Novels," Virginia Woolf's perceptive short account (1440), makes us wish vainly that she had undertaken a fuller study of Hardy's genius.

Among longer studies of Hardy's entire corpus, which furthered interest in and study of his works, A. P. Webb's A BIBLIOGRAPHY OF THE WORKS OF THOMAS HARDY may stand first. Lascelles Abercrombie, THOMAS HARDY: A CRITICAL STUDY, emphasized Hardy's novels, but Abercrombie felt that Hardy's philosophical and psychological poems were an undeniable achievement and that *The Dynasts* was a great summation of the novels. Ernest Brennecke, Jr. mined his 1926 Columbia University Ph.D. dissertation for two books on Hardy: THE LIFE OF THOMAS HARDY and THOMAS HARDY'S UNIVERSE: A STUDY OF A POET'S MIND. Samuel C. Chew's THOMAS HARDY: POET AND NOVELIST stressed Hardy as a late Victorian in view of his fictional technique. Henry Charles Duffin in Thomas Hardy: A Study of the Wessex Novels, Poems and The Dynasts largely substituted summary for analysis. The two volumes Florence Emily Hardy published under her name (1275) actually gave the world Hardy's own assessment of his life.

Further proof of the widening interest in Hardy's writings is the quantity of extra-insular Hardy studies in this period, most of them American, German, and French. Books already discussed by Chase, Brennecke, and Chew will suffice to show the ground-swell of early-century interest in Hardy's novels and poems in America. On the continent, however, interest centered on Hardy's novels. French and German periodical writers often acclaimed Hardy's skill as novelist (415, 419, 437, 438). Book-length studies of Hardy in French or German in this period are largely dissertations, e.g., Richard Taufkirch, Die Romankunst von Thomas Hardy. Pierre d'Exideuil's Le Couple Humain dans l'Oeuvre de Thomas Hardy Essai sur la Sexualité dans les Romans, Contes et Poèmes du Wessex, a sensitive, insightful study, however, was not a university degree by-product.

At the same time that Hardy's critical, if not always popular, fame was spreading in other countries, in England he was acquiring a kind of fame which he had not enjoyed earlier. As Edward Thomas first observed (738) Hardy allowed, even actively encouraged, the identification of the original towns, buildings, monuments and scenes he alluded to in his novels. By so doing Hardy, intentionally or otherwise, encouraged the growth of a "Hardy of Wessex" cult which dedicated itself to touring Wessex to see "Tess's Country," trying to locate the original of Little Hintock in *Woodlanders* (even Hardy tried unsuccessfully to "find" it), or wander through the pages of Casterbridge's counterpart, Dorchester. The first of the Wessex pilgrims was C. J. Hankinson (376). In a long series of writings he, perhaps more than anyone, popularized and publicized the Hardy tour. Wessex, the book he and Walter Tyndale wrote, was both attractive and useful. But it was Wilkinson Sherren, The Wessex of Romance, and Bertram C. A. Windle, The Wessex of Thomas Hardy (1902), who had established the pattern followed by, among others, Charles Harper (442), Robert T. Hopkins (875), and Hermann Lea (644); their books were one part Wessex guidebook, one part summary of Hardy's plots, and one part local folklore. Probably the most reputable of the lot is Lea's Thomas Hardy's Wessex, since Hardy worked closely with its author on assigning identifications. These books still retain value for latter-day Wessex pilgrims but have outlived whatever scholarly interest they may have had. F. Outwin Saxelby's A Thomas Hardy Dictionary may derive from some of the same impulses as those just mentioned, but its emphasis is squarely on

Hardy's art not Hardy's Wessex, and therefore retains considerable value as an aid to identifying or recalling to mind minor points in Hardy's works.

After the unusual outpouring of tribute and interest in Hardy during the last years of his life, a contraction of interest in him and his works after his death was inevitable. Hardy died quietly, leaving behind, as far as anyone then knew, neither scandal, mystery, nor a bulk of unpublished material. While virtually all the histories, guidebooks, and textbooks published in these years pay their tithe of respect to Hardy, substantial Hardy studies are relatively scarce. The books by C. J. Hankinson, THOMAS HARDY, O.M.: THE MAN, HIS WORKS, AND THE LAND OF WESSEX, and William R. Rutland, THOMAS HARDY: A STUDY OF HIS WRITINGS AND THEIR BACKGROUND, were competent studies. Ruth Firor, FOLKWAYS IN THOMAS HARDY, amassed an abundance of material to document Hardy's deep awareness of Wessex lore.

Hardy's reputation as novelist and poet was both challenged and defended in these years. Some younger writers especially felt that Hardy was overrated, that the importance of his works was fading as the Victorian period receded. Ford Madox Ford, THE ENGLISH NOVEL, could only inanely credit Hardy with contributing to the swell of insignificant "novels of commerce," and T. S. Eliot, AFTER STRANGE GODS: A PRIMER OF MODERN HERESY, sharply criticized Hardy as a great talent unrestrained by tradition or audience. Chief among the defenders of Hardy's fiction was D. H. Lawrence, whose several essays on Hardy (gathered in "Study of Thomas Hardy" in PHOENIX: THE POSTHUMOUS PAPERS OF D. H. LAWRENCE) was perhaps the first to recognize the fierce dichotomies between simple instinctual life and complex intellectualism in Hardy's characters. Carl J. Weber was a prolific Hardy defender. His tracing and publication of the surviving piece of the unpublished *Poor Man* was a contribution to knowledge of Hardy's career. His HARDY AT COLBY: A CHECKLIST OF THE WRITINGS BY AND ABOUT THOMAS HARDY NOW IN THE LIBRARY OF COLBY COLLEGE was a useful compilation and a preliminary to his more extensive projects in the following decade.

Generally Hardy's poetry fared better than his novels in this period. Hardy's poems—a select few at least—appeared regularly in the textbooks and anthologies of the period; Hardy was always discussed in the many commentaries on Victorian and contemporary poetry. F. R. Leavis, NEW BEARINGS IN ENGLISH POETRY: A STUDY OF THE CONTEMPORARY SITUATION, saw Hardy as a Victorian poet whose few great poems were the product of powerful personal urging. Arthur McDowall, THOMAS HARDY: A CRITICAL STUDY, studied all Hardy's work based on the thesis that Hardy was "greater as a poet than as anything else."

In at least one quarter—German universities—the interest in Hardy, as a subject for dissertations, did not flag. In 1934, the three published are representative of this interest and of the nature of the investigation: Ilse Griesbach, DAS TRAGISCHE WELTGEFÜHL ALS GESTALTUNGSPRINZIP IN THOMAS HARDYS WESSEXROMANEN UNTER HINEINBEZIEHUNG SHAKESPEARE IN SEINER LEAR UND MACBETH-PERIODE (The Tragic Universal Sentiment as Structural Principle in Thomas Hardy's Wessex Novels in Relation to Shakespeare in His Lear and Macbeth Period); Josef Hartman, ARCHITEKTUR IN DEN ROMANEN THOMAS HARDYS (Architecture in the Novels of Thomas Hardy); Guenther Wilmsen, THOMAS HARDY ALS IMPRESSIONISTISCHER LANDSCHAFTSMALER (Thomas Hardy as Impressionistic Landscape Painter).

The 1940 Hardy centenary observances make a suitable beginning date for the last phase of secondary material. Some of the many articles published on Hardy that year remind us of the many studies of Hardy and his work that wanted writing. Carl Weber's THE FIRST HUNDRED YEARS OF THOMAS HARDY 1840–1940: A CENTENARY BIBLIOGRAPHY OF HARDIANA was the first sizeable secondary bibliography, as well as a guide to probably the finest Hardy collection in the United States—the one amassed under Weber's supervision at Colby College, Waterville, Maine. SOUTHERN REVIEW devoted the whole of its summer 1940 issue to Hardy. The fourteen provocative essays, by such American and English men of letters as W. H. Auden, Jacques Barzun, R. P. Blackmur, Bonamy Dobrée, F. R. Leavis, Katherine Anne Porter, and John Crowe Ransom, did much to revivify interest in Hardy.

A major gap in Hardy studies, a thorough biography, was capably filled by Carl Weber, HARDY OF WESSEX: HIS LIFE AND LITERARY CAREER, and Evelyn Hardy, THOMAS HARDY: A CRITICAL BIOGRAPHY. The work of future biographers and critics has been made easier by Harold Orel, THOMAS HARDY'S PERSONAL WRITINGS: PREFACES, LITERARY OPINIONS, REMINISCENCES; Evelyn Hardy, THOMAS HARDY'S NOTEBOOKS, AND SOME LETTERS FROM JULIA AUGUSTA MARTIN; and Carl Weber, THE LETTERS OF THOMAS HARDY, TRANSCRIBED FROM THE ORIGINAL AUTOGRAPHS NOW IN THE COLBY COLLEGE LIBRARY. (Professor R. L. Purdy is said to be preparing an edition of Hardy's extant letters.) Future biographers must also be indebted to the series of more than sixty monographs on the life of Thomas Hardy, issued regularly since 1962 under the general editorship of J. Stevens Cox, for raising questions about aspects of Hardy's life—most notably the possibility of Hardy's having fathered an illegitimate son (see Lois Deacon, TRYPHENA AND THOMAS HARDY).

Richard Little Purdy, THOMAS HARDY: A BIBLIOGRAPHICAL STUDY, published probably the most basic tool for students of Hardy's work—a reliable primary bibliography. Among the numerous book-length studies of these years many need to be mentioned: Edmund Blunden, THOMAS HARDY; Richard C. Carpenter, THOMAS HARDY; Irving Howe, THOMAS HARDY; Roy Morrell, THOMAS HARDY: THE WILL AND THE WAY; F. B. Pinion, A HARDY COMPANION: A GUIDE TO THE WORKS OF THOMAS HARDY AND THEIR BACKGROUND; Carl J. Weber, HARDY AND THE LADY FROM MADISON SQUARE; Carl J. Weber, HARDY IN AMERICA: A STUDY OF THOMAS HARDY AND HIS AMERICAN READERS; Harvey Curtis Webster, ON A DARKLING PLAIN: THE ART AND THOUGHT OF THOMAS HARDY; and George Wing, HARDY.

In this phase as in the earlier ones, Hardy's stepchild—the novel—continued to arouse far more critical and popular interest than his poetry. Thus book-length studies of this aspect of Hardy's art are quite common in these years—Douglas Brown, THOMAS HARDY; David Cecil, HARDY THE NOVELIST: AN ESSAY IN CRITICISM; Albert Guérard, THOMAS HARDY: THE NOVELS AND STORIES; Desmond Hawkins, THOMAS HARDY; and Benjamin Sankey, THE MAJOR NOVELS OF THOMAS HARDY.

An important reflection of the continuing interest in Hardy is the number of different editions of a few select novels which appear on the lists of major American and English publishers. Among those of the 1950s were Albert J. Guérard (ed), *Tess of the d'Urbervilles,* and Carl J. Weber (ed), *The Woodlanders* and *Jude the Obscure.* In the 1960s, Norton issued, in the Norton Critical Editions, James Gindin (ed), THOMAS HARDY: THE RETURN OF THE NATIVE: AN AUTHORITATIVE TEXT, BACKGROUND, CRITICISM; and Scott Elledge (ed), THOMAS HARDY: TESS OF THE D'URBERVILLES: AN AUTHORITATIVE TEXT, HARDY AND THE NOVEL, CRITICISM. Houghton Mifflin in the Riverside Edition series offered William E. Buckler (ed), *Tess of the d'Urbervilles*; Robert B. Heilman (ed), *The Mayor of Casterbridge*; Irving Howe (ed), *Jude the Obscure*; and A. Walton Litz (ed), *The Return of the Native.* Harper and Row in the Perennial Classic series had Robert B. Heilman (ed), *Jude the Obscure*; Frederick R. Karl (ed), *The Life and Death of The Mayor of Casterbridge*; Arnold Kettle (ed), *Tess of the d'Urbervilles*; and John Paterson (ed), *The Return of the Native.*

But even if Hardy as novelist continued to be the major subject of scholarly and critical concern in these years, his poetry and drama received valuable reconsideration. Three critics examined *The Collected Poems of Thomas Hardy*: Samuel Hynes, THE PATTERN OF HARDY'S POETRY; Kenneth Marsden, THE POEMS OF THOMAS HARDY: A CRITICAL INTRODUCTION; and James G. Southworth, THE POETRY OF THOMAS HARDY. Hardy's long-undervalued, misunderstood epic received three indispensable reconsiderations: J. O. Bailey, THOMAS HARDY AND THE COSMIC MIND; Harold Orel, THOMAS HARDY'S EPIC DRAMA: A STUDY OF "THE DYNASTS"; and Walter F. Wright, THE SHAPING OF THE DYNASTS: A STUDY IN THOMAS HARDY. Even Hardy's few works for the theater received their share of limelight in two works by Marguerite Roberts: HARDY'S POETIC DRAMA AND THE THEATRE and TESS IN THE THEATRE: TWO DRAMATIZATIONS OF "TESS OF THE D'URBERVILLES" BY THOMAS HARDY, ONE BY LORIMER STODDARD.

Since 1969, the appearance of two books, J. O. Bailey's THE POETRY OF THOMAS HARDY: A HANDBOOK AND COMMENTARY—already an indispensable aid to consideration of Hardy's poems—and Jean Brooks's THOMAS HARDY: THE POETIC STRUCTURE, suggests, perhaps, one of the major tasks yet to be achieved in Hardy criticism: the study of the unity and wholeness of Hardy's vision, regardless of the genre in which he chose to write. Other major Hardy studies since 1969, which include Bert G. Hornback, THE METAPHOR OF CHANCE: VISION AND TECHNIQUE IN THE WORKS OF THOMAS HARDY; J. Hillis Miller, THOMAS HARDY: DISTANCE AND DESIRE; Michael Millgate, THOMAS HARDY: HIS CAREER AS A NOVELIST; F. R. Southerington, HARDY'S VISION OF MAN; and J. I. M. Stewart, THOMAS HARDY: A CRITICAL BIOGRAPHY, suggest that the life and works of the Wessex creator remain as provocative as ever.

The Bibliography

1 "Books: *Desperate Remedies*," SPECTATOR (Lond), XLIV (22 April 1871), 481–83.

The anonymity is fortunate for the author; too bad the publishers could not conceal their identity. The book contains no fine or original characters, "no display except of the brute kind, no pictures of Christian virtue." Intricacies of plot show no "transcendent talent," but the author has a talent for "catching and fixing phases of peasant life" and for communicating "sensitiveness to scenic and atmospheric effects." The author's powers "might and ought to be extended, instead of being prostituted to the purpose of idle prying into the ways of wickedness."

2 *"Desperate Remedies,"* SATURDAY REVIEW (Lond), XXXII (30 Sept 1871), 441–42.

"Evolution of character" is the essence of *Desperate Remedies*, this "remarkable story . . . by a nameless author." Cytheria and Miss Aldcliffe are studies of unusual merit, the men are less perfect. H does not indulge in the monstrous for its own sake, though Marston, the villain, may be overdrawn. The progression through time units to the intense description of the burning of the Three Tranters Inn is excellent and convincing. The author delights in *sententiae* a little too often.

3 "Novels of the Week," ATHENAEUM, No. 2266 (1 April 1871), 339.

The knowledge of female toilette displayed in the descriptions might suggest that the author of *Desperate Remedies* is a woman, but some of the expressions in the novel are so coarse that one can hardly believe them to come from an English lady. The plot is intricately worked out, characterization is good, and the parish clerk is really worthy of George Eliot. The author shows great potential.

1872

4 "Current Literature: *Under the Greenwood Tree*," SPECTATOR (Lond), XLV (2 Nov 1872), 1403.

Especially in its dialogue, the novel is indebted to George Eliot. Although "the conversation is out of tune" in places, it is "a very creditable work."

5 [Moule, Horace M.]. *"Under the Greenwood Tree,"* SATURDAY REVIEW (Lond), XXXIV (28 Sept 1872), 417–18.

Under the Greenwood Tree is "a series of rural pictures full of life and genuine coloring," and shows "unusual merit in its own special line," "humour and keen observation," and a "genuine air of the country." Sketches around the figure of "tranter" Dewy are the staple of the book. Reuben's wisdom and old William's defense of the parson are excellent reading. Interior descriptions justify H's reference to the Dutch school on the title-page. The love passages of Dick and Fancy are prolonged, and the countryfolk sometimes talk too much like H, two minor weak points.

6 "Novels of the Week," ATHENAEUM, No. 2329 (15 June 1972), 748.

Under the Greenwood Tree shows many of the fine qualities displayed in *Desperate Remedies*. The excellent descriptions of rustic life become even more vital and vibrant in this second work. The author handles a romantic theme with great skill, but the dialogue of the common people is at times unbelievable.

7 [Review of *Under the Greenwood Tree*], PALL MALL GAZETTE, 5 July 1872 [not seen in this form]; rptd in THOMAS HARDY AND HIS READERS: A SELECTION OF CONTEMPORARY REVIEWS, ed by Laurence Lerner and John Holmstrom (1968), pp. 18–19.

Under the Greenwood Tree has "freshness and originality," but the "humble heroes and heroines of the tale are much too shrewd, and say too many good things, to be truthful representatives of their prototypes in real life." The conversations between members of the choir are excellent; the love story "is considerably marred by an episode regarding the vicar which destroys the simple character of the tale."

1873

8 "Books: *A Pair of Blue Eyes*," SPECTATOR (Lond), XLVI (28 June 1873), 831–32.

H has made "rapid strides." *A Pair of Blue Eyes* shows "not only quick observation and sparkling humor and true moral instinct, but a delicate and subtle analysis of varieties of characters and moods of feeling, a poet's sympathy with human passion when tuned to its sweetest or saddest notes, and an artist's eye for every aspect of nature." The story is "powerful, well-proportioned in its parts, and of varied and deep interest, yet not too harrowing for pleasure." A happier ending would "sacrifice some of the true artistic consistency and dramatic effect." Characters are "revealed" rather than "told": Elfride exhibits a "subtle union of the extremest purity of conduct and intention, with a timidity which, in her loving and ardent nature, suggests prevarication and duplicity." Asks to "hear of Hardy soon, but not too soon again."

9 Browne, W. H. "*A Pair of Blue Eyes*," SOUTHERN MAGAZINE (Baltimore), XIII (Sept 1873), 365–71.

The book is written in a more serious vein than *Under the Greenwood Tree* but has much of the vivacity and light graceful touch. No intricacies of plot, no crowding of the canvas: a few figures are well-drawn, there is an easy sequence of incident and a touch or two of strong passion stir the depths of the heart.

10 "Novels of the Week," ATHENAEUM, No. 2383 (28 June 1873), 820.

The heroine of *A Pair of Blue Eyes* is "a very distinct, if not a very substantial, character, and there is no lack of individuality about the people who surround her. Mr. Hardy's feminine ideal is not lofty, though perilously attractive, as the story shows."

11 "*A Pair of Blue Eyes*," SATURDAY REVIEW (Lond), XXXVI (2 Aug 1873), 158–59.

A Pair of Blue Eyes is "one of the most artistically constructed among recent novels" and, aside from minor poor word choices, is a "thoroughly matured work of its kind." It is not a picture of passion defying social barriers, but a portrait of what the laws of society are and will remain. Like George Eliot, H depicts a ruthless tragedy of circumstance. The earliest scene in the Endelstow vault borrows from HAMLET but is full of genuine touches.

12 "Recent Novels: *Under the Greenwood Tree*," NATION (NY), XVII (10 July 1873), 27.

"It is such a charming little tale that those who are going off for the summer ... cannot do better than slip this volume into their trunks."

1874

13 "Editor's Literary Record," HARPER'S NEW MONTHLY MAG-
AZINE, XLIX (June 1874), 136.

Desperate Remedies, a "somewhat complicated and tragical tale, is an enlarged and laboriously constructed illustration of the admonition, 'Be sure
your sin will find you out.' "

14 [Hutton, R. H.]. "Books: *Far From the Madding Crowd,*"
SPECTATOR (Lond), XLVII (19 Dec 1874), 1597–99.

The novel is a "production of a very high order of ability and humor, . . .
the nearest equivalent to actual experience which a great many of us are
ever likely to boast of." Characters are too vivacious and interesting to be
real; their intellectual banter impossible in a peasant. Style is "an exaggeration of George Eliot," but, unlike H, she "never confuses her own ideas with
those of her dramatic figures." Reader seems never to know "the background of his characters." The hero and heroine are stock figures. H is "too
clever—preposterously clever—where the world is stupid, too original where
he ought to be accommodating himself to the monotonous habits of a world
which is built on usage. It is a rare kind of mistake."

15 [Hutton, R. H.]. "Books: Some of the Magazines," SPECTATOR
(Lond), XLVII (3 Jan 1874), 22.

Far From the Madding Crowd is appearing serially in the CORNHILL MAG-
AZINE. If it is not by George Eliot, "there is a new light among novelists."
CORNHILL offers "a high intellectual treat."

16 James, Henry. "Hardy's *Far From the Madding Crowd,*" NA-
TION (NY), XIX (24 Dec 1874), 423–24; rptd in LITERARY RE-
VIEWS AND ESSAYS BY HENRY JAMES, ed by Albert Mordell (NY:
Twayne Publishers, 1957), pp. 291–97.

When H's novel was published it received such favorable declarations it was
thought that "either George Eliot had written it or George Eliot had found
her match." In reality, however, H's "superficial novel is really a curious
imitation" of Eliot's better work. Its style is verbose and redundant, its narrative is diffuse and inartistic, its author lacks a sense of proportion or
composition. "Everything human in the book strikes us as factitious and in-
substantial; the only things we believe in are the sheep and the dogs."

17 "Novels of the Week," ATHENAEUM, No. 2458 (5 Dec 1874),
747.

H's "recklessness" and "coarseness" often "neutralize" his vigorous qualities of description, plot construction, and "quaint humour." He continues

to put quite unbelievable expressions in the mouths of common people. There is still hope for H's greatness to unfold. The influence of George Eliot is quite plain. H should "hold his peace for at least two years, revise with extreme care, and refrain from publishing in magazines."

18 [Review of *Far From the Madding Crowd*], EXAMINER, 5 Dec 1874 [not seen in this form]; rptd in THOMAS HARDY AND HIS READERS: A SELECTION OF CONTEMPORARY REVIEWS, ed by Laurence Lerner and John Holmstrom (1968), pp. 24–25.

The supposition that *Far From the Madding Crowd* was written by George Eliot is possible only when reading a fragment. Viewed as a whole, H's style is distinctive and identifiable. He is less a preacher and more a dramatist, more interested in unconscious motivation than great lessons.

1875

19 [Alden, H. M.]. "Editor's Literary Record," HARPER'S NEW MONTHLY MAGAZINE, L (March 1875), 598.

Judging from *Far From the Madding Crowd*, "H has studied the works of George Eliot to good purpose, but the indefinite something in the master is wanting in the disciple."

20 "Belles Lettres," WESTMINSTER REVIEW, XLVII (Jan 1875), 265–67.

Far From the Madding Crowd in many respects bears favorable comparison with ADAM BEDE. In his handling of Sgt. Troy, H showed better judgment than George Eliot in her treatment of Arthur Donnithorne. Chief fault of *Madding Crowd* is its sensationalism, "a bastard substitute" for true art.

21 Boucher, Léon. "Le roman pastorale en Angleterre" (The Pastoral Novel in England), REVUE DES DEUX MONDES, 18 Dec 1875, pp. 838–66.

The past twenty years, the critic has been confronted with a legion of facile novelists. Among the few good ones, to this point, George Eliot held sway, but she now has a rival in H. In *Desperate Remedies*, H began by sacrificing to false gods, following Miss Braddon and Wilkie Collins in the genre of the "sensational." H did prove he could handle the character of a woman in a realistic story. However, the novel is not a success because solutions are too off-hand, and the picture is all too grim, dark-passion, and improbable. These faults don't characterize *Under the Greenwood Tree*. The story of the minister Maybold and Miss Fancy Day recalls Boileau's LUTRIN. The rustic figures make the idyll and call to mind the farmers of George

Eliot. They express their thoughts in the form of burlesque philosophizing between a puff of tobacco and a swig of cold cider, and make the most trivial consequences extraordinary. H's narrative maintains the life of the country, its traditions and customs. The characters may be too humorous, too vivacious, but perhaps the English rural character is this way. *A Pair of Blue Eyes* is a strong study of feminine character, a subtle analysis of delicate emotions, and has a poet's sympathy for those caught in passion. H has constructed scenes full of imagination, observation, and novelty. The scene of Knight awaiting the return or death of Elfride is a superior one enhanced with details of fossil rocks that elicit despair and misfortune. H uses peasant gaiety to temper the grimness of this remarkable novel.

Far From the Madding Crowd is perhaps thought of as inferior because an amusing story with dramatic situations is not present. H returned to the traditional pastoral novel, which is often boring; but by true observation, a profound passion, a fresh poetic approach, and a powerful style, he transformed it into an almost original creation. The story recalls the fable, "Beauty and the Beast," but H has given it distinction and novelty. The idyll is modern: Bathsheba is not Galatea, nor the vibrant, vulgar country girls of JOSEPH ANDREWS. She is a young woman of the "new" England. Edgeworth, Burney, and Austen could not approach her. H had the ingenious idea of taking from the country an independent young girl who has a pastoral truthfulness but who is unique and interesting. She retains a certain element of the savage. She is a coquette who is able to choose. She develops Oak's character, his patience, his pride, his ever-present humor, and his fortitude. At the moment tragedy seems to get the upper hand, H stops the analysis of man's passions and reverts to the elements of the environment.

To judge H only as a story teller is to miss his talent for breadth of observation and moral philosophy. *Madding Crowd* is a work of simple construction, but of great imagination. In H's pastoral there is a complete tableau of English rustic life. The drama of "the grand passion" is the first level; the second is the peasants as the tragic chorus commenting on events and characters. The action is restrained and psychological analysis is considerable. The characters are studied and their treatment is astonishing and goes beyond Thackeray. H does not take a position for or against his characters; he explains them. Such a method can be carried to extremes, but H employs it in legitimate measure. *Madding Crowd* is not a novel of the usual day-to-day class. If H continues to write with the same care, the same virile elegance, he will find a place apart from the crowd. [In French.]

22 [Broome, Frederick Napier]. "Recent Novels," TIMES (Lond), 25 Jan 1875, p. 4; rptd in THOMAS HARDY AND HIS READERS: A SELECTION OF CONTEMPORARY REVIEWS, ed by Laurence Lerner and John Holmstrom (1968), pp. 38–39.

Far From the Madding Crowd bears out the promise of *A Pair of Blue Eyes* of H's "possessing a certain vein of original thought, and a delicate perceptive faculty, which transforms . . . the matter-of-fact prosaic details of everyday life into an idyl or a pastoral poem." The reader suspects that H is, "consciously or unconsciously, imitating George Eliot's phraseology and style."

23 "Culture and Progress," SCRIBNER'S MONTHLY, IX (March 1875), 637.

Far From the Madding Crowd "is one of the most unique of modern novels." H can maintain suspense well. The quaint and colorful minor characters remind one of Dickens. Bathsheba is a good study of woman. The novel as a whole is weak in the middle. H is not a master of the grotesque.

24 *"Far From the Madding Crowd,"* LITERARY WORLD (Boston) V (Jan 1875), 114–15.

Although H's characterization in *Far From the Madding Crowd* is not powerful, his delineation of rural life is vivid and energetic. His generally sombre style is relieved by "occasional gems of wit and arch expression," but it is often obscure and wordy. The novel's outstanding attributes are its representation of rural English life and its fascinating story.

25 *"Far From the Madding Crowd,"* SATURDAY REVIEW (Lond), XXIX (9 Jan 1875), 57–58.

Far From the Madding Crowd shows promise, like H's earlier novels, though it is marred by bad writing, clumsy metaphors, mannerisms and affectation; the first half of the book is best. The delicate contrivance of Joseph Poorgrass's drunken imitation of the Bathsheba-Troy scene at Fanny's coffin shows H's tremendous skill. Some of the major scenes in the book are ruined by H's diction and his tendency to force thoughts into the mouths of cheer-faced shepherd lads.

26 Lang, A[ndrew]. "Literature," ACADEMY, VII (2 Jan 1875), 9–10.

"*Far From the Madding Crowd* is so clever a novel, so original in atmosphere and in character, that its brilliant qualities are likely to neutralise the glare of its equally prominent faults." With a philosopher's eye H scrutinizes a country district, trying to extract a philosophy from this crossroad-of-time setting where the old and the new meet. It is an ideal situation for the novelist, but he makes of it somewhat less than an ideal novel. H shows "an original and admirable treatment of nature," but the main persons of the drama are not fully successful because the characters lack a fullness of design.

27 [Review of *Far From the Madding Crowd*], MANCHESTER GUARDIAN, 24 Feb 1875 [not seen in this form]; rptd in THOMAS

Hardy and His Readers: A Selection of Contemporary Reviews, ed by Laurence Lerner and John Holmstrom (1968), pp. 39–40.

The figures in this "pastoral idyll" are "perfect, solid, and substantial"; only "Oak's love is rather too high-toned for the general pitch of the work."

28 [Review of *Far From the Madding Crowd*], Observer, 3 Jan 1875 [not seen in this form]; rptd in Thomas Hardy and His Readers: A Selection of Contemporary Reviews, ed by Laurence Lerner and John Holmstrom (1968), pp. 33–36.

It is ridiculous to suggest that *Far From the Madding Crowd* was written by George Eliot. It is an imitation of her, recognizable by its lack of understanding of human nature. H ought to avoid the philosophical reflections with which he fills his novel because his reflections are commonplaces. His characters and events are mere puppets. H could write a better novel; he has a keen eye for Nature, a sly humor, and a talent for description. What he lacks is depth, especially in portraying character.

1876

29 [Alden, H. M.]. "Editor's Literary Record," Harper's New Monthly Magazine, LIII (Aug 1876), 468.

The Hand of Ethelberta may be read "with no intellectual effort, and very little emotional excitement." The reader enjoys the "improbable story" of the heroine's life.

30 "Belles Lettres," Westminster Review, L (July 1876), 281.

The Hand of Ethelberta is a book that "will sustain Mr. Hardy's reputation."

31 "Books: *The Hand of Ethelberta*," Spectator (Lond), XLIX (22 April 1876), 530–32.

"A more entertaining book has not been published for many years." H is "very original and very skillful," but none of the characters are memorable; they are "vivacious shadows, who amuse us without impressing us." Ethelberta is too contradictory to be real. Although redeemed by H's humor, it is only a "fable illustrating the vices and weaknesses of the upper ten thousand, rather than a picture of the most characteristic figures in the intellectual society of modern London."

32 "Culture and Progress," Scribner's Monthly, XIII (Nov 1876), 135–36.

Ethelberta is really a "repulsive" creature. In *The Hand of Ethelberta*, there is "a lack of grasp, or organized plot . . . and there is a superabundance of padding." "All his books are tentative, after the manner of a beginner." H must write more carefully.

33 *"The Hand of Ethelberta,"* LITERARY WORLD (Boston), VII (June 1876), 4.

Despite a few good passages, *The Hand of Ethelberta* shows that H is less successful with urban than with rural comedy.

34 *"The Hand of Ethelberta,"* SATURDAY REVIEW (Lond), XLI (6 May 1876), 592–93.

The Hand of Ethelberta is not up to the tragic power of H's previous books and is unworthy of him. H's style is affected and unrealistic, and the diction and ideas of the lower characters are not convincing. The plot is entertaining but improbable. The scenes between two of Ethelberta's lovers, Neigh and Ladywell, are humorous.

35 "Novels of the Week," ATHENAEUM, No. 2529 (15 April 1876), 523.

In choosing to become a "modern-romantic" H has chosen a type of fiction "distinctly inferior" to that of the realist. Ethelberta could be a lady from IVANHOE. Some of the dialogue, however, "might be the language of an ostler in Shakespeare, but would it be heard nowadays at a 'Wessex' inn?" His grammar and sentence structure show signs of haste.

36 Saintsbury, George. "New Novels," ACADEMY, IX (13 May 1876), 453–54.

Many readers of H's earlier novels were attracted by "the laboured eccentricity" of his style. *The Hand of Ethelberta*, however, shows much less of this "topsyturvication" of language and thought than does *Far From the Madding Crowd*, for instance, and is, consequently, less wearisome. The character of Ethelberta is "disturbingly unsubstantial," although less so than the other characters. "We should say that it [the novel] suffers from a scrappiness which is a frequent drawback to novels written for periodicals. Nevertheless there is a good deal of power about it."

1877

[No entries for this year.]

1878

37 Henley, W[illiam] E[rnest]. "New Novels," ACADEMY, XIV (30 Nov 1878), 517.

Though *The Return of the Native* possesses "a certain Hugoesque quality of insincerity," H does have a definite theory of what his novels should be. His talent for analysis and description is so powerful that his several lesser talents are well concealed. H handles his subject with an impersonal aloofness that is the result of his peculiar mind, which knows itself better than human nature.

38 "Novels of the Week," ATHENAEUM, No. 2665 (23 Nov 1878), 654.

The Return of the Native is a disappointment to those who have followed H's fine development. This novel indicates, more than any of his others, that he has not as yet developed to the point where his literary expression equals his obviously keen perception of human relations. [H replied in ibid, 30 Nov 1878.]

39 "Recent Novels," TIMES (Lond), 5 Dec 1878, p. 3.

It is difficult to be interested in such entirely foreign people as appear in *The Return of the Native*. H's peculiarity of language is carried too far. The graphic scenes and descriptions, however, make reading it worthwhile.

40 "Thomas Hardy," LITERARY WORLD (Boston), IX (Aug 1878), 46.

[Biographical sketch.]

1879

41 [Alden, H. M.]. "Editor's Literary Record," HARPER's NEW MONTHLY MAGAZINE (NY), LVIII (March 1879), 627–28.

The Return of the Native is "of more than average artistic merit." "The story is powerfully scenic rather than regularly and continuously dramatic."

42 B., M. B. "Table Talk," LITERARY WORLD (Boston), X (15 Feb 1879), 61.

Contrary to the opinion expressed in "*The Return of the Native*," ibid (1 Feb 1879), 37, there is no ambiguity in the title of *The Return of the Native*, since the "native" clearly is Clym Yeobright.

43 "Belles Lettres," WESTMINSTER REVIEW, LV (Jan 1879), 280.
The Return of the Native shows that H "possesses nearly every qualification of the novelist."

44 "Contemporary Literature: IV. Novelists," BLACKWOOD'S MAGAZINE, CXXV (March 1879), 338.
The Return of the Native "might have been a clever parody" of H's earlier novels. There is "a labouring after originality" which turns into the "air of affectation." Wherever the plain would do, he chooses rather the far-fetched.

45 "The Contributors' Club," ATLANTIC MONTHLY, XLIV (Nov 1879), 672–74.
"Hardy does not receive from contemporary criticism the attention which is his due." Besides the characteristic qualities which are found in his other novels, *The Return of the Native* possesses a "more philosophical range." The fascinating setting of Egdon Heath is populated by rustics worthy of Shakespeare's touch, and "higher characters" who "are all touched with some hue of their wild surroundings." Clym Yeobright is "a typical spirit of today," "a tragic figure," a "modern reformer . . . shown . . . [in a] fresh and unhackneyed . . . light," unaffected and unexaggerated. Though H is "accused of taking a low estimate of women," he is rather "keenly appreciative of the feminine situation as well as temperament."

46 "Culture and Progress," SCRIBNER'S MONTHLY, XVII (April 1879), 910–11.
The descriptive sections of *The Return of the Native* are the most numerous, prolix to an extent, but necessarily so. H's overuse of simile causes wordiness of another, weaker sort. H actually pads. The rustics are Shakespearean.

47 "Current Fiction," LITERARY WORLD (Boston), X (25 Oct 1879), 341.
H's short story, "The Distracted Young Preacher," is a capital trifle, light and amusing.

48 [Hutton, R. H.?]. "Books: *The Return of the Native*," SPECTATOR (Lond), LII (8 Feb 1879), 181–82.
H has written a "story of singular power and interest, and in the highest degree vivid," but with two great defects: characters are composites rather than "true pictures of rustic life," and the "significance of human destiny" is lowered to the level of mere "dreariness" by "making human passion in general common-place and poor." H puts his own thoughts, in literary diction, in the mouths of his peasants. They, in turn, are "puppets of a sort of

fate," and "tragedy is almost impossible." He conveys "a mood in which there seems to be no room for freedom, no great heights, no great depths in human life, only the ups and downs of a dark necessity, in which men play the parts of mere offsprings of the physical universe, and are governed by forces and tides no less inscrutable." H is at his best in natural descriptions, in which he proves to be "not only a striking novelist, but in essence at least, a fine poet."

49 "Mr. Hardy's Novels," NEW QUARTERLY MAGAZINE, ns II (July and Oct 1879), 412–31.

The Return of the Native "presents a new phase, and perhaps a new departure in the development of Mr. Hardy's genius." Although "a more serious work" than its predecessors, it is not a " 'stronger' " one. *Native* is "less spontaneous" and "suggests a more definite [authorial] intention." The death of Mrs. Yeobright is "morally stained." When, near the end of Eustacia's life, "a definite moral sense is introduced into her nature, it is transposed from its original key." H "has not had all the courage of his imagination . . . having conceived her [Eustacia] for a larger scale, he has modified her to suit a small one." Clym is "the first of Mr. Hardy's characters who is actuated by any large appreciation of human duty." Thus it seems that "imagination and intellect are fighting for mastery in Mr. Hardy's work." There is a danger that "the consciousness of the motive [will] paralyse the inspiration" in H's future novels.

50 [Preston, Harriet W.]. "The Contributors' Club," ATLANTIC MONTHLY, XLIII (Feb 1879), 260–62.

It is regrettable that more attention is not given to H. There is a soberness about his novels which does not in the least detract from his skills of description and characterization, but rather accentuates them.

51 "Recent Novels: *The Return of the Native,*" NATION (NY), XXVIII (27 Feb 1879), 155.

This is "another of Hardy's peculiar studies . . . in rustic English life." Eustacia "reminds one forcibly of Madame Bovary."

52 "*The Return of the Native* and Other Novels," ATLANTIC MONTHLY, XLIII (April 1879), 500–502.

The heath in this novel is a perfect example of H's remarkable use of scenery. It is not a conventional background, or a mirror of character emotions; it is an omnipresent force: "the heath precedes everything, determines everything, outlasts everything. . . . Over and above this tyranny of place under which Mr. Hardy's people labor, there is a crushing tyranny of circumstance." H's tragedies, however, never break down into melodrama.

53 "*The Return of the Native,*" INTERNATIONAL REVIEW, VI (Feb 1879), 211–12.

H and Blackmore are the "finest of living novelists" other than George Eliot. H's characters suggest Shakespeare's. *The Return of the Native* "shows that grand impartiality in the delineating of character which is the attribute of our best dramatists." The "minutest shades of individual character are realized" in a most striking manner.

54 *"The Return of the Native,"* Literary World (Boston) X (1 Feb 1879), 37.

Both in the characterization of Eustacia and Wildeve, and in the description of Egdon Heath, H shows his power in creating "picturesque unloveliness." But the dissection of the principal characters is too painful; the reader can only admire—not love—the author as a result. [See M. B. B., "Table Talk," ibid (15 Feb 1879), 61.]

55 *"The Return of the Native,"* Saturday Review (Lond), XLVII (4 Jan 1879), 23–24.

The plot of *The Return of the Native* is unpleasing and the rugged simplicity of the subject is artificial. H's affected mannerisms make his style look like literary gymnastics. The major characters are unfortunate inventions. The dialogues of the country-folk, however, are unrivaled and H's description of the landscape is distinctive. The gambling scene is particularly powerful.

1880

56 "Books: Mr. Hardy's New Novel," Spectator (Lond), LIII (18 Dec 1880), 1627–28.

"A novelist born, not made," H is "observant, truthful, humorous, and at once masculine and shy." Never missing "the comic aspect of a situation or episode," he does not enforce it "by a coarse or unsympathetic touch." His one fault is a tendency to "magnify and elaborate trifles" and thus create an "impression of thinness." Neither H nor his characters are suited to high tragedy. *The Trumpet-Major* "is conceived and put together with capital ingenuity." If H never does worse, "he will maintain a literary level which any contemporary writer of English prose fiction might be glad to attain."

57 "Novels of the Week," Athenaeum, No. 2769 (20 Nov 1880), 672.

The Trumpet-Major shows that though H may lack the power "of enthralling the reader's interest," he is second to none "in the art of making one see his scenes and know his characters." John Loveday is the best character H has drawn.

58 Saintsbury, George. "New Novels," ACADEMY, XVIII (11 Dec 1880), 420.

H laid aside much of his extravagant phraseology in writing *The Trumpet-Major* and confined himself to less pretentious diction. The novel moves at a slow pace and, in fact, the true merit of the novel cannot be fully appreciated until the last page is read. The main characters are well sketched, and the novel taken in its entirety is worthy of praise.

59 *"The Trumpet-Major,"* SATURDAY REVIEW (Lond), L (6 Nov 1880), 588–89.

The Trumpet-Major is a fine study of the character of John Loveday. Group scenes, conversations, and character development are good, particularly in the party honoring the regiment and the explanation of Miss Johnson's flight. H's use of terms such as "eye-sockets" when he could have said "eyes" forces an affected ugliness on the reader.

1881

60 [Alden, H. M.]. "Editor's Literary Record," HARPER'S NEW MONTHLY MAGAZINE, LXII (Feb 1881), 474.

[Review of *The Trumpet-Major*, barely a mention.]

61 "Belles Lettres," WESTMINSTER REVIEW, LIX (Jan 1881), 327.

The Trumpet-Major is "decidedly the best story which Mr. Hardy has yet written." But he makes his rustics too clever.

62 "Contemporary Literature: Novels of the Quarter," BRITISH QUARTERLY REVIEW, LXXIII (Jan 1881), 114–19, espec 116–17.

In *The Trumpet-Major* H "seems to have completely realized what he intended; which is, in one respect, a drawback, since . . . he proscribes ideals to a considerable extent, and . . . does not aim high."

63 "Current Fiction," LITERARY WORLD (Boston), XII (15 Jan 1881), 25.

The Trumpet-Major, thanks to its amusing characters and setting, is a more pleasing story than *The Return of the Native*.

64 "Novels of the Week," ATHENAEUM, No. 2827 (31 Dec 1881), 899–900.

H's gallery of women seems to indicate that he is trying to exemplify "the Virgilian dictum about the nature of women." He has presented his heroines in various positions and lights; "but all have the common fault of their sex, they cannot make up their minds." *A Laodicean* adds another portrait to H's gallery.

65 "Recent Novels," NATION (NY), XXXII (6 Jan 1881), 16–17.

The Trumpet-Major has the virtues and failings of H's earlier novels. H's style is "peculiar to the point of eccentricity."

1882

---

66 "At the Theatres," NEW YORK MIRROR, ns VII (22 April 1882), 2.

The dramatic version of *Far From the Madding Crowd* gives the playgoer "a mutilated and unsatisfactory outline of one of the most charming pastoral stories in the English language." Mr. Cazauran "is a dramatic tinker"; he used neither the scissors nor the pen skillfully.

67 Barker, Arthur. "New Articles, Etc.," ACADEMY, XXI (7 Jan 1882), 5.

H's latest novel, *A Laodicean*, seems to be a conventional love-tale. His descriptions are effective, but his realistic dialogue, though perhaps true to life, detracts from, and certainly cannot be called a part of, the purposes of art.

68 "Books: *A Laodicean*," SPECTATOR (Lond), LV (4 March 1882), 296–97.

Paula Power, like other H heroines, is a composite and has no "living original." The concentration on technical aspects of architecture is unfortunate.

69 Cook, Dutton. "The Case of Mr. Pinero," THEATRE, 1 April 1882, pp. 202–4.

Although Arthur Wing Pinero claims to have conceived the idea for *The Squire* before reading *Far From the Madding Crowd*, he did indeed use H's novel as a source. There are many points of resemblance [listed for comparison]. However, Pinero did not see the actual manuscript of H–Comyn Carr's dramatization of the novel.

70 Cook, Dutton, J. Mortimer, and A[rthur] W[ing] Pinero. "Our Symposium: Plays, Plagiarism, and Mr. Pinero," THEATRE, 1 Feb 1882, pp. 65–73.

Dutton Cook: Pinero is obviously indebted to H's *Far From the Madding Crowd*; however, the charge of plagiarism lodged by H's co-author, Comyn Carr, is not justified. Pinero did not see the manuscript of the H–Comyn Carr version of the play. J. Mortimer: Recently it has become commonplace for English dramatists to rewrite foreign works and pass them off as original creations. Equally reprehensible is the borrowing from English novels and then suppressing the source. This practice is unethical and borders on plagiarism. Arthur Wing Pinero: The plot for THE SQUIRE was set before Pinero read *Far From the Madding Crowd*. The two works are quite different. Finally, had Pinero desired to hide his debt he could have done so easily. An established dramatist need not plagiarize in order to write a successful play.

> **71** "Current Fiction," LITERARY WORLD (Boston), XIII (16 Dec 1882), 461.

Two on a Tower is a bad novel, tasteless and outrageous.

> **72** "Current Literature," LITERARY WORLD (Boston), XIII (28 Jan 1882), 26–27.

The lack of his characteristic subtlety and humor makes *A Laodicean* the weakest of the novels H has written.

> **73** D., H. M. "A Liverpool *Premiere*," WHITEHALL REVIEW, XII (2 March 1882), 14.

The "similarity, or coincidence" between Pinero's play THE SQUIRE and H's *Far From the Madding Crowd* is evident. The adaptation of the novel for the stage "is unquestionably a success. . . . It is a thoroughly wholesome drama, and sweetly idyllic."

> **74** "Drama: *Far From the Madding Crowd*," ATHENAEUM, No. 2836 (4 March 1882), 293.

H's and Carr's version of *Far From the Madding Crowd* "is certainly good." The public can now judge whether Pinero borrowed from H's novel in writing THE SQUIRE.

> **75** *"Far From the Madding Crowd*," ERA, 4 March 1882, p. 8.

The dramatization of H's *Far From the Madding Crowd* was a "gratifying success." There were several changes in the stage version as compared to the novel. "In the written story the villainous husband, Sergeant Troy, is slain by one of . . . [Bathesheba's] former admirers." The drama introduces a new character, Will Robin, who slays Troy. In both versions, Gabriel Oak ends up winning Bathesheba. "The construction of the plot [in the drama] is particularly ingenious and effective, bringing into prominence many of the most interesting scenes embodied in the novel."

76 *"Far From the Madding Crowd,"* Theatre (Lond), 1 April 1882, pp. 244–46.

The play is similar to Arthur Wing Pinero's The Squire which was obviously taken from the same source—H's novel. However, the two plays are quite different. The more carefully constructed Pinero version is pastoral and idyllic, while the H–Comyn Carr version tends to be melodramatic. [Review of the H–Comyn Carr dramatization of *Far From the Madding Crowd* produced at the Prince of Wales Theatre in Liverpool.]

77 Jacobs, Charles P. "Will Mr. Hardy Explain?" Critic (NY), II (28 Jan 1882), 25–26.

The twenty-third chapter of *The Trumpet-Major* contains passages that are so much like passages in Judge Longstreet's Georgia Scenes that the similarity cannot be accidental.

78 *"A Laodicean,"* Critic (NY), II (25 Feb 1882), 53–54.

A Laodicean is disappointing because Paula is an unworthy heroine who has an insignificant love affair with Somerset. Furthermore, the "side-lights" which usually make H's novels worthwhile cannot be found in this book.

79 *"A Laodicean,"* Saturday Review (Lond), LIII (14 Jan 1882), 53–54.

Unlike anything H has done, *A Laodicean* has little rusticity; it may be a new departure for H in the wrong direction. The main characters are not completely explained. The minor figures, Miss De Stancy, Dare, and Havill, are good. Some episodes in the plot are not convincing. The middle-aged Captain behaves oddly, and Paula Power shows a strangely undemonstrative passion for George Somerset.

80 "Mr. Hardy's Novels," Academy, XXI (18 Feb 1882), 120–21.

H occasionally borrowed passages for his novels without crediting his sources. The text of chapter 5 of *A Laodicean* and pp. 381–82 of Quarterly Review, XLIX, match closely, as do passages in the texts of *The Trumpet-Major* and Longstreet's Georgia Scenes.

81 "Novels of the Week," Athenaeum, No. 2873 (18 Nov 1882), 658.

In *Two on a Tower* "the rustics are as Shakespearean as ever; but we must still take leave to doubt whether one Dorsetshire village ever produced quite so many Touchstones at one and the same time."

82 "Recent Novels: *A Laodicean,*" Nation (NY), XXXIV (3 Jan 1882), 18–19.

"Mr. Hardy is an ingenious novelist." [Pure plot summary.]

83 Spoor, Charles T. "Plagiarism on a Plagiarist," NATION (NY), XXXIV (19 Jan 1882), 53.

H borrowed a section from "The Turf" [QUARTERLY REVIEW, XLIX (1833), 381] in composing his description of Sir William de Stancy in *A Laodicean*.

84 "THE SQUIRE," OUR PLAY-BOX, 1 Feb 1882, pp. 107–9.

As Dutton Cook has pointed out, Arthur Wing Pinero's THE SQUIRE was taken from H's *Far From the Madding Crowd*. Pinero may have dramatized the novel more successfully than H could have, but the similarities are too obvious to be attributed to coincidence. [Review of THE SQUIRE, produced at the St. James Theatre, London. See Dutton Cook, J. Mortimer, and Arthur Wing Pinero, "Our Symposium: Plays, Plagiarism, and Mr. Pinero," THEATRE, 1 Feb 1882, pp. 65–73.]

85 *"Two on a Tower,"* SATURDAY REVIEW (Lond), LIV (18 Nov 1882), 674–75.

Two on a Tower is a disappointing work. H's analysis of mentality falls flat because he uses the "affectation of profundity" to express Lady Constantine's commonplace notions. "There is too much incongruity in the treatment, too little explanation of motives and reconciling of seeming discrepancies." Lady Constantine's marriage to the Bishop under peculiar circumstances is contrived and "an extremely repulsive element" in the book. The sayings of the country-folk compensate for the "mingled dullness and eccentricity of the greater part of the book." The astronomical conversations are striking and dramatic.

86 Wedmore, Frederick. "The Acting in THE SQUIRE," ACADEMY, XXI (4 Feb 1882), 91–92.

The acting was "distinctly good," but the piece was somewhat disappointing; it captured only the mechanics and not the genius of *Far From the Madding Crowd*. It was a second-rate play based on a first-rate novel. The skill of stage knowledge is evident, but the play lacks study of character, especially country character.

87 Wedmore, Frederick. *"Far From the Madding Crowd* at the Globe Theatre," ACADEMY, XXI (13 May 1882), 348.

Compared to Pinero's THE SQUIRE this play is a close following of the novel, not a shallow echo. THE SQUIRE is a better piece of play-writing, but H's play is a more true rendition of the setting and characters of the novel. One flaw is the replacement of Boldwood with Will Robin, who avenges his sister's death. This is a melodramatic substitution for a fine dramatic and artistic element in the novel.

1883

88 "Books: *Two on a Tower*," SPECTATOR (Lond), LVI (3 Feb 1883), 154.
"There is not a single gleam of probability in the plot, and what good end can be served by violating all natural motives in order to produce such unpleasant results?" Lady Viviette's passion for Swithin St. Cleve "approaches the repulsive." This is H's worst book.

89 [Ellis, Havelock]. "Thomas Hardy's Novels," WESTMINSTER REVIEW, LXIII (April 1883), 334–64; rptd as part of the long article in FROM MARLOWE TO SHAW: THE STUDIES, 1876–1936, IN ENGLISH LITERATURE OF HAVELOCK ELLIS (1950).
H's women have "something elemental, something *demonic* about them." For H the individual self "is an untamed instinctive creature, eager and yet shy, which is compelled to satisfy its own moderate desires for happiness before it can reflect its joyousness on others." *Far From the Madding Crowd* is perhaps Hardy's finest novel but is damaged by his abuse "of the splendid dramatic power" he commanded. *A Laodicean*, better than any other of his early novels, "succeeds so entirely in satisfying the reader's emotional sense." H's novels are "all love stories," but he has "little or nothing to say about either morals or passion, and yet thinks love is the chief business of life."

90 Engel, Eduard. GESCHICHTE DER ENGLISCHEN LITTERATUR VON IHREN ANFÄNGEN BIS AUF DIE NEUESTE ZEIT MIT EINEM ANHANG DER AMERIKANISCHEN LITTERATUR (History of English Literature From Its Beginnings to the Present With a Postscript on American Literature) (Leipzig: Wilhelm Friedrich, 1883), pp. 565–66.
Far From the Madding Crowd is comparable to the best novels of Thackeray and Dickens. [In German.]

91 Kegan, Paul C. "The Rustic of George Eliot and Thomas Hardy," MERRY ENGLAND, May 1883, pp. 40–51.
These are novelists whose strength "has chiefly lain in touching Mother Earth"; they fail in their "portraiture of the fashionable world." Eliot sees the pathos of the common laborer, but her "profound sympathy" is an examination from the outside. H gives us "natural men and women." Eliot and H agree that "pagan impulses" is the religion of the pure unmixed rustic.

92 "Recent Novels: *The Romantic Adventures of a Milkmaid*," NATION (NY), XXXVII (20 Sept 1883), 255.

H's heroine has adventures like those in a fairy tale—to a point. The mysterious nobleman, who "ought by rights to carry her off in the end," disappears, and the milkmaid "subjects herself to the yoke of a prosaic . . . marriage."

93 "Recent Novels: *Two on a Tower*," NATION (NY), XXXVI (11 Jan 1883), 42–43.

The novel is "a strange mixture of love and astronomy." The novel presents us "an obscurity about Hardy's intentions" in writing it: was it to explore the "relations of love and astronomy?"

94 "Romantic Adventures of a Milkmaid," LITERARY WORLD (Boston), XIV (28 July 1883), 245.

This is a weak, inconsequential, unnatural story. The reader lays the story aside with the feeling that the last mouthful is the least palatable of all.

1884

[No entries for this year.]

1885

95 Purves, James. "Mr. Thomas Hardy's Rustics," TIME: A MONTHLY MAGAZINE, ns I (June 1885), 715–28.

H is "the best portrayer of our English rustics" because of the humor, realism, and completeness of his portraits of them.

1886

96 [Alden, H. M.]. "Editor's Study—I," HARPER'S NEW MONTHLY MAGAZINE, LXXIII (Nov 1886), 961–62.

[Concedes H the use of the wife-sale to gain the reader's attention in *The Mayor of Casterbridge*.] H "has never achieved anything more skillful or valuable in its way than the recognition and development" of Henchard's troubles. H's "first sense of people is apparently not a literary sense, but something very much more natural." *Mayor* is "not inferior to any other story of Mr. Hardy's in its grasp of character."

97 B., H. "London Letter," CRITIC (NY), IX (17 July 1886), 30–31.
The Mayor of Casterbridge is a "disappointment."

98 "Belles Lettres," WESTMINSTER REVIEW, LXX (July 1886), 300.
The Mayor of Casterbridge displays "consummate art in describing persons and places." Henchard "is a grand study, which has not . . . its prototype in fiction."

99 "Celebrities at Home: No. CCCCXL. Mr. Thomas Hardy at Max Gate, Dorchester," WORLD, 17 Feb 1886, pp. 6–7.
H wondered "whether his literary principles will go the way of his architectural canons." As a student of architecture H believed there was but one true style of architecture: thirteenth-century Gothic. " 'Now, where has thirteenth-century architecture gone?' " H queried. [Detailed description of Max Gate and the numerous Roman antiquities which adorned it.]

100 [Hutton, R. H.]. "Books: *The Mayor of Casterbridge*," SPECTATOR (Lond), LIX (5 June 1886), 752–53.
H "has not given us a more powerful study than that of Michael Henchard." Not a "man of character," as H claimed, but "a man of large nature and depth of passion, who is yet subject to the most fitful influences." Because he lacked "fixity of mind," he "ran mostly to waste." H's "fashionable pessimism" is, however, inappropriate to the "homely scenery and characters." H, unfortunately, used "character to mould circumstance," rather than "circumstance to chasten and purify character." Elizabeth-Jane is effectively portrayed, but in a "lower tone of vitality" and on a "higher plane of self-restraint." "We cannot express too warmly our admiration for the art with which that stalwart and wayward nature [Henchard's] has been delineated."

101 "List of New Books," ATHENAEUM, 15 May 1886, p. 645.
Publication of *The Mayor of Casterbridge* is announced.

102 "Minor Fiction," LITERARY WORLD (Boston), XVII (12 June 1886), 198.
The Mayor of Casterbridge is a bold charcoal drawing from the hand of a master. The book has much of H's characteristic quality—the charm, the pathos, the humor and the cleverly hit-off country folk with their odd conceits of thought and speech.

103 "Novels of the Week," ATHENAEUM, No. 3057 (29 May 1886), 711.

H has not quite reached the previously hoped-for heights as a novelist. He is a keen observer of the human situation, a gifted story-teller and plot-constructor. Though not as popular as *The Trumpet-Major, The Mayor of Casterbridge* shows all these qualities. H still insists, however, on using his "far-fetched and unpleasant similes and epithets" and continues to make his peasants sound like Greek philosophers.

104 Payne, W. M. "Recent Fiction," DIAL, VII (July 1886), 67–68.

H's *The Mayor of Casterbridge* "is of the most careful sort and the acuteness of his observation deserves unstinted praise . . . his characters excite the curiosity, but rarely the sympathy of the reader." Although the surroundings are described in realistic terms, the characters "are essentially unreal."

105 R., A. M. F. "A Letter from London," LITERARY WORLD (Boston), XVII (24 July 1886), 249.

H has left his favorite moors of Dorset to live, for a time, in London. There has been of late an unhappy pause, a hiatus in H's fame. Now, in *The Mayor of Casterbridge* he has again made a great and striking success.

106 "Recent Novels: *The Mayor of Casterbridge*," NATION (NY), XLIII (12 Aug 1886), 142.

"Scene by scene . . . the tale is deeply impressive; but . . . it has too many catastrophes in it, whether deaths or deliverances."

107 "Reviews," CRITIC (NY), IX (3 July 1886), 5.

The Mayor of Casterbridge is an "entertaining story" with "much human nature."

108 "Some New Novels," BOOK BUYER, ns III (July 1886), 243.

In *The Mayor of Casterbridge*, Henchard is "one of the most powerful and most interesting of Mr. Hardy's creations." The "style is pure" and the book is "a fine story."

109 "Three Novels," SATURDAY REVIEW (Lond), LXI (29 May 1886), 757.

The Mayor of Casterbridge is not equal to *Far From the Madding Crowd*. Henchard and Farfrae are unreal. The story is slight and uninteresting, and too improbable. No character is capable of arousing interest in his unconvincing passions. The description of Casterbridge and the portrayal of peasants are H's strongest points, best seen in Solomon Longways, the séance, and the "skimmington."

1887

110 [Alden, H. M.]. "Editor's Study—IV," HARPER'S NEW MONTHLY MAGAZINE, LXXV (July 1887), 317–18.

Half of *The Woodlanders* (the study of village folk) reminds the reader of George Eliot; half (the manipulation of events) recalls Charles Reade. Grace's "husband is extremely well found, and his character is discovered to the reader with a subtle effect of unconsciousness on the author's part which is very remarkable."

111 Baxter, Lucy. THE LIFE OF WILLIAM BARNES (Lond: Macmillan, 1887), pp. 151–52.

H's poem "The Collector Cleans his Picture" (in *Late Lyrics and Earlier*) draws upon the experience of his friend, the amateur picture-restorer William Barnes.

112 "Belles Lettres," LONDON QUARTERLY AND HOLBORN REVIEW, LXVIII (July 1887), 382.

In *The Woodlanders,* "the description of the Dorset peasantry, as to their character and manners, and the painting of the local scenery, may be perfect; but the moral of the story is very bad." "Neither into the consciousness of the husband nor even (monstrous to say) of the wife does any thought of the moral enormity, the sin against divine and human law, against all that is sacred and all that is decent, involved in the husband's flagrant and callous and long-continued infidelity, seem to have dawned. Her feelings were cruelly hurt and needed to be healed; that is all."

113 "Belles Lettres," WESTMINSTER REVIEW, CXXVIII (June 1887), 384.

The Woodlanders is set apart from the common category of novels by "something in the texture of the writing . . . 'suggestiveness,' 'thoughtfulness,' or 'pregnancy of style.' " Its perusal is a rare intellectual pleasure.

114 [Hutton, R. H.]. "Books: *The Woodlanders,*" SPECTATOR (Lond), LX (26 March 1887), 419–20.

The novel is powerful and disagreeable: "a picture of shameless falsehood, levity, and infidelity, followed by no true repentance, and yet crowned at the end with perfect success." The book was "written with an indifference to the moral effect it conveys." H is "as usual stronger in his pictures of genuine rural life than in any other part of his story." The "best study in the book is that of the vacillating and restless old timber merchant, Melbury." The only pleasant feature is H's description of the woodlands. There is "more serious fault [to be found here] with H's moral standard than in anything that he has published since *Ethelberta's Hand* [sic]."

115 "A Letter from England," LITERARY WORLD (Boston), XVIII (11 June 1887), 184–85.

The Woodlanders is a masterpiece of beauty and irony; a book to analyze, to understand, to remember.

116 "New Novels," SATURDAY REVIEW (Lond), LXIII (2 April 1887), 484–85.

The Woodlanders is rich and human. Winterborne is H's most sympathetic character, and Grace's description of him in comparison to Fitzpiers is "subtle and original." Two persons from the world of fashion throw the primitive society into discord through the "impassioned drama of their romance." The book is flawed, however; the first several chapters after H's strong opening chapters are labored in language. H's vacillation between an exact facsimile of village talk and the use of pure town talk leads to some false-sounding phrases in the mouths of his peasants. Giles Winterborne is too much a phase of village civilization and not quite enough of an individual.

117 "Novels of the Week," ATHENAEUM, No. 3100 (26 March 1887), 414.

H's style in *The Woodlanders* seems to show that he is in a new period of development, less sensational, less "broadly comic." "In point of construction his more recent stories are excellent," but the "general drift of the story is melancholy, and its ending unsatisfactory."

118 Patmore, Coventry. "Thomas Hardy," ST. JAMES'S GAZETTE, XIV (2 April 1887), 6.

The Woodlanders is not up to H's usual standard. Fitzpiers and Mrs. Charmond "are throughout repulsive," and the "whole interest of the story is spoilt by our being expected to believe" in the reformation of Fitzpiers. In his earlier novels H evoked "a tenderness, reality and force." *Under the Greenwood Tree*, as a prose idyll, ranks with THE VICAR OF WAKEFIELD. H's "love of nature is so passionate and observant . . . [that he is] wasting his powers . . . by expending them upon prose."

119 Payne, W. M. "Recent Fiction," DIAL, VIII (July 1887), 68.

The Woodlanders ought to be a tragedy but fails from lack of seriousness. "The story is tragic enough, but the accessories are not in keeping." "To say that people act thus in real life does not justify their so acting in the novel, at least upon the principles of any higher school of fiction than the photographic one."

120 "Recent Novels: *The Woodlanders*," NATION (NY), XLIV (19 May 1887), 430.

Grace Melbury "affects us unpleasantly, like a noxious weed." She is "Anna Karenina called to a lower state of life." H exalts her "spirituality."

121 Stevenson, Robert Louis. "A Humble Remonstrance," MEM-ORIES AND PORTRAITS (Lond: Chatto & Windus, 1887); rptd (NY: Bigelow, 1906); (NY: Scribner's, 1915); and (NY: Scribner's, 1920), pp. 269–70.

A Pair of Blue Eyes illustrates that the dramatic novel is founded on "one of the passionate *cruces* of life."

122 Wallace, William. "New Novels," ACADEMY, XXXI (9 April 1887), 251–52.

The theme of *The Woodlanders* is the consequence of "The Unfulfilled Intention" in the human situation. The Unfulfilled Intention is that perpetual condition of human relationships which, while lending variety to life, also lends a variety to H's tragic presentations.

123 *"The Woodlanders,"* LITERARY WORLD (Boston), XVIII (14 May 1887), 149–50.

H's admirers will deplore that the optimism expressed in his earlier fictions has descended to a pessimism which is, at least, depressing. *The Woodlanders* arouses keen sympathies on the part of the reader but leaves him, at the end, baffled, stupified, cast down. Marty South is a supremely successful embodiment of homely, faithful love, one which touches sublimity. It is love, if we do not utterly mistake the author's meaning, that conquers at last, and seeing this, we can understand H's calm underlying purpose which may be easily mistaken for indifference, but which is simply the deliberateness of the true artist working toward the solution of a definite problem in that great mystery called life.

1888

124 "Belles Lettres," WESTMINSTER REVIEW, CXXX (July 1888), 115.

Wessex Tales has the piquancy and the personal charm of H's other writings. The world of H's short fiction is "homely and rugged, but never commonplace; intensely real, yet highly idyllic and poetical."

125 "Books: Mr. Hardy's Wessex Stories," SPECTATOR (Lond), LXI (28 July 1888), 1037–38.

Wessex Tales is a collection of "admirable little tales, in which, by their variety and power, the reader's interest is kept up to a high pitch throughout." In "The Three Strangers" "we are brought face to face with perhaps one of the most curious . . . happily ending of that ghastly series of narratives which delight in taking the hangman as their hero." "The Distracted

Preacher" is a "thrilling smuggler's story of daring ingenuity mingled with much which is irresistably comic, and led up to by a gradual unfolding and mutual recognition of character on the part of the two chief actors which make the whole stand out before us with striking reality."

126 Bowker, R. R. "London as a Literary Centre," HARPER'S NEW MONTHLY MAGAZINE, LXXVII (June 1888), 8–9.

H relies "almost entirely" on "the strong impressions of youth." He "hesitates to revisit places seen in childhood, and so fixed in his imagination, lest verification may disillusionize." H lets his characters work out their own destiny.

127 Moore, George. CONFESSIONS OF A YOUNG MAN (Lond: Swan Sonnenschein, Lowry, 1888), pp. 264–70.

"Hardy seems to me to bear about the same relation to George Eliot as Jules Breton does to Millet—a vulgarization never offensive and executed with ability." [Hostile criticism of H's fiction in general, though mainly concerned with *Far From the Madding Crowd*. For the defense of H against Moore's attack, see John Middleton Murry, WRAP ME UP IN MY AUBUSSON CARPET (1924).]

128 "Novels of the Week," ATHENAEUM, No. 2769 (20 Nov 1880), 672.

The Trumpet-Major shows that though H may lack the power "of enthralling the reader's interest," he is second to none "in the art of making one see his scenes and know his characters." John Loveday is the best character H has drawn.

129 Stern, Adolf. GESCHICHTE DER WELTLITERATUR (History of World Literature) (Stuttgart: Rieger'sche Verlagsbuchhandlung, 1888), p. 832.

Like German or Italian regionalists, H presents a comparable view of peasant life through realistic descriptions. Earlier works are admirable but not masterpieces of world literature. [In German.]

1889

130 Barrie, J. M. "Thomas Hardy: The Historian of Wessex," CONTEMPORARY REVIEW (Lond), LVI (July 1889), 57–66; rptd in ECLECTIC MAGAZINE OF FOREIGN LITERATURE, CXIII, ns L (Aug 1889), 258–65.

Life has affected H in three ways: the provincial world of his youth has retained its hold on him; his ideas about young women have become fixed; his conception of human tragedy has been developed. The London professional world must be known to H, but it is strange to the Wessex he knows by heart. H's theory of women is that, on the subject of matrimony, no woman knows her own mind, and this is why H is not popular at Mudie's. As a stylist, H ranks higher than any contemporary novelist.

Desperate Remedies is only a study in other people's methods. *The Hand of Ethelberta, Two on a Tower,* and *A Laodicean* are society novels, and the view of society is preposterous. *Under the Greenwood Tree* is not H's greatest book, but from the appearance of Dick Dewey to the nightingale scene, it is his most perfect—nothing jars. After *Far From the Madding Crowd*, H's novels give the simple rustic characters the effect of puppets, but Oak, Troy, the two Lovedays, and Henchard are not priggish like many heroes of the society novels. The manly Englishman Troy does not preach a moral, even though the moral is beaten into Bathsheba's heart. H shows many multi-lovered women. "If Gabriel remained faithful to Bathsheba, Eustacia would court him on the spot. Elfride might elope with Somerset, get secretly engaged to Troy, and subsequently marry Henchard." [Clever and fresh.]

131 "Literarische Notizen," (Literary Notes), DEUTSCHE RUND-SCHAU, LIX (1889), 158–59.

Aside from the occasional nature descriptions and portrayals of peasant life, *The Woodlanders* is tedious reading. [In German.]

1890

---

132 Cotterell, George. "New Novels," ACADEMY, XXXVIII (2 Aug 1890), 88.

THREE NOTABLE STORIES contains one by the Marquis of Lorne, the second by Mrs. Alexander, and the last by H. H's "Melancholy Hussar" "is as melancholy as its title. This is not a defect, however, for a story ought to answer to its name." There is in all three a great deal of unreality.

133 [Gosse, Edmund William]. "The SPEAKER's Gallery: Thomas Hardy," SPEAKER (Lond), II (13 Sept 1890), 295–96.

Neither H nor Meredith "has the great novel-reading public with them; each enlists the bulk of his readers from the class of male adult persons, and each is the peculiar favourite, in his own generation, of the literary and critical minority." H's portrayal of Dorset with its "interesting and wholly unexhausted population" has a "Shakespearian richness of humor" that "has never, perhaps, been fully appreciated." Men enjoy his "feminine realism." Unlike the "demure, ingenuous, practically inhuman type of heroine" common in current fiction, H's "women are molded of the same flesh as his men," and some of them are actually "of the coming-on disposition." "The Three Strangers" is his most complete short story because "the tension of its wild emotion" raises common scenes of ludicrous humor "to the heights of tragedy." H "is one of the very few living English writers who can be measured with the great masters without sinking into insignificance."

134 Kipling, Rudyard. "The Rhyme of Three Captains," ATHENAEUM, No. 3293 (6 Dec 1890), 776–77.
[Poem attacking H et al for their defense (ATHENAEUM, 22 Nov 1890, p. 701) of Harper and Bros. whom Kipling had charged with piracy.]

135 "New Novels," LITERARY WORLD (Lond), ns XLII (25 July 1890), 74.
In THREE NOTABLE STORIES, by the Marquis of Lorne, Mrs. Alexander, and H, H's "Melancholy Hussar" is the most complete and "notable" of the tales.

136 Rutherford, Mildred. "Thomas Hardy," ENGLISH AUTHORS: A HAND-BOOK OF ENGLISH LITERATURE (Atlanta, Ga: Constitution Book, 1890), p. 722.
[Scanty biographical sketch—worthless.]

137 Steuart, John A. LETTERS TO LIVING AUTHORS (Lond: Sampson Low; NY: United States Book Co., 1890), pp. 101–16.
H's novels are both realistic and idealistic. Since they are never hampered by theories, they contain touches of romance, of inconsistencies, and of the Greek spirit.

1891

138 "Contemporary Literature," NATIONAL REVIEW (Lond), XVII (Aug 1891), 845.
In *A Group of Noble Dames* H is unrecognizable except for his ingenuity of invention, however mechanical and strained in this work. H's plots are unhackneyed, but the heroine is the same in all the stories, and all ten male narrators show H's "unnecessary coarseness." Only two stories, "The First Countess of Wessex" and "The Duchess of Hamptonshire," and two of the ten heroines are not ignoble or worse, following the ugly realistic manner.

"Barbara of the House of Grebe" is "revolting in its forced and hysterical materialism."

139 "Editor's Study," HARPER'S NEW MONTHLY MAGAZINE, LXXXIII (Sept 1891), 641–42.

American Puritans are to be warned against *A Group of Noble Dames* and the passions exhibited by H's "beautiful pagans," who, in their peasant simplicity, pursue men at will, catch them, and have large families.

140 "Fiction," LITERARY WORLD (Boston), XXII (1 Aug 1891), 257.

Though there is humor and vitality in *A Group of Noble Dames*, the book is neither artistically nor morally pleasing.

141 "Fiction," SPEAKER (Lond), III (6 June 1891), 683.

A Group of Noble Dames is the "least satisfactory" of all of H's books; its "chief novelty" is "the exclusion of the humorous rustic," not "the assumption of any fresh material." In the novels, "strange and romantic characters" treated with "consummate skill" make the reader forget the "absurdity" of the plots. "In these shorter stories, H has not the space" to execute this "maneuver."

142 "*A Group of Noble Dames*," LITERARY WORLD (Lond), XLIII (12 June 1891), 556–58.

A Group of Noble Dames is a collection of "old-world romances" wherein H portrays human nature on a social plane somewhat higher than usual. The dames themselves, while not always attractive, are "all interesting, and sometimes not a little puzzling." Although the tales are sometimes cynical, and "Barbara of the House of Grebe" is "too gruesome and heartless for all tastes," the general strength and distinction of the collection would be "impossible to deny."

143 Karpeles, Gustav. ALLGEMEINE GESCHICHTE DER LITTER-ATUR VON IHREN ANFÄNGEN BIS AUF DIE GEGENWART (General History of Literature From Its Beginnings to the Present) (Berlin: G. Grote'sche Verlagsbuchhandlung, 1891), II, 283.

[Passing reference to H's portrayal of English peasant life.] [In German.]

144 Kirk, John Foster. "Thomas Hardy," ALLIBONE'S DICTIONARY (Phila: Lippincott, 1891), III, 764–65.

[Conventional survey of H's schooling and career. Gives extracts from reviews of H's novels and some general criticism.]

145 Minto, Professor [William]. "The Work of Thomas Hardy," BOOKMAN (Lond), I (Dec 1891), 99–101.

Though H is now deemed the greater artist, it is not surprising that *Far From the Madding Crowd* was first thought to be written by George Eliot especially when one looks closely at the opening chapters. Besides a similarity in characterization, they both use "learned scientific language" in description. Perhaps H is not more popular because his psychological examinations into the affairs of man and woman only attract the "meditative" reader.

146 "Modern Men: Thomas Hardy," NATIONAL OBSERVER, V (Feb 1891), 301–2.

The monotonous whine of the sentimentalist is inaudible in H's work, yet there is melancholy in almost every page. His genius is lucent and vigorous, but he chooses to surround himself with a sombre atmosphere. H's rustics are humorous people, and yet he looks on the rustic life very much as Millet did. H shows rare originality in his delineation of character. His view of women is sometimes cynical, yet it is full of tenderness. Will his fame endure? The foundation on which it is erected seems to be entirely stable.

147 "Mr. Hardy's New Novel," SPEAKER (Lond), IV (26 Dec 1891), 770–71.

In *Tess of the d'Urbervilles,* H paints the common folk "with the minuteness, the loving care, the sympathy, the instinctive rightness which characterize his genius." He has never drawn "a sweeter heroine." Tess may have been created to "show the consequences of the heroine's strain of aristocratic blood in her life as a peasant," but H is careful not to make this intention obtrusive. He succeeds in "the most difficult of all the tasks which the writer of fiction can attempt—the portraiture of a living woman." The "inexorable" fate of Tess is "powerful and valuable as a contribution to the ethical education of the world."

148 "Mr. Thomas Hardy," LITERARY OPINIONS, Aug 1891, p. 41.

H's work stands apart from other important novelists in its boldness and freshness. He is the master of rustics as Thackeray is of snobs or Dickens of cockneys. His women are nasty, but he will endure as a great writer.

149 "New Books and Reprints," SATURDAY REVIEW (Lond), LXXI (20 June 1891), 757–58.

A Group of Noble Dames, a "literary freak" by H, is like "the shorter tales of Boccaccio in which the plot is stated like the theorem of a proposition in Euclid. You must work in the characters, and colour the scenery for yourself—as Chaucer and Shakespeare did." "The Marchioness of Stonehenge" is one of the stories that would be admirable for a dramatic writer.

150 "Novels of the Week," ATHENAEUM, No. 3323 (4 July 1891), 35–36.

Wessex has offered H an inexhaustible supply of characters, scenes, and events. "*A Group of Noble Dames* is a collection of short stories about Wessex ladies." Though each story shows those qualities which make H a great novelist, "the scope of the stories hardly gives an opportunity for that homely rustic humour of which Mr. Hardy is a master."

151 "Recent Novels: *A Group of Noble Dames*," NATION (NY), LIII (23 July 1891), 72.

These stories "are told with an inborn gift for story-telling which seems to cost the teller neither study nor effort."

152 [Review of *Tess of the d'Urbervilles*], DAILY CHRONICLE, 28 Dec 1891 [not seen in this form]; rptd in THOMAS HARDY AND HIS READERS: A SELECTION OF CONTEMPORARY REVIEWS, ed by Laurence Lerner and John Holmstrom (1968), pp. 62–63.

Tess of the d'Urbervilles "is as pitiless and tragic in its intensity as the old Greek dramas." Tess's life story is "to the last degree painful"; she falls too easily into Alec's snare. However, "Wessex life and character have never found so graphic a delineator as in Mr. Hardy." Although one wishes H had chosen "a more pleasant subject," "he treats it in a masterly manner."

153 [Review of *Tess of the d'Urbervilles*], PALL MALL GAZETTE, 31 Dec 1891 [not seen in this form]; rptd in THOMAS HARDY AND HIS READERS: A SELECTION OF CONTEMPORARY REVIEWS, ed by Laurence Lerner and John Holmstrom (1968), pp. 64–65.

H's *Tess of the d'Urbervilles* is "a grim Christmas gift," in his "most fateful vein"—like *The Return of the Native*—"with an artistic result of concentrated tragedy such as is rarely to be found in the modern novel." H has "never exercised it [his art] more powerfully . . . than in this most moving presentment of a 'pure woman.'" Angel Clare, however, "is not altogether a convincing creation." The portrait of Tess contains "intimate and profound interpretations of the woman's heart . . . done to death, not by slanderous tongues, but by the tyranny of man, of nature, which makes woman emotionally subject to man, and of social circumstances."

154 "Six Volumes of Short Stories," BOOK BUYER, ns VIII (July 1891), 262.

A Group of Noble Dames is enhanced by "a strong air of reality" utilizing "fresh color and much art." The variety of incident and character make each story "almost a novelette."

155 Une Vieille Baderne. "The Editor of THE DAILY CHRONICLE," DAILY CHRONICLE, 30 Dec 1891 [not seen in this form]; rptd in

THOMAS HARDY AND HIS READERS: A SELECTION OF CONTEMPO-
RARY REVIEWS, ed by Laurence Lerner and John Holmstrom
(1968), pp. 63–64.

In *Tess of the d'Urbervilles*, H "has sounded a depth of unrelieved, relentless darkness that . . . seems hardly in keeping with the general tendency of our Age." There is "a remarkable resemblance between the heroine" of H's novel "and the heroine of a novel that was published by M. Marcel Prévost a little more than two years ago." Mme. Jaufre's husband, however, "is more human than Tess's, and M. Marcel Prévost's novel consequently finishes in a far more satisfactory manner than Mr. Hardy's Aeschylian drama."

156 Wallace, William. "New Novels," ACADEMY, XL (22 Aug
1891), 153.

A Group of Noble Dames is a volume of stories told in a "Decameronian" manner. Each story is unmistakably H's in style and theme. There is clever plot construction, and the dominating theme of the tragedy of fate is ever-present.

157 [Zupitza, Julius]. "Beurteilungen und kurze Anzeigen" (Appraisals and Short Notices), ARCHIV FÜR DAS STUDIUM DER
NEUEREN SPRACHEN, LXXXVII (1891), 321–25.

A Group of Noble Dames is similar to Boccaccio's DECAMERON in style and content. [In German.]

1892

---

158 Adams, Francis. "Some Recent Novels," FORTNIGHTLY RE-
VIEW, LVIII (1 July 1892), 19–22.

The style of *Tess of the d'Ubervilles* is variable. While H is capable of moving passages and descriptions, he falls too often into the cheapest conventions of the popular novelists. All the milkmaids falling in love with the same virtuous young man is sickening. Tess's language is much too lofty for so uneducated a girl. Had H received good criticism for his early efforts, he might have overcome his stylistic defects which render *Tess* a failure. The author's greatest ability is showing the interrelationship of a character and the scene in which he moves.

159 The Baron de Book-Worms. "Our Booking-Office," PUNCH,
CII (27 Feb 1892), 108; rptd in THOMAS HARDY AND HIS READ-
ERS: A SELECTION OF CONTEMPORARY REVIEWS, ed by Laurence
Lerner and John Holmstrom (1968), pp. 83–85.

The one great weakness of *Tess of the d'Urbervilles* is the "stage-scoundrel" character of Alec d'Urberville, who is "absurdly melodramatic."

160 "Belles Lettres," WESTMINSTER REVIEW, CXXXVII (March 1892), 347–48.

The heroine of *Tess of the d'Urbervilles* is "one of the most beautiful creations that Mr. Hardy has given to fictive literature."

161 Blathwayt, Raymond. "A Chat with the Author of *Tess*," BLACK AND WHITE, IV (27 Aug 1892), 238–40.

H appears as a gentle man with a pleasing personality. A happy ending for *Tess of the d'Urbervilles*, H says, would have been a " 'ghastly unreality!' " H was usually familiar with real-life characters before putting them in his fiction. When he wrote *Tess* he wanted to give only the facts, not a judgment, of human nature and the demands put on men and women.

162 "A Chat With Mr. Hardy," BOOK BUYER, ns IX (May 1892), 153.

Tess of the d'Urbervilles was given a sad ending " 'because I could not help myself.' " She could not have been reconciled with Angel because " 'he would have inevitably thrown her fall in her face.' " " 'Justice is satisfied,' " however, by her violent death and the accompanying " 'reparation for her sins.' " She was a "pure woman" until her last fall when " 'she was as a mere corpse drifting in the water to her end—an absolutely irresponsible being.' " Many of H's characters are taken from real life, and simple country people are interesting to write about because many of them "are the representatives of a magnificent antiquity." [Interview, reprinted from BOOK-MAN, issue not noted. Important.]

163 Copeland, C. T. "Recent American and English Fiction," ATLANTIC MONTHLY, LXIX (May 1892), 697–702.

Tess of the d'Urbervilles "is a veritable tragedy, as the Greeks understood and practised tragedy." A thorough discussion of the novel will show that it is just as much a testimony for a deterministic as for a non-deterministic universe. It seems almost a "Hopkinsian" attempt at reconciliation of the two. It is unfortunate that the American edition, besides omitting the preface, omits one of the most moving chapters that can be found in modern literature—the "I baptize thee, Sorrow" chapter. The novel is structurally perfect. But the confinement to one isolated country serves to cramp H's philosophy into mere casuistry.

164 "Culture and Anarchy," NATIONAL OBSERVER, VII (16 April 1892), 555.

Mrs. Humphry Ward's DAVID GRIEVE is supposedly a "novel with a purpose," but she has erred in trying to write a novel at all. H's case, in *Tess of the d'Urbervilles*, is different: it is true that his de-Christianized heroine is an adultress out-and-out. But H is not guilty of fin-de-siècle foolishness and abomination. Some curious factor in the sexual problem has been the motive of nearly all his novels. He has done the art of fiction yeoman service in volunteering to reconquer for the novelist a province of clean, legitimate, and serviceable material.

165 "Fiction: *Tess of the d'Urbervilles*," LITERARY WORLD (Boston), XXIII (13 Feb 1892), 58.

Of late, H has fallen into a vein of fiction which we lament. Tess begins her life in an unlawful connection with a man whom she does not love but who dominates her will. She finally murders him and is justly hanged for it, leaving us not very sorry for her. Tess's career ignores the plain, unwritten instincts of morality.

166 Gosse, Edmund. "The Tyranny of the Novel," NATIONAL REVIEW (Lond), XIX (April 1892), 163–75.

The novel does not reflect an effeminate civilization; if women read H, it is because men have told them that they must. The reception of *Tess of the d'Urbervilles* proves the freedom of the English novelist to say whatever he wishes. H's depiction of Dorsetshire dairy farms in *Tess* is of the highest value, and more thorough than that of the apple culture in *The Woodlanders*.

167 Greenwood, Frederick. "The Genius of Thomas Hardy," ILLUSTRATED LONDON NEWS, CI (1 Oct 1892), 431.

H has an eye "lensed like a microscope," with the enlarging power of perception that Dickens had. H sometimes writes with a too-busy descriptive pen, but he excels in the portrayal of country life.

168 H., C. L. "Letters to the Editor: *Tess of the d'Urbervilles*," SPECTATOR (Lond), LXVIII (30 Jan 1892), 167.

The "apparently coarse word" used by Tess no longer carries its coarse dialectical connotations. It is now "spoken by the most modest to imply a company of slatternly, bickering, and generally unpleasant women."

169 Hannigan, D. F. "The Latest Development of English Fiction," WESTMINSTER REVIEW, CXXXVIII (Dec 1892), 655–59.

Tess of the d'Urbervilles "is a monumental work," "the greatest work of fiction produced in England since George Eliot died." [Reply to Andrew Lang's strictures on *Tess* in NEW REVIEW, Feb 1892.]

170 Hodgson, W. Earl. "A Prig in the Elysian Fields," NATIONAL REVIEW (Lond), XIX (April 1892), 191–99.

[Satire of *Tess of the d'Urbervilles*. Angel Clare is a didactic prig who bores Tess and her father by arguing against the application of moral terms to his acts for the reason that the creator deterministically adjusted his character. Mentions Mrs. Oliphant's attack on Clare (perhaps "The Old Saloon . . ." BLACKWOOD'S MAGAZINE, CLI (March 1892), 464–74).]

171 [Hutton, R. H.]. "Books: Mr. Hardy's *Tess of the d'Urbervilles*," SPECTATOR (Lond), LXVIII (23 Jan 1892), 121–22.

H has written "one of his most powerful novels to illustrate his conviction that not only is there no Providence guiding individual men and women in the right way, but that there is something like a malign fate which draws them out of the right way into the wrong." Tess was not a "pure woman," as H declared. She had "pure instincts" but no "deep sense of fidelity" to them. H illustrates "what every Christian would admit: that if fine natures will not faithfully adhere to such genuine instincts as they have, they may deteriorate, and will deteriorate, in consequence of that faithlessness." Reader's "mind rebels against the steady assumptions of the author, and shrinks from the untrue picture of a universe so blank and Godless." H's view "proceeds from the pantheistic conception that impulse is the law of the universe, and that will . . . is a non-existent fiction."

172 i [pseud of Gleeson White]. "To Thomas Hardy, Esq.," LETTERS TO EMINENT HANDS (Derby: Frank Murray, 1892), pp. 62–66.

H applied the art of the French novelists to the English novel of incident. The English readers instinctively hate H's novels because they hate Art. Though H employs strained events, his characters are entirely human. He treats characters that are common in the world but ignored by other writers. H's greatest success is his use of landscape, atmosphere and the seasons. He uses the common and real to achieve what other writers achieve only with the unscientific and impossible.

173 "In the Library," BOOK BUYER, ns IX (April 1892), 107–8.

The "romantic and realistic schools" of novel-writing: H and Mrs. Ward, who "portray life as they find it," represent the latter; R. L. Stevenson, whose works allow us "to escape from the sewer-gas, the typhus germs, the filthy streets," the former. [Conventional complaint against unhappy endings, as in *Tess of the d'Urbervilles*.]

174 Lang, Andrew. "At the Sign of the Ship," LONGMAN'S MAGAZINE, XXI (Nov 1892), 100–106.

Tess "is a rural Clarissa Harlowe." Angel and Alec are not credible characters, and the language is also inappropriate. H places pretentious scientific terms where they do not belong, for example, in Mrs. Durbeyfield's and Alec's vocabularies. So "for its forbidding conception, for its apparent unreality, for its defects of style, so provokingly superfluous—*Tess of the d'Urbervilles* failed to captivate me." [Also see Lang's original review of *Tess*, "Literature and the Drama," NEW REVIEW, VII (Feb 1892), 247–49, to which H replied in ILLUSTRATED LONDON NEWS, to which Lang's present piece is a reply.]

175 Lang, Andrew. "Literature and the Drama," NEW REVIEW, VII (Feb 1892), 247–49.

The conclusion of *Tess of the d'Urbervilles* is rather improbable in our age of halfpenny newspapers and appeals to the British public. The phrase "The President of the Immortals" is particularly jarring. If there be a God, who can think of him seriously as a malicious fiend? And if there be none, the expression is meaningless. There are moral passages of great beauty in *Tess*; the style is pellucid with a few exceptions. [H responded in ILLUSTRATED LONDON NEWS, and Lang replied in "At the Sign of the Ship," LONGMAN'S MAGAZINE, XXI (Nov 1892), 100–106.]

176 "A Letter from Mr. Thomas Hardy," CRITIC (NY), XXI (10 Sept 1892), 134.

[H's denial that he deliberately suppressed, in the American edition of *Tess of the d'Urbervilles*, the explanatory preface which appears in the English editions. It was, he claims, a matter of circumstances "over which I had no control at the time."]

177 "Literature," CRITIC (NY), XXI (9 July 1892), 13–14.

Tess of the d'Urbervilles, a novel of "absorbing and unflagging" interest, is marred by H's effort to defend Tess as a "pure" woman.

178 Little, James Stanley. "Mr. Hardy's *Tess*," LITERARY WORLD (Lond), XLV (29 April 1892), 412.

In *Tess of the d'Urbervilles*, H emphasizes "the terrible risks the purest women encounter in daily life." Doubtless the more conventional readers will question Tess's purity, but few will quarrel with the "pictorial vividness and truth" of the novel.

179 Little, J[ames] Stanley. "Some Aspects and Tendencies of Current Fiction," LIBRARY REVIEW, I (April 1892), 57–71, espec 62–71.

The central idea of *Tess of the d'Urbervilles* is " 'in the ill-judged execution of the well-judged plan of things the call seldom produces the comer, the man to love rarely coincides with the hour of loving.' " Thus Tess can be defended as a "pure woman." With *Tess*, H "has knocked another nail into the coffin of an uncharitable . . . and archaic moral ordinance" that a woman who has once had a lover must always have one. The novel is "pathetic, tragic, soul-stirring to the very depths."

180 "The Lounger," CRITIC (NY), XVII (16 April 1892), 229.

In an interview H revealed that he hated "the optimistic grin"; he visited a place before attempting to describe it; he drew his characters from real life; he believed country people have "far more sentiment and romance than the class above them."

181 Morris, Mowbray. "Culture and Anarchy," QUARTERLY RE-VIEW, CLXXIV (April 1892), 317–43.

Tess is not a "pure woman." It appears that the beginning of the novel was meant to illustrate the law of heredity, but Tess then acts too implausibly —returning to Alec after Angel's departure—to carry on that idea. "Mr. Hardy has told an extremely disagreeable story in an extremely disagreeable manner, which is not rendered less so by his affectation of expounding a great moral law, or by the ridiculous character of some of the scenes into which this affectation plunges the reader." H's early humor has departed, and he attempts too much moralizing. H has misread or forgotten the Greek and Elizabethan dramas "if he conceives that there is any analogy between their great handling of tragic motives and this clumsy sordid tale of boorish brutality and lust." The rustics are caricatures, but they are "extremely amusing caricatures, and founded, moreover, as Dickens's are founded, in the essential facts of humanity." H and Mrs. Ward have taken too seriously the attitude of the times, and so they waste their energies in attempting to inculcate reforms.

182 "Mr. Andrew Lang and Mr. Thomas Hardy," ILLUSTRATED LONDON NEWS, CI (5 Nov 1892), 579.

Lang finally confesses that he must defer to the public opinion and consider *Tess of the d'Urbervilles* a masterpiece. Still he considers the language of the characters frequently inappropriate. Alec's reference to his child as a "babe" is an example "of unreality as if one were reading a morally squalid fairy tale."

183 "Mr. Hardy's New Novel," TIMES (Lond), 13 Jan 1892, p. 13.

Tess of the d'Urbervilles is H's greatest novel; a novel daring in the treatment of conventional ideas; a novel sad and tragic. Tess, the pure woman of the title, challenges convention which denies her purity with its own corruption. *Tess* is tragic because happiness is "missed by a hair's-breadth." Tess knows her misfortune but understands no lapse of innocence in herself. When her husband-to-be reveals some small London dissipation, Tess counter-reveals with her lapse, imagining she will be accepted in the same spirit in which she accepted. The idyllic description of place and characters of the farm and field are too "Arcadian." However, the peasants' fatalism and grim sense of fact is always present.

184 "Mr. Hardy's *Tess of the d'Urbervilles*," REVIEW OF REVIEWS (NY), V (Feb 1892), 200.

H's novel "can hardly fail to take rank as its author's greatest work" to date. The influence of French realism "is strong both for good and ill" in the novel, and H may have sacrificed "the higher truth of imagination for a . . . lower kind of fidelity to the ignoble facts of life." Nonetheless *"Tess of the d'Urbervilles* is truly a great work" and gives the impression "of a cretive personality in some ways greater than the thing created."

185 "New Books. *Tess of the d'Urbervilles*," BOOKMAN (Lond), I (Feb 1892), 179–80.

Those who read *Tess of the d'Urbervilles* as a moral treatise misread H's greatest achievement. Indeed, the novel contains philosophical elements, but H is primarily concerned with depicting the tragic life of Tess and defending her purity to the last.

186 "News Notes," BOOKMAN (Lond), III (Oct 1892), 6.

"The opinions of novelists on novels are always very interesting, whether one agrees with them or not. Mr. Hardy is known specially to admire the writings of George Gissing." [Slight.]

187 Newton-Robinson, Janetta. "A Study of Mr. Thomas Hardy," WESTMINSTER REVIEW, CXXXVII (Feb 1892), 153–64.

Tess's nature is "charged with inarticulate poetry." She is elemental, "superior to all accidents of station or errors of inexperience." "She exists in a state of dreamy exaltation." H's intensity leads him to introduce melodramatic incidents, distasteful details, or bizarre happenings to create an impression which "resembles . . . some weird medieval grotesque." "Mr. Hardy has no direct descent from any other novelist."

188 "Novels," SATURDAY REVIEW (Lond), LXIII (16 Jan 1892), 73–74.

"There is not one single touch of nature in John Durbeyfield or in any other character" in *Tess of the d'Urbervilles*. "The sequence of lightning and thunder is not more prompt than that of cause and effect" in H's stories, as seen in Durbeyfield's destruction of his family. H's suggestions concerning the sexuality of Tess's appearance and about Mrs. Durbeyfield's character render the novel "very disagreeable." H's grammar is not good, and "it must be conceded, Mr. Hardy tells an unpleasant story in a very unpleasant way." "Few people will deny the terrible dreariness of this tale, which, except during the few hours spent with cows, has not a gleam of sunshine anywhere."

189 "Novels of the Week," ATHENAEUM, No. 3350 (9 Jan 1892), 49–50.

It was Huxley who compared life to playing chess with a devious and brutal opponent; this is the attitude of life H presents in *Tess of the d'Urbervilles*. The game is intricately planned and skillfully presented by H. Though many of H's disagreeable habits are present, we must rate *Tess* "high amongst the achievement of Victorian novelists."

190 [Oliphant, M.O.W.?]. "The Old Saloon: *Tess of the d'Urbervilles*," BLACKWOOD'S MAGAZINE, CLI (March 1892), 464–74.

Tess of the d'Urbervilles is the best of H's novels to date, although the author "is not one of our first favorites in fiction" because of his anti-religion and his obsessive interest in the "relations between the sexes." There are serious implausibilities of characters and plot, but the sense of life is genuine. Tess, moreover, is not always consistent; when she leaves Alec and goes to Angel Clare she is not behaving as "A Pure Woman" would. [Alternately fatuous and intelligent.]

191 [Page, Thomas Nelson]. "Editor's Study, I," HARPER'S NEW MONTHLY MAGAZINE, LXXXV (June 1892), 152–53.

None of H's novels before *Tess of the d'Urbervilles* gave "such exquisite landscapes." But there is a certain scientific jargon which has "a slight effect of strain, if not of artificiality." H's effort to show that English writers can deal with passion "has a little of the air of a *tour de force*." H makes Tess act in uncharacteristic fashion in her return to Alec and in her "last moral insensibility to crime."

192 Payne, W. M. "Recent Fiction," DIAL, XII (April 1892), 424.

Tess of the d'Urbervilles has many melodramatic qualities. It is a "tribute to . . . [H's] art that he can succeed in attaching our sympathies to such a character or arousing our interest in such a preposterous series of events." There are certain echoes of Ibsen. The manner of the book is realism; its method is that of photography.

193 "Recent Fiction," BOOK BUYER, ns IX (March 1892), 68–69.

Tess of the d'Urbervilles, if not the best novel of 1891, is one of the author's best stories. The portrayal of Tess, the "tragic undercurrent" caused by her seduction, the love scenes, the pictures of country life, and the characters of Tess's mother and father are all done with great artistry.

194 "Recent Fiction," NATION (NY), LIV (28 April 1892), 325–26.

The subtitle of *Tess of the d'Urbervilles* is misleading and immoral. Tess, far from being pure, is a weak and sensual woman. D'Urberville is an incorrigible rogue; Angel Clare, in fact, is the only moral character in the novel; who, rather than being overly severe and narrow-minded, is indeed a good, just and reasonable man. *Tess*, in short, is as profoundly immoral and dangerous a book as a young person can read.

195 [Rhys, Ernest?]. " 'Hodge' As I Know Him: A Talk With Mr. Thomas Hardy," PALL MALL GAZETTE, LIV (2 Jan 1892), 1–2.

H observed that village life is dull because small freeholders have moved away; villagers enjoy fiction-romance. H has seen many of his characters walking in Wessex and believes them to be representative of antiquity.

196 Sharp, William. "Thomas Hardy and His Novels," FORUM, XIII (July 1892), 583–93; rptd in BOOK NEWS MONTHLY, XII (March 1894), 274–76.

H at his best is one of England's most remarkable novelists, but his popularity is "independent of the literary value . . . of his work." He is a "profound realist," robust of thought and speech. His style is not appreciated because of its austere dignity. His genius is inevitable, sombre, pervasive, and unobtrusive. Though H is profoundly sad, he is not a pessimist. Even his first novels show his originality. *Under the Greenwood Tree* is unique, purely English, vivid. *Far From the Madding Crowd* shows his whole art. *The Return of the Native* is his masterpiece. *The Woodlanders* is a "nobly wrought" book. *Tess of the d'Urbervilles* is the most mature and powerful expression of H's genius and is deeply human. Tess is "as *living* a woman as there is in fiction."

197 "Sylvanus Urban." "Table Talk," GENTLEMAN'S MAGAZINE, CCLXXIII (Sept 1892), 321.

Despite the charm of the rural scenes, *Tess of the d'Urbervilles* is not a great novel. The influence of French realism is too strong; it overpowers the attractiveness of the English nature painting. H was quite bold in permitting his virtuous heroine to be seduced twice. The realism of Tess's slaying Alec is like Pauline Blanchard's murder of her husband in the presentation given recently by Sarah Bernhardt.

198 *"Tess of the d'Urbervilles,"* LITERARY WORLD (Boston), XXIII (4 June 1892), 192–93.

Nothing in *Tess of the d'Urbervilles* is more astonishing than the acceptance, by critics and readers, of the assertion contained in the subtitle. H acquits the prisoner at the bar when neither testimony nor plea has been heard. No woman, unless born and reared in the midst of vice, could remain pure in spirit through the vicissitudes of Tess. Her return to Alec cancels the subtitle of the story, makes it presumptuous and profoundly immoral. With the vitally important exception noted, the romance is very strong in construction. More than once, a too elaborate phrase gives a tint over-subtle for the local color. There are, indeed, great qualities and great defects in *Tess*.

199 "Thomas Hardy," BOOK BUYER, ns IX (May 1892), 151–53.

H begins writing immediately after breakfast, and, if he should happen to go out before his day's work is finished, he cannot return to his writing until after sunset. Most of his work represents a second writing, although "many chapters of his stories have been printed exactly as they were first written." H's job as acting magistrate brings him into contact with the hardships and misfortunes of people.

200 "Thomas Hardy's Latest Novel," INDEPENDENT (NY), XLIV (25 Feb 1892), 276.

"Tess was not a pure woman." She merits the reader's sympathy, but she is unquestionably "defiled" by her two affairs with Alec. Moreover, *Tess of the d'Urbervilles* as a whole does little to "refine and ennoble." It was written for no purpose of reforming wayward humanity, but simply as a sensationalistic commercial venture. In spite of its "noisome" elements, however, it is, in point of craftsmanship and power, "well-nigh perfect."

201 "Thomas Hardy's Wessex," BOOKMAN (Lond), I (March 1892), 26–28.

[The usual tour through H country identifying "localities, partially veiled by fictitious names" in H's work.]

202 Trent, W. P. "The Novels of Thomas Hardy," SEWANEE RE-VIEW, I (Nov 1892), 1–25.

Tess of the d'Urbervilles is "the greatest tragedy since Shakespeare." H is a great novelist for four reasons: he has great and individual style, power of describing and interpreting inanimate nature, power as a narrator, and power of characterization.

203 Truman, Joseph. "Tess and Angel Clare," BOOKMAN (Lond), II (April 1892), 11.

[A poem attempting a sympathetic evocation of H's "vision of despair" in *Tess of the d'Urbervilles.*]

204 Watson, W[illiam]. "Literature," ACADEMY, XLI (6 Feb 1892), 125–26; rptd as "Mr. Thomas Hardy's *Tess of the d'Urber-villes*," in EXCURSIONS IN CRITICISM (Lond: Mathews & Lane; NY: Macmillan, 1893), pp. 70–80.

The tragedy of *Tess of the d'Urbervilles* is H's greatest achievement. The theme of the book is the penalty paid by the innocent for the misdeeds of the wicked. The agony H expresses over the tragedy of human misfortune is equal to the agony he expresses over the unjust and unnatural qualities of inflexible social mores, customs, and unwritten laws.

205 Zupitza, Julius. "Beurteilungen und kurze Anzeigen" (Appraisals and Short Notices), ARCHIV FÜR DAS STUDIUM DER NEUEREN SPRACHEN, LXXXVIII (1892), 217–18.

In *Tess of the d'Urbervilles*, H should present his female protagonists in a more favorable light. [Plot summary.] [In German.]

1893

206 Chesson, W. H. *"Tess,"* LITERARY WORLD (Lond), ns XLVIII (28 July 1893), 78.

Physically, Tess was the mate of Alec; spiritually, she was the wife of Angel. This radical division of her self precluded any facile resolution of the plot and ultimately forced the murder and hanging. [See R. K. Elliot and Harriet Waters Preston (1893).]

207 Elliot, Robert Kerr. "Tess," LITERARY WORLD (Lond), ns XLVIII (21 July 1893), 62.

Harriet Waters Preston's expression "a paroxysm of blind rage" refers not to the death of Tess but to her fall. [Simply a clarification of Harriet Waters Preston's "probable intent," which was evidently misconstrued by W. H. Chesson, judging from his letter in ibid (28 July 1893), 78.]

208 Hannigan, D. F. "Prospective Transformation of the Novel," WESTMINSTER REVIEW, CXL (Aug 1893), 256–60.

H is a "genuinely realistic" novelist, but in nearly all his books he falls into "errors of romanticism," or melodrama. The criticism of *Tess of the d'Urbervilles* as coarse or objectionable is "essentially idiotic." "It is not Mr. Hardy but Mr. Rider Haggard that should be exorcised."

209 "New Novels and New Editions," LITERARY WORLD (Lond), XLVIII (28 July 1893), 74.

The Mayor of Casterbridge, while it may not "in its analysis of character and strong dramatic situation equal some of his later works," is interesting and "exciting from the outset."

210 "Notes About Authors," LITERARY WORLD (Lond), XLVII (28 April 1893), 392.

[Biographical and bibliographical sketch.]

211 Preston, Harriet Waters. "Thomas Hardy," CENTURY, ns XXIV (July 1893), 352–59; partly rptd in REVIEW OF REVIEWS (NY), VIII (Aug 1893), 211; rptd as "A Woman's View of Tess," in THOMAS HARDY AND HIS READERS: A SELECTION OF CONTEMPORARY REVIEWS, ed by Laurence Lerner and John Holmstrom (1968), with errors in date of REVIEW OF REVIEWS appearance.

Until the publication of *Tess of the d'Urbervilles,* H was only half appreciated. In *Under the Greenwood Tree* H first used the chorus of rustics that has become so characteristic and successful. H is like Shakespeare in the reproduction of their speech and humor. In *A Pair of Blue Eyes* H first tried the recurrent theme of "the capacity for headlong and devouring passion of an innocent but ardent woman, the capacity for sheer brutality of a baffled and angry man, and the helpless slavery to circumstance of them both." The common complaint that *Far From the Madding Crowd* is too sensational is unjust because even H did not invent catastrophes more horrible than what actually occur. In *The Return of the Native, The Mayor of Casterbridge*, and *Tess*, H is "positively epic." *Native* ranks with KING LEAR and THE MASTER OF RAVENSWOOD as "unadulterated tragedy." Henchard in *Mayor* ranks with Oedipus and Siegfried in the proportions of the conflict within him between good and evil and in his defeat by exterior forces. The characters of Lady Constantine in *Two on a Tower* and Felice Charmond in *The Woodlanders* are "pathological" and suited only for "a professional book." H's descriptions in *Woodlanders* are "Vergilian." In *Tess*, H leaves the role of artist only and "adopts a cause." Through nearly the entire story —Tess's early fall, her penance, her life on the dairy, her rejection by Angel Clare, her wretchedness as an abandoned wife—the reader is convinced of Tess's essential goodness. But when she yields a second time to her "now doubly repulsive seducer," the novel is ruined, and the subsequent events become "mere vulgar horrors, gratuitously insulting to the already outraged feelings of the deeply disappointed reader." [See W. H. Chesson and R. K. Elliott (1893).]

212 Stevenson, Robert Louis. "Mr. Stevenson on Himself and His Contemporaries," CRITIC (NY), XXII (17 June 1893), 407–8.
[Stevenson acknowledged that he enjoyed reading H but "could not manage" *Tess of the d'Urbervilles*.]

1894

213 [Alden, Henry M.]. "Thomas Hardy," HARPER'S WEEKLY, XXXVIII (8 Dec 1894) [not seen in this form]; rptd in THOMAS HARDY AND HIS READERS: A SELECTION OF CONTEMPORARY CRITICISM, ed by Laurence Lerner and John Holmstrom (1968), pp. 104–7.
H's purpose is always "to deal with simple hearts in the common conditions of life." In order to understand his moral attitude one must accept the limits he sets up. He is not primarily a philosopher or preacher. One can demand nothing of him but truth. Tess suffers without rescue for the sake of truth; that is, because it is her destiny in H's view of the " 'grimness of the general human situation.' " Although H is not trying to moralize, his novel is totally

in keeping with Christianity. While he does not illustrate the reconciling principle of regeneration, he does not preclude it, and offers no other. [Alden, an editor of HARPER'S WEEKLY, bowdlerized H's *Tess* for serial publication.]

214 Av[eling, Edward]. "Pis'ma iz Anglii" (Letters from England), RUSSKOE BOGATSTVO, Jan 1894, pp. 73–76.

Life's Little Ironies is the work of "a writer whom we consider to be one of the most remarkable of the contemporary English belletrists." Each of the first eight stories is "full of life" and "deals with some event which is intended to serve as an illustration of the author's main idea and to reaffirm the eternal truth that we are toys in the hands of fate." Those critics who have attacked H for indecent sexual allusions are wrong: the same kind of thing is to be found in the "SPECTATOR 180 years ago." "In all of Hardy's works, one is struck by his remarkable powers of observation. . . . Every character, every situation is sketched vividly and distinctly, so that it is impossible to substitute one character for another, as is the case with some other writers." [In Russian.]

215 "Books: *Life's Little Ironies*," SPECTATOR (Lond), LXXII (21 April 1894), 537–39.

The plots "would have furnished an ordinary writer with far better material." Irony "lies in the fact that the very actions which were to have brought happiness, gratified ambitions, or at least a quiet conscience in their train, really bring nothing but increased misery and despair." "Stern impersonal directness" leaves "upon the reader's mind a dreary feeling of inevitableness as he follows the chain being remorselessly forged for its victims," who are in some "unknown Power's employ." Females are flawed by "a touch of vulgarity." "H's control of the English language must always arouse genuine admiration."

216 Dolman, Frederick. "An Evening with Thomas Hardy," YOUNG MAN, VIII (Jan–Dec 1894), 75–79.

" 'I don't believe in that idea of a man's imaginative powers becoming naturally exhausted; I believe . . . a man could go on writing till his physical strength gave out. . . . The great secret is, perhaps, for a writer to be content with the life he was leading when he made his first success.' " To H the drama "is an inferior form of art." H expected criticism in writing *Tess of the d'Urbervilles* but " 'the criticism has not come from the people I expected. . . . As a matter of fact, my tone has been the same in regard to moral questions for the twenty years or more I have been writing. From the very beginning I resolved to speak out.' " Someone suggested to H that Tess " 'illustrated the evil that may be done by suddenly destroying a man's faith as Clare did Alec's through Tess handing on his opinions. But I fear the author was Balaam in that.' "

217 Godfrey, Dan, with Olga Nethersole. "Mr. Thomas Hardy," CABINET PORTRAIT GALLERY, Part 57 (June 1894), 65–67. [Brief biography.]

218 "In One Volume," SPEAKER (Lond), IX (17 March 1894), 314–15.

The stories of *Life's Little Ironies* are of "unequal merit, one or two, indeed, being distinctly inferior" to H's ordinary work, but overall, his "genius is to be recognized." They all have "a certain ironical turn that has of late become more and more the prevailing note" in H's writing.

219 Johnson, Lionel. THE ART OF THOMAS HARDY (Lond: Mathews & Lane; NY: Dodd, Mead, 1894; Lond: Lane; NY: Dodd, Mead, 1895; "to which is added a chapter on the poetry, by J. E. Barton and a bibliography by John Lane . . .," Lond: Lane; NY: Dodd, Mead, 1923 [qv]); rvd and rptd (NY: Dodd, Mead, 1928).

H's well-designed novels are characterized by richness of detail, a concern with "modern subtleties of emotion and of thought," economy in the use of words, and accuracy of description. Each of these novels deals with one great theme: "Wessex, and its people." In dealing with Wessex, H shows his concern for the past *and* present of an English county. Taking us into a definite sphere, he impresses on us a sense of the familiarity of his scenes and, in his best novels, creates an atmosphere which has a meditative quality. Immersed in this atmosphere are heroes capable of "a wise passiveness," rustics who are both naturally ignorant and shrewdly humorous, and a variety of people who are "natural growths of the soil." The rustics are of particular interest in that they are barely affected by city life, are Shakespearean, and are fatalistic. Despite a certain "mental immobility," they display their fatalistic ideas "racily and richly" and are clearly in harmony with their surroundings. In contrast, other characters are clearly "at variance with the fundamental principles and crowning issues" of their lives. This is true of the three classes of Wessex characters "most worthy of consideration": the country heroes and lovers, the variety of women, and the attractive youths. Frequently in the novels the strongest of these are brought into contact with people superior to them in education, but inferior to them "in strength and firmness of nature." When love influences these contrasting types, a pattern develops: the action of the novel quickens and the actors engage in conflicts marked by strong attraction and strong repulsion. Although this pattern may vary from novel to novel, each novel has something in common with every other novel: either a discord is resolved into a harmony, or harmony is broken by a discord. The country heroes, the lovers, the various women, the youths, the "excellent divines," and the multitude of other Wessex characters are all affected by both the harmony and the discord. Furthermore, the effect is felt keenly, since H never courts popular tastes and is always ardently sincere. Despite this sincerity, faults can be detected in the novels. Occasionally H will use "fitful phrases" or, as in *Tess of the d'Urbervilles*, include inartistic and obscure remarks and inconsistencies. Also, since he denies that man has a conscience, his arguments are "made sterile" and his determinism strikes the reader as "haunting and disenchanting."

220 "Joseph Kirkland," DIAL, XVI (16 May 1894), 293.

Kirkland, the minor American realist, was an "enthusiastic admirer" of H's work and his own success was along lines laid down by that novelist.

221 "Literarische Notizen" (Literary Notes), DEUTSCHE RUNDSCHAU, LXXIX (1894), 158–59.

In *Tess of the d'Urbervilles*, H treats his theme realistically, but provides poor character motivation. [In German.]

222 "Literature," CRITIC (NY), XXIX (5 May 1894), 298–99.

Despite H's genius *Life's Little Ironies* is an unpleasant book. H plays Jove, laughing "at the feeble woes of mortals . . . and with a cynic smile on his lips [laying] bare to all the world their pathos and uncompromising misery." "There is nothing more harrowing in modern literature, and we regret that we have ever read this book, so much has it affected us."

223 Macdonell, Annie. THOMAS HARDY (Lond: Hodder & Stoughton, 1894; NY: Dodd, Mead, 1895).

H is best approached without specific reference to the various traditions of the English novel or even to his own historical and intellectual milieu, for he is largely independent of either. All his fiction is uniquely his own. His early work achieves a kind of "pictorial unity" of effect, but his mature novels move toward the structural unity of a five-act form. Throughout his fiction, however, both the pictorial quality and the form serve as "illustration and commentary" supporting a basically "poetic" idea or intention. His handling of character might also be called "poetic," for his people are never completely and exclusively realistic. They always have enough of the abstract or unusual about them to make them more than transcripts of life. His rustics in particular are not the result of any "phonographic" capturing of behavior or speech; they are, rather, representations of rustic speech and thought in the abstract. In spite of his poetic intention, however, H has, in the creation of character as in all other aspects of his fiction, remained aloof from the fashionable moralistic tendency in the novel. He doesn't argue; he simply creates. His most persistent theme is perhaps the destructive nature of passion, but in his view passion is not wrong, only tragic—for it is ever "unsatisfied."

224 "New Fiction," BOOK BUYER, ns XI (April 1894), 131–32.
In *Life's Little Ironies* "Mr. Hardy has compressed as the druggists do in convenient tablets the truth and bitterness of Fate." It may be welcomed by those tired of the "metaphysical romance of the time."

225 "Novels and Stories," SATURDAY REVIEW (Lond), LXXVII (31 March 1894), 339–41, espec 340.
In *Life's Little Ironies* "the ironies that appear 'little' to the remote spectator are shrewd, cutting, and great to the victims." The most trenchant and affecting story is "Tragedy of Two Ambitions," which makes the most effective use of the humor inherent in life's ironies to be found in any of the stories. In the appended sketches, "A Few Crusted Characters," H appears again as the delightful creator of Joseph Poorgrass and the *Wessex Tales*.

226 "Novels and Tales," NATIONAL OBSERVER, XI (10 March 1894), 429.
A great deal of *Life's Little Ironies* is excellent. The issues H deals with are tragic even if the tragedy is homespun. The last three tales are the best. The issues are plain, the passions elemental. There is none of the paradox that disfigured *Tess of the d'Urbervilles*. The style is reticent and sober. The stories are models of their kind.

227 "Novels of the Week," ATHENAEUM, No. 3465 (24 March 1894), 367.
H "who excels pre-eminently in those little half-sketched glimpses that suggest the whole situation" but do not reveal the situation completely, rather leaving the mind free to play with the "weirdly powerful" glimpses, has created in *Life's Little Ironies* some "magnificently sombre pictures of Wessex life." In the second part of the book, "A Few Crusted Characters," we find some delightfully humorous stories, not quite so ominous as the first part.

228 Owen, R. "A Thomas Hardy Choir," OUTLOOK (NY), L (16 June 1894), 1095–97.
[A description of a church choir of instrumentalists that survived into the 1890s similar to several H described, especially that of *Under the Greenwood Tree*.]

229 Payne, W. M. "Recent Fiction," DIAL, XVI (16 June 1894), 367.
Life's Little Ironies contains "a score of tales and character sketches" of "people who would be absolutely uninteresting in hands of any less a master."

230 Raymond, Walter. "Mr. Thomas Hardy's New Book," BOOK-MAN (Lond), VI (April 1894), 18–19.

One finds in the collection of stories which make up *Life's Little Ironies* the same fine qualities which mark H's longer works: "delicacy of diction, the sweetness of simple English, the purity and charm of style." The stories are filled with irony, humor, pathos, and excellent characterization.

231 S., D. "The Bookmarker: A New Book by Thomas Hardy," TO-DAY, II (10 March 1894), 138–39.

The short stories in *Life's Little Ironies* are "quite Chaucerian in their humour and power of characterization." If the volume had been a novel, it might have created "as great a stir as *Tess*."

232 St. George, George. "*Life's Little Ironies*," LITERARY WORLD (Lond), XLIX (23 March 1894), 259–60.

H's stories in *Life's Little Ironies*, like his novels, have a strange reticence; an impersonality which at once reveals and denies the author's personal involvement in their action. Such a quality denies H some popularity with the average reader, but along with his tragic sense, his power of description, and his gift for humor, it makes his stories "more modern, more *fin de siècle*."

233 Saintsbury, George. "New Novels," ACADEMY, XLV (2 June 1894), 453.

Life's Little Ironies shows that as long as H dwells on "pessimist-realist" themes, his talents will be better revealed and more appreciated in short stories than in longer works.

234 "Table Talk," LITERARY WORLD (Lond), XLIX (11 May 1894), 437.

The stories in *Life's Little Ironies* are dangerous for a " 'girl,' in the old-fashioned sense of the word," to read. "The whole atmosphere is full of sensuality."

235 Y., G. [pseud of Robert Lynd]. "In the d'Urberville Country," BOOKMAN (Lond), VI (May 1894), 46–48.

A wanderer through Wessex is inevitably struck by its strange mixture of fiction and reality. The reality is in the places and monuments which distinguish this land; the fiction is in the knowledge that the things have been shaped into distinction by the writing of one man.

236 Zupitza, Julius. "Beurteilungen und kurze Anzeigen" (Appraisals and Short Notices), ARCHIV FÜR DAS STUDIUM DER NEUEREN SPRACHEN, XCIII (1894), 35–51.

Life's Little Ironies can be highly recommended to all adults but, like *A Group of Noble Dames* and *Tess of the d'Urbervilles*, it was not written for children. [In German.]

1895

237 Another Woman. " 'The New Hardy,' " NATIONAL OBSERVER, XIV (1 June 1895), 82.

"Poor Tess! 'Of course she wasn't' what the reviewer [author of "The New Hardy," ibid (18 May 1895), 11–12] is thinking of. Yet she was not *a pure woman* for all that—just a woman, and nothing else."

238 "Briefer Mention," DIAL, XIX (1 July 1895), 24.

"Of much interest is the prefatory note in which Hardy tells how he came to naturalize the term 'Wessex' in modern English for purposes of descriptive topography." [Description of a new edition of Harper's *Far From the Madding Crowd.*]

239 Dolman, Frederick. "The Wife of Thomas Hardy," LADIES' HOME JOURNAL, XII (May 1895), 5.

H met and married Emma Gifford when he was helping to restore a church in Devonshire. She encouraged him to turn to literature, made a fair publisher's copy of *Desperate Remedies* for him, and also kept notebooks for him of his future fictional characters.

240 Gilder, Jeannette. "Thomas Hardy Makes a New Departure," WORLD (NY), 8 Dec 1895, p. 33.

"What has gone wrong with the hand that wrote *Far From the Madding Crowd?*" *Jude the Obscure* "is almost the worst book I have ever read." The book's coarseness is beyond belief. Jude and Arabella are "beast[s]"; Sue is "impossible"; Father Time is an "absurdity." H's mind "seems to run to pigs—animal and human" in the novel. "When I finished the story I opened the windows and let in the fresh air . . . and I said 'Thank God for Kipling and Stevenson, Barrie and Mrs. Humphry Ward . . . four great writers who never trailed their talents in the dirt.' "

241 [Gilder, Jeannette L.]. "Hardy the Degenerate," WORLD (NY), 13 Nov 1895 [not seen in this form]; rptd in THOMAS HARDY AND HIS READERS: A SELECTION OF CONTEMPORARY REVIEWS, ed by Laurence Lerner and John Holmstrom (1968), p. 113.

H's realism in *Jude the Obscure* is "not merely gratuitous, but disgusting." That it is directed to adult readers is no excuse; British men and women are not interested in the butchering of pigs. A bad blend of Zola and Tolstoy. [Also see Jeannette Gilder, "Thomas Hardy Makes a New Departure," WORLD (NY), 8 Dec 1895, p. 33; and Paul Lemperly (pub and ed), JUDE THE OBSCURE: A LETTER AND A FOREWORD (1917).]

242 Howells, W. D. "Life and Letters," Harper's Weekly, XXXIX (7 Dec 1895), 1156; rptd in Thomas Hardy and His Readers: A Selection of Contemporary Reviews, ed by Laurence Lerner and John Holmstrom (1968), pp. 115–17.

In *Jude the Obscure* H returns to the Greek mode of tragedy, linking the present with the pre-Christian world where there is no Providence, only Fate. The character of Jude is always dignified, and even such a fool as Sue is pitiable. The book may be morbid, but it is true. However unpleasant the events, they are true to the human condition. If it seems to challenge certain customs, such questioning is healthy.

243 Howells, William Dean. My Literary Passions (NY: Harper, 1895), p. 182.

"I love even the faults of Hardy, I will let him play me any trick he chooses. His people live very close to the heart of nature, and no one, unless it is Tourguenief, gives you a richer and sweeter sense of her unity with human nature. Hardy is a great poet as well as a great humorist, and if he were not a great artist also his humor would be enough to endear him to me."

244 Japp, Alexander H. "Two Pairs of Novelists," Cassell's Family Magazine, XXI (June 1895), 530–31.

H's novels portray, "so far as their individual pictures are concerned, the truest photographs of peasant life in Dorsetshire and round about it." H attains his insight "by living among the people, entering into their life and ways; by an educated sympathy realising their feelings, and so comprehending their actions."

245 "Jude the Obscene," Pall Mall Gazette, 12 Nov 1895 [not seen in this form]; rptd in Thomas Hardy and His Readers: A Selection of Contemporary Reviews, ed by Laurence Lerner and John Holmstrom (1968), pp. 109–11.

For lovers of H, *Jude the Obscure* is worth little more than tears, a book full of "dirt, drivel, and damnation," and unrelieved gloom.

246 "Literature," Critic (NY), XXVII (28 Dec 1895), 437. [Review of "Hearts Insurgents," the version of *Jude the Obscure* serialized in Harper's Magazine. The reviewer is mainly concerned about protecting young people—especially young girls—from "contamination" by the book, which he considers pathological, full of "morbid animality . . . sickening to an ordinarily decent mind."]

247 "The Lounger," Critic (NY), XXVIII (4 Jan 1895), 12. [Notes adverse reception that *Jude the Obscure* is receiving.]

248 *"The Mayor of Casterbridge,"* LITERARY WORLD REVIEW (Boston), XXVI (10 Aug 1895), 244.

The complexly constructed plot of *The Mayor of Casterbridge* is ably sustained by the complexities of its characters, especially the striking figure of Michael Henchard. By the novel's end, Henchard has suffered enough, however, and ought to have been saved from a bitter death.

249 "Messrs. Osgood, McIlvaine's New Books," BOOKSELLING, I (Dec 1895), 14.

In *Jude the Obscure,* "more than in all his other works, the atmosphere is charged with inexpressible potentialities." H's construction of *Jude* is "artistically perfect."

250 "The New Hardy," NATIONAL OBSERVER, XIV (18 May 1895), 11–12.

"Angel Clare may be defined as a 'sweep' . . . [a] dirty, low, despicable [person]." But H's calling Tess "A Pure Woman" was an error: "as innocent folk would say 'she wasn't.' " [See Another Woman, ibid (1 June 1895), 82.]

251 "Novel Notes," BOOKMAN (Lond), VIII (May 1895), 54–55.

Gissing is "one of the very few novelists, besides Mr. Hardy, who dares to endow his attractive heroines with real life faults, not only magnificent and interesting vices."

252 "Novels of the Week," ATHENAEUM, No. 3552 (23 Nov 1895), 709–10.

If one thought it profitable to study the bad books of great writers in order to give them more insight into the writer's better works, one should study *Jude the Obscure.* "Destiny" is a characteristic background for many Hardy novels. In *Jude,* however, H tried to make fate an active element in the foreground of the novel; by doing so he has destroyed the tragic effect. Another element which destroys the effect is Jude's obscure character: how can one feel the tragedy of a man he does not understand?

253 "A Radical Change in *Jude the Obscure,"* CRITIC (NY), XXVIII (11 Jan 1895), 29.

[Two letters observe that in *Hearts Insurgent* Sue's children were adopted. Ed comments that H seems to have made a "radical change" for publication of the serial version.]

254 [Review of *Jude the Obscure*], DAILY TELEGRAPH (Lond), 1 Nov 1895 [not seen in this form]; rptd in part in THOMAS HARDY

AND HIS READERS: A SELECTION OF CONTEMPORARY REVIEWS, ed by Laurence Lerner and John Holmstrom (1968), p. 107. Although it is unquestionably a "masterpiece," *Jude the Obscure* is dominated by an unrelieved "prevailing gloom" not typical of H's earlier novels.

255 [Review of *Jude the Obscure*], MANCHESTER GUARDIAN, 13 Nov 1895 [not seen in this form]; rptd in THOMAS HARDY AND HIS READERS: A SELECTION OF CONTEMPORARY REVIEWS, ed by Laurence Lerner and John Holmstrom (1968), pp. 111–12.

Arabella is "revoltingly coarse"; Sue Bridehead is "revoltingly refined," and Jude is "contemptibly weak, unstable." The book is full of "insulting things . . . about marriage, religion, and all the obligations and relations of life which most people hold sacred." Nothing relieves the sordidness; there is no recognizable purpose, and no reason not to forget this novel as quickly as possible.

256 [Review of *Jude the Obscure*], MORNING POST, 7 Nov 1895 [not seen in this form]; rptd in THOMAS HARDY AND HIS READERS: A SELECTION OF CONTEMPORARY REVIEWS, ed by Laurence Lerner and John Holmstrom (1968), pp. 107–9.

There are only two apparent points to *Jude the Obscure*: if you marry the wrong person you'll probably be unhappy, and the forces of convention are strong in ruining the plans of even the most liberated people. It is hard to imagine what good could have been expected of such a novel. The chapter describing the attraction of Jude to Sue is the worst of many bad chapters. Sue Bridehead is "distinctly abnormal."

257 [Review of *Jude the Obscure*], SUN (NY), 20 Nov 1895 [not seen in this form]; rptd in THOMAS HARDY AND HIS READERS: A SELECTION OF CONTEMPORARY REVIEWS, ed by Laurence Lerner and John Holmstrom (1968), p. 114.

Only H's reputation for sincerity and conscientiousness could have saved *Jude the Obscure* from condemnation. Sordid, gloomy and unnecessarily coarse, it can do no good, and may do much harm.

258 Robinson, Edwin Arlington. "For a Book by Thomas Hardy," CRITIC (NY), XXVII (23 Nov 1895), 348; rptd in THOMAS HARDY AND HIS READERS: A SELECTION OF CONTEMPORARY REVIEWS, ed by Laurence Lerner and John Holmstrom (1968), p. 114.

["Written before the appearance of *Hearts Insurgents* (i.e. *Jude the Obscure*)," according to the editors of CRITIC, the poem comments on "a magic twilight" through which is heard a "grand sad song," "mirth and woe."]

259 "Table Talk," LITERARY WORLD (Lond), LII (27 Sept 1895), 220–21.

Hearts Insurgent [Jude the Obscure] is reported to be suffering the "indignity" of " 'Bowdlerising' " for American readers; the same happened with *Tess of the d'Urbervilles,* and H may console himself with the thought that the process may increase sales of the unexpurgated version when it appears in book form.

260 "Thomas Hardy Reprinted," LITERARY WORLD (Boston), XXVI (7 Sept 1895), 282.

A Pair of Blue Eyes is exciting and memorable; *Far From the Madding Crowd* has succeeded in creating a whole new literary country: Wessex.

261 T[hompson], A. H. "Thomas Hardy," EAGLE (St. John's College, Cambridge), XIX (Dec 1895), 36–61.

H's claim to immortality is already well established. He has the clearest conception of form of all English writers. The men and women in his novels are "pendant pictures to be hung side by side." The chief fault of H's art is "its tendency to improbability."

262 Weiss, August. "Thomas Hardy," DIE GEGENWART, XXXIX (1895), 204–5.

Literature which is to stand the test of time must direct art into new channels either through its content or mode of expression. H never succeeded in doing this and therefore cannot be included with the best novelists. It is not enough for an author to be imaginative and poetic. A minimum criterion demands that an author be able to write a logical and convincing story. The plot and character motivation of *Tess of the d'Urbervilles* and *The Mayor of Casterbridge* are illogical and incredible. H's novels may be read to pass away the idle hours of the day but are not worth the trouble of an exhaustive analysis. [In German.]

263 *"The Wessex Novels,"* BOOKMAN (Lond), VIII (May 1895), 50–51.

One of the more interesting features of *The Wessex Novels* is H's map of Wessex. It is a useful illustration which guides the reader in his verbal meanderings through Wessex.

1896

---

264 Allen, John Barrow. "New Novels," ACADEMY, XLIX (15 Feb 1896), 134.

For *Jude the Obscure* H might "be allowed the compliment of exemption from criticism." Yet one might ask, "What are the limits of realism?" and "Does Mr. Hardy over-step these limits?" Though he is true to nature, "mere imitation of nature is confessedly not synonymous with art."

265 Aronstein, Philipp. "Die englische Prosadichtung der Gegenwart" (English Prose Fiction of the Present), FREIE BÜHNE FÜR MODERNES LEBEN [NEUE RUNDSCHAU], No. 2 (1896), 679–87, espec 685–86.

[Essentially the same as his "Thomas Hardy," MAGAZIN FÜR LITERATUR, LXV, No. 43 (24 Oct 1896), 1316.] [In German.]

266 Aronstein, Philipp. "Thomas Hardy," MAGAZIN FÜR LITERATUR, LXV (24 Oct 1896), 1316.

H is worthy of being compared to Dickens, Charlotte Brontë, and George Eliot. As novelist, H was a composite: a historian of Wessex, a nature artist, a portrayer of character, and a philosopher. The construction of H's plots is frequently careless, and his presentation is sometimes of such tedious length that the interest is lost. But H compensates for this defect by his wealth of original characters. H's *Weltanschauung* is that of a highly cultivated peasant. H can be considered as George Eliot's successor, struggling to free the English people from the prison of puritanism and the hard, unfriendly *Weltanschauung* of Calvinism. [In German.]

267 Butler, A. J. "Mr. Hardy as a Decadent," NATIONAL REVIEW (Lond), XXVII (May 1896), 384–90.

In *Jude the Obscure* H has chosen to depict the "night-cart" side of nature and repress his natural faculty for genially depicting nature's humorous side. H's fame has always been greater among writers than readers, and he is not an over-rapid producer; *Far From the Madding Crowd* is H's first book to be taken into drawing rooms. *The Return of the Native* shows fully H's capacity for describing natural scenery and coloring it with mood. *Jude* shows the one-sided realism which suppresses any aspect of life other than squalid unredeemed tragedy. H's subject matter is offensively gross, such as the foul details of the pig-killing scene in *Jude*.

268 "Chronicle and Comment," BOOKMAN (NY), III (March 1895), 1–2.

[Caricature and four short notes speculating on the publication and critical reception of *Jude the Obscure*.]

269 Douglas, Sir George. "On Some Critics of *Jude the Obscure*," BOOKMAN (Lond), IX (Jan 1896), 120–22.

The unconscientious criticisms made of *Jude the Obscure* call for a revaluation of critical standards. A novel by one of the most distinguished writers of the age deserves serious consideration and cautious response, however much in opposition the critic might be to the writer's moral stance.

270 Ellis, Havelock. "Concerning *Jude the Obscure*," SAVOY, VI (Oct 1896), 35–49; rptd as CONCERNING JUDE THE OBSCURE (Lond: Ulysses Bookshop, 1931); and as part of the long article in FROM MARLOWE TO SHAW: THE STUDIES, 1876–1936, IN ENGLISH LITERATURE OF HAVELOCK ELLIS (1950).

H brought realism back to the English novel after Scott had ruined fiction with his fantasies and romance. The greatness of H lies not (as often argued) in his treatment of Wessex, but in his psychological penetration of the female mind. An artist must treat morality as a segment of the wholeness of life which he tries to present, and he must not—as George Eliot did— prostitute art for mere moralizing. The subtitle of *Tess of the d'Urbervilles* invites the limitation of a moral evaluation alone, while *Jude the Obscure*, though also concerned with questions of love and marriage, escapes becoming a sermon. Unfortunately both works are marred by bloody melodrama (the deaths of Alec and Jude's children) which is out of place in a modern, serious novel. H's pictures of the natural man and woman in conflict with social conventions are not immoral but profoundly real; rather than being suppressed, his works should be read by the young as well as the mature so that false romantic notions may be dispelled.

271 Ellwanger, G. H. "The Landscape of Thomas Hardy," IDYLLISTS OF THE COUNTRY-SIDE (Lond: Bell; NY: Dodd, Mead, 1896), pp. 85–119.

As a prose-writer concerned with representing nature in his novels, H's greatness lay in his making landscapes alive and in his sympathy with the characters of the stories. [Mainly a lush description of the countryside of the Wessex novels and poems.]

272 Gosse, Sir Edmund. CRITICAL KIT KATS (Lond: Heinemann; NY: Dodd, Mead, 1896; Lond: Heinemann, 1913; NY: Scribner's, 1914), pp. [v]–vii, 298.

[Gosse dedicates this book to H "for the sake of the comrade, not the critic," as a landmark of an "inestimably precious" friendship.] The only new book R. L. Stevenson wished to take with him to America was H's *The Woodlanders*, which he had to scour London for the Sunday afternoon before leaving.

273 Gosse, Edmund William. "Mr. Hardy's New Novel," COSMOPOLIS, I (Jan 1896), 60–69.

H is not a perfect writer. *Jude the Obscure* is a study of four lives drawn with almost mathematical rigidity. The "marriage question" is fashionable among writers this year. Two threads of action intertwine in the novel: the contrast between the ideal life Jude wished for and the real life he was fated to lead and second, the rectilinear puzzle of sexual relations of the four principal characters. It is difficult to see what part Oxford has in Jude's destruction, or how H can excuse the diatribes against the university. The scene at Commemoration is true and vivid, but H should not take sides with his unhappy hero. The plot is a ghastly story, but a novelist of H's distinction may treat what themes he will. The *vita sexualis* of Sue is the central interest of the book. Her picture is admirable; she is a poor, maimed "degenerate," ignorant of herself and of the perversion of her instincts, full of febrile illusions, ready to dramatize her empty life and play at loving, though she cannot love. It is a terrible study in pathology, but of the splendid success of it, there cannot be two opinions. H should not force his talent and should not give way to chimerical outbursts of what is falsely termed philosophy. The conversations of his semi-educated characters are terrible. Jude and Sue, that minx, speak a sort of University Extension jargon that breaks the heart.

274 Hannigan, D. F. "Mr. Thomas Hardy's Latest Novel," WESTMINSTER REVIEW, CXLII (Feb 1896), 136–39.

Although H's sympathies "are manifestly with the French naturalistic school of fiction," he is not one of them: "through all that Mr. Hardy has written vibrates a passionate chivalry" which has no parallel in French realism. H's heroines are ideals, "etherialized beings—fays, sirens, who disguise themselves as farmeresses"—free from the "vice of . . . feminine masculinity." *Jude the Obscure* is not H's greatest work, but "the best English novel . . . since *Tess*." Hardy is "the greatest living English writer of fiction."

275 "The Home and Haunts of *Tess of the d'Urbervilles*," PICTURE MAGAZINE, No. 39 (March 1896), 160–61.

[Account of certain real-life scenes which figure prominently in *Tess of the d'Urbervilles*.]

276 "In Thomas Hardy's Country," TEMPLE BAR MAGAZINE, CVIII (May 1896), 150–53.

[Recollection of a holiday visit to some real-life settings H employed in his novels.]

277 Johnson, M. "Thomas Hardy's Novels," PRIMITIVE METHODIST QUARTERLY REVIEW, ns XVIII (Jan 1896), 30–40.

"Poetical rather than psychological, his [H's] work rests nevertheless on a sound basis of thought and analysis." His masterpieces are *Far From the Madding Crowd*, *Return of the Native* and *Tess of the d'Urbervilles*. In *Tess*, after having carried his heroine "safely, reverently, and almost triumphantly," through her sorrowful life to the point where she could retreat " 'from life without shame,' " H is suddenly "seized with a paroxysm of rage against his own creation, and with one violent blow . . . despoils it of . . . symmetry and meaning." Tess's yielding to Alec a second time ruins the novel "artistically no less than morally." H's imagination is unusually powerful and vivid. He achieves "the very highest distinction in the creation of memorable characters." His greatest successes are his "subtle characters, or such as are easily stirred by the winds of impulse or caprice." As an interpreter of nature H "has no equal among English writers."

278 *"Jude the Obscure,"* LITERARY WORLD (Boston), XXVII (11 Jan 1896), 3.

Jude the Obscure is a powerful tragedy but not fit for "general reading." H lays bear the anatomy of suffering, but the effect is too powerful and the suffering too painful: the anatomy becomes vivisection.

279 LeGallienne, Richard. RETROSPECTIVE REVIEWS. 2 vols (Lond: Lane; NY: Dodd, Mead, 1896), I, 12–15; II, 80–83, 149–53; rptd from unidentified reviews.

Dec 1891: The problems of diction in *Tess of the d'Urbervilles* seem to be the result of "sudden moments of self-consciousness in the midst of . . . creative flow, as also [of] the imperfect digestion of certain modern science and philosophy which is becoming painfully obtrusive through the apple-cheek outline of Mr. Hardy's work." Such words as "dolorifuge," "prestidigitation," "heliolatries" are inappropriately used. March 1894: *Life's Little Ironies* and some novels and poems have "a certain coarseness of touch in the love-making." H's use of the phrase " 'let it be lips' " at the climax of a love scene in " On the Western Circuit" should be replaced by a more "honest and straightforward phrase" such as " 'give me your mouth.' " Oct 1894: [Review of Lionel Johnson's THE ART OF THOMAS HARDY (1894).]

280 LeGallienne, Richard. "Wanderings in Bookland," IDLER, IX (Feb 1896), 114–15.

Jude and Sue have their lapses into unreality, but the novel remains perhaps the most powerful and moving picture of human life which H has given us. No doubt the picture is darker than reality. Such pessimism is only half true of life as a whole. Too many reviewers have treated *Jude the Obscure* as polemic against marriage: the novel is an indictment of much older and crueler laws, the laws of the universe. Mrs. Oliphant in BLACKWOOD'S MAGAZINE has been grossly unjust and exceedingly pointless in her clumsy attack upon H. Her insinuation that H has deliberately catered to unclean appetites is either very malignant or very mistaken.

281 Linne, H. "Ein Besuch bei Thomas Hardy" (A Visit with Thomas Hardy), DIE GEGENWART, XLIX (16 May 1896), 307–9.
H said that *Tess of the d'Urbervilles* could not be published until 1891 "since the English public was not, so to speak, ripe for it" in 1889. H would calmly give both *Tess* and *Jude the Obscure* "into the hands of every young girl." The main idea of *Jude* is " 'Can you call women weak when you see how men become slaves, commit sins, die on their account?' " [Account of an interview in which H spoke at length about his intentions, circumstances of composition and publication of *Tess* and *Jude*. Interesting but suspect: H so rarely said anything of significance about his works, let alone to a casual visitor, that the faithfulness of this interview may be questioned.] [In German.]

282 "Literature: Fiction," CRITIC (NY), XXVIII (9 May 1896), 336.
[Charges H again (Charles P. Jacobs, "Will Mr. Hardy Explain?" ibid [28 Jan 1882], 25–26) with plagiarizing Longstreet's GEORGIA SCENES in *The Trumpet-Major*.]

283 "The Lounger," CRITIC (NY), XXVIII (4 Jan 1896), 12.
[Deplores *Jude the Obscure* as "objectionable," but notes the appreciation by ANIMAL'S FRIEND (not seen) of H's merciful reaction against pig-sticking.]

284 "The Lounger," CRITIC (NY), XXVIII (13 June 1896), 429.
[Answer to "Thomas Hardy; His Genius in the Wessex Novels," NEW YORK DAILY TRIBUNE, 7 June 1896, p. 26.] The author of the TRIBUNE article is impertinent in saying that *Tess of the d'Urbervilles* and *Jude the Obscure* are no more indelicate than the preconceptions which the reader brings to them.

285 M., A. "New Books: *Jude the Obscure*," BOOKMAN (Lond), IX (Jan 1896), 123–24.
The reader's opinion about the "purpose" of the tragedy of *Jude the Obscure* will depend upon his separate opinions of the major characters, Jude and Sue. The character of Sue is drawn in an exaggerated fashion and is thus rather unconvincing. Jude, however, comes from the roots of H's spirit and imagination.

286 Mortimer, Geoffrey. "*Jude the Obscure*," FREE REVIEW (Lond), V (Jan 1896), 387–401.
Jude the Obscure is "the supreme achievement of a great artist in the broad and splendid maturity of a notable career." There is something of the Titan

in H for writing *Jude* and "grit in the man who publishes it." "Very few novelists have so well succeeded in bringing themselves *en rapport*" with the common man. [Mostly a plot summary.]

287 "New Editions," LITERARY WORLD (Boston), XXVII (31 Oct 1896), 367.

H's *Wessex Tales* are enjoyable rural stories quite free of the author's recent vein of pathological eroticism.

288 O[liphant], M. O. W. "The Anti-Marriage League," BLACK-WOOD'S MAGAZINE, CLIX (Jan 1896), 137–42; rptd in THOMAS HARDY AND HIS READERS: A SELECTION OF CONTEMPORARY REVIEWS, ed by Laurence Lerner and John Holmstrom (1968), pp. 126–30.

H has used his genius for the dissemination of wickedness. *Jude the Obscure* is a work of "grossness, indecency, and horror," and shows what "art can come to when given over to the exposition of the unclean." H's purpose must have been to show what "destructive and ruinous creatures" women are and to promote "an assault on the stronghold of marriage." Men are passive, victims of women and of fate. H seems to suggest that the hanging of children is the best way to remove the principal obstruction to the abolition of marriage.

289 Payne, W. M. "Recent Fiction," DIAL, XX (1 Feb 1896), 76–77.

Jude the Obscure "bade fair to equal, if not surpass, any of the author's previous achievements." But instead it seems to be a "bitter tirade against the fundamental institutions of society." "Between the noble tragedy which performs for us the Aristotelian function of purging the soul of baseness and such tragedy as Mr. Hardy gives us . . : there is a world-wide difference."

290 P[eck], [Harry Thurston]. "Chronicle and Comment," BOOKMAN (NY), II (Jan 1896), 374–75.

Though H's actual writing habits are irregular, he is very meticulous in revising and preparing the final form of a work. One exception to this rule appeared in a proof where H had a character mount the same hill twice without bringing him down. H replied simply that the second "up" should have read "down."

291 Peck, Harry Thurston. "A Novel of Lubricity," BOOKMAN (NY), II (Jan 1896), 427–29.

Jude the Obscure is "both a moral monstrosity and an outrage upon art." H has introduced "a stream of indecency" which is not found in his earlier novels. In *Jude* H tried to incorporate elements of realism as well as romance. But he has failed, for the novel "neither teaches a truthful lesson, nor is it true to life." H's introduction of this grossness, after the novel was published in a periodical, shows the inconsistency of his theory of art and literature. Jude is "the studied satyriasis of approaching senility, suggesting the morbidly curious imaginings of a masochist or some other form of sexual pervert."

292 Quiller-Couch, Sir Arthur Thomas. "Mr. George Moore," ADVENTURES IN CRITICISM (Lond: Cassell, 1896), pp. 357–61; rptd (NY: Putnam, 1925), pp. 196–99.

The heroine of ESTHER WATERS is more heroic than the heroine of *Tess of the d'Urbervilles,* and Esther's story is informed with a saner philosophy of life. "The story of *Tess,* in which a poor servant-girl is allowed to grapple with her destiny and, after a fashion, to defeat it, is felt . . . to be absolutely inevitable."

293 "A Radical Change in *Jude the Obscure,*" CRITIC (NY), XXVIII (11 Jan 1896), 29.

[Gives two letters denying an earlier reviewer's allegation that Sue was mother of her and Jude's two children. The editors of CRITIC reply that the "radical change" was made in *Hearts Insurgent* by the editor of HARPER'S.]

294 "A Review and Criticism of the Latest Book from the Pen of Thomas Hardy, the Famous English Novelist," OUR DAY (Lond), XVI (Feb 1896), 101–4.

Jude the Obscure, which might be dismissed as obscene had it been written by an unknown, is particularly dangerous because of H's fame. Unconcerned with the effect he might have on innocent minds, H has "disgusted the world with his wallowing in the mire."

295 [Review of *Jude the Obscure*], ILLUSTRATED LONDON NEWS, 11 Jan 1896 [not seen in this form]; rptd in THOMAS HARDY AND HIS READERS: A SELECTION OF CONTEMPORARY REVIEWS, ed by Laurence Lerner and John Holmstrom (1968), pp. 124–26.

H's genius can be seen in his ability to make tragedy in three lives cast a pall over the whole world. The power of the novel is almost destroyed by the doctor's comment that murder and suicide among unnatural children is becoming common due to the " 'universal wish not to live.' " The idea of Little Father Time as a philosopher is ridiculous. The marriage-divorce-remarriage confusion comes close to being ridiculous also, but the novel is a work of genius.

296 Segrè, Carlo. "L'ultimo romanzo di Thomas Hardy" (The Latest Novel of Thomas Hardy), NUOVA ANTOLOGIA, CXLVII (16 June 1896), 620–40.

Jude the Obscure is immoral. The immorality springs not from its realism, but from its conceptual framework. *Jude* is not a novel of manners nor of character. It is a *roman à thèse,* and the thesis is obnoxious. Man is shown as oppressed by destiny and society alike so that he must necessarily suffocate his natural desires, his spontaneous inclinations, and all that offers him happiness. What is pernicious in H's presentation is the despair. H nowhere broaches a remedy for oppression, nor a possible reform of society. Furthermore, he reverses the values which have sustained mankind for centuries. For H, virtue consists not in sacrifice, but in surrender to impulse. H is a vigorous and technically gifted writer, and there are thus several sequences in his work which excite admiration. But for the most part, *Jude* reads like a frenzied dream, sprung from a deranged and feverish night. [In Italian.]

297 Selby, Thomas G. "Thomas Hardy," THE THEOLOGY OF MODERN FICTION, BEING THE TWENTY-SIXTH FERNLEY LECTURE, DELIVERED IN LIVERPOOL, JULY, 1896 (Lond: Charles H. Kelly, 1896), pp. 88–130.

[A viciously doctrinaire examination of the theological implications of H's novels. The following excerpts are typical: "A prince in modern literature, attired in the noblest purple and fine linen, this author has a curious mania for exploiting sewers and acting Parisian ragman. Filth and defilement he faces with the calm, unshrinkable countenance of a Local Board labourer." After allowing that H is "no gay, laughing Silenus of romping wickedness; but a Silenus with a broken heart," Selby continues: "This gifted man has made his home in the slime-pits of Siddim, as early ascetics betook themselves to the caves of the wilderness, and has studiously cultivated the most lachrymose and intractable types of pessimism that a morbid ingenuity can devise."]

298 "Thomas Hardy from an Italian Standpoint," REVIEW OF REVIEWS (NY), XIV (Aug 1896), 229.

Carlo Segrè, in NUOVA ANTOLOGIA, CXLVII (16 June 1896), objects strongly to *Jude the Obscure.* It is immoral and immodest about its immorality—unlike the reticence of Fielding and Smollett. H's "object is to show that man is nothing more than the necessary victim of his social surroundings." Sections of the book, however, command one's admiration.

299 "Thomas Hardy; His Genius in the Wessex Novels," NEW YORK DAILY TRIBUNE, LVI (7 June 1896), 26.

The natural and uninterrupted development from the first novel to the last shows inexperienced natures confused between the dictates of society and their own inner convictions but achieving the glory of renunciation and the transfiguring power of unblemished love. Characters, setting, and methodology are "the envelope in which Hardy passes on his inspiration" and seem "almost trifling beside the beauty of the inspiration itself." [See "The Lounger," CRITIC (NY), XXV (13 June 1896), 429.]

300 Trent, W. P. "Mr. Thomas Hardy," CITIZEN (Philadelphia), I (Feb 1896), 284–86.

H can be counted the greatest living novelist because of his ability to create two great characters (Tess Durbeyfield and Joseph Poorgrass); because of his power of description; because of his "fund of humour"; because he is an artist; and because he has a story to tell.

301 "Two Novels: *Jude the Obscure,* THE EMANCIPATED," NATION (NY), LXII (6 Feb 1896), 123–24.

H's attitude toward the problems involved in his novel "is as obscure as Jude." He is very bitter about marriage, and "seems to stand as an advocate for celibacy and the extinction of the race."

302 Tyrrell, Robert Yelverton. "*Jude the Obscure,*" FORTNIGHTLY REVIEW, LXV (1 June 1896), 859–64.

Jude the Obscure shows a falling off from *Tess of the d'Urbervilles* "not only in conception but in execution." H's powers have either "undergone a sad deterioration . . . or he has determined to try the patience of his public . . . to see whether they will accept a treatise on sexual pathology." His dramatic faculty has deserted him, and his descriptive powers are not conspicuously present. The novel may be classed with the fiction of Sex and New Woman. The "occasional sparks which glow into sustained splendour" cannot save the book: "even an enchanted palace would be vitiated by a whiff from the atmosphere of the POT BOUILLE or GERMINAL." The SATURDAY REVIEW is incorrect in saying that sex is secondary in the novel: "The book is steeped in sex." Sue is "an incurably morbid organism" and her "greensickness" should not be dwelt on. She is a flirt; both she and Jude would still have been dissatisfied if marriage as an institution were done away with. The characters are "not distinctly conceived" because of the "vagueness of the theme." The book is a "dismal treatise."

303 [Untitled Editorial] YORKSHIRE POST, June 1896, p. 4.

"There is not in the whole range of Victorian literature a series of novels more unwholesome in their tone and drift" than H's Wessex novels. One hesitates to give H's novels to the young because of "the soreheaded railing against God and Nature that runs through almost every page of his books." Are not H "and his brood of misanthropic disciples [e.g. Grant Allen] rightly called the Decadents?" H bases his conclusions about God on extremely rare cases, "mere curiosities" which can hardly stand as "proofs that a maleficent Providence . . . delights to torture its creatures."

304 Wakefield, William Walsham Howe, Bishop of. "Thomas Hardy," YORKSHIRE POST, 8 June 1896, p. 4.

"I bought a copy of one of Mr. Hardy's novels, but was so disgusted with its insolence and indecency that I threw it into the fire."

305 [Wells, H. G.]. "*Jude the Obscure,*" SATURDAY REVIEW (Lond), LXXXI (8 Feb 1896), 153–54.

Jude the Obscure is a "great novel," and "its main theme is not sexual at all." Three passages are noted carefully, Jude's view of the legendary Churchminster after his aunt's scolding, his letter of refusal from T. Tetuphenay, and the "grimly magnificent passage" concerning the death of Jude and his final lament, "the voice of the educated proletarian, speaking more distinctly than it has ever spoken before in English literature." [An enthusiastic defense of H's greatness and the quest theme in *Jude,* in opposition to "a band of public informers against indecorum."]

306 Zangwill, I. "Without Prejudice," CHAPBOOK, IV (15 Jan 1896), 238–46; rptd in PALL MALL MAGAZINE, VIII (Feb 1896), 327–36, espec 332–34.

Jude the Obscure is a strange mixture of weaknesses and strengths. Throughout, the artistry of the novel displays some highly disappointing moments. For example, one finds it difficult to accept the postulate on which the novel is based. "Despite the author's uneasy explanations, I find it improbable that Sue, a girl with her pretty eyes wide open, with a pagan feeling of the joy of life, should give herself to a stuffy old schoolmaster." Further, H does not allow his characters to evolve their own inevitable destinies. Intermingled with and opposed to these flaws is H's brilliant workmanship and fertile imagination. Moreover, the sense of injustice with which the novel is imbued has a powerful effect. In spite of the weaknesses that the novel exhibits, one is encouraged by its greatness to "hope that Hardy will yet write the epic of the modern, . . . some book that . . . shall carry on their [*Tess of the d'Urberville's* and *Jude's*] splendid promise and link their high artistic purpose to unfaltering and immortal achievement."

1897

307 Brandl, A. "Thomas Hardy und Rudyard Kipling" (Thomas Hardy and Rudyard Kipling), COSMOPOLIS, VI (May 1897), 579–94.

H missed his mark and should have followed the examples of Auerbach and Rosegger rather than engaging himself in a form of naturalism which makes

Zola look tame. H is a moralist at heart and cannot avoid being didactic. The naturalistic intention of *Jude the Obscure* is ruined when H punishes the sinner drastically and rewards the righteous with a submissive wife. [In German.]

308 "The Comedy of a Curse," LITERARY WORLD (Lond), LV (26 March 1897), 283–85.

Although H insists on mentioning a "breach of morality" which is "quite unnecessary to the story," *The Well-Beloved* is still without the "grosser traits" which scandalized readers of *Tess of the d'Urbervilles* and *Jude the Obscure*. It has, in addition, more of humor and narrative interest than did its two most recent predecessors. *Well-Beloved* is not of H's greatest novels, but it is "vastly above the average of what passes muster among modern novels."

309 Douglas, George. "*The Well-Beloved*," BOOKMAN (NY), V (May 1897), 247–48.

H's later novels resemble those of George Eliot because they were both influenced by the thinking of "the age of Huxleyism, or of Positivism." Eliot marked the beginning of that age, Hardy the end. *The Well-Beloved*, an earlier work than *Jude the Obscure* though it was published later, shows the qualities which distinguished H's earlier works. The landscape which he created for this story compares with Egdon Heath. Among his heroines the first, Avice Caro, must be considered one of his best portrayals. The story begins as a delightful romance, but ends with a "mechanical working out of a plot." This later characteristic suggests, perhaps, the influence of "the French Symbolists."

310 "The Drama: *Tess of the d'Urbervilles*," CRITIC (NY), XXX (6, 13 March 1897), 171–72, 185–86.

[Praises Mr. Lorimer Stoddard's dramatization of *Tess of the d'Urbervilles*. Special appreciation for Mrs. Minnie Fiske as Tess (with picture).]

311 Gosse, Edmund. "Mr. Hardy's New Novel," ST. JAMES'S GAZETTE, XXXIV (31 March 1897), 5–6.

The Well-Beloved is a "graceful, playful, episodical" book. It has been treated harshly by critics because of H's choice of subject: the volatile idealist hero who changes his mind about his beloved *before* marriage and the volatile heroine. If H "will write about human nature . . . he must take the consequences."

312 "Literature," ATHENAEUM, No. 3624 (10 April 1897), 471.

The Well-Beloved is a "Sketch of a Temperament." The story has no hidden moral or latent meaning beyond that of character exposition.

313 MacArthur, Henry. "Realism and Romance: Thomas Hardy and Robert Louis Stevenson," REALISM AND ROMANCE AND OTHER ESSAYS (Edinburgh: Hunter, 1897), pp. 1–33.

H is the leading representative of the realist school, whose distinguishing marks are as follows: he keeps to the present day and within the limits of the possible; his fiction depends, for its interest, upon character rather than upon incident; he chooses and treats subjects boldly and unconventionally; he aims at painting real men and women.

314 Murray, David Christie. "My Contemporaries in Fiction: Thomas Hardy," CANADIAN MAGAZINE, IX (May 1897), 38–41; rptd as "Under French Encouragement—Thomas Hardy," in MY CONTEMPORARIES IN FICTION (Lond: Chatto & Windus, 1897), pp. 71–84.

However sincere and honest his intentions, H is likely to be encouraging the spread of hysteria among women by portraying it romantically in his latest novels. There are certain subjects it is a crime to mention; a fiction writer ought to be "harmless." H is damaging his own art by joining the French movement toward license. [Self-evident nonsense.]

315 Paul, Herbert. "The Apotheosis of the Novel Under Queen Victoria," NINETEENTH CENTURY AND AFTER, XLI (May 1897), 787–88.

Critics at first attributed *Far From the Madding Crowd* to George Eliot, though there is no similarity of style and characters. H's peasants are more real than Mrs. Poyser, but H's country (in the novels) is more real than the characters. Though *Tess of the d'Urbervilles* and *Jude the Obscure* have tragic power (and both are below the level of *The Return of the Native* and *The Mayor of Casterbridge*), and *The Hand of Ethelberta* is a "delightfully quaint piece of humor," vintage H can only be seen in *The Woodlanders*, where "every tree is a character, and the people are a set-off to the summer."

316 Payne, W. M. "Recent Fiction," DIAL, XXII (16 May 1897), 307–8.

In *The Well-Beloved,* it is "distinctly a temperament and not a character that is presented . . . a man who all his life is in love with love rather than any particular woman." This may seem nothing more than a sophisticated way of describing the natural fickleness of the average man; but there is a difference, and a failure to comprehend it is a failure to get the author's point of view. H's novel is not comic despite its situation, "and it is a signal triumph of his art that the reader is not moved to mirth."

317 Phelps, William Lyon. "Incomparable Wessex, Again," BOOK BUYER, ns XIV (May 1897), 410–12.

The Well-Beloved "may not be a great book" but it is "not a bad book" either, and it is a relief after the "detestable *Jude*." Out of the seemingly absurd plot, H has built a story of "sustained interest," "beautiful description," some "natural dialogues," and "considerable elemental force." H's pessimism is "basal, but quiet," and his style "has not in the least fallen off." [More valuable as evidence of Phelps's standards than as comment on the novel.]

318 "Reviews: Mr. Hardy's New Novel," ACADEMY, LI (27 March 1897), 345–46.

In the Wessex novels which preceded *The Well-Beloved*, H had the critics at a disadvantage. They were forced to agree that "Wessex is the home of such fatalistic, impulsive, grave, godless people as the men and women whose interplay of passions makes these wonderful Wessex novels." This latest novel, however, is peculiar, besides having a setting different from that of his earlier pieces, in that H, the usually silent creator, does not refrain from comment on the situation which he creates. Dramatic progression is an admirable aspect of this novel; however, the theme would have been more effective in a short story.

319 Sholl, Anna McClure. "Thomas Hardy," LIBRARY OF THE WORLD'S BEST LITERATURE, ed by Charles Dudley Warner (NY: Peale & Hill, 1897)), XVII, 6933–38.

The keynote of H's work is the effect of circumstances upon "man's war with the lower elements in his nature." These circumstances often cause H's "lovable" characters to be defeated. [A major portion of this article consists of plot summaries of novels.]

320 Shorter, Clement K. VICTORIAN LITERATURE. (NY: Dodd, Mead, 1897), p. 68.

Using the Dorsetshire landscape in *Far From the Madding Crowd*, *Tess of the d'Urbervilles*, *The Return of the Native*, and *The Woodlanders*, H became a great novelist.

321 "Thomas Hardy's New Novel," LITERARY DIGEST, XV (15 May 1897), 70–71.

The Pursuit of the Well-Beloved is more agreeable reading than *Jude the Obscure*.

322 Traill, H. D. "The Literature of the Victorian Era," FORT-NIGHTLY REVIEW, LXVII (May 1897), 835.

H is in the "foremost place among English novelists" but it is "irritating to note that the inspiration of his finest and strongest novel [*Jude the Obscure*] is derived from that everlasting sex problem." Meredith, H, and Stevenson "are three great names in the literature of English fiction."

323 *"The Well-Beloved,"* CRITIC (NY), XXX (May 1897), 300.
The Well-Beloved is not one of H's strong performances. "You cannot carve a cherry-stone with a hatchet. A book with such a theme ought to be rich in subtlety, in reflection, in atmosphere, but *The Well-Beloved* is thin, meagre and bony."

324 *"The Well-Beloved,"* LITERARY WORLD (Boston), XXVIII (15 May 1897), 156–57.
Only its charming style saves *The Well-Beloved* from complete dullness.

325 Williams, Duane. "The Teaching of Thomas Hardy," UNIVERSITY MAGAZINE, VIII (1 June 1897), 253–58.
[Essay draws frequently upon *Jude the Obscure* and *The Well-Beloved* to illustrate the author's contention that H is a populizer of "evolutional ethics" and a critic of outmoded institutions.]

1898

326 Clark, Richard H. "GEORGIA SCENES and *Trumpet-Major*," MEMOIRS OF JUDGE RICHARD H. CLARK, ed by Lollie Belle Wylie (Atlanta, Ga: Franklin Printing and Publishing, 1898), pp. 235–42.
Oliver H. Prince was traditionally held to be the author of the militia scene Augustus Longstreet printed in his GEORGIA SCENES. H plagiarized from GEORGIA SCENES in writing his own *The Trumpet-Major*, believing that the obscurity of Longstreet's book would prevent detection.

327 Johnson, Lionel [Pigot]. "Mr. Thomas Hardy," ACADEMY, LV (12 Nov 1898), 251–52; rptd as "Mr. Hardy's Later Prose," in POST LIMINIUM (Lond: Matthews; NY: Kennerley, 1912), pp. 142–50; partly in OUTLOOK (NY), LXI (4 Feb 1899), 265.
H is a "patient, poetical artist, who portrays the workings of life under certain conditions of nature, society, tradition, dear and familiar to his heart's experience. . . . The Mr. Hardy of our preference is a writer of impassioned and beautiful solemnity. The Mr. Hardy of our occasional dislike is a writer of querulous questioning of universal meaning." But "he is not a difficult, an obscure writer: he is certainly exacting." *The Return of the Native, The Mayor of Casterbridge*, and *The Woodlanders* deserve the "place of honor" over *Tess of the d'Urbervilles* and *Jude the Obscure*. In the earlier works H is more steady and certain of his thoughts. He has neither the subtlety of Henry James nor the "deliberate intellectuality" of George Eliot.

328 "The Lounger," CRITIC (NY), XXXIII (Dec 1898), 438–39. General praise of the Dorsetshire man who "has taught his native country to realize itself in literature," with a portrait by Mrs. Will Rothenstein.

329 Ryan, W. P. "A Lunar Elopement: The Key to Allen Gaunt's Defection," LITERARY LONDON: ITS LIGHTS AND COMEDIES (Lond: Smithers, 1898), pp. 40–48.

H, only a temporary convert "to the mad, bad revolutionary faith of the mid-nineties," now "is going back disappointed and chastened in spirit to the fiction of his earlier manner." [Contains a parody-poem describing H's bidding farewell to the "Madding Crowd of the Maudlin emotions,/O sweet, sinning Sex!"]

330 Vincent, Leon H. "Thomas Hardy," THE BIBLIOTAPH AND OTHER PEOPLE (Boston & NY: Houghton Mifflin, 1898), pp. 80–112.

H has intimate knowledge of "an immense number of interesting things." He knows all sorts of people, many facets of nature. Not merely does he tell a story well, but also he reveals to the reader the mystery in common life through his keen observation and natural dialogue. Fortunately, he does not, though he could, make a naturalistic chronicle of minutiae. H also manifests humor through wit, through description, and through character portrayal. He also displays some melancholy, but sympathy as well; he sees life as it is. His books also convey "spaciousness." Recommends *The Woodlanders* and *The Return of the Native* to new acquaintances of H.

331 *"Wessex Poems and Other Verses,"* LITERATURE, III (31 Dec 1898), 615–16.

H's poems show the sardonic, bitter humor his readers now expect of him but, despite occasional felicities, his pessimistic ideas might be expressed as well in prose.

1899

332 Adams, Francis. "Some Recent Novels," ESSAYS IN MODERNITY (Lond: Lane, 1899), pp. 158–65.

H lapses into "the cheapest conventional style of the average popular novelist" and the dairymaids in *Tess of the d'Urbervilles* do not talk like dairymaids. H excels at creating characters who fit into their natural surroundings and succeeds in catching "the sob of the earth's suffering." H's faults are due to an uncritical reading public that praised his faults and condemned his virtues.

333 Bickley, A. C. "Parsons in Fiction XXV: Thomas Hardy," CHURCH GAZETTE, 30 Dec 1899, p. 293; 6 Jan 1900, p. 321.

"Once [you are] bitten by the Hardy fever, it lasts a lifetime." Even if you don't like it, you cannot help reading his next work. H is in some ways the most difficult of modern novelists to analyze. While *Under the Greenwood Tree* is an unqualified success, *Far From the Madding Crowd* is too much "written by contract" and is spoiled by the inartistic ending. H never gives us a "good" woman. His treatment of women corresponds to his treatment of religion. Though he does not hold them up to contempt nor treat them with indifference, their influence is never orthodox. H is supreme in his neglect of parsons, and when he portrays them he is unsympathetic even if he is fair. Tess, though purportedly an "orthodox" Christian, is really thoroughly pagan. The treatment of religion and the clergy in *Two on a Tower* should have seriously damaged H's reputation. We have to turn to *Greenwood Tree* for an honorable treatment of the parson.

334 "The Career of the Novel," PURITAN, VI (July 1899), 341–44.

Tess of the d'Urbervilles raised a storm of hostile criticism, "and essays were written and sermons preached to prove its teachings uplifting or degrading, as the writer or preacher happened to see them." H is not a "cheap cynic . . . there is such a wealth of poetry and such keeness of insight into human nature in his works that the fatalistic touch cannot destroy their charm and power." *The Return of the Native* and *The Woodlanders* are ranked higher by most critics than *Tess* or *Jude the Obscure*.

335 Columbine, W. B. "The Poems of Thomas Hardy," WESTMINSTER REVIEW, CLII (Aug 1899), 180–84.

In *Wessex Poems*, H's verse "is nearly always good, readable, and interesting [enough] . . . to give him an honourable place amongst the minor poets of our time."

336 "Form in Poetry," LITERATURE, IV (4 March 1899), 217–18.

Wessex Poems, though "independently good of their kind and characteristic of Mr. Hardy's individuality to a remarkable degree," had something unusual about them; they lack form. The publication will later be interpreted by "professors of literary history" as "a signal example of the temporary success of a violent protest against the cultivation of form in verse."

337 "George Meredith and Thomas Hardy," BOOKMAN (NY), IX (April 1899), 146–49.

Wessex Poems contains not great, but good, interesting poetry, like that which fills H's novels. A sensitive, unselfconscious man, H takes all criticism seriously. [Article contains a summary of "How I Built Myself A House" and relates a story (apocryphal) of how H was engaged to write a serial for CORNHILL which became *Far From the Madding Crowd*.]

338 Harper, Charles G. THE EXETER ROAD: THE STORY OF THE WEST OF ENGLAND HIGHWAY (Lond: Chapman & Hall, 1899), pp. 155, 166, 268, 276, 279.
[Passing reference is made to *The Mayor of Casterbridge*, "On the Western Circuit," and *Under the Greenwood Tree* in this account of the road from London, through the heart of H's Wessex, to Exeter.]

339 Holland, Clive [pseud of Charles James Hankinson]. "Thomas Hardy's Country: Scenes from the Wessex Novels," BOOKMAN (NY), IX (June–Aug 1899), 328–40, 410–23, 519–27.
[Holland uses the novels as commentary for a series of black and white pictures of H country. Holland thus furnishes permanent record of non-change, and notes on H's literary usage of it. In depicting real locale, H was as meticulous as any naturalist.]

340 Johnson, Lionel. "Mr. Hardy's Poems," OUTLOOK (Lond), III (28 Jan 1899), 822–23.
In the fifty poems of *Wessex Poems* there are passion, humor, wistfulness, grimness, tenderness, but never joy, the radiant and invincible. "The Impercipient," though, softens and sweetens the whole. Browning might be proud of "The Burghers" and "My Cicely." *Wessex Poems* is cruel to Wessex, which is not a wholly Leopardian land. Like Marcus Aurelius, H's verse "drives at practice" and never dallies over a prettiness or a wayside charm.

341 Kendall, May. "Pessimism and Thomas Hardy's Poems," LONDON QUARTERLY REVIEW, ns XCI (April 1899), 223–34.
H's "verdict on life" is a gloomy one, yet shows the need for Christian strength in the present age. "Where there is unselfish service, even if the outlook seems gloomy, there is faith." "Amabel" shows the decay of a love that is purely egotistic. "To a Friend" and "The Slow Nature" show H's stronger mood, with the loyalty of God reflected in disfigured humanity. Many of H's middle-aged enthusiasts are misled from the gospel of optimism founded on character into a feeling of the vainness of protestation.

342 Ling, William. "Mr. Kipling and the Pirate," OUTLOOK, (Lond), IV (30 Sept 1899), 277–78.
There is a hidden meaning in Kipling's less known ballad "The Rhyme of The Three Captain's," first published in the ATHENAEUM in 1891. Kipling, having had some difficulties with a well-known publishing firm in America, met three eminent novelists at Ballestier's literary club in London. The three captains, identified in a line at the end of the ballad ". . . the bezant is hard, ay, and black," are of course Sir Walter Besant, William Black and H.

343 "The Literary Week," ACADEMY, LVI (7 Jan 1899), 5.
In his poems H often uses the Dorsetshire dialect. The poet Mr. Edward A. Irving also uses dialect to emphasize his poetic pathos.

344 "Literature," ATHENAEUM, No. 3716 (14 Jan 1899), 41–42.
The most poetically successful moments in *Wessex Poems and Other Verses* are those that concentrate on "this curiously intense and somewhat dismal vision of life," the same vision which pervades H's novels. It is a somewhat narrow range of vision, but within it the poet is "voicing a mature and deliberate judgement on life."

345 "The Lounger," CRITIC (NY), XXXIV (Feb 1899), 127.
H's Wessex poems are "not as excellent technically" as the poems of the present laureate. They show a "want of style" as in "She at his Funeral" and "I Look into My Glass."

346 Macdonell, Annie. "Thomas Hardy's Wessex Poems," BOOK-MAN (Lond), XV (Feb 1899), 139–41.
The poet of the Wessex Poems is the poet who often revealed himself in the Wessex Novels. H's prosody is imperfect, but he is always understandable. The ideas and sentiments are the same as those found in his prose, but more concentrated. It is H's "intensity of expression" which necessitated his switch from prose to verse. Ever present in the poetry is H's "uncompromising grip of hard fact" and a "wistful tenderness for life in the grip of fact's tyranny."

347 [Milne, James?]. "Shall Stonehenge Go? Only to the Nation, says Mr. Thomas Hardy. A Talk with the Novelist," DAILY CHRONICLE (Lond), 24 Aug 1899.
If this national relic must be sold, the nation should purchase it and about 2,000 acres of Salisbury plain. H confesses to a "liking for the state of dim conjecture in which we stand in regard to its [Stonehenge's] history."

348 Nicoll, William Robertson. "Notes on English Style in the Victorian Period: V—Thomas Hardy," BOOKMAN (NY), X (Oct 1899), 147–48.
H's recent volume of poems indicates that his theory of the universe, unique among "great writers," had been developed early in his life, but came to be expressed explicitly only in his later works. H is the self-appointed spokesman for those who suffer the abuse of fickle "superior powers." "Hardy has given form and substance and body to the complaints which the ancient poets uttered in hint and shadow."

349 Oliphant, James. VICTORIAN NOVELISTS (Lond: Blackie, 1899), p. 229.
H, if he should write any more novels, "will not show any greater capacity for sustained and consistent portraiture than he has done," and therefore "he can never claim a place among the greatest novelists."

350 Payne, W. M. "Recent Poetry," DIAL, XXVI (16 April 1899), 274–75.

H's *Wessex Poems* "display much rugged strength and an occasional flash of beauty, but are evidently nothing more than literary diversions." At times "they exhibit qualities that almost persuade us a true poet was lost when Mr. Hardy became a novelist."

351 "Reviews: Mr. Hardy As A Poet," Academy, LVI (14 Jan 1899), 43–44.

"All his life [H] has been drawing the English peasant, most unpoetical of peasants, with a realism faithful to his stolidity, coarseness, and absense of any romance save that of destiny, which is present in all things ruled by Fate." Although H's powerful style and ponderous themes might seem best suited to the ballad, the form he used for most of the poems in *Wessex Poems and Other Verses*, H shows his best poetic talent in the "lyrical and personal poems of the opening section." As a poet, as well as a novelist, H has something to say to his readers.

352 "Some Forgotten First Contributions," Bookman (Lond), XVI (April 1899), 6.

Chambers Journal published the first works of several famous authors at a time when magazine competition was less sophisticated than it is now. Among the early contributors was H who published "How I Built Myself a House," in the March 1865 issue.

353 "Thomas Hardy as Poet," Saturday Review (Lond), LXXXVII (7 Jan 1899), 19.

Wessex Poems is a "curious and slipshod volume" full of "slovenly . . . uncouth verses, stilted in sentiment, poorly conceived and worse wrought." H should have burned the bulk of it, though a few poems like "Neutral Tones" and "Heiress and Architect" forecast H's mature strength. "I look into my Glass" is a veritable poem, that will outlive the rest of the book.

354 "*Wessex Poems*," Literary World (Boston), XXX (18 March 1899), 86–87.

As a novelist turned poet, Meredith is superior to H: only H's name on the title page stirs interest in the perfunctory verses of *Wessex Poems*.

355 Wilson, Samuel Law. "The Theology of Thomas Hardy," The Theology of Modern Literature (Edinburgh: Clark, 1899), pp. 381–408.

One of "the most saddening spectacles" of late nineteenth century literature is H, "a very prince in literature, concentrating attention on the shadiness and seaminess of life, exploiting sewers and cesspools, dabbling in beastliness and putrefaction." This emphasis stems from "a sincere, but perverted and mistaken, conception of his mission as an artist." In book after book H has written to show "that the common feelings of humanity against se-

duction, adultery, and murder are no inherent part of the nature of things."
[Bitter vilification of *all* of H's art based solely on Wilson's horror-struck
response to *Tess of the d'Urbervilles* and *Jude the Obscure*.]

356 Zangwill, Louis. "In the World of Art and Letters," Cos-
MOPOLITAN, XXVI (March 1899), 582–83.
H's poetry is great "in the same degree as his prose romances."

1900

357 Beale, Sophia. "Woolbridge Manor, the Home of the Turbervilles," TEMPLE BAR MAGAZINE, CXX (May 1900), 106–9.
Near Wool, the station for Lulworth, may be found the original places that
H selected for some of the scenes in *Tess of the d'Urbervilles*. In the Manor
house may yet be seen the "terrible portraits of two women of the seventeenth century" whose visages so disturbed Tess and Angel. The legend of
the Turberville coach is also drawn from life. At some little distance from
Wool are the ruins of Bindon Abbey, which include "several sculptured stone
coffin slabs . . . [and] one shaped out in mummy form, in which we can
imagine poor Tess being laid by her sleep-walking husband."

358 Beerbohm, Max. "*Tess*, the Footlights and the O.U.D.S.,"
SATURDAY REVIEW (Lond), LXXXIX (3 March 1900), 264–65.
To read a novel in an illustrated edition is bad enough, but to watch the
dramatized version of a book which you love is agony. Mrs. Lewis Waller,
who plays the part of Tess at the Coronet Theatre is an intelligent, powerful
actress, but her face, her voice, her manner on the stage have nothing to do
with H's Tess. Such characters as Angel Clare demand of a dramatist an
extraordinary amount of skill. Mr. H. A. Kennedy's conscience will be
pricking him! *Tess of the d'Urbervilles*, more than most books, should have
been saved from the stage.

359 Blaze de Bury, Yetta. "Thomas Hardy," LES ROMANCIERS
ANGLAIS CONTEMPORAINS (CONTEMPORARY ENGLISH NOVELISTS)
(Paris: Perria, 1900), pp. 53–64.
[Much plot summary and little criticism, mainly limited to *Far From the
Madding Crowd*, *Tess of the d'Urbervilles*, and *Jude the Obscure*. There is
a dubious comparison of Tess and Angel with Marguerite and Mephistopheles in Goethe's FAUST; but a perceptive comment on Arabella as the
most logical character in *Jude*, for Arabella sticks to her grossness or character pattern throughout the book, whereas Jude and Susan are volatile
creatures evidencing H's grasp of indecisiveness.] [In French.]

360 Brown, Vincent. "Thomas Hardy: An Enthusiasm," ACADEMY, LVIII (10 March 1900), 208.

[A dialogue between a young man and an older man. The enthusiasm the young man has for H is expressed in his praise of H's humanistic attitude toward life, his ability as a poet, and his control of the novel as an ideal medium for the expression of his philosophical and moral thoughts.]

361 Champneys, Basil. MEMOIRS AND CORRESPONDENCE OF COVENTRY PATMORE. 2 vols (Lond: George Bell, 1900), II, 261–263.

[Patmore's correspondence includes a letter to H (1875) praising his novels, especially *A Pair of Blue Eyes*, and one from H (1886), in which the novelist thanks Patmore for a recent article on the Dorset poet, William Barnes.]

362 Douglas, Sir George. "Wessex Novels," BOOKMAN (Lond), XVIII (Jan 1900), 110–12.

Two qualities which distinguish H's works are "the essential truth and vitality of his characters, and his mastery of English prose."

363 Pène-Huette, L. "Thomas Hardy," NOUVELLE REVUE INTERNATIONALE, XXXIII (15 Nov 1900), 536–42.

H seems to have a panoramic overview of society which is legitimate enough, but the inner recesses of experience and the whole domain of the psychological escape him. H commits the fallacy of "general ideas." He has little or no appreciation of particularities. The plots of his novels remain always artificial, and are just excuses for his philosophizing. H's main characters are rigid and implausible; only his rural landscapes really "live." His platform for social change, especially in the area of marriage legislation, could only be realized in a perfectly homogeneous society. [In French.]

364 "Some Recent Novels of Manners," EDINBURGH REVIEW, CXCII (July 1900), 211–12.

In writing his novels of manners, H concerned himself with individual characters, not whole groups of less strongly particularized figures.

365 Sturmer, Herbert H. "In Hardy's Wessex . . . ," SPEAKER (Lond), ns II (15, 22 Sept 1900), 643, 670–71; ns III (6, 20 Oct 1900), 8–9, 38–39, 61–62; ns IV (3 Aug 1901), 497–98; ns V (20 Oct 1901), 38–39; rptd in LIVING AGE, CXXVII (Oct–Dec 1900), 260–61, 395–98, 457–59, 844–45.

[Describes places used in H's fiction: Dorchester ("Casterbridge"), the Isle of Portland (used in *The Well-Beloved*), Wareham ("Inglebury"), the Isle of Pierbeck (used in *Tess of the d'Urbervilles* and *The Hand of Ethelberta*), Sherborne ("Sherton Abbas"), and Poole ("Havenpool").]

366 Tinsley, William. "Thomas Hardy," RANDOM RECOLLECTIONS OF AN OLD PUBLISHER. 2 vols (Lond: Simpkin, 1900), I, 126–28.

With *Under the Greenwood Tree*, "I felt sure I had got hold of the best little prose idyll I had ever read." Yet it would not sell. "Even though it is as pure and sweet as new-mown hay, it just lacks the touch of sentiment that lady novel-readers most admire." *A Pair of Blue Eyes* "was by far the weakest of the three books I published of his [H]." H told Tinsley that "unless writing fiction paid him well, he should not go on with it; but it did pay him, and very well indeed."

1901

367 Abernathy, Julian W. "The Invasion of Realism," EDUCATION XXI (April 1901), 467–74.

There has been, over the past few decades, an increasing emphasis on the substitution of concrete fact for abstract thought, reality for ideality, investigation for imagination. This tendency has been manifested in literature by an "invasion" of realistic techniques. "Realism is a great principle in art, and was much needed in giving substance and sanity to fiction; but, like every great principle of reform, it has suffered from the excesses of its exponents, who have perverted it into an instrument of degrading coarseness irreconcilable with the true principles of art." In this respect, fiction is an especially guilty art form. *Tess of the d'Urbervilles* exhibits a "pervasive grossness which leaves the reader with a heavy, morbid, shuddering sense of the coarseness of the clay out of which humanity can be made . . . The beauties of Hardy's novel *Tess* are like the roses in Rappacini's garden, whose perfume was poisonous."

368 Archer, William. "Real Conversations: Conversation I.— With Mr. Thomas Hardy," CRITIC (NY), XXXVIII (April 1901), 309–18.

[A rambling dialogue about H's knowledge of Wessex, his disbelief in the supernatural, the nature of his pessimism, and other topics.]

369 "Current Literature," LITERATURE, IX (28 Dec 1901), 604.

Despite occasional good passages and rough-hewn grace, *Poems of the Past and the Present* does not show H's compete mastery of poetic art.

370 E., F. Y. "Afterthoughts in Verse," SPEAKER (Lond) ns V (21 Dec 1901), 342–43.

H's verses "are, in great part, translated prose"; he does "some violence to his ideas in adjusting them to a form chosen quite independently of them." H "is poetical; that is to say, he is not quite a poet." Neither this volume nor *Wessex Poems* "entirely deserves the name of poetry in the sense of excellent verse." [Review of *Poems of the Past and of the Present*.]

> **371** Gosse, Edmund William. "The Historical Place of Mr. Meredith and Mr. Hardy," INTERNATIONAL QUARTERLY, IV (Sept 1901), 299–323.

Under the Greenwood Tree is H's SHAVING OF SHAGPAT; it is an experiment carried out with complete success, which the author never thought fit to repeat. *A Pair of Blue Eyes* is tragedy, indeed, but conducted with a lighthearted extravagance of plot which is not favorable to our pleasure in it. Elfride is the least comprehensible of H's heroines. With *The Hand of Ethelberta* H made a violent effort to free himself from the bondage of Wessex and try new pastures. A certain unreality broods over the novel; the characters are "*ombres chinoises.*" The central position in the fiction of the end of the nineteenth century belongs to *The Return of the Native*; no other modern novel, out of France or Russia, is pervaded with so serene a sense of unity.

> **372** Gwynn, Stephen. "Literature Portraits.—IX. Mr. Thomas Hardy," LITERATURE, IX (6 July 1901), 4–8.

H's fame grew slowly, and, unlike Stevenson or Kipling, he never acquired a large popular audience. His architectural training colors all his works. *Jude the Obscure* shows most clearly H's conception of the tragic triumph of man's lower instincts over his higher. He has established himself as the foremost prose-poet of nature (though his poetry itself is inferior).

> **373** Hammerton, Sir John Alexander (ed). THE PASSING OF VICTORIA: THE POET'S TRIBUTE (Lond: Horace Marshall & Son, 1901), pp. 15, 178.

[H's "V. R.: A Reverie" is printed; a note of thanks to the author of *Tess of the d'Urbervilles* and to the editor of the TIMES for granting permission for the poem to be included appears.]

> **374** Hankinson, Charles James [Clive Holland]. "In Thomas Hardy's Country," BLACK AND WHITE, XXII (10 Aug 1901), 192–93.

Wessex is not a "mystic" country like Ruritania; it appears on no map, but it lives in H's novels and mainly in the county of Dorset. Many of the tales have their chief scenes within a girdle of forty miles, with Dorchester for its center. [Nine photographs illustrate scenes from two novels: *Tess of the d'Urbervilles* and *Two on a Tower*.]

375 Holland, Clive [pseud of C. J. Hankinson]. "A Pilgrimage to Wessex," CRITIC (NY), XXXIX (Aug 1901), 136–44.

[Claims to be the "first authorized statement ever published concerning the topographical features of the most famous of the Wessex novels." Describes a tour of Wessex, supported by a map of the route and eight photographs, including one of H.]

376 Holland, Clive [pseud of C. J. Hankinson]. "A Pilgrimage to Wessex: Thomas Hardy's Country," SKETCH, XXXIV (10 July 1901), 473; possibly rptd for the Whitefriars Club as a pamphlet (Lond: Lund, 1901).

The Whitefriars made a pilgrimage to Wessex on 20 June 1901 in order to see the world so brilliantly described in H's novels, and to visit H. Because Wessex is still "steeped deep in traditions and customs," a visit there allows one to "trace many of the scenes of the novels."

377 Holland, Clive [pseud of C. J. Hankinson]. "Thomas Hardy: The Man, His Books, and the Land of Wessex," BOOKMAN (Lond), XXI (Nov 1901), 46–50.

[Thin biographical sketch.]

378 Howells, W. D. "Mr. Thomas Hardy's Bathsheba Everdene and Paula Power," HEROINES OF FICTION. 2 vols (NY: Harper, 1901), II, 193–210.

Though the reader can understand Bathsheba's mind in *Far From the Madding Crowd*, something mysterious remains unexplained that makes her character masterfully drawn. She has great common-sense, but when her heart rules her head she is less admirable, although not less real. Paula Power in *A Laodicean* is as vivid and as completely "Hardyesque" as Bathsheba but comes to the reader through the busy backdrop of society. In the character and actions of Sue Bridehead in *Jude the Obscure*, H voiced his strongest praise for "the womanly," but this novel cannot be used to illustrate a critical point without the critic's having to share the disapprobation which the author received.

379 Howells, W. D. "Mr. Thomas Hardy's Heroines," HEROINES OF FICTION. 2 vols (NY: Harper, 1901), II, 177–92.

H's heroines are all of a type. In varying degrees, all are at the mercy of external forces. Though some, like Bathsheba Everdene in *Far From the Madding Crowd*, demonstrate a significant amount of self-will, it is ultimately futile. They act in response to earthy, unconscious impulses and are only temporarily and incompletely committed to moral law. Totally unlike American women, they are untouched by Puritanism. The character of Tess in *Tess of the d'Urbervilles* seems inconsistent, the product of two different conceptions, although this would be difficult to prove. Eustacia Vye in *The Return of the Native* is the most sordid and selfish of H's heroines, so much so that the reader is not interested in the vague circumstances that brought her to Egdon Heath. Contrastingly, it is possible to be affectionately interested in Elfride Swancourt in *A Pair of Blue Eyes* because, despite her recklessness, she is genuinely unselfish.

380 Lee, Elizabeth. "Englischer Brief" (English Letter), DAS LITERARISCHE ECHO, IV (Dec 1901), 406.
Poems of the Past and the Present reveals that H has further entrenched himself in a gloomy view of life. Although H is not a poet, he is still able to lend his thoughts great power and beauty of expression. [In German.]

381 "The Lounger," CRITIC (NY), XXXIX (Oct 1901), 292.
[Notes that *Poems of the Past and the Present* is to be published.]

382 [Mallock, W. H.]. "The Popular Novel," QUARTERLY REVIEW, CXCIV (July 1901), 244–73.
The only genuinely great novelists in England at present are Meredith and H. Both use the novel to express their philosophy, and both have noticeable defects. Both have limited practical knowledge, and this handicaps them. H is great as long as he deals with Wessex, and the remarkable qualities of the philosophy in his novels are second only to those in George Eliot's work; this philosophic bent is, however, not glaring. H's style, "the clearness, the directness, the illuminated originality of vision," is unlike Meredith's, and it is excellently suited for his portrayal of Wessex. Although his focus may seem narrow, "the universalising quality of his genius has made this province a kingdom." Neither novelist is popular at the present time, although they have a small group of discriminating admirers.

383 "Mr. Thomas Hardy," LITERARY WORLD (Lond), LXIII (21 June, 1901), 588.
H's novelistic career falls into two distinct phases: the work before *Tess of the d'Urbervilles*, in which he was "an interpreter of nature" and of "rural life"; and that after *Tess*, in which he exhibits "the chilling pessimism which reduces men and women to automata." *Tess* is "the battle-ground on which the conflict seems to have been fought," and the victory, unfortunately, seems to have gone to philosophy rather than to art.

384 "New Books," BOOKMAN (Lond), XXI (Nov 1901), 41.
"Thomas Hardy's theory that the immortals make sport of human beings goes back to Greek Tragedy." It was revived again in the eighteenth century with the book, A FREE INQUIRY INTO THE NATURE AND ORIGIN OF EVIL, by Soame Jenyns. Dr. Johnson made a famous review of it.

385 "New Novels," BOOKMAN (Lond), XXI (Nov 1901), 40.
[About a paragraph of the manuscript of *Tess of the d'Urbervilles* is reproduced showing several revisions.]

386 "Reviews: Mr. Hardy's New Poems," ACADEMY, LXI (23 Nov 1901), 475–76.
Poems of the Past and the Present shows H as a "serious sympathiser with human nature, a disillusioned observer of life, a frustrated reacher after divine purposes." These characteristics do not, however, make him a good poet. "Mr Hardy is too self conscious, too deliberately rhetorical, too monotonously disenchanted, for the word poet to spring to our lips at all in connection with this book. There is more of sheer poetry in his novels."

387 Tomson, Arthur. "Dorchester," ART JOURNAL, No. 758 (Aug 1901), 231–35.
[An article and sketches by Tomson on H country. Tomson noted fragments of old Roman walls and pavements, the remains of an amphitheater (Maumbury Rings) and a man-made hill (Mai Dun). He found Dorchester's rural qualities inspiring.]

1902

388 Ackermann, Richard. KURZE GESCHICHTE DER ENGLISCHEN LITTERATUR IN DEN GRUNDZÜGEN IHRER ENTWICKLUNG (Short History of English Literature in the Development of Its Principles) (Stuttgart and Zweibrücken: Fritz Lehrmann, 1902), p. 141.
[Associates H, Trollope, and Mrs. Craik as authors of society novels.] [In German.]

389 "As Others See Us: Mr. Thomas Hardy," PALL MALL MAGAZINE, XXVIII (Oct 1902), 254.
H was a tranquil man who was indifferent to the external world and who did not speak freely. He preferred Dorsetshire to London and loved "his own meditations best of all." [Includes photo.]

390 "Books: Thomas Hardy's *Poems of the Past and the Present,*" SPECTATOR (Lond), LXXXVIII (5 April 1902), 516–17.
"Poetry is not his proper medium. He does not move easily in it." At times, however, H's verse has "a haunting rhythm and a wild, eerie, melancholy timbre and ring all of his own." A "realist," H "prefers the seamy to the

smooth side of life" and has "a morbid taste for the ghastly and the gruesome." With all the mental equipment of a poet, "H is barely a poet." He is "best as a prose poet."

391 Boynton, H. W. "Books New and Old," ATLANTIC MONTHLY, LXXXIX (Feb 1902), 280–81.

The "voice of resonant joy [found in Mr. Henley's springtime poetry] is altogether lacking in Mr. Hardy's muse [in *Poems of the Past and the Present*], who is indeed a heathen rather than a pagan, or so we might say if we were sure of her existence. For Mr. Hardy's verse is, after all, a by product, clearly a left-hand mode of expression. His use of metre is ingenious rather than flexible or musical."

392 Brunnemann, Anna. "Thomas Hardy," DIE GEGENWART, LXI (10 May 1902), 294–98.

[Biographical sketch of H. Plot summaries and commentary on *Tess of the d'Urbervilles* and *Jude the Obscure*. Brief discussion of *Poems of the Past and the Present*.] [In German.]

393 DeCasseres, Benjamin. "Thomas Hardy's Women," BOOKMAN (NY), XVI (Oct 1902), 131–33.

The characters in H's novels live in a world like that which Sophocles developed in his dramas: people are objects controlled by irrational powers. From an age of widely differing philosophical thoughts, H gleaned a concept of life which was largely pessimistic. H's characters must be understood in the context of this view of life. [Mainly references to *The Mayor of Casterbridge* and *The Return of the Native*.]

394 Douglas, Sir George. "A New Note of Poetic Melancholy," BOOKMAN (Lond), XXI (Jan 1902), 131–33.

In both form and diction, the *Poems of the Past and the Present* is superior to the *Wessex Poems*. H's pessimism is comparable to the outlook of Shelley, Leopardi, and James Thomson, though none of these is as profound as H.

395 "Echo der Zeitschriften" (Echo of the Periodicals), DAS LITERARISCHE ECHO, IV (Feb 1902), 615–16.

Jude the Obscure is H's masterpiece: sincere, bitter, and thought-provoking. [In German.]

396 "The English Novel in the Nineteenth Century," EDINBURGH REVIEW, CXCVI (Oct 1902), 502–3.

In H, "the most representative figure among modern novelists, . . . the factor of sex bulks big and ugly." The romance of Jude's life is learning; sex is his stumbling block. H's "sombre genius" is now expressing itself in verse, and he has tried drama experimentally.

397 Frye, Prosser Hall. "Nature and Thomas Hardy," INDEPEN-
DENT (NY), LIV (10 July 1902), 1657–59; rptd in LITERARY RE-
VIEWS AND CRITICISMS (NY: Putnam, 1908), pp. 104–13.

H is a novelist of nature. Of all his books, *The Return of the Native* is undoubtedly the one that displays him at the best advantage. *Tess of the
d'Urbervilles* suffers, among other drawbacks, from its incongruous clutter
of erotico-psychological generalizations. H has only continued the tradition
of J. J. Rousseau. There is a mixture in his plots of pity and malice which
resembles the profound duplicity of the Greek tragic spirit and the moral
ambiguity of Victor Hugo's "tragic grotesque." But there is no pathos in
him, because there is no mirth. Even his laughter is dull, brutal, and discordant.

398 Grein, J. T. "Stage Society: *The Three Wayfarers*. A Legendary Trifle in One Act by Thomas Hardy," DRAMATIC CRITICISM
1900–1901 (Lond: Greening, 1902), III, 54–56.

The 1892 dramatization of H's "The Three Strangers" is praiseworthy. The
production was marred by slovenly acting.

399 Hodgkinson, L. "Things and other Things: Letters to Living
Authors—VII. Mr. Thomas Hardy," GOOD WORDS, XLIII (Sept
1902), 673–74.

Many of H's novels are quite good, especially when he is describing nature,
but too often his lack of good taste mars his artistry, as in *Tess of the
d'Urbervilles*, *Jude the Obscure*, and *Two on a Tower*.

400 Howells, W. D. "Some New Volumes of Verse," NORTH
AMERICAN REVIEW, CLXXIV (Jan 1902), 140–41.

Pessimism is justifiable and if it is increased pessimism which has made
Poems of the Past and the Present better than *Wessex Poems*, one must
wish it to abound in H more and more. H writes verse as he writes prose,
and those who do not enjoy his thinking will not enjoy his singing.

401 Ison, Letitia E. "Things and other Things: Letters to Living
Authors—VII. Mr. Thomas Hardy," GOOD WORDS, XLIII (Sept
1902), 676–78.

As a comic writer, H excels at both rural and urban humor, though only
in his country stories can he exercise his faculty for verbal impressionism.
He should shun the coarseness of his recent productions, especially *Jude the
Obscure,* and return to "the sweet smell of woods and fields."

402 Johnson, M. "Mr. Hardy's Poetry and Philosophy of Life,"
PRIMITIVE METHODIST QUARTERLY REVIEW, XXX (July 1902),
381–94.

H, unlike some other novelists who wrote poems, remains a poet even in his poems, but "their mechanism is . . . odd." There is "a sort of fumbling after expression . . . an incompleteness of accomplishment . . . seldom to be found in work of such inherent merit." H "is entirely dependent for his inspiration upon the . . . somewhat dismal vision of life." His hopelessness is no pose, "but a general condition of mind" reached by sincere study "and expressed with great power and lucidity."

403 "The Literary Week," ACADEMY, LXIII (11 Oct 1902), 384.
An article in the NEW YORK BOOKMAN criticized the theme of overpowering fate and the passive female characterizations in H's novels. This would apply well to his later works, but not to his earlier pieces, such as *The Woodlanders* and *Under the Greenwood Tree*, which will, in the future, be appreciated more than the thematically ponderous later works.

404 "Literature." ATHENAEUM, No. 3871 (4 Jan 1902), 6–7.
H's *Wessex Poems and Other Verses* was perplexing because of the inconsistent poetic skills presented. *Poems of the Past and the Present* shows even fewer moments of poetic inspiration and talent. "The diction is persistently clumsy, full of ugly neologisms, with neither the simplicity of untutored song nor that of consummate art." The best poems are those inspired by H's perpetual preoccupation—the tragic irony of life, "the expression of which is by turns grim, cynical, melancholy, resigned, and which more than once arises, in intention at least, to the sublimity of an indictment."

405 Meyerfeld, Max. "Aus de englischen Bücherwelt" (From the English World of Books), DAS LITERARISCHE ECHO, IV (1902), 1240.
With *Poems of the Past and the Present* H has restored the personal art of proclamation in poetry. He treats the enduring questions, transforms nature into a grim plaintiff, and presents the total misery of mankind. [In German.]

406 Meyerfeld, Max. "Echo der Zeitschriften" (Echo of the Periodicals), DAS LITERARISCHE ECHO, IV (1902), 928–29.
Jude the Obscure is far too advanced for its age. Moral justice has not become legal justice, and H presents the conflict of these opposing forces. There is no shortage of mistakes, inaccuracies, and misunderstandings in the German translation. In short, "hands off." [In German.]

407 "Modern Pessimism," QUARTERLY REVIEW, CXCVI (Oct 1902), 621–46, espec 636–40.
H and George Eliot "head a long list of British novelists, distinguished by the grave sincerity and severity with which they depict the darker aspects of modern life, the most recent of whom is the author of that grim and power-

ful tale, THE HOUSE WITH THE GREEN SHUTTERS [George Douglas Brown]." H is especially emphatic on the fate which controls capriciously men's destinies and is unlike George Eliot in this respect, for her characters always receive their just deserts and are not hounded by relentless fate. Duty to persevere makes H's pessimism noble, and it "suggests the enthusiasm of self-surrender as taught by Hartmann."

408 "Out of the Deep," SATURDAY REVIEW (Lond), XCIII (11 Jan 1902), 49.

As *Poems of the Past and the Present* shows, "so far as it is possible to be a poet without having a singing voice, Mr. Hardy is a poet, and a profoundly interesting one." A "melancholy sincerity . . . gives much of its quality to a book otherwise of very varying merit." H has carefully studied the technique of verse "and he has a command of very difficult metres."

409 Payne, W. M. "Recent Poetry," DIAL, XXXII (1 May 1902), 314–20, espec 314–16.

Poems of the Past and the Present justifies the conclusions drawn from H's first volume of poems: it has an "incisive way of laying bare the very heart of life." It is the work of a man who cared little for technique and did not have a singing voice. The book deepens our respect for H's intellectual force; all the poems have something well worth saying. H has "an abundance of ideas that come only to the man who has meditated deeply upon the most serious problems."

410 Pitt, J. "Things and other Things: Letters to Living Authors— VII. Mr. Thomas Hardy," GOOD WORDS, XLIII (Sept 1902), 674–76.

H is much better as a novelist than as a poet or short story writer. But even though *Tess of the d'Urbervilles* and *Jude the Obscure* especially are great tragedies, the philosophy which underlies them is unhealthy.

411 "Realism," WESTMINSTER REVIEW, CLVIII (Sept 1902), 339.

"The typical English realists are perhaps George Moore and George Gissing; Thomas Hardy has some of the characteristics of the realists, but he is not one of them."

412 "Recent Poetry," LITERARY WORLD (Boston), XXXIII (1 Feb 1902), 23.

H's *Poems of the Past and the Present* is not first-rate verse, but despite occasional roughness and faults is distinctly good.

413 "Recent Poetry," NATION (NY), LXXIV (23 Jan 1902), 76. "There is at any rate a solid Saxon grapple of thought" in *Poems of the Past and the Present*.

414 Sherren, Wilkinson. THE WESSEX OF ROMANCE (Lond: Francis Griffiths, 1902); rvd ed (Lond: Griffiths, 1908).
[A useful guide to H's world, especially Part VII which gives a glossary of Wessex terms and a list of identified place names. The first part is discussion of Wessex people with interesting anecdotes drawn from H's novels. The second part is a general discussion of H's life and work, readable but not profound or detailed. The largest section describes Wessex places and towns. Also gives synopses and character lists for all the novels. Concludes with bibliography of H's writings to 1908. Too derivative from novels. Readable but perhaps slightly juvenile. Main use is identifying places in novels.]

415 Shindler, Robert. "Thomson—Hardy," NEUPHILOLOGISCHE VORTRÄGE UND ABHANDLUNG, II (1902), 64–71; trans and rptd as "Thomson. Hardy," in ON CERTAIN ASPECTS OF RECENT ENGLISH LITERATURE (Leipzig: B. G. Teubner, 1902), pp. 59–72 [Sammlung Neuphilogogischer Vorträge und Abhandlungen, II].
In his later works, H has made clear "that his aim is not to justify the ways of God to man, but to vilify them." In *The Mayor of Casterbridge* H does not depict a man whose character led him to triumphant success—as the subtitle promises—but "the reverse side of the picture." He shows "a man of firm will and indomitable energy . . . qualities [which] bring [Henchard] down to hopeless and abject misery." Finally, H's world-view seems to be: "we can at least recognise our sad position, curb all impracticable ideals and impossible ambitions, and avoid increasing our unhappiness by recriminations." [In German.]

416 "Some Poets, Old and New," HARPER'S WEEKLY, XLVI (11 Jan 1902), 52.
[Brief impressionistic appreciation of *Wessex Poems* and *Poems of the Past and the Present*.]

417 Thomas, Edith M. "Some Recent Verse," CRITIC (NY), XL (March 1902), 261–63.
H is unpopular with the General Reader because of the "lack of lyrical quality in his verse." The General Reader is frightened by H's willingness to face all of the possibilities of "the soul's destiny."

418 Windle, Bertram C. A. THE WESSEX OF THOMAS HARDY (Lond: Lane, 1902).
[Traces the topography in H's novels, first by working from Casterbridge in one direction at a time, then, more generally, by considering each novel separately.]

1903

419 Davray, Henry D. "Lettres anglaises" (English Letters), MERCURE DE FRANCE, XLVI (April 1903), 264–65.
H's novels are suddenly gaining recognition. His work may still be less popular than Marie Corelli's or Hall Caine's, but he will be remembered when these authors are forgotten. Three of his novels so far have been translated into French. A new complete English edition of his works is being published. [In French.]

420 Hammerton, J. A. (ed). STEVENSONIA (Lond: Grant Richards, 1903); rptd (Edinburgh: John Grant, 1910), pp. 82, 265.
[The editor comments on Stevenson's love of *The Woodlanders* and quotes Jesse A. Steuart who says only H understood the writing of short stories as well as Stevenson.]

421 MacMichael, J. Holden. " 'Welter,' " NOTES AND QUERIES, 9th ser XII (25 July 1903), 74.
H's use of the word "welter" in his poem "The Pine Planters" calls to mind Milton's use in LYCIDAS and HYMN ON THE NATIVITY.

422 N., A. "Dual Personalities," LITERARY WORLD (Lond), ns LXVIII (21 Aug 1903), 128–29.
H's limitations as a poet spring primarily from his lack of "sympathetic imagination." His message is "the gospel of endurance," and he appears unable to put an optimistic construction on his experience.

423 Nevinson, Henry W. "Thomas Hardy," ENGLISH ILLUSTRATED MAGAZINE, ns XXIX (June 1903), 280–85.
To Wordsworth and H, nature was not pleasant; it was a necessary condition of mankind. Against this natural background, H shows the development of passionate characters. For him, character was fate. [Contains a useful bibliography, including articles about H from 1879 to 1903.]

424 "New Editions and Reprints," LITERARY WORLD (Lond), ns LXVII (30 Jan 1903), 107.
Although H is often gloomy and pessimistic, readers with taste will prefer his darker philosophical novels to the "mere sensational imaginings" which are designed either to shock or to soothe.

425 "New Editions and Reprints," LITERARY WORLD (Lond), ns LXV (14 March 1903), 248.
Under the Greenwood Tree is "rich in the colourings of rural life, deft in characterisation and healthy in its whole atmosphere."

426 "New Editions and Reprints," LITERARY WORLD (Lond), ns LXVII (10 April 1903), 344.

Two persistent objections to H's work should be put aside. The first, that his heroes and heroines are too lowly to merit our interest, is made by the sort of reader who cares only for "fast people in high stations" and not by the person "whose tastes need be considered." The second, that H's pessimism is a wrong-headed, distorted view of life, is a vacuous misrepresentation.

427 "New Editions and Reprints," LITERARY WORLD (Lond), ns LXVII (26 June 1903), 609.

The latest six volumes in the Popular Uniform Edition reveal something of H's range and offer a counterdose to those who would charge him with exclusively morbid tastes. Several of them are pleasantly humorous love-stories. H's skill with the short story is also displayed in the collections here reprinted.

428 "New Editions and Reprints," LITERARY WORLD (Lond), ns LXVIII (4 Sept 1903), 162.

[Notice of the appearance of *Under the Greenwood Tree* and *The Well-Beloved*—the last volumes in Macmillan's "Popular Uniform Edition."]

429 Nicoll, William Robertson. "Thomas Hardy," CHAMBERS' CYCLOPEDIA OF ENGLISH LITERATURE (Phila: Lippincott, 1903), III, 680–83.

[Sketch of life and works, with excerpt from *The Return of the Native* and the poem "Valenciennes" included; photograph by Elliott & Fry attached.]

430 S[horter], C[lement] K. "A Literary Letter," SPHERE (Lond), 24 Oct 1903, p. 84.

H "told me that his earliest influence in the direction of realism was obtained from Crabbe's work."

431 T. "Personal Sketches: XXI—Thomas Hardy," LITERARY WORLD (Lond), ns LXVII (6 March 1903), 223–24.

H's relative lack of conventional education enables him to retain "more humanity and originality" than many of his contemporaries. The fact that he was an architect is "distinctly visible in his story-building." He never seems quite at home in the crush of society, seeming to prefer the role of detached observer. H's comparative unpopularity is the result of the middle class's lack of sympathy for the rural existence which abounds in his work. In addition they miss the melodrama, the happy endings, the "wicked duke and the beautiful duchess." The great writers and thinkers of the day, however, recognize H as a master.

432 Turnbull, M. M. "Two Delineators of Wessex," GENTLE-
MAN'S MAGAZINE, CCXCV (Nov 1903), 469–79.
Though William Barnes was the first literary spokesman for the Wessex
peasantry, H's concern with pessimistic philosophy made him the greater
artist. He was able to realize fully the artistic potential Barnes first detected.
However, H's stature is limited ultimately by his failure to show in his
novels the religious faith by which men must live.

1904

433 Beerbohm, Max. "Thomas Hardy as a Panoramatist," SATUR-
DAY REVIEW (Lond), XCVII (30 Jan 1904), 136–38.
Working in a different genre, H has with *The Dynasts* created the "first
modern work of dramatic fiction in which freewill is denied to the characters." H's treatment of men as mere "electrons" and his inclusion into this
pattern of great figures in history makes *Dynasts* "a noble achievement."
The irony of the play is most clearly seen in the contrast between limited
human vision and the far-reaching panorama seen by the eternally watching
gods. H had to "wrestle for his effects" because his poetry reveals itself
"more surely and firmly through the medium of prose than through the
medium of rhyme and meter." H's drama "expresses itself better through
narration than through dialogue and stage directions."

434 Bennett, Arnold. "My Literary Heresies," T. P.'s WEEKLY, IV
(23 Sept 1904), 392.
H created a new kind of novel, distinct from the realistic of Richardson and
the romantic of Scott: "it contains a new beauty, a new thrill for the amateurs of beauty: it does not 'derive.' " *Tess of the d'Urbervilles* and *Jude
the Obscure* are not H's great books; "they are sign[s] of decadence."

435 "Books: Mr. Hardy's Drama," SPECTATOR (Lond), XCII
(20 Feb 1904), 293–94.
The Dynasts, written as an epic, is for the study not the stage. It shows
"events which shook the world as a kind of puppet show behind which
moves the force which the author chooses to call the 'Immanent Will,'
ruthless and incomprehensible." H's "hard Pyrrhonism" makes the Immanent Will "a thousandfold more distant from humanity than the Fate of
other poets." Peasant characters are "as real as life itself," but great men
are only "brooding shadows." Spirits never speak "without expressing a

banal thought in the worst verse." Metrics are "halting, turgid, and singularly lacking in music"; rhythms are "weak and improverished." "The work of a poet," but "rarely poetry."

436 "Books New and Old," Atlantic Monthly, XCIII (May 1904), 713.
The Dynasts has a logical continuity; it is filled with historical information, but it contains neither people nor poetry. *Dynasts* proves H to be less a poet than his poems do. He is trying to work in an alien field of literary endeavor.

437 Brunnemann, Anna. "Thomas Hardy," Aus Fremden Zungen, V (15 April 1904), 81–84.
In *Tess of the d'Urbervilles* and *Jude the Obscure,* H asserted his individuality. He is one of the few contemporary English writers to treat moral and social problems in a bold and individual manner. H's earlier novels, however, have their own particular charm. The people, customs, and incidents of Wessex inspired H's creativity. From this regional environment stems H's philosophy that the individual is subservient to eternal laws, that his bread is earned by the sweat of his brow, that sorrow comes like joy only less often, and that life is full of irony. [In German.]

438 Davray, Henry D. "Lettres anglaises" ("English Letters"), Mercure de France, L (April 1904), 263–64.
H, whose fame as novelist is well-established in England, has just created a sensation in the literary world. Under the disconcerting title of *The Dynasts,* he has published the first part of what he calls, "A Drama of the Napoleonic Wars." Since he has obviously no intention of having it performed on the stage, one wonders why he chose the dramatic medium and why long passages are in verse. At first, one is tempted to mock and condemn the whole daring enterprise. But, owing to its state of incompletion, it is probably too early to pronounce on the subject. [In French.]

439 "Drama," Athenaeum, No. 3978 (23 Jan 1904), 123.
The first part of *The Dynasts* shows elements of Shakespearean history and Greek tragedy. It has a particular "connexion with Hellenic drama, in that whatever is not explicit in the fable is assumed to exist in the minds of the public." Outside the element of the novel, H is unpoetic and unartistic.

440 "*The Dynasts*: A Suggestion," Times Literary Supplement (Lond), 29 Jan 1904, p. 30.
One cannot classify *The Dynasts* with other plays, but it is not a new form; rather, it is quasi-dramatic. It is a bad relation of means to ends to write a play meant only to be read. One cannot rely on the imagination of spectators either because the most important part of a play is action. The best

way to stage *Dynasts* would be as a puppet show, since H conceived it that way. [H replied (ibid, 5 Feb 1904, pp. 36–37) that the reviewer was too absolute. Literature cannot be thus prescribed. Also, the form of stage-play is not unnatural for reading; it is an "instinctive, primitive narrative shape." The form of *Dynasts* is the only one suitable for what the author wanted to do.]

441 *"The Dynasts* and the Puppets," TIMES LITERARY SUPPLE-MENT (Lond), 12 Feb 1904, p. 46.

H did not like the suggestion that *The Dynasts* could be performed as a puppet show, but it would be perfectly in harmony with his philosophical intent. There would be problems of performance; but *Dynasts* is playable, and H argues against his own interest in saying that it is only for reading. [H replied (ibid, 19 Feb 1904, p. 53) that the critic's real objection is not so much to the form as the philosophy, but there is really nothing new in it—it is as old as predestination.]

442 Harper, Charles. THE HARDY COUNTRY: LITERARY LAND-MARKS OF THE WESSEX NOVELS (Lond: A. & C. Black, 1904, 1911, 1925).

Wessex is H's own creation, an expansion of Dorsetshire to nearly the same boundaries as the ancient kingdom of Wessex. Fawley Magma and Christminster are identified with *Jude the Obscure,* the latter being Oxford. *A Pair of Blue Eyes* takes us far beyond Wessex, but the borders are vague, says H. "Castle Boterel" may be found on maps as Boscastle. [Then follows an exploration of the Wessex of H, starting with Winchester (Wintoncester), running through Pentridge (Tess's Trantridge), Swanage (Ethelberta's Knollsea), Weymouth (Budmouth), etc., with travelogue descriptions and historical notes.]

443 Holland, Clive [pseud of Charles James Hankinson]. "The Work of Frederick Whitehead, a Painter of Thomas Hardy's Wessex," STUDIO (Lond), XXXII (July 1904), 105–16.

Wessex has "come to be a 'Hardy' country." Whitehead, whose best paintings are of Wessex landscapes, is a "singularly sympathetic interpreter" of the district. He paints many scenes described by H, especially those from *Tess of the d'Urbervilles* and *The Return of the Native.*

444 L., L. L. *"The Dynasts,"* T. P.'s WEEKLY, IV (29 Jan 1904), 149.

The Dynasts, Part I, is more "cosmic" than a drama of history, particularly in the Phantom Intelligences, who are "like the chorus of Greek drama," but "emanations of 'the all-urging Will.' " The work creates "the atmosphere of prophecy, a shadowy foreboding, as it were, of future, but inevitable, catastrophes."

445 Lea, Hermann. A HANDBOOK TO THE WESSEX COUNTRY OF MR. THOMAS HARDY'S NOVELS AND POEMS (Lond: Kegan Paul, Trench, Trubner, [1904]); rptd (Bournemouth: Holland Rowbottom, "Graphic" Office, 1906).

[Sketch maps and photographs; like much of Lea's other work in this vein.]

446 Lee, Elizabeth. "Englischer Brief" (English Letter), DAS LITERARISCHE ECHO, Sept 1904, p. 1660.

[In reviewing *Time's Laughingstocks,* Lee restates the plot of "The Revisitation."] [In German.]

447 Macdonell, A. "Mr. Hardy's Experiment," BOOKMAN (Lond), XXV (Feb 1904), 221–23.

H deserves a conscientious appraisal of his experimental work, *The Dynasts.* But the problem in criticizing the work is in deciding upon a basis for criticism. The open-endedness of the work is an immediate barrier to judgment, and one is left to comment arbitrarily.

448 "Mr. Thomas Hardy's Drama," TIMES LITERARY SUPPLEMENT (Lond), 15 Jan 1904, pp. 11–12.

In *The Dynasts,* why did H, a master of prose narrative and poetry, try the dramatic form, which is readable only when it has human qualities? The only human beings are the four rustics; the other seventy-odd have no personality, do not suffer or develop. But these are superficial matters: when the next two parts appear it may become clear that H is not writing about men but nations, or Fate. Most damning to dramatic effect are the Phantom Intelligences, who prevent us from sympathizing with characters whose lives are meaningless.

449 [Newbolt, Sir Henry]. "*The Dynasts,*" MONTHLY REVIEW, XIV (March 1904), 1–12.

In Part I of *The Dynasts,* the "hero [is] the English nation." H's manner is "rigidly impersonal," but this is "not due to any lack of high imaginative power." H's Phantom Intelligences are "no more than personified moods of the human mind in criticism." *Dynasts* presents us H's "serious and reasoned creed, set out with extraordinary skill and impressiveness." H's "real subject" is "the Creator, not the creature." The play's thesis "involves a denial of Free Will," but the point of his argument "is to prove . . . the impossibility of justifying the ways of God to man." Perhaps H erred in naming "The Immanent Will" because Will is possessed only by reasoning creatures. If all life is the outcome of a single Cause, however unreasoning, "how can any impulse or acquirement come to it [life] from Chance?" H seems "purposely to have turned away" from facing some of the difficulties produced by his philosophic system. He sees the Will as an "unneeded" faculty, yet "if the sense of will is an illusion [to mankind] it is an absolutely perfect one."

450 Ortensi, Ulisse. "Letterati Contemporanei: Thomas Hardy" (Contemporary Letters: Thomas Hardy), EMPORIUM, XX (July 1904), 100–108.

[An enthusiastic presentation of H's works to the Italian reading public, with lengthy translated quotations and summaries of his novels. Contains the facsimile reproduction of H's reply to Arnoldo Cervesato's inquiry about "new idealism" in European literature (published in "Primavere d'idee").] [In Italian.]

451 Payne, W. M. "Two Poetic Dramas," DIAL, XXXVI (16 May 1904), 319–21.

The Dynasts is like Richard Strauss's symphonic poems which try to embody a metaphysical system in the endeavor to "express a philosophy of history in a closet-drama." Not successful, but interesting, *Dynasts* adds little to our insight of Napoleonic wars "but does much to illuminate the point of view from which its author contemplates the significant happenings in the tragic comedy of human life." The Phantom Intelligences are very important—they give the work its distinctive character. H's blank verse is unlike that of any other writer. First six acts will hopefully be completed. "So grandiose a plan, conceived by so forceful and distinguished a writer, could not suffer frustration without the world being left the poorer."

452 Peabody, Josephine Preston. "Books Reviewed—Fact and Fiction," CRITIC (NY), XLIV (May 1904), 469–70.

The Dynasts is "interesting," but it "does not justify its method" and is "dry and unbeautiful."

453 Prilipp, Beda. "Heimatkunst im modernen englischen Roman" (Local Color in the Modern English Novel), DIE GRENZBOTEN, LXIII: 3 (1904), 89–98, espec 90–94.

H's art is bitter, profound, and melancholy. Treatment of nature, association of characters with landscape, and portrayal of women are superb in H's novels. [In German.]

454 "Recent Poetry," NATION (NY), LXXVIII (25 Feb 1904), 153–54.

The Dynasts is "uncouth and forbidding." H's panoramic, "quasi-poetic vision . . . gives *The Dynasts* unity and—for all its uncouthness—power."

455 "Reviews: A Vast Venture," ACADEMY, LXVI (23 Jan 1904), 95.

The Dynasts is "a vast venture" in poetic drama. H lacks, however, the poetic flexibility and experience needed for the successful accomplishment of such a tremendous undertaking. His combination of realism and abstraction does not blend. "If it were worked out in that medium of the novel wherein he is a master, we might have an imposing and enthralling trilogy of novels."

456 "Thomas Hardy's Drama," Literary World (Lond), ns LXIX (12 Feb 1904), 139–40.

The Dynasts is an unsatisfactory result following close on H's desertion of what he is best fitted by his genius to do. H's spirits are the most interesting personages of the drama. Especially disheartening is "the poverty of the blank verse." With few exceptions, H, a writer fond of and capable of producing poetry, has somehow contrived to keep poetry out of *Dynasts*, "putting in its place matter almost prosier than prose."

457 "Thomas Hardy's Genius," Literary World (Lond), ns LXX (29 July 1904), 88.

A course of reading H's novels will "alleviate the symptoms" of that mental disease "known to experts as megalomania, and popularly as 'swelled head.' " H's emphasis on fate and the uncertainties of life cautions us against rejoicing in our achievements or security. Even H's happy endings sometimes fail, as in *The Mayor of Casterbridge*—perhaps "the grimmest of Thomas Hardy's stories"—"to lift the curtain of gloom." No novelist of the Victorian period "bears the stamp of genius more unmistakably" than H.

458 [Walkley, Arthur Bingham]. "Mr. Thomas Hardy's Drama," Times Literary Supplement (Lond), 4 Jan 1904, pp. 11–12; rptd, "with alterations," as *"The Dynasts* and the Puppets," in Drama and Life (Lond: Methuen, 1907), pp. 106–14.

The Dynasts is a tale of "the dead facts of a school book history" rather than a drama, and its characters are mere "puppets." "The additional grip and vividness that may perhaps be gained at certain moments by the author's rejection of all the aids offered by the common form of narrative are no compensation for the difficulties he courts and the extra demands on the imagination of the reader." In the first six acts, only four characters are seen. "They talk just enough to advance the historical action and say the things that tradition reports them to have said, and fight in dumb show." "They are puppets, dancing on strings, helpless, impersonal agents of the clockwork thought of a blind and unreasoning It." *Dynasts* supposedly dramatizes the Napoleonic Wars but "here there is nothing to fight and we see not men but puppets."

459 Wright, Edward. "The Novels of Thomas Hardy," Quarterly Review, CXCIX (April 1904), 499–523.

H created in the English novel "a well-knit drama instead of the string of episodes which once it was." H's rustics are more genuine than Wordsworth's. "They are supposed to unite the enervating fatalism that distinguishes Mr. Hardy with a power of silent, grave endurance in adversity that a Roman Stoic would have admired." H's rural characters are more admirable than the urban dwellers in the tales, and many of his women are "nobly conceived." Marty South is a more moving figure than Tess. *Under the Greenwood Tree* provides evidence that H was not entirely joyless. H's dramatic power "is especially displayed in *The Return of the Native,* which in construction is his best work." *The Woodlanders* is the tragic version of the theme of *Greenwood Tree. Tess of the d'Urbervilles* is similar to ADAM BEDE, yet there is a "profound dissimilarity of treatment" in the two works. H's "defect is artificiality." *Tess,* however it is marred, "remains a melodramatic novel excelling in wild pathos and poetic beauty." "He prefers images which convey emotions to images which create pictures in the mind." *Jude the Obscure* "is another of Mr. Hardy's essays in metaphysics." Jude is "Schopenhauer's perfidious lover . . . [and he] is also intended to personify the more gratifying idea of the rapid extinction of the human race by degeneration."

1905

---

460 Bates, Ernest Sutherland. "The Optimism of Thomas Hardy," INTERNATIONAL JOURNAL OF ETHICS, XV (July 1905), 469–85.
There are two sorts of optimism, docile and heroic. For H the Supreme Reality is to be found in a Universal Mind which is above the inconsistency of self-consciousness with its self-contradictory functions of volition and moral agency. Throughout his works, there runs an ever-increasing emphasis upon the sorrow and suffering of life, an ever-increasing passion in the doubt and denial of the goodness of God. While it is plain that H proves nothing, he gives vital expression to an important philosophic temper of the nineteenth century. Egdon Heath in *The Return of the Native* stands as H's supreme personification of the Infinite in terms of natural phenomena. For him life-giving and life-destroying earth is also life-beautifying. H is a true Immanentalist: certainly the Immanent Will is less forbidding than at first it seemed to be. H is no materialist; the weakness to be found in his view, if weakness there be, lies in his extreme idealism, in his assertion of purity of purpose as the sole criterion of purity of deed. Here H is too optimistic for us all to follow him.

461 "Forces: XVIII.—Thomas Hardy, Novelist and Poet," T. P.'s Weekly, V (30 June 1905), 813–14.

H's "frankness in the treatment of the sex question" and his "unconventional attitude regarding life in general" are derived from "the native frankness of the peasants among whom he dwelt." In his poetry, as in his novels, there is "the same nicety of construction, deep thought, and happy phrasing when dealing with Nature or Nature's children." He believed that "beauty of form is as essential to a masterpiece of literature as it is to one of painting or sculpture." His "shepherds," especially Gabriel Oak, have "a stern and silent power of endurance" caused by "something of the fatalism which distinguishes so much of H's work and H himself."

462 Heath, F. R., and Sidney Heath. Dorchester (Dorset), and Its Surroundings, With a Foreword by Thomas Hardy and a Chapter upon the Country Walks round Dorchester by the late Henry J. Moule, M.A. [The Homeland Handbooks, No. 46] (Dorchester: F. G. Longman; Lond: The Homeland Association, 1905–1906), pp. 10, 11, 12, 23, 31, 35, 36, 52, 53, 59, 60–65, 66–76, 80, 98, 113–14.

[Brief account of H's life and works, comments on " 'Wessex' and 'Casterbridge,' " lists places mentioned in H's novels.]

463 Holland, Clive [pseud of C. J. Hankinson]. "Thomas Hardy, and the Land of Wessex," Pall Mall Magazine, XXXVI (Nov 1905), 530–42.

[Essay comments on and illustrates typical scenes in and around Dorset that H used in his novels. Usual Clive Holland procedure: accepts without question the premise that whatever H claimed to be the original for some created character, building, or landscape could infallibly be identified as a real "thing" to be chatted about and photographed.]

464 Lee, Vernon [pseud of Violet Paget]. "Of Hardy and Meredith," Westminster Gazette, 20 July 1905, pp. 1–2.

Unlike French novelists who are born "in possession of a complete craft," modern English novelists like Meredith and H have "no knowledge, save what each can work out for himself, of the actual business of novel-making." In H's and Meredith's novels "all that attempts to be . . . deliberately arranged for the sake of illusion . . . is thin, unreal, sometimes absurd." *Tess of the d'Urbervilles* is characteristic: the important action in the book is not the human one but "the world's life of the seasons, which the dramatis personae symbolise." The book's memorable episodes—the haloed figures returning from the dance, the wounded pheasants, "the new Adam and Eve at daybreak"—are incidents "whose importance exists only for the passionate fancy which the writer communicates to the reader."

465 MacArthur, James. "Books and Bookmen," HARPER'S WEEKLY, XLIX (14 Oct 1905), 1486.

The Wessex Edition of H's novels is to appear soon. It is in H's portraits of women that "we feel most his reality and endowment of fascination." H portrays his feminine characters with "relentless fidelity."

466 Meyerfeld, Max. "Englischer Bücher" (English Books), DAS LITERARISCHE ECHO, III (1 Jan 1905), 474–75.

The Dynasts is a waxwork drama which deserves to be preserved as a curiosity in the literary Chamber of Horrors. The only consolation is that H, like Grillparzer, might bury this work so as to surprise posterity. [In German.]

467 Nevinson, Henry Wood. BOOKS AND PERSONALITIES (Lond: Lane, 1905), pp. 169–78.

Wordsworth and H; the comparison seems strange, yet inevitable. Both love the mankind that lies close to the breasts of earth; they never lose sight of this ancient world, full of strange history, full of unconscious influences and associations. No writer has so penetrating a sense of place as H does; with a sense of construction rightly called architectural, H shows the development of a soul. The end is often sorrow, and the finer the workmanship, the deeper the gravity and the gloom. The titlepage of *The Dynasts* is somewhat ironic and defiant: three volumes, nineteen acts! This drama departs absolutely from all dramatic rules; it is far more like the second part of FAUST than anything else. But the vision does not reveal a series of symbolic figures like FAUST. Never since Lilliput was imagined have we seen the great fortunes and crises of humanity so reduced in size. The vision opens, and we see them spread out before us like little toys. So, with laughter of irony and tears of pity joined, H enacts before us this puppet show of earthly greatness.

468 "Thomas Hardy and the Stage," GRAND MAGAZINE, Aug 1905, p. 96.

Since *The Three Wayfarers* was unsuccessful as a play, H concluded that plays are inferior to novels "as a form of literary art." However, he is aware of the influence the stage can exercise over man's feelings.

469 "Thomas Hardy on the Stage," BOSTON EVENING TRANSCRIPT, 20 Sept 1905, p. 5.

Despite the dramatic nature of H's novels, few have appeared in dramatic versions. H himself dramatized, with Comyns Carr, *Far From the Madding Crowd*, which was produced in London in Feb 1882. He also dramatized "The Three Strangers," which was produced in London in June 1903. *Tess of the d'Urbervilles* was first produced in Stodard's version in New York in March 1897—a version which W. D. Howells called one of the great modern tragedies.

470 Trent, W. P. (ed). SOUTHERN WRITERS: SELECTIONS IN PROSE AND VERSE (NY: Macmillan, 1905), p. 122.
[H is mentioned in the introduction to Augustus Baldwin Longstreet's "The Horse-Swap" in connection with "The Militia Drill" written for GEORGIA SCENES by Oliver Millhouse Prince, a friend of Longstreet—a paper which H "either directly imitated or else strikingly paralleled . . . in *The Trumpet-Major*."]

1906

471 B., M. E. "Some Women Characters of Thomas Hardy," OB-SERVER AND CHRONICLE (Bournemouth), 3 Feb 1906.
H's women are less real than his men, with one or two exceptions. He creates two classes of women, the intellectual and the domestic. The heroine of *Tess of the d'Urbervilles* is H's finest female portrait. [Brief, detailed analysis of H's women follows.]

472 "Current Literature: Mr. Hardy's *Dynasts*," SPECTATOR (Lond), XCVI (7 April 1906), 545.
The Dynasts: Part the Second "shows the same merits and weaknesses as . . . Part I. . . . Blank verse tends to be spasmodic and unrhythmical, and the lyrics suffer from a deplorable lack of music." Despite its faults, there is "a curious sublimity about the very immensity of the scheme" which shows "Europe like a map on a child's slate, and the great protagonists as puppets in the grip of destiny."

473 Davray, Henri. "Lettres anglaises" (English Letters), MER-CURE DE FRANCE, LX (15 April 1906), 611–12.
"Each . . . evocative sentence [in *The Dynasts*] sweeps the spirit [of the reader] to dizzying heights whence he contemplates a fantastic spectacle, unbelievable" yet at the same time "real." From these heights one sees the "indifferent Forces" which make the history of the world. [In French.]

474 Dutton, George Burwell. "The Making of a Portrait," WIL-LIAMS LITERARY MONTHLY, XXII (Oct 1906–1907), 122–30.
Emotionally, Tess is quick-tempered, magnetic, sensuous, loving, passionate. Tess's "gloomy philosophy" led her to drift passively through life. Her views are consistent with her experience in life; H's error, however, is "the essential untruth of his picture of life, in which [nearly] every incident . . . tells against the upward strivings of human nature." Despite her early Christian training, her belief in Christianity is not deep-rooted.

475 *"The Dynasts,"* NATION (NY), LXXXII (19 April 1906), 325.

The gift of panoramic vision revealed in Part I of *The Dynasts* reappears in Part II, while H's philosophy of history becomes still clearer. Furthermore, Part II surpasses Part I in that it contains more prose and less unconvincing supernatural machinery. A final judgment on the meaning of the work as a whole, however, must be reserved until the publication of Part III.

476 *"The Dynasts,"* OUTLOOK (Lond), XVII (7 April 1906), 808.

The second part of *The Dynasts* deepens the impression that H is not enough of a poet to make his vast project succeed. The work is "absolutely hopeless as a poem," and a great waste of a skilled writer's time.

477 *"The Dynasts*: Mr. Hardy's Napoleonic Drama,"* T. P.'s WEEKLY, VIII (23 Feb 1906), 231.

In the second part of *The Dynasts*, the battle of Jena "has for its stage Europe and for its dramatis personae the war lords of the earth." Stage directions are given "as from Olympus," "utterly detached from personal feeling." More of "a panorama" than an actual drama, "the armies advance against each other like shadows in a dream." *Dynasts* "closes with the incongruous impression that the incarnation of the Immanent Will [Napoleon] will be sacrificed to the comfort of George IV."

478 *"The Dynasts*: Part II. . . ,"* INDEPENDENT, LX (5 April 1906), 807–9.

H views history as a naturalist might, peering through his field glass at a swarming ant hill. It is not drama: it is natural history, only the ants happen to be men and women. It is too inhuman or extrahuman. The strange "stage directions" have all the impressiveness of H's matchless prose.

479 Hebb, John. "Mr. Thomas Hardy and Restoration," NOTES AND QUERIES, 10th ser VI (10 Nov 1906), 365.

In 1863, H received a prize from the Royal Institute of British Architects for his essay on "The Application of Terra-Cotta to Modern Architecture." H assisted in the restoration, which he later regretted, of several churches in his native country.

480 Henneman, John Bell. "The Dramatic Novel: George Meredith and Thomas Hardy," READER, VIII (Nov 1906), 680–85.

Both Meredith and H use dramatic methods to emphasize the development and change of characters in crisis. H uses comic relief, uncanny situations, and "the little thing that alters destiny." H has more epic sweep. But his "rhetoric and love for color, his intense dramatic feeling, may run away with him." He loves simple people and is pagan in his oneness with nature. Both he and Meredith are poets by nature and both treat the sex problem.

481 Holland, Clive [pseud of C. J. Hankinson], with Walter Tyndale. Wessex (Lond: Adam & Charles Black, 1906), pp. 95, 178, 179, 180, 246, 256.
[Unusual among books on Wessex topography because of the seventy-five very fine *color* illustrations by Tyndale, many of them landscapes, buildings, or towns from H's novels. The effect of seeing Wessex in color is uncanny, perhaps because H has so thoroughly "painted" Wessex for us in drab, twilight tints. No criticism of the literature.]

482 Hyatt, Alfred H. (ed). The Pocket Thomas Hardy, Being Selections from the Wessex Novels and Poems of Thomas Hardy (Lond: Chatto & Windus, 1906), pp. viii, 312.
[A selection of "familiar characters," descriptive scenes, and "striking incidents" from the novels, plus selected poems. No editorial comment.]

483 "The Lounger," Critic (NY), XLVIII (April 1906), 292–93.
H has turned his "spendid talents" from writing novels "to writing plays that no one reads and that are unactable." Yet H's novels have been successfully dramatized.

484 "The Lounger," Critic (NY), XLVIII (April 1906), 300.
[One-sentence comment on *The Dynasts*, "almost too much literature and not enough play."]

485 Maitland, F. W. The Life and Letters of Leslie Stephen (Lond: Duckworth, 1906), pp. 263–64.
[H, in a letter of 23 March 1875, describes a call on Stephen at his house in Southwell Gardens for the purpose of witnessing Stephen's signature to a deed renunciatory of holy orders. They conversed on systems of religion and metaphysics in Stephen's "Stylites study."]

486 Meyerfeld, Max. "Echo der Zeitschriften" (Echo of the Periodicals), Das Literarische Echo, VIII (1906), 519.
Life's Little Ironies belongs with the best English short stories. The pleasing *leitmotif* of the tragic-ironic or the comic-tragic view of life is excellently handled. H employed the Falken Theory [?] and still maintained his freedom of fantasy. H's novellas are not overburdened with psychology or emotion. [In German.]

487 Moss, Mary. "The Novels of Thomas Hardy," Atlantic Monthly, XCVIII (Sept 1906), 354–67.

Criticism of H's novels has been somewhat adversely affected by his too-close identification with the Wessex setting. His novels show a gradual improvement of method and a definite assertion of the meaning he perceives in life. *Tess of the d'Urbervilles* and *Jude the Obscure* are the culmination of this development. He has shown the importance of the individual character in facing the problems of life. H's contribution to English prose is similar to Tennyson's contribution to English poetry: both retain a romantic atmosphere without losing factual substantiality.

488 Nicoll, W. Robertson, and Thomas Seccombe. THE BOOKMAN ILLUSTRATED HISTORY OF ENGLISH LITERATURE. 2 vols (Lond: Hodder & Stoughton, 1906), II, 520.
The Mayor of Casterbridge, The Woodlanders, and *Tess of the d'Urbervilles* are "great novels of tragic character and import," in which love, life's great necessity, is "converted . . . to a source of torment." H is "a master of impressionistic English."

489 Orr, Lyndon. "Thomas Hardy and Longstreet," BOOKMAN (NY), XII (Feb 1906), 635–36.
H probably plagiarized from A. B. Longstreet's GEORGIA SCENES passage about drilling raw recruits (H uses it in *The Trumpet-Major*, chap 23). [Orr furnishes parallel passages from the two works and comments ironically about "literary coincidences."]

490 Payne, W. M. "Recent English Poetry," DIAL, XL (16 May 1906), 325–26.
The second section of *The Dynasts* now published. The poetry comes from the Phantom Intelligences, a grim story of poetry but impressive. "It requires a superhuman degree of fortitude to accept this view of the mystery of life, yet no other seems vouchsafed to the inquiring eye of our poet, and he makes us feel, while under the spell of his imaginative vision, as if all the others were but tricks of our self-delusion."

491 [Peck, Harry Thurston]. "Longstreet vs. Hardy," BOOKMAN (NY), XXIII (April 1906), 121–22.
The narrative GEORGIA SCENES, which contains the passage very much like one in H's novel *The Trumpet-Major*, was first published around 1836. The similarity was perhaps due to a passage contained in an English school reader which H used as a student.

492 Ross, Robert. "The Drama: A Close Time for the Peasants," ACADEMY, LXX (3 March 1906), 206–7.
The Dynasts proves H to be "not merely a great novelist but an essayist, a poet and a dramatist and I might add, an acute historical critic." The flaws

of the drama are in its "incongruities" and "wilful discords." It is "a great imperfect work of art."

493 Roz, Firmin. "Thomas Hardy," REVUE DES DEUX MONDES, 5eme Serie XXXIV (1 July 1906), 176–207.

Life's Little Ironies could be given as a title to any of H's fourteen novels; it tells of the cruelty, the bitter flavor seasoned with misanthropy, disdain, and revolt that is to be found in them. Throughout his pictures of love, his satires of society, his evocations of nature, H always seems to have in view the fundamental dramatic irony of our lives and destinies. Technically, H is a wonderful realist. We find in him a grasp of life, a sharpness of vision, a strength and lightness of touch, a magic power to conjure up the real that is so much admired in Flaubert, Daudet, de Maupassant. [In French.]

494 Rutherford, Mildred Lewis. THE SOUTH IN HISTORY AND LITERATURE (Atlanta, Ga.: Franklin-Turner, 1906; 1907), p. 159.

The Trumpet-Major resembles Augustus Longstreet's MILITIA DRILL.

495 Stronach, George. "Plagiarism or—Coincidence?— III," SCOTTISH REVIEW, 11 Jan 1906, p. 41.

Edmund Gosse claimed that "execution" or style placed *The Trumpet-Major* " 'beyond plagiarism.' " Hence "extraordinary resemblances" between passages in that novel and A. B. Longstreet's GEORGIA SCENES only show that you may, "steal what you like, but give it 'style.' Then you are perfectly safe."

496 Symons, Arthur. "A Note on the Genius of Thomas Hardy," SATURDAY REVIEW (Lond), CII (29 Sept 1906), 391–92; rptd in LIVING AGE, CCLI (8 Dec 1906), 634–36; and in FIGURES OF SEVERAL CENTURIES (NY: Dutton, 1916), pp. 207–15, with minor revisions.

As one rereads H, the story-teller becomes a philosopher, the cynic becomes a poet, closer to the earth than to the people and shows nature's aloofness from man. *The Mayor of Casterbridge* is rereadable, even though it has too much story, because H's sense of life as growth out of the ground is an interpretive vision which appeals after the facts of the plot are known. Only emotion can cause H to throw off the natural lethargy of his style. In *The Return of the Native*, H's scrupulous study of the effect of emotion on inanimate objects and his intense preoccupation with visual experience causes him to notice things even while assuring the reader that the characters do not see them. This "seeing to excess" spoils major scenes, like the scene before the mirror between Clym and Eustacia, in which the language becomes unconvincingly brittle.

497 "Thomas Hardy's Panoramic Drama," CURRENT LITERATURE, XL (May 1906), 522–23.

Critics are more respectful to the second volume of *The Dynasts* than they were to the first, which seemed to lack form and finish. H's argument with A. B. Walkley, in the TIMES (Lond), over the difference between playable plays and plays for "mental performance" may be responsible for the increased respect. William Archer, in the London TRIBUNE, notes the "fascinating series of dissolving views, or glimpses of history seen through the medium of a peculiar poetic temperament," but feels that the philosophy of a blindly mischievous Immanent Will is disastrous to the play. The London OUTLOOK shares this position; the TIMES LITERARY SUPPLEMENT, however, comments unfavorably on the poetical side of the play. Americans, including the EVENING POST (NY) and H. W. Boynton in the TIMES SATURDAY REVIEW (NY), criticize the work more roughly, particularly in respect to H's choice of poetry as a medium and his workmanship. [Mainly a review of reviews, not all accessible for inclusion in this bibliography.]

498 Trent, W. P. "Thomas Hardy's *Dynasts*," FORUM, XXXVIII (July 1906), 86–94.

H "was never anything less than bold." It is not surprising "to find him announcing on his title page that his drama, when completed, will consist of three parts, nineteen acts, and one hundred and thirty scenes." H was striving for modernity in "outlook and expression"; thus he labeled "the First or Fundamental Entity" as It. In his verse, however, "lyrical charm is almost completely absent, and lyrical power is almost frustrated, save exceptionally, by a strained diction and rhythmical roughness that are often distracting and not infrequently distressing." Yet despite the choric narrators and the erratic verse, *The Dynasts* "is a remarkably able book, whether or not it is a successful drama or a great poem." "There is some good, and a great deal of passable, verse, . . . some excellent prose . . . and a continuous manifestation of imagination and intelligence."

499 Treves, Frederick. HIGHWAYS AND BYWAYS IN DORSET (Lond: Macmillan, 1906), pp. 30, 39, 158, 162, 164, 171, 211, 361.

[Passing references.]

1907

500 "The British Novel as an Institution," EDINBURGH REVIEW, CCV (July 1907), 126.

H is noted as a modern novelist who does not want to make anyone better or worse; rather he seeks only to record life as it strikes him. [H mentioned briefly in a long essay on THE WORKS OF MRS. GASKELL (1906).]

501 Hirn, Yrjö. "Thomas Hardy," Finsk Tidskrift for Vitter-
het, Konst och Politik, LXII: 2 (1907), 91–108.
Certain typical characters and even some typical situations recur in H's
novels, but locality (Wessex) is the main recurring element. The description of the locale is effective enough to give the reader the illusion that he
himself knows all these places. H has not only described the nature of his
locale but has also given a description of the ways of the inhabitants that
amounts to ethnographic monographs. Thus he gives detailed descriptions
of cattle raising (*Tess of the d'Urbervilles*), sheep raising (*Far From
the Madding Crowd*), forestry (*The Woodlanders*), bee-keeping (*Under the
Greenwood Tree*), stone cutting (*The Well-Beloved*), and smuggling ("The
Distracted Preacher" in *Wessex Tales*). The "common people," however,
form only the background in H's novels. His principals come from higher
social classes or (and these are his best characters) from the social border-
land between the common people and the upper classes. The conflicts resulting from this uncertain social position form a constantly recurring theme
in his works. Where the class contrasts are not so evident, the conflict is
nevertheless basically the same: the heroines are more attracted to those
who can satisfy their vanity than to honest but simple men. The source of
all the calamities in most of the Wessex novels is the relationship between
man and woman, often treated with an openness which one would not expect to find in a nineteenth-century English novel. H's heroines are not
idealized, but neither are they the product of an anti-feminine mind. They
are fickle and inconsistent in contrast to the male characters—their victims—who consistently act according to their principles. The irrational in
woman represents the irrationality in life itself—here H's concept of woman
coincides with his notion of fate. But fate is not only fickle, it is also ironic:
all his works could be characterized as studies in the comical or tragic ironies of life. Apparently H has tried to make his novels as upsetting and as
unrelentingly pessimistic as possible. But in spite of this, the effect always
seems to be the same: the depressing impressions are not the ones that remain uppermost in one's memory. This is due to H's treatment of the surroundings in which the plot takes place. The simple people who with their
naive conversations and intermezzos interrupt the main plot are treated
without the bitterness and pessimistic irony that characterize H's philosophy.
[In Swedish.]

502 Hoare, George Barnard. "Mr. Thomas Hardy and Tennyson,"
Academy, LXXII (19 Jan 1907), 75.
The comparison of H's New Year verses with verses by Tennyson printed in
the 5 Jan issue of Academy is unfortunate. Their attitudes and tones are
completely different. Tennyson believed in an ideal of love: "he was not a
poet of pessimism. . . . Mr. Hardy has looked so long on the tragic side of
life . . . that it has become to him the only fact . . . the comparison of
Hardy and Tennyson is odious."

503 "Is Thomas Hardy Overestimated?" CURRENT LITERATURE, XLIII (Sept 1907), 290–92.

Among other articles on H's current reputation, Lindsay Garrett's attack, "The Essence of Hardyism," MONTHLY REVIEW, XXVII (June 1907), 59–67, mentions the slow action and labored "realism" of *Tess of the d'Urbervilles* and *Jude the Obscure*. Wilfred Randell ["The Hardy Critic," ACADEMY (Lond), LXXIII (6 July 1907), 656–57] believes that Garrett misses the over-all scope of the work in his concern with trivia. An editor ["Thomas Hardy," TIMES SATURDAY REVIEW OF BOOKS, 20 July 1907, 454] calls *Jude* and *Tess* worthless and "nauseating in their decadent realism and salacity."

504 Kellner, Leon. DIE ENGLISCHE LITERATUR IM ZEITALTER DER KÖNIGIN VIKTORIA (English Literature in the Period of Queen Victoria) (Leipzig: Tauchnitz, 1907), pp. 22, 24, 529, 561–64; 2nd rvd and enlgd ed as DIE ENGLISCHE LITERATUR DER NEUESTEN ZEIT VON DICKENS BIS SHAW (Modern English Literature from Dickens to Shaw) (Leipzig: Tauchnitz, 1921), pp. 35, 37, 324–27.

H is a master of English regionalism, a realist who gained and lost fame because of his realism. [In German.]

505 Lea, Hermann. "Some Dorset Superstitions," in MEMORIALS OF OLD DORSET, ed by T. Perkins and H. Pentin (Lond: Bemrose, 1907) [not seen in this form]; rptd as SOME DORSET SUPERSTITIONS (Mount Durand, St. Peter Port, Guernsey: Toucan P, 1969).

[A collection of anecdotes about the hag-ridden (*hagrod* of Dorset) in Dorset and the methods of exorcising them. Also see J. Stevens Cox (pub and general editor), Monographs on the Life of Thomas Hardy (1962).]

506 "The Literary Week," ACADEMY, LXXII (5 Jan 1907), 3.

There is in H's New Year poem a similarity to Tennyson's poem, "By an Evolutionist." H, however, does not have a religious tradition behind his thoughts on the subject as Tennyson had.

507 Nicoll, William Robertson. "Thomas Hardy," in HISTORY OF ENGLISH LITERATURE, by W. Robertson Nicoll and Thomas Seccombe (NY: Dodd, Mead, 1907), III, 1247–50.

The clear-eyed realism with which H controls his incidents and abjures those happy endings so dear to the English novel-reader imparts a melancholy tinge to all his best work. He has gained from Sand, the Brontës, Hawthorne, and George Eliot. He is a master of impressionistic English.

508 "The Pessimism of Thomas Hardy," NATION (Lond), I (27 July 1907), 795–96; rptd in LIVING AGE (Boston), CCLV (19 Oct 1907), 180–82.

H tests modern dogmas of social life and finds them all inadequate to men and women wakened from the medieval dream of man's sinfulness by the touch of modern skepticism, which, in itself, provides no answers for them. Like Sue Fawley in her ruminations, H's characters blame not man, but the first cause. "Men, on the whole, are, like all the growing, sentient things in nature, good and noble in their impulses till they are thwarted by society and opposing consciences." Men are burdened with sorrows they do not deserve and are kinder to one another than the gods are to them, a principle seen in Marty South's lyric sorrow.

509 Prilipp, Beda. "Echo der Zeitschriften" (Echo of the Periodicals), DAS LITERARISCHE ECHO, IX (Nov 1907), 1248–49.

In *The Dynasts* H has reached the zenith of his art and deserves to be compared with Shakespeare and the Greek tragedians. [In German.]

510 Prilipp, Beda. "Thomas Hardys Napoleonsdrama" (Thomas Hardy's Napoleon Drama), DIE GRENZBOTEN, LXVI (18 April 1907), 130–36.

[An excellent seven-page description of *The Dynasts*.] [In German.]

511 Randell, Wilfrid L. "The Hardy Critic," ACADEMY, LXXIII (6 July 1907), 656–57.

H is a novelist; he is also a poet and a philosopher. Since all three characters are in action when he writes, he quite naturally puts some distance between his works and some of his readers. The critic Lindsay Garrett [in MONTHLY REVIEW (not seen)] has not shortened the distance. He criticizes the "futile realism" in H's novels without knowing what function realism serves in any novel, much less an H novel. "Overloaded descriptions" and "descriptive digressions" are terms Garrett uses to describe H's descriptions of nature so vital to his works that the removal of any part of them would be like removing one of the main characters. "No other writer has ever used descriptions with such absolute skill to elicit and represent the moods of the human mind." The comparison Garrett makes between H and Wilkie Collins is absurd.

512 "Thomas Hardy," ALMA MATER: ABERDEEN UNIVERSITY MAGAZINE, XXIV (28 Nov 1907), 63.

To H "belongs that most honourable achievement—to have gained the favour and esteem of the public without having sacrificed one handful of incense on the altar of popularity." H's descriptions of Nature "connect in a curious subtle way the history and minds of his characters with the natural scenes they move in, and the natural forces which enter from their surroundings into their souls." According to H's philosophy "we are trammelled in the unyielding meshes of Fate; for us there is no escape."

513 "Thomas Hardy," NEW YORK TIMES SATURDAY REVIEW OF BOOKS, 20 July 1907, p. 454.

H always uses description for a definite purpose, always as "background for human drama." H's plots are "dashing and engrossing, splendidly conceived and executed with skill." H creates scenes which have intense dramatic interest. Examples of these qualities are found in the intrigue, the changed identities, and the midnight procession of *Desperate Remedies;* the precipice scene in *A Pair of Blue Eyes*; the gargoyle episode in *Far From the Madding Crowd*; the gambling by the light of fireflies and the frying out of the adder's oil in *The Return of the Native*; the return of the sailor in *The Mayor of Casterbridge*. H remains detached from his works, breathing life into the characters and then letting them work out their destiny. H has no heroes. It is unfortunate that H is only known to some by *Tess of the d'Urbervilles* and *Jude the Obscure*, "two worthless books, nauseating in their false and decadent 'realism' and salacity."

514 Wülker, Richard. GESCHICHTE DER ENGLISCHEN LITERATUR VON DEN ÄLTESTEN ZEITEN BIS ZUR GEGENWART (History of English Literature from the Earliest Times to the Present). 2 vols; 2nd rvd and enlgd ed (Leipzig: Verlag des Bibliographischen Instituts, 1907), II, 361–64.

H is influenced by French, Russian, and Norwegian realism and naturalism and the philosophy of Taine. H's dramatic power, captivating language, and unembittered tragedy make him a modern novelist. [In German.]

1908

515 Boynton, H. W. "Thomas Hardy's *The Dynasts*," BOOKMAN (NY), XXVII (July 1908), 486–88.

In the preface to *The Dynasts* H admits that the work has little in common with an ordinary stage play. Indeed, the author's own reference to it as a "panoramic show" is, perhaps, the most appropriate label. His blank verse is rather bad, and his stage machinery seems ridiculous. The best thing that can be said about the work is that it is successful when considered in the framework—"panoramic show"—which H created to contain his ideas.

516 Davray, Henry D. "Lettres anglaises" (English Letters), MERCURE DE FRANCE, LXXIII (1 May 1908), 166–67.

The Dynasts will remain one of the most perplexing works in English literature. Such an effort deserves more than respect; it imposes a careful, meditative reading. H's verse will appear inferior to his admirable prose stage-directions; his philosophy will seem too pessimistic, but the whole massive work commands admiration. [In French.]

517 De la Mare, Walter. *"The Dynasts,"* BOOKMAN (Lond), XXXIV (June 1908), 110–12.

H exhibits such intensity of imagination in *The Dynasts* that the critic feels incapable of making an intelligent commentary on that monumental work. Beneath the intensity and within the vastness, however, the H of Wessex can be perceived. The final judgment of *Dynasts* will be made not by critics but by time.

518 "Drama," ATHENAEUM, No. 4203 (16 May 1908), 615.

Those who would have had H abandon his colossal enterprise, *The Dynasts*, "would have missed a manifestation of its author's mind and talent which is a singularly impressive work of art." It is a conscious portrayal of despair; yet, at times, "the pessimist gives place to the indignant humanist." Considering the expansive topic, the work as a whole is a structural masterpiece.

519 "Drama," WESTMINSTER REVIEW, CLXIX (May 1908), 605–6.

The Dynasts, a drama to be staged only in the reader's imagination, is "a very powerful production." "We are prepared to treasure his [H's] *Dynasts* as one of his best services to our literature."

520 *"The Dynasts,"* NATION (NY), LXXXVI (16 April 1908), 353–54.

Despite a superficial roughness of language, Part III of *The Dynasts* presents nothing less than a new "justification of the ways of God to man," although the justification is somewhat tentative. The panoramic yet poetic stage directions and the monstrous verse forms so well tailored to the subject matter provide the vehicle for the expression of H's philosophy. The quality of Part III overshadows that of the preceding parts and gives coherence to the whole.

521 *"The Dynasts,"* NEW YORK TIMES SATURDAY REVIEW OF BOOKS, 2 May 1908, pp. 249–50.

The Dynasts must be placed with the "noblest creations in literature." It is clearly written and easy to follow. The magnitude and seriousness of the work do not prevent it from presenting a realistic and intimate picture of life. The "sense of unity of the human drama" is the wonder of this work. This unity lies in the relationship of the human beings to a type of Unconscious Immanent Will which oversees man's life. The humans, possessing a false sense of their own importance, are in reality puppets of this Will. The conception of a Fate unconscious of itself, the vision of history as the "palpitation of the anatomy of a slumbering cosmic brain" has never been conceived by an imaginative writer, nor "put in such ghastly vividness by a pantheistic philosopher."

522 Fiedler, H. G. "Englischer Brief" (English Letter), DAS LITERARISCHE ECHO, X (1908), 1559–61.

The Dynasts is reminiscent of Grabbe's NAPOLEON, ODER DIE HUNDERT TAGE, Goethe's "Prologue im Himmel" from FAUST, and Schopenhauer's DIE WELT ALS WILLE UND VORSTELLUNG. It is a brave experiment which deserves a prominent place in the history of Napoleonic writings. [In German.]

523 Hind, C[harles] Lewis. "Thomas Hardy," THE DIARY OF A LOOKER-ON (NY: Lane, 1908), pp. 40–46.

[Impressions of *Tess of the d'Urbervilles* and various poems.]

524 "Mr. Hardy's Drama," ACADEMY, LXXIV (14 March 1908), 555–57.

H's drama possesses "the one quality which could make so large and various a thing coherently vital; it has philosophical unity." In this drama of the Napoleonic Wars, "he gives us a philosophical conception of the vast era, and suggests an interpretation of its national movements—indeed, of human progress itself."

525 "Mr. Hardy's *Dynasts*," EDINBURGH REVIEW, CCVII (April 1908), 421–39.

The verse-forms in *The Dynasts* are awkward experiments. The prose in the work is much superior. The negative philosophy of the author is not appropriate for imaginative creation which by its nature can treat only positive viewpoints. As a result *Dynasts* is greatly weakened.

526 "Mr. Hardy's Napoleonic Epic," GUARDIAN, 11 March 1908, p. 425.

Part III of *The Dynasts* lacks the intensity of the two earlier parts, but it is as rich in detail and as faithful to history as Parts I and II were. The poem is without doubt the first epic of the Napoleonic War and should not be regarded as a play since it is obviously unstageable.

527 "Mr. Hardy's World Drama," T. P.'s WEEKLY, IX (6 March 1908), 299.

In the third part of *The Dynasts*, the "direct unerring prose" of the stage directions supplies "much that is necessarily lacking in H's verse." In no other work has H more clearly shown "his mastery of English prose."

528 "On Ugliness in Fiction," EDINBURGH REVIEW, CCVII (April 1908), 448–52.

The contemporary trend favors stories describing unpleasant or ugly events as H's "An Imaginative Woman," "The Withered Arm," and *Tess of the d'Urbervilles* show. The plot of *Tess* is fabricated of "treachery, immorality, deceit, fatuousness, relapse, revenge, and murder."

529 Payne, W. M. "*The Dynasts*," DIAL, XLIV (16 May 1908), 307–9.

The last section of *The Dynasts* makes us aware of a precipitation of the elements—aesthetic, ethical, and philosophic—held in the solution, and "we feel that a great task has been worthily performed." Whatever later criticism may say about the faults of the work, "there will always remain the sense of a great conception, powerfully presented and endowed by its creator with a strange kind of life." H can sometimes force poetry to his will, but we feel, as with Emerson and Whitman, an "obstinate determination not to submit to its formal restraints." H's philosophy embodies the central doctrine of Schopenhauer, but the essential difference is that H provides for the possibility of will becoming conscious and acquiring a positive purpose wherewith to shape a more rational world.

530 Scott-James, R. A. "The Pessimism of Thomas Hardy," MODERNISM AND ROMANCE (Lond: Lane, 1908), pp. 57–68.

H's pessimism stems from the realization that there is something beyond nature—God, Fate?—that arbitrarily governs man and influences nature to defeat man. His major characters—indeed trouble-prone—are all questioners imbued more or less with the modern doubting spirit. They see that it is easier not to live. And they are not to blame for their suffering, for the whole social scheme works to make us miserable [not in *The Mayor of Casterbridge, Far From the Madding Crowd*]. God is either defeated or hostile to man. Fate is negative. Men are positive (see Marty South's lyrical eulogy to a dead man who had never loved her).

531 "SELECT POEMS," ATHENAEUM, II (26 Dec 1908), 815–16.

H's introductory essay, "regarded as a penetrative analysis . . . is noteworthy, even if it does not move us to enthusiasm." [Review of collection of poems by William Barnes, ed by Thomas Hardy.]

532 "Thomas Hardy," T. P.'s WEEKLY, XII (11 Dec 1908), 764.

Though H was unable to attend a performance of *The Trumpet-Major* staged at Max Gate by his neighbors, he "must have felt very deeply the compliment." He "has been taken to the heart of Wessex because it has assimilated his books," and particularly "their humorous features." H's feeling for Wessex was that of "a countryman born and bred."

533 "Thomas Hardy's Latest Production—Magnum Opus or Monstrosity?" CURRENT LITERATURE, XLIV (June 1908), 659–62.

H's "great metrical drama for mental performance" is praised by [W. B. Hale?] in "*The Dynasts*," NEW YORK TIMES SATURDAY REVIEW OF BOOKS, 2 May 1908, pp. 249–50, for its detail and unified conception. "Mr. Hardy's *Dynasts*," EDINBURGH REVIEW, CCVII (April 1908), 421–39, feels that the influence of H's philosophy on the drama is negative, but that it is the "most notable literary achievement" of the last quarter century. The EVENING POST [not located] notes the concluding optimism of the work. [Chiefly citations of current criticism on *The Dynasts*.]

534 Thommen, E. "Ein Führer in Englischen Dingen" (A Leader in English Things), SCHWEIZERISCHE LEHRERZEITUNG (Schweizerischer Lehrerverein; Pestalozzium in Zürich), No. 7 (1908), 58–61.
[Journalistic praise of *Life's Little Ironies*.] [In German.]

1909

535 Bennett, Arnold. "Tendencies of Modern Literature," T. P.'s WEEKLY, XIV (Dec 1909), 7–10.
It is improbable that any contemporary figure will dominate English letters, because of the vastness and diversity of the reading public. Novels now have more technical freedom and show a greater "sense of social responsibility"; in contrast to the modern school, "H seldom meddles with social principles."

536 Burton, Richard. MASTERS OF THE ENGLISH NOVEL: A STUDY OF PRINCIPLES AND PERSONALITIES (NY: Holt, 1909), pp. 13, 21, 110, 152, 262–79.
H's novels of the middle period are superior to *Tess of the d'Urbervilles* and *Jude the Obscure*, as the former have no "definite, aggressive theme" and avoid didacticism. *Jude*, which has no English prototype, is French (i.e. Zolaesque) in its "literary genealogy." H is one of the best "two or three" English novelists in the art of female characterization.

537 Chesterton, G. K. [No title], ILLUSTRATED LONDON NEWS, CXXXIV (22 May 1909), 728.
"The death of George Meredith is the real end of the Nineteenth Century, not that empty date that came at the close of 1899." "Mr. Hardy is wholly of our own generation, which is a very unpleasant thing to be." H sees an evil purpose in nature, and "this is far as possible from the plenitude and rational optimism of Meredith."

538 Durrant, Wilfred S. "The Disciple of Destiny," FORTNIGHTLY REVIEW, XCI (June 1909), 1117–24.

H is a great writer both in prose and poetry. *Jude the Obscure* is the "greatest and most misunderstood of his novels." His work "has created an epoch," because he "is the modern exponent of the guiding principles of ancient Greek tragedy." *Jude* is in the spirit of Aeschylus: Fate and "gloomy grandeur." Also in H's outlook on life he resembles Hebrew prophets. The keynote of *Jude's* construction is unity of action; the keynote of subject matter the "essential misery of human life." His weakness is that he is too pessimistic, too one-sided.

539 " 'An Evening with Thomas Hardy's Rustics,' " DORSET YEARBOOK, 1909–1910, pp. 33–35.
[Report of lecture-recital given by Mr. R. Gregory on H's employment of typical Dorset rustic types and dialect in his novels.]

540 Fiedler, H. G. "Englischer Brief" (English Letter), DAS LITERARISCHE ECHO, XII (Dec 1909), 430.
Time's Laughingstocks shows the old master at the height of his ability without any trace of withered strength. [In German.]

541 "Life and Letters," ACADEMY, LXXVI (23 Jan 1909), 701.
H is a better poet than might be suggested by his poem, "The House of Hospitalities," which is printed in the NEW QUARTERLY for January. He must find his proper element.

542 Nevinson, Henry Wood. "The Son of Earth," ESSAYS IN FREEDOM AND REBELLION (Lond: Duckworth, 1909), pp. 283–89; rptd (New Haven: Yale UP, 1921), pp. 93–99.
One of H's own illustrations to his *Wessex Poems* is very characteristic of Wessex with its Roman road, the distant sea, the little town, and the lonely figure of a sentry dressed in the uniform of Napoleon's time. In all of H's works, there is something of the grave simplicity of places where man has lived long in close relationship to the ground and to the seasons. In H himself one seems to detect the shy animal of heaths and woods: the sensitivity that drove him to the description of pig-killing in *Jude the Obscure* and prompted his protest against the use of horses upon the battlefield during the Boer War. Pity and irony—not mockery and scorn—are the themes of his poetry. We could compare H to Wordsworth; in spite of their country themes, neither H nor Wordsworth has any connection with idyllic art, but both are seeking the "aristocracy of passion" (Walter Pater). Since Wordsworth's death, no one better than H has heard the still, sad music of humanity with so fine an ear and expressed it so poignantly. [Article based on material identical to that used in BOOKS AND PERSONALITIES (1905).]

543 Newbolt, Henry. "A New Departure in English Poetry," QUARTERLY REVIEW, CCX (Jan 1909), 193–209; rptd in LIVING

AGE, CCLX (27 Feb 1909), 544–54; and in STUDIES, GREEN AND GRAY (NY: Nelson, 1926), pp. 193–209.

The Dynasts shows that there are still great paths to travel in poetry. H had to cope with the difficulties inherent in treating the epic theme of Napoleonic times dramatically; this dilemma he solved by taking "for his theatre . . . the reader's mind; for the commentary his own." H's philosophy and his sometimes too prosaic verse are handicaps. There are rapid scene shifts from the earthly to the aerial. H brings freshness to Nelson's death scene, and his indoor scenes are as well handled as those on the battlefields. H "masters both sense and feeling," and the "Phantom Intelligences" provide an appeal to the intellect. Over and over the injustice of an order which forces suffering upon men while denying them free will is emphasized. "When a man of genius formulates a new system of theology in poetry, the poetry is apt to survive the theology."

544 Phelps, William Lyon. "The Novels of Thomas Hardy," NORTH AMERICAN REVIEW, CXC (Oct 1909), 502–14; rptd in ESSAYS ON MODERN NOVELISTS (NY: Macmillan, 1910), pp. 33–55.

H is an architect of the novel. *Desperate Remedies* resembles the *plan* of a good novel. What marred the splendid *Tess of the d'Urbervilles* ruined *Jude the Obscure*. H executed Tess not as Shakespeare hanged Cordelia, but because he was bound to see his thesis through. Animalism, which had partially disfigured *Tess*, became gross and revolting in *Jude*. After finishing one of H's novels, one has the delight of waking from a horrible dream.

545 Seccombe, Thomas. "Books and Bookmen," READERS' RE-VIEW, II (March 1909), 25.

The Dynasts "makes us the heirs of nearly a hundred years accumulated study of the greatest upheaval in modern history."

546 "Thomas Hardy," ACADEMY, LXXVI (27 Feb 1909), 823–26.

Those who label H "a cynic and a misanthrope and a pessimist" do so indiscriminately and thoughtlessly. H himself has stated, "my practical philosophy is distinctly meliorist."

547 "Thomas Hardy," LIVING AGE, CCLXI (1 May 1909), 302–9.

H shows too much detachment to be labeled "pessimist" and nothing else. Too frequently critics forget works like *Under the Greenwood Tree*. H also has a gift for utilizing natural phenomena, and *The Trumpet-Major* shows such scenery "beautifully suggested." H is also an excellent historian of ancient customs and ceremonies. *Tess of the d'Urbervilles* is his masterpiece. H's women are "beloved for their sensuous charm."

1910

548 Adcock, A. St. John. "Thomas Hardy's Poems," BOOKMAN (Lond), XXXVII (Feb 1910), 236–37.

In *Time's Laughingstocks* H is similar to George Crabbe: both wrote of rural England with precise realism, and both embodied in their poetry a strongly-felt pessimism. H's poetry is great in its stern grasp of truth but limited by the monochromatic hue of its pessimistic outlook.

549 Barclay, H. D. "The Man and His Message.—No. XVI: Thomas Hardy and His Criticism of Life," T. P.'S WEEKLY, XV (10 June 1910), 738, 740.

Although H has confined himself to certain areas and types of characters, he is not a "limited specialist" but a writer of universal appeal who bridges "the gulf between what is poetry and logic." He can be compared to Euripides, for both "possess the same ancient love of natural beauty, a tender regard for the honest, homeloving country folk, and apparently, the same dislike of town life." H's pessimism is even stronger than that of Euripides, but his "intellectual irony" is tempered "by the humanity which really possesses his heart."

550 Bense, J. F. "*Tess of the d'Urbervilles*," NOTES AND QUERIES, 11th ser II (30 July 1910), 96.

A legend referred to in *Tess of the d'Urbervilles* is the well-known one of Pygmalion (Ov. '*Met*' X, 243).

551 "Books: Mr. Hardy's Poems," SPECTATOR (Lond), CIV (29 Jan 1910), 155.

Time's Laughingstocks, after the "defects of ear and style" in *The Dynasts*, is a pleasant surprise. H proves himself "a master of the ballad." His subjects are grimly pessimistic, but it is "wonderful poetry." If not his finest medium, H uses verse "like a master."

552 Burrow, Charles Kennett. "An Hour with a Poet: II, Thomas Hardy," T. P.'S MAGAZINE, I (Dec 1910), 273–75.

H's view that "matter . . . being created, has to look after itself" explains his extraordinary use of coincidence, "which is a kind of organic fatalism," and his "fatalism of passion." But since "aspiration, hope, the vision and the dream are essential to great poetry," H is not a great poet.

553 Chapman, Edward Mortimer. "The Newer Fiction," ENGLISH LITERATURE IN ACCOUNT WITH RELIGION, 1800–1900 (Boston: Houghton Mifflin, 1910), pp. 47, 533–58.

H's pessimism ruined his art. *Jude the Obscure* is especially "feeble and extravagant." [Condemns H for his religious opinions.]

554 Dawson, E. P. "Thomas Hardy—The Modern Greek," YALE LITERARY MAGAZINE, LXXV (April 1910), 356–59.
"Like Homer, Hardy is the patriot of an antique land"; he alone has been able to interpret "the memory-haunted Wessex." The essence of H's creed is fatalism: "in his eyes men are but puppets struggling . . . against an overwhelming flood."

555 "Dorchester and the 'Creator' of Casterbridge," DORSET COUNTY CHRONICLE, 24 Nov 1910, p. 5.
[Account of the ceremony granting H the Freedom of the Borough.]

556 *"Far From the Madding Crowd* in London!" DORSET YEAR-BOOK, 1910–1911, pp. 32–36.
The London production by the Dorchester Debating Society of *Far From the Madding Crowd* proved that Mr. A. H. Evans "has produced a capital Dorset entertainment in his dramatisation" of the novel.

557 Foote, G. W. "Views and Opinions," FREETHINKER, XXX (12 June 1910), 1–2.
Although the press and the general public are reluctant to admit it, H was a freethinker. His poems illustrate his free thought, his pessimism, and his humanitarianism.

558 Hauser, Otto. WELTGESCHICHTE DER LITERATUR (World History of Literature) (Leipzig and Vienna: Bibliographisches Institut, 1910), II, 71, 75.
[Brief plot summaries of *Tess of the d'Urbervilles* and *Jude the Obscure*.] H is the successor of Meredith and Moore. [In German.]

559 Hewlett, M. *"Time's Laughingstocks,"* ENGLISH REVIEW, IV (March 1910), 639–43.
The rhythm and tone of *Time's Laughingstocks* catch the essence of H's Wessex. The poems show a Greek simplicity and freedom from useless ornament, and a philosophy of fatalism and acceptance. The ultimate ancestor of H's verse is the broadside ballad.

560 "Literature," ATHENAEUM, No. 4289 (8 Jan 1910), 34–35.
It is regrettable that a writer of H's talents should confine his poetic talents in *Time's Laughingstocks and Other Verses* "to subjects on the whole so narrow." Since poetry aims at expressing the beauty of nature in terms of "human life and human ideals," it is tragic when a poet such as H, motivated by thoughts of beauty, turns to nature and finds "that an abiding

beauty is not what is mainly to be found there, and that ideals are so seldom realized that it is hypocrisy to be serious about them." H's language is appropriate, considering the artist's disillusioned mind. "The temper he writes in is exactly that which could alone give credibility, artistic justice, and a natural appeal to the point of view he is expressing."

561 Macmillan, Alexander. LIFE AND LETTERS OF ALEXANDER MACMILLAN, ed by Charles L. Graves (Lond: Macmillan, 1910), pp. 288–92.

In *The Poor Man and the Lady*, H's satire of Londoners, "especially the upper classes, [is] . . . sharp, clear, incisive, and in many respects true, but . . . wholly dark." The violence of H's attack, "the wholesale blackening of a class" is without the balance and fairness of a Thackeray. "It is inconceivable to me that any considerable number of human beings—God's creatures —should be so bad without going to utter wreck in a week." The poetical qualities of certain scenes, the power and insight of others are admirable, and H is "a writer who seems to me, at least potentially, of considerable mark, of power and purpose." [Reprints Macmillan's long letter—some 1,000 words—of 10 Aug 1868 criticizing the MS of *Poor Man*. A tantalizing piece that makes one wish H had preserved *in toto* his apparently very angry first effort in fiction.]

562 "Mr. Hardy's New Poems," LIVING AGE, CCLXIV (29 Jan 1910), 306–10.

The poems of *Time's Laughingstocks* do not betray H's age. They show "a quiet wonder, tenderness, and silence." The sonnets, like those of Meredith and Shakespeare, "show a wonderful power of getting some momentary intellectual or emotional experience subtly and exactly shaped upon the paper, but Mr. Hardy is not primarily a poet, and consequently his sonnets have not that music of the mind of which the most crabbed problem hardly ever robs Shakespeare." The ballads are the most impressive pieces in the volume, and they remind one of the novels in "that old sense of the vastness of time and the littleness of human doings and sufferings."

563 Phelps, William Lyon. "Thomas Hardy," ESSAYS ON MODERN NOVELISTS (NY: Macmillan, 1910), pp. 33–55.

H's "constructive skill" and sense of humor are unmatched by his contemporaries. The same is true of his pessimism. Since this pessimism springs from a tenderness felt for all living creatures, it is a virtue. It is a virtue, also, because it is "fundamental and sincere," impersonal, and free from cynicism. Furthermore, it is balanced by an "unexcelled" sense of humor.

564 Randell, Wilfrid L. "Reviews: *The Dynasts*," ACADEMY, LXXIX (24 Dec 1910), 616–18.

"The scope of the whole thing is simply tremendous; the effect is profoundly moving, spectacular, magnificent."

565 Symons, Arthur. "Thomas Hardy," ENCYCLOPAEDIA BRITAN-NICA. 11th ed (Cambridge: Cambridge UP, 1910), XII, 946–47.

H is a fatalist who sees the "principle of life" working in the world as nature, and in humanity as sex. Thus he presents a natural world that means more to him than man and presents women who are interesting but dangerous. In addition, he presents peasants who are rooted in the earth.

566 "Thomas Hardy. An Appreciation on the Occasion of his Seventieth Birthday," BOOKMAN (Lond), XXXVIII (June 1910), 122–23.

H, novelist of the Victorian age and poet of the Edwardian, showed how the ideals of one age could be realized as the realities of another by an honest appraisal of the facts of nature. His works revealed the fallacies of the former age and the necessity of a more factual interpretation of life to avoid the same fallacies in the age to come.

567 "Thomas Hardy's New Poems," ACADEMY, LXXVIII (12 March 1910), 249–50.

H has moments of poetic genius; if only he could sustain the moments. "Mr. Hardy's poems are sung by the Spirit Ironic, and are filled with the sense of the vastness of time, and the littleness of human suffering and endeavour, and the pity of it." [Review of *Time's Laughingstocks*.]

568 "Thomas Hardy, O. M.," WORLD'S WORK (Lond), XVI (Aug 1910), 239–40.

"There has been no more popular act of the new reign than the bestowal of the Order of Merit" on H. Often rumored that a new H novel is to be published, but H "seems determined to be true to his own conversion to poetry."

569 *"Time's Laughingstocks,"* SATURDAY REVIEW (Lond), CIX (15 Jan 1910), 78.

H's indifference to poetic vocabulary and his lyrical freedom express his personality. "This direct observation of actual things is the sheet-anchor of the fully matured artist." "The Farm-Woman's Winter" gains its strength from a small descriptive phrase. "New Year's Eve," one of his boldest poems, shows the mystical side of the world in the vein of *The Dynasts*.

1911

570 Cazamian, Louis. "Le problème intellectuel" (The Intellectual Problem), L'ANGLETERRE MODERNE, SON EVOLUTION (Modern England, Its Evolution) (Paris: Flammarion, 1911, 1914, 1918, 1930), espec p. 329.

Among England's transitional thinkers and writers, James Thomson and H are modern pessimists, who are peculiarly sensitive to the turbulence of the uprooted intellectual in England. [In French.]

571 Craigie, Mrs. Pearl Mary Theresa. THE LIFE OF JOHN OLIVER HOBBES TOLD IN HER CORRESPONDENCE WITH NUMEROUS FRIENDS. With a biographical sketch by her father John Morgan Richards and an Introduction by The Right Rev. Bishop Welldon (Lond: John Murray, 1911), pp. 94, 97, 106, 109, 141, 153, 200.

Jude the Obscure is a great book: "Its construction is superb; its literary art, classic." It is "finer than *Tess*," despite its painful subject. [Denies resemblance of her work to H's in a letter (10 Nov 1896) to Unwin, in response to a CHRONICLE review. Prints a letter from H to Craigie (11 April 1897), letter from Craigie to H (18 Dec 1898), acknowledging gift of a book of poems and comparing *Jude* with Michaelangelo's "Last Judgment"; letter to H (14 March 1899). Letter from Craigie to Gosse (5 April 1904) praises H's recording of yeoman speech.]

572 Dawson, William James, and Coningsby W. Dawson. THE GREAT ENGLISH NOVELISTS (NY: Harper, 1911), II, 20–22.

The last of the Victorian novelists, a much greater artist than George Eliot or Meredith, is H. He builds his story with the keenest kind of mathematical accuracy and with the most meticulous attention to detail. Like Sophocles, he sees the end from the beginning and approaches it by deliberate and calculated stages. He has also the Sophoclean sense for the inevitableness of events. In certain facts which appear trivial, he finds the seeds of distant but tremendous tragedy. He is above all a realist, but one who sees things in their essence rather than their surfaces. Dealing constantly with natures really dignified in spite of humble social conditions, his books have not only the spirit but the gravity of Greek drama. For the most part, his books are absolutely truthful transcripts of life, if they are approached without the prejudices of optimism or pessimism. But, however they may affect the reader, no one can deny them greatness which comes from bigness of theme, profound convictions, and patient and deliberate art.

573 Drinkwater, John. "The Loom of the Poets: to Thomas Hardy," POEMS OF MEN AND HOURS (Lond: Nutt, 1911); rptd in POEMS, 1908–1914 (Lond: Sidgwick & Jackson, 1917; 1923), pp. 40–41.

H is a great writer for expressing what he sees and not giving in to his audience's demand for jollity. [Two sonnets.]

574 Fehr, Bernhard. "Zur Evolution des modernen englischen Romans" (On the Evolution of the Modern English Novel), GER-

MANISCH-ROMANISCHE MONATSSCHRIFT, III (1911), 384–597, espec 593.

Kipling and H are the most accomplished and artistic representatives of the intellectual tendency in the English novel. [In German.]

575 Garwood, Helen. THOMAS HARDY: AN ILLUSTRATION OF THE PHILOSOPHY OF SCHOPENHAUER (Phila: John C. Winston, 1911); University of Pennsylvania dissertation, 1909. [Not seen.]

576 Hedgcock, F. A. THOMAS HARDY: PENSEUR ET ARTISTE (Thomas Hardy: Thinker and Artist) (Paris: Librairie Hachette, [1911]); University of Paris dissertation.

H's life was centered in Wessex. The scenes and places of Wessex influenced his character, as his work. The intellectual climate in London influenced him in free thought, the study of the arts, the first attempts at writing.

H's pessimism has two sources: the inability of man confronted with combinations of events and the loneliness of man in the midst of change and in the midst of the mass of individual consciences. Idealism presents our interior reality and shows the futility of effort. Art is the consoler, and the expression of thought is the only way of attaining immortality. Certain of the "Wessex" poems contain H's expression of his temperament. Literature was for him a way of stating the sorrow of being.

H searched for a method, as can be seen in "How I Built Myself a House." The first novel, *Desperate Remedies*, is excessively romanesque. He demonstrated a preoccupation with bizarre contingencies, and his spirit was somewhat naturalistic. It is also realistic in that it recognizes instinct as an integral part of human character and life as a physiological fact. Observation is weak in this novel, and the peasants furnish the best character studies. There is evidence of philosophic reflection. It lacks continuity of ideas and is interesting only as it contains the germ of the better qualities of the author.

Under the Greenwood Tree returns to the country and has the qualities H developed in the family atmosphere. He employs realism, and the novel remains artistic and does not become photographic. There is an instinctive sympathy for plants and animals, a natural pantheism arising out of his rural education. The novel is gay with a slight note of sadness. *The Trumpet-Major* is a true pastoral and not a realistic study. Pessimism surfaces in *A Pair of Blue Eyes*. Happiness is only somewhat accessible to men in the face of their impotence before destiny. It is a study of moral causation in the genre of George Eliot's novels. The denouement is attributable to causes exterior to the characters. These happenings show an irony in life comparable with that of the Greek drama. H, because he can observe facts and complete the observation by imagination, cannot be classified as a naturalistic novelist.

H affirms his fatalism. *The Return of the Native* presents likenesses between Eustacia Vye and Madame Bovary. H does not believe in free will and for him, to live is to suffer. *Two on a Tower* pushes the force of chance to its extreme limits, and H demonstrates a certain primitive temperament. The work was a critical failure because of H's critical attitude toward religion and his frank expression. The novel marked a high point in H's fatalistic approach. In *Life's Little Ironies* H moves toward determinism. The result is that H superimposes Christian doctrines on the superstitions of the locale and combines the two more positively. There is a sense of the mystery of life peculiar to H. The novels of H are fundamentally metaphysical as his attitude opposes the experimental. There is in him a primitive streak that goes back to ancient Dorset. There are resemblances between H and Greek drama. H's strong sensitivity to the primitive spirit in nature also separates him from his compatriots. His later novels become more didactic along a line of progression marked by his use of nature.

The Mayor of Casterbridge is a study of character. A man is impotent before interior forces. His philosophic attitude is resignation, in which negative moral H finds value. H is troubled by two problems at this time: the position of man in the universe and religious beliefs. These problems are found in *Tess of the d'Urbervilles*. It protests the system of things, the First Cause devoid of sympathy for its creatures, society's aggravation of the evils of existence. H, however, confuses and contradicts. There is a change to a more subjective style with too much recrimination and too little frankness. H finds himself between his artistic tendencies and his philosophical leanings. There is quality in the portraits and the scenes.

Jude the Obscure exaggerates the faults of *Tess*. It is a criticism of marriage, and on this point H is anarchic. His thesis fails because it is predicated on exceptional characters. He tries to be experimental. His ideas on marriage belong to his pessimism. The novel marks the last stage of development; thought conquered the artist and because of excessive thought, the novel lacks vitality.

The Hand of Ethelberta is a social study and is not believable. Its excessive romanticism does not serve as social study, and it is weak and exaggerated in its portraits. *The Well-Beloved* is a fantasy.

The interaction of one sex with the other, the movements of the vital force to continue the human race, the conflict between man's intelligence and the will to live of the universe, are universal themes. These are not social themes and do not need the machinations of great houses to exemplify. The rural locale is most suited to reinforce the message of the work. Love, which for H is not an idealized passion but rather sexual attraction, is the base of all his works. His heroines can be classified from this point of view. Man's character is an acquired value. Modern man wavers between intelligence and instinct. The peasants have philosophic value in his work. They represent the conditions of the good earth and lead to the conclusion that intelligence is sickness. They also have artistic value since through them he produces his realistic studies, entertaining and true.

H is at home with nature and his work reveals the desire to penetrate its secret. In the search he shows his familial background and the force of his long association with the natural. His perceptions of nature are alive and his artistic regard completes his knowledge. He demonstrates his knowledge of the fields, animals, birds, and such knowledge is doubled by the poet in him. From this arises his natural pantheism. His pessimism arises from natural conflict, confusion, and blind effort. It is seen in the spirit of modern man out of harmony with nature. H is not a mystic.

The Dynasts synthesizes the ideas on which all H's works are based. There are points of contact with Schopenhauer, and his influence is a possibility. H attributes the evil of man to metaphysical causes. Pessimists generally adopt an individual point of view while optimists adopt a universal point of view. The viewpoint is the result of the temper of the social milieu of the thinker. His education and life form his way of seeing existence and determine the moral tone of his work. This moral in the final analysis is an aspect of Buddhism.

As a writer H was long on aesthetic sense but short on form. His manner of composition is dramatic. He does subordinate his secondary characters; concentrate interest in a small group of which the principal figure is always a woman; maintain unity of action. He does suppress details and compress time. The action is limited to a single plot. Atmosphere and symbolism abound. This technique was acquired little by little and probably was influenced by Greek drama. Psychological presentation of character and life was not H's strong point. H's style is very individualistic, and he is principally concerned with accuracy. This accuracy explains his use of technical terms from architecture, painting, science. Juxtaposed in H's own way, all these words become his vocabulary. He contrasts in phrase: one the simple and natural, the other intellectual and complexly constructed. His vocabulary is also latinized, which betrays the student and the thinker. There is poetry in his style which is marked by fullness, imagination, and artistic penetration.

H's value goes far beyond that of the regional novelist. The region gave him the materials and the great freedom of expression. He is a realist but with some artistic tendencies incompatible with realistic theory. As a thinker, he stands with the great modern pessimists. As a writer he is the greatest English tragic writer of the nineteenth-century. [Despite inaccuracies and H's indignation on the publication of this book, Hedgcock has many insightful things to say about H.] [In French.]

577 Lee, Vernon [pseud of Violet Paget]. "The Handling of Words: T. Hardy," ENGLISH REVIEW, IX (Sept 1911), 231–41; rptd in THE HANDLING OF WORDS AND OTHER STUDIES IN LITERARY PSYCHOLOGY (Lond: Lane, 1923; NY: Dodd, Mead, 1923; Lincoln, Nebraska: University of Nebraska P, 1968), pp. 222–41.

In *Tess of the d'Urbervilles*, H's use of many adjectives is the result of imprecise thought, recording all that he can say about a thing rather than including only relevant detail. Inappropriate metaphors in the description of the valleys as Tess descends to the dairy reveal wavering interest, and, though they may add to the meaning, the pastoral impression H is trying to convey does not gain through them. All of this means that the reader does not need to pay careful attention to the reading, and part of H's popularity may be due to this indulgence of lazy readers. Movement in literature, as in all art, requires the attention of the mind to "the activities of measuring, comparing and unifying," and depends on carefully correlated levels of action and logical processes. The description here analyzed not only lacks "complexity of tense and logical form" but is unnecessarily qualified, suggesting a lack of commitment and energy. But the impression of slovenliness which dominates perhaps contributes to the picture of "sensual life among lush vegetation" that H was attempting, and perhaps shows H to be beyond trifling demands for logic among his readers.

578 Machen, Arthur. "The Dorchester Players," ACADEMY, LXXXI (25 Nov 1911), 657–58.

The performances by the Dorchester Players of *The Three Wayfarers* and *The Distracted Preacher* captured the romantic country which H described in his novels.

579 Mair, G[eorge] H[erbert]. "The Novel," ENGLISH LITERATURE: MODERN (Lond: Williams & Norgate, 1911), pp. 212–36, espec 229–30.

H introduced contemporary Russian pessimism into England. He chose peasant characters because their actions more clearly represent their inner life. He shows that man's fate is nothing [?] more than chance.

580 "The *Mellstock Quire* in Town," DORSET YEARBOOK, 1911–1912, pp. 41–55.

The London production by The Dorchester Debating Society of A. H. Evans's adaptation of *Under the Greenwood Tree* is "the most charming Wessex comedy which has ever come into the glare of the footlights."

581 Noyes, Alfred. "The Poetry of Thomas Hardy," NORTH AMERICAN REVIEW, CXCIV (July 1911), 96–105.
"The Darkling Thrush" is one of the finest lyrics in the world. In the first stanza, the landscape represents the vast intellectual and spiritual period that closed with the nineteenth century, but there is no overemphasis of the symbol. The first two parts of *The Dynasts* were badly received; the publication of the third part revealed the structural perfection, the scientific precision and lucidity, the biting irony, the symbolism of the whole work. H's pessimism is like that of Shakespeare's tragedies. As in the grave-digger's scene, in H's poetry we are shown the skull beneath the face of beauty.

582 "The Poetry of Thomas Hardy," ACADEMY, LXXX (25 March 1911), 350–51.
It is difficult to judge H as a poet because of his dominance as a novelist. The two disciplines overlap somewhat. But "a man who is a poet in prose is not likely to miss being something of a poet in verse, too." Structurally H's poems possess mathematical precision. At times, however, this precision seems strained or forced. His tone of "ruthless pessimism" is ever present, but he never moves out of the realm of reality. There is some humor in his poetry, and some of the rustic description characteristic of his Wessex novels finds its way into his verses also.

583 Saxelby, F. Outwin. A THOMAS HARDY DICTIONARY: THE CHARACTERS AND SCENES OF THE NOVELS AND POEMS ALPHABETICALLY ARRANGED AND DESCRIBED (Lond: Routledge & Kegan Paul; NY: Dutton, 1911); rptd (NY: Humanities P, 1962).
[Contains primary and secondary bibliographies, list of Wessex place names, synopses of the plots of the novels, and a dictionary which identifies references in H's prose and poetry.]

584 Sherren, Wilkinson. "Literary Geography: II.—The Wessex of Thomas Hardy," T. P.'s WEEKLY, XVIII (27 Oct 1911), 531.
Jude the Obscure, "that unjustly maligned tragedy of the artistic temperament, clean as a rain-washed night, in comparison with pornographic fiction of recent years," is practically the only great novel of the Wessex series "that is not in inspiration directly derived from Dorset."

585 Skillington, S. H. "T. P.'s Competition No. I: Who is the Best Writer of Short Stories, and Why?: Thomas Hardy," T. P.'s WEEKLY, XVIII (8 Dec 1911), 724.
H's prose has a "dignity and beauty, derived from the Authorized Version of the Scriptures and what is most worthy in literature." He has "a closeness to

nature and man, a freedom from affectation, and a grim perception of the ironies of Fate." His stories fall into two categories: those which "interpret the old fashioned, rustic world," and those in which "human beings are brought together, by the ironies of Chance, into most piquant relationship, and are carried along by the nature of the situation to a heart-breaking entanglement."

586 Williams, Harold. "Thomas Hardy (1840)," Two CENTURIES OF THE ENGLISH NOVEL (Lond: Smith, Elder, 1911), pp. 283–303. A point of unity between H and Meredith is their profound sympathy for human nature. But while Meredith's fellow sympathy is for mankind, H "centres our interest in the individual." H has peopled "our imagination with a new world of intensely living personalities." H's belief that after his death *Jude the Obscure* will be his only enduring work "shows the proverbial inability of the author to judge his own work." "The unity of all sentient life," past and present, is a major aspect of H's imagination. "Not even Schopenhauer has made us feel so forcibly the continuity of human life in its generations." In depicting man and nature, H stresses that man "works for his living upon the bosom of the great mother earth, and draws his sustenance from her." Although his landscapes rarely smile, his pictures of nature are not haunted by any weak melancholy. His imagination from the first is "severe and impressive." Despite the stigmatizing of *Tess of the d'Urbervilles* and *Jude* as immoral, H is "above all things, an austere moralist." Life may signify nothing, but H's "faith in the present is securely founded." Simplicity marks H's "faculty for design and composition."

1912

587 A. "Thomas Hardy," T. P.'s WEEKLY, XX (30 Aug 1912), 268.
H "dared to draw the shroud from the decaying corpse in our midst," revealing "unholy unions" that are a "hidden contamination of the feast of Life." He knew the female soul is revolted by "that which is unholy, untrue, unreal," and he understood that "the spiritual reality must precede the physical act," but he did not "really close the door to hope."

588 A. "Thomas Hardy: What is to be Learnt from His Works: The Prince of Pessimists," T. P.'s WEEKLY, XX (2 Aug 1912), 143.
Like Mephistopheles in FAUST, H expresses the "grand and stoical despair" of a "shadow-spectre—the haunting 'other self' of the human ever seeking

to drag the real self from its God-like destiny, yet ever foiled and frustrated." Because he *"forces* the human spirit out of the granite limitations of the mental concept which it has built about itself to obscure the light, Hardy— the Prince of Pessimists—will be among the Immortals."

589 Abercrombie, Lascelles. THOMAS HARDY: A CRITICAL STUDY (Lond: Secker, 1912; NY: Kennerley, 1927); rptd (NY: Russell & Russell, 1964).

H's novels, controlled by a metaphysic, are unmatched for perfection of form. They include characters who are not puppets, but who ultimately obey a peculiar fate. In some novels, these characters, the product of "a great psychological imagination," are simultaneously individuals and members of a group. In general, they are part of a well-controlled world and of plots which are characteristically rich in incident. Other important characteristics of the Wessex novels include humor, beautiful pictures of country life, nature, and language which is limited since only the dialect exerts potential or exciting force. In H's "minor" works—*Desperate Remedies, A Pair of Blue Eyes, The Hand of Ethelberta, A Laodicean,* and *The Well-Beloved*—powerfully imagined individuals are missing. Furthermore, the "annexes"—the short stories, *The Trumpet-Major, Two on a Tower,* and *Under the Greenwood Tree*—are mere decorations and experiments. However, *A Few Crusted Characters* is a "little masterpiece," *Tower* has beauty of drama and character, and *Greenwood Tree* is skillfully controlled. But in these works H does not go deep, as he does in the novels of "dramatic form"—*Far From the Madding Crowd, The Return of the Native, The Mayor of Casterbridge,* and *The Woodlanders.* In these novels the characters possess the vigor of the earth and demonstrate that Wessex life is capable of "passing into tragedy." Since they deal with the history of the relationship of groups of people, they are more complex than *Tess of the d'Urbervilles* and *Jude the Obscure.* These two works are novels of "epic form." They allow H to include the gloss of his own opinion. They are major achievements. At first glance, the poems do not seem to match the fiction in achievement, but *Time's Laughingstocks* is a genuine addition to poetry. The philosophical and psychological poems in general are an undeniable achievement. Of an even higher order is the "characteristic poem of our age," *The Dynasts.* This epic-drama is a great summation of the novels.

590 B., T. "Thomas Hardy: What is to be Learnt from His Works: Not Elevating," T. P.'s WEEKLY, XX (2 Aug 1912), 143.

In H's work there is "much in each volume which I should be very sorry for my daughters to read, or my sons either, for that matter." Earlier correspondent's comparison of H to Dickens, Scott, Thackery, or Meredith is "a most unwarrantable slight on the illustrious dead."

591 Beach, Joseph Warren. "News for Bibliophiles," NATION (NY), XCIV (25 Jan 1912), 82–83.

Although a very early work, *The Romantic Adventures of a Milkmaid,* first published in the GRAPHIC "Summer Number" for 1883, is not altogether unworthy of H. It shares the Wessex setting of his later and greater works, and Margery, the milkmaid, may be said in many ways to foreshadow Tess.

592 Beach, Joseph Warren. "News for Bibliophiles," NATION (NY), XCIV (1 Feb 1912), 107.

Another little story, "What the Shepherd Saw," apparently abandoned by H, was printed in the Seaside Library (No. 1155), probably without authority. The tale is reminiscent of *Far From the Madding Crowd* in that it is seen through the eyes of a sheepboy in a hut. Even in this early effort, H emphasizes the tragic side of life and the inevitability of fate.

593 "Books: Novels of Character and Environment," SPECTATOR (Lond), CIX (7 Sept 1912), 335–37.

Pessimistic philosophy is the great flaw in H's work. The "normal mind" views life from neither "an entirely optimistic nor from an entirely pessimistic viewpoint," and great art is "representative of life, not critical of it." Man as a free agent "may be an illusion," but "life compels us to accept" it. *The Return of the Native* is H's most complete "representation of life," because of its "intuitive sympathy with humanity in all its moods," its humor and warmth. H's pessimism "is only a habit of thought, a weariness with life that comes upon all of us sometimes, if it does not remain with us always; and that, too, springs from his sympathy with mankind, from the depth and richness of his emotional nature."

594 Brown, Curtis. "Thomas Hardy in his Home: Interview with the Novelist," SPRINGFIELD WEEKLY REPUBLICAN, 1 Feb 1912, p. 13.

Asked why he was so pessimistic a writer, H replied " 'if one lives long enough one realizes that happiness is very ephemeral.' " Furthermore, " 'there's too much sham optimism, humbugging and even cruel optimism' " at present. Pessimism, even if exaggerated, " 'leaves one, at least, on the safe side.' " To H there was too much sentiment in most fiction, therefore " 'somebody [must] write a little mercilessly—although, of course, it's painful to have to do it.' "

595 "Coroner." "The Prince of Pessimists: Views of Coroner and Working Man," T. P.'s WEEKLY, XX (16 Aug 1912), 205.

H critics, accustomed to "mother's milk" and "sentimental paste," suffer "internal disruptions" when they partake of "the unholy fleshpot containing the element of Truth." They are men "too long steeped in traditions" who dislike H because he "has not given the usual happy ending to his stories in accordance with the wish that all must come right in the end, a wish prompted by the belief in a compensating life in the future."

596 Cramb, Meyrick G. H. "T. P.'s Letter Box: Thomas Hardy and His Faith," T. P.'s WEEKLY, XX (19 July 1912), 88.

H's "new religion" is a "negation of all other religions" that expresses not simple pessimism but "a grand and stoical despair." Life is "a marred and incomplete design," and no power of good guides the world. The "incessant warring" of plants and animals makes nature "as blood guilty as the most criminal men"; all living things are "component parts of one suffering whole, the result of one chance disaster or one unpurposed sin."

597 Dickinson, Thomas Herbert. "Thomas Hardy's *The Dynasts,*" NORTH AMERICAN REVIEW, CXCV (April 1912), 526–42.

The Dynasts is a work of the first magnitude. The stage production was as far as possible from H's idea: mental performance is the most important factor of a great play. H is most original in his supernatural and cosmogonic machinery. This is a drama of the unseen as much as of the seen, and it purports to objectify the hidden purposes and tendencies of the ages as much as the actions and motives of men. The diction, both prose and verse, is masterful.

598 Dunton, E. "Thomas Hardy: Death—Only the Way Out," T. P.'s WEEKLY, XX (9 Aug 1912), 172.

H is "a gentle stoic" who depicts life from the evidence of the senses, not from the "evidence of our higher *instincts,* of our moments of exalted desires, of our insatiable thirst for happiness and for a definite goal." His works do not teach the irrelevance of good and evil but rather "the inevitability of punishment following ignorance and sin, even to the fourth generation." It is more rational to look on life as "a schoolmaster preparing us for a higher form or for another place in the university" and on death as "the only possible way out of the limitations of a worn-out or outgrown body."

599 Fehr, Bernhard. STREIFZÜGE DURCH DIE NEUESTE ENGLISCHE LITERATUR (Rambles Through the Most Recent English Literature) (Strassbourg: Karl J. Truebner, 1912), pp. 78–81, 160–62.

"A Tragedy of Two Ambitions" is a masterpiece of composition. H's style is accumulative—working from a mass of detail towards a conclusion. [Contrasts Meredith's and H's philosophy.] H is incapable of treating true humor, for although we may laugh at times, there is always tragedy waiting to take the foreground. [Includes a biography and lists H's works.] [In German.]

600 "Fiction," ATHENAEUM, No. 4433 (12 Oct 1912), 414.
Two more additions to the Wessex Edition (*The Trumpet-Major* and *Two on a Tower*) show H, in the former, "the *sacer vates* of the yeoman class," and in the latter, a champion for freedom in literature. It is astonishing to think today that at one time *Two on a Tower* was considered "improper" and a satire on the Established Church.

601 "Fiction," ATHENAEUM, No. 4437 (9 Nov 1912), 553.
H's *A Group of Noble Dames* is very realistic, "but we miss the rustic humour of his best books." *The Well-Beloved* is a fantasy.

602 "Fiction," ATHENAEUM, No. 4441 (7 Dec 1912), 689–90.
Desperate Remedies and *The Hand of Ethelberta* have been added to the Wessex Edition. A recent note by H about *Remedies* tells us that it "contains reflections and sentiments derived from the *Wessex Poems* and others which the author had already written, but could not get in print." *Ethelberta* shows that H "is seldom so happy among the upper orders as he is among the peasantry."

603 Fitch, George Hamlin. "Thomas Hardy and his Tragic Tales of Wessex," MODERN ENGLISH BOOKS OF POWER (San Francisco: Elder, 1912), pp. 131–39.
H is the greatest living English fiction writer. But because of harsh criticism of *Jude the Obscure*, he has turned to writing only poetry. H's novels are always fresh, big, genuine. He has no equal in realistic pessimism, in showing the power of nature, in insight into the nature of women. He is one of the greatest story-tellers the world has seen. His stories are never forced; they move with simplicity, clarity, and directness.

604 Forsyth, Peter Taylor. "The Pessimism of Thomas Hardy," LIVING AGE, CCLXXV (23 Nov 1912), 458–73.
Pessimism is more Christian than optimism, but it ignores sin, redemption, and personality. H sees men as the sport of some divinity who does not know or understand suffering. Although H's works have the tragic note, they don't have the tragic motive—i.e., they don't inspire us to overcome fate. In short, H faces some of the facts, but not the "distilled revelationary truth from the total past." The best thing about H and other pessimistic writers is that they "force us to see in Christ's cross not a preliminary of salvation, nor the totem of a sect, but salvation itself."

605 "General," ATHENAEUM, No. 4444 (28 Dec 1912), 783.
A Laodicean completes the prose works of the Wessex Edition. It is not a particularly good novel because it was written during a period of illness. The volume of poems in the Wessex Edition shows that H "can write a

rousing war song, but he is most at home when he is carving into sharply pointed verse the sorrows and bitter ironies of life."

606 Greenlaw, Edwin. A SYLLABUS OF ENGLISH LITERATURE (Chicago: B. H. Sanborn, 1912), p. 302.

The Return of the Native and *Tess of the d'Urbervilles* best illustrate H's method and theory of life. He uses minute realism in his studies of Wessex life. His work marks the chasm that separates Wordsworth's confidence in Nature from modern skepticism. H is distinguished for skill in characterization, mastery of plot, and precision of style.

607 "Hardy's Allusions," SATURDAY REVIEW (Lond), CXIII (22 June 1912), 781–82.

The new Preface matter of the Wessex Edition is worth attention. Local vernacular, Shakespeare, and recent science, as well as H's study of detail and style in paintings all influenced H's style. H's architectural training is the origin of Bathsheba's barn. H's use of classical allusions is not at all encouraging to the shallow reader, for H shows a terseness which is puzzling to the outsider. Herodotus, Terence, and Lucretius supply mottoes for *The Hand of Ethelberta,* while the title of chapter 4 of *Far From the Madding Crowd,* from the satires of Horace, presages the death following the Troy-Boldwood clash.

608 Harper, J. Henry. THE HOUSE OF HARPER: A CENTURY OF PUBLISHING IN FRANKLIN SQUARE (NY & Lond: Harper & Bros, 1912), pp. 112, 492, 528–33, 534, 616–17, 631.

[Harper's expression of admiration for H to Henry Holt at a dinner at the University Club, New York, resulted in Holt's offer to "exchange authors"—H for William E. Norris. Harper accepted the offer and from that time on Harper published all of Hardy's novels. Harper helped H decide on the title of *The Return of the Native,* worked closely with H during the serialization of *Tess of the d'Urbervilles* by HARPER'S BAZAAR, and during the serialization of *Hearts Insurgent* (later changed to *Jude the Obscure*) in HARPER'S MAGAZINE. H rewrote one chapter and made modifications in order that *Jude* "contain nothing which could not be read aloud in any family circle." Attacks on *Jude* by the American press made H fearful that a prospective stage production of *Tess* might be prejudiced. H introduced Harper to George du Maurier in January 1896. H joined Walter Besant and William Black in a public statement of confidence in the honor and fairness of Harper and Brothers after they had been accused of pirating some six stories of Rudyard Kipling (ATHENAEUM, 22 Nov 1890). Letters from H to Harper of June 1883, August 1894, December 1895, January 1896 reprinted.]

609 Holliday, Carl. "Thomas Hardy," English Fiction from the Fifth to the Twentieth Century (NY: Century, 1912), pp. 361–66, 369, 399.

H is a "pandiabolist" and "determinist" of the naturalistic school of fiction whose greatest work is *Tess of the d'Urbervilles*. H's pessimism is superficial beside " 'the plenitude and rational optimism of [George] Meredith.' " H's chief distinction as a novelist is a "language rarely equalled in 19th century prose."

610 "Literary Gossip," Athenaeum, No. 4415 (8 June 1912), 656.

Upon receiving a gold medal from the Royal Society of Literature on his seventy-second birthday, H commented on the need to encourage young writers and stated his displeasure with the increase of slipshod writing resulting from the influence of journalism, American journals in particular.

611 "The Love of Good Writing," Nation (NY), XCIV (20 June 1912), 608–9.

H's address to the Royal Society of Literature upon the reception of a gold medal on his seventy-second birthday stressed the need to perpetuate a taste for "real literature" in the reading public and the importance of an author's satisfaction in his own good work. H pointed out that there had been a deterioration in style in his own day which he attributed to hurried writing, the lower standards of American journals, and a general indifference to form. H maintained that the shortest way to achieve good prose was through the discipline of good verse. In spite of the predominantly pessimistic tone of his comments, however, H concluded his speech by affirming his belief that "pure," that is, good or "real" literature, would ultimately vindicate itself.

612 Mahony, Justin J. "Thomas Hardy: What is to be Learnt from His Works: Thomas Hardy as a Writer," T. P.'s Weekly, XX (2 Aug 1912), 143.

George Eliot is greater than H because she, unlike H, has "the power to inspire noble thoughts and high ideals." "Surely we are all of us too well acquainted with the imperfections of humanity to desire that they shall be thrown at us without any apparent or intelligent motive to teach us a lesson." [See F.H.T., "T. P.'s Letter Box: Hardy and Eliot," ibid (26 July 1912), 120.]

613 Meredith, George. Letters of George Meredith, ed by his son (NY: Scribner, 1912), II, 448.

Tess of the d'Urbervilles "is open to criticism, but excellent and very interesting." The Dairy Farm is fascinating, but Tess and Alec's meeting again is a depression of power. H did not sustain his minute method. The story is too hurried. Tess becomes a "smudge in vapour." [Letter to Frederick Greenwood, 23 Feb 1892.]

614 "Mr. Hardy on Literature, A Plea for Pure English," TIMES (Lond), 4 June 1912, p. 7.

H's speech of acceptance of the gold medal of the Royal Society of Literature, presented to him on his seventy-second birthday by Henry Newbolt and W. B. Yeats, laments "the appalling increase every day of slipshod writing," then praises poetry as the clearest way to convey ideas. He concludes with a quotation on the immortality of "poesy" from the George Sands novel ANDRÉ.

615 Paine, Albert Bigelow. MARK TWAIN: A BIOGRAPHY (NY: Harper, 1912), II, 747; III, 1253, 1567, 1571.

H and Mark Twain admired one another.

616 Powell, G. H. "The Weird of Wessex," OXFORD AND CAMBRIDGE REVIEW, XXII (Aug 1912), 55–70.

H comes among us as a reformer, a revolutionary; his Wessex, presumably typifying a larger world, is presented under a somber grey aspect, varied only by patches of Stygian darkness. His *Life's Little Ironies* should be called "Life's Appalling Fiasco." H shows cold-blooded inhumanity in the delineation of characters like Elizabeth-Jane. When distributing his wretched dole of happiness he is like a family solicitor dealing out a carefully limited allowance to some spendthrift ne'er-do-well. The embittered and portentous gravity of H's pronouncements on life such as "happiness is but an occasional episode in the general drama of pain," is both awkward English and demoralizing rationalization. H is in a chronic "tantrum" with the Deity, but being a genius, he cannot, curiously enough, help painting living characters which we have to defend against the cranky author of their being. The poem "After the Club-Dance" is an elaborate pathetic fallacy, with an insufferable conclusion, "they too have done the same" which is neither poetry nor sense. H is not showing pessimism, but cantankerous ill-temper. The superfluous acid of the novels drained off in crude and uncertain lyrics contributes very little to the enrichment of life. [A slashing attack.]

617 R[andell], W[ilfrid] L. "Reviews: The Smaller Wessex," ACADEMY, LXXXIII (26 Oct 1912), 535–36.

The structures of H's novels fall into two general categories: those whose plot structure flows naturally, e.g., *Tess of the d'Urbervilles* and *The Return of the Native;* the second type of construction, found in some fewer of H's novels, is strained, the incidents are forced into a plot disrupting the realistic flow as in *Two on a Tower*. "We may note . . . as a remarkable characteristic of nearly all his novels, the range and remoteness of his allusions and metaphors." One needs to be versed in various scientific and artistic disciplines to appreciate "all the subtle touches." H has often, and justly, been compared with Meredith.

618 R[andell], W[ilfrid] L. "The Wessex Novels," ACADEMY, LXXXII (29 June 1912), 805.
H "cared as little as did Meredith for popular acclamation, . . . neither seeking praise nor avoiding blame." The Wessex novels will endure time's criticism.

619 "A Reader." "Thomas Hardy: What is to be Learnt from His Works: The Blood Guilt (?) of Flowers and Animals," T. P.'s WEEKLY, XX (2 Aug 1912), 143.
[Attacks as "monstrous" the view expressed by M. G. H. Cramb in an earlier letter (19 July 1912) that H offers a "new religion" of despair and a fatalistic notion that man shares "blood guilt" with animals and flowers.] "Poor, innocent, herbiferous animals to be so maligned! And has the scent of the rose or lily anything of blood guilt in it?" The present age surpasses all others in human "benevolence and charity." England can do without people who share Mr. Cramb's "ignorant, inhuman ideas."

620 Rideing, William H. "Lady Helier and Thomas Hardy," MANY CELEBRITIES AND A FEW OTHERS (Garden City, NY: Doubleday, Page; Lond: Nash, 1912), pp. 280–88.
[In brief conversations with H, Rideing was left with the impression that H could be genial while suggesting the universe is doomed.]

621 Roz, Firmin. "M. Thomas Hardy," LE ROMAN ANGLAIS CONTEMPORAIN (The Contemporary English Novel) (Paris: Libraire Hachette, 1912), pp. 57–106.
H is, fundamentally, an ironist, his stories principally love stories whose most interesting characters are young women trapped by ironic circumstances. These circumstances are often created by the audacity or whimsy of the women themselves, as in the case of Bathsheba Everdene, Eustacia Vye, or Sue Bridehead. All of H's novels employ the love triangle, or extensions of the love triangle. A second major concern, connected with the element of love, is the effect of social convention and prejudice upon sensitive, aspiring individuals. *Tess of the d'Urbervilles* and *Jude the Obscure* explore the tragic consequences of the struggle between the individual and the restraints his society imposes upon him. H's characters can be grouped according to the degree to which they possess freedom from or enslavement to social convention. Farmer Boldwood, Jude Fawley,

Troy, Fitzpiers, Wildeve, Angel Clare, as well as H's fascinating heroines, are in their different ways responsive to the values of conventional society. H's truly heroic characters—Oak, Venn, Winterborne—are strong, wise, and somehow free of social constraint. [In French.]

622 S., C. K. "A Literary Letter: The New Edition of Thomas Hardy's Works," SPHERE (Lond), LIX (18 May 1912), 158.
[An announcement of the publication of the Wessex Edition which praises the format, the superior printing, and the new "General Preface."]

623 Salviris, Jacob [pseud of Jessie Georgina Sime]. "A Reading of the Wessex Novels," WESTMINSTER REVIEW, CLXXVIII (Oct 1912), 400–412; rptd in THOMAS HARDY OF THE WESSEX NOVELS: AN ESSAY AND BIOGRAPHICAL NOTE (Montreal: Louis Carriér, 1928), pp. 23–53.
H has "the rare courage to show us people with the ordinary share of human inconsistency." H's style lacks "formal beauty [but] it has that rarer attribute, sincerity." In his early works "we get the very spirit of [his] . . . age—the spirit of troubled questioning and quick sympathy, together with the underlying suggestion of belief in happiness and beauty." But in his later novels, "he set out consciously to address his own time," and "impaired the effect of his message." H's chief limitation as novelist was his lack of a "hearty, ungrudging belief in himself or in his fellows." Even characters like Giles, Gabriel, and Diggory—for all their triumph over adversity —"lacked the quality of eager and ardent giving." Hence, H fails to provide us "that feeling of *expansion* . . . which . . . is the crown of art." Even his humor is saturnine, "almost always of the grim kind." H's novelistic career has three phases: in the first (*Under the Greenwood Tree, Far From the Madding Crowd*) his characters are "young, hopeful and ready to meet [happiness] halfway." *The Return of the Native* is transition to the second phase (*The Mayor of Casterbridge, The Woodlanders*), in which his "men and women expect from the beginning very little of life." In the third phase (*Tess of the d'Urbervilles, Jude the Obscure, The Well-Beloved, Life's Little Ironies*) H's power of understanding predominates over that of affection; from the beginning his characters lack a "capacity for healthy enjoyment." It is a pity the later novels have attracted so much attention. Like Meredith and Kipling, H "lost the power of enjoyment, satisfaction, happiness, in creating" as he grew older.

624 Schüdderkopf, A. W. "Englischer Brief" (English Letter), DAS LITERARISCHE ECHO, XIV (April 1912), 999.
In "God's Funeral," FORTNIGHTLY REVIEW, March 1912, pp. 397–99, H has not forfeited his poetic strength and beauty. This poem develops in allegorical form H's conception of God. [In German.]

625 Schüdderkopf, A. W. "Englischer Brief" (English Letter), Das Literarische Echo, XIV (May 1912), 1293.
The Wessex Edition of the Works of Thomas Hardy in Prose and Verse, a new edition of H's novels, is to be published by Macmillan. [In German.]

626 Schüdderkopf, A. W. "Englischer Brief" (English Letter), Das Literarische Echo, XV (May 1912 [?]), 855.
The Wessex Edition of the Works of Thomas Hardy in Prose and Verse is now complete. The last two volumes contain *The Dynasts*—a drama for "mental performance"—and *Time's Laughingstocks*—poems which in content and pathos remind the reader of H's major novels. [In German.]

627 Sherren, Wilkinson. "Thomas Hardy, O. M.: The Man Behind the Books," T. P.'s Weekly, XX (23 Aug 1912), 231.
"The sophistication of town life" enabled H to recognize "the romantic possibilities of the 'old, ancient' land of his birth." The homage he receives at Dorchester is only his due, and "the dispersal of his manuscripts is a mournful reminder that his work as a novelist is done."

628 "Some Books of the Week: *Tess of the d'Urbervilles* and *Far From the Madding Crowd*," Spectator (Lond), CVIII (18 May 1912), 804.
[Brief notice of Volumes I and II of the Wessex Edition, which describes H's "Preface" and general "format."]

629 T., F. H. "T. P.'s Letter Box: Hardy and Eliot," T. P.'s Weekly, XX (26 July 1912), 120.
[Refers to a letter by J. J. M., in T. P.'s Weekly, 21 June 1912 (not seen).] The contention that George Eliot "affords intense emotion and that Hardy is merely interesting" is a "personal opinion only." "Just as one obtains a better view of a picture from a distance," so "the next generation" will be in a better position to judge these writers. [See Justin J. Mahony, "Thomas Hardy: What is to be Learnt from His Works: Thomas Hardy as a Writer," ibid (2 Aug 1912), 143.]

630 Taufkirch, Richard. Die Romankunst von Thomas Hardy (Thomas Hardy's Art of the Novel) (Frankfurt/Main: Knauer, 1912); University of Marburg dissertation.
[Examines H's literary activity and criticism, his theory and technique of novel writing, the general characteristics of H's art, the motifs, the meaning of Wessex for the novels, and H's place in English literature.] The critics have done the author an injustice, for they have often been content with expressing their bias and dislikes without being aware of the artistic laws of the novel. The author's originality makes it difficult to place him in

any literary movement. Although H is not a pessimist who purposely seeks to express the gloomy side of human experience in an effort to show that human life is intolerable, the author occasionally sees too much unhappiness. The source of H's particular power rests in the treatment of Wessex, and his art diminishes when he leaves Wessex. Although such a setting has prevented a wide circulation of the works, perceptive readers should be able to recognize that H's local observations have a universal meaning which gives insight into human nature and human life. H is the most significant contemporary English novelist. [The German critical interest in H is greatly indebted to Richard Taufkirch. Aside from this being the first Hardian dissertation in Germany, it also provided the stimulus for almost all future dissertations.] [In German.]

631 Thom, Arthur F. "A Tremendous Genius," T. P.'s WEEKLY, XX (9 Aug 1912), 172.
Contrary to Meyrick Cramb's assertion, H was no thorough-going pessimist. [See "T. P.'s Letter Box: Thomas Hardy and His Faith," T. P.'s WEEKLY, XX (19 July 1912), 88.]

632 "Thomas Hardy at Home," ENGLISH ILLUSTRATED MAGAZINE. XLVII (June 1912), 276–80.
In response to a question, "Is not optimism a useful and sane philosophy?" H retorted, " 'There's too much sham optimism, humbugging and even cruel optimism.' "

633 "Topics of the Day: Literature and Journalism," SPECTATOR (Lond), CVIII (8 June 1912), 900–901.
[Article defending journalism against H's attack in a speech delivered before the Royal Society of Literature.]

634 Wallis, J. "The Prince of Pessimists: Views of Coroner and Working Man: Not Juvenile Fiction," T. P.'s WEEKLY, XX (16 Aug 1912), 205.
[Disagrees with an opinion expressed by T. B. in "Thomas Hardy: What is to be Learnt from His Works: Not Elevating," ibid (2 Aug 1912), 143, condemning H because he is not suitable reading for children.] He does not write for "boys and girls." He writes "of men and women, for men and women, and he writes what he knows to be true." Courageous enough to "put it down in plain language," H is not afraid "of accidentally wounding the delicate susceptibilities of some."

635 "The Wessex Drama," EDINBURGH REVIEW, CCXV (Jan 1912), 93–112.
H sees the world as a connected series of pictures. H is akin to Wordsworth in descriptions of nature, but H always describes outer nature. Though his

love is Wessex drama, he would not be appreciated in Wessex (his characters and dialect might seem demeaning). His attitude toward life is "pathological," part of an age of decadence. The obsession with sex which characterizes his Wessex drama is "physiologically painful," and its psychology is more French than English. H is decadent in seeing only misery in human life.

636 "The Wessex Hardy," BOOKMAN (NY), XXXV (July 1912), 462–63.

The Wessex Edition has a prefatory note by H in which he explains that the Wessex Country has provided everything needed "for one man's literary purpose."

1913

637 Bailey, John. "Thomas Hardy," BOOKMAN (Lond), XLV (Dec 1913), 143–44.

What makes H the greatest living English novelist, besides his instinctive technical talents and his mastery of the English language, is his truthfulness. He shows us truth without the affectation of social customs. He tries to depict man in a simple, elemental world. The stories of *A Changed Man* are products of H's immature years. The setting of the stories is Wessex, and, indeed, the only "contemporary rivals to the peasants of Wessex are perhaps Mr. Kipling's private soldiers."

638 Beerbohm, Max. "A Sequelula to *The Dynasts*," A CHRISTMAS GARLAND (NY: Dutton, 1913), 59–73.

[A parody of *The Dynasts* accusing H of inappropriate language, especially in his penchant for Latinisms (e.g. "Life's impulsion by Incognizance"), cowardice in giving up novel-writing because of *Jude the Obscure*'s reception, parasitism in attempting to describe the Napoleonic Wars, and apparent presumption in deeming "incognizant/An infinitely higher than ourselves." His denial of free will, and his themes of pessimism and fatalism are also made fun of.] [Generally heavy-handed.]

639 Busse, Carl. GESCHICHTE DER WELTLITERATUR (History of World Literature) (Bielefeld and Leipzig: Velhagen & Klasing, 1913), II, 432.

H is a naturalist and psychological realist, especially on the evidence of *Tess of the d'Urbervilles* and *Jude the Obscure*. [In German.]

640 Chesterton, Gilbert Keith. "Great Victorian Novelists," THE VICTORIAN AGE IN LITERATURE (NY: Holt; Lond: William & Norgate, 1913), pp. 138–39, 143–45.

Both Meredith and H disagreed with the orthodox religion of the English village. They were, however, opposed in their disagreement. Meredith's view was a pantheistic, pagan one of nature; H's was an "unnatural" view of nature. Outside of the "Victorian City" there were two naturalistic paths open—"One went upward through a tangled but living forest to lonely but healthy hills: the other went down to a swamp." Meredith took the former; H, the latter. The god of H is almost personal because he is made poisonous. H's concept of an anthropormorphic God comes out of his atheism—he needs to personify a God to "give Him a piece of his mind." Nature is always seen as the betrayer and the ruin of H's women as opposed to Meredith's portrayal of nature as a saver. When these two artists lose artistic control, Meredith becomes comic, almost farcical; H becomes funny in an extravagant depression—a sort of cruel humor, as in the black flag episode in *Tess of the d'Urbervilles.*

641 Clark, James M. "The English Novel, 1870–1910," GERMANISCH-ROMANISCHE MONATSSCHRIFT, V (1913), 670–72.

In *Tess of the d'Urbervilles* H treats problems of sex with delicacy quite equal to that of Hebbel in GYGES UND SEIN RING.

642 "A Happy Surprise: Mr. Hardy's Short Stories," TIMES LITERARY SUPPLEMENT (Lond), 30 Oct 1913, p. 479.

A Changed Man is a "happy surprise" after the fifteen years since H's last novel. The stories are ironic, and every one has "an astringent tang." The more lifelike they are, as they "descend the social ladder," the more the irony thickens. With the men and women of his own Wessex, H is not genial, and in at least three stories he seems to have been vindictive or sardonic, as in "The Grave by the Handpost," toward his erring characters. Death and nature are his servants. Why is he so disinclined to "humour and pacify, to make happy, his puppets"?

643 Jackson, Holbrook. THE EIGHTEEN NINETIES (Lond: Grant Richards; NY: Knopf, 1913), pp. 38–39, 216–17, 221–23; rptd (Harmondsworth: Penguin, 1939), pp. 36, 37, 218, 223, 225.

In the 1890s H was gaining a wide popularity. H's *Tess of the d'Urbervilles, Jude the Obscure,* and *Wessex Poems,* all published in the 1890s, represent a new phase of his art. *Jude* was representative of "the new fiction" which sought to "undermine morality not only because it was immoral, but because it was 'morbid,' 'neurotic,' and 'diseased.' "

644 Lea, Hermann. THOMAS HARDY'S WESSEX (Lond: Macmillan, 1913; 1925).

The object of the book is "to depict the Wessex country of Thomas Hardy, with a view to discovering the real places which serve as bases for the descriptions of scenery and backgrounds given us in the novels and poems." Though not accountable for identification of characters or architectural features with possible originals, "natural configurations . . . are, for the most part, so faithfully pictured that we may venture to be almost dogmatic in reconciling them with their counterparts." Nevertheless, descriptions given in the novels and poems "must be regarded in their totality as those of imaginative places," for "the exact Wessex of the books exists nowhere outside them." For example, Casterbridge is not Dorchester, but the presentment of Casterbridge is "undoubtedly founded on salient traits in the real town." [The book is arranged in four parts: (1) Novels of Character and Environment (*Tess of the d'Urbervilles, Far From the Madding Crowd, Jude the Obscure, The Return of the Native, The Mayor of Casterbridge, The Woodlanders, Under the Greenwood Tree, Life's Little Ironies . . . and A Few Crusted Characters, Wessex Tales*); (2) Romances and Fantasies (*A Pair of Blue Eyes, The Trumpet-Major, The Well-Beloved, A Group of Noble Dames*); (3) Novels of Ingenuity (*Desperate Remedies, The Hand of Ethelbertha, A Laodicean*); (4) Poetical Works (*Wessex Poems, Poems of the Past and the Present, The Dynasts, Time's Laughingstocks*). Included are 240 photographs and illustrations and a map of the Wessex of the novels and poems. Lea's method is to paraphrase the action of the novels, italicizing place names in the novels and giving parenthetically the names of actual places to which places in the novels are thought to correspond.]

645 "Love in Fiction. (Turgenev and Hardy)," TIMES LITERARY SUPPLEMENT (Lond), 30 Oct 1913, pp. 490–91.

Although the love-novel is an exotic in the garden of literature, many have been written. In *Jude the Obscure* love is presented as a riddle while Jude ponders on the fact of Sue's sex—if she had gotten over this, Sue would have been a wonderful comrade.

646 "Mr. Hardy's Stories," ATHENAEUM, No. 4488 (1 Nov 1913), 488.

The stories of *A Changed Man* are further variations on H's favorite theme of "the mockery of human destinies." H has made the Wessex setting romantic, but more importantly, he has made it a miniature cosmos wherein "malevolent spirits" dwell and from which he derives universal meanings. Every entity in the natural scheme becomes an integral part of the whole and contributes to the meaning of the whole. In this respect *The Return of the Native* is the most perfect example of H's skill.

647 Randell, Wilfrid L. "The Modern Laureate," ACADEMY, LXXXIV (14 June 1913), 740.

The position of poet laureate in England has slipped into obscurity, and the death of the laureate Alfred Austin has not stimulated any great interest to revive the dignity of the position. Mr. Kipling and H have both shown their worth. As for Mr. Kipling, "the blend of colloquial with Imperial would be too distressing." And as for H, "we feel that the satirist who wrote, 'The president of the Immortals has ended his sport with Tess,' is not one to trust in times of national need."

648 Randell, Wilfrid L. "Mystic and Realist," ACADEMY, LXXXIV (22 Feb 1913), 228.

H's continual use of metaphor suggests that he constantly sees beyond the object itself; the metaphor is peculiarly necessary for H because of his uncommon insight.

649 Saintsbury, George Edward Bateman. THE ENGLISH NOVEL (Lond: Dent; NY: Dutton, 1913), pp. 274–76.

H and Meredith warrant discussion among non-living writers because they are superior and thus don't present problems. There is a "note of a certain perversity" in both because they "endeavor to be peculiar in thought, in style, in choice of subject, in handling of it; in short, in general attitude." There is a hint perhaps of "Romantic degeneration" in this wish to be different, but both are to be appreciated especially for not stooping to their audience and waiting for taste to change to suit them.

650 Schelling, Felix E. THE ENGLISH LYRIC (Boston and NY: Houghton Mifflin, 1913), p. 273.

Both H and A. E. Housman are fatalists who have a sense of the "oppression of reality."

651 Schüdderkopf, A. W. "Englischer Brief" (English Letter), DAS LITERARISCHE ECHO, XVI (Dec 1913), 418.

A Changed Man and Other Tales is original and characteristic of H's pessimistic view of life. This publication is a noteworthy literary event of 1913. [In German.]

652 Scott-James, R. A. PERSONALITY IN LITERATURE (Lond: Secker, 1913; NY: Holt, 1932); rptd (Freeport, NY: Books for Libraries, 1968), pp. 180, 205, 206.

H was a fatalist who had a "definite philosophical interpretation of the Universe."

653 Thomas, Edward. "Thomas Hardy of Dorchester," POETRY AND DRAMA, I (1913), 180–84.

H's poetry has a rustic quality which is connected with blind fate, careless nature, and man's manipulation by the Immanent Will, verging on superstition and obsession. The woodland, beauty, truth, antiquity were H's consolations, all "mightier than his superstitions." [Review of *Wessex Poems, Poems of the Past and the Present, The Dynasts*, and *Time's Laughingstocks.*]

654 "T. P.'s Referendum: Who shall be Laureate?" T. P.'s WEEKLY, XXII (18 July 1913), 73.
[Readers elected Kipling the winner and H fourth behind Alice Meynell and John Masefield.]

655 *"The Trumpet-Major* in Town," DORSET YEARBOOK, 1913–1914, pp. 46–54.
The Dorchester Debating Society produced *The Trumpet-Major* in London; it is a "bright, amusing play, full of picturesque movement and funny incident."

656 V., R. "Thomas Hardy: A Coincidence," NOTES AND QUERIES, 11th ser VIII (20 Dec 1913), 481.
The beginning of chap 12 of *Desperate Remedies* is almost word for word the opening part of chap 23 of *The Trumpet-Major*. Did H forget he had already used this neat piece of description? Or is it a coincidence?

657 Whibley, Charles. "Thomas Hardy," BLACKWOOD'S MAGAZINE, CXCIII (June 1913), 823–31; rptd in LIVING AGE, CCLXXVIII (12 July 1913), 96–103.
[Uncritical appreciation on the publication of the Wessex Edition.]

1914

---

658 Aronstein, Philipp. "Thomas Hardy," GERMANISCH-ROMANISCHE MONATSSCHRIFT, VI (1914), 160–76, 219–35.
H was a poet like Emerson who lacked the gift of song, of rhyme, and of harmony. *The Dynasts* has historical value, but the language—though thought-provoking—is clumsy, contains too many coined words, and is seldom poetic. *Desperate Remedies, Under the Greenwood Tree*, and *A Pair of Blue Eyes* are apprentice novels. The Wessex Novels are H's greatest contribution to world literature. H is a master of the short story, and *A Group of Noble Dames* deserves to be compared with the short stories of Boccaccio, Chaucer, and William Morris. The bonds of English puritanism were broken by H, who was not subservient to moral codes. It is difficult to classify H as a realist or naturalist. He is an artist who has transcended genres. [In German.]

659 Barnes, J. H. Forty Years on the Stage: Others (Principally) and Myself (Lond: Chapman & Hall, 1914), pp. 28, 31–32, 134–35, 276.

The charming actress Mrs. Scott-Siddons was the "Rosalind" of H's "To an Impersonator of Rosalind" and "The Two Rosalinds" (in *Time's Laughingstocks*). In J. Comyns Carr's dramatization of *Far From the Madding Crowd,* performed 29 April 1882, at the Globe in London, Barnes played the part of Sergeant Troy.

660 "Briefer Mention," Dial, LVI (16 Jan 1914), 74.

"Now that Mr. Hardy remains in unquestioned solitary prominence among living English writers, it is particularly desirable that his more fugitive work [e.g., *A Changed Man and Other Stories*] should be made easily accessible."

661 "*The Dynasts* at the Kingsway Theatre," Athenaeum, No. 4544 (28 Nov 1914), 572.

Granville Barker has shown that the greatness and strength of *The Dynasts* exists in H's unconventional dramatic techniques. It must be appreciated primarily "as a visible and audible creation." In many ways the stage restricts the expansive proportions of the work. The play itself has a particular emotional appeal to the English mind of the present day.

662 "*The Dynasts* on the Stage," Times Literary Supplement (Lond), 10 Dec 1914, pp. 545–46.

The epic poem is successful not only to the reader's imaginative sensibilities but also to the audience's theatrical expectations. Stage production proves "what justice, what essential rightness there is in his conception of characters and situations." Blank verse of H's poetic drama is appropriate to the momentous action. Reader and chorus need to be more impersonal, with less "acting"; the words should be spoken and heard as music. Granville Barker's production is faithful to the poet's temperament and displays a swiftness of succession, absence of realism, and a good choice of scenes.

663 [Fitzgerald, E.] "Mr. Hardy's New Poems," Times Literary Supplement (Lond), 19 Nov 1914, p. 514; rptd in Living Age, CCLXXXIV (2 Jan 1915), 55–57.

Poems included in *Satires of Circumstance* are beautiful in spite of the despondency. Most poems in the section entitled "Satires of Circumstance" should have been prose because it seems that they contain themes about which the whole truth cannot be told in poetry. H seems too much a devil's advocate. He sees man's hope, fears it is in vain, and loves man for hoping.

664 Gardiner, Alfred. "Thomas Hardy," Prophets, Priests and Kings (Lond: Dent, 1914), pp. 203–11.

H is properly obscure because it was necessary to his art. His pilgrimage through life leads us into ever deeper shadow, yet it is a marvelous journey. Nature is the chief actor in his drama, in which poor humanity plays its sad part. His concept is the complement to Wordsworth's—the spirit of Night broods over it, as he is the antithesis of Meredith and the Millet of literature. We do not remember his "semi-barbaric women" but his peasants, the simple and humble lives. There is no hope in his work; the unity of his achievement comes from the subordination of his art to his metaphysics.

665 Jackson, Holbrook. "The Book of the Week: Thomas Hardy and *The Dynasts*," T. P.'s WEEKLY, XXIV (5 Dec 1914), 595–96.
The Dynasts portrays not only great men and women but also the "historically nameless soldiers and peasants without whom even Napoleon could not have played pitch and toss with empires and dynasties." Surpassing even PROMETHEUS UNBOUND and ATALANTA IN CALYDON, the work "stands alone in English literature" because it "bridges epic poetry and drama, combining the two and making peace, as it were, with two ages." The work captures "precisely the spirit one meets with to-day" in the confrontation with the "demi-Napoleon of Prussia." The naturalness of his art "even tricks one into faith with those very artificial beings called 'Phantom Intelligences.'" A Greek chorus provides the means to express personal opinions of his characters, but H creates the effect of "seemingly triumphant impartiality." He deserves "tolerance and pity" because for him "man is a fate-led creature, moving at the direction of an unknowable force which he calls the Immanent Will."

666 "Literature," ATHENAEUM, No. 4544 (28 Nov 1914), 552.
H's theme of the irony in human existence has become a burden to his poetic endeavors. For this reason the poems of *Satires of Circumstance* are infrequently successful. At times, however, we can perceive "that though he holds the foundations of deistic belief to have been finally undermined, he can still find some hope for the future of humanity."

667 "Marriage of the Greatest Living Author Mr. Thomas Hardy, O. M. and Miss Florence Dugdale," ENFIELD GAZETTE, 13 Feb 1914 [not seen in this form]; rptd as "Marriage of Thomas Hardy and Florence Dugdale," in HARDYANA II: A FURTHER COLLECTION OF SHORT MEMORABILIA AND OTHER MATTERS OF HARDY INTEREST, ed by J. Stevens Cox (Mount Durand, St. Peter Port, Guernsey: Toucan P, 1969), pp. 220–23.
[A description of the wedding ceremony; general praise of his work, especially of *The Dynasts*; expresses general preference for his descriptive writing over his poetry. Also see J. Stevens Cox (pub and general editor), Monographs on the Life of Thomas Hardy (1962).]

668 "Mr. Hardy's New Poems," SATURDAY REVIEW (Lond), CXVIII (21 Nov 1914), 535–36.

In *Satires of Circumstance* H's message is that man's inhumanity must not be added to the inhumanity of nature. H's poems are not easily quotable because of his' "ascetic indifference to surface style." "Ah, are you Digging on my Grave?" is terse and austerely beautiful, particularly in the last few lines. "At the Draper's" is one of the grimmest and most deadly of the "satires," while "Channel Firing" shows H's wide, simple view and an indifference to modern things. "Tolerance" echoes Browning and shows how H's philosophy leads toward pity and love. H's presentation of mothers squabbling over new-laid drainpipes is not a sneer at humanity but a statement of the "necessity for comfort and compassion."

669 "Mr. Hardy's New Poems," TIMES LITERARY SUPPLEMENT (Lond), 19 Nov 1914, p. 514.

H's poems, like Meredith's, react against "over-poetical poetry," but their "verse, even when it seems crabbed or morose or tantalizing, is still thoroughly poetic in form." H's poetry, though despondent, still has "unexpected beauty." The "Satires" in *Satires of Circumstance* would have been better told in prose, because not enough can be said in verse. "Poems of 1912–1913" are better. Even in his bitterest disappointment H seems to have faith even though it may be in vain.

670 "Mr. Thomas Hardy's Unholy Joy," ACADEMY, LXXXVII (28 Nov 1914), 476–77.

In *Satires of Circumstance*, H continues his preoccupation with the gloomy and sordid; this, however, does not detract from his qualities as a poet. "Mr. Hardy is concerned with the vivid presentation of moods," the success of which is due to his extraordinary concentration. "Our own relief comes from the imagining of a certain unholy joy in the poet as he fashions some very bitter and deadly stanzas, smiling genially—so we may be permitted to think—at the shudder of his readers."

671 "The Soldiers of Thomas Hardy," TIMES LITERARY SUPPLEMENT (Lond), 27 Aug 1914, p. 401.

H is unusual among modern novelists in his realistic soldiers, who are as natural as Shakespeare's. Sgt. Troy is a feckless charmer, but not unsympathetic; John Loveday is an excellent character. H's short stories "A Tradition of Eighteen Hundred and Four" and "The Melancholy Hussar" also give insights into war and soldiers.

672 Squire, John Collings. "Kingsway Theater: *The Dynasts*," NEW STATESMAN, IV (5 Dec 1914), 224.

Mr. Barker's stage version of H's "Napoleonic Revue" is a success. He has made *The Dynasts* a workable play.

673 Stephens, James. "An Essay in Cubes," ENGLISH REVIEW, XVII (April 1914), 89.

Jude the Obscure is a novel dealing with horrifying events, but the effect is not morbid or perverse since H is sincerely presenting reality as he sees it. Yet the novelist was a pessimist: i.e., "a man lacking in mental courage." H's timorous and pessimistic mind prevents him from being considered a great artist, for "no poet was ever cruel or timorous in his mind."

674 Strachey, Lytton. "Mr. Hardy's New Poems," NEW STATESMAN, IV (19 Dec 1914), 269–71; rptd in CHARACTERS AND COMMENTARIES (NY: Harcourt, Brace, 1933), pp. 181–86; and in LITERARY ESSAYS (NY: Harcourt, Brace, & World, 1949), pp. 220–25.

Satires of Circumstance, Lyrics and Reveries is a very interesting, if baffling book, seemingly designed to disprove aesthetic theorists who insist on harmony and beauty in poetry. H's book is full of cumbersome expressions, clumsy metres, flat, prosaic turns of speech. The originality of this poetry is that it bears everywhere the impress of a master of prose fiction. H's poems are unique by their utter lack of romanticism. The subject-matter of these poems also reveals the novelist, especially the remarkable group of "fifteen glimpses." It is easy to imagine the scene in "Ah, are you Digging on my Grave?" as the turning-point in a realistic psychological novel. If there is joy in these pages, it is joy that is long since dead; and if there are smiles, they are sardonical.

675 Thomas, Edward. "Three Wessex Poets," IN PURSUIT OF SPRING (Lond: Nelson, 1914), pp. 180–98, espec 192–98.

The rustic, old-fashioned nature of H's verse allows him to "mingle elements unexpectedly." A related feature is H's "tyrannous obsession of the blindness of Fate, the carelessness of Nature, and the insignificance of Man." In *The Dynasts* H's obsession with man's powerlessness is "so powerful that only a very great talent could have rescued anything uninjured from the weight of it."

676 "Topics of the Day: *The Dynasts* at the Kingsway," SPECTATOR (Lond), CXIII (12 Dec 1914), 839–40.

A "literary drama," which does not belong on the stage. H "seized the Napoleonic wars as a pretext for the exposition of his views upon the folly of human endeavor, the inevitability of human destiny, and the horrors of life generally." Blank verse "seems to choke his imagination and is the main cause of the feeble characterization." Little of H left in the production: his "gloomy and bittter metaphysics" are converted, through scene selection, to harmonize with patriotic feelings of the present day.

677 West, Rebecca. "Hardy's *Dynasts* Staged," NEW REPUBLIC, I (26 Dec 1914), 25–26.

The production of *The Dynasts* lacks the power of the earth which is found in the original, "as though one had the most beautiful poem in the world read to one in a mumbling undertone."

678 Wiegler, Paul. GESCHICHTE DER FREMDSPRACHIGEN WELT-LITERATUR (History of Foreign World Literature) (Munich: Ernst Heimeran, 1914), p. 436.

[Associates H with Wessex and as the author of *Tess of the d'Urbervilles* and *Jude the Obscure*.] [In German.]

679 Williams, Harold. "The Wessex Novels of Thomas Hardy," NORTH AMERICAN REVIEW, CXCIX (Jan 1914), 120–34.

Whatever may be the *motif* underlying H's tales or the improbability of plots in his minor books, he can claim to have invested the tragedy of the individual with universal significance. The temper of mind which leads H to read the older generations in the face of living men and women is a manifestation of Schopenhauer's tendency to lend a mood of universality to individual life-stories. H is keenly conscious of the monotony of repetition which communicates itself to the mind of country people. He is a pessimist with a deep and rich vein of humor. Only five novels stand in a distinctive place above H's other books: *Far From the Madding Crowd*, *The Return of the Native*, *The Mayor of Casterbridge*, *The Woodlanders*, and *Tess of the d'Urbervilles*.

680 "*The Woodlanders*: The Most Successful of The Dorset Plays is Given in London," DORSET YEARBOOK, 1914–1915, pp. 88–93.

The London production by The Hardy Players of *The Woodlanders* is "the most successful of the Hardy plays imported from the Mother County."

1915

681 Abercrombie, Lascelles. "The War and the Poets," QUARTERLY REVIEW, CCXXIV (Oct 1915), 394–414, espec 409–14.

H's "Song of the Soldiers" is a "marching song" of the best sort in English literature. It is a "rider" to the magnificence of *The Dynasts*, and it "contradicts directly the stark sceptical conclusion" of the longer work.

682 Binyon, Laurence. "The Art of Thomas Hardy," BOOKMAN (Lond), XLVII (Feb 1915), 143–44.

H is certainly not unlike most artists in that he feels compelled to express inward passions. But why he should try to express his bitterness in lyric form is a curious question. The result is "something disconcerting; the mechanism of a stanza creaks and groans with the pressure of its working." There is, nevertheless, a "tenderness that is very deep in the texture of his art."

683 "Books: Mr. Hardy's Later Poems," SPECTATOR (Lond), CXIV (2 Jan 1915), 19–21.

Satires of Circumstance, in an "autumnal and elegaic" tone, displays the "sickness rather than the soundness of life." Although H's "technique is often halting and clumsy and his style lacking in distinction," still "he says what he means with a force and concentration unattainable in prose." "Not a singer, or a consoler, or a prophet; he stands with his back to the future, immersed in tragic retrospect."

684 Fitzgerald, Ellen. "A Modern Epic of War," POETRY, V (March 1915), 288–93.

H's *The Dynasts* is a modern epic in that it uses all possible devices to show the horror and irony of war. "At best, the poem sings a kind of august pity that such a madness as war is the story of the ages."

685 Fletcher, John Gould. "Thomas Hardy's Poetry: An American View," POETRY, V (March 1915), 43–49.

H ranks close to Shakespeare in poetic talent.

686 Freeman, John. "Poetry, Prophecy and the War: Thomas Hardy's *Dynasts*," NINETEENTH CENTURY AND AFTER, LXXVII (May 1915), 644–47.

The Dynasts confirms H's achievement as a poet. Its message has a universal interest, for it not only deals directly with the Napoleonic upheaval, a matter of great historical importance, but with H's philosophical view of human life and destiny at the mercy of blind forces, as well. The technical superiority of H's verse combines with the nobility of his subject to make *Dynasts* a rare instance of a great creative work informed by an ironic spirit.

687 Leacroft, Eric. "Authors of To-Day: II. Mr. Thomas Hardy," KINGSWAY ("The Literary Supplement"), 12 May 1915, pp. i–ii.

The "chief flower" that flourishes in H's atmosphere is "the Hardy woman." She "is made to be compromised." She will have bad luck, but most of her difficulties can be traced to her own failings. She vacillates, is secretly dissatisfied with her surroundings: "she responds like a child to bright colours." In the beginning of her story we are invited to admire "the virtuous sedateness of her maiden state," then H compels "her to fall in love with a man who is socially in a different class." The pervading motive of the novels is "man's indifference to nature," not vice versa. H's characters ignore the earth with "amazing, full-blooded indifference."

688 Lyon, Harris Merton. "A Nineteen-act Play," GREEN BOOK, XIII (April 1915), 595–98.

In *The Dynasts* H shows his great talent as a motion picture scenario writer, for his vast drama, which captures the essence of the Napoleonic wars without the usual sentimentality, is organized around juxtapositions of large and small scenes, and rapid changes of location. In Granville-Barker's recent production, the huge difficulties in staging were overcome. Even the off-stage spirits and prose stage directions were convincingly presented by actors.

689 Macdonald, John F. "English Life and the English Stage," FORTNIGHTLY REVIEW, CIII (1915), 350–55.

The Dynasts, as staged by Granville-Barker, is topical in its emphasis on war, Britain vs. Europe. The play is done without battle-scenes, in subdued light, with scarcely any scenery. Production gives us an eloquent picture of England one hundred years ago, and shows that her indomitable spirit has not changed.

690 "Mr. Hardy's New Poems," LIVING AGE, CCLXXXIV (2 Jan 1915), 55–57.

Meredith and H write at the end of the Romantic movement, and they try to "impart some of the virtues of prose to poetry." Many of H's poems are musical, but the fifteen *Satires of Circumstance* would have been better in prose, for verse does not allow the expansive, psychological consideration essential for a complete comprehension of any of these situations.

691 Newton, Alfred Edward. "Amenities of Book-Collecting," ATLANTIC MONTHLY, CXV (March 1915), 339; rptd in THE AMENITIES OF BOOK COLLECTING (Boston: Atlantic Monthly P, 1918), pp. 11–13.

[Facsimile of an autograph letter of H to his first publisher Tinsley, showing that H financed the publication of *Desperate Remedies* himself.]

692 "P." "My Famous Schoolfellows," SUNDAY AT HOME, May 1915, pp. 621–24.

"P" and H were close boyhood chums. H and his mother "thought the world of each other." Even as a youngster H "knew every house in Stinsford" and was "ever ready to have a word with the parson [or] the blacksmith."

693 Powys, John Cowper. "Thomas Hardy," VISIONS AND RE-VISIONS (NY: Shaw, 1915), pp. 213–23.

Two spirits in H, "one infinitely sorrowful and tender, the other whimsical, selfish and malign," account for his greatness. He does not trifle with subjects of passing interest but concerns himself with the eternal. [Impressionism at its worst.]

694 "Satires of Circumstance," NATION (NY), C (4 Feb 1915), 139.

Although *Satires of Circumstance* often treats unpleasant or grotesque subject matter—ghosts, dreams, graves, and the disenchantment of old age—and does so in rough and dissonant verse forms, the vigor and the vivid imagination of the author overcomes these faults. H's philosophy is disheartening, but his intellect is stimulating.

695 Thompson, Flora. "Travel Talk: The Hardy Country," T. P.'s WEEKLY, XXVI (21 Aug 1915), 188.

The journey to Weymouth "places at least a century between the traveller and ordinary town life." Weymouth is H's "Budmouth Regis"—the seagate and metropolis of Wessex. A short distance away lies Sutton Poyntz, "the Overcombe of *The Trumpet-Major.*"

696 Walmsley, J. R. "Thomas Hardy and Victor Hugo," NOTES AND QUERIES, 11th ser XII (25 Sept 1915), 240.

[Request for copy of lines from H's two stanzas called "From Victor Hugo" in the original French.]

697 Willcox, Louise [Collier]. "Thomas Hardy," NORTH AMERICAN REVIEW, CCI (March 1915), 423–29.

H's much-proclaimed pessimism is really due to the fact that he becomes vocal chiefly at the sight of tragedy. The deliberate circumscription of environment (Wessex) has indeed been one of H's chief gains: he has made a locality live. In the portrayal of women he has but two rivals in English literature, Shakespeare and Meredith. *Two on a Tower,* overlooked by many critics, deserves far greater praise than it has ever won.

1916

698 Bulloch, J. M. "Hardy's 'The Three Strangers,' " NOTES AND QUERIES, 12th ser II (25 Nov 1916), 427.

H's bibliographers have failed to notice that an episode in this story has been set to music by Mr. Balfour Gardiner: "Shepherd Fennel's Dance."

699 Child, Harold [Hannyngton]. THOMAS HARDY (NY: Holt, 1916).

H's central purpose was to describe "the struggles of individual human wills against the power that rules the world, . . . a force neither good nor evil, and indifferent to man's feelings." H's greatness lies in his "double vision of man's greatness and man's futility," and in his "unswerving rectitude" in presenting that vision. *The Dynasts* is in "a sense" the "perfect flower of Hardy the poet and of Hardy the novelist."

700 Clark, John Scott. "Thomas Hardy," A STUDY OF ENGLISH AND AMERICAN WRITERS (NY: Row, Peterson, 1916), III, 599–613.

H's pessimistic realism is actually "French realism . . . [with a] tincture of animalism in *Tess* and [a] revolting quintessence of it in *Jude*." [Largely a synthesis of critical opinion on such aspects of H's art as pessimism, social revolt, dramatic background, and rustic humor.]

701 D. "Thomas Hardy," SATURDAY REVIEW (Lond), CXXI (1 April 1916), 323–24.

"In Time of 'the Breaking of Nations' " has lines which seem "small" and the thesis appears ordinary, but it shows a deep, long-lasting light rather than a hard, sharp, readily available flash. "Beeny Cliff" and "Castle Boterel" are "poems of universal significance in their presentation of love, death, and time."

702 Danielson, Henry. THE FIRST EDITIONS OF THE WRITINGS OF THOMAS HARDY AND THEIR VALUES: A BIBLIOGRAPHICAL HANDBOOK FOR COLLECTORS, BOOKSELLERS, LIBRARIANS AND OTHERS (Lond: Allen & Unwin, 1916).

[Bibliographical descriptions of H's first and collected editions to 1916.]

703 Duffin, Henry Charles. THOMAS HARDY: A STUDY OF THE WESSEX NOVELS, POEMS, AND THE DYNASTS (Manchester: Manchester UP; NY: Longmans Green, 1916); 2nd ed, with appendix on poems and *The Dynasts* (NY: Longmans Green, 1921); 3rd ed, rvd (London: Longmans, 1937); rvd and enlgd (Manchester: Manchester UP, 1938).

Part I: [Running commentary on the novels in chronological order, outlining plots, discussing characters, evaluating novels individually and comparatively.] The art of *The Return of the Native* is more studied than that of *Far From the Madding Crowd*, Elizabeth-Jane in *The Mayor of Casterbridge* is perhaps the subtlest of all H's pictures of women, *Tess of the d'Urbervilles* is the climax of the novels, *Jude the Obscure* is a maturer work but not digested. Minor novels are "rests" between great novels. Part II: Art of the Novels: H is master in range, variety, and significance, in character-drawing of both men and women. The highest aspect of character is the soul's tragedy. H's great achievement is to have found this among ordinary people of earth, earthly. Great characters are neither types nor individuals but "universals"; H is an Idealist in characterization. Plot, Scene, Event: H writes novels of unified artistic structure, conveying a moral lesson built around a central love situation that can be usually diagrammed as rhomboid. Every novel is an answer to the question: "Given certain characters in certain situations, and allowing for the irony of fate, what will happen?" H is a master of great dramatic scenes and has some great psychological revelatory sentences, such as Marty South's at the end of *The Woodlanders*. H used the marvelous, in Diggory Venn, the setting of *Two on a Tower*; coincidences, deliberately used and rooted in his philosophy, are ironic and show power of Chance. Nature: H's tragedies are set in all-consoling beauty of Nature, except for Egdon; personification of Nature is outstanding in H. Descriptions are very effective and observant and placed in emotional connection with events. H's humor is mostly rustic. Stylistically H is essentially writing "emanation of his mind." Part III: Philosophy of Novels: Irony of fate is the primary doctrine, often cruel. *Mayor* and *Return* are bitter novels preeminently showing irony of fate. There is a power that hampers and hinders man, a concept due in part to the transitional situation of the last quarter of nineteenth century when men are trying to find God. H's view of man: Of four qualities that rule—Passion, Reason, Emotion, Instinct—H sees all operative; he does not emphasize instinct except in critical moments when men and women appeal to instinctive selves. H's women range through variety of personality, from great to minor, ordinary women being inferior to men but uncommon women much superior. H sees society as oppressive through sexual conventions, as with Clare's view of Tess and the marital restrictions in *Jude*. H's View of Life: Temperamentally pessimistic, but based on a metaphysic not contemptuous of man.

The Dynasts: A unique, primarily historical work, not glorifying war. H has a sense of dramatic unity, great power, vastness, and conveys feeling of war in totality, as well as in individual incidents. The portrait of Napoleon is effective, but not an epic hero. The drama uses history to express artistic conception of life. Phantom Intelligences display "original greatness of great writer." Viewpoint high above scene is important. The doctrine of Immanent Will poses philosophical problems.

Poems: The keynote is found in love-poems. H is not a great poet, too concerned with life here on earth, but has valuable qualities. Love-poems are intense, especially those of 1912–1913, more lyrical than IN MEMORIAM. The poems help us to understand the dominance of love in novels. H lacks "poetic form," has instead "intellectual form"; content is always interesting, verse-technique often lacking. H is best in ballad-form, sonnet, song. Much poetry is merely prose. There is bitter irony in narrative poems, chiefly concerned with man-woman relationships. About ten poems are outstanding. Hardian metaphysic is evident in the poems, but no volume of eight is worth one chapter of major novels.

704 Esdaile, Arundell. "A Short Bibliography of Thomas Hardy's Principal Works," in THOMAS HARDY, by Harold Child (NY: Holt, 1916), pp. 119–25.

[A brief bibliography of English and American editions of H's works to 1915, confined wholly to first appearances in volume form and collected definitive editions. Intermediate editions and unreprinted stories are not listed.]

705 Freeman, John. "Thomas Hardy," THE MODERNS: ESSAYS IN LITERARY CRITICISM (Lond: Robert Scott, 1916; NY: Crowell, 1917), pp. 103–59.

H is unique in many ways but also typically English. He cannot be called a pessimist; his work shows force of native unsophisticated character. It is curiously unequal, good alternating with bad. *The Trumpet-Major* is a bit below the best but shows some of the finest qualities, "unsuspected watchers" and power of description. Sometimes he is too scientific rather than imaginative in description. *Trumpet-Major* is not the best novel because the level of the story is low, and it has too much coincidence; better that the novel should disguise the fact that it is a conventional illusion. *A Pair of Blue Eyes* is better but has "a singular note of externality," like an essay upon a novel, even in the fine passage of Knight on the cliff. *Far From the Madding Crowd* is superior and has few weaknesses. The character of Oak lends "steadfastness" to the book. In later novels, theses obtrude, though not in *The Return of the Native*, which is finer than *The Woodlanders* for this reason. H's profound human sympathy sometimes leads him to excesses of bitterness, as in *Tess of the d'Urbervilles*, "a study in unrelieved sorrow," and in *Jude the Obscure*, of "unrelieved horror." H loads the dice against Tess; truth does not demand such resentment against life. The tragedy arises more from defects of character than from the Immortals. *Jude* is a "dismal book" because of the tyranny of convention and complete lack of any sweetness to relieve horror. H's *Wessex Poems* reiterate gloomy themes of the novels, a melancholy that breathes through the most beautiful of the verses; there is brooding intensity without the compensating interludes that appear in novels. H shows an almost inexorable rigidity of sorrowful attitude, slightly relieved in later volumes of poems by gentleness and humor. *Satires of Circumstance* disappoints because of its perverse irony. The sharpness and gauntness of H's verse make his constant theme of deceit and desire more powerful and more paralyzing. The over-all impression is one of great lyrical gifts, moral earnestness, emphasis on common lives, originality and vitality of form, perfectly adapted to matter. H is master of rhyme and music of verse. *The Dynasts* is immense in scope, of profound importance whether viewed as drama or philosophy, and ends significantly on a note of hope, unlike other works. It is fundamentally English despite its continental vastness and metaphysical reach. H seems Elizabethan in his singular power, combined with careless technique, his imaginative intensity, and like Emily Brontë or Dostoevsky.

706 "Great Houses of Letters. II. Max Gate, Dorchester, Where Thomas Hardy Wrote his Wessex Novels," BOOKMAN (NY), XLIV (Nov 1916), 238–39.

[A thumbnail sketch of Dorchester with a few comments about the architecture of Max Gate.]

707 "Mr. Hardy's Muse," SATURDAY REVIEW (Lond), CXXII (21 Oct 1916), 394–95.

The chief treasure in *Selected Poems of Thomas Hardy* is a series of poems dated from 1912 to 1913; there is a certain time sequence about the series which is impressive.

708 Phelps, William Lyon. "The Advance of the English Novel," BOOKMAN (NY), XLIII (April 1916), 173–80; rptd as "Meredith and Hardy," in THE ADVANCE OF THE ENGLISH NOVEL (NY: Dodd, Mead, 1919), pp. 173, 187–91.

No living writer is H's equal in prose fiction. H's efforts in other genres are regrettable. Ten novels may be categorized as works of genius, but *Jude the Obscure* is excepted because of "hysterical exaggeration." Installment publication affected H's work; he is skillful in the use of suspense; his work is characterized by scientific objectivity and pessimism.

709 "The Poetry of Mr. Hardy," TIMES LITERARY SUPPLEMENT (Lond), 23 Nov 1916, pp. 553–54.

In the midst of tremendous world tragedy one can still read H's poems because he knows better than anyone else how tragedy affects individuals. Though English and a local writer, he is one to whom nationality and locality matter least. H knows better than younger contemporaries how to unite originality and the traditional, individual and universal. Both a "writer with something to say and an artist with something to make which should be made beautifully."

710 "*Selected Poems of Thomas Hardy*," BOOKMAN (Lond), LI (Dec 1916), 106.

In *Selected Poems*, there is no "lyric spontaneity." H is "more careful of the form of poetry than of its language."

711 Shaw, C. G. "Thomas Hardy and the Ancient Anguish of the Earth," METHODIST REVIEW, XCVIII (March 1916), 235–47.

H habitually tried to demodernize his mind, and thus to revel in a naive world-order. Unfortunately, he carried back to the primitive order much of the reflectiveness peculiar to modern life; hence his art, which should be idyllic, becomes satirical. *Jude the Obscure, Tess of the d'Urbervilles, The Return of the Native* and *The Woodlanders* compose H's great square; they are unified works in which God, man, and the world look from one to another and strive with one another. H's "You shall be born" is the Spanish skepticism of Calderon over again. Without attempting to frame a conception of Godhead, H views the Deity as a cosmic Demiurge toiling amid the stubbornness of disobedient things. He is not far from James or Bergson. The worst flaw in H's art is a pessimism which has no pity about it. Unlike Dostoevsky, H is not acquainted with grief. His lack of sympathy is also lack of insight. H has not wholly succeeded in touching the human soul in its paradoxical and painful exhibition of life on earth.

712 S[horter], C[lement] K. "A Literary Letter," SPHERE (Lond), 15 July 1916, p. 66.

An American friend has sent "a very rare 'first edition' " of H's FELLOW-TOWNSMEN, as published with A STRANGE GUEST in the Seaside Library in the United States. It is not strictly a piracy since "there was no American copyright when it appeared serially in England in 1879."

713 S[horter], C[lement] K. "A Literary Letter," SPHERE (Lond), 16 Dec 1916, p. 210.

[Supports Henry Danielson's contention that *The Romantic Adventures of a Milkmaid* was first published in the United States in 1883, offering three "first editions" as evidence.]

714 Webb, A. P. A BIBLIOGRAPHY OF THE WORKS OF THOMAS HARDY (Lond: Frank Hollings, 1916).

[A primary and a selected secondary bibliography.]

1917

715 Berle, Lina Wright. GEORGE ELIOT AND THOMAS HARDY: A CONTRAST (NY: Kennerley; Lond: Kennerley, 1917); rptd (Folcroft, Pa: Folcroft, 1969).

H contrasts George Eliot in a number of ways. First of all, while he concentrates on the grosser elements of life, she emphasizes the relationship of the spiritual to the material. Secondly, while H is indifferent to morality, Eliot displays a moral purpose. Thirdly, while H's women are degenerate "weak" sisters" who "drain the vitality of those about them," Eliot's women are occasionally ideal and only rarely sinful. Fourthly, while H's "men of straw" are defined in terms of the effect that physical traits have on character, Eliot's men—only occasionally rendered successfully—are defined in terms of the effect that mental traits have on character. Fifthly, while H focuses on sordid, brutal passions, Eliot never loses sight of the "beauty and freshness and charm of love." These two writers have in common little other than that the main characters of each are men of straw and the minor characters, men; that they both present old age in a complex, subtle manner. Ultimately, H must be judged a reactionary: he believes that man must preserve what currently exists since fate allows him to do little more. In contrast, Eliot is a radical: she is identified with progress and change.

716 Blathwayt, Raymond. THROUGH LIFE AND ROUND THE WORLD, BEING THE STORY OF MY LIFE (NY: Dutton, 1917), pp. 171–74.

H had received many letters from readers urging him to contrive a happy marriage for Tess, but he felt that such an ending would be dishonest to the "logical and inevitable tragedy" of her upbringing and heredity. Angel Clare was too sensitive for her anyway and would not have remained faithful to her for many months. Tess and many of the other characters in that novel were drawn from life. [Blathwayt met H in 1892, shortly after the publication of *Tess of the d'Urbervilles*.]

717 Brunius, August Georg. "Thomas Hardy och hans nya diktsamlingar" (Thomas Hardy and His New Collection of Poetry), ANSIKTEN OCH MASKER. MODERN LITERATUR, KONST OCH TEATER (Faces and Masks: Modern Literature, Art and Theatre) (Stockholm: Norstedt, 1917), pp. 36–45.

The poetry of H's old age, that published since 1898, is more truly artistic and gives evidence of greater insight than any of his earlier works. *Time's Laughingstocks* and *Satires of Circumstance*—the work of a man over seventy—are far superior to his earlier poetry. Conflict and irony, colored with tragedy or bitter humor, are still the central themes, but he now has a richer psychological insight. H has developed a greater frankness and does not mince words. In "The Levelled Churchyard" he shows an understanding of peasant psychology like that of Shakespeare and Burns. H's tone is somewhat similar to that of the Swedish poet, Fröding; his ability to illuminate a whole situation in one small scene is reminiscent of Ibsen. [Many poems and novels illustrate Brunius's thesis.] [In Swedish.]

718 Colum, Padraic. "Robert Bridges and Thomas Hardy," NEW REPUBLIC, XII (11 Aug 1917), 47–49.

H is a "disgruntled stoic," lyrical in expressing love denied and racked by the reiteration of what is mechanic in the universe, "hacking out forms to fit his very personal conceptions" or taking jigs from the ballad singers. In *Time's Laughingstocks*, H's intuition of internal (human) poetic rhythms allows "A Trampwoman's Tragedy" to be spoken as dramatic poetry in verse. "The Flirt's Tragedy" is "hacked out verse"—one monotonous rhyme linking thirty stanzas. "The Noble Lady's Tale" exemplifies poems in "ill-fitting forms," where "emotion has not made the mold, but has been forced into a form that happened to be in Hardy's mind at the time."

719 Courtney, W[illiam] L[eonard] [pseud of Walter Lenard]. "Mr. Thomas Hardy and Aeschylus: I," FORTNIGHTLY REVIEW, CVII (1 March 1917), 464–77; "Mr. Thomas Hardy and Aeschylus: II," ibid (2 April 1917), 629–40; rptd in OLD SAWS AND MODERN INSTANCES (Lond: Chapman & Hall, 1918), pp. 1–30. "There is a great deal of Aeschylus in . . . Hardy—a certain ruggedness, austerity, elevation, a definite philosophical scheme at the back of all his creations." H, like Aeschylus, is a true "bard, a seer, a prophet" and a dramatist: one who does not, like a priest, seek "to reconcile men to God" but "to justify God to men." A central problem to H was how "to reconcile what Science tells us about the Cosmos with the revelations of Christianity." How can we find room for a Divine Providence in a materialistic universe? H's answer is to substitute a new conception of Godhead: the Immanent Will, the unconscious, omnipotent source of all. H introduces the Spirit World in *The Dynasts* not because it helps explain "how [earthly] things happen by linking them on to the exercise of conscious Wills," since H's is "a world of Necessity and Automatism," but to "express human feeling or supply human comment." H is "far more element" than the "inhuman . . . creed expressed through the Immanent Will." In his references to mankind, H "shows an unwonted tenderness, which goes beyond the limits of his scientific creed."

720 Cunliffe, J. W. (ed). "Introduction," *The Return of the Native* (NY: Scribner's, 1917), pp. xi–xvi.
This novel is H's first great tragedy, perhaps his greatest. In form and spirit it approximates Greek tragedy more closely than any other of his works. It is unified by a pervasive sense of destiny, and this philosophic unity is supported by the subordinate unities of time, a year and a day, and place, Egdon Heath. Throughout, the peasantry serve as a chorus commenting upon and supplementing the actions of the principals. Of the characters, Eustacia and Diggory are the most fascinating and complex. The marriage of Diggory and Thomasin is "natural enough" and does not blur the effect of the tragedy. [Includes incomplete and inaccurate list of H's periodical contributions.]

721 Follett, Helen Thomas, and Wilson Follett. "The Historian of Wessex," ATLANTIC MONTHLY, CXX (Sept 1917), 356–66.

H's later pessimism is "simply the extension of his earlier temperamental bias toward appreciation of incongruity." H's "idylls," (*Under the Greenwood Tree, Far From the Madding Crowd, A Pair of Blue Eyes, The Woodlanders*) show the "subtly pessimistic bent" of H's mind. In the seventies H found humanity "a sorry spectacle, but still rather a lark; in the eighties, a forlorn hope; in the nineties, a desperate failure." *Jude the Obscure* illustrates a familiar artistic fallacy: "the attempt to prove a general truth about life by imagined facts."

722 Gärdes, Johannes. "Literaturbericht und Anzeigen" (Literature Report and Notices), ZEITSCHRIFT FÜR FRANZÖSISCHEN UND ENGLISCHEN UNTERRICHT, XVI (1917), 67.

Few essential characteristics of H's poetic personality appear in *Life's Little Ironies*. The stories illustrate H's individuality. [In German.]

723 Gilder, Jeannette L. "Dear Mr. Hardy" [two letters], in JUDE THE OBSCURE: A LETTER AND A FOREWORD, ed and pub by Paul Lemperly (Lakewood, Ohio: ptd for pvt circulation, 1917), [unpaginated].

[The first letter to H, dated 13 July 1896, requests an interview with H to give him an opportunity to respond to her "Thomas Hardy Makes A New Departure," WORLD (NY), 8 Dec 1895, p. 33, and claiming that her harsh review "was written in no unfriendly spirit." The second letter acknowledges H's courteous refusal to be interviewed.]

724 Gosse, Sir Edmund. THE LIFE OF ALGERNON CHARLES SWINBURNE (Lond: Macmillan, 1917), pp. 5, 282.

Toward end of his life, Swinburne wrote to H that his father had served as a midshipman under Collingwood.

725 Kilmer, Joyce. "Introduction," *The Mayor of Casterbridge* (NY: Modern Library, 1917), pp. xi–xiv.

H's fatalism is clearer in *The Mayor of Casterbridge* than anywhere else. It is not at all the joyous pagan fatalism of the classical period but a paganism obsessed with the idea of pain and death. H's God is a stern, avenging Hebrew God. H was an evangelist eager to spread the word that man is hopeless and undeserving of pity.

726 Lemperly, Paul (ed and pub). JUDE THE OBSCURE: A LETTER AND A FOREWORD (Lakewood, Ohio; ptd for pvt circulation, 1917). Contents: abstracted separately under date of first publication: P. L., [Note] [not abstracted]; Clement Shorter, "Foreword" (1917); Jeannette L. Gilder, "Dear Mr. Hardy" [two letters]

(1917); Thomas Hardy, "Letter by Thomas Hardy" [not abstracted].

[The pamphlet puts together materials involving Gilder's damning review of *Jude the Obscure*, her request to interview H, and H's refusal to be interviewed.]

727 Meiberger, C. R. "Wessex Edition . . . ," ENGLISCHE STUDIEN, LI (1917–1918), 284–87.

[Merely a description of the Wessex Edition; no significant critical remarks.]

728 Meiberger, C. R. "*The Woodlanders* by Thomas Hardy," ENGLISCHE STUDIEN, LI (1917–1918), 226–47.

[General, uncritical discussion, mostly about the characters of the novel.]

729 "Mr. Hardy's New Poems," COUNTRY LIFE, 8 Dec 1917, pp. 22, 24.

[A favorable review of *Moments of Vision*.]

730 "No More; Too Late; Farewell," SATURDAY REVIEW (Lond), CXXIV (22 Dec 1917), 507.

H is too much shrouded in gloom. His verse is not equal to his novels; but he is a pioneer in the use of natural detail and science, and his rhythm is abrupt and strange. Much of *Moments of Vision* is drawn from more normal earlier poetry. The most striking poems are the ghostly visions, as the "Glimpse" of the "Maid with Red Hair." "In Time of 'the Breaking of Nations' " is an assertion of endless romance, while "The Blinded Bird" recalls H's *Under the Greenwood Tree*. " Something that Saved Him" rises to equal Browning's "Instans Tyrannus."

731 Phelps, William Lyon. "The Advance of English Poetry in the Twentieth Century," BOOKMAN (NY), XLVI (Oct 1917), 125–35.

H's prose is superior to his poetry, which lacks real poetic power. *The Dynasts* is an "epical illustration of German pessimism"; in general, H's verse lacks appropriate elevation, perhaps because H was more interested in ideas than in the expression of feelings.

732 "The Poetry of Mr. Hardy," LIVING AGE, CCXCII (13 Jan 1917), 98–102.

As *Selected Poems of Thomas Hardy* shows, H is like Scott in conveying local color, but the tragedies of the Wessex folk are those of "helpless atoms whirled they know not where in a vast and mysterious universe." H is a "master in the matter of poetry, but in its form only a very highly gifted amateur."

733 "The Poetry of Thomas Hardy," TIMES LITERARY SUPPLEMENT (Lond), 13 Dec 1917, p. 603.

The poems of *Moments of Vision* show as much individuality as H's other poems. H's level of achievement is very even. He questions first and last things with "wistful perception." The themes of his poetry may be tragic or trivial but are always prompted by human experience.

734 Sherman, Stuart P[ratt]. ON CONTEMPORARY LITERATURE (NY: Holt, 1917), pp. 167, 259, 270, 277.
In H's novels, Nature is one of the forces which make the Wessex people "pitiful antagonists of destiny."

735 Shorter, Clement. "Foreword" [a letter to Paul Lemperly], in JUDE THE OBSCURE: A LETTER AND A FOREWORD, ed and pub by Paul Lemperly (Lakewood, Ohio: ptd for pvt circulation, 1917), [unpaginated].
[Notes Jeannette Gilder, usually a "very kindly woman," was tactless to ask H for an interview in the light of her vitriolic review of *Jude the Obscure* in "Thomas Hardy Makes A New Departure," WORLD (NY), 8 Dec 1895, p. 3. H "hates the whole practice of interviewing." Includes Jeannette L. Gilder, "Dear Mr. Hardy," two letters to H (1917).]

736 S[horter], C[lement[K. "A Literary Letter," SPHERE (Lond), 27 Jan 1917, p. 82.
[Lists five early American editions of H's *The Romantic Adventures of a Milkmaid*. Information supplied to Shorter by A. P. C. Griffin, Chief Assistant Librarian of the Library of Congress.]

737 Squire, J. C. "Thomas Hardy's Verse," LAND AND WATER, 13 Dec 1917, p. 17.
H's later poems are "extraordinarily powerful, original in language rhythm and shape" and "enormously finer" than his earlier poems. Most of H's non-narrative poems are finer than the narrative poems. "Regret for the past" is the dominating mood of these poems. Monotony is a weakness of many of H's poems. "Time after time he writes what is virtually the same poem, but the constant freshness and poignancy of his feeling makes it always new."

738 Thomas, Edward. "Thomas Hardy," A LITERARY PILGRIM IN ENGLAND (NY: Dodd, Mead, 1917), pp. 144–54.
In his novels H makes "a double impression by the sound rusticity of many characters, and by his own solitary, brooding, strongly-coloured mind dominating men and landscape." It is regrettable that H allowed, even encouraged, the identification of the originals for his towns, buildings and landscapes, since this process "stand[s] in the way of perfect pleasure" in the narratives. His poems, however, are not harmed by this process.

739 Utter, Robert Palfrey. "The Work of Thomas Hardy," Se-wanee Review, XXV (April 1917), 129–38; rptd in Pearls and Pepper (New Haven: Yale UP, 1924), pp. 178–93.
H belongs to "the age when the hero was a god." He has a Saxon, ninth-century outlook in his conception of a dark fate, in his use of nature in connection with fate, in the beauty of character developed in struggle, and in the epic quality of his work.

1918

740 B., W. L. "Thomas Hardy," New East (Tokyo), III (Oct 1918), 353–54.
H's last three novels are all "variations on his favourite tragic theme, the pitiful condition of man in a cosmic scheme so vast that the governing or life-creating Power is hardly aware of his existence." H uses woman "as the tool of his blind and purposeless Nature."

741 Bickley, Francis. "Hardy's Poems," Bookman (Lond), LIV (April 1918), 12–13.
Because of H's elusive poetic qualities, it will be difficult to place him in literary history. He possesses the potential qualities and elements which produce poetry, but he lacks sufficient "fervor." He is a skillful prosodist, but his metrics are oftentimes strained. While his novels are often poetic his poems lack the power to lift them into the realm of pure poetry.

742 "Books: Some Recent Verse," Spectator (Lond), CXX (16 March 1918), 287–88.
In *Moments of Vision and Miscellaneous Verses*, H's vision is a "mirror" which "reveals the skeleton at the feast." At times he has a "tenderness for the old faith and something like a longing that it might prove true." "After-wards" might be an epitaph on H, "as one who used to notice the glory of May and the ways of shy birds."

743 Chislett, William. "The Major Note in Thomas Hardy," The Classical Influence in English Literature in the Nine-teenth Century (Boston: Stratford, 1918), pp. 142–50.
[A rambling discussion of the novels, short stories, and poems. H's chief affinity is not with Sophocles but with the "romantic Aeschylus."]

744 Follett, Helen Thomas, and Wilson Follett. "Thomas Hardy," Some Modern Novelists: Appreciations and Estimates (NY: Holt, 1918), pp. 127–50.

It is unfortunate that criticism of H resolves itself into discussions of *Jude the Obscure*. His pessimism is not all of H. "When we look for . . . continuity in Hardy, we find it in his art, not in his philosophy. The development of his art is a growth; that of his philosophy is a change." Pessimism is an extension of his temperamental bias toward incongruity. This pessimism is subtly seen in the tragi-comic idylls, "a cadence marred by a half-inaudible discord." Endings of *Under the Greenwood Tree* and *Far From the Madding Crowd* show this tendency: "their resultant taste is bitter-sweet, like that of life." H's judgments of women "are censorious in the extreme"; he also adds "an almost lyrical sense of the cruelty of Time." H progressed from feeling humanity a "sorry spectacle," to a "forlorn hope," to "a desperate failure." *Jude* is a "nightmare" wherein "man's very powers of hope, of faith, of resistance have become agents of tragedy." "There is no bitterness in the Wessex Novels to be compared with the bitterness of this final paradox, that the one greatest evil in the cosmos is the goodness in man's soul." The book is weakened by H's stacking the ironic cards against Jude. Pessimism is one of the extreme absurdities denied to literature; only by faith in life can great tragedy be achieved: we must believe that good overcome by evil is the exception, not the normal course of events. *Tess of the d'Urbervilles* shows H creating tragedy because of Tess's greatness of heart. H's pessimism is the outcome of "his susceptibility to the moral emotions"; he "gnashed his teeth at life" because it hurt "fellow-creatures whom he loved." But H's genius is most irresistible in the comic order. Folk customs and characters are delightful, but most important for structural comic qualities and incongruity of situation like that of the Elizabethans. Superb example of this "rough chiaroscuro" is in chapters culminating in the major crisis of *Madding Crowd*. Another great quality of H is his "scientific detachment" where he makes, as in *The Return of the Native*, "microcosm of personality a stage for the interplay of almost cosmic forces." H is, finally, a unique phenomenon in his age, his largeness towers above all other novelists.

745 George, W. L. A Novelist on Novels (Lond: Collins Sons, 1918); also as Literary Chapters (Boston: Little, Brown, 1918), pp. 44, 45, 106, 129.

H's later work did not decline because he "drew back from the battle of letters." H is one of five writers in England (with Conrad, Galsworthy, Bennett and Wells) to "hold without challenge the premier position." H is "the only notable living exponent" of "a purely narrative style" in an age of great "social complexity." The hero of H's *Jude the Obscure* is not fully developed just because his "sex adventures" are described; there "is more truth in one page of Madame Bovary than in the shackled works of Mr. Hardy."

746 Gosse, Edmund. "Mr. Hardy's Lyrical Poems," Edinburgh Review, CCXXVII (April 1918), 272–93; rptd as "The Lyrical

Poetry of Thomas Hardy," in SOME DIVERSIONS OF A MAN OF LET-
TERS (Lond: Heinemann; NY: Scribner's, 1919), pp. 233–58.
H's poetry is not a mere subsidiary or appendage to his novels. In spite of his
silence of forty years, he labored, like Swinburne, at a revolution against
the optimism and superficial sweetness of his age. Historically, in his earliest
pieces, we find the germ of almost everything he wrote; however, here and
there, we find also an extreme difficulty of utterance ("At a Bridal"); the
series "She to Him" give clearest promise of what was coming. In 1875,
Coventry Patmore, a complete stranger, wrote to ask him to write poetry.
This period saw the first conception of *The Dynasts* and of his narratives,
or short Wessex ballads.

His *Poems of the Past and the Present* (1902) could not but be disappointing, they were produced in three years as compared with the thirty years of
Wessex Poems. His set of poems composed in Rome were not so interesting, for he seems languid when he leaves Wessex. Another section was
severely metaphysical: God has forgotten the existence of earth and left all
human life to be the plaything of blind chance. Eight years later, *Time's
Laughingstocks* confirmed the high promises of the *Wessex Poems*; the
"laughingstocks" are fifteen stories of division and isolation, of failures in
passion, of the treason of physical decay. We find the poet here entirely
emancipated from convention, especially in the narrative pieces which are
often Wessex novels distilled into a wine-glass ("Rose-Ann," "The Vam-
pirine-Fair"). It cannot be said that *Satires of Circumstance* is as satisfactory; in this volume, the ugliness of experience is more accentuated than
it is elsewhere, and it is flung in our face with less compunction. We can
assume that H was passing through a mental crisis when he wrote them.
These poems are monotonously sinister, the strongest poem of disillusion
being "The Newcomer's Wife," with the terrible abruptness of its last stanza.
Moments of Vision, published in the fourth year of the war, shows a remarkable recovery of spirit. Much of it is wholly detached from the bitterness of satire and exhibits an infinite delicacy of pathos.

H is apt to clog his lines with consonants, but most of what is called his
harshness should rather be called bareness, and is the result of a revolt
against Keats's prescription of "loading the rifts with ore." It is in narrative
pieces that his metrical imagination is most triumphant ("My Cicely,"
"Friends Beyond," etc.). The conception of life revealed in his verses displays very exactly the bent of his temperament—pessimism. But that pessimism is directed towards an observation of others. Unlike Crabbe, to
whom he might be compared, H has none of the instinct of a preacher; his
disdain of sentimentality renders him insensible to the imagined sympathy of
Nature. We find in his poetry a violent reaction against the poetry of ego-

tistic optimism of the Romantic school in England. ("Life offers—to deny.") His originality consists also in offering notations of human touches hitherto excluded from the realm of poetry; whatever the poverty of the incident, he commonly redeems it by the oddity of his observation ("The Pedigree"). H holds that the immortality of a dead man resides in the memory of the living; he sees the dead as a crowd of slowly vanishing phantoms. What seemed harsh at the beginning was his peculiar and personal mode of interpreting his thought to the world.

747 Hogben, Launcelot. "Thomas Hardy and Democracy," So-CIALIST REVIEW (Lond), XV (April–June 1918), 159–63.
H's "essential greatness" lies in his recognition "that an understanding of human emotions is quite inadequate without an appreciation of the social influences that mould them." The novels mirror with great vividness the "disquietude born of the adjustment of the social organism to the machine process." H "diagnoses the *maladie de siècle*, and he does not leave you with the feeling that it is an incurable disease." The "clear and persistent note" of H's work is avoidable tragedy—"the sheer sacrifice of creative possibilities to the cruelty and stupidity of unwarrantable class and sex barriers." The *Wessex Tales* are the "most valuable index of our time" because "they touch the very pulse of the social conscience in the machine age of capitalism."

748 Leonhard, L. "Englischer Brief" (English Letter), DAS LITERARISCHE ECHO, XX (May 1918), 987–88.
With *Moments of Vision* H has restored British poetry. His prominent tone is pessimistic, as illustrated by "I Journeyed" ["His Country"?]. [In German.]

749 Moore, Edward [pseud of Edwin Muir]. "Mr. Thomas Hardy," WE MODERNS: ENIGMAS AND GUESSES (Lond: Allen & Unwin, 1918), pp. 186–87; rptd, as by Edwin Muir and with introduction by H. L. Mencken (NY: Knopf, 1920), pp. 194–95.
Creation is an intensification of the pangs of Love and Love's last indignity. Love's ultimate is to torture its victims, caring not who is pained. H's books are filled with such torment of Love, and his main indictment of Life is against Love—in this H is a great decadent. H is great not by his theories, but by his art. [Some passages reprinted from NEW AGE.]

750 "Mr. Hardy's Poems," ATHENAEUM, No. 4625 (Jan 1918), 33–34.
H is one of the group of poets who are trying to revive poetic appreciation. H has obviously been influenced by Browning, but his view of life is considerably one-sided. *Moments of Vision*, though greatly imbued with H's

pessimistic philosophy, "is the truthful record of a man's soul." And even in his darkest moments, glimmerings of faith shine through.

751 Nairne, A. "The Poetry of Thomas Hardy," CHURCH QUARTERLY REVIEW, LXXXVII (Oct 1918), 150–54; rptd in LIVING AGE, CCCII (19 July 1919), 175–78.

Moments of Vision and Miscellaneous Verses and *Selected Poetry of Thomas Hardy* reveal H's love for men and nature and a "severe" faith, tempered by a few signs of optimism.

752 Phelps, William Lyon. "Some Contrasts—Henley, Thompson, Hardy, Kipling," THE ADVANCE OF ENGLISH POETRY IN THE TWENTIETH CENTURY (NY: Dodd, Mead, 1918), pp. 14–28, 66–67.

H, like Meredith, writes poetry distinctly twentieth-century in matter and manner—and thinks it superior to his novels. *The Dynasts* is an "epic illustration of doctrines of pessimism"; its architectonics are admirable. H's poetry is concerned with giving God "a decent burial, with fitting obsequies." His poetry often has dramatic power, lacks grace and movement; uninspired, too consciously crafted by "a master of prose who has learned the technique of verse." [Brief comparison of H's and Housman's view of life and faith in pessimism. The usual exasperating Phelps: some acute observations marred by failure to analyze at length and a tone of condescension.]

753 "The Poetry of Thomas Hardy," LIVING AGE, CCXCVI (26 Jan 1918), 202–7.

H's poetry is "singularly continuous in its spirit and character." The philosophic view of nature comes out most clearly in the descriptive aspects. A sense of destiny pervades the poems of *Moments of Vision*. This volume seems more personal than some of the earlier ones. H and Browning are alike in their interest in the dramatic and the "meetings and partings of fate, its conjunctions and mistimings. Both, in their unvarnished speech, seem to laugh at the mysteries of poetic diction, though they set their plain language to an elaborate rhyme-structure." H is never really obscure, but he does not leave us with a wealth of sensuous imagery as Keats does.

754 Quiller-Couch, Sir Arthur. "The Poetry of Thomas Hardy," STUDIES IN LITERATURE: FIRST SERIES (NY: Putnam, Cambridge UP, 1918), pp. 189–211.

H's poetic muse is "predominantly melancholy," but never faded, jejune, effete, or sentimental. The "curious, haunting, countrified lilt" of H's best poetry is the expression of a countryman's mind "piled high with history and local tradition," privy to the secrets of woodland and meadow. H is "the most genuine, most autochthonous of living writers." He is also a man whose uncompromising pessimism is balanced by a "strangely tender" heart whose sympathy goes out to the suffering of animal (e.g., "The Blinded Bird") and human (e.g., *Tess of the d'Urbervilles*) alike. *The Dynasts* is "the grandest poetic structure planned and raised in England in our time" and deserves comparison with Tolstoy's WAR AND PEACE.

755 Shanks, Edward. "Our London Letter," DIAL, LXIV (31 Jan 1918), 104–5.

"A glorious collection [*Moments of Vision*] of over one hundred and fifty new poems, not one of which is not thoroughly characteristic, none of which are without merit, and a large proportion of which are in his very best manner." H "continues to perform miracles with a style which would at once sink any other poet." The reader comes away from these poems with "only delight" at the power of the poetry, which mitigates its profound gloom.

756 Stewart, H[erbert] L[eslie]. "Thomas Hardy as an Artist of Character," UNIVERSITY MAGAZINE (Montreal), XVII (April 1918), 247–61.

H's marked distaste for the upper classes and for artificial pedigrees prompted him to portray aristocrats in his novels as a decadent, unpleasant lot, often reduced to two-dimensional caricatures. His real understanding and affection is reserved for the unsophisticated villagers who appear as features in a landscape which shapes their destiny. Although gentle humor and incisive psychological insight mark H's treatment of his central characters, his women too often seem to be pliable victims of sexual drives and neuroses.

757 Stewart, Herbert Leslie. "Thomas Hardy as a Teacher of his Age," NORTH AMERICAN REVIEW, CCVIII (Oct 1918), 584–96.

The Wessex Novels are, from one point of view, one prolonged argument about Providence. H is persuaded that there is no moral guidance of human affairs and that no plan of righteousness is being fulfilled. In a great passage in *The Return of the Native* (II), we have a precise inversion of the teaching of Wordsworth. H is not a herald of revolt against conventional morality: he does not belong to the silly tribe that exhausts itself in denouncing "convention." His skepticism is far more thorough, his despair more complete. The critics who charge H with pessimism or fleshliness have missed the real mark. It is true to say that H often exaggerates, and it is not unfair to call *Jude the Obscure* an hysterical performance. H's real weakness lies in an astonishing paradox: we have on one hand a clear-cut cosmic theory, and on the other hand, a fierce moral protest. But if the protest is well-grounded the theory must be false and vice versa. H has at least once recognized this difficulty: in "New Year's Eve," where God is questioned about His reasons for making so painful a world. The reply given is that no purpose, either good or bad, was ever entertained.

1919

758 Aiken, Conrad. "Preface," Two Wessex Tales (Boston: Four Seas, 1919), pp. 7–9.
H is a "merciless, a passionate ironist."

759 Cunliffe, John William. "Thomas Hardy," English Literature During The Last Half Century (NY: Macmillan, 1919), pp. 40–58; rptd (1923), pp. 42–62.
Under the Greenwood Tree "caught charm of . . . secluded England"; *A Pair of Blue Eyes* depended "more on plot than on character." *Far From the Madding Crowd* shows a firm grasp of character as well as rustic humor and pathos. *The Return of the Native* is the "first and perhaps the most perfect combination of what may be called the tragic and idyllic elements of his genius." Eustacia is doomed to tragedy by circumstance, exemplified in Egdon Heath. The austerity of the novel is "happily mitigated by its picturesque setting." Succeeding novels show a falling-off until *The Mayor of Casterbridge*; Henchard is "one of the most original characters in fiction, and his fate is worked out with overwhelming power." *The Woodlanders* has charm, but *Tess of the d'Urbervilles*, H's greatest novel, "gives fuller voice to the author's passionate indignation at injustice, human and divine." It is "a notable work of art, springing from deep feeling, nobly planned, and, on the whole, masterfully executed." In *Jude the Obscure*, "pessimistic philosophy submerges art." H's poems have been neglected, and the general preference for his fiction is justified. One thing that "moves the poet to a kind of cheerfulness is triumphant indulgence in sexual desire." *The Dynasts* combines the method of Shakespeare's history plays with that of Goethe's Faust but lacks humor and is too long. There is a contradiction in philosophy which gives the Will absolute control and yet ascribes to men production of new designs that may awaken It. H protested the idea that he was a pessimist: he called himself an evolutionary meliorist instead. Still, his "main themes are ironies and illusions of life." It is not surprising that he should be considered pessimistic. "His attitude towards human suffering is intensely sympathetic, and very far from cynical; his keen sensibility is matched with kindness."

760 Edward, Ralph. "Some Emendations in the Poetry of Mr. Hardy," Times Literary Supplement (Lond), 18 Dec 1919, pp. 767–68.
H's poetry "contains a number of notable emendations" that show his "fastidious care" in seeking out the best expression. Such poems as "San Sebastian," "My Cicely," "The Dance at the Phoenix" show many signif-

icant changes. Sometimes H ameliorates his philosophy; some of his changes do not seem as felicitous as originals, but he was very careful about the finish of his poetry.

761 Fairley, Barker. "Notes on the Form of *The Dynasts*," PUB-LICATIONS OF THE MODERN LANGUAGE ASSOCIATION, XXXIV (Sept 1919), 401–15.

The Dynasts is the "most distinguished chapter in the development of explicit forms of poetic commentary" in which "explicit device probes the implicit substance." "Apparent formlessness" in *Dynasts* actually "achieves its marvellous inwardness by externalizing its forms of expression," in spite of shortcomings in diction. The work combines the tradition of the epic (its comprehensive and fundamental mode) with the metaphysical (in the supernatural scenes) and with historical drama (in the human scenes), thus achieving a formal novelty—ticketing and compartmentalizing to arrive at a sense of discontinuous experience. There is a contrast of the Years and the Pities, the two major spirits connecting 130 separate sequences. *The Return of the Native,* the "richest in substance" of H's novels, shows a tendency to "implicitness" of comment different from the tendency to "explicitness" in *Dynasts* as a pre-eminently philosophical poem.

762 "From Novelist to Poet: Thomas Hardy and his Verse," BOOKMAN'S JOURNAL, I (12 Dec 1919), 147.

While it has been said that the upheaval of the Nineties "made for a fuller and wider appreciation of Hardy's genius," the reverse is true. H, "in fighting always for truth and freedom, . . . made much easier the way" of the decadents. [Review of *The Poetical Works of Thomas Hardy* (Lond: Macmillan, 1919).]

763 Johnson, Austen H. "The Poetry of Thomas Hardy," SATURDAY REVIEW (Lond), CXXVIII (29 Nov 1919), 511.

[Letter objecting to "flabby sentimentality" of review in ibid (15 Nov 1919).] The critic has ignored H's "mastery of varied metre." H may be pessimistic, "but there is no note of despair . . . the struggle is always worth while, life is always great and important."

764 Korten, Hertha. THOMAS HARDYS NAPOLEON DICHTUNG, THE DYNASTS. IHRE ABHÄNGIGKEIT VON SCHOPENHAUER. IHR EINFLUSS AUF GERHART HAUPTMANN (Thomas Hardy's Napoleon Story, *The Dynasts.* Its Dependence on Schopenhauer. Its Influence on Gerhart Hauptmann) (Bonn: Georgi, 1919); University of Rostock dissertation.

The Dynasts shows H's limited artistic ability, H's failure to acknowledge Schopenhauer's WELT ALS WILLE UND VORSTELLUNG as his primary source, and H's unfortunate influence on Gerhart Hauptmann's FESTSPIEL IN DEUTSCHEN REIMEN. For Germans, *Dynasts* has a twofold interest: it illustrates the world-wide influence of German thought on a foreign literature and explains why FESTSPIEL IN DEUTSCHEN REIMEN was never popular in Germany. [In German.]

765 "Literary Intelligence," LONDON MERCURY, I (Dec 1919), 135–36.

[Describes the manuscript volume of original poems presented to H on his eightieth birthday by a number of poets.]

766 Lynd, Robert. "Mr. Thomas Hardy," OLD AND NEW MASTERS (Lond: Unwin; NY: Scribner, 1919); rptd (Freeport, NY: Books for Libraries P, 1970), pp. 234–49; probably published a little earlier as two periodical pieces [not identified].

H's poetry, while admirable for its "bleak sincerity," lacks "imaginative energy," is marred by its narrow range of subject and technique, and unfortunately dramatizes only the meaningless miseries of life. [Two-part essay: "His Genius as a Poet" and "A Poet in Winter." Lynd seems to assume that a lyric poet is obliged to treat the joys and triumphs of life.]

767 Maxwell, M. E. "The Gifts of Thomas Hardy," BOON MONTHLY, March 1919, pp. 281–83.

We thank H for Wessex, birds, his presentation of the seasons, his treatment of labor, his courageous philosophy. [Includes a brief bibliography.]

768 "Mr. Hardy's Lyrics," TIMES LITERARY SUPPLEMENT (Lond), 27 Nov 1919, pp. 681–82.

All H's poems are "haunted by the presence of their writer." They are close to experience yet dramatic, as he "weav[es] make-believe out of the actual." He makes poetry out of an innumerable variety of commonplace experiences—"self-forgotten, he lives in the created." More precise term for him than realist would be "realizationist." Although his philosophy is "tart and acrid" and his God "phantasmal and remote," the poet is not. Spartan as his philosophy is, it confers "light, energy, and even peace on us." [Review of *Collected Poems*.]

769 M[urry], J[ohn] M[iddleton]. "The Poetry of Mr. Hardy," ATHENAEUM, No. 2200 (7 Nov 1919), 1147; rptd as "The Poetry of Mr. Hardy," ASPECTS OF LITERATURE (Lond: Collins; NY: Knopf, 1920), pp. 121–38, with a Postscript.

"There have been many poets among us in the last fifty years" who have not "this compulsive power" illustrated in *Collected Poems* (1919). "The secret is not hard to find. Not one of them is adequate to what we know and have suffered. . . . Therefore we deliberately set Mr. Hardy among these."

770 Nairne, A. "The Poetry of Thomas Hardy," LIVING AGE, CCCII (19 July 1919), 175–78.

The poems of *Moments of Vision*, which at first seemed "too tersely, masterfully carved, too naked," now seem rare in workmanship, intimate in speech.

771 Phelps, William Lyon. READING THE BIBLE (NY: Macmillan, 1919), pp. 120–22.

[Discussion of the Bible as literature and in literature. H's "Jezreel" (London TIMES, 1918) mentioned because of the recent conquest of Palestine and its description of the presence of the past in the present.]

772 Philips, Charles. "The Hardy Optimist," CATHOLIC WORLD, CVIII (March 1919), 762–66.

While H is generally regarded as the arch pessimist of English literature, the optimist can see in H's constant puzzling over life the suggestion of at least a seeking after God: "as long as Hardy rebels, protests . . . just so long do we love him though he be blind (though not for his blindness!); for just so long does he postulate and presuppose a bitter and a higher Power capable of regulating the affairs of suffering humanity."

773 "The Poetry of Thomas Hardy," SATURDAY REVIEW (Lond), CXXVIII (15 Nov 1919), 459–60.

H's mechanistic realism shows the delusion that "facts" are really the only truth. H's bitterness and his reputation as a novelist pose difficulties in assessing his verse, but "whatever Mr. Hardy's writing, susceptible to scansion, is, it is not poetry." "At a Bridal" (1866) is charming. "In the Cemetery" (1911) shows that "since he cannot have life, as the other [Lucifer] may not have Heaven, he will strip it to rags."

774 Squire, John Collings. "Other People's Books," BOOKS IN GENERAL (Lond: Heinemann, 1919), pp. 168–72.

H, a good poet who became increasingly a good "metrist," is so gloomy in *Wessex Poems* that he presents "life as Thomas Hardy makes it" rather than life as he sees it.

775 Steinbach, Agnes. "Der Pessimismus bei Th. Hardy und Schopenhauer. Ein Vergleich Ihrer Weltanschauung" (The Pessimism in T. Hardy and Schopenhauer. A Comparison of Their World View). Unpublished dissertation, University of Bonn, 1919.

[Listed in Lawrence F. McNamee, DISSERTATIONS IN ENGLISH AND AMERICAN LITERATURE (NY and Lond: Bowker, 1968).] [In German.]

776 Zachrisson, Robert Eugen. "Thomas Hardy, en Författare värd Nobel-pris. Den Engelska Litteraturen Konsekvent Förbigangen . . ." (Thomas Hardy, An Author Worthy of a Nobel Prize, English Literature Since the Beginning), DAGENS NYHETER, 19 Nov 1919, p. 9.

England has four authors deserving the Nobel Prize in Literature: Shaw, Galsworthy, Wells and H. Of these, H is the most deserving. His masterly description of characters, his firm and artistic plot construction, his magnificent descriptions of nature, the philosophical and psychological depth coupled with an exquisite use of the language make H's novels immortal masterpieces. H is the Schopenhauer of fiction. To him the world is ruled by blind and irrational will. People are puppets which perish in their quest to assert themselves. The basic theme in his fiction is phantoms chasing a phantom. But H is not exclusively negative: an appeal to human compassion is found throughout his work. [In Swedish.]

1920

777 A., L. "Thomas Hardy: A French View," ATHENAEUM, No. 4727 (3 Dec 1920), 771.

Julie Bertrand's comment on H's lack of popularity on the continent was probably made with only his prose in mind. Most English critics hold H's verse the best representation of his talent.

778 Abercrombie, Lascelles. "New Books: Hardy the Poet," LIVERPOOL POST AND MERCURY (28 Jan 1920), p. 9.

"The only relationship between Hardy the poet and Hardy the novelist is that we can very well see the same man doing two totally different things." His poetry will live: "he makes lyrical poetry do things it never came near before." [Review of *Collected Poems*.]

779 Alexander, Grace. "Thomas Hardy, Wizard of Wessex," NEW REPUBLIC, XXIII (18 Aug 1920), 335–36.

H's pictures of nature, the creations of a poet-dramatist, are the most significant element in his novels. The two storms in *Far From the Madding Crowd* show H's use of weather at its most dramatic. The vastness of *The Return of the Native* is on the order of Shakespeare's KING LEAR, and H's use of the lower classes and chivalric treatment of women are part of this scheme.

780 "Amateurs Who Surpassed Professionals in a Great Epic-Drama," CURRENT OPINION, LXVIII (May 1920), 643–45.

The recent Oxford amateur performance of *The Dynasts* was more successful than Granville-Barker's professional production and demonstrated clearly that H's masterpiece—at least in the non-supernatural parts—is eminently dramatic, thanks to the vigor of its language.

781 Anderson, John Davis. "In Praise of the Greatness of Thomas Hardy," BOSTON EVENING TRANSCRIPT, 2 June 1920, pt. 3, p. 3.
[Praises H's closeness to nature, the truth of his fictional characters.]

782 Anderson, Sherwood, et al. "Felicitate Thomas Hardy," NEW YORK TIMES, 2 June 1920, p. 3.
[The cable to H on his eightieth birthday read: " 'The following American writers congratulate you upon your living contribution to our literature— Sherwood Anderson, James Branch Cabell, Van Wyck Brooks, Theodore Dreiser, Robert Frost, Joseph Hergesheimer, Vachel Lindsay, Amy Lowell, H. L. Mencken, James Oppenheim, Edwin Arlington Robinson, Carl Sandburg, Sara Teasdale, Louis Untermeyer, B. W. Huebsch.' "]

783 Bernbaum, Ernest. "Introduction," GULLIVER'S TRAVELS (NY: Harcourt, Brace, 1920), p. xv.
When Swift sees the difference between the human ideal and the human reality, his reaction is indignation. But in a pessimist like H "the note is that of pity; naturally enough, for if man is inherently incapable of virtue and happiness, we can be but sorry for him, and we have no justification for scorn and anger."

784 Bertrand, Julie. "Thomas Hardy," ATHENAEUM, No. 4731 (31 Dec 1920), 900.
[Letter to ed in response to Lettie Cole, "Thomas Hardy: A French View," ibid, No. 4727 (3 Dec 1920), 771. Apologies for the lack of appreciation on the continent for the verses of H, Meredith, Kipling, and other English writers.]

785 Bertrand, Julie. "Thomas Hardy: A French View," ATHENAEUM, No. 4726 (26 Nov 1920), 739.
Though, indeed, H's novels present an "acute perception of realities of life" and though H himself has led the "crusade against formalities of morality," his works are too subjective and too personal to be appreciated by a foreign mind. Considering his narrow subject matter and subtlety of expression, would H have been worthy of the Nobel Prize?

786 Betts, Edward W. "Thomas Hardy: A French View," ATHENAEUM, No. 4728 (10 Dec 1920), 820.
The passage from Walter Scott which introduces *Desperate Remedies* lends an irony to Julie Bertrand's statement [ibid, No. 4726 (26 Nov 1920), 739]

about the unsubstantiality of H's characters. The statement emphasizes the greater difficulty in creating a romantic character than in creating a realistic one. This "serves to show that Mr. Hardy's method is part of his literary aim."

787 Blythe, Samuel G. "Great Men Who Have Met Me," SATURDAY EVENING POST, XCII (17 April 1920), 18–19, 152, 155, 159.
[An ironic account of a meeting with H which parodies his reticence, his love of isolation, and his knowledge of nature lore.]

788 "Books of the Month," LONDON MERCURY, I (Jan 1920), 333–34.
"In the history of English literature Mr. Hardy will rank above many of the supposedly established classics. He is a great poet." [Review of *Collected Poems of Thomas Hardy*.]

789 Chew, Samuel C. "Homage to Thomas Hardy," NEW REPUBLIC, XXIII (2 June 1920), 22–26.
H's local background and its influence, his development from a writer of "sensation" to one of "tragic anticipation," and his determinism and realism cast light on his canon. H gradually arrived at an explicit statement of his view of life, as seen in one short paragraph of comment by Sue in *Jude the Obscure* and in the "tentative metaphysic" seen throughout *The Dynasts*. H's personal background, Von Hartmann's Philosophy of the Unconscious, and Zola, are noticeable influences. Sue Bridehead's recognition of the automatic First Cause and H's representation of the contention between the Will-to-Live and the Will-not-to-Live in man are central. "The Self—and this is more remarkable because of the passionate practical individualism of the novels—is made subordinate to the Whole; the particular parcels of the Will are seen as portions of its Immanence."

790 Child, Harold [Hannyngton]. "Thomas Hardy," BOOKMAN (Lond), LVIII (June 1920), 101–3.
H's lyric poems are finding just criticism, and his work, *The Dynasts*, has been acclaimed a masterpiece, a brilliant structure in which all "the component parts of his mind" are expressed. Some people still insist upon reading *Jude the Obscure* as an autobiographical work. Many refuse to see the courage which he expresses in his suffering people—suffering which he sees as an inevitable part of nature.

791 Cole, Lettie. "Thomas Hardy: A French View," ATHENAEUM, No. 4727 (3 Dec 1920), 771.
Julie Bertrand's criticism [ibid, No. 4726 (26 Nov 1920), 739] that H speaks through his characters is not true. He writes of those whom he knows best, and these portrayals offer much to Englishmen and must offer as much

to those interested in the English character. To the objective French mind, H's characters must seem indistinct; but these characters are, nevertheless, portrayals of real characters who are slowly disappearing.

792 Compton-Rickett, Arthur. A HISTORY OF ENGLISH LITER-ATURE (Lond: Jack, 1920), pp. 29, 406, 541–46, 552, 553, 578, 658, 677.

H's forte as a novelist was his keen scientific description of nature, as opposed to the description of the complexities of urban social life, a field in which Meredith triumphed. His best character analyses are of simple primitive types, especially females, who are ultimately unimportant in comparison to the overwhelming force of nature. H's style is clear and unpretentious, direct and sincere, even though his prose suffers sometimes from a certain stiffness. Though H showed us a world of gloom "needlessly intensified," in which the happy side of life is excluded, his works are not immoral: his coarseness is that of nature herself.

793 "Correspondence: Thomas Hardy in France," ATHENAEUM, No. 4721 (22 Oct 1920), 563.

H is better known on the continent than a recent note suggests. Not only has *Far From the Madding Crowd* been translated into French, but also *The Trumpet-Major, Jude the Obscure, Tess of the d'Urbervilles* and some of the stories from *Life's Little Ironies*. Some fine criticism has been written by French reviewers.

794 D., F. H. "Hardy's Casterbridge: *The Return of the Native* Staged," BOOKMAN'S JOURNAL, III (26 Nov 1920), 79.

[Account of a visit to Dorset and of witnessing a performance of *The Return of the Native*. Though the play could not approach the novel in depth, the dramatic interpretation of H's rustics was very effective.]

795 Dark, Sidney. "Thomas Hardy's Napoleon," JOHN O'LONDON'S WEEKLY, III (11 Sept 1920), 638.

The Dynasts is H's culminating achievement and is "unrivalled in our generation." H's conviction that this world is tragically unintelligible is behind all his works. He portrays Napoleon as an "upstart" and a toy of the Will.

796 Ellis, Stewart Marsh. GEORGE MEREDITH: HIS LIFE AND FRIENDS IN RELATION TO HIS WORK (NY: Dodd, Mead, 1920), pp. 7, 186, 208–10, 307, 314.

Though Meredith read and rejected H's lost first novel, *The Poor Man and the Lady*, he took enough interest in the young writer—later to be his chief rival—to advise him to write another tale, less satiric and more eventful. The two writers remained friendly, and in 1895 H remarked that without Meredith's encouragement he would never have abandoned architecture for art.

797 "The Epic of Tragic History," NATION (Lond), XXVI (14 Feb 1920), 668–69.

The Dynasts, as staged at Oxford, leaves out much of the truly poignant material from "the greatest of English historical epics." The comic peasants, drawn on the Shakespearian model, overbear the tragedy of the original. "What was most wanting was the supernatural or spiritual side . . . the very soul of the poet's conception." H received a standing ovation.

798 Erskins, John. "The Novels of Thomas Hardy," NEW YORK POST BOOK REVIEW, 5 June 1920, pp. 1, 13.

"The popularity of Hardy's novels is testimony to the lasting appeal of melodrama." His fiction "glorifies the ministrations of the village gossip without altering them beyond recognition." H developed into an art "such village gossip, with the same insistencies on uncertain but unescapable adventures of sex, the same connoisseurship . . . unwilling to spoil the incident by explaining it." The tales in *Wessex Tales* and *Life's Little Ironies* exhibited "the seeds" of all of H's fiction. In H's novels "the sketches of *Wessex Tales* and *Ironies* are only repeated on a larger scale and with greater richness of tone; they remain sketches still and they preserve in a form of beauty the gossip rather than the portrait of life." The "frankness and abruptness" of the characters in H's early novels revealed his inexperience in developing "the melodrama of village gossip." With experience H learned to make "the frankness of his characters more persuading, not less abrupt."

799 Ewart, Wilfrid. *"The Return of the Native* at Dorchester," COUNTRY LIFE, CL (27 Nov 1920), 692–93.

[Review of a dramatic version of *The Return of the Native* produced by the Hardy Players at Dorchester.]

800 Fairley, Barker. "Thomas Hardy's Lyrical Poems," CANADIAN BOOKMAN, II (July 1920), 18–22.

H's lyrical poetry did much to bring about the change in "the reader's notion of what is or rather what is not lyrical poetry." The diction of *Wessex Poems* is "archaic, scientific prosaic at will." Typical of H's whole series of poems, the "Poems of 1912–13" are "full of the poignant accents of common speech." In H's more subtle poems, he "lets the subject shape itself, so in his rhythms he seems unwilling to cultivate any other cadences than those that come out of natural scenes and speech." His narrative poems "surprise us by their brevity." His philosophical poems "enlarge the field of English poetry, extending it to include metaphysic of a more abstract kind." In H's personal lyric, "metaphysics becomes almost a mythology in which . . . Mother Nature vainly seeks to cover up her deficiency." The forbidding aspect of many of H's poems is diminished, "for a single drop of hope from Hardy is worth gallons of another man's inborn optimism."

801 Fletcher, John Gould. "The Black Rock: To Thomas Hardy," YALE REVIEW, ns IX (July 1920), 727–31; rptd in ibid, ns XVII (April 1928), 447–51.
[A poem praising H for "the force of your patience" and "your grim silent struggle."]

802 Foster, Joshua James. WESSEX WORTHIES (Lond: Dickinson, 1920), pp. 4, 19, 74, 81–83, 141.
[Passing references; Introduction by H.]

803 Foster, Maxwell E. "For Hardy Speaks No Word Foolishly," YALE LITERARY MAGAZINE, LXXXVI (Dec 1920), 95–98.
To the question, how can an all-knowing, all-loving God permit such misery in life, H's first answer was "a Caliban is God." Out of his contemplation after this discovery came "A Plaint to Man" and "God's Funeral"—poems which accept "the Fact of life," and urge man to make the best of it.

804 Freeman, John. "The Poetry of Thomas Hardy," BOOKMAN (Lond), LVII (Jan 1920), 139–41.
Writing poetry for more than a half century, H touches "the fluent formalism of the Victorian period," and "the much-exploring, zestful activity of the latest Georgian poets." Yet he has remained uninfluenced by the changing attitudes of his contemporaries. His poetry is that of a mature man with a profound introspective nature. His poems are the expressions of his personality, but they have a universal significance.

805 Gilbert-Cooper, Everard G. "The Debt of Mr. Thomas Hardy to Indian Philosophy," HINDUSTAN REVIEW, XLI (March 1920), 196–203.
The germs of H's outlook on life are either identical with, or derived from, Indian philosophy. The leading ideas of the nineteenth-century European philosophy of pessimism were derived from a study of Buddhism. Schopenhauer freely acknowledged his debt to the philosophy of Buddha, and H's debt to Schopenhauer, were it not confessed, is obvious. The Indian conception of *Karma* (fate), the central idea of all Indian thought, seems to agree closely with H's ideas on fate. Another Indian conception, that of *Maya* (illusion), finds its place in H's scheme. *Maya* emphasizes the unreality of matter, the illusory character of external objects.

806 "The Great Tragedian of Modern English Letters," CURRENT OPINION, LXIX (Aug 1920), 236–38.
As a writer H remains a puzzling but monumental figure whose pessimism flouts the current of the age. His early humor has turned to bitterness, but he has lost neither his closeness to the rustic countryside nor his command of formal beauty. He reiterates that man is not at the center of the universe,

but an occasional note of hope saves his work from complete despair. [This essay borrows heavily and openly from Samuel Chew's "Homage to Thomas Hardy," NEW REPUBLIC, XXIII (2 June 1920), 22–26.]

807 Harrison, Frederick. "Novissima Verba," FORTNIGHTLY REVIEW, ns CVII (Feb 1920), 180–84.

The Dynasts is a Miltonic world-drama much superior to any of the productions of Tennyson or Swinburne. H's lyric poems touch upon all levels and aspects of Wessex and are all pitched in a minor key. Yet they are too tragic, for the author's concentration on the graveyard part of life blinds him to all other concerns.

808 James, Henry. THE LETTERS OF HENRY JAMES. 2 vols, ed by Percy Lubbock (Lond: Macmillan, 1920), I, 194, 204; II, 111 (NY: Scribner's, 1920), I, 190, 200; II, 108.

To Robert Louis Stevenson (19 March 1892): "The good Thomas Hardy has scored a great success with *Tess of the d'Urbervilles*, which is chock-full of faults and falsity and yet has a singular beauty and charm." To Robert Louis Stevenson (17 February 1893): "Most refreshing, even while not wholly convincing, was the cool trade-wind (is the trade-wind cool?) of your criticism of some of 'ces messieurs.' I grant you Hardy with all my heart." To Miss Ellen Emmet (2 November 1908): A portrait was "done" by Jacques Blanche, the same artist who painted H. H's portrait was "a rather wondrous thing."

809 Mason, Stuart. "An Unknown Magazine Article by Thomas Hardy," ATHENAEUM, No. 4723 (5 Nov 1920), 627.

In the advertisements of a weekly periodical, LIGHT, 1878, H is listed as a contributor; the British Museum does not have a copy of the periodical in question. Perhaps someone will discover a lost poem or story by H "buried in the files of an extinct and obscure publication."

810 Mavrogordato, John (trans). "Thomas Hardy," ATHENAEUM, No. 4729 (17 Dec 1920), 848.

[A translation of a Greek poem by Kostès Palamas entitled, "Tess of the d'Urbervilles." A paean to Tess and the artist who created her, and a condemnation of a world which reflects the injustice Tess suffered.]

811 "Mr. Hardy's 80th Birthday," ATHENAEUM, No. 4701 (4 June 1920), 737–38.

On his eightieth birthday H was honored by the English Society of Authors wherein he served as president. He was praised for his guidance and counsel while holding the office which was once held by Tennyson and by Meredith.

812 "Mr. Thomas Hardy and the Mummers," BOOKMAN'S JOURNAL, III (31 Dec 1920), 168.

At Christmas there was a performance of the mumming scene from *The Return of the Native* for H at Max Gate.

813 Muddiman, Bernard. THE MEN OF THE NINETIES (Lond: Danielson, 1920), pp. 8, 12, 55, 57, 69, 76, 131.

Although H was a major Victorian, he really does not belong to the Victorian movement; in fact, he helped smash the fetters of Victorian fiction. Although younger writers do not approach the greatness of H, Hubert Crackanthorpe in "Antony Garstin's Courtship" approaches H at his bitterest and most pessimistic. Zola influenced H to beget *Jude the Obscure*.

814 Neilson, William Allen, and Ashley Horace Thorndike. A HISTORY OF ENGLISH LITERATURE (NY: Macmillan, 1920, 1935), pp. 410–11, 416, 431, 439.

H's attitude toward life "is one of despair." [Mostly passing references.]

815 "Notes and Comments," ATHENAEUM, No. 4720 (15 Oct 1920), 509.

A translation of a novel by the Nobel Prize winning author, Knut Hamsun, shows that he was deserving of the prize, though not as good a novelist as H, who it was hoped would receive the award. H has a rare quality which is probably not easily grasped by foreign readers because much is lost in translation.

816 O'London, John. "Mr. Hardy Celebrates His 80th Birthday," NEW YORK TIMES, 6 June 1920, V, p. 298.

H's first published work was "How I Built Myself A House." His training as an architect has colored most of his novels, especially *Jude the Obscure*. Max Gate was placed on a Roman cemetery: excavations for the driveway unearthed treasures such as skeletons of soldiers from the time of Hadrian, a skeleton of a Roman lady whose hair brooch H kept as a souvenir, etc.

817 Parker, W. M. "The Genius of Thomas Hardy," NINETEENTH CENTURY AND AFTER, LXXXVIII (July 1920), 63–71.

For forty years H's name has stood for that of "the greatest deliberative genius." His great constructive ability can be seen in at least eight outstanding novels, all of which have memorable characters and scenes, tragic choruses of peasants, etc. *The Return of the Native* is H's *magnum opus*; *Jude the Obscure*, by contrast, is shockingly inartistic. Opening of *Native* is operatic, akin to prelude of TRISTAN UND ISOLDE. *The Dynasts* is a work of genius also, because of great characters and felicitious speeches; it is, to date, the great poetic work of the twentieth century. [Slight.]

818 Parker, W. M. "Thomas Hardy," ATHENAEUM, No. 4729 (17 Dec 1920), 848.

[Replies to Julie Bertrand's contention ("Thomas Hardy," ibid, No. 4726 [26 Nov 1920], 739) that the unpopularity of H on the continent results from the unreality of his characters. By visiting "Hardy Country" one will find that they are indeed real.]

819 Phelps, William Lyon. "The First Time I Read a Novel by Hardy," YALE LITERARY MAGAZINE, LXXXVI (Dec 1920), 89–91.

A Pair of Blue Eyes is "a fool's paradise" for a reader who expects a happy ending. Even if one tries, midway through the novel, to imagine a painful ending he "will not be ingenious enough to devise any scheme so cruel as the actual conclusion." But although painful at first, the study of H's art is rewarding: it quickens the imagination, enlarges the circle of one's thought.

820 Phillpotts, Eden. "To Thomas Hardy," ATHENAEUM, No. 4701 (4 June 1920), 729; rptd in LIVING AGE, CCCVI (17 July 1920), trans into French by Georgette Camille.

[Poem characterizing H as a "steadfast master" who reveals "the invincible predestinate."]

821 Powell, Charles. THE POETS IN THE NURSERY. Introduction by John Drinkwater (Lond and NY: Lane, 1920), pp. 11, 38–41.

[The introduction contains a reference to H's "fibrous verse" and "sifting intelligence"; a parody of *The Dynasts* called "Old Mother Hubbard."]

822 Raymond, E. T. [pseud of Edward Raymond Thompson]. "Portraits of the 'Nineties: XII—Thomas Hardy," OUTLOOK (Lond), XLVI (4 Dec 1920), 564–66; rptd in PORTRAITS OF THE NINETIES (NY: Scribner, 1921) pp. 211–20.

In all H's work "the first quality is power of design, and the second form and discipline in expression." H "stands for the idea of vertical extension; he shows us that on a half-acre plot we can reach the centre of everything."

823 Rolleston, Thomas William. "Life and Death: Considerations on a Poem of Thomas Hardy," HIBBERT JOURNAL, XVIII (Jan 1920), 275–88.

"During Wind and Rain" is a world-tragedy in four stanzas, the poetic expression of the universal tragedy of death.

824 Rothenstein, William (ed). "Thomas Hardy, O. M.," TWENTY-FOUR PORTRAITS . . . WITH CRITICAL APPRECIATIONS BY VARIOUS HANDS (Lond: Allen & Unwin, 1920), pp. [56]–[58].

[Laudatory account of H the "Singer . . . Storyteller, Philosopher, and Patriot," who "for range of vision and grasp of life stands with Shakespeare, Wordsworth and Browning."]

825 Sassoon, Siegfried. "Thomas Hardy as Poet," VANITY FAIR, XIV (May 1920), 63, 106; also in PATRICIAN, June 1920 [not seen].

In H's poems there is "profound pity underlying his apparent pessimism."

826 Stark, Harold. "The Letter that Kills," YALE LITERARY MAGAZINE, LXXXVI (Dec 1920), 91–94.

Mankind is controlled by "an indifferent being with no sense of justice." And though we try "we cannot win against our evil star." Even Sue and Jude, "who lived out the letter of these laws of marriage," found no peace.

827 Sturgeon, Mary C. "Thomas Hardy," STUDIES OF CONTEMPORARY POETS (Lond: George G. Harrap, 1920, rvd and enlgd), pp. 368–80.

H is well-beloved, not certainly for winsomeness but for modernity, for flexibility of thought. H's method is scientific, observing and recording, thus producing fragments and verbal experiments. But the fragments merge in *The Dynasts* to reveal an intellectual, cosmic philosophy which views the universe as "a vast unconscious force, a single energy, working blindly and automatically toward some possible goal of ultimate consciousness." Thus the end result is a note of hope, a denial of evil power. Also, in later lyrics is joy, tenderness, feeling, a general mellowing.

828 Swinnerton, Frank. "The Art of the Novel," BOOKMAN (NY), L (Jan 1920), 411–17.

Art implies design, "an imaginative conception of the whole." H was the first English novelist to combine originality and spontaneity with artistic discipline. [Very general appreciation.]

829 Symons, Arthur. "Thomas Hardy," DIAL, LXVIII (Jan 1920), 66–70.

In *Poems of the Past and the Present*, every poem says something "in a slow, twisted, and sometimes enigmatic manner, without obvious charm, but with some arresting quality," something brooding, obscure, half-inarticulate. H is a poet who is "sorry for Nature," "as if he had sap in his veins instead of blood." The atmosphere is mysterious, almost terrifying. "Nearly the whole book shivers with winter." H's verse is uncertain; some of his experiments are remarkable. Though his verse does not sing, he is a poet, "and a profoundly interesting one." In *The Dynasts*, H's philosophy of despair is boldly presented. There is the disadvantage of too much distance, but H comes down to earth for some of the best moments where the "scenes grow warm with natural emotion."

830 "Thomas Hardy," BOOKMAN'S JOURNAL, II (4 June 1920), 84.

H is an artist who limited his talents by trying to explain life when he might have accepted it or embraced it. His novels are great within his limited perspective; as for his poetry, it might be said he was "a poet in spite of himself."

831 "Thomas Hardy," MERCURE DE FRANCE, CXLI (July 1920), 278–79.

H belongs to a family of remote French origins, which perhaps accounts for the fact that his heroines have been called more French than English. [In French.]

832 "Thomas Hardy of Wessex," OUTLOOK (NY), CXXV (23 June 1920), 369.

H's Wessex novels created a semi-imaginary kingdom, after Meredith coaxed H into fiction. H is now back at work on verse, and *The Dynasts* is great, although "to the general reader, turgid in form and over-subtle in philosophical content."

833 Tyndale, Walter. HARDY COUNTRY: WATER-COLOURS (Lond: Black, [1920]).

[Twenty paintings of actual Wessex scenes which inspired H's fiction.]

834 Williams, Harold. "The Passage of the Centuries," OUT- LINES OF MODERN ENGLISH LITERATURE, 1890–1914 (Lond: Sidgwick & Jackson, 1920), pp. 66–73.

Although H's novels "are already classics in the backward of time" his poems are clearly "post-Victorian." The range of imagination in *The Dynasts* is impressive. H's aim was "to set forth the Napoleonic epoch as an instantaneous imaginative vision of Europe and to impress upon the reader its philosophical significance." Judged as a poem, however, "it fails, save in brief passages." But "the prose passages are simple and vigorous." H's shorter poems impress by "range and variety of content." "The emotion of Mr. Hardy's poetry is that of a strong personality, too deep to break out into feeling which has no essential relation to the whole attitude of his mind and thought toward the problems of life and nature." "Almost every poem makes us feel that the thought is greater than the expression."

835 Williamson, Claude C. H. "The Pessimism of Thomas Hardy," WRITERS OF THREE CENTURIES, 1789–1914 (Lond: Grant Richards, 1920), pp. 314–21.

H's view of life is so serious that he seems to have "the mind and, therefore, the imagination of a child, heavily burdened with a personal responsibility unknown to the compromising and dexterous adult." His pessimism "is directed towards an observation of ethics, not towards an analysis of self." H's inconsistency is that "of a simple man, who refuses to take refuge from facts . . . in a philosophy contrived for the purpose." H was "a strangely sensitive emotional soul, deeply touched with pity for life, and pity for all who live."

836 Zachrisson, Robert Eugen. "Ett Sammanträffande med Thomas Hardy och Wells" (A Meeting with Thomas Hardy and Wells), DAGENS NYHETER, 9 Nov 1920, p. 5.

Behind H's pessimistic outlook one can detect a practical worldly wisdom which unites with the Christian tenets summarized in the Sermon on the Mount with its strict insistence on the humbling of the flesh. The driving force in both cases is love for suffering humanity. On this higher plane H's rationalism and Christian faith meet. [In Swedish.]

1921

837 Beach, Joseph Warren. "Bowdlerized Versions of Hardy," PUBLICATIONS OF THE MODERN LANGUAGE ASSOCIATION OF AMERICA, XXXVI (Dec 1921), 632–43.

Nothing better shows H's "respect for the public taste . . . than his great delicacy . . . —not to say his conventionality—in regard to matters of sex." [Surveys many instances of changes H made in the serial versions of the novels when they appeared in book form to support this thesis.]

838 Brennecke, Ernest, Jr. "Thomas Hardy, Today," NEW YORK TIMES BOOK REVIEW, 5 June 1921, p. 12.

H is a poet "who is exceedingly responsive to the life about him."

839 Canby, Henry Seidel. "The Novelist of Pity," NEW YORK EVENING POST LITERARY REVIEW, 9 July 1921, pp. 1–2; rptd in DEFINITIONS: ESSAYS IN CONTEMPORARY CRITICISM [First Series] (NY: Harcourt, Brace, 1922), pp. 269–77; and in THOMAS HARDY: NOTES ON HIS LIFE AND WORK (NY: Harper, 1925), pp. 5–11.

To call H a pessimist is incorrect, for he is one who "sees clearly that the sufferer is more intelligible than his fate," and it is "pity for the individual, not despair of the race" that is his motive. H is a stylist in fiction only in his "sadder passages." [Includes a report of an unrevealing interview with H.]

840 Chevalley, Abel. LE ROMAN ANGLAIS DE NOTRE TEMPS (The Modern English Novel) (Lond: Humphrey Milford; Lond: Oxford, 1921), pp. 20, 24–27, 51–53, 56, 59, 65–71, 82, 141, 153, 210, 250.

Intent on recording what he had seen with his own eyes, H wrote about unconventional country heroes living in an unidealized country setting. These heroes appear in well-constructed novels which reveal their author's pessimism and great concern for humanity. [In French.]

841 Chew, Samuel C. THOMAS HARDY: POET AND NOVELIST (NY: Knopf, 1921; 1928).

H's technique is not innovative, but Victorian. Stylistically, he was "willing to sacrifice elegance and grace to precision." H is knowledgeable about Wessex, Nature, rural occupations, customs, and superstitions. The peasants in his novels form a distinct class—close to the earth and "at ease in their world." H advocates divorce and is realistic about love: "a physical passion, a sexual attraction, carrying with it the hope, but only the hope, of a permanent bond of affection based on common interests and common ideas." He is generally bitter toward women, who are portrayed as fickle, passionate, never sweet, and lacking self-control. Men are either sensualists, rigid intellectualists, or an "honest middle group . . . who subordinate desire to the other demands of life." H's poetry will outlast his prose. His poems are a series of impressions; they are not didactic.

842 Davis, F. Hadland. "The Music of Thomas Hardy," MUSICAL TIMES, LXII (1 April 1921), 255–58.

All of H's works except *Jude the Obscure* are full of jolly rustic songs. The Mellstock choir in *Under the Greenwood Tree* is the best known musical group in H, but the songs in *Tess of the d'Urbervilles*, *The Dynasts*, and *The Trumpet-Major* (all of which have received musical settings) should not be forgotten. Perhaps H's most moving use of music is at the conclusion of his last novel, where Jude lies dying as the happy Christminster crowds sing their traditional songs.

843 Day, Clarence, Jr. THE CROW'S NEST (NY: Knopf, 1921), pp. 77–83.

"Dying howls, of all kinds, are his speciality." He enjoys presenting the horrors he perceives. Their poignancy, their chilling effect on his audience matters less to him than the personal thrill he feels at discovering some new evidence of malignancy in the scheme of things. His pessimism, then, is essentially self-centered and dishonest. [Flippant tone; more entertaining than persuasive.]

844 Evoe [pseud of E. V. Knox, of "Punch"]. PARODIES REGAINED (Lond: Methuen, 1921), pp. 109–18.

[A skit about H and Alfred Noyes, entitled "The Two Shepherds": the brightminded Noyes and the gloomy H exchange songs (Noyes offers a cloying romantic lyric entitled "Sailing," H a pessimistic ballad entitled

"The False Wife"); their opposing views established, they join to sing a sad-happy ballad of one Corporal Henry Tullidge.]

845 Ewart, Wilfrid. "Thomas Hardy and Our Own Time," NINE-TEENTH CENTURY AND AFTER, XC (Sept 1921), 427–37.
H depicts in the English peasantry a universal sense of impending doom and finality which is in close accord with our own time. Both in his poetry and in his novels, H has given voice to the "what must be" mood of England today. "His [H's] description of Egdon Heath is an unforeseen yet monumental tribute to the cataclysmic aftermath of [the battle of the Somme]."

846 Harding, Henry. "In Hardyland: 'Egdon Heath' and 'Rainbarrow,'" EDUCATIONAL TIMES, LXXIII (April 1921), 169–70.
[The usual guide to interesting sights in H country.]

847 Hind, Charles Lewis. "Thomas Hardy," AUTHORS AND I (NY & Lond: Lane, 1921), pp. 114–18.
H is a "profound critic of life . . ., a pessimist tinged with irony." [Hind recalls a visit to Max Gate shortly after the publication of *Jude the Obscure*, and H's firm resolution to write no more novels.]

848 Hopkins, Robert Thurston. "The Dorset Folks and Dorset Ways: Thomas Hardy's Characters in Real Life," BOOKMAN'S JOURNAL, IV (5 Aug 1921), 238.
A visitor to Dorset will still find much of the humor, charm, and many of the habits of the country folk which H described in his works.

849 Kilmer, Joyce. "Note on Thomas Hardy," THE CIRCUS, AND OTHER ESSAYS (NY: Doran, 1921), pp. 268–74.
H's dominant idea that happiness is the exception and sorrow the rule proves the falseness of the "common and absurd" idea that he is a pagan. It is his propagandistic insistence on this idea which mars the artistic value of his work. He is so intent on announcing his belief that he becomes evangelical. H is a true realist and has a sense of beauty and humor.

850 King, Marianne. "Temperamental Pessimism in Thomas Hardy," PACIFIC REVIEW, I (March 1921), 530–42.
H was able to see the universe as indifferent toward man without falling into the error of considering it malignant. In his novels, the central cause of misery lies in man's "stupidity and ignorance." His heroes and heroines struggle against out-worn mental attitudes rather than a malignant fate. However, the melioristic possibilities of such a view are often overshadowed by the "temperamental pessimism" which grows out of H's intense sympathy for all suffering.

851 "The Literary World of Today," BOSTON EVENING TRAN-SCRIPT, 5 Feb 1921, p. 7.
H's popularity is limited because he is a serious critic of life.

852 "A Memorable Dorset Night: Visit of the Hardy Players to London," DORSET YEARBOOK, 1921, pp. 65–75.
The London production by the Hardy Players of *The Return of the Native* "added fresh laurels to the Hardy Players."

853 Murry, John Middleton. "Wrap Me Up In My Aubusson Carpet," ADELPHI (Lond), I (April 1921), 951–58, espec 955–58; rptd as WRAP ME UP IN MY AUBUSSON CARPET (NY: Greenberg, 1924).
George Moore uses his writing talents to criticize H unjustly. "For this 'criticism' of Mr. Hardy is not criticism . . .; it is simply the spluttering of venom." Moore's criticism of H stems from his envy of H's genius. "In his [Moore's] treatment of Mr. Hardy he has surpassed his own previous triumphs in envy and vulgarity."

854 Tomlinson, H. M. "The England of Hardy," NEW REPUBLIC, XXV (12 Jan 1921), 190–92.
The opening of *The Return of the Native* suggests a view of England at its origin. There is more of the gist, the native vitality, in H's work than in all the cablegrams sent to Americans to describe the present position of England.

855 Whitfield, A. Stanton. THOMAS HARDY: THE ARTIST, THE MAN AND THE DISCIPLE OF DESTINY. Introduction by Sir John Alexander Cockburn (Lond: Grant Richards, 1921); given as a lecture before La Société Internationale de Philologie, Science et Beaux-Arts, 11 April 1921.
H's technical, philosophic, and stylistic range are all the more remarkable when one considers that eleven of his best works spring from the same basic inspiration—his close observation of human life set against the backdrop of the Wessex landscape. This close study, coupled with his reading of Darwin, led to his powerful vision of the continuity between man and nature. His honesty to this vision has lost him some readers, for he "is not a writer for moral cowards and mental invalids." His finest achievements are his tragic novels, of which *Tess of the d'Urbervilles* is the most finished and *Jude the Obscure* the most profound. His poetry is much more personal; it helps us to "understand the man." Like the tragic novels, however, the poetry has an intensity sometimes "painful to the faithful and orthodox." The most complete representation of his vision of life is *The Dynasts*, a work "so stupendous in conception . . . that it almost seems to have been written for an audience of the gods."

1922

856 Anderson, John D. "Hardy, First of Moderns," NEW YORK TIMES BOOK REVIEW, 28 May 1922, p. 10.
As novelist, H's aim is truth; he ranks with Crabbe as a stern word-painter. His descriptions are part of the story and cannot be omitted. The effect of his art is to open the eyes of readers to the wonder in common life and in familiar objects of daily contact. The novels, better than the poems, show to their fullest the tragedies and woes of human existence.

857 Baum, Paull F. "As to Sources," LITERARY REVIEW (NY), III (9 Sept 1922), 18.
At the time of writing *The Dynasts*, H was unacquainted with the ideas of Schopenhauer. A letter from Gosse proves this and adds that H is still fairly unfamiliar with the German's writings. Another theory exploded is that Hauptmann was influenced by *Dynasts* in the "Festspiel in deutschen Reimen." Thus the arguments in Hertha Korten's dissertation are proved invalid.

858 Beach, Joseph Warren. THE TECHNIQUE OF THOMAS HARDY (Chicago: University of Chicago P, 1922); rptd (NY: Russell & Russell, 1962).
H's writing career was very uneven, as is suggested by the fact that he wrote a number of failures after having written *The Return of the Native*. Although it is impossible to determine why his novels did not steadily improve, it can be stated that his best novels—*Native, Tess of the d'Urbervilles,* and *Jude the Obscure*—are those that are dramatic. In lesser achievements such as *Desperate Remedies,* the emphasis is almost entirely on plot, and there is a heavy reliance on mechanical devices he employs elsewhere to his disadvantage: coincidence, mystery, and surprise. In fact, neither this novel nor its successor, *Under the Greenwood Tree,* anticipates the mature H in the way that *Far From the Madding Crowd* does. In this later novel H was successful for the first time because he made use of Wessex, presented a "very attractive piece of Wessex humanity," and provided a "mellow consistency" of tone. Nevertheless, *Madding Crowd* is not as successful as *Native,* a tragedy of irreconcilable ideas which present "a succession of tensions." In this novel H dispenses with the use of mechanical contrivance, observes unity of tone, place, and time and arranges the action around a "balance and reaction of forces expressible almost in algebraic formulas." It is surprising that this great success was followed by a series of failures—*The Hand of Ethelberta, A Laodicean, The Trumpet-Major, Two on a Tower, The Romantic Adventures of a Milkmaid,* and *The Well-Beloved*—and that these failures were followed by *The Mayor of Casterbridge* and *The Woodlanders,* two

novels which represent a partial recovery of the genius displayed in *Native*. The extent of this recovery is suggested by H's honest treatment of human nature in *Mayor* and use of poetry in *Woodlanders*, while the failure in both novels is clearly seen in the use of minor coincidences, overheard conversations, and surprising turns of events. Ultimately both novels fall short of "the dramatic ideal" because of faulty plots and must, therefore, be contrasted to *Tess* and *Jude*, two great novels commendable for their plots. In the former H controls the plot by concerning himself with "the struggle of weakness and innocence in the clutch of circumstance," a struggle which is not created by opposing wills as in earlier novels but exists instead in Tess's breast. Since Tess is a character who has beauty and strength of personality, the pathos of her intense suffering ultimately makes Tess H's greatest achievement. Nearly as great is *Jude*, a novel in which "everything that happens is characteristic and full of meaning." Although this novel has neither the beauty nor the heroic character of *Tess*, it is outstanding in its "pitiless search for the truth," its avoidance of melodrama, and its adherence to what is true of human nature.

859 Binyon, Laurence. "Mr. Hardy's New Poems," BOOKMAN (Lond), LXII (July 1922), 167–68.
Late Lyrics and Earlier shows that H's artistic genius did not " 'get faint and low' with advancing years." The poems leave a strong impression of "music that constantly finds direct or indirect expression." However, H is not a "melodious poet." Two qualities—"his over-present consciousness of the problems of existence" and "his structural definition, his scrupulous aversion from easy smoothness"—prevent H's verse "from obeying more than occasionally the pure singing impulse." H was not a pessimist, for "no true pessimist would still be singing at eighty, with a glorious record of creativeness behind him." *Late Lyrics* is prefaced by an " 'Apology' " which repudiates H's alleged " 'pessimism.' "

860 Canby, Henry S. "Ideas and Poetry," LITERARY REVIEW (NY), III (7 Oct 1922), 84.
In *Late Lyrics and Earlier*, H shows himself ahead of his own generation "with a mind rationalized by science at work upon a world which stirred in him very different emotions from those sanctioned by standard poetry."

861 Chase, Mary Ellen. "A Comparative Study of Several Versions of Thomas Hardy's Novels, *The Mayor of Casterbridge*, *Tess of the d'Urbervilles*, and *Jude the Obscure*." Unpublished dissertation, University of Minnesota, 1922.
[Listed in Lawrence F. McNamee, DISSERTATIONS IN ENGLISH AND AMERICAN LITERATURE (NY and Lond: Bowker, 1968). See Chase, FROM SERIAL TO NOVEL (1927).]

862 Chew, Samuel C. "The Poems of 'An Ancient,'" New Republic, XXXI (19 July 1922), 226–27.

No poems of *Late Lyrics and Earlier* are of quite the perfection of some in earlier volumes, but the average of excellence is about the same. The charity under H's irony is closer to the surface, as in "The Whitewashed Wall." H's technique is often rugged, and sometimes faulty, but "a harsh and halting presentation of sharply felt emotion, of keenly imagined situation, of sternly confronted opinion is more tolerable and durable than the emptiness of Swinburnian music."

863 Darton, F[rederick] J[oseph] Harvey. The Soul of Dorset (Boston and NY: Houghton Mifflin, 1922), pp. 41, 247–48, 299–300, 305.

H's characters, mastery of local dialect, intimate familiarity with topography, and sense of Wessex history make his work a very close index of the Dorset of his day and of the age just preceding his.

864 Dibelius, Wilhelm. England (Stuttgart and Berlin: Deutsche Verlags-anstalt, 1922); trans by Mary Agnes Hamilton, with an introduction by A. D. Lindsay (Lond: J. Cape; NY: Harpers, 1930), I, 188.

The Mayor of Casterbridge illustrates the idea of the renaissance man in modern fiction. [In German.]

865 Ellis, Stewart Marsh. "Current Literature," Fortnightly Review, ns CXII (2 Oct 1922), 692–97; rptd as "Thomas Hardy: His Lyrics," Mainly Victorian (Lond: Hutchinson, [1925]), pp. 245–51.

In the "Apology" prefacing *Late Lyrics and Earlier*, H rightly rejects claims that his works are pessimistic. With only a few exceptions, the poems of this volume—like all his other verses—present a view of life which is true and faithful to human experience rather than pessimistic.

866 Fletcher, John Gould. "Mr. Hardy's Good-bye," Freeman (NY), VI (18 Oct 1922), 139.

Late Lyrics and Earlier can be approached sentimentally or critically. The critical interest is somewhat less, though, for it is not to be expected that a man of eighty-two will break new grounds. We have a gleaning, an interspersal of scattered pieces which their author once either overlooked or found unsuitable. He is not a Victorian poet; he has the genius of a classical poet, a Greek become rustic. There is little in this book to remind us of that other, starker, H. But what there is, is immensely significant. Nothing suggests the querulousness of old age. But he should have spared us the last poem. It is a pity to see a Tolstoyan mood like this crop up in so fine an artist as H.

867 Garnett, Edward. "Some Remarks on Fiction," FRIDAY NIGHTS (Lond: Cape; NY: Knopf, 1922), p. 252; rvd (Lond: Cape, 1929), p. 194.

[List of English "writers of creative originality:" Joseph Conrad, H. G. Wells, R. Kipling, H, John Galsworthy, and Arnold Bennett.]

868 Golding, Louis. "Mr. Hardy and the New Poetry," SATURDAY REVIEW (Lond), CXXXIII (24 June 1922), 649–50; abstracted as "A Young Poet and an Old One," LIVING AGE, CCCXIV (5 Aug 1922), 367–68.

H is a poet of the tomb. His point blank negation of Romantic optimism annoyed his contemporaries. H's prognostication, in the "Apology" for *Late Lyrics and Earlier*, of a "new Dark Age" of "free" verse and "free" morals is wrong.

869 Grey, Rowland [pseud of Lillian Kate Brown]. "Certain Women of Thomas Hardy," FORTNIGHTLY REVIEW, CXVIII (2 Oct 1922), 677–91.

The "splendid vitality" of H's heroines "is indubitable"; they rank next to Shakespeare's. Both Barrie and Hedgecock miss complexity and variety of H's heroines. There are different types of women in the major novels, including those who are not passionate lovers: Marty South, Thomasin Yeobright, Elizabeth Jane, Lucetta. Marty and Tess show the "ideal love" that Hedgecock finds wanting in H's heroines. One cannot find a truer portrait gallery of women than in H.

870 Hewlett, Maurice. "The Root of Poesy," EXTEMPORARY ESSAYS (NY: Oxford UP, 1922), pp. 72–76.

In *Late Lyrics and Earlier*, H's poetry is too much concerned with loss and disillusionment; he seems more resentful than regretful. He speaks too much with his head and not enough with his heart. The best poems are narrative, but when he laments lost opportunity and contrasts past and present "to their mutual disadvantage," we lose interest. His intellectual approach to tragedy transforms it into a sour humor.

871 Hewlett, Maurice. "The Root of Poesy: Mr. Hardy's Muse," TIMES (Lond), 8 June 1922, p. 14.

As his novels abundantly show, H "can be as perverse as the best of us, and is perfectly incurable." H's complaints about the " 'glacial judgments' " critics meted out to his poems are unwarranted. In *Satires of Circumstance* some poems "fairly revolted the reader." Poems like "The Collector Cleans . . ." and "The Wood Fire" are ugly intellectual fantasies.

872 Holmes, Eric. WANDERINGS IN WESSEX (Lond: Robert Scott, 1922), pp. 119–27.

[Travels through the area of the "southern realm," touching on many places in H's writing—Winchester, Dorchester, Dorset—but not connected specifically with H.]

873 Hone, Joseph M. "Mr. Hardy's New Volume: A Duality of Selves," TIMES (Lond), 23 May 1922, p. 16.

Late Lyrics and Earlier shows that there are two H's: a leading self and a following self. Best poetry comes from the assertive element in H's powerful personality. Poems show great diversity and originality. [Denies that H is "the versifier of borrowed pessimism."]

874 Hone, Joseph Maunsell. "The Poetry of Mr. Hardy," LONDON MERCURY, V (Feb 1922), 396–405.

H's "obtrusive philosophical ideas" are especially evident in *The Dynasts*. "Mr. Hardy is a sentimental poet at his best," who cultivates "old recollection for its own sake."

875 Hopkins, Robert Thurston. THOMAS HARDY'S DORSET (Lond: Palmer; NY: Appleton, 1922).

Dorset folk are solid, genial, lovers of good cider. Superstitions are disappearing, but belief in witchcraft was once prevalent, as we see in H's story "The Withered Arm." [Pilgrimage to many towns and places which are originals for H's settings: Shaftesbury (Shaston), Vale of Blackmoor, Blandford (Shottsford), Dorchester, Bere Regis (Kingsbere), and so on. Describes an encounter with a man who saw ghosts in Woolpit House. Story of Farmer Dribblecombe, who defied the rector who wanted to change an old custom. Extensive description of Dorchester; Roman remains, including the Mai Dun; taverns, houses, bridges, etc. connected with the novels and stories; Higher Bockhampton, H's birthplace; influence of the environment on H. Chronicle of H's novels.] H's poems are not always appreciated; they have their own qualities of originality and strength. His philosophy is not cynical; he himself characterized it as search for truth. [Gives an account of the life of William Barnes, his work with language, revival of dialect, his poems and their understanding of the pathos of common life. Describes an encounter with a thatcher and his explanation of his ancient craft, the church at Bere Regis, related to *Tess of the d'Urbervilles*; history of the Turbervilles and meeting with an old poacher, descendant of the family and a hardy ruffian, superstitions of the people at Bere Regis; a visit to Weymouth (Budmouth); visits to Poole and Swanage, associated with *The Hand of Ethelberta*; further rambles through the Dorset country, with only tenuous connections with H.]

876 LeGallienne, Richard. "Thomas Hardy's Apology and Lyrics," NEW YORK TIMES BOOK REVIEW, 24 Sept 1922, p. 4.

Poetry and art have begun to replace religion: a philosophy which underlies H's lyrics. H's skills have not diminished through the years. H again uses verse to record experiences, as a poetic commonplace book. The grim humor of "The Two Wives" and the imaginatively vivid phrasing of "The Woman I met" are impressive.

877 Lynd, Robert. "Mr. Thomas Hardy Defends Himself," NEW STATESMAN, XVII (3 June 1922), 240–41.

H is impatient of criticism in his "Apology" to *Late Lyrics and Earlier*. It is not out of malice that critics point out the defects of authors. H complains that he is "roughly handled," but there are two key-creaks in H's poetry, at times so loud that they interfere with the music. First, he uses words as though they were not jewels but fragments blasted from the rock of language. The second criticism is H's pessimistic outlook; the rainfall in H's verse is excessive.

878 Lynd, Robert. "The Uses of Poetry," in SHAKESPEARE TO HARDY, ed by A[lgernon] Methuen (Lond: Methuen, 1922), pp. ix–xxvii.

[Only incidental references to H. Reprints six H poems.]

879 M., H. W. "The Apology of Thomas Hardy," NATION AND ATHENAEUM (Lond), XXXI (3 June 1922), 345–46.

In *Late Lyrics and Earlier,* H creates "ghostly music" which is second only to Poe's. H is a supreme English artist. His comments on society are well worth considering.

880 Macy, John. "Thomas Hardy," THE CRITICAL GAME (NY: Boni & Liveright, 1922), pp. 237–44.

H brought the English novel into close affinity with the French and the Russians. In *The Dynasts* he created a new mythology; it is the greatest epic since WAR AND PEACE. But in reaction against the saccharine optimism of his contemporaries he comes close to falsifying life. He is not [?] a realist; he is a great romantic, incurably superstitious.

881 Meissner, Paul. "Der Bauer in der englischen Literatur" (The Farmer in English Literature), BONNER STUDIEN ZUR ENG-LISCHEN PHILOLOGIE (Bonn Studies in English Philology) (Bonn: Peter Hanstein, 1922), pp. 159–96.

H has brought regional literature to its zenith, surpassing the works of Wordsworth, Crabbe, the Brontës, and George Eliot. The term pessimist does an injustice to H whose Weltanschauung is far more complex. H is an apostle of truth and has chosen Wessex as his medium. Central to all Hardian thought is the opposition of the intellect and the will. This disharmony is the source of all man's conflicts. Attempting to solve this conflict

H examined nature, which is the key to this problem. There are two essential aspects involved in H's treatment of nature: (1) nature as an organism with its own soul and (2) the affinity of man and nature. [Discusses H's technique and focuses upon H's realistic descriptions and subjectivity. Treats the spiritual life of the characters—their naive piety, fetishisms and super-stitions. Concentrates on the practical life of the peasant (his joy in holidays, alcohol) and the relationship of the characters.] [In German.]

882 Meylan, Paul. "In the Country of Thomas Hardy," HARPER'S MONTHLY MAGAZINE, CXLIV (April 1922), [Unpaged].
[Drawings of scenes from H's novels. "Weatherby" Cottage (*Far From the Madding Crowd*); Wollbridge house, Norman Church, and Bingdon Abbey of *Tess of the d'Urbervilles*; view of Corfe Castle, the "Corvsgate" of *The Hand of Ethelberta*.]

883 "Mr. Hardy's Poems," TIMES LITERARY SUPPLEMENT (Lond), 1 June 1922, p. 359.
The "Apology" in *Late Lyrics and Earlier* is important for its objection to the charge of pessimism. The poems, from all periods of H's verse, show the "high level of his own peculiar accomplishment." Unlike Romantics, H is concerned with the causes of emotion rather than emotion itself. His effort "is to draw the incident in its essence and particularity."

884 "Mr. Thomas Hardy's Apologia," CONTEMPORARY REVIEW, CXXII (Sept 1922), 400–402.
The poems in *Late Lyrics and Earlier* are melancholy but are "true poetry, true pictures, full of deep thoughts." In his apology, H says that his "pes-simism" is merely a questioning of reality, and, foreseeing a new Dark Age in poetry, issues a trumpet-call to the church. His poem on the armistice slaps the conventional optimist.

885 Murry, John Middleton. THE PROBLEM OF STYLE (Lond: Oxford UP, 1922); rptd (Lond: Oxford Paperbacks, 1960), pp. 24, 29, 32, 48–50, 52–53, 96–97, 138–39.
The simple case of achieved literary art, that is, conscious control by the discipline of metre and rhythm over the perturbing emotion (vision of death, eternity, etc) to lift the poem above the plane of sensational reaction is ex-emplified by "A Broken Appointment." Discursive thinking never plays a dominant part in the most philosophical novelists such as H. H is both a realist and a romantic. In *Tess of the d'Urbervilles*, H's treatment of Tess and Angel Clare is beyond rational explanation. It is H's power to gather up the sense and significance of human life into a story of a woman's love for man. For H, the greatest living master of English literature, the novel form went against the grain; H preferred poetry, and his later years show astonishing poetical achievements. Unable to accept current poetic forms,

H resurrected the dead form of poetic drama. *The Dynasts* is unwieldly because it disciplines severely the true creative impulse. In the last stanza of "Neutral Tones" H successfully finds a symbol that compels the mind of the reader to share the emotion H intended him to share. Insofar as "the grand style" requires appropriate thoughts and emotions, H has the "grand style" as Milton had it.

886 Phelps, William Lyon. "As I Like It," SCRIBNER'S MAGAZINE, LXXII (Nov 1922), 629; rptd in As I LIKE IT (NY: Scribner's, 1923), pp. 40–43.

H's poems in *Late Lyrics and Earlier* show an old man's splendid vitality. The prose preface belies a persecution. H should not resent the label "pessimist," for it is not one of dishonor. H's kindness and gentleness to all living things demonstrates that he is not so unfeeling, however, as the term "pessimist" might imply.

887 Powys, Llewelyn. "Glimpses of Thomas Hardy," DIAL, LXXII (May 1922), 286–90.

[Powys reminisces about seeing H when he was a boy; H's comments on church architecture, his interest in country dances; later at Max Gate and Dorchester, sights reminded Powys of H's novels. H was full of interesting conversation concerning Keats and other subjects.]

888 Pyre, J. F. A. "Introduction," *The Mayor of Casterbridge*, ed by J. F. A. Pyre (NY: Harper, 1922), pp. ix–xxxii.

H's genius found itself in novels. *Far From the Madding Crowd, Tess of the d'Urbervilles, The Mayor of Casterbridge, The Return of the Native, Jude the Obscure* are best. Characteristics of H's novels include: dramatic method, coincidences and parallelisms, picturesque settings, and extravagant action. Harmony is noted between natural setting, rustics, and main action. *Native* is most gorgeous of the novels, but *Mayor* is the noblest; its grandeur stems not from the setting, as in *Native*, but from the moral impressiveness of the central human figure. In *Mayor*, H does not suffer from an overconcern with sexual impulses: "One yearns for the fist of a Henchard to bang a little manliness into Jude."

In *The Woodlanders*, irony derives from purely human factors. *Tess* has great scenes and is the most vital and adorable of H's women, but the whole is melodramatic and journalistic. *Jude* is unnecessarily sordid and hopeless to the point of morbidity. [Pyre objects to naturalism as a school.]

H's style is not excitable; he relies more than other novelists on specific locality stamped with seriousness and veracity. Stories hinge on relationships between main characters and surroundings, and they reach after first principles. Characters move naturally, logically, and fatally to cosmic dilemma. Our inherent impulse to satisfy innate desires lies at the root of our problems. Those who demand much of life are overthrown by a natural sequence of disastrous coincidences. Circumstances and hereditary instinct combine to baffle the strugglings of our "voluntary and rational and better selves."

H is a positive thinker who refuses to seek consolations unwarranted by Nature. He teaches renunciation and passivism, but apathetic acceptance is not the final answer. H's interest is where "the ourselves" is alone with the "not ourselves." He enlarges our perception of life.

889 Squire, John Collings. "Poetry," LONDON MERCURY, VI (July 1922), 317–18.
Late Lyrics and Earlier merits high praise; H is better now than he was at sixty.

890 William-Ellis, A. "Poets and Poetry: Mr. Thomas Hardy as Poet," SPECTATOR (Lond), CXXIX (8 July 1922), 54.
In *Late Lyrics and Earlier* we see "an admirable brain expressing itself comparatively badly." H "has not conquered the resources of his medium." The "witty and ironic apology," or preface, is "worth all the pages of verse added together."

1923

891 Abercrombie, Lascelles. "Mr. Hardy's Play," NATION AND ATHENAEUM, XXXIV (29 Dec 1923), 491.
In *The Famous Tragedy of the Queen of Cornwall,* H reduces the splendid story to "passionless, naïve simplicity" in which the two Iseults confront each other with the abstract enmity of two eternally opposite natures. Not one of the great versions of the story, this play is "a sort of epitome of its author's idiosyncrasies." H invests the "simplified action with language of harsh and intricate oddity."

892 Adcock, Arthur St. John. "Thomas Hardy," GODS OF MODERN GRUB STREET (NY: Stokes, 1923), pp. 3–9.
The critics killed H, the novelist, and "from the ashes of the novelist, Phoenix-like, rose Thomas Hardy, the poet." *Under the Greenwood Tree* has more charm than any of H's tales, except *The Trumpet-Major.* The distinctive H touch can be seen in the sketches of country life, the characterizations, the precise style, the realism, and the humor and irony. Though

H's irony and view of realism grow more bitter as he grows older, his compassion and understanding of human weaknesses grow more bitter in capacity also. *Tess of the d'Urbervilles* and *Jude the Obscure* place H as one of the world's greatest novelists. H's grim, stoical philosophy of life is implicit in his novels. His novels are "joined by a religion of nature." Men and women are victims of heredity and environment—pawns of time. There was a controversy over the "morality" in *Tess*. Though H's view is less conventional, in the long run it is more noble and fundamental than that view of the orthodox religion of the time. H has little faith in humanity, but infinite compassion. He depicted the irony in life especially well. There was a public outcry at *Jude,* when H's talents were at their zenith. H then turned to poetry and exhibited his sincere, but sombre, philosophy of life in *The Dynasts*. There are no literary ancestors for H's literary style. He stands in a class of his own and few followers of H can imitate him well.

893 Anderson Galleries. LIBRARY OF JOHN QUINN: PART TWO [D–H] (NY: Anderson Galleries, 1923), pp. 375–81.
[One-paragraph biographical sketch; H items 3766–3834 listed in sale 1783.]

894 Armstrong, Martin. "Poets and Poetry: TRISTRAM AND ISEULT," SPECTATOR (Lond), CXXXI (8 Dec 1923), 904.
The Famous Tragedy of the Queen of Cornwall is a "masterly piece of construction," in that H chooses "the psychological moment when events are rushing together to the final catastrophe" and yet manages to supply the "antecedent facts at once completely and with extraordinary economy." A "real and moving" play, despite "an occasional dryness to the poetry."

895 Arns, Karl. "Bemerkungen zu Hardys Lyrik" (Observations on Hardy's Lyrics), ZEITSCHRIFT FÜR FRANZÖSISCHEN UND ENGLISCHEN UNTERICHT (Berlin), XXII: 3 (1923), 264–77.
H cannot be classified, but he is a highly talented and versatile artist. [Five or six examples from H's poetry support the following chapters: (1) supernatural motivation, (2) the deterioration of lifeless things, (3) optimism, (4) humor, (5) the mixture of optimism and pessimism, (6) the problem of the enslavement of the human will, (7) the formulation of questions concerning humanity, life, and the world, (8) the death motif, (9) love poems, and (10) the portrayal of married life.] [In German.]

896 Avancini, Bianca. "L'Arte di Thomas Hardy" (The Art of Thomas Hardy), ATHENAEUM (Pavia, Italy), ns I (Oct 1923), 280–88.
Like the Italian writers Giovanni Verga, Grazia Deledda, Marino Moretti, and others, H was by choice a regional writer: in Wessex he created a real countryside in which his marionette-like figures act out their tragic lives.

Like those of Balzac and Zola, H's characters often recur in different novels or poems. H was best at creating female protagonists; complex males like Jude or Fitzpiers are rather rare. Humor is confined to H's lesser figures, for the author sees little happiness possible in human life. In his gravity and gray style, H resembles Bazin, but he lacks that writer's faith in religion. Instead, for H the gods make sport of man's suffering, and life ends in nothingness. The divine and the providential are missing from H, and his unalleviated pitiless pessimism constricts the breadth of his artistic vision. [In Italian.]

897 Bagshaw, William. "Thomas Hardy," Manchester Quarterly, CLXVI (April 1923), 99–114.

The philosophy implicit in H's works is neither optimistic nor pessimistic: "it is rather one of futility and hopelessness." Compared with Nietzsche's and Schopenhauer's, H's "cosmic will is not a will; it is a routine," a kind of "great forsightless mechanism." H's genius is essentially poetic, and "he is most a poet when writing prose; for he has not the instinctive mastery of poetic technique of the great poet." In *The Woodlanders* and *The Mayor of Casterbridge,* H's novelistic powers are at their height. H's conception of life "is disheartening and sad"; "he has not given a fair innings to lucky accidents and happy chances."

898 Bailey, John. The Continuity of Letters (Lond: Oxford UP, 1923), pp. 234–37.

The great historical figures of H's *The Dynasts* are generally "far less successful creations in Mr. Hardy's hands than the crowds, the common soldiers, and the obscure people." Except in some of the lyrics, "Thomas Hardy has elected not to be a poet in *The Dynasts.*" He fails to clothe great men in great poetry. "To the understanding of Napoleon, the poet of *The Dynasts* contributes nothing."

899 Barton, J. E. "The Poetry of Thomas Hardy," in The Art of Thomas Hardy, by Lionel Johnson (Lond: Lane; NY: Dodd, Mead, 1923, "to which is added a chapter on the poetry, by J. E. Barton, and a bibliography by John Lane . . ."); rvd and rptd (NY: Dodd, Mead, 1928); rptd as The Poetry of Thomas Hardy (Mount Durand, St. Peter Port, Guernsey: Toucan P, 1969).

No poet surpasses H in writing from experience. He is not spontaneous, but careful and precise. He is neither sentimental nor a practitioner of the "shallow Bohemianism" of the rebellious poetasters. "Clear emotion" through "restrained expression" makes H a great poet. His use of realistic detail, understatement, gruesome irony and humor, concrete images, and "poetic observation" add to the effectiveness of his poems. The "central Hardy . . . assigns eternal value to great moments of experience." "To encounter supreme moments unwittingly . . . is tragic": this is H's basic theme. Stylistically, H avoids both obscurity and any set poetic diction, prefering to be a "cosmopolitan among words." He utilizes architectural training and is influenced by the "free continuous rhythm" of old English music. [For other Toucan Press pamphlets see J. Stevens Cox (pub and general editor), Monographs on the Life of Thomas Hardy (1962).]

> **900** Bleibtreu, Karl. GESCHICHTE DER ENGLISCHEN LITERATUR MIT EINSCHLUSS DER AMERIKANISCHEN (History of English Literature, including American) (Bern & Leipzig: E. Bircher, 1923), p. 543.

[Confused H with Arthur Sherburne Hardy.] [In German.]

> **901** Brennecke, Ernest, Jr. "Thomas Hardy's First Real Play," NEW YORK TIMES BOOK REVIEW, 30 Dec 1923, p. 6.

The Famous Tragedy of the Queen of Cornwall gave no "great sweep" like *The Dynasts*; no "thrill" as in *The Return of the Native*, partly because of distractions: "crashing stage machinery and audible promptings, ill-fitting costumes." The play follows strictly Aristotle's ART OF POETRY, and while not H's crowning achievement when measured against *Dynasts*, is a great accomplishment for a man of 83.

> **902** Brown, Ivor. "At Dorchester," SATURDAY REVIEW (Lond), CXXXVI (8 Dec 1923), 613–14.

The weakness of *The Famous Tragedy of the Queen of Cornwall* does not lie in dramatic values or philosophy but in the combination of rare and strained words with a prosaic diction that approaches bathos. "The clash of Mark, Tristan, and the two Iseults at Tintagel comes with brief violence, and is shot through with the author's violent compassion." "O Jan! O Jan! O Jan!" was based on H's memories of the play-acting of an old Wessex ditty. *The Play of Saint George* fits into a H evening because he described how it should be done in *The Return of the Native*.

> **903** Collison-Morley, Lacy. "Pessimism and Poetry," EDINBURGH REVIEW, CCXXXVII (April 1923), 338.

The calm and reflective H and the passionate James Thomson are related to the pessimistic Italian poet Leopardi.

> **904** Cosens, W. B. "The Hardy Players and *The Famous Tragedy of the Queen of Cornwall,*" DORSET COUNTY CHRONICLE, 6 Dec 1923, p. 3.

"Long live the Hardy players and confusion to their critics, who are destructive of progress in literary education!"

> **905** Davis, Frederick Hadland. "The Hardy Players," DRAMA, XIII (Aug–Sept 1923), 359–60.

One can enjoy the H plays, "especially their song, dance and rustic humour, but when we see one it is like . . . looking at a picture through a cloud of smoke." The best of the H plays is *The Mellstock Quire*. [Contains comments on the eight H plays produced between 1909–1920.]

906 Davis, F. Hadland. "The Women of Thomas Hardy," DORSET YEARBOOK, 1923, pp. 44–49.

"Tess is the one woman in the Wessex novels whose creation is for all time." Her character, "intensely human and . . . loyal," makes her "supremely memorable." Jude is wrong in his accusation of Sue as unfeminine: "She was a woman to her finger-tips, but she regarded love as a rollicking adventure." In the end, Marty South "rises to a sublimity that places her near Tess herself." The best of H's women "are those who are most conscious of the blight [of this world] . . . of the inexorable struggle that in the end proves too strong for them."

907 " 'A Desperate Remedy,' " DORSET YEARBOOK, 1923, pp. 106–12.

For the London production by The Hardy Players of *Desperate Remedies* the adapter, Mr. Tilley, preferred to emphasize the comic and minimize the melodramatic and tragic aspect of H's novel.

908 Döll, Martha. DIE VERWENDUNG DER MUNDART BEI THOMAS HARDY (The Use of Speech in Thomas Hardy) (Giessen: Otto Meyer, 1923); Giessen University dissertation.

Investigates phonetics—vowels and consonants—and the accidence of articles, nouns, adjectives, pronouns, and verbs of the Dorset dialect in *Under the Greenwood Tree, A Pair of Blue Eyes, The Hand of Ethelberta, The Trumpet-Major, The Mayor of Casterbridge, Life's Little Ironies, Tess of the d'Urbervilles* and *Jude the Obscure*. [An important linguistic contribution.] [In German.]

909 Douglas, James. "The Sad Error of Thomas Hardy," DAILY EXPRESS, 3 Feb 1923, p. 6.

That H's verdict on Mrs. Thompson and on God in "On the Portrait of a Woman about to be Hanged" is wrong will be demonstrated by the author in the next day's SUNDAY EXPRESS [not seen]. Mrs. Thompson is a Tess, not a Clytaemnestra.

910 Fehr, Bernhard. DIE ENGLISCHE LITERATUR DES 19. UND 20. JAHRHUNDERTS (English Literature of the 19th and 20th Centuries) (Berlin: Akademische Verlagsgesellschaft Athenaion, 1923), pp. 49, 253, 313, 320, 343, 358–66, 367, 368, 372, 374, 376, 427–28, 461–63, 471, 483, 485, 508.

Both in his shorter works and in his long accomplishment, *The Dynasts,* H's works show fate, or the individual's idiosyncratic errors of judgment, bringing anguish and disaster. But the pain is compensated for by the art with which H renders his pessimistic impressions of life. [Most extensive treatment of H in German histories of English literature.] [In German.]

911 Fisher, W. E. "Thomas Hardy, Novelist of Country Life," HOLBORN REVIEW, XIV (Oct 1923), 433–43.

H had "unique gifts as a delineator of rural life." He had "a wide sympathy with the varying manifestations of nature," and a "closeness and accuracy of observation rivalled only by the power and fidelity with which he describes what he beholds." H's weakness is that "he is too fond of beholding nature through his . . . own gloomy moods." H's country man is "burlesqued." The country man is "seldom as stupid as Hardy makes him, or as entertaining." However H "is not indifferent to the aspirations of the intelligent country man," as seen in *Jude the Obscure*. The secret of H's fame lies in the fact "that he has made Rural England, intelligible and vocal; and portrayed the short and simple annals of its poor in stories of thrilling power."

912 Furniss, Harry. "Thomas Hardy," STRAND MAGAZINE (Lond), LXVI (Sept 1923), 252–56.

Although "naturally uncommunicative," H is unassuming and kind. None of the many portraits of H which hang in his house do him justice. Apparently H "thinks more of the painter than of himself." Along with Thackeray, he feels that "a man of fifty cannot possibly take an interest in young people's love affairs." His smile reveals a keen sense of humor, a surprising quality for one "who is said to be by nature a pessimist." Having worked for seven years as an architect in London, H knew the city well. Contrary to the opinions of some critics, he did not write of Dorset only through ignorance of London. Although many of his characters seem to be based on real people, he stated: "The most truthful characters in fiction are the purely imaginary." H's reticence is due to his distaste for hero worship, which he considers a "modern disease" caused by "the annual invasion of Americans." Only H himself, with his power of character drawing, could describe himself properly.

913 Gorman, Herbert Sherman. "Hardy and Housman," THE PROCESSION OF MASKS (Boston: B. J. Brimmer, 1923), pp. 171–83.

H and Housman both have deep "consciousness of the dark and serious business of life." Housman is less ironic, his nature not so robust. H recognizes the futility of existence but not tearfully, as does Housman. But both were rebels to the great tradition of mellifluous Victorian poetry and observed life as it was. H was more disturbed over life and its mystery, accepted actualities but was far from pessimism, was instead ironic on a higher plane than pessimism. Pessimism in Housman is translated into a "beautiful and lyrical mood." H is more cerebral, "dominated by the conscious prodding of inquiring will." Housman's verse is felicitous and beautiful in its simplicity, though his "lightfoot lads" are always in the shadow of death. H's Wessex lads suffer disillusionment rather than death. "With an acrid penetration the poet pierces the mask of things and touches the white bone behind." H is an ironic tragedian, Housman a romantic and lyrical tragedian. It is sad to think that they consider their writing of poetry ended, but "they were true to their art . . . an uncompromising achievement of beauty as they saw it."

914 Gorman, Herbert S. "Poems and Lyrics," OUTLOOK (NY), CXXXIII (3 Jan 1923), 35–36.

Late Lyrics and Earlier is H's "best book of poems." H's irony is armor against the futility of life, as in "Epitaph," and his "cold acceptance of actualities" makes him a realist, rejecting mellifluous Victorianism. Where the intellect forces into his poems, H delivers an unspontaneous, broken melody. "The Whitewashed Wall," "On a Discovered Curl of Hair," and "A Woman Driving" have a stark note which approaches the majesty of ancient Greek utterance.

915 Gosse, Edmund. "Mr. Hardy's Tragedy," SUNDAY TIMES (Lond), 18 Nov 1923, p. 8.

The Famous Tragedy of the Queen of Cornwall is "a wonderful performance"—not "a work in the grand style," but "a dramatic interlude in one act."

916 Graves, Robert. "Mr. Hardy and the Pleated Skirt," NATION (Lond), XXXIII (7 July 1923), 451–52; also in NEW REPUBLIC, XXXVIII (12 March 1924), 77–79.

Pleated skirts and H's poetry are returning to style. H's bafflement in a confused age makes him popular again. For H, "whatever may be wrong with Heaven, Earth is honest and wholesome." [Review of *Collected Poems*.]

917 "The Hardy Play," DORSET COUNTY CHRONICLE, 6 Dec 1923, pp. 2–3.

[Staggeringly detailed account of preparation and performance of *The Famous Tragedy of the Queen of Cornwall* by the Hardy Players.]

918 Johnson, Harry. "The Architectural Poems of Thomas Hardy," ARCHITECT'S JOURNAL, 19 Sept 1923, p. 415.

H uses architectural terms more often in his early than in his late poems. In using these terms, he reveals a deep understanding of architecture.

919 Lane, John. "A Bibliography of First Editions [1865–1922]," in THE ART OF THOMAS HARDY, by Lionel Johnson (Lond: Lane; NY: Dodd, Mead, 1923, "to which is added a chapter on the poetry, by J. E. Barton, and a bibliography by John Lane . . ."); rvd and rptd (NY: Dodd, Mead, 1928).

[Superseded by Richard Purdy, THOMAS HARDY: A BIBLIOGRAPHICAL STUDY (1954).]

920 McKie, George [Macfarland]. "Thomas Hardy: Studies in the Modern English Novel," UNIVERSITY OF NORTH CAROLINA EXTENSION BULLETIN: CORRESPONDENCE COURSES, 1923–24, III (1 Sept 1923), pp. 11–12.

[Descriptive brochure in which H is listed second among a group of sixteen British novelists since George Eliot. Included is a brief outline for study and discussion of H's novels.]

921 Mais, Stuart Petre Brodie. "The Poetry of Thomas Hardy," FROM SHAKESPEARE TO O. HENRY (Lond: Richards, 1923); rptd (Freeport, NY: Books for Libraries P [Essay Index Reprint Series], 1968), pp. 282–99.

H is among the first three poets of his age. In his poetry we find his philosophy crystallized, the characteristic pessimism softened. Only in "In Tenebris" does his alienation show, and that is only a mood which passes quickly. Of all the poets of his age he was the most sensitive to the appeal of beauty. Unpoetic words seem used for some secret purpose.

922 Mais, Stuart Petre Brodie. "Thomas Hardy," SOME MODERN AUTHORS (Lond: Grant Richards; NY: Dodd, Mead, 1923), pp. 227–37.

H recognizes the function of poetry as the application of ideas to life. There is a lyrical note in his poetry quite different from the usual idea of H. His poems show much optimism.

923 Milne, James. "Thomas Hardy and the Younger Writers," GRAPHIC, CVIII (17 Nov 1923), 736.

[Qualified praise of *The Famous Tragedy of the Queen of Cornwall*. Includes two of H's drawings of Tintagel Castle.]

924 Moore, George. "George Moore and John Freeman," DIAL (NY), LXXV (Oct 1923), 341–62; rptd as chaps 4–5 in CONVERSATIONS IN EBURY STREET (Lond: Heinemann, 1924), pp. 84–109; and as chaps 5–6 in the "Carra Edition" (NY: Boni & Liveright, 1924), pp. 111–36.

Shelley wrote the best nineteenth-century prose and "Mr. Hardy . . . the worst." In *Tess of the d'Urbervilles,* "the woods and fields . . . are never before our eyes." Tess's confession to Angel demands "soul-revealing words," not H's "abrupt retreat into the past definite." The retreat is due to H's "lack of invention, [or] brain paralysis." [See J. M. Murry's defense of H against Moore in "Wrap Me Up In My Aubusson Carpet," ADELPHI (Lond), I (April 1921), 951–58, espec 955–58.]

925 "Mr. Hardy's New Play," DORSET COUNTY CHRONICLE, 29 Nov 1923, p. 8.

The Famous Tragedy of the Queen of Cornwall is impressive because of "the nobility of its verse, the poignant pathos of the tragedy. . . . The loveliness of the lyrics alone makes the play a priceless heritage of English literature."

926 Müller, Karl Otto. "Das Naturgefühl bei Thomas Hardy im Zusammenhang mit seiner Weltanschauung" (The Attitude toward Nature in Thomas Hardy in Connection with His World View). Unpublished dissertation, University of Jena, 1923.

H employed the sense of sight, smell, hearing, and touch in describing nature. The author's philosophy is bound with his blind devotion to nature and his belief in the Immanent Will. [In German.]

927 "A Mummer's Play." SATURDAY REVIEW (Lond), CXXXVI (29 Dec 1923), 704–5.

In *The Famous Tragedy of the Queen of Cornwall,* H's simulated incompetence is not successfully pseudo-primitive. A few of the lyrics are better than the blank verse but are without the starkness of H at his best. The grouping of the characters, with Mark confronted by the two Iseults in succession, is not as effective in the book as it must be on the stage.

928 Murry, John Middleton. "The Poetry of Thomas Hardy," NEW YORK TIMES BOOK REVIEW, 29 July 1923, p. 5.

All of the poems in *The Collected Poems of Thomas Hardy* have "spiritual honesty." H has faced problems of life and set them down honestly and courageously. Each poem shows loyalty to himself and therefore universal loyalty. As did Shakespeare in his dark period, H finds solace in loyalty.

929 Nevinson, Henry Wood. CHANGES AND CHANCES (Lond: Nisbet; NY: Harcourt, Brace, [1923]), pp. 307–8.

In 1903, H had a peculiar grey-white face like one soon to die; many wrinkles, eyes bluish grey. H spoke of London society and also of early days in Dorset; hangmen, flogging of men and children; stories of magic. [Leslie Stephen insisted upon having a material explanation.]

930 Noyes, Alfred. "Hardy, the Master," Evening News (Lond), 15 Nov 1923.

"The Queen of Cornwall is an interesting experiment; for Mr. Hardy has gone straight back to the beginning of the English drama" to adopt the "method and scheme of the morality plays of the fourteenth century." However, *The Famous Tragedy of the Queen of Cornwall* differs in that "it deals, not with allegorical figures of personification, but with strongly-characterised human figures, and that there is . . . an extraordinary amount of action, psychological as well as physical." In *Queen*, H has given another "object-lesson to those amazing latter-day exponents of English literature who labour under the delusion that the master-writer is one who owes nothing to the past; or is not derivate." H is "at his greatest when he is portraying human character in the medium where he is supreme and among the immortals" and where "he is simply giving a faithful picture of Nature in her larger respect."

931 Noyes, Alfred. "To Thomas Hardy on his Eighty-Third Birthday: Poem," Times (Lond), 3 June 1923, p. 185; rptd in Living Age, CCCXVIII (21 July 1923), 185.

H provides a "breath of hope" in his poetry "for his wrestling soul/Through agonies of denial postulates/All that young eyes affirm." "By his grief for love and hope brought low/Proves that the Highest ne'er would have it so."

932 Phelps, William Lyon. "As I Like It," Scribner's Magazine, LXXIII (June 1923), 758–59; rptd in As I Like It (NY: Scribner's, 1923), pp. 180–82, espec 182.

H, along with Conrad, W. J. Locke, William McFee, and Arthur S. Hardy, has profited as a creative writer from his study of mathematics. H's appearance in a fairly joyous anthology of poems may seem incongruous, but "The Year's Awakening" is an inspiring poem. [Very little of value to the H student here. A review of Mrs. Waldo Richards's High Tide.]

933 Powys, Llewelyn. "Thomas Hardy," Thirteen Worthies (Lond: Richards, 1923), pp. 181–92; rptd, with a preface by Van Wyck Brooks (Freeport, NY: Books for Libraries P, 1966), pp. 209–21.

H's art is dependent on the environment from which he came. His outlook is that of a simple man whose experiences have taught him a "tough, idiosyncratic, earth-bound philosophy." This attitude is conveyed in the technique as well as in the content of his verse.

934 "Primus." "Tramping with Tess," Open Air, June 1923, pp. 4–8.

[Account of a six-day tramp in Tess's country. Illustrated by photographs taken during the visit.]

935 "The Prince and the Poet," LITERARY DIGEST, LXXVIII (25 Aug 1923), 26–27; rptd in LIVING AGE, CCCXVIII (15 Sept 1923), 516–19.

The Prince of Wales visited H at Max Gate. H was not essentially a pessimistic writer, for he pictured man's noble struggle with adverse circumstances. Choruses from *The Dynasts*, set to music especially for the Prince's visit, were sung by village children's choirs as the party approached Dorchester. *Desperate Remedies* was "an experiment in character and form, and not devoid of the characteristics of his temper and thought."

936 Proust, Marcel. A LA RECHERCHE DU TEMPS PERDU (Remembrance of Times Past) (Paris: Gaston Gallimard, 1923), XII, 218 [La Prisionière]; trans by Carl J. Weber as "authentic Proof of Hardy's Genius," in COLBY MERCURY, VI (May 1938), 181.

Characteristic traits which function like musical phrases give authentic proof of genius, as in H's parallelisms and "stone mason's geometry." [In French.]

937 Purdy, Richard L. "*The Famous Tragedy of the Queen of Cornwall*," YALE LITERARY MAGAZINE, LXXXIX (Dec 1923), 114–15.

H's version of this old story "lies closer [in spirit] to Gottfried of Strasburg, and the traditional Celtic story of 'Tristram and Iseult' than many we have had of late." H "has held his position of eminence for almost fifty years and . . . in . . . *Queen* . . . his power has not been lost!"

938 Ralli, Augustus John. "The Heart of the Wessex Novels," NORTH AMERICAN REVIEW, CCXVII (May 1923), 688–97; rptd in CRITIQUES (Lond: Longmans, Green, 1927), pp. 37–48.

[Simple-minded survey of some of the beauties of H's novels.]

939 Reed, A. W. "Thomas Hardy and the Poetic Mind," CHURCH QUARTERLY REVIEW, XCV (Jan 1923), 342–47.

Late Lyrics and Earlier shows that "poetry is what the poet makes of his subject." The volume is courageous; and H is an optimist without illusions. H's rough and ruthless irony compares with that of Housman. The narratives are better than the lyrics.

940 Royde-Smith, N. G. "The Hardy Players at Dorchester," WEEKLY WESTMINSTER, ns I (8 Dec 1923), 178–79.

With *The Famous Tragedy of the Queen of Cornwall* H wished "to write such a simple play as his untrained and ingenuous fellow-townsmen" could perform. The play's blank verse, "fierce, uncompromising often arrestingly colloquial," however, proved too great a challenge for The Hardy Players.

941 Russell, Constance. "Mr. T. Hardy's *Queen of Cornwall*," NOTES AND QUERIES, 13th ser I (8 Dec 1923), 448–49.
[On the Iseult legend and various mentions of it in medieval literature.]

942 Schirmer, W. F. DER ENGLISCHEN ROMAN DER NEUESTEN ZEIT (The Modern English Novel) (Heidelberg: C. Winter, 1923), pp. 54, 59, 64.
Although H and Kipling deserve to be esteemed, their prose is, nevertheless, characteristic of the past generation. [In German.]

943 Selver, P. "Englischer Brief" (English Letter), DAS LITERARISCHE ECHO, XXV (April 1923), 732–33.
Late Lyrics and Earlier contains splendid verses! It gives the impression of a very lonely person—reminiscent of Browning. "According to the Mighty Working" illustrates H's sharp, noble style. [In German.]

944 Spencer, Walter T. FORTY YEARS IN MY BOOKSHOP, ed with introduction by Thomas Moult (Boston & NY: Houghton Mifflin, 1923), pp. 238–40.
[Spencer recalls request from H (c. 1903?) for a Latin Vulgate text; Spencer requested H's signature on a collection of his works being assembled for a charitable cause in America; Spencer recalls unsold copies of H's *Desperate Remedies, Under the Greenwood Tree* and *A Pair of Blue Eyes* (published by John Tinsley) being hawked by "a barrow man . . . under a naptha light on Saturday evenings at the corner of Jackson's Road, Holloway Road."]

945 Squire, John Collings. "Poetry," LONDON MERCURY, IX (Dec 1923), 202.
The Famous Tragedy of the Queen of Cornwall is "too short and broken for any great emotional intensity . . .; its full effect will only be discoverable when it is performed."

946 Stevens, Edwin J. "Impressions of The Hardy Players' Visit to London," DORSET YEARBOOK, 1923, pp. 112–15.
The Hardy Players have attained "notoriety throughout the country . . . not for the brilliance of our acting, but because of the Master hand whose writings we are permitted to portray."

947 "Thomas Hardy at Work," LIVING AGE, CCCXVIII (1 Sept 1923), 428.
[Brief comments on the visit of the Prince of Wales to Max Gate. A description of the study used by H and of his rigorous work schedule follow.]

948 "Tristram and the Mummers," Times Literary Supplement (Lond), 15 Nov 1923, p. 767.

H, long fascinated with the story of Iseult and Tristram, tells it "neither prettified nor brutalized" but "firmly and finely" in *The Famous Tragedy of the Queen of Cornwall*. The distinguishing quality of the play's sentiment is "manly pity." H neither blames nor excuses the lovers, who are not just weak-willed but compelled by fate, reminiscent of Greek tragedy. The characterization is excellent; the play is intended for very simple production.

949 Van Doren, Mark. "Lyrics and Magic," Nation (NY), CXVI (31 Jan 1923), 125.

Late Lyrics and Earlier reinforces H's reputation as the most interesting, living English poet. The harsh involutions of rhythm and the abstruse diction add to the wisdom and wit in the poems, while the conscious and sombre vocabulary reflects the depth of H's philosophy. The best part of the collection is the lyrics.

950 Vinciguerra, Mario. "Note di letteratura inglese: Tomaso Hardy" (Notes on English Literature: Thomas Hardy), Concilio: Revista Mensile de Cultura e Letteratura, I (1923), 59–62; possibly rptd as "Precursori: Thomas Hardy" (Precursors: Thomas Hardy), in Romantici e Decadenti Inglesi (English Romantics and Decadents) (Foligno: Campitelli, [1926]), pp. 147–54 [not seen].

H's negativity is "destructive" and "anarchic." In his work, woman is consistently the instrument whereby Destiny represses man. For H, "love . . . is a concrete and manifest reprisal, a simplification of life's tragic struggle." H affords us only one glimpse of Victorian sentimentality: he envies the ignorant, since they can persist in illusion and think life is happy. [In Italian.]

951 Wood, Butler. " 'Break o' the Day' song mentioned in *Tess of the d'Urbervilles*," Notes and Queries, 13th ser I (14 July 1923), 29.

H was unable to provide requested information on this song, except that he heard "snatches of it when a boy."

952 Zachrisson, Robert Eugen. "Stil och Personlighet i Thomas Hardy's Diktning" (Style and Personality in Thomas Hardy's Writing), Edda (1923), 57–98.

H was an independent and original writer, an inborn mystic, and a man of great contradictions: a Christian without belief, a pessimist and also an optimist, local and yet universal. As novelist H was greatest as a tragedian. He was not cruel for the sake of cruelty. Along with his pessimism he had a love for suffering humanity. He attempted to resolve the struggle between the mysticism of his childhood and the rationalism of his maturity. *The Selected Poems of Thomas Hardy* show that H has a sensitive ear and a facility in linguistic expression which produces a harmony of form and content. He is master builder in words; he has universality of theme and richness of style. [In Swedish.]

1924

953 Aldington, Richard. "Conrad and Hardy," LITERARY REVIEW (NY), V (6 Sept 1924), 8.
"The extraordinary reputation of Mr. Hardy as a novelist is something of a mystery to me." H cannot tell a good story, and he is no artist in words. *Tess of the d'Urbervilles* and *Jude the Obscure* are crude melodrama, as George Moore has pointed out. H's style "is never particularly beautiful and is sometimes almost clumsy." Conrad is a much greater stylist than H.

954 Bevan, William. "The Making of Thomas Hardy, O. M.: Unsolved Problems of his Life and Art," T.P.'S AND CASSELL'S WEEKLY, 22 March 1924, p. 779.
Was H born with the vision that always saw "the cloud above and the clod beneath?" If not, "how did the real Hardy come into being?" To those who know H, there are really "two Hardys": one a cheerful, unassuming, sociable antiquarian, and the other a man "of indomitable will power, of warring and intense passions, of profound melancholy." Must there not have been "some tremendous disillusionments which . . . coloured Hardy's view . . . of life . . .?" Architecture may have been one of them, as *A Laodicean* suggests. Another may have been friendship, as *A Pair of Blue Eyes* suggests.

955 Brennecke, Ernest, Jr. THOMAS HARDY'S UNIVERSE: A STUDY OF A POET'S MIND (Boston: Small, Maynard; Lond: T. Fisher Unwin, 1924); rptd (NY: Russell & Russell, 1966); included in "Thomas Hardy's Universe, and the Life of Thomas Hardy," Columbia University dissertation, 1926.
H, a philosopher by nature, gradually developed "a consistent world-view," a world-view developed "through the notions of Chance and Time, Circumstances, Fate, Nature, Providence, Nemesis, and Will, tinged with metaphysical idealism." That Schopenhauer helped to shape this view ultimately is clear, for H subscribes to the same set of beliefs as the philosopher. Thus both men believe that the Will is indivisible, both advocate Idealistic

Monism, both argue that religion satisfies the "innate metaphysical need" of men who wonder, both plead for a humane attitude towards animals. Ultimately both contend that all the great world movements are manifestations of the Will. Thus, although man does what he wants to do, he wants to do what he does because he is what he is. Furthermore, no essential change of character is possible, as Henchard demonstrates. If actions change from one time to another, this is only because the individual has acquired a fuller understanding of his motives. In saying this, both H and Schopenhauer are subscribing to fatalism, to a view of the universe as "an immense automatic clockwork." In fact, everything is done without purpose, since everything is governed by the Will, a force which controls reason while remaining unconscious. *The Dynasts* and especially the novels of H confirm this; they show that man is a willing rather than a thinking being. Thus, although man has an unlimited capacity for consciousness, he is made to live out a life governed by an unconscious and indifferent Will. H is, then, pessimistic as is Schopenhauer who contends that life "is essentially suffering," but this pessimism does not rule out an occasional but "decided gleam of hope" for both men. Thus H and Schopenhauer, feeling the "*horror vacui*," advocate a positive morality. The philosopher "extols pity and compassion as the basis of a true morality" and the novelist-poet, also advocating pity, hopes that the Immanent Will will gradually become conscious.

956 Cazamian, Louis, and Emile Legouis. HISTOIRE DE LA LITTÉRATURE ANGLAISE (History of English Literature) (Paris: Hachette, 1924); pub as A HISTORY OF ENGLISH LITERATURE. Vol I: "The Middle Ages and the Renascence (650–1660)," by Emile Legouis, trans by Helen Douglas Irvine; Vol II: "Modern Times (1660–1914)," by Louis Cazamian, trans by W. D. MacInnes and the Author (NY: Macmillan, 1927); new ed, rvd and reset, two vols in one (NY: Macmillan, 1929), pp. 1259, 1281, 1283–90, 1238*n*, 1317, 1346, 1367, 1381, 1388, 1389.

The optimism of a preceding age disappears, and science is the source of despair. H weaves the fabric of pessimism in close contact with a joyless earth. H's pessimism acknowledges the mechanical conception of things as an intellectual truth. H denies happiness founded on critical reason and so condemns modern civilization. Because H was brought up in the profession of architect, he has a sense of volumes and balance and knows the process of artistic refining. He knows material and aesthetic character of its outlines. He is influenced by history, and all rests on the Victorian mind: "positive data, a respect for science, curiosity as to the cosmic and human past." He settles into directly opposed beliefs revealed through powerful concrete experiences. Science is joyless. His taste led him to Dorsetshire. H's books ignore new facts of the present-day world and go to the eternal hills and moors which light up the true relationship between the universe and man. H's philosophy grows out of reflection and experience and later turns to the immanent will of Schopenauer. Humans are crushed by blind nature, chance, error of desire.

Far From the Madding Crowd, The Return of the Native, The Mayor of Casterbridge, The Woodlanders, Tess of the d'Urbervilles, Jude the Obscure display the originality of H's temperament. In realistic and psychological terms the dramatic struggle between man and evil takes place. The novels are provincial and rustic. The plots are not simple but grow out of elementary passions. As H progresses he shifts the construction of his novels to the inner world: moral drama crossed incessantly by accidents. Fatal chance is the "third party in all relationships of human beings." Chance expresses cruelty in the universe; reveals laws that the self-deceived individuals ignore; becomes the chastisement of selfishness of every life. Yet there are strong-willed souls who struggle against pain and disease of thought, such as Clym, Henchard, or Jude. H's characters are not drawn with faultless art, but they are "laboriously constructed." He is an architect rather than a poet. H's backgrounds are inspired. They are precise, and his impressions owe nothing to literature. H's descriptions call up immobility, and in this symbolic breadth, they carry the philosophy. H's pessimism is his most instinctive sensibility and imbues all his visions. In *Jude* and *Tess* H renounces alleviation. In his poems H is compact. The beauty is in the concentration. This austere poetry is one of the most vigorous and personal in modern English literature. They are pessimistic. *The Dynasts*, a work of the broadest scope, is unequaled. [Contains a bibliography of the works and editions of H to 1928. Abstract based on 1929 ed.] [In French.]

957 Chew, Samuel C. "Isot Ma Drue, Isot M'Amie," NEW RE-PUBLIC, XXXVIII (27 Feb 1924), 23–24.
In *The Famous Tragedy of the Queen of Cornwall,* the two legends of Iseult are ingeniously telescoped, but the harsh and halting style and uncouth neologisms make the play unpleasant. The prologue, epilogue, and one or two lyrics suggest the naked elemental quality of the story, but most of the play smoulders under the "scoriae of words and rhythms."

958 Darton, F. J. Harvey. "Thomas Hardy's Birthplace: The Literary Shrine of Dorset," T. P.'s AND CASSELL'S WEEKLY, 6 Dec 1924, p. 260.
"In a ten-mile circle around Dorchester lived half of H's characters, stand half his scenes." He "*felt* the places and the people; they are part of whatever he bids them to be; they are not mere descriptive words." Like a chorus in *The Dynasts*, H "has interpreted them, yet without losing intimacy."

959 Drinkwater, John (ed). THE OUTLINE OF LITERATURE (Lond: Newnes, 1924); rvd and extended by Hugh Pollock and Campbell Nairne (Lond: Newnes, 1940); rvd by Horace Shipp (Lond: Newnes, 1950), pp. 552, 658, 685, 694–702.

The greatest achievement of H as novelist was making the English countryside a chorus in his books; judged by this criterion, *The Return of the Native* is his masterpiece. Pathos and poignancy dominate all his works in prose and verse.

960 Fairley, Barker. "The Modern Consciousness in English Literature," ESSAYS AND STUDIES BY MEMBERS OF THE ENGLISH ASSOCIATION, IX (1924), 126–44.

Like most other modern writers, the works of H show a division in the modern consciousness, in his case one between the conscious and the unconscious forces in human life. Shakespeare contrasts man and nature only to indicate their ultimate harmony, but H reveals, on a metaphysical level, the separation between man and nature. Writers like H may appear to foster chaos and not artistic order, but only by treating the modern consciousness as divided can they be honest about their age.

961 Fletcher, John Gould. "The Spirit of Thomas Hardy," YALE REVIEW, ns XIII (Jan 1924), 322–33.

A close connection subsists between H's poetry and fiction: *The Return of the Native* is "a tone-poem"; in *Tess of the d'Urbervilles* "the extreme simplicity of the plot structure . . . recalls . . . the technique of many old ballads." H's work "could never have come into being without the support of a definite philosophy." H is a fatalist: "he sees all phenomena . . . as controlled and ordered by a single Immanent Will." But H also "seeks some means of escape from the logical consequences" of this view of life. Of H's greater novels only in *Tess*, "through the lavish beauty and pathos" H lavishes on Tess, are we allowed "to suspend slightly our judgment on the 'intolerable scheme of things.' " In the poems, H's "narrow fatalism" is overpowered by his sense of tragic triumph, as in Nelson's death in *The Dynasts*. H's achievement is important enough to be compared with Tolstoy, Dostoevski, Ibsen and Nietzsche—the leading nineteenth-century literary figures.

962 Fournier-Pargoire, Jeanne. "La poésie de Thomas Hardy" (The Poetry of Thomas Hardy), REVUE DE L'ENSEIGNEMENT DES LANGUES VIVANTES, XLI (1924), 297–300.

H the novelist is recognized in France as a first-rank artist, but H the poet is still almost entirely unknown. And yet the French public, with the antecedents of Vigny and the modern realist school, is in a sense far better prepared to receive and appreciate H's bitterness and dark strength than the Tennyson-reared English public. The bulk of H's poetry is dramatic poetry; his characters may be mere abstractions (like Nature, Life, Time, Hap, they are passive entities, like puppets "in a sporting hand"), but the realist who wrote *Tess of the d'Urbervilles* and *Jude the Obscure* also borrows his dramas from everyday life, never attenuating or idealizing. But he does show, even in his most desperate poems, the same conclusion Pascal and Vigny have drawn, that "man is nobler than the universe," hence the human interest of H's poetry. [In French.]

963 Freeman, John. ENGLISH PORTRAITS AND ESSAYS (Lond: Hodder & Stoughton, 1924), p. 7–8.

G. K. Chesterton once remarked that the atheistic H was like the village idiot ranting at the sun.

964 Guedalla, Philip. "Mr. Thomas Hardy," A GALLERY (Lond: Constable, 1924), pp. 53–61; rptd in MEN OF LETTERS [Collected Essays of Philip Guedalla, I] (Lond: Hodder & Stoughton, [1927]), pp. 49–61; rptd from unidentified periodical pieces.

British veneration for venerable celebrities is an unhappy tendency, but H has refused to be "caught and stuffed." He insists on continuing to write. He is not the last of any species, including Victorian, but a contemporary. Even in stories laid in the past, there is nothing old-fashioned except perhaps the manner of some of the girls. He is not out-of-date in his philosophy. His withdrawal into poetry is blameless, but *The Dynasts* shows he is still great; it is an "achievement on the fullest scale."

965 "The Hardy Players in Town," DORSET YEARBOOK, 1924, pp. 110–15.

The London production by The Hardy Players of *The Famous Tragedy of the Queen of Cornwall,* is "a play admirable in itself in every way," shows that the play's essential energy works through a machinery of fine artistic investment and restraint. The atmosphere of doom woven by the "Greek chorus" is most successful.

966 Henderson, Archibald. "Mr. Hardy Achieves a Second Immortality," LITERARY DIGEST INTERNATIONAL BOOK REVIEW, II (April 1924), 372–74.

The Dynasts and *The Famous Tragedy of the Queen of Cornwall* show that H is still vigorous and capable of great writing. Much of his work is poor (*The Well-Beloved, The Hand of Ethelberta*), but three qualities give permanence to H's fiction: (1) "a minute, intense, profound preoccupation with the rural life and setting"; (2) "a profound sense of form—the artist's mould for the plastic stuff of character and circumstance"; and (3) "the peculiar, yet fundamentally honest, interpretation of human destiny which he exhibits."

967 Henderson, Archibald. "Thomas Hardy in a New Role," FORUM, LXXI (June 1924), 783–90.

There is much interest in H's new play, *The Famous Tragedy of the Queen of Cornwall,* described by H as "a new version of an old story arranged as a play for mummers." H had had the play in mind for many years. The Dorchester performance was not very satisfactory; the chanters, who are supposed to carry the weight of narration for the very condensed story, were not understandable, and the form of Greek tragedy imposed too much compression on the incidents. The play is not really for "mummers," but "is a close-knit drama which would tax the utmost resources of dramatic and dramaturgic art for successful production." The Hardy Players were up to the level of amateur theatricals, but the play demands more than that.

968 Holmberg, Olle. "Thomas Hardy," LITTERÄRT (Stockholm: Bonnier, 1924), pp. 129–45.

One remembers H's characters not for *what* they are but rather for *where* they are and for what happens to them. One can distinguish between them only on the basis of their fates and their surroundings. Within this rural framework H's novels acquire their calm, sad character. As man grows up in a milieu, he also grows up attached to his work. Almost every one of H's novels is built around a trade or occupation, and the details of everyday work fit like cogs into a machine where the other cogs are the personages and the plots. When H turns from nature to man, from milieu to fate, the idyllist becomes a tragedian: Life is hard and death is empty. H's concept of tragedy is closer to that of the Greeks than to that of Shakespeare or Schiller: man is predestined to suffering. Tragedy strikes from without, sudden and meaningless. But though the nature of H's tragedy is the same as in Euripides, the subject is not. H does not associate suffering with greatness. The misfortunes are bitter, not sublime; fate could as well take the form of pinpricks as the thrust of a lance. Michael Henchard recapitulates the fate of Oedipus. *Tess of the d'Urbervilles* closes with a quote from Aeschylus, and the young heroine's end has much in common with the queenly end of Antigone. Beyond the Greeks, Shakespeare, and the Old Testament, one sometimes can discern a touch of another kind of literature: the *Schicksal*-tragedies and novels à la Eugène Sue, serialized stories with the typical ingredients of mistaken identities, unexpected coincidences, bigamy, revealed secrets, strange disappearances, etc. H has ennobled the old sentimental and scary topics, but he has not been able to do without the basic ingredients. H's novels are built of fates put into a milieu of nature and work. His characters are figures in the landscape, carriers of the plot and of the sad, soft wisdom. [In Swedish.]

969 Holmes, Rev. John Haynes. "Anatole France's Successor," NEW YORK TIMES BOOK REVIEW, 16 Nov 1924, p. 12.
H is the greatest poet since Milton, but the Frenchman Romain Rolland is the true successor to France.

970 Jordan-Smith, P. "Thomas Hardy," ON STRANGE ALTARS (NY: Boni, 1924), pp. 80–97.
H's personality is almost Shakespearean; he leads us into the presence of the tragic and makes a gesture significant of profound pity. Although labeled a realist, we are unable to escape a feeling that immanent everywhere in his universe is the miraculous. By knowing one background, Wessex, he is able to set his stage with the power of a Greek dramatist. His novels are autochthonous. He knows very well the interplay of the tragic and of the trivial. He sees man a victim of unseen forces both within and without (Henchard and Tess). He knows the value of simplicity without pretense and the wisdom that comes with the homely life; his "intruders" (in nearly every case, a "gentleman" or a "lady") have no depth of love, no constancy of passion. In his judgment upon the indifference of the universe and the blindness of our nature, H is certainly no optimist; neither is he a pessimist, for he has been purged of bitterness through pity. The darkness that overhangs his books is not that which comes from a certain blindness to the good in human hearts; it is born of a frank recognition of the discrepancy between what one longs for and what one receives, for example, H's poem "Going and Staying," which is somewhat reminiscent of Heine's "Prolog."

971 Lucas, F. L. "Masefield, Hardy, Symons," NEW STATESMAN, XXII (2 Feb 1924), 484–85.
The Famous Tragedy of the Queen of Cornwall has a quietness of tone, an absence of striving, designed to suit the mummers' manner; it is the calm of a veteran writer who needs to strain no more. It is a rather dull piece except for the bewitching frontispiece.

972 Marshall, Archibald. "*Under the Greenwood Tree*," LITERARY DIGEST INTERNATIONAL BOOK REVIEW, II (Feb 1924), 187, 236.
Under the Greenwood Tree "is packed full of humor and the tenderness that comes from love and knowledge." Perhaps this is the "most enjoyable" of all H's books. "The story is nothing apart from its characters, and those characters are, with only one exception, taken from the English peasantry, of whom Hardy is the Laureate." "Rich, racy humor" abounds in this book. Henry James is wrong in condemning H's style. H uses more "Romance words" to convey his meaning, and they give to the fiction what becomes "peculiarly his voice."

973 Martin, Dorothy [Mrs. L. C.]. "Thomas Hardy's Lyrics,"
FREEMAN (NY), VIII (30 Jan and 6 Feb 1924), 490–92, 515–16.
H is a conscientious, successful and original metrist. Even in his early
verse he turned his back to the melodious flow of Victorians. He fashions
poetry of an austere, architectural order. Since economy and precision are
H's outstanding characteristics, it is not surprising that he allows hard,
jagged consonants to clog his lines. He is more successful in the old ballad-
metres, which he adjusts to his modern themes while infusing them with
much of their native energy and swing ("The Workbox," "The Well-
Beloved"). It is significant of H's interest in form that the first poem of his
first book of verse is a sapphic ode. He tried the "terza rima" more frequently ("In a Cathedral City," "A Plaint to Man") because of the effect
of organic growth and progression inherent in its design. He failed distinctly
in "The Alarm," which gives the effect of prose cut into lengths and rhymed.
In "I Said to Love," form and emotion dilate and dwindle in perfect harmony.

The strong beat of his poetry is often akin to the vigorous rhythm of old
psalm-tunes, dialect, and folk-song ("In Time of 'the Breaking of Nations' "). In "Voices from Things Growing in a Churchyard," in the midst
of longer lines which rise and fall like the wind, come the three short
reiterated lines with their sharp click and rattle as of dry bones. Condensa-
tion of time and thought can be perilous for H as in *Satires of Circumstance*
which contain lines of full "potted history," little more than prosaic doggerel. H, intellectually far ahead of his time in the nineteenth-century, is the
prophet of the poetry of the twentieth; he does for this time of philosophical
disintegration and probing what the "metaphysical" poets did for the
Jacobean and Caroline era.

974 Montenegro, E. "Estudios sobre la novela inglesa: George
Meredith y Thomas Hardy" (Studies in the English Novel: George
Meredith and Thomas Hardy), NOSOTROS, XLVII (1924), 181–
92.
A close association with the country inspired the art and informed the
vision of both George Meredith and H, but while it led Meredith to a
courageous optimism, it led H to a moral nihilism. More than any other
contemporary novelist, moreover, H approaches the Hellenic ideal in his
conception of the divine beauty of the land. This love, however, is just one
aspect of his vision. H's conception of an inexorable governing diety
envelops him and his work in a somber pessimism unique in the annals of
English literature. H's scientific and artistic education, moreover, explains
the classically severe and ordered beauty of his work, of which *Tess of the
d'Urbervilles* is the masterpiece. Finally, in *Tess* and indeed in all of his

novels, the bitter moral is that the innocent are punished and the guilty escape with public sanction at the least: no matter how insignificant, every man is linked with the eternal truths. [In Spanish.]

975 Morgan, John H[artman]. JOHN, VISCOUNT MORLEY: AN APPRECIATION AND SOME REMINISCENCES (Lond: John Murray; Boston & NY: Houghton Mifflin, 1924), pp. v, 23, 31, 52, 84, 136, 180.

"[I] was the cause of his writing another and a better" novel after rejecting his first. Lord Morley's "admiration for Hardy . . . was wholehearted and complete." [Mostly passing references.]

976 Morris, Lloyd. "Mr. Hardy's Version of a Famous Love Story," LITERARY DIGEST INTERNATIONAL BOOK REVIEW, II (Jan 1924), 111, 113.

"It was almost inevitable that Thomas Hardy should finally turn to the legend of Tristram and Iseult." In *The Famous Tragedy of the Queen of Cornwall,* H makes the lovers the victims of destiny. They are like modern people, also subject to fate's will. Despite compression and restraint in treating action, the characters are good. H worked on the play from 1916 to 1923. He "has written for the ear, the emotions, and the imagination rather than the eye."

977 Muir, Edwin. "The Novels of Mr. Hardy," LITERARY REVIEW (NY), IV (7 June 1924), 801–2.

All H's characters are similar: "They all stand by themselves, and the immediate protagonist is fate," of a particularly Hardyan kind: while "the Greek fate was inevitable, the final expression of law, . . . Mr. Hardy's fate is deliberately perverse." H views man as noble, the universe as mean. He gives his characters "the emotions which have always moved mankind—those few passions, fears, and hopes which are universal." "In his portrayal of the moods of nature and of woman he is marvelously true; in great scenes of passion and of calamity, where any philosophy, deterministic or consoling, seems equally idle, he writes as if he were the impersonal mouthpiece of the sorrow and desire of humanity."

978 "Nobel Prize for Hardy," NEW YORK TIMES, 4 May 1924, II, p. 2.

John Macy, publicity chairman of the P.E.N. Club, announced that New York Club had wired John Galsworthy and Anatole France (presidents of British and French P.E.N. Clubs) asking them to help urge H upon Sweden as candidate for the Nobel Prize.

979 Parker, W. M. "Christmas With Thomas Hardy," FORTNIGHTLY REVIEW, CXVI (Dec 1924), 804–16.

Various Christmas scenes in H's novels and stories are suitable for reading during the season, especially those in *Under the Greenwood Tree.* H used Christmas scenes for fun, drama, and pathos.

980 Parker, W. M. "The Jubilee of *Far From the Madding Crowd*," CORNHILL MAGAZINE, ns LVI (Jan 1924), 119–26.
"Nothing quite like *Far From the Madding Crowd* was written before 1874." [Surveys the beauties of the novel and the critical reception it received.]

981 Parker, W. M. ON THE TRACK OF THE WESSEX NOVELS. A GUIDE TO THE HARDY COUNTRY (Poole, England: J. Looker, 1924).
[In a guidebook "meant to assist visitors to Dorset," Parker cites the many parallels between the fictitious places in the Wessex novels and the actual places in Dorset. For example, Dorchester is the basis of Casterbridge, St. Thomas is the place where Sue and Phillotson are said to have married, and Lulworth Cove is where Troy went for a swim.]

982 Purdy, Richard L. "On a Portrait of Thomas Hardy," YALE LITERARY MAGAZINE, LXXXIX (March 1924), 233–36.
After the appearance of *Far From the Madding Crowd*, H was marked as a pessimist "with an almost casual simplicity." In the next twenty years H's novels were interpreted with "an absolute misconstruction of the spirit which brooded over them and their author." There is need of a new evaluation of H. In his championship "of the essential elevation and nobility of man's soul, of the grandeur of the human struggle . . . there is something which transcends the barren limits of the pessimist."

983 Richards, I. A. PRINCIPLES OF LITERARY CRITICISM (Lond: Kegan Paul, Trench, Trubner; NY: Harcourt, Brace, 1924; 1930), pp. 114, 129, 130, 197.
[Four references to H to illustrate points about literary criticism.]

984 Sanden, Gertrud von. "Die Väter des modernen Romans in England" (The Fathers of the Modern English Novel), DIE HILFE, No. 20 (1924), 367–69, espec 367.
[General, short survey of H's life and works.] [In German.]

985 Shafer, Robert. FROM BEOWULF TO THOMAS HARDY (Garden City, NY: Doubleday, Page, 1924), II, 757.
[A brief sketch of H's life, career, and reputation introduces eleven pages of his poems.]

986 Sherman, Stuart P. "Thomas Hardy," MEN OF LETTERS (NY: Rudge, 1924), pp. 75–76.

More than a recorder, H interpreted and created a world of splendor as well as blight, ruled by a paradoxical God. His heroes are stalwart, his heroines dangerously beautiful, and their love ruined by chance and human frailty.

987 Smith, Robert Metcalf. "The Philosophy in Thomas Hardy's Poetry," NORTH AMERICAN REVIEW, CCXX (Dec 1924), 330–40.
To understand H's philosophy, the poetry is indispensable. His efforts to answer the age-old problem of "the presence of evil and the incongruity of penalizing the irresponsible" fall into two groups: those poems that question the orthodox theism of H's early years and the statements in *The Dynasts*. In many poems H questioned the three attributes of Power, Wisdom and Love with which the Creator has been endowed (cf. the word *unwittingly* in "By the Earth's Corpse"). After bidding farewell to Christian comfort, H ceased to attempt to reconcile life with the Deity of tradition and began working out his own constructive philosophy. In "Nature's Questioning," he ventured several proposals, all equally somber. Retaining his former denial of omniscience, H suggested that the cosmic flow of circumstance is the working of an Immanent Will, all-powerful, but blind and purposeless ("The Lacking Sense," "Doom and She"). The great tragedy for mankind lies in the chance development of sentience. There are two hopes, a practical and a metaphysical. The first is "evolutionary meliorism" (versus "pessimism"); the second may gradually appear as the "sleep-worker" becomes conscious and, perceiving Its misdoings, will " 'fashion all things fair,' " and "patiently adjust, amend, and heal."

988 "Sprache und Literatur" (Language and Literature), BEI-BLATT ZUR ANGLIA, June 1924, pp. 175–81.
In *The Famous Tragedy of the Queen of Cornwall,* H's style is unpretentious, plain, and artistic. As in the novels, H displays his aptitude for symbolic representation, his faithfulness to a region, and his awareness of women's psychology. H is less pessimistic in this work. [In German.]

989 Stewart, Agnes. "*The Dynasts*: A Psychological Interpretation," ENGLISH REVIEW, XXXVIII (May 1924), 666–80.
Modern psychology has demonstrated the significance for the individual of an unresolved split between passion and reason; H has shown this same split on an epic scale in his treatment of the ten crucial years of the Napoleonic Wars. In *The Dynasts* the poet treats the evolution of all of Europe in terms of this conflict between passion and reason. Napoleon becomes the instrument of his own defeat, for H's intuition led him to portray the Will as man's own, not some outward force. The evolution that this epic portrays is therefore not mechanistic, but creative, thanks to H's instinctual grasp of the action he portrays.

990 "Theatre Arts Bookshelf: Other New Books: *The Famous Tragedy of the Queen of Cornwall*," THEATRE ARTS (NY), VIII (April 1924), 281.

This "one-act poetic playing version" of Tristram and Iseult does not increase H's "stature as a poet," but it is another tribute to the power of the story.

991 "Thomas Hardy and the Nobel Prize," LIVING AGE, CCCXXI (21 June 1924), 1212.

Since Yeats has been awarded the Nobel Prize, it seems unfair that H has not yet been the recipient of such an honor. The charge of pessimism is also unfair if one recalls the admiration accorded Strindberg. "An inability to appreciate Hardy could only be explained by an inability to appreciate good literature altogether, or by sheer ignorance."

992 Tomlinson, May. "*Jude the Obscure*," SOUTH ATLANTIC QUARTERLY, XXIII (Oct 1924), 335–46.

Sue was unique to the reader in 1896 because "she was a curious mixture of fearlessness and sensitiveness." Arabella is "careless." Phillotson is admirable. There is no good reason for Sue and Jude's objecting to the marriage ceremony. There is "an all-pervading sweetness" which brightens the dark scenes in the story, and the easy style shows the work of a master.

993 Van Doren, Mark. "Thomas Hardy's Tristram," NATION (NY), CXVIII (9 Jan 1924), 38.

Since the Tristram legend was a local one, it was a natural choice for H in *The Famous Tragedy of the Queen of Cornwall*. Although the story has been reduced to the barest minimum, the book succeeds as beautiful and intense poetry.

994 Veldkamp, J. "The Tristram-legend and Thomas Hardy," NEOPHILOLOGUS, IX (July 1924), 286–93.

H uses Bédier's Tristram legend rather than Malory's and adds his own pessimistic view of marriage to make *The Famous Tragedy of the Queen of Cornwall*. Swinburne's view of Tristram and Iseult as victims of fate also attracted H. In some lines of the story H's view of dark, blind fate is jarring. H speaks with the voice of twentieth-century realism more than with that of medieval romanticism.

995 Wade, John Donald. AUGUSTUS BALDWIN LONGSTREET (NY: Macmillan, 1924), pp. 178–80.

The similarity of passages in Longstreet's GEORGIA SCENES (1835) and *The Trumpet-Major* did not result from H's deliberate plagiarism of Longstreet. H said he used C. H. Gifford, HISTORY OF THE WARS OCCASIONED BY THE FRENCH REVOLUTION (Lond: 1817). Ultimately a source common to Longstreet and Gifford—perhaps a sketch by Oliver Prince—caused the illusion that H had stolen from GEORGIA SCENES.

996 West, Rebecca. "Interpreters of Their Age," SATURDAY REVIEW OF LITERATURE, I (16 Aug 1924), 41–42.
H's novels are of "unequal merit," and he had little influence on the life of his time; novels like *The Well-Beloved* show no aesthetic quality. His priestly sacramental quality makes him greater than Shaw, however, because he shows the modern sense of meaningless tragedy awaiting the common man. [Most of the essay is a review of Forster's PASSAGE TO INDIA.]

997 Whitmore, Charles E. "Mr. Hardy's *Dynasts* as Tragic Drama," MODERN LANGUAGE NOTES, XXXIX (Dec 1924), 455–60.
The Dynasts has a place in the general current of dramatic tradition. The main artistic effect of the play is achieved in the first part. *Dynasts* parallels medieval French drama—the PASSION of Arnoul Greban—and oratorio—in the use of "Spirits" as soloists and chorus, entering "from nowhere"—both of which are distinct early Christian forms.

998 "Why Thomas Hardy Did Not Get the Nobel Prize," LIVING AGE, CCCXX (23 Feb 1924), 381–82.
H has not been the recipient of the prize because "his dark naturalism, with its deterministic psychology and pessimistic outlook, does not fulfill the requirements," i.e., the "idealistic direction" clause stipulated by Nobel. H also has technical strikes against him: "His form is heavy and restrained. The development of his action is often unreasonably slow, and the atmosphere heavy with its gloomy monotony." Contemporary admiration for H is exaggerated.

999 Williams, Randall. THE WESSEX NOVELS OF THOMAS HARDY: AN APPRECIATIVE STUDY (Lond: Dent, 1924).
H recognizes in all his tragedies "the necessity for obedience to moral law" but is always compassionate in his treatment. H was a master of the short tale as well as the novel. He uses selectivity, impressionism, and irony. In the novels of ingenuity (*Desperate Remedies, The Hand of Ethelberta* and *A Laodicean*) the plots are mechanically contrived. *Ethelberta* is the worst of H's productions. The form of his works shows the hand of the architect; his character and scenic delineation, that of the painter; his sensitivity to Nature's sounds, that of the musician; and his wide range of sympathies, that of one cognizant of "the beauty of human character." "Hardy is faithful to those principles which make for what is noble, beautiful, and permanent in artistic expression." H's novels center around strong, independent,

highly individual women. He is "one of the most faithful and chivalrous delineators of woman's mind and character." H is "unequalled except when we think of Shakespeare, in representing with piquancy and geniality a phase of English rural life which is now moribund." The "author seeks to reveal to us the intrinsic power of cosmic forces, the inmost Necessity and Truth of natural laws which men find incomprehensible but to which they must submit." "He finds that the tragedy of life springs from the fact that man possesses an impulse of self-determination whose origin is wrapt in mystery and whose operation is that of tragic revolt against an implacable law of Necessity controlling man's instincts and aspirations." "His temperament is the result of the adjustment of these qualities—humour, picturesqueness, and poetry."

1000 Wyeth, N. C. "Illustration for Hardy's Poem 'The Midnight Revel,' " McCall's Magazine, LII (Dec 1924), 8–9.
[Two-page color illustration of nine startled carolers, with lanterns and instruments, encountering a towering "figure against the moon" on Egdon Heath. Wyeth has given the diaphanous creature two antennae and a billowing cape.]

1925

1001 Abercrombie, Lascelles. The Idea of Great Poetry (Lond: Martin Secker, 1925), pp. 154–57.
Although *The Dynasts* will someday be compared "with the great poems of Europe," the depiction of individuals as no more than "fingers" of a capricious and impersonal Will prevents it from having the effect of a Paradise Lost or an Iliad. For since it denies personal life, "no kind of personal life could ever be its symbol."

1002 "An Amendment to the Dramatization of *Tess*," Notes and Queries, CXLIX (14 Nov 1925), 344.
H's admirers have persuaded him to add a new scene to the play showing Tess and her family on the verge of starvation and explaining the reasons that forced Tess to throw herself upon Alec.

1003 Bauch, Reinhold. Englishes Lesebuch zur Einführung in Kultur und Geistesleben (English Reader: An Introduction to Culture and Spiritual Life) (Dresden: L. Ehlermann, 1925), pp. 246–49.
H's scenes of rural life and solemn intense style give substance to such abstractions as silence, loveliness, night, dawn, noon, and twilight. H's pes-

simism springs from his sense of nature's inherent cruelty and man's wanton cruelty. H continuously shows that human life is governed by inscrutable forces and that man is a victim of time and fate. [In German.]

1004 Bennett, Arnold. "Tributes from American and English Writers," THOMAS HARDY: NOTES ON HIS LIFE AND WORK (NY: Harper, [1925]), p. 17.

H "is one of the world's greatest writers of any period." He has published nothing "that does not show great creative and emotional power, and nothing that is not beautiful."

1005 Bithell, Jethro. "Thomas Hardy, Poète" (Thomas Hardy, Poet), THOMAS HARDY: POÈMES: (Thomas Hardy: Poems), trans by J. Fournier-Pargoire (Paris: Librairie de France, 1925), pp. i–vii; rptd as "An Introduction to Thomas Hardy's Poetry," COLBY MERCURY, VI (May 1935), 36–40, trans from French by Catherine C. Laughton.

H's poems help to clarify the sense of pessimism which suffuses his novels because the poems outline his attitude toward many of the themes and ideas which he treats in the novels. The poems are particularly helpful in understanding his views on Christianity and on sexual morality. From "Lausanne—In Gibbon's Old Garden," "Panthera," and other poems, we learn that H was clearly not an orthodox Christian; but it is equally clear that he was not an atheist. Except in his rare moods of defiance, he is a saddened agnostic. From others of his poems, we can deduce his attitude toward sexual morality. He was not a free-love advocate; indeed, it appears that he held the typically British view that marriage is sacred, for marital infidelity invariably leads to tragedy in his work. In part, however, he blames the unconscious cosmic force for the pain which derives from sexual desire, and he always has great compassion for those who are driven by passion. [Contains French prose translations of sixty-one H poems.] [In French.]

1006 Boas, Ralph Philip. AN INTRODUCTION TO THE STUDY OF LITERATURE (NY: Harcourt, Brace, 1925), pp. 68, 209, 243.

H was influenced by French realism in expressing his pessimistic view of nature. While creating a realistic picture of the peasants of "Wessex," he simultaneously developed his philosophy of the uncertain destiny of men. He wrote *Tess of the d'Urbervilles* primarily to express this idea. At times his characters, which seem drawn primarily to illustrate his pessimistic theme, are weak.

1007 Boyd, Ernest Augustus. "A New Way With Old Masterpieces. VI—Thomas Hardy," HARPER'S MONTHLY MAGAZINE, CLI (July 1925), 234–45; rptd in LITERARY BLASPHEMIES (NY & Lond: Harper, 1927), pp. 227–55.

H, on the evidence of the poems from his first years in London, "was undisturbed by the turmoil of the sixties." *"Desperate Remedies* was everything that a mid-Victorian best-seller ought to be," but it went unnoticed. H's novels have survived while those of George Eliot have disappeared from view. H "was very conscious of that condition of puerility and insincerity into which the English novel declined during the Victorian era." The novelists who preceded H emasculated the novel and divorced it from "all sense of reality." H "belongs to our own time primarily because of the implied, rather than the expressed ideas that underlie his treatment of his characters." "In his ironical detachment and his sense of reality this last of the Victorians was preeminently un-Victorian."

> **1008** Brennecke, Ernest. "The Introduction," LIFE AND ART, By Thomas Hardy, ed by Ernest Brennecke (NY: Greenberg, 1925), pp. 1–6.

Although H's "reminiscential and critical writings" are minor compared to his imaginative works, they are valuable in that they reveal his personality. They reveal that H had a "keen sensibility and excellent sense."

> **1009** Brennecke, Ernest, Jr. THE LIFE OF THOMAS HARDY (NY: Greenberg, 1925); included in "Thomas Hardy's Universe, and the Life of Thomas Hardy," Columbia University dissertation, 1926.

H was descended from Norman nobility on his father's side and from "the solid, intelligent, independent English yeomanry" on his mother's side. From the Hardys he acquired "his detached realization of all-too-human motives"; from his mother he gained affection for the soil, humanitarianism, and artistic truths. The influence of the land he inhabited enabled him to impart to his writing a "flavor of genuine reality" which was enhanced by the ability to use dialect acquired from William Barnes. In general, H was influenced by whatever he came in contact with because he had a "preternaturally active and retentive" mind. This mind caused him to see readily that the gap between his and his father's generation was widening and that the Hardys had declined socially. As a result, he developed an inferiority complex. A worthless formal education did nothing to counter this nor did his contact with the young ladies for whom he, as a boy, wrote love letters. Hoping to establish himself in the world, he began work as an architect under John Hicks. That the influence of architecture remained with him all his life is confirmed by the fact that more than one Wessex character is an architect and by the fact that all of H's works reveal a concern for form. Thus architecture, as well as music and painting, contributed to making H a poet and novelist. As a poet, he was not initially successful. In the years 1863–1870, he failed to publish the poems which foreshadow later works in dealing with fatalism, chance, disillusionment, and time. In the poems in general, "sense" predominates over "sound" in the choice of words, and the influence of Shelley and Browning can be detected. In the poems of 1865–1870, "a generally complete and entirely Hardyan attitude towards the world" is reflected, but the world was not yet ready to accept this attitude. The poet was forced to become a novelist and, after suppressing his first novel, published *Desperate Remedies* and *Under the Greenwood Tree* without material success. In 1873, he began earning money from *Far From the Madding Crowd*. Influenced by the Bible and particularly by Aeschylus, he wrote novels until 1895 when *Jude the Obscure* was published. In all of his novels, the content is of primary importance. It follows naturally, then, that H is not concerned with smoothness of style, but rather with gaining "insight into the workings of the human heart" and with revealing the truth. When he returned to writing poems, he showed these same concerns. Thus his guiding principle was to use "the exact and precise word for the expression of an idea." He wrote not melodic, but pungent poems that employ form perfectly suited to subject matter. Despite this, critics have been reluctant to accept him as a poet. They have, however, gradually come to admire *The Dynasts,* an epic-drama in which there is both human and philosophical action. Despite the pessimism of this distinctly Aeschylean work and of his other works, H sees himself not as cynical, but as photographic.

1010 Burdett, Osbert. THE BEARDSLEY PERIOD (NY: Boni & Liveright, 1925), pp. 33–34, 96, 113, 205–6, 227–28, 281.
H is an author who makes "a virtue of Necessity" by writing great tragic novels in a period of dark disillusionment, inviting us "to recognize the beauty of a tragic conception of human life."

1011 Chave, Penrhyn. "The Tragedy of Tess," T. P.'s AND CASSELL'S WEEKLY, 16 May 1925, p. 103.
"*Tess* is the story of Eve reversed"—"Man the Betrayer, dominant, heedless, captious . . . and . . . Woman who Pays, receptive, patient, staunch." She is the victim of man and man-made laws. Alec and Angel, though widely different in outlook and temperament, "react upon Tess to the same hideous effect": Alec by his lack, Angel by his excess, of ideals. As Jack Durbeyfield's encounter with the Parson and Tess's with Alec shows, "a superior upbringing bears within it the seed of . . . tyranny, however unconscious or . . . well-intentioned."

1012 Collins, H. P. MODERN POETRY (Lond: Jonathan Cape, [1925]), pp. 90–96.
Tess of the d'Urbervilles and the corpus of H's poetry indicate H's modernity. H looks back to an age of certainty now passed away; he is divided "between hope in mankind and regret for the loss of a more primitive solace." H does not exaggerate "the iniquity of things" even when portraying the universe as adverse and presents psychological peculiarities, as in Angel Clare, whose perverse priggishness is shown "as part of a vast spiritual action."

THOMAS HARDY

1013 Courtney, W. L. [pseud of Walter Lenard]. " 'The Most Modern of the Moderns,' " THOMAS HARDY: NOTES ON HIS LIFE AND WORK (NY: Harper, [1925]), pp. 25–26.
"Victorian as a descriptive epithet seems in no sense to be applicable" to H: "he is a Georgian poet—a seer, a prophet, a philosopher."

1014 Cox, A. G. "The Hardy Players," LOCAL GOVERNMENT SERVICE, X (Sept 1925), 216–17.
[Detailed account of genesis and activities of The Hardy Players 1908–1925.]

1015 Darton, F. J. H. "Thomas Hardy's Birthplace," LIVING AGE, CCCXXIV (7 Feb 1925), 303–5.
Near H's birthplace in Lower Bockhampton, near Dorchester, are all the natural phenomena found in the Wessex novels. There are also "those churches whose architecture influenced Hardy as a young man." H "has *felt* the places and people; they are part of him . . . they are not mere descriptive words."

1016 Deutsch, Babette. "Thomas Hardy," NEW YORK HERALD TRIBUNE BOOKS, 24 May 1925, p. 5.
The essays on literature in LIFE AND ART, ed by Ernest Brennecke (1925), show H's view of the novel as organic and realistic and as having a "sound" effect on the reader's mind. Pieces such as "How I Built Myself a House" are too undistinguished to justify reprinting. [Also reviews Brennecke's THE LIFE OF THOMAS HARDY (1925).]

1017 Dreiser, Theodore. "Tributes from American and English Writers," THOMAS HARDY: NOTES ON HIS LIFE AND WORK (NY: Harper, [1925]), p. 15.
"Mentally and emotionally and as a painter of the human scene he [H] seems to me to outrank most of his contemporaries. I rank him with but one other really—Feodor Dostoievsky."

1018 Edgett, Edwin F. "The Voice of Thomas Hardy Through the Years," BOSTON EVENING TRANSCRIPT, 21 Feb 1925, p. 3.
H is primarily a novelist, rather than a poet, as LIFE AND ART by Thomas Hardy, ed by Ernest Brennecke, Jr. (1925) shows.

1019 Frierson, William C. L'INFLUENCE DU NATURALISME FRANÇAIS SUR LES ROMANCIERS ANGLAIS DE 1855 À 1900 (The Influence of French Naturalism on the English Novelists From 1885 to 1900) (Paris: Giard, 1925), pp. 15–18, 21, 53, 71, 109, 163, 164, 244, 252, 254, 255, 257, 258, 259, 268.
In general H's style and his use of intrigue plots, melodrama, and coin-

238

cidences tie him to earlier English novelists, while his pessimism and irony sharply distinguish him from preceding moralists like George Eliot and mark his affinity with contemporary continental writers. Yet his adherence to these older modes of plotting make quite justifiable his rejecting the suggestion that his novels imitated French realism. [In French.]

1020 Gilbert, Katherine. "Hardy and the Weak Spectator," RE-VIEWER (Chapel Hill, NC), V (July 1925), 9–25.
H's novels are difficult to fully appreciate because of their "depth," "thickness," and "shape." [A silly, simple-minded article.]

1021 Gosse, Edmund. "Mr. Hardy's Poems," SUNDAY TIMES (Lond), 13 Dec 1925, p. 8.
Human Shows, Far Phantasies, Songs, and Trifles reveals "a brooding and dejected temperament left during extreme old age in possession of a cerebral acuity rarely equalled." H may object to being called a pessimist, but in this volume he rejects all hope, all "faith in the accomplishment of promises human or divine." It is difficult to establish the connection between "his creative power and his theoretical passivity."

1022 Grey, Rowland [pseud of Lilian Kate Rowland-Brown]. "Christmas in Wessex," CORNHILL MAGAZINE, LVIII (Jan 1925), 26–33.
[Assembles numerous references to Christmas in H's works to show the sad wistfulness "as to the great miracle" which is "intensely English."]

1023 Grey, R. [pseud of Lilian Kate Rowland-Brown]. "The 'jeune premier' and Thomas Hardy," BOOKMAN (Lond), LXIX (Dec 1925), 151–55.
Because the center of attention in H's novels is usually on female characters does not mean that H's male characters are less artfully created.

1024 Grimsditch, Herbert Borthwick. CHARACTER AND ENVIRON-MENT IN THE NOVELS OF THOMAS HARDY (Lond: H. F. & G. Witherby, 1925; NY: Russell & Russell, 1962).
Although H's primary purpose is artistic, one must examine his philosophy in order to understand him. Man is ruled by the working of Immanent Will, so that there is a clash between his concept of himself as free and his determined nature. H is sympathetic toward his characters, even villains. He is a pessimist who feels life is best borne by stoic resignation. He has both a scientific and an artistic vision; out of strife between them he creates his art. Environment plays a large part in shaping character, in cooperation with inward biases. The aim of the study is to consider principal characters as they are molded by environment, producing a clash between individual

and immutable destiny. Tess shows the influence of a bad home-life in her foolish father, scheming mother, and position of leadership forced on her. This is both the beginning of her trouble and culminating factor in bringing about her final surrender. [See a similar combined influence of heredity and environment in Jude and in Dare (*A Laodicean*), somewhat less so in many other characters.] Natural surroundings affect Tess, Sue, and others; landscape is often an actor in drama. H relates detail of scene with characters, as with the shearing-barn in *Far From the Madding Crowd,* Egdon Heath, and Eustacia. Countrymen have qualities of reserve and stoicism which H admires: strength of character is drawn from the soil and combined with innate culture (Winterborne, Oak). Opposing this are a few portraits of country sordidness (Arabella). H's intimate knowledge of rural life is seen in his peasants, where is shown higher realism of interpretation. H loves dialect and old ways which are being corrupted by modernity. Historical and genealogical background are important in novels, particularly in *Tess of the d'Urbervilles.* The struggle between medievalism and modernity are exemplified in Paula Power. Intellectual influences are evident in more highly educated people, and the conflict this engenders between emotion and thought can be seen in Elfride. Most intellectual men are repellent—Knight, Angel Clare, Clym Yeobright, Fitzpiers—because of their alienation from natural feeling. H was keenly conscious of the power of convention and opposed to it in general, especially in theology, where honesty, justice, and generosity should outweigh dogma. *Tess* and *Jude the Obscure* are the great studies of the clash between social and natural law. The final environmental influence is that of occupation, where the problem is to determine whether or not H kept too closely to types. There are five groups of occupations to consider: men of agriculture, soldiers and sailors, men of business, and leisured, professional men. The influence of responsibility for the farm is not sufficient to counteract Bathsheba's emotional nature, whereas Oak shows how occupation can mold character effectively. H admires thoroughness and efficiency in any work. H generally treats soldiers and sailors romantically. Henchard is an unsuccessful man of business because of his rigidity; Farfrae succeeds through his poise. The leisured are treated ineffectively. H does not distort character and event; his theory is drawn from his observations of man undaunted, bearing trouble with fortitude.

1025 Hall, J. A. "The 'Thing' of Mr. Hardy's Poetry," ADELPHI, III (Oct 1925), 364–67.

In all of his poetry, H refers the evils he sees to a "First Cause" only. His refusal to consider second causes (e.g., individual free will) invalidates many poems. His theology is in "apparent conflict" with orthodox Christianity but is characteristic of his Wessex background. [Valuable ideas, but inadequately defended.]

1026 Hammerton, J. A. "The Art of Thomas Hardy," AN OUT-
LINE OF ENGLISH LITERATURE (Lond: Educational Book Co.,
1925), pp. 31, 52, 102.
[Casual references.]

1027 Harper & Brothers. THOMAS HARDY: NOTES ON HIS LIFE
AND WORK (NY: Harper, [1925]).
Contents, abstracted separately by author, all in 1928, except as noted:
Henry S. Canby, "The Novelist of Pity," rptd from NEW YORK EVENING
POST LITERARY REVIEW, 9 July 1921, pp. 1–2; Sinclair Lewis, "Tributes
from American and English Writers"; Theodore Dreiser, "Tributes from
American and English Writers"; W. J. Locke, "Tributes from American and
English Writers"; Arnold Bennett, "Tributes from American and English
Writers"; Frank Swinnerton, "Tributes from American and English Writ-
ers"; W. L. Courtney, " 'The Most Modern of the Moderns' "; Booth Tark-
ington, "Tributes from American and English Writers"; and Sheila
Kaye-Smith, "Tributes from American and English Writers."

1028 Harper, George McLean. "Hardy, Hudson, and Housman,"
SCRIBNER'S MAGAZINE, LXXVIII (Aug 1925), 151–57.
H's poems raise religious questions, and they also, under the scientific bent
of the author, "record the actual life of men and women . . . creatively."
Although *The Dynasts* aspires to epic proportions, the small details therein
give it its natural qualities. H's philosophy is the unique element of the poem,
and this philosophy is "faith reduced to a minimum." H has, however, an
"immense relish for life." He is distressed at human misery, for so often
it results from a misdirection of love.

1029 Hind, C. Lewis. "Two Poets: Thomas Hardy and Flecker,"
OUTLOOK (NY), CXXXIX (25 Feb 1925), 297.
H's pessimism is so honest and sincere in its truthful presentation that it
becomes optimism. Henry James commented, "Cannot something be done
to mollify the action of the critics against *Jude*? It will end in Hardy ceasing
to write novels, I fear." *The Woodlanders, Tess of the d'Urbervilles*, and
Jude the Obscure are more pleasing than *The Dynasts*, which Abercrombie
so highly regards.

1030 Houghton, M. "The Women of the Wessex Novels," HOL-
BORN REVIEW, LXVII (Oct 1925), 433–42.
One remembers H's novels primarily because of the women characters that
fill their pages. "It is not so much that they are creatures of circumstance
impelled by destiny to become (in so many cases) the chief victims in a
succession of tragic events, but that they are for the most part beings at
variance with their natural surroundings." While the actions of these women

largely determine events, those actions are conditioned by an environment to which they are, for the most part, ill-suited. Very often we find pity and its kindred sentiments directing our reaction to these women. Throughout the pages of H's novels, there appears an almost wistful entreaty on behalf of the "weaker sex."

1031 *"Human Shows,"* TIMES LITERARY SUPPLEMENT (Lond), 3 Dec 1925, p. 829.

H is eighty-five yet still fully himself and able to express that self for us. The poems in *Human Shows, Far Phantasies, Songs, and Trifles* are brief lyrics in his customary vein. H still does not believe in happiness; all the poems show the perversity of Fate and ironies that are often tragic. The last word here is resignation and silence, not meliorism. The grave beauty of these poems shows H's genius.

1032 "The Journeyman." "Round and About Sincerity," ADELPHI, III (Sept 1925), 296–301.

Horace Thorogood [not seen] fails to realize that H and H. M. Tomlinson write pessimistically because they have real love for their fellow men; they refuse to let sentiment blind them to the unpleasant reality they see in human experience.

1033 Kaye-Smith, Sheila. "Tributes from American and English Writers," THOMAS HARDY: NOTES ON HIS LIFE AND WORK (NY: Harper, [1925]), p. 13.

H, "the last of the great Victorians," "has given us a portrait gallery of Immortals," and has what the Victorians lacked, "a sense of the personality of place."

1034 Kingsgate, John. *"Tess* and Thomas Hardy, New Facts about His Life in London," GRAPHIC (Lond), CXII (5 Sept 1925), 377.

[Gives some interesting details about H's days in London between 1863 and 1867; extracts from the minutes of the "Royal Society of British Architects," the different addresses of the young H in London; a drawing by Alan Stapleton of No. 16, Westbourne Park Villas; two illustrations reproduced from GRAPHIC of 1891 for *Tess of the d'Urbervilles* by G. Borough Johnson, one of Herkomer's pupils.]

1035 Lefèvre, Frédéric. "Une Heure avec Thomas Hardy" (An Hour with Thomas Hardy), LES NOUVELLES LITTÉRAIRES, 21 Feb 1925; trans and rptd in LIVING AGE, CCCXXV (11 April 1925), 98–103.

"It is, I suppose, impossible to form a serious opinion about contemporary French literature as a whole without making a thorough study of Thomas

Hardy's work." Although H was eighty-four at the time of this interview, he displayed "amazing vitality." H said, " 'I think . . . we are entering on a dark age whose port of entry was the abominable war we have just lived through.' " H also said he believed that the world's dogmas are disappearing. He dreamed " 'of an alliance between religions freed from dogmas. The religion which ought to be preserved if the world is not to perish absolutely and which we must achieve if the world is not to perish, an alliance of rationalism and religion, would be created by poetry.' " H said he thinks the third part of *The Dynasts* is superior to the other two. When H was thinking about *Dynasts*, he read WAR AND PEACE. He praised Anatole France as a great artist; he has read his HISTOIRE COMIQUE, which he finds terribly ironic. [In French.]

1036 Lewis, Sinclair. "Tributes from American and English Writers," THOMAS HARDY: NOTES ON HIS LIFE AND WORK (NY: Harper, [1925]), pp. 13–14.
H "is probably the greatest living novelist." In H's work one finds "great and original vision charged with warm humaneness."

1037 Locke, W. J. "Tributes from American and English Writers," THOMAS HARDY: NOTES ON HIS LIFE AND WORK (NY: Harper, [1925]), pp. 15–16.
"No man living has achieved the stern marble beauty of Hardy's prose" because H was the greatest novelist of the nineteenth-century.

1038 Lowell, Amy. JOHN KEATS (Boston: Houghton Mifflin, 1925), I, 6.
[Refers to H's hypothesis—as related in a letter by Mrs. H to Lowell—that a family named Keats who, in H's boyhood lived two or three miles from Dorchester, were related to John Keats.]

1039 MacAffee, Helen. "Among the New Books: Saint Joan and Other Plays," YALE REVIEW, ns XIV (Jan 1925), 386–87.
In *The Famous Tragedy of The Queen of Cornwall*, Tristram and Iseult "are conjured from the tomb and are brought before us 'in ghostly grave array.' " It is not a great work, but "it is nevertheless adumbrated by his [H's] tragic genius."

1040 McKay, Roy. "The Philosophy of Thomas Hardy," MODERN CHURCHMAN, XV (June 1925), 125–34.
The label "pessimist" has often been hurled at H. For him, the world has not been evolved by a conscious force, as "Hap" and "The Blow" show. The animal creation and lesser forms of life are not cursed with consciousness of the workings of the Unconscious Will, but man is able to see that it is the

same force at work in nature that controls his own actions. But how is it that an Unconscious Force has evolved a conscious will in man? H's inadequate explanation is that consciousness in man is the work of inexplicable chance. In the Wessex novels the happiest characters are to be found among the rustics. His is not a very happy picture of man, but it depicts the potential nobility of man. H is essentially an artist and not a philosopher.

1041 Morley, Edith, and John Buchan. "Thomas Hardy: The End of the Century," A HISTORY OF ENGLISH LITERATURE, ed by John Buchan (Lond: Nelson, 1925), pp. 558–61.

"The structure of Mr. Hardy's plots is almost always admirable." His style "is as a rule clear, terse, and austere. . . ." He is "a master of style" who avoids "rant, 'fine writing,' and excess of all kinds, while he succeeds in expressing deep emotion and passion." [Broad, superficial survey.]

1042 "Mr. Thomas Hardy Sees *Tess*," SPHERE (Lond), CIII (12 Dec 1925), 329.

[A photo of H watching a performance of the dramatic version of *Tess of the d'Urbervilles* (play) performed at his home by the London company.]

1043 Nevinson, Henry Wood. MORE CHANGES, MORE CHANCES (Lond: Nisbet; NY: Harcourt, Brace, [1925]), pp. 165, 179–81, 404.

On 26 April 1906, H saw Gorki's play "The Bezsemenoffs." H volunteered a few remarks on the entire futility of American criticism, said *Tess of the d'Urbervilles* sold best of his works and *Far From the Madding Crowd* next best. He enjoyed concerts better than theaters and thought Tchaikowsky's music had exactly the note of unrest that fit our century. H's intense sensitivity to other people's pain explains the horrible fascination some subjects, like hanging, had on him.

1044 "On Hardy's Chair of Literature," TIMES (Lond), 26 May 1925, p. 17.

The proposal to name University College at Southampton, when it should become a university, the University of Wessex and establish a Thomas Hardy Chair of English Literature is endorsed by several distinguished men, including E. K. Chambers, Arthur Quiller-Couch, and the Duke of Wellington. It is an appropriate idea because H "revealed" in Wessex "an imaginative vision of the whole of human life" and because the sphere of influence of the university-to-be is the same as the territory of Wessex.

1045 Phelps, William Lyon. "Thomas Hardy," SATURDAY REVIEW OF LITERATURE, I (6 June 1925), 808.

H was an uncompromising pessimist in the face of great worldly success. "The Profitable Reading of Fiction" (1888) leads one to suppose that H would find contemporary frankness of a low order of creativity. The "Chorus of the Pities" and such supernatural baggage are a "good deal of a bore" in *The Dynasts*. In a personal conversation H said that *A Laodicean* "contained more of his personal experience than any other of his books." [Freely rendered personal opinions, quotations from the prose, and some personal reminiscence. Review of LIFE AND ART, ed by Ernest Brennecke (1925).]

1046 Ritter, Otto. "Thomas Hardy und Victorien Sardou" (Thomas Hardy and Victorian Sardou), ENGLISCHE STUDIEN, LIX (Feb 1925), 159–60.

There are striking similarities between the sequence of events leading to Tess's marriage to Angel and a similar one in Sardou's drama FERNANDE (1870). H was not directly dependent on Sardou's play, but H, a good student of French, may have known and been influenced by it. [In German.]

1047 Schweikert, H. C. (ed). SHORT STORIES (NY: Harcourt, Brace, 1925), pp. 348–49.

[A brief sketch of H's life is used as an introduction to "The Three Strangers."]

1048 Shand, John. "Tess of the Melville Bros.," NEW STATESMAN, XXV (26 Sept 1925), 662–63.

Though H wrote the adaptation of *Tess of the d'Urbervilles* and sanctioned its production, the dramatic form of the novel loses the irony and inner tensions which make *Tess* great art. The individual actors have performed their parts well but have not made the adaptation convincing.

1049 Shanks, Edward. "Two Innovators," SATURDAY REVIEW (Lond), CXL (19 Dec 1925), 740–41.

In *Human Shows, Far Phantasies, Songs, and Trifles*, H's pessimism is "much more exuberant and tonic in its nature than one expects from a settled pessimism." H loves life, even though he sees death behind it. In practice, H is "the most fertile inventor of stanza-forms in all English literature." [The other "innovator" is Robert Bridges.]

1050 Solomon, Max. "Zur Naturbehandlung in Thomas Hardys Romanen" (The Use of Nature in Thomas Hardy's Novels). Unpublished dissertation, University of Giessen, 1925.

[Illustrates through numerous quotations H's nature descriptions and metaphors. Attempts to define the relationship between man and nature in *Far From the Madding Crowd, The Woodlanders, Tess of the d'Urbervilles*, and *The Return of the Native*.] [Incomplete and superficial.] [In German.]

1051 Squire, John Collings. "Chronicles: the Drama," LONDON MERCURY, XII (Oct 1925), 650–51.

[Mixed praise and blame of H's dramatic adaptation of *Tess of the d'Urbervilles* at the Barnes Theatre, 1925.]

1052 Squire, J. C. *"Human Shows,"* OBSERVER (Lond), 6 Dec 1925, p. 4.

H's new volume, *Human Shows, Far Phantasies, Songs, and Trifles,* defies the supposition that only younger poets can produce great lyrics. This volume differs from H's earlier poetry in only two aspects: he is not so dogmatic in asserting that life is governed by an ironic destiny and his poetic technique has "advanced slightly." Although he is "pre-occupied with change, with transience and death," the backgrounds of his lyrics continue to describe the rich beauty of rural Wessex.

1053 Squire, J. C. "Thomas Hardy's Early Poems," T. P.'S AND CASSELL'S WEEKLY, 28 March 1925, p. 831.

Selected Poems of Thomas Hardy displays H's view of life, "never the morbidity of the decadent, nor the cultivated gloom of the sombre poseur" but a belief "in making the most of life." H's poems "might be regarded as a kind of pessimistic complement of Browning's."

1054 Steinbach, Agnes. "Thomas Hardy und Schopenhauer" (Thomas Hardy and Schopenhauer), ANGLICA: UNTERSUCHUNG ZUR ENGLISCHEN PHILOLOGIE [A. Brandl z. 70 Geb.] (Anglica: Studies in English Philology [on A. Brandl's 70th Birthday]) (Leipzig: Mayer & Müller, 1925), pp. 434–47.

Schopenhauer provided H with a philosophical system which crystallized his own beliefs, i.e., the meaning and purpose of life, the problems of the individual towards society, the isolation of the individual, and the problem of love between man and woman. H moved beyond the limitations of Schopenhauer and denied life itself. [In German.]

1055 Swinnerton, Frank. "Tributes from American and English Writers," THOMAS HARDY: NOTES ON HIS LIFE AND WORK (NY: Harper, [1925]), pp. 18–19.

H is the "greatest of all English novelists." Life in H's books is not merely depicted or analyzed, "it is created anew, so powerful is [H's] imagination."

1056 Tarkington, Booth. "Tributes from American and English Writers," THOMAS HARDY: NOTES ON HIS LIFE AND WORK (NY: Harper, [1925]), p. 12.

H is modern in that he "wrote of everything; moreover Hardy wrote of everything beautifully."

1057 Taylor, Coley. "Thomas Hardy's Essays," WORLD TOMORROW, VIII (March 1925), 88.

The essays in THOMAS HARDY'S LIFE AND ART, ed by Ernest Brennecke (1925), are not among H's best work.

1058 "This Week's Books," SPECTATOR (Lond), CXXXV (19 Dec 1925), 1145.

In *Human Shows, Far Phantasies, Songs, and Trifles*, "half a dozen poems are among Hardy's best." They more than compensate for the others which are awkward or mechanical.

1059 "Thomas Hardy on the Art of the Novel," NEW YORK TIMES BOOK REVIEW, 1 March 1925, p. 7.

THOMAS HARDY'S LIFE AND ART, by Ernest Brennecke (1925), except for one or two essays by H on the art of fiction, is motley and unimportant. In one essay, H blames the influence of the popular magazine and circulating library for not permitting free treatment of life and sex; in another, he limits the "scientific approach" to writing to the pre-writing stage of the observation of phenomena. H, in recent years, has become "disturbed" at the formlessness of the modern novel.

1060 "Thomas Hardy, Poet," NATION (NY), CXXI (23 Sept 1925), 319.

A careful consideration of H's work as both a poet and a novelist places him in the forefront of English poetry and gives the public every reason to expect that his new book, *Human Shows, Far Phantasies, Songs, and Trifles*, will be as fine as the rest of his work, if not the culmination of it.

1061 "Thomas Hardy Writes to the American Red Cross," BIBLIO, V (Nov–Dec 1925), 857.

[H praised the organization as one of the few signs that material progress in the last century has not wholly outdistanced moral progress.]

1062 Van Doren, Carl and Mark Van Doren. AMERICAN AND BRITISH LITERATURE SINCE 1890 (NY & Lond: Century, 1925), pp. 144–49, 242–47, 324–25.

"Robinson had been studying Thomas Hardy for his strong hold on common life." The great novelist became "the most distinguished of living English poets," profound and interesting, penetrating life and human nature "beyond the point where life can be declared either good or bad." In narrative poems, H "shows human beings in the grip of relentless fortune, tricked and betrayed by indifferent nature." H's poetry has philosophy, atmosphere, beauty, rich vocabulary, rugged meter, even happiness. H, "Noyes, and Masefield . . . sang the pity of slaughter." H, "though his work as a novelist was nearly finished by 1890 . . . has generally been regarded as the greatest novelist of the age, particularly for the unity of his place, tone, and ideas." *The Dynasts* is a "lone masterpiece," "a panorama of mighty sweep." H creates abstractions to reflect his philosophy. The reader is given a god-like perspective. [Suggestions for study: standard text, criticism, and selected poems. Standard text of *Dynasts* listed.]

1063 Van Doren, Carl. "Anatole France and Thomas Hardy," CENTURY MAGAZINE, ns LXXXVII (Jan 1925), 418–23.
While Anatole France seems "a citizen of all the world," H seems "a symbol and a distillation of England." Even so, they are concerned with the same topics, such as "Who or what . . . governs the world." H, "for all his disillusion," "is still incurably theological."

1064 Wedmore, Sir Frederick. "Thomas Hardy's Poems," CERTAIN COMMENTS (Lond: Selwyn & Blount, 1925), pp. 72–74; probably rptd from MANCHESTER GUARDIAN or TIMES LITERARY SUPPLEMENT (Lond) [unidentified in this form].
Satires of Circumstance is neither the best nor the worst. *Time's Laughingstocks* are more the real H—courageous, ironic, tolerant, tender. The new volume has "fertility in invention" and "wonderful descriptive passages" but is occasionaly "gratuitously depressing." The best group is "Poems of 1912 and 1913," which are "admirably intimate." The most popular now will be the Postscript, a song of soldiers "struck out of the heart of a patriot."

1065 Weygandt, Cornelius. "The Mastery of Thomas Hardy," A CENTURY OF THE ENGLISH NOVEL (NY: Century, 1925), pp. 211–28.
Eliot passes on the tradition of English novel to H, H to Phillpotts, Phillpotts to Sheila Kaye-Smith. Wessex appears in DANIEL DERONDA in progress 1873, and thus may pre-date *Far From the Madding Crowd*, pub 1874. "The Mastery of Thomas Hardy": H's "writing discloses a completer understanding and interpretation of an English community than . . . any other." H has a wide range of characters, an understanding of the life of Wessex, a memory for folk-lore and anecdote, an objectivity, and wide sympathy and tolerance. His characters are of many sorts: peasants, artists, worldly ladies. His heroines "surrender quickly to impulse," to the mating instinct. H "is resolutely the presenter of a province"—Wessex, and few characters are not of Wessex origin. [A discussion of the novels follows.] H "has never written better than in *The Return of the Native.*" In his greater novels "his writing is almost always clear, well balanced and rhythmical." Only in earlier work and thesis novels does the style stumble and drag; at its best in dialect. *Jude the Obscure* disappointingly falls short of tragedy and becomes a pathological case study. H is pessimistic but claims to be a meliorist, with even a glint of hope in *The Dynasts*. H does not give reasons for abandoning the novel with *Jude* (*The Well-Beloved* appeared serially earlier): he may have

wished not to hurt the public further, he may have been disappointed at the reception of the book, he may have wished to complete a philosophy of life by another medium, or he may simply have wished to return to verse. *Dynasts* is beyond fathoming. The great H is the teller of stories— either in verse or prose. H "has been a classic for half a century." He is unlike the Russians, but English to the core "of the stock of Scott and Shakespeare and Chaucer." Nine contemporary groups: "The Hardians are Phillpotts, 'Zack,' and Charles Lee among the late Victorians, and Bullock, 'John Trevena' and Sheila Kaye-Smith in more recent years." During the first quarter of the century, we had H and Conrad of top rank and can be thankful for George Moore. [A study based upon two critical standards: the method of presentation and comparison of novels of same subject and power. H is mentioned in various respects with Scott, Meredith, Austen, Chaucer, Shakespeare, Stevenson, Moore, Lawrence, Eliot, Conrad, Thackeray, Dickens, Brontë, Aeschylus, Cervantes, Goethe, and Ibsen.]

1066 Wildhagen, Karl. Der Englische Volkscharakter. Seine Natürlichen und Historischen Grundlagen (The English Folk-Character. Its Natural and Historical Bases) (Leipzig: Akademische Verlagsgesellschaft, 1925), pp. 58, 60.
[H is mentioned in connection with authors who illustrate the idea of the self-made man and writers who bind the will of their fictional characters to nature.] [In German.]

1067 Willcocks, M[ary] P[atricia]. "Thomas Hardy," Between the Old World and the New (Lond: Allen & Unwin, [1925]), pp. 331–51.
The "one divine mystery of Hardy's world" is that man "the blind agent of a blind Force sees what its creator saw not—the pain and wrong of the whole." Man, through sex, "has worked up so far, only to find himself in a blind alley." "Life is, then, a mere tournament of the frustrated." "Hardy's Fate is all made up of perversity." Fate is a "great cat" who sports with helpless, bewildered beetles—men. Nemesis is an important idea to H since all his rebels are bound to be struck down. Regarding Fate or Destiny, H "has done nothing more than carry into literature the great peasant formula 'it was to be.'"

1068 Williams, Harold. Modern English Writers: Being a Study of Imaginative Literature 1890–1914. 3rd ed (Lond: Sidgwick & Jackson, 1925), pp. 24, 77–90, 294, 339, 386, 392–93, 479, 491.
"Mr. Thomas Hardy, for example, as a novelist virtually finished his work many years since, but his poetry is of fresh significance, and derives in nothing from the Victorian traditions." Poetry "has that large note of uni-

THOMAS HARDY

versality, that boldness of imaginative conception which sets it apart . . .
despite . . . limitations in the graces of the poetic art." *Wessex Poems,
Poems of the Past and the Present, Time's Laughingstocks, The Dynasts*:
the last has the "architectural faculty," "great and small are . . . seen with a
single eye." The appeal is not dramatic, nor poetic, but intellectual. It illustrates deterministic concepts. "At least thirty poems, and probably more, in
the miscellaneous collections were written before any of the novels appeared." H is greater as a novelist than poet. He has impressive range and
variety: "sonnets, dramatic monologues, psychological studies, speculative
poems, poems of pilgrimage, poems of war, dialect poems, love lyrics, song,
ballads, humorous poems and epigrams." H's work is imbued with strong
personality and philosophical implications. A melancholy sense of pity and
consciousness of irony of time run throughout the works. The sonnets are
characterized by disillusion in love, *mésalliance* and a "Shakespearian
breadth of conception and thought." Much of his best poetry is in dramatic
monologue. No charming metrist, H has an individualistic style. The note
of melancholy is not depressing, but reasoned pessimism. He presents a large
number of psychological studies of character; the theme is the irony of time.
Love lyrics are as intellectual as passionate. Few are in dialect. He "is first
and foremost an artist endowed with a profoundly original vision of human
life." "There is a reality wider than the poem." Housman, like H, believed
in a philosophy of disbelief, in "stoic faith in the courage to endure." Meredith and H use the novel as vehicle for systems of thought, a growing modern
tendency. Dowson's prose is, like H's, about life's little ironies, but differs
in treatment and is more sentimental. Bennett's treatment of characters is
realistic like H's, but he never achieves the detachment and fuller meaning of
H. Eden Phillpotts and John Trevena at their best approach H. Phillpotts's
model for Dartmoor life was H, but his "mind is complex, his ideas sophisticated" and his "intention is unfulfilled." "In the Wessex novels the composition is equivalent to the original inspiration." James and H are both
narrow in range, but H is more significant because "he pierces to what man
is." American local color novelists do not have H's "whence and whither of
the whole race of man." They merely seek realistic rendering.

1069 Woodward, Kathleen. "Thomas Hardy Cleaves to His Solitude," NEW YORK TIMES, 22 Nov 1925, IV, p. 14.
As H approaches his eighty-fifth birthday, he is more of a recluse than ever.
A shy, ordinary-looking little man, he avoids human contact to court the
muse of sadness. In an interview, he talked of slipshod American writing
and its influence on British journalism. Dorsetshire pays little attention to
him.

1070 Woolf, Leonard. "The World of Books: Jug Jug to Dirty
Ears," NATION AND ATHENAEUM, XXXVIII (5 Dec 1925), 354.

H, as *Human Shows, Far Phantasies, Songs, and Trifles* shows, is one of the spiritual parents of the modern generation of poets. "Any little old song" is tuned until "it bears the imprint of that queer, original personality."

1926

1071 Allen, Hervey. "English and Choctaw," NORTH AMERICAN REVIEW, CCXXIII (June–Aug 1926), 360–62.

Human Shows, Far Phantasies, Songs, and Trifles continues without a change the themes treated in the rest of H's poetry: the result is one of the most profound comments on the dance of shadow shapes in the human comedy of our tongue. Each poem manages to include within itself at least one complete life history from swaddling clothes to shroud. By turning to the imaginative shorthand of poetry, H has produced a whole galaxy of characters and comments in which his novels are only one solar system.

1072 "Another Dram Discussed," NEW YORK TIMES, 18 June 1926, p. 22.

H has revived the old semantic crux of Hamlet's "dram of eale." H suggests it is a blundered spelling of "e'll" or "ill" [editor suggests "evil" as another alternative].

1073 "Any Wife to Any Genius," NEW YORK TIMES, 4 Oct 1926, p. 22.

Mrs. H is doing writing also but is keeping it in her desk and is not competing with her husband. [Editor approves her action but hopes she will sometime give insight into her husband's character.]

1074 Aronstein, Ph. (ed). A THOMAS HARDY READER: EINE AUSWAHL AUS THOMAS HARDY'S PROSA UND DICHTUNG (A Selection from Thomas Hardy's Prose and Poetry) (Leipzig: Tauchnitz, 1926).

[A selection of H's short stories, scenes from the novels and *The Dynasts*, and the poems. Includes pronouncing gazetteer of proper nouns, explanatory notes, and an English-German glossary.] [In German.]

1075 Beer, Thomas. THE MAUVE DECADE (NY: Knopf, 1926), pp. 181, 215, 246.

H is part of the background of the American Nineties because of the publication of *Jude the Obscure* in HARPER'S. [Passing mention.]

1076 Benson, Arthur. THE DIARY OF ARTHUR CHRISTOPHER BENSON. 4th ed, ed by Percy Lubbock (Lond: Hutchinson, 1926), pp. 81–82, 254, 259–61, 281.

[Records two meetings with H: one in 1904 when H discussed Newman (the APOLOGIA is the work of a poet, not a logician, according to H) and one in 1913 when the novelist commented on his religious feelings, and the loss he felt for his first wife which he recorded in the poems of that year.]

1077 Brennecke, Ernest. "Thomas Hardy's Universe, and the Life of Thomas Hardy." Unpublished dissertation, Columbia University, 1926.

[Listed in Lawrence F. McNamee, DISSERTATIONS IN ENGLISH AND AMERICAN LITERATURE (NY & Lond: Bowker, 1968)]; combines THOMAS HARDY'S UNIVERSE: A STUDY OF A POET'S MIND (1924) and THE LIFE OF THOMAS HARDY (1925).

1078 Brown, Ivor. "The Theatre: Sliced Hardy," SATURDAY REVIEW (Lond), CXLII (18 Sept 1926), 311.

Because the drama of *The Mayor of Casterbridge* is in the war of attrition between Henchard and the world, this novel adapts much less readily to the stage than did *Tess of the d'Urbervilles*, which has a plot full of surging climaxes that make for good theater. Drinkwater's adaptation is much too choppy; the seventeen different scenes interrupt the flow of the story and destroy the greatness of H's novel. [Review of John Drinkwater's unpublished dramatic adaptation of *Mayor*.]

1079 Buchan, John. HOMILIES AND RECREATIONS (Lond, Edinburgh, & NY: Nelson; Boston: Houghton Mifflin, 1926), pp. 17, 50, 200–202.

H's careful and accurate sketching of the Wessex country provides "a familiar and recognizable stage" for his works and sharpens their sense of verisimilitude.

1080 Calverton, V. P. SEX EXPRESSION IN LITERATURE (NY: Boni & Liveright, 1926), pp. 244–46, 262–63.

H's pessimism was the result of a bourgeois interpretation of Darwin, but his sexual realism was anti-bourgeois, a product of personal candidness not social aggressiveness. [Vague.]

1081 Carr, Alice Vansittart (Strettel) [Mrs. J. Comyns]. MRS. J. COMYNS CARR'S REMINISCENCES, ed by Eve Adam (Lond: Hutchinson, 1926), pp. 76–79.

Joe Comyns and H produced *Far From the Madding Crowd* in Liverpool to offset H's displeasure over the Hare-Kendal production of Pinero's THE SQUIRE, which had resemblances to H's novel, at the St. James Theatre in

London. The Comyns-H production went well after some amusing episodes due to H's inexperience with theatrical ventures; plans for a London production at the Globe fell through, for THE SQUIRE was too successful. [J. Comyns was a new producer, having previously been editor of ENGLISH ILLUSTRATED MAGAZINE and a drama critic for PALL MALL GAZETTE.]

1082 Christensen, Glenn J. "The Thomas Hardy Collection," PRINCETON UNIVERSITY LIBRARY CHRONICLE, VIII (Nov 1926), 24–27.
Addition of the Morris Parrish collection makes Princeton a center for H textual studies. Parrish Library had: a full set of American and English first editions of the Wessex novels; two of the novels in serial form; first collected editions of poems and short stories (with many in the magazine or newspapers in which they first appeared); more than half of H's essays and articles (including two copies of "How I Built Myself A House"); thirty programs from performances of H's plays; H's chief anti-war contributions in copies of KING ALBERT'S BOOK, THE BOOK OF FRANCE, and THE BOOK OF THE HOMELESS; some war-time items in small private printings; letters from Mrs. H to Parrish; biographies; and critical studies of H's work. Since Princeton had a few first issues of the novels, files of nineteenth-century periodicals containing most of the H serials and the 1895–1897 and 1911–1912 collected editions of H's works, only MSS, would be needed to do textual analyses of H's writings.

1083 Coffin, Henry Sloane. WHAT TO PREACH (NY: Doran; NY: Harper, 1926; Lond: Hodder & Stoughton, [1927], NY: Richard R. Smith, 1930), p. 168.
The two ineffectual ministers who fail to aid Tess and Clare in *Tess of the d'Urbervilles* exemplify ministers who fail to observe and reflect upon damnation acting itself out in human life. [Warrack Lectures for 1926 in New College, Edinburgh and in colleges of United Free Church of Scotland in Glasgow and Aberdeen; Russell Lectures at Auburn Seminar; Swander Lectures at the Theological Seminar of the Reformed Church in the United States at Lancaster, Pa.]

1084 Davison, Edward. "Thomas Hardy, 85 Years Young," LITERARY REVIEW (NY), VI (23 Jan 1926), 1–2.
Human Shows, Far Phantasies, Songs, and Trifles, like H's other volumes of verse, is dominated by works which evince his rationalistic bent. The "most surprising" aspect of the volume, however, is that H has retained into old age the same intellectual vigor, spareness of language, and delicacy of description that characterized his early poetry. He is "one of the most considerable poets since Tennyson."

1085 De Casseres, Benjamin. "Thomas Hardy," Forty Immortals (NY: Lawren, 1926), pp. 34–50.

H is a master fatalist, a supreme ironist. No artist has seen deeper into life, none has been more "fearless, inexorable, or sincere" than H. H "occupies the same place in modern imaginative literature that Sophocles does in dramatic literature." He stands "rooted in his age," in the center of nineteenth-century intellectual activity. H's women are always the victims of destiny. Social law is constantly "in conspiracy against their souls." H sees no distinction between "good" and "bad" men and women. Moral principles are matters of time and circumstance. The fate of H's heroines is often decided by "incidental," "trivial" events. His characters are "corks on a current." "Overhead is the vast dome of grey nature; beneath, insects that crawl to their appointed dooms."

1086 Drew, Elizabeth. The Modern Novel: Some Aspects of Contemporary Fiction (Lond: Cape, 1926), pp. 18, 69.

H transmuted his perception of the pettiness and insignificance of life into the grandeur of enduring art and enlightened the reading public about the real motives and emotions of human beings.

1087 Drinkwater, John. A Book for Bookmen (Lond: Dulau, 1926; NY: Doran, 1927), pp. 175, 181–85, 201.

H wished to visit Robert Stephen Hawker, the Cornish poet, but when he went to Morwenstow in 1875, intending to call on him, H heard "the passing bell announcing Hawker's death, which had taken place at Plymouth." H made a selection of Barnes's poems in Dorset dialect and "discusses Barnes's dialect with unrivalled authority." H also printed four other poems in "Common English" in his selection. Comment on Gosse's library, contains "a presentation copy of the first edition of *The Dynasts,* with the very rare 1903 title page to the first volume."

1088 Drinkwater, John. Mayor of Casterbridge [For reviews of this 1926 unpublished dramatic adaptation of H's *The Mayor of Casterbridge,* see H. Shipp, "The Novel and the Play," English Review, XLIII (Oct 1926), 469–71; Ivor Brown, "The Theatre: Sliced Hardy," Saturday Review (Lond), CXLII (18 Sept 1926), 311; and N. G. Royde-Smith, "The Drama: The Material for Plays," Outlook (Lond), LVIII (18 Sept 1926), 267.]

1089 Ellis, S. M. "Current Literature," Fortnightly Review, ns CXIX (Jan 1926), 140–42.

Human Shows, Far Phantasies, Songs, and Trifles reveals the aging author's awareness that the paths of life lead to death, which H conveys with brave resignation. His compassion is more in evidence for animals than for men.

1090 Freeman, John. "Human and Half-Human Shows," BOOK-MAN (Lond), LXIX (Jan 1926), 197–99.

At eighty-five H, as a poet, remains, "more resolute in conformity to the Hardy conviction than ever, more securely self-expressive than ever." Yet the sardonic humor which he sees in the human situations he describes is, in fact, simply part of the same quality which is innate in the English humor, a humor which often turns to melancholy, or even the grotesque.

1091 Goodspeed, Helen. "Far Phantasies," NEW REPUBLIC, XLVI (3 March 1926), 52.

The poems of *Human Shows, Far Phantasies, Songs, and Trifles* show the H we know: unpretentious, sensitive, too conscious of the world's mal-adjustments, visited by the ghosts of dead tragedies, haunted by the vision of an ultimate Ideal. H's "wry utterances" are "freely put in resistant forms."

1092 Grey, Rowland [pseud of Lillian Kate Rowland-Brown]. "Woman in the Poetry of Thomas Hardy," FORTNIGHTLY REVIEW, CXIX (Jan 1926), 34–46.

H's poetry shows woman as the "eternal feminine"; women are paramount but not Venus Victrix. *The Dynasts* has a gallery of women who are puppets in the hands of Fate, like the other characters, but there are different characterizations, from the nude woman who jumped from the stricken *Achille* and swam to the English boats, to the "cleverest intriguer of her time," Madam Metternich. *Dynasts* "leaves the conviction that the world is a poor place for women, though they are essential to its existence." H's shorter poems present great variety of women, especially fallen and unfaithful ones, "their clean-cut clearness of outline invariable." Barrie was wrong that H's women are all of one type. He shows us Jezebel but also a human picture of Mary in retelling in his own way the legend of Panthera. H is "still loyal to the mainspring of his inspiration."

1093 Haggard, Sir Henry Rider. THE DAYS OF MY LIFE: AN AUTOBIOGRAPHY, ed by C. J. Longman (Lond: Longmans, Green, 1926), I, 272–73; II, 214.

H read a review of his last novel [*Jude the Obscure*?] at the Savile Club [in 1896?]. After reading it, H exclaimed: " 'There's a nice thing to say about a man!' 'Well, I'll never write another novel.' " H observed King Edward's body lying in state in Westminster Hall in 1910.

1094 Heath, Frederick. "A Stranger at Max Gate," LITERARY DIGEST, LXXIX (12 June 1926), 34.

[This poem in five stanzas tells about H's quiet home and about his pleasant hospitality to the author of the poem. The narrator recalls H's saying,

"Youth's joy is hope." He says that the old writer speaks in the "Twin voice of Shakespeare talking of the world."]

1095 Herring, Robert. "Poetry," London Mercury, XIII (Feb 1926), 434–35.
Though in *Human Shows, Far Phantasies, Songs, and Trifles* H's verse is flawed, his "deep virtues" as a poet merit high praise.

1096 Hopkins, R. Thurston. "Thomas Hardy and his Dorset Home," Books of the Month, June 1926, pp. i–iii.
H had a "hot, nervous life" in him. In a conversation H denied having a philosophy. In a novel, H said, the search for truth should transcend pessimism, meliorism, and optimism. [Impressions and anecdotes about H by his neighbors and Dorset rustics.]

1097 Hutchison, Percy A. "An Elder Poet and A Young One Greet the New Year," New York Times Book Review, 2 Jan 1926, p. 14.
Though most of H's poems in *Human Shows, Far Phantasies, Songs, and Trifles* are from his late period, they are as mature (but no more) than those from earlier volumes. H the poet will be forgotten while H the novelist will live, but H could have been a major poet had he devoted his life to that art. Like Donne and Browning, he admires cacophony but lacks their compensation for its use. The volume includes wit, humor, tenderness—most poems are in the lyrical vein. All poems could have benefited from more careful craftsmanship.

1098 Johnson, William Savage. "Hardy the Poet," Saturday Review of Literature, III (7 Aug 1926), 19.
Human Shows, Far Phantasies, Songs, and Trifles of 1925 is like "Hap" of 1866 but with a difference; it is "full of realistic pictures" rather than the escape poetry of other contemporaries. Old philosophical ideas are expressed in new ways in "Sine Prole," "Genetrix Laesa," and "The Aerolite." Hope is reaffirmed, as in *The Dynasts*, in one of the most interesting of the new poems, "Xenophanes, the Monist of Colophon"; consolations for man as a victim of cynic circumstance appear in the simple substance of human values in "Any Little Old Song" and "A Leader of Fashion." "Life and Death at Sunrise" is redolent of Wessex soil, true to the idiosyncracies of humanity, yet universal.

1099 King, Robert Wylie. "The Lyrical Poems of Thomas Hardy," London Mercury, XV (Dec 1926), 157–70.
H's lyrics in variety of subject-matter and in mastery of a highly individual technique "are among the most interesting in the language." The lyrics are remarkably uniform from first to last. The early "Neutral Tones" is similar

in technique and "flavour" to the very late *The Famous Tragedy of the Queen of Cornwall.* Nevertheless H "possessed almost unlimited variety of form." [Groups H's poems by subject-matter, showing the many general topics and the great variety of sub-topics.]

1100 Lalou, René. PANORAMA DE LA LITTÉRATURE ANGLAISE CONTEMPORAINE (Panorama of Contemporary English Literature). 9eme Edition (Paris: Kra, 1926).

H arrived on the literary scene with *Under the Greenwood Tree.* H is naturally associated with pessimism in England. H saw without illusion and with icy detachment, earthy dramas that could instill a holy terror especially in the impotent and the delicate. Such a world is one born under a fated star. All the efforts of civilization have failed to develop conscience. At thirty, H confirmed his pessimism and cloistered himself in Dorset. In 1872, his first novel, *Greenwood Tree,* was situated there. Two years later *Far From the Madding Crowd* appeared with the name taken from Gray's "Elegy." During this time he defined the locale of Wessex (Southwest England) over which the imaginary Christminster (Oxford) kept watch. H devoted fifteen novels to Wessex, writing according to the prescripts of a regional novelist. His work has a certain rightness which discovers in a restricted locale the quality of a universal "pathetique." George Eliot had prepared the public to receive H's first works; thus, the English were not disconcerted by his philosophy and realism. H added to such weight the irony of humor. He put together the most minute observation and an infallible touch in execution. His architectural studies gave him the precise qualities of sense of line and volume, solidity, the rightness of construction. The novels are vast scapes of plastic art, in musical terms, symphonies of woods and lands. A work such as *The Return of the Native* appeared bathed in the sinister light of an inexorable and eternal fatalism.

Psychology is not essential to H's work. All the characters are constructed robustly but laboriously and are not greatly varied with the exception of Jude and Sue, who is extremely complex. H injects himself often, sometimes heavily, to explain. H is the observer of a cruel destiny, a mechanism at the heart of life, that pleases to torment simple beings. Human error has two sources: human folly and events which detour a planned way, a simple gesture turned to catastrophe. The peasants and farmers, becoming the marionettes of destiny, acquire tragic relief.

H is a master of the description of nature. His scenes of farmers working are picturesque and majestic and better when he describes the nature of the visible human countenance, however much desolated. Using the song of the wind, the play of light, the sounds of the night, the interplay upon the earth,

H evokes a country scene that is quasi-immutable in which each reply, each happening is mysterious. H has the precision of a geometrician and the powerful magic of the great poet. The hill at Norcombe and the heath at Egdon are unforgettably beautiful. H's contemporary landscape carries the same prestige as the land where Macbeth met the three sisters.

H's two greats are *Tess of the d'Urbervilles* and *Jude the Obscure*. *Tess* is the story of a pure woman, faithfully represented, which justifies H's definition of the novel as: "an attempt to give artistic form to a series of real events." Nowhere does he present the heroine as the seduced and abandoned girl who pays a social debt. "A novel is an impression rather than an argument," says H. Nor is the vanity of present justice denounced or the cruelty of destiny playing with human lives. *Tess* alarmed the puritan public. Five years later H published *Jude* with the epigraph: "the letter kills." Jude, a peasant of Wessex who aspires to the intellectual life, and his cousin Sue, who is a torment to his faith, H has made into a drama of the fatal battle between the letter and the spirit. *Jude* is a tragedy of impossible ends which denounces the cruelty of love and culture on a level with the book of Job. H presents a condemnation of all modern thought. Opinion did not follow H, and he abandoned the novel and returned to poetry.

The Dynasts, a drama of the Napoleonic wars in three parts, nineteen acts, and 300 scenes, is an epic action, an intellectual exercise, which is Shakespearean in its breadth, diversity of character, and simultaneous use of verse and prose. H's verse is bland and monotonous. The work comes alive only in its animated characters and the sincerity of inspiration. In *Dynasts* a ray of hope breaks through as it does in a number of other poems less lyrical than intellectual and dramatic. Their originality lies in the fragile note of confidence: the earth is created for the joy of man which is possible if man abandons his beliefs and illusions and recreates his birthright to have a new reality to feed his joy. [Note on pp. 108–9 contains a brief biographical sketch and a bibliography of his principal novels.] [In French.]

1101 Lawrence, Isabelle Wentworth. "The Human Shows of Thomas Hardy," BOSTON EVENING TRANSCRIPT, 2 Jan 1926, pt. 6, p. 4.

The theme of H's *Human Shows, Far Phantasies, Songs, and Trifles* is the "essential but terrible loneliness of the individual human soul."

1102 LeGallienne, Richard. THE ROMANTIC 90's (Garden City, NY: Doubleday, Page, 1926), pp. 67, 195.

[H mentioned in passing as England's own "apostle of 'naturalism.' " Some articles collected in this volume first appeared in SATURDAY EVENING POST.]

1926: 1101-1106

1103 "Literature," A.L.A. BOOKLIST, XXII (March 1926), 243.
Human Shows, Far Phantasies, Songs, and Trifles is generally "realistic, and contains the germ of many a superbly ironical or tragic story," although some "are indeed 'far phantasies,' lyrical and imaginative."

1104 Lowe, Orton. "The Poetry Corner: Thomas Hardy," SCHOLASTIC, IX (18 Sept 1926), 12.
H can be "one of the most delicately beautiful lyricists in the language." [Brief introduction to a group of H poems.]

1105 Lowes, John Livingston. "Two Readings of Earth," YALE REVIEW, ns XV (April 1926), 515–39; rptd in OF READING BOOKS (Lond: Constable, 1930); ESSAYS IN APPRECIATION (Boston: Houghton Mifflin, 1936), pp. 119–56; rptd (Port Washington, NY: Kennikat P, 1967), pp. 121–56.
The Wessex Poems show H's world of contrasting light and dark, solitary dark figures against endless space, and men and women infinitesimal and yet elemental in the universe. It is a world of dawn, dusk, and night representing phantom potentialities and presences. Light and shadow throw unusual meanings over scenes and people. Night contains the relentless forces which determine man's fate. Infinite time and space form the background for the insignificant activities of tiny man. Measureless Past is an eternally present force in human destiny. *The Dynasts* is unrivaled in literature for the grandeur of its conception. It is vividly pictorial. The key to the power of *Dynasts* lies in the blind mindlessness of the primal force, haunted by its dream of man. Meredith's bright, unhaunted world contrasts with H's, but both writers see death as only one of the many changes of earth. Wind in H is ambiguous; in Meredith it is a glorious, cleansing force. Meredith's earth listens and responds to the starry universe as if it is a winged thing; H's listens and broods. The sense of union of man and earth is important in Meredith, for earth becomes spiritual through man. But for H man is only the fantasy of a disordered mindlessness.

1106 Lucas, Frank L. "The Triumph of Time," NEW STATESMAN, XXVI (23 Jan 1926), 448–49.
Human Shows, Far Phantasies, Songs, and Trifles brings "a strange, tangled mood . . . painful, yet thrilled; saddened, yet exhilarated." Turning to H after Wordsworth, "I become conscious of an intense relief that such suppressions [the failure to speak truth about God] have no longer to be made." H's poetry "never flatters or falters with the truth." H's style, a "strange, rough dialect," is appropriate to his subject: "the things of every day." Much of H's writing "has consisted in . . . stringing together distant moments into a necklace of flashing irony."

1107 McNutt, Roy D. "A Visit to Mr. Thomas Hardy," DAL-HOUSIE REVIEW, VI (April 1926), 51–55.

A visit with H shows his gentle, unassuming manner but also his essential genius. People of Dorchester respect his privacy. H said *A Pair of Blue Eyes* was the favorite among his novels. H was fond of Jane Austen and Dickens; he had much in common with the latter: Dickens did for London what H has for Wessex.

1108 Macy, John. "Hardy and the Nobel Prize," SATURDAY RE-VIEW OF LITERATURE, II (6 March 1926), 616.

H, "the greatest living man of letters," should receive the Nobel prize.

1109 Manly, John Matthews. "Thomas Hardy," ENGLISH PROSE AND POETRY (Boston: Ginn, 1926, rvd ed), p. 861.

H was more profound and universal than any other writer of his day. He wrote beautiful, intense prose. [Poems rptd, pp. 679–85.]

1110 Marble, Annie Russell. "Hardy Again," SATURDAY REVIEW OF LITERATURE, II (15 May 1926), 796.

H would be omitted from Nobel prize recognition for three reasons: his late recognition, his fatalism rather than "idealism," and the lack of a prestigious nominating academy, all at variance with prevailing award principles. *The Dynasts* is, however, a "glorious epic with a final note of idealistic surmise."

1111 Maynard, Theodore. "The Poetry of Thomas Hardy," CATHOLIC WORLD, CXXIII (April 1926), 46–54.

Though H's genius accomplished "prodigies in verse" it is "most naturally itself when it works in prose." There is an unfinished quality to H's verse: "the perfect adjustment [between form and substance] has not been effected." H's few perfect poems are all simple lyrics, e.g. "When I Set Out for Lyonesse," "The Oxen," "The Darkling Thrush." Many of H's poems are " 'broken arcs'; but even these so often have a grandeur and nobility that can rarely be found in more perfectly finished things."

1112 Moore, M. "Memory's Immortal Gear," DIAL, LXXX (May 1926), 417–21.

In *Human Shows, Far Phantasies, Songs, and Trifles*, H shows keen observation, awareness, intense particularity, and originality in the characterizing of nature. One perceives always "a justly dramatic interest in the significance of what seems insignificant." One must accept as poetic certain apparently unpermissible plots. H can "feel as well as look at cosmic malady." He is a craftsman with his own distinctive technical idiom which he has mastered, but he is even more a seer than a craftsman.

1113 Morgan, Charles. "Drinkwater's Dramatization of Hardy's *Mayor*," NEW YORK TIMES, 2 Oct 1926, VIII, p. 2.

The dramatization was faithful to H's novel, superbly acted and staged, but the play was dead. The novel, a work of art, was the story's final form: the play is hollow by comparison.

1114 Partridge, Eric. "Thomas Hardy: The Novelist," A CRITICAL MEDLEY (Paris: Librairie Ancienne Honoré Champion, 1926), pp. 77–86.

H's morality is not obscured by a pessimism rooted in irony and concern with operations of chance. H's novels achieve the concrete universal, for he "sees further than most men into the hearts of men and things" with keen psychological insight and a "deep, liberal sympathy." Joy and humor are present along with gloom. H excels at characterization. [Takes issue with Chesterton on H's ideas of God and nature.] Architecture of plots avoids intricacy; the style is poetic, "vigorous, sinewy, and picturesque." [An introduction concentrating on *Tess of the d'Urbervilles* and *Jude the Obscure*. Comparisons with Meredith, Bennett, Phillpotts. Liberal use of quotation from H and others. Impressionistic, sensible, often perceptive.]

1115 Pearson, Edmund. "The Book Table: Poetry," OUTLOOK (NY), CXLII (17 March 1926), 424–25.

Among the fragments of West Country description and wonderful examples of lyric art in *Human Shows, Far Phantasies, Songs, and Trifles*, there are "five or six really important poems." Some technical experiments in rhythms and verse forms are successful, others unfortunate. "Waiting Both" is true poetry.

1116 [Pearson, Hesketh]. THE WHISPERING GALLERY: BEING LEAVES FROM A DIPLOMAT'S DIARY (Lond: Lane, 1926), pp. 99, 122–24.

H is one of those upon whom the general public has bestowed a "strange halo of sanctity." Impressions gained from a week-end visit include H's unconcern with himself and interest in everyday matters, another incongruity of the "dismal" outlook and the pleasant old gentleman appearance. A remembered epigram stands for all his life and works: "Fate stalks us with depressing monotony from womb to tomb, and, when we are least expecting it, deals us a series of crushing blows from behind. Though the rays of intermittent happiness are permitted to play on us for our greater undoing, we are marked down for miserable ends." [Flip.]

1117 Phelps, William Lyon. "Using Graphic Algebra on Thomas Hardy," LITERARY DIGEST INTERNATIONAL BOOK REVIEW, IV (Jan 1926), 109, 111.

A graph reveals when H's novels were published and how they may be ranked. *Desperate Remedies* is the worst, and *Jude the Obscure* is next to it. The best, in descending order, are *The Return of the Native, Tess of the d'Urbervilles, The Woodlanders*, and *Far From the Madding Crowd*. [There is a great deal of Phelps's pretensions to humor here and very little worthwhile comment on H.]

1118 Phillips, R. Le Clerc. "Gifted Couples Run Risks of Rival Glory," NEW YORK TIMES, 21 Nov 1926, VIII, p. 18.
[While commenting on several gifted couples, Phillips notes that Mrs. H won't publish her poetry, rather is satisfied to live in the reflected glory of H.]

1119 Royde-Smith, N. G. "The Drama: The Material for Plays," OUTLOOK (Lond), LVIII (18 Sept 1926), 267.
Despite good individual performances by the actors, John Drinkwater's adaptation of *The Mayor of Casterbridge* sacrifices a great novel for a poor drama. Many of the scenes in H's novel take place outside; the play is confined to indoor sets, and thus loses the impact of many of the best episodes in the novel. [Review of John Drinkwater's unpublished dramatic adaptation of *Mayor*.]

1120 Sassoon, Siegfried. "Thomas Hardy," GREAT NAMES: BEING AN ANTHOLOGY OF ENGLISH AND AMERICAN LITERATURE (NY: Dial P, 1926), pp. 270–71.
"In his short poems he fuses all that he has learned from the past and endured in the present in a supreme imaginative vision, with masterly and original craft in words and a powerful and subtle ironic sense."

1121 Scherr, Johannes. ILLUSTRIERTE GESCHICHTE DER WELT-LITERATUR (Illustrated History of World Literature). 11th ed, rvd and enlgd by Dr. Ludwig Lang (Stuttgart: Dieck, 1926–1927), p. 112.
H is England's best representative of regional literature. [In German.]

1122 Shafer, Robert. "Thomas Hardy," CHRISTIANITY AND NATURALISM (New Haven: Yale UP, 1926), pp. 235–81.
Although H saw himself as an evolutionary meliorist, he came increasingly to believe in deterministic monism. Ultimately he professed that chance determines everything, that the universe is a "mechanism," that life is futile and empty, and that men are puppets. Consequently, he found naturalism credible. Thus he accepted the view that man, in that he has a dual nature, is swayed by both wrong and "divine" impulses. However, since the latter are man-made, man should obey only his "strongest, universal impulses." In saying this, H in effect "resigned his humanity."

1123 Shanks, Edward. "The 'New' Poetry, 1911–1925: a Survey," QUARTERLY REVIEW, CCXLVI (Jan 1926), 138–53.

H and Housman were "premature Georgians." They moved away from the worn imitation of Tennyson and Swinburne: H *"compelling* words to evoke such emotions as he chose, and Mr. Housman expressing lyrical feeling in a simple, epigrammatic, almost lapidary style" yet neither has been revolutionary.

1124 Shipp, H. "The Novel and the Play," ENGLISH REVIEW, XLIII (Oct 1926), 469–71.

Though the cinematic cutting back and forth between different time-sequences is an interesting experiment in dramatizing H's *The Mayor of Casterbridge,* Drinkwater's adaptation blurs the novelist's presentation of fate dominating human life. Nonetheless this stage version of H's novel is superior dramatically to the author's own adaptation of *Tess of the d'Urbervilles.* [Review of John Drinkwater's unpublished dramatic adaptation of *Mayor.*]

1125 Smith, Alexander Brent. "The Place of Music in the Works of Thomas Hardy," STUDIES AND CAPRICES (Lond: Methuen, 1926), pp. 164–71.

H, unlike most men of letters, is able in his works to make the various art forms "a real part of human life." Thus we find "that his love of astronomy is in a certain sense a love of architectural immensities; that he is equally capable of regarding a fine tune in terms of a Gothic arch as he is of admiring a fine building as a masterly symphonic stone-poem. His method as an artist is . . . [to take] as his stand-point the common knowledge of mankind such as any normal person without any particular technical knowledge can comprehend; then, having established this position, he occasionally throws the brilliance of his own intellect upon it, thereby revealing the myriad thoughts that lie behind."

1126 "Thomas Hardy—A Man of Solitude," WORLD REVIEW (Chicago), II (8 March 1926), 56–57.

H's "shyness has an arrogance about it, as if it came from fear that a warm, reckless human contact . . . might rob him of his . . . classic pessimism."

1127 Valakis, Apollo P. D. "The MOIRA of Aeschylus and the Immanent Will of Thomas Hardy," CLASSICAL JOURNAL, XXI (March 1926), 431–42.

Perhaps because of their occasional similarities in diction, Aeschylus and H have often been thought to share a similar vision of mankind. But there is little resemblance either in language or philosophy. H's fitful vocabulary intrudes upon his reader and lacks the unvarying stateliness of Aeschylus. Furthermore, the Greek tragedian affirmed a universe in which both men and gods could make good prevail over evil. H's god or Immanent Will cannot derive from the MOIRA of the Greeks since H believed in a blind, purposeless power foreign to Greek conceptions of the world. The contrast between the two writers is no more clear than in their most famous female creations: Tess and Antigone. Tess goes to her pathetic death because H wills it so; Antigone achieves a truly tragic end because Aeschylus shows us that she dies for something worth the suffering, and in this way rouses sympathy for his heroine.

1128 Van Doren, Mark. "First Glance," NATION (NY), CXXII (20 Jan 1926), 64.

In spite of the fact that most of the poems in *Human Shows, Far Phantasies, Songs, and Trifles* are bad, it nevertheless furthers the opinion that H is the most considerable living British poet. The flaws in the poems are merely aspects of a yet undefined central virtue rising out of H's ability to create within himself an infinite variety of human moods. Above all, the poems are consistently readable, always interesting.

1129 Van Doren, Mark. "The Still Visible World," NEW YORK HERALD TRIBUNE BOOK REVIEW, 24 Jan 1926, p. 6.

In *Human Shows, Far Phantasies, Songs, and Trifles,* H, who has always been a lyric poet at heart, repeatedly exhibits the characteristic quality of his poetry: he "grasps with an almost pathetic intensity at the tangible facts of earth lest they escape with him into that void in which, presumably, there are no arts and no remembrances."

1130 Vowinckel, Ernst. DER ENGLISCHE ROMAN DER NEUESTEN ZEIT UND GEGENWART (The English Novel of Recent and Present Time) (Berlin: Herbig, 1926), pp. 131–38.

H is a deterministic realist. H presents an aesthetic as well as organic harmony between life and man. His works deserve to be considered as the highest form of metaphysical art. [In German.]

1131 Wilkinson, Marguerite. "Thomas Hardy's Gallery of Portraits," LITERARY DIGEST INTERNATIONAL BOOK REVIEW, IV (Sept 1926), 628, 630.

Human Shows, Far Phantasies, Songs, and Trifles reveals again the strength and essential honesty which have informed all H's best work, qualities which allow him to make poetry of what should be dull, boring, or sentimental material. He is "one of the few poets who know . . . that Nature is austerely beautiful, but seldom pretty except in details and particles."

1132 Wolfe, Humbert. *"Human Shows: Far Phantasies* by Thomas Hardy," NEW CRITERION, IV (April 1926), 384–88, espec 384–86. The power of the earth does not appear in H's poetry, although his novels "breathe, like the world at night, deeply and slowly" and neither assert nor seek. H's poetry "stubbornly argues," and H expects his poems "to invest themselves in loveliness without any assistance from him," as he is indifferent to shape. Death, "to him the natural disaster which consummates the tragedy of life," is used this way in much of the poetry. Even though H's poetry is uninspiring, *The Dynasts* is a true epic.

1133 Wood, William. "Hardy and the Nobel Prize," SATURDAY REVIEW OF LITERATURE (NY), II (27 March 1926), 666.
John Macy's suggestion (ibid [6 March 1926], 616) that H should receive the Nobel prize is sound, but the Nobel committee decided not to consider fully-established major writers.

1927

1134 Aas, L. THOMAS HARDY OG HANS DIGTNING (Thomas Hardy and His Work) (Copenhagen: Haase, 1927).
[Chapters on Wessex, the novels and short stories, the poems, *The Dynasts*, and H's thought. Not seen, but reviewed by W. Worster, "Thomas Hardy," BOOKMAN (Lond), LXX (July 1928), 220–21, as being rather extensive than intensive, chiefly a compilation of data and opinion rather than an interpretation of H's work.] [In Danish.]

1135 Arns, Karl. "Hardys neue Lyrik" (Hardy's New Lyrics), ZEITSCHRIFT FÜR FRANZÖSISCHEN UND ENGLISCHEN UNTERRICHT, XXVI (1927), 175–86.
H's poetry is natural and spontaneous. It reveals a simple manner of expression, repetition, and variation. H's metrical versatility and his ability to realize his artistic purpose is stronger in the later poems. An examination of the content of these poems reveals that H is not a pessimist in the true sense of the word. [In German.]

1136 Arns, Karl. "Thomas Hardy, *Human Shows* . . .," ENGLISCHE STUDIEN, LXI (May 1927), 299–301.
It won't do to call H a pessimist. The ground-tone of his verse is tragic and earnest, but he believes in love, a great true love, as that for his first wife. [In German.]

1137 Austin, Frederic. THREE WESSEX SONGS (Lond: Boosey, 1927).
[Musical settings of "When I Set Out for Lyonesse," "Though Dynasties Pass," and "The Fiddler."]

1138 Braybrooke, Patrick. THOMAS HARDY AND HIS PHILOSOPHY (Phila: Lippincott, 1927).
H's philosophy "is certainly, I think, melancholy. It may even be morbid." H's thought did not evolve: "Mr. Hardy, in my opinion, adopts precisely the same stand-point to life in his early works as he does in his later volumes. All through his works his quarrel with life asserts itself. There is never the slightest indication that Mr. Hardy has any intention of growing out of his gloom." One difference between H's prose and his verse is that while both are somber, gloomy, pessimistic, deterministic, and materialistic, the poetry contains "an amused satirical vein which is not very apparent in the prose works."

1139 Brebner, J. Bartlet (ed), et al. CLASSICS OF THE WESTERN WORLD (Chicago: American Library Assoc., 1927); 2nd ed rvd (1934), pp. 114–15.
[Recommends *The Dynasts, Time's Laughingstocks, Satires of Circumstance*, and *The Return of the Native*. Under "Additional" list are: *Under the Greenwood Tree, The Woodlanders, The Mayor of Casterbridge*, and *Jude the Obscure*.]

1140 Browne, P. H. A COLLECTION OF THE WRITINGS OF THOMAS HARDY, 1927. . . . (Chicago: P. H. Browne, 1927).
[A Chicago bookseller's mimeographed catalog of works by and about H.]

1141 Chase, Mary Ellen. THOMAS HARDY FROM SERIAL TO NOVEL (Minneapolis: University of Minnesota P, 1927).
[Compares serial versions of *The Mayor of Casterbridge, Tess of the d'Urbervilles*, and *Jude the Obscure* to their book versions, primarily to reveal bowdlerizations made for Victorian serial readers. Many significant changes.] *Mayor*: in serial Henchard had married Lucetta out of gratitude for saving his life, in novel they had had an illicit affair; serial readers' desire for sensationalism caused H in serial to lengthen battle with the bull and to have Farfrae come upon Henchard and Lucetta in the amphitheater. *Tess*: in serial Alec wins Tess through sham wedding, in book by seduction; the baptism of Sorrow is not in the serial; serial and novel have different sequences of letters by Angel and Tess; in serial Tess is not accosted by Alec in Kingsbere Church; in serial Tess and Alec do not share the same apartment in Sandbourne. *Jude*: in serial Arabella tricks Jude into marrying her by making him jealous with a feigned lover, in the book she seduces him and tells him she is pregnant; in serial Jude and Arabella do not spend the night together in Aldbrickham after meeting in Christminster; in serial Jude

and Sue live in different houses, they eventually adopt a child rather than have two of their own, and Sue is not pregnant when Father Time commits murder and suicide. [This pioneering textual study is marred by vagueness as to which edition of the book text she is referring to at several points.]

1142 Cross, W. L. "The Contemporary Novel," DEVELOPMENT OF THE ENGLISH NOVEL (NY: Macmillan, 1927), pp. 272–80.
H is the "best English representation" of philosophical realism. He uses people from the lower walks of life, where conduct is undisguised, as subjects. His language aims at "exact and felicitous expression of his ideas and emotions." *Tess of the d'Urbervilles* is "his mightiest production," a tragedy belonging to these "*fin de siécle days.*" It reverses the assumption of English tragedy that the hero must commit some deed for which he suffers. Tess's only weakness is the result of heredity and environment, coincidence and happenstance, not her will. H and other philosophical realists fail to account for the human feeling that we are free.

1143 Fehr, Bernhard. ENGLISCHE PROSA VON 1880 BIS ZUR GEGENWART (English Prose from 1880 to the Present) (Berlin: B. G. Trübner, 1927), pp. 11, 22, 23, 45, 106, 107, 127–31.
[Compares H to English naturalists. Criticizes H's characterizations and praises his sensual descriptions.] [In German.]

1144 Fletcher, John Gould. "Perennial Hardy," SATURDAY REVIEW OF LITERATURE, III (12 Feb 1927), 576–77.
H's reputation as a poet, apart from *The Dynasts*, will stand on *Satires of Circumstance* and *Moments of Vision* plus some random poems—all of H's work English to its marrow. There is no prevailing unity of subject matter. H is an impressionist in vision and an individualist in philosophy—neither one currently in favor. His style is magnificent, despite his occasional flounderings into rusticity and is adapted to his brooding reflective type of mind. "On a Midsummer Eve" is notable for its simplicity; "Satires of Circumstance" for asperity; "Two Rosalinds" for complexity. [Review of *The Collected Poems of Thomas Hardy* (1926).]

1145 Flower, Newman. "Hardy's Mother's Quips," NEW YORK TIMES BOOK REVIEW, 2 Oct 1927, p. 18.
Mrs. H thought Americans were brainless lunatics. When they asked for a straw from the thatched roof she told them they could buy a load for the pound note they often insisted she take. She remarked about them: "Do they not suppose that my roof has been thatched since Tom was born?"

1146 Fogelquist, Torsten. "Thomas Hardy," TYPER OCH TÄNKESÄTT (Types and Trends of Thought) (Stockholm: Albert Bonniers, 1927), pp. 148–56.

Only when H became a patriarch in England did his novels become popular in Sweden. His first Swedish translations went virtually unnoticed because of the Gallic tastes of critics like Levertin, but by the 1920s new translations began to win him admirers in Sweden. His books are heavily descriptive, but not naturalistic in the Continental way, for he disliked Zolaesque fascination with details and preferred the more idealized and philosophical prose of earlier English writers. Rich and vital as his landscapes and characters (especially women) are, the lack of psychological reality and the ever-present burden of preconceived theories and complex plots weakens the effect of his novels. Despite the influence of Schopenhauer and naturalism, H's work verges ultimately on the romantic. [In Swedish.]

1147 Forster, E. M. ASPECTS OF THE NOVEL (Lond: Edward Arnold; NY: Harcourt, Brace, 1927), pp. 140–42, 198.

Sometimes a plot triumphs too completely in H's work. He seems to be a poet and conceives of his novels from a great height. He arranges events with emphasis on causality. This works for him in *The Dynasts*, but in the novel medium he never "catches humanity in its teeth."

1148 Forzato-Spezia, B. "Thomas Hardy," STIRPE (1927), pp. 713–15.

After the great figures of the Victorian period, such as Tennyson, Browning, Rossetti, Swinburne, the erroneous opinion exists that a period ensued that could only produce mediocre work. The period of the industrialization and democratization of society with the rapid diffusion of ideas and influences would suffocate imagination in the name of science. Two profound novelists, H and Meredith, anchored a new spirit. Both are romantics in characterization and austerity, but both deal with a sacred reality to which men owe obedience but not servitude. H puts aside the influence of industrialism and modern thought and concentrates on agrarian conservatism, the peasant tradition. Great Britain follows the new horizon of industrialism, the postulates and influences of new theories of life, geology, biology, chemistry which are creating a new phenomenon of the world. All this is contrapuntal to H's fundamental conception, which is deterministic and pessimistic. The pessimism of H presents a fundamental tragic vision, sorrowful and funereal, sincere in a passion which is a tremendous resonance of the human spirit. H's work is never freed by cheerfulness.

In poetry, H attempts a grand line, lyrical in his poetic quest in *The Dynasts* which demonstrates the new and characteristic depth in contemporary lyricism. The general character of the work is calm, sad, and has a sense of hope with a touch of disgust and despair. A critic of life, he did not see any resolution for the problem of misery. He searched for an eternal design and found an immense mechanism guiding human destiny. H had a sense of sympathy for man. The human tragedy is illumined by a quality of joy sought by H in abandonment to communion with nature, the unchangeable and consoling element of the world.

Fatalism of desperate sadness forms the *leitmotif* of his poetry. The element of tragedy is not relieved by any principle of living, love, or hope of remedy: man is determined and is not morally free, not held responsible for his own action, and always moves to a desperate conclusion.

The originality of his technique consists in the faithful expression of passionate feeling, custom, and manners. The result is a lyric expression, vigorous and new. H is a strong voice in prose and poetry. [In Italian.]

1149 Hansford, F. E. "Literary Diversions: The Early Environment of Thomas Hardy," SCHOOLMASTER AND WOMAN TEACHER'S CHRONICLE, CXII (2 June 1927), 1112, 1114.
H's novels display a sensitiveness to nature and an appreciation of Wessex dialect that can be traced to his childhood in Upper Bockhampton. [First of two articles. See F. E. Hansford, "Some Formative Influences on Thomas Hardy's Art," ibid (16 June 1927), 1212, 1229.]

1150 Hansford, F. E. "Some Formative Influences on Thomas Hardy's Art," SCHOOLMASTER AND WOMAN TEACHER'S CHRONICLE, CXII (16 June 1927), 1212, 1229.
The experiences of H's early manhood left their mark upon his novels. The solitude of the Great Heath set the mood of many works, especially *The Return of the Native*, and his architectural studies influenced both the setting of the novels and H's choice of the architect-hero who appears in several works. [Second of two articles. See F. E. Hansford, "Literary Diversions: The Early Environment of Thomas Hardy," ibid (2 June 1927), 1112, 1114.]

1151 Harris, Frank. "Thomas Hardy," LATEST CONTEMPORARY PORTRAITS (NY: Macaulay, 1927), pp. 150–61.
In the later Eighties, H was unaffected, simple, and sincere. If you said anything worthwhile, he would stop and dwell on it, and his thoughts bred a certain melancholy sadness in him. His philosophy, his thoughts on life and living were soul-revealing. He was preoccupied, indeed almost obsessed, by thoughts of death and the undiscovered country, and above all by the transitoriness of human affairs. The best part of H's intelligence was his courage: he could not cozen himself with the foolish optimism that all is for the best. However, H was always being overpraised, his faults and weaknesses overlooked. He is too far divorced from reality, too much an idealist and poet, and at heart, overpowered by the tragedy of the world and the fleeting show

of human life. It was astounding to find that H was being ranked with Meredith as one of the Immortals. He is indeed astonishingly articulate in prose and verse, but he has little or nothing of any value to say.

1152 Hitchcock, Helen. "An Aspect of Hardy," VASSAR JOURNAL OF UNDERGRADUATE STUDIES, II (May 1927), 88–96.

H has "the prime requirement for the artist": the power to *see*, which encompasses "visual accuracy and emotional realization." H's deep interest in painting and architecture is apparent in his novels. "His novels are a series of pictures . . . great figure-pieces where background, figures, light, color and perspective all receive . . . careful development."

1153 Mainsard, Joseph. "La Pensée de Thomas Hardy" (The Thought of Thomas Hardy), ETUDES, CXCI (20 May 1927), 439–61.

In place of God, H posits "a strange idol, a blind unconscious Will." The laws governing brute Nature control man as well. The late-phase H is best understood in terms of Schopenhauer. In *The Dynasts*, H offers a tentative solution to mankind's dilemma. The solution is modeled along the lines of Schopenhauerean thought. In man, Will "knows" itself and its own hideousness for the first time. Will, through the empirical egos of individual men, can pierce through this phenomenology of evil, and contemplate the mystic world beyond appearances. This mystic world is characterized by an aesthetic unity that can calm the mind. [In French.]

1154 Mayoux, J. J. "La Fatalité Intérieure dans les Romans de Thomas Hardy" (Interior Fatality in the Novels of Thomas Hardy), REVUE ANGLO-AMÉRICAINE, IV (Feb 1927), 208–19.

H's *Weltanschauung* must be seen in the context of its historical milieu. It is an "anti-optimism" reacting against Victorian optimism. The typical Victorian believed in evolutionary meliorism. H likewise believes in evolution, but reverses the values: he sees human consciousness as an evolutionary "breakthrough" but as a "breakthrough" to misery. Nature, in and through man, is for the first time conscious of its own hopeless predicament. [In French.]

1155 Myers, Walter L. THE LATER REALISM (Chicago: University of Chicago P, 1927), pp. 60–61, 80, 103–4, 110–11, 141–43.

In *The Mayor of Casterbridge*, Michael Henchard represents an early approach to incongruity. H was more interested in large movements than specific, unqualified truths. Realism in H's characterizations is enriched by philosophical and poetical elements. Such extra-realism later become commonplace. Milieu is an important element in H's characterization. His personal description varies from the perfunctory to the highly detailed. A tendency toward less reflection, greater consciousness of scene, and the use of trivial details represents the influence of French naturalism. [An early recognition of the complex nature of H's realistic mode.]

1156 Palmer, C. H. "The Religion of Thomas Hardy's Wessex," AMERICAN CHURCH MONTHLY, XXI (Aug 1927), 425–29.

"If poor Tess had had a good parish priest in whom she might have confided," instead of the one who refused to bury her irregularly baptized baby, "how different might her fate have been!" [Officious and mechanical piosity.]

1157 Priestley, J. B. THE ENGLISH NOVEL (Lond: Nelson, 1927, 1935); rptd (Lond: Ernest Benn [Essex Library], 1931), pp. 99, 107–14, 124.

H was "a dour but pitiful pessimist" who wrote philosophical novels about simple rural people fostered by their "special environment." Since H manipulated these characters and allowed malevolent Nature to play games with them, he often falsified life. He was, however, a great novelist because he structured his novels, controlled atmosphere perfectly, and had a sense of drama.

1158 Proust, Marcel. LES CAHIERS MARCEL PROUST (Memorials of Marcel Proust). 8 vols (Paris: Gallimard, 1927–1935), I (HOMMAGE À MARCEL PROUST) (In Honor of Marcel Proust) (1927); relevant letter in MARCEL PROUST: LETTRES ET CONVERSATIONS (Marcel Proust: Letters and Conversations), ed by Robert de Billy (Paris: Editions de Portiques, 1930), pp. 180–81; included in LETTERS OF MARCEL PROUST, trans and ed by Mina Curtiss (NY: Random House, 1949), pp. 204–5.

Letter to Robert de Billy (ca. Dec 1909): *The Well-Beloved* is "very beautiful" and "slightly resembles what I am doing (only it is a thousand times better). . . . It doesn't even lack that slight touch of the grotesque which is an essential part of all great works." [Also see Klaus Dryer, "Proust on Hardy," COLBY MERCURY, VII (Dec 1941)—not listed here.] [In French.]

1159 Pure, Simon [pseud of Frank Arthur Swinnerton]. "The Londoner; Mr. Shaw, Mr. Hardy, and the Nobel Prize," BOOKMAN (NY), LXIV (Feb 1927), 720–21.

The fact that Mr. Shaw received the Nobel Prize rather than H makes one take note that H's notoriety is dwindling, and Mr. Shaw's is obviously increasing—on the national level. H's reputation as a pessimist may have also been a factor which prevented him from receiving the prize.

1160 Rann, Ernest H. "The Hardy Country," THE HOMELAND OF ENGLISH AUTHORS (Lond: Methuen; NY: Dutton [1927]), pp. 68–95.

[Tour of "the new Wessex," i.e. draws the usual parallels between real towns and sights and those in H's novels, stories, and poems.]

1161 Ruhrmann, Friedrich G. "Studien zur Geschichte und Charakteristik des Refrains in der englischen Literatur." (Studies in the History and Characteristics of the Refrain in English Literature), ANGLISTIK FORSCHUNGEN (English Studies) (Heidelberg: Carl Winters, 1927), p. 176.

[Lists H with great Victorian writers.] [In German.]

1162 Salberg, Gerda. THOMAS HARDYS FRAUEN IM LICHTE SEINER WELTANSCHAUUNG (Thomas Hardy's Women in the Light of His World View) (Mulhouse: Editions "Alsatia," 1927); University of Zurich dissertation.

The characterization of Eustacia, Tess, and Sue reveals that H was interested primarily in the psychological and intellectual conflicts of his female characters and not in their physical or social needs. [In German.]

1163 Schultheis, L. M. "Thomas Hardy," DER TÜRMER, XXX (Oct 1927–March 1928), 489.

H, one of the most impressive English authors, is almost unknown in Germany. His greatest contribution to literature stems from an inner association with his native Dorset. H is one of the few authors on the other side of the channel who could not disregard the kinship of the German and English people. [In German.]

1164 Shanks, Edward. "Hardy and the 'New' Poetry," SECOND ESSAYS ON LITERATURE (Lond: Collins, 1927), pp. 112–14.

H and A. E. Housman are poets who, in different ways, "turned from the exhausted and etiolated Tennysonian manner and from that Swinburnian manner which was so fatally easy for any imitator to acquire and so impossible for any imitator to put to the smallest living use." Their turn "implies a turn to reality, . . . and each contributed a new method of using language, Hardy *compelling* words to evoke such emotions as he chose."

1165 Symons, Arthur. A STUDY OF THOMAS HARDY (Lond: Charles J. Sawyer, 1927).

"In all his work, Hardy is concerned with one thing, seen under two aspects: not civilization, not manners, but the principal of life itself, invisibly realized as Sex, seen visibly in the world as what we call Nature." H is "a fatalist and he studies the workings of fate in the chief living and disturbing influence of life, woman." [Discussion of *A Pair of Blue Eyes, A Laodicean, Jude the Obscure, The Return of the Native.*]

1166 Trueblood, C. K. "The Poetry of Thomas Hardy," DIAL, LXXXII (June 1927), 522–25.

H's greatest sympathies are for life's most living moments; his themes naturally come from the realms of passion. He is not a pessimist, nor an optimist, but compassionate, exacting "a full look at the worst. One should not mistake composure for resignation, or sombreness for surrender." His narrative lyrics are not as effective as his novels. The lyrics voicing a single personal feeling are superior, but they do not sing and lack a variety of feeling. H's diction is original but "buffets our expectations." [Review of *Collected Poems*.]

1167 Weltzien, Erich. DIE GEBÄRDEN DER FURCHT IN THOMAS HARDYS WESSEX-ROMANEN (The Face of Fear in Thomas Hardy's Wessex Novels) (Berlin: Willfried Deyhle, 1927); University of Griefswald dissertation.

Fear is illustrated in the protagonists, their cries for help, their unsuccessful attempts to escape, their search for shelter, and their involuntary involvement in unalterable circumstances. Characters belonging to the middle and upper classes—Clym Yeobright and Angel Clare—are almost free from fear or at least from the outward appearance of this feeling. [Weltzien summarized his contention in a letter to H on 28 March 1927. H answered on 18 April 1928: "In respect of the question you put—whether the men of the middle and upper classes here are almost free from fear—I am not able to give a definite reply, but I am inclined to think that they feel it whenever occasion arises, much as other men do, but have acquired a habit of not expressing it outwardly."] [In German.]

1168 Winterich, John T. A PRIMER OF BOOK COLLECTION (NY: Greenberg, 1927), pp. ix–x, 15, 64, 105–6, 153, 182–94; rvd (NY: Greenberg, 1935), pp. 50, 212–22, 239, 243–54. [Reference to the rarity of the first edition of Part I, *The Dynasts* (1903).]

H may become as much a collector's item as Dickens. Association copies, except by major authors like Dickens, Thackeray, or H, are not necessarily expensive. H collectors would welcome announcements from dealers not only of the rare London, 1871 *Desperate Remedies*, but also any new volumes, association copies, or sales and would resent advice from the dealer to collect Conrad instead of H. Collectors use the best bibliographies available, like Wise on Conrad and A. P. Webb and Henry Danielson on H. [Compares prices of *Desperate Remedies, Under the Greenwood Tree, A Pair of Blue Eyes, The Hand of Ethelberta, Far From the Madding Crowd, The Return of the Native, The Trumpet-Major, Two on a Tower, The Mayor of Casterbridge, The Woodlanders, Wessex Tales, Tess of the d'Urbervilles* and *The Dynasts* as estimated by Danielson in 1916 with actual prices at the McCutcheon sale in 1925, an increase of nine hundred percent on the average.]

1928

1169 Aas, L. "Thomas Hardy," URD, 21 Jan 1928, p. 33. [Obit.] [In Norwegian.]

1170 "Abbey Burial for Mr. Hardy," MORNING POST (Lond), 13 Jan 1928, p. 9.
The burial of H will take place at the Abbey at two o'clock Monday afternoon. [Contains messages from the King and Queen and the Prince of Wales to Mrs. H, and her replies.]

1171 "The Abbey Mourners," SUNDAY TIMES (Lond), 22 Jan 1928, p. 13.
A limited number of the general public will be admitted to H's Westminster Abbey funeral service.

1172 " 'Aberdeen' Ms," ABERDEEN UNIVERSITY REVIEW, XV (March 1928), 142.
The holograph manuscript of the short poem "Aberdeen" and H's accompanying letter have been given to the Aberdeen University Library by Theodore Watt, editor of ALMA MATER, which printed the poem in Sept 1906. The poem was written in April 1905, on the occasion of H's receiving the LL.D.

1173 Adcock, [Arthur] St. John. "Thomas Hardy," BOOKMAN (Lond), LXXIII (Feb 1928), 263–66.
Unlike Dickens, who was a man of the town, H was a man of the country, expressing a "contemplative spirit." "His novels are not ethical treatises," nor "scientific exposition of universal law"; rather, they are descriptions of life as H perceives it. It is not pessimism which one finds in his works; "it is the simple hard truth about life." As a poet, however, he fails. He was much more a poet in his novels.

1174 Alexander, Hooper. "Hardy's Plagiarism," NEW REPUBLIC, LIV (29 Feb 1928), 71.
H is said to have plagiarized an account of a militia drill in *The Trumpet-Major* from A. B. Longstreet's GEORGIA SCENES. The sketch comes originally from an actual incident recorded in 1820 by Oliver Prince.

1175 "Architecture and Thomas Hardy," ARCHITECT AND BUILDING NEWS (Lond), CXIX (20 Jan 1928), 119–21, 139, 147.
H started his literary career "after some fifteen years in the study of architecture." H's architectural training enriched and colored his literary works and rendered him "capable of descriptive work, . . . craftsmanship, well-

thought-out plan, well-wrought construction, and rigid economy of means" which characterize his work. H also sympathized with "the fate that overtakes buildings" from either continuous use or neglect. In *Far From the Madding Crowd*, H takes great pain describing the Great Barn, a noble medieval building. In *A Laodicean*, "the hero is an architect, [and] the 'second villain' is an architect." The central figure in *Jude the Obscure* is a stone mason—a "kindred spirit" to an architect.

1176 "At Max Gate," SUNDAY TIMES (Lond), 15 Jan 1928, p. 13. [A description of the hearse leaving Max Gate with H's body.]

1177 Barton, J. E. "The Genius of Thomas Hardy," BRISTOL TIMES AND MIRROR, 14 Jan 1928 [not seen in this form]; rptd as THE GENIUS OF THOMAS HARDY (Mount Durand, St. Peter Port, Guernsey: Toucan P, 1969) [bound in with No. 56, as No. 57 of the Monographs on the Life, Times and Works of Thomas Hardy Series].

Of all great figures in English literature, H had the greatest staying power and most consistent artistry. He was the unconscious and instinctive interpreter of nineteenth-century thought, and the only one able to embody in his art the barely conscious Victorian notion that man was not the center of the universe. H's ideas, rather than those of the political economists and professors, remain because they represent the change in outlook that went on under the surface in the Victorian era. He was not a cynic in the sense of denying the great virtues. He was a pessimist in not accepting easy answers, yet he constantly testified to life's grandeur. Unblinded by conventional "book-culture," H developed a poetic style that reveals a new beauty of the language. [Also see J. Stevens Cox (pub and general editor), Monographs on the Life of Thomas Hardy (1962).]

1178 Bauer, Gérard. "Le coeur et les cendres de Thomas Hardy" (The Heart and the Ashes of Thomas Hardy), L'ECHO DE PARIS, 19 Jan 1928.

The pomp and circumstance of H's funeral rites at Westminster Abbey and Stinsford came as a shock to us, for H never was a conformist and remained anti-Victorian to the end. Is Meredith's wish in LORD ORMONT near fulfillment? "English people have many things to learn, and above all, not to be frightened by ideas." [In French.]

1179 Bent, Silas. "Death and the Newspapers," NEW REPUBLIC, LIII (25 Jan 1928), 274–75.

[H's obituaries received half the space in five New York newspapers of that given to the execution of Ruth Snyder for murder of her corset-salesman lover.]

1180 Blanche, Jacques-Emile. "Souvenirs sur Thomas Hardy" (Recollections of Thomas Hardy), Les Nouvelles Littéraires, 21 Jan 1928, pp. 1–2; rptd in Mes Modèles: Barrès—Hardy—James—Gide—Moore (My Models: Barrès—Hardy—James—Gide—Moore) (Paris: Librairie Stock, 1928), pp. 77–90.

H was a shy little man who seemed not to belong to the "high society" life of the London "season." By 1900 he had only a kind of regional fame and very few people knew his works in France. During the sittings, H asked questions about the Napoleonic myth in France as he was then preparing what was to be *The Dynasts*. [Recollections by the man who painted the portrait of H now at the Tate Gallery.] [In French.]

1181 Blei, Franz. "Thomas Hardy," Erzählerkunst. Ein Almanach Auf Das Jahr 1927 (The Story-Teller's Art: An Almanac of the Year 1927), ed by Hans Reisiger (Leipzig: Paul List, 1928), pp. 80–83.

Germany has not accepted H. *Tess of the d'Urbervilles* is his best work and illustrates H's philosophy that life cannot be explained, that man knows only what is probable and never what is real, that a work of art is essentially unreal, for truth is only that which is experienced. H has his peculiarities, is somewhat difficult but original. [In German.]

1182 Boas, F. S. "A Lecture and its Sequel," Wessex: An Annual Record, I (June 1928), 27–28.

[Account of an ironical occurrence: Boas heard of H's second marriage moments after hearing a lecturer expound on the thesis that "women, as depicted by Hardy, are a disturbing and harassing influence."]

1183 Bombe, Walter. "Thomas Hardy," Deutsche Kunstwart, XLI (April 1928) 62–63.

Not themes but the power of presentation accounts for H's greatness. H was equally esteemed as a novelist, poet, and dramatist. George Bernard Shaw thought H was more articulate in poetry than prose, and Arnold Bennett believed that *The Dynasts* was superior to Tolstoy's War and Peace. [In German.]

1184 "Books: Death of Hardy," Time (Chicago), XI (23 Jan 1928), 30–31.

"The quiet tides of the country (Wessex), the slow changes of the land and its people, were a solemn whisper always ringing in his ears." H's reputation is due to "an intense sincerity, unconcerned with merely literary effects, a profound, pitying pessimism, a relentless humanism which condemns the disorderly deities who make men's lives sterile and without joy." H brought "to life out of darkness many harvests of bitter, golden grain."

1185 Boston, Noel. "Church Music a Hundred Years Ago," SIGN, XXIV (Dec 1928), 163.

H's description of church string and wind bands in the early nineteenth-century in *Under the Greenwood Tree* is vivid and accurately reflects the supplanting of the bands by harmoniums and barrel-organs.

1186 Boughton, Rutland. "A Musical Association with Thomas Hardy," MUSICAL NEWS AND HERALD, LXXIII (15 Feb 1928), 33–34.

In considering a musical setting of *The Famous Tragedy of the Queen of Cornwall* "the unrelieved grimness of the tragedy" posed a problem for the composer: a "weakness . . . would result from continuously playing on a single series of emotions." The difficulty was surmounted by inserting six H poems and by making substantial cuts in the play—all with H's approval.

1187 Boylesve, René. "Thomas Hardy," LA REVUE NOUVELLE, Nos. 38–39 (Jan–Feb 1928), 57–59.

We suspend disbelief when reading H's novels. Their characters are first only characters; then, as we identify with them, they become characters plus an aspect of ourselves; finally they become wholly symbols of ourselves, of mankind, and of the human condition. [In French.]

1188 Brash, W. B. "Thomas Hardy: June 2, 1840—Jan. 11, 1928," LONDON QUARTERLY REVIEW, CXLIX (April 1928), 145–57.

A poetic novelist in the great English tradition, H is "Hardy of Wessex, not of Westminster" in his six great tragic novels. H, however, "asks a little too much from extreme and odd coincidences." "His noblest characters become regal through their suffering, and are crowned with a crown of thorns." In *Tess of the d'Urbervilles,* there is a unity of compact surroundings and properly chosen local characters, part of the planning and symmetry in H's novels which comes from his architectural experience.

1189 Brooks, H. G. "A Hardy Tour Through Wessex," SCHOOL-MISTRESS, 21 June 1928, pp. 395, 410.

[Suggested itinerary for an eighty-mile auto trip through Wessex.]

1190 Bullet, Gerald. "Thomas Hardy: 1840–1928," LITERARY GUIDE, ns CCLXXX (Feb 1928), 32–33.

H's flaws are mere spots on a sun. Though our sons may react against him, later generations will honor him. His genius is barely recognized on the continent. He is for England "in the company of Shakespeare, Dickens and but few others." He was a Victorian in conflict with his age.

1191 Bulloch, J. M. "Thomas Hardy and Aberdeen," ABERDEEN UNIVERSITY REVIEW, XV (March 1928), 141–42.

Aberdeen was the first university "to recognise Hardy's genius" when it presented him with an honorary LL.D. degrees in 1905. H remembered the school as always having "a curiously romantic aspect." [Personal reminiscence by a member of the party present at the ceremony.]

1192 Burrell, Martin. "Two English Poets," BETWIXT HEAVEN AND CHARING CROSS (Toronto: Macmillan, 1928); rptd (Freeport, NY: Books for Libraries P, 1968), pp. 43–54.

H's poetry, for all its occasional clumsiness and its unevenness, is his most authentic artistic expression. In his verse, more clearly than in his fiction, we can see the intensely individualized, radically skeptical, essentially tragic and compassionate vision which culminates in the "spaciousness" and "freedom of movement" of *The Dynasts*, his masterpiece. [H treated with, but not compared or contrasted to, Masefield. Conventional appreciation.]

1193 Busse, Kurt. "Thomas Hardy und Wir" (Thomas Hardy and We), PREUSSISCHE JAHRBÜCHER, CCXI (March 1928), 359–61.

The great names in nineteenth-century English prose—Lamb, Emily Brontë, and H—"to us are all virtually unknown." H's style is a unique mixture of spontaneous originality and wide-reaching humanistic education. In form and conception, his works are bourgeois and Victorian, but H turned his back on the city which the era's culture created in order to plant himself and his art in peasant soil. If Germans are ever to appreciate H's works, a series of translations of his novels, and a film version of *The Dynasts* is essential. [In German.]

1194 C., M. "Thomas Hardy," OXFORD MAGAZINE, XLVI (18 March 1928), 407–8.

The height of incongruity was reached in the burial of H in Westminster Abbey. The Abbey is at least a Christian burial-place, while the Power that rules H's universe is malevolent, spiteful, capricious. This itself explains partly the rise of H's popularity in his later years—a popularity which will wane ere long.

1195 C., S. C. (B/C.). "The d'Urbervilles' Claim to Arms," NOTES AND QUERIES, CLIV (25 Feb 1928), 140.

[Reply to Parson Tringham, "The d'Urbervilles' Claim to Arms," ibid (11 Feb 1928), 101.] By applying to the College of Arms, Tess's brother could gain access to the numerous records of information on an ancestor who bore arms prior to 1415. Parish registers commenced in 1538.

1196 [Canby, Henry Seidel]. "He Carried On," SATURDAY REVIEW OF LITERATURE, IV (21 Jan 1928), 529, 532; rptd in AMERICAN ESTIMATES (NY: Harcourt, Brace, 1929), pp. 53–56; and in DESIGNED FOR READING (NY: Macmillan, 1934), pp. 165–67.

H is the "only Victorian spokesman for both the nineteenth and the twentieth century." His moral earnestness and pessimism shot through with pity are identical with the thinking of other Victorians, though he came to different conclusions he is not a behaviorist. Such interests as H's will renew their power after the present materialist age.

1197 Catalogne, Gérard de. "Ce que fut la vie de Thomas Hardy" (What the Life of Thomas Hardy was Like), LES NOUVELLES LITTÉRAIRES, 14 Jan 1928, p. 7.
H was a novelist, a poet and a philosopher; the beginning of his career was marked by his abandonment of the Christian faith; this coincided with his loss of the childhood world which he later tried to recapture as an artist. [In French.]

1198 Catalogne, Gérard de. LE MESSAGE DE THOMAS HARDY (The Message of Thomas Hardy) (Paris: Librairie de France, [1928]).
What the sea was to Conrad, Wessex was to H. At his hand he found clear evidence of the Roman past, strikingly poetic place-names, the vital primitivism of the fields and heaths, the durable simplicity of rustic life, and the possibility of achieving, through only minor manipulations of fact, a sense of mystery without mysticism. He exploited these natural characteristics of the region, and with them as a solid basis, he was able to achieve at once an artistic and a philosophic synthesis of the visible and the invisible, the natural and the supernatural. *The Dynasts* is the most perfect artistic fusion of the two and is, at the same time, H's most complete response to the "grand pourquoi" of the universe. [Preface by François Mauriac. Rather comprehensive biographical sketch; bibliography, including French translations. Repeats some of the anecdotes about H's first wife found in Jacques-Emile Blanche, MES MODÈLES (1928).] [In French.]

1199 Chang, Hsin-Hai. "A Chinese Estimate of Hardy's Poetry," HIBBERT JOURNAL, XXVII (Oct 1928), 78–92.
The leading thought underlying all of H's work is that life is a tragedy, an inevitable conflict between the human will and the Immanent Will. The misfortune of human existence is that it has a will. Callousness is the characteristic of H's destiny. There is only a superficial similarity between H and Schopenhauer or Leopardi. H's attitude toward the problem of life is therefore often a negative one; he is always crying for the state of the unborn; death seems to be preferred to all forms of human existence. However, the exclusion of an evil consciousness from H's Immanent Will makes it possible for the recognition of the existence of Hope. In H the human will is always a very strong assertive power. H's religious views are not Christian; in "God's Funeral" and "The Impercipient," H is left helpless in the face of those "obstinate questionings . . . which come to all thinking minds." H is, if anything, fundamental, and if he seems to emphasize misery

and suffering, it is because they are the great realities of our modern existence.

1200 Chesterton, Gilbert Keith. "On Thomas Hardy," GENERALLY SPEAKING (Lond: Methuen, 1928), pp. 245–50; (NY: Dodd, Mead, 1929), pp. 285–91; rptd (Freeport, NY: Books for Libraries P [Essay Index Reprint Series], 1968), pp. 285–91.

H loves concrete descriptions, mistakenly labeled "atmosphere" by critics. His scenes are not flat, but three-dimensional like a stage. H has the last reverberations of the Greek tragedy, though his view of life is more than tragic irony; it approaches torturers' mockery. His pessimism had two roots: subconscious sorrow for the dying fields in English agriculture and the old heathen sense of doom, returned in the Puritan form of damnation which took away man's free will in Calvinism. For example, H's view of the heroine in *Tess of the d'Urbervilles* is that she was predestined to be damned—he doesn't damn the people who treat her so badly. His religious views are not agnostic or atheistic but more a demonic mania in which he conceived a cosmic center responsible for everything, and then reproached this center angrily. He mellowed in later life—as a person, he was always humane and humble.

1201 Chesterton, G. K. "Thomas Hardy," ILLUSTRATED LONDON NEWS, CLXXII (21 Jan 1928), 94.

H had great modesty. H's novels and poems "might be called the practical jokes of a pessimist." H's pessimism had two roots: (1) "the neglect and decay of English agriculture," and (2) "the final effect of the strange interlude of Calvinism." H's pessimism "was a strange sort of demonic monism, which conceived a cosmic center immediately responsible for the most minute and remote results of everything, and which he was always angrily reproaching with its responsibility." "Between these two things, the subconscious sorrow of the dying fields and the old heathen sense of doom, that had returned to England in the Puritan form of damnation, Hardy grew up as the heir of tragedy." [Obit.]

1202 Chevalley, A. "Thomas Hardy," REVUE DE PARIS, XXXV (1 Feb 1928), 697–707.

H's main function in contemporary literary history was to be a living protest against the illusions of his times; first in his youth, when he discarded the prevalent "Victorian" conception of life; later, as a mature novelist, when he reacted against the new utopia of progress. He was essentially a non-conformist and the words "pessimism," "fatalism" that were hurled at him came from people who resented his dissenter's attitude in the fields of morals and science. H's so-called "pessimism" was only a case of inverted optimism; unfortunately, three generations of English and American critics have failed to notice it, and the Continental ones have done no better. It is too early to judge his poetry, but his fiction can be divided into four main categories: first, his minor romances (from *Desperate Remedies* to *The Well-Beloved*); second, his side-altars (*Under the Greenwood Tree* and the short stories); third, the four polyphonies (*Far From the Madding Crowd, The Return of the Native, The Mayor of Casterbridge* and *The Woodlanders*); finally, the two great symphonies (*Tess of the d'Urbervilles* and *Jude the Obscure*). [In French.]

1203 Chew, Samuel. "Thomas Hardy's Winter Words in a Wintry Mood," NEW YORK EVENING POST, 8 Dec 1928, p. 10.
The prevailing atmosphere in *Winter Words* is bleak and wintry although some poems are lighter.

1204 Chislett, William, Jr. "New Gods for Old," MODERNS AND NEAR MODERNS (NY: Graften P, 1928), pp. 171–80.
Even though new writers in the recent history of English Literature, such as H, have tried to create within their work new mythologies, the old classical mythology has withstood the pressure of the newer myths. This indicates the flexibility of our literature; it can encompass both the old and the new.

1205 Church, Richard. "The Last Sheaf from Wessex," SPECTATOR (Lond), CXLI (6 Oct 1928), 443–45.
Poems of *Winter Words* evince "a very subtle and very substantial delight in life." H's "pose of despair . . . was only a paradoxical expression of his delight in life." Pessimism is "a mask shielding his powerful and agonized sensibility." Last work retains "dramatic genius" and "youthful lyricism controlled by sixty years of technical practice."

1206 Church, Richard. "Thomas Hardy," SPECTATOR (Lond), CXL (21 Jan 1928), 71–72.
H's novels and poems, good and bad, are the product of a "continually inspired artist"; each work is "informed by the same quality, the same idea, and conceived on the same aesthetic plane." His theme is man's dependence upon "the silent tides of external fate." All great writers, in expressing "the divine in man," have "defined and accentuated it by an insistence on the external darkness." H's pessimism is "proof of his poetic strength. . . . His lyrical genius is so prolific that it has grown and wooded into the tree-like form of the epic, of which his novels are the branches and his *The Dynasts* the main trunk."

1207 Clarke, George Herbert. "Thomas Hardy," DALHOUSIE REVIEW, VIII (April 1928), 1–15.

Since H was universally admired at his death, it is fitting that he should lie in the Abbey. H was a truly religious man, not a pessimist, as the Nobel Prize committee thought in denying him the prize. H's pessimism is only an ingredient in his work; he "sought to imagine that which he knows." Intellectually honest, he insisted on his "obstinate questionings." It would be more accurate to term him a "malo-meliorist," considering life largely evil but hoping for its improvement. H's poetry may become more significant to us than his fiction. Its chief theme is love—its imperfections and worth. The philosophical poems are preferable to the psychological poems. *The Dynasts* is a great work.

1208 Clodd, Edward. "Hardy's Waterloo Lyric," TIMES LITERARY SUPPLEMENT (Lond), 2 Feb 1928, p. 80.
[Contains extract of a letter, dated 20 Feb 1908, from H to Edward Clodd referring to " 'the fauna of Waterloo field on the eve of the battle . . .' " in the "Chorus of the Years" lyric (Act VI, scene viii). H stated that this particular page now strikes him " 'as being the most original,' " in *The Dynasts*.]

1209 Cock, Albert A. "Thomas Hardy at Max Gate: Some Reminiscences," WESSEX: AN ANNUAL RECORD, I (June 1928), 45–47.
H respected John Morley as " 'honest all through.' " Receiving the Order of Merit gave H "evident pride and delight." In 1922 H related that because of the Treaty of Versailles he could not write as hopefully as he had earlier at the close of *The Dynasts*.

1210 Cohen, Chapman. "Views and Opinions," FREETHINKER, XLVIII (22 Jan 1928), 49–50.
H, a writer whose prose is superior to his poetry, was a freethinker who did not believe in the Christian deity or in Christian doctrines. Accordingly, his burial in Westminster Abbey is an insult.

1211 Collins, Vere H. "Intimate Talks with Hardy," T. P.'s WEEKLY, IX (4 and 11 Feb 1928), 501–2, 548–49, 560; rptd in part in BOOKMAN (NY), LXVII (March 1928), 1–6; excerpts in BOOK LEAGUE MONTHLY, II (Dec 1928), 180–85; in fullest form in TALKS WITH THOMAS HARDY AT MAX GATE, 1920–1922 (Lond: Duckworth; NY: Doubleday, Doran, 1928).
[H was a cordial man and a good conversationalist who expressed interest in a variety of subjects. He was interested particularly in the "book trade" and in commenting on lines from his own poetry. He was resentful of intrusions into his private life and criticized F. A. Hedgcock's THOMAS HARDY: PENSEUR ET ARTISTE (1911), which was both personal and inaccurate. Based on six conversations presented in dramatic form.]

1212 Colum, Padraic. "The Poetry of Thomas Hardy," BOOK LEAGUE MONTHLY, I (Dec 1928), 3–7.

H, a poet who was also a seer, wrote mellow poems full of sights and sounds. Using his ability to tell "stories in verse that are condensed novels," he revealed both a love of life and a "tragic sense of life," but no philosophy or "views."

1213 Colvin, Ian. "Thomas Hardy," MORNING POST (Lond), 16 Jan 1928, p. 8; rptd in LIVING AGE, CCCXXXIV (15 Feb 1928), 337; and LITERARY DIGEST, XCVI (18 Feb 1928), 32.

[Verse elegy proclaiming that H's spirit now "homes along to Egdon Heath/ the Hintocks and Kingsbere" in the company of Tess, Clym, Gabriel, Jude, Sue, Marty, and Giles.]

1214 Conacher, W. M. *"Jude the Obscure*—A Study," QUEEN'S QUARTERLY, XXXV (Autumn 1928), 529–40.

The novel fails because of H's perverse tendency to make things "go unnecessarily awry." He is unfair in his portrayal of Shaston and Christminster; Jude is unnaturally naive and has an ill-defined vocation, and H allows his hero to mistake material success for the true joys of learning and scholarship. Finally, Sue Bridehead anticipates the twentieth-century woman and pays a high price for being ahead of her time.

1215 C[onacher], W. M. "Thomas Hardy—Regional Novelist," QUEEN'S QUARTERLY, XXXV (Feb 1928), 271–87.

H's strength lies in his ability to depict the subtle intricacies of nature, the homely rituals of rural life, and characters who are at home in this milieu. He viewed town life with suspicion. Even in his later novels, the characterization of men like Michael Henchard and Jude Fawley owe much of their significance to setting.

1216 Cowley, Rev. Mr. H. G. B. "Inquiring American 'Paul Pry' to Hardy," NEW YORK TIMES, 16 Jan 1928, p. 14.

An American wanted to know why he couldn't find the items in Stinsford, the Mellstock of *Under the Greenwood Tree.* H reportedly told the Vicar to say that *Greenwood Tree* was a work of fiction and, "as in most works of fiction scenes are invented." H also said, "I may say that I never heard or saw the old choir and players or my grandfather, who died before I was born."

1217 Crawford, Jack R. "Thomas Hardy," WHAT TO READ IN ENGLISH LITERATURE (NY: Putnam, 1928), pp. 285–88.

H was "a mind disillusioned," able to present tragedy with the Greek sense. His universality and greatness free him from the often-made charge of pessimism. Rather than depressing, he enlarges his readers' view. H believes that character and environment mold a person's fate. We control our lives, well or badly, subject only to environmental obstacles. H's novels are simple in structure, with firm, austere plots. His poetry, though not as often praised, must not be neglected.

1218 Crawford, S. J. "The Wessex of Thomas Hardy," WESSEX: AN ANNUAL RECORD, I (June 1928), 65–81.

In the employment of typical Wessex scenes, customs, beliefs, and inhabitants, the connection between region and author is so intimate in H's works "that it is difficult to decide whether Wessex created Hardy, or Hardy created Wessex."

1219 Cristofaro, C. "Tommaso Hardy" (Thomas Hardy), RASSEGNA NAZIONALE, 3rd ser I (Jan 1928), 11–15.

H's novels bespeak one great theme: humankind must submit to its tragic fate, yet retain serenity. H is best understood when contrasted with that other great Victorian, George Meredith. The former is a pessimist and the latter an agitated idealist. Both profess the cult of Nature but impute to it opposite functions. Nature intervenes to save the heroines of Meredith, but to ruin those of H. [In Italian.]

1220 Crouch, Henry C. "George Moore Lets Statement Stand," NEW YORK TIMES, 22 April 1928, p. 6.

George Moore refused to retract his view that H knew nothing about human nature. H should be "considered more like a country schoolmaster" than a master of English country life.

1221 Daudet, Léon. ECRIVAINS ET ARTISTES, IV (Writers and Artists, IV) (Paris: Editions du Capitole, 1928), p. 83–92.

H's rejection of the female figure as a redemptive force is the underlying cause of his pessimism. In *Jude the Obscure*, his masterpiece, Sue is the final statement of his disenchantment with womankind. [In French.]

1222 Daudet, Léon. "Sur Thomas Hardy" (On Thomas Hardy), L'ACTION FRANÇAISE, 16 Jan 1928.

H wrote at least one masterpiece, *Jude the Obscure*, in which three pages—the death of Little Father Time—reach absolute despair and anguish. The portrait of Sue Bridehead is disappointing. The pessimist in art is usually a woman-hater, and Ibsen, Schopenhauer, and H are to be pitied for their attitude towards women. The fact that H abandoned the medium of fiction for that of poetry in spite of the fact that he never was a real poet, proves that his "malaise" was that of the man without women. [In French.]

1223 Davis, F. Hadland. "Thomas Hardy and the Sea," BLUE PETER, May 1928, pp. 98–99.

Though related to Nelson's famous Captain, "few writers have written less of the sea" than H. There are only isolated references to the sea and ships in the novels. Robert Loveday is the only sea-faring character in the Wessex novels; Mrs. Lizzy Newberry in "The Distracted Preacher" warns sailors. H's portrayal of Nelson in *The Dynasts* is "not a study faithful in every detail to well-authenticated facts."

1224 Davray, Henry D. "Lettres anglaises" (English Letters), MERCURE DE FRANCE, CCII (15 Feb 1928), 5–19.

Was H "the last of the Great Victorians," as many obituary notices published these days in England would have it? If the term "Victorian" is to be equated with emotional inertia, intellectual passivity, British "stolidity," then it is sure that H was no Victorian. In fact he was a latent insurgent against Victorianism which he found embodied in the person of his first wife. His inspiration, instead of being Victorian, is more akin to the French realistic and naturalistic schools, but his freedom of expression was less important than that accorded to the French writers of the same period. The first novel he wrote, *The Poor Man and the Lady*, may have been inspired by this feeling of intellectual and moral oppression. [In French.]

1225 "Death of Mr. Thomas Hardy," DAILY TELEGRAPH (Lond), 12 Jan 1928, pp. 10–12.

H was a great novelist by virtue of his ability to tell a story. He builds up his narrative "with true architectural skill." H took great care in developing male characters who were "staunch, patient, strong men," and female characters who were "capricious, impatient, vain, but lovable, bringing havoc into men's lives." *The Return of the Native* "represents the top-note of his great achievements." *Tess of the d'Urbervilles* "is vitiated to some extent by the distasteful priggishness of the hero." *Tess*'s "artistic merit is further diminished by the insinuation of didactic argument." *Jude the Obscure* may be said to be "the finest sex-novel ever written." *Jude* is inspired with the "wild frenzy of anger at the power of women to work havoc in a man's life." H's volumes of poetry "showed with each new outburst an astounding fertility of invention and command over metrical forms."

1226 "The Death of Mr. Thomas Hardy . . . ," NEW STATESMAN, XXX (14 Jan 1928), 421.

With H died the sole surviving representative of nineteenth-century literature. He was altogether a Victorian. All the work by which H will be remembered was done before Queen Victoria died. Some time must elapse before a balanced judgment of his contribution to literature can be offered. *The Dynasts* may not last, but *Tess of the d'Urbervilles* will remain.

1227 Deutsch, Babette. "Poets and Poetasters," BOOKMAN (NY), LXVIII (Dec 1928), 472.

Winter Words contains neither meaningful or significant thoughts, nor artful poetic technique. Altogether it is a disappointing collection.

1228 Dixon, W. MacNeile. "A Memoir of John S. Smart," SHAKESPEARE: TRUTH AND TRADITION (Lond: Edward Arnold, 1928), pp. 9–10.

An example of Smart's quiet irony in literary criticism: "The phrase, 'President of the Immortals' has indeed been translated from Aeschylus; but 'ended his sport' is Hardy's own."

1229 Douglas, Sir George. "Some Recollections and Reflections," HIBBERT JOURNAL, XXVI (April 1928), 385–98.

Emma H and H were as well assorted as most of the happily married couples that one comes across in life. Each had sacrificed something to the other. H's work appears to range itself naturally into three groups: a period of pure artistic creation (*Desperate Remedies, The Woodlanders*), a didactic or propaganda period (*Tess of the d'Urbervilles* and *Jude the Obscure*), and a period of self-revelation (the poetry). In the six volumes of H's lyrical poems, the ballads are the most striking. The autobiographical poems will probably be most eagerly sought out by the devoted Hardian, but they remain baffling and cryptic.

1230 DuBos, Charles. "Quelque traits du visage de Hardy" (Some Features of Hardy's Vision), LA REVUE NOUVELLE, Jan–Feb 1928, pp. 115–39; rptd in APPROXIMATIONS, IV (Paris: Correa, 1930), pp. 125–64.

H's opening description of Egdon Heath is an epiphany of his vision: all mankind, in H's eyes, is "slighted and enduring," and the genius of H is, like Egdon, "colossal and mysterious in its swarthy monotony." The eternal relativity of things in this world, the blindness of its moving force, and H's architectural orientation in his conception of the structure of both the universe and his art are other aspects of H's vision, which are also stressed in *The Return of the Native*. This and all of H's works, moreover, are permeated with a bitter and austere awareness of the omnipresence of destiny, an awareness nurtured by his sense of the ancient, the primitive. This sense, in turn, reveals something invariable and unchanging in H's temperament which is, nonetheless, altogether modern in the sense of having an uncompromising honesty of soul which encompasses the totality of experience. H's belief in destiny, however, should not be misconstrued. Not a pessimist, H is rather a naturalist in the ancient and cosmic sense of that term. The legitimacy of H's point of view as a novelist and as a poet lies in his lines from "In Tenebris," "if way to the Better there be, it exacts a full look at the worst." [In French.]

1231 "Echo der Zeitungen: Thomas Hardy" (Newspaper Echo: Thomas Hardy), Literatur, XXX (March 1928), 333–34.
[Reprint of obituaries by Kurt von Stutterheim, Berliner Tageblatt, 24, and Paul Cohen-Portheim, Frankfurter Zeitung, 64.] C–P: The division of H's remains symbolizes H's own two-mindedness: his heart belonged to Wessex, in London he led a quiet, unobtrusive life. KVS: [Hasty summary of H's pessimistic world-view.] [In German.]

1232 Elliott, George R. "Hardy's Poetry and the Ghostly Moving Picture," South Atlantic Quarterly, XXVII (July 1928), 280–91.
H's pessimism should not be taken too seriously. *The Dynasts* may be viewed as a "sheer moving picture—episodic, grotesque, pathetic, flittering, ghostly." The poem is "an epic of pity," and one must think of it as a great ghostly series of film scenes.

1233 Elliott, G[eorge] R[oy]. "Spectral Etching in the Poetry of Thomas Hardy," Publications of the Modern Language Association, XLIII (Dec 1928), 1185–95; rptd in The Cycle of Modern Poetry (Princeton: Princeton UP, 1929), pp. 91–111.
The poems' ghostly nimbus is a natural emanation from the sincere and simple center. H sympathizes with the universe too much to see it as really sinister. He articulated the poetic remains of the nineteenth-century— Wordsworthian wonder coupled with the Shelleyan vision of life as a single network of emotion. H's yearning for harmony, an elegaic scanning of the gloomy universe, is disguised in his "realism." Awe and pity overflow in *The Dynasts*, and H becomes thinly monotonous.

1234 Ellis, S. M. "Hardy's Lost Novel," Sunday Times (Lond), 5 Feb 1928, p. 10.
George Meredith read *The Poor Man and the Lady* for Chapman and Hall and rejected it. He may also have read and rejected *Desperate Remedies*. H and Meredith later became friends. [See Edmund Gosse, "The World of Books: Thomas Hardy's Lost Novel," Sunday Times (Lond), 22 Jan 1928, p. 8; and George A. Macmillan, "Hardy's Lost Novel," ibid (Lond), 29 Jan 1928, p. 14.]

1235 Ellis, Stewart Marsh. "Thomas Hardy: Some Personal Recollections," Fortnightly Review, ns CXXIII (March 1928), 393–406.
H was modest about his genius and "his immense achievement," and he always showed "gentle courtesy and kindness." Yet he was at the time "the unchallenged head of literature in England." H talked about Ainsworth, "the most powerful literary influence of his boyhood," and his fondness for

historical romances of G. P. R. James and James Grant, also his dislike for Stevenson and Scott. H also admired Housman's SHROPSHIRE LAD, and thought Sheila Kaye-Smith clever but not informed about peasant life. "The Melancholy Hussar" was based on an incident related to him and his interest in the threatened invasion of Napoleon in 1804. H often talked of his love and appreciation of his dog "Wessex" and cats and his regard for all of nature. H was very active in his later years: he was in no way a "pessimist" but a man who realized "the sad impermanence of all mortal things." He was shy and sensitive, did not like strangers, but was not "depressed" nor were his eyes "full of pain." He had an excellent sense of humor. He was a very considerate, kind, and simple man.

1236 "An Estimate of Hardy," NEW YORK TIMES, 16 June 1928, p. 16.

George King, in "Thomas Hardy: Novelist and Poet," CORNHILL MAGAZINE, LXIV (March 1928), 278–91, is wrong in equating H and Scott. America has forgotten Scott.

1237 Exideuil, Pierre d'. LE COUPLE HUMAIN DANS L'OEUVRE DE THOMAS HARDY; ESSAI SUR LA SEXUALITÉ DANS LES ROMANS, CONTES ET POÈMES DU WESSEX (Paris: La Revue Nouvelle, 1928); as THE HUMAN PAIR IN THE WORKS OF THOMAS HARDY; AN ESSAY ON THE SEXUAL PROBLEM AS TREATED IN THE WESSEX NOVELS, TALES AND POEMS, trans by Felix W. Crosse, with an Introduction by Havelock Ellis [qv, 1930] (Lond: Humphrey Toulmin, 1930).

Chap 1: Focus of the work is on the human pair, but it treats the theme of infinite dimensions revealing permanent laws of mind and feeling; it uses the philosophical and historical method as well as the aesthetic. One must assess H's pessimism on its own merits. Studies of H have overlooked his place in English realism and naturalism. Chap 2: H shows the force of physiological necessity that brings men and women together. He possesses the gift of discovering the elementary nucleus in the pair. *Jude the Obscure* and *Tess of the d'Urbervilles* show this most clearly. H crushes Victorian sentimentality under the weight of truth. He was probably affected by naturalism, as shown by detail, environmental determinism, anthropomorphism. Chap 3: H shows the pair desiring and suffering in an indifferent universe. He drew nourishment from Schopenhauer's pessimism but never departed from his "personal quarrel with God"; he was more an "eradicator of illusions" than despair. H knew simple happiness. Chap 4: The conflict between sexes shows the power of destiny: love is born and runs its course in an atmosphere of struggle, intensified by cunning, coquetry, seductions, deceit. It is without solution because of disparate functions of men and women. No sooner is a couple called into being than it is faced with danger from others. The human situation is paralleled in Nature: past vs. present. Everywhere the couple shows the "same will to live, same need for domination." Chap 5: Love is a will that projects itself against every being within reach, but people must have right individual natures for reaction to take place. H found most sincere expression of love in people close to earth, peasants, where love retains elemental force—thus he stays in Wessex. The relation between sexes is the main problem, two people drawn together by an irresistible attraction of passion. The lover is a despot. Suddenness, finality, and fatalism characterize the love-story, yet H also shows softness, nuances of atmosphere of love. Chap 6: H seems to show attraction governed by frivolous causes, but really it comes from essential forces of the world. Eustacia (*The Return of the Native*) and Boldwood (*Far from the Madding Crowd*) show this. As in Darwin's theory of sexual selection, H sees man and woman responding to the "mighty voice of the race," a determinism for which reason cannot account. Chap 7: H's women are spontaneous, ruled by Nature rather than intelligence. Tess is the most complete expression of H's conception of woman. H is attracted by crises which "show how far passion may be effective in bringing about transformation." H's women are inevitably led astray by instinct, but his ideal is represented by the "triple alliance of beauty, purity, and intelligence." Except for Elizabeth-Jane, his women are creatures of love. Chap 8: Social aspects of conflict of sexes: marriage is a grievous joke in H, contrary to Victorian idealization. H records rather than combats it, but exposes disaster of incompatibility "which a malignant destiny has found it pleasant to arrange." "Conjugal happiness can only be attained through an understanding based on mutual concessions." Marriage should not be an indissoluble tie. H saw woman as victim both of Nature and society. Chap 9: Force of circumstance also determines the fortunes of the pair, a "studied complicity of atmosphere," as at Talbothays Dairy. No matter how close to melodrama H comes he is saved by the common humanity of his characters. H discovers the unity of life and the permanence of things, the antinomy between the human condition and external conditions. Chap 10: Poems are filled with tales of passion leading to grief, trenchant and brutal. "The destiny of the pair is always tragic," the same motifs as in novels but told concisely with no softening effect. Chap 11: Conflict between the pair comes from basic psychological differences between men and women, an endless antagonism. H shows us that real happiness rests upon accepting the truth "without reticence," and his characters do not pursue this ideal tenaciously. H finds the only answer to the pair's unhappy existence is negation, not reproducing. Chap 12: H's kingdom is Wessex, and he left his native earth only to rise to the plane of metaphysics. Appendices: (I) Freud and H—no direct influence, but H was a Freudian before Freud: love is the great psychological motive force. (II) Visit with H. [In French.]

1238 Exideuil, Pierre d'. "La Vision des *Dynastes*" (The Vision of *The Dynasts*), LA REVUE NOUVELLE, Nos. 38–39 (Jan–Feb 1928), 105–10.

The Dynasts combines the traditions of the Nordic epic (BEOWULF, etc.)

and the classical Greek epic. H adds to these several elements derived from modern philosophy. For example, he updates the ancient motif of the "Fates" by converting it into the "Immanent Will" of Schopenhauer. [In French.]

1239 Faulkner, Edwin. "The Poetry of Thomas Hardy," DECA-CHORD, IV (March–April 1928), 56–61.
H is akin to Wordsworth in his ability to endow the simple acts of humble people with great dignity. He is stoic, yet brotherly, and his realism has a sort of sympathetic irony.

1240 Fehr, Bernhard. "Thomas Hardy," NEUE ZÜRICHER ZEITUNG, 17 Jan 1928, p. 84.
H is the last great Victorian novelist after Scott, Dickens, and Thackeray. His finest works are the Wessex novels. H's profession as an architect, his native environment, affinity with nature, and love for his fellowman were factors which influenced his tragic view of life. [In German.]

1241 Fernandez, Ramon. "Le romancier" (The Novelist), LA REVUE NOUVELLE, Nos. 38–39 (Jan–Feb 1928), 84–96.
H is a "realist" and "naturalist," but not of the kind associated with Zola and the whole French Naturalist school. The latter presents objects as "massive," "raw," and lacking "in transparency," so the human spirit "collides" against them. H's objects are transparent, so his "thought" reflects through them. H symbolizes interior psychic phenomena in and through his use of "geographical" and "geometric" space. H's pessimism is a "sidereal stoicism." Man is subject to Nature's architectonic laws; he is incorporated into a "transhuman, or rather, prehuman, nature." [In French.]

1242 Flower, Newman. "In His Wessex Home: A Sheaf of Memories," SUNDAY TIMES (Lond), 15 Jan 1928, pp. 12, 17.
H's greatness was "adorned by his extreme simplicity," and he "seemed to me as ageless as the Wessex that had bred him." He was a great lover of animals; his dog "Wessex" once bit John Galsworthy. Florence, his second wife, had protected him "from the aggressive attack of unknown admirers."

1243 Ford, Ford Madox. "Declined with Thanks," NEW YORK HERALD TRIBUNE BOOKS, 24 June 1928, pp. 1, 6.
ENGLISH REVIEW was first planned in order to print H's "A Sunday Morning Tragedy," which was rejected everywhere else in England because of its subject: an unwed, pregnant girl.

1244 Ford, Ford Madox. "Thomas Hardy, O. M. Obit 11 January, 1928," NEW YORK HERALD TRIBUNE BOOKS, 22 Jan 1928, pp. 1–3.

At a house party all averred their faith, and H said that he was a member of the Church of England. H's talents as a novelist are recognizable, but he was relieved to turn to poetry when his need for money was filled, as he had been in contention with the first Mrs. H over the course of the later novels. Although his poems are "almost uniformly somber," they are tragic rather than harrowing. H's work, generally, is "fatalistic, gloomy, darkling, and determined, it accepts the dictates of fate and faces the universe erect, with the determination to keep all on going, as says the Kentish peasant, and then to keep all on!"

1245 "Forged Hardy MS," MORNING POST (Lond), 20 Feb 1928, p. 12.
[Thomas J. Wise (quoted as an "expert") discovered that a MS, supposedly by H, was a forgery.]

1246 Fowler, John Henry. THE NOVELS OF THOMAS HARDY (Lond: Oxford UP, 1928) (English Association Pamphlet 71).
The particular effect of H's novels comes not only from their location in one part of England but also from the author's knowledge of science and history. H realized that science revealed a universe hostile to man and that archaeology demonstrated the long history of man's conflict with his environment. His novels are informed by a sense of man's past suffering and of his pain in an indifferent universe. H sometimes makes chance too prominent, but his novels remain great because his sympathy is always with his characters. [Shallow.]

1247 Freeman, John. "Thomas Hardy," LONDON MERCURY, XVII (March 1928), 532–44.
H is loved for his melancholy, his "central virtue." H's conception of God as the Antagonist derives from his melancholy, but his ironic detachment prevented him from becoming a pessimist (except in *Jude the Obscure* and *Satires of Circumstance*, both "strictly 'eccentric' "). All of his characteristic ideas and techniques are most explicitly revealed in *The Dynasts*, a poem "which has no parallel, and which for scope and genius can only be compared with Tolstoi's WAR AND PEACE." The greatness of H's prose, on the other hand, rests in the large quantity of mixed excellence and failure. [Rambling and impressionistic.]

1248 "French Estimate," MORNING POST (Lond), 13 Jan 1928, p. 8.
[Quotations from the French press's obituary notices.]

1249 Fuess, Claude Moore. "Thomas Hardy Among the Immortals," BOSTON EVENING TRANSCRIPT [Book Sect], 28 Jan 1928, pp. 1, 5.
[Lengthy obituary notice of H.]

1250 Galpin, Stanley I. " 'He Was Very Kind to Me': Thomas Hardy, O. M.," DORSET YEARBOOK, 1928, pp. 3–9.

H "never spared himself the trouble" of revising poems of his which had appeared in print "if he thought it necessary and desirable." H "was very kind to me. May he rest in peace."

1251 Garland, Hamlin. BACK-TRAILERS FROM THE MIDDLE BORDER (NY: Macmillan, 1928), pp. 292–94.

In his later years H spoke openly of his novels as "income producers" and made clear his preference for his verse. He denied that there was any technique in his prose; conversely, he wished critics would pay greater attention to the techniques he employed in his poetry.

1252 Garland, Hamlin. "Thomas Hardy," NEW YORK TIMES, 23 Jan 1928, p. 17.

In his speech at West Side Unitarian Forum, 22 Jan 1928, Garland said H was a "genius in triumphing over the social barriers of England." He said that "though Hardy was born in a thatched-roof cottage he was buried in Westminster Abbey." [Report of Garland's speech.]

1253 Garstang, A. H. "The Humour of Thomas Hardy," FORTNIGHTLY REVIEW, ns CXIII (Feb 1928), 205–9.

Those who have only cursory acquaintance with the Wessex novels may not know the importance of H's humor, but "those touches of drollery that relieve the pessimism of the most sombre of his stories form an essential, and not the least engaging, part of the literary personality of the narrator." Humor is found in different ways in the three classes of novel: the rustic idyll like *Under the Greenwood Tree*, the comedy of society like *The Hand of Ethelberta*, and the tragedies like *The Return of the Native*. H is not at his best in the second class; his true inspiration lay in the countryside, and his rustic characters provide most of the humor. We see this in his descriptions, his appreciation of the good things of life (the beer of *The Trumpet-Major*, for example), and the exact way he hits off country characters. "A sense of humour is an integral constituent of the genius of all great tragedians. Hardy shares it with the greatest of those Immortals whose ranks he has joined."

1254 Garvin, J. L. "The Victorian Epic: Myths and Truths: From PICKWICK to Pessimism: Why the Golden Years Return," OBSERVER (Lond), 15 Jan 1928, p. 12.

H's death, it has been argued, closed the Victorian age. Yet the age was so diverse, so full of contradiction and change, that its influence continues to be felt everywhere in the world of letters. Still, H's death does suggest that the age has become part of the past, and there is a certain absurdity in continuing to attack Victorian follies while forgetting Victorian virtues and complexity.

1255 Gibson, Wilfrid. "Hardy's Last Poems," BOOKMAN (Lond), LXXV (Nov 1928), 107–8.

H continues to chide critics who call his poems "gloomy and pessimistic." But how can anyone come to an alternative conclusion? H has a sense of humor, but he does not use it as a controlling attitude which might save his poems from becoming morbid. His intricate rhyme schemes are often stultifying. He is not a stylist. To appreciate H's poems one must learn to overlook technical flaws and concentrate on his curious themes. [Review of *Winter Words.*]

1256 Gibson, Wilfrid. "Hardy's Short Stories," BOOKMAN (Lond), LXXIV (June 1928), 148–49.

H is far from being a flawless stylist. Rather, he "too often wrote carelessly and perfunctorily." It was in the spirit and exuberance of his story-telling that his real genius was expressed. But in spite of this spirit of narration, his themes revealed his mental preoccupation with "sterility."

1257 Gilbert, Ariadne. "In Thomas Hardy's World," ST. NICHOLAS: MAGAZINE FOR BOYS AND GIRLS, LV (March 1928), 357–58, 409.

H is not an author for young people; "his work was too consistently gloomy." *Tess of the d'Urbervilles* outclasses all H's other books "in its piled-up agony." [Also refers to appealing, cheerful sections in H's works.]

1258 Gillbard, Richard. "Thomas Hardy," SUNDAY TIMES (Lond), 22 Jan 1928, p. 12.

H and John Morley "were fast friends." They shared " 'the twilight view of life.' "

1259 Gillet, Louis. "Thomas Hardy," REVUE DES DEUX MONDES, XLIII (1 Feb 1928), 704–5.

Nothing was less provincial than H's Wessex Novels. In *The Dynasts* H revealed himself as a much better thinker than Tolstoy. His lesson is one of pity and courage and protest against "man's inhumanity to man." [Obit.] [In French.]

1260 Gosse, Edmund William. "The Lost Novel of Thomas Hardy," BOOKMAN'S JOURNAL, 3rd ser XV (1928), 194–98.

[Account of Gosse's conversation with H about *The Poor Man and the Lady*. Nothing new. Excerpts from Gosse's "The World of Books," SUNDAY TIMES (Lond), 22 Jan 1928, p. 8.]

1261 Gosse, Edmund. "Mr. Hardy's Last Poem," Times (Lond), 13 Sept 1928, p. 13.

[Prints a letter written to Gosse three weeks before H's death. H's last poem was begun in 1925 and was published in the Times, Christmas Eve, 1927. Also reprints telegrams of condolence sent to Mrs. H from the King, dignitaries, men of letters.]

1262 Gosse, Edmund. "Thomas Hardy, 1840–1928: A Vacant Throne: The Writer and the Man," Sunday Times (Lond), 15 Jan 1928, p. 12.

H had completely finished his work before he died; it was the "presence of the man himself" as a "representative of living English literature" that was missed after his death. H's work strikes a balance; he was "equally distinguished in the two arts of prose and verse."

1263 Gosse, Edmund. "The World of Books: Thomas Hardy's Lost Novel," Sunday Times (Lond), 22 Jan 1928, p. 8.

H destroyed the manuscript of *The Poor Man and the Lady* because he was conscious of its "crudity and imperfection." The only interesting thing about the novel, H said, "was that it showed a wonderful insight into female character. I don't know how that came about." [See news report on Gosse's disclosure in "Hardy's Lost Novel," ibid, p. 15.]

1264 Grabo, Carl H. The Technique of the Novel (NY: Scribner's, 1928), pp. 113–33, 174–75, 250.

H's use of mischance in advancing the plot of *The Return of the Native* is not to be dismissed as overplotting but rather as the reflection of a philosophy which "calls the world to note we are the sport of destiny manipulating chance, and that fate may hang upon the most trivial incident." H is "essentially a Calvinist who has substituted the Devil for God in a fatalistic universe. The coincidences upon which he depends are perverted miracles."

1265 "Un grand écrivain britannique" (A Great British Writer), L'Illustration, CLXX (21 Jan 1928), 73.

H's art is characterized by the truth of his Balzac-like descriptions and characters. [Obit.] [In French.]

1266 Graves, Robert. "Robert Graves on Thomas Hardy," Sphere (Lond), CXII (28 Jan 1928), 129.

[An account of several meetings with H. There are several interesting details concerning H's life and work.]

1267 Grenzow, Daisy. "The Last of the Victorians," World Review (Chicago), V (30 Jan 1928), 261.

"Fierce individualism," not pessimism, is the dominating characteristic of H's work. This quality—of great value to H as novelist—might, however, have proved a weakness had he concentrated on poetry.

1268 Grierson, H[erbert] J[ohn] C[lifford]. "The Nineties," LYRICAL POETRY FROM BLAKE TO HARDY (Lond: Hogarth P, 1928); rptd in LYRICAL POETRY OF THE NINETEENTH CENTURY (NY: Harcourt, 1929), pp. 122–59.

H's poetry evidences a kind of "suppressed romanticism" which cuts through the awkwardness of diction and rhythm and justifies the verse as a "clear statement of the poet's feeling." Along with Kipling and Housman, H the poet represents the "final subsidence of the romantic wave which had traversed the century."

1269 Gwynn, S. "Ebb and Flow," FORTNIGHTLY REVIEW, CXIII (1 March 1928), 416–25.

The honor paid H at his funeral "answered to all men's judgment of what was due to a great man, not only for his own sake, but as a tribute to the generation which had in him its last illustrious survivor." Nevertheless there was irony in the burial of his ashes at Westminster while his heart was taken out and buried at Dorchester, especially for a man "whose living mind had so often dwelt on the normal process of creative transformation from one mould into another of animated dust." H was not a Victorian but belonged to an England "much rather of Shakespeare's or Milton's." Unlike his contemporaries he has no gospel to preach and "is more truly the contemporary of the post-war young who like so well to be reminded of what the Victorians liked to ignore." Despite his lack of style and the bitter tang that comes into his humor, H is more like Shakespeare than any other writer, because of his strength, "the sap, the vital force, the mass and momentum of his thought." [Obit.]

1270 "Hail and Farewell," MORNING POST (Lond), 16 Jan 1928, p. 8.

H "was of that race of genius which is too big for society or class, fashion or time, and embraces humanity." Although he was often called pessimist and pagan, he was in some ways a "characteristic product of our Christian faith and culture."

1271 Hale, Will T. "Thomas Hardy the Novelist," INDIANA UNIVERSITY ALUMNI QUARTERLY, XV (April 1928), 199–200.

H is a great writer who shocked the public by his outspokenness, his pessimism, his fatalism, and his arraignment of Providence. He gained greatness because of his loyalty to the truth, his ability to reveal the charm of the countryside, his "architectonic skill," and his ability to create characters who are "real men and women."

1272 Hangest, G. d'. "Méditation avec Thomas Hardy sur la dignité humaine" (A Meditation with Thomas Hardy on Human Dignity), LA REVUE NOUVELLE, Nos. 38–39 (Jan–Feb 1928), 97–104.

H's theory of the cosmos is often misunderstood. Though the two prime forces of the cosmos, Nature and human consciousness, are necessarily locked in combat with each other, they derive at bottom from the same regulatory laws. The essence of the cosmos is unitary and organic. On the phenomenal level, the very harshness of Nature is designed so as to provoke man into greatness and dignity. [In French.]

1273 Hansford, F. E. "A Heart of Pity," SCHOOLMASTER AND WOMAN TEACHER'S CHRONICLE, CXIV (22 March 1928), 573.
H's legacy to the Royal Society for the Prevention of Cruelty to Animals should come as no surprise. His sympathy for animals who suffer unnecessarily at the hands of man is evident throughout his writings.

1274 "Hardy and the Rainbarrow," MANCHESTER GUARDIAN WEEKLY, 20 Jan 1928, p. 56.
H wanted no elaborate funeral and only a simple column—if anything—for a memorial.

1275 Hardy, Florence Emily [Dugdale]. THE EARLY LIFE OF THOMAS HARDY, 1840–1891 (NY & Lond: Macmillan, 1928); re-issued with THE LATER YEARS OF THOMAS HARDY, 1892–1928 [1930] in two vols (Lond & NY: Macmillan, 1933); rptd, two vols in one, as THE LIFE OF THOMAS HARDY, 1840–1928 (NY: St. Martin's P; Lond: Macmillan, 1962).
[Although published as a biography, these volumes are essentially autobiographies dictated by H to his second wife. Despite omissions of much material that was burned before and at H's death, these volumes still remain an essential mine of primary information. Because these volumes are considered as primary works, abstracts of selected reviews are given under pertinent dates of publication.]

1276 Hardy, Florence E. [On Thomas Hardy Chair of Literature], WESSEX: AN ANNUAL RECORD, I (June 1928), 6.
H was "deeply interested in the endeavours to establish the University of Wessex, and was much gratified by the proposal to found a 'Thomas Hardy' Chair of Literature."

1277 "Hardy's First Publisher," MANCHESTER GUARDIAN WEEKLY, 20 Jan 1928, p. 46.
Tinsley published H's first three novels. He advised H to go to another publisher when H said that £300 had been offered for his next MSS, *Far From the Madding Crowd.*

1278 "Hardy's Last Poems," TIMES LITERARY SUPPLEMENT (Lond), 4 Oct 1928, p. 705.

Winter Words is a "crisp and vigorous sheaf of verse" hardly suggesting H was nearer ninety than eighty. Poems show an expected continuity; in a note H protests against charge of pessimism and warns that his verse "attempts no consistent philosophy." There is considerable variety in these poems, even some humor, but their general tone is gloomy.

1279 Heath, Frederick. "A Note on Thomas Hardy," BERMONDSEY BOOK, V (March–May 1928), 57–63.

H possessed a philosophy of life at a very early age, and he had one of the most ordered minds of his time. The tragic ground-bass of pity and irony is present throughout the choruses of *The Dynasts*, the poems, and the novels. *Dynasts* is H's masterpiece; the subject is man's own terrible stupidity: war. H's irony is for the overlords, "the President of the Immortals" and the Will weaving with "skilled unmindfulness," but his pity and compassion are for the little people. A note of hope, at the very end, does prophesy the coming of an age of truth, a realization that the universe as it exists for us is God's only revelation to mankind. H's pessimism might well be called optimism.

1280 Hellens, Franz. "Actualité de Thomas Hardy" (Present Interest in Thomas Hardy), LA REVUE NOUVELLE, Nos. 38–39 (Jan–Feb 1928), 111–14.

The younger generation of writers can profit from a study of H. Unlike them, H is not consciously imagistic nor is he preoccupied with style as such. Rather, he keeps his eye steadily trained on humanity and chooses the most direct and simplest way of putting his observations into words. When one has something really meaningful to say, style comes naturally and of its own accord. Nor is H a pessimist. He just describes the forces which really govern life. In a word, he is truthful. [In French.]

1281 Hellstrom, Gustav. "Thomas Hardy och Odödligheten" (Thomas Hardy and Immortality), DAGENS NYHETER, 1 Feb 1928, pp. 4–5.

H's view of life was most un-English. It had more in common with Leonod Andreyev's desperate fatalism than with any English code of "fair play" or "give a poor fellow a chance." [Obit.] [In Swedish.]

1282 Holland, Clive [pseud of C. J. Hankinson]. "The Charm of Hardy's Wessex," NEW PHOTOGRAPHER, X (20 Feb 1928), 498–99.

[Illustrated account of places in Wessex H used in his works.]

1283 Holland, Clive [pseud of C. J. Hankinson]. "The Hardy Country," WINDSOR MAGAZINE, LXVIII (June 1928), 77–83.

297

[Chatty travel essay, identifying certain buildings and sites in Wessex that correspond to similar ones in H's fiction.]

1284 Holland, Clive [pseud of C. J. Hankinson]. "Thomas Hardy and Wessex," BOOKMAN (Lond), LXXIII (Feb 1928), 267–70.
When asked whether or not he would choose to be born, H replied, "No, surely not." If this defined a pessimist, then H admitted he was one. But H could not understand why his works were labeled pessimistic when he was simply trying to show "man's inhumanity to man."

1285 Holland, Clive [pseud of C. J. Hankinson]. "Thomas Hardy as I Knew Him," LAND-MARK, X (Jan 1928), 75–77.
H remains indisputably the great novelist of English rural life and the interpreter of the countryside. There were two Thomas Hardys: one, a delightful, cultured companion, witty, full of quaint lore; and the other H who showed himself first to those who sought unduly to lionize him.

1286 Hopkins, R. Thurston. "Thomas Hardy," BOOKS OF THE MONTH, Feb 1928, pp. i–v.
H, not a victim of the abnormalities that plague authorship, was characterized by serene detachment, great sympathy, unyielding courage. Though his poems may not possess the kind of "form" of beauty that critics call the true quality of poetry, he is capable of giving us an "immortal wound." H's novels are devoid of modern intellectual trickery that substitutes for thought and emotion. H was a stoic who looked too hard at the worst, but always with truthfulness to life.

1287 Hutchison, Percy A. "Hardy's Last Verses Are Gnarled and Powerful," NEW YORK TIMES BOOK REVIEW, 9 Dec 1928, p. 2.
The poems in *Winter Words in Various Moods and Metres* flout the usual qualifications for poetry but still bear a stamp of greatness. H can be compared only to Wordsworth as a lyricist. H is an economical poet; he makes one word do the work of two. In this respect Robert Frost learned from H's example.

1288 Hutchison, Percy. "Thomas Hardy: The Shakespeare of the English Novel," NEW YORK TIMES BOOK REVIEW, 29 Jan 1928, pp. 3, 16.
H is to the novel what Shakespeare is to drama—a great tragedian. *Under the Greenwood Tree* shows H's later theme: fate working through love/sex. H turned to poems to dramatize ideas ("In the Nuptial Chamber" has the same theme as *Jude the Obscure* and *The Return of the Native*). *The Dynasts* handles man's dilemma, as does *Tess of the d'Urbervilles*, and the ironic concluding scenes in both are parallel. H has determinism, but pessimism is inherent in his dramas. *Tess* is his best work because of singleness of effect; in *Native* and *Jude*, this effect is diffused by too many plots and

characters. Despite fine scenes in *Dynasts*, H is a better novelist than poet. His sense of poetic form is good, but his utterance is faulty. Still, a good "toughness of fibre" characterizes the poems.

1289 "Ibsen, Hardy and Man's Salvation," CHRISTIAN CENTURY, XLV (12 April 1928), 466–67.

Like Ibsen and the Greek tragedians, H believed that events are "causally determined" and therefore wrote pessimistically to "depict the legitimate and inescapable consequences of conduct."

1290 "In the Abbey," SUNDAY TIMES (Lond), 15 Jan 1928, p. 13.

[A description of the Poet's Corner in Westminster Abbey where H is to be buried.]

1291 Jaloux, Edmond. "Le Pessimisme de Thomas Hardy" (The Pessimism of Thomas Hardy), LA REVUE NOUVELLE, Nos. 38–39 (Jan–Feb 1928), 71–74.

We never can know a man's "true biography," because it is interior. We may surmise that the Darwinian revolution conditioned H's theories about determinism. However, Darwin's influence could never have been so great unless H was innately receptive to it. H was born with a "dolorous sensibility." The plots of H's novels are sometimes developed from documented facts. For example, the selling of a woman at the beginning of *The Mayor of Casterbridge* is based on a real-life incident. However, fiction is not supposed to build its case on unusual events, even if factual in some analogous way; rather, fiction should deal with events that can "recur quite frequently." It so happens that man does not suffer perpetually and inexorably. He sometimes has fun, forgets his troubles, and thus "saves" himself. H ignores this phenomenon and thus misrepresents reality. [In French.]

1292 Jaloux, Edmond. "Thomas Hardy," CANDIDE, 19 Jan 1928, p. 3.

H was the last of the great European novelists. He leaves us three masterpieces: *Tess of the d'Urbervilles*, *Jude the Obscure* and *The Mayor of Casterbridge*; the rest of his fiction is indifferent, but he was a great poet, as he proved in *The Dynasts*. His thought is dominated by an implacable determinism; he must have been a very unhappy man indeed. [In French.]

1293 Jiriczek, O. L. "Zum Thema Maternal Impression" (On the Theme of Maternal Impression), BEIBLATT ZUR ANGLIA, XXXIX (March 1928), 87–88.

H's story "An Imaginative Woman" corroborates the theory of "Maternal Impression," as described by P. Fijn van Draat, "Maternal Impression," ANGLIA, L (1926), 287–90 [not seen]—that a mother's frightful visual impressions can mar an unborn child. [In German.]

1294 Johnson, Harry. "Thomas Hardy," ARCHITECTURAL RE-VIEW, LXIV (Feb 1928), 58–59.
"Whatever the medium—even colour—never can one imagine Hardy's working in any other than neutral tones." [Trifling.]

1295 Kennedy, Thomas J. "The Novels of Thomas Hardy," CENTRAL LITERARY MAGAZINE, April 1928, pp. 219–26.
The unevenness of H's work may be explained by his lack of effectiveness in writing of sophisticated, cultured, comfortable people. *Far From the Madding Crowd* is the most satisfying of the Wessex novels because of its balanced interplay of character, emotion, and circumstance, and its even distribution of realistic, comic, and tragic elements. *Tess of the d'Urbervilles* is propagandistic. *Jude the Obscure* exhibits H's often-repeated failure: while in great literature tragedy is followed by exaltation, H leaves us in hopeless despair.

1296 King, George. "Thomas Hardy; Novelist and Poet," CORNHILL MAGAZINE, ns LXIV (March 1928), 278–91.
H's several volumes of verse make "the gloom of his later novels" more visible. H's shorter poems "can scarcely be accounted more than incidental to his" reputation. [Obit.] [Survey of H's life and works.]

1297 Knickerbocker, Frances Wentworth. "The Victorianness of Thomas Hardy," SEWANEE REVIEW, XXVI (July–Sept 1928), 310–25.
Some of "the root ideas" of H's work "are themes that were beaten out of the struggles of those fighting [eighteen] sixties and seventies." H's protest against the romantic conception of a beneficent Nature "is the very voice of mid-nineteenth-century rationalism." Tess and Jude are "victim[s] of social convention." H's social criticism, however, "outran his time"; only Mill and Meredith anticipated him "in claiming for women a large freedom to live and love." H could not share the "faith in progress toward a better social order," either. In his dealings with the "overworld," the "voice of the seventies" sounds unmistakably. H's agnosticism is, however, rarely argumentative.

1298 Knowles, David. "The Thought and Art of Thomas Hardy," DUBLIN REVIEW, CLXXXIII (Oct 1928), 208–18.
H's "gloomy outlook on life" probably sprang from his "godless view of the universe." In his darkest period H suggested not only that endeavor is useless "but that the fight is against a malicious power." His more common suggestion, however, is that man is part of "the irresistable movement of the universe." While H "tilts the scale against his creatures," the world remains "tantalizingly lovely."

1299 [Krans, Horatio S.]. "Thomas Hardy," THE NEW INTERNATIONAL ENCYCLOPAEDIA. 2nd ed (NY: Dodd, Mead, 1928), X, 691–92.
[Sketch of life and works of H as "realistic novelist."]

1300 L., S. R. "The 'Dorchester Plays,' Some Personal Reminiscences," MORNING POST (Lond), 13 Jan 1928, p. 8.
H wrote *The Dynasts* "without any care for theatrical feasibilities" because "his prime had belonged to a day when the theatre was not ready for him." But H had no disregard for the Victorian theater: "he had a relish even for the tawdry glamour of the old Adelphi melodramas."

1301 "The Last of the Great Victorians," DAILY TELEGRAPH (Lond), 12 Jan 1928.
"Thomas Hardy [was] not merely the last of the great Victorians, but one of those rare spirits who have made a permanent contribution to literature." H was never "obsessed by trivialities." His themes are "richly divergent . . . and his views are enlivened with a caustic humor that . . . [is] 'refreshingly horrid.' " All of H's poems "display a mind deeply impregnated with pity for man's tragedy." His male characters are masculine and "distinguished by great fidelity." H's female characters are "lovable" for the most part as well as "capricious, evasive, and vain." "He will be read for all times because he dwelt upon themes that will interest man for all time." "To love Hardy it is not necessary to agree with his conclusions, but to deny his genius because his message was not one of comfort and hope is to display a spirit of cowardice."

1302 Levy, Oscar. "Thomas Hardy and Friedrich Nietzsche," OUTLOOK (Lond), LXI (18 Feb 1928), 217–18.
We can now understand why H would not, or could not, appreciate Nietzsche, whose fame unjust war propaganda could only temporarily damage, but not finally arrest: H's remained the Calvinistic attitude to life, Nietzsche's was the Hellenic. H has the *horror fati*, Nietzsche proclaims the *amor fati*. [Unconvincing.]

1303 "London Students' Tribute," SUNDAY TIMES (Lond), 15 Jan 1928, p. 13.
A memorial service will be held for H at the City Literary Institute on 18 Jan 1928.

1304 Loomis, Roger S., and Thomas Hardy. THE PLAY OF SAINT GEORGE (NY: Samuel French, 1928).
[Prints H's version of the mummer's play mentioned in *The Return of the Native,* and a "Modernized Version" by Loomis.]

1305 Lösch, Olga. DAS NATURGEFÜHL BEI GEORGE ELIOT UND THOMAS HARDY (Feeling for Nature in George Eliot and Thomas Hardy) (Giessen: J. Christ, 1928); University of Giessen dissertation; also in BEITRÄGE ZUR ERFORSCHUNG DER SPRACHE UND KULTUR ENGLANDS UND NORDAMERIKAS, V (Giessen: J. Christ, 1928), 88–180.

[Tripartite structure: (1) H's language, particular natural phenomena, relationship between man and nature, and the association of nature and action; (2) collection of H's personal remarks on nature; (3) essence, structure, and purpose of H's descriptions. Primary sources are *The Woodlanders* and *Far From the Madding Crowd*.] [In German.]

1306 Lucas, E. V. THE COLVINS AND THEIR FRIENDS (Lond: Methuen, 1928), pp. 318–20.

[Mentions of H and H's letters to Keats's biographer Colvin identifying where Keats landed on the "Wessex coast."]

1307 M., A. N. "Thomas Hardy," MANCHESTER GUARDIAN WEEKLY, 20 Jan 1928, p. 52.

H's early architectural training contributed to the growth of unity in his fiction. A writer like Meredith, on the other hand, lives on because of "vital and passionate scenes."

1308 MacCarthy, Desmond. "Thomas Hardy," SATURDAY REVIEW OF LITERATURE, V (1 Dec 1928), 421–22.

The man in this "objective life," Florence Hardy's EARLY LIFE OF THOMAS HARDY (1928), seems the same as the older H to be met at Max Gate. Tiny incidents in his uneventful life blossomed into poems long afterward. H commented that Fielding seems to have forgotten that Tom Jones's Molly was woman; human nature was to H the most serious of themes. Of *Tess of the d'Urbervilles* H said, " 'If I had known that book was going to make such an impression, I would have made it a *really good book*.' " H admired Browning, was pleased that Swinburne liked "The Slow Nature," and, in his own readings, emphasized the meter. [Comments on the EARLY LIFE correspond, although unintentionally, with our knowledge of H's relationship to the work, a number of personal reminiscences are included.]

1309 McDowall, Arthur S. "Thomas Hardy's Poetry," TIMES LITERARY SUPPLEMENT (Lond), 26 Jan 1928, pp. 49–50.

H's poetry has "a strong, continuous idiosyncrasy." H saw poetry as the "vehicle for the last, concentrated truth of things." Poetry is both an exploration of reality and an adventure of imagination. H had a "Balzacian ambition" to embrace all cardinal situations; his primary trait was the "contrast and comprehension of opposites." H is a philosophical poet because he explores man's predicament by implication. He is a tragic ironist; inexorable change is his main theme.

1310 McGrath, Fergal. "The Pessimism of Thomas Hardy," STUDIES (Dublin), XVII (1928), 29–38.

H is a consistent pessimist whose determinism is not metaphysically precise. Man is hindered by a "hateless Immanent Will" (*The Dynasts*), by the sport of the "President of the Immortals" (*Tess of the d'Urbervilles*), or by the fight with circumstances (*The Mayor of Casterbridge*). Because of its "all-pervadingness" and its "bitterness," this *is* H's philosophy. The importance of philosophy lies in the flaws it causes in H's novels: an air of unreality (*Mayor*), unwearying invocation of coincidence, and unnecessary delays in action to permit the author to philosophize. *Dynasts* would be improved as drama if speeches of all spirits except Rumour were ignored. As writer, H owes to his philosophy of life "whatever littleness may be found in one so great."

1311 McGrath, Fergal, S. J. "Reviews," STUDIES (Dublin), XVII (Sept 1928), 504–5.

H's reputation as a novelist will remain great because "the short story never loses a certain suggestion of the ephemeral." His stories "have all the power of his novels: wealth of description, quaint lore of the Wessex countryside, shrewd psychology." Moreover, they are not "blemished" by the "intruding presence of the Fate motif." His stories come to a "natural, unadorned conclusion." They are less pessimistic than the novels but still present a "low estimate of human nature and all that has to do with human love and married life." "It was a strange 'little irony' that H, who certainly had a heart for the suffering ones of the earth, should not have realised that by his ruthless shattering of the remnants of human ideals, he was only helping to submerge yet more hopelessly those whom some of his pages would seem to show that he was sincerely trying to lift up." [Review of *The Short Stories of Thomas Hardy* includes the stories originally published in *Wessex Tales*, *Life's Little Ironies*, *A Group of Noble Dames*, and *A Changed Man*.]

1312 Macmillan, George A. "Hardy's Lost Novel," SUNDAY TIMES (Lond), 29 Jan 1928, p. 14.

Edmund Gosse referred to Alexander Macmillan's letter to H rejecting his first novel (*The Poor Man and the Lady*). [Morley's comment and Alexander Macmillan's letter follow. See Edmund Gosse, "The World of Books: Hardy's Lost Novel," SUNDAY TIMES (Lond), 22 Jan 1928, p. 8.]

1313 Macy, John. "The Two-Fold Genius of Hardy," BOOKMAN (NY), LXVII (April 1928), 134–39.

The genius of H is found in both his poetry and his prose, though in both one finds a conflict between the Fate of Character (personal flaws) and the Fate of Circumstance (the predetermination of the universe, which overrides character). Despite this confusion, H deserves praise for bringing to an end the "Pippa Passes optimism" of the Victorians and turning literature in the direction of greater realism. [Obit.]

1314 Macy, John. "The World of Thomas Hardy," BOOK LEAGUE MONTHLY, I (Dec 1928), 149–59.

Although he was a great writer, H wrote loosely constructed novels having plots made unnecessarily complicated by accidents and coincidences. However, these faults are more than compensated for by his ability to create characters who are "always living, pitiable, lovable, even fascinating"; by his ability to tell a good story; and by his ability to deal sympathetically, but without sentimentality, with peasants.

1315 Mansfield, Katherine. THE LETTERS OF KATHERINE MANSFIELD, ed by J. Middleton Murry (Lond: Constable, 1928), I, 192, 309, 314; II, 114–15, 146, 150, 266; rptd (NY: Knopf, 1929), I, 170, 274, 278; II, 384, 411, 414, 514.

The Well-Beloved is "appallingly bad" and the style preposterous. Poetic dramas of the future will be like *The Dynasts*: "*As if* for the stage and yet not to be played." H's poems are "almost intolerably near to one . . . that love and regret touched so lightly—that autumn tone." [Casual remarks about H in letters written between 1918 and 1922.]

1316 Mantripp, J. C. "Thomas Hardy's *The Dynasts*," HOLBORN REVIEW, LXX (April 1928), 157–68.

The entire thematic drift of *The Dynasts* is to suggest that human effort is meaningless; that which seems to give this human existence direction is discovered to be purposeless. "As literature *The Dynasts* is a shining example of the power of genius to bring amorphous materials into reasonable shape and give them purposeful meaning." The primary means by which this is achieved is the use of devices such as humor and, more importantly, effective poetry in the drama. The meaning, for its part, is largely centered on the equation of God and the Immanent Will, a Being which shows "no personality, with the warm wealth of love, as the goal of the seemingly purposeless process." "However, where Hardy reads failure we must win triumph, and prepare the path for God's victory and man's."

1317 Margoliouth, H. M. "A Note on Hardy's 'Philosophy,' " WESSEX: AN ANNUAL RECORD, I (June 1928), 29–30.

"I deprecate the application of philosophical names to a poet who explicitly disclaims to be any setter-forth of doctrines." In his later works, blind Chance yields to the unconsciously working All-Immanent Will. Man with his struggling consciousness "seems to have an unhappy superiority to the Higher Powers." One of H's "faint hopes" is Sincerity.

1318 Martin, G. Currie. "Thomas Hardy and the English Bible," BOOKMAN (Lond), LXXIV (April 1928), 24–26.
H was fascinated by the language of the Bible, and he could use quotations from it with great effectiveness. The influence of biblical thought and the use of biblical references is most clearly seen in *The Return of the Native, The Mayor of Casterbridge, Tess of the d'Urbervilles,* and *Jude the Obscure.*

1319 Maxwell, Donald. THE LANDSCAPE OF THOMAS HARDY (Lond: Cassell, 1928).
[Reproductions of a series of drawings to illustrate scenes from the novels; one Wessex scene was reproduced in BOSTON EVENING TRANSCRIPT, 12 Jan 1929, p. 2 (Book Sect).]

1320 Mayoux, J. J. "L'amour dans les Romans de Thomas Hardy [I]" (Love in the Novels of Thomas Hardy [I]), REVUE ANGLO-AMÉRICAINE, V (Feb 1928), 201–18.
"The cycle of love, in the traditional conception, would be: I see her, I love her; for Thomas Hardy it is: I love, I see her, I love her. In one case the point of departure is this pure circumstance: I see her. In the other, this state is purely interior: I love, that is to say, I am in a state of love." [In French.]

1321 Mayoux, J. J. "L'amour dans les Romans de Thomas Hardy [II]" (Love in the Novels of Thomas Hardy [II]), REVUE ANGLO-AMÉRICAINE, V (April 1928), 331–39.
H's women, more than his men, reveal their essence in and through love. A woman is essentially receptive. Before loving, she loves to be loved. For H, the male imagination is Platonic and abstract; the woman's is concrete and emotional. [In French.]

1322 "Men and Events: Thomas Hardy," WORLD TODAY, LI (Feb 1928), 244–45.
H "might not have achieved even . . . moderate popularity . . . had it not been for the almost accidental success" of *Tess of the d'Urbervilles,* which was not one of his best novels. H "was exclusively an artist—ruthless in the pursuit of truth, austere, often bitter, seldom sentimental." H never made terms with the public. [Obit.]

1323 Monroe, Harriet. "Thomas Hardy," POETRY, XXXI (March 1928), 326–32.
Victorian in birth, H belonged to the twentieth century by austerity of art, style (drawn from John Donne and folk balladists of Wessex), tone (irony)

and skepticism towards creeds. *The Dynasts* is a great poem, despite excessive length, because it presents truths in "harshly swinging rhythms." A dominant note in H's poems is frustration at change, blamed generally on Fate, but "he looked facts in the face as did no other Victorian." But H's gloom is becoming tedious.

1324 Moore, John R. "Thomas Hardy the Man," INDIANA UNIVERSITY ALUMNI QUARTERLY, XV (April 1928), 197–99.
[A brief biographical sketch which emphasizes H's lineage, family, and achievements.]

1325 Morgan, Charles. "Thomas Hardy," NEW YORK TIMES, 29 Jan 1928, VIII, p. 2.
H "was both aware and unaware of his own preeminence. He was at once greatly proud and astonishingly humble."

1326 Morgan, J. H. "Lord Morley and Thomas Hardy," SUNDAY TIMES (Lond), 5 Feb 1928, p. 10.
H and John Morley were friends for many years. [See Richard Gillbard, "Thomas Hardy," SUNDAY TIMES (Lond), 22 Jan 1928, p. 12.]

1327 Morley, Christopher. "Touch Wood," SATURDAY REVIEW OF LITERATURE, IV (21 Jan 1928), 533; rptd in DESIGNED FOR READING (NY: Macmillan, 1934), pp. 118–22; and with an added Part II not in the original or other printings in OFF THE DEEP END (NY: Doubleday, Doran, 1928), pp. 125–36.
News of H's death brings thoughts of plain and elemental things. H's stoic loving-kindness was not pessimism, just questioning. He "ran the scale of all observations," speaking for the mute in the Chorus of Years or Pities just as in the Wessex milkmaid. He turned to poetry to better express himself, not to escape criticism. "One could not have easily explained to any visitor that in burning a pile of trash in the back lot one was trying to pay honor to Thomas Hardy; but so it was." [II only] H's collected poems are "tabloid in their emphasis on the morbid, the comic, the melodramatic," but they show H's "deep naïveté." Some of his best verse is light *vers de société*, though it happens to be rustic society. His coincidences are sometimes architecturally methodical. Time is his chief problem. *Tess of the d'Urbervilles* and *Jude the Obscure* are the chief and only major sellers upon the news of his death.

1328 Morris, Lloyd. "Hardy, the Great Pagan," OPEN COURT, XLII (June 1928), 382–84.
Lacking a sense of "purposive continuity" in human life, H saw the world as a place of unrelieved suffering. This unbalanced view leaves the reader with a sense of horror.

1329 "Mr. Hardy's Funeral," OBSERVER (Lond), 15 Jan 1928, p. 13.
[A description of the funeral services at Westminster Abbey and at Stinsford.] [Obit.]

1330 "Mr. Hardy's Will," OBSERVER (Lond), 26 Feb 1928, p. 9.
H's estate of £91,000 was probated. Lloyd's Bank is named as general executor, and his wife and Sydney Cockerell are named literary executors. His estate was divided among relatives, various libraries and museums, and selected charities.

1331 "Mr. Thomas Hardy," SATURDAY REVIEW (Lond), CXLV (14 Jan 1928), 30–31.
H's poetic vision is the source of the lasting power in his novels, where there is "something epical to the tragic stories" which is not seen in the over-contrived ironies in the poems. In H's poetry, word choices and thoughts are recalcitrant to meter and hostile to the emotional atmosphere. *Far From the Madding Crowd* and *The Return of the Native* are fine novels. *Jude the Obscure* is "the least prejudiced presentation of sex relations ever written in English," although this was forgotten in the moral uproar; *Jude* also shows H's overworking of circumstantial irony. *The Dynasts* is "a stupendous thing, awkward and labored in many places." [Obit.]

1332 "Mr. Thomas Hardy—Death Last Night at Dorchester," TIMES (Lond), 12 Jan 1928, p. 12.
H died at Max Gate shortly after 9 pm on 11 Jan. He had been sick since 12 Dec. His robust constitution enabled him to make a long fight against illness. Among the last things read aloud to him were some poems by de la Mare.

1333 Muir, Edwin. THE STRUCTURE OF THE NOVEL (Lond: Hogarth P, 1928; 1957; NY: Harcourt, Brace, 1929), pp. 42, 48–50, 65, 66–68, 71–72, 143, 147, 148.
H's fault, less than Merimée's, is that his figures exist only in relation to the situation. They are lifeless, moved by fate. H's power of invention gives living movement in spite of the plot. H's figures are elemental, moving in a space that is undifferentiated and universal. The power of his landscapes is drawn from nature directly, and his characters are bound by strong ties to each other and the earth. *The Return of the Native* is a dramatic novel because it gives prescience of something definite to come. *Tess of the d'Urbervilles* and *The Mayor of Casterbridge* also illustrate the technique of the dramatic novel. [Some obvious self-contradictions on H's character-drawing and the particularity or universality of landscape.]

1334 Murray, Alison D. BURROW'S GUIDE TO WESSEX, THE HARDY COUNTRY (Lond: Burrow, 1928).

"Wessex as a land of literary pilgrimage is associated with Thomas Hardy in a sense which is notably different from the association of Warwickshire with Shakespeare or of Scotland with Burns and Scott. In Shakespeareland and the Scott and Burns countries, it is the personality of the 'presiding genius' that dominates the place. It is otherwise in Wessex. There, the people 'bodied forth' by the imagination of Thomas Hardy seem to loom larger than their creator. The pilgrim follows the footsteps of Tess, Jude, Henchard, Bathsheba Everdene, Gabriel Oak, Eustacia Vye, and other Hardy characters as if they once actually moved about in the flesh; he visits the Manor House where the fictitious Tess spent her tragic honeymoon and made her confession to Angel Clare, just as he would visit the shrine of a real and famous man in some other literary 'province'—such as Burns's cottage or Shakespeare's birthplace." [Index of H's place names with identifications of actual counterparts; interesting advertisements of taverns, restaurants, hotels, and so on; cover drawing of H's birthplace.]

1335 The Editor [John Middleton Murry]. "Notes and Comments: Thomas Hardy: Hardy and the English Church," NEW ADELPHI, I (March 1928), 193–94.
The unflinching integrity of H's statement, "If way to the better there be, it exacts a full look at the worst," which jeopardized his reputation thirty years ago, shows him as "perfectly simple" and makes the burial of his heart at Stinsford appropriate. H said that he considered entering the Church of England, and he probably regarded himself as a Church of England man, for he was one of the most Christian minds of the age, in spite of his pessimism.

1336 Murry, J. Middleton. "The Supremacy of Thomas Hardy," NEW ADELPHI, I (March 1928), 219–24; rptd as "La Suprématie de Thomas Hardy," trans into French by G. d'Hangest, in REVUE HEBDOMADAIRE, XXXVII (28 Jan 1928), 413–23; and in LA REVUE NOUVELLE (Paris), Feb 1928, pp. 62–70.
H conquered his popularity inch by inch from unwilling critics and readers, for he was painful to read because of his pessimism. His peculiar autochthonous Englishness lies in his creative power and his provincialism, in both of which he is comparable to Shakespeare. The amazing speculative crescendo from *The Return of the Native* to *Jude the Obscure* to *The Dynasts* shows his Shakespearian capacity to see the problem of human life. For Shakespeare, the realm was the Elizabethan playhouse, for H, the Victorian novel—areas almost comparable in their audience. [In English/French.]

1337 "Musings without Method: Thomas Hardy, the Shakespeare of our Time," BLACKWOOD'S MAGAZINE, CCXXIII (March 1928), 429–32.
H was not a pessimist. He did not "invent unhappiness for the mere love of it"; rather, "there was in him a streak of the *macabre*." [Obit.]

1338 "Nation's Homage to Thomas Hardy," MORNING POST (Lond), 16 Jan 1928, p. 9.
[Detailed summary of the cremation at Woking and the Abbey Ceremony.]

1339 "Nation's Homage to Thomas Hardy," SUNDAY TIMES (Lond), 15 Jan 1928, p. 13.
[Obit.]

1340 "Nation's Homage to Thomas Hardy," TIMES (Lond), 17 Jan 1928, p. 15.
[Description of H's burial service.]

1341 Neel, Philippe. "Thomas Hardy," EUROPE, 15 March 1928, pp. 398–404.
H is primarily a poet, especially in his descriptions. It is absurd to describe him as a pessimistic writer; he was full of pity for mankind; his mystical testament, *The Dynasts*, ends on a note of hope. [Obit.]

1342 Neilson, Francis. "Thomas Hardy's 'Pessimism,' " UNITY (Chicago), CI (5 March 1928), 22–23.
"Hardy was no pessimist." Someone of a later generation may even assert that "he was an optimist, for he saw Wessex folk as they are and he made them live in his works."

1343 "Neuerscheinungen der erzählenden Literatur" (Recent Narrative Literature), BÜCHEREI UND BILDUNGSPFLEGE, VII:1 (1928), 54–55.
One cannot love *Tess of the d'Urbervilles*. Despite H's description of scenery, his logical presentation of characters, the sympathy he excites on behalf of the protagonist, and the construction of the narrative, it is a dismal book. *Tess* is only for larger libraries. [In German.]

1344 Nevinson, Henry W. "Hardy, Cruelty's Foe and Lover of Country," SUN (Baltimore), 30 Jan 1928.
H wrote "long and beautiful" novels, a great epic-drama, and "unmusical lyrics." In these works he displays sensitivity to cruelty, compassion, a love of the country, and "an attraction to spirits touched from their birth by something alien." [Largely a personal reminiscence.]

1345 Nicholas, Rev. D. J., B. D. "Thomas Hardy: A Rebellious Spirit," BROTHERHOOD WORLD, IV (April–June 1928), 162–65.
Sympathy with human suffering and loyalty toward man made H a rebel toward God. H "sorrowed more for mankind than mankind did for itself." He could not find any real differences between man's misfortunes and his sins, for everything was "due to the decree of the Fates."

1346 Nitchie, Elizabeth. The Criticism of Literature (NY: Macmillan, 1928), pp. 49, 60, 100, 115, 163, 234, 247.

H's use of scene is an "excellent illustration" of the possibility open to the novelist to use description to intensify and set off the feelings of his characters. [Passing references—useless.]

1347 "Notes on Rare Books," New York Times, 24 April 1928, III, p. 24.

[Descriptive bibliographical details on Yale exhibition of H's works: autograph MS of *Far From the Madding Crowd* from A. E. Newton collection, errors in Purdy's catalogue description of several items; lament at lack of H items at Yale (most of these are from private collections).]

1348 Observator. "At Random," Observer (Lond), 15 Jan 1928, p. 11.

H was buried in Westminster Abbey against his wishes. If H had not suddenly switched from prose to verse in his mid-fifties, his reputation would not have been so great. Had he devoted himself exclusively to either novels or poetry, he would not have become a legend. The only two possible successors to H as the head of English letters are George Bernard Shaw and George Moore. Both seem too rebellious to be pictured as O.M. H was always young at heart. [Obit.]

1349 O'Connor, T. P. "Men, Women, and Memories: Thomas Hardy—Sir Alfred Temple—Sir Harry Barnston," Sunday Times (Lond), 15 Jan 1928, p. 11.

H's philosophy was a reflection of his "personal characteristics and experiences: his writing was melancholy because he was melancholy." He "inherited the gift of story-telling" from his mother. "Compassion was the great note of Hardy's character and of Hardy's work."

1350 O'Connor, T. P. "Men, Women, and Memories: Thomas Hardy's Funeral—De Lesseps—Miss Kahn—Sir John Simon," Sunday Times (Lond), 22 Jan 1928, p. 13.

Fred B. Fisher, H's family doctor, says in a letter that the entire Hardy family could "tell stories" and that H submitted his novels to his first wife who "revised them pretty freely."

1351 O'Connor, T. P. "Personal Traits of Thomas Hardy," Daily Telegraph (Lond), 13 Jan 1928; rptd as "Thomas Hardy As I Knew Him," Living Age, CCCXXXIV (1 March 1928), 454–57; and as a separate pamphlet, Personal Traits of Thomas Hardy (Mount Durand, St. Peter Port, Guernsey: Toucan P, 1969).

H was "essentially a lonely man"; he had no interest in the world of London; "he was born melancholy." *Tess of the d'Urbervilles* has "the splendour of the tragedy evolved from the genius of Hardy." It is "the greatest plea for woman that was ever written." The man personally gave the impression of "unlifting melancholy." *Far From the Madding Crowd* was the first work to give "indication of the great literary force that had come into the world." Mrs. H's philosophy was in sharp contrast to H's. She referred to him as " 'very vain and very selfish.' " She was the least suitable companion for him. [Also see J. Stevens Cox (pub and general editor), Monographs on the Life of Thomas Hardy (1962).]

1352 Olivero, Frederico. "On Thomas Hardy," POETRY REVIEW, XIX (Feb–March 1928), 107–15.

H's art is characterized by "chasteness of style and form, felicitious phrasing, and lyrical scene painting." Through all of it, however, one sees "the endless misery of life in all its forms."

1353 O'Rourke, M. R. "Thomas Hardy, O. M.," MONTH, CLII (Sept 1928), 205–12.

H was not an antagonist of religion, as many of his religious friends will testify. His lyric poems show an honest wrestling with God, and should not be condemned out of hand by religious apologists like G. K. Chesterton. Verbal architecture and detailed observation of life make his lyrics memorable. [Memorial tribute.]

1354 Palmer, C. H. "Thomas Hardy and the Church," NEW AMERICAN CHURCH MONTHLY, XXII (1928), 153–58.

While one can find moments in H's novels where his attitude toward the Church could almost be said to be favorable, he is, for the most part, concerned with a detraction of it. This is especially true of his two greatest works, *Tess of the d'Urbervilles* and *Jude the Obscure*. In *Tess*, "Hardy gives vent to the most pessimistic of his views of life and the Christian religion." He reserves his most vicious attacks on the Church for *Jude*. Moreover, strains of his displeasure with the Church occur throughout his poetry. In spite of all this, there are passages which make one think: "the man that wrote that must have known what true worship is."

1355 Parker, W. M. "A Visit To Hardy: The Great Victorian on Pessimism," EVENING NEWS (Glasgow), 13 Jan 1928.

The dignity and the creative genius of H's works truly make him the last of the great Victorians. He had a keen insight into the lives of his characters and "the paradoxial condition of man." His art is characterized by courage and the "truth as he saw it." However, H relied too much on ingenuity, which oftentimes had to be created by use of "Chance and Fate." H was a lonely and isolated person, but he was not a pessimist.

1356 "Parson Tringham." "The d'Urbervilles' Claim to Arms," Notes and Queries, CLIV (11 Feb 1928), 101.

If Tess's father had had a son who had wished to repossess the family arms, would it be possible to obtain them and if so, how?

1357 P[atterson], I[sabel] M. "Turns with a Bookworm," New York Herald Tribune Books, IV (11 March 1928), 23.

Might *The Mayor of Casterbridge* have come from an idea used in a popular ballad? There is one using the wife-selling theme in a collection of street-ballads from the 1830s in the New York Public Library. H has contrived neat retributive justice, although real husbands in such stories were probably insensitive to their guilt.

1358 Perkins, Joycelyn. "Dickens Funeral Recalled by Recent Hardy Ceremonies," New York Times, 5 Feb 1928, III, p. 5.

Though H was buried with pomp and circumstance, Dickens was buried without prior notice to the public.

1359 "Personal and Otherwise," Harper's Monthly Magazine, CLVI (March 1928), 526.

[The editor refers to H's poem, "A Gentleman's Second-Hand Suit" (published this issue, p. 443) as having been received a month before H's death. "It was one of the last poems—if not actually the last—written by him." The editor cites H's many contributions to Harper's—including the serial *Heart's Insurgent (Jude the Obscure)*.]

1360 Phelps, William Lyon. "A Thomas Hardy Memorial," Saturday Review of Literature, IV (21 April 1928), 785.

[Requests donations to create a memorial to H, who was so important to literature as a novelist and poet. Conventional appreciation and fund-raising statement.]

1361 Phelps, William Lyon. "Thomas Hardy's Fifteen Novels," Forum, LXXIX (March 1928), 436–47.

H is the "most notable of English ambidextrous writers," famous both for prose and poetry. After thirty years, we are able to consider his novels with as much detachment as those of George Eliot. The worst is *Desperate Remedies*, with *Jude the Obscure* next; the best are *The Return of the Native* and *Tess of the d'Urbervilles*, with *The Woodlanders* a close third. His great novels have superb construction, lifelike characters, adequate style, and the temper of tragedy. H was mistaken in thinking the modern mind was bent toward pessimism; people are enjoying life as never before. *The Mayor of Casterbridge* is not great because H was not objective, and bad luck was too consistent; *Woodlanders* is "the most beautiful and the most noble" of the novels, and *Tess* is "a masterpiece." *Jude* "is a pseudo-masterpiece, written not in the glow of artistic creation, but in the heat of anger." "The book is written in such a key and in such a mood as to be lacking in that serenity which is the final grace of great art."

1362 Pinto, Vivian de Sola. "Foreward," WESSEX: AN ANNUAL RECORD, I (June 1928), 4–5.

"The *Wessex* of the novels, the poems and *The Dynasts* . . . exists as an intellectual and spiritual fact." "It is appropriate that the first number of WESSEX should commemorate Thomas Hardy," for in *Jude the Obscure* he shows the terrible disillusion that follows when a young man's dreams of higher education are not realized.

1363 Pinto, Vivian de Sola. "Thomas Hardy," WESSEX: AN ANNUAL RECORD, I (June 1928), 16–20.

H was "the last great novelist of the nineteenth century and the first great poet of the twentieth." The "qualities that constitute the chief attractions" of H's novels—his knowledge of landscape, tragic philosophy, his ardent pity and intense admiration for man's heroism and spiritual beauty—"are the qualities of a great poet." Like Shakespeare, H has "the power of giving a universal quality to things which are intensely local." *The Dynasts* is "the supreme achievement of modern English poetry" and "triumphantly solves" the problem of how to write "a poem on a grand scale, which is moving and profound without being too remote from contemporary life."

1364 "Poet's Modesty," MORNING POST (Lond), 13 Jan 1928, p. 8.

H's modesty is illustrated by his enclosing a stamped, self-addressed envelope with a poem he submitted to a London magazine the year before he died.

1365 Potter, Norris. "The Burial of Thomas Hardy," COLBY ECHO, XXXI (2 May 1928).

[This poem is a tribute on. the death of H. He will be remembered by his works despite the fact that he was a pessimist.]

1366 Powys, John Cowper. "Thomas Hardy and his Times," CURRENT HISTORY, XXVII (March 1928), 829–31.

H's fiction was largely unaffected by the historical events of his era, one of England's "most momentous epochs." "The Wessex novels form a kind of classic viaduct from the ponderous forums of the Victorian age to the hurly-burly of the modern market place." [Numerous inaccuracies; see C. J. Weber, " 'History' as It Is Written," COLBY MERCURY, V (Feb 1934), 37–40.]

1367 Powys, Llewellyn. "Thomas Hardy," NEW YORK HERALD TRIBUNE BOOKS, 22 Jan 1928, p. 3.

H's place among the immortals will always remain unchallenged. "He waged war against conventional prejudices because he detected the unnecessary cruelty they inflicted upon a race already sufficiently ill-used."

1368 Prilipp, Beda. "Thomas Hardy," HOCHLAND, XXV (March 1928), 671–73.
H is the historian of English authors, a scholar and philosopher. [Attention is drawn to H's treatment of nature, women, irony, and Immanent Will.] [Obit.] [In German.]

1369 Puaux, René. "Thomas Hardy," REVUE DE FRANCE, VIII (1 Feb 1928), 572–76.
H will remain a great novelist, in spite of his weak style. [Obit.] [In French.]

1370 Puccio, Guido. "Il solitario del Wessex: Tommaso Hardy" (The Hermit of Wessex: Thomas Hardy), RASSEGNA ITALIANA, XXI (March 1928), 212–18.
H's characters live as real, suffering persons: all readers who have tasted suffering can identify with them. In the face of suffering and a blind, brutal cosmos, H still maintains the classical calmness of the true artist. [In Italian.]

1371 Purdy, R. L. THOMAS HARDY MEMORIAL EXHIBITION (Catalogue of a Memorial Exhibition of First Editions, Autograph Letters and Manuscripts) (New Haven: Yale UP, 1928).
[Contains brief descriptions and histories of 146 first editions, manuscripts, autograph letters and "accessories" which appeared at a memorial exhibition of H's works. In each instance, the lender's name is cited. Forty-one pages.]

1372 R., J. A. "Thomas Hardy, Pessimist," SCOTTISH EDUCATIONAL JOURNAL, XI (27 July 1928), 830.
Recent estimations of H have tended to interpret his pessimism "in the most optimistic light." They try to show that "pity and admiration" work in H's art to exalt it "above any conventionally-conceived definition of pessimism." But his last novels and "practically his entire poetic output . . . seem all to tighten the net of pessimism about the unbowed head of Hardy." His conception of life, "The Martyrdom of Man," is pessimistic to the core.

1373 Rendall, Vernon. "Thomas Hardy, O. M.," ENGLISH REVIEW, XLVI (Feb 1928), 192–95.
Hailed as the last of the Victorians, H was as unlike them as was Swinburne. Instead he created from the real world of the peasants and dealt with authentic passions and disasters of hopes unrealized. While George Eliot was moral, H was human. *The Mayor of Casterbridge* is a Greek tragedy, enhanced by H's taste for anything ancient in England. His novels are better than his poetry. [Obit.]

1374 Robertson, Stewart A. "Mr. Hardy's Scotsman," SCOTTISH EDUCATIONAL JOURNAL, XI (27 April 1928), 458, 471.

H constrains his characters into scenes which are "made for the reader, and are not inevitable to the characters." Farfrae "is no Scot: he is a Robot." His speech is good "English English, until his creator bids him halt and say a Scots word or sing a stave of a Scots song."

1375 Russell, J. A. "The Poetry of Thomas Hardy," NIEUWE GIDS, XLIII (Dec 1928), 611–25.

Whether or not H is a pessimist or fatalist, he showed that man achieves independence only through the possession of "some belief, some philosophy which has the driving power of a passionate conviction." Victory does not lie in success, "but in steadfast holding by whatever belief is in your heart." H possesses the feeling and thought of a major poet. He "staked his whole poetic reputation on his profound personal exploration of the cosmic problem." His attitude as a poet, that is, has a far more philosophic cast than is common.

1376 Sackville-West, V. "Hardy's Poems," NATION AND ATHENAEUM (Lond), XLIV (13 Oct 1928), 54.

Winter Words resembles H's other poetry: his "landscape was always wintry." His stiff, uncomfortable diction and presentation match the winter season and fit the man closely, once one is accustomed to them.

1377 Saintsbury, George. TALES FROM FLAUBERT (Lond: Grayson & Grayson, 1928); rptd in PREFACES AND ESSAYS (Lond: Macmillan, 1933), p. 421.

Perhaps *The Dynasts* was influenced by Flaubert.

1378 "Scene at Stinsford," MORNING POST (Lond), 17 Jan 1928, p. 10.

[Account of the service and burial of H's heart in Stinsford.]

1379 Schlumberger, Jean. "Thomas Hardy poète tragique" (Thomas Hardy, the Tragic Poet), LA REVUE NOUVELLE, Nos. 38–39, (Jan–Feb 1928), 75–78.

H's work belongs to the genre of tragic drama, and not of the novel. And despite the bleak despair, his work affords its audience a kind of compensation or relief, as even tragic drama must. This compensation is a sense of human "grandeur." "The tragedy of his books is quite analogous to that which dominates the life of sailors and confers on it, even in its failures, . . . a nobility unknown to the bourgeoisie." [In French.]

1380 Scott-James, Rolfe A. THE MAKING OF LITERATURE (Lond: Secker, 1928, 1930; NY: Holt, 1930), pp. 64, 70, 190–91, 267.

H's characters are, like Eliot's, Meredith's, James's, "subservient to a pattern of life." The ancient Greeks "would have shrunk" from the grim story of *Jude the Obscure* where blameless men are tortured for no reason. H's scenes are never just visual but also aural (e.g., *Far From the Madding Crowd*).

1381 Shanks, E. "Hardy's Reply to His Reviewers," John O'London's Weekly, XX (27 Oct 1928), 103.

Preface to the posthumous volume *Winter Words* shows H's "unbounded attachment to life" and his protest against the reviewers who found his last collection "wholly gloomy and pessimistic," in the reviewer's words. In his poetry H shows "a robust, powerful, and invigorating acceptance of the things that happen."

1382 Shanks, Edward. "Songs of Joy," Saturday Review (Lond), CXLVI (10 Nov 1928), 610.

H is "omnivorous" in his love of life, in keeping with his disclaimer of pessimism found in the draft preface to *Winter Words*. His admiration of the strange passes of life appears in the grotesque tragedy of "The Gap in the White." H likes life revealed in ironic contrasts; "very often one term of the contrast is suppressed" to deepen the impression.

1383 Shanks, Edward. "Thomas Hardy," Saturday Review (Lond), CXLV (21 April 1928), 495.

H's reputation will be subject to reactions; his poems are presently exalted at the expense of his prose. Yet the touch of the inevitable in the prose compels admiration. As *The Short Stories of Thomas Hardy* shows, H, like Wordsworth, is a great writer who can write badly, as in the immoderate and pungently odd plot of "For Conscience' Sake." H handles words with the maladroitness of Shaw, but there is some marvelously concise description in "The Three Strangers."

1384 Shaw, George Bernard. "Thomas Hardy's Death," Daily News (Lond), 12 Jan 1928.

[George Bernard Shaw admits his shock upon learning of H's death. He says that he and H were on "very friendly terms" and that he likes H's poetry better than H's prose.]

1385 Sheppard, Alfred Tresidder. "A Glimpse of Thomas Hardy," Bookman (Lond), LXXIII (March 1928), 319–20.

H commented that his second wife had been a great inspiration to him, particularly in the writing of his later poems. He was noted for never giving a direct answer to a question about his works. He, in fact, disliked discussing his own works.

1386 Sheppard, Alfred T. "Thomas Hardy," SUNDAY TIMES (Lond), 22 Jan 1928, p. 12.

H was a truly compassionate man. [Also, an account is given of an execution of pirates that H mentioned in relation to his life in London.]

1387 Shuster, George N. "Thomas Hardy," CATHOLIC WORLD, (March 1928), 721–29.

One of the earmarks of an H novel is the presence of a metaphysical power: "an intuition of the whole drama of human existence over and above a grasp of individual comedies and tragedies." A major flaw in the Wessex novels regarding this metaphysical power is that H resorts too much to chance. An emphasis on the role of chance in the drama of existence is not conducive to a truly metaphysical view of the universe. H's approach to existence, however, is eminently acceptable as a prelude to the "redemptive affirmations" of the Catholic faith. Thus, while the ideal philosophic novelist would use H's view of life, he would also transcend it: "to the extent that a religious novelist would perfect the view of life that Hardy sponsored and would then add, as a consequence of assenting to the reality of God, an equivalent vision of spiritual existence, he would approximate to the ideal."

1388 Siddhanta, N. K. "Thomas Hardy," MODERN REVIEW (Calcutta), XLIII (Feb 1928), 191–95.

[The usual summary of life and works.] [Obit.]

1389 Sime, A. H. Moncur. "Thomas Hardy and Music," MUSICAL OPINION, LI (Sept 1928), 1178–79.

Although it may be true H "is not specially interested" in "music proper— as an art and an end in itself," he repeatedly speaks of music in his prose and poetry. "Hardy's language [in his poems] is often-times picturesque, full of colour, and motion, tuneful, and never far away from what is symmetrical and intrinsically musical."

1390 "Sir James Barrie," SUNDAY TIMES (Lond), 15 Jan 1928, p. 13.

James T. Barrie and T. L. Gilmour were the only two witnesses at H's cremation.

1391 Smart, John Semple. SHAKESPEARE: TRUTH AND TRADITION (Lond: E. Arnold; NY: Longmans, 1928), pp. 169–70.

[In proving Shakespeare was well-educated enough to have written the plays, Smart cites other "uneducated" English writers, including Dickens, Meredith, Stevenson, and H. H is mentioned as quoting a phrase from Aeschylus's PROMETHEUS BOUND in *Tess of the d'Urbervilles* and thus paralleling Shakespeare's alluding to Sophocles's AJAX.]

1392 Soupault, Philippe. [Thomas Hardy], EUROPE, 15 March 1928, pp. 404–6.

H considered himself, at the beginning of his literary career, a kind of "amateur"; he did not belong to the literary world of his time, like Proust, and was never interested in literary fashion. As early as 1908, the French critic Valery Larbaud indicated the importance of *The Dynasts*, in CE VICE IMPUNI, LA LECTURE. . . . H did not have a good style; he was a great writer but not a great artist; like Tolstoy, whom he resembles very much, he is one of the greatest writers of the nineteenth-century.

1393 Spies, Heinrich. KULTUR UND SPRACHE IM NUEN ENGLAND (Culture and Language in Modern England) (Berlin & Leipzig: B. G. Trübner, 1928), pp. 13, 88, 120, 141.

The turn of the twentieth-century was characterized by many "isms" which were already expressed in the literature of preceding decades. In *The Woodlanders* and *Tess of the d'Urbervilles*, H attacks these categories. [In German.]

1394 Squire, J. C. "Thomas Hardy," OBSERVER (Lond), 15 Jan 1928, p. 14.

H "was the most lively of philosophical pessimists and the cheerfulest man that ever frequented a churchyard." The tendency to dwell upon the tragic and ironic tone of his novels and poems often overshadows the fact that H never lost his lively interest in the world around him and that the dark mood of his works is tempered by his brilliant "panorama of rustic life." He may someday be remembered more for his poetry than for his novels, though they too have the qualities of greatness.

1395 S[tepney], G. H. "This Idle Show," BROTHERHOOD WORLD, IV (April–June 1928), 146–48.

The world is not an idle show. Though H "neglected the only justification of God's ways that ever appealed to the heart of man," he is a Christian. His words are dangers to minds not so strong as his.

1396 Steuart, John A. "Thomas Hardy," SUNDAY TIMES (Lond), 22 Jan 1928, p. 12.

Long after *Far From the Madding Crowd* appeared, H "was almost utterly neglected." When *Tess of the d'Urbervilles* appeared in book form, H "was probably the most abused man in England."

1397 Strickland, Roger. "The Genius That Was Hardy's," NEW YORK TIMES, 22 Jan 1928, III, p. 5.

Disagrees with editorial obituary of 13 Jan 1928; feels H's analogies in *The Return of the Native* are not tortured and do not destroy mood but rather heighten and accentuate it. H, in fact, didn't say enough through analogy; he consciously leaves gaps for readers to fill in. This allusiveness is H's genius. All of H's women have something of Mona Lisa; all of his men something of Jesus. H hints much, declares little.

1398 Swinnerton, Frank. "Hardy Mourned as Greatest English Writer of Times," CHICAGO DAILY TRIBUNE, 28 Jan 1928, p. 10. "The death of Thomas Hardy has taken from us the greatest modern English writer." No one is left to take his place because his work has a "uniqueness of its own." Although H's works had some defects, they were "creative" in every sense of the word. Mrs. H's biography of H will probably be authentic in every fact, but "his true memorial will eventually be found . . . in the body of work which he himself produced."

1399 "Thomas Hardy," DIAL, LXXIV (Feb 1928), 179–80. H's "martyr-like sincerity drew the world as an undertow toward true vision and respect." The region around Max Gate is rich with commemorations. The seclusion of the graves of members of his family is now his. [Obit.]

1400 "Thomas Hardy," NATION (NY), CXXVI (25 Jan 1928), 84–85. Whether one praises the poems or the novels, H's greatest value will prove to be for his contemporaries, for his vision was informed by purely nineteenth-century attitudes. The discrepancy between desire and destiny was the central conflict in H's life, and he explored reality through literature in his attempt to resolve it. Even though he is still recognized as a master of the narrative mode, his poetry of the past thirty years has far eclipsed his novels. Ultimately, however, his position as a great artist is secure if only because his character, and finally his literature, developed out of his temperament. [Obit.]

1401 "Thomas Hardy," NEW REPUBLIC, LIII (25 Jan 1928), 260–61. H was the last survivor of the Victorian Age. Poems such as "Hap" show the pessimism of *Tess of the d'Urbervilles* and *The Mayor of Casterbridge* to be a creed, not merely an aristic device. H's renunciation of his position as a leading novelist, "because the public would not agree with the artist as to the limitations of his esthetic creed, was in itself unprecedented," in 1895. In *Tess*, geology and biology emphasize the brevity and triviality of man's place in the world. Tess and her companion "crawling like flies between the upturned face of earth and the downturned face of sky, typify man's place in nature." [Obit.]

1402 "Thomas Hardy," NEW YORK TIMES, 13 Jan 1928, p. 22. H's achievement "took the meal out of the mouth" of fiction, revealed his "conviction . . . of the sombre fate of mankind." His faults are "deplorable infelicities of style," too many philosophical digressions (especially in *Tess of the d'Urbervilles* and *Jude the Obscure*); he was melodramatic, too reliant on chance, a bit of a misogynist. His virtues are the fusion of scene and character; he never bores, "never wastes words on insignificant characters." H was the last large star of the Victorian era, but a bit pedantic at times, as in *The Return of the Native*. [Obit.]

> **1403** "Thomas Hardy," OUTLOOK (Lond), LXI (21 Jan 1928), 74–75.

It is presumptuous to assign to such a figure as H his place in thought or in literature, but he has wielded and welded our tongue like no man since Milton. His work alone gives unity to a changeful epoch. He strove first with his mother-tongue and next with the temper of his age, until he molded both to his sovereign will.

> **1404** "Thomas Hardy," REVIEW OF REVIEWS (NY), LXXVII (March 1928), 319–20.

H's work "had linked the Nineteenth and Twentieth Centuries." *A Pair of Blue Eyes* was tremendous. *Tess of the d'Urbervilles* spread his fame throughout England and to America. [Obit.]

> **1405** "Thomas Hardy," TIMES (Lond), 12 Jan 1928, p. 13.

H won his great reputation through patience and courage; he eschewed a facile popularity. His philosophy of "no abstract or dilettante theorizing [was] an energetic conviction . . . too stern and melancholy to rouse flippant applause." H sees the greatness in man. We must finally attribute his popularity to his national epic, *The Dynasts*, with its unpretentiousness, its masculinity, and its atmosphere of quiet endurance.

> **1406** "Thomas Hardy: An Appreciation," WORLD WIDE (Montreal), XXVIII (4 Feb 1928), 95; perhaps rptd from A. N. M.'s "Thomas Hardy," MANCHESTER GUARDIAN WEEKLY, 20 Jan 1928, p. 52 [not confirmed].

"The mood in which Shakespeare . . . brooded over all . . . undeserved, unchecked . . . suffering became perennial in Hardy till his whole genius was tinged with a bitter compassion." H is a great man "because he has given to the outward face and the common life of a great tract of rural England . . . a kind of monumental and storied quality of reality."

> **1407** "Thomas Hardy and 'Anti-Scrape,'" TIMES LITERARY SUPPLEMENT (Lond), 23 Feb 1928, p. 129.

H perhaps gave up architecture because of what he saw was being done to ancient buildings. At any rate he was a member of the Society for Protection of Ancient Buildings (dubbed Anti-Scrape by William Morris) for forty-eight years. His paper "Memories of Church Restoration," read at a meeting in 1906 by Col. Balfour, also three letters to Anti-Scrape not in his handwriting but with his signature, throw valuable light on H's attitudes. H later repented his early part in "restoration" that did not preserve ancient buildings.

1408 "Thomas Hardy Buried," MORNING POST (Lond), 17 Jan 1928, pp. 9–10.
[Detailed account of the church ceremonies at the Abbey and Stinsford, and the burials.]

1409 "Thomas Hardy: His Heart in Wessex; His Ashes in the Abbey," ILLUSTRATED LONDON NEWS, CLXXII (21 Jan 1928), 95–97.
[Photographs of the solemnities connected with H's funeral constitute the major portion of this article.] [Obit.]

1410 "Thomas Hardy, J.P., O.M., D.Litt., LL.D.," PROCEEDINGS OF THE DORSET NATURAL HISTORY AND ANTIQUARIAN FIELD CLUB, XLIX (1928), xxv–xxix.
H was active in the Dorset Field Club from 1881–1893. He was vice president of the Dorset County Museum "from 1918 onwards, and his interest in it continued until his death."

1411 "Thomas Hardy, Last of the Victorians," LITERARY DIGEST, XCVI (4 Feb 1928), 36–41.
H's cousin Teresa Hardy states that H should have worked at architecture instead of fiction; part of Tess's character was based on herself. [Obit., containing a discussion of H's burial, and a brief biography and character testimonials taken from newspapers.]

1412 "Thomas Hardy: The Greatest Writer of his Time," TIMES (Lond), 12 Jan 1928, p. 14.
H at his death was the greatest writer of his time, the "most impressive personality among the authors of our day." From a teller of powerful tales of passion he developed into a philosophical novelist, isolated by his theory of life. But he won his way to recognition with his own manner as a poet and epic dramatist.

1413 "Thomas Hardy's Early Years in A Memoir By His Wife," NEW YORK TIMES BOOK REVIEW, 11 Nov 1928, p. 3.
[THE EARLY YEARS OF THOMAS HARDY, by Florence E. Hardy (1928), is a mine of information in the notes. Praises H for liberalizing English novel.]

1414 "Thomas Hardy's Will," MORNING POST (Lond), 27 Feb 1928, p. 8.
H left an estate of £91,707. [Presents details of H's will.]

1415 "Thomas Hardy's Will," New York Times, 25 Feb 1928, p. 5.

H left an estate of $450,000 with stipulations as follows: Max Gate and a $3000 annuity to his widow, trust funds for his widow and his brother and sister, the remainder (one-half) to found a college in Wessex or, if it is unestablished in five years, to go for scholarships to Magdalene College, Cambridge. Unpublished MS, letters and documents are left to literary executors to dispose of as they choose.

1416 "Thos. Hardy," Sunday Times (Lond), 22 Jan 1928, p. 15.

The temporary inscription on H's commemorative stone in Westminster Abbey reads "Thos." instead of "Thomas." The full name will appear on the permanent slab.

1417 Tomlinson, H. M. "Hardy at Max Gate," Saturday Review of Literature, IV (11 Feb 1928), 585–87; rptd and rvd in Out of Soundings (NY & Lond: Harper, 1931), pp. 232, 255–82.

Contemporaries cannot offer impartial criticism of the works as art apart from the man. H's brooding sorrow was his "life-long error." H once spoke of the unfavorable reception of his last novels, but only humorously and tolerantly. H, like Shakespeare, had innocent divination into people. H was traditionally English, no other author was more so.

1418 "Turns with a Bookworm," New York Herald Tribune Books, 11 March 1928, p. 23.

[Answer to a query whether H made up the story for *The Mayor of Casterbridge*: H did not make it up, but the author of the column cannot remember where H's comments on this fact may be found.]

1419 Twitchett, E. G. "Poetry," London Mercury, XIX (Dec 1928), 203–5.

H did not express a harmonious philosophy in his works, and his prevailing mood was not gloomy ("delicate regret," was his "prevailing mood for twenty years"). *Winter Words* is "not Hardy's greatest book, but it is one of his most interesting."

1420 Van Doren, Carl. "Thomas Hardy," Outlook (NY), CXLVIII (25 Jan 1928), 154.

H, like Shakespeare, brought "dead pageant of his native region to life," and he shaped and colored the universe poetically. But H shaped his with his mind. His victims are earthbound, possessing shorter chains than Shakespeare's. Wessex will exist forever as H shaped and imagined it. Division of H's remains did not exist in his life. H's "brain was no less native than his heart to the soil by which he loved to be bound." [Obit.]

1421 Van Doren, Mark. "April and December," NATION (NY), CXXVII (12 Dec 1928), 662.

Florence Hardy's THE EARLY LIFE OF THOMAS HARDY: 1840–1891 (1928) is indispensable for the factual information it gives, but it is disappointing in that it reveals no personal disillusionment to which H's tragic view of life might be attributed. The only frustration that H seemed to have encountered was that the universe failed to meet his expectations—"nothing bears out in practice what it promises incipiently." Some of the tales which H heard as a young man are repeated here. *Winter Words* is just one more example of the amazing variety H could produce within a single mood. It is as interesting and as significant as the preceding volumes.

1422 Van Doren, Mark. "Last Words of Thomas Hardy," NEW YORK HERALD TRIBUNE BOOKS, V (23 Dec 1928), 3.

Winter Words is a "worthy successor" to H's other volumes, "both in its badness—which it would seem from a note somewhere in Hardy's biography was deliberate—and in its several excellencies." The introduction is characteristic, disclaiming the charge of pessimism and the existence of any organized philosophical approach.

1423 Van Doren, Mark. "Thomas Hardy, Poet," NATION (NY), CXXVI (8 Feb 1928), 151–52; rptd in MODERN WRITERS AT WORK, ed by J. K. Piercy (NY: Macmillan, 1930), pp. 170–74.

The principle reason for H's stature as a poet is that his poems are interesting. In fact, H's only competitor for first place among twentieth-century British poets is William Butler Yeats, whose poems are in some respects more admirable but not as interesting. Because of H's background as a novelist, he had a unique way of seeing and describing things in his poetry. This grounding in prose narrative is also evident in the stories which so often appear in his poems.

1424 Vaudoyer, Jean-Louis. "Souvenirs d'une lecture" (Memories of a Reading), LA REVUE NOUVELLE, Nos. 38–39 (Jan–Feb 1928), 79–82.

[When Vaudoyer was at the Front during World War I, he read *Tess of the d'Urbervilles* in his spare time. H depicts Tess in so life-like a fashion that she walked in Vaudoyer's imagination constantly.] [In French.]

1425 W., R. W. G. "Hardy and Animals," NEW YORK TIMES, 22 Jan 1928, III, p. 5.

[Quotes H's poem about a baby watching a wagtail drink from a ford: wagtail drinks while a bull, horse, and dog pass by, but flees at the sight of "perfect gentleman."]

1426 Walpole, Hugh. "Hardy—the Man and the Poet," SPEC-TATOR (Lond), CXLI (3 Nov 1928), 657.

Florence Hardy's THE EARLY LIFE OF THOMAS HARDY: 1840–1891 (1928) links "fact to fact, making the background clear, but doing no more than that": the "one inevitable right way" of writing H's biography. Possessed of "crudity" and "enthusiasm," H was close to life. Always a poet at heart and "never at ease in the technique of the novel," his "creative zest" carried him over his "animosity" to the form and enabled him to produce great works of fiction. A "poet by desire, novelist by compulsion, creator by divine inheritance."

1427 [Wells, H. G.?]. "Thomas Hardy: Last of the Victorians," LITERARY DIGEST, XC (4 Feb 1928), 36, 41.

According to H's cousin Teresa, H used actual people (herself among them) for his fictional characters. Some parts of Teresa's personality appear in *Tess of the d'Urbervilles* and *Under the Greenwood Tree*. The funeral at Dorchester was attended by people similar to characters in the novels. H's physical appearance belied his "gigantic intellectual stature." When pointed out to H. G. Wells, Wells ejaculated, "What? Not that little gray man!" Public opinion toward H has recently grown quite favorable, as opposed to the low esteem in which he was held in the days of *Tess* and *Jude the Obscure*.

1428 [Wells, T. B.]. "Personal and Otherwise," HARPER'S MONTHLY MAGAZINE, CLVI (March 1928), 526.

H's poem reached HARPER'S before his death. May have been his last written poem. "We publish it in proud and grateful recollection of his long association with the house of Harper."

1429 Weltzien, Erich. "Thomas Hardys Heimatkunst" (Thomas Hardy's Regional Art), NEUE JAHRBÜCHER FÜR WISSENSCHAFT UND JUGENDBILDUNG, IV (1928), 288–303.

[Fine general introduction to H's regional art. Primary attention given to the Wessex novels. Discussion of the interrelationship of landscape, seasons, time of day, customs, and the inhabitants of the city and the village, stressing a unity of existence bound to nature.] [In German.]

1430 Westminster Abbey. THE FUNERAL SERVICE OF THE LATE THOMAS HARDY, O.M., MONDAY, JANUARY 16TH, 1928. 2 P.M. (Lond: Vacher, 1928).

[Before the Service: J. S. Bach's "Choral Preludes" and B. Harwood's "Requiem Aeternam." Order of Service: "The Sentences" (John. 11: 25–26; Job. 19: 25–27; I Timothy. 6: 7; Job. 1: 21; Psalm XXIII); "The Lesson" (Eccles. 44: 1–15); Procession of Clergy and Mourners to the Grave, S. S. Wesley's "Thou wilt keep him in perfect peace" being sung;

after grave side proceedings, "Lead, kindly Light," The Nunc Dimittis, The Blessing. After the service: Handel's "The Dead March in Saul."]

1431 "A Westminster Abbey Irony," LITERARY DIGEST, XCVI (11 Feb 1928), 29.

There is irony in H's burial in Westminster Abbey because he held the same "artistic theology" as Meredith, whose remains were denied burial there. Had H died during the controversy over *Tess of the d'Urbervilles* and *Jude the Obscure*, he might have been kept out of the Abbey. But now that he is remembered more for *The Mayor of Casterbridge*, *The Return of the Native*, and *The Woodlanders*, "that glorious book in which you can hear the sap running in the trees," he has gained admittance.

1432 Weygandt, Cornelius. TUESDAYS AT TEN (Phila: University of Pennsylvania P, 1928), pp. 8, 41, 62, 67, 71, 87, 131, 190, 264, 281, 288, 294, 296, 297, 311, 313.

[Comparison of H's works and characteristics to works of other authors of similar works, passim.] Pinero, Wilde, Shaw, Barrie, Dunsany are not of the same stature as H or Conrad. [An essay on a porcupine, purportedly "an illustration of coincidence from a lecture on Thomas Hardy," does not mention H and omits the lecture.] "Mr. Stephens as a poet in verse is but a minor poet . . . and of only a slender talent as compared to such majors as Mr. Hardy." H has "fidelity to country life." W. H. Hudson is comparable to H in "sense of the past" and "the power to recall it." Masefield has sponsors in Chaucer, Whitman; H in tales of wayfaring and of tragedy. Joe, in DAUBER, "is like Jude in his artistic feeling and his sensitiveness" but is not cursed by women or drink, nor does he have the "compensating strength." In THE DAFFODIL FIELDS, Mary is an exceptional woman, as Sue is in *Jude the Obscure*. In THE TRAGEDY OF NAN the desperate circumstances of the heroine are as vivid as in *Tess of the d'Urbervilles*, but the tone is "not so gloomy as Hardy's." Masefield totally lacks irony, differentiating him from H, "the greatest ironist of our time."

1433 Widows, Margharita. ENGLISH LITERATURE (Lond: Chatto & Windus, 1928), pp. 294–95.

[Brief consideration of H's place in literature, noting his pessimism, "pagan outlook," and "Christian sensitiveness to suffering." Mentions *Tess of the d'Urbervilles*, *Jude the Obscure*, *The Woodlanders*, *Under the Greenwood Tree*, and *The Dynasts*. Superficial.]

1434 Wild, Friedrich. DIE ENGLISCHE LITERATUR DER GEGEN-WART SEIT 1870: DRAMA UND ROMAN (English Literature of the Present Since 1870: Drama and Novel) (Wiesbaden: Droskuren Verlag, 1928), pp. 118–21, 159–68, and passim.

In *The Dynasts*, "the real hero . . . is England as represented by Pitt, Nelson and Wellington." The dumb shows and, even more, the mass scenes are reminiscent of cinema techniques. The dominant tone of *The Famous Tragedy of the Queen of Cornwall* is that of the mournful complaint over the irreclaimable past, not the triumph of love over death. To describe H's novels as folk-art and to praise his realistic description of landscape is to describe only one side of his creativity, since H's novels embody an idealistic philosophy which derives from Schopenhauer. The motive of fickleness, faithlessness or the divisibility of love present in many of H's novels is bound up with the Immanent Will, who stands over the characters and intervenes in their lives. Similarly, in *The Return of the Native,* the heath is more than only a symbol; it is the destiny of its children like Eustacia and Clym. *The Mayor of Casterbridge* "is the expression of the most hopeless pessimism, of an idea of fatalistic retribution." *Tess of the d'Urbervilles* and *Jude the Obscure*, "genuine tragedies," are shot through with Schopenhauer's *Weltanschauung*. Jude's fate has, from the beginning, "been written in the stars." [In German.]

1435 Williams, Orlo. "*Far From the Madding Crowd*," NEW ADELPHI, II (Dec 1928–Feb 1929), 128–39.
Far From the Madding Crowd is only occasionally marred in phraseology by the outcroppings of H's hard, rocky intellectualism. H's "privileged intimacy with the face and features of the Earth" makes every aspect of familiar countryside counterpoint human themes or processes, much as Conrad's works use the sea. Bathsheba and Gabriel are fine, but Troy with his stilted diction and bravura of swordplay in the hollow is difficult to swallow whole. H, "without seeking falsely to ennoble what is ignoble, has used for an effective contrast with death in misery the sensual stoicism of the country that is rooted in life, the dynamic principle of an agricultural community."

1436 Windle, Bertram C. A. "Thomas Hardy as I Knew Him," COMMONWEAL, VII (Feb 1928), 1006–7.
[Records a few conversations with H concerning the geographical background of his novels and the nature of his pessimism. H said about the latter: " 'I am so constituted that, when it begins to rain, I find it impossible to believe that it will ever be fine again.' "]

1437 Wolfe, Humbert. DIALOGUES AND MONOLOGUES (Lond: Gollancz, 1928), pp. 23, 86–89, 92, 178.
An author's views color his story: "You can't imagine Thomas Hardy writing TRAVELS WITH A DONKEY or Robert Louis Stevenson *Jude the Obscure*." H, for "sometime past has been conceded a place as a fixed star almost beyond criticism." H authoritatively uses his own country. Life is

wanting. Rhythm in H is highly individual but prosaic. H does not sing and is therefore no poet. H gives the "movement of earth itself" a kind of music. The test of poetry does not apply well to H, Yeats, or Kipling. How can it be applied to contemporaries? There are no Public Servants in Eliot, C. Brontë, Reade, Meredith, or H.

1438 Woolf, Leonard. "Thomas Hardy," NATION AND ATHE-NAEUM, XLII (21 Jan 1928), 597–98.
H's "novels are in the full English tradition, solid works built about a story" in which character, humor, description, and philosophy are accessories. As George Moore says, H does not "write well," but his novels have the qualities which he describes in Egdon Heath: "majestic without severity" and "grand in their simplicity." H's mixture of genius and simplicity is shown through his anecdote about a dinner with Galsworthy, Shaw, Wells, and Barrie. [Obit.]

1439 Woolf, Virginia. "Half of Thomas Hardy," NATION AND ATHENAEUM, XLIV (24 Nov 1928), 289; rptd in NEW RE-PUBLIC, LVII (5 Dec 1928), 70–72; and in THE CAPTAIN'S DEATH-BED AND OTHER ESSAYS, ed by Leonard Woolf (NY: Harcourt, 1950), pp. 62–68.
H had an aversion to books about himself. With his decision to write novels, H felt he must behave as novelists do; "he must frequent dinners and clubs and crushes. He must keep a note-book." H's early novel-writing was much influenced by others' opinions of his work, but he finally decided to be himself. The result was *Tess of the d'Urbervilles*. [Commentary on Florence Hardy's THE EARLY LIFE OF THOMAS HARDY (1928), mainly dictated by H.]

1440 Woolf, Virginia. "Thomas Hardy's Novels," TIMES LITER-ARY SUPPLEMENT (Lond), 19 Jan 1928, pp. 33–34; rptd as "The Novels of Thomas Hardy," in THE SECOND COMMON READER (Lond: Hogarth P, 1932), pp. 245–57; rptd (NY: Harcourt, Brace, 1932), pp. 266–80; and rptd (Lond: Penguin Books, 1944), pp. 186–96.
When H lived "there was a king among us and now we are without." He left seventeen volumes of fiction as a guide "to distinguish between those qualities which are and those which are not still forces in the life of the present moment." H can be described as an "unconscious writer" whose "moments of vision" caused "passages of astonishing beauty and force" in every book he wrote. *Far From the Madding Crowd* gives a deep sense of the physical world and shows that "man's existence is ringed by a landscape which, while it exists apart, yet confers a deep and solemn beauty upon his drama." Three or four characters dominate each novel and "attract the

force of the elements." While H's women characters suffer through dependence on others, men suffer through "conflict with fate." In each novel love is a "catastrophe," happening "suddenly and overwhelmingly." *Jude the Obscure* is the only novel which could "fairly" condemn H as a pessimist. *The Mayor of Casterbridge* is not pessimistic, although it contains as much misery as *Jude*.

1441 Wyatt, A. J., and Henry Clay. MODERN ENGLISH LITERATURE: 1798–1919 (Lond: University Tutorial P, 1928), pp. 174–77, 195–96, 205, 216–17.

H's work was comparatively cheerful at first but as the years passed more of "the bitter pessimism of the time entered into his novels." H is a "writer with a philosophy"—fate becomes malignant. "Wordsworth's deity immanent in the great comforter nature has become a mocking devil." H's hero is typically "the toy of the forces of heredity and environment." "In imaginative range and intellectual nobility the greatest of modern poets is [Hardy]."

1442 Zachrisson, Robert Eugen. "Trollkarlen fran Wessex" (The Wizard of Wessex), MODERN ENGELSK VARLDSASKADNING I LITTERATURENS SPEGEL (Uppsala & Stockholm: Almqvist & Wiksells, 1928), pp. 9–60; trans and rptd as "Thomas Hardy as Man, Writer, and Philosopher: An Appreciation With a Swedish Hardy Bibliography," STUDIER I MODERN SPRAKVETENSKAP UTGIVNA AV NYFOLOGISKA SALLSKAPET I STOCKHOLM, X (1928), 131–59; and as a separate pamphlet (Uppsala: Almqvist & Wiksells, 1928).

To understand and appreciate H, one must remember the writer's artistic temperament, the social milieu of the time, and the author's outlook on life. H's temperament was melancholy but not necessarily pessimistic because his characters always reach out for life with a vitality that conquers disaster. His failure to receive the Nobel Prize in 1921 [Zachrisson proposed him for it] can partly be blamed on the social milieu in England. Statements from Professors W. Ker, W. Raleigh, Sir Edmund Gosse, and Sir Arthur Quiller-Couch assert that H should have received the prize. Sweden itself suffered a loss of prestige because of the failure to award the Nobel Prize to him. Outside of England, H was best known in Scandinavia and was consistently praised by Scandinavian, German, and French critics.

All the characteristics of H's philosophy are revealed in his earliest poems, some of which are cited. His twilight view of life was due to a melancholy disposition, despair over the ironies of life and compassion for suffering. He was not influenced by Schopenhauer. The sad fate of H's heroes is due not necessarily to fate but often to weakness of will (Tess, for example). This book is "one of the finest novels in all literature." An outstanding example of H's literary style at its best and his worship of nature is the description of Egdon Heath. [At the end of the article is a bibliography of other articles on H in Swedish. This article is interesting because it includes Zachrisson's personal impressions of H following a meeting in Weymouth in 1920 and statements on H by important literary critics.] [In Swedish/English.]

1929

1443 Abercrombie, Lascelles. "Thomas Hardy," ENCYCLOPAEDIA BRITANNICA, 14th ed (Lond & NY: Encyclopaedia Britannica, 1929), XI, 192–93.
H deals with "the principle of life itself" (as seen in sex and nature) not civilization or manners. His French view of women is subtle and cruel; he has "thoroughly a man's point of view" and is still an apologist for women. Three periods in his career: fiction, *The Dynasts*, lyrical poetry.

1444 Arns, Karl. "Hardys letzte Gedicht" (Hardy's Last Poems), ZEITSCHRIFT FUR FRANZOSISCHEN UND ENGLISCHEN UNTERRICHT, XXVIII (1929), 612–16.
Under no circumstance can H be labeled as a pessimist in the strict sense of the word. There is a persistent elegiac and melancholy quality in his verse as if he were saying, "Lo, I have borne my burden." H is not obsessed with one idea or mood. He is able to present a happy feeling; he is humorous, satirical, cynical. H can write of death without being bitter and of the tragedy of love. In H's last volume of poetry he does not present new themes; yet, the fact that he was able to give new form and color to old themes is evidence enough of his originality and poetic ability. [In German.]

1445 "Barrie Reviews Hardy," LITERARY DIGEST, C (2 Feb 1929), 22.
Barrie first met H in a club in Piccadilly. H never desired fame, although he "could easily be hurt, by not ill-intended pens." H's love for Shelley dated from an early age. [Trivial.]

1446 Baugh, Albert C. "Introduction," *The Return of the Native* (NY: Macmillan, 1929 [1928]), pp. ix–xxi.
H's career is partly reflected in Stephen Smith (*A Pair of Blue Eyes*) and Springrove (*Desperate Remedies*). H's detailed knowledge of great Greek dramatists and Shakespeare was a major influence. The interaction of char-

acters and setting in *Native* is impressive. However great *Tess of the d'Urbervilles* and *Jude the Obscure* are, "it is doubtful whether on artistic grounds time will continue to give them a place besides those consummate works of fiction, *Far From the Madding Crowd, Native,* and *The Mayor of Casterbridge.*" H is not a pessimist in the simplest sense; he "insists on facing squarely what he believes to be the facts of life."

1447 Bensusan, Samuel L. "Thomas Hardy," QUARTERLY REVIEW, CCLIII (Oct 1929), 313–29.

H, annoyed by misconceptions about his life which had been printed, gave Florence Hardy corrective materials to right matters in THE EARLY LIFE OF THOMAS HARDY (1928). H's memory was clear in his later years, but the volume is "admirably reticent." He loved the old times in Dorset, like those portrayed at the beginning of *Under the Greenwood Tree.* "In the practice of his art a sense of drama was innate, his stage was always prepared carefully before the first figure took the boards, and all the changes suggest that they had been thought out beforehand." He frequently contemplated dramatizations of his novels, but he usually was deterred by a demand for what he considered unwarranted changes. H's work is uneven. His characters are plausible, and even the minor ones are surprisingly alive as they appear in various Wessex scenes.

1448 Braybrooke, Patrick. "Thomas Hardy," PHILOSOPHIES IN MODERN FICTION (Lond: Daniel, 1929), pp. 35–40.

H is deeply pessimistic, deterministic, and atheistic, but he treats those who are victims of circumstances with kindness.

1449 Burchardt, Carl. "Thomas Hardys livsyn" (Thomas Hardy's View of Life), VOR VERDEN, VI (Oct 1929), 500–504.

H's view of life is that of a realist rather than a pessimist; he is not disillusioned, but illusionless. H did not want to be labeled with a single word, yet his poetry does indeed reflect his philosophy. In his early poems he emphasizes fortune's indifference to man and the transitory quality of human life. Nothing is sure but that life is meaningless; God is a de-personalized thing and men are mere puppets in the hands of a universal will—a theory set forth in *The Dynasts.* The poem "To Sincerity" is evidence of H's positive view of life, his faith in man's ability to shape a higher destiny. The love poems are poems of memory in which confused emotions of the past are now viewed with clarity. H's temperament was by nature tragic. But the tragic view is not completely synonymous with pessimism, which does not allow for the rise as well as the fall of man's fortunes—the theme of many of H's poems. Because he believed it was impossible for humans to intervene in nature's world, H was branded a pessimist. It is surprising that the indictment should have bothered him in the least. [In Norwegian.]

1450 Bush, Douglas. "Hobnobbing with Eminent Authors," BOOKMAN (NY), LXX (Sept 1929), 55.
[Bush could never muster the courage to ask to see H. When he did visit Max Gate he took a picture of it.]

1451 Bush, Douglas. "The Varied Hues of Pessimism," DALHOUSIE REVIEW, IX (Oct 1929), 271–81.
H is not a "modern pessimist," for, like Arnold, his pessimism is not founded on the certainty that science shows man to be a purposeless atom. Arnold and H are much more alike than ordinarily thought; they exemplify universal melancholy rather than religious disillusionment. H is not philosophical and tends toward pathos and sentimentalism rather than tragedy, but *The Mayor of Casterbridge* is a possible exception. Arnold is more classical and humanistic. H is a humanitarian whose world is one of "undisciplined emotion." Arnold appeals to "that inner life of discipline and self-dependence, and to that calm possession of the soul which, if seldom achieved, must yet always be the goal and reward of such discipline." Arnold is thus the greater poet, his work has an "organic unity and wholeness" and his quality is due to "the sad lucidity of soul with which he seeks for truth."

1452 Chilton, Eleanor Carrol, and Herbert Agar. THE GARMENT OF PRAISE (NY: Doubleday, Doran, 1929), pp. 311–24.
H's statement that he was a meliorist might have been one of his "little ironies." For, indeed, his work is the expression of a distinct fatalist. *The Dynasts* is a clear statement of H's belief that in the scheme of nature, human nature and human life are both painful and inconsequential. The most man could attain, H believed, was a noble stature in the midst of his predicament. This is the theme of *Tess of the d'Urbervilles*.

1453 Colum, Padraic. "Thomas Hardy, Poet," IRISH STATESMAN, XII (20 July 1929), 390–92.
H was a "deeply and widely learned" man as well as a poet who was a "seer." His poetry reflected his "love of life" and his strong desire for "what life held." "A grace has been added to his poetry because he loved the things that have been shaped by men's hands." H's poetry leaves a strong sense of "clear sights and sounds." H's verse has an "odd knowledgeableness, a quaint mastery of the craft" which is surprising in the work of a village poet.

1454 D., T. M. "Durnovarian Reminiscences: Thomas Hardy and The Wessex Novels; Interlopers at the Knap," DORSET YEARBOOK, 1929, pp. 143–44.
H confessed having forgotten who Higgins, the carpenter in *Desperate Remedies*, was: "Dickens himself could not easily have bettered Hardy's account of Higgin's home."

1455 Dobrée, Bonamy. "Thomas Hardy," THE LAMP AND THE LUTE: STUDIES IN SIX MODERN AUTHORS (Oxford: Clarendon P, 1929), pp. 21–44; rptd in ENGLISH CRITICAL ESSAYS: TWENTIETH CENTURY, ed by Phyllis M. Jones (Lond: Humphrey Milford, 1933), pp. 326–50.

H's tragic view is redeemed by his human richness and proffered sympathy. Like Aeschylus, H sees tragedy as occurring to firm and strong people, but for H, the tragic flaw is in the universe, not in man. Though his novels are notable for their irony and their portrayal of man and nature, *The Dynasts* remains his masterpiece.

1456 Fisher, John S. "The Fairs and Showmen of Thomas Hardy," WORLD'S FAIR, 19 Jan 1929, p. 10.

H's books "are full of little pictures of the fairs and showmen who provided the few extra pleasures of the rustics in Hardy's youth."

1457 Fletcher, John Gould. "Thomas Hardy," BOOKMAN (NY), LXIII (Feb 1929), 621.

[Poem emphasizing H's "power to bear/Testimony to mankind of man's dark mystery."]

1458 Ford, Ford Madox. THE ENGLISH NOVEL (Phila: Lippincott, 1929), p. 118.

H contributed to the swell of insignificant "novels of commerce." [Noteworthy only for this single and singular absurdity.]

1459 Freeman, John. "The Early Life of Thomas Hardy," LONDON MERCURY, XIX (Feb 1929), 400–407; rptd in LIVING AGE, CCCXXXVI (May 1929), 192–95.

[Review of Florence Hardy's THE EARLY LIFE OF THOMAS HARDY (1928); nothing new.]

1460 Hansford, Frederick E. "Thomas Hardy and Animal Suffering," ANIMALS' FRIEND, XXXV (Feb 1929), 54–55.

H, "always interested in . . . the work of societies devoted to the protection of dumb creatures," was deeply sensitive to animal suffering, as his works show.

1461 Holland, Clive [pseud of C. J. Hankinson]. "A Fair in Wessex," MORNING POST AND GAZETTEER (Lond), 24 Sept 1929, p. 10.

A fair held annually for two or three days in the third or fourth week of September at Bere Regis is one of the few surviving examples of the fairs H described in his novels.

1462 Hubbell, Jay B. THE ENJOYMENT OF LITERATURE (NY: Macmillan, 1929), pp. 58–60, 83–84.

A study of H's *The Return of the Native* reveals a masterly employment of practically all the uses of setting. Egdon Heath is the main character in the story. The Greek conception of Fate is embodied in the environment. No other novel handles so skillfully the spirit of place. W. L. Phelps's comments on H's pessimism: "After finishing one of Mr. Hardy's novels, one has all the delight of waking from an impressive but horrible dream, and feeling through the dissolving vision the real friendliness of the good old earth."

1463 Huscher, Herbert. "Über Eigenart und Ursprung des englischen Naturgefühls" (Concerning the Type and Origin of the English Feeling for Nature), KÖLNER ANGLISTISCHE ARBEITEN, V (1929), 5–39, espec 20–22.

H was not as popular in Germany as Meredith or Hamsun. [In German.]

1464 K[elly], B[lanche] M. "*Winter Words in Various Moods and Metres*," CATHOLIC WORLD, CXXIX (June 1929), 366–67.

The poems contain unaccustomed pathos and familiar irony. The kind of majesty with which H treats folk tragedies in prose is absent from his verse. At least one poem is blasphemous, several are willfully pagan. A few are genuine poems but no lyric rapture.

1465 Lemperly, Paul. AMONG MY BOOKS (Cleveland: The Rowfant Club, 1929), pp. 24, 26, 39, 55–57.

[Mention is made of Lemperly's holding the following H items: a first edition of *Under the Greenwood Tree* containing, in the first volume, H's original signed agreement of 22 April 1872 with Tinsley for sale of copyright, and in the second an autograph letter dated 3 Jan 1875 attempting to recover the copyright for "any sum"; a first edition of *Wessex Tales* inscribed to Robert Browning in 1888; a copy of H's *Two on a Tower* inscribed to Paul Lemperly; a copy of H's "G. M.: A Reminscence" (1927).]

1466 Loane, George Green. "*The Dynasts* and the N.E.D.," TIMES LITERARY SUPPLEMENT (Lond), 14 Feb 1929, p. 118.

N.E.D. editors should consider a supplement which would contain words used in *The Dynasts* either in different senses or new words. Some of many such words are "cess," "comb," "cymballed," and "Fleshings."

1467 Lovett, Robert Morss. "Biography," BOOKMAN (NY), LXIX (March 1929), 96–98.

THE EARLY LIFE OF THOMAS HARDY by Florence Emily Hardy (1928), is a valuable aid "in interpreting his work through his experience of life." The work is unsatisfactory in that it does not reveal enough about H's "intellectual experience." Religion, music, a fascination for the macabre, and solitude are a few of the aspects of his life which were important in his youth and which became significant in his writing and retained importance in his later life.

1468 [Lurie, Charles N.]. "Thomas Hardy," NEW INTERNATIONAL YEAR BOOK: A COMPENDIUM OF THE WORLD'S PROGRESS FOR THE YEAR 1928, ed by Herbert T. Wade (NY: Dodd, Mead, 1929), pp. 321–22.
[Sketch of H's life and works.]

1469 Magnus, Philip M. "Poetry and Society Since Tennyson," EDINBURGH REVIEW, CCXLIX (April 1929), 303–4.
Despite the uneven quality of the whole body of H's poetry, his experiments in new forms were more successful than Housman's attempts to escape the influence of Tennysonian lushness.

1470 Meissner, Paul. "Die Überwindung des 19. Jahrhunderts im Denken von Samuel Butler" (The Conquest of the Nineteenth Century in the Thought of Samuel Butler), GERMANISCH-ROMANISCHE MONATSSCHRIFT, XVII (1929), 205–20, espec 206.
Schopenhauer's philosophy or H's poetry are clear examples of a *Weltanschauung* which sees in all occurrences only the working of a blind and unreasonable Will. [In German.]

1471 Newton, A. Edward. THOMAS HARDY, NOVELIST OR POET? (Phila: pvtly ptd, 1929).
[Based on original and unpublished manuscripts in the libraries of Paul Lemperly and the author, gives facsimiles of H's letters in the "Oak Knoll" library: H's letters to the American journalist Jeannette L. Gilder; the facsimile of an inscription by H in the first edition of *Jude the Obscure,* written Oct 1904, which shows that ten years after publication the *Jude* incident still rankled.]

1472 Olivero, Frederico. "The Poetry of Hardy," POETRY REVIEW, XX (Jan–Feb 1929), 1–22.
H deals with the unjust suffering of humanity. "He is a follower of Wordsworth in so much that he does not look for ornate words, but uses a plain, everyday language," and his poetry is also very musical. He uses traditional meters in many forms, and he is attentive to form, despite some evidence of clumsiness. He uses "word-pictures" in his poems and novels, and he is especially fond of "odd and striking similes." The rural imagery is especially good. [Some very good critical comment.]

1473 O'Neill, George. "Poetry from Four Men," OUTLOOK (NY), CLI (16 Jan 1929), 110–11, 114, 120, espec 110.

In *Winter Words*, H's poems labor under the obvious use of devices to obtain ironic effects. Prose ideas are distorted to fit a confining and falsified medium, and the result is "disappointing."

1474 Parker, W. M. "My Visit to Thomas Hardy," CORNHILL MAGAZINE, LXVI (Feb 1929), 149–57; expanded as A VISIT TO THOMAS HARDY (Beaminster, Dorset: Toucan P, 1966).

[A descriptive reminiscence of the writer's visit to H at Max Gate in Sept 1920. Appendix: "Five Letters from Florence Hardy to W. M. Parker." Also see J. Stevens Cox (pub and general editor), Monographs on the Life of Thomas Hardy (1962).]

1475 Phare, E. E. "Hardy as a Humanitarian," CAMBRIDGE REVIEW, L (3 May 1929), 410–11.

Though he often adopts an omniscient/omnipotent stance in his novels, H feels compassion for the human condition and treats men and women with extreme tenderness. This humanitarianism in the face of an impersonal cosmos prevents the reader's discomfort and disgust with the otherwise pessimistic tone of H's novels.

1476 Phelps, William Lyon. "As I Like It," SCRIBNER'S MAGAZINE, LXXV (Feb 1929), 221–23.

With THE EARLY LIFE OF THOMAS HARDY (1928), Mrs. H has written what approaches an "ideal biography." H "was born old," and so he was always sympathetic but never jovial. The great scenes in the novels are those of man in his aloneness. *Winter Words* bears out H's resigned and retiring outlook on life.

1477 Purdy, Richard L. "A 1905 *Dynasts*," TIMES LITERARY SUPPLEMENT (Lond), 14 Feb 1929, p. 118.

A rare copy of the first 1905 edition of *The Dynasts* with uncanceled title page turned up in the library of Phillips Exeter Academy.

1478 Quiller-Couch, Sir Arthur. STUDIES LITERATURE: THIRD SERIES (Cambridge: Cambridge UP, 1929), p. 51.

[Lecture on "The Journals of Dorothy Wordsworth" begins with reference to "the extreme indelicacy of our newspaper press during the week after the death of that great and simple countryman, Thomas Hardy." Without stating his reason, Quiller-Couch "swear[s] that nothing could have been falser or unjuster to all that [H] ever meant, wished or stood for than the strangling sobs of the British Press in Westminster Abbey over the writer of *Under the Greenwood Tree*." Without stating specifically why, in the case of H, Quiller-Couch calls for temperate control of curiosity concerning the lives of great authors. Apparently the British press's coverage of H's life in the wake of his funeral had not been in keeping with H's lifelong reticence about his personal affairs.]

1479 Reilly, Joseph J[ohn]. "The Short Stories of Thomas Hardy," CATHOLIC WORLD, CXXVIII (Jan 1929), 407–15; rptd in OF BOOKS AND MEN (NY: Julian Messner, 1942), pp. 117–29.

H was the master of form in writing great short stories. In fact, all of the stories show the marks of H's genius: constructive skill, vitality, power of characterization, vigor, and vividness. Furthermore, these stories reveal H's ability to handle chance adroitly, to deal with humor, and to make us sympathetic with his women.

1480 Richards, I. A. "Poem XI," PRACTICAL CRITICISM: A STUDY OF LITERARY JUDGMENT (Lond: Kegan Paul, 1929), pp. 147–53.
[Detailed analysis of student reaction to H's "George Meredith."]

1481 Roberts, Morris. HENRY JAMES'S CRITICISM (Cambridge: Harvard UP, 1929), pp. 33–34.

In reviewing *Far From the Madding Crowd*, James called it a merely clever, superficial imitation of George Eliot; "the suspicion that he was dealing with anything more than the average novel of the day never crossed his mind apparently."

1482 Russell, J. A. "*The Dynasts*: Thomas Hardy's Epic-Drama," NIEUWE GIDS, XLIV (Aug 1929), 158–66.
[Simple précis of the poem—no analysis or criticism.]

1483 Sanders, Gerald DeWitt, John Herbert Nelson, and M. L. Rosenthal (eds). CHIEF MODERN POETS OF ENGLAND AND AMERICA (NY: Macmillan, 1929; 1936), p. 3; rptd as CHIEF MODERN POETS OF BRITAIN AND AMERICA (NY: Macmillan, 1970), pp. 3–5.
[Brief references to H's pessimism, fatalism, and command of language are followed by forty-one pages of his poetry.]

1484 Selver, P. "Englischer Brief" (English Letter), DAS LITERARISCHE ECHO, XXXI (1929), 477.
In THE EARLY LIFE OF THOMAS HARDY, by Florence Hardy (1928), one learns to know H as a novelist. [In German.]

1485 Sencourt, Robert Esmonde. THE LIFE OF GEORGE MEREDITH (Lond: Chapman & Hall, 1929), pp. viii, 154–55, 193, 303.
Meredith's letters to Mlle. Hilda de Longueuil were printed in NINETEENTH CENTURY, CIII (Feb 1928), in conjunction with H's reminiscence. In Jan

1869, Meredith rejected H's *The Poor Man and the Lady* for Chapman & Hall but offered "encouraging but acute" criticism—ended "oppressed by his twilight view of life." Leslie Stephen got Stevenson, H, Gosse, et al to contribute to CORNHILL, which he edited 1871–1882. [H's tribute to Meredith quoted.]

1486 "Shaw and Hardy Write to Henry Arthur Jones," LIVING AGE, CCCXXXVII (1 Sept 1929), 30.

Mrs. Doris Thorne, Jones's daughter, has recently released some documents she is using in writing the life of her father. H would now write *Tess of the d'Urbervilles* differently than he did thirty years earlier.

1487 Sholl, Anna McClure. "Thomas Hardy," THE COLUMBIA UNIVERSITY COURSE IN LITERATURE, ed by John W. Cunliffe and others (NY: Columbia UP, 1929), XV, 59–64, 64–87.

Since H presents not life itself but his own theory of life, he is free to make his unconsciously witty rustics, his good men, and his "real" women suffer more than they should. Controlled by chance and circumstance, these characters can hope for no more than a compromise with life. [Selections from *Under the Greenwood Tree, Far From the Madding Crowd,* and *The Return of the Native,* pp. 64–87.]

1488 Slaughter, Gertrude E. T. "Hardy's Poetry," THE COLUMBIA UNIVERSITY COURSE IN LITERATURE: WRITERS OF MODERN ENGLAND (NY: Columbia UP, 1929), XV, 87–91, 91–105.

H's shorter poems and *The Dynasts* portray "the unequal struggle between individuals and the force of destiny." [Act VII, scenes vii and viii of *Dynasts* reprinted.]

1489 Swaffer, Hannen. "Tess in the Grill-Room," SUNDAY EXPRESS (Lond), 28 July 1929, p. 5.

Mrs. Bugler held her London audience despite her utter ingenuousness as an actress. She is "a natural actress, one . . . who has soaked herself in the part of a heroine . . . and then . . . just carried on with her life."

1490 Swann, George Rogers. "Hardy and the Dualism of Will and Idea," in "Philosophical Parallelisms in Six English Novelists"; University of Pennsylvania dissertation, 1929; pub as PHILOSOPHICAL PARALLELISMS IN SIX ENGLISH NOVELISTS (Folcroft, Pennsylvania: Folcroft P, 1969), pp. 110–38.

H derived from Schopenhauer the belief that the Universe is irrational. To illustrate this belief he wrote novels structured around "a central conditioning character" whose existence is complicated by "new personal factors" which produce unpredictable results. An "ethical structure" results from a combination of "the outer maladjustment and the inner defect" of the character. When the character seeks to escape from the "outer circumstance," an ethical complication results. It is neither this complication nor the unpredictability of action that leads to a character's defeat, rather it is the character's inner defect. Nevertheless, no one is to be blamed for his actions, since biological and moral good oppose one another. In fact, there is opposition everywhere with the result that the inner and outer lives become exclusive, and a dualism arises. Thus, the only basis of ethical behavior is resignation. [This essay has numerous errors and a style so garbled its content is at times impossible to comprehend.]

1491 Trueblood, C. K. "A Tragedian of Sentience," DIAL, LXXXIV (Feb 1929), 150–54.

Poems of *Winter Words* show H is not a pessimist and Florence Hardy's THE EARLY LIFE OF THOMAS HARDY (1928) that he was always a poet. In his novels H was not interested in manners but in the substance of life. He made no concessions against his own feelings. Carried on "life as an emotion." EARLY LIFE'S strength is in its consistency with novels and poems.

1492 Van Dyke, Henry. "*Tess of the d'Urbervilles,*" THE MAN BEHIND THE BOOK: ESSAYS IN UNDERSTANDING (NY: Scribner's, 1929), pp. 283–305.

In H's novels it is the plot, "the strange web of circumstance, the predestined accidental meeting, the fatal coincidence, the secret betrayed by a passing gust of wind, the mystery disclosed by a momentary gleam of light —in short, the game which fate plays with us mortals, that holds the central phase in each book." The gloom of H's novels is "singularly impersonal"— a reflection on the general pitifulness and helplessness of the human lot as he sees it, a picture of the futility of human life at large, entangled in a web of unknown fates, and vainly struggling to escape." The "noble inconsistency" (between a concern for "the well being of society" and his belief in naturalism) of H's philosophy gives human interest to his novels. *Tess of the d'Urbervilles* reflects "his most intense personal feeling" and "marks the height of his tragic power." As a vindication of Tess, the story is sublime but "as an indictment of God, it fails." God did not kill Tess; the guilt of her death lies between two human beings. [Includes the recollection of a meeting with H during which he overtly indicated *Tess* was his favorite book.]

1493 Vicar of Stinsford Parish. "Stinsford and the Hardy Family," SOMERSET AND DORSET NOTES AND QUERIES, XIX (1929), 106–10.

The H family tradition "that they were connected with the Hardys of Portisham and thus distantly were collateral kinsmen to Admiral Sir Thomas Masterman Hardy, Bart, Nelson's flag captain on the Victory" is one "founded upon fact." [Contains a "Pedigree of Mr. Thomas Hardy" tracing his ancestry to 1540.]

1494 Weltzien, Erich. "Thomas Hardys Anschauung vom Immanenten Willen" (Thomas Hardy's View of the Immanent Will), NEUE JAHRBÜCHER FÜR WISSENSCHAFT UND JUGENDBILDUNG, V (1929), 451–65.
[Well-articulated presentation of H's concept of the Immanent Will. Substantiated primarily from *The Dynasts* with numerous references to H's poetry, e.g. "God-Forgotten," "The Unborn," "To an Unborn Pauper Child," "Hap," "Nature's Questioning," and "In a London Flat."] [In German.]

1495 Wise, Thomas James. A BROWNING LIBRARY: A CATALOGUE OF PRINTED BOOKS, MANUSCRIPTS AND AUTOGRAPH LETTERS BY ROBERT BROWNING AND ELIZABETH BARRETT BROWNING COLLECTED BY THOMAS JAMES WISE (Lond: pvtly ptd, 1929).
[Between pp. 118–19 is a facsimile of a holograph letter from H to Edmund Gosse, 3 June 1899, concerning the paradox of "Smug Christian optimism" in the works of a "seer." Perhaps it was "bait to get the rest of him taken." On p. 119, the date of the letter is inaccurately reproduced as 3 March 1899, and "leading" is substituted for "literary."]

1496 Woolf, Virginia. "Phases of Fiction," BOOKMAN (NY), LXIX (June 1929), 407–8.
H is a poet of fiction but an imperfect novelist. *Far From the Madding Crowd* lacks control, has an incoherence not found in Proust, Austen, or Tolstoy. H is too fully charged with "sense of poetry" but has "too limited or imperfect a sympathy with human beings to express it through that channel." In H, the impersonal element—fate, the gods—dominates the people, but they can't express the poetry H feels, "their psychology is inadequate," and "thus the expression is left to the writer, who assumes a character apart from his people and cannot return to them with perfect ease when the time comes." Characters are wooden, melodramatic because the author is separate from them. The result is incoherence.

1930

1497 Benson, E. F. As WE WERE: A VICTORIAN PEEP SHOW (Lond: Longmans, Green, 1930), pp. 275, 284–85.
"The critic who does not perceive that the Wessex novels are great literature . . . demonstrates his own deficiency."

1498 Bliss, Howard. "Thomas Hardy's Inscriptions," TIMES LITERARY SUPPLEMENT (Lond), 2 Jan 1930, p. 12.
Books for sale bearing inscriptions from H to Peter Cushing, Patrick Hastings, and Curtis Shalley are not genuine judging from handwriting and testimony of Mrs. H.

1499 Bryan, John Ingram. THE PHILOSOPHY OF ENGLISH LITERATURE (Tokyo: Marusen, 1930), pp. 256–58, 307.
H, influenced by George Eliot, is an example "of what the world would be like without faith." He is engaged in a battle between a philosophy of faith and philosophy of the senses. He shrinks from any concept of immensity. He remains content "with a company of limited moral and intellectual beings thru whose imaginary experiences he attempted an estimate of reality." None of his characters is great or noble; his heroines are sensual and stupid. His poetry reflects the same pessimistic philosophy of the universe found in his novels. "His verse is not real poetry, because it has no joyous or singing quality, nor of the buoyance of true life. . . . To the Hardy school of fiction and poetry there is but one goal: distrust of the integrity of the universe."

1500 Burdett, Osbert. "The Hardy Biography," LONDON MERCURY, XXII (July 1930), 250–57.
[Mainly a summary of the first volume of THE EARLY LIFE OF THOMAS HARDY and LATER YEARS OF THOMAS HARDY, by Florence Emily Hardy (1928, 1930). No evaluation of the books is offered, except to praise them as "admirable."]

1501 Cunliffe, John W. "Thomas Hardy," CENTURY READINGS IN THE ENGLISH NOVEL (NY: Century, 1930), pp. 397–423.
Since the time when he abandoned novel-writing, H's reputation as a novelist has risen, and he has kept a hold on the twentieth-century reader more firmly than any other Victorian novelist. His modest beginnings gave little promise of this. His novels are of quaint country folk and contain a rather dark view of man's struggles against circumstance. [With references, mainly, to *The Return of the Native*.]

1502 Davis, Frederick Hadland. "The Simplicity of Thomas Hardy," LITERARY GUIDE, ns CCCCIX (July 1930), 120.
H's humility parallels the greatness of his accomplishments. H disavowed "rationality" as a discipline, and he cannot be thought of as a profound thinker. "The simplicity of Hardy is indicated in his belief that war on a vast scale is impossible to-day."

1503 Edgett, Edwin F. "About Books and Authors," BOSTON EVENING TRANSCRIPT [Book Section], 17 May 1930, p. 2.

Mrs. H's claim in THE LATER YEARS OF THOMAS HARDY (1930) that H's turning to poetry was good is incorrect. LATER YEARS is not a biography, but "materials for a biography."

1504 Eliot, T. S. "Poetry and Propaganda," BOOKMAN (NY), LXX (Feb 1930), 595–602.

H is an example of a writer whose work is based on a "mechanistic philosophy of science." Unfortunately this philosophy was a bad one. H would have been a better writer had he had a better philosophy, or none at all. "Hardy has exploited determinism to extract his esthetic values from the contemplation of a world in which values do not count."

1505 Ellis, Havelock. "Introduction," THE HUMAN PAIR IN THE WORKS OF THOMAS HARDY . . ., by Pierre d'Exideuil, trans by Felix W. Crosse (Lond: Humphrey Toulmin, 1930; see French ed under 1928); rptd as "Thomas Hardy and the Human Pair," in VIEWS AND REVIEWS, 2nd ser (Boston: Houghton Mifflin, 1932), pp. 181–89.

H is neither an optimist nor a pessimist but an observer of the tragedy and comedy of life which often has its edge at the point of sex. It is appropriate that a French critic should analyze this element in H's work. H presents the problem of love between modern man and more elemental woman.

1506 Fisher, F. B. "Some Recollections of Thomas Hardy," CHRIST CHURCH COLLEGE (Cawnpore) MAGAZINE, XXIV (March 1930); rptd in LIFE IN THOMAS HARDY'S DORCHESTER 1888–1908, by C. M. Fisher (Beaminster, Dorset: Toucan P, 1965), pp. 21–24.

H's mother's favorite book was Dante's COMEDIA, and "she was the fount of her son's genius." [Also see J. Stevens Cox (pub and general editor), Monographs on the Life of Thomas Hardy (1962).]

1507 Gardner, W. H. SOME THOUGHTS ON *The Mayor of Casterbridge* [English Association Pamphlets, No. 77] (Oxford: Oxford UP, 1930; Folcroft, Pa: Folcroft P, 1969).

Although *The Mayor of Casterbridge* has been attacked by some critics, it is a great novel. Evidence of this is that it meets the " 'three fundamental rules of design' " established by Arnold Bennett: the interest of the novel is centralized; the interest of the novel is maintained; the plot of the novel is kept throughout " 'in the same convention.' " In addition, the novel's "textural qualities," including setting, style, and the influence of environment, contribute to its greatness. Ultimately, however, it is Henchard who establishes the novel as great. Engaging in a struggle with Farfrae which illustrates that character is fate, he, like Lear, causes the reader to identify with him and share the alternations of pity and disgust elicited by his actions.

1508 Graves, Robert. GOOD-BYE TO ALL THAT: AN AUTOBI-OGRAPHY (NY: Jonathan Cape & Harrison Smith, 1930), pp. 360–65.

In conversation, H spoke about religion, politics, and the war. He offered remarks on his literary practice: "I have never in my life taken more than three, or perhaps four drafts for a poem. I am afraid of it losing its freshness"; "wrote novels by time-table, but that poetry was always accidental, and perhaps for that reason I prized it more highly." H "spoke disparagingly of his novels," but there were chapters he admired. He disliked autograph-hunters and regarded professional critics as parasites. He had no early literary influences except for books lent him by fellow-apprentice architects.

1509 Guha-Thakurta, P. "Thomas Hardy," CALCUTTA REVIEW, 3rd ser XXXVI (Sept 1930), 376–85.

H suffers from much unjust criticism. His pessimism, which is "both philosophic and temperamental," is not unalloyed. Man has an infinite capacity to struggle and endure, and H has both a sense of the law of the universe and a sense of pity. Ultimately "the intention of the heart" determines the status of his characters.

1510 Hamblen, Emily S. ON THE MINOR PROPHECIES OF WILLIAM BLAKE (Lond & Toronto: Dent; NY: Dutton, 1930), pp. 43–44.

A passage from H's *The Woodlanders* illustrates "that mystical union with nature" enjoyed to the full by Boehme, Thoreau, and Blake. [*The Woodlanders*, Chap 44, passage beginning "The casual glimpses" and ending "not from that of the spectator."]

1511 Hammerton, J. A. BARRIE: THE STORY OF A GENIUS (NY: Dodd, Mead, 1930), pp. 449, 473, 478, 487.

Since H was unable to attend awarding of honorary LL.D. at St. Andrews, it was conferred in his absence. Roberston Nicoll, Ellen Terry, and Barrie were similarly honored at the same time. H's death ended one of Barrie's most precious friendships. H visited London rarely in his later years, but Barrie's home was the main attraction for him. Barrie bore the casket of H's ashes from Dorchester to Westminster Abbey. Barrie gave a "long and noble tribute" to H. H never desired his fame and had to be pushed into Elysium by its guardian angel.

1512 Hardy, Florence Emily [Dugdale]. THE LATER YEARS OF THOMAS HARDY, 1892–1928 (NY & Lond: Macmillan, 1930); reissued with THE EARLY LIFE OF THOMAS HARDY, 1840–1891 [1928] in two vols (Lond & NY: Macmillan, 1933); rptd, two vols in one, as THE LIFE OF THOMAS HARDY, 1840–1928 (NY: St. Martin's P; Lond: Macmillan, 1962).

[Although published as a biography, these volumes are essentially auto-biographies dictated by H to his second wife. Despite omissions of much material that was burned before and at H's death, these volumes still remain an essential mine of primary information. Because these volumes are considered as primary works, abstracts of selected reviews are given under pertinent dates of publication.]

1513 Harvey, Sir Paul. THE OXFORD COMPANION TO ENGLISH LITERATURE (Oxford: Clarendon P, 1932), pp. 108, 153, 219–20, 247, 280, 289, 350–51, 352–53, 364, 422, 444–45, 507, 510, 563, 583, 661–62, 738, 776, 806–7, 810, 820, 829, 841, 843, 850, 854, 858, 866.

[Identifies the chief characters in H's novels, gives brief plot summaries of the major novels and *The Dynasts*, and gives a short biographical sketch and a categorized list of H's works.]

1514 Hutchison, Percy A. "When Hardy Foreswore Fiction for Poetry," NEW YORK TIMES BOOK REVIEW, 11 May 1930, p. 5.

In THE LATER YEARS OF THOMAS HARDY, 1892–1928 (1930), by Florence E. Hardy, Mrs. H made judicious use of H's diaries to give a picture of H the philosopher and artist, but H the man shines through also. The key to all of H—man, philosopher, and artist—is insistence on worthiness. This volume, with EARLIER YEARS (1928), forms "one of the most distinguished biographies anywhere to be found."

1515 Jiriczek, Otto L. "Sprache und Literatur" (Language and Literature), ANGLIA BEIBLATT, XLI (6 Nov 1930), 321–27.

THE EARLY LIFE OF THOMAS HARDY and THE LATER YEARS OF THOMAS HARDY, by Florence Hardy (1928, 1930), provide information which H would not communicate earlier. The books do not, however, orient the wealth of incidents in H's life to his creative work. The index is incomplete. [In German.]

1516 Jones, Doris. TAKING THE CURTAIN CALL (NY: Macmillan, 1930), pp. 50, 141, 220, 236, 312.

H, a friend of Henry Arthur Jones, attended opening night of TRIUMPH OF PHILISTINES. H questioned Jones about financial terms for plays. H was willing to sign protest against retention of Censor, although the matter concerned him, as a "mere book-author" (in 1909), less than it did dramatists. Conferring of Order of Merit on H (1910) led Jones to wonder if he might not have been recognized if he had written novels rather than plays. H asked for advice on having a copyright performance of dramatic version of *Tess of the d'Urbervilles* in London at same time it appeared in New York.

1517 "Kicking the Classics," LITERARY DIGEST, CIV (8 March 1930), 17.

Dickens, H, and Charles Kingsley are considered as somewhat more than fallible. "Hardy wrote about upper-class life (in *Tess of the d'Urbervilles*), which he didn't understand, and made a conventional villain of Alec. . . . The excitement over *Tess* in the nineties was due to its defiance of Victorian delicacy."

1518 Knight, G. Wilson. THE WHEEL OF FIRE: ESSAYS IN INTER-PRETATION OF SHAKESPEARE'S SOMBRE TRAGEDIES (Lond: Oxford UP, 1930), p. 197.

The world of LEAR is "rooted in nature, firmly as a [H] novel."

1519 Lacey, Charles. "Reminiscences of an Old Durnovarian," DORSET YEARBOOK, 1930 [not seen in this form]; rptd as MEMORIES OF THOMAS HARDY AS A SCHOOLBOY. With additional notes of Hardy interest by C. D. Austin, Charles Lacey's Grandson (Mount Durand, St. Peter Port, Guernsey: Toucan P, 1968).

At the British School in Greyhound Yard, Dorchester, H was "one of the cleverest pupils." [Almost wholly anecdotes unrelated to H. Additional note by C. D. Austin, trivial and not abstracted. Also see J. Stevens Cox (pub and general editor), Monographs on the Life of Thomas Hardy (1962).]

1520 Laing, Alexander. "Hardy and Housman Again," SATURDAY REVIEW OF LITERATURE, VI (5 July 1930), 1180.

Margaret Woodbridge's letter ["Housman and Hardy," ibid (17 May 1930), 1055] is unwarranted. By one chain of reasoning H might have copied Housman rather than the other way around, but the case is too unclear for any finding.

1521 Lucas, F. L. "The Last of the Victorian Poets," LISTENER, III (11 June 1930), 1034–35.

Other poets are but shadows of reality beside the authenticity of H. This is true partly because H grew up in a rude environment and was never young. He has a stern sense of reality and a saddened sense of time.

1522 Lucas, F[rank] L[aurence]. "Thomas Hardy," EIGHT VICTORIAN POETS (Cambridge: Cambridge UP, 1930), pp. 133–51; rvd and enlgd as TEN VICTORIAN POETS (Lond: Cambridge UP; NY: Macmillan, 1940, 1948), pp. 183–99.

Unlike most poets, H brings us not a dream but a vision "of that reality more vivid than our own." He writes not to create illusion but to destroy it. H's truthfulness is evident in his sincerity and intellectual honesty. To H nature was both radiantly beautiful and "a blind fiend." In all he wrote H's personality is evident—essentially his compassion.

1523 Mais, S. P. B. "Thomas Hardy: A Picture of the Man," DAILY TELEGRAPH (Lond), 29 April 1930.

Florence Hardy's THE LATER YEARS OF THOMAS HARDY (1930) is dignified, "never trivial," and "allows the subject of the memoir to be as far as possible self-revelatory." "It traces the stages by which he changes from the most abused to the most honored of English authors." It also sheds light on the workings of H's mind. The biography reveals H's deeply religious nature, his "bird-like alertness and eagerness about everything and . . . his extraordinary capacity for friendship." It also shows that H was not "driven from prose to poetry by the clamour of the critics." "The truth about him is that he was as far from being a pessimist as he was from being an atheist." H was a "meliorist" with a very "inquisitive and penetrating mind [which] prevented him from being an optimist."

1524 Miller, George Morey. THE VICTORIAN PERIOD (NY: Scribner, 1930), pp. xix, xlviii–xlix, lvii–lviii, lx, 493–94.

H is not properly speaking, a Victorian. Like other pessimists of the age, H had no confidence in any satisfactory solution to then current problems. He is more markedly pessimistic in his novels than in his poetry. In his view of evolutionary science, the reign of law is wholly hostile to man, containing no external force for righteousness. [Reprints selected H poetry, pp. 303–12.]

1525 Olivero, Frederico. AN INTRODUCTION TO HARDY (Torino, Italy: Fratelli Bocca Editori, 1930).

H is linked to the Elizabethan dramatists: "he is essentially dramatic in building up his plots, in contrasting characters, in disposing scenes and episodes." H "is consistent in his pessimistic outlook throughout his work. It is a conception born of intellectual pride." Even so, H's final view "is one of sympathetic comprehension and profound pity." "His lovers are slaves, dying slowly in the thraldom of passion." *Jude the Obscure* and *Tess of the d'Urbervilles* "are the result of utter despondency in the consideration of human affairs." But there is a sharp contradiction between H's ethical conception and his hopes. Although in H's novels we only see "fragments of the universal design . . . nevertheless we are induced to think that these events are determined by a divine power." H's moral sense is "far more evident that his mystic thought." Although man is "a free and responsible agent . . . he [H] represents him as apparently a slave of circumstance," and often of his passions. [Surveys H's work under these headings: "His World," "Symbolism and Fancy," "Ground-Thoughts," "Mysticism," "Ethics," "Love and Passion," "Humour," "Characters," "Nature," "Plot," "Form," "Poems and Dramas." Badly proofread, superficial.]

1526 Pitfield, Robert L. "In the Footsteps of Tess d'Urberville," General Magazine and Historical Chronicle [University of Pennsylvania], XXXII (July 1930), 497–507.

[Describes Tess's travels about Wessex from the "vacant house" in the New Forest to Stonehenge. This is a sentimental and over-written travel-piece which adds little to our knowledge of H or *Tess of the d'Urbervilles*.]

1527 Podewils, Clemens. "Thomas Hardy, ein Rückblick" (Thomas Hardy: A Backward Glance), Abendland Monatshefte, V (1930), 200–203.

H is not popular in Germany. The penetration of English sensational literature has resulted in the overestimated worth of novelists of lesser rank and has hindered the literary reputation of prominent novelists. Although H's regionalism is of a high artistic order, it is, nevertheless, limited to a particular area and cannot be fully appreciated by foreigners. H's poetry alone—with its sharp observations of nature and life, powerful expression and beauty of language—could bring H a prominent place in literary history. H has bridged the classics and the moderns, not merely physically but artistically with his polished psychology, heightened tension, and sincere, unbiased poetic realism. [In German.]

1528 Scripture, E. W. "Versformeln und Betonungsprinzipien bei Hardy und Kipling" (Verse Forms and Accentual Principles in Hardy and Kipling), Neueren Sprachen, XXXVIII (Feb 1930), 122–26.

Since "the verse forms [a poet uses] are expressions of the unconscious inner life," it is natural that those of Kipling and H differ sharply. H wrote [in response to Scripture], " 'In respect of the questions [you asked] I regret to say that I am unable to answer them and can only suggest in a general way that I write poems because I cannot help it.' " [In German.]

1529 Shand, John. "Bodysnatchers of Literature," English Review, L (June 1930), 734–40.

For a variety of reasons, novels adapted for the stage are not successful dramatic works. John Drinkwater's adaptation of H's *The Mayor of Casterbridge* contained too many scenes (seventeen), which caused too many interruptions for scenic changes. H's own adaptation of *Tess of the d'Urbervilles* reduced the richly allusive texture of that novel to a mere flat tale of seduction in which Tess is ruined not by Destiny but by the scheming villain Alec d'Urberville.

1530 Shaw, William B. "The World of Books: Biography 1930 Style," Review of Reviews (NY), LXXI (June 1930), 12, 14.

The attacks upon *Jude the Obscure* probably caused H to turn to poetry. In Florence Hardy's The Later Years of Thomas Hardy (1930), extensive use is made of H's own comments in letters and notes. His meetings with writers such as Swinburne, Meredith, Wells, and Yeats are chronicled. [This tells little that would interest the already informed H scholar.]

1531 Sparks, James. "Puddleton Volunteer Broadside," SOMERSET AND DORSET NOTES AND QUERIES, XX (1930), 58–60.
"Volunteer 34, Thomas Hardy . . . was the grandfather of the great Wessex poet-novelist."

1532 Squire, J. C. "Introduction," THE ASHLEY LIBRARY. A CATALOGUE OF PRINTED BOOKS, MANUSCRIPTS AND AUTOGRAPH LETTERS, collected by Thomas James Wise (Lond: Dunedin, 1930), X, x–xi, 120–34; rptd (NY: William H. Smith, Jr., 1934), pp. 69–71.
[Cites a letter to Edward Clodd in which H writes favorably of Gibbon's style; suggests H was utterly truthful, genial, and "even jolly." Pages 120–33 of the Catalogue contain descriptions of H's novels, volumes of poetry, and letters, as well as photographs of title pages and letters.]

1533 Squire, John Collings. "Thomas Hardy," SUNDAY MORNINGS (Lond: Heinemann, 1930), pp. 289–300.
In his last years H was a vital, "very loveable" man, interested in younger poets, in world affairs, gracious and considerate toward the author on his visits to Max Gate. The somewhat grim tone of much of H's poetry and fiction has misled critics into thinking H a morbid person. "He was the most lively of philosophical pessimists and the cheerfulest man that ever frequented churchyards." [Dated 15 Jan 1928.]

1534 Stanley, Charleton Wellesley. "The Poetry of Thomas Hardy," NINETEENTH CENTURY AND AFTER, CVIII (Aug 1930), 266–80.
H's poetic corpus is larger than Tennyson's, but H—"one of the great English poets"—is unrecognized by the critics because he can't be conveniently pigeonholed. Aside from *The Dynasts*, H's work is predominantly lyrical in form. The predominant theme is death—but many poems are also humorous. There are many fine dramatic and narrative poems also. In style, subject and form, H has immense variety. *Dynasts* is a "completely new and original work of art" because H is the first poet to use the ideas of nineteenth-century science. In originality, H can only be compared to Lucretius, but H has a humanity the Roman lacks.

1535 Stopes, Marie C. "To Thomas Hardy, O. M.," NATION AND ATHENAEUM, XLVI (29 March 1930), 893.
[Poem. H won three fames. *Jude the Obscure*, once scorned, is now honored.]

1536 Sykes, Gerald. "The Best is Yet to Be," New Republic, LXIV (24 Sept 1930), 160–61.

Florence Hardy's The Later Years of Thomas Hardy, 1892–1928 (1930) and The Early Life of Thomas Hardy (1928), "form one of the most discreet and reticent testimonies." It is ironic that the great pessimist spent his later life happily and died happily. The character of H's wife is shown in the reticence of the work.

1537 Thompson, Alan Reynolds. "Biography," Bookman (NY), LXXI (Aug 1930), 553.

In Florence Hardy's The Later Years of Thomas Hardy (1930), Mrs. H has refrained from revealing facts about her personal relationship with her husband and has concentrated on describing those facts of H's life which influenced his writing.

1538 Ufer, Hanna. Über die Kompositionelle Bedeutung der Natur bei Thomas Hardy (On the Structural Significance of Nature in Thomas Hardy) (Oberviechtach: Forstner, 1930); University of Marburg dissertation.

[Explores H's use of nature as an artistic creation in *Far From the Madding Crowd*, *The Return of the Native*, and *Tess of the d'Urbervilles*. Considers H's approach to nature, the importance of nature, the relationship of nature and man, and the structural significance of nature in the novels. Preference is given to *Native* because nature unifies the temporal and the spiritual, the motif and the idea, and the objective and the subjective and thereby fulfills H's goal that "a novel should be an organism." Original scholarship.] [In German.]

1539 Untermeyer, Louis (ed). "Thomas Hardy," Modern British Poetry, 3rd rvd ed (NY: Harcourt, Brace, [ca. 1930]), pp. 128–45.

H was no pessimist: "actually the poet was an unorthodox moralist whose heart went out to the things, people and elements he loved." H denied no God but sensed design in chaos. His poetic resources are seemingly endless. He commanded an unusually wide variety of poetic moods, personae, and meters.

1540 Van Doren, Mark. "Hardy's Other Life," Nation (NY), CXXX (11 June 1930), 680.

Florence Hardy's The Later Years of Thomas Hardy: 1892–1928 (1930) is simply a chronicle of H's thoughts and actions as recorded in his journal, focusing on the reasons for his shift from prose to poetry at the age of fifty-five. Unfortunately, the book fails to explore the reasons for H's inclination to tragedy.

1541 Van Doren, Mark. "Thomas Hardy Veiled," NATION (NY), CXXXI (29 Oct 1930), 475.
The hero of CAKES AND ALE, Edward Driffield, is assumed by everyone to be H. Driffield should not, however, be read literally as H in all respects. But even at that, the character does increase our understanding of H. [Review of W. Somerset Maugham, CAKES AND ALE: or THE SKELETON IN THE CUPBOARD (1930).]

1542 Wagenknecht, Edward. "Thomas Hardy: An Authorized Record," VIRGINIA QUARTERLY REVIEW, VI (Oct 1930), 621–24. [Florence Emily Hardy's THE EARLY LIFE OF THOMAS HARDY (1928) and THE LATER YEARS OF THOMAS HARDY (1930) (there is no awareness expressed that the work is H's) is a "record" rather than a "biography" from which emerges "the image of an extraordinarily sensitive, extraordinarily humane and thoughtful man."]

1543 Williams, Charles. "Thomas Hardy," POETRY AT PRESENT (Oxford: Clarendon P, 1930), pp. [vii], 1–17, 32, 41, 57, 82, 92, [149], 153.
H's use of prosaic and obsolete words and forced meter is part of the charm of his poetry. H is more than propagandist and theologian. He has a romantic mind, but unlike Shelley "satisfied it by creating out of his own emotional protest a world where all protest is valueless." He enlarged English verse by introducing "states of mind as causing and expressing distress." His poems are not all irony and sorrow; some are wistful, happy in a subdued way, gravely thoughtful, even fun, covering a wide scope. But beneath all is the invariable, the philosophy as expressed in "Hap" and *The Dynasts*. He imbues the antilogy with emotion and creates a classic universe in which lies some hope. "His reputation is assured of permanence, for him rather than by any other poet the romantic Muse has achieved, without losing her own character, a triumph of classical art." "Mr. Hardy has invented a god to argue with; Mr. Housman dismisses the First Cause." Kipling, H, and most poets write badly occasionally. Yeats, unlike H and others, is of undisputed classic importance. H has riches; de la Mare, richness. Contemporary poets write frequently of nothing. H says, "somewhere consciousness shall cease"; de la Mare charges "nothing with beauty and significance." H, as a man of one idea, sees clearly; Abercrombie, as a man of many ideas, is more obscure. Abercrombie's dramatic poems, though ironical, are unlike H's in that the outcome is unpredictable.

1544 Wise, Thomas James. THE ASHLEY LIBRARY. A CATALOGUE OF PRINTED BOOKS, MANUSCRIPTS AND AUTOGRAPH LETTERS, collected by Thomas J. Wise. 11 vols (Lond: pvtly ptd, 1930), X, 120–34.

[A descriptive bibliography of twenty-four H items in the Wise collection, with facsimile reproductions of title pages and A.L.S.]

1545 Woodbridge, Margaret. "Housman and Hardy," SATURDAY REVIEW OF LITERATURE, VI (17 May 1930), 1055.
There is a similarity between Housman's "No. XXVI" in LAST POEMS and H's "The Division" in *Time's Laughingstocks*. H's influence is evident. [See the response by Alexander Laing, "Hardy and Housman Again," SATURDAY REVIEW OF LITERATURE, VI (5 July 1930), 1180.]

1931

1546 "The American Memorial to Thomas Hardy," DORSET COUNTY CHRONICLE AND SOMERSETSHIRE GAZETTE, 16 April 1931, p. 7.
"Nowhere in the world is Hardy's genius more admired than in the United States," hence the American memorial to H at his birthplace is appropriate.

1547 Boas, Ralph Philip. THE STUDY AND APPRECIATION OF LITERATURE (NY: Harcourt, Brace, 1931), pp. 100, 108, 109, 111, 124, 131, 134, 137, 142–43, 317–18.
"The careful, intimate zest with which Thomas Hardy individualizes Egdon Heath in *The Return of the Native* sets the reader brooding upon the permanence of nature in a world of change, and makes the incidents in the story of little importance in a scale of cosmic values." H's novels are "full of a sense of the brooding, immutable Earth upon which human beings end in futility." *Tess of the d'Urbervilles* illustrates H's idea that "a human being who is pure in heart may nevertheless come to disaster through the sheer malignity of fate." H deeply considered the great ethical questions. "His characters do not think, as do Meredith's, but their author thinks and in the movement of the people in the Wessex novels, so calmly desperate, so gravely passionate, may be seen the mind of a creator." H's point of view was pessimistic. "He adopted the technique of the realists: first, to present faithful pictures of peasant life in southwestern England, as in *The Woodlanders* and *Far From the Madding Crowd*; and second, to develop his thesis of the insignificance of human suffering in the face of an unconcerned Destiny and an unmoved Nature, as in *Tess of the d'Urbervilles* and *The Return of the Native*." [Limited to general remarks on H, chiefly to place him in perspective.]

1548 Broadus, Edmund Kemper. THE STORY OF ENGLISH LITER-
ATURE (NY: Macmillan, 1931), pp. 529–33, 607–13.
Although H believed that a "blind Force" moves the world, he did not complain but instead, calmly accepted life. This calm acceptance resulted in
poems and novels which are seldom cheerful but are never hard, cynical, or
callous. In the plain, simple poems especially, he displays pity and tenderness for human suffering.

1549 Charteris, Sir Evan. THE LIFE AND LETTERS OF SIR EDMUND
GOSSE (NY: Harper, 1931), pp. 107, 140, 141, 154, 198, 200,
204, 223, 279, 295, 296, 309, 316, 345, 346, 367, 416, 417, 441,
456, 497, 500.
[Contains thirteen letters of Gosse to H. Most are quite gossipy and show
Gosse, whose friendship with H covered several decades, extending his
sympathy to the novelist when his works were unfavorably received. Gosse
praises *Tess of the d'Urbervilles* as a great work and predicts that H will
someday be considered a great poet.]

1550 Compton, Charles H. "Who Reads Thomas Hardy?" JOUR-
NAL OF ADULT EDUCATION, III (Jan 1931), 72–76; rptd, with additions, in WHO READS WHAT? (NY: Wilson, 1935), pp. 35–52.
A survey by the St. Louis Public Library reveals that H is read by blue- and
white-collar workers as well as professionals. Of all occupational groups,
more stenographers had read H than any other group—the stenographers
preferred *Tess of the d'Urbervilles*. Bookkeepers preferred *The Return of
the Native*, and *Far From the Madding Crowd* was the most popular novel
among builders and painters, *A Pair of Blue Eyes* among the hairdressers,
and *Under the Greenwood Tree* among unskilled workers. The preferences
were about the same for doctors and lawyers, and icemen and janitors alike.
The comments reprinted from some of those surveyed indicate that H's
popularity stems from his sympathetic understanding of the human situation.

1551 Coppard, A. E. "On First Getting Into Print," COLOPHON,
Part VI (May 1931) [unpaged].
"The Son's Veto" in *Life's Little Ironies* made it clear to Coppard that his
real mission was to write stories, not poetry.

1552 Danchin, F. C. "La Biographie de Thomas Hardy" (The
Biography of Thomas Hardy), REVUE DE L'ENSEIGNEMENT DES
LANGUES VIVANTES, XLVIII (Aug 1931), 337–47; ibid (Oct
1931), 385–95.
What we hear in Mrs. H's biography is H's own voice, intermingled now and
then with that of privileged witnesses; the biographer's interventions are

almost too rare. For a French reader, one psychological trait of H's emerges pre-eminently from this book, his extraordinary "sensitivity." H often gives the impression of being a country-bred brother of Shelley, by his uncommon keenness of perception, whether it be visual or auditive. In spite of the fact that H's life does not seem to have been marked by exceptional afflictions, H tended to assume the sufferings of others, men or beasts, in a way that was almost Christian. His pessimism was temperamental rather than theoretical; pessimism was typically the atmosphere he moved in, not an organized "harmonious" philosophy. The religious element in his work is as strong as the anti-religious one ("The Oxen," "God's Funeral"). H's literary career offers the challenging mystery of his double avocation of novelist and poet. His sudden shift to poetry is generally assigned to the furor created by *Jude the Obscure*; the explanation, however, is a weak one. H's biography helps us understand the fundamental timidity which underlies H's decision. Poetry seemed a more prudent tactical choice than fiction to H, more in keeping with his temperament. [In French.]

1553 "Did Hardy Sham?" LITERARY DIGEST, CX (19 Sept 1931), 16.

Barrie thinks that H was no pessimist. He also tells how H seemed dead at the time of his birth, was dropped by the doctor into a basket, and was saved only because a curious woman picked the child out of the basket. This was H's only sham in life, and for the remainder there was no more faltering.

1554 Eastman, Max. THE LITERARY MIND (NY: Scribner, 1931), pp. 146, 328n.

In *The Dynasts*, H "keeps only a faint-hearted pretense" of treating the history of the Napoleonic wars. Much of the mystery H makes with his "Impersonated Abstractions" has now been lifted by a study of underlying economic forces. The attempt to really understand history has become the affair of prose writers, and H is a poet. Agnes Stewart defended H, saying that his message came from his unconscious mind.

1555 Firor, Ruth. FOLKWAYS IN THOMAS HARDY (Phila: University of Pennsylvania, 1931; NY: Barnes, 1962); University of Pennsylvania dissertation.

H "worked with a collaborator, the folk." Omens and premonitions play a large part in the fortunes of his people. His books would be too gloomy, but for his sympathy with his characters. There are few good omens: the swarming bees in *Under the Greenwood Tree* and Christian Cantle being with a caul. Bad omens: stumbling of Napoleon's horse in *The Dynasts,* unlucky days, crowing of the cock on Tess's wedding day. [Many examples of all kinds of folklore devices from the works.] Divination about marriage or death, special cakes, Bible and key, sowing hempseed, are used to reveal character, Bathsheba's capriciousness. [Among types of folklore devices: ghosts and fairy lore, burial customs, magic and witchcraft, folk medicine ("The Withered Arm" recalls the scapegoat ceremony), mandrake lore, weather lore, seasonal festivals and customs, sports and pastimes.] H's use of folk humor is keenly perceptive. He also makes use of folk law (lore of betrothal and marriage, wife-sale, skimmington ride, traditions and executions, lifehold as law, hiring fairs). [Still the most encyclopedic study of this subject.]

1556 Halperin, Maurice. "Le Sort Implacable: *The Queen of Cornwall* de Thomas Hardy" (Implacable Fate: *The Queen of Cornwall*, by Thomas Hardy), LE ROMAN DE TRISTAN ET ISEUT DANS LA LITTÉRATURE ANGLO-AMÉRICAINE AU XIXe ET AU XXe SIÈCLES (The Novel About Tristan and Isolde in Anglo-American Literature of the 19th and 20th Centuries) (Paris: Jouve, 1931), pp. 98–106; University of Paris dissertation.
H draws upon the versions of Thomas and Malory but presents the conventional episodes of the legend in a bold and original manner. H insists upon an implacable fate which pursues the lovers to their deaths. H is a fatalist, and in this ancient Celtic legend, he has found a wholly pure fatalistic theme. As in his great drama *The Dynasts*, this tragedy is steeped in an atmosphere of inexorable tragedy. [In French.]

1557 Hickson, Elizabeth. VERSIFICATION OF THOMAS HARDY (Phila: pvtly ptd, 1931); University of Pennsylvania dissertation.
H was interested in poetry early in life. He felt poetry consists of making most of any subject. His own life is interwoven in poems: Love of Nature, for example, study of Latin and Greek, courtship, music. [Poems are classified according to subject, viz., 148 on Philosophy, 132 on Woman, and these are subdivided—Woman: Loyal, Fickle, Vain, etc. Settings are classified: Country 334, Churches 37, etc.] H is a master of form, with architectural influence of "cunning irregularity." He is adept at rhythmical variations [these classified, with many examples]. Rhyme is varied [stanzaic forms classified]. [Analysis of style and diction, the versification of *The Dynasts*, and the Appendix has tables, stanza patterns, diction, etc.]

1558 Holland, Clive [pseud of C. J. Hankinson]. "A Literary Pilgrimage by Car," BOOKMAN (Lond), LXXX (June 1931), 147–52.
[This pleasantly-written piece contributes little new to that hoary subject, H's "geography." Not worth reading.]

1559 Horrocks, A. J. "Thomas Hardy's Analysis of Human Nature, A Psychological Study of the Wessex Novels." Unpublished dissertation, University of London (External), 1931.

[Listed in Lawrence F. McNamee, DISSERTATIONS IN ENGLISH AND AMERICAN LITERATURE (NY and Lond: Bowker, 1968).]

1560 Kassner, Rudolf. "Thomas Hardy," CORONA (Munich), II: 3 (1931), 323–40; rptd in TRANSFIGURATION (Erlenbech–Zurich: Eugene Rentsch, 1946), pp. 251–74.

The absence of an ironic relationship between the author and his protagonists is responsible for H's powerful characterizations. Unlike Hamsun, Chekhov, or Thomas Mann, H does not attempt to hide himself in his protagonists. Few authors apply such vital juxtaposition of characters as H. There is a literary affinity between Goethe's WAHLVERWANDTSCHAFTEN and H's "A Tragedy of Two Ambitions." There are few finer collections of novelle than *A Group of Noble Dames*. [In German.]

1561 Knight, Grant Cochran. THE NOVEL IN ENGLISH (NY: Richard R. Smith, 1931), pp. 130, 165, 210, 225, 226, 233–48, 260, 353.

Among nineteenth-century British novelists, only Emily Brontë's "doubt as to this being a well-ordered world" anticipates H's pitiless "attack on Victorianism . . . in his reaction against a philosophy of acquiescence and confidence." H's best novels—*The Return of the Native, Tess of the d'Urbervilles, The Mayor of Casterbridge,* and *Jude the Obscure*—embody his supreme characteristic, . . . the insistence upon the fell power of circumstance, upon the power of accident, soil, prejudice, and obstinacy, to involve people in disaster."

1562 Lehmann, Karl. "Thomas Hardy: *The Dynasts,*" DIE AUFFASSUNG UND GESTALTUNG DES NAPOLEON PROBLEMS IM ENGLISCHEN DRAMA (The Conception and Embodiment of the Napoleon Problem in English Drama) (Erlangen: Karl Döres, 1931), pp. 47–69; University of Erlangen dissertation.

"As Goethe almost at the end of his life created with FAUST the crowning of his life's work, so Hardy wished to crown his *Weltanschauung* with *The Dynasts.*" The Spirits of the Years seem at times "an incarnation, even a personification of the Immanent Will." The Spirits of the Pities most closely resembles the ancient Greek Chorus. [Largely a summary-description of *Dynasts.*] [In German.]

1563 McCarthy, Desmond. "The Bubble Reputation," LIVING AGE, CCCXL (Oct 1931), 164.

[McCarthy ironically advises H's friendly readers to desert him before his reputation collapses. Having liked him for his profound tragic sense and "lovely originality," his readers can burst the bubble of his reputation by noting the crudeness of his style, the melodrama of the novels, and the "quaint, lamenting tunes" of his poems.]

1564 McDowall, Arthur [Sydney]. THOMAS HARDY: A CRITICAL STUDY (Lond: Faber & Faber, 1931).

H was "greater as a poet than as anything else, yet not exclusively as the poet of his verse." It may be argued that the novels, even more than the poetry, give evidence of the poetic cast of his mind, for they show the full range of his temperament and his keen attention to both the detail and the larger patterns of life. H was religious in that he was always concerned with ultimate things, but his devotion to truth, derived in part from the post-Darwinian climate of thought in which he reached maturity, marks a kind of scientific attitude which modifies and sometimes overwhelms the religious. Of H's great novels, only *Far From the Madding Crowd* is not a tragedy. The others, *The Return of the Native, The Mayor of Casterbridge, The Woodlanders, Tess of the d'Urbervilles,* and *Jude the Obscure,* exploit the "spirit of place" which he discovered in the first and show a developing sense of tragic form which culminates in the hard and direct movement of *Jude* to its inevitable ending. While none of H's novels is without humor and even lightness, it is his essentially tragic vision in these books which marks his greatness. H's poetry is clearly the product of the same mind and temperament which produced the great novels, and in *The Dynasts*, perhaps more than anywhere else, we can see the poetic bent of his mind. The drama is before all else a "great vision" poetically conceived. In the shorter poems we see once again H's unswerving devotion to truth mixed with an intimacy, as in the superb "Poems of 1912–13," which it seems almost rude to overhear. His poetic technique shows the craftsman in him, but in verse as in prose he aims first at sincerity and truth and only second at craft.

1565 Milne, James. A WINDOW IN FLEET STREET (Lond: Murray, 1931), pp. 117, 253–66, 278, 297.

H esteemed *The Dynasts* and his later poetry more than he did his Wessex novels. The threatened loss of Stonehenge prompted a visit to H, who had used the setting in *Tess of the d'Urbervilles.* Stonehenge and a visit to the church at Adleburgh showed H's innate religion.

1566 Newton, Alfred Edward. A THOMAS HARDY MEMORIAL ("Oak Knoll," Daylesford, Berwyn P. O., Pa: pvtly ptd, 1931).

[Describes the erection of a granite shaft on Egdon Heath to the memory of H in 1931 and gives extracts from the press on the occasion.]

1567 Parker, W. M. "Three Years Ago: When Thomas Hardy Passed Onwards," DORSET YEARBOOK, 1931, pp. 5–9.

"Alas! there will be no return of *this native.*" [Memorial essay.]

1568 "Rebecca West Proves a Beatitude," LITERARY DIGEST, CVIII (21 Feb 1931), 18–19.

West thinks that H couldn't have been the model for Driffield in Maugham's CAKES AND ALE because H was too respectable; he came from the yeoman classes and aspired to be above criticism. " 'He was angry when people would not accept his novels and poetry, but that was because he thought that what he said was true and ought to be known.' "

1569 Rhodes, A. J. "The Wessex of the Hardy Novels," LISTENER, V (3 June 1931), Supplement xi–xii.
The imaginative "tour" of the Dorset countryside is most helpful in identifying places which figure in the Wessex geography.

1570 Rhys, Ernest. EVERYMAN REMEMBERS (Lond: J. M. Dent, 1931), pp. 113, 178–87; (NY: Cosmopolitan Book Corp., 1931), pp. 311–18.
Lionel Johnson once said at the Rhymer's Club that H could, with a word, construct the whole aspect of a place or give the whole manner and presence of a man. [A brief, uninformative account of meetings with H.]

1571 Rothenstein, William. MEN AND MEMORIES: RECOLLECTIONS OF WILLIAM ROTHENSTEIN, 1872–1900. 2 vols (Lond: Faber & Faber, 1931–1932), I, 48, 207, 268, 302–3, 304; II, 26, 86, 134, 138, 164–65, 167, 173, 219, 290, 322, 343.
H was so disturbed at the reception of *Jude the Obscure*, which he had recently published, "that he declared he would never write another novel." The feeling about his portrait of Oxford in the novel was so strong that "he scarcely liked going to the Athenaeum." "Hardy resented the constant charge of pessimism made against him; he tried to depict man's life, its beauty and ugliness, its generosity and meanness. Far from darkening the picture, had he told the truth about village life, no one would have stood it, he said." H was a "quiet and unassuming" man with "a small dark bilberry eye which he cocked at you unexpectedly." In response to the receipt of THE AGRICULTURAL LABORER, H recalls details of the peasant revolt and of the "hungry forties," concluding with the observation that "things are a little the other way now [ca. 1910], for the farm labourers are very comfortable, and better off than the London poor." A sketch of H was included in a public exhibition of 1912. [Rothenstein visited H and his wife at Max Gate in 1915, made several drawings of him, and studied with H the latter's sketches for *Wessex Poems*.] H said that he had planted the trees around his house himself and that "they began to sigh directly the roots touched the soil" [observation similar to that made by Marty South in *The Woodlanders*]. [Quotes a poem by Beerbohm—"Thomas Hardy and A. E. Housman."]

1572 St. Clair, George. "Is Hardy, the Poet, a Pessimist?" NEW MEXICO QUARTERLY, I (Nov 1931), 307–21.

The poems in each volume of H's verse may be divided into three categories —poems of sorrow and sadness, poems of resignation, and poems of cheer. For example, in *Wessex Poems*, twenty-two are sorrowful, twenty-three are resigned, and five are cheerful; in *Poems of the Past and the Present*, forty-four are sad, forty-five are resigned, ten are cheerful. *The Dynasts*, because of its undercurrent of hope, exhibits fatalism but not pessimism. In terms of total percentages, excluding *Dynasts,* there are 795 poems, fourteen percent of which are cheerful, fifty-two percent of which are resigned, and thirty-four percent of which are sad. Given these statistics, while H "has never been able to reconcile life's inconsistencies," although he has wanted to, "the light of hope has flickered in him," therefore he is not a pessimist.

1573 Salomon, Louis B. THE DEVIL TAKE HER: A STUDY OF THE REBELLIOUS LOVER IN ENGLISH POETRY (Phila: University of Pennsylvania P, 1931), pp. 64, 106–7, 181–82, 304, 318.
While abjuring love, H commemorates its passing away.

1574 "Thomas Hardy," DER GROSSE BROCKHAUS (The Large Brockhaus [Encyclopedia]) (Leipzig: F. A. Brockhaus, 1931), VIII, 177–78.
[In addition to listing Hardian works and criticisms, this encyclopedia expresses what is considered most characteristic of H: his interest in architecture, his preoccupation with fate, his characterizations—especially of women—, and his descriptions of nature.] [In German.]

1575 "A Thomas Hardy Memorial," DORSET COUNTY CHRONICLE AND SOMERSETSHIRE GAZETTE, 23 April 1931, p. 3.
[Detailed account of the unveiling of the American memorial to H, including texts of speeches by John Livingstone Lowes, St. John Hornby, W. J. Fare, and a poem by A. C. Cox.]

1576 Van Doren, Carl. "Introduction," *The Return of the Native* ([NY]: Literary Guild, [1931?]), pp. [i]–iv.
H is not "to be judged by a dry, literal realism" any more than Shakespeare, yet *The Return of the Native* "can still be considered a great novel." Essentially, H was a tragic poet. Thus he gave the Heath "a kind of character, a monstrous will." The novel's most convincing character is Mrs. Yeobright, "who is a tragic victim . . . because she is caught between the doomed Clym and the doomed Eustacia."

1577 Ward, A. C. FOUNDATIONS OF ENGLISH PROSE (Lond: Bell, 1931), pp. 71–72, 74–78, 109, 123.
H's novels are dissimilar from those of other English novels in their representation of the tragedy of life, in the total sense of completion H's novels

give, in their monumental stature, and in the importance of their background.

1578 West, Rebecca. "Blessed are the Pure in Heart," Outlook (NY), CLVII (28 Jan 1931), 132–33, 156; reviewed and cited in "Rebecca West Proves a Beatitude," Literary Digest, CVIII (21 Feb 1931), 18–19; rptd in Ventures in Contemporary Reading (NY: Longmans, 1932), pp. 19–25.

H was an "intensely respectable little man," who looked as if he was half a yeoman and half a laboring man. [Anecdotes are used to show the innocent simplicity of H. Useless.]

1579 West, Rebecca. "Two Kinds of Memory," The Strange Necessity: Essays and Reviews (Lond: Cape, 1931), pp. 243–56, 258–61, 262, 267, 296.

H's poems have exactitude, restraint, compression, but also too frequently deal with the macabre. Shorter works are tainted with "eccentric morbidity." In "briefer composition . . . there obtruded on him his habitual perplexity as to what art could possibly be about." H recollected true stories for the sake of entertainment and wisdom which were uncustomary, contrary to what he found subconsciously pleasurable. Sitwell's writing suffers from inexactitude and lack of factual constraint in which H excels, but H's writing suffers from "his ignorance of his own nature, his tendency to present the abnormal phases of his being as if they were the normal." [Attacks Agnes Repplier's "The Fortunate Poets," which compares H's rejection of World War I to Viscount Morley's as one of " 'resentment at an imperfect but not altogether worthless civilization.' "] H deplored war but was no pacifist. Steeped in English tradition, he knew the vulnerability of the island kingdom. "The greatness of Thomas Hardy was very largely due to the intensity with which he has learned such lessons as were taught him by the soil where he was born." H resented life and the limitations of man's will, but "there never was a great writer who more completely swallowed civilization . . . than Thomas Hardy." *Tess of the d'Urbervilles* and *Jude the Obscure* scandalized the age, not as reform documents but as tragedies which challenged Victorian optimism. He was not a revolutionary, but a traditionalist. [From reviews of S. Sitwell's All Summer in a Day: American Criticism, ed by Drake; and the "new collected edition" of H's poems.]

1580 Wild, Friedrich. Die Englische Literatur der Gegenwart Seit 1870: Versdichtungen (English Literature of the Present Since 1870: Poetry) (Leipzig: Dioskuren Verlag, 1931), pp. 15, 140–43, 151, 169, 171, 183, 186, 234, 248.

Poetry for H is "the exploration of reality." But in nature he saw no hidden design or higher plan: "he recognizes only blind forces in nature which parcel out joy and sorrow without choice or purpose." The tragic irony of

his poems springs from his conception of nature as "blindly ruling fate."
H's "*Weltanschauung* has often been compared with Schopenhauer's, of
which, however, Hardy knew for a long time only the most basic principles."
[In German.]

> **1581** Wolfe, Humbert. GEORGE MOORE (Lond: Thornton Butter-
> worth, 1931), p. xiv.

H's death "was saluted [by the Press] with almost as much apparent emotion
as that of a Divisional General who had never prevailed in any engagement."
By predestining his characters and not his story Moore avoided H's "ludicrous irregularities."

> **1582** Zachrisson, Robert Eugen. "Thomas Hardy's Twilight View
> of Life," STUDIER I MODERN SPRAKVETENSKAP, XI (1931), 217–
> 33; rptd as a separate pamphlet (Uppsala & Stockholm: Almqvist
> & Wiksells, 1931).

H's view of life was based not so much on personal experience or philosophical meditation as on his innate temperament. Excerpts from H's diary
of the 1860s show his dissatisfaction with life, his distrust of women, his
indifference toward religion and his lack of self-confidence. The two reasons
for his dissatisfaction with life are the cruelty of nature and his inability to
believe in a merciful creator, themes which are dealt with in these early
poems: "She, to Him," "At a Bridal," "Hap," "Heiress and Architect,"
"The Two Men." In the passage from *A Pair of Blue Eyes* where Knight is
suspended between heaven and earth clinging to a rock, nature is inimical
to man.

Because H's twilight view of life must have been innate to his temperament,
he was bound to give expression to it to be true to himself. He denied being a
pessimist, yet did write in that vein. However, it was merely the conflict
between his artistic viewpoint and his humanitarian beliefs. He reveals his
true greatness when he deals with life as an entity containing both sorrows
and joys. In his poetry there is too little of the double vision of life which
brightens the mood of the novels.

1932

> **1583** Arns, Karl. "Proviktorianismus und Antiviktorianismus in
> der neuen englischen Literatur" (Pro- and Anti-Victorianism in
> Modern Literature), ENGLISCHE STUDIEN, LIX (1932), 284, 292.

[Passing reference to H's pessimism.] [In German.]

1584 Atherton, Gertrude. ADVENTURES OF A NOVELIST (NY: Liveright, 1932), pp. 170–71, 234, 263–64.

H confided that he had insomnia " 'and went from bed to bed all night.' " In the London of the 1890s it was "superfluous to mention Meredith or Hardy" in a list of famous authors. T. P. O'Connor blamed H's "pessimistic nature" on Mrs. H. "No doubt Hardy went out so constantly to be rid of her!" But H himself "was anything but great in personality." [Interesting picture of H in society.]

1585 Beach, Joseph Warren. THE TWENTIETH CENTURY NOVEL: STUDIES IN TECHNIQUE (NY: Century, 1932), pp. 11, 39, 140–44, 186, 330, 331.

H is even more Victorian than Meredith. He is fond of mystery and complications of plot; the coincidences that upset the plans and betray the best intentions of his characters. This use of coincidence is H's "Dark Angel" that gives a quaint and almost ridiculous air to *Two on a Tower* and *The Mayor of Casterbridge*. Occasionally H gets impatient with the complications and tells rather than shows in his weaker novels. H's greatness lies in the association of the events with the settings in which they occur. The scenes are harmonious with the emotions involved. In his settings, H appeals to our sense of reality, our sense of beauty, and our sympathetic emotions. The appeal of setting is strongest in those novels set in H's native "Wessex." *Far From the Madding Crowd* is an example of the passions of the heart taking their color and tone from the pictures of pastoral life H draws. H constantly shows "the inseparableness of people" from their natural setting. He is objective (camera-like) and interprets in terms of human feelings, the things he observes. *The Return of the Native* best illustrates H's greatness in the association of story and setting. Each character is determined by his attitude towards Egdon Heath. Something similar is true in *The Woodlanders, Tess of the d'Urbervilles,* and *Jude the Obscure.* In the last two novels, the effect is heightened by the fact that the novels are centered upon one character, but neither of these novels is as remarkable in unity of place as *Native.* We can exclude "Aftercourses," which was H's concession to an editor's demand for a happy ending and is not included in H's original design. In story-telling, H proceeds on lines diametrically opposed to those of Henry James.

1586 Bennett, Arnold. THE JOURNALS OF ARNOLD BENNETT. 3 vols. (London: Cassell, 1932–1933), I, 7, 28, 96, 103; II, 103, 202, 203, 250, 285, 289; III, 18, 21, 149, 171, 252, 253, 254, 256.

In *The Trumpet-Major*, H employs "an excessively slow method of narration." H at a London gathering in 1917 contended that "a tale must be unusual and the people interesting" and, despite his becoming involved "in the meshes of applications and instances," he kept his head and came out quite well. George Moore "has no use for Hardy," whom he called " 'Hardy the villager.' " *Tess of the d'Urbervilles* "is really a very impressive master-piece; and its faults are quite trifling."

1587 Benson, E. F. As We Are: A Modern Revue (Lond: Longmans, Green, 1932), p. 262.

Tess of the d'Urbervilles was regarded in the 1890s "as the sort of book that should not be left about, lest a pure-minded girl might pick it up and suffer instant corruption."

1588 Bescou, Yves. "La Tragédie de l'échec dans *Jude l'Obscur* et dans *Tess d'Urbervilles*" (The Tragedy of Failure in *Jude the Obscure* and *Tess of the d'Urbervilles*), Revue de L'enseigne-ment des Langues Vivantes, XLIX (Aug 1932), 337–43.

H's emphasis on human failure in his main fiction is nowadays regarded by some critics as detrimental to his work. And yet the study of failure in *Tess of the d'Urbervilles* and *Jude the Obscure* is in itself an admirable lesson in compassion. Like the character of Hélène created by Jean d'Agrève (M. de Vogüé), Tess and Jude belong to that race of people who were born to love, not to domineer. Instead of a world ruled by ruthless instinctual impulses, H would have the universe governed by Pity. [In French.]

1589 Biggs, John R., and James E. Masters. Shaftesbury: The Shaston of Thomas Hardy, Twelve Wood-Engravings (Shaftesbury: High House P, 1932).

[Contains wood-engravings of scenes in and around Shaftesbury, including the Shaftesbury Infants School, identified as Phillotson's school in *Jude the Obscure*, and "Old-Grove's Place," where Sue and Phillotson lived. H did not invent the name of Shaston; it is an earlier name still found on mile-stones.]

1590 Blunden, Edmund. "Thomas Hardy," in The Great Vic-torians, ed by H. J. Massingham and Hugh Massingham (NY: Doubleday, Doran, 1932), pp. 219–25.

[The personal reminiscences of social visits with H in 1922 and 1923 are superficial.]

1591 Brockington, A. Allen. Browning and the Twentieth Century (Lond: Oxford UP, 1932); rptd (NY: Russell & Russell, 1963), pp. 11, 86, 87*n*3, 88, 89, 90, 156, 178, 198, 199, 200, 216, 217, 218, 219, 221, 222–24.

Although Robert Browning's influence on H was so great that The Ring and The Book can be called the "stimulus" for *The Dynasts*, H was no optimist. In fact, he reacted against optimism so vigorously that ultimately he had to defend himself against those who accused him of "gloom and pessimism."

1592 Brown, Alec. "Inward and Outward Dialogue," Dublin Magazine, ns VII (April 1932), 33–39.

H used "passages of artificial and stilted dialogue" in his novels and lyric poems. They bar our easy progress through the work, but H manages—with the narrative sweep of the novels, and his dedication to "the absolute exclusion of all the more graceful . . . surface aspects of life"—to carry us through.

1593 Carswell, Catherine. The Savage Pilgrimage (Lond: Chatto & Windus, 1932); rvd ed (Lond: Secker, 1932); rptd (Lond: Secker & Warburg, 1951), p. 22.

In 1914 D. H. Lawrence was asked by a publisher to do a study of H which was to run about 15,000 words. [Apparently "Study of Thomas Hardy," Phoenix (1936).]

1594 Eliot, T. S. Selected Essays, 1917–1932 (NY: Harcourt, Brace, 1932), pp. 68, 252.

[Discounts H's conscious use of Sophocles in *Jude the Obscure*; H lacked the seventeenth-century virtues of wit and magniloquence.]

1595 Goodale, Ralph Hinsdale. "Schopenhauer and Pessimism in Nineteenth Century English Literature," Publications of the Modern Language Association, XLVII (March 1932), 241–61, espec 249, 252–53, 259.

Schopenhauer and Hartmann influenced H, according to a letter to Miss Helen Garwood [cited in Helen Garwood, "Thomas Hardy: An Illustration of the Philosophy of Schopenhauer" (1911)]. The two philosophers have a greater impact on *The Dynasts* than on any previous work in English literature. "Hap," however, shows typical H pessimism prior to any likely Schopenhauer influence in point of his theories that the will, behind objective phenomena, is irrational. There is probably a "sympathy" of viewpoint rather than direct influence.

1596 Graham, Joe. "Plagiaristic Plays," Cornhill, ser 3 LXXII (June 1932), 653–71.

[Notes H's charge in 1881 that Arthur Pinero's The Squire was plagiarized from an earlier dramatization by H and Comyns Carr of *Far From the Madding Crowd*. No legal battle ensued; Hardy and Carr produced a rival version.]

1597 Grove, Frederick Philip. "Thomas Hardy: A Critical Examination of a Typical Novel and his Shorter Poems," University of Toronto Quarterly, I (July 1932), 490–507.

Although they were among the greatest educators of the nineteenth-century, Ibsen and Tolstoy "stand dwarfed" by H. While Tolstoy questioned social justice, and Ibsen questioned "conventional remedies for social ills," H questioned "the value of life itself." He believed "all things are fundamentally wrong; they can become right only through man's victory over God." In his later novels, and particularly in *The Return of the Native*, characters are "removed from the soil from which they sprang" and elevated to a plane of universal values where "most of the old and standard values are inverted." H's verse is not predominately lyrical but "novelistic" in its "dramatic" intention and "cynical view of human nature." This "cosmic negation pauses" with the possibility that "God is amenable to education." There remains in H "a hope that ultimately man will make himself and the best of his spirit the real master of this world who carries the work of creation to the point of moral perfection."

1598 Gutbier, Elizabeth. PSYCHOLOGISCH–ÄSTHETISCHE STUDIEN ZU TRISTANDICHTUNGEN DER NEUEREN ENGLISCHEN LITERATUR (Psychological–Aesthetic Studies of the Tristan Poems of Modern English Literature) (Erlangen: Döres, 1932.)
The playing-out of *The Famous Tragedy of the Queen of Cornwall* is disturbed by H's repeated reaching back to earlier happenings: the drama pursues no direct line but creates the impression of a spiral. [Essay compares and contrasts the handling of various aspects of the Tristan-Isolde story by seven recent authors.] [In German.]

1599 Handsacre, Alan. "Freethought in Fiction. II," FREE-THINKER, LII (6 March 1932), 148–49.
H combines great ideas with "meticulous detail" in fiction which is characterized by "mastery of proportion," faithfulness to nature and human nature, and a matchless style.

1600 Handsacre, Alan. "Freethought in Fiction. III," FREE-THINKER, LII (13 March 1932), 171–72.
Although H's poetry has been called pessimistic, gloomy, and too perfect technically, it can be described more accurately as combining realism and symbolism; as being sad, but not gloomy; as fusing courage and caution, art and craft.

1601 Hiett, Herbert R. "Comparisons and Contrasts in the Philosophy of George Eliot and Thomas Hardy." Unpublished dissertation, University of Maryland, 1932.

1602 Hobson, Harold. "Thomas Hardy and the Drama," CHRISTIAN SCIENCE MONITOR, 30 July 1932, p. 9.
When *Tess of the d'Urbervilles* was performed in London, H was unable to attend. Consequently, the entire company performed it for him privately in his home. According to Gwen Davies [the young woman who played Tess],

H preferred *Jude the Obscure* to *Tess*. Oxford did not treat indigent young men as unkindly as H implied in *Jude*.

1603 Lafourcade, Georges. SWINBURNE: A LITERARY BIOGRAPHY (NY: William Morrow, 1932), p. 139.

[Six lines of H's elegy to Swinburne, "A Singer Asleep" (1909), quoted to illustrate how Swinburne's verse shocked his contemporaries.]

1604 Lavrin, Janko. "Thomas Hardy and the Continent," NEW ENGLISH WEEKLY, 13 Oct 1932, pp. 616–17.

H's position as an international author is restricted by his pure regional roots and setting. Besides that, a cultivated reader often stumbles over the walking tempo of his novels. His characters, however, become universal and are appreciated on the continent. H's "voluptuous pessimism" is not popular with continental readers who expect optimism from the English. On the continent H "will probably never be more than a cult of Literary connoisseurs and a subject for Doctor's degrees."

1605 Leavis, F. R. NEW BEARINGS IN ENGLISH POETRY: A STUDY OF THE CONTEMPORARY SITUATION (Lond: Chatto & Windus, 1932), pp. 56–62; rptd (Ann Arbor: University of Michigan P; Toronto: Ambassador Books, 1960).

H is a Victorian poet of simple attitudes and outlook whose greatness lies in "the integrity with which he accepted the conclusion, enforced, he believed, by science, that nature is indifferent to human values, in the completeness of his recognition, and in the purity and adequacy of his response." H is a naive poet of "precritical innocence" whose great poems (and they are few in proportion to his abundant output) are the product of "triumph of character," that is, of a powerful personal urging that enables him to transform his "innocent awkwardness." Examples of great poems are the following: "After a Journey," "The Voice," "The Self-Unseeing," "A Broken Appointment," "Neutral Tones," "During Wind and Rain."

1606 Loane, George Green. "Hardy and N.E.D.," TIMES LITERARY SUPPLEMENT (Lond), 21 Jan 1932, p. 44.

[List of words used by H in *The Collected Poems of Thomas Hardy* either not given in the N.E.D., used in a different sense, or not in use in the nineteenth-century. Some examples: baldachine, blinkered, bygo, fellowdike, wauzing.]

1607 Lovett, Robert Morss, and Helen Sard Hughes. THE HISTORY OF THE NOVEL IN ENGLAND (Lond, Toronto: George G. Harrap; NY & Boston: Houghton Mifflin, [1932]), pp. 313–25.

In contrast with Meredith, for whom "the struggle of humanity is that of man with man, . . . a desperate but never hopeless warfare," in H's world "man is far from his cosmic importance" and "the element of healthful, hopeful combat Hardy refuses to admit." In *The Return of the Native*, the Heath "typifies the enduring force of nature against which man vainly pits his puny strength." "Meredith uses nature to exalt his characters: Hardy, to reduce them to the inconsequence of vermin." Henchard's remarks "have given rise to the notion that Hardy's order of the universe was malevolent rather than merely indifferent toward man." H uses pessimism not solely for artistic reasons; it springs from his personal belief, "one which questions . . . the spiritual values of knowledge, human love, renunciation and death."

1608 Lucas, E. V. READING, WRITING, AND REMEMBERING: A LITERARY RECORD (Lond: Methuen, 1932), pp. 84, 190, 320–22.
[Brief references. Reprints "The Rencontre," E. V. Knox's (e.g. "Evoe's") parody of H's poetry.]

1609 Masters, James E. "Foreword," SHAFTESBURY: THE SHASTON OF THOMAS HARDY, TWELVE WOOD-ENGRAVINGS, by John R. Biggs and James E. Masters (Shaftesbury: High House P, 1932).
H's description of Shaftesbury in *Jude the Obscure* is "one of the finest . . . ever penned." Some structures and much of the mood in Part IV of *Jude* "still exist and may easily be found and recognised from Hardy's description of them." [The engravings, in stark black and white, follow on double-folded recto pages; short commentaries, mentioning H's descriptions five times, are on the verso.]

1610 Neugebauer, Paul. SCHOPENHAUER IN ENGLAND: MIT BESONDERER BERÜCKSICHTIGUNG SEINES EINFLUSSES AUF DIE ENGLISCHE LITERATUR (Schopenhauer in England: With Special Regard to His Influence on English Literature) (Berlin: Doktordruck-Graphisches Institut Paul Funk, 1932), pp. 33–39.
H's Weltanschauung is not original. From *Desperate Remedies* through *Jude the Obscure*, Schopenhauer's hovering spirit is present. *The Return of the Native* could not be more Schopenhauerian had the German philosopher written the novel. The similarities of thought and expression in *The Dynasts* remove every doubt that H knew Schopenhauer and knew him well. [In German.]

1611 Newbolt, Sir Henry John. MY WORLD AS IN MY TIME (Lond: Faber & Faber, 1932), pp. 282–89.
H's reviewers have been largely women, especially in America; surely editors ought to know that the subject of *The Dynasts* "can hardly be expected to appeal to women" (13 March 1904). The philosophy advanced in *Dynasts* is "tentative" only (9 Feb 1906). H had "periodic fright lest he should

never live to finish the book." As for the title-page, H had thought of "a mental drama, a vision drama, a closet drama, an epical drama, etc . . . or a Chronicle poem of the Napoleonic Wars under the similitude of a drama." The lines of the After-Scene, in which the Pities bring hope into the darkness of the world, are H's acknowledgment of the criticism of two or three of his friends. [The two notes Newbolt added to his "A New Departure in English Poetry," QUARTERLY REVIEW, CCX (Jan 1909), 193–209, where he criticized H's style were written at the suggestion of the editor, George Pruthero. H received such plain-speaking from a young man in a very easy manner. Extracts from a correspondence with H that lasted more than twenty-five years and started with Newbolt's article for QUARTERLY REVIEW.]

1612 Norman, Sylva. "Thomas Hardy," in THE GREAT VICTORIANS, ed by H. J. Massingham and Hugh Massingham (NY: Doubleday, Doran, 1932), pp. 209–25, with "Hitherto unpublished" reminiscences by Edmund Blunden, pp. 219–25.

The characteristics that make H's writing unique were condemned by his contemporaries and are taken for granted now. He had to cater to gentility and sentimentality while still trying to stir up curiosity. *Tess of the d'Urbervilles* and *Jude the Obscure* are keys to H's growth as a novelist and show the shift in his attention from the personal to the universal. H's insistence on cosmic scheme ruins *Jude*. H's own voice intrudes in the characters of Jude and Sue. Tess is his last freely individual character. In *The Dynasts* he is free from current fashions. [Blunden's are superficial personal reminiscences of social visits with H in 1922 and 1923.]

1613 Parrott, Thomas Marc, and Willard Thorp (eds). POETRY OF THE TRANSITION: 1850–1914 (NY: Oxford UP, 1932), pp. 411–15.

H will be remembered not as a pessimist, but as a man who wrote simple, sincere, and realistic poems which represent a departure from the standards of Victorian poetry. [Mostly biographical data used to introduce thirteen pages of H's poetry.]

1614 Peake, Leslie S. "Thomas Hardy as a Religious Teacher," METHODIST LEADER, 28 July 1932.

Like Meredith, H could not accept the doctrine of personal immortality, but this was for H "a matter of regret, rather than something in which he could glory." H "bids us seek Truth and strive to do our duty even when . . . our faith in the Highest is dim."

1615 Pickering, Ernest. A BRIEF SURVEY OF ENGLISH LITERATURE (Lond: Harrap, 1932), pp. 12, 130, 131–34, 152–53, 155, 175, 187.

H, the last and greatest of the Victorian novelists, wrote skillfully constructed novels which contain irony and humor. These novels, like the poetry, reveal H's "lack of optimism."

1616 Pirkhofer, Anton. "Studien zur Romantechnik Thomas Hardy" (Studies in Thomas Hardy's Novelistic Technique). Unpublished dissertation, University of Innsbruck, 1932.
[Justifies H's classification of his works by examining their structure and characterizations. Worthless.] [In German.]

1617 Price, Lawrence Marsden. THE RECEPTION OF ENGLISH LITERATURE IN GERMANY (Berkeley: University of California P, 1932); rptd as ENGLISH LITERATURE IN GERMANY (Berkeley: University of California P [PUBLICATIONS IN MODERN PHILOLOGY, XXXVII], 1953); trans by Maxwell E. Knight as DIE AUFNAHME ENGLISCHER LITERATUR IN DEUTSCHLAND 1500–1960 (Bern & Munich: Francke Verlag, 1961), pp. 369–70; and rptd as THE RECEPTION OF ENGLISH LITERATURE IN GERMANY 1500–1960 (Chapel Hill: University of North Carolina P [NORTH CAROLINA STUDIES IN COMPARATIVE LITERATURE, No. 39], 1966).
The reception of H in Germany was delayed because his fatalistic philosophy stood in the way of a reception of him as an artist. His debt to Schopenhauer and influence on Hauptmann were discussed in a dissertation in 1919, but Gosse's denigration of H as a reader of Schopenhauer is combined with Hauptmann's insistence that he knew of *The Dynasts* only by reputation.

1618 Reilly, Joseph J[ohn]. "Bazin and Hardy: Some Comparisons and a Contrast," DEAR PRUE'S HUSBAND AND OTHER PEOPLE (NY: Macmillan, 1932); rptd (Freeport, NY: Books for Libraries P, 1968), pp. 237–62.
H and René Bazin are similar in that each crowds his novels with incidents; each uses Nature to reflect a character's mood; each uses a limited geographical space; and each is decidedly virile, stylistically. However, H contrasts Bazin in that he "found no joy" in an enigmatic world, whereas Bazin was unable to react pessimistically to a world governed by "divine order."

1619 Ridder-Barzin, Louise de. LE PESSIMISME DE THOMAS HARDY (The Pessimism of Thomas Hardy) (Bruxelles: Travaux de la faculté de philosophie et lettres de l'Université de Bruxelles, Tome III, 1932).
H's sense of pessimism can be understood best by a careful examination of all his novels and poems. Though at times his pessimism resembles Greek

or German ideas, his conception of destiny as proceeding by a slow, over-whelming series of light touches (as opposed to a sudden catastrophe) is entirely his own. At times destiny passes beyond impersonality and affects man as if it were a wicked personal force, taking pleasure in the pain it causes. H was quite correct in rejecting the arguments of those who categorized him as a thinker in the school of Schopenhauer; though he was aware of the German thinker, he remained always an author rather than a philosopher. Furthermore, he was affected to a much greater degree than hitherto realized by nineteenth-century English philosophical developments. His pessimism, rather than drawing on German metaphysics, carried to the honest conclusions the scientific materialism popularized in England by writers like Huxley and Spencer. [Includes a bibliography, pp. 189–92, which records French and Italian studies as well as many in English.] [In French.]

1620 Roberts, Morley. "Meetings with Some Men of Letters," QUEEN'S QUARTERLY, XXXIX (Feb 1932), 62–80.
Henry James was unimpressed by H, both as a person and as an author. He may well have dismissed H as an amateur.

1621 Rutland, William R. *"Jude the Obscure,"* TIMES LITERARY SUPPLEMENT (Lond), 22 Dec 1932, p. 977.
The rapidly growing literature on H has no survey of the corpus of H criticism, and the history of H's reputation remains to be written. [Rutland was unable to find the source of remark from Bishop of Wakefield quoted in Florence Hardy's THE LATER YEARS OF THOMAS HARDY (1930) that he had thrown *Jude the Obscure* into fire.] [See William Walsham Howe, Bishop of Wakefield, "Thomas Hardy," YORKSHIRE POST, 8 June 1896, p. 4.]

1622 Rutland, William R. THOMAS HARDY: CONFÉRENCE INAU-GURALE (Thomas Hardy: Inaugural Lecture) (Faite en Séance Publique le 14 Janvier 1932 à l'Université de Lausanne) (Montreux: Ch. Corbaz, [1932]).
H is essentially English in that his work reflects the continuity of English life and literature. H's novels are unique for their poetic and dramatic qualities, his poetry for its success in conveying the inexpressible. [In French.]

1623 "Stet." "Thomas Hardy as Poet," WEEK-END REVIEW, VI (3 Sept 1932), 261.
The Collected Poems of Thomas Hardy is "a book into which [people of a certain temper] may look at times for grim pleasures not easily to be found elsewhere." And H's "strange, crumbling yet resistant poetry will endure in a quantity adequate to their needs."

1624 Stevenson, Lionel. "Thomas Hardy," DARWIN AMONG THE POETS (Chicago: University of Chicago P, 1932), pp. 237–97.
Darwin, a gloomy temperament, and a conscious desire to counteract his contemporaries' optimism caused H to become a pessimist. As a pessimist, he rejected orthodox ideas about God and immortality, called belief in good an illusion, and asserted that man has no advantage over other natural phenomena. Both God and Nature are indifferent and are, in reality, only symbols. The force that controls everything is the Immanent Will, an unconscious force which has a general purpose but no direction. Hence, while there is continued change, there is no progress and can be none unless the Will awakens.

1625 Stillman, Clara G. SAMUEL BUTLER, A MID-VICTORIAN (NY: Viking P, 1932), pp. 7, 156.
H. like Samuel Butler, sees things from the modern point of view.

1626 Strong, Archibald Thomas. "The Poetry of Thomas Hardy," FOUR STUDIES, ed with a memoir by R. C. Bald (Adelaide: Preece, 1932), pp. 81–101.
H is a "true Victorian in his preoccupation with the significance of life, in his strenuous desire to wring meaning out of the riddle of the universe." With H "the tragic sense was from first to last interfused with the ironic." To H nature was a Sphinx, "blind, inscrutable, and utterly indifferent," and in the contest between man's "suffering and aspiration" and "Nature's indifferent exquisiteness," H found "the ironic and . . . tragic significance of life." In *The Dynasts* too, one sees "the tragic interpretation of life, clashing sometimes, and sometimes blending with the ironic." His sense of the ironic prevented romantic heightening, "moral unction and sentimentalism."

1627 Vogt, Frieda. THOMAS HARDYS NATURANSICHT IN SEINEN ROMANEN (Thomas Hardy's View of Nature in His Novels) (Hamburg: Friederichsen de Gruyter, 1932); University of Hamburg dissertation.
[Stresses the unity between man and nature, H's naive and spontaneous portrayal of nature, and H's ability to contrast the past and present forms of English rural life. Value restricted to German readers. Clear, concise, but not original.] [In German.]

1628 [Weber, Carl J. (photographer and compiler)]. CASTERBRIDGE (Fairfield, Maine: Fairfield Publishing, 1932).
[Contains photographs, corresponding to scenes in *The Mayor of Casterbridge,* and relevant passages from the novel.]

1629 Weiner, Joyce. "Four Novels of Hardy: Some Second Impressions," CONTEMPORARY REVIEW, CXLII (Aug 1932), 229–36.

H wrote four great tragic novels, dealing with waste, circumstance, relentless change, and ambition. The lyric element of the true epic is never absent for long from any of them, and their situations, characters, and descriptive passages show an "autumnal" tinge. *Jude the Obscure* possesses some beauty through "the unity and consistency of colouring, even where that colouring is in sepia and half tones" in the love passages between Sue and Jude. *The Mayor of Casterbridge* is not as spacious as *Jude*, for the characters are stationary and the action tightly woven around them. Henchard dominates what is essentially a dramatic lyric, a form as characteristic of H's fiction as of his poetry. *The Return of the Native* has a satiric element comparable to H's poem "Moth Signal." The description is purposefully thrown out of proportion. *Tess of the d'Urbervilles* shows fewer faults of detail than *Native* and triumphs over its melodramatic material by treating its subject with such intensity that the work creates its own style.

1933

1630 Arns, Karl. LITERATUR UND LEBEN IM HEUTIGEN ENGLAND (Literature and Life in Present-day England) (Leipzig: Emil Rohmkopf, 1933), pp. 18, 19, 96.
H was not a part of the mid-Victorian tradition. H resembles certain women regional novelists. H is superior to Housman as an interpreter of life. [In German.]

1631 Baillie, John. AND THE LIFE EVERLASTING (NY: Scribner, 1933), pp. 228, 343.
H represents "a radical and consequent pessimism."

1632 Bardi, Pietro. STORIA DELLA LETTERATURA INGLESE (History of English Literature) (Bari: Gius. Laterza & Figli, 1933), pp. 197–98.
H's early novels (to 1873) are fantasies with but slight plots. From 1874 to 1896, however, was a period of more intense realism in which he emphasized almost exclusively the classic struggle between man and evil. Both his novels and his poems arise from the same inspirations and have almost equal bases in his intimate knowledge of the English countryside. *The Dynasts* is his major work. [Errors in dating *Desperate Remedies* and *Dynasts*.] [In Italian.]

1633 Bissell, Frederick Olds. FIELDING'S THEORY OF THE NOVEL (Ithaca: Cornell UP, 1933); rptd (NY: Cooper Square, 1969), pp. 40, 43, 55, 64, 78–79.

H is like Henry Fielding in his use of chapter titles and in making coincidence credible but is unlike him in being aloof from his readers and in using purple passages effectively.

1634 Brittain, Vera. TESTAMENT OF YOUTH: AN AUTOBIOGRAPHICAL STUDY OF THE YEARS 1900–1925 (NY: Macmillan, 1933), pp. 113, 202, 382–83.
[Brief recollections of Tess of the d'Urbervilles and "In Time of 'the Breaking of Nations' " read in youth.]

1635 Cecil, Lord David. SIR WALTER SCOTT (Lond: Constable, 1933), pp. 16, 25, 27, 32, 33, 55.
[Scattered references to Tess of the d'Urbervilles, H's descriptive powers, his characters, comedy and tragedy in his works.]

1636 Chambers, E. K. THE ENGLISH FOLK-PLAY (Oxford: Clarendon P, 1933).
[A discussion of the folk-play ST. GEORGE AND THE DRAGON and the traditions associated with it, which H used in The Return of the Native.]

1637 Churchill, Winston. "Tess of the d'Urbervilles," BOSTON HERALD, 7 May 1933, p. 5; probably the same as "The World's Great Stories: No. 5 Tess of the d'Urbervilles," NEWS OF THE WORLD (Lond), 5 Feb 1933, pp. 5–6.
"Here is tragedy, sublime, inexorable, annihilating." [Mostly plot summary.]

1638 Coffin, Henry Sloane. WHAT MEN ARE ASKING (Nashville, Tenn: Cokesbury P, 1933), pp. 123, 160, 161, 181.
H found in his old age that the universe was no longer as "nonchalant" as he formerly had thought it, for he came to realize that "life cared for me."

1639 Collins, Norman. "Meredith and Hardy," THE FACTS OF FICTION (NY: Dutton, 1933), pp. 207–27.
Meredith and H have in common a theory of life which they express in their novels. Meredith holds an intellectually (rather than passionately) optimistic view of life. H, especially in Tess of the d'Urbervilles and Jude the Obscure, presents a passionately-felt pessimism which sees man subdued by a fate "remorseless as a steam-roller." In expressing his rebellion against contemporary society, H sometimes commits artistic blunders, as in Tess, where the reader feels the author rather than fate hounds the heroine to her grave. H is very much like Ibsen in that both see society and religion built on deceit; both had the ability, not given to realists like Gissing, to make a single character suggest the experience of all mankind, and both adopted philosophical positions which now appear very dated.

1640 Compton-Rickett, Arthur. I LOOK BACK: MEMORIES OF FIFTY YEARS (Lond: Jenkins, 1933), pp. 13, 176–86.

H's work reflects only half of him. He was inordinately sensitive to pain and tragedy, but he had a vital sense of humor and almost continuous good spirits. He was a generous, kind, and unpretentious man. Of all his characters, Tess was the most real to H. He always spoke of her "as if speaking about a friend." He related that she was a composite of three actual women: a waitress in a tea-shop at Weymouth and two Dorchester girls. H always insisted that his poetry was his most important artistic product, and he saw the hostile reception accorded *Tess of the d'Urbervilles* and *Jude the Obscure* as ample evidence that the reviewers agreed with his judgment.

1641 Cunliffe, John William. ENGLISH LITERATURE IN THE TWENTIETH CENTURY (NY: Macmillan, 1933), pp. 22–25, 40–42, 201–2, 273.

H's avoidance of contact with the public made him an appealing and romantic figure. His dark, fatalistic philosophy fell in with the temper of the time more readily than Meredith's optimism. His poetic drama, *The Dynasts*, was regarded as a remarkable achievement for a man in his sixties. It is a combination of the method of Shakespeare's history plays and that of Goethe's FAUST, but with less humor than either. Although he attempts to escape being known as a fatalist, certain tendencies of thought recur in his novels and poems. His tone in later poems is one of gentle resignation. His themes continue to be life's disappointments and illusions. But he is intensely sympathetic and far from cynical. H abandoned novel-writing in disgust over popular taste and critical restrictions.

1642 Cunliffe, John W. PICTURED STORY OF ENGLISH LITERATURE (NY: Appleton-Century, 1933), pp. 363–66.

In H's early novels, we find two kinds of interest—an idyllic strain picturing the charm of country life and a more sensational melodramatic element. But in his later novels a pessimistic philosophy produced tragic endings. His merits as a writer of popular fiction were quickly recognized and his reputation continued to grow. His poetry was even more pessimistic than his novels and lacked the color and humor of his prose.

1643 Drinkwater, John. "Thomas Hardy," SUMMER HARVEST: POEMS 1924–1933 (Lond: Sidgwick & Jackson, 1933), pp. 90–93.

H's poetry gives us hope for years to come. [Poetic eulogy on H's eighty-fifth birthday.]

1644 Edgar, Pelham. "Thomas Hardy," THE ART OF THE NOVEL: FROM 1700 TO THE PRESENT TIME (NY: Macmillan, 1933), pp. 28, 32, 33, 151, 163, 164–71, 174, 180, 250, 275, 276, 294, 335, 354.

The Woodlanders represents both H's weaknesses (inability to render sophisticated personages, unreal circumstantiality of plot) and his strengths (poetry and power of descriptive passages, realistic rendering of rustic characters).

1645 Evans, Ifor. ENGLISH POETRY IN THE LATER NINETEENTH CENTURY (Lond: Methuen, 1933), pp. 178–94; 2nd ed, rvd (1966), 205–25.

Though H's skill in poetics increased over his long career, his vision remained unchanged. His best poetry usually embodies an investigation of human psychology in a boldly stark diction, though there is much variety of style and content in his masterpiece, *The Dynasts.*

1646 Frauwallner, E., H. Giebisch, and H. Heinzel (eds). DIE WELTLITERATUR: BIOGRAPHISCHES, LITERARHISTORISCHES UND BIBLIOGRAPHES LEXIKON IN ÜBERSICHTEN UND STICHWÖRTERN (World Literature: Biographical, Literary-Historical and Bibliographical Dictionary with Abstracts and Keywords) (Vienna: Verlag Bruder Hollinek, 1933), II, 681–82.

H is noted for his characterization of women and his fatalistic philosophy. *Tess of the d'Urbervilles* is his best novel. [Includes biography, works, and criticism.] [In German.]

1647 Günther, Hildegard. DAS VERHEIMLICHUNGS-, HOCHZEITS-, UND BRIEFMOTIV IN DEN ROMANEN THOMAS HARDYS (The Motif of Concealment, Marriage, and Letters in Thomas Hardy's Novels) (Halle: Eduard Klinz, 1933); University of Halle dissertation.

Through the employment of various motifs, H was able to limit his action, intensify his portrayal, and create a "living organism." Concealment, letters, and marriage are three such motifs which—to a greater or lesser extent—were used in all of H's novels. The author's genius is exhibited in his ability in concentration or limitation. H's interest in architecture was an important influence and enabled him to accomplish his literary ideal. He is capable of organizing his plots clearly and of restricting episodes to achieve a dramatic tension which had previously been restricted to the stage. [Excellent scholarship.] [In German.]

1648 Hamilton, Cosmo. "Thomas Hardy," PEOPLE WORTH TALKING ABOUT (NY: McBride, 1933), pp. 245–52.

It is ironic that H, at the frail age of eighty, should receive the adulation of his land, after enduring years of insignificance, and so hurt by atrocious criticism that he had given up writing novels. After years of neglect, he suddenly found himself in the unique position of being considered a classic author while still alive. When he first gave up architecture for writing, he had a bad beginning, but after publishing a few works, he gained the support of both critics and the public and remained at the top until publishing *Jude the Obscure*, at which time he fell into disfavor with the critics. Throughout his life he remained modest, sensitive, and unaffected.

1649 Hiller, Hedwig. THOMAS HARDY, SEINE ENTWICKLUNG ALS ROMANCIER (Thomas Hardy: His Development as a Novelist) (Tübingen: Eugen Göbel, 1933); University of Tübingen dissertation.

[Divided into six chapters: (1) biography, (2) H seen through his works, (3) method—relation to the public and the novel genre, melodramatic tendencies, the progression from incident to character portrayal, characteristic traits of the works, influence of architecture, theory of the novel, and H's relation to realism, (4) nature, (5) Weltanschauung, (6) comparison with other Victorian novelists.] The unifying element in H's work is his search for truth. In the later novels H's method is more realistic, while his themes are increasingly naturalistic. He outgrows his romantic tendencies and becomes prey to the pessimistic thought of Hartmann and Schopenhauer. Characteristic of H is his employment of nature and history as vehicles for transcending a regional microcosm and presenting the depth and breadth of a macrocosm. [Clear, perceptive, and sympathetic introduction to H.] [In German.]

1650 Holland, Clive [pseud of C. J. Hankinson]. THOMAS HARDY, O. M.: THE MAN, HIS WORKS, AND THE LAND OF WESSEX (Lond: Jenkins, 1933).

H was an introspective and retiring man, although much appreciated late in life. He was not descended from peasants but from Le Hardis of Jersey; in fact, the germ of *The Dynasts* may be in his pride of ancestry and military antecedents. His mother, a woman of natural culture, encouraged H's reading and writing. His early life was influenced by the semi-genteel atmosphere of home and the rougher life of out-of-doors, which gave him a detached attitude toward peasants. Schooling was less important to his education than reading and direct observation. [Conventional survey of H's schooling, apprenticeship to Hicks, assistantship to Blomfield, the early writing of poems, visits to art galleries, his marriage, the writing of the novels, building of Max Gate.] Mrs. H presided over the household, a gracious woman whom H may have found "tiresome." Following the publication of *Tess of the d'Urbervilles*, H was much distracted by reviews and letters, but the novel was a great success. *Jude the Obscure* created a storm of controversy but also received some appreciation, which pleased H. H traveled abroad and made several English journeys, began to revise poems he had written over the years, felt novel-writing was no longer for him (partly because of the prudery that limited his work), and refused to write criticism of other novelists (Fielding and Dickens). *Wessex Poems* was not very favorably received, the reviewers not realizing that H had been writing poetry for many years and had his own theory about it. *Dynasts* was too difficult to be favorably received by most reviewers, not to H's surprise. His literary friends appreciated it. H disliked interviews and refused honors from the government, not wishing to be limited if he wished to criticize; he did accept other honors, including the presidency of the Society of Dorset Men and Honorary Freeman of Dorchester, LL.D. from Aberdeen. An opera based on *Tess* was produced and a dramatic version of *Far From the Madding Crowd*. An address by H on his being elected Freeman comments on changes that have come over Dorchester, how the old is giving way to the new. His manuscripts, at the request of Sydney Cockerell, were distributed to various museums and libraries. H wrote "Convergence of the Twain" to aid the fund for relief of the sufferers from the *Titanic*. The death of Mrs. H deeply affected him. During the first World War, H was a member of a group of literary men who presented the Allies' case to neutral countries and wrote several war poems. Needing companionship, he married Florence Dugdale. After the war, he wrote and published more poems, received more honors, but led an essentially peaceful life and was in failing health for a time. He recovered his vigor toward the end of his life and engaged in many activities in his last years. H will be known to most readers for his pictures of rustic life and of nature in the novels. His poems come close to the heart of the ballad as a natural growth, but his masterwork is *Dynasts*, which established him as one of the greatest poets of the century. His contribution to the novel was in changing it from discursive to architectural. In comparison to Meredith, he is more popular though less the finished artist. He is the most local of all distinguished writers, essentially of the soil of Wessex. [Holland describes "Four Seasons of Wessex," and, with historical observations, the scenes (settings) of five of the novels: Dorchester, Weymouth, Isle of Portland, a Wessex farm, Greenhill Fair. Traces in detail the various settings of *Tess*, following plot, and of Isle of Portland (called the Isle of Slingers) in *The Well-Beloved*.]

1651 L[ucas], E. V. "T. H.," PUNCH, CLXXXV (9 Aug 1933), 154.

The inscription, "T. H. 1844," on the pyramid at Portland Bill, does not stand for "Hardy" but for "Trinity House."

1652 McCarthy, Lillah [Lady Keeble]. MYSELF AND MY FRIENDS (Lond: T. Butterworth; NY: Dutton, 1933), pp. 101–4, 179, 201, 202, 214, 230, 270–71.

[Lillah McCarthy, a leading actress of the London Theatre, ruminates on dramatizations of H's novels and tells of the peaceful benefit to her of the stoicism of his art.]

1653 Mackenzie, Compton. "George Meredith and Thomas Hardy," LITERATURE IN MY TIME (Lond: Rich & Cowan, 1933), pp. 46–52.

By 1900 H was replacing Meredith as the great English novelist of the late nineteenth-century.

1654 Monro, Alida. "Introduction," RECENT POETRY 1923–1933 (Lond: Gerald Howe, 1933), pp. v–x.

Charlotte Mew's poem "Fin de Fête" was copied out by H and found among his papers after his death. [MS version reproduced on p. 92.]

1655 N., D. K. "Thomas Hardy in Russian Translation," ADELPHI, ns V (Jan 1933), 277–79.

In 1931 H's only work translated into Russian by the Soviets was *Tess of the d'Urbervilles*. Although the writers of the foreword (Lunacharski) and preface (Eugene Lann) criticize H for being loath to let go of his illusions about the past, he is praised as "one of the outstanding figures of the last days of the bourgeois world." [Interesting.]

1656 Newton, A. Edward. END PAPERS: LITERARY RECOLLECTIONS (Boston: Little Brown, 1933), pp. 39, 71–73.

["The Voice of the Admiral," a dialect skit, "with apologies to the Shade of Thomas Hardy," describing the "honkonkerable" thirst that compelled the crew of the "Victory" to drink the cask of grog in which the corpse of Nelson had been "set hupright with 'is 'ed between 'is knees and spirits poured hover him to keep 'im sweet." Brief reference to *Under the Greenwood Tree*.]

1657 O'Neill, Burke, S. J. "The Pessimism of Thomas Hardy," THOUGHT, VII (March 1933), 619–36.

H's writing is "both a manifestation and a cause" of the "modern preoccupation with the problem of evil." His pessimism derives from a conception of "the First Cause as one, limited in power, or cruel, or unknowing." However, he did show "a profound charity towards all mankind; a humane sympathy for its sorrow." Clym Yeobright best represents H's doctrine of "fatalistic submission to circumstance." H's poetry develops the same "twilight view of life" expressed in the novels: "this unsatisfactory earth and the evil-wracked dwellers thereof are gradually dying out, slowly sinking into a sea of oblivion." *The Dynasts* depicts "all mankind in the grip of circumstance"; "it is contrary to human reason for man to believe that his liberty is an illusion."

1658 Ray, Margaret. "Bibliography," in THE ART OF THE NOVEL, by Pelham Edgar (NY: Macmillan, 1933), pp. 417–20.
[Bibliography of H's work and criticism on it.]

1659 Robinson, Herbert Spencer. "Thomas Hardy," in AUTHORS TODAY AND YESTERDAY, ed by Stanley J. Kunitz (NY: Wilson, 1933), pp. 291–96.
[A brief biographical sketch of H and a very brief bibliography.]

1660 Sharp, Evelyn [pseud of Mrs. H. W. Nevinson]. UNFINISHED ADVENTURE: SELECTED REMINISCENCES FROM AN ENGLISH-WOMAN'S LIFE (Lond: Lane, 1933), pp. 95–99.
H is modest, has a taste for the macabre, and is uneasy in society.

1661 Stoll, Elmer E. ART AND ARTIFICE IN SHAKESPEARE (Cambridge: Cambridge UP, 1933), p. 72.
In *The Mayor of Casterbridge* there is "an arbitrary contrast" in that Henchard is both single and married.

1662 "Thomas Hardy," MEYERS BLITZ-LEXIKON (Meyer's Quick-Reference Dictionary) 3rd ed, rvd (Leipzig: Bibliographisches Institut Ag., 1933), p. 246.
H is an English realist born 1840, died 1928. [In German.]

1663 Tugwell, Rexford Guy. "Meditation in Stinsford Churchyard," COLUMBIA UNIVERSITY QUARTERLY, XXV (June 1933), 97–106.
H's simplicity of line and careful under-ornamentation belong to the writer first and do not come out of any architectural influence. H's pessimistic view of man's small capacity to deal with the land comes from his rural background in combination with his Dorchester surroundings and the influence of the classics. "This is what the novels mean, where *The Dynasts* tends, and where the lyrics end." H retreats into comedy where the whole divine inconsequence can be transmuted into literature. H was very much a part of the Dorchester neighborhood and the people among whom he lived.

1664 Wakefield, Catherine F. "The Anglo-Saxon Philosophy in BEOWULF and Thomas Hardy," COLBY MERCURY, IV (May 1933), 34–41.
Although H's philosophy is generally "that of such minds as are described in BEOWULF" (insofar as H's god is like Wyrd), H does possess a "passionate sympathy for mankind" which leads him to protest vehemently against Fate's potency, and thus, taken together with his perception of the loveliness of particular aspects in nature and his "tendency toward optimism" differentiates his ideas from theirs.

1665 Watts, Nevile. " 'Poiêsis' and the Modern World," DUBLIN REVIEW, CXCIII (Oct 1933), 245–57.

The real H is an idealist, "the chanter of the joy that lies behind the human tragedy."

1666 Weber, Carl J. IN THE LAND OF THE D'URBERVILLES (Fairfield, Maine: Fairfield Publishing, 1933).

[Contains photographs by the author, which correspond to scenes in *Tess of the d'Urbervilles*, and relevant passages from the novel.]

1667 Webster, H. C. "Borrowings in *Tess of the d'Urbervilles*," MODERN LANGUAGE NOTES, XLVIII (Nov 1933), 459–62.

H copied five descriptive passages in *Tess of the d'Urbervilles*, with little alteration, from articles he had published earlier, one from the NEW QUARTERLY MAGAZINE and four from the DORSETSHIRE LABOURER.

1934

1668 Aldred, Cyril. "Introduction," *The Woodlanders*, ed by Cyril Aldred (Lond: Macmillan [Scholar's Library], 1934), pp. vii–xvii.

H's tragic vision is rooted in his observation of the tension between the new scientific knowledge and the older inherited wisdom. In *The Woodlanders*, Grace, Fitzpiers, and Felice are the representatives of modern sophistication while rustic security is reflected in Melbury, Giles, and Marty. [Includes notes, study, and essay questions and a biographical sketch with errors in dating.]

1669 Armstrong, A. Joseph. INTIMATE GLIMPSES FROM BROWNING'S LETTER FILE (Waco, Texas: Baylor University, 1934 [Baylor University's "Browning Interests," Series Eight]), pp. 81–82.

[Transcript of letter, dated 23 June 1879, to Browning from W. H. Pollock asking Browning to join the Rabelais Society cites H as one of the original members.]

1670 Baker, Bernard Granville. "Cavalrymen in Thomas Hardy's Novels," OLD CAVALRY STATIONS (Lond: Heath Cranton, 1934), pp. 70–74.

"Wessex conjures up visions of characters [the Trumpet-Major and Sergeant Troy] created by Thomas Hardy and of the countryside from which he called them to take their place among the Immortals." Places like Exeter

[Exonbury] and Salisbury [Melchester] were locales for not only horses but racing, beer, and good times. [An old horse soldier gives the history of cavalry stations in England. He cites *The Trumpet-Major* and *Far From the Madding Crowd*.]

1671 Boas, Ralph P., and Edwin Smith. ENJOYMENT OF LITERATURE (NY: Harcourt, Brace, 1934), pp. 102, 189, 207, 225, 239–40, 270, 321, 516–18.

H is a great realist whose philosophical views led him to excessive melodrama and forced characterizations.

1672 Budke, Willi. DIE DARSTELLUNG DER FRAU BEI THOMAS HARDY, UNTER BESONDER BERÜCKSICHTIGUNG SCHOPENHAUERS (Thomas Hardy's Representation of Women, With Particular Regard to Schopenhauer's) (Bochum-Langendeer: Heinrich Poppinghaus, 1934); University of Münster dissertation.

H's heroines fall into three categories: 1) the altruists—Cytherea (*Desperate Remedies*), Paula (*A Laodicean*), Viviette (*Two on a Tower*), Elizabeth-Jane (*The Mayor of Casterbridge*), Tess (*Tess of the d'Urbervilles*), and Avice (*The Well-Beloved*); 2) the egoists—Fancy (*Under the Greenwood Tree*), Elfrida (*A Pair of Blue Eyes*), Bathsheba (*Far From the Madding Crowd*), Ethelberta (*The Hand of Ethelberta*), Eustacia (*The Return of the Native*), Anne (*The Trumpet-Major*), Grace (*The Woodlanders*), and Arabella (*Jude the Obscure*); 3) the altruistic egoists—Sue Bridehead (*Jude*). [Imaginative and interesting.] [In German.]

1673 Bullough, Geoffrey. THE TREND OF MODERN POETRY (Edinburgh & Lond: Oliver & Boyd, 1934), pp. 3–5, 54, 56.

In H's best poems, he has an "apprehension that man's powers of feeling and thought brought with them a unique capacity for suffering in a world of inscrutable laws." H learned his use of everyday idiom and dramatic technique from Browning. His poems show intellectual acceptance of the new world of Darwin, Shopenhauer, and the biblical critics, but "his heart rebelled against the 'vast Imbecility' of life." The "unresolved tension" between the ideal and the actual resulted in the "ruggedness, grotesquerie, and occasional banality" of H's verse. H was a regional poet like Housman, Yeats, and Kipling.

1674 Burrell, Martin. "Thomas Hardy's Wessex," CRUMBS ARE ALSO BREAD (Toronto: Macmillan, 1934), pp. 128–40.

[Account of a visit to Dorset in 1929. Only scanty references to H.]

1675 Cazamian, Louis. "L'Angleterre du Sud: Hampshire, Berkshire, Wiltshire, Dorsetshire; Ile de Wight" (South England: Hampshire, Berkshire, Wiltshire, Dorsetshire; Isle of Wight), LA GRANDE

BRETAGNE (Great Britain) (Paris: Didier, 1934), pp. 121–46, espec 121–27.

H's "austere and powerful dramas" are a reincarnation of the old Wessex region to which the author has given the boundaries of the original. H has, through his obsession with the past and the use of a severe landscape, made the settings of his stories most mysterious and imposing. [In French.]

1676 Chapman, Frank. "Hardy the Novelist," SCRUTINY, III (June 1934), 22–37; reissued (Lond: Cambridge UP, 1963).

H was accepted as great in England, but he lacked standing on the continent. He is considered great because of "his philosophy of life and tragic world-outlook" and his powers of characterization.

To note the style in H's verse is important. It seems the poems of the second order have usually been chosen to illustrate H's philosophy. The style is " 'literary,' pedantic and, at the same time, *gauche*." These same elements of style are in the great poems, i.e, "After a Journey," "Neutral Tones," "A Broken Appointment," "The Voice." In the poems, personal feeling is concentrated and intense; in the novels the effect is cumulative. "Friends Beyond" is full of H's typical traits: the odd, facetious phrase; the moral couched in "stilted and pedantic language"; and the dialect. It contains the elements of H's work: "the rural scene, the habit of contemplation, the strange vocabulary, and the habitual bent of mind, labeled, as a rule 'Philosophy' "; the complete lack of development. These conditions are paralleled in the novels. H's sensibility is in his style. The immediate personal feeling is the source of the greatness in the poems, but this cannot be paralleled in the novel, so an approximation must be looked for, that is, the cumulative effect.

H's prose is clumsy when aiming at impressiveness, which for H is to be "literary," the erudite word over the simple one. H pulls in the display of knowledge with his references. Though too often disastrous, they are an integral part of his style. They are typical of him and his naive ideas of scholarship and education. They are sequel to the ponderous words he habitually uses. H's simple and straightforward writing is the rustic dialogue. It is highly stylized, intentional and careful. H's personal knowledge, the solid habitual background of experience, takes the place of reminiscence, the success of the second order poems. The further H removes himself from his background, the less successful he is.

The philosophy in the novels parallels the poems. The philosophy is lacking in *Under the Greenwood Tree* and is what makes the novel facetious in tone. *The Trumpet-Major* is successful because the essential background is there;

the fatalism is present and the conviction that "things will never come right." It is founded on local reminiscences and the characters are villagers of varying rank. *The Dynasts* is ponderous and without vitality, except in a few scenes. H was not in possession of a truly philosophical mind and was incapable of real thinking. His blind 'immanent will' attests to this. *Dynasts* is hundreds of intervening pages made up of incredibly bad blank verse and dull prose descriptions in the form of stage directions of a long series of battles and conferences.

In the novels, when the philosophic attitude remains in the background, it gives atmosphere and unity; "it stands for Hardy's essential character, his constancy of bent, the sense of fate, and the level of seriousness at which he contemplates human life." When it is direct, it is tedious and unconvincing as in a long chain of improbable circumstances to point a moral or bring about tragedy or in a crude form of symbolism such as the child, Father Time. H's symbolism of implicit meaning is more successful than the marriages of Jude and Arabella and of Jude and Sue. The physical aspect of the union is catastrophe, and H's moral is Victorian—'the wages of sin is death.' Victorianism is part of H's strength: stolid, static, simple. His pessimism implies firm and solid positions that are without doubt and conflict. H's prose takes on vital impressiveness when his "most vital interests and attitudes are engaged." H's style is as unyielding as his attitude.

1677 Coffin, Henry Sloane. GOD'S TURN (NY: Harper, 1934), pp. 21, 27, 78.
For H the world we live in is a "non-chalant universe" in which Christian faith is not possible. It is the "on-going of the world" for H which makes man's existence so painful; H would like to see a "stationary heaven or earth."

1678 "Colby Mercury Lists Letters of Hardy," BOSTON EVENING TRANSCRIPT, 4 Dec 1934, p. 7.
[Note on the first published list of Hardy's letters, compiled by Carl J. Weber.]

1679 Cowley, Malcolm. EXILE'S RETURN: A NARRATIVE OF IDEAS (NY: Norton, 1934); rvd as A LITERARY ODYSSEY OF THE 1920s (NY: Viking P, 1951), p. 20.
The "exiles," in "a desperate search for guidance," read Kipling, Stevenson, Meredith, H, Gissing, Conrad, Wilde and Shaw.

1680 Cunliffe, John William. "Mid-Victorian Novelists," LEADERS OF THE VICTORIAN REVOLUTION (NY: Appleton-Century, [ca. 1934]), pp. 215–27.

The atmosphere of H's novels contrasts with that of Meredith's. H's characters are victims of circumstance, and his novels are therefore less hopeful than Meredith's. And yet H's own life was a peculiarly fortunate one, both personally and professionally. H's novelistic purpose was to produce the grandeur and unity of a Sophoclean tragedy. He is set apart from the realists of his day by his combination of universals in human nature and uncommonness of events.

1681 Davidson, Carter. POETRY: ITS APPRECIATION AND ENJOYMENT (NY: Harcourt, Brace, 1934), pp. 95, 114, 197.
"The realistic poet centers his attention upon personality, and makes the characters live richly for the reader." This is the method of H in *Satires of Circumstance*. "Through an Olympian calm, perceiving the inevitable outcome against the indifference of the universe, the tragedian may raise tragedy to the level of philosophy, as fatalists from the Greeks to Thomas Hardy have done." H and other naturalistic pessimists hold a fatalistic view of nature.

1682 Eliot, Thomas Stearns. AFTER STRANGE GODS: A PRIMER OF MODERN HERESY (NY: Harcourt, Brace; Lond: Faber & Faber, 1934), pp. 59–62; first given as the Page-Barbour Lecture at University of Virginia, 1933; rptd in POINTS OF VIEW (Lond: Faber & Faber, 1941).
H is one of the most unfortunate examples of a great talent unrestrained by tradition or his audience, and thus expressing an inner self which was not a "wholesome or edifying matter of communication." His style "touches sublimity without ever having passed through the stage of being good." In giving rein to the emotions of his character, he vents his own emotions and betrays his want of ideas. Whatever popularity he acquired came from his flattering the vulgar notion that emotion for its own sake is good. Finally his over-plotted novels are weak in leaving nothing to nature.

1683 Finger, Charles J. AFTER THE GREAT COMPANIONS (NY: Dutton, 1934), pp. 272–79.
H's style has "magnificent construction and sweep." His writing is for the "discriminating, who dread emotional poverty and seek the significant thing behind appearances." H's books which are excellent for reading aloud: *Tess of the d'Urbervilles, The Mayor of Casterbridge, Life's Little Ironies, Far From the Madding Crowd, Jude the Obscure*.

1684 Fosdick, H. E. SECRET OF VICTORIOUS LIVING (NY: Harper, 1934), p. 146.
H's loss of Christian faith is shown in such lines as "the dreaming, dark dumb Thing/That turns the handle of this idle Show!" and implies loss of "awareness of deep interior resources."

1685 "French Epigrams," TIMES LITERARY SUPPLEMENT (Lond), 2 Aug 1934, p. 534.
H's poem "Smith of Stoke" [i.e. "Epitaph on a Pessimist"] who lives without a dame is an epigram "after the French."

1686 Garland, Hamlin. "Thomas Hardy's Birthplace," AFTERNOON NEIGHBORS (NY: Macmillan, 1934), pp. 85–99.
Dorchester is a neat market-town. [Describes Max Gate and the elderly H.] H spoke of Barrie and his living in London, which H could not stand because of visitors. H liked visits from American professors but was surprised that a book on his technique [J. W. Beach (1922)] was about prose rather than poetry, since prose just came of itself. H would not answer questions about locales of his novels. He called some of the novels "historical." H liked Howells as person, thought Bret Harte a good portrayer of the West, admired Conrad but said he was "not English in any sense," admired Masefield as a good friend and "great poet." [Garland thought it remarkable that H should come from such surroundings as his remote, small, cramped birthplace.]

1687 Gill, W. Walter. "Lucetta's House at Casterbridge," NOTES AND QUERIES, CLXVI (16 June 1934), 422–23.
[Excerpt from the DORSET COUNTY CHRONICLE, 29 May 1834, about the "large and ancient house at the corner of South Street and Durngate Lane," described as Lucetta's house in *The Mayor of Casterbridge*.]

1688 Griesbach, Ilse. DAS TRAGISCHE WELTGEFÜHL ALS GESTALTUNGSPRINZIP IN THOMAS HARDYS WESSEXROMANEN UNTER HINEINBEZIEHUNG SHAKESPEARE IN SEINER LEAR UND MACBETH-PERIODE (The Tragic Universal Sentiment as Structural Principle in Thomas Hardy's Wessex Novels in Relation to Shakespeare in His Lear and Macbeth Period) (Bochum-Langendeer: H. Poppinghaus, 1934); University of Marburg dissertation.
[H's female characterizations, concept of mutibility, and direct quotations from Shakespeare confirm a literary affinity. In chapters 2 and 3 H's Weltanschauung and dramatic technique are defined. *The Return of the Native* and *Tess of the d'Urbervilles* are compared to LEAR and MACBETH in chapters 4 through 6. The concluding chapter summarizes Shakespeare's and H's concept of tragedy with respect to the German Weltanschauung. Orthodox, clear, and well-documented. Deserves a prominent place in German Hardian scholarship.] [In German.]

1689 "Hardy's 'Greenwood Tree,'" OBSERVER (Lond), 16 Sept 1934, p. 25.
The old beech that gave the title to *Under the Greenwood Tree* became diseased and was cut down and sold for firewood.

1690 Hartman, Josef. ARCHITEKTUR IN DEN ROMANEN THOMAS HARDYS (Architecture in the Novels of Thomas Hardy) (Bochum-Langendeer: H. Poppinghaus, 1934); University of Münster dissertation.

[Reveals how H's interest in architecture found expression in the novels. The architecture of the 1860s and H's own experience as an architect are related in chapters 1 and 2. Chapter 3 analyzes the architects and stonemasons portrayed in *Desperate Remedies, Under the Greenwood Tree, A Pair of Blue Eyes, Far From the Madding Crowd, A Laodicean,* and *Jude the Obscure.* Descriptions of churches, secular buildings, nature, the body, and objects illustrate H's architectural technique. Interesting and informative.] [In German.]

1691 Hartwick, Harry. THE FOREGROUND OF AMERICAN FICTION (NY: American Book Co., 1934), pp. 43, 318.

To Stephen Crane, H seemed "a gigantic writer." W. D. Howells's book MY LITERARY PASSIONS, dealing with authors "I must call my masters," includes H.

1692 House, Homer Clyde, and Susan Emolyn Harman. COLLEGE RHETORIC: WITH PRACTICE LEAVES (NY: Prentice-Hall, 1934), pp. 274–75.

With reference to a passage from *Under the Greenwood Tree,* "the delicate art of Thomas Hardy fuses the moods of skies and heaths and woods with those of his human characters as to make them seem part and parcel of one another."

1693 Hübner, Walter. DIE ENGLISCHE DICHTUNG IN DER SCHULE: GRUNDZÜGE EINER INTERPRETATIONSLEHRE (English Literature in School: Outlines of an Interpretation Method) (Leipzig: Quelle & Meyer, 1934), p. 218.

H, Sheila Kaye-Smith, James Barrie, R. L. Stevenson, and Kipling are forerunners of Knut Hamsun and Johan Bojer who best expressed the Germanic feeling for nature. [In German.]

1694 Hunt, Cecil. SHORT STORIES: HOW TO WRITE THEM (Lond: Harrap, 1934), pp. 50, 149.

[Passing reference to H's skill as a delineator of pastoral setting, and to *Tess of the d'Urbervilles.*]

1695 Kent, William. LONDON FOR SHAKESPEARE LOVERS (Lond: Methuen, 1934), pp. vii, 117.

[H is mentioned, and his "To Shakespeare after Three Hundred Years" quoted in part.]

1696 Legouis, Émile. COURTE HISTOIRE DE LA LITTÉRATURE ANGLAISE (Oxford: Clarendon P, 1934); trans by V. F. Boyson and J. Coulson as A SHORT HISTORY OF ENGLISH LITERATURE (Oxford: Clarendon P, 1934), pp. 363, 365–67.

H, with John Davidson, Ernest Dowson, and A. E. Housman, is a "pessimist," a "poet of disillusionment." "His work [his fiction] is tinged with the pessimism of Schopenhauer, and presents striking analogies with the French naturalistic writing of Flaubert and Zola." [In French.]

1697 Lewis, Sinclair. WORK OF ART (NY: Doubleday, Doran, 1934), p. 115.

[*Jude the Obscure* is alluded to in connection with the character Myron: "Yet if this Yankee Jude was obscure enough, he could not be awed into remaining so."]

1698 Luccock, Halford E. CONTEMPORARY AMERICAN LITERATURE AND RELIGION (Chicago: Willett & Clark, 1934), pp. 17, 57.

The post–World War I era "has not been what history will call a great age." For H, "to whom is usually awarded the crown of pessimism," it is "a dark and dreary age." In H "man was a marionette in whom free will was a mocking delusion." But this view "did not ordinarily involve belief in fatalism," rather in "the blind action of physical forces."

1699 MacIntyre, Carlyle, and Edward Bock (eds). ELEMENTS OF DISCOURSE IN ENGLISH LITERATURE (NY: Macmillan, 1934), pp. 292–97.

[Contains examples of descriptive, narrative, and expository writing, including H's "Anna, Lady Baxby" from *A Group of Noble Dames*.]

1700 Parry, D. A. "Hardy's 'Greenwood Tree,'" OBSERVER (Lond), 23 Sept 1934, p. 12.

A previous issue of the OBSERVER incorrectly stated that the tree referred to in the title of H's novel had been cut down. The real model for H's "Greenwood Tree" is still standing. [See "Hardy's 'Greenwood Tree,'" OBSERVER (Lond), 16 Sept 1934, p. 25.]

1701 Phelps, William Lyon. WHAT I LIKE IN POETRY (NY: Scribner, 1934), pp. 9, 11, 41, 56–57, 118–19, 218.

[An anthology including three of H's poems and brief references to H.]

1702 Pinto, Vivian de Sola. "Introduction," *The Mayor of Casterbridge*, ed with introduction and notes by Vivian de Sola Pinto (Lond: Macmillan, 1934), pp. ix–xix.

While developing the thesis that the modern spirit works to the disadvantage of the heroic Wessex peasants, H presents simultaneously what is commonplace and tragic, what is universal and local. This is particularly true of *The Mayor of Casterbridge* which presents poignantly "the sense of living in an imagined locality."

1703 Powys, John Cowper. AUTOBIOGRAPY (Lond: Lane; NY: Simon & Schuster, 1934), pp. 206, 209–11, 262, 282–83; new ed, with an introduction by J. B. Priestly (Lond: Macdonald, 1967).
[A brief description of a meeting with H, who alluded to Wordsworth's "pious optimism" and praised Poe's "Ulalume."]

1704 Powys, John Cowper. WEYMOUTH SANDS (Lond: Macdonald; NY: Simon & Schuster, 1934); new ed, with prefatory note by E. R. H. Harvey (Lond: Macdonald, 1963).
[Powys's novel gives brief references to H by name.]

1705 Quiller-Couch, Sir Arthur. "The Earlier Novels of Thomas Hardy," THE POET AS CITIZEN AND OTHER PAPERS (Cambridge: Cambridge UP, 1934; NY: Macmillan, 1935), pp. 36, 37, 38, 177, 178, 185, 191, 196, 197–217.
It is refreshing to turn from the poetry of 1934 with its "air of aloof condescension," to H and his "hope and trust in the young." Though it is difficult "to grope with Hardy through a twilight between two worlds, one dead, the other powerless to be born," H continued to trust in youth and was able to achieve, in old age, a poem "that trafficked with event and fate, with the beginnings of a nation, with the universal scheme of things." The "pessimism in these dark uncertain days" of 1934 does not derive from H, who finds tragedy (as Shakespeare did) in the nobility of his characters. During a visit to the Dorset dialect poet, Barnes talked extensively of H's upbringing, marriage, and literary prospects. "Hardy's questioning, ironic verse and method" derives from Barnes. H, with Richard Jeffries, is the initiator in English fiction of "that sensitive and 'subjective' intimacy with the country-side" later cultivated by W. H. Hudson and Edward Thomas. In contrast to the active denouncing by Blake, E. B. Browning, and Ruskin of "the ruin of our lovely valleys and streams," H and Jeffries offered a "new outlook on the rural inheritance." Until H, English poetry and fiction, with the occasional exception of G. Eliot, had neglected the rural life in favor of social themes or romantic adventure. H's earlier fiction, from *The Poor Man and the Lady* to *Two on a Tower*, reveals his deeply felt need to write a fiction of manners or a romantic fiction uncongenial to his best talents. Thus his vacillation between the sensational *Desperate Remedies* and the pastoral *Under the Greenwood Tree*, between the rustic *Far From the Madding Crowd* and the comic *The Hand of Ethelberta*, between *The*

Return of the Native and *A Laodicean*. *Tower* "just misses the idyllic best by stilted talk between amorous lips."

1706 Rendall, Vernon. WILD FLOWERS IN LITERATURE (Lond: Scholartis P, 1934), pp. 32, 38, 47, 63, 64, 167, 176, 185, 227, 252, 298, 304, 317, 325, 332, 347, 356.
[H's use of flowers in his poetry and novels.]

1707 Richards, I. A. COLERIDGE ON IMAGINATION (Lond: Kegan Paul, Trench, Trubner, 1934), pp. 95, 142.
One of H's characteristic structures is arranging "a series of imaginative passages" "(as beads on a string) in the mode of Fancy."

1708 Sedgwick, Henry Dwight. DAN CHAUCER: AN INTRODUCTION TO THE POET, HIS POETRY, AND HIS TIMES (Indianapolis: Bobbs-Merrill, 1934), pp. 344, 354.
H's "The Three Strangers" is an example of a great short story. H might have drawn Chaucer's Poor Parson.

1709 Sisson, Charles J. "The Mythical Sorrows of Shakespeare," PROCEEDINGS OF THE BRITISH ACADEMY, XX (Lond: Oxford UP, 1934), p. 65; rptd as THE MYTHICAL SORROWS OF SHAKESPEARE (Lond: Humphrey Milford, 1934), p. 23.
H said that it is impossible to write good books about cheerful people.

1710 Smith, Fred. "Hardy: The Poet of Life at its Worst," PERSONALIST, XV (Winter 1934), 32–38.
H really had no philosophy. "The vastness of things was beyond his comprehension." He considered the universe "capricious" and "mean." He could be crushing when "dealing with the cherished creeds of men" because "for him God was defeated by his own creation." H's merit and defect was that [he] "vowed himself to melancholy as a nun to her virginity. In every episode of life, according to Hardy, there is reason for wailing." H was popular because "the English like their poetry sad." [This writer neglects the possibility that there was a pleasant moment in anything written by H.]

1711 Smith, Warren Hunting. ARCHITECTURE IN ENGLISH FICTION (New Haven: Yale UP; Lond: Oxford UP, 1934), pp. 205, 215.
[Passing reference to *The Woodlanders* (chap 4) and *Two on a Tower*.]

1712 Stephens, James, Edwin L. Beck, and Royall H. Snow (eds). VICTORIAN AND LATER POETS (NY: American Book Co., 1934), pp. 911–24, 1136*ff*.
H's work may be divided into three stages: novel writing, which includes lighter and traditional forms and more somber forms emphasizing man's

conflict with nature; the writing of *The Dynasts*, which was the culmination of H's artistic and philosophical thoughts; the writing of lyric poetry—poetry which showed an originality of technique. With H's death the last link to the Victorian era was broken.

1713 Swinnerton, Frank. THE GEORGIAN SCENE: A LITERARY PANORAMA (NY: Farrar & Rinehart, 1934), pp. 8–10, 12, 25, 177, 255, 285, 289, 320.

In 1906 H succeeded Meredith to the post of literature's Grand Old Man; however, though his work as novelist was long complete, his reputation was not to reach its climax until about 1920. H was the victim of the criticisms of George Moore who rather unfairly based them upon isolated passages or single poems. In 1910 H was unquestionably "the living writer who held highest place as a poet." *The Dynasts* was regarded the most majestic poetic creation of the age, and H's lyrics had their defenders among poets and critics.

1714 Thouless, Priscilla. "Thomas Hardy—*The Dynasts*," MODERN POETIC DRAMA (Oxford: Basil Blackwell, 1934), pp. 115–25. "Hardy's pessimism was fundamental and involved distrust of the foundations on which life itself is built, the creative and reproductive instinct." He had "an acute perception of the sorrow of life" which arose from the evolution of a species of man "too sensitive to bear with the rude shocks of life." In *The Dynasts* H dramatized "the eternal disharmony of human life, the desires and aspirations of man in conflict with the force of fate." Although the spirit of the universe is a "blind unfeeling force," the Spirits of the Pities and Ironic Spirits "express the revolt in the human mind against the impersonality of fate," the "unconquerable irrational hope of men's minds." These spirits lend unity to the vast design of the play, "an extraordinary architectural achievement," but the play has a vital weakness: the diction of the verse. Nevertheless *Dynasts* "is described as a great work and does indeed give an impression of majesty" because of the "greatness of Hardy's cosmic vision, partly due to the keenness of his visual imagination." Despite dreary patches, H's prose "at times attains to greatness," so that the verse scenes seem greater than they are.

1715 Untermeyer, Louis, and Carter Davidson. POETRY: ITS APPRECIATION AND ENJOYMENT (NY: Harcourt, Brace, 1934), pp. 95, 114, 197.

H is realistic in *Satires of Circumstance*. If the reader "can attain an Olympian calm and perceive the inevitable outcome against the indifference of the universe, he may raise tragedy to the level of philosophy, as fatalists, from the Greeks to Thomas Hardy, have done." Of the different poetic views with respect to nature, Meredith's and H's (a naturalistic pessimist) are terrestrial, somewhat utilitarian, and fatalistic and reveal nature as "impersonal, the embodiment of unchangeable law."

1716 Walley, Harold R., and J. Harold Wilson. THE ANATOMY OF LITERATURE (NY: Farrar & Rinehart, 1934), pp. 6, 85, 92. [Passing references.]

1717 Walsh, Michael. "Christmas From Crashaw to Chesterton," CATHOLIC WORLD, CXL (Dec 1934), 292-96, espec 295.

Given H's "agnosticism, his sarcastic references to Providence," it is remarkable that he wrote the poem "The Oxen." Perhaps H, despite his fatalism, ultimately realized "that his philosophy lacked everything, that the house, yea, the city of his literature was defective in its fundamentals." H, in remembering the legend in conjunction with his childhood, may, like Wordsworth, have had an intuition of immortality.

1718 Ward, A. C. THE FROLIC AND THE GENTLE: A CENTENARY STUDY OF CHARLES LAMB (Lond: Methuen, 1934), pp. 162–64.

There "is a slight resemblance in two respects between Lamb's tale [ROSAMUND GRAY] and Hardy's *Tess*," the similarity of the heroes' names [Allan Clare and Angel Clare], and both violations occur at night and out-of-doors.

1719 Weber, Carl J. "A Careful Chronology," WRITER (Boston), XLVI (July 1934), 236–37.

Although no dates appear in *Tess of the d'Urbervilles* "in the author's mind it was all . . . definitely timed." Tess was born in November 1867; the night in The Chase was 27 September 1884; etc. [Weber presents no evidence to support this chronology.]

1720 [Weber, Carl J.]. "The Colby Collection of Hardy's Letters," COLBY MERCURY, VI (Dec 1934), 11–16.

[Lists 156 H letters "available, either in manuscript or in print, at Colby College."]

1721 Weber, Carl J. "From Barchester to Melchester," COLBY COLLEGE BULLETIN, XXXIII (May 1934), 3–27; rptd in IN THOMAS HARDY'S WORKSHOP (Waterville, Maine: Colby College [Colby Monographs, No. 6], 1934), pp. 3–27.

The fiction, autobiography, and literary life of Anthony Trollope may have had significant impact on H's life and fiction. H may have taken the clue for Michael Henchard from Trollope's remarks about his father in his AUTOBIOGRAPHY; Trollope's Barsetshire may have suggested Wessex place-names to H; Trollope's timid presentation of a fallen woman in THE VICAR OF BULLHAMPTON may have incited H to write *Tess of the d'Urbervilles*. "Did he learn from Trollope how the public rewards honesty in a writer?"

1722 [Weber, Carl J.]. " 'History' as It Is Written," COLBY MERCURY, V (Feb 1934), 34–40.
[Points out six errors of fact in recent discussions of *Tess of the d'Urbervilles* and *Far From the Madding Crowd*. Valuable corrections of *Tess*'s printing history.]

1723 W[eber], C[arl] J. "Mrs. Grundy's Wheel-Barrow," COLBY MERCURY, V (May 1934), 56–57.
[Notes a revision in *Tess of the d'Urbervilles* to accommodate the sensibilities of an editor of GRAPHIC.]

1724 [Weber, Carl J.]. " 'A New Kind of Beauty,' " COLBY MERCURY, V (Feb 1934), 33.
Tess of the d'Urbervilles and "The Lost Pyx" preserve two different stories of the origin of an apparently medieval pillar above the Vale of Blackmore.

1725 Weber, Carl J. "Notes and Observations: A Note on the Manuscript Names of Hardy's Characters," REVIEW OF ENGLISH STUDIES (Lond), X (Oct 1934), 456–59.
Characters "seem born to their names," but the names should not be interpreted as symbols because his manuscripts show that H repeatedly changed them. His place-names are mainly "done from the real" and should be read as "genuine Wessex products."

1726 Weber, Carl J. "On the Dismemberment of *Tess*," SATURDAY REVIEW OF LITERATURE, XI (24 Nov 1934), 308.
One *Tess of the d'Urbervilles* chapter, "The Midnight Baptism: A Study in Christianity," appeared originally in FORTNIGHTLY REVIEW (May 1891); it was not purged from the printing of *Tess* in the GRAPHIC to end up in SCOTS OBSERVER, as Florence Hardy says. Another chapter leading to Tess's seduction, which was dropped for serial publication and ended up in the NATIONAL OBSERVER, probably led to the error.

1727 Weber, Carl J. "Shakespeare's Twin-Voice Again," SHAKESPEARE ASSOCIATION BULLETIN, IX (July 1934), 162–63.
[Gives additional items as evidence of H's indebtedness to Shakespeare to supplement Weber's "Twin-Voice of Shakespeare," ibid (April 1934), 91–97.]

1728 Weber, Carl J. "Thomas Hardy's 'Aeschylean Phrase,' " CLASSICAL JOURNAL, XXIX (April 1934), 533–35.
The source of H's phrase, "The President of the Immortals had ended his sport with Tess," is a translation of Aeschylus by Theodore Alois Buckley made in 1849. H had presumably kept the book for thirty years.

1729 Weber, Carl J. "A Trip to Brazil: The Historian of Wessex Goes Abroad," COLBY COLLEGE BULLETIN, XXXIII (May 1934), pp. 29–63; rptd in IN THOMAS HARDY'S WORKSHOP (Waterville, Maine: Colby College [Colby Monographs, No. 6], 1934), pp. 29–63; possibly rptd as "Brazil as it is in Thomas Hardy's Novel," REVUE ANGLO-AMERICAINE [not seen].

H's depiction of the region of Brazil, around Curitiba, in *Tess of the d'Urbervilles*, is grossly inaccurate. The real city lacks the clayey soil, the excessive rainfall and heat, the unhealthy climate which broke the mind and body of Angel Clare. H seems to have based his depiction not on the mountainous region in which Curitiba lies, but on the low-lying plain of the Amazon River—some two thousand miles north.

1730 Weber, Carl J. "Twin-Voice of Shakespeare," SHAKESPEARE ASSOCIATION BULLETIN, IX (April 1934), 91–97.

George Moore's unkind reference to H as not nearly approaching the greatness of Shakespeare is unsound. H's devotion and indebtedness to Shakespeare's writings is immense, and it has not yet been properly assessed. The most direct debt appears in H's numerous borrowings of quotations from the plays. [Also see Carl J. Weber, "Shakespeare's Twin-Voice Again," ibid (July 1934), 162–63.]

1731 Wells, H. G. EXPERIMENT IN AUTOBIOGRAPHY (NY: Macmillan, 1934), p. 118.

Life as a draper's shopman was insupportable; Latin, as for Jude, was a "symbol of mental emancipation."

1732 Wharton, Edith. A BACKWARD GLANCE (NY & Lond: Appleton-Century, 1934); rptd (NY: Scribner's, 1964), pp. 215–16.

During several meetings, H was "remote and uncommunicative," but his silence seemed due to "an unconquerable shyness rather than to the great man's disdain for humbler neighbours." Although he recounted a few incidents of having to make changes in some of his works before their publication, "he seemed to take little interest in the literary movements of the day, or in fact in any critical discussion of his craft," and "he was completely enclosed in his own creative dream, through which I imagine few voices or influences reached him."

1733 Wilmsen, Guenther. THOMAS HARDY ALS IMPRESSIONISTISCHER LANDSCHAFTSMALER (Thomas Hardy as Impressionistic Landscape Painter) (Düsseldorf: G. H. Nolte, 1934); University of Marburg dissertation.

"Naturalistic impressionism" is characteristic of H's earlier novels and corresponds with the *pleinairist* painters. Light, color, and movement are inextricably mingled as in the paintings of Monet. H is also capable of psychological-impressionism by removing all colors and contours and seeing the psychic through the author's eyes. Impressionism assumes a symbolic importance in *The Return of the Native* and is clearly illustrated in *Tess of the d'Urbervilles*. [In German.]

1734 Wingfield-Stratford, Esmé. THE VICTORIAN AFTERMATH (NY: William Morrow, 1934), pp. 145, 157, 173.

Meredith and James resorted to artificiality in their expression of the psychological; others, like H, reproduced reality with fidelity to accomplish the same end. "Wessex novels . . . are not only profound studies of the human soul in conflict with destiny, but also serve as a unique historic memorial of the Wessex countryside." In the Edwardian period, thought became journalized, and greatness and serious purpose in writing were denigrated, except in survivals like H with *The Dynasts*. Galsworthy, as a sympathetic observer, has "none of Thomas Hardy's high stoicism in the face of destiny."

1735 Yendell, N. C. "On the Pessimism of Thomas Hardy," POETRY REVIEW, XXV (July–Aug 1934), 289–93.

H's era forces on one the idea that there is no immortality. In *The Dynasts*, however, is a hopeful note. [Most of the article consists of the breast-beating of a firm believer in immortality.]

1935

1736 Aldred, Cyril. "Introduction," *Far From the Madding Crowd*, ed by Cyril Aldred (Lond: Macmillan, 1935), pp. vii–xix. [The text follows the Wessex Edition except that the preface is abridged. Contains a short survey of H's fiction, a sensible commentary on the novel, and a brief account of H's life.]

1737 Blumenfeld, Ralph D. "The Father of *Tess*," R. D. B.'s PROCESSION (NY: Macmillan, 1935), pp. 187–90.

H's statement at a social gathering that the writer of fiction must adhere to the factual elements of life seemed inconsistent with the writer's own practice at the time, which was being criticized by the realists as too unreal. He was also, however, being criticized by the idealists for being too factual.

1738 Cecil, David. EARLY VICTORIAN NOVELISTS (Indianapolis: Bobbs-Merrill, 1935), pp. 42, 70, 161, 184–86, 236–38, 265, 270, 336.

H, in different ways, resembles four Victorian novelists. Like Dickens, he portrayed the society in which he grew up; like Emily Brontë, he was concerned with the questions of man, nature, and free will; like Mrs. Gaskell, rustic scenes were his forte. Finally, like Thackeray, H's style was always personal and idiosyncratic. [Slight.]

1739 Chew, Samuel C. "A Fragment of Hardy," NEW YORK HERALD TRIBUNE BOOKS, 16 June 1935, p. 9.

An Indiscretion in the Life of an Heiress, ed by C. J. Weber, is a pallid little story which will add nothing to H's fame. H regarded this lengthy excerpt from *The Poor Man and the Lady* as negligible, and the longer book, with its advanced opinions and satiric tone, was rejected by the publishers.

1740 Cockerell, Sir Sydney. "Early Hardy Stories," TIMES LITERARY SUPPLEMENT (Lond), 14 March 1935, p. 160.

H's executors did not approve the printing of a limited edition of *An Indiscretion in the Life of an Heiress*, announced in TIMES (Lond), 4 March 1935. Mrs. H agreed that it should not be reprinted and refused permission to the Rowfant Club. Mrs. H also arranged in 1929, however, for a reprint of "Old Mrs. Chundle" (to which Cockerell also objected). [H. Lawson Lewis, "Early Hardy Stories," ibid, 9 May 1935, p. 301, corrects typographical errors in Cockerell's letter.]

1741 Drew, Elizabeth. THE ENJOYMENT OF LITERATURE (NY: Norton, 1935), pp. 132, 167–71, 215.

The Dynasts is the only modern epic, a vast work of dignified but desolate blank verse which makes up in its sweep for what it lacks in subtlety.

1742 Elliott, Albert Pettigrew. FATALISM IN THE WORKS OF THOMAS HARDY (Phila: pvtly ptd, 1935); rptd (NY: Russell & Russell, 1966); University of Pennsylvania dissertation, 1932.

H was not an exacting philosopher, and his ideas about pessimism cannot be treated as philosophy, but as adjuncts to his art. His dark view of the universe came from his childhood sickness and especially his religious doubts; they permeate his works from his earliest writings. Man's misery H blamed on fate, and his anatomy of fate's workings showed this in five areas: Chance and Coincidence, Nature, Time, Woman, and Convention— many examples may be displayed for each area. H devised the Immanent Will as a hopeful wish for some happiness in the future. [Text and bibliography corrupted by errors, on which see Carl J. Weber's review, with a list of errors, in MODERN LANGUAGE NOTES, LI (Nov 1936), 481–82; the 1966 reprinting is apparently without correction of errors.]

1743 Heseltine, Guy. "Thomas Hardy and Religion," WESSEX: AN ANNUAL RECORD, III (May 1935), 85–89.

H realized "that Christianity did not hang on temporary details that expediency might modify, and that the practice of an early few . . . could not be binding on the [later] multitudes." H was sympathetic towards efforts to modify the Prayer Book Services by " 'dropping preternatural assumptions.' " He was very disappointed at the appearance of a new Prayer Book which did not fulfill these expectations.

1744 Katayama, Shun. "Shisō No Hattatsu" (The Development of Hardy's Thought), STUDIES IN ENGLISH LITERATURE (Tokyo), XV (April 1935), 194–207.

Periods in H's life suggest the development of H's original idea that *feeling* will evolve. 1881–1890 was H's darkest period; 1891–1899, a less dark period; and 1900–1928, the period of hope. In the first period H found no salvation for human agony as long as human beings were under the control of a God who is God in the world of unconsciousness, human consciousness having abnormally developed to the extent that human beings could no longer bear the human condition. The first period ended with the idea that *feeling* would evolve but with no progress towards its realization. Thus we find H's "literature of disaster," in which feeling is born in human beings without the awareness or permission of individual will. The second period, while full of melancholy, resentment, and indignation, offers some slight hope in the attitude of confronting the worst. That is, the human animal, for the first time, finds a way at least to look at the idea of *Will*, to discover that Will and human beings are part of one flesh. This realization leads to H's third period and the awakening of Will, as in *The Dynasts*. H extricated himself from the Agony of Will through the power of art, a philosophy partly agnostic and partly melioristically evolutionary. He came to feel that a portion of Will, a portion of the human being, had already become conscious through evolution. [In Japanese.]

1745 Ledoux, Louis V. "Robinson and Hardy," SATURDAY REVIEW OF LITERATURE, XII (11 May 1935), 11.

Robinson's "For a Book by Thomas Hardy" appeared in THE TORRENT AND THE NIGHT BEFORE and THE CHILDREN OF THE NIGHT but was not included in later volumes of collected poems. [A response to Carl Weber, "Two Sonnets," SATURDAY REVIEW OF LITERATURE, XI (27 April 1935), 648.]

1746 Lillard, Richard Gordon. "Irony in Hardy and Conrad," PUBLICATIONS OF THE MODERN LANGUAGE ASSOCIATION, L (March 1935), 316–22.

Irony is pervasive as a leitmotif. H, classically oriented, sees tragic collectivism on Earth, and his more objective, systematic, dramatic use of irony is in keeping with his thesis about life. Irony and character are best fused in *Far From the Madding Crowd, The Return of the Native, The Woodlanders, The Hand of Ethelberta, A Laodicean*—*Native* has ironies best justified; *The Dynasts'* ironies are unconvincing. There are three bases for irony: concealments by fate or other men, as in *Tess of the d'Urbervilles* and *The Mayor of Casterbridge*; coincidence and brute chance, integral to H, as in *Jude the Obscure*; and the appeal to the sense of justice in the reader, often accentuated with rigidly selective bits of realism.

1747 Linn, James Weber, and Houghton Wells Taylor. A FORE-WORD TO FICTION (NY: Appleton-Century, 1935), pp. 49–50, 122–36.

H had a strong feeling for background and scene as formative influences. Environment is not seen scientifically, but metaphysically as a powerful force in an indifferent or hostile universe. Accidents have universal significance. H adds poeticized setting to heighten the reality of character. In *Tess of the d'Urbervilles* H departs from omniscience in the dramatic scenes to mark all important steps in the plot and to provide emotion, always adding narrative comment. He changes narrative method twice to offstage drama in order to enhance Tess's eventual submission to Alec d'Urberville and the killing of Alec. Omniscience allows him considerable flexibility of method, including objective, psychological, and dramatic focus. The detailed development of Tess's seduction provides for clear understanding of Tess's character before the primary basis for tragedy—her love for Angel Clare—begins. [A fairly early recognition of H's subtle use of angle of narration.]

1748 Marrot, H. V. THE LIFE AND LETTERS OF JOHN GALS-WORTHY (Lond: Heinemann, 1935; NY: Scribner's, 1936), pp. 217, 264, 416, 419, 438, 458, 459, 462, 465, 469, 480, 481, 494, 507, 510, 549, 550, 578, 699.

Letter of 24 March 1916: H will do a rare thing if he can make adequate dramatic versions of his novels. *The Dynasts* should be read straight through; it is "a very fine affair." Letter of 27 March 1916: *Dynasts* is stupendous. Letter of 28 Sept 1915: H is a "nice, alert old fellow." [Gives 13 letters from H and ten other passages by H, indexed p. 813.]

1749 Morley, Christopher. "An Indiscretion," SATURDAY REVIEW OF LITERATURE, XI (16 March 1935), 551.

In *An Indiscretion in the Life of an Heiress*, ed by Carl J. Weber (1935), "the ironical title, and an occasional phrase of brooding power, show the genuine gristle of Hardy; but mostly it has the savor of tripe." H's interest is in satirizing a social fetich not in writing a credible story. The reader must accept H's assumptions, such as the assumed—and probably true at that time—social gulf between squire and townspeople. The novel is really an indiscretion in the life of a novelist.

1750 Oman, John. "The Book of Proverbs," RELIGION IN LIFE, IV (Summer 1935), 336.

"Had the writer of Proverbs had the privilege of reading Hardy's *Tess* . . . he would, I think, have said that she lacked the wisdom to discern the depths of right action and the highest quality of true award. . . . The wise are the morally discerning, and there are disasters they do avoid. As a protest against harsh external human judgment Hardy is right and of the quality of Job."

1751 Osgood, Charles G. THE VOICE OF ENGLAND: A HISTORY OF ENGLISH LITERATURE (NY: Harper, 1935), pp. 555–59.

In his tragedies, H "seems resolved to overweight the tragic weakness of his characters against their virtues." His "impression" was that life's accidents, human character and will "are shaped and propelled by an inscrutable and aimless Destiny or Super-Will." But H was partial when it came to recording this impression: the accidents and coincidences of his fiction are "almost without exception . . . unlucky." As poet, H is at his best "when he touches 'Wessex.' " Although *The Dynasts* often is compared with PARADISE LOST, FAUST, and Aeschylus's PROMETHEUS, its matter was "too new to have undergone the age-long ripening and maturing process, the human handling" characteristic of the great classics. Too, Milton and Aeschylus had an advantage denied H: "grand ideas current in their time with which to work —the positive convictions of many agreeing minds."

1752 Payne, L. W. "Thomas Hardy's Lost Novel is Traced," DALLAS MORNING NEWS, 24 March 1935, p. 232.

[Account of the vicissitudes of *The Poor Man and the Lady* and *An Indiscretion in the Life of an Heiress*, ed by Carl J. Weber (1935).]

1753 Powys, Llewelyn. DORSET ESSAYS (Lond: Lane, 1935), pp. 1, 72–74, 183–87; partly rptd in EARTH MEMORIES (NY: Norton, 1938), pp. 209–11.

[Musings on the relationship between H's work and Dorsetshire, and on the appropriateness of H's burial place in Stinsford churchyard. Useless.]

1754 Purdy, R. L. "The Thomas Hardy Collection," YALE UNIVERSITY LIBRARY GAZETTE, X (July 1935), 8–9.

[Description of the collection—consisiting primarily of first editions—given Yale by Henry C. Taylor. The collection includes a number of autographed letters and several sheets of proof.]

1755 Schloesser, Anselm. DIE ENGLISCHE LITERATUR IN DEUTSCHLAND VON 1895 BIS 1934 (English Literature in Germany from 1895 to 1934) (Jena: Frommannschen Bachhandlung Walter Biedermann, 1935), pp. 121–22, 142, 143.

[Examines reasons for H's limited reception in Germany and suggests that perhaps if H's less pessimistic works had been the first to be presented in Germany, the Germans might have recognized H's artistic ability and been less harsh in criticizing his philosophy.] [In German.]

1756 Sperry, Willard L. WORDSWORTH'S ANTI-CLIMAX (Cambridge: Harvard UP, 1935), pp. 175–76.
The first eight books of THE PRELUDE are like the opening of *The Return of the Native*.

1757 Spurgeon, Caroline F. E. SHAKESPEARE'S IMAGERY AND WHAT IT TELLS US (Cambridge: Cambridge UP, 1935); rptd (Boston: Beacon Paperback, 1958), p. 384.
[Mentions, in passing, H's "To Shakespeare after 300 Years."]

1758 Wagenknecht, Edward. MARK TWAIN: THE MAN AND HIS WORK (New Haven: Yale UP, 1935), pp. 42, 190–91.
Concerning religion, H and Twain were poles apart. Both writers "found it impossible to accept the religious beliefs of [their] contemporaries," but H "has always a fine reverence for belief," a result of "his background, his early associations, his training in ecclesiastical architecture." In H "there is nothing of the iconoclast." Twain, on the other hand, "knows no Church."

1759 Waugh, Arthur. ONE MAN'S ROAD (Lond: Chapman & Hall, 1935), pp. 186–89.
Kipling attacked Walter Besant, William Black, and H in a poem entitled "The Rhyme of the Three Captains." H used to visit Gosse; he was "punctiliously considerate, never by word or look suggesting any consciousness of his own distinction." [Literary gossip.]

1760 Weber, Carl J. "Care and Carelessness in Hardy," MODERN LANGUAGE NOTES, L (Jan 1935), 41–43.
Several instances in the manuscripts of *Tess of the d'Urbervilles* and *Far From the Madding Crowd* attest to H's concern for factually accurate detail in his writing.

1761 Weber, Carl J. (ed). COLBY NOTES ON "FAR FROM THE MADDING CROWD," BY MEMBERS OF THE CLASS IN "ENGLISH 30" AT COLBY COLLEGE. (Waterville, Maine: Colby College Department of English, 1935).
[Some useful and interesting notes explaining obscure references, words, ideas in the novel.]

1762 Weber, Carl J. "E. A. Robinson and Hardy," NATION (NY), CXL (1 May 1935), 508.

[Letter asking readers for any insights or information on a poem by Edwin Arlington Robinson, "For a Book by Thomas Hardy." The poem is reprinted. Also see Louis V. Ledoux, "Robinson and Hardy," SATURDAY REVIEW OF LITERATURE, XII (11 May 1935), 11.]

1763 Weber, Carl J. "Hardy's First Novel," NEW YORK HERALD TRIBUNE BOOKS, 14 July 1935, p. 15.

Mr. Chew makes three incorrect statements in his review. First, Weber's edition of H's first novel is not in competition with Mrs. H's edition, which is private only. Second, H did not forget the novel after Meredith refused it; a reference in a letter dated 8 June 1869 indicates that he had sent it elsewhere. Third, H did not forget the book but talked to friends about it and referred, in 1921, to its publication in final form. [See Samuel Chew's "A Fragment of Hardy," NEW YORK HERALD TRIBUNE BOOKS, 16 June 1935, p. 9.]

1764 Weber, Carl J. "Hardy's Lost Novel," AN INDISCRETION IN THE LIFE OF AN HEIRESS, ed with introduction and notes by Carl J. Weber (Baltimore: Johns Hopkins P, 1935), pp. 1–20; rptd (NY: Russell & Russell, 1965), pp. 1–20.

[Reviews the known history of *The Poor Man and the Lady* as revealed by Edmund Gosse, "Thomas Hardy's Lost Novel," TIMES (Lond), 22 Jan 1928; Vere H. Collins, TALKS WITH THOMAS HARDY AT MAX GATE (1928); Florence Emily Hardy, THE EARLY LIFE OF THOMAS HARDY (1928); Charles L. Graves, THE LIFE AND LETTERS OF ALEXANDER MACMILLAN (1910); passages in Mrs. H's "biography" citing George Meredith and John Morley.] The "lost" novel was dismembered and portions used in *Desperate Remedies, Under the Greenwood Tree*, and in the story "An Indiscretion in the Life of an Heiress." [For various printings of this story in periodicals and separately, see Richard L. Purdy, THOMAS HARDY: A BIBLIOGRAPHICAL STUDY (1954), pp. 274–76; W. R. Rutland, THOMAS HARDY: A STUDY OF HIS WRITINGS AND THEIR BACKGROUND (1938), pp. 111–33, also provides a detailed discussion of the "lost" novel. Weber reprints his text from the NEW QUARTERLY MAGAZINE printing.]

1765 Weber, Carl J. "In Thomas Hardy's Handwriting: A Record of Sixty-two Years in the Colby Collection of Hardy Manuscripts," COLBY MERCURY, VI (Feb 1935), 18–19.

[Lists twenty-six items, some in manuscript.]

1766 Weber, Carl J. (ed). "Notes and Comments," *Tess of the d'Urbervilles* (NY: Harper, [1935]), pp. 509–46.

[Useful explanations and comments on H's text.]

1767 [Weber, Carl J.]. "Recent Additions to the Colby Hardy Collection," COLBY MERCURY, VI (May 1935), 28–36.

Records the donation of "almost the entire correspondence that passed from Hardy to his friend Sir Edmund Gosse" and the Lemperly donation of "Hardy criticisms, reviews, press notices, etc., etc."

1768 Weber, Carl J. "Thomas Hardy's 'Song in *The Woodlanders*,' " ENGLISH LITERARY HISTORY, II (Nov 1935), 242–45. J. Middleton Murry referred to "the song in *The Woodlanders*" in a discussion of H, but there are really *three* poems in that novel—and none is by H. Nor does this mysterious song appear in any edition or magazine version of the novel. Murry was confused by a printing error in a volume of H's verse. After the publication of the novel, H wrote a poem reflecting on a certain passage in *Woodlanders*. He named the poem "In a Wood," subtitling it "Vide *The Woodlanders*," to indicate the relationship. In the volume *Selected Poems of Thomas Hardy*, "Vide" was misread and misprinted "From"; the error was undetected and thus perpetuated in *The Collected Poems of Thomas Hardy*.

1769 Weber, Carl J. "Two Sonnets," SATURDAY REVIEW OF LITERATURE, XI (27 April 1935), 648. Two poems by E. A. Robinson bear on H. What happened to Robinson's "For a Book by Thomas Hardy" from CRITIC (NY), XXVII (23 Nov 1895), 348? Is "A Christmas Sonnet: For One in Doubt" (1928) a rejection of H's pessimism? Is it foolish to recall that both poets wrote about Tristram? [The first question is answered by Louis Ledoux, "Robinson and Hardy," SATURDAY REVIEW OF LITERATURE, XII (11 May 1935), 11.]

1770 Zimmerman, Isabella C. "A Study of Thomas Hardy's Theory of Love." Unpublished dissertation, University of Southern California, 1935. [Listed in Lawrence F. McNamee, DISSERTATIONS IN ENGLISH AND AMERICAN LITERATURE (NY and Lond: Bowker, 1968).]

1936

1771 Abercrombie, Lascelles. "Thomas Hardy's *The Dynasts*," PROCEEDINGS OF THE ROYAL INSTITUTION OF GREAT BRITAIN, XXIX, Part III (1936), 444–62. *The Dynasts* is "Hardy's greatest single achievement" and, except for THE TESTAMENT OF BEAUTY, "the greatest single achievement in recent English literature." It is as a great epic poem that *Dynasts* must be judged: it has "grandeur in scope," "reality of matter," and "importance of significance." It surpasses other Victorian epics like IDYLLS OF THE KING and THE RING

AND THE BOOK by its reality, by "the poet's sense that he was dealing with real matters [which] enters into the whole spirit of the poem." In the company of the great epics, however, *Dynasts'* "capital defect" is evident— "Hardy is not one of the great artists in language." The poem's greatness lies "in its imagination; not in the craftsmanship by which his imagination is wrought into language." The form H evolved for *Dynasts* enabled him to carry the great inspiration which had produced the Wessex novels on into a further stage of development. In this vast chronicle play H could at last state "his idea of life in a perfectly explicit and undisguised manner," using the Phantom Intelligences. But it is a play without a hero: "all men are equally the instruments of destiny." The philosophy of the play is "the purest determinism."

1772 Atkins, Elizabeth. EDNA ST. VINCENT MILLAY AND HER TIMES (Chicago: University of Chicago P, 1936), pp. 11, 84, 85, 253.

H's novels show the tone of melancholy amusement of a late-Elizabethan writer, but the tone is vitiated by his obtrusive philosophical comments. His plots seem forced and contrived. On the other hand, his poetry successfully combines thought and expression, showing him as a "true tragic humorist."

1773 Bates, H. E. "Joseph Conrad and Thomas Hardy," THE ENGLISH NOVELISTS: A SURVEY OF THE NOVEL BY TWENTY CONTEMPORARY NOVELISTS, ed by Derek Verschoyle (Lond: Chatto & Windus, 1936), pp. 229–44.

H's heavy prose and contrived causality make him, as George Moore said, "a second-class writer." H was, however, a master of atmosphere. Tess is H's one character who transcends the plot and "lives on beyond her doom and the pages of the book." H demands that we judge Tess on moral standards, but since morality is relative and ever-changing, he is now dated. Conrad, in his "gorgeous verbosity," emotional development, pictorial style, cosmopolitan attitudes, and disregard for plot is the far better writer. [Dated and factually unreliable, but often perceptive.]

1774 Beach, Joseph W. THE CONCEPT OF NATURE IN NINE-TEENTH-CENTURY ENGLISH POETRY (NY: Macmillan, 1936), pp. 503–21.

H "heralds the disappearance from English poetry of nature." H is opposed to Wordsworth in his naturalism and optimism. H's somber philosophy is revealed in the prevailing somberness of nature in his poetry and in his novels. Distress is caused in H's novels when natural impulses are balked by artificial codes of conduct. Nature herself in H is full of cruelty, for example, the fate of the Durbeyfield children in *Tess of the d'Urbervilles* and Sue's misery in *Jude the Obscure*. The flaw in the terrestial scheme is that

" 'What was good for God's birds was bad for God's gardener,' " as in *Jude* and *The Return of the Native*. In *The Mayor of Casterbridge*, H is more a scientific determinist. In *Tess* and in *The Woodlanders*, fate is seen as a series of unavoidable coincidences. In H's poems there is a hostility of circumstance to men's desires and aspirations. The final term chosen by H for designating the unity and directing power of the universe is (from Schopenhauer) The Immanent Will. The Darwinian theory of evolution underlies all of H's general speculation. In *Poems of the Past and the Present* the evolution of the mind is by sheer blunder—Mother Nature is blind and dumb.

1775 Behr, Amelie Von. DER TYPEN-KONFLIKT IN THOMAS HARDYS ROMANEN (The Type-Conflict in Thomas Hardy's Novels) (Marburg: Hermann Bauer, 1936); University of Marburg dissertation.

By recognizing the differences between such novels as *Desperate Remedies*, *The Return of the Native*, and *Jude the Obscure*, the novels can be classified on the basis of the protagonists' relationship to life. Those works which H referred to as "novels of ingenuity" or "romances and phantasies" can be labeled *Weltflucht* novels. The Wessex novels or "novels of character and environment" can be subdivided into the *Weltbild* category, which includes *Far From the Madding Crowd*, *Native*, *The Mayor of Casterbridge*, and *The Woodlanders*. *Tess of the d'Urbervilles* and *Jude*, however, are *Weltklage* novels. The reader can best accept H's philosophy in the *Weltbild* works. Here, through "loving kindness," man, in his relationship with his fellowman, is able to solve his problem. The *Weltflucht* novels present unbelievable characters, and the *Weltklage* novels are distorted by the author's lack of pathos. Because of these three distinct world views, H's basic themes, e.g. the conflict of the urban and rural type, are manifested in distinct ways. [In German.]

1776 Bliemal, Bernhard. VERKETTUNG VON DICHTER UND WERK BEI THOMAS HARDY (The Linking of Poet and Work: Thomas Hardy) (Ohlau in Schleswig: Eschenhagen, 1936); University of Breslau dissertation.

The statement that "there is more autobiography in a hundred lines of Mr. Hardy's poetry than in all the novels" is incorrect. [Chapter 3 analyzes the function of time in the Wessex novels—the passage of days and years, the relation of the sun, moon, plants, and animals to time.] [In German.]

1777 Blyton, W. J. "A Sojourn Among Giants," CORNHILL, CLIII (Feb 1936), 238–47.

H's is a "substantial world," and although his novels are often limp in style, taste, and technique, his place in literature is likely to grow more and more secure.

1778 Brickell, Herschel. "How Thomas Hardy Was Accused of Plagiarism," New York Post, 24 June 1936, p. 15.

H was once accused of plagiarism in connection with a passage in *The Trumpet-Major* which closely resembled a scene in Longstreet's Georgia Scenes. "Hardy finally admitted that he had taken some of his material from Gifford's History of the War With Napoleon."

1779 Brown, David. "Some Rejected Poems of Edwin Arlington Robinson," American Literature, VII (Jan 1936), 395–414, espec 409–10.

"For a Book by Thomas Hardy" is "an acceptance of the 'modern English novel' " in the same spirit as the poet's defense of Zola. Although it is a rather good poem, Robinson rejected it from the 1921 edition, perhaps because "he had changed his opinion of Hardy."

1780 Buck, Philo M., Jr. "The Immanent Will and Its Design," The World's Great Age (NY: Macmillan, 1936), pp. 331–56.

H's works make a fitting close for the nineteenth-century. Unlike Ibsen and his contemporaries, H is not interested in society but rather "man's eternal debt to the universe and man's debt to his neighbor." His vision sees the world as "a welter of futile doing," of man "as an ironic jest, in a universe unconscious of the jest." H's double interest in human nature and "cosmic background" are best illustrated in *The Dynasts*. [Generally conventional reading of H's ideas; diffuse but literate.]

1781 Canby, Henry Seidel. Seven Years' Harvest: Notes on Contemporary Literature (NY: Farrar & Rinehart, 1936), pp. 35, 36, 114, 202, 215.

[Alludes to H's use of rural characters, and his skill in "projecting" personalities. Trivial.]

1782 Cecil, David. "Hardy's Wessex," Listener, XVI (16 Sept 1936), 537–39.

Of prime importance in H's novels is "the relation between man and the impersonal forces of chance and nature." Hence natural surroundings play an unusually important role. The H country has a special charm "which comes from the unique way it combines man and nature": the region is sparsely populated; one is conscious of elemental nature; evidences of past generations are abundant.

1783 Chase, Mary Ellen. A Goodly Fellowship (NY: Macmillan, 1936).

[Miss Chase, who wrote her doctoral dissertation on H, once wrote to the novelist suggesting that his view of the world was too dark.]

1784 Chase, Mary Ellen. THIS ENGLAND (NY: Macmillan, 1936). [Gives a word-picture of H's "Wessex" in Chapter 5 of this book of essays on England. Slight.]

1785 Chesterton, G. K. THE AUTOBIOGRAPHY OF G. K. CHESTERTON (NY: Sheed & Ward, 1936), pp. 173, 174, 285–87, 291. H lacked one essential element of the Greek tragedians who influenced him: hubris. [Chesterton denies that his famous phrase about H, the "village atheist brooding over the village idiot," was meant to impugn the author, whom Chesterton says he respected for H's modesty and sincere atheism.]

1786 Ehrsam, Theodore G., Robert H. Deily, and Robert M. Smith (comps). BIBLIOGRAPHIES OF TWELVE VICTORIAN AUTHORS (NY: Wilson, 1936), pp. 91–125. [Chronological outline of publications; alphabetical lists of bibliographical material and of biographical and critical works. Unfortunately marred by many errors.]

1787 F., P. "Rural Authors—39: Thomas Hardy," COUNTRYMAN, XXIV (July 1936), 525–28. H's work is characterized by an intimacy with nature and an inability to understand those who are apart from the soil. [Includes a letter from Hardy to Masefield on 18 Nov 1924.]

1788 Finzi, Gerald. EARTH AND AIR AND RAIN, MUSICAL SETTING FOR TEN MORE HARDY POEMS (Lond: Boosey & Hawkes, 1936). [Self-explanatory.]

1789 Ford, Ford Madox. "Mr. Ford Replies," AMERICAN MERCURY, XXXIX (Nov 1936), xx, xxii. [Defends most of the points to which C. J. Weber objected in a letter, "Fact vs. Fiction," ibid, xiv, xx.]

1790 Ford, Ford Madox. "Thomas Hardy," AMERICAN MERCURY, XXXVIII (Aug 1936), 438–48. [Loose, sketchy reminiscences of H—more horn-blowing for Ford than recollection of H.]

1791 Freeman, John. JOHN FREEMAN'S LETTERS, ed by Gertrude Freeman and Sir John Squire (Lond: Macmillan, 1936), pp. 173, 263. [A poem by Freeman in a letter to Mrs. H of Sept 1927 (?).]

1792 Haines, Helen E. "Elective Affinities for Librarians," LIBRARY JOURNAL (NY), LXI (July 1936), 527–28.

The Dynasts remains comparatively unknown to American readers. The epic has far greater potency today than when it appeared. It could be compared with Benet's epic JOHN BROWN'S BODY, for it illuminates, as well as interprets, history.

1793 Hänsch, Marie-Luise. DIE SPRACHKUNSTLERISCHE GESTALTUNG BEI THOMAS HARDY: STILSTUDIEN ZU "TESS OF THE D'URBERVILLES" (Rhetorical Structure in Thomas Hardy: Stylistic Studies of *Tess of the d'Urbervilles*) (Marburg: G. Braun, 1936); University of Marburg dissertation; in NEUEREN SPRACHEN, Beiheft No. 31 (1936).

H's style was influenced by that characteristic of the earlier nineteenth century, as evidenced by his rhetorical asides to the reader. His predilection for stilted expression also goes against the modern tendency towards simplicity. Modern English prose favors clarity (its highest principle is concrete images): therefore, modern stylists make little use of the more rational antitheses. But H uses antitheses frequently. H's style, characterized by impressionistic and descriptive elements, is a mirror of the man; H was both very impressionable and equipped with a strong reflective capacity. The characteristic note of his style, then, may be called "bound-impressionism"; the limiting or qualifying of sense-impressions by his reflective remarks. In his style and philosophy H is un-English: his fondness for long sentences and learned words and his pessimistic-fatalistic philosophy ("the basic English attitude toward life is optimistic and more practical") set him apart from the English tradition. [In German.]

1794 Henderson, Philip. THE NOVEL TODAY: STUDIES IN CONTEMPORARY ATTITUDES (Lond: Lane, 1936), pp. 32–34.
[Discusses inconclusively T. S. Eliot's harsh treatment of H in AFTER STRANGE GODS (1934).]

1795 Hone, Joseph. THE LIFE OF GEORGE MOORE (Lond: Gollancz, 1936), pp. 194–95, 376, 385, 408.
Moore was gratified by SPECTATOR's placing ESTHER WATERS above H's *Tess of the d'Urbervilles*. Moore read *Tess* while writing ESTHER, and the scene in which Angel carries Tess over the plain "increased the distaste for [H] which he had shown in the CONFESSIONS." Moore disliked H's " 'machine-made plots' " and continued his attack on the Wessex Novels in CONVERSATIONS IN EBURY STREET. [See Moore, "George Moore and John Freeman," DIAL (NY), LXXV (Oct 1923), 341–62.]

1796 Kunitz, Stanley J., and Howard Haycraft (eds). BRITISH AUTHORS OF THE NINETEENTH CENTURY (NY: H. W. Wilson, 1936), pp. 36–37, 275–78.
[The entry on William Barnes quotes from H's obituary notice in ATHENAEUM: the entry on H is a full, balanced account of H's life and works.]

1797 Lawrence, D. H. "Study of Thomas Hardy," PHOENIX: THE POSTHUMOUS PAPERS OF D. H. LAWRENCE, ed by Edward D. McDonald (Lond: Heinemann, 1936); rptd (1961); and (NY: Viking P, 1936), pp. 398–516; Chap 3 pub as "Six Novels of Thomas Hardy and the Real Tragedy," BOOK COLLECTOR'S QUARTERLY, V (Jan–March 1932), 44–61; and with slight variations in JOHN O'LONDON'S WEEKLY, XXVI (12 and 19 March 1932); part of Chap 5 rptd as "Hardy's 'Predilection d'Artiste,' " in HARDY: A COLLECTION OF CRITICAL ESSAYS, ed by Albert J. Guérard (Englewood Cliffs, NJ: Prentice-Hall, 1963), pp. 46–51; Chap 9 is the basis for "Sue Bridehead," in HARDY: A COLLECTION of CRITICAL ESSAYS, ed by Albert J. Guérard (Englewood Cliffs, NJ: Prentice-Hall, 1963), pp. 71–76.

Poppies and phoenixes represent the eternal dichotomy between man's common-sense self-preservation and imagination as beauty, excess. The final aim of all living beings is full achievement of self. All of H's heroes and heroines are struggling for being; "taking a wild flight into flower," they explode out of the conventional. H's tragedy comes from the clash of this explosion with the code of self-preservation, of convention, in themselves more than society. Each of the novels shows the development of this theme [brief sketches from *Desperate Remedies* to *The Return of the Native*, the first important tragic novel]. Eustacia wants self-realization; Clym escapes from it; both are sidetracked. Only the conformists remain. The real stuff of tragedy is the Heath—the instinctive life, the "deep black source." Clym's error is in denying this life within himself. Egdon brought it to him in Eustacia (who was life), but he was all on the surface, did not understand that she was the "powerful eternal origin." There is a constant revelation in H of human lives set against primal natural background: the "vast morality of life itself," which is opposed to man's little morality. H's characters, like Tolstoy's, are punished by a little mechanical system rather than by a great fate as in Shakespeare or Sophocles. The tragedies of Eustacia, Tess, Sue, and Jude are that they did not abide by the greater morality and take what they wanted. There is always excess, brimming-over. Man was made for this, not for work which is the activity of the machine —safe, predictable, imprisoning when he would be free. One can see H's characters as degrees of individuation. H has the *predilection d'artiste* for aristocrats and moral antagonism to them because they can be individual. But they must die, both because of H's bourgeois taint and their own "germ of death." H's condemnation goes against himself, thus he must give his individualist a weakness. Troy, Clym, Tess, Jude have a "weak life-flow" and cannot break away; unlike Oedipus or Macbeth, they are destroyed by conformity rather than passion. Interaction of male and female is as an axle (male) turning upon a hub (female) and is begetter of *all* life, not just physical. All men seek the female principle, providing stability. "Life consists in the dual form of the Will-to-Motion and the Will-to-Inertia," and the religious effort of Man is to balance them. All artists fascinated by antinomy between Law and Love, Flesh and Spirit. H believes in Law but destroys the primeval Law of Female Principle. Women he approves are not Female but the passive echo of Male: Tess, for example, respects right of others to be, although they do not respect hers. While Alec, recognizing the female in himself, betrays her femaleness, Angel is just the opposite, i.e., averse to the female in himself. In turn, both make Tess despise the deep Female in herself. Tess is aristocratic, and aristocratic men and women are "exceedingly personal," regarding their own desires. Jude is "Tess turned roundabout," containing two principles, while Arabella and Sue are like Alec and Angel. Arabella is a kind of aristocrat in her arrogance, taking but not giving. Two kinds of love are represented—that which uses woman, and that which sees her as Unknown, through which man discovers self. The first combines pride with fear of the Female—makes woman jaded, devitalizes a race; the second vitalizes, gives man a sense of the All, the Inexhaustible Embrace. Arabella represents the female side of the first attitude but brings out the male in Jude, makes him stronger. Sue's will is male: she identifies with the male principle, suppressing the Female, wanting to live only in the mind. Jude wants more than sexual release from her; he wants to penetrate into the Unknown. His exhaustion is from consciousness, hers is from body. Man must reconcile Law and Love. [Many references to *Far From the Madding Crowd, Native, Jude the Obscure, Tess of the d'Urbervilles.*]

1798 Reynolds, Ernest. EARLY VICTORIAN DRAMA (1830–1870) (Cambridge, England: W. Heffer, 1936); rptd (NY: Benjamin Blom, 1965), p. 13.

"After 1870 there was a revival in drama. But the novel had come to stay as the main channel of literary expression. Hardy was one of the great tragic writers in the world's literature, yet he chose the novel form, and not the drama. . . . We prefer to weep over *Tess* in the seclusion of our armchairs."

1799 Rideout, John G. "Hardy's Last Words on *The Dynasts,*" COLBY MERCURY, VI (June 1936), 85–87.

[First publication in English of H's preface for a French translation, with a note from a French editor. H's preface stresses the drama's applicability to France and Napoleon.]

1800 Schönfeld, Herbert. "Kurze Anzeigen" (Short Notices), LITERATUR, XXXVIII (1936), 386.

A Group of Noble Dames is a well-modulated book which contains a touch of sarcasm and yet refrains from cynicism. It is a moral work but not censorious, a little boring but not tiring because of its subtleties. The translation is ineffective. [In German.]

1801 Schumacher, Margot. BIOLOGISCHE PROBLEME IN THOMAS HARDYS WERK (Biological Problems in Thomas Hardy's Work) (Munich: R. Mayr, 1936); University of Bonn dissertation.
[Over one hundred biological terms are defined, qualified, and applied to H's novels. Themes considered are: (1) man and nature, (2) reflective individual reactions—primarily of a physical nature, (3) metaphysical moods of behavior for the entire organism, (4) the individual man as an entity, and (5) the meaning of life.] [In German.]

1802 Targ, William, and Harry F. Marks. TEN THOUSAND RARE BOOKS AND THEIR PRICES (NY: Harry F. Marks, 1936).
[Lists twenty-two vols or sets of works by H that sold between 1927 and 1936 for more than $10 per book.]

1803 Venn, Florence. "More Trumpeting," COLOPHON, ns II (Oct 1936), 133.
[A correction of Carl J. Weber's assertion in "A Connecticut Yankee in King Alfred's Country," ibid, I (April 1936), 525–35, that H got the tale of Captain Clodpole's drill from C. H. Gifford, who got it from O. H. Prince through A. B. Longstreet. H admittedly took the story from Gifford, but Gifford derived it directly from John Lambert's TRAVELS THROUGH CANADA AND THE UNITED STATES, which first appeared in 1810.]

1804 Weber, Carl J. "A Connecticut Yankee in King Alfred's Country," COLOPHON, ns I (April 1936), 525–35.
The similarity between H's militia drill in *The Trumpet-Major* and that in a chapter in A. B. Longstreet's GEORGIA SCENES is traceable to an anonymously published satire by Oliver Prince. H's use of the scene, which he took from Gifford's HISTORY OF THE WARS OCCASIONED BY THE FRENCH REVOLUTION (1817), brought on an accusation of plagiarism which ultimately caused him to add a note explaining the origin of the scene. [For further notes on the origin of this scene see Carl Weber's "A Ghost from a Barber Shop," NEW COLOPHON, ns I (April 1948), 185–89.]

1805 Weber, Carl J. " 'The Cottage Lights of Wessex,' " COLBY MERCURY, VI (Feb 1936), 64–67.
[Traces the origins of H's impact on the life of Edwin Arlington Robinson.]

1806 Weber, Carl J. "Fact vs. Fiction," AMERICAN MERCURY, XXXIX (Nov 1936), xiv, xx.
[Points out numerous "errors" in F. M. Ford's "Thomas Hardy," ibid, XXXVIII (Aug 1936), 438–48.]

1807 Weber, Carl J. HARDY AT COLBY: A CHECK-LIST OF THE WRITINGS BY AND ABOUT THOMAS HARDY NOW IN THE LIBRARY

of Colby College (Waterville, Maine: Colby College Library, 1936).
[This bibliography lists prose writings, published verse, letters by H, items in H's handwriting, and books and articles about H.]

1808 Weber, Carl J. "Last Notes on Hardy's First Novel," Colby Mercury, VI (June 1936), 89–93.
[New annotations for *An Indiscretion in the Life of an Heiress* confirming it as an adaptation of *The Poor Man and the Lady*. Homeric echoes in *Tess of the d'Urbervilles* are elaborated.]

1809 Weber, Carl J. "Lowell's 'Dead Rat in the Wall,' " New England Quarterly, IX (Sept 1936), 468–72.
According to Edmund Gosse in a letter to W. D. Howells, H was upset over an interview (1886) in which J. R. Lowell supposedly criticized H's person and style of writing. The identity of the interviewer had been lost with time, though Lowell described his infidelity "like a dead rat in the wall, —an awful stink and no cure." Lowell had talked confidentially with Julian Hawthorne in October 1886, and Hawthorne published the substance of the conversation as an interview in the New York World under the title, "Lowell in A Chatty Mood." However, Lowell was credited with only two statements about H: that he had tried to read *Two on a Tower* "but couldn't get on with it" and that afterwards he had met H—who was "small and unassuming in appearance" and "did not look like the genius of tradition."

1810 Webster, Harvey C. "The Development of Thomas Hardy's Philosophic Thinking, 1840–1895." Unpublished dissertation, University of Michigan, 1936.
[Listed in Lawrence F. McNamee, Dissertations in English and American Literature (NY and Lond: Bowker, 1968).]

1811 Weygandt, Cornelius. The Time of Tennyson (NY: Appleton-Century, 1936), passim.
H helped widen the scope of poetry. H's "A Trampwoman's Tragedy" is indebted to Wordsworth's concern for the humble. H was "fellowly" compared to Tennyson. H is among the major poets on the basis of new notes, beauty of a new kind, a unique vision of life, wide scope of subject, and universality of appeal. Browning's The Ring and The Book is comparable to H's *The Dynasts* in awing by its "stupendousness." Browning's dramatic monologues are comparable to H's in expressing only the speaker's sentiments, not the author's. But Browning is less memorable than H because of belabored philosophical analysis. Arnold's pessimism is weary, not "leavened with irony," as in H. Arnold's sad melancholy falls short of the effect of H's "numbing irony." William Barnes's idyllic poems in dialect

are contrasted with H's range from "broad comedy to desolating tragedy," written with only the suggestion of dialect. Barnes's "Woak Hill" is most like H. H in "The Fire at Tranter Sweatley's" has written a kindred study to T. E. Brown's provincial Manx versified novels of peasant life. Brown's Manx girls are as attractive as H's Wessex girls, but "better fated." If one praises a poet against his "predecessors of like kind, . . . one is less likely to err. . . . Looking so at Yeats and Hardy . . . A. E. Housman and Ralph Hodgson, one cannot write down as of less than first moment the time in which they wrote."

1812 Wright, Whitney. "An Index to Hardy's Poems," COLBY MERCURY, VI (June 1936), 94–100.
[An alphabetical index to *Collected Poems* and *Winter Words*.]

1813 Young, G. M. VICTORIAN ENGLAND: PORTRAIT OF AN AGE (Lond: Oxford UP, 1936), pp. 61, 166, 202, 204, 206, 208, 210, 212.
[Reference to Sue Bridehead as a Queen's scholar at Salisbury Training College. "Hardy and Rider Haggard, observers of unquestionable competence, agreed that village tradition came to an end about 1865." Chronological Table: Floruit, 1875, H. Dates of H's major works given.]

1937

1814 Abercrombie, Lascelles. "Thomas Hardy," DICTIONARY OF NATIONAL BIOGRAPHY: 1922–1930, ed by J. R. H. Weaver (Lond: Oxford UP, 1937), pp. 392–97.
The Dynasts is by far H's "greatest single achievement, and the fullest and most complete expression of his genius." [Concise biography, bibliography, and critical judgments. Expansion of BRITANNICA, 14th ed, article, with some repetition.]

1815 Adams, Randolph G. "Still Trumpeting," COLOPHON, ns II (Winter 1937), 284.
The ultimate origin of the drill scene in *The Trumpet-Major* is in Lambert's TRAVELS, published in Charleston, S. C. in 1810, which, according to a statement found only in the rare first edition of this work, appropriated the scene from a local periodical.

1816 Asquith, Herbert. MOMENTS OF MEMORY (Lond: Hutchinson, 1937), pp. 172–73.

H was impressed by T. E. Lawrence, especially his description of his treatment by the Turks. In answer to whether any living author would be known in five hundred years, H replied, " 'Someone whose name we have never heard.' " H was once considered as a potential peer; H had a low opinion of politicians.

1817 Blanche, Jacques-Emile. PORTRAITS OF A LIFETIME: THE LATE VICTORIAN ERA, THE EDWARDIAN PAGEANT: 1870–1914, trans and ed by Walter Clement (Lond: J. M. Dent, 1937), pp. 145, 164, 177–82, 189.

According to George Moore, H created "sentimental postcards." Emma Hardy was not H's "evil genius," as T. P. O'Connor said, but H was "manifestly Jude." H is unaffected, non-literary.

1818 Blyton, W. J. ENGLISH CAVALCADE (Lond: Murray, 1937), pp. 1, 27, 40, 62, 140–43, 307.

[The usual "literary Pilgrim" approach to a description of H country.]

1819 Brooks, Philip. "Notes on Rare Books," NEW YORK TIMES BOOK REVIEW, 19 Dec 1937, p. 19.

Sotheby's sale of the library of Sir James M. Barrie included MSS of H's "Before Marching and After," and two books belonging to H which Mrs. H gave to Barrie: a volume of Shelley which H carried around and annotated in early days as an architect and THE BOY'S OWN BOOK: A COMPLETE ENCYCLOPEDIA OF ALL THE DIVERSIONS . . . OF BOYHOOD & YOUTH. Barrie's note on the latter tells of H's saving pennies at age twelve to buy it.

1820 Burke, A. E. "Hardy and Hudson," TIMES LITERARY SUPPLEMENT (Lond), 3 July 1937, p. 496.

There is a similarity between W. H. Hudson's observation of a thrush who enjoys gloomy weather in NATURE IN DOWNLAND, printed in 1900, the same year H's "Darkling Thrush" was published. Thus H may have seen his thrush in Hudson's book, not in nature.

1821 Bush, Douglas. MYTHOLOGY AND THE ROMANTIC TRADITION IN ENGLISH POETRY (Cambridge: Harvard UP, 1937), pp. 316, 340, 349, 457.

Meredith may well come to be viewed as a more significant writer than H because H's philosophy has ceased to be an impressive world view. *The Dynasts* could not have been written without the precedent of Greek tragedy. [Very little said about H directly—referred to only in allusions and comparisons.]

1822 Castelli, Alberto. THOMAS HARDY POETA: SAGGIO D'INTERPRETAZIONE (Thomas Hardy The Poet: An Interpretive Essay) (Milano: Societa Editrice, 1937).

Although H's poetry presents no philosophic system, it is philosophical in its attempt to deal with the fundamental questions of Man's relationship to God, Nature, Christ, and Art. H's struggle to understand these concepts convinced him of their fallibility and consequently became a primary basis for both his social iconoclasm and his artistic creation. [In Italian.]

1823 Compton-Rickett, Arthur. PORTRAITS AND PERSONALITIES (Lond: Selwyn & Blount, 1937), pp. 21–32.

H was avowedly inconsistent. Unsympathetic critics, however, have blamed him for a lack of philosophic consistency, a quality to which he never aspired. Critics have unfortunately ignored H's greatness as a humorist and consequently a major aspect of his personality—his jollity.

1824 Davidson, Donald (ed). BRITISH POETRY OF THE EIGHTEEN-NINETIES (Garden City, NY: Doubleday, Doran, 1937), pp. xli–xlii, lxiv–lxv, 230–32.

H's poems have a "Saxon stauchness" which sets them apart from the products of the Decadents. They exhibit not self-pity but pity for all of suffering man. Technically, they avoid the merely decorative and emphasize the "native Gothic irregularity" of English verse.

1825 The Enquiring Layman. "Thomas Hardy's *The Dynasts*," OUTLINE [supplement to JOHN O'LONDON'S WEEKLY], (1, 8, 15 and 22 Jan 1937), 585–86, 621–22, 657–58, and 695–96.

The novels of H are preferable to the philosophical convolutions of *The Dynasts*. [Hardly more than a bare summary.]

1826 Flower, Newman. "The Wife of a Genius: Recollections of Mrs. Hardy," SUNDAY TIMES (Lond), 24 Oct 1937, p. 10.

Florence H, H's second wife, "put years on to his ageing life. But for her, much of his later poetical work would never have been written. He would have laid down his pen too soon." It is not true that before their marriage she was "his secretary"; she was a "friend of his first wife."

1827 Ford, Ford Madox. "Thomas Hardy," PORTRAITS FROM LIFE (Boston: Houghton Mifflin; Chicago: Regnery, 1937), pp. 120–42.

H treated his early novels and short stories indifferently and wasted good subjects. *Jude the Obscure* is his masterpiece and shows a skill only the poems match. H never wanted to be a novelist and cared little for his novels.

1828 Funke, Otto. DIE SCHWEIZ UND DIE ENGLISCHE LITERATUR (Switzerland and English Literature) (Bern: A. Francke, 1937), p. 55.

[Passing reference to H as an author who traveled in Switzerland.] [In German.]

1829 Hamilton, G. Rostrevor. POETRY AND CONTEMPLATION: A NEW PREFACE TO POETICS (NY: Macmillan; Cambridge: Cambridge UP, 1937), pp. 55, 111.
[H mentioned.]

1830 Lawrence, Arnold Walter (ed). T. E. LAWRENCE BY HIS FRIENDS (NY: Doubleday, Doran, 1937), pp. 334–35, 440, 488.
[In addition to passing reference to H, whom Lawrence admired immensely, the books of H included in Lawrence's library are listed.]

1831 Lucas, Frank Laurence. THE DECLINE AND FALL OF THE ROMANTIC IDEAL (NY: Macmillan, 1937), pp. 145, 147–50, 154, 221, 280.
To the end of his life H remained "one of the greatest of all English romancers despite his incomparable honesty of mind." As a poet H is "worth many Shelleys"; H "was a master builder, who built houses that stood; whereas Shelley's handling of material things only landed him at the bottom of the Gulf of Spezzia."

1832 MacMinn, Ney. "Thomas Hardy, Scientific Determinist and Artist," CREATIVE THINKERS: ORIENTATION FOR MODERN TIMES (Division 2, part 2) (Chicago: Delphian Society, 1937), pp. 588–642.
[Sketchy survey of life and works.]

1833 Martin, Houston. "With Letters from Housman," YALE REVIEW, XXVI (Winter 1937), 283–303.
H's favorite Housman poem was XXVII in A SHROPSHIRE LAD. According to Mrs. H, Housman and H never talked about Housman's poems.

1834 Meusel, Marie Antoine Magdalene. THOMAS HARDY UND DIE BIBEL. EIN BIETRAG ZUR ENGLISCHEN LITERATUR UND KULTURGESCHICHTE (Thomas Hardy and the Bible. A Contribution to English Literature and Cultural History) (Kiel: Schmidt & Klaunig, 1937); University of Kiel dissertation.
[Part I contrasts H's religion with the Old and New Testament. The latter is absent in H's novels. Like the author of THE SONG OF SONGS, H does not turn to a higher order or an afterlife to solve man's problems. H's solution rests in man's love for his fellowman as expressed in I Corinthians 13; yet, this love is not performed in obedience to God's commandment but in the name of humanity. Part II considers the number of allusions to places, situations, and characters in the Bible which deeply influenced H.] [In German.]

1835 Miller, Edwin S. "Hardy's Venerable Drama," Studies in English Literature (Tokyo), XVII (Oct 1937), 568–81.
The St. George play performed in *The Return of the Native* is remarkably faithful to the traditional St. George folk-drama. Though it omits much of the elaboration found in the various analogues, H's version displays many points common to the fifty extant versions of the play.

1836 Minning, Ruth. Der Heimatroman des 20. Jahrhunderts in Süd-England und Wales (The Regional Novel in the 20th Century in South England and Wales) (Bleicherode: Carl Nieft, 1937), pp. 10–11.
[Restricted primarily to minor regional novelists who were influenced by H.] [In German.]

1837 Molson, Hugh. "The Philosophies of Hardy and Housman," Quarterly Review, CCLXVIII (April 1937), 205–13.
H and Housman admired each other's works. "This spectacle of life affects the two poets in somewhat different ways: Hardy, the humanitarian, is affected by the pity of it all, while Housman, the realist, seeks the most reasonable way to face both life and death." Housman was not so concerned to "illustrate the wretchedness of man's lot." He vacillates between the Epicurean and Stoic philosophies according to his mood and does not choose between them. Both writers feel that capital punishment is "necessary in human legislation, unjustifiable in divine." H, unlike Housman, longed for the solace of religion while being an agnostic (cf. "The Impercipient"). "Hardy wanted the dogmas of the Church broadened to reconcile faith and reason, the first being necessary for the solace of man's spirit, the second for the satisfaction of his mind." Friendship and love are themes which interest both poets, but each approaches them with a different outlook.

1838 Muller, Herbert J. "Thomas Hardy," Modern Fiction: A Study of Values (NY: McGraw-Hill, 1937), pp. 136–58.
H, "the first great tragic novelist in England," stands apart from his predecessors and contemporaries whose limited views fell short of his cosmic view, containing within it both pessimism and idealism. H was among the first to capture "the full impact of the new forces at work." He was on the defensive against his age's complacency; this defensiveness, expressed in the novels as pessimism and arbitrary irony, became the chief threat to his art. Yet H's defensiveness never succumbed to cynicism. His handling of rustics in their acts of human kindness (like the peasant who cares for the dying Henchard) represents the other side of his cosmic view. "He insists . . . that man is nobler than the will that creates and controls him." H's essential understanding of "the primary elements of human character" pro-

vides consolation in his tragic novels as idealism and pessimism balance his art.

1839 Paton, J. M. "Thomas Hardy's *Under the Greenwood Tree*," SCHOOL (University of Toronto, Ontario College of Education), XXVI (Dec 1937), 311–15.

Under the Greenwood Tree "clearly illustrates the principles of good writing" which H expressed in his literary essays. It has organic form; it evokes the beauty of rural Wessex; and it treats the conflict between ancient tradition and modern rootlessness which is central to H's major novels. These virtues earn *Greenwood Tree* a place among his major novels, those H classes as novels of character and environment.

1840 Phillips, H. C. B. "Nineteenth Century Literature: Bookshop Practice: Talks on Books and the Bookshop—No. 18," PUBLISHERS' CIRCULAR AND PUBLISHER AND BOOKSELLER, 10 April 1937, pp. 556–57; 17 April 1937, pp. 589–90.

H's sense of history and his closeness to nature, evident throughout his novels, are the product of his Wessex heritage. His ability to translate the minute events of his region into actions of universal significance allowed him to develop his tragic view of life. H's poetry is of the first rank; *The Dynasts* alone would place him among the major figures in English literature. [A very general introduction to H's works, punctuated by long quotes.]

1841 Pratt, E. J. "Introduction," *Under the Greenwood Tree*, ed with an introduction by E. J. Pratt (Toronto: Macmillan, 1937; St. Martin's Classics, 1938), pp. ix–xxiii.

Since H wrote pessimistic tragedies which relate what is local to what is universal, *Under the Greenwood Tree* is not a characteristic work. However, it is similar to other Wessex novels in that it contains noteworthy scenic descriptions, a distinct atmosphere, and humorous rustic characters.

1842 Routh, Harold Victor. "Hardy Sets Himself to Reveal the Inadequacy of Life and Reveals the Inadequacy of Culture," TOWARD THE TWENTIETH CENTURY (Cambridge: Cambridge UP, 1937), pp. 316–30.

Despite a prosperous career as novelist and poet, H "proved himself to be the most confirmed pessimist of his age." H's poetry is experimental in that it represents his attempt to "feel" certain "abstract notions" that make up modernism. The cerebral quality of H's poetry, the tendency of so many of his poems to illustrate a particular idea, is H's substitute for religion. But he is not at home with this "acquired culture": "modern culture will not serve as this artist's religion." Humanitarianism is the most persistent sentiment in his verse, and its source is disillusionment and an attendant fear for himself and his fellow man. "His poetry may be epitomized as paradox leading to pity." This pervasive sense of pity stems from the view that "man is too highly developed to inhabit this world." H's novels envision man emerging from a background spun out of nature, which is to him a "mysteriously cruel and inhuman power" whose creatures must struggle to survive just as man must struggle to be happy. Just as seeds, insects, and animals live at the mercy of accidents, man's desire for fellow-feeling and love is always being undermined by chance.

1843 Rutland, W. R. "The Sources of *The Dynasts*," TIMES LITERARY SUPPLEMENT (Lond), 13 Nov 1937, p. 866.
H did not provide a list of his sources, but his library at Max Gate contained a collection of less than one hundred well-chosen volumes covering the field. Important are works by Thiers, Capefigue, Lanfrey.

1844 Schirmer, Walter F. GESCHICHTE DER ENGLISCHEN UND AMERIKANISCHEN LITERATUR VON DEN ANFÄNGEN BIS ZUR GEGENWART (History of English and American Literature From the Beginnings to the Present) (Halle/Saale: Max Niemeyer, 1937), pp. 545, 546, 577–78, 650; 2nd ed (Tübingen: Max Niemeyer, 1954), II, 145, 169–71, 173, 176, 211, 223, 228, 263, 274; 3rd ed (Tübingen: Max Niemeyer, 1960), II, 148, 173–75, 177, 180, 204, 217, 230, 234, 236, 281, 294, 331.
[The first ed contains passing references to H. The second and third eds contain plot summaries of H's works as well as numerous comparisons to other Victorian authors.] [In German.]

1845 Symons, Katharine E., et al. ALFRED EDWARD HOUSMAN: RECOLLECTIONS BY KATHARINE E. SYMONS, A. W. POLLARD, LAURENCE HOUSMAN, R. W. CHAMBERS, ALAN KER, A. S. F. GOW, JOHN SPARROW (NY: Holt, 1937), pp. 40, 48.
"Some Reminscences" by A. W. Pollard: "Among novelists his favorite was Thomas Hardy, and I think Hardy's influence went far deeper than Arnold's." " 'Shropshire Lad' Year—and After" by Laurence Housman: "That small book of poems has given to many Shropshire place-names an added romance comparable to that which attaches to the place-names of Thomas Hardy's novels."

1846 Towne, Charles H. "There Was Only One Mrs. Fiske," STAGE (NY), XIV (Jan 1937), 110–12.
Mrs. Fiske's brilliance in the title role of *Tess of the d'Urbervilles* [play] insured her reputation.

1847 Waldock, A. J. A. "Thomas Hardy and *The Dynasts*," JAMES, JOYCE, AND OTHERS (Lond: Williams & Norgate, 1937), pp. 53–78.

H's six major novels show a "gradual darkening of tone" from the tragedy-touched pastoral *Far From the Madding Crowd* to the extinguishing of "the last gleams of the exaltation of tragedy" in *Tess of the d'Urbervilles* and *Jude the Obscure*. In *The Dynasts*, H gave full expression of the conception of a "Somnambulist First Cause" mentioned by Sue in *Jude*. *Dynasts* lacks the anger and bitterness of *Tess* and *Jude*, but "humanity has dwindled to an insignificance." H's use of scenic effects prefigures the cinema.

1848 Weber, Carl J. "Browning and Hardy," SATURDAY REVIEW OF LITERATURE, XV (27 March 1937), 9.

Where is the letter H wrote to Browning in May 1888 with his gift of *Wessex Tales*? [Weber answered himself in "Pessimist to Optimist," ibid, XVIII (7 May 1938), 9, 21.]

1849 Weber, Carl J. "Introduction," *Far From the Madding Crowd*, ed by Carl J. Weber (NY: Oxford UP, 1937; 1941; rvd, 1948), pp. vii–xviii; rptd, essentially, in Rinehart Editions (NY: Rinehart, 1959), pp. v–xx.

H's first attempt at fiction, *The Poor Man and the Lady*, was abridged and published under a new title, *An Indiscretion in the Life of an Heiress*. "No other English novelist has been so successful with so limited a stage," and "no one since Shakespeare has been so successful in describing the English agricultural laborer." "There is no evidence that Thomas Hardy and Pinero got their respective plots for *Far From the Madding Crowd* and THE SQUIRE from the same source, although the novel and the play have similar plots."

1850 Weber, Carl J. ON THOMAS HARDY'S BIRTHDAY: CATALOGUE OF AN EXHIBITION (Waterville, Maine: Colby College Library, 1937).

[Lists and comments on 200 items which represent "every important title produced in H's career."]

1851 Weber, Carl J. "Plagiarism and Thomas Hardy," COLOPHON, ns II (Summer 1937), 443–54.

An H–Carr idea was "stolen" by A. W. Pinero according to H letters to the TIMES (Lond) and the DAILY NEWS (Lond) on 2 Jan 1882. *Far From the Madding Crowd* was ruined for stage adaptation by Pinero's THE SQUIRE, although H's adaptation played London and Liverpool in 1882. H dropped the matter when an article appeared in the ACADEMY on plagiarism in *The Trumpet-Major* and Charles F. T. Spoor announced H's plagiarism in *A Laodicean* from Charles Apperly's "The Turf," review of A TREATISE on the Care of the English Race Horse, in Quarterly Review, XLIX (1833) [p. 414, in the American edition].

1852 Weygandt, Cornelius. The Time of Yeats: English Poetry of Today Against an American Background (NY: Appleton-Century, 1937), passim.
Perhaps Hawthorne's Zenobia has some connection with Eustacia Vye. "Hardy's Practice of the Higher Provincialism": H gives more of the country folk and their environment than any other writer—customs, architecture, landscape, humor, sympathy, "the dignity and inexhaustible humanity of the common man." [Tangential comparisons to Bridges, Hewlett, Phillpotts, Yeats, Johnson, Stephens, and Francis Ledwidge.] "The Penetration of Thomas Hardy": "Thomas Hardy is a great poet by reason of his power of penetration to the realities of things." Interest in people and native candor save verse from being mere propaganda. He wrote verse from 1860 but did not publish until 1901. The first volume is deficient, but the next is memorable. H's world of verse is unique and unprecedented. Later volumes are less propagandistic but have more second-rate poems. H's knowledge of life was broad, and his "ability to get at the heart of a situation amounts almost to divination." He wrote of Wessex, of the countryside, ritual, customs; but he also presents a somber new philosophy. He "looked backward in things of the heart, and forward in things of the mind." The irony of injustice is the prevailing tone, but H was not entirely pessimistic nor is his verse completely reflective of personal belief. Much is dramatic. *The Dynasts* is the most comprehensively analytical with some insights and an epic sweep, but it is a magnificent failure. His poetry of little things is the greatest. Some subjects are death, the English countryside, dogs, tributes to other poets, women, love, marriage. H's greatness lies in the "sense of largeness and luminousness" in his verse, "in a nature of the broadest tolerance and of the deepest insight," "compassionate" and "clear-visioned" with a "knowledge of life." [Further tangential references in connection with Charles Doughty, Bottomley, Masefield, Gibson, Lascelles Abercrombie, Edward Thomas, Drinkwater, Coppard, Charlotte Mew, Blunden, and C. Day Lewis.]

1853 Winters, Yvor. "Robert Bridges and Elizabeth Daryush," American Review, VIII (Jan 1937), 353–67, espec 353.
"Bridges and Hardy must be regarded as the two most impressive writers of poetry in something like two centuries." At his best H "offers a kind of summation of folk wisdom: it is his power and his limitation."

1854 Yeats, W. B. (ed). The Oxford Book of Modern Verse: 1892–1935 (NY: Oxford UP, 1937), pp. v, vii, xiii, xxxix, 7–10.

In the Eighties, H was still unpublished. "Ballad of Reading Gaol" has been pruned to a "stark realism" akin to H. "Thomas Hardy, though his work lacked technical accomplishment, made the necessary corrections [reaction from rhetoric] through his mastery of the impersonal objective scene." Hopkins's "influence has replaced that of Hardy and Bridges." [The following poems reprinted: "Weathers," "Snow in the Suburbs," "The Night of Trafalgar," "Former Beauties."]

1938

1855 [Adams, F. B.]. "Observations by the Ordinary Seaman," COLOPHON, ns III (Spring 1938), 313–16.
[According to CHAP BOOK PRODUCTION IN THE UNITED STATES, 1870 TO 1891 by Raymond Howard Shove (Urbana: University of Illinois Library, 1937) [not seen], many H editions were published in the United States before they were published in Great Britain, and H novels were published in cheap series throughout the period covered.]

1856 Adams, Randolph G. "Hardy vs. Pinero," COLOPHON, ns III (Spring 1938), 307.
According to a letter from E. N. Sanders to Carl Weber, Pinero's denial of plagiarism charges concerning *Far From the Madding Crowd* should be modified by the knowledge that Pinero read the work very early in the period in which his own THE SQUIRE was written; thus he may have borrowed more than he thought.

1857 Baker, Ernest A. THE HISTORY OF THE ENGLISH NOVEL (Lond: Witherby, 1938), IX, 11–96, espec pp. 11–22, 28–51, 52–86.
Meredith and H differed in many ways, some of them fundamental. The difference is like the break between two literary epochs. H's "chief character is man, and the play Existence." Both accepted THE ORIGIN OF SPECIES, but H accepted the whole theory, including natural selection. Meredith believed in free will. Meredith was not obsessed with the inexorable working of natural laws. Fiction in this time became used as a vehicle for social criticism and philosophic thought. From the first, H's novels had a critical attitude towards the world. In *The Return of the Native*, H piles up coincidences, maneuvering hostile forces. This maneuvering disfigured H's later works. H believed in the extraordinary as the right subject for fiction, but the " 'uncommoness must be in the events,' the people must be as ordinary as possible." Characteristics of H's novels include some melodrama, the

confutation of free will, nature interwoven with the story, and the disillusionment with life. *The Trumpet-Major* is one exception which is concerned with good nature and happiness. In H's later works, the influence of Greek tragedy is apparent. H's short stories are inferior to his novels. H's novels became more and more philosophic statements of the human dilemma. H used primarily three types of characters: (a) protagonists, who were often more abstract symbols than real people; (b) "cogs in the machine"—characters who are instrumental to the plot; and (c) a chorus of rustics.

1858 Blyton, W. J. "Hardy Chiefly: And Others," WE ARE OBSERVED (Lond: Murray, 1938), pp. 3, 6, 15, 199, 207–35, 319.

H, whose creed is expressed by Marty South at the end of *The Woodlanders*, believed in fidelity, love, humor, and pity. He loved the open country and Nature; created "superb country characters"; saw that man was "within Nature and a working portion of it"; had a sense of the past; and dealt with how destiny treated people.

1859 Chakravarty, Amiya. THE DYNASTS AND THE POST-WAR AGE IN POETRY (Lond: Oxford UP, 1938).

"Hardy's *The Dynasts* was chosen as a promontory from whence to view the turbulent stretches of modern verse." Through *The Dynasts* one is able to see the beginning of the complexities of the modern mind and the link that binds H with the moderns.

1860 Cockerell, Sydney. "Hardy's Library," TIMES LIBRARY SUPPLEMENT (Lond), 17 Sept 1938, p. 598.

[Sydney and Mrs. H, in "tidying up" H's library, labeled H's books with black and red labels. Subsequently Mrs: H bequeathed some of the books to the Dorchester Museum. Others were sold to Hodgson and included Mrs. H's books and others of small account, which booksellers have marked with imitation labels: original red labels were for books with H's signature or notes, black were for other selected books.]

1861 Colling, Alfred. LE ROMANCIER DE LA FATALITÉ: THOMAS HARDY (The Novelist of Fatality: Thomas Hardy) (Paris: Emile-Paul, 1938).

To an unusual degree, H's works show the effects of the genetic and environmental forces which made up the man. The sensitivity, sincerity, humility and melancholy which mark H's treatment of essentially rustic materials all have a readily traceable origin in his own life. [An impressionistic critical biography cast in the form of a dreamlike visitation to the Wessex of H's youth and of the novels. Numerous typographical and factual errors.] [In French.]

1862 Cruse, Amy. AFTER THE VICTORIANS (Lond: Allen & Unwin, 1938), pp. 128, 150, 173, 177, 178–80, 185, 186, 214, 242.

H was at first well received by the English reading public, but his dark and unhappy novels, beginning with *Far From the Madding Crowd*, lost him his wide popularity. The publication of *Tess of the d'Urbervilles* brought him back to general attention because of the strong opposition to that novel, though some critics—Besant, Gosse, and Mrs. Humphrey Ward, among others—praised it as a masterpiece. The furor over *Jude the Obscure* was even greater, comparable only to the outcry over Swinburne's 1866 POEMS AND BALLADS. Only Havelock Ellis among the better-known critics spoke favorably of the last of H's novels. Probably many of H's admirers in the nineteenth century read him only for the thrills of melodrama; Hall Caine and Maria Corelli, the principal purveyors of sensations for the late century reading classes, were more popular and influential than either H or Meredith. Only in the twentieth century, after the publication of *The Dynasts*, was H regarded as one of the great English classics, appreciated by all classes of readers for his sympathetic grasp of human predicaments. However, Edwardian high society tended to deprecate his novels since these dealt with common people.

1863 Ford, Ford Madox. MIGHTIER THAN THE SWORD (Lond: Allen & Unwin, 1938), pp. 123–44.

H's short stories and novels mangled many beautiful subjects, H usually dropping the story just when a genuine novelist would have found it interesting. *Jude* is his best book, where his avocation becomes an art, comes alive. H was a great poet, never a novelist. Though he attacked the heartless Establishment in *Jude*, H remained a Believer. When H turned to poetry, he felt free and shaved off his beard. H's poetry forms a "great landscape of the human heart." [In Ford's youth, H was a classic, which Ford did not read. He avoided *Tess of the d'Urbervilles* because it had too much uplift, from the unorthodox point of view. When he met H, Ford had written THE BROWN OWL; H commented on onomatopoeia and quoted an example from Latin. Mrs. H called on Garnett to persuade H to burn the MS of *Jude the Obscure*. H was kind to young Ford. On a visit to Max Gate, H was away and Mrs. H read her poems to Ford. Much later Ford was introduced to H as a poet by reading "A Sunday Morning Tragedy," which CORNHILL refused to print. Ford realized what H's real excellence was.]

1864 Fullington, James F., Harry B. Reed, and Julia Norton McCorkle. THE NEW COLLEGE OMNIBUS (NY: Harcourt, Brace, 1938), pp. 901–7.

Despite its roughness, H's verse has its beauty. Unlike many other nineteenth-century poets, H realized that nature was not beneficent but just another source of human strife; he knew that mere indifference lay under its surface beauty. In poems like the *Satires of Circumstance*, H reveals the "other side" of Victorian religious and moral conventions, yet throughout his works, he always admired man struggling against the trammels of nature and society.

1865 Hamlin, Arthur T. "The Howells Collection," HARVARD LIBRARY NOTES, III (May 1938), 147–53.
Several arresting letters addressed to William Dean Howells by H are to be found in the Howells Collection now at Harvard.

1866 Heath, Sidney. "The Laureate Quality in Thomas Hardy," DORSET COUNTY CHRONICLE, 13 Oct 1938, p. 3.
Although H seemed preoccupied with the great problems of human destiny, he could write occasional verse of high quality—as his "in memoriam" poems on Swinburne and Meredith show. Thus there is an often overlooked " 'laureate' quality" to his verse.

1867 Hicks, Granville. "Was Thomas Hardy a Pessimist?" EDUCATIONAL FORUM, II (Nov 1938), 58–67.
H's position—he saw "no evidence of a power not ourselves that makes for righteousness"—was "that of virtually all materialists," but he put unusual stress on the role of consciousness in the creation of man's misery. Before deciding whether the irremediable ill outweighs the good in human life, man should set about ridding the world of its "thousand remediable ills." H labored to this end by means of his art. The "devotion to truth is Hardy's clearest claim to the name of meliorist." After H gave up writing novels, he continued to serve Truth as a poet. Yet many of H's utterances in prose and verse seem to belie his meliorism. These bursts of despair show that H's meliorism, while perhaps a consistently-held view, was certainly not a consistently-maintained attitude of mind. The problem for H may have been that although he believed in remedying many of the world's ills, he found no program or party with which he could collaborate. Then, too, his sensitivity and lack of self-confidence made an immersion in party politics impossible. H was a meliorist subject to fits of pessimism.

1868 Hoare, Dorothy M[ackenzie]. "The Tragic in Hardy and Conrad," SOME STUDIES IN THE MODERN NOVEL (Lond: Chatto & Windus, 1938; Phila: Dufour Editions, 1953), pp. 131–32.
H, with Conrad, is "important as having, in contrast with most of the writers of this century, a profound tragic sense. Both deflect tragedy a little, into a new course, by a subtle alteration of its elements; H, by an emphasis on both bitterness and pity; Conrad, by a combination of romanticism and irony."

1869 Hodgson and Co. THE LIBRARY OF THOMAS HARDY, O. M. With books and autograph letters, the property of the late Mrs. Thomas Hardy (Lond: Hodgson and Co, 26 May 1938); rptd as THE LIBRARY OF THOMAS HARDY, O. M., ed by J. Stevens Cox (Mount Durand, St. Peter Port, Guernsey: Toucan P, 1968.)
[A reprint of the catalogue of H's library as sold by Messrs. Hodgson and Co. on 26 May 1938. It lists 309 items. Also see J. Stevens Cox (pub and general editor), Monographs on the Life of Thomas Hardy (1962).]

1870 Holst, Imogen. GUSTAV HOLST (Lond: Oxford UP, 1938), pp. 126–28, 130–31, 140–41, 164, 169.
Holst, a close friend of H, was inspired to the composition of his EGDON HEATH symphony (1927–1928) by reading *The Return of the Native* and by a walk over Egdon Heath at Easter, 1926. EGDON HEATH is Holst's homage to H; it is the "product of years of knowing Hardy and his books and that desolate stretch of country between Wool and Bere Regis." EGDON HEATH had its first London performance in Feb 1928.

1871 Housman, Lawrence. MY BROTHER, A. E. HOUSMAN (Lond: Cape; NY: Scribner's, 1938), pp. 72, 85.
Housman "felt affection and high admiration for some of [H's] novels and a few of his poems." H was Housman's "outstanding favourite among contemporary novelists."

1872 Lang, Varley. "Crabbe and *Tess of the d'Urbervilles*," MODERN LANGUAGE NOTES, LIII (May 1938), 369–70.
George Crabbe's "The Maid's Story" in TALES OF THE HALL, "surprisingly analogous" to *Tess of the d'Urbervilles*, provides a possible explanation for Alec d'Urberville's unmotivated conversion to "zealous piety."

1873 Lawrence, T. E. THE LETTERS OF T. E. LAWRENCE, ed by David Garnett (Lond: Cape, 1938; NY: Doubleday, Doran, 1939), pp. 408, 424, 427, 429, 430, 441, 442, 460, 471, 473, 475, 482, 498, 503, 564–67, 574, 578, 582, 592, 593, 667, 668, 869; letters to and from H also in ATLANTIC MONTHLY, CLXIII (1939), 331–32.
[Lawrence, who met H in the 1920s and corresponded occasionally with Mrs. H, found the old writer quite friendly to those he knew and trusted. Mrs. H had approached Lawrence (as Lawrence hints) to edit H's recollections.]

1874 Leibert, Vera. "*Far From the Madding Crowd* on the American Stage," COLOPHON, ns III (Summer 1938), 377–82.
A. R. Cazauran adapted H's complex novel with scissors rather than with a pen. It was reduced to a contrived absurdity that ran for two weeks only at

the Union Square Theater in New York. Clara Morris made a disappointing Bathsheba. [Contains a full-page reproduction of the opening-night program of 17 April 1882.]

1875 Lemperly, Paul. BOOKS AND I (Cleveland: The Rowfant Club, 1938), pp. 47–51.

[Comments on the following H rarities: an advance copy of volume 1 of *The Dynasts* (dated 1903 rather than 1904 like the usual first editions); the copy of *Wessex Tales* presented by H to Browning on the latter's seventy-sixth birthday; *The Convergence of the Twain* (perhaps "the rarest Hardy first edition" because it was published in only ten copies in 1912); H's personal copies of Tennyson's IDYLLS OF THE KING, and PSALMS AND HYMNS (given Lemperly by Mrs. H in 1937); the sale of H's volume of Shelley's poems and of his THE BOY'S OWN BOOK: A COMPLETE ENCYCLOPEDIA OF ALL THE DIVERSIONS.]

1876 Littmann, Hildegard. DAS DICHTERISCHE BILD IN DER LYRIK GEORGE MEREDITHS UND THOMAS HARDYS IN ZUSAMMENHANG MIT IHRER WELTANSCHAUUNG (The Poetic Image in the Lyrics of George Meredith and Thomas Hardy in Connection with Their World-View) (Berlin: Furst, 1938); University of Bonn dissertation; rptd as "Die Metapher in Merediths und Hardys Lyrik" (The Metaphor in Meredith's and Hardy's Lyrics), SCHWEIZER ANGLISTISCHE ARBEITEN, VI (1938), 5–485, espec 259–485.

[Treats H's poetic representation of the superhuman forces (i.e. time, fate, chance, change, death, nature, Mother Earth, God, and the Immanent Will) and Nature (sun, moon, stars, the heavens, rain, snow, plants). Juxtaposes H's and Meredith's verses and compares and contrasts their views towards man, propagation, change, death, progress, evolution, self-determination, sorrow, love, women, beauty, and laughter.] [In German.]

1877 Meissner, Paul. ENGLISCHE LITERATURGESCHICHTE: ROMANTIK UND VIKTORIANISMUS (English Literary History: Romanticism and Victorianism) (Berlin: Walter de Grunter, 1938), III, 29, 139, 142.

H should be remembered as a regional novelist and associated with Moore, Conrad, and Kipling for helping to break the bonds of Victorian sentiment. [In German.]

1878 Moore, John. "Thomas Hardy's Moors," DALHOUSIE REVIEW, XVIII (1938), 185–88.

H's moors, especially Egdon Heath, serve to embody his metaphysic of man both as experiencing fate and striving to ascend; they are "co-weavers of Time in the web of human destiny." H does not *paint* his scene but *reveals* it.

1879 "Notes on Sales: Nineteenth Century First Editions," Times Literary Supplement (Lond), 23 April 1938, p. 284.

A copy of *Tess of the d'Urbervilles* was incorrectly described as a first edition rather than second, but several other firsts were on sale at Sotheby's, including *Under the Greenwood Tree* at forty pounds and *The Return of the Native* at eighteen pounds.

1880 Pearman, Marjorie. "Scenes and Scenery in Hardy's England," Dorset Yearbook, 1938, pp. 54–58.

Old customs survive in Wessex because it was until recently "completely isolated by . . . beautiful hills and by lack of suitable transportation." In *The Return of the Native* "local scenery dominates the lives of the characters . . . more than in any other [novel] . . . he wrote."

1881 Pirkhofer, A. "Zur Einheit des dichterischen Impulses in Thomas Hardys Kunsttheorie und Dichtung" (On the Unity of the Poetic Impulse in Thomas Hardy's Artistic Theory and Poetry), Germanisch-Romanische Monatsschrift, XXVI (1938), 232–46.

[Attempts to formulate H's theory of art from several statements in H's biography.] [In German.]

1882 Pound, Ezra. Guide to Kulchur (Norfolk, Conn: New Directions, 1938), pp. 284–89, 290–95, 302.

H, a poet who writes so clearly there is nothing for the explaining critic to do, is an excellent narrative writer. He is like Swinburne, Henry James, and the pre-Raphelites in being disgusted with the social estimates of his era.

1883 Powys, John Cowper. The Pleasures of Literature (Lond: Cassell, 1938), pp. 137, 140, 528, 605–23; also in Enjoyment of Literature (NY: Simon & Schuster, 1938), pp. 433–50.

H's pessimism, the result of his "indignant sympathy with a suffering world," is related to a philosophy of life based on "defiance and pity." This defiance and pity is a natural response in a person who saw that existence is based on a struggle for survival, who saw that everyone is the victim of the "nature of the Universe." Since everyone is a victim, it follows naturally that H uses his "rigidly-planned" plots to suggest the relentlessness of fate.

1884 R., H. "Max Gate: Memories of Thomas Hardy's Home," Birmingham Post, 15 June 1938.

Max Gate, recently purchased by H's sister Kate, is no longer the lonely country house. It has close neighbors and is only isolated by the trees which H planted years ago. The house and grounds have undergone some changes but all are in keeping with H's plans.

1885 Rhodes, Geoffrey. "About Wessex," SUNDAY AT HOME, Dec 1938, pp. 131–34.

The great charm of Dorset is that "it is a calm backwater" full of charming scenes. "The Romans were wise . . . when they chose this province for some of their more important settlements." One of H's "touches of genius" was to "restore the ancient Saxon kingdom of Wessex" and use it for his novels.

1886 Rutland, W. R. "Thomas Hardy." Dissertation, Oxford University, 1938; pub as THOMAS HARDY: A STUDY OF HIS WRITINGS AND THEIR BACKGROUND (1938).

[Listed in Lawrence F. McNamee, DISSERTATIONS IN ENGLISH AND AMERICAN LITERATURE (NY & Lond: Bowker, 1968)]

1887 Rutland, William R. THOMAS HARDY (Lond: Blackie [Order of Merit Series], 1938).

[A critical biography in five chapters (Youth in Dorset; Between Architecture and Literature; The Novelist; The Poet; Some Friendships) considerably indebted to the same author's THOMAS HARDY: A STUDY OF HIS WRITINGS AND THEIR BACKGROUND (1938). Chap 5 ("Some Friendships") describes H's association with the Moule family, T. W. H. Tolbort, William Barnes, Leslie Stephen, A. C. Swinburne, Edward Clodd, Anne Proctor, Florence Henniker, Edmund Gosse, and others.]

1888 Rutland, William R. THOMAS HARDY: A STUDY OF HIS WRITINGS AND THEIR BACKGROUND (Oxford: Blackwell, 1938).

The "essential characteristic" of H's art is to show the "emotional history of two infinitesimal lives" against "the stupendous background of the stellar universe." This "elemental antilogy has its roots in H's temperament, but also in the influence on him of the Authorized Version of the Bible, the Book of Common Prayer, the drama of Sophocles and Aeschylus, as well as the writings of Darwin, Huxley, Spencer, Mill, and Swinburne, to mention only the most prominent. [Chaps 1–3 ("Influence of Early Reading," "Hardy and the Classics," "The Background of Hardy's Thought") are concerned with the background to H's writings. Chaps 4–7 treat historically the writings themselves ("Hardy's Early Writings," "The Novels: 1875–1891," "*Tess* and *Jude*," "The Poems and *The Dynasts*.") Also three appendices: "Letter on *Poor Man and the Lady* (from Alexander Macmillan to Thomas Hardy)," "List of Hardy's Writings," "List of Hardyana."]

1889 Vandiver, E. P., Jr. "Hardy and Shakespeare Again," SHAKESPEARE ASSOCIATION QUARTERLY, XIII (April 1938), 87–95.

[Supplements two articles by Carl J. Weber: "Twin-Voice of Shakespeare," ibid, IX (April 1934), 91–97 and "Shakespeare's Twin-Voice Again," ibid,

IX (July 1934), 162–63. *A Pair of Blue Eyes* "abounds" in Shakespearean allusions, as lists of allusions, with page references to the Wessex novels and the poems, show.]

1890 Weber, Carl J. "Chronology in Hardy's Novels," PUBLICATIONS OF THE MODERN LANGUAGE ASSOCIATION, LIII (March 1938), 314–20.

"Calendrical facts" help us recognize that ten of H's novels have complete and segregated geographic atmosphere and time sense and sequence, although there is overlapping in *Jude the Obscure* and *The Well-Beloved*. In this group of Wessex novels, H made a historical study of the nineteenth century as accurate as his topographical observations. Time, the archsatirist, is shown in his progress through the century. In *The Return of the Native* and *Far From the Madding Crowd*, calendar dates even coincide with days of the week correctly. [Relatively interesting and with chronological lists, but there are some inaccuracies as noted in John Emery's "Chronology in Hardy's *Return of the Native*," PMLA, LIV (June 1939), 618–20.]

1891 Weber, Carl J. "A Jekyll and Hyde Exhibition," COLBY MERCURY, VI (May 1938), 182–88.

T. J. Wise's pamphlet NOTES ON "THE DYNASTS" [not seen] contains four letters from H to Edward Clodd.

1892 Weber, Carl J. "On Browning's Birthday," COLBY MERCURY, VI (May 1938), 177–80.

H presented an inscribed copy of *Wessex Tales* to Browning on Browning's seventy-sixth birthday and sent with it a letter [reprinted]. [Catalogue of Colby Exhibit of associated items.]

1893 Weber, Carl J. "Pessimist to Optimist," SATURDAY REVIEW OF LITERATURE, XVIII (7 May 1938), 9, 21.

H sent his *Wessex Tales* to Browning in 1888 with a letter hoping that he would find one in the lot to his liking; the letter and books have ended up in various places. [Response to Weber's own inquiry in "Browning and Hardy," ibid, XV (27 March 1937), 9.]

1894 Weber, Carl J. "Setting a Time Piece," COLOPHON, ns III (Winter 1938), 139–41.

From 1874 to 1935 Jan Coggan's watch, in *Far From the Madding Crowd*, chap 32, struck one o'clock twice, but Weber's 1937 edition makes it strike one–two, as it did originally.

1895 Weber, Carl J. " 'The Sound of Cornish Waves Cold Upon Cornish Rocks,' " COLBY MERCURY, VI (Nov 1938), 215–16.

E. A. Robinson's TRISTRAM may contain an echo of *The Famous Tragedy of the Queen of Cornwall.* [Conjecture; filler.]

1896 Weber, Carl J. "Thomas Hardy in America," COLOPHON, ns III (Summer 1938), 383–405.

America is good H country. The zeal for publishing and collecting his works goes back to the first appearance of his name on the title page of one of his works, Holt's edition of *Under the Greenwood Tree* in 1873. There were numerous American piratings and a long list of H editions can be compiled. Manuscripts in the United States, like the draft of "Squire Petrick's Lady," show some of H's deletions for popular taste.

1897 Weber, Carl J. "Three-score Years of Egdon Heath," COLBY MERCURY, VI (Feb 1938), 149–55.

[Catalogue of sixtieth anniversary exhibition of books and papers connected with *The Return of the Native.*]

1898 Wentworth, H. "Some Manuscripts of Thomas Hardy," DAILY ATHENAEUM, 29 April 1938, p. 8.

H's original manuscripts "are about evenly divided between private collectors and museums."

1899 Wilson, Knox. "Clym Yeobright's Song," ENGLISH JOURNAL, XXVII (Nov 1938), 773.

[A metrical English translation of the French song which Clym sings in Book IV of *The Return of the Native.*]

1939

1900 Anderson, Marcia Lee. "Hardy's Debt to Webster in *The Return of the Native,*" MODERN LANGUAGE NOTES, LIV (Nov 1939), 497–501.

A quarrel between Clym and Eustacia in *The Return of the Native* (Book V, chap 3) was inspired directly by the quarrel between Brachiano and Vittoria in THE WHITE DEVIL (IV, ii).

1901 Bugler, Gertrude. "Hardy at Max Gate," LISTENER, XXI (29 June 1939), 1375–76.

Although much has been made of H's "sad philosophy and pessimistic attitude to life," he seemed "always a man of smiles and kindness; he was anything but the morose, grim, cynical man often pictured." [Reminiscence by the woman who played Tess and other H heroines in Dorset and London productions.]

1902 Ellis, Havelock. MY LIFE: THE AUTOBIOGRAPHY OF HAVE-LOCK ELLIS (Boston: Houghton Mifflin, 1939), pp. 97, 189–91.
[In preparation for "Thomas Hardy's Novels," Ellis read all H had written, and he visited Dorset. Ellis wrote, "I dwell on this essay because . . . it was in writing it that I learnt to write." It was accepted for publication by the WESTMINSTER REVIEW, LXIII (April 1883). Ellis received almost immediately a letter from H saying: "I consider this essay a remarkable paper in many ways, and can truly say that the writing itself, with its charm of style, and variety of allusion, occupied my mind . . . far more than the fact that my own unmethodical books were its subject-matter."

1903 Emery, John P., and Carl J. Weber. "Chronology in Hardy's *Return of the Native*," PUBLICATIONS OF THE MODERN LANGUAGE ASSOCIATION, LIV (June 1939), 618–19, 620.
There are several calendrical slips in *The Return of the Native*, and the action covers two and a half years (contrary to Weber's chronology ["Chronology in Hardy's Novels," ibid, LIII (March 1938), 314–20]). [Weber's rejoinder]: H's footnote in the 1912 edition allows us to see the time span as intended to be shorter than it appears.

1904 "Fatal Age for Poets," DAILY TELEGRAPH (Lond), 11 May 1939, p. 12.
John Masefield remarked at the opening of the H memorial at the Dorset County Museum that H's best work was done after he was fifty and that the *Wessex Poems* are the most powerful influence for good on English poetry since Browning.

1905 Forster, E. M. "Woodlanders on Devi," NEW STATESMAN AND NATION, XVII (6 May 1939), 679–80.
[An interesting account of the reading of H's *The Woodlanders* when Forster was in India living in a semi-derelict palace, during the hot season. "Trees, trees, undergrowth, English trees! How that book rustles with them!" Devi was a sacred hill: one day, as E. M. Forster raised his eyes to it, the trees he had been reading about transplanted themselves to its slopes and hung for a moment in a film of green. . . . Not a vision; only a pleasant literary fancy.]

1906 "Hardy at Dorchester," TIMES (Lond), 11 May 1939, p. 15.
Mrs. H showed imagination and good sense in establishing the H Memorial Room. The visitor feels continuity and a sense of survival of H in Dorchester surroundings. Visitors will "be looking at the birthplace of his most consummate achievement and his greatest to the world"—*The Dynasts* and his poems.

1907 Hicks, Granville. "The Pessimism of Thomas Hardy," FIGURES OF TRANSITION: A STUDY OF BRITISH LITERATURE AT THE END OF THE NINETEENTH CENTURY (NY: Macmillan, 1939), pp. 109–44.

The "figures of transition" are Morris, H, Butler, Gissing, Wilde, and Kipling. James Thomson's "City of Dreadful Night" expresses a pessimism whose chief spokesman H would be. H's pessimism is both the product of new modes of thought and of his temperament and situation. He was driven by science to see the Cause of things as "neither moral nor immoral, but *un*moral," and this was accompanied by a sense of social inferiority and by a tendency to isolate himself. But fundamentally, H was as he himself claimed—a meliorist rather than a pessimist in his plea throughout his works against " ' man's inhumanity to man,' to woman, and to the lower animals."

1908 Horwill, H. W. "A Thomas Hardy Memorial Room," NEW YORK TIMES BOOK REVIEW, 4 June 1939, p. 8.

At the opening of the Thomas Hardy Memorial Room in Dorset County Museum, containing a collection of MSS and personal relics, John Masefield spoke of his intimate knowledge of H. Masefield said H was a "vital personality" and traced H's maturity through novel, epic, and lyric, noting how H resembled Ibsen, except that Ibsen moved from poetry to prose.

1909 "The Inspiration of Hardy," TIMES (Lond), 11 May 1939, p. 17.

At the opening of the Thomas Hardy Memorial Room at Dorset County Museum, John Masefield said he first thought H conformed to his idea of a Chinese philosopher—pale, gentle, aware of mass suffering, wise and pessimistic; on later acquaintance, he came to regard H as a vital personality full of passion and great depth of feeling. H continued to mature past the age of seventy.

1910 Meissner, Paul. ENGLISCHE LITERATURGESCHICHTE: DAS 20. JAHRHUNDERT (English Literary History: The 20th Century) (Berlin: Walter de Grunter, 1939), IV, 21–24, 35, 53–54, 59, 86, 109, 127.

Regionalism transcends reality and becomes metaphysical under H's pen. H's poetry is inferior to his prose. The success of *The Dynasts* is in inverse proportion to its symbolism. [In German.]

1911 Muchnic, Helen. "Thomas Hardy and Thomas Mann," SMITH COLLEGE STUDIES IN MODERN LANGUAGES, XXI (1939–1940), 130–43; rptd in THE STATURE OF THOMAS MANN, ed by

Charles Neider (Norfolk, Conn: New Directions, 1947), pp. 265–78.

H is not so great an author as Mann, but Mann seems to answer the questions that H asked. While H was annoyed with all attempts to interpret his writings as having a consistent philosophy, Mann accepted his position as prophet of his day. H's "impressions" are unified, but they express a stark dualism in thought. Mann's view is not so pitying: compare Henchard's defeated "I must suffer, I perceive" and Hans Castorp's "challenge" to the elements. The verb "to happen" (cf. the poem "Hap") is as essential in H's idiom as it is inappropriate to Mann's. These two ironists differ also in their estimates of human capacities. For H the history of humanity presents the spectacle of complete loss and waste. But Mann sees in it an extraordinary tenaciousness. For H death is simply the ceasing of an individual existence; for Mann death is linked to life in an indivisible process of birth, decay, and rebirth. The fundamental difference between the two writers springs from the dualism implicit in all H's perceptions and the integration characteristic of Mann.

1912 Murphree, A. A., and C. F. Strauch. "The Chronology of *The Return of the Native*," MODERN LANGUAGE NOTES, LIV (Nov 1939) 491–97.

Carl J. Weber's assertions that H not only had before him a " 'calendar for the year 1842' " but that " 'his careful attention to dates' " is due to his early training as an architect are questionable. There are "many instances where he [H] apparently quite lost sight of the calendar if he had one." These inconsistencies suggest that perhaps "too much had been made of Hardy's 'blue-print habits.' "

1913 "Notes and News: Masefield on Thomas Hardy," BULLETIN OF THE JOHN RYLANDS LIBRARY, XXIII (Oct 1939), 362.

At the opening of an H memorial room in Dorchester, Masefield asserted that H had a potent influence on young poets and that he exemplified "that rare maturity which defies the advance of years."

1914 Osawa, Mamoru. "Hardy and the German Men-of-Letters," STUDIES IN ENGLISH LITERATURE (Tokyo), XIX (Oct 1939), 504–44.

H "had unusual sympathy for German civilization"; he admired German music and painting, and he studied the "representative philosophers of Germany." He also drew on the work of such German poets as Goethe, Schiller, Richter, Schlegel, Novalis, Börne and Heine. [Basically a hasty survey of references to German writers culled from H's works, with more substantial treatment of H's debt to Heine and Schopenhauer.]

1915 Partington, Wilfred. FORGING AHEAD: THE TRUE STORY OF THE UPWARD PROGRESS OF THOMAS JAMES WISE . . . . (NY: Putnam's, 1939), pp. 85, 98, 102, 197–98, 207, 274.
[Six brief references to H, including his reading of Swinburne and comment on the mystery of Browning's character. Retells a Florence H description of how Clement King Shorter prevailed on H's courtesy and obtained an original manuscript.]

1916 Phelps, William Lyon. AUTOBIOGRAPHY WITH LETTERS (NY: Oxford UP, 1939), pp. 204, 205, 322, 389–404, 426, 551–52, 570, 571, 573, 576, 681, 803, 813, 816, 818, 823, 827.
In private conversations H expressed his belief that a novelist should tell a story. He revealed, also, that *A Laodicean* contained more facts of his own life than any other novel. [In general, this is a record of people's brief comments on H. Thus, Henry James derides H, Florence H describes the look of "radiant triumph" on his face in death, and William Phelps says H "had less of hypocrisy than of anything else."]

1917 Pinto, Vivian de Sola. "Realism in English Poetry," ESSAYS AND STUDIES BY MEMBERS OF THE ENGLISH ASSOCIATION, XXV (1939), 81–100.
H and Housman lived in an age like the seventeenth century in that the advance of science fostered realism, but neither could react optimistically. Both became poets of the "tragedy of the lonely individual in a non-moral universe." H owes much of his poetic realism to George Crabbe, but he had a bent for philosophy not found in the earlier poet.

1918 Pirkhofer, A. "Von Thomas Hardys Bild der Gegenwart" (Of Thomas Hardy's Picture of the Present), ZEITSCHRIFT FÜR NEUSPRACHLICHEN UNTERRICHT, XXXVIII (1939), 145–50.
H's moral and intellectual tendencies overburden his novels. H's prudery, lofty rhetoric and eclecticism are not in vogue; yet his employment of folklore and portrayal of the Wessex region are eternally artistic. [In German.]

1919 Powys, Llewelyn. "Recollections of Thomas Hardy," VIRGINIA QUARTERLY REVIEW, XV (Winter 1939), 425–34.
[A recounting of associations with H between approximately 1890 and 1928 which reveal H's views on a variety of topics: traditional dance, humane treatment of animals, genealogy of John Keats (a humorous incident which brought H's wrath down on Powys because Powys inadvertently put Amy Lowell on H's trail), Frank Norris. Also sharply drawn sketches of H, Emma Lavinia, and Florence Emily Hardy, as well as of the interior of Max Gate.]

1920 Rothenstein, William. SINCE FIFTY: MEN AND MEMORIES, 1922–1938 (Lond: Faber & Faber, 1939), pp. 10, 12, 79, 99–106, 107, 254, 264, 266, 286.

[Chap 7, "A Hardy Project," describes H's burial in Westminster Abbey, which Rothenstein witnessed and sketched with the intention of attempting a composition on the subject. But he was forced to abandon the "Project" because he was unable to persuade all of H's pallbearers (among whom were Barrie, Shaw, Kipling, Housman, Gosse and Galsworthy) to sit for him. Includes a curious tribute to H by T. E. Lawrence: "He was so by himself, so characteristic a man, that each contact with him was an experience. I went each time, nervously: and came away gladly, saying, 'It's all right.' That's the spirit in which most of us R.A.F. fellows go up into the air."]

1921 Sandison, Helen. "An Elizabethan Basis for a Hardy Tale?" PUBLICATIONS OF THE MODERN LANGUAGE ASSOCIATION, LIV (June 1939), 610–12.

"The First Countess of Wessex" in *A Group of Noble Dames* parallels the marriage of Douglas Howard to Arthur Gorges in 1584. Two Dorchester traditions mingle in the tale as H tells it. H's squire departs from his Tudor prototype, Mr. Horner. [See also C. J. Weber, "An Elizabethan Basis for a Hardy Tale—an Addendum," ibid, LVI (June 1941), 598–600.]

1922 [Smith, Joseph C. ?]. "New Hardy Items Presented to Colby," NEW YORK TIMES, 8 Jan 1939, II, p. 8.

[Description of gift of seventeen volumes of H novels all autographed by H and annotated by Betty and Rebekah Owen who knew him for twenty years.]

1923 Squire, Sir John. WATER-MUSIC, OR, A FORTNIGHT OF BLISS (Lond: Heinemann, 1939), pp. 222–26.

[Delightful account of two of the author's many visits with H between 1914 and 1928. On the first occasion, Sir John was reprimanded by the second Mrs. H for keeping H over a bottle of claret long beyond his regular bedtime. She insisted that upon future visits he would sleep at a hotel. On the second, Squire introduced John Goss, a then well-known singer of traditional songs. This meeting produced duets which H sang with great joy and feeling, at times with tears in his eyes. Upon H's death shortly thereafter, Squire, in a fit of revulsion at the separation of H's heart from his body for burial, wrote a macabre ballad ("Hardy in Our Abbey") recommending "a further distribution of parts."]

1924 Syrett, Netta. THE SHELTERING TREE (Lond: Geoffrey Bles, 1939), pp. 194–96.

[Chap 15 recalls the author's meeting with H on one occasion in the early 1900s when H was trying to rent rooms in London. H, very much in the care of Florence Emily Dugdale (then his secretary), is recalled as "gentle and simple," "a little, slight man with a fresh-coloured, rather sad face."]

1925 "Thomas Hardy's Study," TIMES (Lond), 10 May 1939, p. 9.

[On the reconstruction of H's study in Dorset County Museum, opened on 10 May by John Masefield. Visitors can look in and see it exactly as it was at Max Gate.]

1926 Tindall, William York. D. H. LAWRENCE & SUSAN HIS COW (NY: Columbia UP, 1939), pp. 32, 51, 93, 201, 203.

"He [Lawrence] called Ibsen, Flaubert, and Hardy 'the Nihilists, the intellectual, hopeless people,' from whose error he hoped mankind was now escaping by way of a religious revival." H was gloomy, Henley joyous over "the idea of mechanism and of life as an accident in matter." Later nineteenth-century writers saw nature, not in the friendly Wordsworthian sense, but as a cruel force. "Thomas Hardy's world was one of fungus and mildew and of cold grey stones upon which poets now declined to sit for fear of parasites." Science had intervened. Lawrence had read H and knew science, but still found nature worshipful as Wordsworth did, though the object differed. Lawrence the novelist imitated H at first and had in common with him "a peculiar sensitivity to . . . the spirit of place." Lawrence failed as a novelist to sacrifice theory and philosophy to vision, as T. S. Eliot said H was able to do.

1927 Titman, Lily. "Thomas Hardy as Musician," CHESTERIAN, XX (July–Aug 1939), 157–62.

[Assembles the usual evidence from H's writings to show how well H knew and loved music.]

1928 Wais, Kurt. DIE GEGENWARTS DICHTUNG DER EUROPAISCHEN VÖLKER (The Contemporary Fiction of the European People) (Berlin: Junker & Dunnhaupt, 1939), pp. 79, 80, 81–82, 115, 133, 135.

[Mentions H in connection with pessimism, regionalism, the post-war poetry, and the psychological novel.] [In German.]

1929 Weber, Carl J. (ed). COLBY NOTES ON "THE WOODLANDERS" (Waterfield, Maine: Fairfield Publishing, 1939).

[Contains primary and secondary bibliographies relating to The Woodlanders and more than 500 separate notes on the novel.]

1930 [Weber, Carl J. ?]. "Hardy Collection Received," LIBRARY JOURNAL, LXIX (1 June 1939), 463.

[Colby College Library has received the Owen Hardy Collection. H deferred to Rebekah Owen's judgment in revising the text of *The Mayor of Casterbridge*.]

1931 Weber, Carl J. "Hardy in America," COLOPHON, new graphic series I (March 1939), 95–96.

["Thomas Hardy in America," ibid, ns III (Summer 1938), 383–404, brought forth a number of new H titles in American imprints, listed here. Further information is requested for the Caxton, Arlington, and Red Letter series.]

1932 Weber, Carl J. "The Jubilee of the 'First Countess of Wessex,'" COLBY MERCURY, VI (Dec 1939), 278–81.

[Catalogue of semi-centennial exhibition at Colby of items associated with this thinly disguised story of the child-marriage of Betty Horner to Stephen Fox in 1736.]

1933 Weber, Carl J. "Notes and Observations: Hardy and *The Woodlanders*," REVIEW OF ENGLISH STUDIES (Lond), XV (July 1939), 330–33.

From the date of the publication of *The Woodlanders* on, "the chorus of praise had been fairly constant." When H said he liked it "as a story," he implied he did not like the characters. Rebekah Owen recorded a conversation with H in her copy of the book which confirms this dislike and identified Mrs. Charmond as "exactly E. L. H." or Emma Lavinia Hardy.

1934 Weber, Carl J. REBEKAH OWEN AND THOMAS HARDY (Waterville, Maine: Colby College Library, 1939).·

[Brief account of the relationship given full treatment in Weber's HARDY AND THE LADY FROM MADISON SQUARE (1952). Contains Rebekah Owen's annotations in her copies of H's novels and poems.]

1935 Weber, Carl J. "Virtue from Wessex: Thomas Hardy," AMERICAN SCHOLAR, VIII (Spring 1939), 211–22.

In H "we have then the spectacle of a tender-hearted little man courageously facing a world ready to despair and offering them his leadership." [Shallow.]

1936 Wedel, Theodore O. "Our Pagan World," THEOLOGY, Nov 1939, pp. 333–43.

H's atheism is "noble," for if he does not compromise with traditional religion, he does not sneer at it; but his alternative, "the human heart's resource alone," does not solve "the hard practical problems of daily living."

1937 Winslow, Donald J. [and Shun Katayama]. "Thomas Hardy in Japan," BOSTON EVENING TRANSCRIPT, 27 Feb 1939, p. 10.
H's popularity has declined in Japan because the peak has been reached in criticism, and H's pessimism is not universally appreciated. Some works of H (longer novels, short stories, and a very few poems) have been translated into Japanese. Some longer works that were abridged for textbooks have been put aside by the educational authorities (along with D. H. Lawrence and James Joyce) as unsound. *Jude the Obscure* and *The Well-Beloved* have interfered with the availability of *Tess of the d'Urbervilles,* a much-liked novel in Japan. H will come back in Japan when the individual ceases to be lost in national purpose. [Excerpts from a letter by Shun Katayama.]

1938 "Yale Library Receives Rare Hardy Manuscript," NEW YORK HERALD TRIBUNE, XCIX (15 May 1939), 15.
H's fair copy of *Human Shows, Far Phantasies, Songs, and Trifles,* in his own hand, was saved by Mrs. H so that the 196-page document could be sent to Yale as a token of appreciation for their display of H material at the time of the author's death.

1940

1939 Aaronson, L. "*Selected Poems of Thomas Hardy,*" NINE-TEENTH CENTURY AND AFTER, CXXVIII (Nov 1940), 492–99.
In *The Selected Poems of Thomas Hardy,* ed by G. M. Young (1940), Young's selections are not sufficiently purposive. Selections from *The Dynasts* are only confusing, and many outstanding individual poems are omitted. "Mr. Young insists [in his introduction] altogether too much upon the Time-spirit in Hardy's poetry." He lacks the quality of drawing "one down into the deepest mysteries of word-meaning," as the greatest poets do. H was divided, inconsistent, and as a result, his incidents and inventions by their contrivance and the sense of the author's presence distract from word meanings. H was a marvelous writer of popular poetry, contributing a sense of historical time and a true Englishness. He is not, however, as Young insists, without self-pity. "If one of the tests of poetic greatness be a compulsive power in the poetry that annihilates all distraction and translates us inevitably into its own world of reality, above all, the distraction that narrows us too physically into awareness of our mortality and the burden of death, Hardy is supreme."

1940 "Ald. T. H. Tilley's Memories of an Intimate Friendship," DORSET COUNTY CHRONICLE AND SWANAGE TIMES, 6 June 1940, p. 1.
[Account of Mr. Tilley's—former mayor of Dorchester—association with H in the production of H plays in Dorset.]

1941 Auden, W. H. "A Literary Transference," SOUTHERN REVIEW (Thomas Hardy Centennial Edition), VI (Summer 1940), 78–86.
[Auden had an adolescent love-affair with H's poems. H comforted Auden, educated his "vision as a human being," and gave him "technical instruction" in writing verse. H was Auden's "poetical father."]

1942 Baker, E. A. "Hardy's *Dynasts*: The Moment for A Performance," TIMES (Lond), 4 Jan 1940, p. 4.
The H centenary could best be honored by a performance of *The Dynasts*, which is a "philosophical drama revealing, behind the visible acts and their immediate results, the fundamental realities of history."

1943 Baker, Howard. "Hardy's Poetic Certitude," SOUTHERN REVIEW (Thomas Hardy Centennial Edition), VI (Summer 1940), 49–63.
The best test of poetry is its humanity, and H (in "Hap") shakes free from half-truths and settles upon hard truth. When H's pessimistic utterances are motivated (they aren't always), poetry emerges. The root of his inspiration is "conflict between love of life and contempt for the world." His subjects are everyday histories of people: for him, the lyric is always dramatic. H's keynote is "deep sad truth," whether in lyrics, *The Dynasts*, or novels.

1944 Baldwin, Earl of Bewdley. "Thomas Hardy," ENGLISH, III: 14 (1940), 57–62.
Like Scott, H will be remembered by the best of his novels and not by his poems. *The Dynasts* will stand for generations. [A speech delivered at Dorchester on the occasion of the H Centenary Celebrations, 2 June 1940. Being not overfond of literary criticism, the Earl gives us his own views of H and his work.]

1945 Barber, Edmund. "Hardy and Hardy's Wessex," COUNTRY LIFE, LXXXVII (8 June 1940), 562–65.
H made the countryside of his childhood the setting for many of his novels, creating a whole fictional province named "Wessex." So real did Wessex become to the author and his readers that H finally printed a map in the end papers of his collected novels which identifies the real and imaginary places in his literary counties.

1946 Barzun, Jacques. "Truth and Poetry in Thomas Hardy," SOUTHERN REVIEW (Thomas Hardy Centennial Edition), VI (Summer 1940), 179–92.

Despite the critics, unity exists in H's writings; old Aristotelian categories of fact and fiction (Truth and Poetry) simply do not apply. H's brand of truth is not narrowly realistic but romantic or imaginative. His people are true; his events are unreal. We object to the events because they, although causeless, effect tragedy. H insists there is lack of adequate cause in human events. Since the imagination of the author has been formed by personal experience, and that of the reader by literary experience, H must educate us to his viewpoint. H reminds us constantly that he treats truth poetically. Critics' problem with H is their attempt to consign him to this or that school, or to measure him by their standards. H, spiritually and intellectually a Romantic and Gothic in his artistic principles, doesn't fit our categories. To him, "Truth and Poetry do not fight a manichean fight which will leave Science or Ignorance master of the field: they merge into each other by degrees and constitute together the sum total of mind-measured reality."

1947 Bentley, Phyllis. "Thomas Hardy as a Regional Novelist," FORTNIGHTLY REVIEW, CXLVII (June 1940), 647–52.

Of the various types of regionalism—from mere local color to the total regionalism that explores locality itself—H is at the "penultimate stage." H describes intensely, has regional characters who are vital in proportion to their closeness to the soil. But his sparing use of dialect indicates a reservation. He does not want "to subordinate the individual to the locale." Plots are not regionally motivated as a rule, except for *The Return of the Native*. His theme is the whole human race and its conditions of existence, as exemplified in Wessex.

1948 Bernard, S. G. "Wessex Celebrates the Hardy Centenary," FIELD, 25 May 1940, pp. 814–15.

[A biographical sketch which stresses H's love of Wessex and Max Gate.]

1949 Bernard, S. G. " 'Wessex,' the Dream Country," ENGLISH DIGEST, Sept 1940, pp. 59–61.

[A brief biography of H commemorating the 100th anniversary of his birth.]

1950 Blackmur, R. P. "The Shorter Poems of Thomas Hardy," SOUTHERN REVIEW (Thomas Hardy Centennial Edition), VI (Summer 1940), 20–48; rptd in LANGUAGE AS GESTURE (NY: Harcourt, Brace, 1952).

H's "poems of ideas in which the poet has violated his sensibility" should be weeded out of the canon. H, his subjects show, had a "scandalous sensibility." H too often dispensed with tradition in verse or "damaged it . . .

by adherence to his personal and crotchety obsessions." Too often H's machinery gets in the way of the poetry. Exceptions are "The Workbox," where formula fits poem and gets incorporated in it; "Last Words to a Dumb Friend," in which H uses violence of intellect but lets violence emerge out of the poem, and some two dozen others. H is a "great example of a sensibility great enough . . . to survive the violation."

1951 Blyton, W. J. "Hardy, After a Century," NATIONAL REVIEW (Lond), CXIV (May 1940), 611–15; rptd in CATHOLIC WORLD, CLII (Dec 1940), 292–95.

Jude the Obscure is a cold fare but the supposed despondency of the other novels is corrected by lovable characters—Oak, Venn, Winterborne, Marty South, and Bathsheba Everdene, all having Biblical counterparts. The "morality" of the books is apt to become dated and a liability. H's historical instinct compensates, however. "In everything but the *genius*, he was the typical late Victorian, country-town archaeologist." "Like many Englishmen, his religion was largely sub-conscious." "Men who March Away" is one of the best of the 1914–1918 war-poems.

1952 Carter, H. S. "County Pride Keeps Hardy Alive," DORSET COUNTY CHRONICLE AND SWANAGE TIMES, 30 May 1940, p. 5.

H's novels offer a rich experience: "Hardy harrows the feelings, racking and torturing his unhappy subjects until the reader is dismayed." "Does Nature never relent? Do we not know life as sometimes radiant, happy and peaceful in its endings?"

1953 "College Library Gets New Books," COLBY ECHO, XLIII (17 Jan 1940), 1, 6.

[Account of recent additions of rare H items to Colby's collection.]

1954 Cottman, Thomas. "Hardy's Attitude Towards Religion," DORSET COUNTY CHRONICLE AND SWANAGE TIMES, 6 June 1940, p. 1.

There is ample evidence in *Jude the Obscure* that in creating Sue and Jude, H had "this conflict [the Tractarian Movement] very much in mind." When love came to Jude "he exactly reflected the intellectual position of the authors of the tracts. Final disappointment came to him." Sue, unlike Jude, was reason personified.

1955 Craig, Hardin, and John W. Dodds. TYPES OF ENGLISH FICTION (NY: Macmillan, 1940), pp. 583–87.

"In the exploitation of a region Scott and Wordsworth are Hardy's only rivals, and perhaps neither of them has quite equaled Hardy in making the land utter its inhabitants." Like Wordsworth, but with additional evidence provided by Darwin and other scientists, H believed "man's lot is a product of his relation to external nature." Despite improbabilities, "there is always plausibility in character." He may have turned to poetry because he felt that "the deeper forces controlling human existence could no longer be satisfactorily expressed through any prose medium." [Reprints "What the Shepherd Saw" as an example of "philosophical realism," pp. 588–608.]

1956 Daiches, David. THE NOVEL AND THE MODERN WORLD (Chicago: University of Chicago P, 1940; rptd 1960), pp. 18, 30, 39, 68, 70.

H uses an indirect method of presenting character in his introduction of Henchard into *The Mayor of Casterbridge*. He emerges from the story itself. Galsworthy, compared with H, is not so tragic but has instead a sense of disturbed compassion.

1957 Daiches, David. POETRY AND THE MODERN WORLD: A STUDY OF POETRY IN ENGLAND BETWEEN 1900 AND 1939 (Chicago: University of Chicago P, 1940), pp. 17–19.

At root H's pessimism springs from his view of Victorian social values. He construed the social scheme of the period to be evil and translated that perception into an ill-founded assertion of cosmic evil.

1958 Dataller, Roger [pseud of A. A. Eaglestone]. THE PLAIN MAN AND THE NOVEL (Lond: Nelson, 1940), pp. 51, 114, 133–38.

"Celestial double-cross" is one of H's favorite devices. In *The Woodlanders*, however, the basic struggle is between Town and Country, between close-to-nature characters like Giles and Marty and "the sophisticated, the artificial" town characters like Mrs. Charmond and Dr. Fitzpiers.

1959 Davidson, Donald. "The Traditional Basis of Thomas Hardy's Fiction," SOUTHERN REVIEW (Thomas Hardy Centennial Edition), VI (Summer 1940), 162–68.

H is misunderstood by most critics because his art and even his own times are foreign to them. Technically, H is a ballad-singer of the novel in a time of artistic self-consciousness, an American of the Southwest-humorist school isolated in Victorian England. H's work is "traditional" but not "literary-traditional," rather the folk-tradition of ballads, dances, country church music. The typical H novel is conceived of as a told (or sung) story, with emphasis on action, not psychology, of character and utilization of folk archetypes: Gabriel Oak—a patient Griselda, Fanny Robin—a deserted maiden, Sergeant Troy—archetype of soldier/sailor in ballads, Tess—deserted maiden who murders her seducer, etc. H's use of coincidence can also be defended, as in traditional tales, as a means of making the story unusual and memorable. H uses the device of changeless characters from traditional literature. These are rustics close to nature who survive; the changeful characters cause trouble and die. H's habit of mind is implicit in plots and characters. He is neither pessimistic nor blasphemous; he is merely the teller of traditional tales.

1960 Dobrée, Bonamy. *"The Dynasts,"* SOUTHERN REVIEW (Thomas Hardy Centennial Edition), VI (Summer 1940), 109–24.
The Dynasts appears timely for a second time. H's mind agrees with the Spirit of Years, his heart with the Pities. H's metaphysics furnish "Intuitive Correlative" to complement "Objective Correlative"; the reader is also torn between Years and Pities. H gives us a new form—Epic-Drama—which enables straight-line plot but requires immense variety in meters and machinery to hold the reader's interest. H keeps eye of imagination continually at work by rapid change of visual scenes. Allegorical characters are also realistic; worlds are distinct but connected; spirits comment on human action and influence it; human panorama succeeds because it moves quickly; poem's form is stamped on our emotions. The work's weaknesses the "Pre-Marlovian" blank verse, echoes of Jacobean drama (couplets to mark the end of scenes), characters speaking out of character (prostitute using blank verse). But the work communicates three things: a "sense of stoicism tempered by love," a "sense of the oneness of living things with the earth," and a "sense of the dignity of man."

1961 Downs, R. B. "Notable Materials added to American Libraries, 1938–39," LIBRARY QUARTERLY, X (1940), 162.
"Colby's Hardy collection—comprising some 3,000 items, including all first editions except two—was strengthened by several collected editions."

1962 Edgar, Pelham. "The Hardy Centenary," QUEEN'S QUARTERLY, XLVII (Autumn 1940), 277–87.
Conformity we shall never find in H, but his detractors have never questioned his burning sincerity. He considered himself a pessimist only in the sense that the great tragic writers from Aeschylus onward could be so defined. H could not perceive any evidence of loving-kindness in the ordering of our fate, but no writer has realized more fully the nobility of the human struggle. If this is pessimism, we must accept the verdict. H's debt to Schopenhauer has been exaggerated. *The Dynasts* is H's greatest contribution to English poetry. His briefer poems remain to be considered: before Gerard Manley Hopkins appeared on the scene, they were a powerful influence on younger writers.

1963 Empson, William. "Thomas Hardy," NEW STATESMAN AND NATION, XX (14 Sept 1940), 263–64.
In *Selected Poems of Thomas Hardy*, ed by G. M. Young (1940), Young's introduction brings out all the points but fails to emphasize H's contradictions. The selection omits eight excellent poems and a working selection

of bad ones. Young's incomprehensible views on rhythm were doubtless the basis of his selection.

1964 Flower, Newman. "Some Memories of Thomas Hardy," DORSET COUNTY CHRONICLE AND SWANAGE TIMES, 30 May 1940, p. 5.
[Account of how Flower came to know H, and of their visits together.]

1965 Gilchrist, Anne G. "Correspondence," MUSIC AND LETTERS, XXI (July 1940), 301–2.
The selection of tunes printed in Edna Sherman's "Thomas Hardy: Lyricist, Symphonist," ibid (April 1940), 143–71, as having been referred to by H in his writings is familiar to those possessing an acquaintance with old fiddler's books. The origin of Nos. 12, 18, 40, 98, 102, and 177 is easy to trace. These old dance-airs are worth studying on account of the social and historical customs or events they reflect.

1966 Grebanier, Bernard D. N., with Stith Thompson. ENGLISH LITERATURE AND ITS BACKGROUNDS (NY: The Cordon Co, 1940), II, 861–63.
[A brief summary of H's life and works with three poems appended: "Rome: At the Pyramid of Cestius, etc," "A Christmas Ghost-Story," and "Ah, are you Digging on my Grave?"]

1967 Grew, Eva Mary. "Thomas Hardy and Music," CHOIR (Lond), XXXI (June 1940), 82–83.
Though H lost his religious faith early in life, the influence of religious music remained with him. From his early years, H was "an essential musician."

1968 Grew, Eva Mary. "Thomas Hardy as Musician," MUSIC AND LETTERS, XXI (April 1940), 120–42.
As a child H was sensitive to music to the point of tears. As he grew up he came to know the local jigs and songs, hymns, chants, and anthems very well and used this knowledge often in his art. He sometimes wrote verse to the inspiration of music, as "Lines to a Movement in Mozart's E-Flat Symphony" shows. Yet H has not shown that for him music was a vast elemental thing, a cosmic power. He could not have written "Abt Vogler." H, an experienced fiddler, often suggests in his poems the frenzy of dancing and its inspiring music. H has the rare Shakespearian power to condense an aural impression into a single word; thus, in *The Mayor of Casterbridge*, he remarks that the milk "*purrs*" into the pails. H's rhythms have been declared unrhythmical, his meters immetrical, and his harmony no harmony at all; however, his lilting "When I Set Out for Lyonesse" and "Shelley's Skylark" prove him well-nigh as gifted as Tennyson in these respects.

1969 Grigson, Geoffrey. "Architecture and Thomas Hardy," Architectural Review, LXXXVIII (1940), 1–2.

H was a man without ambition, "able to conceive ideas . . . and mature them slowly." H was probably miscast as an architect. But even if H's "architectural talent was mediocre, he had that sense of human history in physical images which architecture needs." For H churches were places sacred to tragedy rather than to God, where an answer had been "pitifully looked for and never found."

1970 Harding, Hy. "The Humour of Thomas Hardy," Dorset Yearbook, 1940, pp. 39–42.

The secret of the humor in H's rustics is that they are like children, "the ignorant quaint children of Arcadia." H's "gift of humour confines itself almost entirely to the Dorset rustic." Education, it would seem, "is destructive of humour."

1971 "Hardy Collection Receives Acclaim In Wide Reviews," Colby Echo, XLIII (8 May 1940), 1, 6.

[Account of the praise accorded Colby College for its H collection.]

1972 Hashiba, Masaichi. "Thomas Hardy's *The Mayor of Casterbridge*: A Study of a Lonely Man," Studies in English Literature (Tokyo), XX (Oct 1940), 486–508.

[An uncritical statement of the obvious qualities of *The Mayor of Casterbridge.*]

1973 Henkin, Leo J. "Evolution and the Idea of Degeneration," Darwinism in the English Novel, 1860–1910 (NY: Corporate P, 1940); rptd (NY: Russell & Russell, 1963), pp. 221–32, espec 223–26.

H saw no hope of man's controlling his own destiny. Man's consciousness developed quite fortuitously and without a place in Nature. Man's tragedy is the result of his ignorance of Nature's indifference to him. *Two on a Tower* and *A Pair of Blue Eyes* point up man's insignificance in space and time.

1974 Hillebrand, Anneliese. Kirchliche Bewegungen Englands Im Spiegel der Modernen Romanliteratur (English Church Movements As Reflected In Modern Fiction) (Lengerich: Lengerischer Handelsdruckerei, 1940), pp. 54–56, 107–8; University of Münster dissertation.

[Considers briefly the religious convictions of Anthony Trollope, Charles Kingsley, George Eliot, C. M. Yonge, Margaret Oliphant, Mrs. H. Ward, Samuel Butler, George Moore, Edna Lyall, Jerome K. Jerome, H, Hall Caine, Marie Corelli, Arthur Quiller-Couch, Lawrence Housman, H. G.

Wells, W. B. Bereford, T. F. Powys, Compton Mackenzie, Hugh Walpole, Gilbert Cannan, May Sinclair, Sheila Kaye-Smith, and Rose Macaulay. H's biography was the primary source for establishing his religious convictions.] The Reverend Clare in *Tess of the d'Urbervilles* illustrates a type of positive evangelism which is frequently found in the novels of George Eliot. [In German.]

1975 Holland, Clive [pseud of C. J. Hankinson]. "Cycle Rides with Hardy," DORSET COUNTY CHRONICLE AND SWANAGE TIMES, 6 June 1940, pp. 1, 8.

H's pessimism was of the intellectual kind, "the rather cynical pessimism of several of the ancient classical writers."

1976 Holland, Clive [pseud of C. J. Hankinson]. "Thomas Hardy, the Man," JOURNAL OF THE ROYAL SOCIETY OF ARTS, LXXXVIII (9 Aug 1940), 779–92.

H once said concerning the location of settings he used in his novels, "You must not assume as a general rule that you may discover the actual place I had in mind. . . . Sometimes two places may have been merged by me in one." The poem "The Lost Pyx—A Medieval Legend" was set on the hill above the Vale of Blackmore, near the "Cross-and-Hand" stone. Mrs. H was a kind woman and a good hostess, but she would have been more suited to the environment of a country vicarage than as the wife of a distinguished man of letters. H's prose rather than his verse will survive the efflux of time.

1977 Hübner, Walter. DIE KUNSTPROSA IM ENGLISCHEN UNTER-RICHT (Imaginative Prose in English Instruction) (Leipzig: Quelle & Meyer, 1940), pp. 155, 161–62.

H's interest in peasant life, his fascination with the landscape, his love for portraying nature, and his sincere sympathy for his characters are reflected in *Wessex Tales* and make these stories typical of H's artistry. [In German.]

1978 Kaplan, Estelle. PHILOSOPHY IN THE POETRY OF EDWIN ARLINGTON ROBINSON (NY: Columbia UP, 1940), pp. 6, 12, 31–33, 52.

E. A. Robinson was influenced by H. He wrote of H's novels: "There is a marvelous mixture of pastoral humor and pathos." "Tragedy is by no means forgotten, though Hardy is not so bloodthirsty as his contemporary Black-more." Robinson saw H's world as struggling against indifferent, albeit neutral forces, representing a type of idealism derived from an examination of evil and error.

1979 Kelliher, Beatrice. "Hardy's Books Marked the End of an Era," NEW HAVEN REGISTER, 2 June 1940, p. 4.

Centennial of H's birth reminds us that he was the last of the great Victorian writers. H's works which will remain great are *Under the Greenwood Tree, Far From the Madding Crowd, The Return of the Native, The Mayor of Casterbridge, Tess of the d'Urbervilles, Jude the Obscure, The Dynasts,* and "In Time of 'the Breaking of Nations.' "

1980 Leavis, F. R. "Hardy the Poet," SOUTHERN REVIEW (Thomas Hardy Centennial Edition), VI (Summer 1940), 87–98.
There is only a handful of H poems worth examining: "Friends Beyond," "Julie-Janes," "The Darkling Thrush," etc., and only six are of major quality: "Neutral Tones," "A Broken Appointment," "The Self-Unseeing," "The Voice," "After a Journey," and "During Wind and Rain." Most of H's poems are prosaic, sing-song efforts, haunted by H coinages and saved, if at all, by H's intensity. "Lack of distinction in Hardy becomes a positive quality."

1981 Leisner, August R. "Sonnets on Hardy," DALHOUSIE REVIEW, XX (1940), 316–18.
[Four sonnets: "He Explains His Choice of Tragedy," "He Speaks of Lovers," "The Woodlanders," and "Houses For Him Were Haunted." Each considers an aspect of H's work and interprets its significance.]

1982 Lovett, Neville. "In Memory of Hardy," TIMES (Lond), 3 June 1940, p. 3.
At the H centenary, celebrated 2 June in Dorchester, the Bishop of Salisbury said that one could understand H's pessimism because H concentrated so much on unhappy things. However, H can still be seen as one who served us in a very Christian way by leading us to "sweeter manners, purer laws."

1983 MacCarthy, Desmond. "Thomas Hardy: the Writer," LISTENER, 6 June 1940, pp. 1086–88.
In fiction H deals with a past epoch; in poetry he approaches the present more directly. "I remember his saying that it was the desire to make a little money that first prompted him to write fiction." H's rustics are preferable to Shakespeare's, "for they never sink into buffoonery. They seem in touch with life in a deeper way than the town-dwellers." H's diction is sometimes clumsy and pedantic.

1984 McCourt, E. A. "Thomas Hardy and War," DALHOUSIE REVIEW, XX (July 1940), 227–34.
H lived through many wars, so when he speaks of war it is with authority. But he belongs neither to jingoist or pacifist schools of poets and speaks with detachment. *The Dynasts* presents the horrors of war with gloomy

resignation. Of the later poems, some are topical, others ironically philosophical, like "The Man he Killed." H was not a pacifist, but he despised aggression. War is, however, inevitable—all are driven by the Immanent Will.

1985 McFadden, G. V. "When I Met Thomas Hardy," DORSET YEARBOOK, 1940, pp. 43–46.
"[I] found in him neither the reticence nor the gloomy pessimism so often associated with his name but merely a kindly homeliness and geniality."

1986 "Many Magnificent Additions To The Hardiana Are In The Colby Library," COLBY ECHO, XLIII (13 March 1940), 1, 6.
[The title says it!]

1987 Meynell, Viola (ed). FRIENDS OF A LIFETIME: LETTERS TO SYDNEY CARLYLE COCKERELL (Lond: Jonathan Cape, 1940), pp. 274–315
[Reprints letters from H to Cockerell covering a period between 1911 and 1925. Contains indications throughout of his thoughts on the war and on various books Cockerell had sent him. Indicates H's desires regarding the disposition of various MSS, specifically "An Imaginative Woman," *Wessex Poems, Time's Laughingstocks, Poems of the Past and the Present, Life's Little Ironies*. Nietzsche and "the school" mistakenly regard life as perfectible, when the best to be hoped for is amelioration; Kant, Schopenhauer, etc., are closer to Christianity than to Nietzsche. During a visit to Tintagel H's vision of "The Famous Tragedy of the Queen of Cornwall" was clouded by the memory of "an Iseult of . . . [his] own"; Masefield's war experiences must have left him quite shaken and will interfere with his writing; Swinburne's intention to stick to the facts in his version of Tristram is amusing; the original need to disguise the location of *A Pair of Blue Eyes* has since been removed by a death. H's comments on *Late Lyrics and Earlier* refer to Cockerell's help in preparing it for publication, the intention of the Preface, and the meaning of some of the poems. Frequent comments indicate H's dissatisfaction upon rereading his own work and his lack of interest in publishing things. Letters from Mrs. H quote H that Crabbe was an important influence on his novel writing and that in other writing Shakespeare, Shelley, and Browning were, and indicate H's reactions to various books they read together. Although mainly by H, this material reveals Cockerell's role in H's career.]

1988 Milner, Gamaliel. "The Religion of Thomas Hardy," MODERN CHURCHMAN, XXX (July 1940), 157–64.
H will interest posterity as the great representative of the closing phase of the Victorian Age. He was not a rationalist but fundamentally a pagan. Young H was brought up in Church of England and did not have any def-

inite belief about the Trinity. A vague agnosticism was the prevailing tone in intellectual circles when young H went to London. There was nothing in H's life to explain the deep undercurrent of pessimism to be noted in the Wessex novels. The sketches of clerical life in his novels are usually drawn with a kindly spirit. *The Mayor of Casterbridge*, the story of King Saul in nineteenth-century life, is tragedy unrelieved. A better motto for *Jude the Obscure* would have been: "The flesh lusteth against the spirit, and the spirit against the flesh." There are signs of exhaustion and weariness in *Jude*.

1989 Mizener, Arthur. "*Jude the Obscure* as a Tragedy," Southern Review (Thomas Hardy Centennial Edition), VI (Summer 1940), 193–213.

H intended to write tragedy in *Jude the Obscure*—idea of "worthy encompassed by the inevitable"—but he identified too generally with the hero and produced a naturalistic novel. The reason: H's conception of truth is historical, not fabulous. H thus becomes the hero of *Jude*, and his world is too time-bound to produce the universal truth of tragedy. "There is no basic unresolvable tension between the real and ideal in his attitude, and there is as a consequence no tragic tension in the formal structure it invokes as its representation." *Jude* is a "history of a worthy man's education." In the novel, Jude learns "the true morality of 'unbiased nature'" but also learns that neither nature nor society recognizes it, to say nothing of attempting to live by it. Since hero's life and death are essentially meaningless, *Jude* cannot be tragedy.

1990 Morley, Christopher. "Soliloquy on Thomas Hardy," Columbia University Quarterly, XXXII (Oct 1940), 206–9.

H's message is that no matter how high we rise or how low we sink, nothing personal is intended by fate for our dismay. H is not merely a pessimist, as he is misrepresented, nor is he a comic, although he has a comic lack of relish for the husband of the species. In the novels, H's "invention was nil," and "his sense of reader psychology was defective." He published poems written at twenty-four at eighty-five, for it was all part of the panorama he was creating. "Great Things" is one of the merriest of the lighter poems. "The Subalterns" is one of H's most beautiful poems, showing even great annihilating forces of life under orders.

1991 Muller, Herbert J. "The Novels of Hardy Today," Southern Review (Thomas Hardy Centennial Edition), VI (Summer 1940), 214–24.

Critics can say nothing new about H's novels; their weaknesses and strengths are clear. Critics too often assail H for not fitting their molds, instead of enjoying his. After the many weaknesses have been seen and the virtues chronicled, H's effect defies analysis. Perhaps it is that he produced "majestic fictions."

1992 O'Rourke, May. "He Was Not Merely English, but England," DORSET COUNTY CHRONICLE AND SWANAGE TIMES, 30 May 1940, p. 5.

"Literature was the breath of life in that household." Life there was placid, homey, satisfying. [Account of Miss O'Rourke's life with the Hardys at Max Gate.]

1993 Pirkhofer, A. "Der Unsterblichkeitsgedanke in Thomas Hardys Gedichte" (Immortality in Thomas Hardy's Poetry), ZEITSCHRIFT FÜR NEUSPRACHLICHEN UNTERRICHT, XXXIX (1940), 175–85.

There are four different expressions of immortality in H's poetry: (1) the materialistic belief in the conservation of energy and substance (the idea of metamorphosis), (2) the biological idea of permanence, (3) spiritual immortality, and (4) the belief that everything is a unified experience. H's *Weltanschauung* and view of man did not change considerably in the course of his long life. H does not express the transferred consciousness of an existing association between the living and the dead, which is typical of Germanic thought. [In German.]

1994 Porter, Katherine Anne. "Notes on a Criticism of Thomas Hardy," SOUTHERN REVIEW (Thomas Hardy Centennial Edition), VI (Summer 1940), 150–61.

H is acceptably "churchy," though he represents a long line of questioners. Contrary to what T. S. Eliot said, H edifies by posing proper questions. H's characters "suffer the tragedy of being, Eliot's by not being." In style, H is not consciously concerned with the phrase, sentence, paragraph, but with over-all effect. This makes his work always memorable, occasionally sublime.

1995 Quiller-Couch, Sir Arthur. "*The Dynasts*," JOHN O'LONDON'S WEEKLY, 7 June 1940, pp. 275–76.

Most of H's reasons for choosing the Napoleonic War as his subject in *The Dynasts* concerned the war's local impact. Despite the controversy, *Dynasts* may be termed a drama, but it contains many faults. The blank verse is often quite bad; the lines given to the spiritual beings, while lyrical, are rarely good; the choruses "exaggerate a quasi-philosophic lingo," and they are monotonous and boring. *Dynasts* is valuable, however, in that it is "the last testament of a great writer."

1996 Ransom, John Crowe. "Honey and Gall," SOUTHERN REVIEW (Thomas Hardy Centennial Edition), VI (Summer 1940), 1–19.

H's poetic corpus—some 1,000 poems—is unparalleled in the literature of irony. H is superior to Housman and Swinburne in his use of irony. H is an uneven poet: there are some awkward and tasteless passages but also some of innocence and spontaneity. H's worst poem is *The Dynasts* because the subject was too exalted for his talents. H was most successful in handling short lyrics. H is a "great minor poet . . . and a poor major poet."

1997 Robinson, Edwin Arlington. SELECTED LETTERS OF EDWIN ARLINGTON ROBINSON, ed by Ridgeley Torrence (NY: Macmillan, 1940), pp. 45, 129, 130, 159, 177.

26 Sept 1901: "From the artist's point of view I cannot place it [ESTHER WATERS] along with Hardy's *Jude the Obscure*, but it has a message without being a sermon and for that reason will live. Nearly all of Hardy will die, I think, though I dislike to think of the funeral of *The Return of the Native*. I should call *Jude*, with all its misery, his one book that is true." 15 Aug 1922: I "doubt if you know what a luce is. It has nothing to do with the lucifugous Thomas Hardy—whose last book of poems, by the way, is most remarkable. Apparently he will take his place among the solid poets of England, which is a pretty good place to take. He and Francis Thompson are, so far as I can see the only real figgers [sic] (both of the second order, I suppose) since Swinburne." 24 Aug 1922: "Hardy's poetry, by the way, fares about as badly with a single reading as that of another spreader of sunshine whom I might drag in." 19 June 1929: "You are entirely wrong about my being steeped in Zola and Hardy when I was young." 11 Sept 1934: "The insects will take over one day."

1998 Rogers, T. H. "How Hardy Solved the Autograph 'Nuisance,' " DORSET COUNTY CHRONICLE AND SWANAGE TIMES, 30 May 1940, p. 5.

H instructed his servants "to sign all letters addressed to him requiring acknowledged receipts."

1999 Rowse, A. L. "Thomas Hardy and North Cornwall," COUNTRY LIFE, LXXXVIII (27 July 1940), 70–72.

After "Wessex," H's favorite spot in England was North Cornwall, where, at St. Juliot, he met his first wife, Emma Gifford. St. Juliot was also the setting for much of the action in *A Pair of Blue Eyes*, which records in fictional form some of H's and Emma's feelings and impressions about the author's first visit to Cornwall as a church-restorer. Though H and Emma never returned to St. Juliot after their marriage, occasional poems refer to Cornwall. Finally the series of poems H wrote in 1912–1913, reflecting upon Emma's death, often take place in St. Juliot, the town of their courtship.

2000 Rush, N. Orwin. A CENTURY OF THOMAS HARDY: CATALOGUE OF A CENTENNIAL EXHIBITION (Waterville, Maine: Colby College Library, 1940).

[Descriptive catalogue of one hundred items from H's home at Max Gate; all the items "bear his signature, his book-plate, or other mark of having been in his own hands in his house."]

2001 Sampson, Ashley. "Hardy & England's Wars," DAILY TELE-GRAPH (Lond), 3 June 1940, p. 4.

The Dynasts is as appropriate to World War II as to the first war. Hardy was not a jingoist but knew that national peril "made keen the edge of men's souls to deeds of real heroism."

2002 Samuel, Viscount. "The Philosophy of Thomas Hardy," JOHN O'LONDON'S WEEKLY, 7 June 1940, pp. 277–78.

H's view of the world was influenced by his own temperament. Even as a child he was sensitive and sympathetic and, as a result, was highly conscious of the suffering around him. Despite his temperament, H preferred to think of himself as a meliorist rather than a pessimist. H also did not like being labeled a philosopher; he claimed his ideas did not comprise a system but a series of impressions. H was, nonetheless, a philosopher. Man in H's world is always being acted upon irrationally; hence, H felt the cosmos must be indifferent and non-rational—it knew neither good nor evil. H did not consider his ideas antithetical to religion, for he wanted an alliance between religion and rationality.

2003 Sassoon, Siegfried. "Hardy As I Knew Him," JOHN O'LONDON'S WEEKLY, 7 June 1940, pp. 269–70.

H was humble, sensitive, respectful, unobtrusive, wise, and still quite active in his eighties. For those who never met H, his character can best be understood by reading his personal poems, for they contain his attitudes toward himself and toward life.

2004 Schwartz, Delmore. "Poetry and Belief in Thomas Hardy," SOUTHERN REVIEW (Thomas Hardy Centennial Edition), VI (Summer 1940), 64–77.

H "believed, in the most literal sense, that the fundamental factor in the nature of things was a 'First or Fundamental Energy,' as he calls it in the foreword to *The Dynasts*." H in the historical sense shows the "conflict between the new scientific view of Life which the nineteenth century produced and the whole attitude toward Life which had been traditional to Western culture"; his views are apparent in such poems as "A Plaint to Man," "God's Funeral," and "The Oxen." The effects of nineteenth-century scientific thought upon H are comparable with similar effects upon Dreiser, Shaw, Lord Russell. I. A. Richards is wrong in his theories about H. H fails in attempting to state his beliefs directly. Not many readers will subscribe to H's beliefs as he held them.

2005 Sherman, Elna. "Music in Thomas Hardy's Life and Work," MUSICAL QUARTERLY (NY), XXVI (Oct 1940), 419–45.

Music was the predominant interest in H's early environment. He reacted with great sensitiveness to music. He learned to play the accordion and the violin. He longed to study music and become an organist. H had seen old tune-books, especially one compiled about 1820 by his grandfather. H bought his own violin in London and enjoyed exploring scores of operas both English and Italian. Much later H recreated from memory an old "folk-play," "*O Jan, O Jan, O Jan*," for The Hardy Players of Dorchester. In 1924 H was conversant with works by Vaughan Williams, Rutland Boughton, Gustav Holst. But the most compelling proof of H's musical susceptibility is to be found in his own work.

2006 Sherman, Elna. "Thomas Hardy: Lyricist, Symphonist," MUSIC AND LETTERS, XXI (April 1940), 143–71.

Throughout his life H was obsessed by the sacred and secular music he had learned in his youth. *Under the Greenwood Tree* reflects a rich musical inheritance. There are about 200 "musical" poems in H's collected poems; all are permeated with music of many moods. Folk material was excellent schooling for H in rhythm, rhyme, melody. Some poems show definitive folk influence, e.g., "The Sergeant's Song" and "The Bridge of Lodi." Others contain allusions to folk music or dancing. Then, there are songs which echo old folk melodies such as "I Said to Love" (which might be a madrigal), "To Lizbie Browne" and "A Song of Hope" and used by H as a composer uses discord, extreme chromaticism, atonality or distortions of rhythm as sources of expression. H's genius was of the type that ripened slowly. His powers increased with the years, like Verdi. The Fore Scene of *The Dynasts* may be likened to a prelude of a vast music-drama or an introduction to a gigantic tone-poem.

2007 Sime, A. H. Moncur. "Thomas Hardy—The Poet," LONDON QUARTERLY AND HOLBORN REVIEW, CLXV (July 1940), 330–38.

H's poetry interprets the beauty of the modern world found under its surface ugliness. Common everyday life appears in "A Kiss" and "The Faded Face." "At a Watering-Place," "In the Room of the Bride-Elect," "At the Altar-Rail," and "The Dance at the Phoenix" bring laughter touched with sadness. "The Stranger's Song" is grotesque humor, but "Shelley's Skylark" and "After the Visit" are exquisite. *The Dynasts* is realistic, unconventional, and artistic; it grips and thrills us, particularly in Napoleon's scenes.

2008 SOUTHERN REVIEW (Thomas Hardy Centennial Issue), VI (Summer 1940).

Contents, listed separately by author, all under 1940: W. H. Auden, "A Literary Transference"; Howard Baker, "Hardy's Poetic Certitude";

Jacques Barzun, "Truth and Poetry in Thomas Hardy"; R. P. Blackmur, "The Shorter Poems of Thomas Hardy"; Donald Davidson, "The Traditional Basis of Thomas Hardy's Fiction"; Bonamy Dobrée, *The Dynasts*"; F. R. Leavis, "Hardy the Poet"; Arthur Mizener, "*Jude the Obscure* as Tragedy"; Herbert J. Muller, "The Novels of Hardy Today"; Katherine Anne Porter, "Notes on a Criticism of Thomas Hardy"; John Crowe Ransom, "Honey and Gall"; Delmore Schwartz, "Poetry and Belief in Thomas Hardy"; Allen Tate, "Hardy's Philosophic Metaphors"; Morton D. Zabel, "Hardy in Defense of His Art: the Aesthetic of Incongruity."

2009 Stoll, Elmer Edgar. SHAKESPEARE AND OTHER MASTERS (Cambridge: Harvard UP, 1940), pp. 86, 88, 92, 329, 403, 404–6, 407.

[References to H's works are used to illustrate points about tragedy.]

2010 Tate, Allen. "Hardy's Philosophic Metaphors," SOUTHERN REVIEW (Thomas Hardy Centennial Edition), VI (Summer 1940), 99–108.

H's intellectual position, Naturalism, determines philosophic metaphors, but his poetic feeling often contradicts or causes metaphors to contradict themselves. In "Nature's Questioning," metaphoric vehicle replaces tenor, causing confusion of meaning. Poem fails because of its "ill-digested" blend of Naturalism, Deism, and Theism. The more direct, less-philosophical poems are best.

2011 "Thomas Hardy," MANCHESTER GUARDIAN WEEKLY, 7 June 1940, p. 438.

The Dynasts is again topical because of another great war involving Europe. H is often ungainly in style, "but his acuteness of vision and force of feeling acted so powerfully upon his flow of words that he achieved more majesty of description in landscape and a truer pathos in his treatment of calamity than a more polished technical equipment ever could have won."

2012 "Thomas Hardy," SCHOLASTIC, XXXVI (20 May 1940), p. 20.

[Centennial essay with the usual clichés.]

2013 "Thomas Hardy: Born June 2, 1840. *The Dynasts*, the Book of the Moment," TIMES LITERARY SUPPLEMENT (Lond), 1 June 1940, pp. 266, 270.

It is twenty-five years since H called on his countrymen to defend England; now the situation is again at hand. *The Dynasts* is the poem of the moment from which many "exemplars of deportment" may be gathered. H was not untrue to his philosophy in calling on patriotism, because he was a dramatic poet, not a single-minded philosopher.

2014 "Thomas Hardy Centenary Will Focus Nationwide Interest on Dorset," Dorset County Chronicle and Swanage Times, 30 May 1940, pp. 3, 5.
[Account of preparations for H centenary.]

2015 Titman, Lily. "An Animal Sympathiser's Centenary," Animals' Friend, XLVI (June 1940), 148.
H "had an intense sympathy for all animals."

2016 Titman, Lily. "A Master's Method," Writer, ns II (June 1940), 91–94.
On the centenary of H's birth we examine his means of garnering material for his writing. He made special visits on occasion to get needed background but more often used experience gleaned through his life, often from the seemingly insignificant.

2017 Titman, L[ily]. "Thomas Hardy as Archaeologist," Country Life, LXXXVII (15 June 1940), 599.
Digging for the foundations at Max Gate revealed Roman ruins, about which H delivered a paper in 1884 to the Dorset Field Club. The essence of that account, even quotations from it, crop up in the description of Casterbridge. Other stories of H's cite local archaeology, too.

2018 Titman, Lily. "Thomas Hardy as Violinist," Strad, LI (June 1940), 43–45.
[About the importance of violin-playing in H's boyhood environment and of his extensive use of it in his poems and fiction.]

2019 Titman, Lily. "The Thomas Hardy Centenary," Methodist Magazine, June 1940, pp. 253–54, 257.
"Hardy's view [of life] seems truly summed up in the words of Tess . . . as she drove the beehives in the cart to Marlott": we live on " 'a blighted one [world].' " [Poor essay. Merely assembles, without purpose, many small instances of "sorrow" and "mockery" from H's novels.]

2020 Titman, Lily. "Thomas Hardy's Sussex Contacts," Sussex County Magazine, XIV (June 1940), 215–19.
"Not inconsiderable, surely, are Thomas Hardy's contacts, direct and indirect, with our own county [Sussex]." H visited Sussex often, knew of its lore, and was acquainted with authors who lived in or came from Sussex.

2021 Tomlinson, H. M. "The Wessex Novels," John O'London's Weekly, 7 June 1940, p. 272.
H was harshly criticized by many critics partly because of his genius— "abuse is a common noise when frustration is felt in supposed rivalry." H had a unique talent for vividly describing nature and his characters. His plots "work out as if designed by fate," and H seldom intervenes.

2022 Walker, S. J. "He Assures the Transience of Evil Things," DORSET COUNTY CHRONICLE AND SWANAGE TIMES, 30 May 1940, p. 5.
For all H's concern with suffering, the action of his novels occurs before "a never-changing background . . . of the loveliness and variety of the English countryside," thereby reminding us that nature remains constant " 'though Dynasties pass.' "

2023 Walpole, Hugh. "Foreword," A BOOKSELLER LOOKS BACK: THE STORY OF THE BAINS (Lond: Macmillan, 1940), p. vii.
[Except for the reference in Hugh Walpole's short foreword, there is, surprisingly, no mention of H among the multitude of literary greats and near-greats mentioned.] "I have seen Andrew Lang and Gosse and Hardy and Rupert Brooke and Asquith and Sassoon and many another in this ship."

2024 Walpole, Hugh. "Two Memories of Thomas Hardy," JOURNAL OF THE ROYAL SOCIETY OF ARTS, LXXXVIII (9 Aug 1940), 792–93.
[At a meeting with H in 1909, Mrs. H never stopped talking. H tried to discourage him [Walpole] from becoming a novelist. A description of the centenary at Stinsford in 1940.]

2025 "War and Thomas Hardy," TIMES (Lond), 1 June 1940, p. 7.
H knew about war from his studies of Napoleon and had great respect for the common soldier. When H took up *The Dynasts* he realized that in war is concentrated both the suffering and the heroism of humanity. In war H could best convey his "brooding over why men, being so essentially good of heart, should do these frightful things to one another." But he was no "supine pacifist" and knew the necessity of fighting evil.

2026 Watson, Herbert. "The Idle Singer of an Empty Day: Reflections on the Hardy Centenary," PORTSMOUTH EVENING NEWS, 5 June 1940, p. 4.
H thought "life and the world were hopelessly bad"—a view that is "hopelessly wrong." By continually proclaiming the dark side of life, such men as H may have helped create the present war. [Mostly nonsense.]

2027 Weaver, John D. "Thomas Hardy's Tragedy Was To Be Misunderstood by His Generation," KANSAS CITY STAR, 6 June 1940, p. 154.
"Hardy was not the first gentle genius to be stoned for his honesty." He was the first great novelist to develop the seduction theme with a degree of accuracy and, in *Tess of the d'Urbervilles*, dared to make a "seduced woman" the heroine. "Victorian readers missed the warmth of *Tess*, caring

for nothing save the fact that a socially improper situation had been described." *Jude the Obscure* is the most deeply tragic of H's works, but readers refused to look beyond the passion.

2028 Weber, Carl J. "The Centenary of Emma Lavinia Gifford," COLBY MERCURY, VII (Nov 1940), 1–8.

[Contains useful biographical detail not provided in HARDY OF WESSEX (1940), mostly concerning her literary efforts. Notes that H's interest in The Mellstock Edition was confined to those works dealing with his first wife ("Poems of 1912–13" and *A Pair of Blue Eyes*). Catalogue of twenty-four items appearing at Colby College Library Exhibition.]

2029 Weber, Carl J. A CENTURY OF THOMAS HARDY: CATALOGUE OF A MEMORIAL EXHIBITION (Waterville, Maine: Colby College Library, 1940).

[A "centennial display" limited to one hundred items from H's Max Gate library.]

2030 Weber, Carl J. "Correspondence," MUSIC AND LETTERS, XXI (July 1940), 302.

[Supplements bibliography in Weber's "Thomas Hardy Music: with a Bibliography," ibid (April 1940), 172–78.]

2031 Weber, Carl J. "Correspondence," MUSIC AND LETTERS, XXI (Oct 1940), 400.

[Supplements bibliography in Weber's "Thomas Hardy Music: with a Bibliography," ibid (April 1940), 172–78.]

2032 Weber, Carl J. THE FIRST HUNDRED YEARS OF THOMAS HARDY 1840–1940: A CENTENARY BIBLIOGRAPHY OF HARDIANA (Waterville, Maine: Colby College Library, 1940).

[Extensive, unannotated secondary bibliography marred by errors in dating, but still a useful checklist.]

2033 Weber, Carl J. "The Hardy Collection at Colby," COLBY ALUMNUS, XXIX (15 April 1940), pp. 5–8.

[Account of the making of the Colby H collection.]

2034 Weber, Carl J. HARDY OF WESSEX: HIS LIFE AND LITERARY CAREER (NY: Columbia UP, 1940); 2nd ed, rvd (NY: Columbia UP; Lond: Routledge & Kegan Paul, 1965).

"Above all, the biographer must remain keenly alert to detect those radical discords which result in literary activity. His task is to unravel the psychological complexity and unrest that find release in a work of art." [Chaps 1–3 deal with H's boyhood, schooling, and architectural apprenticeship; Chap 4 deals with H's efforts to teach himself the art of fiction and his writing of *The Poor Man and the Lady* and *Desperate Remedies*. Chap 5 deals with his courtship of and marriage to Emma Gifford. Chaps 6–8 deal with the publication of H's novels, through *The Return of the Native*. Chap 9 concerns "An Indiscretion in the Life of an Heiress," the early short stories, H's interest in the drama, the controversy concerning the source of H's *Far From the Madding Crowd* and Pinero's THE SQUIRE, and the publication of *Two on a Tower*. Chap 10 deals with *The Mayor of Casterbridge*, some essays and stories, and Chap 11 with *The Woodlanders*. Chap 12 gives considerable detail on *Tess of the d'Urbervilles*. Then follows a chapter on copyright problems, American piracies, H's engaging in the controversy begun by Kipling, and the writing of *The Well-Beloved*. Chap 14, once more in considerable detail, deals with *Jude the Obscure*. The last six chapters concern marital problems, the writing of poetry (with a chapter on *The Dynasts*), and his second marriage. Particularly valuable in the first edition of Weber's book, many being omitted in the second edition, are the thirteen appendices. Despite Weber's erudition, this biography is lamentably deficient in analytical insight. The second edition is not significantly revised.]

2035 Weber, Carl J. "A Hardy Thought," SATURDAY REVIEW OF LITERATURE, XXII (25 May 1940), 11.
H apparently foresaw his burial in the Poets' Corner of Westminster Abbey judging by his spacing of letters in his design for his burial tablet at St. Juliot Church, Cornwall.

2036 Weber, Carl J. "Introduction," REVENGE IS SWEET: TWO SHORT STORIES BY THOMAS HARDY (Waterville, Maine: Colby College Library, 1940), pp. 7–16.
The fact that H did not include all his stories in the four volumes he published does not mean "that Hardy intended to suppress them" but that either he had forgotten about them or could not locate copies of certain stories. [Account of five H stories—"Destiny and a Blue Cloak," "Our Exploits at West Poley," "The Intruder," "The Doctor's Legend," and "Old Mrs. Chundle"—which he sent to American publishers but did not include in collected editions. Book contains "Destiny" and "Legend."]

2037 Weber, Carl J. "The Restoration of Hardy's Starved Goldfinch," PUBLICATIONS OF THE MODERN LANGUAGE ASSOCIATION, LV (June 1940), 617–19.
The Owen sisters convinced H that Henchard's return to the wedding and the starvation of the bird did not weaken *The Mayor of Casterbridge*, and the episode was returned to the 1895 edition. It was not, as Mary Ellen Chase supposes, removed as "melodramatic."

2038 [Weber, Carl J.]. "Thomas Hardy in America (Supplement No. 2)," COLOPHON, new graphic series I (Jan 1940), 100.
"The latest crop of American Hardiana" adds a few items to the bibliography of H publications under American imprints in ibid, ns III (Summer 1938), 383–405; and "Hardy in America," ibid, new graphic series I (March 1939), 95–96.

2039 Weber, Carl J. "Thomas Hardy Music: with a Bibliography" [and further letters concerning Thomas Hardy music], MUSIC AND LETTERS, XXI (April 1940), 172–78; (July 1940), 302; (Oct 1940), 400; XXII (April 1941), 197; (July 1941), 298; XXIII (Jan 1942), 98–99; included in HARDY MUSIC AT COLBY: A CHECK-LIST COMPILED WITH AN INTRODUCTION (Waterville, Maine: Colby College Library, 1945).
"The Maid of Keinton Mandeville," first published in *Late Lyrics and Earlier*, 1922, was H's tribute to Sir Henry Bishop's tune for "Should he Upbraid," declared by him the most marvelous song in English music. Throughout his life H searched for an elusive dance-tune he had heard when he was sixteen. This unending hunt, futile though it proved to be, is typical of the poet's life-long devotion to music. The first H poem set to music was "The Stranger's Song: as sung by Mr. Charles Charrington in the play *The Three Wayfarers.*" [A list of about 120 items based upon the Thomas Hardy Collection in the library of Colby College (Waterville, Maine), completed by further letters, is given in an appendix.]

2040 Wells, Henry W. NEW POETS FROM OLD: A STUDY OF LITERARY GENETICS (NY: Columbia P, 1940), passim.
[This study does not deal with the archaistic and historical influences, like H, because they are obvious and rare.] In the chapter "The Heritage of Technique," H is studied as giving renewed dignity to the use of dialect in verse. Realism, psychological analysis, seeking beauty through truth are characteristics of poet-physicians Browning, Meredith, and H. Theirs is the analytic tradition. H analyzes destiny herself and "performs an autopsy on a defunct universe." In the chapter "The Heritage of Form," H is represented as reviving the hereditary rhythms of rondeau and troilet and blank verse. Realism, psychological analysis, seeking beauty through truth are ballad, which satisfied his love for narrative and fulfilled the public demand for compression; the dialogue, both between people and inanimate objects; the objective monologue, especially in sonnet form; the elegy in graveyard meditations and stoical interpretations of death; and the true song, such as "Weathers." Aiken's poetry in idealization, misanthropy, nostalgic mysticism, and dark stoicism "are natural developments of the art and philosophy of the romantic school from Coleridge and Poe to James Thomson and Thomas Hardy."

2041 Willis, Irene Cooper. "Thomas Hardy," NEW STATESMAN AND NATION, XIX (1 June 1940), 698–99.
[An uninteresting, conventional account of H's life.]

2042 [Wilson, Carroll A.]. A DESCRIPTIVE CATALOGUE OF THE GROLIER CLUB CENTENARY EXHIBITION 1940 OF THE WORKS OF THOMAS HARDY, O. M. 1840–1928 (Waterville, Maine: Colby College Library, 1940).
[Brief foreword by Wilson followed by a description of 268 items exhibited —first editions, autographed editions, MSS, A.L.S., and memorabilia. Many are from Wilson's collection (see 1950).]

2043 Young, G. M. "Introduction," *Selected Poems of Thomas Hardy*, ed by G. M. Young (Lond: Macmillan, 1940; 1960), pp. ix–xxxiv; rptd as "Thomas Hardy," in LAST ESSAYS (Lond: Rupert Hart-Davis, 1950), pp. 258–81.
Much of H's verse is casual. Yet, he brought to it "the ancient music of rural England," as William Barnes did before him. His diction, however, is often "ungainly," a result of an imperfect education, an "untrained taste," and a propensity to follow "unfortunate models," particularly classical prose. His prose career ended in 1895 (except for *The Well-Beloved*), and after that he wrote verse, nearly one thousand pieces in the collected edition. This selection attempts to reproduce the poetic personality of H, a poet of place, of local incident, and of reflection. *The Dynasts*, an example of Titanism or revolt against an unjust order, resulted from the effect of Darwin, Mill, Huxley, and Spencer who "forced the imagination of their time into a monistic habit of thought." Pessimism, without the Titan view, can become propaganda. The inspiration for *Dynasts* emerged from place. In form it harmonizes the "variety of Shakespearean History" with "the epic progress of Aeschylean trilogy." H's world cannot be synthesized— the disproportion between man's aspirations and the impersonality of the Immanent Will. Yet his pessimism is not one of despair but one of speculation that a consciousness will one day transform the Immanent Will. "In Tenebris" is the keynote of his philosophy. H was of no school and created none. He stands alone in "unpretentious integrity" bringing home the scenes and thought of Victorian and Late Victorian life. [Text: over one hundred selections.]

2044 Zabel, Morton D. "Hardy in Defense of His Art: the Aesthetic of Incongruity," SOUTHERN REVIEW (Thomas Hardy Centennial Edition), VI (Summer 1940), 125–49; rewritten with the same title for CRAFT AND CHARACTER (1957).
H, a product of discordant nineteenth-century forces, coined an aesthetic to defend himself against critics. This aesthetic justified his limitations: for

variety in life and poetry he used occasional, inexact rhymes and meters. His defense of "casual vitality" is linked to significance of chance and accident in life. H, like Browning, disliked the perfect in art, preferred to depict "seemings" of man. H's art is consciously artless; he disliked the artful but lifeless renderings of James and Moore. H saw endless dichotomy in life and transferred it to fiction and poetry but thought his efforts always "tentative," whether examining men and manners (*Jude the Obscure*) or the cosmos (*The Dynasts*). H's dichotomies approximate Schopenhauer's, but H was more optimistic. Like Shaw, H believed in creative evolution: hence his emphasis on "seemings," "tentativeness," "emergent forces," etc. "Seemings" permit contrivances which shake credulity but also permit H to effect "startling touches of weirdness" and "strokes of the most exquisite tenderness." By precept and example, H protests against Naturalism/Realism's "slice of life" and the aesthetic novels of James, Flaubert, and Moore. All his works depict conflicts in the artist and thus exhibit sincerity and life.

1941

2045 "Adventures of a Novel: *Tess* After Fifty Years: Thomas Hardy and the Public Outcry," TIMES LITERARY SUPPLEMENT (Lond), 5 July 1941, pp. 322, 325.
Publication of *Tess of the d'Urbervilles* in serial form brought strong reactions because readers were caught up by the novel's realism: it is H's most English novel. Readers of the higher class were misled into thinking it false because they were ignorant of the mores of country folk. Lionel Johnson complained about the philosophy, first that it was not art and then, contradictorily, that it was not consistent.

2046 Aliesch, Peter. STUDIEN ZU THOMAS HARDYS PROSASTIL (Studies in Thomas Hardy's Prose Style) (Schiers: A-G. Buchdruckerei, 1941); University of Bern dissertation.
H's prose style is natural. He conceived of it as a means rather than an end in itself. Hence its asymmetry and occasional uncouthness reflect not carelessness but an unmannered and almost unconscious submission of language to the demands of theme. [In German.]

2047 Arns, Karl. GRUNDRISS DER GESCHICHTE DER ENGLISCHEN LITERATUR VON 1832 BIS ZUR GEGENWART (Outline of the History of English Literature From 1832 to the Present) (Paderborn: F. Schöningh, 1941), pp. 14, 17, 73, 74, 75, 82, 89–95, 125, 159, 162, 195.

H's *Weltanschauung* contrasts with typical Victorian optimism, prudery, and self-complacency and is alien to the German temperament. H therefore was accorded a limited reception in Germany. [In German.]

2048 Bates, H. E. The Modern Short Story: A Critical Survey (Boston: The Writer, 1941), pp. 37–43, 81–82, 169, 217.
H's "heavily Latinized, abstract prose" and penchant for "moral teaching" were too weighty for the short story. In such hands as H's the short story "is choked crudely to death." H's failure to be effectively pictorial is like that of a man "trying to paint a picture with a dictionary." H's "philosophical vapourings" and "spiritual anguish" are unreal to the modern reader, but the pig-sticking in *Jude the Obscure*, the wife sale in *The Mayor of Casterbridge*, and Tess working in the turnip field and praying with the children are scenes that will always be vivid. The English short-story suffered from "arrested development" because of the parochialism (evidenced by the reception of *Tess of the d'Urbervilles* and *Jude*) of that country. [Opinionated but astute criticism of the short story; well-put if conventional comments on H's novels; little on his short fiction.]

2049 Bax, Clifford. "On Style in Some of the Older Writers," Yale Review, XXX (June 1941), 734–48.
"While H had not [George] Moore's gift of making words glide and shimmer along the page . . . [H's] gnarled and oaken style, both in verse and in prose, nobly expresses a noble nature."

2050 Bentley, Phyllis. "England in Her Fiction," Library Journal (NY), LXVI (Sept 1941), 697.
The characters in H's novels cover the whole range of Wessex inhabitants from Lord Luxellian down to poor old Granfer Cantle; the nearer the character is to the soil, the more sucessful H is in drawing it, often with a racy humor.

2051 Bentley, Phyllis. The English Regional Novel (Lond: Allen & Unwin, 1941); rptd (NY: Haskell House, 1966), pp. 23–28.
With H comes the first record of a "projected series" of local novels (in an unidentified quote from H in 1874). There is more sight and sound of the chosen region in H's novels than in other English regional novels. The local color goes beyond setting into plot, becoming part of the cause of the action. Agreeableness in character depends on closeness to the soil of the region. H's sparing use of dialect illustrates the limit of his commitment to local color. The nature of his characters is more important than the precise representation of dialect; H refuses to "subordinate the individual to the locale." His themes are not regional; he uses decidedly local elements to depict the universal.

2052 "Books in Brief Review," COLLEGE ENGLISH, II (May 1941), p. 815.

Claire Leighton is familiar with H's country, and her beautiful engravings for *Under the Greenwood Tree* will delight lovers of H.

2053 Cargill, Oscar. INTELLECTUAL AMERICA: IDEAS ON THE MARCH (NY: Macmillan, 1941), pp. 42, 63, 69–77, 83, 84, 99, 107, 112, 114, 125, 138, 269, 300.

Even in his finest novels, *The Return of the Native* and *Tess of the d'Urbervilles*, H's passionate engagement with his characters prevents him from treating them with the critical detachment that distinguishes the naturalism of Flaubert. While Flaubert sees both the virtues and faults of Emma and Charles, H is so concerned with attacking God and Fate that he fails to see the faults in Tess and Jude. His naturalism is less pure than that of the French writers, who scoffed at the notion that God or Fate was responsible for the results of human action.

Despite the narrative improbabilities H's novels are susceptible to, *Jude the Obscure* shows that he no longer pictured his protagonists as pure in mind or god-like in beauty. Perhaps his greatest influence on the English novel was his frank treatment of sex.

2054 Chew, Samuel C. (ed). TENNYSON: REPRESENTATIVE POEMS (NY: Odyssey P, 1941), pp. 157, 325, 369.

[Suggests the following thematic comparisons and contrasts between works of H and Tennyson: *The Famous Tragedy of the Queen of Cornwall* and "The Last Tournament" (the Tristram legend); "At a Lunar Eclipse" and section 23 of IN MEMORIAM; "The Darkling Thrush" and section 88 of IN MEMORIAM.]

2055 Farley, Philip J. "Pattern, Structure, and Form in the Novels of Thomas Hardy." Unpublished dissertation, University of California (Berkeley), 1941.

[Listed in Lawrence F. McNamee, DISSERTATIONS IN ENGLISH AND AMERICAN LITERATURE (NY and Lond: Bowker, 1968).]

2056 Fehr, Bernhard. VON ENGLANDS GEISTIGEN BESTÄNDEN: AUSGEWÄHLTE AUFSÄTZE (On England's Spiritual Constants: Selected Essays) (Frauenfeld: Hubert, 1941), pp. 143–48.

[Focuses on H's tragic sense of life.] [In German.]

2057 Fortescue, Lady Winifred. "THERE'S ROSEMARY . . . THERE'S RUE . . ." (Boston: Houghton Mifflin, 1941), 110.

H made a sinister impression on Lady Winifred when she met the author at a garden party at Max Gate. [A very peripheral anecdote.]

2058 Ghent, Percy. "Thomas Hardy Note Is Mainly Concerned with Canadian Babe," EVENING TELEGRAM (Toronto), 8 Sept 1941, p. 6.
[The MS of *Far From the Madding Crowd* was sold in 1941 as part of the Newton Collection. Contains a brief biographical sketch. Reprints a 21 Sept 1907 letter to John Moule in which H states his "conscientious objection" to being the godfather of Moule's son.]

2059 "Hardy Collection Now At Wesleyan," COLBY ECHO, XLIV (7 May 1941), 1, 6.
[Account of Colby's loan of H material to Wesleyan University for an exhibit commemorating the fiftieth anniversary of the publication of *Tess of the d'Urbervilles*.]

2060 Hobson, Harold. "A London Letter," CHRISTIAN SCIENCE MONITOR, 1 March 1941, p. 11.
Claire Leighton has captured H's later mood of tragic sublimity and includes it in her engravings for *Under the Greenwood Tree*, a more idyllic, untroubled novel. [Review of Macmillan's 1940 ed of *Greenwood Tree*.]

2061 Horwill, Herbert. "The Hardy Country Recorded Here," BALTIMORE SUN, 23 Feb 1941, p. 10.
[Interview with Claire Leighton about her woodcuts for *Under the Greenwood Tree* (Macmillan, 1940). All the illustrations were prepared from memories of the H country and were made in her apartment in Baltimore.]

2062 Horwill, Herbert W. "News and Views of Literary London," NEW YORK TIMES BOOK REVIEW, 18 May 1941, p. 8.
Under the Greenwood Tree was a popular choice by contestants for inclusion in a list of three "entirely happy" books in the English language. It was not on the winning list, and the editor of the contest does not think H ever wrote an entirely happy book.

2063 Lord, David. "Thomas Hardy: Poet Laureate of Animal Lovers," OUR DUMB ANIMALS, LXXIV (Feb 1941), 35.
"If Thomas Hardy had left no other claim to immortality than . . . [his] animal poems, he would still be assured a high place in the Valhalla of the poets."

2064 Mackail, Denis. THE STORY OF J.M.B. (Lond: Peter Davies, 1941), pp. 7, 117, 147, 155, 210, 241, 334, 433, 473, 501, 508, 537, 545, 558, 570, 572, 612, 647.
Barrie saw in H qualities which even H didn't recognize. He considered H almost a God of literature, and his personal acquaintance with him never diminished his opinion.

2065 Nevinson, Henry W. THOMAS HARDY (Lond: Allen & Unwin, 1941).

[The first part of this pamphlet is devoted to personal memories (drawn mainly from already published articles and notes); the rest is devoted to the teller of tales, to the poems, and finally, to *The Dynasts*.] H disliked being called a novelist; his novels might be divided into "Comparatively cheerful" and "Profoundly sad." There is much in *Tess of the d'Urbervilles*, as in H's finest books, that is incredible: for example, Angel's rejection of Tess on his wedding-night. *Jude the Obscure* is a tremendous story full of pity and fear, perhaps too horrible. The purpose of the book is not university reform or the removal of shameful inequalities of class and wealth: there are the more intimate problems of love and marriage. H rejected "free verse"; but his meters are often strange, his sounds harsh, his expression crabbed—far removed from the melody of Tennyson. H's personality lies partly revealed in nearly all that he wrote, but only a few of his poems are personal; e.g. "Afterwards." The charge of pessimism moved H to indignation (cf. "Apology" in *Late Lyrics and Earlier*). But it is true that Browning's resolute optimism often appeared rather forced. Bertrand Russell may have been scientifically right in saying: "It is only on the firm foundation of unyielding despair that the soul's habitation henceforth alone can be safely built." H pronounced *Dynasts* on the analogy of "dynamite" and "dynamic," ignoring the Greek short quantity. The Immanent Will expresses the same idea as Schopenhauer's "Willie" or Bergson's "Elan vital." There is a note of deliverance in the last line of *Dynasts*. In 1922, H confessed that he should not have written it after the World War.

2066 Olivier, Edith. COUNTRY MOODS AND TENSES: A NON-GRAMMARIAN'S CHAPBOOK (Lond: Batsford, 1941), pp. 62–64.

"There is no stretch of land in England which a writer has made so completely his own" as Wessex.

2067 Peel, J. H. B. "A Century of Thomas Hardy," POETRY REVIEW, XXXII (March–April 1941), 89–93.

H, "a product of the Victorian age," is still quite topical. He possesses definite intellectual tendencies, but they do not constitute a system of philosophy. The Second World War ended any optimistic hopes H might have entertained about the world's future. His last years cannot have been so serene as his wife would have us believe. There are, however, comic touches in most of the novels, and some "of the most charming humour in our language is to be found in *Under the Greenwood Tree*, that true finding of *metier* after Meredith's fatal advice to find a 'plot' had brought forth the over-dramatic *Desperate Remedies* (full though that book is of future greatness)."

2068 Pritchett, V. S. "Books in General," NEW STATESMAN AND NATION, XXI (31 May 1941), 557.

A novelist's choice of character and story changes but little between his first and his last book. In *Under the Greenwood Tree* and *Jude the Obscure,* only age separates the pastoral from the tract. Sue Bridehead is one of the consequences of being Fancy Day, and Jude is a Dick Dewy become conscious of his obscurity: and all is a variation of H's first marriage. H was the only Victorian novelist to have paid any attention to science, to have had, like Zola, his imagination enlarged by Darwinism. In *Greenwood Tree,* there is a visual vividness, and the talk of the cottagers is taken, rich and crooked, from their very mouths. In *Jude,* the vividness has gone; there appears instead a faculty of instant abstraction. Towns, people, country have become generalized, as if Time has seized them. *Jude* is, in part, a tract on marriage laws; Victorians thought they could get rid of conventions without damaging the basis of the society which produced the conventions.

2069 "The Rare Book Corner," COLBY ALUMNUS, XXX (15 April 1941), 17.
[Account of a group of H books owned by Rebekah Owen just added to the Colby collection—"all bearing Miss Owen's characteristic notes, photographs, clippings, letters and other memoranda."]

2070 Sadleir, Michael. "Hardy's Magazine Editors," TIMES LITERARY SUPPLEMENT (Lond), 12 July 1941, p. 335.
H's magazine editors were more prudish than his publishers, but the reverse was the case when Le Fanu published Rhoda Broughton's NOT WISELY BUT TOO WELL in DUBLIN UNIVERSITY MAGAZINE—publishers later refused it.

2071 Samson, George. "Thomas Hardy," THE CONCISE CAMBRIDGE HISTORY OF ENGLISH LITERATURE (Cambridge: Cambridge UP; NY: Macmillan, 1941), pp. 808–10, 948.
[Summary of H's life and works.]

2072 Strauch, Carl F. MAP OF EGDON HEATH (Bethlehem, Pa.: pvtly ptd, 1941).
[One-page map charting the important movements and locations of *The Return of the Native,* "based partially on Hardy's map, but chiefly on the text."]

2073 Weber, Carl J. "Ainsworth and Thomas Hardy," REVIEW OF ENGLISH STUDIES (Lond), XVII (April 1941), 193–200.
Ainsworth "revived for a nineteenth century public the terrors which had thrilled the readers of Mrs. Radcliffe," and he had a "profound influence" on H, particularly on his nature descriptions. Ainsworth "taught him how to describe a storm," but both have stilted dialogue. "The shadow of William Harrison Ainsworth falls across many of the pages" of the Wessex novels.

2074 Weber, Carl J. "Correspondence," MUSIC AND LETTERS, XXII (April 1941), 197; included in HARDY MUSIC AT COLBY: A CHECK-LIST COMPILED WITH AN INTRODUCTION (Waterville, Maine: Colby College Library, 1945).
[Supplements C. J. Weber, "Thomas Hardy Music: with a Bibliography," ibid, XXI (April 1940), 172–78, and subsequent issues.]

2075 Weber, Carl J. "Correspondence," MUSIC AND LETTERS, XXII (July 1941), 298.
[Supplements bibliography in Weber's "Thomas Hardy Music: with a Bibliography," ibid, XXI (April 1940), 172–78.]

2076 Weber, Carl J. "An Elizabethan Basis for a Hardy Tale?—an addendum," PUBLICATIONS OF THE MODERN LANGUAGE ASSOCIATION, LVI (June 1941), 598–600.
[See Helen Sandison, "An Elizabethan Basis for a Hardy Tale?" ibid, LIV (June 1939), 610–12.] "The First Countess of Wessex" is really about Betty Horner, the second source mentioned by Sandison, with some chance oral mergings from the Elizabethan source. Personal letters from a woman who knew H when he wrote the tale confirm this. [Although based on impeccable evidence, this is dully pedantic nit-picking of less interest than the original item.]

2077 Weber, Carl J. THE JUBILEE OF TESS 1891–1941: CATALOGUE OF AN EXHIBITION (Waterville, Maine: Colby College Library, 1941).
[Items exhibited included a few MSS leaves, and fifty different editions of the novel (English, American, and foreign), with explanatory notes and comment.]

2078 Wilson, Carroll A. "Some Hardy Corrections and Notes," COLBY MERCURY, VII (Dec 1941), 73–76.
[Corrections of Carroll A. Wilson, A DESCRIPTIVE CATALOGUE OF THE GROLIER CLUB CENTENARY EXHIBITION 1940 OF THE WORKS OF THOMAS HARDY, O. M. 1840–1928 (1940) and notes on "the year's additional bibliographical Hardy crop on The Wilson farm!"]

1942

2079 Barrie, J. M. LETTERS OF J. M. BARRIE, ed by Viola Meynell (Lond: Davies, 1942; NY: Scribner's, 1947), pp. 4, 5, 10, 65, 67, 75, 146, 150, 151, 152–54, 160–62, 170, 175–76, 214, 262, 283.

[Letters to various persons]. Meredith remarked that he cannot endure *Tess of the d'Urbervilles* and that H will need to do two novels as good as the old ones before he forgives this one [to A. Quiller-Couch, 26 June 1892]; "*Tess* was right, because it was Hardy's natural output" [to A. Quiller-Couch, 25 Dec 1893]; H has dramatized *Tess*, and "when a man dramatises his troubles begin" [to A. Quiller-Couch, 23 March 1896]; H at 85 much interested in the production of his play *Tess* [to Charles Scribner, 20 Sept 1925]. [Exchanges with Mrs. H on H's health, her "biography" of H, H's popularity]: H "could not look out at a window without seeing something that had never been seen before"; the most striking thing in the LIFE "is that his life was a preparation for *The Dynasts*." [3 Feb 1928]. [Barrie was a frequent, much-liked visitor.]

2080 Blunden, Edmund. THOMAS HARDY (Lond: Macmillan, 1942); rptd (Lond: Macmillan Pocket Library, 1951).
H would have been successful as a biographer, literary critic, or rural historian. H may have stopped writing fiction because he had lost the ability to interject the "unexpected" into his stories, as evidenced by *Jude the Obscure*'s "precision and purpose." [Little original criticism; valuable chiefly for inclusion of contemporary reviews and for efforts to sketch the literary milieu when H was writing. Only two chapters on novels, especially *A Pair of Blue Eyes*.]

2081 Collins, V. H. "The Love Poetry of Thomas Hardy," ESSAYS AND STUDIES BY MEMBERS OF THE ENGLISH ASSOCIATION, XXVIII (1942), 69–83.
H's main preoccupation in his poetry is love, "used in a wide sense." Besides desire, courting, and consummation, the poetry includes "jealousy, unreciprocated or otherwise frustrated love, disillusion, disunion, ill-mating, inconstancy, loss, and other reactions and complications." In three collections of poems, totaling over 800, 340 are love poems, even though H was in his seventies when the last two volumes were published. "Moreover the supremacy of the love interest in Hardy's poetry often comes out indirectly in what is not primarily . . . a love poem." "A characteristic of Hardy's poetry is that it so often gives the woman's point of view." But affairs of the heart are of greatest importance to H's men also. "For the most part throughout the love poems—however varied the setting, the characters, the situation—the predominant note is of dissatisfaction, regret, unhappiness. The subject of very many of them is the death of a loved person." "Love begins with pain, or leads to pain, or ends in pain. . . . It is because love means so much in Hardy's scale of values that unhappiness on that plane is so intolerable. Life has potentially so much to give, but it 'offers only to deny.' "

2082 Gerould, Gordon Hall. THE PATTERNS OF ENGLISH AND AMERICAN FICTION: A HISTORY (Boston: Little, Brown, 1942), pp. 384–93.

H, an individualist interpreter, should not be judged by representational standards. Because his settings are accurately described, we should not expect the same verisimilitude in character where he interprets human emotions poetically. Though he was baffled and confused when he reasoned, he had "extraordinarily keen and delicate perceptions," intuitive knowledge, and a native gift for story-telling. H's early life gave him a chance to observe country people, but he had a certain detachment from them because of his aim to be a professional man. Life in London not being very promising, he was determined to become a writer. Meredith read his first novel, advised him not to publish. H imitated Wilkie Collins in *Desperate Remedies* and learned how to manage narrative. The next three novels were successful, although some reviewers always looked askance at them when they came out. As he continued, the "misgivings of many earnest people" about the morality of his work were realized in *Tess of the d'Urbervilles*. H felt criticism keenly but wrote *Jude the Obscure* in the spirit of defiance. H turned to poetry, won renown, especially with *The Dynasts* which is not so great as some critics would have us believe, a "pretentious and empty" work. Admirers of H have done him a disservice; it is time for a more sober evaluation. Eustacia is not developed consistently as a character; Henchard is poorly motivated; *Tess* shows the manipulation of events. H was good when he showed a sensitive interpretation of life but not when he dealt with sophisticated people. His art was highly stylized, not realistic. His power is in making us see, hear, and feel his events. *Jude* is especially poor because H abandoned his usual method of linking the actions of men to the operations of nature. [The "soberer evaluation" Gerould demanded has taken place and reversed many of Gerould's judgments.]

2083 H., R. "Tree-Voices," NOTES AND QUERIES, CLXXXIII (5 Dec 1942), 345.

[Suggests a parallel between CONINGSBY and *Under the Greenwood Tree*, about the varied voices of trees under the wind.]

2084 Horwill, Herbert W. "News From Literary London," NEW YORK TIMES BOOK REVIEW, 27 Sept 1942, p. 29.

Adam Fox, professor of poetry at Oxford, said of H that he "will come to be regarded as poet of the highest order when his novels are forgotten."

2085 Kenmore, Dallas. "Thomas Hardy and the Human Drama," POETRY REVIEW, XXXIII (Nov–Dec 1942), 345–50.

Browning and H are akin in their interests in "the vagaries of the Spirit," and to label H a pessimist is as irrelevant as labeling Browning an optimist. H is a "poet of pity," for he profoundly sympathizes with man's struggle against fate. One may deduce from many poems that H's life was not so uneventful as is generally believed.

2086 Kernahan, Coulson. "The 'Pessimism' of Thomas Hardy," LONDON QUARTERLY AND HOLBORN REVIEW, CLXVII (July 1942), 276–83.
While Mrs. Arthur Henniker did not think H pessimistic on the basis of the pathetic "To an Unborn Pauper Child," he was. H received his criticism of *Tess of the d'Urbervilles* as having a melodramatic ending without excitement. H also collaborated with Mrs. Henniker on IN SCARLET AND GREY, adding a "wing" to the architecture of the book which more properly belongs in *Life's Little Ironies*.

2087 Newbolt, Lady Margaret. THE LATER LIFE AND LETTERS OF SIR HENRY JOHN NEWBOLT (Lond: Faber & Faber, 1942), pp. 121–22, 165–66, 185–86, 199, 240, 370.
H's acceptance of a gold medal for literature from Newbolt and William Butler Yeats in June 1912 was strangely uneasy; H thought solitude and seclusion necessary for the artist; he thought oral tradition superior, as historical record, to written documents. [Newbolt repeats his earlier estimate of H and of *The Dynasts*.]

2088 Orwell, George [pseud of Eric Blair]. "Thomas Hardy Looks at War," TRIBUNE (Lond), 18 Sept 1942, p. 13.
The Dynasts shows "that even a half-lunatic view of life will do as a basis for literature provided it is sincerely held." H was attracted by the "huge and meaningless suffering" of the Napoleonic Wars, and the form he chose to depict it gave a freer rein to "his strange mystical pessimism" than a novel could. H's handling of the Waterloo sequence "leaves one with the feeling that *The Dynasts* is one of the very few genuine tragedies . . . written in our time." The story is moving "because personal ambition is tragic against a background of fatalism."

2089 Parrish, M. L. "Adventures in Reading and Collecting Victorian Authors," PRINCETON UNIVERSITY LIBRARY CHRONICLE, III (Feb 1942), 35.
On the shelves of H's study were represented the works of every English poet. In another room were copies of first editions of every book he had written, all in their original binding except *A Pair of Blue Eyes*. The copy of *Desperate Remedies* was pristine, the only one known in blue cloth.

2090 Pritchett, V[ictor] S[awson]. "The First and Last of Hardy," IN MY GOOD BOOKS (Lond: Chatto & Windus, 1942), pp. 99–106; rptd (Port Washington, NY: Kennikat P, 1970).
Only superficial differences separate *Under the Greenwood Tree* from *Jude the Obscure*. H knows country life from inside; he neither laughs at it nor

poeticizes it. H's imagination was enlarged by Darwin to recreate "the human ritual." H depicts the realism of man as part of the mass, of humdrum circumstance, thus the importance of journeys which show H as master of circumstance, because he is master of the movement of people. *Jude* suffers from authorial intrusion and shows H at his worst in attacking convention. [Unsustained but not uninteresting impressionism.]

2091 Reaver, J. Russell. "*The Dynasts* of Thomas Hardy," BULLETIN OF THE CITADEL, VI (Nov 1942), 41–45.

The Dynasts contains "an explicit summary of the philosophy implied in his [H's] novels." Napoleon "is conceived as a symbol of Hardy's fundamental philosophy of life." He is at times aware of "the controlling power of the Immanent Will," and he at last "wonders if human effort has any final significance." Man here has no power to act either for good or evil; he is "a mere chip of wood in the whirlpool of circumstance."

2092 Richards, Grant. HOUSMAN, 1897–1936 (NY: Oxford UP, 1942), pp. 8, 169, 246, 247, 269, 271, 290, 334, 337, 339, 341, 381.

Housman, who admired H as a person and as a writer, was influenced by H's pessimism.

2093 Richards, Mary C. "Irony in Thomas Hardy." Unpublished dissertation, University of California (Berkeley), 1942.

[Listed in Lawrence F. McNamee, DISSERTATIONS IN ENGLISH AND AMERICAN LITERATURE (NY & Lond: Bowker, 1968).]

2094 Sagar, S. "Chesterton and Hardy," WEEKLY REVIEW, XXXVI (17 Dec 1942), 139–41.

"Behind the façade of the Wessex novels . . . is a background of mental confusion." The tendency of H's characters to "throw up the sponge at the slightest obstacle" detracts from the tragedy in H's novels. H's "philosophy of despair can be traced to a too intense brooding over the unfortunate exceptions, those instances where the hand of the potter seems to have slipped."

2095 Sassoon, Siegfried. "*The Dynasts* in War-Time," SPECTATOR (Lond), CLXVIII (6 Feb 1942), 127–28.

"A panoramic masterpiece which shows us all in relation to our tormented chapter in history," *The Dynasts* "can help us towards a sense of proportion and perspective when we try to acclimatise and adapt our minds to the biological struggle for survival in which we are involved."

2096 Tomlinson, Philip. "Hardy as the Spirit of Pity," TIMES LITERARY SUPPLEMENT (Lond), 21 Feb 1942, p. 86.

Reading *The Dynasts* at this time brings consolation, even confidence. H had faith in the "unconquerable spirit of the British people in adversity."

2097 Wagenknecht, Edward. " 'Pessimism' in Hardy and Conrad," COLLEGE ENGLISH, III (March 1942), 546–54.
Neither H nor Conrad can be adequately described as a pessimist. H has respect for humanity, and his pity is all-embracing. Neither views the world as friendly to man, but theirs is not the world of the moral nihilist. Their works are the results of creative, intuitive personalities which do not work in a systematic way.

2098 Weber, Carl J. "A. J. Cronin and Thomas Hardy," COLLEGE ENGLISH, III (March 1942), 590.
Cronin denies the allegation that the main character of his novel, HATTER'S CASTLE, derived from H and claims that his knowledge of H is limited to a few pages of *Jude the Obscure*.

2099 Weber, Carl J. "Correspondence," MUSIC AND LETTERS, XXIII (Jan 1942), 98–99; included in HARDY MUSIC AT COLBY: A CHECK-LIST COMPILED WITH AN INTRODUCTION (Waterville, Maine: Colby College Library, 1945).
[Supplements C. J. Weber, "Thomas Hardy Music: with a Bibliography," ibid, XXI (April 1940), 172–78, and subsequent issues.]

2100 Weber, Carl J. "From Belmount Hall to Colby," COLBY MERCURY, VII (May 1942), 85–93.
[A list of fifty-eight H association items given to the Colby College Library.]

2101 Weber, Carl J. "Hardy's First Christmas Story," THE THIEVES WHO COULDN'T HELP SNEEZING (Waterville, Maine: Colby College Library, 1942).
"The Thieves Who Couldn't Help Sneezing" may be H's "first short story of any kind." It *may* be the story H alluded to in a letter in November 1871. Asked for a Christmas contribution in 1877, H "may have quickly revised it [the earlier tale] into this fable tale of a boy-hero."

2102 Weber, Carl J. "Hardy's Grim Note in *The Return of the Native*," PAPERS OF THE BIBLIOGRAPHICAL SOCIETY OF AMERICA, XXXVI (Dec 1942), 37–45.
The full bibliographical listing of *The Return of the Native* editions shows the 1912 edition to be "definitive." It contains H's footnote showing his original conception of the novel as more pessimistic than the final version: Thomasin and Venn were married only to suit the demands of serial publication.

2103 Weber, Carl J. "Housman and Hardy—And Maine," BULLETIN OF THE MAINE LIBRARY ASSOCIATION, III (May 1942), 7–9.
Housman "was a great admirer" of H. Despite his " 'high admiration for some of his [H's] novels,' " however, Housman's library in 1932 contained " 'not many.' "

2104 Weber, Carl J. "Thomas Hardy and His New England Editors," NEW ENGLAND QUARTERLY, XV (1942), 681–99.
Despite some protests by readers, W. D. Howells as editor of ATLANTIC MONTHLY ignored H's work, even failed to answer H's letter offering serial rights to *The Trumpet-Major* and gave only a hasty and superficial reading to H's novels late in life. Thomas Bailey Aldrich ran one serial installment of *Far From the Madding Crowd* in EVERY SATURDAY (24 Oct 1874); as editor of ATLANTIC, Aldrich serialized *Two on a Tower* (1882) with limited popular success—though it was sufficient to encourage some nineteen American pirated editions within the next twenty years. After American charges of plagiarism in *Trumpet-Major*, H wrote Aldrich details of his borrowings from Gifford, but Aldrich chose not to publish the letter. In 1884, H offered *The Woodlanders* to Aldrich for ATLANTIC but was turned down.

2105 Weber, Carl J. THOMAS HARDY IN MAINE (Portland, Maine: Southworth-Anthoensen P, 1942).
"Throughout his [H's] life he met rebuff, ridicule, and vilification at the hands of English publishers, English readers, and English critics." Yet H "was more honored in Maine than in Mayfair."

2106 Winslow, Donald J. "Thomas Hardy, His British and American Critics." Unpublished dissertation, Boston University, 1942.
[Listed in Lawrence F. McNamee, DISSERTATIONS IN ENGLISH AND AMERICAN LITERATURE (NY & Lond: Bowker, 1968).]

2107 Winterich, John T. "How This Book Came To Be," *The Return of the Native* (NY: Heritage P, 1942), v–viii.
The Return of the Native "is certainly Hardy's most representative novel."

1943

2108 Braybrooke, Patrick. "Thomas Hardy: A Consideration," DORSET YEARBOOK, 1943–1944, pp. 24–27.
H's standpoint is the same in his earlier and later volumes. He fails to prove from his characters that his "deplorable deity" exists. Rather, his characters

cause their own suffering. H "seemed to be pleased to indulge in a kind of dualism" regarding the human will. While some of his characters lack a will, others have plenty and "plenty of opportunity of using it to their own disadvantage." H "invested sorrow and melancholy with genius."

2109 Carr, Mildred Refo. THOMAS HARDY (Baltimore: Enoch Pratt Free Library, 1943).
[Typical biographical sketch with negligible critical comment.]

2110 Cecil, David. HARDY THE NOVELIST: AN ESSAY IN CRITICISM (Lond: Constable, 1943; Indianapolis: Bobbs-Merrill, 1946); given as the Clark Lecture at Cambridge, 1942.
H's artistic range was conditioned by the circumstances of an early life lived in a world so elemental that passions became obsessions. Thus in his novels Nature is often a leading character, and the most living characters are those who reside in the country. The stories of these characters are presented as folk tales by an author whose imagination was turned to the past and whose range was limited by his "angle of vantage." What this angle of vantage resulted in was a gloomy view of the world; a conception of the universe as "a huge impersonal machine"; a presentation of man, helpless in the face of circumstances, struggling against Fate in the form of love and chance. Such a view of man and the world indicates that H was intellectually advanced. It does not prepare us to discover that aesthetically "he was a man of the past," a man who, like Scott, liked a story to be a story. In telling his stories, H always displays an "individual" imagination made powerful by being true to nature, by being poetic, and by dealing with the strange and grotesque. In fact H, unlike most writers, is able to be poetic while telling a good story. Furthermore, he is able to tell a story in pictures and thus is able both to establish atmosphere and to keep our interest engaged. He is also able to create entire scenes that are symbolic, to create settings that stand for the universe. These settings or landscapes, seen in terms of both time and space, are important not in themselves but because of the figures who always populate them. These figures, like the landscape, are representative of more than themselves. They are basic types who stand in for an entire species. Unlike many other fictitious characters, they are conceived in relation to a destiny and are made alive not only by their actions but also by their conversations. The very good ones are particularly well drawn, but the intellectuals, the great ladies, and the villains are seldom convincing. It is here that H shows a major weakness: he can create only a few different types. He reveals other weaknesses: he is a faulty craftsman, his themes are often too simple, he violates probability, he writes outside his range, he repeats himself, he overdoes his use of chance, he twists the plot to suit his purpose, he preaches. Despite all this, we learn that "we do not just admire Hardy; we love him." This is due partly to the fact that, in choosing not to be a craftsman, his deliberate uncouthness reveals to the reader the man

471

behind the works. This man is "the last representative of the tradition and spirit of the Elizabethan drama," a man willing to tell a sensational tale but also willing "to rise to the boldest flights of imagination." He captivates the reader by presenting a gradually darkening mood while remaining "one of the most Christian spirits who ever lived," despite the fact that he could not believe "the Christian hope."

2111 "Christmas Once and Now," TIMES LITERARY SUPPLEMENT (Lond), 13 Nov 1943, p. 547.
Mummers visited Max Gate to perform *The Play of Saint George* for H on his eightieth Christmas.

2112 Clemens, Cyril. "My Chat With Thomas Hardy," DALHOUSIE REVIEW, XXIII (1943), 87–94.
[General conversation with eighty-five-year-old H, principally on other writers: Mark Twain, whom H once met and talked with; Fenimore Cooper, admired for his Indians; Galsworthy, to whom H suggested the genealogical tree in his Forsyte novels; Housman, a mutual admiration; Stevenson, who enjoyed *The Woodlanders*; and Poe, said by H to have influenced his own work.]

2113 Eden, Helen Parry. "The Genius of Thomas Hardy," PUNCH, CCIV (14 April 1943), 318.
"An Elizabethan *manqué*, Hardy's was a poetic and a dramatic genius whose vision, complicated by the Victorian approach, gained in poignancy what it lost in grandeur." [Review of David Cecil, HARDY THE NOVELIST (1943).]

2114 Edmonds, J. E. "Hardy Has It Correctly," TIMES LITERARY SUPPLEMENT (Lond), 27 Feb 1943, p. 103.
H has the name of the river where Napoleon escaped correct in *The Dynasts*: Beresina, not Beresinay.

2115 Ekeberg, Gladys W. "The English Novel as a Vehicle of Tragedy, Richardson Through Hardy." Unpublished dissertation, University of Wisconsin, 1943.

2116 "Ellery Queen Builds Collection of Rare Detective Short Stories," PUBLISHERS' WEEKLY, 20 Nov 1943, pp. 1946–49.
Ellery Queen includes the U.S. single volume and the British double volume first editions of *Wessex Tales* among his great collection of detective stories.

2117 Esdaile, Katherine. "Hardy's Names," TIMES LITERARY SUPPLEMENT (Lond), 30 Jan 1943, p. 55.
The name Angel appears on a "fine mural monument" dated 1723 in Stinsford Church to commemorate sons of Angel Audeley. No doubt H named Angel Clare from this source.

2118 "The Impossible Name," TIMES LITERARY SUPPLEMENT (Lond), 23 Jan 1943, p. 43.

H was not always good at choosing names. In *The Woodlanders* H couples the perfect names, Giles Winterborne and Marty South, with the unfortunate creations Felice Charmond and Edred Fitzpiers. His most serious misjudgment comes in *Jude the Obscure* with his use of the name "Tetuphenay," a serious blot and a sign of "warped judgment."

2119 Mais, S. P. B. "Thomas Hardy," QUEEN, 25 Aug 1943, p. 22.

H is "one of the most satisfying of all authors to read in war-time" because "he is never vapid or trivial" and because "he delights in depicting, and is successful in depicting good characters."

2120 "Memorabilia," NOTES AND QUERIES, CLXXXV (17 July 1943), 31.

The Henry St. George of Henry James's "The Lesson of the Master" might well stand for H; James accepted Gosse's view that H had published mostly good and mostly bad novels alternately, and he did not care very much for H's work anyway.

2121 Moody, Wm. Vaughan, and Robert Morss Lovett. A HISTORY OF ENGLISH LITERATURE "New and Enlarged Edition" (NY: Scribner's, 1943), pp. 96, 340, 368, 370–72, 385, 412–14.

H's art is in sharp contrast to George Meredith's. To the latter, "man is all-important," and the struggle of humanity "is always capable of yielding glorious victory"; to H "man is of the smallest importance," and H's world is devoid of "healthful, hopeful combat." H is one of the most powerful of twentieth-century poets.

2122 "Morals and Masterpieces," TIMES LITERARY SUPPLEMENT (Lond), 4 Dec 1943, p. 583.

The recently published National Book Council lecture of Dr. Temple, Archbishop of Canterbury, emphasizes that he considers *Tess of the d'Urbervilles* "among the worst books ever committed to paper" because it does not matter whether or not she is a "pure woman." The attitude that a masterpiece must have the proper morality as far as the reader is concerned is inadmissible as an aesthetic criterion. Artists embody their ideas in their art, which is not a matter of decoration.

2123 Morgan, Charles. THE HOUSE OF MACMILLAN (1843–1943) (Lond: Macmillan, 1943), pp. 41, 54, 58, 87–100, 102, 125, 135, 145, 152–62, 212, 224, 226, 231.

[Reprints several letters between H and Alexander Macmillan and traces the progress of relations between author and firm from their initial rejection of *The Poor Man and the Lady* to H's joining the Macmillan fold and after. John Morley's reader's report, dated Sept 1871, on *Under the Greenwood Tree* praises the story, recommends that H study the work of George Sand and not let "realism grow out of proportion to his fancy."]

2124 Nayler, John. "W. F. Tillotson's Rejection of *Tess*," TIMES LITERARY SUPPLEMENT (Lond), 26 June 1943, p 307.

Tillotson's set *Tess of the d'Urbervilles* in type before reading it because they trusted their known authors to provide suitable work. When Tillotson saw proofs he was taken aback and asked H to make changes. H refused and suggested canceling the contract. There were no hard feelings, and Tillotson published *The Well-Beloved*. [Letter from Richard Purdy enclosing the letter from Nayler, who was secretary to W. F. Tillotson when *Tess* contract was canceled.]

2125 Pearson, Hesketh. CONAN DOYLE (Lond: Methuen, 1943), p. 105; rptd (NY: Walker, 1961), pp. 142–43.

Meredith, not H, was an idol of his fellow writers in the Nineties because H was not respectable enough; H's turn came later.

2126 Purdy, Richard L. "George Gissing at Max Gate, 1895," YALE UNIVERSITY LIBRARY GAZETTE, XVII (1943), 51–52.

"His [Gissing's] portrait of Hardy is startling in its imperceptions." Yet Gissing's "half-truths are significant" in suggesting "the painful and embittered years of *Tess of the d'Urbervilles* and *Jude the Obscure*." [Reprints letter from George Gissing to his brother Algernon regarding visit to Max Gate in 1895.]

2127 Purdy, Richard L. "Ms. Adventures of *Tess*," TIMES LITERARY SUPPLEMENT (Lond), 6 March 1943, p. 120; 26 June 1943, p. 307.

Tess of the d'Urbervilles seems to have been started as early as the autumn of 1888, and half of it was set up by Tillotson and Son as early as Sept 1889. H withdrew it and, after its rejection by MURRAY'S MAGAZINE and MACMILLAN'S MAGAZINE because of the frankness of some of its scenes, bowdlerized it for the GRAPHIC.

2128 Purdy, Richard L. "A Source for Hardy's 'A Committee-Man of "The Terror," ' " MODERN LANGUAGE NOTES, LVIII (Nov 1943), 554–55.

The source of H's "A Committee-Man of 'The Terror' " was Lady Elizabeth Talbot's letter to her sister Lady Harriot Fox-Strangways, which appeared in THE JOURNAL OF MARY FRAMPTON.

2129 Reed, Henry. "The Making of *The Dynasts*," PENGUIN NEW WRITING, No. 18 (July–Sept 1943), 136–47.

The Dynasts justifies and fulfills H's life as an artist, since its story and philosophy had built up slowly throughout H's life. The "Intelligences" *"are the insight and the vision of the work . . . the ruler of the universe [is] an unconscious all-pervading Immanent Will."* The work resembles ULYSSES: in both works an artist labored "to reconcile under a great architectural discipline all that its author 'knew,' " and "to solve linguistic problems." H used five languages in *Dynasts*: the prose of the stage-directions, the colloquial prose of some dialogues, the straightforward blank verse for the earth-bound parts, and the two "levels" of speech in the choruses—the "special lingo" (parodied by Beerbohm) and the lyric choruses. H's managing of the vast and complex story reminds us of the advantage the Greeks enjoyed in knowing a story beforehand. *Dynasts* is a work of great originality and power.

2130 Sagar, S. "Hardy did Harm," CATHOLIC WORLD, CLVI (Feb 1943), 614–15.

H's pessimistic view of the universe is the result of mental confusion similar to that of the pagans. However, the pagan gods did not see men as playthings, as H's gods do, and the pagans themselves did not become disturbed at the irrationality of the universe. H's despair is the result of an overconcern for "the unfortunate exceptions" who seem to suffer unnecessarily. Because of this overconcern, H ultimately came to view the entire cosmos as hostile. H's philosophy of despair is, essentially, a misperception of the world, and consequently, it is harmful to those who accept it as true.

2131 Stowell, Gordon. "From Trafalgar to Waterloo," RADIO TIMES (Lond), LXXXI (15 Oct 1943), 1, 4, 8, 12, 16.

The immortals are the leading figures in *The Dynasts*. Except for its length, the drama "might almost have been written . . . with broadcasting in mind."

2132 Temple, William, Archbishop of Canterbury. THE RESOURCES AND INFLUENCE OF ENGLISH LITERATURE (Lond: National Book Council, 1943), p. 16; The First Annual Lecture of the National Book Council, delivered 21 May 1943.

If one is to learn from a work of art, it must not be based on principles that clash with one's own. H's *Tess of the d'Urbervilles* is one of the worst books ever written, despite H's artistic power, because it creates a sense of uselessness in life which is "the greatest disservice any man can render to his fellows."

2133 Wagenknecht, Edward. "Hardy and the Cosmic Drama," CAVALCADE OF THE ENGLISH NOVEL (NY: Holt, Rinehart & Winston, 1943; 1954; 1967), pp. 352–72.

H's novels are quite Elizabethan, rooted in folk art. His real achievement began with *Under the Greenwood Tree*. Egdon Heath is the real hero of

The Return of the Native. The use of scene to determine the lives of the characters is technically interesting in *Tess of the d'Urbervilles* and *Far From the Madding Crowd* as well as *Native.* The *Mayor of Casterbridge* began a tendency to focus on one leading character, which came to full development in *Jude the Obscure* and especially in *Tess.* Tess is too pure to be typical of any class. *Jude* is the culmination of H's pessimism and gloom. It is perverse, containing scenes of unrelieved horror. H is not a didactic writer; thus *Jude* is not typical. His works are not based on a philosophical system, and none can be deduced from them. H gave up fiction because he had nothing further to say in fiction.

2134 Weber, Carl J. "Hardy Gifts From the Russian Government to the Colby Library," NEW YORK TIMES BOOK REVIEW, 18 April 1943, pp. 2, 33.
In 1937–1938, upon request, the Russian government sent Colby a Russian translation of *Tess of the d'Urbervilles*; remembering this, in 1943, they also sent a Russian edition of *Far From the Madding Crowd*.

2135 [Weber, Carl J.]. "Hardy's Popularity," COLBY LIBRARY QUARTERLY, I (March 1943), 27–29.
[Lists and partially reprints recent tributes and other evidence of continually increasing popularity, including editions.]

2136 [Weber, Carl J.]. "Harte and Hardy," COLBY LIBRARY QUARTERLY, I (Oct 1943), 57–58.
[Reprints a letter from Bret Harte to Nelly Goodrich and Harte's description of H as "a singularly unpretending-looking man, and indeed resembling anything but an author in manner and speech."]

2137 Weber, Carl J. "Henry James and Thomas Hardy," MARK TWAIN QUARTERLY, V (Spring 1943), 3–4.
Though H and James both published their first stories anonymously in 1865, they became very different writers: H wrote of the simple people, James of the cultivated. Although they met occasionally, they never altogether appreciated each other's art.

2138 Weber, Carl J. "Introduction," *The Three Wayfarers* (by Thomas Hardy), ed by Carl J. Weber (NY: Scholars' Facsimiles and Reprints, 1943), pp. vi–xvi.
It was James Barrie's encouragement that led to H's dramatization of "The Three Strangers" as *The Three Wayfarers.* The play shows "Hardy's genius for vivid presentation of character and of striking dramatic situation."

2139 Weber, Carl J. "A Masquerade of Noble Dames," PUBLICATIONS OF THE MODERN LANGUAGE ASSOCIATION, LVIII (June 1943), 558–63.

"Dame the Ninth" was published in three separate places disguised by minor alterations in names and phraseology—"The Impulsive Lady of Croome Castle," LIGHT (1878), "Emmeline, or Passion vs. Principle," INDEPENDENT (NY) (1884), and as one of *A Group of Noble Dames* (1896 and after). Another of the collection was also published in an earlier version.

1944

2140 Blunden, Edmund. "Thoughts of Thomas Hardy," SHELLS BY A STREAM (Lond: Macmillan, 1944), p. 21.
H was one who "looked aware of a vaster threne of decline,/And considered a law of all life," but who "lovingly regarded" the fate of a leaf. [A poem.]

2141 Gifford, Gordon. "The First Mrs. Thomas Hardy," TIMES LITERARY SUPPLEMENT (Lond), 1 Jan 1944, p. 7.
David Cecil's statement that H's first marriage was unhappy is not accurate. There were differences over *Jude the Obscure,* but Emma helped with all the other novels.

2142 Gregory, Horace, and Marya Zaturenska. "The Vein of Comedy in E. A. Robinson's Poetry," BOOKMAN (NY), I (Fall 1944), 43–64, espec 61–62.
Robinson's contribution "was comparable in quality" to H's. Both men exemplified a "beautifully trained gift of reawakening emotion through the art of scrupulously unadorned understatement." [One of a number of comparisons with other literary figures.]

2143 Haines, F. H. "Thomas Hardy as Poet," DORSET YEARBOOK, 1944–1945, pp. 18–25.
"Hardy accepted Hartmann's theory of the Unconscious Will . . . as a working hypothesis . . . in his poetry." But as he said in *The Dynasts,* this Will would evolve until it became conscious.

2144 Honig, Camille. "In Search of Thomas Hardy," NEW STATESMAN AND NATION, XXVII (10 June 1944), 384–85.
[Interviews of H's postman and barber in 1939, with a glimpse at the new occupants of Max Gate—nice people who don't care for H. The barber said: "Some people say he was a bit queer in the head. But I think he was just strange, like the books he wrote."]

2145 Ignoto. "Blunders in Quotations," NOTES AND QUERIES, CLXXXVII (22 April 1944), 208.

In *Jude the Obscure,* the hero's first view of Christminster City gives him visions and dreams of famous men; one of them exclaims: "Beautiful city! So *valuable,* so lovely." Not "valuable," but "venerable" should be read.

2146 Lewis, Cecil Day. "The Shorter Poems of Thomas Hardy," BELL (Dublin), VIII (Sept 1944), 513–25.

H's verse is colored by a "mild relish for respectability," his gossip-loving nature, and a rich musical heritage. H wrote many flawed poems that are dull or have "indigestible subjects." Poems bear the mark of the struggle between the peasant and the genius, between the life of orthodoxy and the unorthodox imagination. H is master of the stanza form and writes with "deliberate roughness." Largely based on the anapest, the poems give us "the pure sincerity of utterance."

2147 M., H. S. "An Anachronism in Thomas Hardy," NOTES AND QUERIES, CLXXXVI (20 May 1944), 246–47.

The heroine quotes a "sensible, new-risen poet" [Browning] and three lines from his poem "The Statue and the Bust," first published in MEN AND WOMEN in 1855. This is anachronistic since the story is supposed to take place in the 1830s.

2148 Munson, Gorham. "Who are Our Favorite Nineteenth-Century Authors?" COLLEGE ENGLISH, V (March 1944), 291–96; also in ENGLISH JOURNAL, XXXIII (March 1944), 113–18.

According to a survey conducted by Mary Barrett [apparently, privately circulated] H is among the twelve favorites, but his popularity is declining.

2149 Purdy, Richard L. "Thomas Hardy and Florence Henniker: The Writing of 'The Spectre of the Real,' " COLBY LIBRARY QUARTERLY, I (Oct 1944), 122–26.

[Details the extent of collaboration, gives details of composition, and notes coolness of reception.]

2150 Roberts, Marguerite. "The Dramatic Element in Hardy's Poetry," QUEEN'S QUARTERLY, LI (Winter 1944–1945), 429–38.

The dramatic element in poetry implies action, struggle, or conflict plus a sense of reality and immediacy. H's ability to grasp a tragic or ironic situation is best shown in three kinds of poems: his occasional poems, the dramatic monologues, and the ballads. In "The Convergence of the Twain" the use of the word "Now!" emphasizes the immediacy of the tragedy. H favored the dramatic monologue, a *genre* established by the Victorian poets. "The Church-Builder" suggests a churchman similar to the one in "The Bishop Orders his Tomb." H is at his best in the ballads, which vary widely in treatment and tone. Most ballads reveal tense, significant figures in passionate action. They are momentary dramas of passionate or ironical human events. The subject-matter is not ideal or romantic: it is sordid, painful, and real. The main emphasis is on action; the incidents speak for themselves; the characters tell their own story.

2151 Roberts, Marguerite. "Hardy and the Theatre." Unpublished dissertation, Radcliffe College, 1944.
[Listed in Lawrence F. McNamee, Dissertations in English and American Literature (NY & Lond: Bowker, 1968).]

2152 Rush, N. Orwin (comp). A Bibliography of the Published Writing of Carl J. Weber (Waterville, Maine: Colby College Library [Colby College Monograph No. 10], 1944).
[A chronological listing of the distinguished H scholar's published writings (200 items).]

2153 [Weber, Carl J.]. Illustrations For *Far From the Madding Crowd* (Fairfield, Maine: Galahad P, 1944).
[Contains photographs of buildings, etc., referred to obliquely in the novel, and a few MS pages.]

2154 Weber, Carl J. " 'The Spectre' after Fifty Years," Colby Library Quarterly, I (Oct 1944), 126–28.
[Catalogue of an exhibition of " 'Spectral' volumes which have survived the half-century."]

2155 "A Wessex Virgil: Barnes' 'Poems of Rural Life,' " Times Literary Supplement (Lond), 1 July 1944, p. 321.
William Barnes, after studying Dorset dialect extensively, pronounced it a better and purer form of English. His collections influenced Tennyson and H, both in poetry and fiction. H sought to revive interest in Barnes with his Select Poems of William Barnes (1908).

2156 Woodbridge, Benjamin M. "Poets and Pessimism: Vigny, Housman *et alii*," Romanic Review, XXV (Feb 1944), 43–51.
Arnold Whitridge's opinion that H was not a genuine pessimist—in "Vigny and Housman, *A Study in Pessimism*," American Scholar, X (Spring 1941), 156–69 [not listed]—is mistaken. *Tess of the d'Urbervilles* and "The Blow" [in *Moments of Vision*] provide evidence contrary to Whitridge's conclusions. [H mentioned in passing.]

1945

2157 Bailey, J. O. "Hardy's 'Imbedded Fossil,' " Studies in Philology, XLII (July 1945), 663–74.

H read widely in the scientific literature of his age, and this reading had a significant influence upon his fiction. Most obvious are the many allusions to astronomy, geology, biology, physics, and other sciences. However, these allusions are not merely decorative for they are important in establishing the mood of key scenes. Further, scientific writing helped shape H's naturalistic treatment of character and his pervasive sense of man's transitory and insignificant place in a universe as immense and timeless as that envisioned by astronomers and geologists.

2158 Ballard, A. E. "Thomas Hardy's *Jude the Obscure*: A Book of Yesterday," WORLD REVIEW (Lond), Dec 1945, pp. 57–59.

Jude the Obscure is not an attack on the convention of matrimony "but on the fallacy of . . . a marriage of reparation, and on public opinion." Jude is "an Achilles of great potentialities, courage and ambition"; his flaw was his inability to resist the call of his sexual appetite. Sue's chief difficulty, too, was weakness—an inability to face the realities of life, to withstand public opinion. Still, Jude and Sue might have found happiness away from Christminster; their decision to remain dooms them to ongoing despair. In the end, "Jude pays over and over again, not merely for a first weakness but for repetitions of it."

2159 Collis, J. S. "Thomas Hardy's *Tess of the d'Urbervilles*: A Book of Yesterday," WORLD REVIEW (Lond), March 1945, pp. 57–59.

"*Tess*, one feels today, is an outrageous book, and should never have been written." Had H relented over Clare as Cervantes relented over Don Quixote, the novel might have been all right, but H did not relent. It is not "the President of the Immortals who had the sport—nay, it was Hardy." The confession scene is "one of the most unbearable scenes in literature." Even for the Victorian period it is "abnormal and absurd." When Angel nearly relents, H instead turns him away: "Hardy loved harrowing and bullying the reader with incidents of this sort." Again H might have relented when Angel leaves Tess, but no, "the *novel* must be served . . . the character must obey orders."

2160 D., C. E. "Hardy's 'In Time of "the Breaking of Nations," ' " EXPLICATOR, III (March 1945), Q 14.

The first six lines of this poem speak of the perdurable vitality of nature, not of the exhaustion of man and nature. Nonetheless, the lines speaking of the lovers, ll. 9–10, seem sentimental and out of place.

2161 Ervine, St. John. "God and My Neighbour," MODERN CHURCHMAN, Sept 1945, pp. 185–95.

H, indifferent or hostile to religion, was sensitive to the Christian message of kindness and pity. "Chronic melancholy" can be seen in *Tess of the d'Ur-*

bervilles and "the coming universal wish not to live" in *Jude the Obscure*. The chorus at the end of *The Dynasts* articulates "the unquenchable hope in the Christian's heart that we shall fulfill the good intentions and live forever in the felicity of God's grace."

2162 Ervine, St. John. "Was Thomas Hardy a Pessimist?" LIS-TENER, XXXIII (19 April 1945), 438–39.
The two most persistent legends about H, that as a boy he was poor and almost illiterate and that he was a pessimist who thought the world to be a pointless muddle, are equally false. His family was quite comfortable; his father was an accomplished musician; his mother was well-read; and his education, though spotty, was "uncommonly" sound. Finally, he was "too inquisitive about life to feel pessimistic about it."

2163 Flower, Newman. THROUGH MY GARDEN GATE (Lond: Cassell, 1945), pp. 50–51.
H quite rightly described himself in "Afterwards" as a man "who used to notice such things," for he once remarked to Flower that his garden looked quite different in the early morning than it did in the day time. [Rather peripheral; Flower is name-dropping his way through a book of reminiscences and short essays.]

2164 Funke, O. EPOCHEN DER NEUEREN ENGLISCHEN LITERATUR (Epochs of Modern English Literature) (Bern: A. Francke, 1945), pp. 217–19.
H is a part of a pessimistic age and reflects it most poignantly in *Tess of the d'Urbervilles*, *Jude the Obscure*, and *The Dynasts*. [In German.]

2165 Gierasch, Walter. "Hardy's 'On the Departure Platform,' " EXPLICATOR, IV (Nov 1945), Item 10.
"On the Departure Platform" is not an indulgence in nostalgia. Rather, the poem shows the speaker's realization that the passing of time has changed the mood of both lovers. Their full confidence, as it once was displayed on the departure platform, cannot be regained. Looking back to this event, the speaker can evaluate it objectively.

2166 Holland, Clive [pseud of C. J. Hankinson]. "When I Cycled and Talked with Hardy," CHAMBERS' JOURNAL, Nov 1945, pp. 571–75.
[Reminiscences of H, recalling his pessimism and kindliness, some of his habits of composition, and his agnosticism.]

2167 Hopkins, Annette B. "*The Dynasts* and the Course of History," SOUTH ATLANTIC QUARTERLY, XLIV (Oct 1945), 432–44.
The Dynasts "shows the universal pattern of power politics in action." The

philosophical view gives the work uniqueness. H views Napoleon, individuals, and armies in a "time-space perspective"; he emphasizes the havoc war wreaks on the natural scene and achieves cinema effect by the progression of scenes.

2168 Jackman, Douglas, M.B.E. THREE HUNDRED YEARS OF BAPTIST WITNESS OF DORCHESTER, 1645–1945 (Dorchester, England: Longmans, 1945), pp. 7–8.
[An account of the Dorford Baptist Church, Dorchester, from its founding in 1645 (by a trooper of Cromwell's army) to its 300th birthday in 1945. It is noted that in 1858 a Mr. Bastow, a "keen Baptist from Bridgport" working in an architect's office in South Street, Dorchester, joined Dorford. Bastow persuaded H, "a very strict Church of England man" of the same office, to attend a prayer meeting at Dorford. However, Bastow and the two young Perkinses (sons of Frederic Perkins, pastor of Dorford) visited a circus then in town and left H waiting for nearly an hour in the vestry of the church.]

2169 Morgan, C. "Bathsheba Everdene," TIMES LITERARY SUPPLEMENT (Lond), 10 Feb 1945, p. 63.
The incident of the valentine in *Far From the Madding Crowd*, an example of H's "imps" of Fate that cause things to happen capriciously, is the mainspring of the plot. It is useless to argue with its realism because it is the way things happen in H. It is inseparably bound up with the character of Bathsheba, whom we remember as good despite her vanity and emotional nature, the truly feminine heroine.

2170 Orcutt, William Dana. "Thomas Hardy—Master of Nature," FROM MY LIBRARY WALLS: A KALEIDOSCOPE OF MEMORIES (NY: Longmans, 1945), pp. 146–49.
"With Hardy scenic descriptions are vital to the story and cannot be separated from the characters or the action of the human figures." H was "certainly the first writer" to break away from Victorian "smugness."

2171 Purdy, Richard L. "Hardy's 'The Sacrilege,' " EXPLICATOR, III (Feb 1945), Item 28.
Though ambiguous, the final stanza of H's "The Sacrilege" is probably the poet's comment, not that of the brother of the church robber. This latter possibility would require an improbable shift in the poem from first to third person narrative.

2172 Schirmer, Walter. KURZE GESCHICHTE DER ENGLISCHEN LITERATUR VON DEN ANFÄNGEN BIS ZUR GEGENWART (Short History of English Literature from the Beginning to the Present)

(Halle/Salle: Max Niemeyer, 1945), pp. 226, 239–40, 243, 275, 280, 291.
[Compares and contrasts H with his contemporaries.] [In German.]

2173 Schröck, Margarethe. DIE WERTWELT THOMAS HARDYS (Thomas Hardy's Value-World). Unpublished dissertation, University of Vienna, 1945.
[A general characterization of H and his works is discussed under five chapter headings: (1) The Kingdom of Man, (2) The Realm of Nature, (3) The Relation between Man and Nature, (4) Artistry, and (5) The Kingdom of the Supernatural. Treats such concepts as H's view of God, the Immanent Will, nature and mother earth, fate and chance, time as a tyrant, death, and the hereafter. Longest and most comprehensive study of H written in German.] [In German.]

2174 Scudder, Harold L., and W. W. G. "Selling a Wife," NOTES AND QUERIES, CLXXXIX (4 March 1945), 123–24; (11 Aug 1945), 64–65.
[Records an instance of the transfer of conjugal rights by way of auction in RETROSPECT OF A LONG LIFE, by S. C. Hall (Lond: 1883), I, 43–44; which is relevant to *The Mayor of Casterbridge*.]

2175 Turner, W. J. "How I Feel About Kipling," KIPLING JOURNAL, XII (Dec 1945), 3–5.
[Praises Kipling's craftsmanship and compares him to H in sincerity and realism, saying that Kipling and H have been butts for the clever because of their independence.]

2176 Van den Bergh, Gerhard. DER PESSIMISMUS BEI THOMAS HARDY, GEORGE CRABBE UND JONATHAN SWIFT (Pessimism in Thomas Hardy, George Crabbe and Jonathan Swift) (Menziken: A. Baumann, 1945); rptd (Menziken: Kolumbus, 1947); University of Zurich dissertation.
"The study of the nature of pessimism of our three authors shows that pessimism does not exclude the impulse to reform but, on the contrary, must precede it." *Jude the Obscure* is a reaction against late-Victorian liberalism, the mechanistic view of culture, and the modern spiritual situation. The wise and intelligent characters of the novel are unconventional and senseless; the stupid ones, however, are conventional and sensible. In H's novels, he blames society because it either forces man to restrain his instincts unconsciously or to express them in unanswerable optimism as something else. In his treatment of love and marriage H turns against Victorian arrogance. The only characters who demand a legal marriage are the lowly-valued Arabella and the mindlessly-conventional Phillotson. Sue and Jude,

who had the courage to be answerable only to their consciences, are broken by the judgment of Society, which demands an entrance-ticket for the theater in which man and woman live together—a ticket which cheapens exactly the most earnestly-meant relations. [In German.]

2177 [Weber, Carl J.]. "Hardy's Deference to His Publishers," COLBY LIBRARY QUARTERLY, I (Jan 1945), 148–50.
A comparison of the 1871 and the 1889 editions of *Desperate Remedies* reveals only trivial differences.

2178 Weber, Carl J. "People Who Read and Write," NEW YORK TIMES BOOK REVIEW, 20 May 1945, p. 19.
An Indiscretion in the Life of an Heiress appeared first in book form in 1935, but it had appeared serially in HARPER'S WEEKLY and LIVING AGE in 1878.

2179 Weber, Carl. "Tragedy and the Good Life," DALHOUSIE REVIEW, XXV (1945), 225–33.
Although in H's novels men suffer because of the nature of the universe, their struggles are heroic. It will not do to say simply, as the Reverend Thomas Saunders said, that H's tragic characters are subject to chance and simply resigned to their fate. The first of these charges will not stand up if we look at characters whose good fortune is the result of character and of those who suffer because of character, like Henchard. The second is even less true and does not apply to such characters as Clym, Gabriel Oak, and Marty South. Saunder's charge that H's tragedies are inferior because they lack hope, can be said equally well of Aeschylus. H's tragedy is "purer" because it dares to question the existence of a moral order and makes man dependent only on his own character.

1946

2180 Bailey, J. O. "Hardy's Mephistophelian Visitants," PUBLICATIONS OF THE MODERN LANGUAGE ASSOCIATION, LXI (Dec 1946), 1146–84.
Characters like Troy in *Far From the Madding Crowd* are satanic intruders who invade stories to alter the course of events, seriously affecting other characters' lives. Diggory Venn, whom H treated with satanic symbolism, is the most impressive of these figures. William Dare, in *A Laodicean*, has a mephistophelian function and is so labeled by his father, in addition to his quoting Satan. Related examples of H's device appear in *The Mayor of*

Casterbridge, The Dynasts, and *Jude the Obscure.* The pattern is explained by H's love of the uncommon in human experience linked with conventional Faust imagery and mummers' plays to depict the operation of will in human life.

2181 Bevan, T. W. "Thomas Hardy's Apology," LONDON QUARTERLY AND HOLBORN REVIEW, CLXXI (July 1946), 255–60.

Although H's life always lacked the final assurance of Christian faith, he was an honest doubter who set out to counteract a too superficial view of life and became the relentless foe of the dishonest doubter and the pretending believer alike. His "Apology" in *Late Lyrics and Earlier* shows that his pessimism was a healthy exploration of reality. He saw in the possible alliance of religion and rationality the prevention of a new Dark Age of superstition. H's poems show a broad range of approaches to man's state: "God-Forgotten" depicts man self-estranged from a concerned God, "The Bedridden Peasant" shows an indifferent God, "The Servant's Quarters" uses a Biblical incident, "The Curate's Kindness" and "The Slow Nature" show gentle laughter, "Time's Laughingstocks" and "The Church-Builder" are grimly humorous, and "Ah, are you Digging on my Grave" strips away all self-delusion. "To Sincerity" and "To a Lady" show H using the same consistent approach in his attack on over-optimism.

2182 Bowra, C[ecil] M[aurice]. THE LYRICAL POETRY OF THOMAS HARDY (Nottingham: Nottingham University, 1946 [Twenty-third Byron Foundation Lecture, 29 Nov 1946]); rptd in INSPIRATION AND POETRY (Lond: Macmillan; NY: St. Martin's P, 1955), pp. 220–41.

H's career falls decisively into two halves. In the second half, he published not only *The Dynasts* but also eight volumes of lyrical verse. He is the most representative English poet between Tennyson and Yeats; as a poet, he is a singular figure. The poets whom he most loved—Crabbe, Scott, Shelley, Keats, Swinburne, Barnes—left no trace on his work. His origins as a true countryman did much to determine his work and outlook. A poem like "Postponement," written in 1866, shows no indebtedness to any predecessor but much that was to be characteristic of his mature style, forty years later. This kind of style bears no relation to the refined, sensitive manner of the great Victorians. H writes poetry with prose words; his verse seems to combine natural ease with conscious elaboration. His poetry is that of the dramatic situation; many poems deal with what would be interesting even in a newspaper—hence, H's realism, his interest in what really happens but also his awareness of the odd, unexpected elements in every human crisis (cf. "The Convergence of the Twain"). He may be the most tragic English poet since Shakespeare, but pessimism is not the clue to the real character of his poetry.

However, at some time he seems to have suffered a terrible shock or disappointment which left an enduring scar (cf. "In the Seventies" and "He Fears his Good Fortune," poems written late in life and published in 1917). It was a collapse of confidence and harmony in himself, the loss of an inner contentment. Although H liked to write about the things that pleased him, he was irresistibly drawn to more disturbing subjects; his sensitiveness increased with the years; his escape was to transform the blows inflicted on his heart into art. For him, poetry was release. Irony was H's response to contrasts and contradictions. This irony took different forms: whimsical fancy in "He Revisits his First School," a harsher kind of mockery in the poem "In Church," ironical pathos in "Drummer Hodge," philosophical poetry in "Beyond the Last Lamp." H's beliefs were those of his time: Darwinism and the scientific study of history had undermined the traditional Christianity of his childhood, but he did not break absolutely with it. H's search for some other system found no final solution; his controversy with official Christianity was part of his quarrel with the universe (cf. "The Blinded Bird"). H seldom creates a myth. His genius was essentially dramatic, especially in the scope of his lyrical poetry. Because he believed that the universe is senseless, he was able to give his characters the tragic dignity which belongs to those who struggle in hopeless causes. He regarded criminals as pathetic creatures of circumstance who deserve pity far more than condemnation (cf. "On the Portrait of a Woman about to be Hanged"). For H in the last resort the responsibility for evil lies not with human beings but with the system of things which makes them act as they do. [An important essay. The first serious treatment of H by a critic of Bowra's stature. Prefigures, in abbreviated form, almost every major theme in criticism of the 1960s.]

2183 Chapple, Joe Mitchell. "As I Remember Thomas Hardy," CHRISTIAN SCIENCE MONITOR [Magazine Section], 26 Jan 1946, p. 5.

[Chatty recollection of a visit with H—nothing special.]

2184 Christensen, Glenn J. "The Thomas Hardy Collection," PRINCETON UNIVERSITY LIBRARY CHRONICLE, VIII (Nov 1946), 24–27.

Morris L. Parrish's Hardy Collection is but a part of a vast collection of Victorian literature left by the bibliophile to Princeton University. It contains a full set of English and American first editions of the Wessex novels; two of the lesser novels in serial form; all the poems and short stories in their first collected editions (and a number of them in the magazines or newspapers where they first appeared); and letters from the second Mrs. H to Mr. Parrish.

2185 Etherington, Michael. "R. D. Blackmore," NEW ENGLISH REVIEW, XIII (1946), 298–306.

[Contains two hitherto unpublished letters by H to the author of Lorna Doone. One of 8 June 1875 describes H's delight at discovering Blackmore's finest novel: "It seems almost absurd that I had never read it before, considering the kind of work I attempted in *Far From the Madding Crowd*." H and Blackmore must later have met through their publisher Marston. The second and shorter letter, dated 4 Nov 1875, refers to H's sending a ballad to the older novelist: Carl J. Weber identifies it with "The Bride-Night Fire," later published in *Wessex Poems*.]

2186 Ferguson, Delancey. "Hardy's 'In Time of "the Breaking of Nations," ' " Explicator, IV (Feb 1946), Item 25.
In response to C. E. D.'s query, ibid, III (March 1945), 4, ll. 9–10 of this poem are not sentimental because they too speak of the perdurable vitality of nature, showing us the love between man and woman will continue.

2187 Flower, Newman. "Walks and Talks with Thomas Hardy," Countryman, XXXIV (Winter 1946), 193–95.
H wrote " 'against bird-catching, performing animals, careless butchering, and the chaining of dogs. . . .' Animals, birds, insects, are here as part of the pageant of our lives. Exactly what part some are intended to play, we do not know." [Accounts of picnics with H in his old age and reminiscences about Wessex, H's dog, and a Persian kitten named Cobby, given to H six months before H's death.]

2188 Gierasch, Walter. "Hardy's 'In Tenebris, I,' " Explicator, IV (April 1946), Item 45.
"In Tenebris, I" shows the irony of bereavement. The speaker attempts, but fails, to solace himself with the belief that the dead cannot die twice— his pain cannot be repeated. The structural monotony of the poem conveys the dullness of the speaker's mind but comes too close to boring the reader.

2189 Grierson, H. J. C., and J. C. Smith. Critical History of English Poetry (Lond: Oxford UP, 1946), pp. 507–11.
H's poems begin by inveighing against the indifference of Nature and the machinery of natural selection and proceed to speak of some ultimate Power behind Nature. Schopenhauer's doctrine of Immanent Will becomes the frame for *The Dynasts*, and the conflict of an Immanent Will that does not know or feel and of man who hopes is engaged. The dominant note of H's poetry is doom. His loyalties are to the humble people, his native county of Dorset, and the language of Wessex.

2190 Laird, John. "Hardy's *The Dynasts*," Philosophical Incursions into English Literature (Lond: Cambridge UP, 1946), pp. 187–204.
The fatalist believes that his affairs and those of his race "are settled . . . not by him or by his race." The determinist believes "every event . . . is

the inevitable result . . . of preceding events and . . . a determinant of what comes later." Predestination arises when fatalism is added to determinism: "all human actions and (so-called) 'struggles' are overridden . . . by super-human causes." These "causes" may predestine personally, unconsciously, or impersonally. *The Dynasts* "heaves uneasily in the wash of these conceptions, never clearly distinguishing their separate currents . . . and offering in consequence a troubled perspective." Although H said he had " 'little eye to a systematized philosophy,' " his extensive use of a "monistic mythology" belies this statement. In practice, the commentary of the Upper Air "is a prolonged dialogue between Y [Ancient Spirit of the Years] and P [Spirit of the Pities], between the new mythology of science . . . and the old outmoded overhumanized Christian world-view." The chief confusion of *Dynasts* concerns "puppetry": helplessness, willessness of characters. "Some of the agents believe themselves masters of their destiny, and some waver." Napoleon's own "wavering fatalism" is "an amalgam of determinism and fatalism" which rarely approaches consistency.

2191 Lowndes, Mrs. Belloc. The Merry Wives of Westminster (Lond: Macmillan, 1946), pp. 116, 136, 147–49, 158–59, 169.

In conversations, H revealed that he wanted to be remembered as a poet, that he felt it was best always to tell the truth, that *Jude the Obscure* is not autobiographical, and that many of his short stories are founded on fact.

2192 McCullough, Bruce. "Thomas Hardy," Representative English Novelists: Defoe to Conrad (NY: Harper, 1946), pp. 231–49.

H did not share the optimism of George Meredith and George Eliot, the writers with whom he is most often associated. He saw the world as malignant and life as a constant struggle between man and nature. He was never a realist [?] and not essentially a moralist, and unlike other writers of the time he resisted [?] the influence of science on fiction. He is more a poet than Meredith or Eliot, less intellectual and more in sympathy with his material. His artistic control is evident everywhere in *The Return of the Native*. His use of setting is more effective than in The Egoist and more subtle than in Middlemarch. Environment works as a force of destiny and man is unconsciously responsive to it. Major characters represent forces of change and struggle; minor characters represent permanence in the midst of change and exert a leveling influence. The novel is a subtle blend of character, action, and setting, humor, and poetry. [Bracketed queries indicate questionable judgments. A somewhat old-fashioned view.]

2193 Oberholzer, Otto. Kleines Lexikon der Weltliteratur (Brief Dictionary of World Literature) (Bern: A. Francke, 1946), I, 143–44.

[Includes works and translations.] [In German.]

2194 Parker, Eileen. "The Regionalism of Thomas Hardy," New Saxon Review, No. 4 (1946), 17–22.

In H's novels the principle of regionalism applied to a conscious philosophy, receives full treatment for the first time. Scott *used* local color; H *creates* it. In re-creating Wessex, H concerns himself with the elements of change ever present in Society and Nature, together with the enduring characteristics of past generations. But the Wessex of H's vision has a grandeur beyond the limits of its locality; its prototype is the Universe itself. Characters like Gabriel Oak, Giles Winterborne or Diggory Venn, are instinct with the woodlands and orchards: they overshadow the shallowness of Troy, Wildeve, and Fitzpiers. With Clym Yeobright, Angel Clare and Henry Knight, H emphasizes the growing conflict between passions and intellect. In re-creating local color, H uses very effectively a kind of supernatural atmosphere, only to be paralleled in some passages of de la Mare. In presenting human frailties among "locals" as comic, H recaptures a Chaucerian quality of sympathetic understanding which creates laughter *with*, rather than *at*, his humorous figure.

2195 Routh, H[arold] V[ictor]. English Literature and Ideas in the Twentieth Century (Lond: Methuen, 1946; NY: Longmans, 1948), pp. 3, 5, 7, 56, 73, 76–77, 80, 82, 83, 119, 150, 151, 155.

H's novels are Victorian in spirit, but his poems belong to both the Victorian and the modern periods. What both the novels and the poems show is a man of stoical outlook responding pessimistically to the results of scientific findings but turning finally to the modern conviction that man's being is rooted in pity and revolt.

2196 Sassoon, Siegfried. Siegfried's Journey: 1916–1920 (NY: Viking P, 1946), pp. 19, 43, 96, 105, 112, 119, 120, 131–39, 143, 149, 156, 159, 179, 180–81, 219–20, 221, 222–24, 226, 231, 253, 265, 289.

H, a physically frail, wizard-like, shy, and modest man, liked to discuss poets and poetry. The more he talked, the more lovable he became, especially when it became clear he was receptive to everyone's ideas. During the conversations he revealed that he would not have written *The Dynasts* if he had foreseen the Great War. H had his aunt's face in mind when describing Tess.

2197 Sherman, George Witter. "Thomas Hardy & The Lower Animals," Prairie Schooner, XX (Winter 1946), 304–9.

H, among the first to read Darwin's The Origin of Species, applied its philosophy to his love of animals, high and low. In his novels, birds, bees, glowworms, rabbits, and horses are treated with sympathy; in essays, he pleads against vivisection; in diary entries, he recalls death of pet dogs; in poems, he is sympathetic with animals. For H, man may be treacherous and hypocritical, animals never.

2198 "Thomas Hardy," SCHWEIZER LEXIKON (Swiss Dictionary) (Zurich: Encyclios Verlag Ag., 1946), III, 1470.
H depicts nature's destruction of human will with Shakespearian strength. [In German.]

2199 [Weber, Carl J.]. "Deep in the Heart of China," COLBY LIBRARY QUARTERLY, I (Jan 1946), 208–9.
Japanese Major General Takeo Imai sent to Colby the now suppressed Japanese translation of *Tess of the d'Urbervilles.*

2200 Weber, Carl J. HARDY IN AMERICA: A STUDY OF THOMAS HARDY AND HIS AMERICAN READERS (Waterville, Maine: Colby College P, 1946).
H was a cultural phenomenon: in many ways he has been a more popular and perhaps a greater writer in America than in England. [Traces in meticulous detail the history of H publication, appreciation, and scholarship in the United States.]

2201 [Weber, Carl J.]. "Jude from Obscurity, via Notoriety, to Fame," COLBY LIBRARY QUARTERLY, I (Jan 1946), 209–15.
[Descriptive list of Colby Semi-Centennial Exhibit of *Jude the Obscure* items includes domestic and foreign editions, material relating to H and Miss Jeanette Gilder who wrote a notorious review, and discussions of the novels.]

2202 Weber, Carl J. "The Manuscript of Hardy's *Two on a Tower,*" PAPERS OF THE BIBLIOGRAPHICAL SOCIETY OF AMERICA, XL (First Quarter 1946), 1–21.
Aldrich's manuscript, salvaged from the 1882 ATLANTIC publication, shows that H's last-minute emendations were not taken into the text and that the style of the American version was freely revised, although no "shocking passages" were deleted as Miss Francis, Aldrich's assistant, once claimed. A third manuscript was probably used for the English edition. The manuscript gives evidence that H's wife acted only as amanuensis.

2203 [Weber, Carl J.]. "A Most Desirable Association Item," COLBY LIBRARY QUARTERLY, I (Jan 1946), 201–8.
Among seven sentimental associations with Colby's copy of Dante Gabriel Rossetti's HAND AND SOUL, printed by William Morris at the Kelmscott Press, is that this copy is inscribed to H by Beatrice Stella Campbell, the actress whose unfulfilled wish it was to play the role of Tess.

2204 Weber, Carl J. "Note," *The Old Clock* (Portland, Maine: Southworth-Athoensen P, 1946).

H wrote "The Old Clock" when he was only fifteen. The poem shows "how truly and fully the boy of fifteen was father of the man of eighty-five.

2205 Wicks, F. C. S. "Thomas Hardy, the Unlabeled," HUMANIST, VI (Summer-Autumn 1946), 66.

H escapes labeling, although he abandoned the idea of an anthropomorphic, fatherly God and speaks of the "Unmoral Cause" of things in a letter to Noyes. H's wife wrote to Noyes that the war finished any idea that there was a fundamental "Wisdom" at the back of things. In answer to the charge that he had a savage, tribal god, H calls himself a "harmless agnostic," but *Two on a Tower* shows "impersonal monsters in the universe."

1947

2206 "The Edwardian Novel," TIMES LITERARY SUPPLEMENT (Lond), 28 June 1947, p. 322.

Reputations fluctuate often because an author's work is out of touch with the times. Later generations make their own estimate. H's twilight as a novelist was delayed by his fame as poet but at his death he passed "into a period of belittlement." People found his kinship with Elizabethan tragic poets melodramatic. Critics are now rediscovering him.

2207 Erskine, John. "Tess, Plaything of Fate," AMERICAN WEEKLY, 12 Oct 1947, p. 2.

When *Tess of the d'Urbervilles* appeared, the reading public was torn between resentment at H's philosophy and sympathy for his heroine. The reason—H couldn't decide what his mission was in art. The novel doesn't need the philosophy. It was H's philosophy "rather than the law which insisted upon Tess's execution."

2208 Gilbert, Katherine. "Recent Poets on Man and His Place," PHILOSOPHICAL REVIEW, LVI (Sept 1947), 469–90, espec 477–80.

The comments from H's overworld in *The Dynasts* "are logically incompatible, as dramatic statements have a right to be." On one hand "values are made nonexistent," on the other, Pity "assigns at the outset a value—a negative one—to all terrestrial history." Man's place in this universe is contradictory: he may be a helpless puppet, but he has feelings—an "intolerable contradiction." But "suffering is not a mechanical event. Either the Universe is different, or man is different from Hardy's picturing."

2209 "Hardy's Earliest Verses," TIMES LITERARY SUPPLEMENT (Lond), 23 Aug 1947, p. 432.

The holograph of "The Household Clock" was written one Sunday morning when he was fifteen, according to H's brother and sister. It was written in pencil on the inside of the door of the grandfather's clock at Higher Bockhampton, signed by H, and dated 19 Dec 1855. [Photo taken by W. H. Cuming of Weymouth.]

2210 Heilman, Robert B. "Sue Bridehead Revisited," ACCENT, VII (Winter 1947), 123–26.

In the subordination of her love to her religious duty, Sue Bridehead resembles Julia Flyte in Waugh's BRIDESHEAD REVISITED, yet the treatment of the two heroines is quite different. H writes from both heart and head about Sue, exploring her difficulties with sympathy. Through her, H questions the religious atmosphere of his day. On the other hand, Waugh uses Julia Flyte to answer questions, not to raise them; she is a much less dramatic character, less credible than Sue because she is used as a counter in a predetermined religious solution. Waugh writes only from the head, and the force of his fiction is impaired thereby.

2211 Herbert, Jane. WE WANDER IN WESSEX (Lond & Melbourne: Ward, Lock, 1947), pp. 147, 174, 176, 178, 179.

[Passing references and photo of burial place in Stinsford of H's heart.]

2212 Holland, Clive [pseud of C. J. Hankinson]. "The Charm of Thomas Hardy's Wessex," DORSET YEARBOOK, 1947–1948, pp. 5–13.

"A visit to Hardy's Wessex has always left me with a vivid impression of his genius as a writer; and the truth and vividness of the portraits he drew of Wessex folk."

2213 Lewis, C[ecil] Day. THE POETIC IMAGE (Lond: Cape; NY: Oxford UP, 1947), pp. 20–21, 33, 87–88, 150–53.

[Quotations from the poetry and notebooks; discussion of poetic quality of H's prose in *Tess of the d'Urbervilles*; analysis of "To an Unborn Pauper Child."]

2214 Liddell, Robert. A TREATISE ON THE NOVEL (Lond: Cape, 1947), pp. 116–21.

Background in H is well done when he relates people to work (Winterborne, Oak). There is no artificially pretty view of nature. Sometimes H overdoes "pre-raphaelite" accuracy, as in the scene at Talbothays where Tess is covered with "country messes" in the weedy garden. The technique of farce tends to overdo detail. The too overpowering scenery diminishes characters, as in Egdon.

2215 Peters, Eric. "Thomas Hardy as Poet," POETRY REVIEW, XXXVIII (Dec 1947), 503–7.
In fiction and poetry H tries always to relate his thoughts and characters to Wessex, and yet he is simultaneously cosmic in outlook. He is honest and straightforward but also possesses a "keen, if somewhat bitter, sense of humor." A strangeness and eeriness pervades many of the poems, and this may have influenced Walter de la Mare. "Modern verse forms owe more to this man's [H's] pioneering than is generally recognized, and he was one of the first to free English poetry from the more rigid conventions." His people show symptoms of repressed and smoldering passions.

2216 Powicke, Frederick Maurice. THREE LECTURES (Lond: Oxford UP, 1947), pp. 72–73.
Displaying a sense of the poetic in history, H wrote under the influence of "local associations" and a "desire for historical truth."

2217 Rosenberg, Bernard. "Hardy's Earliest Poem," TIMES LITERARY SUPPLEMENT (Lond), 27 Sept 1947, p. 497.
H's earliest poem, "The Household Clock," was published as a song written by A. Sedgwick, copyrighted in the United States in 1853. Both words and music are presumably by Sedgwick. Perhaps he and young H owed something to an "original" author.

2218 Sherman, George Witter. "Thomas Hardy and the Reform League," NOTES AND QUERIES, CXCII (6 Sept 1947), 383–84.
The Reform League was located on the ground-floor rooms of 8 Adelphi Terrace, where H was employed as a Gothic draughtsman by the aristocratic architect Blomfield. May not H's quarrel with the organization of human society, as exemplified in his legendary first novel, have taken on some of the "political tinge" alluded to by Rutland [THOMAS HARDY (1938), p. 126] from his acquaintance with the Reform League underneath Blomfield's offices?

2219 Southworth, James Granville. THE POETRY OF THOMAS HARDY (NY: Columbia UP, 1947); rvd ed (1966).
H is a poet whose roots and sympathies were not with the Victorian poets but "with the scientists: Darwin, Huxley, Mill, and others who began in the 1850s to upset so-called Victorian complacency," and a poet whose aesthetic is governed by "the purity of his reaction to form as an object of emotion rather than as a means of suggesting emotion or conveying information." [Part I ("The Thing Said") of this tripartite study deals with Love, Woman, God, Free Will, and Fate and attempts to synthesize H's poetic aesthetic with his poetic thought. Part II ("The Way of Saying It") treats

Diction, Imagery, Prosody, Architectonics, and Nature in an attempt to demonstrate H's consciousness of technique and method. Part III ("The Achievement") attempts to measure H's accomplishment "as a poet, not as a thinker." Also, five appendices: "THE ORIGIN OF SPECIES," "The Revised Version of the Bible," "Music," and "Hardy's Humaneness."]

2220 Stallman, Robert W. "Hardy's Hour Glass Novel," SEWANEE REVIEW, LV (April–June 1947), 283–96; rptd in THE HOUSE THAT JAMES BUILT AND OTHER LITERARY STUDIES (East Lansing: Michigan State UP, 1961), pp. 53–63.

The hourglass is both an emblem of structure and a symbol in *The Return of the Native*. As symbol, it equals real time (Eustacia) versus clock-time or calendar time (Thomasin). Structurally, there are seven hourglasses (reverse turns) in the novel, as well as extra-structural hourglass-reversals. All of H's novels are geometrically constructed; most depend upon reversed triangles or hourglasses.

2221 Tindall, William York. FORCES IN MODERN BRITISH LITERATURE 1885–1946 (NY: Knopf, 1947), passim.

Charles M. Doughty is "of the rough-hewn tribe of Hardy." "With Housman and Hardy, E. M. Forster belongs among the prewar ironists." H and others signed a petition to free Vizetelly. "Like Hardy, Conrad considered man's consciousness his tragedy. Like Hardy, he had a gloomy temper." [Mainly comparison and contrast with other authors of the period with respect to the major forces upon it.] Writers of the H school who used landscape as background for melodrama were Eden Phillpotts, Sheila Kaye-Smith, D. H. Lawrence, Mary Webb, and John Cowper Powys. [H's *The Mayor of Casterbridge*, *The Woodlanders*, *Tess of the d'Urbervilles*, *Jude the Obscure* and *The Dynasts* are discussed under the heading "The Troughs of Zolaism" (determinism).] Zola saw cause and effect; H chance. H learned from science—Darwin, Spencer, and Colenso—and interpreted Greek fate as chance. His novels "are tragedies of Darwin's man in Newton's universe and Mrs. Grundy's parlor." "Their power comes from the feeling with which Hardy contemplated human significance and insignificance, their irony from the disparity he found between chance and will, their density from love of native soil." [Discussion of *Tess, Jude,* H's lyrics, and *Dynasts* follows.] Poems fail; they are technically deficient. "But form and mood happily conspire" in *Dynasts*, "his most successful work."

2222 Trewin, J. C. "In Other Words," ILLUSTRATED LONDON NEWS, 7 June 1947, p. 614.

Ronald Gow's stage adaptation of *Tess of the d'Urbervilles* is an unusually good one. Most of the dramatic adaptations of H have been unsuccessful.

Dickens, Thackeray, the Brontës, and Trollope have also been poorly staged. Gow "has both brought Tess to the theatre and kept her at the core of Hardy's Wessex."

2223 Vallins, G. H. " 'Hardy the Poet,' " METHODIST RECORDER, 13 March 1947, p. 7.

Although H's novels are popular, H is more the poet than the novelist. His favorite poetic themes are "chance and change." H's other themes are thwarted or illicit love, the impact of war, and a desire for religious conviction. The common characteristics of his poetry include irony, bitterness, pity, and sympathy for animals. H's style is often rough and broken but suits his purposes well.

2224 Van Doren, Mark. "Homage to Three," KENYON REVIEW, IX (Winter 1947), 70.

[Verse tribute to H, Emily Dickinson, and Homer. H was "The last man that remembered the country singing,/And first to call it pitiful."]

2225 [Weber, Carl J.]. "Hardy Additions," COLBY LIBRARY QUARTERLY, II (Aug 1947), 46–49.

Eight more American editions of works by H have been added to the Colby College Hardy Collection and to the bibliography of American imprints of H's work.

2226 Weber, Carl J. "Not Hardy's Verse," SUN (NY), 1 Oct 1947, p. 24.

"The Old Clock," which the SUN attributed to H, is in reality by Charles Swain, a Manchester poet born in 1803.

2227 [Weber, Carl J.]. "Notes and Memoranda," COLBY LIBRARY QUARTERLY, II (Aug 1947), 49–52.

[Notes receipt of a book from H's library.]

2228 [Weber, Carl J.]. "Recent Gifts to the Colby Library," COLBY LIBRARY QUARTERLY, II (Feb 1947), 13–16.

Twenty-four items have been added to the Hardy Collection.

2229 [Weber, Carl J.]. "Some Recent Gifts," COLBY LIBRARY QUARTERLY, II (Nov 1947), 66–67.

[Notes the addition of numerous books from H's library and one autograph letter to the collection of the Colby College Library. The letter, to the Rev. John Oliver, answers an inquiry about *The Dynasts*.]

2230 Webster, Harvey Curtis. "Hardy as Thinker," TIGER'S EYE, I (Dec 1947), 49–60.

H's philosophic development went from High Church to determinism to the inconsistent position of meliorism and pessimism to a final resolution. He perpetually tried to resolve moral and natural law. "The inconsistencies within [H's] philosophy do hurt the totality of effect of the novels." The poems which present H's central philosophy are more successful than any of his novels written during the period in which he was struggling to reconcile meliorism and pessimism. *The Dynasts*, the consummation of his thought, approaches "the deepest insight of man about man and his universe."

2231 Webster, Harvey Curtis. ON A DARKLING PLAIN: THE ART AND THOUGHT OF THOMAS HARDY (Chicago: University of Chicago P, 1947); rptd (Hamden, Conn: Archon Books, 1964).
H was initially a traditional Anglican but became antitheistic about 1863, primarily through the influence of THE ORIGIN OF SPECIES and ESSAYS AND REVIEWS and of Moule. Disillusionment with people and with finding a vocation tinged his early poems and novels with pessimism. Chance, social conditions, and sexual determinism are the three threads that run in varying degrees through all his novels. Despite H's marriage, his early novels reflect the elements above, perhaps as a result of Leslie Stephen's determinism, which reinforced H's own thinking. *The Return of the Native* is artistically the best of these novels in character creation, dramatic structure, and singleness of effect. Philosophically, however, the texture of the novels varies, sometimes through antilogy. "Hardy approaches most nearly the position of the meliorist. Believing that there is much irremediable evil in the world, he nevertheless believes in the possibility of a slow progress that will ultimately do away with those evils, mostly social, that do not inhere in the nature of things." The later novels become increasingly deterministic and more aimed at social ills. By 1902, he had reconciled the conflicting ideas of free will and determinism. "Through man's conscious awareness he can control and change those parts of the universe which are products of his consciousness (i.e., society) even if he cannot overcome or change for the present the unconscious portions of the universe or the unconscious (i.e., emotional) parts of himself. Ultimately, perhaps, consciousness will inform the entire Will." H was not influenced by Schopenhauer until after 1886. Even then Von Hartmann impressed him more. H's inconsistencies are those of the artist exploring "new manifestations of reality." "During the first fifty-five years of his life, Hardy was continually in search of philosophical congruity." *The Dynasts* is the culmination of that effort. It "represents man's insight into his place in the universe as no other modern epic does." "Hardy is not the greatest thinker of modern times or the greatest artist. But no man of letters of our period, with the exception of Thomas Mann, has so well combined the function of the thinker with the function of the artist."

1948

2232 Bebbington, W. G. THE ORIGINAL MANUSCRIPT OF THOMAS HARDY'S THE TRUMPET-MAJOR: A STUDY WITH PHOTOGRAPHS (Windsor: Luff & Sons [ca 1948]).
[In order to "help those who cannot have the good fortune of seeing the ms. for themselves," the pamphlet presents variant readings of the chapter headings, chapter divisions, names of characters and places, and passages of the text as well as photographic reproductions of four pages from the MS.]

2233 Breyer, Bernard R. "The Element of Occasionality in the Poetry of Thomas Hardy." Unpublished dissertation, University of Virginia, 1948.
[Listed in Lawrence F. McNamee, DISSERTATIONS IN ENGLISH AND AMERICAN LITERATURE (NY & Lond: Bowker, 1968).]

2234 Burian, Orhan. "An Introduction to Hardy's Novels," ANNALES DE L'UNIVERSITÉ D'ANKARA, III (1948–1949), 441–522.
The critical emphasis upon H's philosophy has unfortunately obscured the tripartite balance of forces at work on the characters in his novels. H's people are affected to differing degrees by their own characters, the conventions of society and the laws of nature, and an obscure destiny.

2235 Child, Harold. "Adventures of a Novel," ESSAYS AND REFLECTIONS (Lond: Cambridge UP, 1948), pp. 64–72.
[A history of *Tess of the d'Urbervilles*—difficulties of publication, necessity of alterations and excisions to meet prudish publisher's standards, and attacks by contemporary readers. Child defends *Tess*. Greatly dependent upon Carl Weber's HARDY OF WESSEX (1940).]

2236 Church, Richard. BRITISH AUTHORS: A 20TH CENTURY GALLERY (Lond: Longmans, Green, 1948).
[A brief discussion of H emphasizing his calm, detached, and contemplative stance toward life.]

2237 Darby, H. C. "The Regional Geography of Thomas Hardy's Wessex," GEOGRAPHICAL REVIEW (NY), XXXVIII (July 1948), 426–43.
In England, the topographical novel, such as Scott's romances, becomes regional with H's novels, whose theme is man and his work on the land. H's prefaces and passages in the novels describe landscape accurately. *Tess of the d'Urbervilles* shows the chalk upland's uninviting aspects, while *Far From the Madding Crowd* shows one of the fertile intervales. "The pictures

Hardy drew take their place in the sequence that stretches from John Coker's survey in the seventeenth century up to the modern accounts of the land utilization of Dorset."

2238 Evans, Sir Ifor. A SHORT HISTORY OF ENGLISH DRAMA (Middlesex: Penguin Books, 1948); 2nd ed, rvd and enlgd (Boston: Houghton Mifflin, 1965), pp. 12, 16, 188.

H's preface to *The Dynasts* and Milton's SAMSON AGONISTES have helped to perpetuate the illusion "that the drama can be appreciated in independence of the theatre." But *Dynasts* "shows a distinct talent for the drama." [Cites H's 1909 comment to the Joint Committee on Stage Plays (Censorship).] In *Dynasts* and *The Tragedy of the Queen of Cornwall*, H "showed . . . that he had genuine dramatic gifts."

2239 Greening, G. W. " 'The Woman Pays,' " DORSET YEARBOOK, 1948–1949, pp. 77–89.

[Account of scenes between Flintcomb-Ash farm ("generally conceded to be Dole's Ash near Puddletrenthide") to Emminster (Beaminster), the route of the heroine's last journey in *Tess of the d'Urbervilles.*]

2240 Grigson, Geoffrey. "Thomas Hardy," THE HARP OF AEOLUS AND OTHER ESSAYS ON ART, LITERATURE AND NATURE (Lond: Routledge, 1948), pp. 123–30.

A brief essay on H's relation to architecture. Although H was a poor draftsman and designer, he was nevertheless a true architect because he began with man.

2241 Holland, Clive [pseud of C. J. Hankinson]. THOMAS HARDY'S WESSEX SCENE (Dorchester: Longmans, 1948).

All his life H had an exceptional memory for events of his youth and stories told by his grandmother and mother. [Gives background of the family lineage, H's youth and early education, his charm and occasional tendency to suddenly withdraw into himself, his indolence as a student, his apprenticeship, his marriages, the publication of his books, and his later aversion to being interviewed and photographed.] "When talking with Hardy, one . . . sensed the fact that in reality, there must be two individuals": a cheerful, communicative person and a melancholy person. [Speculates on reasons for this self-division, with reference to the fictive architect in *A Laodicean*, to his first marriage to an "unsuited" wife, and to a discussion between H and Sarah Grand.] H accepted being called a pessimist if it meant agreement with Sophocles that " 'not to be born is best.' " H wanted to believe " 'in what is known as the supernatural.' " [When the evidence of biography and history fails, Holland turns to the novels for "evidence" to support his assertions. Much rambling anecdotage. Chaps 2 through 6 deal with the towns, countryside, landmarks, and historical associations of H's Wessex. Chap 7 deals with "The Scenes and Stories of Some Representative Novels" with special reference to *The Trumpet-Major, Far From the Madding Crowd, Tess of the d'Urbervilles, Two on a Tower, The Well-Beloved, The Mayor of Casterbridge, Under the Greenwood Tree, The Woodlanders*. An appendix lists "Localities of the Novels," includes "Topographical Index (A)," "Topographical Index (B)," and a place-name index to the entire book. Eighteen illustrations are based on original drawing by Douglas Snowdon.]

2242 Horsman, E. A. "The Language of *The Dynasts*," DURHAM UNIVERSITY JOURNAL, ns X (Dec 1948), 11–16.
Although H's language can be traced to several sources, *The Dynasts* succeeds in spite of its language rather than because of it. Many of H's archaisms are found only in older English dialects, but a large number are borrowed out of the lively traffic in words between the seventeenth and nineteenth centuries, particularly the use of abstract nouns in concrete senses and the prolific formulation of compounds. H's colloquialisms, used as deliberately as are his archaisms, brusquely and awkwardly emphasize the common humanity of great men and even give a "macabre vulgarity" to the comments of the Spirit Sinister. The use of scientific words is organically related to H's theme, as are the negative prefixes which depict "human misery in the purely negative terms which befit the unknowable." Too many word formations, however, are unsuccessful for the language as a whole to improve the play. [Well-documented.]

2243 Lavalette, Robert. LITERATURGESCHICHTE DER WELT (Literary History of the World) (Zurich: Orell Füssli, 1948), p. 416.
ULYSSES was created from the literary tradition of H, Gissing, and Conrad. [In German.]

2244 MacLiesh, Fleming. "Thomas Hardy: His Art and Thought," NEW YORK TIMES BOOK REVIEW, 28 March 1948, p. 6.
H "was compelled to evolve a personal philosophy and metaphysic without any large or established frame of reference—a process extremely damaging, if not fatal, to an artist." [Review of Harvey Curtis Webster, ON A DARKLING PLAIN (1947).]

2245 Manly, John M., and Edith Rickert. CONTEMPORARY BRITISH LITERATURE. 3rd ed, rvd and enlgd, by Fred B. Millett (NY: Harcourt, Brace, 1948 [earlier eds: 1921, 1928, 1935]), pp. 17, 21, 69–71, 261–68.
H and Meredith brought about a change of tone in the treatment of family life and sex. H's style often contains much "clumsily awkward and some-

times downright bad writing." H became a "more accurate interpreter of the time spirit than either the muscular poets or the aesthetes" and "one of the most impressive poets of the age." He accepted the full implications of scientific determinism, but he extends compassion to all human life. He "resorted to crusty and crabbed diction and rhythms, but he was capable of intense lyricism." His supreme achievement is *The Dynasts*, the range of whose tone and manner "is extreme." [Bibliography lists works by H and five pages of writings about him, nearly all included in the present bibliography.]

2246 Marchand, Leslie A. "The Symington Collection," JOURNAL OF THE RUTGERS UNIVERSITY LIBRARY, XII (Dec 1948), 1–15.
The Symington collection, lately acquired by the Rutgers University Library, contains many H items, among which are two letters complaining of Andrew Lang's review of *Tess of the d'Urbervilles* and Lang's own point of view in another letter, and large files of copies of H's letters to his personal friends, mostly unpublished.

2247 Möller-Boldt, Günther Peter. "Soziale Probleme in Thomas Hardys Romanen und Kurzgeschichten" (Social Problems in Thomas Hardy's Novels and Short Stories). Unpublished dissertation, University of Hamburg, 1948.
Do social problems exist in H's novels and short stories? If so, what kind of problems, and how are they assessed? Is H a social critic; what does he criticize; what is the form of his criticism? H is a didactic artist. [In German.]

2248 P., F. "J. R. Lowell and Hardy," NOTES AND QUERIES, CXCIII (27 Nov 1948), 523.
In 1886, Julian Hawthorne printed a conversation with Lowell about English affairs in a New York paper. H was very much wounded by what Lowell was reported to have said about his personal appearance. [See Edmund Blunden, THOMAS HARDY (1942), p. 47.]

2249 Parker, W. M. "Hardy's Scott Quotation," SCOTSMAN (Edinburgh), 10 May 1948, p. 4.
The quotation on the title page of *Desperate Remedies* is from Sir Walter Scott's 1830 introduction to THE MONASTERY, with "slight variants." H wrote that in nature courses of adventures are "connected with each other by having happened to the same individual"; Scott had written that such events "are only connected with each other by having happened to be witnessed by the same individuals."

2250 Peirce, Walter. "Hardy's Lady Susan and the First Countess of Wessex," COLBY LIBRARY QUARTERLY, II (Feb 1948), 77–82.

In both "The First Countess of Wessex" and "The Noble Lady Speaks" ["The Noble Lady's Tale"?], the fictional circumstances are for the most part a thinly-disguised historical narrative of the lives of Susanna Strangways-Horner and her granddaughter, Lady Susan Fox-Strangways. Given H's conviction that "history and fiction should not be mixed," H's intention in departing from the discernible facts must remain a matter for conjecture.

2251 Randall, David A., and Carl J. Weber. "The Court of Appeals; Appeal No. 6 Thomas Hardy [by Weber]; Answer to Appeal No. 6 [by Randall]," NEW COLOPHON, I (Jan 1948), 84–85.

The publisher Holt sent H the "Leisure Hour Series" in 1873, including the *Far From the Madding Crowd?* Were these reproductions of the original novels of Turgenev. When did this same series first include illustrations in illustrations in CORNHILL, drawn by Miss Helen Paterson whose work H admired highly? Holt added twelve illustrations by Miss Paterson in 1876 with the margins trimmed and on thin paper so that they could be bound into the same bindings used for the 1874 and 1875 editions.

2252 Rolland, Romain. CHOIX DE LETTRES À MALWIDA VON MEYSENBUG (Selected Letters to Malwida Von Meysenbug), établi par Marie Romain Rolland (Paris: Albin Michel, 1948), pp. 202, 209.

[In a letter of 24 Feb 1897, Rolland mentions that his sister has just completed a translation of H's *Tess of the d'Urbervilles* and is seeking a publisher (Paris: Hachette, 1901). In a second letter of 23 June 1827, Rolland mentions that Mlle. Rolland's translation rights for *Tess* (which was then appearing in the JOURNAL DES DÉBATS) were being challenged by another translator claiming exclusive translation rights. Mlle. Rolland, according to Rolland, possessed the exclusive permission of H.] [In French.]

2253 Sassoon, Siegfried. MEREDITH (NY: Viking P; Lond: Constable, 1948), pp. 69–70, 72, 73, 116, 117, 127, 198, 228–30, 232, 237–38, 255, 256.

Meredith first met H in 1869 when, as a reader for Chapman & Hall, he read the manuscript of *The Poor Man and the Lady*. H made a public expression of gratitude for the encouragement shown him by Meredith at this time, at a banquet of the Omar Khayyam Club, July 1895. In a letter of 1905 to Edmund Gosse, Meredith mentions a visit from H, then states: "I am always glad to see him, and have regrets at his going; for the double reason, that I like him, and am afflicted by his twilight view of life."

2254 Sherman, George Witter. "The Influence of London on *The Dynasts*," PUBLICATIONS OF THE MODERN LANGUAGE ASSOCIATION, LXIII (Sept 1948), 1017–28.

H's hypersensitivity to crowds from an 1865 London experience and his life in London in the 1860s generally, molded his view of somnambulistic traits in the unconscious mind of the mass of humanity. His idiosyncratic conception of history and the metaphysic of the drama come from his pre-Schopenhauer vision of "the intolerable antilogy of making figments feel." His notebooks show him to have been studying humanity; his treatment of the mass of men comes out of his disgust with the upper classes seen at Lord Carnarvon's gatherings.

2255 Stewart, J. I. M. "The Integrity of Hardy," ESSAYS AND STUDIES BY MEMBERS OF THE ENGLISH ASSOCIATION, ns I (1948), 1–27.

T. S. Eliot in AFTER STRANGE GODS (1934) cites H as an example of the modern author who seeks to impose his morbid view of the world upon his audience because he is obsessed with his own personality. But H is scarcely morbid; he was a good man who portrayed honest people striving to be good themselves. He was an ethical idealist, not a pervert like some of his contemporaries. His morbidity was not the result of his obsession with himself but an accurate reflection of the contemporary intellectual climate. The cruelty he portrays in his novels is not sadism; it is rather his objective picture of how men suffer in an indifferent universe. The final effect of his work is not despair but awe at the vitality of mankind.

2256 Tate, Allen. "Hardy's Philosophic Metaphors," ON THE LIMITS OF POETRY (NY: Swallow P, 1948), pp. 185–96.

The Alexandrines in "Nature's Questioning" are extremely successful lines; the entire rhythmic effect proves H's mastery of technique. The metaphors are probably characteristic of H's philosophical poetry: vehicle replaces tenor, and intelligible meaning is limited. H's abstractions are generally unsubstantiated by experience. When H is least philosophical he shows the greatest freedom of sensibility of which he is capable. His philosophy is a rough mixture of Schopenhauer, Darwin, Spencer and eighteenth-century Deism which he could not integrate into his experience.

2257 Van Doren, Mark. "Thomas Hardy, Poet," NEW POEMS (NY: William Sloane, 1948), p. 49.

[Van Doren's poem, on the theme of paradox, suggests the hopelessness and bleakness of H's outlook but also the life, warmth, and beauty in H's works.]

2258 Weber, Carl J. "A Ghost from a Barber Shop," NEW COLOPHON, ns I (April 1948), 185–89; condensed under "The New Colophon," in COLBY LIBRARY QUARTERLY, 2nd ser (1948), 117–20.

Further information has been added to H's "plagiarism" of his drill scene in *The Trumpet-Major* from A. B. Longstreet [discussed in Weber's "A

Connecticut Yankee in King Alfred's Country," COLOPHON, ns I (April 1936), 525–35.] Oliver H. Prince's lampoon of the Georgia militia, appearing in the WASHINGTON MONITOR (Georgia), 6 June 1807, was reprinted as "The Ghost of Baron Steuben" in the SALEM BARBER SHOP (Mass), Sept 1807, where John Lambert saw it and carried it in his TRAVELS THROUGH LOWER CANADA AND THE UNITED STATES IN THE YEARS 1806, 1807, AND 1808 (Lond) (1810) to Gifford's HISTORY OF THE WARS (1817), H's source for his Wessex militia drill. The piecing together of this chain exonerates H of plagiarizing from Longstreet's GEORGIA SCENES.

2259 [Weber, Carl J.]. "Miscellaneous Notes," COLBY LIBRARY QUARTERLY, II (Feb 1948), 82–84.
Manuscripts of musical settings by Walter Peirce for "The Ruined Maid" and Katherine E. O'Brien for "When I Set Out for Lyonesse" have been presented to the Colby Library.

2260 Weber, Carl J. "Thomas Hardy as College Student," COLBY LIBRARY QUARTERLY, II (Aug 1948), 113–15.
H's copy of a textbook, HALF-HOURS OF FRENCH TRANSLATION, shows that he attended classes at King's College, London, in the fall and winter terms of 1865–1866. The book reveals that H was not studious, but many of the passages underlined are echoed in H's later work.

2261 [Weber, Carl J.]. "With Admiration and Love," COLBY LIBRARY QUARTERLY, II (May 1948), 85–108.
[A list of one hundred association items in the Colby Library, including twenty-five H items.]

2262 Webster, Harvey C. "Introduction to *The Mayor of Casterbridge*," *The Mayor of Casterbridge* (NY: Rinehart, 1948), pp. v–x.
The Mayor of Casterbridge "is a better balanced book than any of its predecessors . . . and the most integrated." "To a degree unparalleled in any of Hardy's earlier novels, his [Henchard's] character is his fate." He is reminiscent of Lear. [Brief biography, general criticism covering H's Victorian limitations and un-Victorian virtues, specific criticism of *Mayor*, and a brief bibliographical note.]

1949

2263 Adams, Frederick B., Jr. "Another Man's Roses," NEW COLOPHON, II (June 1949), 107–12.

"Two Roses" was a poem printed in Hogg's LONDON SOCIETY magazine over H's name, although submitted by another person. H was upset over the forgery both because it appeared in 1882 when he was having other troubles with plagiarism and because he was jealous of his poetic reputation, as he hoped to return to poetry once novels had provided him the financial means to do so. The London FIGARO printed an announcement of the forgery, including the line "Mr. Thomas Hardy never writes trash," which H underlined in the clipping in his scrapbook.

2264 Anschutz, Herbert Leo. "The Road to Nirvana: A Study of Thomas Hardy's Novels and Poems, With Special Emphasis Upon the Autobiographic and Artistic Significance of *The Well-Beloved* Viewed in the Light of Schopenhauer's THE WORLD AS WILL AND IDEA and The Metaphysics of the Love of the Sexes." Unpublished dissertation, University of Washington, 1949.

In an attempt to resolve the doubt and confusion which followed his loss of religious belief, H turned to Schopenhauerian transcendentalism. *The Well-Beloved* presents H's philosophy at the stage of development which it had reached in the 1890s and therefore could not have been an early work resuscitated for publication. The novel is also autobiographical in that Pierston is H, Marcia Bencomb is Emma, and Pierston's "fugitive love affairs" are "those of Hardy himself."

2265 Bertocci, Angelo Philip. CHARLES DUBOS AND ENGLISH LITERATURE (NY: King's Crown P, 1949), pp. 5, 154, 193, 211–18, 238, 240, 247, 257.

Charles DuBos was one of the first French critics to rank H "among the supreme novelists" because his works possessed "le sens de la vie en général." DuBos shared H's "cosmic point of view."

2266 Blankenagel, John C. "A Note on Hardy's *Tess of the d'Urbervilles* and Goethe's FAUST," GERMAN QUARTERLY, XXII (Nov 1949), 202–3.

In *Tess of the d'Urbervilles*, H evaluates the beauty of human character as lying in its will more than its accomplishments, which is consistent with Goethe's view of human character seen in the hero of FAUST. [A further parallel to those cited in J. O. Bailey, "Hardy's Mephistophelian Visitants," PMLA, LXI (Dec 1946), 1146–84.]

2267 Daniels, Diana P. "More Than a Book," CHRISTIAN SCIENCE MONITOR, 16 June 1949, p. 11.

H did not wish to be remembered for either "gloom or greatness." *Under the Greenwood Tree* is typical: the characters are not fated; the forces that surround them are not cruel forces. The tale shows "human pluck and constancy."

2268 Gordan, John D. "First Fruits: An Exhibition of First Books by English Authors in the Henry W. and Albert Berg Collection, Part II," BULLETIN OF THE NEW YORK PUBLIC LIBRARY, LIII (May 1949), 241.

The Berg Collection has two rare issues of *Desperate Remedies* (Lond: Tinsley, 1871): one "in the binding advertising TINSLEY'S MAGAZINE is contrasted with another volume which does not have this stamping." It also has an autograph letter from H to William Tinsley [3 Jan 1872] in which H asks for an accounting of the sales of *Remedies* and warns of a possible delay in completing *Under the Greenwood Tree* unless he receives an accounting.

2269 Guérard, Albert. THOMAS HARDY: THE NOVELS AND STORIES (Cambridge: Harvard UP, 1949).

H is not a craftsman but a traditional teller of tales and great poet who practiced fiction waywardly. He has a rich imagination and plodding intellect. The critics have over-schematized his work. H needs revaluation because most of his critics belong to a generation which held to different standards for the novel. They did not care for the grotesque and macabre in H. We now see the demonic in human nature and value foreshortening. The modern novel emphasizes sensation and wants to express a vision of world. In H we now are attracted by qualities that disturbed older critics, as we care less for those once praised. The academic tendency to make H a somber philosopher obscures H as tale-spinner and humorist. *The Dynasts* is badly distorted by treating it as philosophy, and even the simplest of novels, under its shadow. Too much reasoning escapes art. Critics also look for a subtle craftsman; H's over-conscious craft is one of his worst weaknesses. H is also intellectually commonplace but not imaginatively. H distorted actual Dorset to achieve his own kind of truth: rural simplicity threatened by urban complexity; intellectuals or aristocrats who disturb or destroy, as in *The Woodlanders* or deracination of Stephen Smith or Jude; evil of class feeling, as in *The Hand of Ethelberta* and *A Laodicean,* even more so in "Squire Petrick's Lady." Attitude toward incompatible marriage of long-standing in H's fiction. H is ambivalent toward rebelliousness. He preferred spontaneity and passion to cold temperament, but still there are contradictions: H's attitude toward society is purely aesthetic. Both first and last novels are problem-novels. But *Jude the Obscure* seems true because of the impressions it gives of unrest and collapse. H's novels were affected by the public's dislike of pessimism and his desire for success. Critics were of little help; H was too willing to take their advice. A knowledge of his life does not assist much in understanding his fiction; the interior life is a mystery. Conflicting impulses in his writing are sacrificed to each other "inevitably and often," between, for example, impulse toward anti-realism and realism. Some impulses are enervating, others energizing because of challenge and difficulty. H tended to relax into easy ways out. Structure was affected by conflicting impulses: H's continuing or changing from the initial impulse after it had been exhausted [e.g., *Desperate Remedies* which has the structure of three or four novels. See, in *Laodicean* and *Two on a Tower*, how the creative impluse fluctuated between comedy and grotesque or from difficult human situations to enervating melodrama]. *The Mayor of Casterbridge* illustrates the use of contrived psychology to prepare for tragedy. The most striking contrast is between realism and anti-realism: indifferently rational realist is always threatened to suppress the haunted poet. Theory triumphs over the imagination most clearly in *The Well-Beloved*. When H is at his best, his poetic imagination prevails. He is sometimes an orthodox realist in details, but he both observes and recreates his world, especially its atmosphere, as in Talbothays. His anti-realism is closest to Dickens but is less concerned with the manic, more with dramatic absurdity. Chance is prevalent, but malignity of events goes beyond nature (*The Romantic Adventures of a Milkmaid*). Occult visitants, Mephistophelean. H is a creator of personality more than an analyst of character, but he still intuitively understood abnormal psychology (shown symbolically). However, he did not manage familiar neuroses well, except for Sue Bridehead's—a complex portrait of sexual maladjustment and moral masochism. H's sympathy prevents her from being unpleasant. Heroes are unaggressive, temperamentally impotent, voyeur-type, modern men. One must distinguish H's rustics from his main characters: rustics are personalities rather than characters, changeless, unsuffering. Rustics become real in poems, where they suffer. Their major characteristic is self-depreciation. H has a great gallery of women characters. He emphasizes women's "impulse to seize the day." Men see the dream behind reality; women take the dream for reality. The early women are feminine personalities; the later ones are genuine characters. They fall into related groups: hedonists, ingenues, sufferers. Types can be traced through the novels, with variants and developments. Henchard is the best male character: the isolated, damned individualist. Jude is not a tragic hero because of his modernity; he does not resist his fate. The portrait suffers from H's stress on the contrast between the ideal and sordid, but Jude is the most human and likeable of H's men, a fully realized life.

2270 Hatch, Benton L. "Notes Toward the Definitive Bibliography of Thomas Hardy's *Poems of the Past and the Present*," COLBY LIBRARY QUARTERLY, II (Nov 1949), 195–98.
[A description of four copies of *Poems of the Past and the Present*. On the basis of dating, collation reveals four issues of the English first edition.]

2271 Knott, Olive. "The Blackmore Vale in Fiction," DORSET YEARBOOK, 1949–1950, pp. 103–5.
Many scenes in *Tess of the d'Urbervilles* and *The Woodlanders* are drawn after real ones in Blackmore Vale.

2272 Knott, Olive. "Casterbridge of the Wessex Novel," DORSET YEARBOOK, 1949–1950, pp. 173–74.
"Thomas Hardy still lives in Dorchester . . . and . . . his characters still frequent their old haunts."

2273 Lock, H. O. "A Note on the Hardy Plays," DORSET YEARBOOK, 1949–1950, pp. 149–51.
[Account of the birth, growth, and demise of the H plays movement in Dorchester, 1908–1928.]

2274 Loewenberg, J. "The Comic as Tragic," DIALOGUES FROM DELPHI (Berkeley & Los Angeles: University of California P, 1949), pp. 1–35.
[Imaginary conversations between H and Meredith, disguised as "Hardith" and "Meredy," on the subject of art, aesthetics, comedy, tragedy, etc., as a means of presenting contrasting points of view.] H's novels are not tragic, only pessimistic: "There can be no tragedy, in the pregnant sense of the term, if men are entirely precluded from determining their own way of life."

2275 Martin, E. W. "Thomas Hardy and the Rural Tradition," BLACKFRIARS, XXX (June 1949), 252–56.
For both his creation of rural characters and his evocation of the countryside, H deserves a high place as a regional novelist. But he failed to understand the common laborer, partly because of his natural aloofness, and partly because his neighbors distrusted his atheism. H never had any real human contact with another person, and his novels reveal this shortcoming. As a regional novelist, he has been followed by Henry Williamson and Llewelyn Powys.

2276 Muir, Edwin. "The Novels of Thomas Hardy," ESSAYS ON LITERATURE AND SOCIETY (Lond: Hogarth P, 1949), pp. 110-19; rvd and enlgd (Cambridge: Harvard UP, 1965), pp. 111–19.
H sees chance and accident ruling a universe that is empty, yet the enemy of man; indifferent, yet deliberately cruel. Man nobly struggles against Nature, is better than Nature, yet is defeated. Since coincidence rules the lives of H's characters, his plots are intricate and tangled. His characters are largely passive and colorless, their best quality a quiet patience by which they rise above the cruelty of fate.

2277 Peirce, Walter. "A Visit to Max Gate," COLBY LIBRARY QUARTERLY, II (Nov 1949), 190–95.

[A record of a conversation with H in 1909, including comment on the similarity between Wessex and Dorsetshire and H's preference for his poetry over his novels.]

2278 Reynolds, Ernest. "Davidson—Hardy's *Dynasts*," MODERN ENGLISH DRAMA: A SURVEY OF THE THEATRE FROM 1900 (Lond: Harrap, 1949), pp. 72–75.

In *The Dynasts*, life is conceived of as a "mournful ant-hill," which is "not a good basis for dramatic effect." The work "is the product of a mind obsessed with the hopelessness of human existence." The play "is an outstanding example of the general deepening of the intellectual gloom of poetic drama in England in the twentieth century."

2279 Richards, Mary Caroline. "Thomas Hardy's Ironic Vision: I," TROLLOPIAN, III (March 1949), 265–79; "Thomas Hardy's Ironic Vision: II," NINETEENTH CENTURY FICTION, IV (June 1949), 21–35.

H "was a great humanitarian who did not have the courage of his instincts and who was held in thrall by the prestige of the new science." [A repetitious and simple-minded consideration of H's use of irony.]

2280 Sherman, George Witter. "The Wheel and the Beast: The Influence of London on Thomas Hardy," NINETEENTH CENTURY FICTION, IV (Dec 1949), 209–19.

During his youth, H spent five years (1862–1867) in London, and his experience there was the basis for the creation of two dominant metaphors in his work. London became for him a Wheel and a Beast. He summed up the "hurry, speech, laughter, moans, cries of little children" as "this hum of the Wheel—the roar of London." At night, the Wheel became a Beast, "a monster whose body had four million heads and eight million eyes." But H did not have the requisite strength to fight the Wheel and the Beast. H incorporated his indignation at the ills of society into his novel *The Poor Man and the Lady*, but George Meredith advised him not to publish it. "London was not material for a novel to him, but only for novel-padding." However, the philosophical disposition which H acquired from his experience in London remained. The images, the Wheel and the Beast, which resulted from this experience would not be extracted from his subconscious, and he used them, in various forms, throughout his work thereafter.

2281 Short, Clarice. "Thomas Hardy and the Military Man," NINETEENTH CENTURY FICTION, IV (Sept 1949), 129–35.

H had both a sympathy and an admiration for the military man. "Although his portrayal of a soldier may indicate weaknesses of character in that man, there is something of awe discernible when Hardy speaks of his martial prowess or his historical significance." The emotional charge that permeates

The Dynasts results largely from H's response to the emotional stimulus of war. In *The Trumpet-Major* and *Far From the Madding Crowd,* H gives leading-character prominence to military men. He studies the non-commissioned officer who has responsibility but also partakes of the danger and hardships of those under him, in *Trumpet-Major. Madding Crowd* concentrates on the impact of military life on the professional soldier and examines the civilian attitude toward this man.

2282 Simon, Irène. "Thomas Hardy," FORMES DU ROMAN ANGLAIS DE DICKENS À JOYCE (Forms of the English Novel From Dickens to Joyce) (Liège: Faculté de Philosophie et Lettres, 1949), pp. 186–215; University of Liège dissertation.

An ominous dark cloud envelops all of H's world, becoming heavier the more one reads. Moments of light and hope only yield to a more intense darkness in a universe where the same cruel destiny that allows creatures to hope is hostile to that hope. Tragedy is the result of man's trying to assert his own individuality in resistance to the general rhythm of the universe. Man tends toward growth and outward movement. In defeat, he learns the uselessness and vanity of his aspirations and the necessity of participating in the universal movement, even without understanding it. Man's destiny is only the most striking example of the absurdity of all creation. All creatures ought to submit to the unfathomable force, recognizing the double law of expansion and submission that is the source of the universal drama. All H's novels are filled with this sense of tragedy that unites the elements of the drama in an austere harmony and grandeur. His work is a cry of indignation at the injustice of fate and a vision of the world in struggle against an immovable and incomprehensible will. The most obvious characteristic is the integration of man and Nature. Whether his characters submit or revolt, they are always simpler elements of a vast whole. The dominant quality is the power of the atmosphere created in the novels. H sees his characters in a context of natural elements whose influence they submit to and whose sense is perceived through them. Inversely, H relates his impressions of Nature back to man and his problems. The unity of man and Nature is emphasized in descriptive passages like that of the Field of Famine in *Tess of the d'Urbervilles* and the tree-planting scene in *The Woodlanders.* At times H's insistence on reading human sentiments into Nature strays toward sentimentality and destroys the tragic effect. He presents his characters rather than describing them, and their attitudes, words and behavior reveal their nature and manner of living. The characters are simple and distinguishable by general human qualities rather than by individual traits. They are moved by elemental passions. For all of the major characters life is a serious business; they ask themselves questions about the universe that are surprising in simple people. For H, art did not exist in faithfulness to the object but in the interpretation and intense expression of the meaning discovered in following his personal vision. The artist must reveal the hidden spirit of things and unveil the intimate life of Nature. *Far From the Madding Crowd* and *Woodlanders* are chronicles where unhappy episodes are related about the lives of a group of characters. *The Return of the Native, Tess,* and *Jude the Obscure* are dramas representing a conflict of wills. Unhappiness comes from the failure to appreciate the rustic life. However melancholy the beauty of Nature and however isolated their lives, the characters live them without shocks as long as they accept the conditions of their existence, as Giles and Marty do in *Woodlanders*. Unhappiness comes from an individual's resistance to the spirit of the place—in trying to remove his daughter from her environment, Melbury destroys her. H tells a story a little in the manner of the popular story-teller who knows the public needs the unexpected and sensational. In some of his minor novels one gets the impression that he is telling a story for children. He likes complications and mysterious situations and does not disdain to use certain stock elements such as the illegitimate child, the return of the prodigal, the secret marriage, and the sudden conversion. These gimmicks are not of great importance in the novels, however. H liked to talk as a philosopher and had a tendency to comment too much on the meaning of his images, replacing the rich and evocative mood with its equivalent abstraction. Such a tendency is all the more regrettable because his philosophy is quite simple. In an effort to speak seriously, H becomes hollow, and at the same time, his diction becomes more abstract and erudite. When his heroes explain their metaphysical thoughts, their tone becomes almost pompous. [In French.]

2283 Weber, Carl J. "Some Letters on Hardy's *Tess,*" JOURNAL OF THE RUTGERS UNIVERSITY LIBRARY, XIII (Dec 1949), 1–6.
H had joined the Saville Club of London in 1878; he was therefore terribly upset when, after the publication of *Tess of the d'Urbervilles,* bitterest criticisms came from Savillans like Andrew Lang, in "Literature and the Drama," NEW REVIEW, VII (Feb 1892), 247–49. In a letter to Clodd, H complained of Lang's "Christian (?) objection (I suppose it is meant to be Christian) to the words 'President of the Immortals' etc. . . . for I distinctly state that the words are paraphrased from Aeschylus." The reference to the "gentleman who turned Christian for half-an-hour the better to express his grief that a disrespectful phrase about the Immortals should have been used" [Preface for a new edition of *Tess*] indicates that H had Lang in mind.

2284 West, Ray B., Jr., and Robert Wooster Stallman. THE ART OF MODERN FICTION (NY: Rinehart, 1949), pp. 594–606, 638.
The Mayor of Casterbridge is closer to classical tragedy, there is more emphasis on the character of Henchard, less on external forces than in

other novels. [Recap of plot.] There are ironic coincidences in action as in OTHELLO, and ironic reversals of situation and scene. The structure is circular; scenic contrast is used to disjoint time (Amphitheater). Only the major figures suffer—Henchard and Lucetta. It is not a true tragedy; omniscient point of view counters Victorian optimism with fatalistic pessimism. Yet chance is not strictly to blame; Henchard is guilty of *hubris*. The novel was written before H took a strictly deterministic view. So, though minor characters seem puppets, Henchard and Lucetta are tragic in the traditional sense. [Questions and Exercises. Biographical note.]

1950

2285 Barrows, Herbert. SUGGESTIONS FOR TEACHING 15 STORIES (Boston: Heath, 1950), pp. 3–5.
The student response to "A Tradition of Eighteen Hundred and Four" is generally centered correctly. It is a storyteller's story, and the reader is asked to listen to a good story. What is striking about human life, or human nature, or a human quality of unusual power, or something in the extreme or vivid test makes the good story. Its effect depends upon the author's careful attention to detail and the interrelationships of its parts. [Explicatory manual published separately as a pamphlet.]

2286 Beach, Joseph Warren. "The Literature of the Nineteenth and Early Twentieth Centuries, 1798 to the First World War," A HISTORY OF ENGLISH LITERATURE, ed by Hardin Craig (NY: Oxford UP, 1950); rptd as ENGLISH LITERATURE OF THE 19TH AND THE EARLY 20TH CENTURIES, 1798 TO THE FIRST WORLD WAR (NY: Collier Books, 1962) ["Volume IV of A HISTORY OF ENGLISH LITERATURE. With a New Preface by Hardin Craig"], pp. 164, 166–68, 172–73, 195, 204, 205–7, 234–35.
H found an idealogy in the Darwinian and Positivistic thought of his day which expressed "the tragic pathos of humanity." His works, therefore, are representative of the "systematic determinism of an age of science." Unlike his fellow Victorian writers with whom he had many things in common, he was not given to didactic moralizing; in this respect he is closer to the writers of the continent. H saw man's development, as it was expressed in Darwinism, as something undesirable in the sense that it made man more and more aware of his tragic condition and his inability to control the blind forces of nature. He used irony as a major device in his poetry. His experimentation with language and verse forms, much of it successful, caused his poetry to suffer various kinds of criticism. Much of his poetry seemed

to be a reaction to the optimism in the poetry of the earlier Victorian poets. H's stories are ever fascinating for their irony. *A Group of Noble Dames* is his most successful group of stories.

2287 Bisson, L. A. "Proust and Hardy: Incidence or Coincidence?" STUDIES IN FRENCH LANGUAGE, LITERATURE AND HISTORY: PRESENTED TO R. L. GRAEME RITCHIE, ed by Charles F. Mackenzie (NY: Cambridge UP, 1950), pp. 24–34.

In 1926 H noted in his diary that there was a similarity between a theme of platonic love which he used in *The Well-Beloved* and a theme in Proust's A LA RECHERCHE DU TEMPS PERDU. It has been suggested that H was insinuating that Proust got his idea from him. H's influence on Proust has been noted several times, but in this instance, evidence shows that Proust had developed his theme of platonic love before he ever had a chance to read H's novel.

2288 Brogan, Howard O. " 'Visible Essences' in *The Mayor of Casterbridge*," JOURNAL OF ENGLISH LITERARY HISTORY, XVII (Dec 1950), 307–23.

While the writing of *The Mayor of Casterbridge* was in progress, H is reported to have said, "My art is to intensify the expression of things . . . so that the heart and inner meaning is made visible." Thus, in both the envelope and main sections of that novel, H especially concentrated on using character, setting, action, structure, and style as "visible essences"; that is, he treated each of these as tools that would concretize abstract thought. "What are called symbols by today's authors were 'visible essences' to Hardy. He employed them with perfect consciousness and for the same reason that all great narrators have always employed them: to achieve the maximum effect possible in his art."

2289 Brown, E. K. RHYTHM IN THE NOVEL (Toronto: University of Toronto P, 1950), pp. 13–16.

The repetition, with variations, of incident and character of H's *The Well-Beloved* is a simple, rigid example of "rhythm" in a novel.

2290 Bush, Douglas. SCIENCE AND ENGLISH POETRY (NY: Oxford UP, 1950), pp. 125, 134–35, 136.

H's basic intellectual position, as defined in the poem "Hap," included a grim interpretation of Victorian scientific opinions, especially evolution and was in keeping with the pessimistic tone of writers like Swinburne and Fitzgerald.

2291 Ellis, Havelock. FROM MARLOWE TO SHAW: THE STUDIES, 1876–1936, IN ENGLISH LITERATURE OF HAVELOCK ELLIS, ed with a foreword by John Gawsworth and a prefatory letter by

Thomas Hardy (Lond: Williams & Norgate, 1950), pp. 230–90; amalgamated from "Thomas Hardy's Novels," WESTMINSTER REVIEW, LXIII (April 1883), 334–64, and "Concerning *Jude the Obscure*," SAVOY, VI (Oct 1896), 35–49, containing essentially the same material.
[See the abstracts of the two periodical items.]

2292 Erzgräber, Willi. "Die Darstellung der Ländlichen Gemeinschaft bei Thomas Hardy (Untersuchung zu Gestalt und Form der Wessexromane)" (The Depiction of the Rural Community by Thomas Hardy [Study of Structure and Form of the Wessex Novels]). Unpublished dissertation, University of Frankfurt, 1950. [Examines the rural communities as presented in *Under the Greenwood Tree, Far From the Madding Crowd, The Return of the Native, The Woodlanders*, and *Tess of the d'Urbervilles*. The specific character of each community, the different relation of each individual in a novel to this rural society, and the various communities' unique social problems are compared and contrasted. In view of the original approach and interesting observations, this dissertation deserves to be printed as a book.] [In German.]

2293 Fiedler, Leslie A. "The Third Thomas Hardy," NATION (NY), CLXXI (2 Sept 1950), 210–11.
As F. R. Leavis and others saw it, "Hardy's hopelessness as a craftsman is compounded by his heretical refusal to take his work quite seriously; in Jamesian terms he is frankly immoral, with his ready-made plots, his endings tailored to popular taste, and his Prefaces with their cynical disavowals of anything that might offend his readers." How then may H be redeemed "in terms useful to current practice and sensibility?" The qualities of "anti-realism" and the "demonic" in his novels offer one way. H's coincidences, far from being "mere intrusive flaws" are "structural devices for foreshortening and dramatizing the essential 'absurdity' of human life." Unlike modern writers who "consciously arrayed the devices of symbolism or depth psychology," H "reached toward the demonic, mythic dimension, and did so *unconsciously*." But H, part naive countryman and part sophisticated thinker and artist, is not completely successful in "evoking the absurd." Could he have treated characters "with the same contempt for probability with which he treated the march of events, he might have produced total novels of the 'absurd' like Kafka or Gide or James Joyce." [Review article on Albert J. Guérard, THOMAS HARDY (1949).]

2294 Fischer, Bernhard. "Freie Wille und Notwendigkeit bei Thomas Hardy" (Free Will and Necessity in Thomas Hardy). Unpublished dissertation, University of Halle, 1950.
[Purpose and thesis are not defined. Unintelligible.] [In German.]

2295 Flower, Sir Newman. JUST AS IT HAPPENED (Lond: Cassell, 1950; NY: Morrow, 1951), pp. 81–108.

[When Flower was young, H seemed an immortal. H lived nearby in Dorset, and Flower often inquired about him. *Under the Greenwood Tree*, read in his teens, had the very life Flower knew in Dorset. Flower tried to see H on his visits to H's mother at Upper Bockhampton. The affection between H and his mother was very deep, although she knew nothing of his fame. Flower met H many years later and became a close friend.] Portraits of H are never exact except the bust by Yoweivitch which shows H's nose as it was. H did not seem to grow old, remained agile and alert to his eighties. H's memory went far back; he recalled the woman who said she had known Keats. Early writing was not successful—H paid Tinsley £15 for deficit on *A Pair of Blue Eyes*. H was drawn toward tragedy but was far from a cold man. H never forgot executions seen when he was young. He could not see the reason in tragic happenings and brooded on these. He was never seen to laugh. H bore the estrangement from Emma for years. When one day they had words and shortly thereafter she fell ill and died, he blamed himself. [Depicts H's method of working at his writing, his self-discipline, the plague of constant visitors, and his death and funeral.]

2296 Grigson, Geoffrey. "The English Novel—VII: Geoffrey Grigson on Thomas Hardy," LISTENER, 2 March 1950, pp. 392–93.

H is extremely uneven in quality; his novels contain too many examples of "stilted language, ill-digested learning, convenient accidents, fantastic transformations, melodramatic plot." *Tess of the d'Urbervilles* and *The Mayor of Casterbridge* are H's masterpieces. He is a more considerable poet than novelist, although his poetic abilities show effectively in the novels.

2297 Grigson, Geoffrey. "The Heart of a Book: *The Mayor of Casterbridge*," LEADER MAGAZINE, VII (3 June 1950), 31–34.

H shows his pessimism in *The Mayor of Casterbridge. Mayor* can be interpreted as a four-act tragedy in which H was not afraid "of making Chance into coincidence." "His novels are a large Department of Coincidence, sometimes outraging (though not in this one so much) our notions of propriety and likelihood." H's over-reliance on "Chance" to direct the action in *Mayor* resulted from its initial form as a serial. "Hardy had contrived to work an incident into each installment," which "had broken off promising each time a further tensity of dramatic entrances."

2298 Guérard, Albert J. "Introduction to *The Return of the Native*," *The Return of the Native*, ed by Albert J. Guérard (NY: Rinehart, [1950]), v–xxii.

H did not "care" about his fiction the way Conrad and James did. H is

primarily a poet. H is an entertainer in his novels. H is historically significant because he gave seriousness to the "old romantic tale of adventure,"
although he was unaware of his significance. H is a great novelist but not a
profound thinker, a realist, or a subtle psychologist or master of the complex novel form. His novels can be divided into four categories: (1)
entertainments—(*The Trumpet-Major, Two on a Tower*); (2) problem
novels—(*The Well-Beloved, The Hand of Ethelberta*); (3) Wessex
romances—(*Far From the Madding Crowd, The Woodlanders*); and (4)
tragedies—(*The Mayor of Casterbridge, Tess of the d'Urbervilles, Jude the
Obscure*). *The Return of the Native* is the most representative of all four
categories.

2299 Guérard, Albert J. "Introduction," *Tess of the d'Urbervilles*
(NY: Harper's Modern Classics, 1950), pp. v–xii.
For the heroine and the victim in *Tess of the d'Urbervilles*, H took the
popular "pure woman" and, from conventional materials, made a great and
restrained novel. He raised popular materials to the level of art. H's production of twenty-two years, from the stylized *Under the Greenwood Tree*
to the bitterness and economy of *Jude the Obscure*, is uneven. The threat
to H's fiction was his tendency to take an abstract view of human beings.
When he wrote *Tess*, H highly idealized his rural female. H's popularity
results from his assumption that "things" are to blame, not men. *Tess* contains many creative collapses which reason cannot justify, but H does
solve difficult problems in several aspects of fiction: the use of reticence,
the functional use of atmosphere, literal realism combined with the "probable impossible," and the treatment of obvious symbolism.

2300 Harrison, J. E. "Hardy's Tragic Synthesis," DURHAM UNI-
VERSITY JOURNAL, ns XII (Dec 1950), 20–26.
H arrived at tragedy incidentally in his progress in pessimism from casual
irony to universal unenviability. Unfortunate coincidences appear in H's
tragic novels as ingeniously as fortunate coincidences appear in the works
of the popular novelists. *Far From the Madding Crowd, The Return of the
Native*, and *The Woodlanders* show suffering distributed throughout a
cross-patterning of relationships, and the central characters are not sufficiently dignified to achieve tragedy. *The Mayor of Casterbridge* shows a
small group of interrelated people all linked to Michael Henchard, who is
isolated in his agony and equal to it. *Tess of the d'Urbervilles* and *Jude the
Obscure* are stories of a single tragic hero, but the latter novel degenerates
into despair. In *Tess*, the scenery does not get out of control to counterpoint the action, but accompanies Tess's tragedy through the foreshadowing
of seasonal changes. H finally over-reaches individual tragedy and goes on
to poetry and the representation of collective nobility found in his "tragedy
of history," *The Dynasts*.

2301 Heath-Stubbs, John. The Darkling Plain (Lond: Eyre & Spottiswoode, 1950), pp. 65, 91–94, 191.

H, like John Clare and William Barnes, is a regionalist; unlike them, he is self-conscious and intellectual. In spite of his intellectual culture, however, H's "sensibility remained that of the unlearned countryman he described." H's deep roots in the regionalist tradition are complemented by the influence of Browning upon him. The unique qualities of H's poetry derive from a "fusion of Browning's dramatic appreciation of the value of situation and his intellectual curiosity, with the countryman's sensibility, . . . nourished on the detailed observation of landscape and the ways of animated nature." H's poetry marks the end of the "traditional poetry of the peasantry," for by the end of the nineteenth century, traditional songs, crafts, and ways of life were dead.

2302 Hübner, Walter. Die Stimmen der Meister: Eine Einführung in Meisterwerke des Englischen Dichtens und Denkens (The Voices of the Master: An Introduction to Masterworks of English Fiction and Thought) (Berlin: Walter de Gruyter, 1950), pp. 276, 366, 376, 492, 496–99, 500, 512, 532.
[Passing references to H and Tess of the d'Urbervilles in characterizing the Victorian age.] [In German.]

2303 Johnson, Maurice. The Sin of Wit: Jonathan Swift As Poet (Syracuse: Syracuse UP, 1950), pp. 130–35.
H, Joyce, and Yeats sometimes showed a predilection for a Swiftian style. "Hardy's deliberately unadorned, disillusioned poetry often unconsciously resembles Swift's." Both had a dry, satirical sense of humor, used homely subjects, wrote often in monologue or dialogue; both used contrast—sudden juxtapositions of the formal and colloquial or the permanent and the fleeting.

2304 Kindermann, Heinz, and Margarette Dietrich. Lexikon der Weltliteratur (Dictionary of World Literature) (Vienna & Stuttgart: Humbolt, 1950), p. 316.
H is the last Victorian novelist of stature. [Lists novels and translations.] [In German.]

2305 Maugham, W. Somerset. "For Maugham It's Cakes and Ale," New York Times Book Review, 19 March 1950, pp. 1, 38.
Edward Driffield (Cakes and Ale) was not modeled on H. [Maugham met H only once, at a dinner party, and found him a "small, gray, tired, retiring man." Maugham knew neither of H's wives. He supposes newspaper writers accused him of using H because H had just died when Cakes and Ale came out.]

2306 Maugham, W. Somerset. "Introduction," CAKES AND ALE (NY: Modern Library, 1950), pp. v–xii.
It was in vain to deny that Edward Driffield in CAKES AND ALE was patterned after H. When the book first came out, the papers immediately made a fuss over the matter, perhaps because H had recently died. They might just as well have chosen Tennyson or Meredith, however.

2307 Meissner, Paul. ENGLISCHE LITERATURGESCHICHTE VON DEN ANFÄNGEN BIS ZUM ERSTEN WELTKRIEG (English Literary History From the Beginnings to the First World War) (Heidelberg: F. H. Kerle, 1950), pp. 112, 115, 119, 130.
[Associates H with other Victorian novelists. Compares and contrasts Meredith's and H's philosophy.] [In German.]

2308 Millet, Fred B. READING FICTION: A METHOD OF ANALYSIS WITH SELECTIONS FOR STUDY (NY: Harper, 1950), pp. 39, 42, 43, 56, 61–62.
H shows "an almost excessive ingenuity" in the multi-linear plot structure of *The Mayor of Casterbridge*. Henchard is put through a complex series of "emotional paces." [Occasional references to H in discussion of novel versus short story form.]

2309 Moore, John Robert. "Two Notes on Thomas Hardy," NINETEENTH CENTURY FICTION, V (Sept 1950), 159–63.
Smithfield Marriages: The wife-selling incidents in *The Mayor of Casterbridge* are very similar to incidents recorded in the historical records of the actual town of Casterbridge and its surrounding territory. It is quite possible that H's episodes derive from an authentic wife-selling incident recorded in SIX MOIS À LONDRES, EN 1816, said to have been written in Paris in 1817. While H's account differs from this latter in certain respects, in others the two are very much alike. Sergeant Troy: The problems critics have had with interpreting the character of the villain in *Far From the Madding Crowd* may very well arise from "Hardy's inadequate knowledge of contemporary life and from his inappropriate use of source material." Often, when he was concerned with Troy, H wandered outside the Wessex area which was so familiar to him. As he moved into this unfamiliar territory, his treatment of Troy often became imprecise. Secondly, while Sergeant Bothwell in OLD MORTALITY was a model for Troy, "almost every quality of Bothwell was copied in Troy only to be degraded."

2310 Newton, William B., Jr. "Thomas Hardy and Naturalism." Unpublished dissertation, University of Chicago, 1950.
[Listed in Lawrence F. McNamee, DISSERTATIONS IN ENGLISH AND AMERICAN LITERATURE (NY & Lond: Bowker, 1968).]

2311 Oehl, Johann Christoph. "Vererbung und Milieu in der Romanen von Thomas Hardy" (Heredity and Environment in the Novels of Thomas Hardy). Unpublished dissertation, University of Vienna, 1950.

The concepts of heredity and environment, as introduced by Darwin and Taine, respectively, greatly influenced H. Heredity is used merely as an aid for character description in *Desperate Remedies, Under the Greenwood Tree, The Trumpet-Major, A Laodicean, Two on a Tower, The Mayor of Casterbridge, The Woodlanders,* and *The Well-Beloved.* In *A Pair of Blue Eyes, Far From the Madding Crowd, The Return of the Native, Tess of the d'Urbervilles,* and *Jude the Obscure,* heredity determines the individual's character. Taine's concept of milieu is restated in the foreword to *Jude.* The manner and extent of this influence is traced in every novel with the exception of *Trumpet-Major, The Hand of Ethelberta, Remedies,* and *Laodicean.* [The objectivity and clarity of this study are to be commended.] [In German.]

2312 Oppel, Horst. DIE KUNST DES ERZÄHLENS IM ENGLISCHEN ROMAN DES 19. JAHRHUNDERTS (The Art of Narrative in the 19th Century English Novel (Bielefeld: F. Eilers, 1950), pp. 62–68.

H contradicts the Victorian optimism and is free from an established aesthetic theory. Like all great artists, H transcends his media. [In German.]

2313 Roberts, Marguerite (ed). TESS IN THE THEATRE: TWO DRAMATIZATIONS OF "TESS OF THE D'URBERVILLES" BY THOMAS HARDY: ONE BY LORIMER STODDARD (Toronto: University of Toronto P, 1950).

"Of all the greater Victorian novelists, Hardy could probably best have taken his place in the theatrical world. . . . Hardy's gifts were essentially dramatic." H was moved to dramatize *Tess of the d'Urbervilles* in 1894–1895 despite earlier unfortunate experiences with the English stage, partly by the renaissance of English drama in the early 1890s and partly by a request for the dramatization from someone in the theatrical world. H's failure to permit his play to be acted until 1924 may be due to his embarrassment caused by "the ambition of a number of leading actresses to play Tess." Then, too, as the Nineties wore on, H came to be more and more engrossed in writing *The Dynasts* and lyric poetry and may have lost interest in the theater. [Traces the composition and performance of the version of *Tess* by Lorimer Stoddard, Hugh Arthur Kennedy's unauthorized version, Baron d'Erlanger's opera, and H's relationship with The Hardy Players.] When H's own version of *Tess* reached the London stage in 1925, H " 'no longer believe[d] in dramatizing novels, and . . . [had] no dramatic ambitions.' "

2314 [Weber, Carl J.]. "Books from Hardy's Max Gate Library," COLBY LIBRARY QUARTERLY, II (Aug 1950), 246–54.
[A list of fifty books from H's library now in the Colby College Library.]

2315 Weber, Carl J. "*Far From the Madding Crowd,*" ENCYCLO-PEDIA AMERICANA (NY: 1950), XI, 16.
[The usual clichés.]

2316 [Weber, Carl J.]. "Thomas Hardy's Chair," COLBY LIBRARY QUARTERLY, II (Nov 1950), 258–60.
[A note of the gift to the Colby Library of the armchair from H's study at Max Gate.]

2317 Weber, Carl J. "The Tragedy in Little Hintock," BOOKER MEMORIAL STUDIES: EIGHT LECTURES ON VICTORIAN LITERATURE IN MEMORY OF JOHN MANNING BOOKER (1881–1948), ed by Shine Hill (Chapel Hill: University of North Carolina P, 1950), pp. 133–53.
H revised *The Woodlanders* four times. The revised editions appeared in print in England almost immediately but did not appear in America until 1912. Since many of the revisions are important in that they "clarify" a scene or a particular character, it is not surprising that critics in England praised the book and critics in America disparaged it. The revised versions are greatly superior to the original.

2318 Wilson, Carroll A. "Thomas Hardy: 1840–1928," THIR-TEEN AUTHOR COLLECTIONS OF THE NINETEENTH CENTURY AND FIVE CENTURIES OF FAMILIAR QUOTATIONS, ed in two vols by Jean C. S. Wilson and David A. Randall (NY: Scribner's, 1950), I, vi, [39]–117.
Descriptive bibliography listing points of the relatively complete first edition collection of H from the library of Carroll A. Wilson, sold after Wilson's death. Contains excerpts from many A. L. S., among which is the following from H to Francis Thompson dated 31 Dec 1891, not noted elsewhere: "Ever since I began to write—certainly ever since I wrote *Two on a Tower* in 1881 I have felt that the doll of English fiction must be demolished, if England is to have a school of fiction at all; and I think great honour is due to DAILY CHRONICLE for frankly recognizing that the development of a more virile type of novel is not incompatible with sound morality."

1951

2319 Assalino, Walter. "Stilkundliche Interpretation von Thomas Hardy: 'A Tragedy of Two Ambitions' " (A Linguistic Interpreta-

tion of Thomas Hardy: "A Tragedy of Two Ambitions"), DIE LEBENDEN FREMDSPRACHEN (Braunschweig), III: 1 (1951), 7–17.
[Examines the linguistic form of "A Tragedy of Two Ambitions" with reference to the protagonist Joshua to illustrate H's ability in unifying form and content.] [In German.]

2320 B., W. G. "Wife-Selling in 19th Century," NOTES AND QUERIES, CXCVI (17 Feb 1951), 82. Other articles on the same subject in CXCVI, pp. 173, 238–39, 283, 327, 348–49, 460, 504.
[Examples of wife-selling.]

2321 Borinski, L. ENGLISCHER GEIST IN DER GESCHICHTE SEINER PROSA (The English Spirit in the History of Its Prose) (Freiburg I. Br.: Herder, 1951), pp. 146–47, 188–89, 195.
[Contrasts H with Fielding, Charlotte Brontë, and Jane Austen. Examines H's regionalism.] [In German.]

2322 Bramley, J. A. "Religion and the Novelists," CONTEMPORARY REVIEW, CLXXX (Dec 1951), 348–53, espec 350–51.
"Unbelief has taken a step forward" from previous novelists, but H is a Christian soul driven to atheism by the preponderence of evil over good in the world, a modern Ecclesiastes unable to accept the Christian hope or its consolation.

2323 Christiansen, D. R. "Thomas Hardy and the Freedom of the Human Will, A Study of His Work with Special Reference to *The Dynasts.*" Unpublished dissertation, University of Manchester, 1951.
[Listed in Lawrence F. McNamee, DISSERTATIONS IN ENGLISH AND AMERICAN LITERATURE (NY & Lond: Bowker, 1968).]

2324 Church, Richard. THE GROWTH OF THE ENGLISH NOVEL (Lond: Methuen, 1951), pp. 2, 3, 128, 165, 168, 187, 189–95, 195.
[Emphasizes H's style and use of rustic characters in a brief description of the novelist's contribution to the English novel. Subjective and impressionistic; more an appreciation than an analysis.]

2325 Clarke, G. H. "*Tess* in the Theatre," QUEEN'S QUARTERLY, LVIII (Spring 1951), 136–38.
H prepared in 1920 a stage version of *Tess of the d'Urbervilles.* As a play, *Tess* lacks the poetry, the delicate symbolism, the artistic integrity, the quiet English countryside charm of the novel and the inevitability of its five-part movement. Dr. Roberts presents the Dorchester and the London

forms of H's texts and also the version by Lorimer Stoddard. [See Marguerite Roberts, TESS IN THE THEATRE (1950).]

2326 Davies, Aneirin Talfan. ["William Barnes, Friend of Thomas Hardy"; original Welsh title unknown], WELSH ANVIL (Aberystwyth) [date unknown]; rptd in SYLWADAU (Comments) (Llandysul, Cardiganshire: Gwasg Aberystwyth, 1951); included in an address to Third Congress of the International Literature Association, Utrecht, 1961; pub in PROCEEDINGS OF THE THIRD CONGRESS OF THE INTERNATIONAL LITERATURE ASSOCIATION ('S-Gravenhage: Mouton, 1962); trans and rptd as WILLIAM BARNES FRIEND OF THOMAS HARDY (Mount Durand, St. Peter Port, Guernsey: Toucan P, 1967).

William Barnes is similar in many ways to Welsh poets. He was inspired by his rural life and was conscious of language. He was attracted to Welsh literature and history by the purity of the language, a goal he held desirable for the English language. The culture of Dorset is comparable to that of Wales. Barnes's poetry was much influenced by the Welsh *cynghanedd*. There is a need for critical study of Barnes's influence on H and through Barnes the influence of Welsh literature on H. [Reprints part of H's introduction to a posthumous volume of Barnes's poetry. Also see J. Stevens Cox (pub and general editor), Monographs on the Life of Thomas Hardy (1962).] [In Welsh.]

2327 Feibleman, James, Alice Leone Moats, and Lyman Bryson. "Hardy: *Tess of the d'Urbervilles*," INVITATION TO LEARNING, I (Fall 1951), 304–11.

Tess is overtly "sexy." Chance and accident are the villains in H's books. Nature is also an important character. H is unlike the Greeks in his attitude toward tragedy, for he does not accept it but is furious about it. The artist in H deals magnificently with the problem confronting Tess.

2328 Gehlo, Heinz. "Hardy und Cervantes" (Hardy and Cervantes). Unpublished dissertation, University of Berlin (Frei), 1951.

[Listed in Lawrence F. McNamee, DISSERTATIONS IN ENGLISH AND AMERICAN LITERATURE (NY & Lond: Bowker, 1968).]

2329 Hawkins, Desmond. THOMAS HARDY (Lond: Arthur Barker, 1951; Denver: Swallow P, 1952 [English Novelists Series]).

With *Far From the Madding Crowd*, there was no doubt a new novelist of first rank had arrived. *Madding Crowd* was the first of H's books to reach out toward tragedy, and the first in which he used "Wessex." H is the "greatest delineator of rural England in prose"; he drew from his experiences with Dorset and its folk. The spirit of balladry is in his work. Wessex was changing in his time, and H was most deeply attuned to life that was passing. H loved peasant music. H was a bright provincial, like Lawrence, and very fastidious. Sue Bridehead represents much of his personality. His London experience added to his Dorset experience, his philosophy and his modernism make him the unique writer he is. His main concept is evolutionary—that the development of consciousness only exacerbates man's problems. H did not preach a return to the simple but accepted evolution as an evil, leading to tragedy. H was an innovator in using the philosophy of modernism in relation to landscape and most importantly "discovered and charted the desert island of sex in the ocean of social confusion." H's novels waver in quality, perhaps because he was not sure of what he wanted to do. *Madding Crowd* was the first novel to pull together all his qualities; after that he veered back and forth. *The Return of the Native* is good, but the next three novels are poor or indifferent; *The Mayor of Casterbridge* is one of the very best; *Tess of the d'Urbervilles* and *Jude the Obscure* are not up to standard. Great achievements are his grand, epic tragedy, which is not to be criticized by canons of realism but poetic intensity, and his superb sense of landscape. Defects are his ordinary plots and his unexciting character-drawing. H developed his own unique type of novel: Wessex scene, infusion of poetic drama into prosaic lives, sureness of touch laying bare human passion. Verisimilitude in characters limited to the ordinary; major figures like Tess and Jude are portraits, inventions. H gains from counterpoint between types of characters, roots major figures in solid humanity. H's plots are spotty, sometimes careless (although the center is clear enough), limited in scope and invention, usually oriented around a love-situation. H's attitude toward sex: a "mode of entry into a more sublime world where the higher sensibility finds its true object." His sympathies are with the heretic, whom love fails and who suffers damnation. Evil comes from "follies of faulty judgment" in sexual matters. H is ambivalent and wants to explain and excuse his characters, thus weakening the proposition. Great conflict is between the real and ideal, culminating in *Jude*'s denial of the real, which nonetheless persists. H's style is impure, an estimate of its worth depending on one's estimate of the importance of impurities. Wordy, often stiff and ungainly, antiquarian, the dialogue is weak. H's besetting sin is solemnity. But he is a "slowly soaring writer" who gathers momentum through the paragraphs. His prose rises to stature in broadly panoramic passages. He needs distance and a wide range. His abandonment of the novel is appropriate; he had exhausted its possibilities, and he was not a born novelist so much as a poet. But we are fortunate that he was deflected into fiction because of his contribution of tragedy to the novel, of life rather than lives. His unique and prophetic vision provides us with great pictures of passion and ruin, firmly rooted in the earth of Wessex. [Appendix outlines plots and characters of novels.]

2330 Hedgcock, Frank A. "Reminiscences of Thomas Hardy," NATIONAL AND ENGLISH REVIEW, CXXXVII (Oct and Nov 1951), 220–28, 289–94.

In two conversations held in 1910, H showed extreme reticence about his personal life but discussed his work freely. H the poet could not believe that the works of H the novelist were worthy of much attention. H liked *The Return of the Native* most, but *Tess of the d'Urbervilles* was probably his best novel, although he had put too much feeling into it to recall it with pleasure. *Jude the Obscure* was really a double tragedy of the sexual misfits, Jude and Sue. H was glad to have his early poems connected with *The Dynasts* in his development as a writer. The first Mrs. H copied the novels by hand, called them "our" work, and said she amended some of them, such as *A Pair of Blue Eyes*. She seemed to prefer the earlier novels. H wished Wells were a better writer, thought Meredith had a little too much style, liked Henry James's shorter works, and thought Stevenson overrated. He admitted that he thought of going into the church more than once in his life.

2331 Kettle, Arnold. "*Tess of the d'Urbervilles*," AN INTRODUCTION TO THE ENGLISH NOVEL VOL. II: HENRY JAMES TO THE PRESENT (Lond: Hutchinson's University Library, 1951; NY: Harper Torchbook, 1960), pp. 49–62.

The subject of *Tess of the d'Urbervilles* is the destruction of the English peasantry. *Tess* is a *roman à thèse* and that thesis is that "in the course of the nineteenth century the disintegration of the peasantry—a process which had its roots deep in the past—had reached its final and tragic stage." Tess's seduction by Alec is symbolic of the historical process, of the exploitation of the working by the ruling class. Tess's destiny is of a social rather than a personal nature, and her story is to be read as a moral fable, i.e., "the expression of a generalized human situation in history and neither . . . a purely personal tragedy nor . . . a philosophic comment on Life in general and the fate of Woman in particular."

2332 Lewis, C[ecil] Day. "The Lyrical Poetry of Thomas Hardy," PROCEEDINGS OF THE BRITISH ACADEMY, XXXVII (1951), 155–74; first read as the Warton Lecture on English Poetry, 6 June 1951; rptd as THE LYRICAL POETRY OF THOMAS HARDY (Lond: Cumberledge, [1957]).

Critics should in general avoid consideration of the personality of a poet in their treatments of his poetry, but it is "extraordinarily difficult, and possibly undesirable, to dissociate Hardy's poetry from his character." Almost all his best poems are "deeply, nakedly personal." However, T. S. Eliot's strictures on H's work on the grounds that it is too personal are misplaced and are really expressions of taste rather than of criticism. F. R. Leavis, on the other hand, recognizes the authenticity of H's personal voice but fails to see the "great technical skill" with which he wrote. Both critics, therefore, give only a partial view of H the poet. The center of his achievement as a poet is the elegaic series, "Poems of 1912–13," in which he fuses his technical skill, the intensely personal themes, and a nostalgia which would have ruined the work of a lesser poet. In this series better than anywhere else, he showed the "ripeness, breadth of mind, charity, honesty," which made it possible for him to be one of the few poets capable of writing great personal poetry.

2333 Morcos, L. "*The Dynasts* of Thomas Hardy." Unpublished dissertation, Trinity University (Dublin), 1951.
[Listed in Lawrence F. McNamee, DISSERTATIONS IN ENGLISH AND AMERICAN LITERATURE (NY & Lond: Bowker, 1968).]

2334 Newton, William. "Chance as Employed by Hardy and the Naturalists," PHILOLOGICAL QUARTERLY, XXX (April 1951), 154–75.
Insisting on the "slice of life" theory, Naturalists denounce the use of chance and accident in fiction; H denied the "slice" theory, insisted upon the validity of chance/accident in fiction. The main difference is in the reading of life: Naturalists delight in science's discoveries, H sees nothing optimistic in science's revelations. But, despite theory, Naturalists used chance/accident and Gothic spectacle in fiction (Zola, in THERESE RAQUIN, GERMINAL, and L'ASSOMMOIR, and Moore, in A MUMMER'S WIFE). H, in *The Mayor of Casterbridge* and the last novels, uses devices of Naturalism (heredity, environment, biological analogy between man and nature, constricting influence of money, physiological organization of characters) but also chance and accident. His use of both is artistically defensible; it is his view of life. Zola's use of chance and spectacle, though non-philosophized, is artistically unnatural; it contradicts his theory.

2335 Newton, William. "Hardy and the Naturalists: Their Use of Physiology," MODERN PHILOLOGY, XLIX (Aug 1951), 28–41.
H, as seen particularly in *Under the Greenwood Tree, The Woodlanders,* and *The Return of the Native*, is closer to the physical realism of Flaubert than to the complicated physiological theories of the Naturalists. He is in favor of "frank and honest treatment of the physiological fact of life"; he carries out aesthetic studies of crumbling aspirations but not of the physiological processes behind. Nature is a control on animal life, which H uses as a psychological analogy. H said he was not well-read in Zola; he reverses mind-body theory found in the Naturalists. *Jude the Obscure* shows a physiological contrast between Sue and Arabella, bodily organizations are seen as controlling forces for the first time.

2336 O'Rourke, May. THE YOUNG THOMAS HARDY. With illustrations by Naomi Lang (Dorchester: Dorset P [Henry Ling, Ltd], 1951); rptd as YOUNG MR. THOMAS HARDY. With an introduction

by Richard Curle (Mount Durand, St. Peter Port, Guernsey: Toucan P, 1966).
[Sketchy survey of H's family, his schooling, the countryside he recalled so vividly in later life, his apprenticeship at Hicks's—mostly drawn from Florence Emily Hardy's LIFE OF THOMAS HARDY (1928, 1930). Also see J. Stevens Cox (pub and general editor), Monographs on the Life of Thomas Hardy (1962).]

2337 Phillpotts, Eden. "Thomas Hardy and Schopenhauer," FROM THE ANGLE OF 88 (Lond: Hutchinson, 1951), pp. 68–76.
H could be either cheerful or gloomy but was always modest and humane. Like Schopenhauer, he believed that compassion was a virtue in a world where man is but one among millions.

2338 Pinto, Vivian de Sola. "Hardy and Housman," CRISIS IN ENGLISH POETRY (Lond: Hutchinson House, 1951), pp. 36–58.
H overcame the crisis in modern poetry by devising techniques to embody in verse both the "voyage without" and the "voyage within." Chiefly through the use of irony, he made explicit man's failure to achieve the perfection he dreamed of. From the beginning of his career, H struck a distinctive note in his verse: the schism of the modern soul. He avoided the richness of Tennyson and Swinburne and sought to open up new kinds of beauty for poetic treatment without giving way to the cult of "beauty in ugliness." His mythology often was unable to express his ideas, and thus his attempts to express universal values frequently failed. But in treating concrete instances of human (and animal) suffering, H reached his highest achievements. Even before Freud's work made poets aware of the subconscious, he had realized its significance, though *The Dynasts* denied that the subconscious in itself is a path to salvation. Housman treated at times the same subjects as H, but, perhaps because he was less in touch with popular culture, his poetry—unlike H's—often falls into rhetorical gesturings or sentimental nostalgia. [A distinctly superior general introduction to H as poet.]

2339 Ransom, John Crowe. "The Poetry of 1900–1950," KENYON REVIEW, XIII (Summer 1951), 445–54.
H, surprisingly, must be named among the five major poets of 1900–1950. The hideous contrast between science's indifferent universe and the gentler affections and decencies of the human spirit was a topical theme in the 1860s but stale when H returned to poetry in the 1900s. Multiplicity of occasions, conventional metrics, and quaint homely words register his experience.

2340 Rockwell, Frederick S. "More About Wife Selling," NINETEENTH CENTURY FICTION, V (March 1951), 329.

Professor's note on wife-selling and *The Mayor of Casterbridge* recalls a passage in Robert Gibbing's COMING DOWN THE WYE, in which an eyewitness gives an account of such an incident. The newspaper report [TIMES (Hereford), 20 May 1876] which is the source for this passage cites several other wife-selling incidents at various times and in various places. [See John Robert Moore's "Two Notes on Thomas Hardy," ibid (Sept 1950), 159–63.]

2341 Rowse, Alfred Leslie. "Thomas Hardy and Max Gate," THE ENGLISH PAST: EVOCATIONS OF PERSONS AND PLACES (NY: Macmillan, 1951), pp. 165–83.
H is disliked and criticized by the people he lived among, yet he is a true and insightful heir of Dorchester. He is a product of the place, and it still recalls him.

2342 Scott-James, R. A. THOMAS HARDY (1840–1928) [Bibliographical Series of Supplements to "British Book News"] (Lond: Longmans, Green, 1951).
H is an observant, sensitive writer who used his early life as the raw material of his art. As a result, Wessex is more vividly realized than any other region described by an English author. Within Wessex, live characters who are influenced, first of all, by their surroundings and, secondly, by love, the passion which is the basis of H's tragedies. These tragedies, although written in an awkward style, are H's greatest achievement. As a group they reveal that H is pessimistic about the "governance of the Universe, but not about human beings." *The Dynasts* not only confirms this but is, in addition, a summing-up of all that H wrote earlier.

2343 Scott-James, Rolfe Arnold. "Some Elder Poets," FIFTY YEARS OF ENGLISH LITERATURE, 1900–1950 (NY: Longmans, Green, 1951), pp. 99–114, espec 99–106.
H is essentially a poet, in prose or poetry, with much in common with Wordsworth, although H is more spontaneous and more comfortable with humble settings. The force of H's poetry, as well as his prose, comes from his handling of Nature, Mankind, and Destiny. In *The Dynasts*, as in *Jude the Obscure*, H's vision of life is a belief in an "unsympathetic First Cause." [A somewhat blurred comparison with WAR AND PEACE.]

2344 Sheppard, John T. "President of the Immortals," MUSIC AT BELMONT, AND OTHER ESSAYS AND ADDRESSES (Lond: Rupert Hart-Davis; NY: Houghton, 1951), pp. 163–78.
The Aeschylean phrase with which H concludes *Tess of the d'Urbervilles* is not a "flourish, an evasion, a parade, in doubtful taste, of scholarship," rather it is a clue to H's deepest thought. Tess's acceptance of her imminent

death is an acceptance of the decree of imperfect human justice. H's controversial phrase is an ironic comment on this but only a conjecture as to the role of a First Cause in Tess's tragedy.

2345 Sherman, G. W. "Hooper Tolbert's Influence upon Thomas Hardy," NOTES AND QUERIES, CXCVI (23 June 1951), 280–81.

The influence of H's friends, like Bastow, Stephen and Moule, has been studied, but Hooper Tolbert's influence continues to be ignored. Tolbert died in 1883 after a promising career in the Indian Civil Service; he had studied under William Barnes.

2346 Strong, L. A. G. "Dorset Hardy," ESSAYS IN CRITICISM, I (Jan 1951), 42–50.

H's unity with his country environment is of major importance, since virtually everything he wrote was informed by his Dorset experience. Because H was a man, mankind, rather than nature, is the focal point in his works. Man is the lens through which all nature and experience are filtered. H's originality and his failure to adopt the accepted norms which dominated nineteenth-century London's literary circles were responsible both for his successes and his failures. Obsessed by the concept of a governing power, H returns again and again to the relationship between man and nature, the relationship that can clearly manifest itself only in a country setting. This is not to imply that H was merely a narrow, rustic genius. His London education, however, only confirmed his loyalty to his native rural surroundings. H was the greatest of the English country writers and one whose devotion to the more primitive style of country life did not blind him to the universal ambiguity of the human condition, even though it restricted his means of portraying that condition.

2347 Thomas, Gilbert. "The Dark Horse: Thomas Hardy," DALHOUSIE REVIEW, XXX (Jan 1951), 403–11.

The response to "God's Funeral" was the attitude which made H, in his own words, "the Dark Horse of English literature." He rejected Christianity with his intellect, yet retained it emotionally, and lived as though the "dream" of Christianity were true. H disliked being called a pessimist, or immoral, yet he was certainly a theoretic pessimist. His stance was largely determined by Darwinism and by a personal determination to anticipate disappointment.

2348 Thomson, G. H. "The Problem of Tragic Form in the Novels of Thomas Hardy." Unpublished dissertation, University of Toronto, 1951.

[Listed in Lawrence F. McNamee, DISSERTATIONS IN ENGLISH AND AMERICAN LITERATURE, SUPP I (NY & Lond: Bowker, 1969).]

2349 Van Doren, Mark. INTRODUCTION TO POETRY (NY: William Sloane Associates, 1951), pp. 98–102, 107–10, 418–26.
The three stanzas of "Drummer Hodge" present three times—present, past, future. "The Roman Road" compares two kinds of time—two lines in space—one historical, the other within memory; the latter seems longer. [Reprints ten poems.]

2350 Wagner, Hans R. DER ENGLISCHE BILDUNGSROMAN BIS IN DER ZEIT DES ERSTEN WELTKRIEGES (The English Developmental Novel Through the First World War) (Bern: A. Francke, 1951), pp. 54–60.
[Discusses the importance of *Jude the Obscure* as a Bildungsroman in literary history. Jude was the first unsuccessful protagonist in this genre.] [In German.]

2351 [Weber, Carl J.]. "Fifty-one Manuscripts: 1451–1951," COLBY LIBRARY QUARTERLY, III (Aug 1951), 37–44.
Among fifty-one manuscripts recently displayed were one H holograph ("A Glimpse from the Train," published in *Late Lyrics* as "Faintheart in a Railway Train"); two essays by Arnold Bennett (on *Tess of the d'Urbervilles* and Mrs. H's "biographical writings"); John Drinkwater's "original rough-draft manuscript" of "Thomas Hardy [on] His Eighty-Fifth Birthday"; Mary Ann Sheldon's musical settings for "First or Last" and "Rose-Ann"; J. G. Banwell's music for "Could he but come to me" from *The Famous Tragedy of the Queen of Cornwall*; Christopher le Fleming's musical settings of "Her Song" and "When I Set Out for Lyonesse"; and John Duke's musical setting for "When I Set Out for Lyonesse."

2352 Weber, Carl J. "Hardy: A Wessex Seesaw; A Classic Revalued: XIV," SATURDAY REVIEW OF LITERATURE, XXXIV (6 Jan 1951), 24–25.
The fixed point in the seesaw is H's genius and personality, the moving ends are the novels such as *The Return of the Native* (now noted as full of faults), and the poetry (which is gaining appreciation even while increasing urbanization disqualifies modern judgments of H as a rural writer). H's poetry is gaining recognition because it shows his essential belief in humanity. Individual optimistic poems may be discussed by themselves, whereas optimistic pages in predominantly pessimistic novels tend to be hidden under the bulk of negative material.

2353 Wright, Elizabeth Cox. METAPHOR SOUND AND MEANING IN BRIDGES' THE TESTAMENT OF BEAUTY (Phila: University of Pennsylvania P, 1951), pp. 21, 120, 196, 270.
"Winters . . . believes Bridges and Hardy to be 'the two most impressive writers of poetry in something like two centuries.' " Bridges's physical world is more detailed, less aerial, more associative through human experience, less

geographical than H is in *The Dynasts*. Beach's book, THE TECHNIQUE OF THOMAS HARDY (1922), is revolutionary criticism which "has insisted that structure is a vital factor in the living *whatness* of the work of art." In the poetic structure of Book II, Bridges considers war in terms of emphasis on the individual. "Hardy would have emphasized the social compulsions, and so made the poem structurally firmer at this point."

1952

2354 "Account of Hermann Lea's Death. Was a Friend of Thomas Hardy," WESTERN GAZETTE, 22 Feb 1952 [not seen in this form]; rptd in THOMAS HARDY THROUGH THE CAMERA'S EYE, ed by J. Stevens Cox (Beaminster, Dorset: Toucan P, 1964), p. 49.
[Also see J. Stevens Cox (pub and general editor), Monographs on the Life of Thomas Hardy (1962).]

2355 "Answers: Farinelli's Singing," NEW YORK TIMES BOOK REVIEW, 13 April 1952, p. 27.
Dan H. Laurence supplied information that Farinelli was the stage name for the eighteenth-century male soprano Carlo Broschi; the princesses are probably offspring of Philip V of Spain, for whom Broschi often sang. [Reply to query of S. M. U. in NEW YORK TIMES BOOK REVIEW, 16 March 1952, p. 35.]

2356 Brooks, Cleanth. "A Note on Thomas Hardy, with Six Poems by Thomas Hardy," HOPKINS REVIEW, V (Summer 1952), 68–79.
H and Browning, as F. M. Ford noted, paved the way for the Imagists. H's secret may lie in his restraint, the "steady undercutting of the vehement statement." There are fifty or sixty superb poems in *The Collected Poems of Thomas Hardy*, but the same blendings appear in both the good and bad poems—effects reminiscent of the country newspaper in the 1840s. H mixes Latinisms and Dorset dialect, odd coinages, and awkward inversions. "Wessex Heights" shows H's restraint. "In Death Divided" shows H's use of rhythm and line length variations. H's powerful handling of the stanza form also appears in "The Going."

2357 Cockerell, Sydney. "Honours to Authors," TIMES LITERARY SUPPLEMENT (Lond), 25 April 1952, p. 281.
[Letter correcting a footnote in Rupert Hart-Davis's biography of Hugh Walpole. H was offered a baronetcy, which he declined. He did accept an O.M. and doctorates from Aberdeen, Cambridge, and Oxford.]

2358 Decker, Clarence R. THE VICTORIAN CONSCIENCE (NY: Twayne Publishers, 1952), pp. 9, 12, 21, 32–33, 99.
The influence on H of French Naturalism is shown in his detailed background, emphasis on environment, minute and unsavory details, and unidealized characters.

2359 Dike, D. A. "A Modern Oedipus: *The Mayor of Casterbridge*," ESSAYS IN CRITICISM, II (April 1952), 169–79.
The tragic pattern in *The Mayor of Casterbridge* is analogous to that in OEDIPUS REX, yet achieves the stature of original expression because it arises naturally out of content. H surpasses reality to establish the archetypal conflicts implicit in the immediate context. The Market is the nineteenth-century equivalent of fate which spins the wheel of fortune. The tragic hero, Henchard, is at once an individual and the servant-leader of the community, a duality which first precipitates, then intensifies, his fall. The relations between the characters, moreover, are influenced by money, with the Market as the symbol around and through which their destinies are fulfilled. In short, instinct and emotion are equated to financial transactions. Ultimately reverting to the ancient model, H depicts alienation and isolation as the penalties for Henchard's sin. Henchard's will is a final judgment on his society, not only by him, but, broadly taken, by H as well. Human destiny is linked with cultural depravity in such a way that blurs the distinction between the guilt and innocence of the individual, and the tragic pattern must continue to repeat itself.

2360 Fairchild, Hoxie N. "The Immediate Source of *The Dynasts*," PUBLICATIONS OF THE MODERN LANGUAGE ASSOCIATION, LXVII (March 1952), 43–64.
Robert Buchanan's THE DRAMA OF KINGS (1871) heavily influenced *The Dynasts*, which first appeared shortly after Buchanan's death. Buchanan's "melioristic humanitarianism" is a subordinate theme in H's more harshly pessimistic treatment, but the vision of Napoleon as a "corrupted champion of liberty" is held in common, and Buchanan's chorus is a crude philosophic and technical sketch of H's Pities. Buchanan's Napoleon has a "Famulus," and H's 1887 notes show Napoleon haunted by a crude Familiar. The title of Buchanan's work appears in H's notes when he comments on the need to infuse his historical realism with supernatural impressiveness. [See also John Cassidy, "The Original Source of Hardy's *Dynasts*," PMLA, LXIX (Dec 1954), 1085–1100.]

2361 Glicksburg, Charles I. "Hardy's Scientific Pessimism," WESTERN HUMANITIES REVIEW, VI (Summer 1952), 273–83.
H accepted the ethical implications of the theory of natural selection, that the best did not always survive. But he refused to infer from this that might

equals right: "He could not get himself to believe that those who actually survived were the fittest—not according to his criteria of what was *humanly most fitting.*"

2362 Holland, Clive [pseud of C. J. Hankinson]. "At Woodbury Hill With Thomas Hardy," FIELD, 1 Nov 1952, p. 734.
[A personal reminiscence in which the author describes a visit to a fair with H, "a warm-hearted and very human personality."]

2363 Lawrence, E. P. *"The Return of the Native,"* in AN INTRODUCTION TO LITERATURE AND THE FINE ARTS, comp by a committee of the Department of Literature and Fine Arts (East Lansing: Michigan State UP, 1952); rptd in THE LAUREATE FRATERNITY: AN INTRODUCTION TO LITERATURE, ed by Adrian H. Jaffe and Herbert Weisinger (Evanston: Row, Peterson, 1960), pp. 264–67.
The Return of the Native is an example of determinism and reflects the influence of Darwinism. The operation of chance and fate in human life is emphasized; all of the characters who consciously strive to be happy are thwarted and punished.

2364 Leavis, F. R. "Reality and Sincerity: Notes in the Analysis of Poetry," SCRUTINY, XIX (Winter 1952–1953), 90–98.
H's poem, "After a Journey," is superior to Alexander Smith's "Barbara" and Emily Brontë's "Cold in the earth."

2365 Lynd, Robert. "A Hardy Heroine," BOOKS AND WRITERS (Lond: Dent, 1952), pp. 178–82; perhaps published earlier in a periodical [not identified].
H's melancholy notwithstanding, his characters are cast in the heroic mold. Bathsheba Everdene in *Far From the Madding Crowd* is great in her wildness, her innocence, and the extent of her suffering.

2366 Marriner, Ernest C. "A Poetic Apostrophe to Hardy," COLBY LIBRARY QUARTERLY, III (May 1952), 86–87.
[Discusses a letter and an annotated poem by W. E. Harker added to Colby's Hardy Collection (23 Nov 1951).] "In his letter Mr. Harker contends that Hardy, instead of being a fatalistic pessimist, was actually a man of deep faith."

2367 Morris, Lloyd, Virgilia Peterson, and Lyman Bryson. "Thomas Hardy: *The Return of the Native,*" INVITATION TO LEARNING, II (Summer 1952), 173–80.
"One might say that Thomas Hardy's attitude toward nature is typical of a certain part of the Victorian tradition." Eustacia is a heroine in a tragic way. Recklessness and passion are the flaws in her character. [The discus-

sion degenerates into a series of rather naive and eccentric impressionistic judgments.]

2368 Peirce, Walter. "An Unpublished Letter of Thomas Hardy," COLBY LIBRARY QUARTERLY, III (May 1952), 91–95.
[Reprints a letter from H to the Duchess of Sutherland (16 Dec 1925), to show H's acquaintance with life among the upper classes. More interesting on her than him.]

2369 Prescott, Orville. "The Novelist's World: 'In Time of "the Breaking of Nations," ' " IN MY OPINION (Indianapolis: Bobbs-Merrill, 1952), pp. 16–21; amalgamated from material published at various dates in the NEW YORK TIMES column "Books of the Times."
The modern world is described in terms of the exciting and stimulating, though discomfiting, work of Darwin, Marx, Freud, and Einstein. In place of the decadent behavior characterizing much of our response to our uncertainty, we need to re-establish standards of ethical conduct as a social force. Human values of the sort in the quoted H poem may be useful reminders of a fundamental system of values and behavior.

2370 Purdy, Richard L. "Introduction," *Our Exploits at West Poley*, by Thomas Hardy (Lond: Oxford UP, 1952), pp. vii–xii.
Our Exploits at West Poley, a story of two boys and a cave, was written by H for a youthful audience. Written in 1883 and published between Nov 1892 and April 1893 in HOUSEHOLD, it is characterized by a "sufficiently apparent moral" and "the familiar touches of the Wessex novels."

2371 Ransom, John Crowe. "Hardy—Old Poet," NEW REPUBLIC, CXXVI (12 May 1952), 16, 30–31.
"There is often in Hardy's poems the visible quaint rightness of a workman going by the rules." Although H usually uses iambic or iambic-anapestic, the dipodic line seen in the hymn books of H's youth appears, the original eight-beat line with a break worked down to two four beaters (and ultimately to four two-beaters which give a full musical pause when the last regular beat is dropped). The pattern of "Friends Beyond" is close to that of "Neutral Tones" in its reflection of the trauma H suffered in London in the 1860s when his faith was blown up. This is Dante's terza rima, an indication of the marriage between the high and the low in H's poetry.

2372 Ray, Gordon N., Carl J. Weber, and John Carter. NINE-TEENTH-CENTURY ENGLISH BOOKS: SOME PROBLEMS IN BIBLI-OGRAPHY (Urbana: University of Illinois P, 1952), pp. ix, 9, 31, 36–45; given as talks in Third Annual Windsor Lectures in Librarianship.

Many editions of H's works were pirated and printed in "debased" form in America.

2373 Reed, Henry. "For Younger Readers," LISTENER, XLVIII (9 Oct 1952), 599–600.
"Exploits" appeared in HOUSEHOLD, an obscure Boston journal, where R. L. Purdy discovered it. It is "genuine Hardy" throughout, with references to Carlyle, Bentham, and nature, all done in a light manner. It is not likely to become a children's classic. [Review of Thomas Hardy, *Our Exploits at West Poley*, ed by Richard L. Purdy (1952).]

2374 Rollins, Cecil A. "Hardy's 'Man of Character' on the Air," COLBY LIBRARY QUARTERLY, III (May 1952), 87–91.
Desmond Hawkins's ten-part radio adaptation of *The Mayor of Caster-bridge* is successful in preserving a vivid sense of time and place, but it concentrates perhaps excessively on incident and insufficiently on character. [Includes photographs of H in 1889 and 1913.]

2375 Sherman, George W. "A Note on One of Thomas Hardy's Poems," COLBY LIBRARY QUARTERLY, III (May 1952), 99–100.
"Nature's Questioning" has its emotional roots in the same observations that [Includes photographs of H in 1899 and 1913.]

2376 Sherman, G. W. "Thomas Hardy and the Agricultural Laborer," NINETEENTH CENTURY FICTION, VII (Sept 1952), 111–18.
H's essay, "The Dorsetshire Labourer" (1879), documents his sympathy with the cause of the agricultural laborers. His own transitional class position as a boy made him sensitive to the plight of these laborers at the hands of the industrial revolution. He found the annihilation of their morale and self-respect the most deplorable of the privations that these people suffered. "In spite of the [eventual] general improvement in the living standards of the agricultural class as a whole, Hardy recognized that there were forces at work which did not originate with agricultural unrest, and which even collective bargaining was powerless to stop." H works his concern with this class into *The Woodlanders* and *Far From the Madding Crowd*. In the former, "the conditions and mental state of the displaced farm tenant is symbolically represented"; in the latter, he traces the lamentable condition of this class as it loses contact with its environment and its cultural roots because of the industrialization process.

2377 Siegel, Paul N. "Hardy's 'Convergence of the Twain,' " EXPLICATOR, XI (Nov 1952), Item 13.
The dominant image of the second section of "The Convergence of the Twain" is the "marriage" between the iceberg and the ship. This "marriage"

is a parody of "the idea of a marriage made in heaven." The section emphasizes subtly the combination of two such alien objects as the ship and the iceberg, made one by the "intimate welding" of the convergence.

2378 Slack, Robert. "Hardy and Rebekah Owen," TIMES LITERARY SUPPLEMENT (Lond), 30 May 1952, p. 361.
The reviewer of Carl J. Weber's HARDY AND THE LADY FROM MADISON SQUARE (1952) failed to mention the central point of the book: Rebekah Owen's influence upon H's fiction. [The reviewer replies that the evidence establishes no significant influence. See original review in TIMES LITERARY SUPPLEMENT (Lond), 25 April 1952.]

2379 Snell, Reginald. "A Self-Plagiarism by Thomas Hardy," ESSAYS IN CRITICISM, II (Jan 1952), 114–17.
Certain portions of the dialogue in *The Famous Tragedy of the Queen of Cornwall* seem out of place and lacking in artistic integrity. This defect is the result of a self-plagiarism by H, that of using, with only slight modifications, the exchange between Elfride Swancourt and Henry Knight in *A Pair of Blue Eyes*. Elfride begs Henry not to leave her, for that which occurs between Tristram and Iseult in a similar situation. [The parallel scenes are appended.]

2380 U., S. M. "Farinelli's Singing," NEW YORK TIMES BOOK REVIEW, 16 March 1952, p. 35.
In chap 5 of *The Return of the Native* H wrote: " 'As with Farinelli's singing before the princesses.' " "Who were the princesses? When did this happen? Who was Farinelli?" [See reply by Dan H. Laurence in NEW YORK TIMES BOOK REVIEW, 13 April 1952, p. 27.]

2381 Wade, Rosalind. "Thomas Hardy is in Demand," ST. MARTIN'S REVIEW, No. 739 (Oct 1952), 311–12.
H's novels continue to be widely read, probably as a result of his power to create a living landscape, of "his tenacious grip on the opening scenes," and of his exaltation of humble people's lives.

2382 Weber, Carl J. HARDY AND THE LADY FROM MADISON SQUARE (Waterville, Maine: Colby College P, 1952).
In preparing the first book edition of *The Mayor of Casterbridge*, H, convinced that it weakened the ending to have Henchard go away twice, removed the caged goldfinch and other material at the end of the serial version. Rebekah Owen and her sister Catherine ultimately convinced H that the original ending was stronger, so he restored it in later editions. Ardent H fan as she was, Rebekah was nevertheless offended by *Jude the Obscure*—and H knew it, as his poem "To a Lady Offended by a Book of the Writer's" [i.e. "To Lady ———. Offended by something the Author had

written" and "To a Lady"] shows. The relationship or friendship between H and Rebekah—which began so propitiously in the 1880s—failed to develop: Rebekah remained a demanding "taker," endlessly asking H to autograph books for her or to answer her pleas for information.

2383 Weber, Carl J. "Hardy as a Writer for Boys," TIMES LITERARY SUPPLEMENT (Lond), 17 Oct 1952, p. 684.

Reviewer's comment on "A Lost Hardy Story" overlooks the fact that "Our Exploits at West Poley" (1883) was not the first story H had written for boys. H had a story, "The Thieves Who Couldn't Help Sneezing," in a Christmas annual for 1877.

2384 [Weber, Carl J.]. "Program of Tranchell's Opera," COLBY LIBRARY QUARTERLY, III (Aug 1952), 115.

[Records the addition to the Colby Hardy Collection of the program for the first performance of Peter Tranchell's highly acclaimed three-act opera *The Mayor of Casterbridge*.]

2385 Weber, Carl J. "Thomas Hardy in Yankeeland," YANKEE MAGAZINE, XVI (May 1952), 42, 46.

[Account of various denizens of "Yankee-land" (e.g. Mary Ellen Chase, E. A. Robinson, Sarah Orne Jewett) who became enthusiastic admirers of H. Some discussion of the H collection at Colby College.]

2386 Woolf, Virginia. A WRITER'S DIARY: BEING EXTRACTS FROM THE DIARY OF VIRGINIA WOOLF, ed by Leonard Woolf (Lond: Hogarth P, 1952), pp. 8, 41, 78, 87, 89–94, 95, 122, 264; rptd (NY: Harcourt, Brace, 1954), pp. 8, 39, 76, 86, 88–93, 94, 120, 263.

5 March 1919: List of authors to be read, including H. 15 Nov 1921: Writing on Henry James's ghost stories for THE TIMES: next must do H. 1 June 1925: Mrs. H says H reads and listens to COMMON READER with " 'great pleasure.' " 9 March 1926: Recording George Moore's observations on H at a party. Moore thought ESTHER WATERS better than *Tess of the d'Urbervilles* and that H could not tell a story. English fiction is the worst part of English literature. 25 July 1926: Visit to H. Mrs. H has sad eyes, is childless, and a receptionist. The dog is most important to her. H is "puffy-cheeked, cheerful," has "a round whitish face, the eyes now faded and rather watery, but the whole aspect cheerful and vigorous," and is an affable host. [Talked of father (Leslie Stephen), and history of the publication of *Far From the Madding Crowd* in CORNHILL'S.] The MS was sold during the war for Red Cross. H no longer liked or recognized London. He is no longer interested in his novels, never took them along with him; he takes more pains with *The Dynasts* (pronounced Dinnasts), wrote poetry from notes of early stuff rejected by publishers, but fair copies are lost. H would

not commit himself on which book of his own he thought best. He talked of de la Mare and T. E. Lawrence. "What impressed me was his freedom, ease and vitality. He seemed very 'Great Victorian' doing the whole thing with a sweep of his hand . . . and setting no great stock by literature." They looked at an engraving of Tess by Herkomer; the story of an old picture is fictitious. Aldous Huxley's book Mrs. H thought clever, but H couldn't recall. Literature is only a far-off amusement to him.

1953

2387 Arnold, Eric. "Hardy's Wessex," NOTES AND QUERIES, CXCVIII (June 1953), 266.
Can readers explain two major discrepancies in *The Trumpet-Major*, related to locations and the general truth of H's picture of the countryside?

2388 Ervine, St. John. "Thomas Hardy and the Maid from Donaghadee," BELFAST TELEGRAPH, 16 July 1953.
[Ervine requests that more evidence be given for the contention that Sarah Grand was the young girl that inspired H's Donaghadee jingle (see Marjorie Spencer's "A Maid from the County Down," BELFAST TELEGRAPH, 13 July 1953. He also suggests that Miss Spencer is mistaken in her belief that H did not know the age of the correspondent who inspired these lines, for the last lines indicate that he was aware of her youth.]

2389 Ervine, St. John. "Who Did Inspire Donaghadee 'Jingle'?" BELFAST TELEGRAPH, 31 July 1953.
[Ervine contends that he has proof in letters that Sarah Grand could not have been the girl who inspired the Donaghadee jingle (see Marjorie Spencer, "A Maid from the County Down," BELFAST TELEGRAPH, 13 July 1953. He mainly recounts the circumstances under which he received the letter in which H mentions the jingle; he suggests that, in place of Sarah Grand, one Mrs. Harwood was responsible for its being written.]

2390 Ervine, St. John. "Who Wrote to Hardy from Donaghadee?" BELFAST TELEGRAPH, 11 Aug 1953.
[Ervine rejects his earlier theory that Mrs. Harwood was H's youthful Donaghadee correspondent (see St. John Ervine, "Who Did Inspire Donaghadee 'Jingle'?" BELFAST TELEGRAPH, 31 July 1953); moreover, he suggests that there is no way of telling who the person was. He concludes the entire issue with: "The matter is not important except as an illustration of the strange way in which a writer's mind works. At any moment, and without intention by anybody, a spark may be struck in his imagination."]

2391 Gwynn, Frederick L. "HAMLET and Hardy," SHAKESPEARE QUARTERLY, IV (April 1953), 207–8.

The closet scene in HAMLET (III, iii, 27) is a "partial source for the bitter accusation by Clym Yeobright of his wife, Eustacia, in Bk. V, ch. III of *The Return of the Native.*" [Unconvincing.]

2392 Heath-Stubbs, John. "Introduction," THE FABER BOOK OF TWENTIETH CENTURY VERSE: AN ANTHOLOGY OF VERSE IN BRITAIN, 1900-1950, ed by John Heath-Stubbs and David Wright (Lond: Faber & Faber, 1953), pp. 21, 22, 24, 25.

H, C. M. Doughty, W. S. Blunt, Kipling, and Bridges "most clearly represent the passage of the English tradition from the Nineteenth to the Twentieth Century." H shares the "pastoral mood" which dominated so much of the poetry from 1900 to 1920 in his "reaching back to an organic past, remembered as a concrete reality, but felt as already dead or dying."

2393 Hecht, Anthony. "Spring for Thomas Hardy," POETRY, LXXXII (April 1953), 17.

[In an H-like poem on spring, Hecht lists H's poetic subjects and praises H's poems on spring.]

2394 Hill, Charles J. "George Meredith and Thomas Hardy," NOTES AND QUERIES, CXCVIII (Feb 1953), 69–71.

Meredith and H were friends "on and off . . . for forty years," but the record of their friendship is very slight. Edmund Gosse acted as a busybody between the two great men in 1905 [see Evan Charteris, THE LIFE AND LETTERS OF SIR EDMUND GOSSE (1931), p. 298]. Their first meeting was early in 1869; then, they met at the Rabelais Club dinner in 1886. There was then a series of meetings at Box Hill and at the Omar-Khayyam Club. H wrote to Meredith on his eightieth birthday. However, H did not really enjoy reading Meredith's novels. On the other hand, Meredith declared: "H is one of the few men I can read." Was H conscious of RHODA FLEMING when he wrote *Tess of the d'Urbervilles*? The seduction theme is the same in both novels, and there is a striking resemblance between the openings of the two stories. Both novels are powerful indictments of respectability.

2395 Holloway, John. THE VICTORIAN SAGE: STUDIES IN ARGUMENT (Lond: Macmillan; NY: St. Martin's P, 1953); rptd (Hamden, Conn: Archon Books, 1962); rptd (NY: Norton Paperback, 1965), pp. 244–89.

H is a philosopher and moralist whose works embody "a definite though unobtrusive sense of values." But H's novels are impressions, not arguments, and their emphasis is on the quality rather than the course of things. H's frequent use of wildly improbable incidents (the lost letter in *Tess of the d'Urbervilles*, the spitting gargoyle in *Far From the Madding Crowd*, for example) are clumsy attempts on H's part to illustrate his belief that the course of things is governed by "a vague thrusting or urging internal force in no pre-destined direction." The quality of things in H's fiction is determined by his idea of Nature, "the working and changing system of the whole world . . . which includes [human activity], profoundly modifies it, and ultimately controls it." H's view is best summarized by the following abstraction: "it is right to live naturally, i.e., to live in continuity with one's whole biological and geographical environment." Those who live in harmony with nature (Gabriel Oak, Diggory Venn, Giles Winterborne, for example) are satisfied with their lot in life. Those who lack continuity with nature (Clym Yeobright, Angel Clare, Jude Fawley, for example) seek a personal, self-created dream. "Most of the novels recount how tragedy sooner or later results from the attempt to abandon the natural pattern of things in pursuit of the dream." *Madding Crowd, The Return of the Native, The Woodlanders*, and *Tess* convey H's impression of the quality of things most completely.

2396 Kilby, Clyde S. POETRY AND LIFE: AN INTRODUCTION TO POETRY (NY: Odyssey P, 1953), pp. 5–6.
"The Fallow Deer at the Lonely House" is a moving reflection of H's interest in "the strange bond between the higher and lower forms of life" and in "the whole mystery" of the universe.

2397 Laaths, Erwin. KNAURS GESCHICHTE DER WELTLITERATUR (Knaur's History of World Literature). 3rd ed (Munich: Th. Knaur, 1953), pp. 611–12.
[Brief mention of H and WUTHERING HEIGHTS.] [In German.]

2398 Laurence, Dan H. "Henry James and Stevenson Discuss 'Vile' *Tess*," COLBY LIBRARY QUARTERLY, III (May 1953), 164–68.
[Reprints in full and for the first time the correspondence relative to *Tess of the d'Urbervilles*, establishes its context, and succinctly charts James's and Stevenson's opinions of H's merits as a novelist. H was aware of their hostility.]

2399 MacCarthy, Desmond. "Hardy," MEMORIES (NY: Oxford UP, 1953), pp. 108–12.
H is both a poet and novelist of equal talent who finds truth in the response to life and sees in it the "profound sense of man's destiny."

2400 Maurer, Oscar. "Leslie Stephen and the CORNHILL MAGAZINE, 1871–82," UNIVERSITY OF TEXAS STUDIES IN ENGLISH, XXXII (1953), 67–95.
Stephen was impressed by *Under the Greenwood Tree* and advised H to

give it a plot suitable for serial publication. The tradition of anonymity in serialized fiction caused *Far From the Madding Crowd* to be attributed to George Eliot. Stephen warned H to treat Fanny's seduction with care. Stephen also warned H about *The Hand of Ethelberta*. H refused to publish *The Return of the Native* in the CORNHILL because of Stephen's qualms about the opening chapters. Stephen was sorry he did not bring out *The Trumpet-Major* in the CORNHILL.

2401 Noyes, Alfred. "A Debate with Hardy," TWO WORLDS FOR MEMORY (Phila & NY: Lippincott, 1953), pp. 147-57.
[Noyes met H only once in London at a party given by Mrs. William Sharp. With respect to Noyes's review of *The Famous Tragedy of the Queen of Cornwall* ("Hardy, the Master," EVENING NEWS [Lond], 15 Nov 1923), H wrote: "I envy you the dispatch by which you could do it in a few hours." In a later controversy about a lecture given by Noyes in 1920 to a London audience, several letters were exchanged. Only H's letters were printed in his biography. Noyes here gives his side of the correspondence, noting he has been unable to understand many passages in H's work because he cannot conceive that the cause of things could be less than the things caused. Noyes apologizes for the phrase "an imbecile jester" as one of those extempore exclamations which do not represent one's opinions as a whole.] [A very weak, maudlin apology.]

2402 Orel, Harold. "*The Dynasts* and PARADISE LOST," SOUTH ATLANTIC QUARTERLY, LII (July 1953), 355–60.
"*The Dynasts* is an unread great poem of our age: with little exaggeration perhaps the greatest." There has been too much wrong-headed criticism of the poem. It is a "repudiation of the epic tradition, as exemplified by Milton's PARADISE LOST" and must be read in that light.

2403 Pike, Royston. "Down the Lane with Thomas Hardy," RATIONALIST ANNUAL, 1953, pp. 22–27.
H was deeply concerned with what he called " 'the immortal puzzle—given the man and woman, how to find a basis for their sexual relation.' " He never fell into the "gross error of thinking of that relation in purely animal terms" nor "maintained that the coming together of man and woman is justified only as a means of perpetuating the species." In his pages there is no "surging sensuousness"; instead, "pity, not passion is the controlling note of all he wrote."

2404 Roche, Charles Edward. "Thomas Hardy and C.-G. Étienne," MODERN LANGUAGE NOTES, LXVIII (March 1953), 173.
Clym Yeobright's song in Book IV, chap 11, of *The Return of the Native* is from Charles-Guillaume Étienne's comic opera, GULISTAN.

2405 S., R. "Origins of British Theatre," THEATRE NOTEBOOK, VII (April–June 1953), 58–60.

The Symondsbury Mummer's play, a performance in four parts whose first part is a "more or less orthodox variant" of the "St. George" play, bears striking similarities to the "St. George" play used in *The Return of the Native*.

2406 Sherman, G. W. "The Source of the Hero's Name in Thomas Hardy's Novelette, *An Indiscretion in the Life of an Heiress*," NOTES AND QUERIES, CXCVIII (Sept 1953), 397–99.

When H cut his youthful novel, *The Poor Man and the Lady* (1868), to the size of a novelette, *An Indiscretion in the Life of an Heiress* (1878), he changed the hero's name, Will Strong, into Egbert Mayne. "Mayne" may have been suggested by the name of the Police Commissioner, Sir Richard Mayne, at the time of the Reform Bill. Egbert was the name of a King of Wessex.

2407 Sherman, G. W. "Thomas Hardy and Professor Edward Beesly," NOTES AND QUERIES, CXCVIII (April 1953), 167–68.

Edward Beesly the Positivist (1831–1913) is mentioned once in H's biography. When did H first meet this man who took part in the organizational meeting of the First International? That H shared the progressive hope for humanity with the reformers of the time and followers of Comte like Beesly is evident from his early poem "1967" (1867). Sir Arthur Quiller-Couch has noted the "economic source" of H's quarrel with society as a young man, and John Morley had thought that the radicalism of his first novel might be detrimental to H's literary career.

2408 Spencer, Marjorie. "A Maid from the County Down," BELFAST TELEGRAPH, 13 July 1953.

[Article suggests that the jingle about Donaghadee appearing in an H poem was inspired by a note written to H about his novels by a young girl, Frances Elizabeth Clarke. Later, under the name of Sarah Grand, she became a novelist and a social reformer; her reputation as novelist rests, for the most part, on a stormily received (because of the sex problems with which it dealt) work, THE HEAVENLY TWINS. See the series of articles (1953) by St. John Ervine.]

2409 Stevenson, Lionel. THE ORDEAL OF GEORGE MEREDITH: A BIOGRAPHY (NY: Scribner's, 1953), pp. 79, 174, 268, 319, 334, 343, 344, 349, 354.

H's association with Meredith, whom he much admired, began in 1869 when Meredith, as reader for Chapman & Hall, advised H against publishing *The Poor Man and the Lady*. H met with Meredith in 1886, 1895, and again in 1905. At this last meeting, Meredith refrained from offering H his private opinion that *The Dynasts* should have been written in prose. Contrasting himself with H, Meredith stated in 1908 that he himself "kept on the causeway between the bogs of optimism and pessimism." At Meredith's death in 1909, hesitation whether to bury Meredith in Westminster Abbey prompted H to remark to Edward Clodd that the Abbey was in need of "a heathen annexe."

2410 Tallmadge, John A. "The Social Ideas of Thomas Hardy," DISSERTATION ABSTRACTS, XIII (1953), 549–50. Unpublished dissertation, New York University, 1953.

2411 Unger, Leonard, and William Van O'Connor. "Thomas Hardy," POEMS FOR STUDY (NY: Rinehart, 1953), pp. 565–76.
A pattern of irony runs through H's poetry; many of his short poems, like "The Newcomer's Wife," are "mechanical formulations of the ironical pattern." In "Nobody Comes," on the other hand, H's sensibility is not violated by any of his favorite ideas. The poem's development "moves toward an increasingly clear focus on the physical and psychological isolation of the speaker."

2412 Van Ghent, Dorothy. "On *Tess of the d'Urbervilles*," THE ENGLISH NOVEL: FORM AND FUNCTION (NY: Holt, Rinehart & Winston, 1953), pp. 195–209; rptd (NY: Harper, 1961), pp. 195–209; and in MODERN BRITISH FICTION: ESSAYS IN CRITICISM, ed by Mark Schorer (NY: Oxford UP, 1961), pp. 30–44.
Although there is intrusive commentary in *Tess of the d'Urbervilles*, the book is a success because of H's "incorruptible feeling for the actual," a feeling which makes "amazingly blunt" symbolism effective. This symbolism and "the dramatic motivation provided by natural earth" are central to the book. Functioning as "a factor of causation," the earth exists also as a "Final Cause" which is complemented by the accidents and coincidences which comprise the narrative pattern of the book. In turn, the accidents and coincidences suggest the necessity of this pattern which is reinforced by "folk instinctivism," "folk fatalism," and "folk music." Ultimately the folk bridge the gap between "mere earth and moral individuality," in that their fatalism is communal and ritual. What they do is symbolic, as is Tess's death at Stonehenge and, in fact, the entire novel. This symbolism "enforces a magical view of life."

2413 Vinson, Grace E. "Diction and Imagery in the Poetry of Thomas Hardy." Unpublished dissertation, University of Wisconsin, 1953.
[Listed in Lawrence F. McNamee, DISSERTATIONS IN ENGLISH AND AMERICAN LITERATURE (NY & Lond: Bowker, 1968).]

2414 Weber, Carl J. "Our Exploits at West Poley," NINETEENTH CENTURY FICTION, VII (March 1953), 307–8.

R. L. Purdy found H's story in HOUSEHOLD, an obscure Boston periodical. *"Our Exploits* has all the familiar [H] characteristics": a vividly presented scene, the "comic eloquence" of the rustic, and a "sensational" plot. It shows H's "usual clumsiness but also his characteristic charm, as well as his skill."

2415 Woolf, Virginia. "Pages from a Diary," ENCOUNTER, I (Oct 1953), 5–11; rptd and expanded in A WRITER'S DIARY, ed by Leonard Woolf (1952) [qv].

1954

2416 Amy, Ernest F. "Laying a Ghost: A Note on Hardy's Plagiarism," NINETEENTH CENTURY FICTION, IX (Sept 1954), 150–53.

Critics have agreed, for the most part, in their castigation of H for the plagiarized passage in *The Trumpet-Major*. However, in an interview, Mrs. H indicated that H was in the habit of keeping notebooks to which he continually referred. It is very likely that when the passage from Gifford's HISTORY OF THE WARS OCCASIONED BY THE FRENCH REVOLUTION caught his eye, "He might well have copied or paraphrased it in a pocket book. If so, when he wrote *Trumpet-Major* years later, he had forgotten that the passage was not his own and lifted it out . . . for the novel." This would also explain the use of other passages in the novels for which H has been accused óf deliberate plagiarism.

2417 Andersen, Carol Reed. "Time, Space and Perspective in Thomas Hardy," NINETEENTH CENTURY FICTION, IX (Dec 1954), 192–208.

By manipulating time, space, and perspective, H uses metaphors of enlargement and diminution, premonition, accumulation, and even metaphors which become direct symbols to complement other facets of the novels. These metaphors, working in contiguity with each other and with more conventional aspects, give a universality to plot and an expanding significance which make the reader's enjoyment critically justified.

2418 Bellman, Samuel I. "Thorstein Veblen: A Descendant of the Mayor of Casterbridge," COLBY LIBRARY QUARTERLY, III (Nov 1954), 265–67.

Not only are Veblen and Michael Henchard strikingly independent of and indifferent to society, but their penciled wills reveal an even more striking similarity: their wish to be "obliterated from the earth in every sense."

2419 Brown, Douglas. THOMAS HARDY (Lond: Longmans, 1954); rptd (Lond: Longmans, 1961).

In his five great novels—*Far From the Madding Crowd, The Return of the Native, The Woodlanders, The Mayor of Casterbridge,* and *Tess of the d'Urbervilles*—H presents "a clash between agricultural and urban modes of life" and traces the drastic decline of the "national agriculture" which results, finally, in the defeat of the peasantry and the collapse of agriculture. In fact, the novels in general comprise "a sustained imagery of agricultural calamity" which begins with the storm in *Madding Crowd* and culminates in the scene at Flintcomb Ash in *Tess*. While the novels include such representatives of agricultural life as Oak, Diggory Venn, Henchard, Giles, and Tess, they also include such "invaders" as Troy, Wildeve, Farfrae, Fitzpiers, and Alec who threaten the stability of the agricultural community. The community withstands the invaders in the earlier novels, but in *Woodlanders* it is defeated when Giles dies and in *Tess* when Tess dies. When in *Jude the Obscure* the "gifted villager" moves into the "civic world," the pattern of decline is completed, and the scene of the action shifts. Despite this shift, the uniqueness of H is evident in *Jude* as it is in all the novels. Thus behind each Wessex novel is H, "the countryman," whose handling of words, phrases, and movement; whose "treatment of country voices and the idiom of local speech"; and whose "rhythm of the ballad-tale" reveal the "man of the soil" who wrote the book. Also revealed are H's view of life as bitter, his belief that the dismay which life produces is at odds with the "steadfastness" of the agricultural community, and his belief that life is tragic. The novelist who records these beliefs is also behind the poems which are "the harvest of the novels." In deceptively simple poems which "extend themselves in the mind," H presents his deepest theme: "the desolation of utter loss." In doing so, he reveals his "poetic personality," which consists of the endowments of the ballad and folk singer, severe honesty, "the impulse of nostalgia," and an ability to render poignantly the "presentness" of the moment.

2420 Cassidy, John A. "The Original Source of Hardy's *Dynasts*," PUBLICATIONS OF THE MODERN LANGUAGE ASSOCIATION, LXIX (Dec 1954), 1085–1100.

Hoxie Fairchild's source study of H's *The Dynasts* and Buchanan's THE DRAMA OF KINGS ultimately leads to Victor Hugo's LA LÉGENDE DES SIÈCLES. "Besides borrowing Hugo's structure and over-all plan, Buchanan also used much of his method and treatment," despite the absence of direct textual similarities. Hugo's mysticism of the 1850s influenced Buchanan in the 1860s. Both works show gloomy forebodings under forced optimism, conceiving of humanity as a single giant individual and giving a speaking voice to abstracts and institutions. [See Hoxie N. Fairchild, "The Immediate Source of *The Dynasts*," ibid, LXVII (March 1952), 43–64.]

2421 Church, Richard. "Thomas Hardy as Revealed in *The Dynasts*," ÉTUDES ANGLAISES, VII (Jan 1954), 70–79; rptd in ESSAYS BY DIVERS HANDS: BEING THE TRANSACTIONS OF THE ROYAL SOCIETY OF LITERATURE, ns XXIX (1958), 1–17.

The Dynasts is on the poetic plane of Dante and Milton; it has the epic simplicity of WAR AND PEACE, and finally, is a religious Aeschylean drama. H's singleness of vision should not be misconstrued as pessimism. H sees the universe as a working organism.

2422 Clifford, Emma. "The Child: The Circus: And *Jude the Obscure*," CAMBRIDGE JOURNAL, VII (June 1954), 531–46.

H's thought was unsystematic; he himself described his ideas as "a confused heap of impressions, like those of a bewildered child at a conjuring show." The children in H's work have received insufficient attention. H associated childhood with "the ultimate horror of human existence." Children see a world like that of the toy-shop or fair, in the abstract, but H's children do not enjoy what they see. Patterns of visual images reflect the horror of the world to "an immature and frightened awareness."

2423 Cockerell, Sydney. " 'Hardy After Fifty Years,' " TIMES LITERARY SUPPLEMENT (Lond), 22 Jan 1954, p. 57.

H was not buried in Westminster Abbey against his wishes, as the author of "Hardy After Fifty Years," TIMES LITERARY SUPPLEMENT (Lond), 15 Jan 1954, pp. 33–35, suggests.

2424 Craig, M. J. " 'Hardy After Fifty Years,' " TIMES LITERARY SUPPLEMENT (Lond), 22 Jan 1954, p. 57.

H did not die the oldest of English poets at eighty-eight. Walter Savage Landor died at eighty-nine. [See "Hardy After Fifty Years," TIMES LITERARY SUPPLEMENT (Lond), 15 Jan 1954, pp. 33–35.]

2425 Edgren, C. Hobart. "A Hardy-Housman Parallel," NOTES AND QUERIES, CXCIX (March 1954), 126–27.

There is a similarity between Housman's "Is my Team Ploughing?" and H's "Ah, are you Digging on my Grave?" Both poems begin with a question; in each, four questions are asked and four answers given. Both poems are concerned with a "triple obsession with death, memory and time"; both are structurally projected on a question-answer basis. It appears that H had Housman's poem in mind when he wrote his poem.

2426 Fielding, K. J. "The Brotherton Collection, The Brotherton Library, University of Leeds: Library Notes," VICTORIAN NEWS-LETTER, No. 6 (Nov 1954), 1.

Eighty letters, 1886–1927, from H to Edmund Gosse are in the collection.

2427 Gwynn, Frederick L., Ralph W. Condee, Arthur O. Lewis, Jr. (eds). THE CASE FOR POETRY: A NEW ANTHOLOGY (NY: Prentice-Hall, 1954), pp. 166–69; 2nd ed as THE CASE FOR POETRY: A CRITICAL ANTHOLOGY (Englewood Cliffs, NJ: Prentice-Hall, 1965), pp. 145–49.

"The Darkling Thrush" may be read as a statement of despair, of hope, or as a "delicately poised expression of optimism and pessimism, skepticism and belief." [First edition prints "The Darkling Thrush" with outlines of explications as well as "The Phantom Horsewoman" and "The Oxen," without critical comment; second edition adds "In Time of 'the Breaking of Nations.' "]

2428 "Hardy After Fifty Years," TIMES LITERARY SUPPLEMENT (Lond), 15 Jan 1954, pp. 33–35.

The language of *The Dynasts* was originally received as unpoetic. One reason is H's weakness in using paraphrases of the statements of historical characters. But H knew what he was doing and avoided mere "style." The Will drives everything, including himself, hence naturalness and artlessness are called for to prevent the sense of characters' having insight into their situations. "Supernatural spectators" speak rich language. Now one can see that the thought of *Dynasts* is more original and metaphorical than it was at first considered. There are blemishes, but H was a poet who knew himself and showed integrity of his work. [See Sydney Cockerell, ibid, 22 Jan 1954, p. 57.]

2429 Hardy, Evelyn. "Hardy and the Phrenologist," JOHN O'LONDON'S WEEKLY, LXIII (26 Feb 1954), 191, 203.

At twenty-four H was fascinated by phrenology and visited "Dr." C. Donovan. The four "Animal Faculties" in which Donovan rated H "large" —adhesiveness, destructiveness, acquisitiveness, and constructiveness—all bear a close relationship to H's personal life and literary work. In "Moral Faculties" H rated high in five. Especially applicable are "comparison" and "causality." H's descriptions utilize similes and metaphors. "As for Hardy's power to question and re-question the tragic fact of existence, no writer, not even Shakespeare, or the Greek tragedians, has studied it so persistently, and sought for an answer so stubbornly as Thomas Hardy."

2430 Hardy, Evelyn. THOMAS HARDY: A CRITICAL BIOGRAPHY (Lond: Hogarth P; NY: St. Martins P, 1954).

Materials for writing about H are voluminous. H's autobiography, as written by his second wife, is a mine of information; it reveals that H had a remarkable and sensitive memory. The Dorset countryside is also an important mine. H was influenced by the problems of his age, a period of spiritual and physical unrest typified by the railway. Changes in the old ways affected him and his writing, though he was not a reformer. His mother, who loved reading, was the basis for Bathsheba. The Hardys loved music, played in church and at country dances. H was a delicate child, precocious and sensitive. Early incidents of a half-frozen bird and wishing he would never grow up remained with him all his life and are used in *Jude the Obscure*. H was imaginatively affected by romantic stories of earlier ladies of the manor in the vicinity, but Julia Augusta Martin was most influential on his life; he attended the school she built. She was his first love. Important were lines from Latin authors reflecting on the uncertainty of life: H's attitudes were set early. H reacted to executions he had seen— man's implacability to man. He learned Greek while an apprentice architect in Dorchester; he was much concerned with the question of adult baptism. Moule advised him on practical grounds to give up the study of Greek, but H went back to it later and had excellent knowledge of it. Tragic dramatists were of greater influence on his thought than Schopenhauer. In London, literary surroundings (opera, plays, dancing) were exciting to him. Worked as architect on church restoration. H's first assignment was overseeing removal of the remains from a graveyard to make way for railway. H studied literature intensively and won architectural prizes; read poetry exclusively for two years; and studied painting in museums (an enduring aspect of his work is his painter's eye). He wrote a number of poems between 1863 and 1867, showing most of his permanent characteristics as a poet. Despair in these poems is shared with other poets like Thomson and Swinburne and resulted from loss of optimistic faith. Mill and Swinburne influenced rebellion against religious concept of a beneficient universe. *The Poor Man and the Lady* shows some of H's later characteristics: good rural scenes, inability to handle society, melodrama and magnificent scenes, attack on social conventions. Not published, part of it later appeared as *An Indiscretion in the Life of an Heiress*, which shows dislike of aristocracy and their heedless power. *Desperate Remedies* is sensational in plot but shows power of characterization and description. The first two novels (along with *A Pair of Blue Eyes*) are typified by death-bed, churchyard scenes, and fantasy life, found in many later novels. All show deep inner tendencies of H's own. Emma Lavinia Gifford was a vital, impulsive, alive person, fond of nature and riding. Their courtship was mostly at a distance, although H got to Cornwall two or three times a year. Although discouraged over his writing, H wrote *Under the Greenwood Tree*, with success. It is a prose idyll, has descriptions reminiscent of Dutch painters, history of old church musicians unlike anything else in English, and reveals H's extreme responsiveness to music. *Blue Eyes* is notable for vivid scenes, especially the Knight clinging to the cliff, and for the quality of its poetical tragedy. The novel shows a changed attitude toward woman (sympathetic), the theme of mis-mating, desertion, and belated return to first love: shows H's personal conflicts. *Far From the Madding Crowd* is his finest early novel, has moving descriptions, shows a love of color and music and a capacity for joy and pain, has poetic similes and metaphors which are especially brilliant. H and Leslie Stephen are similar in many ways, although Stephen's loss of religious faith was easier for him. Success of *Madding Crowd* enabled H to marry. He made a serious study of style, developing his own tendencies. *The Hand of Ethelberta* was not a success but has some important points—social criticism, Ethelberta's independence. *The Return of the Native* is the most pagan of H's books. Egdon Heath is not only a protagonist but related to the Immanent Will; characters are emanations of the Heath. In London, H met important literary and artistic people. *The Trumpet-Major*, a new departure, is part historical, part local tradition; a delicate, charming book with wonderfully sensuous descriptions of food and drink, and cinematic technique. During long illness H dictated *A Laodicean*, the weakest of his books, but autobiographical. H pondered the relation between emotional and scientific attitudes toward life. He wrote many short stories from 1879–1900; the best are the "Withered Arm" and the "Fiddler of the Reels." *Two on a Tower* has the theme of an ordinary man loving the lady of the manor and shows fascination with stars, sense of desolation. *The Mayor of Casterbridge* is unique in its powerful and complex man-protagonist. By this time H decided stoicism was the only proper attitude. *Mayor* is remorseless; Henchard is driven by inner destructive forces he does not comprehend. *The Woodlanders* shows understanding of growing things, wonderful descriptions of nature. A transitional novel, looking ahead to *Jude* in treatment of marriage, it is pastoral in a classical sense. H often visited London, admired late Turner paintings; in many ways H is much like Turner in suppressed violence of his nature. During travels in Italy, H became interested in pagan past. *A Group of Noble Dames* shows interest in genealogy, as does *Tess of the d'Urbervilles*. *Tess* is basically didactic. H went back to his early reading of Greek tragedians and Darwin, Huxley, Mill. Tess is a complex character with a strain of martyrdom. This beautiful book has wonderful descriptions, lyrical imagery, many threads from H's past, people known. H is intensely sympathetic toward suffering at this time. *Jude* is a novel of the war between flesh and spirit, contrasts. Violent reactions to it were due to bitterness of disillusionment more than attacks on conventions. D. H. Lawrence says that *Jude* is not a real tragedy because characters do not really rebel against fate, only society. *The Well-Beloved* is a fantasy; H was long intrigued both with Platonic Idea and Portland. Unhappiness in marriage is important to attitude in the last novels and poems of this period; Emma became increasingly eccentric and egotistical, verging on insanity. H wrote a fine series of poems expressing his love and remorse. *The Dynasts* shows lifelong interest in Napoleonic period and in philosophic themes, but it is especially notable for the realism he could not put in his novels and stories. Spirits enabled him to penetrate behind appearances to the "substance of things not seen." An examination of the MS demonstrates the poet's mind at work. *Dynasts* is a magnificent accomplishment. Florence Dugdale was an invaluable helpmate in his old age. H continued lyric poetry, concerned with love and death, also narrative and philosophical, dealing with the why of existence and the problem of pain. The spirit of his poetry is irony and pity. H was not interested in success.

2431 Holland, Norman. *"Jude the Obscure*: Hardy's Symbolic Indictment of Christianity," Nineteenth Century Fiction, IX (June 1954), 50–60.

Jude the Obscure marks the transition in H's writing from fiction to poetry, from depicting people and events realistically to transforming them into non-realistic symbols. The animal imagery surrounding Arabella Donn is one of the most obvious of the clusters of images which center on Jewish, Christian, and pagan religious symbols. Another prominent group is that which focuses on the characters' names and their almost allegorical interrelationships. Especially notable in this regard is the Christ-figure of Little Father Time, and much of the imagery coalesces around his "crucifixion." The location of his death, Christminster, has been established in the first chapters as the "heavenly Jerusalem" and the repository of all of Jude's highest aspirations. Furthermore, Sue's frigidity imparts an aura of virginity to her, even in motherhood. The final tragedy is intensified by the convergence of several clusters of religious images. Jude, the Jew, is left bitter and unredeemed, while Sue, the pagan, is seduced from the pursual of broad, classical ethics to restrictive Victorian conventionality. The self-styled Christian society in which these characters fulfill their destinies lauds self-sacrifice yet renders it futile, largely through the imposition of a stultifying and artificial moral code, totally unrelated to the concept of Christian love and tolerance. H's message is quite clear: the only Christian ideal worthy of preservation is not that of self-sacrifice but rather that of the love for one's fellow man that makes life tolerable.

2432 Knott, Olive. "The Philosophy of Hardy," Dorset Yearbook, 1954–1955, p. 26.

"Unable to reconcile the suffering of humanity with the existence of a loving God, he [H] erects a deity of his own imagination for whom the vicissitudes of mortals provide a sportive pastime." H's supposed pessimism is rather "an awareness": "he loved humanity and would fain have offered it the solace which he sought in vain."

2433 Korg, Jacob. "Hardy's *The Dynasts*: A Prophecy," SOUTH ATLANTIC QUARTERLY, LIII (Jan 1954), 24–32.
A source for *The Dynasts* is Robert Buchanan's A DRAMA OF KINGS. The poem compares in technique with the cinematic excellences of GONE WITH THE WIND. It is a "premonition of this mass abdication of the will which makes it impossible to think of war as serving any human ends."

2434 Leclaire, Lucien. LE ROMAN RÉGIONALISTE DANS LES ÎLES BRITANNIQUES 1800–1950 (The Regional Novel in the British Isles 1800–1950) (Paris: Société d'édition "Les Belles Lettres," 1954).
H is the first to dedicate a group of novels to a certain region, under the name of Wessex. The first occurrence is in *Far From the Madding Crowd*. H's intention, however, was to use the precision of local detail to give unity to the scene but a single story was not enough for his objective. The idea "Wessex" precedes the term which gives order to the composition, has significance but does not give the interpretation. H speaks as an architect and "archaeologue." As both he contributes to the design and the depiction: dimension, passing states, forms, and nuances. H's observations of nature are rich, but most especially of the sounds of nature. Prehistoric traces and Roman remains have an importance in the action. The characters are essential to the region. The region of the sea and field dependent on the seasons is important since Tess, Giles Winterborne, Henchard, etc. need contact with the fields and woods to live and die. The total effect is that of truth. Also, there is an element of separation between H and the region. There are terrible and tragic events, but beauty, peace, etc. should also be natural. H's philosophy moves his novels to irrevocable destruction. All is reduced, however, to the rapport between the destiny of man and the fact of his existence. H's people possess the earth and through their contact with it acquire a fatalism without indignation.

[Listed with H as graphic regional novelists: Richard Doddridge Blackmore, William Black, William Alexander, Mary Linskill, Peter Magennis, Richard Jeffries, Elizabeth Owens Blackburne, Richard Dowling, Sabine Baring-Gould, Charles Gibbon, David Christie Murray, William Westall, Annie Swan (pseud of Mrs. Burnett-Jones), Amelia Barr, Sir Hall Caine, Wesley Guard Lyttle, Emily Lawless, Robert Louis Stevenson, Walter Raymond. H is the point of comparison for the above.

Listed with H as regional, but sentimental, novelists: Sir James Matthew Barrie, Sir Arthur Quiller-Couch, Edith Oenone Somerville, Joseph Henry Pearce, William Edward Tirebuck, Jane Barlow, Joseph Smith Fletcher, Charles Allen Clarke, Samuel Rutherford Crockett, Gabriel Setoun, Howard Pease, James Keighley Snowden, M. E. Francis (pseud of Mrs. Francis Blundell), Henry Dawson Lowry, Seumas MacManus, Shan Bullock,

Joseph Hocking, Ian Maclaren (pseud of Rev. John Watson), Fiona McCleod (pseud of William Sharp), James Marshall Mather, Katherine Tynan, David Storrar Meldrum, Patrick Augustine Sheehan, John Ackworth (pseud of Rev. Frederick R. Smith), Jane Helen Findlater, Mary Findlater, Mary Hamilton, Neil Munro, Joseph Laing Waugh, Eden Phillpotts, James Prior.

Regional realists influenced to some degree by H: Archibald MacIlroy, Allen Raine (pseud of Anna Adeliza Beynon), Haliwell Sutcliffe, Gwendoline Keats, Violet Hobhouse, Matilda Barbara Betham Edwards, Mrs. Henry Dudeney, Omre Angus (pseud of John C. Higginbotham), J. Henry Harris, Dorothea Conyers, George Douglas (pseud of George Douglas Brown), George Bourne, Joseph Keating, Stephen Lucius Gwynn, A. P. A. O'Gara (pseud of W. R. MacDermott), Violet Jacob, John Joy Bell, George Moore, William Buckley, John Weyman, Rev. Joseph Guinan, John Trevena (pseud of Ernest George Henham), Jan Stewer (pseud of Albert John Coles), George Birmingham (pseud of Rev. James Owen Hannay), Edward C. Booth, Florence Bone, Lynn Doyle (pseud of Leslie Alexander Montgomery), Sheila Kaye-Smith, Hugh Seymour Walpole, Frances Elizabeth Crichton, Seumas O'Kelly, Dr. McIntyre de Rothesay (pseud of John Brandane), Stephen Andrew (pseud of Dr. Frank Layton), James Bryce (pseud of Alexander Anderson), Tickner Edwards, W. Cribb, J. Macdougall Hay.

Novelists of interpretative regionalism who demonstrate resemblance to H: David Herbert Lawrence, William Riley, Dermot O'Bryne, Horace Annesley Vachell, George Woden, Frederick Niven, Francis Brett Young, Alexander Irvine, Constance Holme, Katherine Frances Purdon, Caradoc Evans, John Cowper Powys, Theodore Francis Powys, Daniel Cokery, Mary Webb, John Heron Lepper, Amy Dawson-Scott, Michael Ireland (pseud of Darrel Figgis), Patrick MacGill, Brinsley MacNamara, Thomas Moult, Dot Allan, John Sillars, John C. Tregarthen, Henry Williamson, Christine Orr, Edward Albert, George Blake, John Smellie Martin, Winifred Hotby, Liam O'Flaherty, L. A. G. Strong, Hilda Vaughan, John Carruthers (pseud of John Y. Th. Greig), Helen G. Davies, Meil Miller Gunn, William Black, Peadar O'Donnell, Ralph Hale Mottram, Margaret Storm Jameson, Harold Webster Freeman, Hubert Quinn, Edith Marjorie Ward, Phyllis Eleanor Bentley, James Lansdale Hodson, Lettice Cooper, Rhys Davies, Harold Heslop, Russell Linklater, Thomas James Morrison, Claire Spencer, Nancy Brysson Morrison, John Cecil Moore, G. Stowell, Margaret Leigh, Adrian Bell, A. G. Street, James Hanley, Samuel Levy Bensusan, Frank O'Connor (pseud of Michael O'Donovan), Ian Macpherson, Sean O'Faolain, John Galt, James Lennox Kerr, Herbert E. Bates, Frederick Cecil Boden, Leo Walmsley, Doreen Wallace, Dorothy Mabel Large, Thomas Thompson,

Walter Greenwood, Roger Dataller, Michael Home, Elizabeth Goudge, Naomi Jacob, Russell Green, Jack Jones, Agnes Romilly White, Pat Mullen, Francis MacManus, Nan C. Rogers, Meta Mayne-Reid, Geraint Goodwin, Margiad Evans, Gwyn Jones, Glyn Jones, Elizabeth Macpherson, Patrick Greer, Lewis Jones, Richard Llewellyn.] [In French.]

2435 Levy, William Turner. "An Introduction to the Poetry of William Barnes," DISSERTATION ABSTRACTS, XIV (1954), 1398. Unpublished dissertation, Columbia University, 1953.

2436 Lüdeke, Henry. DIE ENGLISCHE LITERATUR: EIN KULTUR-HISTORISCHER UMRISS (English Literature: A Cultural-Historical Outline) (Munich: Lehnen, 1954), pp. 96–97, 124.
H increases Meredith's tragic sentiment. [In German.]

2437 P., H. "The Poet Keats and Lulworth Cove," DORSET YEAR-BOOK, 1954–1955, p. 134.
H believed "that Keats was related to a family who lived not far from Dorchester."

2438 Paterson, John. *The Return of the Native*: A Study in the Genesis and Development of a Novel," DISSERTATION ABSTRACTS, XIV (1954), 1216; University of Michigan dissertation; rvd as THE MAKING OF THE RETURN OF THE NATIVE (Berkeley & Los Angeles: University of California P, 1960).
The manuscript of *The Return of the Native* had its origin as an Ur-novel. A study of this manuscript and the serial text reveals that originally Eustacia was Satanic in a more than metaphorical sense; Clym was intended to function as Thomasin's brother; classical motives did not predominate; Diggory Venn and Captain Vye were social equals. Seemingly the novel was to have dealt with rural melodrama rather than romantic love and aspirations. When H revised the serial text for the first edition in Nov 1878, he made a number of changes. Thus, Diggory is transformed from an "uncouth countryman to middle-class dairy-farmer" and is made less grotesque; "the contours of Mrs. Yeobright's character" are softened; Damon is presented as a young man rather than an adult philanderer; Eustacia is made less Satanic; Clym is presented unsuccessfully as a hero in the tradition of the Greeks; greater prominence is given to sexual implications. In general, the first edition "sought to counteract the damaging influences of haste, pressure and censorship" which had caused H to suppress in the manuscript and the serial edition whatever was morally discreditable. When preparing the Uniform Edition of 1895, H made additional changes, some of which consolidated the changes made in the first edition and others of which added new dimensions to the novel. Thus, Diggory is defined more vaguely and eventually acquires a "symbolic function." Clym, formerly a jeweler's assistant, be-

comes a jeweler's manager. Eustacia is not only less Satanic but also acquires a new dimension by being identified for the first time "with the brilliant and mysterious civilization of ancient Greece." In the Uniform Edition, as well as in the Wessex Edition of 1912, H revealed a special interest in Eustacia, but in the latter edition his main objective was "to readjust the half-real, half-imaginary landscape in the novel." In achieving this objective, it became clear that H was a better artist than he cared to admit. Ultimately, his effectiveness in revising refutes the standard charge that he was too obvious and mechanical in his method. In particular, the symmetry of *Native* cannot "be ascribed to the mechanical influence of a blueprint or an outline," since not even the quartet of lovers was part of a preconceived plan: Clym was to have been Thomasin's brother. Furthermore, the additions and revisions suggest that "a critically aware intelligence" provided at least a minor note in creating a novel which was amplified and particularized until it offered symbolic comment. Ultimately, H achieved a rational comprehension of the materials he used in *Native*.

2439 Pentin, The Rev. Canon Herbert. "Thomas Hardy and Milton Abbey," COLBY LIBRARY QUARTERLY, III (Nov 1954), 262–64.

H had particular interest in the history and lore of Milton Abbey and in Dorset songs and doggerel rhymes generally. [Reprints H's letter of 23 Feb 1905 on the subject.]

2440 Purdy, Richard Little. THOMAS HARDY: A BIBLIOGRAPHICAL STUDY (Lond, NY, Toronto: Oxford UP, 1954); rptd (1968).

[The book contains four chief divisions: "Editions Principes," "Collected Editions," "Uncollected Contributions to Books, Periodicals, and Newspapers," and "Appendixes." Notes concerning conditions under which the novels were written and identifying characters, incidents, and places in the poems are especially helpful. Location of MSS under each appropriate work is an aid to studies of a textual nature. The standard bibliographical tool for H students.]

2441 Shawe-Taylor, Desmond. "Britten and Hardy," NEW STATESMAN AND NATION, XLVII (30 Jan 1954), 127–28.

Before Britten, only Gerald Finzi and John Ireland have set H's poems to music. H's simplicity is coupled with much that is comical, quaint and crude; his verses are an old curiosity shop where fine pieces of local ware lie side by side with commercial gimcrack. Benjamin Britten's song cycle, including eight H songs, is called WINTER WORDS (among them "Wagtail and Baby," "The Little Old Table," "The Choirmaster's Burial," and "Before Life and After").

2442 Slack, Robert C. "A Variorum Edition of Thomas Hardy's *Jude the Obscure*," PITTSBURGH UNIVERSITY GRADUATE SCHOOL ABSTRACTS, L (1954), 8–11. Unpublished dissertation, University of Pittsburgh, 1953.

2443 Spivey, Ted R. "Thomas Hardy's Tragic Hero," NINE-TEENTH CENTURY FICTION, IX (Dec 1954), 179–91.

H's tragic heroes are, to a great degree, responsible for his greatness. A complex attitude characterizes a tragic hero; he must at once defy and accept his downfall. This "demands not only a passionate spirit but also an imaginative intellect that realizes the enormity of the forces of evil." In H's work, Tess, Henchard and Sue all display this attitude. Moreover, the forces that effect the downfall of the tragic hero must come from within as well as from without. Tess, Sue, Jude, Henchard, Clym, and Eustacia all possess tragic flaws which, in addition to outside forces, lead to their downfall. A great deal of our appreciation of some of H's characters as tragic heroes must spring from our recognition of them as romantic heroes "whose desires are never fulfilled, but whose spirits, in the best traditions of tragedy, are never crushed." Eustacia is perhaps the most fully developed of this type in H. For H, tragedy consists in having foiled the romantic hero's bid for a higher spiritual state, while his spirit remains undaunted.

2444 Stephen, Leslie. "Six Letters of Leslie Stephen as Editor of the CORNHILL Relating to *Far From the Madding Crowd*," in THOMAS HARDY: A BIBLIOGRAPHICAL STUDY, by Richard L. Purdy (1954), Appendix II, pp. 336–39.

[Contains one letter written in 1872 after Stephen had read *Under the Greenwood Tree*, inviting H to offer a story to the CORNHILL. Other letters, dated 1874, deal with the publication of *Far From the Madding Crowd*, suggesting abridgment of certain passages to allow for the exigencies of magazine publication and apologizing for necessary prudery, especially regarding the cause of the death of Fanny Robin and the possible omission of the baby, "in the interest of a stupid public, not from my own taste."]

2445 "Thomas Hardy," DER GROSSE BROCKHAUS (The Large Brockhaus [Encyclopedia]) (Wiesbaden: F. A. Brockhaus, 1954), V, 263.

Wessex is the background for H's tragic philosophy. [Works and criticisms listed.] [In German.]

2446 "Thomas Hardy," DER GROSSE HERDER (The Large Herder [Encyclopedia]) (Freiburg: Herder, 1954), IV, 625.

Fate plays an important part in H's masterfully described Wessex. [Includes portrait, dates, list of novels and their translations.] [In German.]

2447 Tillyard, E. M. W. THE ENGLISH EPIC AND ITS BACK-GROUND (Lond: Chatto & Windus, 1954), pp. 14, 531.
[Mentions *The Dynasts* as being of epic scope, though Tillyard excludes the dramatic from his study.]

2448 [Weber, Carl J.]. " 'Coaching' an Illustrator," COLBY LIBRARY QUARTERLY, III (May 1954), 229–30.
[Reprints a letter of 5 June 1885 from Arthur Locker, editor of GRAPHIC, to Robert Barnes concerning his assignment to prepare illustrations for the magazine's serialization of *The Mayor of Casterbridge*. Two of H's suggestions appear in the letter, as well as recent praise of Barnes's work.]

2449 [Weber, Carl J.]. "Hardy's Burial," COLBY LIBRARY QUAR-TERLY, III (Nov 1954), 268.
Sir Sydney Cockerell's statement that "Thomas Hardy was *not* opposed to the idea of burial in Westminster Abbey" is correct, as H's design for his own memorial tablet in St. Juliot Church, Cornwall, shows.

2450 Weber, Carl J. (ed). THE LETTERS OF THOMAS HARDY, TRANSCRIBED FROM THE ORIGINAL AUTOGRAPHS NOW IN THE COLBY COLLEGE LIBRARY, ed with an introduction and notes by Carl J. Weber (Waterville, Maine: Colby College P, 1954); rptd NY: Kraus, 1970).
[Weber supplies headnotes, commentary, and copious notes relating the letters to H's works and life. The letters cover the period from 1873 to 1927. The list of recipients and the index are most useful.]

2451 [Weber, Carl J.]. "Russian Translations of Hardy," COLBY LIBRARY QUARTERLY, III (Aug 1954), 253–56.
[A rebuttal of Kenneth E. Harper and Bradford A. Booth's article "Russian Translations of Nineteenth Century Fiction," NINETEENTH CENTURY FIC-TION, VIII (Dec 1953), 187–97, listing only an 1893 translation of *Tess of the d'Urbervilles*. It is not safe to claim H's best works have been ne-glected in Russia, or in the Slavic countries generally.]

2452 [Weber, Carl J.]. "*Tess* Since 'Forty-one," COLBY LIBRARY QUARTERLY, III (May 1954), 232–34.
[Besides listing fourteen additions to the Colby materials on *Tess of the d'Urbervilles* since the fiftieth anniversary listing in the catalogue, THE JUBILEE OF TESS (1941), the author tells of an abortive plan for an edition to be illustrated with his photographs. Autographed picture of H is at end of issue.]

2453 White, Sydney J. "Shaston: the Ancient British Pallador," DORSET YEARBOOK, 1954–1955, pp. 163–64.

H "must have been fond of this beautiful view [illustration] from Castle Hill, Shaftesbury" which he called "Shaston" in *Jude the Obscure*.

2454 White, Sydney J. "Thomas Hardy's Casterbridge," DORSET YEARBOOK, 1954–1955, pp. 61–64.
[Guide to some scenes in Dorchester which correspond to those in *The Mayor of Casterbridge*.]

1955

2455 Allen, Walter. THE ENGLISH NOVEL (Lond: Phoenix House, 1954), pp. 232–46; also (NY: Dutton, 1955), pp. 100, 260, 285–304.
H's view of life, which dictates the way we react to his characters, is implicit in each sentence he writes. H's prose is fresher than George Eliot's. His peasants are simple. H is primarily a storyteller; his strength lies in the fact that he is a country man. Like Scott, his characters live in history—part of the earth that has changed little over the centuries. Social life in his novels scarcely exists; his characters stand in relation to other things—the weather, seasons, etc. There is not often individuality in H's novels. H was intellectually advanced for his time in showing the changing times and holding a pessimistic view of religion. H's greatness is due to the combination of his philosophical pessimism and his habit of seeing human behavior in its most abiding aspects. H rises to tragedy in his arraignment of the universe. His cosmic view raises *The Return of the Native* to the level of tragedy. In H, "the only characters who need fear no fall are those already down." A key to H's mind is in the characterizations of *Native*. H's faults are that his plots sometimes "creak," his villains are "melodramatic," and his prose is often "clumsy."

2456 Baker, James R. "Thematic Ambiguity in *The Mayor of Casterbridge*," TWENTIETH CENTURY LITERATURE, I (April 1955), 13–16.
The novel's fault is that Henchard is a "unique case" who fails to provide an "adequate basis for Hardy's concluding generalization." The work's conclusion should be modified to read: "Life is a general drama of pain *for the moral deviate*," because Henchard is "as much a victim of adverse circumstance as he is of moral conscience." Since the cause of Henchard's downfall is ambiguous, we are left with the question: "Is man's suffering due merely to circumstance, or is it due to his moral flaws?" H probably intended the former, but he made his "symbolic victim" more acceptable to readers by showing that he "was culpable on the moral level."

2457 Bartlett, Phyllis. "Hardy's Shelley," Keats-Shelley Journal, IV (Winter 1955), 15–29.

An examination of H's copy of Queen Mab and Other Poems and especially of H's markings of Prometheus Unbound shows that H was especially interested in Shelley's active verbs and descriptions of natural phenomena and that H probably re-read Prometheus Unbound before beginning *The Dynasts*. In ideas, the Shelleyan sense of pity appealed to H, as did Shelley's view of the tyranny of custom, such as marriage bonds, religion, etc. Shelley's interest in science also was akin to H's; both were evolutionary meliorists.

2458 Bartlett, Phyllis. " 'Seraph of Heaven': A Shelleyan Dream in Hardy's Fiction," Publications of the Modern Language Association, LXX (Sept 1955), 624–35.

H's 1866 underlinings in Shelley show his concern with the platonic ideal of perfection lodging in separate beautiful women, as seen in "Epipsychidion." *The Well-Beloved* employs such a philosophy, and Robert Trewe, in "An Imaginative Woman," pursues this calamitous ideal. Sue Bridehead is H's "mature" study of the Shelleyan woman who sees herself more as seraph than fleshly human being and wishes to emanate an "ideal and remote radiance." H does not deplore Sue but rather the collapse of her reasoning power in the face of social convention.

2459 Clifford, E. A. "Thomas Hardy's View of History." Unpublished dissertation, Bristol University, 1955.

[Listed in Lawrence F. McNamee, Dissertations in English and American Literature (NY & Lond: Bowker, 1968).]

2460 De la Mare, Walter. "Meeting Thomas Hardy," Listener, LIII (29 April 1955), 756–57.

"Hardy was not wholly within his novels." Nor do Chesterton's and George Moore's comments truly present H as he was. He was quite courteous and modest. He enjoyed showing de la Mare his home and parts of the nearby "Wessex" countryside.

2461 Ervine, St. John. "Portrait of Thomas Hardy," Listener, LIV (8 Sept 1955), 371–72.

H was neither so antisocial nor so pessimistic as many now think. He turned from fiction to poetry not because of the outcry against *Jude the Obscure* but because poetry had always been his first love. The construction of the novels shows that H never forgot his early architectural interests.

2462 Guérard, Albert J. "Introduction," *Tess of the d'Urbervilles*, by Thomas Hardy (NY: Washington Square P, 1955), pp. v–viii; rptd in Twentieth Century Interpretations of Tess of the d'Urbervilles, ed by Albert J. LaValley (Englewood Cliffs, NJ: Prentice-Hall, 1969).

In *Tess of the d'Urbervilles*, H succeeds in creating a "fine unforced sympathy and natural humility . . . in the face of basic human difficulties." In doing so he set himself apart from Dickens, Thackeray, Eliot and Trollope who were all, "in some sense, patronizing: patronizing toward their characters or their readers or both." In *Tess*, H wrote his first best seller, which was to become, in due time, one of the great English novels.

2463 Hardy, Evelyn (ed). THOMAS HARDY'S NOTEBOOKS, AND SOME LETTERS FROM JULIA AUGUSTA MARTIN (Lond: Hogarth P, 1955).

The first notebook covers the period from 1867 to 1920, the second, the period from 1921 to 1928, and the fragment of a third (notebook for *The Trumpet-Major*) covers the 1878–1880 period. The Martin-H letters were written from 1863 to 1887. The notebooks were screened and edited by H in 1921 and 1923, and H drew heavily on the second when writing THE LATER YEARS, by Florence Hardy (1930). The notebooks are "in no sense unreserved records of emotional or intellectual experiences," rather they are unpolished nuggets of thoughts, details of rural and social life, comments on poetic contemporaries, passing thoughts and observations. [Also included in this volume are the only extant letters to H from his boyhood lady of the manor, Julia Augusta Martin, wife of Francis Pitney Brouncker Martin of Kingston Maurward, near Stinsford. The letters reveal that H learned his letters at the knee of Julia Augusta who built and staffed, at her own expense, a school for the neighboring children but seemed to have selected young H as her favorite.]

2464 Hough, Graham. "The Novel as Exploration," LISTENER, LIII (20 Jan 1955), 111, 114–15.

In the last eighty years, there has been a change in attitude on the part of some novelists toward the proper function of their art. The novel ceases to be solely entertainment and becomes something of an exploration. The novelist as explorer attempts to "discover the undercurrents of feeling that are present in his time but have not yet come to the surface." The explorer-novelist is interested in some aspect of the human condition, and often he momentarily abandons the advancement of plot in order to explore his own vision. "Hardy sees his characters as tiny, insignificant specks. Yet these infinitely small and feeble creatures have a consciousness that can in some measure apprehend the enormous whole. This is Hardy's problem, and to get this into the framework of a novel is something outside the range of novelist as entertainer."

2465 Hübner, Walter. EPOCHEN DER ENGLISCHEN LITERATUR (Epochs of English Literature) (Frankfurt/Main, Berlin, Bonn: Moritz Diesterweg, 1955), pp. 100, 102, 105, 111.

Among innovators of the Victorian era, H rejected the positive correlation between evolution and improvement, broadened the scope of the regional novel, challenged sentimental optimism, and helped establish the psychological novel. [In German.]

2466 Johnson, Wendell Stacy. "Some Functions of Poetic Form," JOURNAL OF AESTHETICS AND ART CRITICISM, XIII (June 1955), 496–506.

"The Convergence of the Twain" is an example "of the embodiment of idea in poetry"; the form mirrors the content.

2467 Kreuzer, James R. ELEMENTS OF POETRY (NY: Macmillan, 1955), pp. 135–36, 161–64, 172–73.

["The Darkling Thrush" is reprinted, with study questions for analysis of imagery; symbolism in "During Wind and Rain" is analyzed; "In Time of 'the Breaking of Nations' " is included "for further analysis."]

2468 Matchett, William H. *"The Woodlanders* or Realism in Sheep's Clothing," NINETEENTH CENTURY FICTION, IX (March 1955), 241–61.

Realistic novels are "those works . . . in which an author has attempted to give his view of reality, provided that the view is one which the readers can accept as coherent, mature and founded on the facts of experience." In much contemporary fiction, however, the artist is not involved with the rendering of his view of reality; rather he uses realistic detail to disguise a vulgar sentimentalism. In *The Woodlanders*, H "attempted to combine the elements in the opposite way, molding a realistic intention to the requirements of a sentimental form." Superficially, H was involved with the interpenetration of four sentimental concerns in the novel (the stories of Marty South, Giles Winterborne, Grace Melbury, and Mrs. Charmond). The ironic coincidences in the novel should be seen in terms of the interaction of these concerns. "The world . . . is so densely packed that every event vibrates through every other and is likely to turn back on itself and destroy what it has created." Moreover, H uses personifications of setting and manipulation of symbol to guide us to the correct interpretation of the novel. "The result lives up to the intention and must be considered a convincing example of a tenable view of reality."

2469 Morcos, Louis. *"The Dynasts* and the Bible," BULLETIN OF ENGLISH STUDIES (Cairo, Egypt), 1955, pp. 29–65.

H's knowledge of the Bible and his early interest in it is reflected in all his works, but he had a particular interest in the Old Testament, especially the Book of Job, which is very apparent in *The Dynasts*. In his drama H deliberately divided Jehovah's and Satan's personalities among a few Spirits. Contrary to the Book of Job, however, H shows no "direct mutual relationships between man and the universe" or man and God. Furthermore "one man on earth is not the centre of interest in *Dynasts* . . . but the greater part of the Continent of Europe." There are many "passages in which Hardy was obviously inspired by Biblical reminiscences"—passages from John, Luke, Matthew, Jeremiah, Ezekiel, and many other books of the Old Testament. Even so H "deliberately cast aside the teaching of the Bible and adopted another way of thinking." "While Hardy carefully avoided any unnecessary allusions to things Christian or Biblical, he fell back, consciously or unconsciously, on Biblical phrases and imagery for literary effect, and for more subtle shades of thought, emotion of description."

2470 Morcos, Louis. "The Manuscript of Thomas Hardy's *The Dynasts*," ANNALS OF THE FACULTY OF ARTS (Ain Shams University, Cairo, Egypt), III (Jan 1955), 1–39.

H made interesting changes in the forescene and afterscene of *The Dynasts* before publishing the work, as examination of the MS in the British Museum shows. Comparison of the two versions shows that the philosophy of *Dynasts* was not cut-and-dried, but "in evolution, at times in abrupt evolution" as H reworked the poem. The changes show that H revised "more to be true to himself than for any other reason." When H began writing *Dynasts,* the conception of the Immanent Will was "in a very nebulous state in his mind"; as the work progressed his conception evolved "until in the afterscene he is forced to abandon it." That is, while H first wrote " 'Consciousness the Will *expanding*,' " his final thought was " 'the Will *informing*,' " which promises that "the world will be delivered" by the radical change in the Will.

2471 Pilkington, Frederick. "Religion in Hardy's Novels," CONTEMPORARY REVIEW, CLXXXVIII (July 1955), 31–35.

H's Wessex characters are victims of the bankruptcy of humanism, their environment, and heredity. Unable to find their way through tribulation, they end in a pagan death. "As a novelist Thomas Hardy reveals man's need for a savior." Jude, Arabella, Tess, and others struggle with a fate which is really H's projection of social change in a blighted world. Although evil overwhelms them, their rejection of the responsibility of Christian faith helps to advance their suffering and destruction. Marty South's final soliloquy shows the power of undying love and faith. Angel Clare's final realization hints at the mystery of life. [Biased, apparently Calvinist.]

2472 Sorensen, Morten. "*Tess* in Icelandic," COLBY LIBRARY QUARTERLY, IV (Aug 1955), 63.

Tess of the d'Urbervilles has been translated into Icelandic by Snaebjörn Jónsson (1954).

2473 Spivey, Ted R. "Two Visions of Character and Fate: A Study of Themes and Major Characters in the Novels of Thomas Hardy and George Eliot," DISSERTATION ABSTRACTS, XV (1955), 127. Unpublished dissertation, University of Minnesota, 1954.

2474 Teets, Bruce E. "Thomas Hardy's *The Dynasts*. A Critical Study." Unpublished dissertation, Duke University, 1955.
[Listed in Lawrence F. McNamee, DISSERTATIONS IN ENGLISH AND AMERICAN LITERATURE (NY & Lond: Bowker, 1968).]

2475 Templeman, W. D. "Hardy's Wife-Selling Incident and a Letter by Warren Hastings," HUNTINGTON LIBRARY QUARTERLY, XVIII (Feb 1955), 183–87.
A letter from Warren Hastings to a kinsman describes an incident of wife-selling very similar to that opening *The Mayor of Casterbridge*. The story is not a certain source, but the events took place near H's "Casterbridge," and it may "have served as at least partial basis" for H's account.

2476 Tunk, Eduard von. ILLUSTRIERTE WELTLITERATURGESCHICHTE (Illustrated World Literary History) (Zurich: Stauffacher, 1955), III, 342–43, 361.
H belongs to the Naturalist school. [Describes each work in a sentence.] [In German.]

2477 Untermeyer, Louis. MAKERS OF THE MODERN WORLD (NY: Simon & Schuster, 1955), pp. 56, 165–69, 206, 277.
Melville's verse, greatly underrated, has the rough meter and gnarled syllables of H. "Hardy never compromised between truth as he saw it and the complacently unctuous taste of his times." "Indifference is . . . at the heart of creation." Fatalism, accident, chance, skepticism, joylessness, but not hopelessness, are elements of his philosophy. "He could not regard a pitiless universe without pity." His prose is "ungainly and his poetry seems clumsy and involved," but he "brought a tart, talk-flavoured idiom to modern poetry; he gave it not only fresh blood but tough sinews." Hopkins's affirmations were replies to the skepticism of H and Housman. Housman's stoicism is reminiscent of H.

2478 [Weber, Carl J.]. "Autograph Letters," COLBY LIBRARY QUARTERLY, IV (Aug 1955), 68–71.
[An annotated transcription of three unpublished H letters given the Colby College Library: to Miss Smith (an American admirer), to the Rev. Herbert Pentin, and to (Clement Shorter?).]

2479 Weber, Carl J. "Hardy Notes," COLBY LIBRARY QUARTERLY, IV (Nov 1955), 84–86.
[A record of the receipt by the Colby College Library of various H items, including a transcript of an autograph letter to John Morley, sent with a copy of H's "The Dorsetshire Labourer."]

2480 Weber, Carl J. "Hermann Lea's Recollections of Thomas Hardy," DORSET YEARBOOK, 1955–1956, pp. 39–48.

H "played an active part, practically amounting to a collaboration," in the preparation of Lea's THOMAS HARDY'S WESSEX (1913). [Gives details of Lea's association with H and their many tours of Wessex together—based on Lea's unpublished recollections in the Dorset County Museum.]

2481 Yarmolinsky, Avrahm. "Hardy Behind the Iron Curtain," COLBY LIBRARY QUARTERLY, IV (Aug 1955), 64–66.
[A catalogue of translations of H's novels into Slavic languages.]

1956

2482 Asquith, Cynthia. "Thomas Hardy at Max Gate," LISTENER, LV (7 June 1956), 753–54.
H resembled a "shrewd, weather-wise farmer," more than he did the creator of *Tess of the d'Urbervilles* and *Jude the Obscure*. His concern about proper burial bordered on the comic at times. He read and admired the poems of Charlotte Mew.

2483 Bailey, J. O. THOMAS HARDY AND THE COSMIC MIND (Chapel Hill: University of North Carolina P; Lond: Oxford UP, 1956); rptd (Chapel Hill: University of North Carolina P, 1966).
The Dynasts shows the influence of Ernst Haeckl's "thoroughgoing determinism" and Eduard Von Hartmann's theory of the Unconscious. Nevertheless, it is not as pessimistic as the novels of the 1890s, as its hopeful conclusion indicates. This conclusion, "a paean of hope," stems naturally from a work which embodies the view that "evolutionary meliorism is possible, that the consciousness may be striving to express itself." The view may be taken as H's. In fact, it is clear that each General Chorus speaks for H. In contrast, it is clear that no one Spirit reflects all of H, although the Spirit of the Years reflects his thought and the Spirit of the Pities, his feelings and temperament. Furthermore, the Spirits collectively develop the thesis of *Dynasts* through a "clash" of opinions. Aided by his clash, H presents his "concept of the Will as unconscious Mind." He presents, also, a belief derived from Von Hartmann—reflection upon sensations and perceptions may lead to decisions to act. In particular, the Spirit of the Pities presents H's view that, informed by human consciousness, the Will may awaken. This leads naturally to the conclusion that gradually consciousness may spread to more and more people. In the future, the Will may be changed by human resistance when man's conscious reflection enables him to choose on the basis of reason rather than impulse. Of course, most characters in *Dynasts* do not serve the Will but are, instead,

subject to it. Notably, Napoleon is "a mechanism of the Will" in that he is "impelled toward power and command" by its "reasonless and insatiable hungers."

2484 Beer, Johannes, Wilhelm Olbrich, and Karl Weitzel (eds). DER ROMANFÜHRER (The Novel Guide), Vol VII (Stuttgart: Anton Hiersemann, 1956).
[Summarizes the plots of *Die Heimkehr* (*The Return of the Native*), *Eine reine Frau* (*Tess of the d'Urbervilles*), and *Juda der Unberühmte* (*Jude the Obscure*).] [In German.]

2485 Bellman, Samuel I. "How 'New' a Woman Was Hardy's Sue Bridehead?" COLBY LIBRARY QUARTERLY, IV (Aug 1956), 137–39.
Although Sue is "remarkable for her self-assertion," hers is not, by any means, the first portrait of a feminist. Aristophanes had described the type, and the "new woman" of the seventeenth and early eighteenth centuries is the subject of a recent critical study. In the nineteenth century, notable portraits appear in such works as Charles Brockden Brown's CLARA HOWARD and Ibsen's A DOLL'S HOUSE.

2486 Bellman, Samuel Irving. "Man As Alien, The Isolation Theme in Thomas Hardy," DISSERTATION ABSTRACTS, XVI (April–June 1956), 960. Unpublished dissertation, Ohio State University, 1955.

2487 Brown, T. J. "English Literary Autographs XIX: Thomas Hardy, 1840–1928," BOOK COLLECTOR, V (Autumn 1956), 249.
The "simple charity and unaffected innate elegance" of H's handwriting is the mark of the man: sensitive but strong. [Commentary on a photograph of a page from *Tess of the d'Urbervilles* MS showing alterations for serialization and three of the five names Tess was successively called.]

2488 Chaikin, Milton. "A Possible Source of Hardy's *The Well-Beloved*," MODERN LANGUAGE NOTES, LXXI (Nov 1956), 496–97.
The pattern of *The Well-Beloved* is borrowed from de Maupassant's FORTE COMME LA MORT (1889). This supports the opinion that H, in his later works, was greatly influenced by the French realists.

2489 Clifford, Emma. "WAR AND PEACE and *The Dynasts*," MODERN PHILOLOGY, LIV (Aug 1956), 33–44.
H's varied uses of Tolstoy materials are impressive. *The Dynasts* was prepared while H was surrounded by source books; the emotional coloring of small episodes and the depiction of Napoleon show debts to Tolstoy.

Tolstoy's treatment of Napoleon's mind as a philosophic problem is taken into the voices of the Spirits in H's work.

2490 Faverty, Frederic (ed). THE VICTORIAN POETS: A GUIDE TO RESEARCH (Cambridge: Harvard UP, 1956), pp. 21, 118, 136, 230–41.
[Useful annotated bibliography of H studies.]

2491 Gerber, Helmut E. "Hardy's 'A Tragedy of Two Ambitions,' " EXPLICATOR, XIV (June 1956), Item 55.
H's short story "A Tragedy of Two Ambitions" is organized by contrasts of light and dark, patterns of irony and symbolism, and incremental repetitions. Two important structural devices are the framing of the narrative by the references to the Epistle to the Hebrews and the repeated appearance of the father.

2492 Green, David Bonnell. "A Source for Hardy's 'The Duchess of Hamptonshire,' " NOTES AND QUERIES, CCI (Feb 1956), 86.
The basic plot in "The Duchess of Hamptonshire" is obviously taken from an experience of H's brother-in-law, the Reverend Caddell Holder. As a young man, Holder had been invited by a charming widow and two days later unknowingly buried her among the cholera victims of the great Bristol plague.

2493 Hardy, Evelyn. "Some Unpublished Poems by Thomas Hardy," LONDON MAGAZINE, III (Jan 1956), 28–39.
H's poetry "contains a number of paradoxes, none of them more curious than this—that it is lyric poetry very often expressed un-lyrically." As in the plots and characters of his novels and in his treatment of religion, H also disdained "conventional poetic expression." Six previously unpublished poems—"The Unplanted Primrose," "To a Bridegroom," "The Hatband," "She Would Welcome Old Tribulations," and "Thoughts from Sophocles" —were not included in *Winter Words*. The themes treated are "neglected love; a young man's fears of matrimony; the unreality and inherent tragedy of stage scenes and relationships; the early extinction of love in the heart of a former suitor, amounting to a threat to the immortality of the loved one; and a lighter comment on the comparative merits of youth and age." That "Sophocles" may have been written in the same year as *Jude the Obscure* and at least one of the "In Tenebris" poems, may account for *Jude*'s deeper tone. "Sophocles" proves that H read OEDIPUS AT COLONUS as well as OEDIPUS REX.

2494 Holmes, Lawrence Richard. "Hardy's 'Her Father,' " EX-PLICATOR, XIV (May 1956), Item 53.

The "cynic ghost" of line thirteen refers to "the voice of experience . . . the image of a former sweetheart for whom the loved had once felt a now suspiciously similar passion." This cynical view of the love's passing may be found also in "Neutral Tones" and other poems in this section of *The Collected Poems of Thomas Hardy*.

2495 Hutchings, Monica. Dorset River (Lond: Macdonald, 1956), pp. 11, 76, 144, 183–84.

[Dorset River is the River Stour, which flows "across some fifty miles of Hardy's countryside" and near which many of H's novels and poems are set. Miss Hutchings follows the Stour from its mouth at Bournemouth to its source, giving a faithful account of bird and plant life on its banks, as well as of towns, buildings, and other landmarks. Passing reference is made to the sale of certain of H's manuscripts by the Society for the Preservation of Ancient Buildings (in 1929?), to H's poem "Wagtail and Baby," and to *Tess of the d'Urbervilles*.]

2496 Hynes, Samuel. "The Pattern of Hardy's Poetry." Columbia University dissertation, 1956; pub as The Pattern of Hardy's Poetry (Chapel Hill: University of North Carolina P, 1961).

The pattern is "the eternal conflict between irreconcilables." H's method is antinomial rather than dialectical because there is no resolution. Style, to H, meant tone rather than literary finish. Antinomialism is reflected in his diction, both particular and abstract. He never developed a characteristic metric. H's metaphors are based on two "worlds"—of light, youth, and life and of dark, age, and death; the latter of which is dominant, the former of which forms a counterpoint (antinomial). H's imagery "produces tone rather than picture." H did not develop as a poet except that he became more characteristically personal, "a narrowing, not an expanding process." H's revisions do not alter the form or meaning of his poems but clarify them and refine the antinomial qualities. In *The Dynasts*, Napoleon is modern man, isolated from fellow men and helpless to change his fate. *Dynasts* has two worlds—human and spirit—to create an antinomy, supported by diction and imagery (as in lyrics); the speech by the Spirit of Pities at the end is not a resolution but only another point of view. *Dynasts* proves that H's antinomial pattern works on a large scale. [Objective and reasoned analysis; well-written.]

2497 Johnson, S. F. "Burke and Hardy," Times Literary Supplement (Lond), 7 Dec 1956, p. 731.

The passage in *The Return of the Native* explaining Mrs. Yeobright's ability to have an insight into life as similar to Blacklock's ability, though blind, to describe colors is a close paraphrase of a passage in Burke's Treatise on the Sublime and the Beautiful. Also, the idea that sublime is "rugged negligence" may have been confirmed by Burke. *Native* may have derived the sublimity ascribed to it from H's careful reading of Burke's treatise.

2498 Liddell, Robert. SOME PRINCIPLES OF FICTION (Lond: Cape, 1956), pp. 43–45.

The fact that there are two contradictory criticisms of a passage from *Far From the Madding Crowd* shows that "we need both 'academic' and 'practical' critics." "Hardy has said what he has to say badly, but not so badly that he has failed to say it: his meaning is significant . . . though expressed in very bad prose."

2499 Little, Bryan. THE MONMOUTH EPISODE (Lond: Werner Laurie, 1956), pp. 30, 194.

[Passing references to the "countryside of Hardy's peasants," to Tess and Gabriel Oak. Chap 2, "The West," is an informative account of society and manners in seventeenth-century Dorset.]

2500 Meynell, Viola (ed). THE BEST OF FRIENDS: FURTHER LETTERS TO SYDNEY CARLYLE COCKERELL (Lond: Rupert Hart-Davis, 1956), pp. v, 24–25, 29, 31–32, 34, 39, 45, 54*n*, 61, 63, 78, 81, 118, 167, 199–200, 224.

Katherine Adams (4 Aug 1920): H is remembered as rough-looking, dressed unlike his fellows, with a keen and alert face and a decided accent; now he looks like a refined, fragile, gentle old man. There was conversation about his books and the performance of *The Dynasts* at Oxford. C. H. St. John Hornby (13 Sept 1922): Sent H a shooting-seat. Walter de la Mare (12 Jan 1928): It is our loss that H is gone, but a saving grace that he was *here*; what he stood for seems to be perishing, and that is perhaps real pessimism. Siegfried Sassoon (30 Oct 1923, 29 Sept 1938, 19 May 1939, 6 June 1940, 12 Dec 1949): H's minor poems betray his everyday voice; a precious thing to carry is the cadence of one's voice in his head; posterity will envy our incommunicable power to enjoy H's verse; St. Juliot's rectory presents visitor with Hardyish atmosphere of long-lost romance; have H's signed Suetonius; H's significance is greater than ever; why did not H marry Anne Thackeray? H was not a memorable talker; H's agnosticism must have pained Emma. Field Marshal Viscount Wavell (9 March 1944): Attended H's funeral. T. H. White (4 Sept 1945): H's firm way with ghosts is admirable. Major Earl Wavell (6 Sept 1953): Cockerell knew H well enough to dissuade him from waxing his moustache.

2501 Miller, Betty. "Kipling's First Novel," CORNHILL, CLXVIII (Spring 1956), 405–12.

[Psychological discussion of THE LIGHT THAT FAILED includes an examination of the close physical and emotional affinities of Masie and Sue Bridehead and of the parallels between the stories of Dick Heldar and Jude.]

2502 Miller, Milton L. "A Comparison of REMEMBRANCE OF
THINGS PAST with Thomas Hardy's *The Well-Beloved*," NOSTAL-
GIA: A PSYCHOANALYTIC STUDY OF MARCEL PROUST (Boston:
Houghton Mifflin, 1956), pp. 116–21.
H's *The Well-Beloved* and Proust's REMEMBRANCE OF THINGS PAST show
clearly that a man's greatest love may be for a phantom of the past.
Fantasies of love for several generations of one person are not uncommon
in psychoanalysis and are a way of dealing with emerging conflicts. H's
hero renounces incestuous love at the cost of artistic inspiration; Proust's
renounces marriage and friendship for the sake of artistic success.

2503 Moynahan, Julian. "*The Mayor of Casterbridge* and the Old
Testament's First Book of Samuel: A Study of Some Literary
Relationships," PUBLICATIONS OF THE MODERN LANGUAGE ASSO-
CIATION, LXXI (March 1956), 118–30.
Henchard's career is connected with the Biblical Saul's through H's "strat-
egy of association" in which Farfrae figures as David. Grain speculation
parallels the Philistine invasion; both Saul and Henchard are victims of
their emotions and have a weakness for music; Henchard ironically tries to
apply the Davidic Psalm CIX to Farfrae, though it applies to himself. The
main action of the novel is framed by this material; H shows that both
kings and men must suffer and decline in the ordinary succession of generations.

2504 Neiman, Gilbert. "Thomas Hardy, Existentialist," TWEN-
TIETH CENTURY LITERATURE, I (Jan 1956), 207–14.
Critics should not attack H for lack of feeling for the "common man" and
inability to see beyond the "mere terrestrial manifestations"; he believed
that "a story must be exceptional enough to justify its telling" and that
because life is absurd "we are self contradictions from the start." H "loved
the world enough to draw it faithfully," and in *The Dynasts*, he, like
Sisyphus, attempted to define life but perhaps failed. Sartre's statement that
"man is a being who makes himself a lack of being in order that there
might be being" admirably describes H.

2505 Neiman, Gilbert. "Was Hardy Anthropomorphic?" TWEN-
TIETH CENTURY LITERATURE, II (July 1956), 86–91.
H was "first a fatalist and then a determinist," but he had also a "mystical
strain" suggested by his belief in the "unrealizability of man's higher desires" and his "eternal search for some meaning in the universe." H's poem
"The Lacking Sense" is "a basic statement of this mystical strain" because
it "equates Nature with God" and compares both to a "Mother," thus
giving "a distinctly anthropomorphic character to both Nature and God."
The poem is not deterministic but "an exquisite statement of the feeling"

which moved him to formulate the "concept of Immanent Will as an explanation of the enigmatic nature of creation." His conception of "Nature as Mother" is close to "the Hindu concept of the Divine Mother," which implies a "duality of destructiveness combined with creative consciousness." In H's poems and novels, women "share the dual aspect of the Divine Mother, they create and destroy," and all men "are of her clay."

2506 O'Connor, Frank. "Thomas Hardy," THE MIRROR IN THE ROADWAY (NY: Knopf, 1956), pp. 237–50.

H is "a fascinating example of historic schizophrenia, standing on the frontier of two cultures"—the vanishing folk and the advancing modern industrial. H took refuge "in the depths of his heart," in his belief in " 'spectres, mysterious voices.' " "More than any other novelist . . . [H] is socially limited and naive." All his faults "are faults of simple-mindedness." Even in *The Mayor of Casterbridge*, "easily his best-planned novel," the plot "overshoots the mark." The two H's were H the serial entertainer and H the poet; the former was concerned with hot, tense character and action, the latter with "the enchanting surface of things." Finding the spectacle of passing life intolerable, H can "contemplate it only as if it were already gone by, its suffering ended. All his characters are treated as though they were already dead."

2507 Oppel, Horst. "Der Einfluss der englischen Literatur auf die Deutsch" (The Influence of English Literature on German), in DEUTSCHE PHILOLOGIE IM AUFRISS (German Philology in Perspective). 2nd ed, ed by Wolfgang Stammler (Berlin, Bielefeld, Munich: Erich Schmidt, 1956), I, 106.

[Assures the German reader that H immortalizes the fiction of the Victorian period.] [In German.]

2508 Reichard, Hugo M. "Hardy's *Tess of the d'Urbervilles*, Chapter XVI," EXPLICATOR, XIV (April 1956), Item 42.

The penultimate paragraph of chap 14 of *Tess of the d'Urbervilles* does not concern the dignity of dairy workers but rather the relationship between them and their animals: both men and animals are subject to death. Thus the vanity of human wishes is shown.

2509 Roppen, Georg. "Darwin and Hardy's Universe," EVOLUTION AND POETIC BELIEF (Oxford: Basil Blackwell, 1956); rptd (Folcroft, Pennsylvania: Folcroft P, 1969), pp. 283–316.

Darwin revealed to H that the natural order is indifferent. Reacting to this, H became the first great Victorian to break from the optimism of Tennyson and Browning. In doing so, he presented a joyless world in which nearly all the characters are defeated in unequal battles with fate. Since fate, or the

Will, is forever unknowable and unmotivated, there is little reason either for joy or hope. Whatever hope there is stems from H's belief that social ills can be corrected and that the Will may evolve a consciousness.

2510 Starr, William T. "Romain Rolland and Thomas Hardy," MODERN LANGUAGE QUARTERLY, XVII (June 1956), 99–103.

The ideal of internationalism figures in Rolland's appreciation of H. He admired *Tess of the d'Urbervilles* early in his career; *Jude the Obscure* later became his favorite. JEAN–CRISTOPHE shows the influence of suicides, among other echoes. The Immanent Will of *The Dynasts* is a sort of life force in the hero in L'AME ENCHANTÉE.

2511 Stevenson, Lionel. "Thomas Hardy," THE VICTORIAN POETS, ed by Frederic E. Faverty (Cambridge, Mass: Harvard UP, 1956), pp. 21, 118, 136, 238–41.

[A brief survey of the best critical, bibliographical, and biographical works on H.]

2512 Swinnerton, Frank. AUTHORS I NEVER MET (Lond: George Allen & Unwin, 1956), pp. 9–15.

[Swinnerton explains that he never sought the acquaintance of H because he thought H's prose style "old-fashioned," because H "had adopted the creaking and malignant gods of Greek tragedy," and because "as a man he was dreary." Others of his time thought H "irreligious and obscene." He lived a retired life and seldom talked. "He just had no interest in his own personality or its social exploitation." He did, however, feel intensely and could call forth emotions buried for years. "Great as his grand prose dramas may be . . . he was first, last, and always a poet." Though meeting him would have wasted H's time, Swinnerton regrets not having done so.]

2513 Ward, A. C. "Thomas Hardy," TWENTIETH CENTURY LITERATURE: 1901–1950. 3rd ed, rvd and enlgd (Lond: Methuen, 1956 [1st ed, 1928]), pp. 7, 35, 99, 154–66, 185, 211, 227*n*.

"Never at any time is Hardy's poetry intoxicating or magical." Its chief characteristic is a " 'satisfying flatness.' " [The usual (and useful) clichés about H's poetry.]

2514 [Weber, Carl J.]. "Among Notable Recent Acquisitions," COLBY LIBRARY QUARTERLY, IV (Nov 1956), 150–52.

Edward Westermarck's HISTORY OF HUMAN MARRIAGE may be important because it was issued—and evidently read—during the year in which H was at work on *Jude the Obscure*.

2515 Weber, Carl J. "Forty Years in an Author's Life: A Dozen Letters (1876–1915) from Thomas Hardy," COLBY LIBRARY QUARTERLY, IV (May 1956), 108–17.

[An annotated transcription of letters to H's American publishers, to editors requesting permission to reprint various of H's poems, and short notes to acquaintances.]

2516 [Weber, Carl J.]. "A Midsummer Gossip on Romance," COLBY LIBRARY QUARTERLY, IV (Aug 1956), 121–37.
[A record of the receipt of a copy of Hardy's *A Laodicean*, which had been used as H's scrapbook. Annotations and letters pasted in.]

2517 [Weber, Carl J.]. "Napoleonic Echoes," COLBY LIBRARY QUARTERLY, IV (Feb 1956), 101–2.
[A record of gifts of Hardiana to the Colby College Library, plus a transcript of a letter by H to the Rev. L. E. V. Filleul noting receipt of a jingle on Napoleon.]

2518 [Weber, Carl J.]. "Other Recent Acquisitions," COLBY LIBRARY QUARTERLY, IV (May 1956), 118–20.
H's markings in his copy of Lucretius's ON THE NATURE OF THINGS may show the beginning of ideas developed in *The Dynasts*.

2519 Weber, Carl J. " 'What's in a Name?'—Or in a Signature?" MANUSCRIPTS, VIII (Spring 1956), 185–88.
In the Mellstock edition of H's works from Max Gate, only one book is cut on every page, *A Pair of Blue Eyes*, which is based on H's romance with his first wife. There are some notes in *The Dynasts* as well. Some H letters are signed "T. Hardy" and some initialed "T. H."

1957

2520 Brogan, Howard O. "Science and Narrative Structure in Austen, Hardy, and Woolf," NINETEENTH CENTURY FICTION, XI (March 1957), 276–87, espec 279–81.
Though Austen's concept of a Newtonian universe, benevolent and objective, enabled her to create the machinery through which a beneficent providence could assert itself, H's concept of an equally absolute and objective universe, though Darwinianly indifferent to man's lot, forced him to establish the machinery through which his characters could struggle and fail. In *The Mayor of Casterbridge*, Henchard is engaged in a Darwinian struggle for the survival of the fittest. He succeeds in the primitive society of bargaining and fairground, but fails in the complex world of machinery, accounting, and management. The new order symbolically enters with the railroad, as Henchard leaves through the fairgrounds. [Sound.]

2521 Clifford, Emma. "The 'Trumpet Major Notebook' and *The Dynasts*," REVIEW OF ENGLISH STUDIES (Lond), ns VIII (May 1957), 149–61.

"The Trumpet Major Notebook" records historical details from the first five years of the nineteenth century, many of which H used in *The Dynasts* and *The Trumpet-Major*. These details "do not appear to be of importance for their own sake; their function is to provide a necessary background to an event in the story." The notebook "provides an interesting practical illustration of H's attitude to historical fact."

2522 Cohen, Joseph. "Owen's 'The Show,'" EXPLICATOR, XVI (Nov 1957), Item 8.

Wilfred Owen's poem "The Show" shows in its handling of war themes the influence of *The Dynasts* and Yeats's dramatic poem "The Shadowy Waters." Owen demonstrates that the blame for war rests with mankind, and he images the slayer and the slain in the same figure.

2523 Davidson, Donald. "Futurism and Archaism in Toynbee and Hardy," STILL REBELS, STILL YANKEES, AND OTHER ESSAYS (Baton Rouge: Louisiana State UP, 1957), pp. 62–83.

Arnold Toynbee's historiological terms, "futurism" and "archaism," provide a useful framework for understanding H's major fiction, in particular *The Mayor of Casterbridge*. In this novel, the two central male characters, Henchard and Farfrae, exemplify the polar opposites of "archaism" and "futurism" respectively, and the conflict of the novel becomes both personal and historical as the new destroys the traditional.

2524 Fackler, Miriam Ernestine. "Death: Idea and Image in Some Later Victorian Lyrists," DISSERTATION ABSTRACTS, XVII (1957), 621–22. Unpublished dissertation, University of Colorado, 1955.

2525 Glicksberg, Charles I. "Fiction and Philosophy," ARIZONA QUARTERLY, XIII (Spring 1957), 5–17, espec 6–7.

H "struggled to reconcile the scientific outlook with the spiritual." He finally came to the conclusion that each man should make his own philosophy out of his own experience.

2526 Goldberg, M. A. "Hardy's Double-Visioned Universe," ESSAYS IN CRITICISM, VII (Oct 1957), 374–82.

H's dual aesthetic of beauty and his dual metaphysic of Reality versus Idealism are fundamental to *The Return of the Native*. There are two kinds of beauty: the Ideal Beauty which appeals to all that is happy and joyous in the accepted sense, and the Real Beauty which appeals to a rarer instinct and which is illustrated by the beauty of Egdon Heath. The first kind of beauty is inconsistent with both emotional maturity and a concommitant grasp of reality. H's concept of beauty is reinforced by his concept of reality as somber tragedy to which he opposes the idealism of unrealized expectations. This relationship between external reality and internal aspirations is the key to H.

2527 Goodhart, Eugene. "Thomas Hardy and the Lyrical Novel," NINETEENTH CENTURY FICTION, XII (Dec 1957), 215–25.
The quality of H's genius was alien to the prevailing literary tradition of the social novel. Although his novels often disclose an incipient social awareness, H is fundamentally opposed to complexity, and values simplicity and directness of manner in his characters. Because H distrusts most social arrangements, the drama in his novels is conceived as an irremediable opposition between the integrity of the individual personality and a corrupt and threatening world. This concentration upon the individual is the result of H's temperamental inclination to poetry. He portrays a poetic reality whose form lies beyond experience, not in it. This orientation, in addition to his almost exclusive concern with man as a creature whose finest instincts are warped by contact with civilization, label H as a Romantic lyric poet. Yet, because he is never free from the doctrinal and mechanical commitments of the novelist, his books reveal the inadequacy of the Romantic conception: nature and society, mutually exclusive in theory, are inextricably united in actuality. The anomaly of H's position is best illustrated by his attitude toward nature. Both a symbol of freedom and a threat to sociey, nature is a force to be both loved and hated. This ambiguity in H is the result of his honest yet unsuccessful search for the truth, and it is also responsible for the uniqueness of his achievement.

2528 Gordan, John D. "New in the Berg Collection: Thomas Hardy. Autograph Manuscript of 'The Three Strangers,'" BULLETIN OF THE NEW YORK PUBLIC LIBRARY, LXI (July 1957), 356.
Despite H's great fame as a poet and a novelist, he also wrote many praiseworthy short stories. H's story "The Three Strangers" is in the Berg Collection, in the manuscript H gave to Sir Sydney Cockerell.

2529 Green, David Bonnell. " 'The Eve of St. Agnes' and *A Pair of Blue Eyes*," NOTES AND QUERIES, CCII (April 1957), 153.
There is a doubtless unconscious reminiscence of "The Eve of St. Agnes" in *A Pair of Blue Eyes*; the moonlit scene in the church at Endelstow is colored by Keatsian spectacles rather than by reality.

2530 Haber, Grace Stevenson. "Echoes from Carlyle's 'Goethe's "Helena" ' in *The Mayor of Casterbridge*," NINETEENTH CENTURY FICTION, XII (June 1957), 89–90.
H's description of Henchard seems, at times, merely transcribed from Carlyle's essay. Henchard is likened to Faust and, as was Faust, to Bellerophon.

At length one suspects that H had seen beyond Faust and discovered Mephistopheles himself in the mayor's "dark pupils . . . [with] a red spark of light in them" and "his red and black visage."

2531 "Hardy's Drawings for a Child," TIMES LITERARY SUPPLEMENT (Lond), 19 July 1957, p. 448.

[A series of pen-and-ink drawings discovered by Evelyn Hardy.] The dates 1885–1887 and superscriptions were added by H when he put his papers in order. The inscription "To Please L. G." is perhaps addressed to Lilian Gifford, his first wife's niece. Drawings are very simplified, "primitive" sketches with some cartoon humor, of Greek classical situations, e.g. Diogenes telling Alexander to stand out of the sunshine and Plato teaching in the Academy.

2532 Hillyer, Robert. "Speaking of Books," NEW YORK TIMES BOOK REVIEW, 3 Feb 1957, p. 2.

It is "hairsplitting" to say that H wasn't pessimistic because his god was not actively malicious. H is a cosmic pessimist in his novels and in *The Dynasts*. His poetry ranges from cosmic to personal pessimism, without the warmth of compassion shown in his novels.

2533 Hoopes, Kathleen R. "Illusion and Reality in *Jude the Obscure*," NINETEENTH CENTURY FICTION, XII (Sept 1957), 154–57.

As a part of his idealization of the real world, Jude created a "ghostly" world and defined his existence in terms of it. Though the divergence between the "real" world and his own made for confusion in his life "as long as he was sustained by the two most inspiring of all his ghosts—the elusive and unattainable Sue Bridehead and the beatific vision of Christminster—life still had meaning for him." With the disintegration of these ghosts, his will to live disappeared. That last pathetic walk with Arabella documents his recognition of his "ghost" world for what it was.

2534 Houghton, Walter E. THE VICTORIAN FRAME OF MIND, 1830–1870 (New Haven & Lond: Yale UP, 1957), pp. 401n, 414.

[Two references, in passing, to H the pessimist.]

2535 Lucas, F. L. TRAGEDY: SERIOUS DRAMA IN RELATION TO ARISTOTLE'S POETICS (Lond: Hogarth P, 1957).

[Passim references. Useless.]

2536 Mallory, Thomas Oliver, Jr. "The Devil and Thomas Hardy: A Study of the Manifestations of Supernatural Evil in Hardy's Fiction," DISSERTATION ABSTRACTS, XVII (1957), 2012–13. Unpublished dissertation, University of Illinois, 1957.

2537 Peterson, Edith Hamilton-Moodie. " 'Symmetric History': A Study of Thought Patterns in the Prose Works of Thomas Hardy," DISSERTATION ABSTRACTS, XVII (1957), 2599. Unpublished dissertation, University of New Mexico, 1957.

Emphasizes H's medievalism in terms of (1) the Saxon "stage," in which Norman and Celtic place names are removed in favor of medieval toponymy or West Saxon place-name elements, (2) the naming of characters which distinguishes Norman conquerors from Saxon underlings, (3) the "nostalgic treatment of medieval ecclesiastical remains, and (4) plots which are "like morality plays without God."

2538 Proctor, Mortimer R. THE ENGLISH UNIVERSITY NOVEL (Berkeley & Los Angeles: University of California P, 1957), pp. 7, 9, 204*n*.

Like so many other major Victorian novelists, H was not a university man, and also, like many others, his gloomy picture is fragmentary not sustained. The reviewer in the ATHENAEUM (23 April 1895) accused H of "scolding and injustice" in the old-fashioned complaint that the universities were the stronghold of the rich. The hero of *Jude the Obscure* feels the sentiment of Christminster; the rebuffs he receives parallel H's own experience.

2539 Purdy, Richard L. "Introduction," *Far From the Madding Crowd*, ed with an introduction and notes by Richard L. Purdy (Boston: Houghton Mifflin, 1957), pp. v–xvii.

H's style does not always equal his poetic vision but in *Far From the Madding Crowd*, "a poet's novel," he is successful. The novel's numerous contrivances reflect its serial publication but also, a "congenial medium" in which H could work.

2540 Sanders, E. N. "Another Hardy Scrapbook," COLBY LIBRARY QUARTERLY, IV (May 1957), 173–77.

[Transcripts of letters from H and his wife, correcting the annotation in "A Midsummer Gossip on Romance," ibid (Aug 1956), 121–37.]

2541 Schmidt, Adelbert. LITERATURGESCHICHTE: WEGE UND WANDLUNGEN MODERNER DICHTUNG (Literary History: Ways and Changes in Modern Fiction) (Salzburg & Stuttgart: Das Berglan Buch, 1957), p. 405.

[Mentions Virginia Woolf's admiration for H.] [In German.]

2542 Shirreff, A. G. " 'The Eve of St. Agnes' and *A Pair of Blue Eyes*," NOTES AND QUERIES, CCII (Nov 1957), 502.

H used Keatsian spectacles, but Browning in his "Blot on the Scutcheon" and Scott with the "Lay of the Last Minstrel" seem to have done so, too, in describing the moonlit scene in the church at Endelstow. [Related, but not directly on H, ibid, CCIII (June 1958), 252.]

2543 Slack, Robert C. "The Text of Hardy's *Jude the Obscure*," NINETEENTH CENTURY FICTION, XI (March 1957), 261–75.
Although *Jude the Obscure* was H's last novel, he did not forget it during his poetry-writing career. He revised the novel for the "New Edition" which Macmillan published in 1903, and for the "Wessex Edition" of 1912. For the "New Edition" of *Jude*, H "emasculated" the passage dealing with the pig's pizzle, corrected an oversight, and made twenty-eight isolated changes in the text. For the "Wessex Edition," H made 206 changes, some of which serve to give Sue Bridehead "more human sympathy" than she possessed earlier; "she is a shade more sympathetic, more elusive, more charming."

2544 Stamm, Rudolf. ENGLISCHE LITERATUR (English Literature) (Bern: A Francke, 1957), II, 336, 338, 344, 358, 362–66.
[Reviews the outstanding criticism of H for a German audience.] [In German.]

2545 [Weber, Carl J.]. "A Gift from Mark Twain's Nephew," COLBY LIBRARY QUARTERLY, IV (Nov 1957), 226–27.
[Receipt of a copy of *Wessex Poems* (Lond: Macmillan, 1903) constitutes an addition to Richard L. Purdy's THOMAS HARDY: A BIBLIOGRAPHICAL STUDY (1954).]

2546 Weber, Carl J. "Hardy's Copy of Schopenhauer," COLBY LIBRARY QUARTERLY, IV (Nov 1957), 217–24.
H's copy of Schopenhauer's FOUR-FOLD ROOT OF THE PRINCIPLE OF SUFFICIENT REASON shows that although H denied the influence of Schopenhauer he was familiar with at least this work. "It" or "The Will" in *The Dynasts* is clearly drawn from Schopenhauer, and the FOUR-FOLD ROOT provides a "summons to us to reexamine the philosophical framework of *The Dynasts*."

2547 Weber, Carl J. "Introduction," *Jude the Obscure* (NY: Harper's, 1957), pp. vii–xvii.
In planning the plot of *Jude the Obscure*, H sought to blend two themes: the "frustrated pursuits of an education" and the problems concerning English marriage and divorce laws. It was pity, not satire, that drove H's pen, pity for the unfortunate Jude—"scourged, disgraced, starved, deserted" —and Sue—"the most complex woman whose portrait Hardy ever attempted." The novel shows that H had the power "to accept tragedy in its starkest and bleakest aspect—tragedy not as divine punishment for wrongdoing . . . but simply and finally, without possibility of repair, as tragedy."

2548 [Weber, Carl J.]. "Recent Gifts to the Library," COLBY LIBRARY QUARTERLY, IV (May 1957), 186–88.

The Colby Library has received a manuscript of FIVE SONGS by Harper McKay, a musical setting for five H poems: "In Time of 'the Breaking of Nations,'" "Waiting Both," "My Spirit will not Haunt the Mound," "The Oxen," and "When I Set Out for Lyonesse."

2549 Weber, Carl J. "Thomas Hardy," VICTORIAN NEWSLETTER, No. 12 (Autumn 1957), 23–24.

[A guide to research giving widely dispersed locations of H MSS for both prose fiction and poems. No complete listing of the locations of letters is available, and consequently no definitive biography can be done.]

2550 [Weber, Carl J.]. "An Unrecorded Hardy Item," COLBY LIBRARY QUARTERLY, IV (May 1957), 177–78.

The Colby Library has received a copy of George Brazile's French translation of "An Imaginative Woman." It was first printed in two installments in REVUE POLITIQUE ET LITTÉRAIRE on 19 and 26 Oct 1912, not in 1918 as had been thought.

2551 Yamamoto, Bunnosuke (ed). BIBLIOGRAPHY OF THOMAS HARDY IN JAPAN; WITH REFERENCE BOOKS IN ENGLAND AND AMERICA, OUTLINES OF HIS PRINCIPAL WORKS (Tokyo: Shinozaki Shorin, [1957]); also see BULLETIN OF THE THOMAS HARDY SOCIETY OF JAPAN, I (1966) [not seen].

[Except for some titles and excerpts, the text of the bibliography is in Japanese. The biographical note and outlines of works are in English. Bibliography—1,119 entries (pp. 1–220). Works about H—154 entries (pp. 221–48). Standard reference works on H in England and America arranged chronologically, titles in English—fifty-five entries (pp. 249–56). Biographical note, note on Wessex and Egdon Heath, an essay, "Humour of Hardy's Characters," by Mono Mitobé, and brief outlines of H's principal prose works and *The Dynasts* (pp. 259–94).] [Partly in Japanese.]

2552 Zabel, Morton Dauwen. "Hardy in Defense of His Art: The Aesthetic of Incongruity," CRAFT AND CHARACTER: TEXTS, METHOD, AND VOCATION IN MODERN FICTION (NY: Viking P, 1957), pp. ix–x, 70–96, 110, 329; rewritten from an article of the same title in SOUTHERN REVIEW, VI (Summer 1940), 125–49; rptd in HARDY: A COLLECTION OF ESSAYS, ed by Albert J. Guérard (1963), pp. 24–45.

New aspects of the work of Dickens, H, Conrad, and James are constantly coming to the fore. H's "theme and vision" have influenced "art and experience in the last eighty years" despite critical distaste. H's unique quality is ambivalence—conformism and skepticism, acceptance and protest, abnormal characters and rudimentary ones, cosmic simplification and confusion. Discordance is central to his works. A product of his times, he nonetheless created a personal aesthetic so as to be apart from it. H's aesthetic defended occasional awkwardness in style and "instinctive and emotional qualities above the intellectual." He opposed both naturalism and aestheticism, favoring rather Coleridge's aim of illusion, something between delusion and falsity. The dichotomy of life, the "dualism of subject and object," is the basis for his conception of tragedy. H, however, was pro-evolution, and behind the seeming negation lies "humanistic hope," "of human worth and dignity," "of will and intelligence." H's metaphysic was tentative, and an incongruity arises from his "attraction toward life and his confusion by it." "He now appears to us as a realist developing toward allegory." The success of both his novels and poetry evolves from sincerity.

1958

2553 Block, Haskell M. "James Joyce and Thomas Hardy," MODERN LANGUAGE QUARTERLY, XIX (Dec 1958), 337–42.
At first Joyce was dissatisfied with H's psychological depiction, but his maturation with his own reading public made him appreciate H more, particularly in terms of integrity and pride of authorship. "A Tragedy of Two Ambitions" disturbed Joyce, due to biographical similarities to his own family. There is common ground in the two authors' widening of the scope of fiction. [Shared relation found through Joyce's comments, not terribly worthwhile on H.]

2554 Cantwell, Robert. "Introduction," *Far From the Madding Crowd* (NY: Heritage P, 1958), pp. i–[xxi].
[The text follows the Macmillan "Wessex" edition of 1912 except that the "Preface" by Hardy is deleted; the emendation suggested by Carl Weber, COLOPHON, ns III (Feb 1938), 139–41, is used. The introduction confuses the conclusion of *Far From the Madding Crowd* with that of *The Return of the Native*. The chief interest of the edition is its illustrations, which may be compared with the original illustrations done for CORNHILL by Helen Patterson.]

2555 Carl, Ralph F. "The Early Critical Writings of Valery Larbaud," KENTUCKY FOREIGN LANGUAGE QUARTERLY, V:1 (1958), 1–11.

The Dynasts considered in its entirety is "the product of a genius." "The faults of the poem lie in a tendency to philosophize too much, in its form, and in the prosaic, sometimes clumsy use of blank verse." [A summary of Larbaud's criticism of H and others, as found in La Phalange, between Aug 1908 and Feb 1914.]

2556 Cary, Joyce. ART AND REALITY: WAYS OF THE CREATIVE PROCESS (NY: Harper, 1958), pp. 168–72.

The dramatic scenes in H's fiction, like Tess at Stonehenge, Henchard's seeing the effigy of himself in the water, and Tess's baptizing her baby, are often symbolic. H skillfully manipulates symbols to control our responses to these scenes from *Tess of the d'Urbervilles* and *The Mayor of Casterbridge*. H contrives his scenes with a skill approaching Shakespeare's.

2557 Coombes, Henry. LITERATURE AND CRITICISM (Lond: Chatto & Windus, 1958), pp. 83–85, 111–15.

In "The Sleep-Worker" H has treated his subject in a "serious and enquiring" way, showing sympathy for human suffering. His language lacks "direct and immediate impressiveness of 'true' poetic thought"; it is labored and abstract. The poem is personal with reserves of strong emotion but no self-pity; its title is appropriate; its images and tone are exact. H is mature; he can "distance" his emotion.

2558 Fricker, Robert. DER MODERNE ENGLISCHE ROMAN (The Modern English Novel) (Göttingen: Vanderhoeck & Ruprecht, 1958), pp. 5–27.

[H is listed with nine late Victorian authors who had the greatest influence on twentieth-century English literature.] [In German.]

2559 Friedman, Norman. "Criticism and the Novel," ANTIOCH REVIEW, XVIII (Fall 1958), 343–70, espec 348–52.

While *The Mayor of Casterbridge* is commonly interpreted as showing Henchard's fall as retribution for selling his wife, "with the exception of the return of the furmity woman and of Newson, the opening section plays practically no causal role at all!" When the rivalry between Henchard and Farfrae develops, Henchard's past "has in effect ceased to operate in any real way." The blame for the usual interpretation is partly H's: "he has so overplotted his story that perhaps his original intention . . . became smothered."

2560 Glasgow, Ellen. LETTERS OF ELLEN GLASGOW, ed with an introduction by Blair Rouse (NY: Harcourt, Brace, 1958), pp. 88, 89, 257, 258.

[Letter to Anne Virginia Bennett (25 Aug 1927): describes visit to the Hardys. Mrs. H is "very shy, but a thoroughly nice sensible woman," and H is an extraordinarily attractive man for his age ("far more modern and advanced than most men of twenty-five, . . . profoundly civilized and sympathetic about animals just as he is in his books"). Letter to Van Wyck Brooks (4 Oct 1939): recalls the spring of 1914 "made unforgettable to me by my meeting with Hardy, . . . the most sympathetic Englishman, and one of the most sympathetic persons I have ever known. Nothing rang hollow in his nature."]

2561 Hammerle, Karl. "Transpositionen aus Shakespeares KING LEAR in Thomas Hardy's *Return of the Native*" (Transpositions from Shakespeare's KING LEAR in Thomas Hardy's *Return of the Native*), in STUDIES IN ENGLISH LANGUAGE AND LITERATURE PRESENTED TO PROFESSOR DR. KARL BRUNNER. . . . (WEINER BEITRÄGE ZUR ENGLISCHEN PHILOLOGIE, LXV) (Vienna & Stuttgart: Braumüller, 1958), pp. 58–73.

H's use of elements of KING LEAR may be called "transpositions," as if H shifted Shakespeare's music in LEAR into another key. One important parallel between the play and the novel is the theme of people who desire only those desired by others, and its opposite, the individual who desires someone who has been rejected. Thus H transposed Cordelia's story—rejected by the Burgundians for her poverty but warmly received by the King of France on account of her rejection—into his novel by showing that Damon desires Eustacia only when he sees that she is about to be possessed by another man and that Diggory is very willing to marry the rejected Thomasin. "The Closed Door," Part IV of the novel, shows another of Shakespeare's influences. Doors are closed in Lear's face by his daughters, and Eustacia fails to admit Mrs. Yeobright. Lear's cry of " 'Filial ingratitude' " has obvious echoes in Mrs. Yeobright's accusation of her son's and daughter-in-law's treatment of her. H's use of Egdon Heath is a further transposition, not an exact copy. There is no violent storm in the novel, but neither is there a Lear to see it as a mirror of his own passionate suffering. [In German.]

2562 Hardy, Evelyn. "Plots for Five Unpublished Short Stories," LONDON MAGAZINE, II (Nov 1958), xi, 33–45.

These skeletons for stories are unique for they tell us something of H's method of working, delineating first the bare bones of facts and characters, later covering them with emotion, imagery, color. "Number One," a sensational story about a school-mistress (cf. Fancy), reveals H's fondness for strange alliances. "Number Two" is a bitter domestic drama of the countryside. "Number Three" is a Christmas story based on incidents in the life of Barthelemon (cf. the poem "Barthélémon at Vauxhall"). This story introduces the Frankenstein theme, very unusual in H. "Number Five" is a set of three drafts for the same story of unrequited love—the first being told by an anonymous narrator, the second by the young man himself, the third by a sparrow. The tale resembles "She at his Funeral" and other early poems. [A rare, recently discovered photograph of H about the time of his marriage in 1874, and a photograph of Maggie Richardson's bust of H are also reproduced.]

2563 Holloway, John. "Hardy's Major Fiction," in FROM JANE AUSTEN TO JOSEPH CONRAD: ESSAYS COLLECTED IN MEMORY OF JAMES T. HILLHOUSE, ed by Robert C. Rathburn and Martin Steinmann, Jr. (Minneapolis: University of Minnesota P, 1958), pp. 234–45; rptd in THE CHARTED MIRROR: LITERARY AND CRITICAL ESSAYS (Lond: Routledge & Kegan Paul, 1960), 94–107.

It is important to see H's deepening gloom in close relation to the passing of the old order in rural England. This view enables one to see H's awareness that the old order lacked essential strengths necessary for it to last. Significant change comes between *The Return of the Native* and *The Mayor of Casterbridge*. In the former, the rural way of life still has revitalizing power; in the latter, Henchard, the only representative of the old order and still possessing a greatness that comes from it, plunges downward to eventual death. By *The Woodlanders*, Henchard's defeated strength has become Marty South's and Giles Winterborne's weak acceptance. By the writing of *Tess of the d'Urbervilles* and *Jude the Obscure*, rural life has become ugly and illustrative of a decline in the old stock. Narrative movement in *Mayor* shows Henchard gradually becoming tamed, as an animal is tamed. Tess is shown as a hunted animal whose flight can be understood in terms of natural history and Darwinian science. This view of H's development suggests that his reason for leaving fiction was his disbelief that what he considered the source of human vitality—the traditional rural order—could survive.

2564 Hyde, William J. "Hardy's View of Realism: A Key to the Rustic Characters," VICTORIAN STUDIES, II (Sept 1958), 451–59.

H's "rustics are both real and unreal by . . . design." H avoided the sheer bestiality of the peasantry, and their economic distress. He made "his selections chiefly from among the 'aristocracy' of the peasant community." His purpose was not merely to photograph reality but through selectivity, to heighten it and "reveal a newly discovered comprehension," to see into " 'the heart of a thing.' "

2565 Klingopulos, G. D. "Hardy's Tales Ancient and Modern," FROM DICKENS TO HARDY, in PENGUIN GUIDE TO ENGLISH LITERATURE, Vol VI, ed by Boris Ford (NY: Penguin Books, 1958), pp. 59, 69, 81, 86, 97, 99, 102, 104, 108, 111, 158, 167, 184, 195, 201, 385, 406–19, 479–80.

All of H's novels "contain evidence, implicit or explicit, of the tension in [his] mind between Dorset and London," of "his attitude of suspense between things ancient and modern." An element of personal involvement in the change that menaces his characters who move in an agricultural setting lends his analysis a special urgency. His great failing as a novelist is "his inability to go beyond stereotypes of character and to deepen the intrinsic development of his plot." H's true genius is more securely represented by his poetry than by his novels, two or three of which should endure as minor classics. He is significant as "one of the most important mediators of continuity between the nineteenth and twentieth centuries," for he has left us in his fiction "a poet's record of ancient ways that were submerged by modern life."

2566 Lewis, C[ecil] Day. "Introduction," *Tess of the d'Urbervilles: A Pure Woman*, ed by C. Day Lewis (Lond, Glasgow: Collins; NY: Norton, 1958), pp. 11–18.
The geographical basis of the plot suggests that Tess is a "graceful, innocent animal" being hunted down by Destiny, human weaknesses, and human institutions. [Biographical sketch and bibliography.]

2567 O'Connor, William Van. "Cosmic Irony in Hardy's 'The Three Strangers,'" ENGLISH JOURNAL, XLVII (May 1958), 248–54, 262.
Typically, H employs cosmic irony to view human actions from a perspective distant in space and time, reducing the significance of our lives. When viewed against an incomprehensible universe, the incongruity of life becomes pathetic and comic. "The Three Strangers" shows us the pathos of the human situation, as the laws man creates try to ruin his happiness. H's ironic viewpoint may be the result of the nineteenth-century doctrine of evolution, which demonstrated man's close relation with lower forms of life, humbling his self-regard. The story itself is not artistically a success because there is no link between the action (or plot) and the meaning. No theme grows organically from the narrative itself.

2568 Raleigh, John Henry. "Victorian Morals and the Modern Novel," PARTISAN REVIEW, XXV (Spring 1958), 244–45, 253–54, 261.
H, Moore, and others broke the pattern of familial censorship of fiction by the Eighties and Nineties. H, Butler, and Lawrence represent the revolt of the workingman against Mrs. Pardiggle of BLEAK HOUSE: "he got drunk, they, surging up also from below, wrote novels" affirming the instinctive ways of life as opposed to "theoretical and restrictive moral preconceptions of the middle class." Butler embodies comedy of this revolt against class consciousness; H embodies its antitype as pastoral and as tragedy. "The world of *Far From the Madding Crowd* and *The Woodlanders* is pretty

much pastoral/idyllic." Tess, however, is surrounded by a "host of 'moral hobgoblins,'" hence suffers tragedy. H, despite affinities with Lawrence, "looks toward the stasis and tragedy, the entrapment of the individual in the hell of his consciousness, that is the province of the later James, of Conrad, of Woolf, of Joyce." H's major impulse toward pessimism came from the Old Testament.

2569 Reinhard-Stocker, Alice. CHARAKTERDARSTELLUNG UND SCHICKSALSGESTALTUNG IN DEN ROMANEN THOMAS HARDYS (Characterization and Fate in Thomas Hardy's Novels) (Winterthur: P. G. Keller, 1958); University of Zurich dissertation.
[Summarizes the philosophical and textual approach to H's characterizations and portrayal of fate. The quotations of H and his protagonists are compared in chap 3. The final chapter treats the relationship between the characters' self-imposed fate and the fate placed upon them by their environment.] [In German.]

2570 Short, Clarice. "In Defense of *Ethelberta*," NINETEENTH CENTURY FICTION, XIII (June 1958), 48–57.
For the most part, critics have not reacted favorably to *The Hand of Ethelberta*. A re-evaluation of it requires "a new approach, namely a careful consideration of what comedy meant to Thomas Hardy. . . . There is evidence in the work that Hardy thought of comedy as being the reverse of tragedy, at least the reverse of his conception of tragedy." This twist is most evident in two aspects of the novel. First, H de-emphasizes, almost to the point of omission, the role of fate, chance, and the "immanent will." Secondly, he fashions the character of his heroine in a different mold from that used for the heroines of his better-known novels. Ethelberta is not marked by those qualities which H considered central to the creation of a tragic effect. For example, she is controlled by her will and reason rather than by her emotions. Moreover, "there are several elements in both the plot and characterization which could easily have slipped over into the material of tragedy if they had been handled differently."

2571 Stedmond, J. M. "Hardy's *Dynasts* and Mythical Method," ENGLISH, XII (Spring 1958), 1–4.
While H in *The Dynasts* made no such elaborate attempt to juxtapose ancient myth and modern concerns as Joyce and Pound were to do later, he did seek to superimpose antique models on recent events. Critics have pointed out parallels between H's epic-drama form and Aeschylus's tragedies, but they have not sensed the *ironic* overtones inherent in H's use of this Aeschylean superstructure. H believed in an order, but an order imposed by an unconscious and apparently purposeless Will; whereas Aeschylus believed in a moral order, in a deity who was both just and merciful. The over-all structural plan is Aeschylean (three parts, three plays of a

trilogy). H's use of the chorus is borrowed from the early Greeks: there is a family relationship between the "Eumenides" and the Spirits Sinister and Ironic. But there is no single tragic hero in H's drama; no more than Milton can he resolve the paradox of free will and an omnipotent creator. The "myth," which H, by implication, contrasts with that of Aeschylus, is peculiarly modern: H foreshadows typical preoccupations of our time.

2572 Weber, Carl J. "Honeysuckles at Princeton: A Sororicidal Investigation," PRINCETON UNIVESITY LIBRARY CHRONICLE, XIX (Winter 1958), 69–81.

The unique "trial" binding copy (three volumes) of the first edition of *Tess of the d'Urbervilles*, acquired by Morris L. Parrish in 1928 and subsequently bequeathed to Princeton University Library, was not, as assumed earlier by the London bookseller J. A. Allen, a presentation copy offered by the first London publisher James Osgood to his sister Irene. Two facts: the Irene Osgood who owned the book before Parrish bought it was not the publisher's sister; the publisher of *Tess* did not present the copy now at Princeton to her.

2573 [Weber, Carl J.]. "An Important Hardy Manuscript," COLBY LIBRARY QUARTERLY, IV (Nov 1958), 303–4.

Receipt of an autograph manuscript of "The Three Tall Men," a poem not in *Collected Poems of Thomas Hardy*, shows that the poem was one of the last written before H's death and makes clear the evolution of the poem into "Three Tall Men."

2574 Weber, Carl J. "Introduction," *The Woodlanders* (NY: Harper's, 1958), pp. v–xix.

The lack of critical and popular esteem for *The Woodlanders* in the United States may be due to the constant re-publication of the "rough-draft wording" of the HARPER'S BAZAR serial version. One effect of this lack of esteem is the failure to see the pivotal position of the novel in H's canon: in writing the novel H came to see "apparently for the first time . . . that man's unhappiness *may* be due, not to blind chance or a malign Fate . . . but to the organization of society, to man-made laws and conventions." Still, the novel contains "traces of *all* his differing ways of looking at the world."

2575 Woods, George B., Homer A. Watt, George K. Anderson, Karl J. Holzknecht. "Thomas Hardy: 1840–1928," THE LITERATURE OF ENGLAND: AN ANTHOLOGY AND A HISTORY. 1936 ed, rvd (Chicago & NY: Scott, Foresman, 1958), pp. 907–15.

H's poems are "exceedingly plain in style, stripped naked of the overdress of [many] . . . Victorian lyrics." He thought his literary function was to bring about melioristic change by assault on "man's inhumanity to man" and by dealing blows at the "robustious swaggering of optimism."

1959

2576 Bailey, J. O. "Hardy's Visions of the Self," STUDIES IN PHILOLOGY, LVI (Jan 1959), 74–101.
In almost all of H's novels there appears a "truepenny apparition," a "vision of the self" which causes "the character to accept responsibility for disasters he had blamed on circumstance." Often the character sees two ghosts, the first a "false ghost" or vision of the self as the character sees himself, the second a "truepenny ghost" of the real self. "Truepenny mirrors of the soul" have three things in common: they appear "in grisly or spectral lights"; they usually include "a reference to some aspect of Christianity, often a lurid image"; and "the substance of each vision lay already in the character's mind, either suppressed below consciousness or denied." While Huxley is the major source of this concept, its exact meaning is unclear for "H had no simple answer for the riddle of the universe." He was a "spokesman for compassion and human hope," yet he felt that happiness was an "occasional episode in a general drama of pain."

2577 Baylen, Joseph G. "A Note on Thomas Hardy and W. T. Stead," MISSISSIPPI QUARTERLY, XII (Fall 1959), 205–6.
Stead asked H for support of a plan of English tours to promote Anglo-Saxon unity. H's favorable reply states that "the idea of a pilgrimage—at any rate to the haunts of the now dead, if not to spots brought into notice by the living—is an interesting one, and in these days when all classes seem to be waiting for a lead in respect of emotions, dreams, views, and religion, might be carried out I should think rationally and systematically." H saw a possible objection in "the mixing together of persons of different classes previously strangers."

2578 Calhoun, Philo. "An Old Architect's Last Draft," COLBY LIBRARY QUARTERLY, V (Dec 1959), 61–66.
In 1923, the octogenarian H designed a war memorial tablet for the Dorchester Post Office—his last public design save the frontispiece of *The Famous Tragedy of the Queen of Cornwall.* As an epitaph, H used the twelfth line of his poem "Embarcation": "None dubious of the cause, none murmuring." This fact is worth recording because it sheds light on the old man's human warmth and hatred of war, even in his last years.

2579 Chapman, Frank. *"Far From the Madding Crowd,"* USE OF ENGLISH, XI (Autumn 1959), 12–15.
Despite its many faults—H's failure to treat emotions seriously, the stilted "literary" style, the lifeless characterization of most of its people—*Far From the Madding Crowd* is still "suitable for school reading" because of

H's employment of a convincing authentic rural background. "The strength of the book . . . is the firm relationship of characters and events to well-known, vividly realised environment."

2580 Clifford, Emma. "Thomas Hardy and the Historians," STUDIES IN PHILOLOGY, LVI (Oct 1959), 654–68.

H's extensive reading of history was "a heavy burden," but he was proud of the historical accuracy of *The Dynasts*. Through his "imaginative awareness," he finds historical reality in the grotesque, dream-like atmosphere of the battlefield. The historians H read—Thiers, Alison, Napier and others—were amateurs like himself, writing history because of a "personal enthusiasm" for the subject and often "with a theme to expound." Comparable passages from H and the historians do not show "that the sources exerted any great influence on *The Dynasts.*" "Each of the historians lives to some extent in his own persuasive imaginary world, and H is by no means at odds with them even in his most imaginative writing." Although the historians did not share his philosophical concepts, such as the "Immanent Will," "they sometimes perceive that there is a kind of life in war itself that transcends and overwhelms the life of man."

2581 Colaco, M. F. "The Pessimism of Thomas Hardy," JOURNAL OF THE UNIVERSITY OF BOMBAY, XXVIII (1959), 126–45.

H's pessimism was "in all likelihood, congenital: the distemper was in his blood, and was . . . intensified . . .by vicarious experience, but also perhaps by the disintegrating philosophies of his time." He made a "sharp distinction . . . between belief in a personal God and a god who is a vague, mythical abstraction such as he himself believed in." Unlike the Christian God, H's gods, "who combine unmeasured power with unlimited irresponsibility," were "fitful, capricious, wayward" and subject to "unpredictable moods, yet capable of nursing implacable resentments." H's characters are "weak, anaemic souls" who are "caught in a vice-like grip," of the gods and are "driven by the pressure of external forces to their ultimate and inevitable doom."

2582 Collie, M. J. "Social Security in Literary Criticism," ESSAYS IN CRITICISM, IX (April 1959), 151–58.

Judgment is a matter of discrimination, not measurement. The unity of organization for which *The Return of the Native* is so highly acclaimed also makes it rigid and, conversely, the lack of a well-organized plot in *Tess of the d'Urbervilles* permits greater depth of insight.

2583 Danby, John F. "*Under the Greenwood Tree*," CRITICAL QUARTERLY, I (Spring 1959), 5–13.

The philosophy of the book is transcendent, although H later said it was not, because the novel shows a story-world as the poet-and-novelist constructs it. The first five chapters are a superb example of H's technique—connecting man, family, community, and the earth. The past is the great leveler in the human romance, and Time, as later in *Jude the Obscure*, is the chief character.

2584 Ellis, H. F. "The Niceties of Plagiarism," ATLANTIC MONTHLY, CCIII (Jan 1959), 76–78.

Authors trying to avoid any accusation of plagiarism can be driven to extremes. Rider Haggard wrote an apology in his book ALLAN QUARTERMAIN because someone had noted a similarity between a scene in his book and a scene in *Far From the Madding Crowd*. Haggard could not distinctly remember, however, if he had ever read H's novel.

2585 Fuchs, Konrad. "Die Integration von Leben und Werk bei Thomas Hardy." (The Integration of Life and Work in Thomas Hardy), NEUEREN SPRACHEN, No. 2 (Feb 1959), 516–22.

In everything H wrote we find "an amalgamation of reality and fiction" so close that we are unable to determine where H deals with factual occurrences or with imaginary ones. This could lead to the induction that H's work is a "fiction," yet H often drew his characters from real people, his scenes from actual places. The fate that befalls his characters befell real people; the social change H pictured in his novels mirrors a rural upheaval that happened in H's lifetime. For all that, characters, places, and happenings in H's novels seem "to come from a dream-world." In this masterful shaping of man and landscape into the characters and setting of his novels, H shows "his genius as a story-teller." [In German.]

2586 Green, David Bonnell. "A New Thomas Hardy Letter," NOTES AND QUERIES, CCIV (Jan 1959), 34–35.

[A short letter from H to E. Pasco on the use of the word "Harlican" in *Jude the Obscure* and on the story of "broaching the Admiral" in *The Dynasts*, a local tradition.]

2587 Green, David Bonnell. "A Shakespearean Allusion in *Far From the Madding Crowd*," SHAKESPEARE QUARTERLY, X (Winter 1959), 129.

In *Far From the Madding Crowd*, chap 18, Gabriel sees Bathsheba's face as *"the uncertain glory of an April day."* H borrows the phrase from TWO GENTLEMEN OF VERONA (I, iii, 85). The borrowing is probably unconscious.

2588 Green, Peter. Kenneth Grahame: A Biography (Cleveland and NY: World Publishing, [1959]), pp. 3, 59, 167, 220–21, 270, 333.

In 1896 Grahame met H on social occasions; Mrs. Grahame and Mrs. H discussed their difficult husbands; the Grahames's child considered a fit theme for an H novel.

2589 "Hardy Hot and Cold," Colby Library Quarterly, V (Dec 1959), 66–69.

Brendan Behan entertained himself while under arrest as an Irish rebel by reading *Under the Greenwood Tree*. A. J. Cronin, on the other hand, expressed his dislike for H by rejecting all contentions that his characters derive from those of the Wessex master.

2590 Herbert, Lucille Oaklander. "History and Tradition in the Novels of Thomas Hardy," Dissertation Abstracts, XIX (1959), 3305. Unpublished dissertation, Cornell University, 1958.

2591 Herman, William R. "Hardy's *Tess of the d'Urbervilles*," Explicator, XVIII (Dec 1959), Item 16.

H's *Tess of the d'Urbervilles* is constructed of a series of concentric temporal and spatial circles, having as their center Tess herself. She tries to escape the power of space and time but is trapped finally at Stonehenge as space and time narrow in upon her. Tess is a passive character, a child of nature.

2592 Hogan, Donald Joseph. "Structural Design in Thomas Hardy's Poetry," Dissertation Abstracts, XX (1959), 2291. Unpublished dissertation, University of Minnesota, 1958.

2593 Hollander, John. "The Metrical Emblem," Kenyon Review, XXI (Spring 1959), 279–96.

H "was possibly the last major poet to write in a long tradition of English versifying whose founding we might assign to Ben Jonson." [Brief mention.]

2594 Hurley, Robert. "A Note on Some Emendations in *Jude the Obscure*," Victorian Newsletter, No. 15 (Spring 1959), 29–30.

H made four emendations in the second ed of *Jude the Obscure*, in conformance with R. Y. Tyrell's attack on *Jude* ["*Jude the Obscure*," Fortnightly Review, LXV (1 June 1896), 857–64]. A more extensive study might reveal H's sensitivity to criticism.

2595 Hynes, Sam. "Hardy and Barnes: Notes on Literary Influence," South Atlantic Quarterly, LVIII (Winter 1959), 44–54.

H does not appear to have been influenced by many of his poetic contemporaries, but he does acknowledge a debt to Barnes. The "poem-as-drama" in H probably derives from Barnes, although Browning might also figure in this background. Some of H's forms seem to derive from Barnes. [Unconvincing.]

2596 Johnson, S. F. "Hardy and Burke's 'Sublime,'" STYLE IN PROSE FICTION: ENGLISH INSTITUTE ESSAYS 1958, ed by Harold C. Martin (NY: Columbia UP, 1959), pp. 55–86.
Edmund Burke's A PHILOSOPHICAL ENQUIRY INTO THE ORIGIN OF OUR IDEAS OF THE SUBLIME AND BEAUTIFUL seems, especially in the case of *The Return of the Native*, to have influenced significantly H's "conception of literary effectiveness." H seems to have used Burke's essay as a handbook in writing *Native*. For example, H's "use of an adder to effect the turning point of his plot" seems to be based on Burke's assertion, among his comments on "Terror," that "serpents and poisonous animals of almost all kinds" are terrible with regard to sight and are thus sublime. H made similar efforts, throughout *Native*, to embody Burke's ideas about "Obscurity," "Power," "Privation," "Vastness," "Infinity," "Sound," "Bodily Pain," and "Ugliness" as sources of sublimity in literature. Hardy achieved a sublime effect in *Native* but failed to achieve a truly tragic one.

2597 Jones, Katherine. "King Mark Disguised as Himself," AMERICAN IMAGO, XVI (Summer 1959), 115–25.
Among the many ancient and modern versions of the Tristram legend, the role of Tristram's uncle, King Mark, varies. In the old versions and in those of Tennyson and H, Mark is cruel, envious, wicked, appearing "to the dreamer—for what else is a poet but a dreamer?—as the parent. But all the subsequent associations point to another Mark, a milder, kinder, better person. . . . This would be the stage Wagner, Swinburne, and Masefield reached." The wicked Mark seems the truer.

2598 King, Montgomery Wordsworth. "Manichaeism in Thomas Hardy," SOUTHERN UNIVERSITY BULLETIN, XLVI (Sept 1959), 135–60 [not seen in this form].
Though there is no evidence that H knew the doctrines of Mani, there are many parallels in H's work with Manichaeism, "a mode of late 19th-century pessimism that followed the fading of the romantic impulse." Characteristics of Manichaeism H's works display include: the concept of the demonic origin of the soul, belief that the world is ruled by a Prince of Darkness, that neither Divine Providence nor the Immanent Will is consistent or rational. [From summary in ABSTRACTS OF ENGLISH STUDIES, V (June 1962), #1385.]

2599 Lea, Frank Alfred. The Life of John Middleton Murry (Lond: Methuen, 1959; 1960), pp. 71, 83, 85, 124, 141, 148, 217, 346.

Murry's tremendous admiration for H amounted almost to " 'monomania.' " For his " 'profound acquiescence' in all experience," Murry viewed H (with Chekhov) as one of the two greatest writers of the twentieth century. Athenaeum, which Murry edited from 1919 to 1921, "sailed under the banner of Hardy." " 'Mr. Hardy can speak for all that is noble in England as no poet since Wordsworth has been able,' " Murry wrote in an editorial of Nov 1920. After first meeting H in May 1921, Murry wrote that he found him to be " 'everything I had dreamed—everything.' " Murry wrote a spirited defense [in Wrap Me Up in My Aubusson Carpet (1924)] of H's novels against the attack of George Moore [see George Moore, "George Moore and John Freeman," Dial (NY), LXXV (Oct 1923), 341–62]. At the birth of his daughter, Katherine, in April 1925, H and Mrs. H were asked to be godparents.

2600 Lowe, Robert Liddell. "Three New Hardy Letters," Modern Language Review, LIV (July 1959), 396–97.

Three unpublished H letters are among the papers of Percy William Bunting (1836–1911), editor of the Contemporary Review from 1822 until his death. The importance of these letters lies in H's comments on the agricultural working man.

2601 Maxwell, J. C. "Hardy's *Our Exploits at West Poley*: A Correction," Notes and Queries, CCIV (March 1959), 113.

In the edition of 1952 (limited ed, p. 94; unlimited ed, p. 106) reproducing the American periodical Household (1892–1893), the American compositor has misread H's handwriting: "I would never ['liever'] have had no water in West Poley forevermore than have lost Steve! said Job."

2602 Paterson, John. "*The Mayor of Casterbridge* as Tragedy," Victorian Studies, III (Dec 1959), 151–72.

The Mayor of Casterbridge, unlike *Tess of the d'Urbervilles* and *Jude the Obscure*, is not preoccupied with nineteenth-century humanistic thought but reverts to traditional moral values. It is archaic in its sociology, psychology, and cosmology and thus approaches Shakespearean and Sophoclean tragedy and becomes "one of the truly remarkable anachronisms in the history of English literature."

2603 Paterson, John. "*The Return of the Native* as Antichristian Document," Nineteenth Century Fiction, XIV (Sept 1959), 111–27.

In the original manuscript of *The Return of the Native*, there is a strong rejection of Christianity. The forceful censorship at the time of the novel's publication, however, forced "underground what evidently threatened to materialize as an open denigration of Christianity." Nevertheless, H retained his anti-Christian note beneath the surface of the novel, and he shows his bias primarily through his characters. Various aspects of Eustacia Vye's character are geared toward the expression of an anti-Christian sentiment, the most sharply defined of which is her "persistent identification as a black witch, the immemorial antagonist of the Christian faith." Clym Yeobright, opposed to Eustacia, is the figure of Christian piety, but as such, he becomes the victim "of a number of highly damaging ironies." The novel exploits the pagan-Christian antithesis, as the subsidiary figures like the reddleman and the peasant chorus show. Diggory Venn is intended to trumpet pre-Christian values and, thus, implicitly criticizes the Christian. The peasants, in their participation in pagan rituals, however unaware they are of exactly what they are doing, also implicitly oppose the Christian.

2604 Peckham, Morse. "Darwinism and Darwinisticism," VICTORIAN STUDIES, III (Sept 1959), 37–38.
The use of accident, control of structure, and ecology in *The Return of the Native* recalls Darwinian thought. "*The Native* exhibits . . . a profoundly Darwinian orientation, even to the implication that we can never fully understand the world in which we live, and our relation to it."

2605 Perkins, David. "Hardy and the Poetry of Isolation," JOURNAL OF ENGLISH LITERARY HISTORY, XXVI (June 1959), 253–70.
H's sensitivity to the tragedy and pathos of existence caused him to feel alienated from his fellow men. His poetry is, to a great extent, an exploration of the isolation theme and an attempt to discover ways out of it. One way out is an unawareness achieved by concentrating solely on that which is immediately before him. A second way out is "an escape from the obsession with sorrow through the visionary imagination, leading one to a knowledge of 'transcendent things,' and making life a blessing by a knowledge of a truth beyond surface appearances." Because of his honesty to his own experience, however, H could take neither of these roads—although he rejected unawareness more readily than the transcendent vision which he distrusted. "But moving within the distrust of the imagination, there is also the questioning, tentative openness of Hardy—a humility which could not finally measure life only against his more programmatic ideas, and an honesty which, while it scrutinized the claims of the imagination, at other times he simply doubted his own capacity for it, feeling himself to be somehow incomplete."

2606 Purdum, Richard. "A Year and a Day in *The Return of the Native*," Notes and Queries, CCIV (Jan 1959), 40.

H apparently employed an element of folk literature (the "twelmonth and a day" of Sir Gawain and the Green Knight, and of the Wife of Bath, in his novel *The Return of the Native*, which begins on Guy Fawkes Day and ends a year and a day later, for the essential story), without understanding its strict original significance.

2607 Slack, Robert C. "Some Characteristics of Hardy's Novels," Six Novelists: Carnegie Series in English, Number Five, ed by William M. Schutte, et al (Pittsburgh: Carnegie Institute of Technology P, 1959), pp. 41–52.

In writing his novels, H was influenced by the pastoral tradition, by Elizabethan and Greek tragedies, and by folk tales and customs. He was also influenced by Essays and Reviews and by The Origin of Species as his pessimism and presentation of an indifferent cosmos suggest. Thus H's novels carry on the traditions of the past while reflecting the present, of which *The Return of the Native* is illustrative. Furthermore, *Jude the Obscure* is evidence that H also anticipated the future.

2608 Stanford, Raney. "Thomas Hardy and Lawrence's The White Peacock," Modern Fiction Studies, V (Spring 1959), 19–28.

Lawrence's real debt to H lies not in "a vague feeling for nature" but in the use of "symbolic scenes as structural devices" and in his interest in feminine psychology. Sue Bridehead is a sado-masochist prevented by social pressure from entering into a mature relationship with another human being. She tries either to master others or to be absorbed by them. [Use of modern psychological theory to justify Sue's behavior. Plausible.]

2609 Swinburne, Algernon Charles. The Swinburne Letters, ed by Cecil Y. Lang. 6 vols (New Haven: Yale UP, 1959–1962); II (1869–1875), 335; V (1883–1890), 191–92; VI (1890–1909), 91, 122, 133, 175.

[(1) To Theodore Watts, 29 Aug 1874: Swinburne refers to chap 42 of *Far From the Madding Crowd* and is shocked by the unseemly reference to the household relations of the Hebrew Carpenter. "If the mystery of our redemption is thus to be associated by ribald writers with the badge of cuckoldom, what wonder that our Laureate should find in the ideal cuckold his type of ideal man?" (2) To H, 12 May 1887: He acknowledges the receipt of a copy of *The Woodlanders* inscribed by H to Swinburne. He has read every book by H, but this one with a double sense of gratification and gratitude. (3) To H, 5 Nov 1895: He acknowledges the gift of *Jude the Obscure*, a beautiful tragedy and terrible in its pathos. The beauty, truth, and terror belong only to H. A man who does such work needs no praise. If H wishes, he may be the "most tragic of poets" in fiction, since no one has written thus since Balzac. (4) To H, 28 March 1897: He acknowledges the receipt of *The Well-Beloved*. (5) To H, 26 Dec 1898: He acknowledges the receipt of *Wessex Poems and Other Verses*. He especially admired the illustrations and the poems "In a Wood," "The Fire at Tranter Sweatley's," "Her Death and After," "The Slow Nature," "The Dance at the Phoenix." (6) To H, 23 Jan [1904]: He acknowledges the gift of *The Dynasts*. He has a double interest because of his father's association with Collingwood and Lady Stanhope. The fifth scene of the second act is delightful and the song at the close of Act V is noble. He hopes H will not abandon work in creative romance even for the field of epic or historic drama.]

2610 Thomas, Henry, and Dana Lee Thomas. "Thomas Hardy," LIVING BIOGRAPHIES OF FAMOUS NOVELISTS (Garden City, NY: Garden City Books, 1959), pp. [292]–305.
[Gives a lively anecdotal biography, recounting key points in his life, emphasizing that H's novels "grew out of the nagging of a woman who didn't love her husband" and "are built largely upon the formula of misdirected love." Recounts the plot of *Tess of the d'Urbervilles*. Attributes H's return to poetry to the adverse critical reaction to *Tess* and *Jude the Obscure* and to the mutilation of his works for periodical publication. "Now at last nobody read him and everybody admired him."]

2611 Van Doren, Mark. "The Poems of Thomas Hardy," FOUR POETS ON POETRY, ed by Don Cameron Allen (Baltimore: Johns Hopkins P, 1959), pp. 83–107.·
H's reputation will rest on *Collected Poems*. The views of the world in these poems are often inconsistent. Time, pain, and gloom "were the three dimensions of his universe." His style is sometimes awkward because he was "interested in nothing but accuracy of statement," which is also art. "Hardy was a musician; he was also an etcher." H deformed and twisted the world into queer shapes after his style, his genius.

2612 Weber, Carl J. THE RISE AND FALL OF JAMES RIPLEY OSGOOD: A BIOGRAPHY (Waterville, Maine: Colby College P, 1959), pp. 15, 209, 231, 235–37, 242–44, 246, 248–52, 254, 259, 261, 262, 265.
"It is quite possible that Osgood was instrumental in steering *The Wood-landers* into the pages of" HARPER'S BAZAR. "Osgood's friendship with Thomas Hardy is of more than passing significance."

2613 Wheeler, Otis B. "Four Versions of *The Return of the Native*," NINETEENTH CENTURY FICTION, XIV (June 1959), 27–44.

Basically, there are four different versions of *The Return of the Native*, "distinguishable on the basis of changes in action, character, and to a slighter degree, setting." A closer attention to the various texts of the novel reveals a fourth distinguishing factor—style. The examination of the various stages in the evolution of the novel as we know it reveals that in the later versions "the main characters are more full-bodied, more plausible; the conflicts are stronger, the plot more tightly knit. The realistic surface, despite minor flaws, is more elaborate and more convincing through his painstaking attention to details of setting, which fuse this novel into the imaginary Wessex, and to details of speech and mannerism in the minor characters, who are responsible for so much of the local color. The style is more direct, emphatic, colloquial, lending speed and interest to the narrative."

1960

2614 Beebe, Maurice, Bonnie Culotta, and Erin Marcus. "Criticism of Thomas Hardy: A Selected Checklist," MODERN FICTION STUDIES, VI (Autumn 1960), 258–79.

[About 450 entries. Emphasis on 1940–1960 criticism and scholarship. Selective, omitting "unpublished dissertations, foreign criticism, reviews and journalistic comment of transitory interest, routine discussions in histories of literature or the novel, and casual references." Includes "a goodly portion . . . to interest the serious teacher and student of Hardy." Three parts: general studies, poetry, individual novels. Part III divided into place in the standard Wessex edition, editions with notes and/or introductions, index to general studies listed in Part I, and special studies not previously cited.] [Very useful.]

2615 Bradley, John Lewis. "An Echo of Tess," TIMES LITERARY SUPPLEMENT (Lond), 9 Sept 1960, p. 577.

The incident which generated H's poem "Night in a Suburb (Near Tooting Common)"—later altered and titled "Beyond the Last Lamp (Near Tooting Common)"—also inspired, twenty years earlier, a passage in *Tess of the d'Urbervilles*, chap 35, where after Tess has admitted her past to Angel Clare, the two walk outside and are observed by a cottager.

2616 Bradley, John Lewis. "A Footnote to Hardy's 'Channel Firing,' " NOTES AND QUERIES, CCV (May 1960), 188–89.

In the last stanza of "Channel Firing," H refers to "Stourton Tower," i.e., King Alfred's Tower in southwest Wiltshire, a brick edifice erected in 1766 to commemorate the spot upon which the standard of King Alfred was raised against the Danes.

2617 Brooks, Cleanth, and Robert Penn Warren. UNDERSTANDING POETRY (NY: Holt, Rinehart & Winston, 1960), pp. 6, 168, 190, 219, 264.

H illustrates his genius as a poet in "Channel Firing" by playing *down* the weird and ghostly element. He mixes the conventional devices for giving a weird effect with "the hungry little church mouse and the cow that is drooling over its cud in the meadow." [Reprints the poems "The Man he Killed," "In Tenebris, I," "Channel Firing," "Wessex Heights," and "The Going."]

2618 Buckler, William E. "Introduction," *Tess of the d'Urbervilles,* ed by William E. Buckler (Boston: Houghton Mifflin, 1960 [Riverside Editions]), pp. v–xvi.

H's essential greatness as a novelist is due to several things. (1) His use of local color. (2) His philosophical ideas. H introduced subjects of popular controversy in his day. H's novels are not argumentative—he reports or shows controversy but does not moralize. For example, the destinies of Tess and Jude are controlled not by blind Gods but by the ambiguous state of the protagonist who feels the "ache of modernism." H presents the problem as characterization, not controversy, in Angel Clare (distinction between morality and religion). (3) His novels do not try to be highly refined technical achievements. H had a feeling of responsibility to his reading public—a story must be "*exceptional* enough to justify its telling." This attitude is a cause of H's popularity. In *Tess of the d'Urbervilles*, for example, H chose an omniscient narrator who was moved almost at will. (4) H's concern with the changes that had greatly altered conditions of life in England in one generation: (a) the decay of the aristocracy and the rise of a new bourgeois class (Stoke–d'Urbervilles), (b) industrialization (the railroad and the threshing machine in *Tess*), (c) the spirit of religious doubt. The religious dilemma as a source of disaster in *Tess* is revealed by the three principals losing their faith in the orthodox church in three different ways.

2619 Carpenter, Richard C. "Hardy's 'Gurgoyles,' " MODERN FICTION STUDIES, VI (Autumn 1960), 223–32.

H's use of the "grotesque" (a "kind of situation, scene, or image which yokes man and his environment together in strange relationships") gives us some of his most effective scenes, as in the description of the "gurgoyle" in *Far From the Madding Crowd* or the picture of the Dutch clock in *Desperate Remedies* with its hanging "entrails." Although it is difficult to speculate on why H utilized the grotesque, we can assess the "aesthetic results." It contributes to H's "anti-realism" by creating a "more penetrating vision" and exemplifying the "emotive meaning" of imagery. By its very obtrusiveness it creates an "enrichment and thickening of the aesthetic texture," like dissonance in music and distortion of perspective in painting. This "dissonance" is also thematic and reveals "the morass which lies beneath" the "green and pleasant land" of H's physical world. It suggests that "decay and laceration are fundamental." [Perceptive illumination of H's aesthetic.]

2620 Cockerell, Sydney. "An Echo of Tess," TIMES LITERARY SUPPLEMENT (Lond), 23 Sept 1960, p. 611.

J. L. Bradley's suggestion (ibid, 9 Sept 1960, p. 577) that "Beyond the Last Lamp" was composed long after *Tess of the d'Urbervilles* cannot be accepted because when H produced a new volume of poems he touched up ones written long before. H said that he would never have "written a word of prose if he could have made a living by verse." The poem was probably written in 1887–1891.

2621 Crompton, Louis. "The Sunburnt God: Ritual and Tragic Myth in *The Return of the Native*," BOSTON UNIVERSITY STUDIES IN ENGLISH, IV (Winter 1960), 229–40.

Generally, the writer of prose fiction has three alternatives open to him. First, he may write prose romance; secondly, "he may imitate epic or dramatic forms"; and finally, he may base his work on some psychological or social theory. In *The Return of the Native*, H uses "all three modes simultaneously as part of a carefully wrought whole." Clym Yeobright and Eustacia Vye are the two main characters in this double tragedy. Clym is something of a messianic figure and thus invites treatment as both a romantic and a tragic hero. H sets up Eustacia as a witch, and consequently she is a romantic figure. However, she is also a queen of high tragedy, suggestive of Cleopatra. Moreover, H's suggestion that both Clym and Eustacia are subject "to biological and economic laws which seriously limit any sense of human responsibility" shows H's realism. "Hardy relates his characters to myth through his romantic archtypes, and solves the problem of the tragic hero's social evaluation by underscoring the Vyes' and Yeobrights' sense of superiority to the general ruck of peasants and small farmers who make up the closed society of the heath." As a naturalist, H turns "the telescope around and show[s] the characters in reduced scale as insignificant figures in a landscape."

2622 Daiches, David. A Critical History of English Literature, 2 vols (NY: Ronald P, 1960), II, 725, 1033–38, 1039, 1073–82, 1128.

The important classes of H's poems are those of "mechanical ironic coincidence," "haunting renderings of an experience fully rendered in verse" and "more generalized poems" which describe an illuminating incident, attitude, or mood. In *The Dynasts* "the ideas . . . remain external, not realized in the texture of the drama." H's novels show some disparity between genius and achievement, but the latter seems greater than "a critical inspection of the talents at work would seem to warrant." As in the case of Faulkner, "it is precisely the author's amateur status as a novelist . . . that gives the writing weight and integrity." "*The Mayor of Casterbridge* is genuine tragedy, and Hardy's most perfectly wrought work of fiction." Nature, civilization, and human character "work on each other continually." Nature does not change, and Henchard regards it as something "that can only be controlled by submitting to it." But Farfrae shows that "man is not as dependent on nature as Henchard . . . imagines." The same weather that ruins Henchard makes Farfrae prosperous. *Tess of the d'Urbervilles* is a remarkable novel containing "some first-rate Hardy; but it is not, taken as a whole, a great tragedy." A clue to interpreting *Jude the Obscure* is "the conflict between flesh and spirit," but the novel's real subject is "the inevitable frustrations of the human condition."

2623 Deen, Leonard W. "Heroism and Pathos in Hardy's *The Return of the Native*," Nineteenth Century Fiction, XV (Dec 1960), 207–19.

H intended Eustacia Vye to be a tragic heroine in the grand tradition, but *The Return of the Native* declines into the pathetic/ironic mode. Egdon is Eustacia's Hell. She is the bitterly enduring hero (like Milton's Satan or Shelley's Prometheus). Clym was conceived of as a Hamlet, an overly spiritualized modern man. As such, he and Eustacia are incompatible. Each also has relationships he cannot escape: Eustacia has Wildeve, and Clym, his mother. After his mother's death, Clym becomes Oedipus the avenger who seeks the answer to his mother's death but instead destroys Eustacia's and his happiness. At the novel's end H indicts Providence for Eustacia's and Wildeve's deaths and Clym's role as mediocre preacher. Though Clym is central at the novel's end, their demise and his decline promote irony and pathos instead of tragic purgation. *Native*, like *Jude the Obscure* and *Tess of the d'Urbervilles*, begins with tragic possibilities but gives only pathos and irony.

2624 Denniston, Robin. "The World of Thomas Hardy," Time and Tide (Lond), XLI (27 Aug 1960), 1010–11.

The BBC serial version of *The Return of the Native* was not effective.

"Without the Wessex scenery and country activity, the human personalities seem as wooden and their motives as obscure as a superficial and cynical reader of H would believe them to be." The novels should be filmed because "his [H's] imagination was cinematic." Writing "never came easily to him"; it was "the compulsion to express the ideas that beset him rather than joy in the use of words that brought him to the point." H's plots "creak" and his style is "homespun at best," though he has "an exactness of phrase, a grim determination not to let prose rhythms interfere with the only words that will fit what he describes." In his poetry, the "emotions batter through with no obvious artifice in their ordering or presentation." "When all is said about the forces of destiny or chance, what remains with H is a quality of love."

2625 Drake, Robert Y., Jr. "*The Woodlanders* as Traditional Pastoral," MODERN FICTION STUDIES, VI (Autumn 1960), 251–57.

When critics refer with condescension to *The Woodlanders* as a pastoral, they are really praising it; true pastoral is not "a 'retreat' from reality" but includes the duality of the natural world and the human heart. Little Hintock is a pastoral community with traditional beliefs, both pagan and Christian. The scenes of pastoral serenity are balanced by descriptions of "subversive forces"—decayed and grotesque nature. The essential conflicts are between pastoral love ("traditionalism") and anti-pastoral love ("modernism"). Giles and Marty are the "true Arcadians"; Edred Fitzpiers embodies the modernist attitude, while Grace Melbury, an "uncommitted" character at first, is sought after by both sides. It is Grace and not Marty who is the heroine of the book and a round whom most of the action moves. Grace, significantly, will not at the end renounce her Arcadian principles, but Fitzpiers, after the reconciliation, does modify his modernist views. Arcadia, meanwhile, lives on in "historical permanence."

2626 Fayen, George S., Jr. "Imagination in the Novels of Thomas Hardy." Unpublished dissertation, Yale University, 1960.
[Listed in Lawrence F. McNamee, DISSERTATIONS IN ENGLISH AND AMERICAN LITERATURE (NY & Lond: Bowker, 1968).]

2627 Frederik, H. F. DIE WELTLITERATUR (World Literature) (Munich: Bogen Verlag, 1960), p. 81.
[Lists H's dates and works. Labels H as the last Victorian who wrote depressing regional novels and poems.] [In German.]

2628 Glicksberg, Charles I. LITERATURE AND RELIGION: A STUDY IN CONFLICT (Dallas: Southern Methodist UP, 1960), pp. 43, 66, 68, 86, 87, 159, 170–71, 209.

H could find no solace in the death experience because he believed that God was "either blind and not aware of what [He] . . . was doing or [He was] an automaton and hence not responsible for [His] . . . actions." The ideological struggle between science and religion "was brought dramatically to a head in Thomas Hardy's poetry, particularly in *The Dynasts*, in which he deliberately refers to God as 'It.' " H conceived that "death ends every-thing," and he could not believe in God's existence. Since all H knows is "that we are born and that we die," he sees no sense in "brooding on the meaning of life, for nothing is gained thereby." For H, the "First Cause, whatever its nature, was neither good nor evil but unmoral." The element of "automatism or blind impulsion in human affairs" impressed H, who was already sympathetic to Schopenhauer. "The one philosophical conviction to which [H] . . . clung stubbornly, both as a poet and as a novelist, was that the First Cause is neither unknowing or immitigably cruel. H "could not conceive of a morality, benign or malevolent, associated with Nature, not even one of which the human mind has no awareness."

2629 Green, David Bonnell. "The First Publication of 'The Spec-tre of the Real,' " LIBRARY, XV (March 1960), 60–61.
The first of six installments of H's "The Spectre of the Real" appeared 15 Nov 1894 in the Philadelphia PRESS. *This* was the first publication, not 17 Nov 1894 in the winter issue of TO-DAY as stated by Prof. Richard L. Purdy in THOMAS HARDY, A BIBLIOGRAPHICAL STUDY (1954). Newspaper syndication often presents problems in determining first publication, since newspapers belonging to the same syndicate may run installments on different dates. Probably "Spectre" was carried in other American news-papers as well as the PRESS. In addition, "A Mere Interlude" was also pub-lished first in the Philadelphia PRESS.

2630 Guenther, Paul F. "Storm and Hardy: a Study in Similarity," KENTUCKY FOREIGN LANGUAGE QUARTERLY, VII (1960), 87–93.
There are obvious similarities worthy of consideration between these two authors, although H and Storm were almost a generation apart. They both discovered the heath-landscape of their countries, but H concerned himself with the rustics of Wessex, whereas Storm's people were small-town bourgeois. H's and Storm's finest writings are tales of social pressure and of the individual's struggle against injustice engendered by differences of classes, family background, or personality. H and Storm share a sort of Pantheism and treat the past as actively experienced life. H's paganism owes much to the Greeks; that of Storm is Germanic. Both writers were at best describing women. Possessed with a love for tribal lore, Storm and H had a strong preference for the supernatural and the uncanny (versus Christian dogmatism). Their writings have an almost

balladic character; this "folksong" mood is closely allied to an interest in music in general.

2631 Hamilton, Horace E. "A Reading of *Tess of the d'Urbervilles*," Essays in Literary History, ed by Rudolf Kirk and C. F. Main (New Brunswick, NJ: Rutgers UP, 1960), pp. 197–216; rptd (NY: Russell & Russell, 1965).

In *Tess of the d'Urbervilles*, H's device of personifying nature is extended to a symbolizing of action and character. "It can be seen throughout [*Tess*] that a complex of symbolic images ramify from two complimentary metaphors: the Biblical-Miltonic Eden and country-England's lost heritage." With the theological and pagan principles interacting, the middle portion of the allegory provides for the "half-resolutions, conflicts, and wrong turns of inevitable tragedy." H sees the two themes as "complementary: the archetypal myth and its protean variations ramifying into a form of natural tragedy. The ratio between the theological symbol, the story, and the wider social analogy is something like that of the musical signature, the melody, and the counterpoint." The elements of this allegory clearly form an implicit pattern which is "indispensable as a justification of otherwise random emphasis on incidents and behavior unharmonious to strictly naturalistic narrative."

2632 Hartig, Paul (ed). Englandkunde (Note on England). 4th rvd and enlgd ed (Frankfurt/Main, Berlin, Bonn: Moritz Diesterweg, 1960), I, 386, 479, 482, 484, 486, 491, 493, 495, 496, 497.

[References to H are from Walter Hübner's Epochen der Englischen Literatur (Epochs of English Literature) (Frankfurt/Main, Berlin, Bonn: Moritz Diesterweg, 1955).] [In German.]

2633 Hodgins, James Raymond. "A Study of the Periodical Reception of the Novels of Thomas Hardy, George Gissing, and George Moore," Dissertation Abstracts, XXI (1960), 196–97. Unpublished dissertation, Michigan State University, 1960.

2634 Holloway, John. "*Tess of the d'Urbervilles* and The Awkward Age," The Charted Mirror: Literary and Critical Essays (Lond: Routledge & Kegan Paul, 1960), pp. 108–18; originally a BBC broadcast.

Tess of the d'Urbervilles (1891) and The Awkward Age (1899) "document a whole period of English life." James's novel portrays the awkwardness of English aristocratic society in the late 1880s and in the 1890s. And just as Kipling's Kim represents "one of the nether worlds beneath the glittering facade of The Awkward Age, *Tess of the d'Urbervilles* represents another: . . . the great late-nineteenth-century rural depression which took two million acres out of cultivation, drove a million people from the farms to the towns, and went on until the war of 1939." James and H in these novels are "drawing upon and representing whole societies: one the city plutocracy, the other the impoverished countryside hidden behind it. But neither has presented . . . a mere neutral slice of life; rather an interaction between the society he has chosen, and a certain distinctive human quality: the Pure Woman for Hardy, Innocence for James."

2635 Hunt, Kellog W. "LORD JIM and *The Return of the Native*: A Contrast," ENGLISH JOURNAL, XLIX (Oct 1960), 447–56.

LORD JIM is a novel of moral evaluation, while *The Return of the Native* is concerned with man's place in the cosmos. Conrad underscores his moral meaning by abstracting his story from space and time: Jim's tale of regeneration could take place anywhere, anytime. The plot of this novel breaks into two halves, failure and success, which are bound together by the theme of moral regeneration. *Native* is inferior to LORD JIM because there is no binding moral theme. Rather the complex plot is held together by a web of casual relationships which do not demonstrate any moral meaning.

2636 Karl, Frederick R. "*The Mayor of Casterbridge*: A New Fiction Defined," MODERN FICTION STUDIES, VI (Autumn 1960), 195–213; rptd in MODERN BRITISH FICTION: ESSAYS IN CRITICISM, ed by Mark Schorer (NY: Oxford UP, 1961), pp. 10–29.

In *The Mayor of Casterbridge* H aimed at a kind of realism different from that of Dickens, Eliot, and Thackeray. The novel is a psychological history, the story of a man who means well but is obsessed by a singular passion that destroys him. Although chance and an array of circumstances contribute, the events which destroy him develop from his own character. Nevertheless, he suffers more than he should and thus qualifies as a nineteenth-century counterpart of an Aeschylean or Euripidean protagonist. He is, ultimately, a "new type of nineteenth-century man," a "split individual" ruled by "a mysterious universe" and "a misdirected will."

2637 [Kent, Christopher]. "Thomas Hardy," LEXIKON DER WELT-LITERATUR IM 20 JAHRHUNDERT (Dictionary of World Literature in the 20th Century) (Freiburg im Breisgau: Herder, 1960) pp. 854–58.

Although for the most part H wrote his novels hastily and under pressure for income's sake, seven of his works belong to the most meaningful achievements of the English novel: *Under the Greenwood Tree, Far From the Madding Crowd, The Return of the Native, The Mayor of Casterbridge, The Woodlanders, Tess of the d'Urbervilles* and *Jude the Obscure.*

What makes his poetry so attractive are the love of English landscape and the depiction of the obstinate uprightness of a mind which is saturated with often painful doubts about man's destiny. [In German.]

2638 McDowell, Frederick P. W. "Hardy's 'Seemings or Personal Impressions': The Symbolic Use of Image and Contrast in *Jude the Obscure*," MODERN FICTION STUDIES, VI (Autumn 1960), 233–50.

Jude the Obscure, despite naturalistic tendencies, is not a "scientific" work but rather one that retains H's "more fluid theory of the art of fiction." The symbols are "not adventitious but organic"; they create an "ineffable . . . significance." H's use of symbols, images, and contrasts creates a book of "spiritual trueness." The book is "a pulsing organism," a "kaleidoscope" where each pattern "continually changes with the angle from which it is viewed"; it is a work of "fluid contours" and "changing vistas of meaning." [An image study; uses 1895 text of the novel.]

2639 Marcus, Mordecai, and Erin Marcus. "Hardy's 'During Wind and Rain,' " EXPLICATOR, XIX (Dec 1960), Item 14.

"During Wind and Rain" is a poem carefully constructed to show compassion in the face of the grief of death. It is a judgment against a view of life which ignores natural limitations, and it should not be read as sentimental.

2640 Marshall, George O., Jr. "Hardy's *Tess* and Ellen Glasgow's BARREN GROUND," TEXAS STUDIES IN LITERATURE AND· LANGUAGE, I (Winter 1960), 517–21.

Glasgow was a "great admirer" of H, and *Tess of the d'Urbervilles* had a "pervasive effect" on her BARREN GROUND. Similarities of "theme, tone, and detail, added to the Calvinistic fatalism permeating each book, suggest that Ellen Glasgow was influenced by Hardy's *Tess* to an extent that perhaps she, herself, was unaware."

2641 Martin, W. R. "Casterbridge and the Organic Community," USE OF ENGLISH, XII (Autumn 1960), 30–35.

Passages describing Casterbridge in *The Mayor of Casterbridge* show that H wants us to contrast the old town with the one beginning to come into existence in the novel. But H does not sentimentalize the old Casterbridge: "Casterbridge was picturesque but its citizens were ludicrously inefficient and naive." Thus nostalgia and amusement counterpoise each other throughout the descriptions. Henchard represents old Casterbridge, Farfrae the new; hence Henchard's downfall shows the individual's helplessness in the face of social change. The death of the old, organic community wrought adverse changes in man's psyche, as Farfrae's "inner coldness, a divorce of behaviour from feeling" shows.

2642 May, Derwent. "The Novelist as Moralist and the Moralist as Critic," ESSAYS IN CRITICISM, X (July 1960), 320–28.
H's theme of "pity for man in the hopelessness of fate" often leads him to distortion; H's novels may exonerate the guilt of his characters by making excuses for them. H makes characters the victims of their actions rather than holding them personally responsible.

2643 Paterson, John. "The Genesis of *Jude the Obscure*," STUDIES IN PHILOLOGY, LVII (Jan 1960), 87–98.
The manuscript discloses that *Jude the Obscure* "must have undergone a basic reorganization." It was originally conceived as a short story describing the suicide of a young man of the lower classes who fails to satisfy his academic ambitions. Among the various manuscript changes in the novel, the most important is the reversal of the roles of Phillotson and Sue Bridehead as inspiration to Jude. Manuscript revisions "suggest that once the novel was launched, the theme with which H started was forced by the dynamics of the author's imagination to give way to another and more dangerous theme, to an attack on the stringency of the marriage laws and on the narrow Christianity responsible for their stringency."

2644 Paterson, John. "The 'Poetics' of *The Return of the Native*," MODERN FICTION STUDIES, VI (Autumn 1960), 214–22.
H's imagination was dominated by the legend and literature of Greece and Rome when he wrote *The Return of the Native*. There are several instances of formal correspondence with Greek tragedy (the observance of the unities, the peasants as chorus, Eustacia's set speech, etc.); but because of the stress on a number of characters, their dubious claim to aristocratic standing, and the complexity of the plot, these classical elements of the form appear as only "arbitrary and ornamental." The novel does parallel Greek tragedy, however, in a "poetic or musical" sense. The accumulation of allusions to classical antiquity, the picturing of Egdon Heath as Tartarus, and the allusions to the novel's main characters as Tartarus's inhabitants display H's immersion in classical legend. Moreover, scenes, characters, and incidents are judged according "to a scale provided by classical history and literature." Eustacia Vye, for instance, inspires allusions to Sappho, the Sphinx, the lotus-eaters, the Delphian oracles, Venus, etc. The Promethean theme, however, contributes the most to the novel's "transfiguration." Several of the characters (Clym, Eustacia, etc.) suggest Prometheus. The fire imagery, utilized in a number of different aspects, is prominent. Although the novel does not use this pattern of clas-

sical allusion and imagery throughout, its predominance shows the concept of "the musical or poetic—i.e., less clearly rational—concept of form favored by modern experimenters in prose fiction."

2645 Piper, Henry Dan. "Fitzgerald, Mark Twain, and Thomas Hardy," FITZGERALD NEWSLETTER, No. 8 (Winter 1960), 31.
H told Cyril Clemens in 1925 that he had "read and been greatly impressed by THIS SIDE OF PARADISE."

2646 Purdy, R. L. "The Authorship of Hardy's Biography," TIMES LITERARY SUPPLEMENT (Lond), 30 Dec 1960, p. 845.
Cyril Clemens's MY CHAT WITH THOMAS HARDY [not seen] is a pastiche of materials from THE LIFE AND LETTERS OF JOHN GALSWORTHY, M'CONNACHIE AND J. M. B., and a New York TIMES account of Purdy's Hardy Centenary Lecture at the Grolier Club. The first revelation of H's authorship of EARLY LIFE and LATER YEARS, by Florence Hardy (1928, 1930), was not in a casual chat in 1940 but in Purdy's bibliography in 1954.

2647 Ransom, John Crowe. "Thomas Hardy's Poems, and the Religious Difficulties of a Naturalist," KENYON REVIEW, XXII (Spring 1960), 169–93.
H has "a metaphysical imagination, in the service of a theological passion." Some of H's small poems "are like terse but sure little dramas." The genre most likely to describe them is the fable. Even *The Dynasts* is "a reinforcement to Hardy's small fables." In his melancholy and irony, H finds "unexpected company" in Browning, although "Hardy thought that Browning's optimism came too cheaply." But on the evidence of certain pieces in ASOLANDO, H felt he had done Browning an injustice. [Rambling and disorganized essay.]

2648 Rosenthal, M. L. "Hopkins, Hardy, and the 'Religion of Art,'" THE MODERN POETS: A CRITICAL INTRODUCTION (NY: Oxford UP, 1960), pp. 20–27.
"The religion of art"—as glimpsed in Rossetti, Swinburne, Pater, Hopkins et al—current after 1870 culminated in Yeats who "won through to . . . passionate detachment, . . . concerned disinterestedness." H, however, failed in his attempts at establishing " 'an alliance between religion . . . and complete rationality . . . by means of the interfusing effect of poetry' " because H "lacks the necessary conviction and the necessary symbols as well."

2649 Schofield, Geoffrey. "Hardy and the Tragic Sense," HUMANIST, XL (May 1960), 136–38.

Though H "represents the darker strands of humanist thought, he reacts negatively to being called a pessimist."

2650 Scott, James Frazier. "The Gothic Element in the Fiction of Thomas Hardy," DISSERTATION ABSTRACTS, XXI (1960), 1556. Unpublished dissertation, University of Kansas, 1960.

2651 Scott, Nathan A., Jr. "The Literary Imagination and the Victorian Crisis of Faith: The Example of Thomas Hardy," JOURNAL OF RELIGION, XL (Oct 1960), 267–81.

The two books which most shaped H's mind were THE ORIGIN OF SPECIES and ESSAYS AND REVIEWS. Darwin was the greater influence, and as late as *The Dynasts*, H pictures a world of natural selection and "fierce struggle." The important events in H's works are always the "utterly gratuitous" ones, and the "absurdity" of chance happenings should remind us of the world of "Gide and Kafka and Camus." Dealing as he did with the "metaphysical crisis," we may call H's writings "religious testimony," not because they offered orthodox solutions, but because they posed religious problems.

2652 Stevenson, Lionel. THE ENGLISH NOVEL: A PANORAMA (Boston: Houghton Mifflin, 1960), pp. 383–89, 390, 402, 404–7, 419, 421–23, 424, 425, 429, 430, 431, 453, 480, 511, 528–29.

H absorbed the sense of an ageless past in the Dorset countryside. He grew up with the patterns of living untouched tradition, but the region was disturbed by rumors of Napoleonic invasion. Music was a formative influence. At twenty-seven he returned to Dorset and started work on a novel. Upon submission to Chapman and Hall it was read by George Meredith, who criticized it as containing radical propaganda and indiscriminate satire. H conformed and produced the intricately structured (á la Collins) *Desperate Remedies*. The work was sensational but contained some poetic sensibility and philosophic meditation. It was given a devastating review in the SPECTATOR. *Under the Greenwood Tree* had the slenderest narrative. A more dramatic situation and a final ironic twist was used in *A Pair of Blue Eyes*. This novel was probably related to H's wooing of a young lady in Cornwall. The worst defect of *Blue Eyes* is the style, which is pretentious and awkward; the conversation is formal and ponderous.

The success of *Greenwood Tree* brought the invitation to serialize for CORNHILL MAGAZINE, and in 1874 *Far From the Madding Crowd* appeared. It contained the idyllic country setting with an adequately dramatic plot. The greatest advance was in characterization. Another serial was requested, and H tried comedy in *The Hand of Ethelberta*. The humor is admirable, but the attempt at social satire suffers from lack of familiarity with the society satirized. *The Return of the Native* brings all H's previous best features together with a mature philosophical outlook: survival is a ruthless struggle; the tragic outcome of the accidental process of development is the human mind because it makes man conscious of his helplessness and gives him hope without the chance of fulfillment; the universe is incalculable in size and with such a background the individual is trivial; persons of fiction are embodiments of the life force struggling futilely against heredity and environment. The novel contributes the imaginative and symbolic use of landscape. H's Wessex novels use a background which enhances emotional effects and symbolizes the timeless, unchanging power of nature. The superstitions perform a similar function. Coincidence is the working of pure chance and is ironic when it rests on the trivial. The ascendancy of blind chance gives H's major novels the fatalistic dignity of Greek tragedy. H sees man dethroned as the favorite of a benevolent creator and thus losing the guarantee of fulfillment. H emphasized the tragic irony of inevitable frustration.

The Trumpet-Major is a romantic story. *A Laodicean* is a serial with an unconvincing plot. *Two on a Tower* is an extreme example of the symbolic use of vast and ageless settings; *The Mayor of Casterbridge* is a study of a strong unstable character whose problem is self-control, and it is the only novel by H that is situated in town; *The Woodlanders* is expressive of the relentless struggle for survival as the primary law of nature, the mechanistic control of human doings. *Tess of the d'Urbervilles* is deterministic and contains improbabilities, and the murder makes the book outrageously immoral. *The Well-Beloved* deals with psychological abnormality on the literal level, but symbolically it is a search for the Platonic ideal. *Jude the Obscure* is deterministic, contains an element of social protest, makes poverty an unavoidable fact of life, and presents the grotesqueness of calamity and black pessimism. [Contains the usual biographical material and pp. 528–29 contain a bibliography of H's novels.]

2653 Stoll, Elmer Edgar. SHAKESPEARE STUDIES (NY: Frederick Unger, 1960), pp. 60, 66, 340, 343, 357, 372.
[A series of unrelated, trivial remarks about H and his works.]

2654 Walcutt, Charles Child. "Character and Coincidence in *The Return of the Native*," TWELVE ORIGINAL ESSAYS ON GREAT ENGLISH NOVELS, ed by Charles Shapiro (Detroit: Wayne State UP, 1960), pp. 153–73; rptd in Walcutt's MEN'S CHANGING MASK: MODES AND METHODS OF CHARACTERIZATION IN FICTION (Minneapolis: University of Minnesota P, 1966).
The images of dark and light prominent in chap 1 of *The Return of the Native* suggest the nature of H's cosmos; mankind, caught in a dark

savage world, can only grope "towards its puzzling ends." But man's chief antagonist is no "diabolical god" who thwarts man by grotesque coincidences. What look like coincidences in the novel are often Freudian errors, like Wildeve's slip in obtaining a marriage license. The tangled lives of Part I are caused not by "an indifferent or incompetent God . . . but [by] human qualities." The Yeobrights possessed a wide stripe of self-destructiveness: Thomasin sacrifices herself to Wildeve; Clym enjoys the torture inflicted on him by his mother and Eustacia. H's characters are so afflicted with these tendencies that their contests against error and mischance "seem more inevitably doomed . . . than those, say, of Othello." The coincidences may modify this fatalistic view of man's character, "but the trouble is that the flaws in the universe do not remove the flaws in the characters."

2655 Webster, Harvey Curtis. "Comments and Queries," VICTORIAN STUDIES, IV (Sept 1960), 90–93.

John Paterson's view of *The Mayor of Casterbridge* as an example of traditional tragedy ("*The Mayor of Casterbridge* as Tragedy," ibid, III [Dec 1959], 151–72) is not entirely correct. H's view was rather " 'The WORTHY encompassed by the INEVITABLE,' " not a justification of God's ways to man. H's novels are all flawed in one way or another. There is no ideal justice in them. *Mayor* is no more tragic than other H novels or novels by other great novelists. "Tragedy . . . makes us understand the noble finiteness of man that can endure the worst, remedy the inevitable, and say 'yes' to what cannot be altered or more than partially comprehended."

1961

2656 Alvarez, A. "Afterword," *Jude the Obscure* (NY: New American Library, 1961), pp. 404–14.

In *Jude the Obscure*, Sue is at times only the projection of one side of Jude's personality. There are not really any heroines in the book, only a hero. The scene in which Jude dresses the soaking-wet Sue in his clothes is the equal of another masterful scene of double identity in Joseph Conrad's "The Secret Sharer."

2657 Barber, Richard [William]. ARTHUR OF ALBION: AN INTRODUCTION TO THE ARTHURIAN LITERATURE AND LEGENDS OF ENGLAND (Lond: Barrie & Rookliff, 1961), pp. 166–68.

H's *The Famous Tragedy of the Queen of Cornwall* is only a "partial success." The addition of the choruses and Merlin's prologue and epilogue "lend weight to the action" but offer only inadequate background exposition. Although "some of the lyrical outbursts are among" H's best poetry, his mixing of the commonplace and poetic is a weakness. H was apparently uncertain whether it should have been a "mummery-play" or a tragedy. [Pointed but unillustrated criticism.]

2658 Beatty, C. J. P. "Two Rare Birds in Hardy's *The Return of the Native*," NOTES AND QUERIES, CCVI (March 1961), 98–99.

H mentions two rare birds in *The Return of the Native,* chap 10: the "cream-coloured courser" and "the bustard." He found information on these birds in his own copy of THE HISTORY AND ANTIQUITIES OF THE COUNTY OF DORSET by John Hutchins, now at the Dorset County Museum.

2659 Booth, Wayne C. THE RHETORIC OF FICTION (Chicago UP, 1961), pp. 27, 114, 126, 187–88, 196, 386, 389.

H is an example of a writer whose philosophical views allegedly obtrude upon his novels in an inartistic way. [Quotes H's defense of *Tess of the d'Urbervilles* on moral grounds to show H's response to his critics.]

2660 Carpenter, Richard C. "Thomas Hardy and the Old Masters," BOSTON UNIVERSITY STUDIES IN ENGLISH, IV (Spring 1961), 18–28.

Although evidences of H's training as an architect have been pointed out in the context and structure of his novels, equal attention has not been paid to the influence of painting. This influence can be seen in the content of his novels, but more important is his adaptation of certain painting techniques to his literary technique. "Perhaps because of the Dutch realists . . . Hardy deals little in color." He concentrates rather on "careful composition, manipulation of the physical point of view, attention to the perspective and lighting of a scene."

2661 Cassis, A. F. "The Tragic Theme in the Works of Thomas Hardy." Unpublished dissertation, Trinity University (Dublin), 1961.

[Listed in Lawrence F. McNamee, DISSERTATIONS IN ENGLISH AND AMERICAN LITERATURE (NY & Lond: Bowker, 1968).]

2662 Cecil, Lord David. "Hardy's Unhappy First Marriage," SUNDAY TIMES [Magazine Section] (Lond), 22 Oct 1961, p. 30.

The volume offers some insights into H's first wife. Her writing style suggests an imaginative side that attracted H to her. Conversely, the snobbishness revealed in her comments together with the sense that she was H's social superior helps explain why their marriage was unhappy. [Review of

Emma Hardy's SOME RECOLLECTIONS: WITH SOME RELEVANT POEMS BY THOMAS HARDY, ed by Evelyn Hardy and Robert Gittings (1961).]

2663 Clifford, Emma. "The Impressionistic View of History in *The Dynasts*," MODERN LANGUAGE QUARTERLY, XXII (March 1961), 21–31.

H's "Anti-realism" in *The Dynasts* arouses our awareness of underlying determinist principles in which actions coexist with dreams. The historical scenes are impressions, defined by The Spirit of the Years as "demonstrations from the back of things." Events are woven into the Immanent Will, a brain-like webwork of event and scene.

2664 Coates, William Ames. "Thomasin and the Reddleman," UNIVERSITY OF CEYLON REVIEW, XIX (April 1961), 61–67.

The present ending of *The Return of the Native* (Thomasin's marrying Diggory Venn) is consistent with the rest of the novel; the ending as originally planned (Thomasin remaining a widow) shows that H failed to understand the dynamics of his own creation. In real life joy and sorrow are mixed; exclusive concentration on either is a falsification of life. [Feeble.]

2665 Coombes, H. "Hardy, de la Mare, and Edward Thomas," THE MODERN AGE [Vol VII of THE PELICAN GUIDE TO ENGLISH LITERATURE, ed by Boris Ford] (Hammondsworth, Middlesex, & Baltimore: Penguin Books, 1961); 2nd ed (1963), pp. 138–53.

H's pessimism was his attempt to understand the world without recourse to pleasant deceptions. While this pessimism led the poet to write some dull philosophical verses, his essential feeling for others, his ability to describe things precisely, and his detailed knowledge of rural life led him to write many sincere and honest poems.

2666 Dale, T. R. "*The Dynasts* and Eduard von Hartmann," NOTES AND QUERIES, CCVI (March 1961), 100–101.

Many critics assume that Hartmann originated the idea of an Unconscious Will of the Universe (in his PHILOSOPHY OF THE UNCONSCIOUS) and that H's repeated statements about his own originality are errors or forgetfulness on the part of an old man. But Hartmann cannot be said to have originated an idea he had hastily dismissed: he wrote "the will itself can *never* become conscious." H's presentation of an unconscious will gradually becoming conscious is therefore directly and essentially opposed to Hartmann's teaching.

2667 Davie, Donald. "Hardy and the *Avant-Garde*," NEW STATESMAN, LXI (20 Oct 1961), 560–61.

Although H's poetry is supposed to show how an indigenous tradition went undisturbed through all the shrillness of the *avant-garde*, did H not write poems like Eliot or Pound, whose meaning is all in the arrangement of their images? "During Wind and Rain," for instance, is but a collection of images. It differs from "The Waste Land" only by H's having used rhythm as an instrument to help the reader pick his way through the images. Of course the H poem *feels* quite different from any *avant-garde* poem: the triviality, the oddity of some of the details. All H's art is in the choice and the arrangement of images, drawn from "literature," just as Pound drew his images from Arnault Daniel or Eliot from Baudelaire.

2668 Drake, Robert Y. "*A Laodicean*: A Note on a Minor Novel," Philological Quarterly, XL (Oct 1961), 602–6.
Despite the thematic war of Traditionalism and Modernism, treated successfully in *The Mayor of Casterbridge* and *The Return of the Native*, *A Laodicean* fails because of its peculiar embodiment in characters. The De Stancys—traditionalists—are a worn-out family; Paula Power and George Somerset—modernists—fight with each other but both also have a desire for Tradition. The issues are not sufficiently clear-cut, but H has "rigged" conflict. "The real conflict is . . . a struggle between the self-possessed (Somerset) and the self-betrayed (the De Stancys) for the uncommitted (Paula)." This conflict is obscured by the promise of a greater one between Traditionalism and Modernism. The novel's power is further dissipated by a loose plot, irrelevant incidents, and the presence of inadequately developed characters.

2669 Elsbree, Langdon. "Tess and the Local Cerealia," Philological Quarterly, XL (Oct 1961), 606–13.
The dance motif in *Tess of the d'Urbervilles* functions both thematically and structurally. Thematically, it emphasizes Tess's youthful ardor and innocence, and her initial desire for Angel Clare as partner, his failure to select her, and the "foreshadowed doom of their marriage"; the farmers' loss of their folk-heritage; and, "in the orgiastic dances at Chaseborough, the farm hands' rootlessness and moral confusion." Structurally, the dance introduces Tess to the reader and Angel Clare to both. The dance also places the novel in a historical moment—"when the farm community . . . has forgotten the meaning and is neglecting the customs of its past."

2670 Fayen, George S., Jr. "Hardy's *The Woodlanders*: Inwardness and Memory," Studies in English Literature, I (Autumn 1961), 81–100.
The Woodlanders "marks a crucial phase in the development of Hardy's imagination." Shelley's influence is seen in *Woodlanders*. There is an

analogy between the plot of the novel and the knotted undergrowth of Little Hintock. "Hardy as narrator persistently indulges in the remembering which shapes the acts of his characters."

2671 Griffin, Ernest G. "Hardy and the Growing Consciousness of the Immanent Will," CAIRO STUDIES IN ENGLISH, 1961–1962, pp. 121–32.

The ending line of *The Dynasts* is neither unprepared for nor a concession not to be regarded seriously. Starting from "the certainty of history," utilizing his background in Greek and English Classics, and not attempting to escape from an evolutionary philosophy, H tries "to see consciousness in the supreme Will so that men might once again hear the prompting of a sublime consciousness and decide to act nobly." The poem, then, does not show the barrenness, but the promise of the present.

2672 Hagan, John. "A Note on the Significance of Diggory Venn," NINETEENTH CENTURY FICTION, XVI (Sept 1961), 147–55.

There is no contradiction between the fact that Venn's actions invariably are harmful to the other characters and the fact that his motives are always benevolent. It is appropriate that Venn possess these two seemingly inconsistent qualities because in doing so he emblematically symbolizes the basic incongruity of the cosmos which, in turn, is "the unifying principle" of the book itself.

2673 Hardy, Emma. SOME RECOLLECTIONS BY EMMA HARDY WITH NOTES BY EVELYN HARDY TOGETHER WITH SOME RELEVANT POEMS BY THOMAS HARDY WITH NOTES BY ROBERT GITTINGS (NY & Lond: Oxford UP, 1961).

[Emma was known as "attractive" as a child rather than intellectual. She describes early houses, delightful atmosphere, Plymouth and The Hoe, band concerts, drills, walks, teas, excursions, dancing, attending church, family music. Grandmother Gifford, a gentlewoman of the old style, had an income which supported the family after father retired as solicitor to live a life of leisure. Reading and family conversation about books included Shakespeare and the Bible. Father was handsome, had a problem with drink, enjoyed gardening. The family moved to Cornwall after grandmother's death. Emma's sister was a companion to an old lady at Tintagel. Her sister married, and she moved with her to St. Juliot Rectory, a poor parish in an isolated and wildly romantic setting. Emma enjoyed riding. When the church needed repair, H came as architect. There were further visits, rambles through the country, Emma riding. An Unseen Benevolence always guided her path. Fourteen relevant poems by H including "Rain on a Grave," "The West-of-Wessex Girl," "Lonely Days," "Beeny Cliff." Appendix: Emma's novel, MAID ON THE SHORE, is related to *A Pair of Blue Eyes*.]

2674 [Hardy, Evelyn, and Robert Gittings] "Introduction," SOME RECOLLECTIONS BY EMMA HARDY WITH NOTES BY EVELYN HARDY TOGETHER WITH SOME RELEVANT POEMS BY THOMAS HARDY WITH NOTES BY ROBERT GITTINGS (NY & Lond: Oxford UP, 1961), pp. ix–xv.

H found the recollections among Emma's papers. They had been estranged for many years. She came from a family of mental eccentricity, and she suffered from delusions. The papers drew H back to the joyful period when they became engaged. The poems he wrote from 1912 to 1928 show his love and remorse that he had not done more for her. Fourteen poems that show the direct influence of Emma's RECOLLECTIONS are appended here. H included about one-fifth of the RECOLLECTIONS in THE EARLY LIFE OF THOMAS HARDY, 1840–1891 (1928), much edited. The merits of the complete collection are Emma's own spontaneity, charm, sharp observation, her feeling for poetry of scene, and for the influence on H's poems.

2675 Houghton, R. E. C. "Hardy and Shakespeare," NOTES AND QUERIES, CCVI (March 1961), 98.

H may have been unconsciously influenced by KING LEAR while he was writing *The Return of the Native*. The crisis in the novel lies in Eustacia's refusal to admit Clym's mother to her house: it is this disappointment and the physical exhaustion from a double journey that bring about Mrs. Yeobright's death. In the play, it is exclusion by his daughters and exposure on a heath that turn Lear mad. There are also some verbal parallels. In the conclusion to a short preface (written in 1895) H fancies that Egdon Heath might have been Lear's heath.

2676 Hyde, William J. "Hardy's Response to the Critics of *Jude*," VICTORIAN NEWSLETTER, No. 19 (Spring 1961), 1–5.

H was not shattered by contemporary response. He made light of some of the most vicious and seemingly ignored favorable critiques of *Jude the Obscure* by eminent writers. Perhaps with *Jude* he deliberately placed "himself in a position in which further prose writing proved undesirable." Thus, he could return to the more pleasurable though less remunerative medium of poetry.

2677 Kayser, Wolfgang. KLEINES LITERARISCHES LEXIKON (Brief Literary Dictionary). 3rd ed (Bern & Munich: A. Francke, 1961), I, 445–46.

H as a pessimist and realist. [Includes works and German translations.] [In German.]

2678 Kelvin, Norman. A TROUBLED EDEN: NATURE AND SOCIETY IN THE WORKS OF GEORGE MEREDITH (Stanford: Stanford UP, 1961), pp. [1], 3, 113, 121, 141, 178, 179, 185–86, 187–88, 212, 213.

Faith in nature's benevolence influenced Meredith as distrust of nature influenced Tennyson, Arnold, and H. Like H, Meredith wanted to be remembered for poetry. Meredith thought nature beneficent; H, Tennyson, Arnold, Mill thought it cruelly impersonal. In *The Dynasts*, H views cosmic indifference as a shocking attack on personality; in "The Woods of Westermain," Meredith did not despair at individual insignificance in the face of cosmic grandeur. Comparison of Nataly in ONE OF OUR CONQUERORS with Sue Bridehead in *Jude the Obscure*: though the differences of conception are enormous, they follow similar paths, both reacting to their initial freedom. Meredith differs in his "romantic myth-making propensity" from H's "almost pathological genius for turning society into a cruelly contrived labyrinth, in which the individual is forced . . . to the ultimate horror mirror casting back the image of a puny victim in his last degradation." Comparison of Matey Weyburn in LORD ORMONT AND HIS AMINTA to Jude Fawley in *Jude*: H uses poverty to crush Jude; Meredith uses poverty as a challenge to Matey, who triumphs where Jude fails to survive. H's characters have no free will, as opposed to Meredith's who create their own destinies. Meredith rejects the fate of original sin and also H's kind: he believes man free through acceptance of nature's laws "to give his life a rationally inspired pattern." Meredith in "My Odes in Contribution to the Song of French History" gives his "conception of the power of Society to harm, to do evil," his substitute for concepts in novels of Balzac, Stendahl, Flaubert, H, and James.

2679 Lewis, C[ecil] Day. "A Half-open Door," LISTENER, LXV (23 Feb 1961), 358–59.

"Dorset is a leading character in his [H's] books." "He was a great master in the education of the heart." H attained a degree of legendary stature in the area.

2680 Lowe, Robert Liddell. "Two Letters of Thomas Hardy to P. W. Bunting," NOTES AND QUERIES, CCVI (March 1961), 99–100.

[Two short letters (1890 and 1891) by H to the editor of the CONTEMPORARY REVIEW, one concerning a possible contribution to the magazine and the other introducing Mrs. Mona Caird.]

2681 McCann, Eleanor. "Blind Will or Blind Hero: Philosophy and Myth in Hardy's *Return of the Native*," CRITICISM, III (Spring 1961), 140–57.

The division between Clym Yeobright's rationality and his passions comes from his half-understood Oedipal relationship with his mother. Clym hovers between full acceptance of natural life, represented by the heath, and "Victorian primness," represented by his mother. His partial blindness suggests his incomplete awareness of these opposite poles of attractions and also recalls the Oedipus story. H was unable to portray the Oedipus story more clearly because it touched upon his own life in his relationship with his mother and the mother-figure, Julia Augusta Martin. Clym's psychological conflict makes him an interesting character, not merely an automaton ultimately dragged under by Fate.

2682 Morcos, Louis. "The Overworld: A Projection of Hardy's Personality," CAIRO STUDIES IN ENGLISH, 1961–1962, pp. 37–93.
The seven Spirits of the Overworld in *The Dynasts* represent divisions in H's own personality. "Intellectually he was a free-thinker, emotionally a fundamentalist." This "dichotomy" reveals itself most clearly in the conflict between the Spirit of the Years and the Spirit of the Pities. And this dichotomy between the head and heart, between the "Immanent Will and the revolt of feeling" is a theme that runs through all of his works. [Some isolated perceptions buried in a labored exposition. Naive "analysis" of H's "personality."]

2683 "Notes on Sales," TIMES LITERARY SUPPLEMENT (Lond), 21 April 1961, p. 256.
On 23 & 24 Feb 1961, Hodgson's sold "autograph drafts of some lyrics by Thomas Hardy, the highest price being £80 paid for a rough draft of 'The three kissing gates,' " thirty-six lines in pencil.

2684 Paterson, John. "Hardy, Faulkner, and the Prosaics of Tragedy," CENTENNIAL REVIEW, V (Spring 1961), 156–75, espec 160–63.
The novel "has not often accommodated the sublime affections and affirmations of tragedy." It is committed "to hold the mirror hard against the surface of life" and is nourished by an "unheroic climate of 'life.' " Nevertheless *The Mayor of Casterbridge* suggests that a novel "may reach to tragedy without ceasing to be a novel." Plot, not character, is predominant in *Mayor*. H's plot, "traditional rather than improvised, fabulous . . . [like the plots of] Oedipus and Lear," "enacts a universal motion . . . greater than and exterior to both the will of character and the bias of environment." The absence of "remorseless psychological analysis" keeps Henchard's "masterful figure" from overshadowing plot: his character "remains to the very end . . . something of a miracle and a mystery." Plot dominates setting, too. Casterbridge does not dwarf Henchard as Egdon dwarfs Clym; there is no "elaborate and exhaustive set description." Though realistic elements do enter the novel—e.g., the nineteenth-century conflict between tradition

and progress and the depiction of nineteenth-century rural life, they too are "assimilated by the tragic structure of the novel."

2685 Patton, John. "An Unpublished Hardy Letter to Millay," COLBY LIBRARY QUARTERLY, V (June 1961), 284–85.
H preferred Edna St. Vincent Millay's verse to her dramas.

2686 Pongs, Hermann. DAS KLEINE LEXIKON DER WELTLITERATUR (The Short Dictionary of World Literature) (Stuttgart: Union Verlag, 1961), pp. 719–20.
H is a dismal realist, depicts the rupture of civilization in Wessex, and was influenced by Schopenhauer. [In German.]

2687 Reeves, James. A SHORT HISTORY OF ENGLISH POETRY, 1340–1940 (Lond: Heinemann, 1961; NY: Dutton, 1964), pp. 158, 206–8.
In H's poetry there is "a certain linguistic archaism, a certain angularity or awkwardness of movement; we are reminded of the influence of Browning, of Meredith, of Swinburne."

2688 Schorer, Mark (ed). MODERN BRITISH FICTION (NY: Oxford UP, 1961).
Contents, abstracted under date of first publication: Frederick R. Karl, "*The Mayor of Casterbridge*: A New Fiction Defined," MODERN FICTION STUDIES, VI (Autumn 1960), 195–213; Dorothy Van Ghent, "On *Tess of the d'Urbervilles*," THE ENGLISH NOVEL: FORM AND FUNCTION (1953); Arthur Mizener, "*Jude the Obscure* as a Tragedy," SOUTHERN REVIEW, VI (Summer 1940), 193–213.

2689 Smart, Alastair. "Pictorial Imagery in the Novels of Thomas Hardy," REVIEW OF ENGLISH STUDIES (Lond), ns XII (1961), 262–80.
H's landscapes are "ominous, desolate, and essentially inimical to man," who is "presented as an insignificant creature pathetically uncertain of his existence and his fate." A "saturation in European art" contributes to his descriptive ability. He "frequently mentions a work of art to make a description precise," "to suggest psychological change," or "for more dramatic effect." [Lists H's references to paintings and their importance, particularly noting the influence of Rembrandt and Turner.] "The richness and evocativeness of H's imagery are to a large extent the natural fruits of exceptional powers of observation; but they also reflect a profound knowledge of the visual arts."

2690 Subramanyam, N. S. "Imagery in Hardy's *The Dynasts*," INDIAN JOURNAL OF ENGLISH STUDIES, II (1961), 125–29.

"In *The Dynasts,* there are three major systems of imagery" used: the analogy of "weaving and spinning," the "mechanical world," "puppetry," "architecture," and "the numerous references to the world of deluded small insects and helpless animals." The "weaving" imagery is the dominating image in *Dynasts.* These images "picture the way the various aspects of creation, the galaxies, the planets, the earth and life on it, are produced by the Immanent Will" and show history as a "closely-webbed development of character and motive."

1962

2691 Atkins, Norman J. HARDY, TESS AND MYSELF. With an introduction by Richard Curle (Beaminster, Dorset: Toucan P, 1962).

In 1919, when H was mainly writing poetry, he was still best liked in his native country for his novels, dramatic versions of which were regularly produced by the Dorchester Debating and Dramatic Society. Max Gate in 1924, when H was 84, was "not a house of fun." Mrs. H recalls an American silent film of *Tess of the d'Urbervilles.* [H thought Atkins portrayed Alec as "being too nice to Tess."] "I [Atkins] had definitely annoyed him [H] and he showed signs of being what I should describe as 'scratchy.' " T. H. Tilley, a retired monument mason who had dramatized *Desperate Remedies* and *The Return of the Native,* "was probably Mr. Hardy's most intimate friend." The production of *Tess* at the Dorchester Corn Exchange and in Weymouth was a considerable success. [Highly detailed reminiscences by the player of Alec, of visits to Max Gate, of famous visitors like Barrie and T. E. Lawrence, of H's fondness for Galsworthy and his lack of interest in Henry James, and of rehearsals and performances of *Tess.* Also see J. Stevens Cox (pub and general editor), Monographs on the Life of Thomas Hardy (1962).]

2692 Bailey, J. O. "Temperament as Motive in *The Return of the Native,*" ENGLISH FICTION IN TRANSITION, V: 2 (1962), 21–29. Temperament rather than Fate or destiny accounts for the major action and the catastrophes which plague the characters in *The Return of the Native.* Little happens by chance; characters are victims of their own "innate forces, emotions, and desires." Factors other than temperament or Fate are "the laws of nature, blind circumstance, and narrow social codes."

2693 Beckman, Richard D. "Irony and Character in the World of Thomas Hardy." Unpublished dissertation, Johns Hopkins University, 1962.

[Listed in Lawrence F. McNamee, DISSERTATIONS IN ENGLISH AND AMERICAN LITERATURE (NY & Lond: Bowker, 1968).]

2694 Bicánić, Sonia. "Writing for the Magazines," STUDIA ROMANICA ET ANGLICA ZAGRABIENSIA, Nos. 13–14 (July–Dec 1962), pp. 13–30.

Investigation of novels serialized in CORNHILL shows the "magazine publication . . . had a definite, discernible and important influence on the form of the great majority of novels." H's experience in writing *Far From the Madding Crowd* shows that Leslie Stephen's desires were influential in shaping the novel. Of the serial's twelve parts, four end very dramatically, three with a noticeable heightening of interest; only four "have no marked serial ending."

2695 Billingsley, Bruce Alder. " 'Take Her Up Tenderly': A Study of the Fallen Woman in the Nineteenth-Century English Novel," DISSERTATION ABSTRACTS, XXIII (Oct–Dec 1962), 1681–82. Unpublished dissertation, University of Texas, 1962.

The fallen woman, as she appears in eight Victorian novels, was always treated sympathetically, and in each case "the double standard and class prejudice" were responsible for her fall. The novelists suggested as a remedy either a "singe standard of purity" or, in the case of H, "a single standard of freedom" for both sexes. Of the seducers, Alec d'Urberville was treated the least sympathetically. [A study of THE HEART OF MIDLOTHIAN, PENDENNIS, DAVID COPPERFIELD, RUTH, ADAM BEDE, RHODA FLEMING, THE VICAR OF BULLHAMPTON, and *Tess of the d'Urbervilles*.]

2696 Bowden, Ann. "The Thomas Hardy Collection," LIBRARY CHRONICLE OF THE UNIVERSITY OF TEXAS, VII (Summer 1962), 6–14.

[Description of the "truly distinguished" H collection at the University of Texas.]

2697 Brick, Allan. "Paradise and Consciousness in *Tess*," NINETEENTH CENTURY FICTION, XVII (Sept 1962), 115–34.

In *Tess of the d'Urbervilles* H depicts love "in the imagery of Biblical Paradise. Here his focus is man's fate under the first covenant in Paradise as compared with that under the new covenant of Christ." Alec "springs into Tess's consciousness for essentially the same reason that Satan springs into Eve's: he is correlative to her yearning for status as divinity—or, in Tess's case, as nobility—and to her natural pride in her beauty." In "Phase the Second" Tess "is a fallen being starting the first phase of real human life with the burden of original sin already upon her." "Phase the Third" is her "true beginning in earth's illusory Eden. Her Adam is Angel Clare, a young man who comes direct from the high gentility to which Tess has aspired." Tess's vision of Angel as her Christ is emphatically not that of the reader, "who after the end of 'Phase the Fourth' sees him as man horribly fallen—the antithesis of Milton's 'second Adam.'" When Angel and Tess are reunited after the murder, "she acts as intercessor and savior, opening him up to the bodily reality which lies within and beyond her mere bodily form."

2698 Briggs, R. C. H. "I Am, Sir, Your Obedient Servant," JOURNAL OF THE WILLIAM MORRIS SOCIETY, I (Winter 1962), 18–27. Sir Sydney Cockerell wrote more than a hundred letters to the Press to point out inaccuracies in a particular article on H. His letters are concise and reveal his interest in many subjects. [The bibliography lists several of his letters that were written concerning inaccuracies dealing with H.]

2699 Brown, Douglas. THOMAS HARDY: THE MAYOR OF CASTERBRIDGE [Studies in English Literature, No. 7.] (Lond: Edward Arnold; Woodbury, NY: Barron's Educational Series; Great Neck, NY: Barron's Educational Series, 1962).
The Mayor of Casterbridge stresses human society rather than individual consciousness. Blending sociological, "fabular," and saga elements, it depicts the passing away of the old rural order, represented by Susan and Henchard, and the rise of a new order, represented by Farfrae and Lucetta. The struggle between the two orders is seen in the struggle between Henchard and Farfrae. Thus, while a major portion of the novel presents a balance between the two orders, eventually Farfrae prospers and Henchard fails. The mayor's defeat is no surprise since the old order has only "doggedness" in its favor, while the new has both machines and "necessary process." Change and machinery combine to defeat the man who represents the "style of life" of an entire community.

2700 Bugler, Gertrude. PERSONAL RECOLLECTIONS OF THOMAS HARDY (Dorchester: The Dorset Natural History and Archaeological Society, 1962); first given as a talk, "My Memories of Thomas Hardy," at the Dorset Evening in the Corn Exchange, Dorchester, 7 April 1959, the MS of eight typed pages is in the Colby College Library; distributed by J. Stevens Cox, this title became the first of the Hardy Monograph Series later published by J. Stevens Cox's Toucan Press.
The Dorchester Debating and Dramatic Society prepared many of the Wessex novels for the stage and acted in the dramatic versions. H allowed The Hardy Players to perform his own dramatization (1895) of *Tess of the d'Urbervilles* in 1924, with Mrs. Bugler as Tess; Frederick Harrison's plans to have Mrs. Bugler play the role at the Haymarket Theatre, London, in 1925, were frustrated; *Tess*, with Mrs. Bugler in the title role, was revived at the Duke of York's Theatre in 1929. [More about Mrs. Bugler's reactions and experiences than about H. Also see J. Stevens Cox (pub and general editor), Monographs on the Life of Thomas Hardy (1962).]

2701 Cox, J. Stevens (pub and general editor). Monographs on the Life of Thomas Hardy (Beaminster, Dorset; later Mount Durand, St. Peter Port, Guernsey: Toucan P, 1962–continuing). [Individual titles are entered by author under year of first publication. The first forty-two titles became the basis for CONCERNING THOMAS HARDY, ed by D. F. Barber (Lond: Charles Skilton, 1968); the first thirty-five titles, with a specially prepared introductory monograph, make up Vol I of THOMAS HARDY: MATERIALS FOR A STUDY OF HIS LIFE, TIMES AND WORKS (1968). Most of the material in Lois Deacon's monographs (Nos. 3, 31, 33, 34, 38, 47, and 62, below) is absorbed in PROVIDENCE AND MR. HARDY, by Lois Deacon and Terry Coleman (Lond: Hutchinson, 1966). Most of F. R. Southerington's monographs (Nos. 28 and 42, below) and other articles have been absorbed in HARDY'S VISION OF MAN (Lond: Chatto & Windus, 1971). Although many items are quite inconsequential, some have serious scholarly interest. The illustrations in nearly all the titles are alone worth the cost. The following titles appeared between 1962 and 1969, the cut-off date for the present bibliography. The series is still continuing in 1971. Volume II of THOMAS HARDY: MORE MATERIALS FOR A STUDY OF HIS LIFE, TIMES AND WORKS will include monographs 36 through 72 and specially prepared introductory material. Both volumes are available bound in buckram.]

1. Bugler, Gertrude. PERSONAL RECOLLECTIONS OF THOMAS HARDY (Dorchester: The Dorset Natural History and Archaeological Society, 1962); first given as a talk, "My Memories of Thomas Hardy," at the Dorset Evening in the Corn Exchange, Dorchester, 7 April 1959, the MS of eight typed pages is in the Colby College Library; distributed by J. Stevens Cox, this title became the first of the Hardy Monograph Series later published by J. Stevens Cox.

2. Atkins, Norman J. HARDY, TESS AND MYSELF. With an introduction by Richard Curle (Beaminster, Dorset: Toucan P, 1962).

3. Deacon, Lois. TRYPHENA AND THOMAS HARDY. With an introduction by Richard Curle and an account of an interview between J. Stevens Cox and Mrs. Eleanor Tryphena Bromell (Beaminster, Dorset: Toucan P, 1962).

4. T[itterington], E[llen] E. THE DOMESTIC LIFE OF THOMAS HARDY (1921–1928). With an introduction by Richard Curle (Beaminster, Dorset: Toucan P, 1963). [Also see Ellen E. Titterington, No. 59, below.]

5. Mills, W. G. THOMAS HARDY AT THE BARBER'S. With an introduction by Richard Curle (Beaminster, Dorset: Toucan P, 1963).

6. Stephens, Bertie Norman.. THOMAS HARDY IN HIS GARDEN. With an introduction by Richard Curle (Beaminster, Dorset: Toucan P, 1963).

7. Voss, Harold Lionel. MOTORING WITH THOMAS HARDY. With an introduction by Richard Curle (Beaminster, Dorset: Toucan P, 1963).

8. O'Rourke, May. THOMAS HARDY: HIS SECRETARY REMEMBERS. With

an appendix, "Louisa Harding," by J. Stevens Cox, and an introduction by Richard Curle (Beaminster, Dorset: Toucan P, 1965).

9. O'Rourke, May. THE YOUNG THOMAS HARDY. With illustrations by Naomi Lang (Dorchester: [Dorset P (Henry Ling Ltd), 1951]); rptd as YOUNG MR. THOMAS HARDY. With an introduction by Richard Curle (Mount Durand, St. Peter Port, Guernsey: Toucan P, 1966).

10. Blunden, Edmund. GUEST OF THOMAS HARDY. With an introduction by Richard Curle (Beaminster, Dorset: Toucan P, 1964).

11. Oliver, Constance M. THOMAS HARDY PROPOSES TO MARY WAIGHT. With an introduction by Richard Curle (Beaminster, Dorset: Toucan P, 1964).

12. Meech, Dorothy M. MEMORIES OF MR AND MRS THOMAS HARDY. With an introduction by Richard Curle (Beaminster, Dorset: Toucan P, 1963).

13. Wessex Redivivus [pseud of H. S. L. Dewar]. THE RETURN OF WESSEX. With an introduction by Richard Curle (Beaminster, Dorset: Toucan P, 1964).

14. [Cox, J. Stevens (ed)]. HARDYANA: A COLLECTION OF SHORT MEMORABILIA AND OTHER MATTERS OF HARDY INTEREST. With an introduction by Richard Curle (Birling, Mount Durand, St. Peter Port, Guernsey: Toucan P, 1967). [Contents abstracted separately by author under year of first publication.]

15. Mardon, J. Vera. THOMAS HARDY AS A MUSICIAN. With an introduction by Richard Curle (Beaminster, Dorset: Toucan P, 1964).

16. Evans, Evelyn L. THE HOMES OF THOMAS HARDY. With an introduction by Richard Curle (Mount Durand, St. Peter Port, Guernsey, 1968).

17. Evans, Evelyn L. MY FATHER PRODUCED HARDY'S PLAYS. With an introduction by Richard Curle (Beaminster, Dorset: Toucan P, 1964).

18. Homer, Christine Wood. THOMAS HARDY AND HIS TWO WIVES. With an introduction by Richard Curle (Beaminster, Dorset: Toucan P, 1964).

19. Scudamore, Joyce. FLORENCE AND THOMAS HARDY: A RETROSPECT. With an introduction by Richard Curle (Beaminster, Dorset: Toucan P, 1964).

20. [Cox, J. Stevens (ed)]. THOMAS HARDY THROUGH THE CAMERA'S EYE. With an introduction by Richard Curle (Beaminster, Dorset: Toucan P, 1964).

21. Minamawa, Saburo. APPRECIATION OF THOMAS HARDY'S WORKS IN JAPAN (Beaminster, Dorset: Toucan P, 1965).

22. Fisher, C. M. LIFE IN THOMAS HARDY'S DORCHESTER 1886–1908. With an appendix, "Some Recollections of Thomas Hardy" (1930) by F. B. Fisher (Beaminster, Dorset: Toucan P, 1965).

23. Parker, W. M. THOMAS HARDY ON MAUMBURY RINGS (Beaminster, Dorset: Toucan P, 1965).

24. Parker, W. M. "My Visit to Thomas Hardy," CORNHILL MAGAZINE,

LXVI (Feb 1929), 149–57; expanded as A VISIT TO THOMAS HARDY (Beaminster, Dorset: Toucan P, 1966).

25. Pinney, Lady Hester. THOMAS HARDY AND THE BIRDSMOORGATE MURDER 1856 (Beaminster, Dorset: Toucan P, 1966).

26. Hardy, Thomas. SOME ROMANO-BRITISH RELICS FOUND AT MAX GATE, DORCHESTER. With an introduction by H. S. L. Dewar [qv] (St. Peter Port, Guernsey: Toucan P, 1966). [H's title, read at the Dorchester Meeting in 1884, is rptd from PROCEEDINGS OF THE DORSET NATURAL HISTORY AND ANTIQUARIAN FIELD CLUB, XI (1890), 78–81.]

27. Moule, Henry. PAUPERS, CRIMINALS AND CHOLERA AT DORCHESTER IN 1854. With an introducton by Stephen Dewar [qv] (Mount Durand, St. Peter Port, Guernsey: Toucan P, 1968). [Reprints two letters addressed to H. R. H. The Prince Consort, first published in the DORSET COUNTY CHRONICLE, 21 and 28 Sept 1854 and collected in EIGHT LETTERS TO HIS ROYAL HIGHNESS PRINCE ALBERT (1855).]

28. Southerington, F. R. THE EARLY HARDYS: AN INTRODUCTORY NOTE (Mount Durand, St. Peter Port, Guernsey: Toucan P, 1968).

29. Hardy, Emma Lavinia. POEMS AND RELIGIOUS EFFUSIONS. With an introduction by Prof. J. O. Bailey (Mount Durand, St. Peter Port, Guernsey: Toucan P, 1966). [Reprints poems and prose from the original editions of ALLEYS (1911) and SPACES (1912).]

30. Davies, Aneirin Talfan. ("William Barnes, Friend of Thomas Hardy") [original Welsh title unknown], WELSH ANVIL (Aberystwyth) [date unknown]; rptd in SYLWADAU (Comments) (Llandysul, Cardiganshire: Gwasg Aberystwyth, 1951); included in an address to the Third Congress of the International Literature Association, Utrecht, 1961; pub in PROCEEDINGS OF THE THIRD CONGRESS OF THE INTERNATIONAL LITERATURE ASSOCIATION ('S-Gravenhage: Mouton, 1962); trans and rptd as WILLIAM BARNES FRIEND OF THOMAS HARDY (Mount Durand, St. Peter Port, Guernsey: Toucan P, 1967).

31. Deacon, Lois. " 'The Chosen' by Thomas Hardy: Five Women in Blend—An Identification," LITERARY REPOSITORY, No. 1 (1966), 2–6; rptd as "THE CHOSEN" BY THOMAS HARDY: FIVE WOMEN IN BLEND—AN IDENTIFICATION (Mount Durand, St. Peter Port, Guernsey: Toucan P, 1966).

32. Phelps, Kenneth. ANNOTATIONS BY THOMAS HARDY IN HIS BIBLES AND PRAYER-BOOK, PRESENTED AGAINST THE BACKGROUND OF HARDY'S LIFE, WORK AND LOVES, WITH NEW LIGHT ON CERTAIN POEMS (Mount Durand, St. Peter Port, Guernsey: Toucan P, 1966).

33. Deacon, Lois. TRYPHENA'S PORTRAIT ALBUM AND OTHER PHOTOGRAPHS OF HARDY INTEREST (Mount Durand, St. Peter Port, Guernsey: Toucan P, 1967).

34. Deacon, Lois. HARDY'S GRANDMOTHER, BETSY, AND HER FAMILY (Mount Durand, St. Peter Port, Guernsey: Toucan P, 1968). [One version

of this title was published in error without covers and without illustrations.]

35. Beatty, C. J. P. STINSFORD—A HARDY CHURCH (Mount Durand, St. Peter Port, Guernsey: Toucan P, 1967).

[Unnumbered]. Cox, J. Stevens (ed). THOMAS HARDY: MATERIALS FOR A STUDY OF HIS LIFE, TIMES AND WORKS (MONOGRAPHS 1–35) (Mount Durand, St. Peter Port, Guernsey: Toucan P, 1968). [This pamphlet was prepared for binding with Monographs 1 to 35 "making Volume One of MATERIALS FOR THE STUDY OF THE LIFE, TIMES AND WORKS OF THOMAS HARDY."]

36. [Cox, J. Stevens (pub).] THOMAS HARDY'S WILL AND OTHER WILLS OF HIS FAMILY (Mount Durand, Guernsey: Toucan P, 1967).

37. Parsons, W. G. L. A "MELLSTOCK QUIRE" BOY'S RECOLLECTION OF THOMAS HARDY (Mount Durand, St. Peter Port, Guernsey: Toucan P, 1967).

38. Deacon, Lois. HARDY'S SUMMER ROMANCE, 1867: AN INTERPRETATION AND A RECONSTRUCTION (Mount Durand, St. Peter Port, Guernsey: Toucan P, 1967).

39. Cox, J. Stevens. IDENTIFICATION OF FICTITIOUS PLACE NAMES IN HARDY'S WORKS (Mount Durand, St. Peter Port, Guernsey: Toucan P, 1968).

40. Farris, Lillie May. MEMORIES OF THE HARDY AND HAND FAMILIES (Mount Durand, St. Peter Port, Guernsey: Toucan P, 1968).

41. Ball, Reginald Lacy. RECOLLECTION OF A VISIT TO THOMAS HARDY (Mount Durand, St. Peter Port, Guernsey: Toucan P, 1968).

42. Southerington, F. R. HARDY'S CHILD: FACT OR FICTION? (Birling, Mount Durand, St. Peter Port, Guernsey: Toucan P, 1968).

43. Stickland, Dorothy. THOMAS HARDY AT CATTISTOCK (Mount Durand, St. Peter Port, Guernsey: Toucan P, 1968).

44. Lacey, Charles. "Reminiscences of an Old Durnovarian," DORSET YEARBOOK (1930) [not seen in this form]; rptd as MEMORIES OF THOMAS HARDY AS A SCHOOLBOY. With additional notes of Hardy interest by C. D. Austin, Charles Lacey's grandson (Mount Durand, St. Peter Port, Guernsey: Toucan P, 1968).

45. Cox, J. Stevens (ed). LETTERS FROM EDEN PHILLPOTTS TO MRS. F. E. HARDY (Mount Durand, St. Peter Port, Guernsey: Toucan P, 1968).

46. Knott, Olive. HARDY'S STURMINSTER HOME (Mount Durand, St. Peter Port, Guernsey: Toucan P, 1968).

47. Deacon, Lois. THE MOULES AND THOMAS HARDY. With an introduction by Canon Edward B. Brooks (Mount Durand, St. Peter Port, Guernsey: Toucan P, 1968); originally given as a lecture during the Hardy Festival, 18 July 1968, in St. George Church, Fordington, Dorchester.

48. Cox, J. Stevens (ed). DORCHESTER IN 1851 (Mount Durand, St.

Peter Port, Guernsey: Toucan P, 1968); rptd from Hunt and Co's DIREC-
TORY OF DORSETSHIRE, 1851 [not seen in this form; see under 1968.]

49. Brinkley, Richard. THOMAS HARDY AS A REGIONAL NOVELIST. With
special reference to *The Return of the Native* (Mount Durand, St. Peter
Port, Guernsey: Toucan P, 1968).

50. Horsfall, Mary. LIFE IN BRIDPORT 1898–1918, PORT BREDY OF
HARDY'S NOVELS (Mount Durand, St. Peter Port, Guernsey: Toucan P,
1969).

51. Last, Edwin A. THOMAS HARDY'S NEIGHBOURS (Mount Durand, St.
Peter Port, Guernsey: Toucan P, 1969).

52. Hodgson and Co. THE LIBRARY OF THOMAS HARDY, O.M. With books
and autograph letters, the property of the late Mrs. Thomas Hardy (Lond:
Hodgson and Co, 26 May 1938); rptd as THE LIBRARY OF THOMAS HARDY,
O.M., ed by J. Stevens Cox (Mount Durand, St. Peter Port, Guernsey:
Toucan P, 1968).

53. Cox, J. Stevens (ed). HARDYANA II: A FURTHER COLLECTION OF
SHORT MEMORABILIA AND OTHER MATTERS OF HARDY INTEREST (Mount
Durand, St. Peter Port, Guernsey: Toucan P, 1969). [Contents abstracted
separately by author under year of first publication.]

54. O'Connor, T. P. "Personal Traits of Thomas Hardy," DAILY TELE-
GRAPH (1928) [not seen in this form]; rptd as PERSONAL TRAITS OF
THOMAS HARDY (Mount Durand, St. Peter Port, Guernsey: Toucan P,
1969).

55. Codd, Alfred Percy. LIFE IN BEAMINSTER (THE EMMINSTER OF
HARDY'S NOVELS) 1864–1910 (Mount Durand, St. Peter Port, Guernsey:
Toucan P, 1969).

56. Barton, J. E. "The Poetry of Thomas Hardy," in THE ART OF THOMAS
HARDY, by Lionel Johnson (Lond: Lane; NY: Dodd, Mead, 1923, "to
which is added a chapter on the poetry, by J. E. Barton"); rptd as THE
POETRY OF THOMAS HARDY (Mount Durand, St. Peter Port, Guernsey:
Toucan P, 1969).

57. Barton, J. E. "The Genius of Thomas Hardy," BRISTOL TIMES AND
MIRROR, 14 Jan 1928 [not seen in this form]; rptd as THE GENIUS OF
THOMAS HARDY (Mount Durand, St. Peter Port, Guernsey: Toucan P,
1969 [bound in with No. 56 as No. 57 under title THE POETRY OF THOMAS
HARDY]).

58. Evans, Evelyn L. ROUND DORSET WITH HARDY (Mount Durand, St.
Peter Port, Guernsey: Toucan P, 1969).

59. Titterington, Ellen E. AFTERTHOUGHTS OF MAX GATE (Mount Durand,
St. Peter Port, Guernsey: Toucan P, 1969); expands THE DOMESTIC LIFE
OF THOMAS HARDY (1921–1928) (1963).

60. Lea, Hermann. "Some Dorset Superstitions," in MEMORIALS OF OLD

DORSET, ed by T. Perkins and H. Pentin (1907); rptd as SOME DORSET SUPERSTITIONS (Mount Durand, St. Peter Port, Guernsey: Toucan P, 1969).

61. Stevens, E. J. HARDY AS I KNEW HIM (Mount Durand, St. Peter Port, Guernsey: Toucan P, 1969); first delivered, in part, on BBC, 16 Aug 1938.

62. Deacon, Lois. HARDY'S TRYPHENA IN TOPSHAM, DEVON (Mount Durand, St. Peter Port, Guernsey: Toucan P, 1969); first presented as a lecture to the Parochial History Section of the Devonshire Association on 6 April 1964.

63. Asquith, Lady Cynthia. THOMAS HARDY AT MAX GATE (Mount Durand, St. Peter Port, Guernsey: Toucan P, 1969); first given as a talk on the Home Service of BBC, 1956.

64. Powys, Llewelyn. SOME MEMORIES OF THOMAS HARDY (Mount Durand, St. Peter Port, Guernsey: Toucan P, 1969).

> **2702** Deacon, Lois. TRYPHENA AND THOMAS HARDY. With an introduction by Richard Curle and an account of an interview between J. Stevens Cox and Mrs. Eleanor Tryphena Bromell (Beaminster, Dorset: Toucan P, 1962); the basis for the full-scale development of the central thesis in PROVIDENCE AND MR. HARDY, by Lois Deacon and Terry Coleman (1966).

On the basis of interviews with Eleanor Tryphena Bromell, daughter of Tryphena Sparks (later Mrs. Charles Frederick Gale), H appears to have been engaged to his cousin Tryphena Sparks from about late summer of 1867 to early July 1872. [This pamphlet is mainly concerned about establishing the "hard facts" of Tryphena's birth, schooling, employment, marriage to Charles Gale, and death. The allusions to H's works in this pamphlet are fairly general; the notes in Appendix I to some of H's poems in the main assert rather than prove allusions to Tryphena. Cox's Appendix II mainly confirms the clearly factual aspects of Deacon's information. Also see J. Stevens Cox (pub and general ed), Monographs on the Life of Thomas Hardy (1962).]

> **2703** Fairchild, Hoxie N. RELIGIOUS TRENDS IN ENGLISH POETRY. 5 vols (V: GODS OF A CHANGING POETRY: 1880–1920) (NY & Lond: Columbia UP, 1962), V, 243–53.

Is not H "a major English poet who, rejecting both faith in God and faith in man, draws his art and his view of life from a despairingly realistic faith in matter?" Yes, but "his naturalism . . . is saturated in the preternatural," and what is still more strange "this resolute atheist is constantly talking about God." H's poems are "startlingly uneven in quality," an index perhaps of H's own philosophical confusion: "in a poet who is trying hard to think, intellectual muddle breeds imaginative muddle." H's poems are damaged by his inconsistent mythology. H conceives of God as absentminded, devoid of consciousness but still possessing "some secret intention" for the universe. The contradiction between H's melioristic and pessimistic poems suggests "his intellectual irresponsibility." Not only are these views "radically incompatible," neither one "achieves consistency within its own boundaries." We are distressed "that this philosophical poet possesses no philosophy at all."

2704 Fairley, Barker. "Two Coincidences," JAHRBUCH DER RAABE-GESELLSCHAFT (Yearbook of the Raabe Society) (Braunschweig: Waisenhaus-Buchdruckerei und Verlag, 1962), pp. 74–77.

Phillotson's refusal in *Jude the Obscure* to force Sue to stay with him when she obviously loves Jude parallels Velten Andres's unconventional behavior in DIE AKTEN DES VOGELSANGS in giving his property away: both men act unconventionally and are criticized by their uncomprehending neighbors. [Useless. The parallel is outrageously far-fetched, and, at best, a coincidence not worth recording. No influence on or by H is suggested.]

2705 Felkin, Elliott. "Days With Thomas Hardy," ENCOUNTER, XVIII (April 1962), 27–33.

In conversations in 1918 and 1919 H remarked that all literature is seen through the personality of the author; it is never truly objective since the selection of relevant facts is the result of a particular subjective choice. Among H's favorite authors were George Eliot (who he says is better understood as a thinker than a story-teller), Meredith and James (he prefers the latter), Shelley, Swinburne, Browning and certain modern writers like Arthur Waley and Shanks. H preferred his poetry to his novels. In writing a novel he had to "make out a case for" his protagonists, even if he realized their defects.

2706 Fischler, Alexander. "Thomas Hardy's Short Stories: Their Relation to Major Trends and Interests in the Criticism of His Work," DISSERTATION ABSTRACTS, XXII (1962), 3199–3200. Unpublished dissertation, University of Washington, 1961.

2707 Gittings, Robert. "Emma Hardy's Recollections," TIMES LITERARY SUPPLEMENT (Lond), 8 June 1962, p. 429.

Distinguishing between actual misspelling or unusual spelling and unintentional spelling resulting from haste or crowded writing is a basic editorial problem. Where the spelling of a word in H's MSS is the result of the latter, it is regularized in SOME RECOLLECTIONS BY EMMA HARDY (1961). No alterations of the MSS were attributed to H himself unless they could be ascribed with certainty. [Letter in response to one from C. J. P. Beatty, "Emma Hardy's Recollections," ibid, 1 June 1962, p. 420 (not listed).]

2708 Gregor, Ian. "The Novel as Moral Protest: *Tess of the d'Urbervilles*," in THE MORAL AND THE STORY, by Ian Gregor and Brian Nicholas (Lond: Faber & Faber, 1962), pp. 123–50.

H finds, in the rural land of Tess, "a community in decay, a tragic vision inviting moral protest." The story of Tess reveals "poverty, class privilege, cruelty, hypocrisy"; therefore, her story is the substance of moral protest. A novel like ADAM BEDE ends with a broken community restored and a social group of friends; *Tess* ends with two exiles who haven't any friends. H was at heart a traditional teller of stories; had "he possessed a greater sophistication, a greater mastery of the 'art of the novel,' *Tess of the d'Urbervilles* and *Jude the Obscure* would not have caused the stir they did." Protest fiction was against H's natural bent as rural story teller. His *Tess* was "about the death of a whole tradition of local life, local folklore, a tradition in which he found the source of his artistic power." H's highly personal mode of fiction, like ballad literature, has a great anonymity about it. To find comparisons with it, we have to look to "poems like Wordsworth's GUILT AND SORROW . . . and to the tales of Crabbe." H realized that the ballad world was passing away, but his art "overlooks, without ever invading, the territory occupied in one direction by the tract and in the other by the pastoral, and it is because he keeps to the space between that his art is a living thing." The ballad world and its gradual disintegration "are the basic elements of Hardy's fiction, and wholly within the compass of his art." The "ballad narrative, together with its frequent and pervasive irony, provide natural channels in which a deterministic philosophy can set." After describing H's novels as the work of a ballad writer, conscious that the ballad world is disintegrating, one should consider "how far this general description illuminates *Tess*, and in particular what light it casts on Hardy's attitude to the central character of the 'pure woman.' " In this novel there is "the art of the ballad writer talking of village life"; there is "the art of the writer who feels that such a world is dying in the shadows of the new industrial society"; and "there is the writer who reflects philosophically on these things." The "total impression that *Tess* leaves on the reader is undeniably one of unity." One of the elements that make up this unity is "the extraordinary vividness and imaginative density with which Tess herself is presented." The dominant unifying images which run through the novel are images of interior states which are visualized in terms of landscape. Tomb and blood imagery also unify the tale. In the Stonehenge scene, Tess is "in effigy, a sacrifice on the tomb of the d'Urbervilles." Tess lives in the ballad world, Alec "is lightly connected to the ballad world of Tess but really 'lives' . . . in the new capitalistic world"; Angel "is lightly connected with that world of Alec's . . . but his real element is that of the Free-Thinker's Hall." In exploring and assessing Tess's situation, H uses a double standard. "His immediate defense is by way of beneficient Nature" which knows no rights or wrongs, but "when Hardy is taking a remoter view, the tragedy is inherent in Nature's 'cruel law'—in the way things are." The thresher scene between Alec and Tess brilliantly presents the pure woman defending her nature. [Quite good, but poorly organized.]

2709 Hardy, Evelyn. "Emma Hardy's Diaries: Some Foreshadow-ings of *The Dynasts*," ENGLISH, XIV (Spring 1962), 9–12.

Emma H's pocket-diaries give us many details that are not to be found in the official biography. From the Wedding Diary (filled with penciled jottings interspersed with lively rough sketches) we learn about two journeys abroad. During the first one, Hardy visited the Père-Lachaise cemetery (Sir Sydney Smith's tomb) and Napoleon's tomb at the Invalides. During the second journey on the Continent, a year and a half after the marriage, H and his wife visited Waterloo; Emma's account is much more detailed than H's mere statement of the fact in his autobiography. The value of Emma's diaries lies in the fact that they fill out what we already know of H's obsession with the Napoleonic theme. They give us some fresh information, nowhere else stated, and they reveal something of Emma's "gay inconsequential charm" which, according to Florence, H's second wife, she retained to the end of her life.

2710 "Hardy's Own Life," TIMES LITERARY SUPPLEMENT (Lond), 6 April 1962, p. 234.

H wrote THE LIFE OF THOMAS HARDY: 1840–1928 [see 1928, 1930] himself; he suppressed some material and manipulated evidence and then destroyed many of the documents on which the LIFE is based.

2711 Hartley, L. P. "The Novelist's Responsibility," ESSAYS AND STUDIES BY MEMBERS OF THE ENGLISH ASSOCIATION, ns XV (1962), 88–100.

H was a revolutionary figure in the history of the English novel, partly because he did not subscribe to contemporary ideas of morality. He never denied that humans acted incorrectly, but he did believe that the universe, not the individual, was at fault for human error.

2712 Heilman, Robert B. "Introduction," *The Mayor of Caster-bridge*, ed with an introduction by Robert B. Heilman (Boston: Riverside P, 1962), pp. v–xxxviii.

H's style is particularly allusive. In *The Mayor of Casterbridge*, antiquity looms over the modern scene. Henchard, like Macbeth, does away with all obstacles to his kingship. For Macbeth's witches, he has Mr. Fall and for the murders he has Jopp. Of all the parallels in the book, the most remarkable is the parallel between Henchard and Lucetta; both are haunted by their past, which remains "immanent in the present." The story of Henchard is archetypal—the past is inescapable. H "has invested a homely business operation with the essential characteristics of tragedy."

2713 Hellstrom, Ward. "A Study of Jude the Obscure," DISSERTATION ABSTRACTS, XXII (1962), 3645. Unpublished dissertation, University of Illinois, 1961.

2714 Hone, Joseph. W. B. YEATS, 1865–1939 (NY & Lond: Macmillan; NY: St. Martin's P, 1962), pp. 113, 184, 357, 371, 455.

Yeats praised Lionel Johnson's book, cared more for his themes about literature than about H in particular. Something is wrong about praising H's style in one better. H attended the performance of Yeats's WHERE THERE IS NOTHING, in London, 1904. Gosse was disappointed, along with other strong supporters of H, that Yeats received the Nobel Prize. Yeats admitted that H "had his moments" as a poet. Yeats chose a H poem for his BBC broadcasts but rejected it.

2715 Jones, Lawrence O. "Theme and Structure in the Novels of Thomas Hardy." Unpublished dissertation, University of California, 1962.

[Listed in Lawrence F. McNamee, DISSERTATIONS IN ENGLISH AND AMERICAN LITERATURE (NY & Lond: Bowker, 1968).]

2716 King, R. W. "Verse and Prose Parallels in the Work of Thomas Hardy," REVIEW OF ENGLISH STUDIES (Lond), ns XIII (Feb 1962), 52–61.

Similarity exists between passages from H's novels and poems, but it is impossible "in the absence of further external evidence" to determine which was written first. H's statement that some of the "verses were turned into prose" and his "faculty" for recalling emotion further confound the issue. [Author analyzes in detail the similarities between chap 35 of *Tess of the d'Urbervilles* and "Beyond the Last Lamp." Summarizes: "It is never safe to jump to conclusions about the priority in time of the prose and poetic versions of such parallel passages."]

2717 Larkin, Philip. "Mrs. Hardy's Memories," CRITICAL QUARTERLY, IV (Spring 1962), 75–79.

EMMA HARDY: SOME RECOLLECTIONS, by Evelyn Hardy and Robert Gittings (1961), is a major addition to H biographical materials. It gives a different view of Emma Hardy than the usual. It is enthusiastic about the courtship. There are parallels between Emma's record and H's poems from 1913.

2718 Lunn, Arnold. "The Technique of the Trumpet," NATIONAL REVIEW (Lond), XIII (25 Sept 1962), 234–35.

THE LIFE OF THOMAS HARDY, 1840–1928, by Florence Hardy (1928, 1930), shows that H was a "confused and reluctant agnostic" who keenly resented Chesterton's comment—"The village atheist brooding over the village idiot"—and the summation of his beliefs by Noyes as "the power behind the universe was an imbecile jester." H responded by writing a biography of himself to be attributed to his wife, a fact hinted at in T. E.

Lawrence's letters and shown by R. L. Purdy in 1954. H's flattering self-portrait, a little like "blowing his own trumpet," is a response to his unduly harsh critics.

2719 McCormick, Benedict, O. F. M. "Thomas Hardy: A Vision and a Prelude," RENASCENCE, XIV (Spring 1962), 155–59.

The "chief quality" of H's art, more than pity and charity, is "sympathy," the ability to "become" the thing described. H and Hopkins (cf. his idea of "thisness") held a Franciscan view of Nature, "an awful reverence and gratitude for things." The submission theme, which we find in all of the Wessex novels, deals with the achieving of sympathy or love with the rest of creation. Unfortunately, H (unlike Hopkins) did not evince a faith in a benevolent God but was forced to "face up to an unredeemed creation." The note of hope in H's works does, however, in the words of George N. Shuster, make his words a " 'wholly permissible prelude to the redemptive affirmations of the Catholic faith.' " [Based on *The Return of the Native*. A challenging initial idea, but sketchily developed.]

2720 Marshall, Percy. "Thomas Hardy," MASTERS OF THE ENG-LISH NOVEL (Lond: Dennis Dobson, 1962), pp. 183–98.

Always the scholar, H asked questions rather than giving answers. His mother and the countryside were two strong influences. There are close resemblances to George Eliot, but H's novels contain none of the orthodox Methodism of Eliot. H's lasting subject was the problem of human relationships within the social context and always exposed to unseen forces. [Typical biography and survey of H's publications and critical reception.]

2721 Morrell, Roy. "An Essay on Criticism," TO DR. HACHIRO YIRASA (Tokyo: International Christian University of Japan, 1962), pp. 825–59; rptd, with changes, in THOMAS HARDY: THE WILL AND THE WAY (1965), pp. 1–29.

John Holloway's summary of H's view, " 'it is right to live naturally,' " even though " 'human choice can exert some influence on the course of things' " has little meaning. H really meant that by knowing the limitations and burdens of life, by taking "an intelligent and honest scrutiny of the difficulties and conditions and loopholes presented by life, man could . . . make something out of this reality." H was a pessimist in that he saw that "no Providence will extricate us from a mess just . . . because 'it can't happen to us.' "

2722 Morrell, Roy. "*Far From the Madding Crowd* As An Intro-duction to Hardy's Novels," STUDIES IN ENGLISH LITERATURE (Tokyo), XXXIX (June 1962), 117–32; rptd in THOMAS HARDY: THE WILL AND THE WAY (1965), pp. 59–72.

In *Far From the Madding Crowd* H showed his real power, and its general "scheme" is typical of H. *Madding Crowd* illustrates H's " 'hard-prosaic' . . . way of writing born of a conviction that the truth must be told, even if it cannot always be told attractively." Also typical of H, the ending of *Madding Crowd* is not "happy-ever-after." H advocates that one should live in accordance with "reality," as Oak does, and not with "nature," as Bathsheba and some other characters do. *Madding Crowd* is full of contrast, often resulting from Chance. It is a good introduction to H's novels because "it is positive, and provides a basis for understanding the irony of the others."

2723 Morrell, Roy. "Hardy in the Tropics: Some Implications of Hardy's Attitude Towards Nature," REVIEW OF ENGLISH LITERATURE, III (Jan 1962), 7–21; absorbed, with changes, in THOMAS HARDY: THE WILL AND THE WAY (1965).

H was neither a nature worshipper nor "bitterly against Nature and all her promptings." Nature, to him, was neutral but full of "flux and reflux" and a continually readjusting equilibrium. For H, men are responsible for their acts; they are not merely acted upon by circumstance. The adaptability of plants is paralleled in humanity by intelligence. H subscribed to "evolutionary meliorism" and in doing so, believed that survival was most likely to be achieved by men through three means of action: the ability to adapt to a "changing world," an attitude of "pessimism" whereby suspicion of the predatory nature of the world provides constant watchfulness, and the use of extra precautions and all "known resources" to prevent disaster. But even more than these, H valued the prospects of survival through co-operation, something which he knew men long for but which they see little of. [Informed and useful.]

2724 Morrell, Roy. "Thomas Hardy: Remorse and Memorials," MAKERERE JOURNAL, No. 6 (1962), 22–37; rptd in THOMAS HARDY: THE WILL AND THE WAY (1965).

A "favourite subject" in H's novels, stories and poems is reality, "sometimes contrasted . . . with the dead past; more often with romance or with appearance." The theme is ever-present in *Tess of the d'Urbervilles*; self-deluders like Angel, Tess, and John Durbeyfield cause their misfortunes by neglecting present possibilities in search of some fairy-castle dream. Despite his reservations about dreamers, H seems to waver at times. Occasionally a character's adoption of a fictitious belief of his beloved may be helpful (e.g. Bathsheba Everdene's father), but usually his characters adopt "a romantic illusion . . . which, instead of preserving the reality of their lives, seems bound to destroy it" (e.g. Margery's dream of the Baron von Xanten). Largely H's characters suffer not because of fateful coincidence, but through their failure to *avoid* trouble: Tess had ample time to discover whether

Angel had read her letter of confession, but she failed to do so. "Barbara of the House of Grebe" shows the "weakness of Barbara's love"—an affection based solely on Willowes's physical beauty, i.e. on outward appearance. Uplandtowers's cruel treatment of her, however, eventually cures her of a morbid fascination with her ideal of Willowes's beauty. In *The Well-Beloved*, "it is the sculpture, the actual stone [i.e. the raw material out of which life is fashioned], that is the central symbol of the novel." The novel "seeks to show that the beautiful appearances which glamourize our lives are devices of cowardice," and that reality is life, and life is courage.

2725 Oba, Keizo. "The Poetry of Thomas Hardy," BULLETIN OF THE THOMAS HARDY SOCIETY OF JAPAN, I (July 1962), 17–34.

[An introductory note on H's poetry, including *The Dynasts*, paying due homage to the poet's lyricism. Stress on H's conception of man as a creation of blind forces utterly careless of their creations.] [In Japanese.]

2726 Pietch, Frances. "The Relationship Between Music and Literature in the Victorian Period: Studies in Browning, Hardy, and Shaw," DISSERTATION ABSTRACTS, XXII (1962). Unpublished dissertation, Northwestern University, 1961.

In the nineteenth century, music was thought to be the art which most directly expressed the emotions. H uses sound patterns as Wagner uses tone: to evoke subtle emotions in his audience. Symbolic sound images function like *leitmotivs*, emphasizing emotional passages and evoking mood. Larger units of sound images form patterns similar to those used by contemporary composers. H's characters are often susceptible to music. [Chap 4 is on H.]

2727 Riesner, Dieter. "Zur Textgeschichte von Hardys Romanen" (On the Textual History of Hardy's Novels), ARCHIV, CXCIX (1962), 398–404.

Unlike other nineteenth-century authors, H scarcely mentioned his frequent and significant revisions of his novels. Research into this promising area of H studies raises significant questions: did H the prose writer wish to be no more than "a good hand at a serial" . . . and did he all his life feel his essential being was that of a poet? "The scarcely imaginable physical labor and self-denial and the continuous demand on his creative faculties demanded by the 20,000 alterations [in the various editions of H's novels] should contradict the often-repeated assertion that novel-writing was only a step-child of his Muse." [Surveys recent criticism dealing with the problem of the genesis of H's novels.] [In German.]

2728 Roberts, James L. "Legend and Symbol in Hardy's 'The Three Strangers'" NINETEENTH CENTURY FICTION, XVII (Sept 1962), 191–94.

The values the rural people of Higher Crowstairs "look for are courage, resourcefulness, shrewdness, and composure"—qualities Timothy Summers possessed. "To hang such a man is a perversion of justice; to escape from such a punishment is a sign of courage and resourcefulness." Summers becomes then a representative of the simple man's triumph over injustice and a symbol of those qualities necessary to life in the country around Higher Crowstairs.

2729 St. John-Stevas, Norman. "The Author's Struggles with the Law," CATHOLIC WORLD, CXCIV (March 1962), 345–50.

When *Tess of the d'Urbervilles* was being serialized, the editor refused to publish the scene in which Angel carries the milkmaids bodily across the stream, so H had them carried in a wheel-barrow. When *Tess* was published in book form, the girls were back in their original positions.

2730 Schweik, Robert C. "Moral Perspective in *Tess of the d'Urbervilles*," COLLEGE ENGLISH, XXIV (Oct 1962), 14–18.

Angel Clare raises crucial questions near the end of *Tess of the d'Urbervilles*. " 'Who was the moral man? Still more pertinently, who was the moral woman?' " Though the novel provides no answer to Clare's questions it does provide "answers which imply limited views and conflicting assumptions about moral reality." The philosophical passages in the novel, often regarded either as keys to H's deeper meaning or as nearly irrelevant abstract moralizing, "appear rather in the context of the novel to provide recognizably limited moral perspectives—partial insights into a much more complex moral reality revealed by the novel as a whole." [See rebuttal by Bernard J. Paris, "A Confusion of Many Standards . . .," NINETEENTH CENTURY FICTION, XXIV (June 1969), 57–79.]

2731 Schweik, Robert C. "Theme, Character, and Perspective in Hardy's *The Return of the Native*," PHILOLOGICAL QUARTERLY, XLI (Oct 1962), 757–67.

H treats the validity of human insight through three characters in different stages of "psychological time": Eustacia is related to "sensuous paganism of the past," Mrs. Yeobright to "common-sense conventionality of the present," and Clym to "thoughtful asceticism of the future." But H also uses a second device of perspective with the characters: each is presented "as an ideal type . . . gifted with some unusual insight into the world, but . . . also described as a victim of circumstances acting on temperament to severely limit and distort that insight." Eustacia's imagination distorts her sense of reality; Mrs. Yeobright can generalize about the world but can't solve specific problems; Clym is enthusiastic about ideas but careless about outward things. The parallel treatment of characters suggests that H believes, with Mill, in relativism, and this gives additional ironic force to Clym's delusive preaching at the novel's end.

2732 Selna, Barbara. "Hardy's *Tess of the d'Urbervilles*," Ex-PLICATOR, XX (Feb 1962), Item 47.

Card imagery pervades *Tess of the d'Urbervilles*. Tess's mother tells her to play her trump—her face—to win over their wealthy "relations," the d'Urbervilles, but Tess saves her real trump—her *heart*—for Angel, whom she really loves.

2733 Sixt, Erika. "Zur Struktur des Romans bei Thomas Hardy" (Thomas Hardy's Conception of the Structure of the Novel). Unpublished dissertation, University of Munich, 1962.

[Listed in Lawrence F. McNamee, DISSERTATIONS IN ENGLISH AND AMERICAN LITERATURE, (NY & Lond: Bowker, 1968).] [In German.]

2734 "Thomas Hardy," DER GROSSE HERDER (The Large Herder [Encyclopedia]) (Freiburg: Herder, 1962), I, 543.

[Essentially the same as 1954 edition.] [In German.]

2735 "Thomas Hardy," MEYERS NEUES LEXIKON (Meyer's New Dictionary) (Leipzig: Bibliographisches Institut, 1962), IV, 20–21.

[Lists collected works. Characterizes H as mainly a regionalist.] [In German.]

2736 Thomson, George H. "The Trumpet Major Chronicle," NINETEENTH CENTURY FICTION, XVII (June 1962), 45–56.

The Trumpet-Major is one of H's experiments in form. "It is especially original in the creation of a time perspective in which the action moves forward but gives rise to a contrary impression of gliding away into the past." The novel succeeds as a chronicle because it offers a series of pictures of Wessex life. Also "it offers a sequence of dramatic actions, and it combines these and contains them within a time perspective stretching far into the past and into the future."

2737 Toliver, Harold E. "The Dance Under the Greenwood Tree: Hardy's Bucolics," NINETEENTH CENTURY FICTION, XVII (June 1962), 57–68.

The recurring dilemma of H's bucolics "is that the desire to escape bucolic life does not in itself create a place to escape to. Poverty, ennui, isolation, and rootlessness circumscribe one's possibilities." *Under the Greenwood Tree* shows the beginnings and hints at the end of the rural land's fight for existence, a fight which will be lost "because it cannot survive critical examination and cannot statisfy the whole, intelligent man." "The choir is the chief symbol for an old order which since ancient times, has bound the individual members of the community in a loose and varied unity." The choir "may represent a disappearing idyllic order, but their clumsiness and crudity, as much as the opposition of new ideas, cause the disintegration of the old ways." "The conclusion reveals an uneasy compromise between old and new elements, a compromise in which each part of the community joins in its own way the dance under the ancient greenwood tree."

2738 Weatherby, Harold L. "Hardy's Art in Transition, a Study of *Jude the Obscure*." Unpublished dissertation, Yale University, 1962.

[Listed in Lawrence F. McNamee, DISSERTATIONS IN ENGLISH AND AMERICAN LITERATURE (NY & Lond: Bowker, 1968).]

2739 Wing, George. "Tess and the Romantic Milkmaid," REVIEW OF ENGLISH LITERATURE, III (Jan 1962), 22–30.

Although written six years apart, there are "prophetic affinities" between the long short story "The Romantic Adventures of a Milkmaid" (1883) and the novel *Tess of the d'Urbervilles*. The former is on the "optimistic side of desperation," while the latter looks without blinking at the world's "worst contingencies." Margery and Tess are "pastoral cousins," although Tess, because of the increased "intensity" of the novel and its tragic framework, is "Margery carried to a frighteningly right conclusion."

2740 Yuill, W. E. " 'Character is Fate': A Note on Thomas Hardy, George Eliot and Novalis," MODERN LANGUAGE REVIEW, LVII (July 1962), 401–2.

The famous statement in *The Mayor of Casterbridge*, "Character is Fate," comes from George Eliot's THE MILL ON THE FLOSS, where one finds: " 'character,' says Novalis, in one of his questionable aphorisms—'character is destiny.' " This confirms the observations by Henry James and other critics that H was dependent on George Eliot.

1963

2741 Bailey, J. O. "Evolutionary Meliorism in the Poetry of Thomas Hardy," STUDIES IN PHILOLOGY, LX (July 1963), 569–87.

Only about fifty of H's poems "treat philosophic questions in a direct way." Most "express moods and impressions of the moment." Nevertheless, it is possible to trace in them three stages of H's philosophical development: in the first phase, influenced by Darwin, the poems "express the pessimistic view that insensate natural law rules the world"; in the second phase, influenced by Schopenhauer, H "tended to personify natural law as the universal Will or as an Unconscious Mind capable of being wakened into consciousness through human agency"; in the last phase, he reaches "evolutionary meliorism," a "hope, at least, that human action can make the circumstances of life and life itself better in ethical quality and in happiness." The cycle culminates in *The Dynasts* where H "sought to work out the process of the wakening of the Will." "Whatever else H might include in the creed of his religion, one article would concern reverence for all life, and one goal would be to develop universal compassion."

2742 Beatty, C. J. P. "The Tranter's Cottage in *Under the Greenwood Tree*," NOTES AND QUERIES, CCVIII (Jan 1963), 26.

By comparing the three textual variants of the description of the tranter's cottage in chap 2 of *Under the Greenwood Tree*, it is possible to find that each time H was making the tranter's cottage resemble his birthplace more and more closely.

2743 Beckman, Richard. "A Character Typology for Hardy's Novels," JOURNAL OF ENGLISH LITERARY HISTORY, XXX (March 1963), 70–87.

In H's novels, four basic types of characters occur: those who accept life without asserting themselves, those who accept life and assert themselves, those who reject life and assert themselves, and finally those decadents who neither accept life nor assert themselves. *The Woodlanders* provides a good example. Winterborne is of the first type, Grace of the second, Fitzpiers of the third, and Felice Charmond of the fourth. These types may be found also in *Far From the Madding Crowd*, *The Return of the Native*, and *The Mayor of Casterbridge*. The typology of *Tess of the d'Urbervilles* and *Jude the Obscure* is more complex, for each title character has elements of all four types, and each is surrounded by a pair of figures—Alec and Angel, Sue and Arabella—who embody opposing elements of these more complex characters.

This typology is related to the four seasons of the year, as H himself suggests in THE LATER YEARS OF THOMAS HARDY, by Florence Hardy (1930), p. 23. The typology relates the characters of the novels to the changing pattern of the seasons, relating human personalities to temporal evolution.

2744 Berry, Minta Sue. "Creation's Groan: Late Nineteenth-Century Thought as Reflected in the Works of Thomas Hardy," DISSERTATION ABSTRACTS, XXIV (1963), 280–81. Unpublished dissertation, Vanderbilt University, 1963.

2745 Dell, Francis G. "Exploring the Thomas Hardy Country: The 'South Wessex' of His Novels is Really Dorset," AMERICAN BOOK COLLECTOR, XIII (Feb 1963), 14–17.

[Conventional description of locations from H's life and works, especially *Tess of the d'Urbervilles*.]

2746 Elsbree, Langdon. "The Breaking Chain: A Study of the Dance in the Novels of Jane Austen, George Eliot, Thomas Hardy, and D. H. Lawrence," DISSERTATION ABSTRACTS, XXIV (1963), 2476. Unpublished dissertation, Claremont Graduate School, 1963.

2747 Forsyth, R. A. "The Conserving Myth of William Barnes," VICTORIAN STUDIES, VI (June 1963), 328–29, 336, 345–46, 347, 350, 353.

Unlike H and George Borrow, Barnes's treatment of country life was limited. He was not interested in fringe characters, like pedlars and gypsies, or in suggestions of cruelty and immorality. He was, however, like H, concerned with the effect of the Enclosure Acts and the loss of the Christian values of rural home life by displacement to cities. [References to *The Mayor of Casterbridge*, the introduction of the horsedrill in agricultural planting.]

2748 Gerber, Helmut E. "Hardy's *The Well-Beloved* as a Comment on the Well-Despised," ENGLISH LANGUAGE NOTES, I (Sept 1963), 48–53.

The subtitle of *The Well-Beloved*, "A Sketch of Artistic Temperament," may be applied to H's own situation as an artist in the 1890s when he was about to give up novel writing, which had been a constant vexation because of censorship and adverse critics, in order to realize his long-repressed desire to write poetry. The contrast between Somers and Pierston in the novel is that between the compromising artist who lowers his standards to win public acceptance, and the sincere creator, like H, who remains true to his own vision. *Well-Beloved* is in effect H's bitter farewell to novel writing, which he felt demanded an onerous restriction of his sincerely felt view of the world.

2749 Gose, Elliott B., Jr. "Psychic Evolution: Darwinism and Initiation in *Tess of the d'Urbervilles*," NINETEENTH CENTURY FICTION, XVIII (Dec 1963), 261–72.

"Hardy's interpretation of two specialized developments in mid-Victorian thought, Darwinism and Anthropology" are central concerns of *Tess of the d'Urbervilles*. In *Tess* H "brings together the evolutionary view of man as a product of nature with the anthropological findings about early man's attempt to control nature through primitive rituals." In the novel, Tess struggles to advance on the scale of psychic evolution so that she may become a fuller individual. While H favored evolution with its sympathy and cooperation, he could not forget natural selection and its competitive lack of compassion: "Man's aggressive nature must be reckoned with, as . . . in Alec's seduction of Tess." After losing her chance of breaking free of Alec's blood seal, "of becoming a fuller individual guided by Angel's high spiritual nature, she reverts first to the peasant level of her family, and then below that to the animal level after she leaves them." The murder of Alec severs their blood bond and "to do it she has to regress as far down the human scale as Alec had in The Chase, back that is to the pagan Druids." Tess has now become a primitive, and her ritual death at Stonehenge "is called for by the dark law of man's earliest relation to nature as much as by any unenlightened social law." Her death demonstrates "the ritual necessities of man's relation to nature."

2750 Griffith, Phillip Malone. "The Image of the Trapped Animal in Hardy's *Tess of the d'Urbervilles*," TULANE STUDIES IN ENGLISH, XIII (1963), 85–94.

Tess of the d'Urbervilles becomes a better and more hopeful book if we can see that the picture of "the trapped animal—an image insistently and consciously patterned throughout the action of the novel"—implies that Tess (a "natural woman") is destroyed by "societal, as opposed to natural, laws." The fact that the image functions powerfully mitigates the attacks on H's didacticism.

2751 Guérard, Albert J. (ed). HARDY: A COLLECTION OF CRITICAL ESSAYS (Englewood Cliffs, NJ: Prentice-Hall, 1963) [Twentieth Century Views].

Contents, abstracted separately under date of first publication: Albert J. Guérard, "Introduction" (1963); Donald Davidson, "The Traditional Basis of Thomas Hardy's Fiction," from SOUTHERN REVIEW, VI (Summer 1940); Morton Dauwen Zabel, "Hardy in Defense of His Art: The Aesthetic of Incongruity," from SOUTHERN REVIEW, VI (Summer 1940); D. H. Lawrence, "Hardy's Prédilection d'artiste," from chap 5 ("Work and the Angel and the Unbegotten Hero") of "A Study of Thomas Hardy," in PHOENIX: THE POSTHUMOUS PAPERS OF D. H. LAWRENCE (1936); John Holloway, "Hardy's Major Fiction," from FROM JANE AUSTEN TO JOSEPH CONRAD, ed by Robert Rathburn and Martin Steinman, Jr. (1958); Albert J. Guérard, "The Women in the Novels," from THOMAS HARDY: THE NOVELS AND THE STORIES (1949); D. H. Lawrence, "Sue Bridehead," from chap 9 ("A Nos Moutons") of "A Study of Thomas Hardy," in PHOENIX: THE POSTHUMOUS PAPERS OF D. H. LAWRENCE (1936); Dorothy Van Ghent, "On *Tess of the d'Urbervilles*," from THE ENGLISH NOVEL: FORM AND FUNCTION (1953); John Paterson, "*The Mayor of Casterbridge* as Tragedy," from VICTORIAN STUDIES, III (Dec 1959); A. Alvarez, "*Jude the Obscure*," from "*Jude the Obscure*: Afterword," in *Jude the Obscure* (NY: New American Library, 1961); Delmore Schwartz, "Poetry and Belief in Thomas Hardy," from SOUTHERN REVIEW, VI (Summer 1940); W. H. Auden, "A Literary Transference," from SOUTHERN REVIEW, VI (Summer 1940); David Perkins, "Hardy and the Poetry of Isolation," from

English Literary History, XXVI (June 1959); Samuel Hynes, "*The Dynasts* as an Example," from The Pattern of Hardy's Poetry (1956, 1961); also included but not abstracted: "Chronology of Important Dates," pp. 175–76; "Notes on the Editor and Authors," p. 177; "Selected Bibliography," pp. 179–80, items listed being abstracted under the dates of first publication.

2752 Guérard, Albert J. "Introduction," Hardy: A Collection of Critical Essays (Englewood Cliffs, NJ: Prentice-Hall, 1963) [Twentieth Century Views], pp. 1–9.

H turned to poetry after twenty-five years of writing novels not so much because of the critical attacks on *Tess of the d'Urbervilles* and *Jude the Obscure*, but because he had completed what he had to say as a novelist. Unlike the poetry, the novels are impersonal. They combine real human beings and fantastic events. There are many opposites in H's world. The novels have always been a problem for critics. [Summarizes points of view in the essays reprinted in this volume.]

2753 Hazen, James Forsyth. "The Imagery and Symbolism of Thomas Hardy's Major Novels," Dissertation Abstracts, XXIV (1963), 1616. Unpublished dissertation, University of Wisconsin, 1963.

2754 Heilman, Robert B. "Hardy's *Mayor* and the Problem of Intention," Criticism, V (Summer 1963), 199–213.

Despite H's careful designing of his fiction "in terms of some special aim or philosophical preoccupation," he often relaxed "the hold of design on character," and thereby "unconsciously surrendered constricting intention to artistic need." H reveals his intentions in *The Mayor of Casterbridge* largely by what he—"as idea-pusher, overt director of the proceedings"—interjects about the characterization of Susan Henchard and Elizabeth-Jane, and "his evaluation of Elizabeth's life as representative of human experience generally." In these areas, much to the benefit of the novel, there is great disparity between H's clear intention and his actual creation. "It is as if there were two Hardy's, one a spontaneous . . . untheorizing storyteller, the other a rigid man of doctrine 'intending' to force upon us a dour view of oppressive circumstance." Despite that, "Hardy's stature as artist is a function of the discrepancy between intention and performance."

2755 Heywood, C. "*The Return of the Native* and Miss Braddon's The Doctor's Wife: A Probable Source," Nineteenth Century Fiction, XVIII (June 1963), 91–94.

H admired Miss Braddon and was acquainted with her novels. The heroine of The Doctor's Wife closely resembles Eustacia Vye. Bookish romanticism "plunges both heroines into infatuation for a traveller who returns to his native province from the Continent." Both heroines dislike their husbands. Wildeve is a close structural parallel to Roland Lansdell, and Clym emerges as a second parallel to Lansdell. "Like Clym, Lansdell wished to 'improve the condition of the farm-labourer' through education . . . and in his romantic pessimism, his rationalism, and his guilt-ridden attachment to the memory of his dead mother . . . he foreshadows Hardy's hero."

2756 Hopcutt, G. C. S. "Religion as Poetry and Ritual," LITERARY GUIDE AND RATIONALIST REVIEW, LXVIII (Oct 1963), 161–62.

H's spirits in *The Dynasts* are "contrivances of the fancy" with hopes for "dramatic plausibility." H's stoical disbelief still allowed his appreciation of the aesthetics of religion.

2757 Hübner, Walter. DAS ENGLISCHE LITERATURWERK: THEORIE UND PRAXIS DER INTERPRETATION (The English Literary Work: Theory and Practice of Interpretation) (Heidelberg: Quelle & Meyer, 1963), pp. 44, 107, 113, 135, 281, 292, 298, 313, 321–22.

[Compares H with numerous English writers, i.e., Richardson, Goldsmith, Swinburne, Shelley, Scott, Meredith, and D. H. Lawrence.] [In German.]

2758 Hurd, Michael. "The Queen of Cornwall," MUSICAL TIMES, CIV (Oct 1963), 700–701.

Though the operatic version of *The Famous Tragedy of the Queen of Cornwall* was produced at the peak of Boughton's career, it has been almost wholly neglected, due mostly to Boughton's idiosyncrasies.

2759 Kramer, Dale. "A Query Concerning the Handwriting in Hardy's Manuscripts," PAPERS OF THE BIBLIOGRAPHICAL SOCIETY OF AMERICA, LVII (Third Quarter 1963), 357–60.

Although it has been assumed that Mrs. Emma H did no more than copy H's writing for him, the merits of her autobiography—"good description, a well-realized faculty of recollection and observation of long-past events, and a readable—even interesting—prose style"—show that it is possible that she revised, of her own accord, "perhaps even complete passages of description." [Kramer gives a possible example of such revision from *The Woodlanders* manuscript but emphasizes that he is just suggesting the possibility and not affirming Emma H's hand in the revision. Kramer also indicates the necessity for more research with other manuscripts, not only by the literary scholar but by a handwriting expert as well. He points out discrepancies in the distinctions between H's handwriting and that of his wife made by Carl J. Weber and Robert Gittings. Since most recent scholarly research is directed at H's manuscripts, it is necessary that the minds behind the stylistic revisions be identified if conclusions about H's craftsmanship are to be valid.]

2760 Kramer, Dale. "Repetition of Imagery in Thomas Hardy," VICTORIAN NEWSLETTER, No. 23 (Spring 1963), 26–27.
H repeated five images in *The Woodlanders* MS elsewhere. H preserved "his creative powers for passages of emotional conflict" by borrowing lesser details from his own work.

2761 Kramer, Dale. "The Textual History of a Novel: Thomas Hardy's *The Woodlanders*." Unpublished dissertation, Western Reserve University, 1963.

2762 Lawrence, T. E. To HIS BIOGRAPHERS, ed by Robert Graves and Liddell Hart (Lond: Cassell, 1963), pp. 25–27, 120.
" 'Do you think old Hardy would let me look at him? He's a proper poet and a fair novelist . . . and it would give me a feeling of another milestone passed if I might meet him.' " " 'There is an unbelievable dignity and ripeness about Hardy.' " " 'They used to call . . . [him] a pessimist. While really he is full of fancy expectations.' " To H " 'every person starts scratch in the life-race.' " [While stationed near Dorchester in the Royal Tank Corps in 1923, Lawrence met H and spent some of his leisure time at Max Gate.]

2763 Marshall, William H. "Motivation in *Tess of the d'Urbervilles*," REVUE DES LANGUES VIVANTS (Bruxelles), XXIX:3 (1963), 224–31.
"Tess . . . has contributed, though involuntarily, to the completion of the sport of 'the President of the Immortals' by an ingrained superstition regarding love and marriage." H stresses that Tess has two husbands—a natural one (Alec) and a legal or social one (Angel). She feels so bound to the first—despite his vile treatment of her and the absence of any legal or religious sanction—that her return to Alec late in the novel is well-motivated. And when Angel's return makes Tess rise from her "emotional lethargy" and to long for a union with Angel, Alec must die, since she unconsciously regards her "marriage" to him "like all marriages, as one that presumably can be broken only by death." The primary forces which conditioned Tess to accept this belief were tradition, religion, and society. She "reveals a fundamental fatalism," a sense of being borne along, against her will, by vast, invisible forces.

2764 Meech, Dorothy M. MEMORIES OF MR AND MRS THOMAS HARDY. With an introduction by Richard Curle (Beaminster, Dorset: Toucan P, 1963).

[Anecdotes, mainly hearsay and gossip received at second hand, by one who never actually met H. Also see J. Stevens Cox (pub and general editor), Monographs on the Life of Thomas Hardy (1962).]

2765 Mills, W. G. THOMAS HARDY AT THE BARBER'S. With an introduction by Richard Curle (Beaminster, Dorset: Toucan P, 1963).

[H's barber recalls H's never tipping or giving presents, his preference to be alone in the barber shop, his disinclination to talk, his wife's bicycling, etc. Also see J. Stevens Cox (pub and general editor), Monographs on the Life of Thomas Hardy (1962).]

2766 Mitchell, Charles. "Hardy's 'Afterwards,'" VICTORIAN POETRY, I (Jan 1963), 68–70.

The "logically unrelated" observations of H's "Afterwards" are "imaginatively integrated"; the images fall into a common pattern relating to death. The poem would seem to say that although life is merely "a momentary stoppage of the steady flow of death" and that life is insignificant, trying to understand life is not insignificant, and the poet's knowledge of this experience is worth "the attention of his readers."

2767 Mizener, Arthur. "The Novel of Doctrine in the Nineteenth Century: Hardy's *Jude the Obscure*," THE SENSE OF LIFE IN THE MODERN NOVEL (Boston: Houghton Mifflin, 1963), pp. 55–77.

Jude the Obscure, "in many ways a novel of great poetic intensity," is a striking example "of how a powerful imagination can be frustrated when the form of the novel . . . is determined, not by the imagination's sense of life, but by some doctrine about life . . . [which permits it] to express only so much of his [the author's] sense of life as is consistent with it." H found some escape from his gloomy awareness of " 'the horror of human and animal life,' " in meliorism—the promise of a fundamental betterment of the human condition in the remote future. But there exists "serious difficulty for the imaginative sense of tragedy" in this kind of hope—it reduces most present-day life to meaningless misery and makes an idealist a foolish dreamer. Yet H puts "the weight of his authority behind Jude's dream," since H believed this ideal *would* be realized in the remote future —and, conversely, that it must *fail* to be realized in his and Jude's own world. H could not accept the idea that his Wessex peasants might even now live in a more blessed state than his city dwellers: the "felicitous moments" that precede the catastrophes in so many H novels are only "a fool's paradise," a prelude to the inescapable misery and destruction of H's present-day world. H is unable "to do the life of ordinary men anything like the justice it deserves." Arabella is a pure villainess, never a real woman with "very real if limited wisdom." In the pig-killing, H emphasizes Jude's sentimental aversion and ignores Arabella's practicality. H's partiality for Jude also shows in his covert criticism of Sue for going back to Phillotson on account of her newly-found religious convictions. Jude's death makes clear "that the conditions of Jude's life were, for Hardy's deepest feelings, Earth's ingrained conditions." Yet H could not say this about the world: his doctrine of meliorism demanded the perfect future state to which Jude's ideal looked.

2768 Morrell, Roy. *"The Dynasts* Reconsidered," MODERN LANGUAGE REVIEW, LVIII (April 1963), 161–71; absorbed, with changes, in THOMAS HARDY: THE WILL AND THE WAY (1965).

The popular view of *The Dynasts* as a key to H's pessimistic philosophy is wrong: H's own efforts show that he could not have believed in the "futility of *all* effort." This view has caused confusion in the interpretation of his novels and deprived them of "tragic force." In *Dynasts* man is always the center of H's picture, and we must read the poem with an eye to this intention. H does not champion the "Will" but blames man's choosing to be a puppet before it. The world is not made comfortable *for* man; but it might be made comfortable *by* man. The poem certainly does not present us with a world in which human endeavor counts for nothing. "The value of discipline, co-operation, and carefully timed effort is recognized clearly. It is a world too in which individual decisions count."

2769 Orel, Harold. THOMAS HARDY'S EPIC DRAMA: A STUDY OF "THE DYNASTS" (Lawrence, Kansas: University of Kansas P, 1963).

The Dynasts is the culmination of H's previous work. H's pessimism is not derived from Schopenhauer or other philosophers; it was shared by most of his literary contemporaries. Edmund Burke's writings on the sublime suggested to H his use of perspective from a height and the disorder of diverse materials; the lack of dramatic unity reflects Burke's idea of obscurity properly conveyed." H is "attempting to define the nature of man's relation to unknown and unknowable forces, and doing so confident in the belief that each poet must write his own definition [of epic] and abide by it." *Dynasts* modifies the "Miltonic relationship between man and God in at least three ways: the celestial machinery, which Hardy chose to invent rather than borrow; the pitiful stature of Napoleon as opposed to the genuine majesty of Adam; and the inability of *The Dynasts* to promise a happy ending." Another deviation from conventional epic is the attitude toward war: H (anti-heroically) says war is insane, bestial, and unnecessary; the ILIAD reveals Homer to be ambivalent (war is cruel but a testing ground). H feels sovereigns are irresponsible. [Useful.]

2770 Parker, W. M. "Hardy's Letters to Sir George Douglas," ENGLISH, XIV (Autumn 1963), 218–25.

The National Library of Scotland acquired, in 1958, a group of unpublished manuscript letters from H to Sir George Brisbane Douglas, ranging from 1887 to 1929. The importance of these H letters is their confidential tone and the variety of interest reflected in them. About *Jude the Obscure* H wrote, "Please don't read it in the magazine, for I have been obliged to make many changes, omissions and glosses." "The marriage question was made the vehicle of tragedy . . . I feel that a bad marriage is one of the direst things on earth, and one of the cruellest things, but beyond that my opinions on that subject are vague enough."

2771 Perrine, Laurence. SOUND AND SENSE: AN INTRODUCTION TO POETRY. 2nd ed (NY: Harcourt, Brace & World, 1963), pp. 20, 21–22, 28, 29, 57, 273.

[Four of H's poems are dealt with in a general introduction to poetry. "The Man he Killed" is analyzed with suggested questions for discussion; "Hap" and "The Subalterns" are supplied with queries for students, and "Afterwards" is reprinted without comment.]

2772 Riesner, Dieter. "Über die Genesis von Thomas Hardys *The Return of the Native*" (On the Genesis of Thomas Hardy's *The Return of the Native*), ARCHIV, CC (April 1963), 53–59.

Although John Paterson's THE MAKING OF THE RETURN OF THE NATIVE (1960) appears to be a brilliant work, it contains inaccuracies. Paterson did not see two editions corrected by H. Paterson misinterprets and over-interprets the telescope and the hourglass symbols in *The Return of the Native*. Also, there are no dramatic changes in Clym's development in the various texts toward a more heroic classical figure. The multifaceted elements of the characters are present in all textual stages. In the main, H's search is for the precise word and the meaningful detail. Also, the topography of *Native* is brought in line with that of other novels earlier than Paterson supposes. H, in his revisions of *Native*, developed no new themes but improved and enriched existing materials. [In German.]

2773 Schill, H. "The Criticism of Thomas Hardy's Novels in England from 1871–1958." Unpublished dissertation, University of London (Birkbeck), 1963.

[Listed in Lawrence F. McNamee, DISSERTATIONS IN ENGLISH AND AMERICAN LITERATURE (NY & Lond: Bowker, 1968).]

2774 Scott, James F. "Thomas Hardy's Use of the Gothic: An Examination of Five Representative Works," NINETEENTH CENTURY FICTION, XVII (March 1963), 363–80.

Although H dismissed Victorian lending-library fare as "literature of quackery" and endorsed the growing candor of late nineteenth-century fiction, his fiction contains a pervasive thread of inspiration drawn from folklore, balladry, and the tale of terror. "Hardy never borrowed subject matter directly from Gothic fiction, but the similarities of theme and tone surely are not accidental." H's protagonists, like those of Gothic fiction, "are baffled and mocked by forces beyond their comprehension or control."

2775 Sirimanne, A. M. G. "A Recapitulatory Test on *Tess of the d'Urbervilles*," EXERCISE EXCHANGE, X (March 1963), 30–31.

[Contains a list of twenty-nine questions on *Tess of the d'Urbervilles* designed to "ensure exactness of knowledge, preliminary to the more conventional essay-type test of critical awareness."]

2776 Smith, D. J. "Music in the Victorian Novel," KENYON REVIEW, XXV (Summer 1963), 517–32.

In his novels, H reflects conventional attitudes and suggests that music comprises a tradition worth preserving. The sequence in *Jude the Obscure* tracing a hymn's authorship, based on a real experience of Louis Spohr, indicates that desire for money is alike in London and among provincials. The sympathetic portrait of the "Mellstock Quire" in *Under the Greenwood Tree* shows the provincial appreciation of the conventional.

2777 Stephens, Bertie Norman. THOMAS HARDY IN HIS GARDEN. With an introduction by Richard Curle (Beaminster, Dorset: Toucan P, 1963).

[H's gardener recalls H's love of privacy and quiet, moods signaled by his not coming down for lunch, his love of wild flowers and young fresh vegetables, the crudeness of bathing facilities, H's fondness for animals and his talking more easily to his dog than to people, the visits of Ramsay Macdonald, Sir James Barrie, Sir Edmund Gosse, and T. E. Lawrence, Mrs. H's burning of "baskets full of the letters and private papers. . . . My impression was she did not want any of the letters or papers to be seen by anyone." "Most Dorchester folk hadn't thought a lot of him. Many had the idea he didn't treat his first wife right." Also see J. Stevens Cox (pub and general editor), Monographs on the Life of Thomas Hardy (1962).]

2778 Stewart, J. I. M. "Thomas Hardy," EIGHT MODERN WRITERS. Vol XII of THE OXFORD HISTORY OF ENGLISH LITERATURE, ed by F. P. Wilson and Bonamy Dobrée (NY: Oxford UP, 1963), pp. 19–70, 188, 191, 212–13, 237, 242, 284, 292, 400, 412, 437, 567, 585; bibliography, pp. 629–38.

H, a countryman of simple birth and an artist of Gothic imagination and critical ingenuousness, shares the ironic plight of the late Victorian age. H's distinction lies in his ability to transfer this "disenchanted vision" into the world of Wessex, a world in which happiness consists in the ignorance of its old-fashioned, innocent people to change a world in which misery consists in the awareness in a few of its people of the possibility of transcending this world. H was at once a commercial novelist who recklessly modified his work at the request of editors and a careful craftsman who revised his work with thoroughgoing devotion. H's poetry, more clearly than his novels, is the product of "the struggle between an intellect subdued to determinism and an imagination nourished upon the Christian assertion of spiritual and moral order." H's first published novel, *Desperate Remedies* (1871), a novel of intrigue imitative of Wilkie Collins, was the product of George Meredith's advice that he scrap the satiric *The Poor Man and the Lady* in favor of a novel with more plot. Adverse criticism of *Remedies* on moral grounds and John Morley's praise of certain rural scenes in the aborted *Poor Man* turned H in yet a new direction. *Under the Greenwood Tree* (1872) is a delicate pastoral idyll, a cheerful comedy in which "what was already the characteristic colouring of his mind" was notably absent. *A Pair of Blue Eyes* (1873), H's "last apprentice piece," combines the "linked coincidences" of *Remedies* with an expanding sense of tragedy. In *Eyes* H faces for the first time what was to be a persisting problem: how to represent convincingly his profound sense of "the incidence upon human destiny of the mere blind recalcitrance of the universe." H's next four major novels—*Far From the Madding Crowd* (1874), *The Return of the Native* (1878), *The Mayor of Casterbridge* (1886), and *The Woodlanders* (1887)—"preserve some amenity" which is absent in *Tess of the d'Urbervilles* (1891) and *Jude the Obscure* (1896). *Madding Crowd* is a "sudden glory" in H's writing in its power "to make us see, in observation of and control over a wide diversity of natural things, and in the perfection of the rustic chorus." A sense of "the fertility in nature" pervades *Madding Crowd*; its people "achieve an equilibrium amid its stresses." In *Native*, however, Egdon Heath is "Nature in its otherness, closed to Mind," typifying "the vast neutral unregarding universe" that forms the theater of human destiny. The tiny individual existences of *Native*, the isolation and insignificance of minute figures moving upon vast spaces, give way to the massive dimensions of Michael Henchard in *Mayor*, H's next major novel. Henchard is H's "most powerful," "most original," character, and his tragedy is "more nearly Shakespearian than is anything else of the kind in Hardy." *Woodlanders* "returns to the method of spreading interest over a group of characters, and of implicating them, this time subtly rather than powerfully, with a natural scene." *Woodlanders* also places new emphasis upon two frequently shown forces: "the keen sense of social distinction possessed by countrymen" and the ready acceptance by countrymen of "the letter of man-made moral law." *Woodlanders* illustrates H's shifting focus: from the relation between man and God to the "merciless intolerance" of relations between man and man. Between 1875 and 1891 H published five novels of minor stature: *The Hand of Ethelberta* (1876), a polite comedy; *A Laodicean* (1881), "Hardy's only unredeemed failure"; *The Trumpet-Major* (1880), a novel set in the Napoleonic period; *Two on a Tower* (1882), "the ironic comedy of a county Venus and a scientifically preoccupied Adonis" that attains tragic dimensions with the heroine's death; and *The Well-Beloved* (1897, but not published until 1902), a story about a man "who has to confess to the woman he would marry that he was the suitor too of her mother and her grandmother." *Tess* and *Jude* are "at once moving and imaginatively insufficient." Undiscriminating application of "his philosophy of the raw deal," produced two novels that, though "formidable and unforgettable," are often "uninspired, dismal, and obscurely but fatally lacking in the final integrity of art." H published poetry steadily from 1898 until his death in 1928: *Wessex Poems* (1898), *Poems of the Past and the Present* (1902), *The Dynasts* (1903–1908), *Time's Laughingstocks* (1909), *Satires of Circumstance* (1914), *Moments of Vision* (1917), *Late Lyrics and Earlier* (1922), *Human Shows, Far Phantasies* (1925), and *Winter Words* (1928). H's poetry is the product of the simple aesthetic of a " 'latent music in the sincere utterance of deep emotion.' " Browning was the most profound literary influence upon his verse, though H could not share Browning's optimism. The love poems of 1913, elegies all to his first wife, are "as great love poetry as any written in English during the first half of the twentieth century." *Dynasts*, H's "longest-considered and most ambitious work," is his "largest achievement" and is "fittingly a work of the historical imagination." His "abundant sense of the past" is the foundation of his merit as poet and novelist.

> **2779** T[itterington], E[llen] E. THE DOMESTIC LIFE OF THOMAS HARDY (1921–1928). With an introduction by Richard Curle (Beaminster, Dorset: Toucan P, 1963); supplemented by Ellen E. Titterington, AFTERTHOUGHTS OF MAX GATE (1969).

[H's parlor-maid gives a very detailed account of the daily routine, H's whims, his stinginess, his obsession with cobwebs, such frequent visitors as Sir James Barrie, Siegfried Sassoon, E. M. Forster, T. E. Lawrence, and others, and the evening of H's death. She particularly notes the gloominess of the house—it "was depressing"; "nobody there was really happy." Also see J. Stevens Cox (pub and general editor), Monographs on the Life of Thomas Hardy (1962).]

> **2780** Voss, Harold Lionel. MOTORING WITH THOMAS HARDY. With an introduction by Richard Curle (Beaminster, Dorset: Toucan P, 1963).

[H's "favourite driver," whose father was also a builder, recalls that he and his family knew the Hs well; on drives, H preferred going to remote "unspoilt" villages and would talk about his memories of these places; Mrs. H always gave a better tip than H. H was saddened whenever the character of one of the old Dorset inns or any other building was altered. H was always calm, never in a temper. "I think the old boy lived as much in the past as he did in the present." Also see J. Stevens Cox (pub and general editor), Monographs on the Life of Thomas Hardy (1962).]

2781 Wade, Rosalind. "Thomas Hardy: The Sources of His Inspiration," CONTEMPORARY REVIEW, CCIV (Nov 1963), 248–53.

The "diversity of emotion and creative insight [of H's literary corpus] appears incompatible with the public image of a Victorian man of letters pursuing a conventional, humdrum routine." Is it, then, reasonable to suppose that the "qualities and actions" of his characters "had their origin in personal experiences and close observation?" From his family, H drew respect for traditions, rituals, and country ways, and for the people who continued to honor them. The "Big Houses" of the neighborhood stocked H's memory with tales of the wealthy. Surely H's love experience—especially with E. L. Gifford and Tryphena Sparks—"proved to be merely contributory to Hardy's inspirational progress." But an awareness of whom he knew as man or boy cannot account for the "amazing depth and variety of his work." Not memory, but "the creative imagination alone was responsible."

2782 Weber, Carl J. (ed). HARDY'S LOVE POEMS (Lond: Macmillan; NY: St. Martin's P, 1963).

Along with Shakespeare's SONNETS and E. B. Browning's SONNETS FROM THE PORTUGUESE, H's love poems are one of the three best series of love poems in English literature.

2783 Weber, Carl J. "He Came from Dorset," VIEWPOINT: CONTEMPORARY ISSUES OF THOUGHT AND LIFE, No. 1 (1963), 14–15.

[Discusses H's remarkably detailed knowledge of the geography and topography of Dorset.]

2784 Wilpert, Gero von (ed). LEXIKON DER WELTLITERATUR: BIOGRAPHISCH-BIBLIOGRAPHISCHES HANDWÖRTERBUCH NACH AUTHOREN UND ANONYMEN WERKEN (Dictionary of World Literature: Biographical-Bibliographical Glossary of Authors and Anonymous Works) (Stuttgart: Alfred Kröner, 1963), p. 554.

[Lists biographical works, criticism. Discusses H's tragic presentation of life.] [In German.]

2785 Wing, George. HARDY (Edinburgh & Lond: Oliver & Boyd, 1963).

In H's "portraiture of women . . . one factor remains constant . . . sexual betrayal, largely, but not always, the result of an incompatible marriage or unhappy alliance." In his stories this theme is "clamorously repetitive" as in "On the Western Circuit" and "Interlopers at the Knap." H's six least successful novels are *A Laodicean, A Pair of Blue Eyes, Desperate Remedies, The Hand of Ethelberta, Two on a Tower,* and *The Well-Beloved.* Among H's minor successes, *Under the Greenwood Tree* is a pastoral love idyll with overtones of betrayal and unhappiness to come. In *Far From the Madding Crowd,* the action rises from the facts that "Bathsheba is irresponsibly flirtatious," and Troy is "aggressively masculine." *The Return of the Native* suffers from "two unfortunate exaggerations": the character of Clym and Egdon Heath. On the other hand, "there is no doubt about the supreme success of Eustacia." Among H's finest novels, *Tess of the d'Urbervilles* is a commentary "on the complexity of sexual morality." In *Jude the Obscure,* which was written in a spirit of great bitterness, "the whole complexity of moral canons is taken to pieces." *The Dynasts* is not "a successful culmination" of H's life work but only "a museum piece . . . artistically more dead than alive." H's "essential poetic force and inspiration" are far more in evidence in his shorter poems.

1964

2786 Alexander, B. J. "Thomas Hardy's *Jude the Obscure*: A Rejection of Traditional Christianity's 'Good' God Theory," SOUTHERN QUARTERLY, III (1964), 74–82.

Jude the Obscure contains the same· lesson as "Hap": "No beneficent providence rules the world." Nature (body and sex) thwarts spirit, and no beneficent deity comes to Jude's aid. Sex (Arabella) subverts him; Jude's own fleshly nature causes him to pursue Sue. The Church loses its meaning for him. Jude wants to be a minister, but no "sympathetic assistance from an understanding God came to strengthen Jude in his attempt to overcome the power of the flesh; and life overcame him." This is H's view of the cosmos.

2787 Beatty, C. J. "The Part Played by Architecture in the Life and Work of Thomas Hardy, with Particular Reference to the Novels." Unpublished dissertation, University of London (External), 1964.

[Listed in Lawrence F. McNamee, DISSERTATIONS IN ENGLISH AND AMERICAN LITERATURE, SUPP I (NY & Lond: Bowker, 1969).]

2788 Beebe, Maurice. IVORY TOWERS AND SACRED FOUNTS: THE ARTIST AS HERO IN FICTION FROM GOETHE TO JOYCE (NY: New York UP, 1964), pp. 18, 98, 99, 250.

H's distinguishing characteristic is his geometrical design and structural parallelism. *Jude the Obscure* is one of the apprentice novels that flourished from 1880 to 1920, like Butler's THE WAY OF ALL FLESH and Maugham's OF HUMAN BONDAGE. In H's *The Well-Beloved*, as in Wyndham Lewis's TARR, Dreiser's THE "GENIUS" and Norris's VANDOVER AND THE BRUTE, the artist-hero is dependent on romantic fulfillment in order to function as an artist.

2789 Blunden, Edmund. GUEST OF THOMAS HARDY. With an introduction by Richard Curle (Beaminster, Dorset: Toucan P, 1964).

On a first visit in 1922, H was courteous, candid, and not as silent as he has been reported to be. H maintained the reviewers could not have cut all the pages of *Late Lyrics and Earlier*. H avoided talking of Robert Louis Stevenson. [Also see J. Stevens Cox (pub and general editor), Monographs on the Life of Thomas Hardy (1962).]

2790 Blunt, Wilfred. COCKERELL: SYDNEY CARLYLE COCKERELL, FRIEND OF RUSKIN AND WILLIAM MORRIS AND DIRECTOR OF THE FITZWILLIAM MUSEUM, CAMBRIDGE (Lond: Hamish & Hamilton, 1964), pp. 97, 98, 142, 153, 155n, 156, 165, 208, 212–23, 261, 268, 269, 271, 272, 295, 372.

[Cockerell, one of H's literary executors, became acquainted with the novelist in 1911 and paid him forty-two visits before H's death. Part II, chap 8 gives a picture of the suspicious and domineering Florence H, who objected violently to a brief and inconsequential flirtation her husband had with a young amateur actress, Gertrude Bugler, in 1920. Cockerell also supervised the distribution of H manuscripts to various British museums.]

2791 Brooks, Cleanth, John T. Purser, and Robert Penn Warren. AN APPROACH TO LITERATURE. 4th ed. (NY: Appleton-Century-Crofts, 1964), pp. 327–28, 334–38, 375–77.

H's "Neutral Tones" has a conversational and meditative tone and shows the poet's fatalistic attitude. In "The Convergence of the Twain," the contrast between various rhythms supports the ironical contrasts in the poem. "The whole poem is a splendid study in the variations of meter which a poet may use, as it is also a fine study in the effective use of contrasts of varying degree and of varying effect." The poem's "round plan . . . is a system of contrasts and fusions of opposites." [Also see earlier variant editions, e.g. 1936, 1939, 1952.]

2792 Carpenter, Richard C. "The Mirror and the Sword: Imagery in *Far From the Madding Crowd*," NINETEENTH CENTURY FICTION, XVIII (March 1964), 331–45.

One of the reasons why H's major novels are major "is precisely that in them Hardy managed to create a fabric of images, repeated and 'concatenated' to deepen and make complex the emotional and conceptual significance" of these novels. "The imagistic design of *Far From the Madding Crowd*, unlike the straightforward structure of its narrative, is fundamentally musical. A motif, announced in an early scene, reappears time after time, sometimes as a leitmotiv attached to similar situations or characters and gaining in significance because of repetition in an expanding milieu, but more often transposed, inverted, taken up by a different character or situation."

2793 Carpenter, Richard C. THOMAS HARDY (NY: Twayne, 1964).

The reticence in handling sexual experience, enforced by public pressure, may have subconsciously stimulated H's skill in creating scenes heavily laden with sexual connotations, as the sword drill scene in *Far From the Madding Crowd*. His familiarity with folk customs and classical tradition, coupled with his philosophic inquisitiveness, stimulated his tendency to view experience mythically. His fiction "is abundant in powerful archetypal situations and symbols." The psychological and mythical elements are important aspects of H's art. Clym Yeobright in *The Return of the Native* is a "Prometheus-Oedipus figure." *The Mayor of Casterbridge* is the working out of the self-destructive impulses of the hero, Michael Henchard; Giles Winterborne in *The Woodlanders* suggests "a Dionysus or Balder the Beautiful whose death signifies the loss of some precious organic vitality to this fallen world." H's poetry relies too heavily upon a philosophy not suited to poetic creativity, though his individuality has left its mark on some masterful poems. [Though Carpenter's heavy reliance on other critics makes his book of limited value to well-read students of H, his study may be a valuable introduction for the beginning reader to the current critical views on the author. Carpenter is best at psychological studies of the characters.]

2794 Cox, J. Stevens (ed). "Identifications of Some Places in Hardy's Works," in THOMAS HARDY THROUGH THE CAMERA'S EYE, ed by J. Stevens Cox (Beaminster, Dorset: Toucan P, 1964), pp. 50–52.

[Identifies several places referred to in *Satires of Circumstance*, *Moments of Vision*, and several stories, some identifications apparently made by H himself for Hermann Lea. Also see IDENTIFICATION OF FICTITIOUS PLACE NAMES IN HARDY'S WORKS, ed by J. Stevens Cox (1968). Also see J.

Stevens Cox (pub and general editor), Monographs on the Life of Thomas Hardy (1962).]

2795 [Cox, J. Stevens (ed)]. THOMAS HARDY THROUGH THE CAMERA'S EYE. With an introduction by Richard Curle (Beaminster, Dorset: Toucan P, 1964).
[Contents, abstracted separately by author or title under date of first publication: Alfred T. D. Scudamore, "Hermann Lea, Friend of Thomas Hardy: A Memoir" (1964); Hermann Lea, "Hermann Lea's Notes for a Biography of Thomas Hardy," ed by J. Stevens Cox (1964); Hermann Lea, "Letters from Lea to Hardy," ed by J. Stevens Cox (1964); Hermann Lea, "Letters from Lea to Sanders," ed by J. Stevens Cox (1964); Hermann Lea, "Notes from Lea to Sanders" (1964); "Account of Hermann Lea's Death. Was a Friend of Thomas Hardy," rptd from WESTERN GAZETTE, 22 Feb 1952 (not seen in this form); "Identifications of Some Places in Hardy's Works," ed by J. Stevens Cox (1964). Not specifically relevant and thus not abstracted separately: "Manuscript Memorandum in the Hand of Alfred Wade Lea," pp. 53–55, essentially a genealogical record of the Lea family; "Dorset Apples," p. 56, a list of apples grown in particular parts of Dorset.] [Also see J. Stevens Cox (pub and general editor), Monographs on the Life of Thomas Hardy (1962).]

2796 Dawson, E. W. "Two 'Flat' Characters in *Jude the Obscure*," LOCK HAVEN REVIEW, No. 6 (1964), 36–44.
Using E. M. Forster's terms (in his ASPECTS OF THE NOVEL), both Father Time and Vilbert are "flat" characters. The former follows a formula like "I see nothing in life which would make it desirable or even tolerable," but he fails artistically because he is not comic and frequently impossible to believe. Although there are successful moments, it is only Jude's and Sue's interactions with him that prevent him from destroying the novel. Vilbert, on the other hand, is comic and "part of the societal INEVITABLE which encompasses Jude." His name suggests "villain," and both he and Arabella are "metaphorically identified with the 'hot mass' and 'the rest.' " His compatability with Arabella is made possible by their both being basically "flat" and insensitive opportunists.

2797 Deacon, Lois. HARDY'S SWEETEST IMAGE: THOMAS HARDY'S POETRY FOR HIS LOST LOVE, TRYPHENA (Ingledene, Chagford, Devon: [pvtly ptd], 1964); in part the basis for several Toucan Press pamphlets and in the main absorbed in PROVIDENCE AND MR. HARDY, by Lois Deacon and Terry Coleman (1966).
The sequence of twenty-six love lyrics in *Time's Laughingstocks* is a central document in the case for H's love affair with his cousin, Tryphena Sparks. The poems record, with great poignancy, the grief and the bliss which

accompanied the courtship, betrothal, and separation of the pair. Beyond this sequence, there are scattered references and allusions in the poetry to support the contention that Tryphena was "the love of Hardy's whole life." [Also see J. Stevens Cox (pub and general editor), Monographs on the Life of Thomas Hardy (1962).]

2798 El-Ayouty, A. Y. "The Novels of Thomas Hardy and Their Relation to His Social Views and Attitudes." Unpublished dissertation, University of Leeds, 1964.

[Listed in Lawrence F. McNamee, DISSERTATIONS IN ENGLISH AND AMERICAN LITERATURE, SUPP I (NY & Lond: Bowker, 1969).]

2799 Evans, Evelyn L. MY FATHER PRODUCED HARDY'S PLAYS. With an introduction by Richard Curle (Beaminster, Dorset: Toucan P, 1964).

In 1908, A. H. Evans first persuaded H to allow a scene from *The Trumpet-Major* to be dramatized and presented in connection with A. M. Broadley's lecture on "Napoleon's Threatened Invasion of England"; H and Evans worked out the outline, and H wrote new lines for the play, produced 18 Nov 1908. The play, unlike the novel, ended happily with wedding bells, on H's insistence. Next (1909), Evans prepared *Far From the Madding Crowd* for the stage, T. H. Tilley having solved some of the staging problems. After Evans, Tilley went on to dramatize and produce *The Return of the Native* (1920), *A Desperate Remedy* (1922), THE MUMMING PLAY OF ST. GEORGE (1923), and A RUSTIC WEDDING SCENE (1924). THE MELLSTOCK QUIRE, based on *Under the Greenwood Tree*, was produced 16 Nov 1910. H's own dramatization (1893) of "The Three Strangers" was produced in 1911 as THE THREE WAYFARERS; with it was produced the dramatic version of "The Distracted Preacher." H had taken a walk-on part in THE FORTY THIEVES when he was in his late twenties in London. H once led a little boy, who was to be Maurice Evans, to safety. H told Evans *The Woodlanders* was his own favorite among the novels. The Dorchester productions were brought to the Cripplegate Institute each December. [Also see J. Stevens Cox (pub and general editor), Monographs on the Life of Thomas Hardy (1962).]

2800 Fayen, George S., Jr. "Thomas Hardy," VICTORIAN FICTION: A GUIDE TO RESEARCH, ed by Lionel Stevenson (Cambridge: Harvard UP, 1964), pp. 349–87.

Almost all the pre-1964 work on H has been recorded, so that now "little needs to be done in Hardy bibliography except to continue recording annually the increasing number of essays on his fiction." The following research guide offers a survey of those important works on H that have already been recorded. [The text of this guide is divided into five categories:

bibliography, edition and texts, biography, general criticism, and studies of individual novels and stories. A running commentary is offered on the important works in each category along with suggestions for further work.]

2801 Gordon, David J. "D. H. Lawrence's Quarrel with Tragedy," PERSPECTIVE, XIII (Winter 1964), 135–50.

Lawrence was fascinated with H's characters but felt H didn't go far enough in "penetrating his characters with a morality of nature," instead, they were "wrestling with mere social convention." In H's early novels, the exceptional people were villains and punished by the community; in later novels, H's sympathies were with "dark villains" (Henchard, Eustacia, Tess, Alec) and withdrawn from "white virgins" (Angel Clare, Sue Bridehead). With Tess and Jude, H "shied away from true tragic depiction"; they have inherent weaknesses, are pathetic rather than tragic. H's error in art is his failure to recognize universal opposites: not social morality vs. natural morality, but polar forces of Natural Morality (Love vs. Law, Male vs. Female, Christ vs. Jehovah, Spirit vs. Flesh). H has an unconscious predilection for one side of being (Love, Male, Spirit, Christ) and a corresponding prejudice against the other (Law, Female, Flesh, Jehovah). H fails to balance these and depicts "inharmonious characters" that are "either too strong or too weak." He frustrates the fulfillment of his characters.

2802 Greshoff, C. J. "A Note on *The Return of the Native*," STANDPUNTE (Cape Town), XVIII (1964), 33–41.

The "profound contradiction which tears . . . [*The Return of the Native*] apart" is that H "the tragic writer first lights . . . the great . . . fires of tragedy, but then Hardy, the novelist, must pour over them the cold water of daily fact . . . without which the novel cannot live but which kills the tragic flames." H's attempt to "reconcile tragedy and the novel" was doomed, for "the novel cannot give expression to the tragic vision of life." The tragic vision must find expression "in a strict and hieratic form removed from the immediate realities of daily living." Even H's employment of traditional themes, forms, and ballad-devices to provide a mythological basis for his story "does nothing to remove . . . the profound and disrupting contradiction born from the antithetical nature of tragedy and the novel." Although H's description of Eustacia creates a vivid impression of a genuinely tragic heroine, when he moves into the realm of factual narrative "he leaves off writing in the heroic key and starts writing in a prosaic key." H's problem was "a novel cannot contain the heroic-tragic Eustacia." Therefore, as novelist, H is forced to "scale down the nature of his heroine." *Native* is reminiscent of MADAME BOVARY, "an un-heroic, un-tragic novel." Eustacia and Wildeve, for all H's insistence on their tragic stature, resemble the prosaic, unheroic Emma and Rodolphe.

2803 Grigson, Geoffrey. "Thomas Hardy," Poets in Their Pride (NY: Basic Books, 1964), pp. 163–75.
[A superficial summary of H's life.]

2804 Gross, Harvey. Sound and Form in Modern Poetry: A Study of Prosody from Thomas Hardy to Robert Lowell (Ann Arbor: University of Michigan P, 1964), pp. 42–48.
The prosody of many poems fails because versification is clumsy, words are forced into metrical patterns, and meters are inappropriate to the subject. In his best poems, H creates a music within traditional metrics that moves psychologically, the experience of the life of feeling.

2805 Guérard, Albert J. "The Illusion of Simplicity: The Shorter Poems of Thomas Hardy," Sewanee Review, LXXII (Summer 1964), 363–88.
Three aspects of H's poetry appeal to the modern reader: sincerity, clarity in expression of ideas, and the spoken quality of the verse. H uses form ironically; the form and the meaning are deliberately incongruous. He deliberately roughens his art and experiments in form and metrics. He doesn't allow "an easy correspondence of spoken phrase and written line." His poems may be categorized as occasional and incidental, ballads and ballad-tragedies, personal lyrics evoking the Wessex past, and poems of pessimism and disillusioned wisdom. Secondary categories and impulses of his poetry are mourning, calm weariness, nostalgia, failure of communication, pleas for numbness of the heart, moments of vision and intuition, and love's becoming tedious.

2806 Hardy, Barbara. The Appropriate Form (Lond: Athlone P, 1964; Lond: Oxford UP, 1965), pp. 6–9, 24, 36, 47–48, 51, 53, 70–75, 81–82, 109, 132, 135, 181.
H, along with Defoe, Charlotte Brontë, and Forster, uses dogmatic form; that is, he fits "the complexity and contradictoriness of life into a predetermined dogmatic pattern." H uses his art "to embody an ideology." "Because of the very nature of the ideology, [his] art shapes character and action in a special way." For example, the action and characters of *Jude the Obscure* "are organized as illustrations of . . . belief in an absence of Providence which allows nature and society to frustrate the individual and create a pattern not significantly different from one which would illustrate a malignant God." Another feature of "ideological form" is "the constant play of opposites," and this is common to H's later novels. According to D. H. Lawrence, H's form suffers because of " 'his clumsy efforts to push events into line with his theory of being.' "

2807 Heilman, Robert B. "Hardy's *Mayor*: Notes on Style," Nineteenth Century Fiction, XVIII (March 1964), 307–29.
Most critics "tend to note the contradiction between the general air of

quality in Hardy's work and the frequent ineptitude of the style." It is possible to identify a number of H's stylistic habits and "thus provide a descriptive account of those unlike strands whose uneasy and irregular interweaving constitutes that singular fabric, Hardy's style." "In using abstract language Hardy often names or describes a situation instead of solidly presenting it and thrusting us into it as a palpable reality"; for instance, Elizabeth-Jane is "too abstract to be convincing." H has, however, a concrete style and with it "he exhibits an extraordinary capacity to be conscious of many kinds of details and to find the specific terms that will render them visible, audible, or tangible and thus evoke a lively response from the reader's imagination." "Hardy's characteristic inconsistency appears, finally, in his style at two opposite poles of the novelist's work. At one he is the omniscient commentator, emphatically present; at the other he disappears as the characters take over in the dialogue." The problem of H's style is its inconsistency.

2808 Hellstrom, Ward. "Hardy's Use of Setting and *Jude the Obscure*," VICTORIAN NEWSLETTER, No. 25 (Spring 1964), 11–13.

The implication in Samuel Chew's THOMAS HARDY (1921) that H was careless of setting in *Jude the Obscure* is wrong. The conflict in *Jude* is no longer with nature, as in H's earlier novels, but with society. Setting with H was consistently a "vital" concern.

2809 Heywood, C. "Miss Braddon's THE DOCTOR'S WIFE," REVUE DE LITTERATURE COMPARÉE, XXXVIII (April/June 1964), 255–61.

The resemblance of *The Return of the Native* to MADAME BOVARY has frequently been noted, but H's slight acquaintance with French novels has argued against a direct borrowing. H did, however, borrow from a mid-Victorian novel, Miss Braddon's THE DOCTOR'S WIFE (1864), which was itself an adaptation of MADAME BOVARY. Comparison of the texts shows the persistence of detailed resemblances in the succession of adaptations. Evidence suggesting that H knew MADAME BOVARY does not emerge; nevertheless, his intellectual position, as shown in the handling of a theme which was evidently fascinating to Victorian readers, more closely approximates Flaubert's than Miss Braddon's.

2810 Hoffman, Russell. "The Idea of the Unconscious in the Novels of Thomas Hardy," DISSERTATION ABSTRACTS, XXIV (1964), 4190. Unpublished dissertation, University of California (Berkeley), 1963.

2811 Homer, Christine Wood. THOMAS HARDY AND HIS TWO WIVES. With an introduction by Richard Curle (Beaminster, Dorset: Toucan P, 1964).

In the 1890s, H and his first wife often went on cycling parties with the Homers and Hermann Lea. About 1900, Lea drove H through the countryside to verify the scenes of the novels for Lea's Thomas Hardy's Wessex (1913). Although shy, H was always kind to young people; H was on the whole a cheerful man who loved a joke. The first Mrs. H would not let people see H if they showed no interest in seeing her; she sought flattery for her indifferent creative efforts. The Hs gave two or three garden parties a year until Mrs. H became more "difficult." H was always polite to his wife, even when she embarrassed him. After H's second marriage, members of his family frequently visited at Max Gate. H was humane and could be generous. H entertained some soldiers during 1914-1918. After H's death, some of his notebooks were burned. [Prints a poem by the first Mrs. H. Also see J. Stevens Cox (pub and general editor), Monographs on the Life of Thomas Hardy (1962).]

> **2812** Hornback, Bert Gerald. "History, Time, and Timelessness in the Novels of Thomas Hardy," Dissertation Abstracts, XXV (1964), 2490–91. Published dissertation, University of Notre Dame, 1964; pub as Metaphor of Chance: Vision and Technique in the Works of Thomas Hardy (Athens, Ohio: Ohio UP, 1971).

> **2813** Horne, Lewis B. "Fawley's Quests: A Reading of *Jude the Obscure*," Tennessee Studies in Literature, IX (1964), 117–27.

Jude the Obscure is an example of Northrop Frye's "romance-quest." "The characters perform not as their mythic counterparts do, but in ironic contrast."

> **2814** Karl, Frederick R. "Thomas Hardy's 'Mayor' and the Changing Novel," An Age of Fiction: The Nineteenth Century British Novel (NY: Farrar, Straus & Giroux, 1964), pp. 295–322; rptd as A Reader's Guide to the Nineteenth Century British Novel (NY: Noonday P, 1965), pp. 295–322.

H created a world in which cosmic misery and despair seem the inevitable result of birth. His is a peculiarly idiosyncratic vision that causes "his characters and plots . . . [to] move in a sphere unknown to his contemporaries, an area of personal anxiety and neurosis that no other Victorian, excepting Dickens in some respects, had attempted to define." H is a symbolic realist, his fiction peculiarly close to that of Flaubert because in it "the actual fact exists prosaically but can nevertheless be projected far beyond the immediate historical situation." Chance ("everything over which man has no control") is the universal symbol of H's personal philosophy. Chance is the will of the universe, the Immanent Will, and man's helplessness before it makes life painful—surcease from pain to be found only through nullification of the individual will. The anxiety and neurosis of his characters—that which makes them more of the twentieth than the nineteenth century—is the product of their anxious quest in a "chance-filled universe" for an individual identity lost in a maze of possibilities. The themes of lost identity and of deception in *The Mayor of Casterbridge* and the indifference or neutrality of the individual will in the novel anticipate, at many points, modern existential beliefs. H's reliance on chance is a recognition of all those factors beyond the control of the conscious self.

2815 Lea, Hermann. Hermann Lea's Notes for a Biography of Thomas Hardy," in THOMAS HARDY THROUGH THE CAMERA'S EYE, ed by J. Stevens Cox (Beaminster, Dorset: Toucan P, 1964), pp. 14–38.
[Random personal reminiscences of H and of Dorset scenes, activities and dialect. Quotes from some letters from H to Lea. Also see J. Stevens Cox (pub and general editor), Monographs on the Life of Thomas Hardy (1962).]

2816 Lea, Hermann. "Letters from Lea to Hardy," in THOMAS HARDY THROUGH THE CAMERA'S EYE, ed by J. Stevens Cox (Beaminster, Dorset: Toucan P, 1964), pp. 39–41.
[Reprints letters written during 1924 regarding publication by Macmillan of Lea's work on H's novels. Also see J. Stevens Cox (pub and general editor), Monographs on the Life of Thomas Hardy (1962).]

2817 Lea, Hermann. "Letters from Lea to Sanders," in THOMAS HARDY THROUGH THE CAMERA'S EYE, ed by J. Stevens Cox (Beaminster, Dorset: Toucan P, 1964), pp. 41–48.
[Reprints letters written between 1940 and 1947 to E. N. Sanders, especially regarding Lord David Cecil's book, HARDY THE NOVELIST (1943), and other works about H. Also see J. Stevens Cox (pub and general editor), Monographs on the Life of Thomas Hardy (1962).]

2818 Lea, Hermann. "Notes from Lea to Sanders," in THOMAS HARDY THROUGH THE CAMERA'S EYE, ed by J. Stevens Cox (Beaminster, Dorset: Toucan P, 1964), pp. 48–49.
[Notes regarding the help given Lea by H in preparing THOMAS HARDY'S WESSEX (1913). Also see J. Stevens Cox (pub and general editor), Monographs on the Life of Thomas Hardy (1962).]

2819 Lewis, C[ecil] Day. "Introduction," *Under the Greenwood Tree or the Mellstock Quire: A Rural Painting of the Dutch School*, ed by C. Day Lewis (Lond & Glasgow: Collins, 1964), 11–18.
In spite of some faults in construction, dialogue, and characterization,

Under the Greenwood Tree is attractive by reason of its solidly realistic presentation of rural life. [Biographical sketch and brief bibliography appended.]

2820 McDowell, Frederick P. W. "In Defense of Arabella: A Note on *Jude the Obscure*," English Language Notes, I (June 1964), 274–80.

A careful look at Arabella's behavior and the images associated with her show this character to be more complex than an allegorical reading of the novel would render her. H neither hated her nor pictured her only as a representation of "Piggishness." She has insight, "human attributes," and other praiseworthy qualities. Though she is selfish, she is frank; though she is vulgar, she possesses "abundant life and amiability"; and although she is not "delicately discriminating," she is shrewd. In creating her, H intended to produce "a shudder among his genteel readers." In her we find not something that can be translated into "abstractions" but rather "multiform impressions of reality and . . . complications of motive." [Perceptive.]

2821 Maddock, Lawrence H. "*Tess of the d'Urbervilles*: The Last Paragraph," CEA Critic, XXVII (Dec 1964), 8.

Since H uses imagery of the sun to describe happy times in Tess's life, the novel ends on a happy note, at least for Liza Lu and Angel Clare who walk off hand in hand as the sun rises.

2822 Mardon, J. Vera. Thomas Hardy as a Musician. With an introduction by Richard Curle and an appendix containing the old Dorset folk song and dance "O Jan! O Jan! O Jan!" now first printed (Beaminster, Dorset: Toucan P, 1964).

H on occasion showed actors in the dramatization of scenes from his novels how to dance the figures in some folk dances and showed the fiddler how a tune should be played. H was a competent musician, chiefly interested in the old tunes and not in classical music. [Mrs. Mardon, a pianist, occasionally accompanied H at Max Gate. She recalls dramatic versions of or scenes from *The Trumpet-Major* (by A. H. Evans, 1908), The Mellstock Quire (Evans's adaptation [1910] of *Under the Greenwood Tree*), The Distracted Preacher (1911) (based on the story "The Distracted Preacher"), *The Return of the Native* (adaptation of 1920, including The Mummers Play), and *The Tragedy of the Queen of Cornwall* (1923). She provides anecdotes of H's fear of "hearty extroverts, especially American ones"; H's writing love letters for some village girls, from which he got his knowledge of how a woman's mind works; the Prince of Wales's visit (1923); and so on. Also see J. Stevens Cox (pub and general editor), Monographs on the Life of Thomas Hardy (1962).]

2823 Marks, William Sowell, III. "The Novel as Puritan Romance: A Comparative Study of Samuel Richardson, the Brontës, Thomas Hardy, and D. H. Lawrence," DISSERTATION ABSTRACTS, XXV (1964), 1214. Unpublished dissertation, Stanford University, 1964.

2824 Nelson, Duncan M. "The Poetry of Thomas Hardy." Unpublished dissertation, Harvard University, 1964.
[Listed in Lawrence F. McNamee, DISSERTATIONS IN ENGLISH AND AMERICAN LITERATURE, SUPP I (NY & Lond: Bowker, 1969).]

2825 Oliver, Constance M. THOMAS HARDY PROPOSES TO MARY WAIGHT. With an introduction by Richard Curle (Beaminster, Dorset: Toucan P, 1964).
[Mary Waight's granddaughter reports H's proposing to her grandmother when H was 22 and the lady was 29; she refused him. Also see J. Stevens Cox (pub and general editor), Monographs on the Life of Thomas Hardy (1962).]

2826 Parish, John E. "Thomas Hardy on the Evidence of Things Unseen," VICTORIAN POETRY, II (Summer 1964), 203–5.
With "mischief bordering on malice," H's "The Impercipient at a Cathedral Service" reduces Wordsworth's ideas on pre-existence in "Ode: Intimations of Immortality" and St. Paul's idea that "faith is the substance of things hoped for" into the notion that "the evidence of things unseen" can be attributed to "childish hallucinations."

2827 Posey, Horace Gadsden, Jr. "*The Dynasts*: Unity in Irony, A Critical Study," DISSERTATION ABSTRACTS, XXIV (April–June 1964), 4682. Unpublished dissertation, University of Wisconsin, 1964.

2828 Riesner, Dieter. "Kunstprosa in der Werkstatt: Hardys *The Mayor of Casterbridge* 1884–1921" (Imaginative Prose in the Workshop: Hardy's *The Mayor of Casterbridge* 1884–1921), FESTSCHRIFT FÜR WALTER HÜBNER (Publication in Honor of Walter Hübner), ed by Dieter Riesner and Helmut Gneuss (Berlin: Erich Schmidt, 1964), pp. 267–326.
H, like few other authors, has suffered from the textual-critical indifference and laziness of his interpreters. The many changes H made in the different editions of his novels—often undertaken with great care and, despite his own disavowal, high artistic sense—have largely been overlooked. Speculative critics have failed to correct their subjective impressions by studying the evolution of the novel and understanding H's artistic intention by study-

ing the genesis of his works. The changes H made in the six versions of the text of *The Mayor of Casterbridge* "represent an astonishing performance of the creative imagination." The recent critical emphasis on the role played by social conditions—i.e. the repeal of the Corn Laws, introduction of machinery into Wessex farming, etc.—overlooks the fact that "cancellations in the manuscript show how unessential external circumstances were for Henchard's tragedy." H first thought of Henchard as a mechanic, a skilled countryman, a future architect, and a woodsman. Study of the *Mayor* manuscript also contradicts the idea that H wrote his novels from a carefully worked-out plan. Instead, H evolved characters, themes, and situations tentatively and experimentally. H's careful alterations of the text of *Mayor* from edition to edition "contradict Hardy's assertion that novel-writing was for him at this time 'mere journey-work' and that he did not concern himself with artistic form." [In German.]

> **2829** Sankey, Benjamin. "Thomas Hardy's Prose Style," SPEC-TRUM, VII (Spring 1964), 52–75; rvd as "Hardy's Prose Style," TWENTIETH CENTURY LITERATURE, XI (April 1965), 3–15; rptd in THE MAJOR NOVELS OF THOMAS HARDY (1965).

H's diction is "unselfconsciously literary" but "exact and wide ranging, capable of naming the tools of a trade or expressing a carefully made observation." He has "noticeable rhythms, but they are prose rhythms, used for emphasis and for tying notions together." His best passages are those describing nature. "Natural cooperation in the plotting" is used to suggest "the fragility of even the best human concerns in a universe governed by laws indifferent to humanity." H's style has "a power of absorption which seems to rule out the danger of incongruity," enabling him to employ "technical principles and terms unusual for a novelist." To present mental events, he has a preference for the use of "impersonal exposition," usually summary or metaphor. "Clarity and breadth of perspective are possible precisely because he sees things in general terms," somewhat like "a Sophoclean chorus," and "the movement from particular to general is accompanied by a gradual intensification of tone." H's prose style is "serious—neither pompous nor affectedly familiar; it seldom makes claims the subject won't support. And above all, it is interesting."

> **2830** Scudamore, Alfred T. D. "Hermann Lea, Friend of Thomas Hardy: A Memoir," in THOMAS HARDY THROUGH THE CAMERA'S EYE, ed by J. Stevens Cox (Beaminster, Dorset: Toucan P, 1964), pp. 9–13.

Hermann Lea and H were very close friends for twenty-nine years, very often visiting each other and riding around Dorset identifying the places mentioned in H's novels. They had a great deal in common. [Random personal reminiscences of Lea by his nephew. Also see J. Stevens Cox (pub and general editor), Monographs on the Life of Thomas Hardy (1962).]

2831 Scudamore, Joyce. FLORENCE AND THOMAS HARDY: A RETROSPECT. With an introduction by Richard Curle (Beaminster, Dorset: Toucan P, 1964).

Mrs. H was a "lonely woman." H resented anyone who "took Mrs. Hardy's attention." Their marriage "must have been more a marriage of convenience than an emotional union." Wessex, Mrs. H's dog, and her pianola caused friction because H did not like noise. H did not want children about Max Gate; he smiled little, and was "self-centred." [Hermann Lea introduced the author to Florence H, with whom she became close friends. Also see J. Stevens Cox (pub and general editor), Monographs on the Life of Thomas Hardy (1962).]

2832 Singh, G. "Thomas Hardy and Leopardi: A Study in Affinity and Contrast," RIVISTA DI LETTERATURE MODERNE E COMPARATE, XVII (March 1964), 120–35.

Between H and Leopardi "there was more of an affinity of outlook . . . than any influence of the one on the other in the matter of . . . artistic expression." The " 'renunciative philosophy' " characteristic of Angel Clare's father and Father Time show H's awareness that there was "an in-fluence in the air both of Schopenhauer and Leopardi." But H's philosophy was really his own, arrived at independently before reading Leopardi. Despite H's efforts in his prefaces "to dissociate himself from the views expressed" in his verse, in reading H's poetry one still feels as if H *were* attempting to create a " 'harmonious philosophy' "—a contradiction between preaching and practice absent from the more candid, consistent, forthright philosophical poetry of the Italian. Leopardi's lament over a garden as "a vast hospital (far more deplorable than a cemetery)" parallels the " 'Unfulfilled Intention' " in the nature imagery of *The Woodlanders*. In *The Dynasts* H's use of "ultra-terrestrial landscape" may also have been inspired by Leopardi.

2833 Spradley, John Olin. "The Contrast of Old and New in the Novels of Thomas Hardy," DISSERTATION ABSTRACTS, XXV (1964), 456. Unpublished dissertation, University of Colorado, 1963.

2834 "Thomas Hardy," MEYERS HANDBUCH ÜBER DIE LITERATUR (Meyer's Handbook on Literature) (Mannheim: Allgemeiner Verlag, 1964), p. 418.

[Biographical data, works of H, short evaluation stressing H's pessimism.] [In German.]

2835 Urwin, G. G. THE MAYOR OF CASTERBRIDGE (NY: Barnes & Noble, 1964).

"In *The Dynasts* Thomas Hardy achieved the climax of his art: it is the

supreme expression of those ideas which had inspired the Wessex novels."
[A casebook on *The Mayor of Casterbridge*, starting with some background
on H and his works, then analyzing style, plot, setting, characters, and
theme, proceeding with a detailed analysis of chap 39, and concluding with
an evaluation in terms of Aristotle's principles of tragedy, which H closely
follows.]

2836 Vandiver, Edward P., Jr. "*The Return of the Native* and
Shakespeare," FURMAN STUDIES, XII (1964), 11–15.

In writing *The Return of the Native* H was influenced by KING LEAR,
OTHELLO, HAMLET, and ANTONY AND CLEOPATRA. Accordingly, Mrs.
Yeobright's exposure to the heat of the sun parallels Lear's exposure to the
storm; Mrs. Yeobright and Lear both complain about the ingratitude of
children; Clym's denunciation of Eustacia parallels Othello's denunciation
of Desdemona; Eustacia remonstrates with Clym for brooding over his
mother's death just as Claudius remonstrates with Hamlet for brooding over
his father's death; Clym, like Antony, wishes he had never known his beloved.

2837 Weber, Carl J. "Hardy's Comet," ENGLISH LANGUAGE
NOTES, I (March 1964), 215–18.

H's sighting of Tebbutt's comet on 25 June 1881 (as recorded in Florence
Hardy's THE EARLY LIFE OF THOMAS HARDY [1928]) accounts for the
subject and many of the details in *Two on a Tower*, which he was asked to
write for ATLANTIC MONTHLY six months later. H's study of American
geography for the novel was less careful. He knew neither the site nor the
size of Cambridge and called it merely "Cambridge, United States." H once
asked Hamlin Garland if Harvard was a girls' school.

2838 Wessex Redivivus [pseud of H. S. L. Dewar]. THE RETURN
OF WESSEX. With an introduction by Richard Curle (Beaminster,
Dorset: Toucan P, 1964).

[A spoof in which the ghost of H's dog reports on life with H. Also see J.
Stevens Cox (pub and general editor), Monographs on the Life of Thomas
Hardy (1962).]

2839 Williams, Raymond. "Thomas Hardy," CRITICAL QUAR-
TERLY, VI (Winter 1964), 341–51.

H is central to the recording of social change from Dickens to Lawrence,
the complicated historical process of upward mobility. Economic problems
of rent, capital, and trade indicate the general exposure of the individual,
and the difficulty of marriage choice is one of the most obvious features of
mobility. The specific failures projected in H's fatalism eventually amount
to a general alienation of man from land and labor. Experience of upward

mobility is obvious in Tess in *Tess of the d'Urbervilles,* Grace in *The Wood-landers,* Clym in *The Return of the Native.* The artifice of conventional pastoral always threatens H's style, more frequently than the often-noticed Latinisms. While H is often patronizingly regarded as a self-educated countryman, he is really a complex, educated observer in a period of radical change. [Excellent statement treating philosophical and biographical under-pinnings of H's style as relevant to the trends of his age and to conscious problems for H as an artist.]

1965

2840 Beards, Richard Douglas. "The Novels of Thomas Hardy and D. H. Lawrence: A Comparative Study," DISSERTATION ABSTRACTS, XXVI (1965), 2743. Unpublished dissertation, University of Washington, 1965.

2841 Buckley, Jerome Hamilton, and George Benjamin Woods (eds). POETRY OF THE VICTORIAN PERIOD. 3rd ed (Chicago: Scott, Foresman, 1965), pp. vii, 918–35, 1054–57.

Browning used living speech, which carried over to "the direct idiom and spoken cadence of Kipling and Hardy and Housman." H's "An Ancient to Ancients" is an appropriate epilogue. [Includes forty-three selections from H, with bibilography, biography, and criticism.]

2842 Christ, Henry I. "Semantics and Thomas Hardy," ENGLISH JOURNAL, LIV (Nov 1965), 738–40.

The protagonists of *The Return of the Native* tend to confuse the real people they encounter with imagined abstractions they have created. Thus, Eustacia imagines a Clym Yeobright with whom she falls in love even before she has met the real Clym. Clym himself falls in love with a self-created image of Eustacia. Mrs. Yeobright has an image of Clym as a successful merchant which she cannot give up. As a result of this in-ability to see the real person behind the imposed image, the protagonists are unable to communicate with one another and bring tragedy down upon themselves.

2843 Clarke, Robert William. "Shadow of a Magnitude: A Study of Hardy's First Five Novels," DISSERTATION ABSTRACTS, XXVI (1965), 3328–29. Unpublished dissertation, University of Wisconsin, 1965.

2844 Connolly, Cyril. THE MODERN MOVEMENT: 100 KEY BOOKS FROM ENGLAND, FRANCE AND AMERICA, 1880–1950 (Lond: Hamish Hamilton, André Deutsch, 1965), p. 32.

"The 'Satires' in this book link Hardy more directly to the Movement than his novels, which had all been steeped in the Victorian tradition. They are Maupassant-like vignettes passed through his great contemplative soul and they strike a new note like the poems about his dead wife in the same volume which concludes with the first war-poem, 'Men who march away,' and contains his much more remarkable poem about the sinking of the *Titanic*—'The Convergence of the Twain.' " [Lists of H's *Satires of Circumstance*.]

2845 Duffin, H. C. "Man and God in Thomas Hardy," ARYAN PATH, XXXVI (May 1965), 215–18.

Like Conrad and Charles Morgan, H had unorthodox religious views, but he was not an atheist. His soul responded to God, but his imagination rejected Him. H's religious views were not finally mystical but came close to Shavian ideas of Creative Evolution.

2846 Elledge, Scott. "Preface," THOMAS HARDY: TESS OF THE D'URBERVILLES: AN AUTHORITATIVE TEXT, HARDY AND THE NOVEL, CRITICISM, ed by Scott Elledge (NY: Norton, 1965 [Norton Critical Edition]), pp. vii–ix.

[Inconsequential except for the dubious assertion that the Wessex Edition is "definitive" and for the puzzling rationale for determining the supposed "authoritative text" of the H novel reprinted in this volume.]

2847 Elledge, Scott (ed). THOMAS HARDY: TESS OF THE D'URBERVILLES: AN AUTHORITATIVE TEXT, HARDY AND THE NOVEL, CRITICISM (NY: Norton, 1965 [Norton Critical Editions]).

Contents, abstracted separately under date of first publication: Scott Elledge, "Preface" (1965); "[Hardy's Autobiography]," from Florence Emily Hardy, THE EARLY LIFE OF THOMAS HARDY, 1840–1891 (1928) and THE LATER YEARS OF THOMAS HARDY, 1892–1928 (1930); "[*Tess* as a Serial]," from Richard Purdy, THOMAS HARDY: A BIBLIOGRAPHICAL STUDY (1954); "[Hardy's Concessions]," from Ian Gregor and Brian Nicholas, THE MORAL AND THE STORY (1962); "[*Tess* in Three Volumes]," from William R. Rutland, THOMAS HARDY: A STUDY OF HIS WRITINGS AND THEIR BACKGROUND (1938); "[Hardy's Revisions]," from Wallace Hildick, WORD FOR WORD: A STUDY OF AUTHORS' ALTERATIONS (1965); "[Later Editions]," from Richard Purdy, THOMAS HARDY: A BIBLIOGRAPHICAL STUDY (1954); "Novels of the Week," ATHENAEUM, No. 3350 (9 Jan 1892); "Mr. Hardy's New Novel," TIMES (Lond), 13 Jan 1892; "Novels," SATURDAY REVIEW (Lond), LXXIII (16 Jan 1892), Andrew Lang, "Literature and the Drama," NEW REVIEW, VI (Feb 1892);

W[illiam] Watson, "Literature," ACADEMY, XLI (6 Feb 1892); "Culture and Anarchy," QUARTERLY REVIEW, CLXXIV (April 1892); Andrew Lang, "At the Sign of the Ship," LONGMAN's MAGAZINE, XXI (Nov 1892); "[RLS and James on *Tess*]," from Dan H. Laurence, "Henry James and Stephenson Discuss 'Vile' *Tess*," COLBY LIBRARY QUARTERLY, Series III (May 1953); "[The Argument]," from Lionel Johnson, THE ART OF THOMAS HARDY (1894); "[Hardy's Moment of Vision]," from Virginia Woolf, "Thomas Hardy's Novels," TIMES LITERARY SUPPLEMENT (Lond), 19 Jan 1928; "[The Male and Female Principles in *Tess of the d'Urbervilles*]," from D. H. Lawrence, chap 9 ("A Nos Moutons") of "A Study of Thomas Hardy," in PHOENIX: THE POSTHUMOUS PAPERS OF D. H. LAWRENCE, ed by Edward D. McDonald (1936); Donald Davidson, "The Traditional Basis of Thomas Hardy's Fiction," SOUTHERN REVIEW, VI (Summer 1940); "[The Elizabethan Tradition and Hardy's Talent]," from Lord David Cecil, HARDY THE NOVELIST (1943); "[Hardy and the Modern Reader: A Revaluation]," from Albert J. Guérard, THOMAS HARDY: THE NOVELS AND STORIES (1949); "[*Tess* as a Moral Fable: A Marxian Interpretation]," from Arnold Kettle, "Thomas Hardy: *Tess of the d'Urbervilles* (1891)," AN INTRODUCTION TO THE ENGLISH NOVEL, II (1951); "[Unifying Metaphors in *Tess of the d'Urbervilles*]," from John Holloway, "Hardy's Major Fiction," in FROM JANE AUSTEN TO JOSEPH CONRAD, ed by Robert C. Rathburn and Martin Steinman, Jr. (1958); "[The Self-Destructive Element in Tess's Character]," from Evelyn Hardy, THOMAS HARDY, A CRITICAL BIOGRAPHY (1954); Ian Gregor, "The Novel as Moral Protest: *Tess of the d'Urbervilles*," in THE MORAL AND THE STORY, by Ian Gregor and Brian Nicholas (1962); "Selected Bibliography," items listed here being abstracted under date of first publication. By H and not abstracted: *Tess of the d'Urbervilles*, "Explanatory Note to the First Edition," "Preface to the Fifth and Later Editions," and ten poems.

2848 Fernando, Lloyd. "Thomas Hardy's Rhetoric of Painting," REVIEW OF ENGLISH LITERATURE, VI (Oct 1965), 62–73.
H's interest in European painting greatly affected *The Return of the Native*. It caused him to produce a rhetoric "unique in the art of the novel." His rhetoric creates "not an evocation of Eustacia, but a painting of her." "Hardy is a spectator before a static object and he writes as an art critic might." An example is his description of Eustacia's mouth—the subject is carefully posed "as a painter's model" might be. The negative aspects of H's pictorial art: "It reduces astonishingly the flexibility of Hardy's language, and has the effect of making his heroine largely immobile." Eustacia does not move; her scene is rearranged. Finally, "his pictures are less pictures of reality than pictures of pictures." In place "of imagination, we have, . . . a disturbing amount of unusable

fantasy; in place of incident we have tableaux; in place of insight into character . . . fine writing."

2849 Fisher, C. M. LIFE IN THOMAS HARDY'S DORCHESTER 1888–1908, with an appendix, "Some Recollections of Thomas Hardy," by F. B. Fisher (1930) [qv] (Beaminster, Dorset: Toucan P, 1965).
[Memories of the physical appearance, transport, and social life of Dorchester and environs. Also see J. Stevens Cox (pub and general editor), Monographs on the Life of Thomas Hardy (1962).]

2850 Fleissner, Robert F. "The Name Jude," VICTORIAN NEWSLETTER, No. 27 (Spring 1965), 24–26.
[A refutation of Norman Holland's "*Jude the Obscure*: Hardy's Symbolic Indictment of Christianity," NINETEENTH CENTURY FICTION, IX (1954), 50–60, and John Paterson's "*The Return of the Native* as Antichristian Document," NINETEENTH CENTURY FICTION, XIV (1959), 111–27, on the basis that Jude's namesake is Saint Jude, thus placing the work "within the framework of Victorian moral ethic" as a "pro-Christian document."]

2851 Friedman, Barton R. " 'When There is Nothing': Hardy's 'Souls of the Slain,' " RENASCENCE, XVII (Spring 1965), 121–27.
H's poetry is still not appreciated or understood. "The Souls of the Slain" is a poem of great depth showing "a total picture of life as Hardy understands it." The language and all the elements of prosody project its theme and amplify H's use of the persona and dream vision. It is a "beautifully cohesive work of art" exhibiting H's "full-look-at-the-worst" theme and invites comparisons with "His Immortality" and "The Contretemps." [Friedman rejects H's own analysis that the poem is a fantasy, believing that Mrs. H wrote the "biography." Perceptive explication, but in isolated fragments.]

2852 Gilbert, Elliott L. "To Whom Does Kipling Speak Today?" KIPLING JOURNAL, XXXII (Dec 1965), 57–58, 64.
In the face of an absurd universe, H's characters are controlled by mechanistic determinism; Kipling's characters have a choice. H believed in no escape from the absurd universe; Kipling believed in "escape from the need to spend life *reacting* to that absurdity."

2853 Gordan, John D. "An Anniversary Exhibition . . .: Thomas Hardy," BULLETIN OF THE NEW YORK PUBLIC LIBRARY, XIX (Nov 1965), 601.
[Brief sketch of H's career followed by a description of a 160-page fragment of MS of *A Pair of Blue Eyes*. Notes other materials in Berg Collection in which H's "three careers" are well-represented.]

2854 Gordan, John D. "Novels in Manuscript . . . : *A Pair of Blue Eyes*," BULLETIN OF THE NEW YORK PUBLIC LIBRARY, LXIX (May 1965), 327–28.

[Brief sketch of H's career prefatory to a description of "heavily worked over" 160 MS pages of *A Pair of Blue Eyes* as written for serialization in TINSLEY'S MAGAZINE.]

2855 Harvey, W. J. CHARACTER AND THE NOVEL (Ithaca, NY: Cornell UP, 1965), pp. 56, 136, 139.

H's rustics are a good example of background characters used as a chorus to the main action. H and Defoe made an effort to give the main character as little freedom of play as possible. H's novels of circumstance are "simple and crude by comparison" to BLEAK HOUSE.

2856 Higgins, Elizabeth J. "Class Consciousness and Class Conflict in the Novels and Tales of Thomas Hardy, O. M.," DISSERTATION ABSTRACTS, XXV (March-April 1965), 5279. Unpublished dissertation, University of California (Los Angeles), 1964.

2857 Hildick, Wallace. "Thomas Hardy," WORD FOR WORD: A STUDY OF AUTHORS' ALTERATIONS WITH EXERCISES (Lond: Faber & Faber, 1965), pp. 109–25.

H poses great problems because he ranges from great poetry to contrived melodrama on the same page. Two facts must be considered in H's alterations: (1) H did not at first take novel-writing seriously, and (2) he had "highly idiosyncratic views about style." Many of H's novels were conceived as serials. The first edition of *The Return of the Native* counteracted the haste, the pressure, and the censorship of serialization. Later, H developed the technique of minimizing the damage. Examples of H's working technique are taken from *Tess of the d'Urbervilles* MS in the British Museum (Add. MS 38, 182).

2858 Howe, Irving. "Hardy as a 'Modern' Novelist," NEW REPUBLIC, CLII (26 June 1965), 19–22; rptd as "Introduction," to *Jude the Obscure* (1965).

H's novel is "modern" because it exists in the inner torments of the hero's psyche and not in a formal tragic realization through historical action. The usual public behavior of characters in novels, as Henchard in *The Mayor of Casterbridge*, is replaced by a speculative treatment of human character showing "the unspoken miseries of daily life with its prolonged isolation or prolonged closeness." Sue Bridehead is also a triumph of psychological portraiture. The structure of *Jude the Obscure* is influenced by depressiveness, and it is a "dramatic fable" much more than a realistic novel; "unity and verisimilitude are subordinated to . . . distended expressiveness." Static tableaux, set-pieces, depth psychology, and linked episodes replace plot.

2859 Howe, Irving (ed). "Introduction," *Jude the Obscure* (Boston: Houghton Mifflin [Riverside Editions], 1965), pp. v–xxiii.

Jude the Obscure is H's most distinctly "modern" work, for its premises are central to modernist literature: "that in our time men wishing to be more than dumb clods must live in permanent doubt and intellectual crisis; that for such men, to whom traditional beliefs are no longer available, life has become inherently problematic; that in the course of their lives they must face even more than the usual allotment of loneliness and anguish; that in their cerebral over-development they run the danger of losing those primary appetites for life which keep the human race going; and that courage, if it is to be found at all, consists in a readiness to accept pain while refusing the comforts of certainty." This deracination of *Jude* is the product of H's gradual realization throughout the novels that the "natural" world, the world of the farmlands, animals, rocks, hills, and woodlands of Wessex, was being permanently eroded by the forces of commerce and industrialism. H's best writing "displays a unique convergence of traditional and modern, the two impulses in a fruitful entanglement, neither in harmony nor struggle but in a kind of sustaining friction one with the other." H shares the uncertainty of the modern world while recognizing the weight and authority of the past. The "modern" element in *Jude* is observable in its characterization and narrative structure. Unlike the characters of Fielding, Jane Austen, Thackeray, or H in his earlier novels— characters whose "inner life . . . is to be inferred from their public behavior, or from the author's analytic synopses"—the character of Jude or of Sue is to be seen "not as a coherent force realizing itself in self-consistent public action, but as an amorphous and ill-charted arena in which irrational impulses conflict with one another." Thus the true action of the novel lies behind the sequence of events occupying the foreground of the novel. The true action of *Jude* is a series of situations, moments, instants of intense revelation (usually involving a confrontation between Jude and Sue) rather than an orderly movement toward an appropriate conclusion.

2860 Hurley, Robert. " 'Crumby' Tess," NOTES AND QUERIES, CCX (Aug 1965), 303.

In the 1906 Harper's (NY) edition of *Tess of the d'Urbervilles* the word "crumby" applied to Tess by Alec (end of chap 5) in the original version was changed to "charming," for the sake of the American readers. The change, however, was not accurate since "crumby" in the English slang of H's day meant "plump, full-figured."

2861 Hyde, William J. "Theoretic and Practical Unconventionality in *Jude the Obscure*," NINETEENTH CENTURY FICTION, XX (Sept 1965), 155–64.

An important concept in *Jude the Obscure* is John Stuart Mill's idea of a fusion of " 'a Greek ideal of self-development, which the Platonic and Christian ideal of self-government blends with, but does not supersede.' " Both Sue and Arabella become inverse parallels in their failure to realize the ideal of Mill. Arabella, not Sue, acts instinctively upon advanced notions of liberty. "The person of strong but uncontrolled feelings reveals one of the major shortcomings to realizing Mill's liberty, for she, in Arabella's case, will invariably invade that domain where true liberty, not license, must restrain itself, trespassing otherwise on 'that which concerns others.' " "At the other extreme stands Sue, her more than sufficient intellect wed to insufficient feeling, marking a shortcoming equally grave to the realization of a full life of liberty."

2862 Jones, Lawrence O. "*Desperate Remedies* and the Victorian Sensation Novel," NINETEENTH CENTURY FICTION, XX (June 1965), 35–50.

Desperate Remedies is an early and unsuccessful resolution of the conflict of H's "idiosyncratic mode of regard" and the conventional mode demanded by his contemporary audience. H wrote a popular sensation novel, but, especially in the first half of the novel, he couldn't suppress Hardyan elements—"the early development of the love situation as an example of the working of sexual selection, the full early development of the major characters, the use of the rustic chorus, the fire scene, the occasional authorial comments." The characters first are shown as divided, not wholly good or bad. But by the end of the book, they are conventional stereotypes of good and evil. After the fire scene, H turns the book back to the sensation novel, with a conventional melodramatic ending. H omits key scenes so that the emphasis is not on a love tangle but on mystery. "Although the clash of tragic and conventional patterns does not lead to a radically divided structure, it does lead to a diminution of the vitality and significance of the fictional world. . . . The real weakness of the book is that [H], after a brief struggle, rejected a potentially vital personal pattern for an oversimplified, melodramatic pattern that did not suit his natural gifts."

2863 Ketcham, Carl H. " 'A Vixen-Voice': Hardy and Thackeray," COLBY LIBRARY QUARTERLY, VII (Sept 1965), 130.

The idea for H's poem "Outside the Window," No. VII of *Satires of Circumstance*, is from an incident described by Thackeray in PENDENNIS.

2864 Kramer, Dale. "Unity of Time in *The Return of the Native*," NOTES AND QUERIES, CCX (Aug 1965), 304–5.

H undoubtedly tried to use the dramatic unities in *The Return of the Native*. Why did he choose a year (or a year and a day, as some critics have suggested [cf. Richard Purdy]) to approximate a day in drama? In Book IV, chap 1, para 1, H establishes this relation by describing seasons on the heath as if they were portions of a single day. The unity of time in the novel is not based upon man's hypersensitive calendar but upon the eternal clock of the seasons. The supposedly unsophisticated novelist utilizes an artificial convention (temporal unity) to clarify and amplify his delineation of man's lonely transience.

2865 Larkin, Philip. "Wanted: Good Hardy Critic," CRITICAL QUARTERLY, VII (Summer 1965), 174–79.

Major twentieth-century critics have neglected H, though his reputation is still relatively high. An extended consideration of the centrality of suffering in H's work should be the first concern of the critic. Morrell rejects the notion, and his work suffers because of it. Weber's work adds some valuable new material but is clumsily written. [Review-article on Roy Morrell's THOMAS HARDY: THE WILL AND THE WAY (1965) and Carl J. Weber's revised HARDY OF WESSEX (1965; see 1940).]

2866 Lawyer, William Robert. "Aesthetics, Criticism, and the Fiction of Thomas Hardy," DISSERTATION ABSTRACTS, XXV 1965), 7245–46. Unpublished dissertation, University of Washington, 1965.

2867 McCullen, J. T., Jr. "Henchard's Sale of Susan in *The Mayor of Casterbridge*," ENGLISH LANGUAGE NOTES, II (March 1965), 217–18.

A parallel to the sale of Susan by Henchard in *The Mayor of Casterbridge* has been recorded by Catherine Milnes Gaskell, bringing to thirteen the total number of recorded wife-sales in nineteenth-century England. In this analogue, the wife desires to be sold, saying "I wants a change."

2868 Malich, Peter de. THOMAS HARDY FROM BEHIND (Dorchester: Melissa P, 1965).

[Not seen, but "copies may be obtained from P. J. Platts, South Walks Rd, Dorchester." Supposedly a satiric attack upon the Toucan Press pamphlets: a mock representation of a rat-catcher's memories of H.]

2869 Mayers, D. E. "Dialectical Structures in Hardy's Poems," VICTORIAN NEWSLETTER, No. 27 (Spring 1965), 15–18.

Samuel Hynes's position in THE PATTERN OF HARDY'S POETRY (1956) that H's formulized pattern is antinomical is incorrect. Actually, the ironist implies a synthesis from his opposition of the thesis to the antithesis. In H's case the synthesizing factor is the Immanent Will. In "The Convergence of the Twain," "the operation of Hardy's transcendent and universal principle of accident is introduced into an appropriate circumstance"; in "The Torn Letter" it becomes "an obtrusive element." "Thus, it is the degree to which H's formula is integrated into the total structure of a poem that largely determines success or failure."

2870 Minakawa, Saburo. APRECIATION OF THOMAS HARDY'S WORKS IN JAPAN (Beaminster, Dorset: Toucan P, 1965).
"Brief Account of Hardyan Studies in Japan": The Japan Hardy Society was founded in 1932; Bunnosuke Yamamoto's BIBLIOGRAPHY OF THOMAS HARDY IN JAPAN was published in 1932 [see 1957] and refers to some commentary on *Far From the Madding Crowd* in an 1890 issue of the magazine KOKUMIN NO TOMO; Shun Katayama's THOMAS HARDY (1934, not seen), critical studies of H's works, marked a further advance in Japanese studies; Mamoru Osawa's APPRECIATION OF HARDYAN LITERATURE (1949, not seen) is a still more advanced standard of "academic research," and Osawa's translations of H's works, especially *Tess of the d'Urbervilles* and *The Return of the Native* further advanced H's reputation in Japan; still more significant are Bunnosuke Yamamoto's two-volume THOMAS HARDY: HIS WORKS AND THOUGHT (1963, 1964; not seen); a large-scale "Hardy Glossary," by ten members of the Japan Hardy Society is in progress. "Character and Circumstances": Japanese readers have a high regard for H's works because of their experience throughout history with "climatic [natural] disasters." H's structural art and the unfolding of his stories "with mathematical formulas" are admirable. H "is not a fatalist, but a man who gives a careful and measured utterance about the grim facts of life." "Traditions, Beliefs, and Differences in Social Standing": Japanese readers sympathize with H's characters who suffer because of oppressive traditions. "Cosmic Ideas": H's insistence on the law of cause and effect "in the fatal chain of occurrences" is a familiar tradition in Japanese literature. Both Japanese strict interpreters of the Bible and those with "a naturalistic view" admire H, mainly for the poetic imagery with which he depicts life. "Humour and Pathos": There is much in H's rustic humor and pathos and in the natural scenes of such novels as *The Woodlanders*, *Native*, and *Madding Crowd* that is familiar to the Japanese reader and admired by him. [Also see J. Stevens Cox (pub and general editor) Monographs on the Life of Thomas Hardy (1962).]

2871 Minakawa, S. MONOGRAPHS ON THE LIFE OF THOMAS HARDY (Tokyo: Kobunsha, 1965).
[Not seen, but reported to be partly in Japanese and with reprints of some of the Toucan Press monographs.] [In Japanese.]

2872 Minerof, Arthur Frederick. "Thomas Hardy's Novels: A Study in Critical Response and Author Response, 1871–1900," DISSERTATION ABSTRACTS, XXVI (Sept–Oct 1965), 1651–52. Unpublished dissertation, New York University, 1963.

2873 Morrell, Roy. THOMAS HARDY: THE WILL AND THE WAY (Singapore: University of Malaya P, 1965); incorporates, in revised form, articles published in 1962 and 1963 [qv].

"The main lines of Hardy criticism . . . [are] misleading." H is not a fatalist or defeatist, despite the occasional philosophical intrusions in his novels, but as he said, a pessimist who believed "a man can be successful in the long run only if he is prepared for the worst contingencies, and happy only if his demands on life are modest." H's works are not gay but neither are they "steeped in . . . fatalistic gloom." They are "a true exploration, a series of 'questionings.' " Above all, H's novels are concerned with personal, human dilemmas, not social problems. The disasters in his novels result not from a "simple fatalistic pattern—an irrevocable mistake followed by disaster" but from "a simple unawareness of the conditions of life." In *Far From the Madding Crowd* H shows the danger of trusting nature (inclinations, emotions). Instead, man must resist what is natural and human—as Oak resists danger, fear of the storm, and warns Bathsheba about Troy. Those who suffer most—Troy, Fanny Robin, Boldwood, and Bathsheba—are ruled by passion, whim. *The Dynasts*, so often cited as the key to H's philosophy of human powerlessness in the hands of the Immanent Will, shows instead that "man is a puppet by his own choice." "Man's one hope . . . was to . . . rely on himself." In *Dynasts*, H "does not present us with a world in which human endeavour counts for nothing. The value of discipline, co-operation, and carefully timed effort is recognized clearly."

2874 Moscinski, Joseph. "The Victorian Woman," VICTORIAN NEWSLETTER, No. 28 (Fall 1965), 26–27.

Jane is the antithesis of Becky, and Dorothea the synthesis. Eustacia is the antithesis of Dorothea. Dorothea accepts reality and accommodates; Eustacia is unable "to accept the exigencies of life." [An application of Jerome H. Buckley's attestation of "the dynamic growth of Victorian prose" " 'as a ceaseless dialectic worked out its design,' " to four Victorian heroines—Becky Sharpe, Jane Eyre, Dorothea Brooke, and Eustacia Vye.]

2875 Neumeyer, Peter F. "The Transfiguring Vision," VICTORIAN POETRY, III (Autumn 1965), 263–66.

The word "transfigure" in H's poem "Former Beauties" makes use of the connotation "to idealize, spiritualize." The women are unable to "remember" and are not spiritualized; H, on the other hand, does, and his "transfiguration is shown by the timeless vision of which [he] writes in this poem." This "transfiguring power of the poetic vision" is the real subject of the poem.

2876 O'Grady, Walter. "On Plot in Modern Fiction: Hardy, James, and Conrad," MODERN FICTION STUDIES, XI (Summer 1965), 107–15.

Plot is the "rate" and "flow" of the external situation of "incident" and the internal situation of "event." James balances event and incident in THE AMBASSADORS and Strether; H emphasizes incident in *Tess of the d'Urbervilles*, but not to the extent of Conrad's Verloc in THE SECRET AGENT. A James novel flows "forward and inward," in contrast to an H or Conrad plot which flows "outward and backward."

2877 O'Rourke, May. THOMAS HARDY: HIS SECRETARY REMEMBERS. With an appendix, "Louisa Harding," by J. Stevens Cox, and an introduction by Richard Curle (Beaminster, Dorset: Toucan P, 1965).

[H's secretary recalls Louisa Harding, with whom H had been in love at a distance as a youth (Cox in Appendix 2 confirms this information) and whom he mentions in several poems; the former residence of the Moules, which was her home for a time, had fond associations for H. On first meeting H in 1918, she found him charming, debonair, and possessed of "a sense of fun." Working for H began in March 1923. Florence H spoke warmly of H's first wife, who had been kind to her. H is shown disturbed by any invasion of his privacy, preferring an orderly, closely regulated patterned life and interested in "the young, new writers." In 1924, Mrs. H had an operation on her throat and was subject to intermittent tension and depression thereafter. H may have been "pensive" but never "morose" or "cynical." H opined that young poets should write "original stuff," not about old poets. He loved children and felt deeply the lack of any of his own. H would not let his secretary type a poem of his which contained a line that might offend a Catholic. Many scattered anecdotes; much on Miss O'Rourke; rather rambling. Also see J. Stevens Cox (pub and general editor), Monographs on the Life of Thomas Hardy (1962).]

2878 Orwen, William R. "Hardy and Burke," AMERICAN NOTES AND QUERIES, III (April 1965), 116–17.

H obviously borrowed passages in Book III, chap 3 of *The Return of the Native* from Edmund Burke's A PHILOSOPHICAL INQUIRY INTO . . . THE SUBLIME AND BEAUTIFUL.

2879 Parker, W. M. THOMAS HARDY ON MAUMBURY RINGS (Beaminster, Dorset: Toucan P, 1965).

H is quite interested in Roman antiquity, especially in Maumbury Rings, which appear in several works. [A transcript, with comments, of H's article for TIMES (Lond), 9 Oct 1908, in which he describes the archaelogical excavations and the history of the amphitheater. Also see J. Stevens Cox (pub and general editor), Monographs on the Life of Thomas Hardy (1962).]

2880 Rice, Phyliss Ann Petty. "Hardy's Irony with Particular Reference to the Short Stories," DISSERTATION ABSTRACTS, XXVI (1965), 2759. Unpublished dissertation, University of Illinois, 1965.

2881 Roberts, Marguerite. HARDY'S POETIC DRAMA AND THE THEATRE (NY: Pageant P, 1965).

As a child H was deeply attracted by music, dance, play-acting and printed drama. H once thought of becoming a playwright. Later, through his friends, he came to have many connections with the theater. "While *The Dynasts* is obviously not a well-made play, it is a drama." H unified his vast design by "writing the drama on three levels: the peasants and people of everyday life, the great historical figures, and the celestial chorus." The drama's greatest flaw "is the lack of human responsibility and human conflict." The work is cinematic in many of its effects. [Long discussion of Granville Barker's adaptation of *Dynasts* for the stage, and its performance in London and Oxford.] In *The Famous Tragedy of the Queen of Cornwall*, H showed he "might have conquered the technique of the commercial stage and have become an expert professional dramatist." [Considerable discussion of the preparation, performance, and reception of *Queen*.]

2882 Sankey, Benjamin. "Hardy's Plotting," TWENTIETH CENTURY LITERATURE, XI (July 1965), 82–97; rptd in THE MAJOR NOVELS OF THOMAS HARDY (1965).

In H's work, the development of "potential opposition among elements in a personality" remains "in doubt until the reader sees exactly what the character is confronted with." Every incident contributes to "the revelation of character." Minor characters exist primarily for "the main argument" and are not "plainly in view" at all times. H's chief method is "narrative logic," with natural description used for reinforcement or emphasis. He does not labor to conceal his manipulation of plot, which is "in part a consequence of the demands made by the serial form." However, H's "plot machinery is not a straightforward expression of his conception of the universe, but rather an intentional exaggeration, even a caricature of it." He "recognizes the existence of a break—a discrepancy between the way things ordinarily operate and the way they may be made to operate to produce special effects."

2883 Sankey, Benjamin. "Henchard and Faust," ENGLISH LANGUAGE NOTES, III (Dec 1965), 123–25.

H's description of Henchard, comparing him to Faust, is borrowed from Carlyle, whose interpretations of Goethe's FAUST "are remarkably similar to those which Hardy later used in his characterization of Henchard." H sees in Henchard the same "innocent selfishness" that Carlyle sees in Faust. On the other hand, Henchard, unlike Faust, has no "intellectual pride" and is given "no provision for . . . ultimate salvation."

2884 Sankey, Benjamin. THE MAJOR NOVELS OF THOMAS HARDY (Denver: Alan Swallow, 1965).

Contents, abstracted separately under first date of publication: "Preface" (1965); "Hardy's Prose Style," SPECTRUM, VII (Spring 1964), 52–75; "Topics and Assumptions" (1965); "Hardy's Plotting," TWENTIETH CENTURY LITERATURE, XI (July 1965), 82–97. [The articles are revised in the book versions.]

2885 Sankey, Benjamin. "Preface," THE MAJOR NOVELS OF THOMAS HARDY (Denver: Alan Swallow, 1965), pp. 7–10.

The study is an attempt to describe H's achievement as a novelist. The four critical problems which will be examined are H's conception of the universe, his arbitrariness of plotting, his problems of style, and the problem of "point of view" in his work. H's "world view" was "generally well reasoned and consistent with the best reasoning of his day on the subjects which interested him." H's critics foolishly attempt to make H fashionable by calling him absurd, try to improve him by "attaching certain anti-naturalistic terms and slogans" to his work, and try to give his novels more dignity by systematically relating them to a traditional form.

2886 Sankey, Benjamin. "Topics and Assumptions," THE MAJOR NOVELS OF THOMAS HARDY (Denver: Alan Swallow, 1965), pp. 24–43.

In *Far From the Madding Crowd* H naturalizes his material, "subordinating the public and moral aspects of his characters to a conception of Nature and human psychology in which external forces and human passions exercise an abrupt and sometimes dangerous energy." The novel sets up "a tension between the moral terms implicit in his judgement of consequences and the theme of human weakness before the powers of nature." Each of his four major characters "is confronted by the unexpected— the sudden effort of a natural emotion, or the sudden recognition of responsibility for an event; of the four, only Gabriel has the mentality necessary to react wisely." The logic of H's plot presupposes a definite morality, for "virtues like those possessed by Oak actually do win out in the long run." H believes that a man is a part "but not a particularly well accommodated part of the natural scheme." Henchard of *The Mayor of Casterbridge* "represents the human will acting on its own, uninfluenced by those qualities, innate or acquired, which normally disguise it and soften its impact." Henchard "sees Nature as an expression of an alien will, which . . . he must confront and defeat." H's guiding logic is "that a man like Henchard will himself set in motion those forces which finally destroy him." In *Mayor*, related to H's conception "of nature as something in itself regular but not predictable or manageable, is a conception of history, in which human society is involved in a perpetual but scarcely recognized system of change, destruction, and adaptation." In *Tess of the d'Urbervilles*, society punishes Tess "not for breaking a moral code but for attempting to live by a personal code of integrity and dignity after her 'fall' had disqualified her for a life on these terms." However, H's point is not that Tess is entirely innocent but rather that her weakness and errors have no logical relationship to her fate. Tess's values are distinguished from those which are endorsed by her parents, society, and nature. H "uses the plot to define situations in which Tess's earnest attempt to do the right thing . . . leads her into difficulties." Tess's world makes no special allowances for her decent set of values, so she is destroyed. "*Jude the Obscure*, like Tess, concerns a situation in which the inert habits and institutions of nineteenth-century England contribute to the destruction of a person whom the reader has been taught to value and like." Jude, Sue, and Phillotson try to be guided by what they consider to be indisputable personal fact, "but there is no way to bring such fact into harmony with the inherited prejudices of society." Sue, like Henchard and Eustacia, "is led by a hostility to the conditions of life so thoroughgoing as to be self-destructive and dangerous to others." The main forces operative within Jude's character are, as in the Clym-Eustacia story, "forced into conflict by the woman he chooses." "Hardy's principles are in keeping with two nineteenth-century movements: the acceptance of a non-anthropomorphic, non-purposive view of Nature; and the humanitarianism (no doubt an outgrowth of Christian ethics) for which human cruelty and nature's cruelty are alike disturbing." Perhaps the most important difference between H's attitude towards human suffering and that of earlier British novelists is that H does not see suffering principally as a consequence of moral evil.

2887 Scott, James F. "Spectacle and Symbol in Thomas Hardy's Fiction," PHILOLOGICAL QUARTERLY, XLIV (Oct 1965), 527–44.
H's symbolism derives from his use of Gothic spectacle, promoted probably by having read Burke on the Sublime. But H seems to have conceived of symbols as an irregular succession of gloomy tableaux and Turneresque murals which he uses to slow down action or, at best, resolve plot problems. In *Far From the Madding Crowd*, a "gothic thunder-

storm" attempts this; in *Jude the Obscure*, double murder-suicide does, but both fail since they lead the reader away from the plot. Some symbolic scenes that work are the meeting of Henchard and his estranged wife at the Roman ring (spectacle reflects character), Jude's first visit to Christminster and Tess's final scene at Stonehenge (encounters between individuals and society), and Egdon Heath as counterpoint to authorial moralizing.

2888 Slack, Robert C. "A Comment on Recent Victorian Scholarship," PENNSYLVANIA COUNCIL OF TEACHERS OF ENGLISH BULLETIN, No. 12 (Dec 1965), 19–30.

Between 1960 and 1964, H received more critical attention than any Victorian writer except Dickens. [The 165 items devoted to H are classified, and the more significant ones are discussed.]

2889 Stanzel, Franz K. "Thomas Hardy: *Tess of the d'Urbervilles*," DER MODERNE ENGLISCHE ROMAN: INTERPRETATIONEN (The Modern English Novel: Interpretations), ed by Horst Oppel (Berlin: Erich Schmidt, 1965), pp. 34–48.

Although chronologically *Tess of the d'Urbervilles* stands at the threshold of a new epoch in the English novel, the novel itself reveals that H's novelistic development ran counter to that of the era—so much so that in many ways *The Return of the Native* is more modern than *Tess*. While the tendency of the modern novel is toward autonomy, both in the world represented in the novel and in the way of depicting that world (i.e. no editorializing by author or his narrator), H in his last two novels chose to write using the older method "in which the narrator is permitted a wide-reaching power of disposition over the fictional world." Because of the worldliness of the narrator, the characters lose a large part of their maturity. H was perhaps too closely involved with his novel's theme than is desirable for a novelist. The subtitle, a result of H's "*saeva indignatio*" directed against the conventional standards which damn women like Tess, is unfortunate; "it chains Tess—even before her entrance into the novel— to a moral phantom, whose omnipresence utterly prevents autonomy both as novel-character and as ethical being." H repeatedly erases the dividing line between the narrator and his characters—which James and other modern authors drew with such painful sharpness. At many points H edited the thoughts of his characters, using his own commentary, without adequately designating it as authorial admixture. [In German.]

2890 Swets, Marinus M. "Understanding Hardy's *The Return of the Native* Through His Poetry," EXERCISE EXCHANGE, XII (April 1965), 4–6.

The study of H can be difficult for the beginner, but his ideas become less mysterious when they are sought in his short poems. Some which express outstanding ideas in *The Return of the Native* are "The Convergence of the Twain," "Waiting Both," "Hap," "In Time of 'the Breaking of Nations,' " "The Man he Killed," "The Darkling Thrush," "At the Draper's," "Ah! are you Digging on my Grave?" "In Church," "At Day-Close in November," and "Winter in Durnover Field."

2891 Tuttleton, June M. "Thomas Hardy and the Christian Religion," Dissertation Abstracts, XXVI (Sept–Oct 1965), 1637. Unpublished dissertation, University of North Carolina (Chapel Hill), 1964.

2892 Wain, John. "Introduction," *The Dynasts*, ed by John Wain (NY: St. Martin's P, 1965), pp. v–xix.

H was "a tragic fatalist, holding it useless to struggle against . . . blind, indifferent destiny . . . he was nevertheless not entirely unwilling to allow the human individual some play." H's artistic problem in planning *The Dynasts* was form. He could not write a novel on the Napoleonic Wars—Tolstoy's War and Peace closed that avenue—the long narrative poem was a dying form, "non-realistic drama . . . he felt inhibited from attempting." Eventually H chose to write "his huge work in accordance with . . . the art of the cinema." "*The Dynasts* is neither a poem, nor a play, nor a story. It is a shooting-script." The work has serious faults: many characters fail to come to life, much of the writing is of poor quality, the fantastic variety of lyric verse forms gives "the impression that the whole enterprise is turning into a hobby, like . . . collecting sea-shells."

2893 Weber, Carl J. "Hardy's Debut—How a Literary 'Career was Determined' One Hundred Years Ago," Papers of the Bibliographical Society of America, LIX (Sept 1965), 319–22.

Although in later years H tended to deprecate "How I Built Myself a House," his first published work, he did confess in an 1878 letter to Literary World (Boston) that the ready acceptance of his " 'first attempt in fiction' " determined his literary career.

2894 Zietlow, Paul Nathan. "The Shorter Poems of Thomas Hardy and Edwin Arlington Robinson: A Study in Contrasts," Dissertation Abstracts, XXVI (1965), 2765. Unpublished dissertation, University of Michigan, 1965.

1966

2895 Alexis, Gerhard T. "Hardy's 'Channel Firing,' 33–36," Explicator, XXIV (March 1966), Item 61.

The last stanza of "Channel Firing" contains three geographical references, two of which—Camelot and Stonehenge—have been clearly explicated. The third, Stourton Tower, has never been related to the poem's meaning, because of lack of identification. Stourton Tower was an eighteenth-century Wessex monument to Alfred the Great, commemorating his arming to fight the Danes in 879. Together then these references refer to three distinct time periods in British history: Stonehenge—prehistory, Stourton Tower—history, and Camelot—legend. These references widen the historical scope of the poem, as well as give it a concrete location, since all three sites are in Wessex, close enough to the coast that naval guns might be heard there.

2896 Armens, Sven. ARCHETYPES OF THE FAMILY IN LITERATURE (Seattle & Lond: University of Washington P, 1966), pp. 194–98, 213.

Just as H sees "the objective reality of darkness *and* the subjective reality of hope in his poem 'Darkling Thrush,' so we see demonstrated in the family both a mode of analytical logic and a form of understanding best described as intuitive (Father concludes this must be done: Mother feels it right to do so)." In the poem, H's thrush "does not *know* what he voices in his song, nor does Hardy, yet we all know that the mere existence of song is itself evidence of natural vitality, of a desire to voice emotion. In this sense, the analogical platitude which associates bird and poet is true." Here the poet has been forced "to turn to certain subtleties of verbalization to achieve his insight."

2897 Bailey, J. O. "Autobiography in Hardy's Poems," ENGLISH LITERATURE IN TRANSITION, IX: 4 (1966), 183.
[Raises numerous questions concerning the factual bases of "Thoughts of Phena," "She at his Funeral," "My Cicely," and "Midnight on the Great Western."]

2898 Bailey, J. O. "Hardy's Poems of Pilgrimage," ENGLISH LITERATURE IN TRANSITION, IX:4 (1966), 190–96.
[The poems from H's visit to Italy in 1887 are discussed chronologically in relation to Baedeker's HANDBOOK FOR TRAVELERS and chap 15 of Florence H's THE EARLY LIFE OF THOMAS HARDY (1928) noting corroborations, inconsistencies, and omissions among the three sources.]

2899 Bailey, J. O. "Introduction," POEMS AND RELIGIOUS EFFUSIONS, by Emma Lavinia Hardy (Mount Durand, St. Peter Port, Guernsey: Toucan P, 1966), pp. [i]–[iii]. [Mrs. H's titles rptd from ALLEYS (Dorchester: Cornhill P, 1911) and SPACES (Dorchester: Cornhill P, 1912).]
The chief interest of Mrs. H's poems is the light they throw on "upwards of a hundred" of H's poems. She seems to have intended to rival him, exhibits

both her own limitations and her joyful spirit. [Also see J. Stevens Cox (pub and general editor), Monographs on the Life of Thomas Hardy (1962).]

2900 Beatty, C. J. P. "Introduction to the Notebook," *The Architectural Notebook of Thomas Hardy*, ed by C. J. P. Beatty (Phila: George S. Macmanus, 1966).

[The notebook, which is here reproduced, is one H kept between 1862 and 1872, the decade in which he was most actively engaged in architecture. Beatty's introduction discusses H's work in architecture and its influence on his novels and poems. The notebook itself comprises a series of sketches and notes concerning projects H was involved in. The introduction contains much valuable biographical information and is most interesting.]

2901 Bohling, Beth. "Why 'Michael Henchard,' " English Journal, LV (Feb 1966), 203–7.

Often H used names for characters in his novels that metaphorically describe those characters. In *The Mayor of Casterbridge*, "Farfrae" signifies the Scotsman's distance from home and from Michael Henchard. "Michael" suggests a kind of royalty and greatness, since it suggests the Biblical archangel, Byzantine and Russian kings, and Wordsworth's poem of that name. It means "who is like God," which suggests that Henchard equates himself with God in assigning to himself penance for the sale of his wife. "Henchard" is more difficult. It may come from "hencher," someone who throws in an underhand motion, jerking the arm against the haunch. This derivation seems appropriate since Henchard, like a hencher, "throws" or acts without forethought, as the impulsive sale of his wife shows.

2902 Boll, T. E. M. "Tess as an Animal in Nature," English Literature in Transition, IX: 4 (1966), 210–11.

[Analyzes *Tess of the d'Urbervilles* by the dichotomy of natural versus social morality. Discusses the imagery of Tess as a "wary animal." There are different connotations of "animal" when Alec speaks of himself.]

2903 Brown, Thomas R. "The Magnificent View; A Study of Mind and Method in Hardy's Wessex Novels," Dissertation Abstracts, XXVII (Oct–Dec 1966), 1360A. Unpublished dissertation, University of Denver, 1966.

2904 Buckley, Jerome Hamilton. The Triumph of Time (Cambridge, Mass: Harvard UP, 1966), pp. 2, 6, 16, 63, 67, 82, 84–85, 100, 104, 108, 116, 158, 169.

H was ambiguous about the question of progress. In the decay of the life of his rural characters he saw a sign of degeneration, yet he hoped that the darkling thrush perceived "some blessed Hope" of which he was unaware. In *Jude the Obscure* H expressed both a sense of progress (in Jude's telling

Sue their ideas were fifty years in advance of society) and a sense of decadence (in the death of Father Time). When in his eighties, the poet, in his "Apology" to *Late Lyrics and Earlier*, renounced forever the ideal of progress, seeing before him only "a new Dark Age." Like many other Victorian novelists and poets, H often showed the people in his poetry finding solace for the present in a happy moment of the past.

2905 Campbell, Harry M. "Tate on Hardy: The Critic as Moralist," CEA CRITIC, XXIX (Nov 1966), 8–9.
Moralism clouds Alan Tate's understanding in ON THE LIMITS OF POETRY (1948) of H's "Nature's Questioning." Tate finds "too close a correlation between what he calls 'philosophical limitations' and poetic weakness."

2906 Carpenter, Richard. "Hardy's Dramatic Narrative Poems," ENGLISH LITERATURE IN TRANSITION, IX: 4 (1966), 185–86.
One-tenth of *The Collected Poems of Thomas Hardy* show the "pattern of plot," conflict or resolution, and length typical of the "dramatic narrative" poem. They "stick close to the method and spirit of the traditional ballad." There is the recurrent theme of sardonic irony toward love and marriage. Their success rests in H's explicitness and economy.

2907 Cavanaugh, William Charles. "The Dramatic Element in the Poetry and Drama of Thomas Hardy," DISSERTATION ABSTRACTS, XXVII (1966), 1027A. Unpublished dissertation, University of Wisconsin, 1966.

2908 Coustillas, Pierre. "Some Unpublished Letters from Gissing to Hardy," ENGLISH LITERATURE IN TRANSITION, IX:4 (1966), 197–209.
Six recently uncovered letters from Gissing to H, spanning a sporadic correspondence of thirteen years, show a respectful affection between them. There is a disparity between what Gissing wrote to H about H's fiction and what he said about it to others.

2909 Daniels, Diana P. "Boy with a Lantern," CHRISTIAN SCIENCE MONITOR, 16 April 1966, p. 8.
[Musings on an H keepsake, a lantern used by H as a boy.]

2910 Deacon, Lois. " 'The Chosen' by Thomas Hardy: Five Women in Blend—An Identification," LITERARY REPOSITORY, No. 1 (1966), 2–6; rptd as "THE CHOSEN" BY THOMAS HARDY: FIVE WOMEN IN BLEND—AN IDENTIFICATION (Mount Durand, St. Peter Port, Guernsey: Toucan P, 1966); absorbed in PROVIDENCE AND MR. HARDY, by Lois Deacon and Terry Coleman (1966).
H cleverly disguised the women in his novels to keep the tragic secret of his relationship with Tryphena Sparks from his family and his biographers. The

women in "The Chosen" appear in the reverse order of his love for them: Florence Emily Hardy; Elizabeth Browne; Mary Waight; Emma Lavinia Hardy; Tryphena Sparks. The sixth or composite woman is not Emma Lavinia Hardy. [Reprints "The Chosen," and contains a bibliography. Also see J. Stevens Cox (pub and general editor), Monographs on the Life of Thomas Hardy (1962).]

2911 Deacon, Lois, and Terry Coleman. PROVIDENCE AND MR. HARDY (Lond: Hutchinson, 1966).

H's cousin, Tryphena Sparks, was "probably the greatest single influence on Hardy as a man and a writer." She and H began a courtship in 1867; by the following year they were betrothed; and by late 1868 Tryphena had given birth to H's son, Randal, who lived secretly with his uncle, Nathaniel Sparks, in Bristol. The engagement lasted until sometime in 1873, when Tryphena returned H's ring. In 1874 H married Emma Gifford, and in 1877, Tryphena married Charles Gale. The particulars of the courtship, the engagement, and the child were initially suggested by the recollections of Tryphena's daughter and are corroborated by additional evidence, including characters, oblique references, and themes in H's novels and poems. In the novels, for example, the high incidence of seductions is partially attributable to the affair with Tryphena. Similarly, several pairs of characters seem to have been drawn from the relationship, particularly Stephen and Elfride, and Jude and Sue. References to Tryphena and the relationship in general persist throughout H's work and confirm the extent of her influence upon him. [Conclusions, particularly those drawn from the works, are largely conjectural and often forced. In addition, the reliability of Eleanor Tryphena Bromell's recollections may be open to question since she was more than eighty years old when she furnished the basic information. Absorbs material published earlier in several Toucan Press pamphlets, for which see J. Stevens Cox (pub and general editor), Monographs on the Life of Thomas Hardy (1962).]

2912 Dewar, H. S. L. "Introduction," *Some Romano-British Relics Found at Max Gate, Dorchester,* by Thomas Hardy (St. Peter Port, Guernsey: Toucan P, 1966).

H, a careful archaeological observer, asked important and still relevant questions. [H's title, read at the Dorchester Meeting in 1884, is rptd from PROCEEDINGS OF THE DORSET NATURAL HISTORY AND ANTIQUARIAN FIELD CLUB, XI (1890), 78–91. Also see J. Stevens Cox (pub and general editor), Monographs on the Life of Thomas Hardy (1962).]

2913 Duerksen, R. A. SHELLEYAN IDEAS IN VICTORIAN LITERATURE (The Hague: Mouton, 1966), pp. 56, 160–65, 200.

Like Shelley, H expressed in his poetry a set of non-Christian, radical ideas about man and society. The two poets had also novel ideas on sex and marriage and agreed in repudiating human institutions as baneful hindrances of natural human activity. Shelley's chief influence was on the form of H's *The Dynasts*, which recalls the earlier poet's PROMETHEUS UNBOUND. Both works share a similar view that man can and must work towards amelioration of his situation.

2914 Ensor, Thomas, & Son. PLAN OF HIGHER & LOWER BOCK-HAMPTON FARMS, STINSFORD, DORCHESTER (Dorchester: pvtly ptd, 1966).
[Auctioneer's detailed plan, six inches to the mile, based on an ordinance survey map.]

2915 Feibleman, James, Alice Leone Moats, Lyman Bryson, Alfred Kazin, David Hardman, George D. Crothers. "Thomas Hardy," INVITATION TO LEARNING: ENGLISH AND AMERICAN NOVELS, ed by George D. Crothers (NY & Lond: Basic Books, 1966), pp. 163–79; broadcast as conversations, between 1950 and 1964, by the CBS Radio Network on "Invitation to Learning."
In spite of the awkwardness of its texture, "the sometimes grotesque and Gothic quality of the plot," and the many characters that are "clay figures," *Tess of the d'Urbervilles* deals superbly with the chief problem: "a woman of great submissiveness and responsiveness who, through a series of accidents, gets into the hands of two men who destroy her and whom she must destroy." *The Mayor of Casterbridge* makes us see the classic "lineaments of human fate: that man is bound by his own character." Yet again and again, the book shows "man's strangeness to himself and to the world in which he lives." *Mayor* is reminiscent of the best of American fiction, in that its people are "strangers to the world." [*Tess* is discussed by James Feibleman, Alice Leone Moats, and Lyman Bryson; *Mayor* is discussed by Alfred Kazin, David Hardman, and George D. Crothers.]

2916 Fischler, Alexander. "Theatrical Techniques in Thomas Hardy's Short Stories," STUDIES IN SHORT FICTION, III (Summer 1966), 435–45.
H often used his settings as a type of stage and assumed the role of director in order to manipulate his characters and thus imply that their fates are part of a universal pattern. Further, he used elaborate stage settings in order to account structurally for his notorious coincidences and to express a view of the world that he could not embody fully in character and action.

2917 Fleissner, Robert F. "A Return to Hardy's Native," CEA CRITIC, XXVIII (June 1966), 7–8.
The Return of the Native is a "naturist" not a "naturalist" novel, since H makes use of country customs, folklore, etc. and emphasizes natural *law* rather than *natural* law. The novel's structure is musically contrapuntal in

that Eustacia and Wildeve receive the pagan justice their acts warrant, whereas Clym obtains Christian mercy.

2918 Fleming, Thomas J. "The Novel of the Future," AMERICA, CXIV (7 May 1966), 654–58.

The novelist of the future must, like H, deal not "with ideas, but with values, with a vision of life." Only in this way may the novelist's perception of life be expressed and the novel saved from competition from other forms, like biography. [H mentioned once, in passing.]

2919 Fraser, G. S. "Edmund Blunden," LONDON MAGAZINE, VI (April 1966), 79–83.

Blunden is the last surviving poet of the school of H, inasmuch as he writes native English poetry of direct and "unadjusted impressions."

2920 Friedman, Alan. "Thomas Hardy: 'Weddings Be Funerals,' "
THE TURN OF THE NOVEL (Lond: Oxford UP, 1966), pp. 38–74.

Against the traditional form, the closed experience of H's *Far From the Madding Crowd*, "we can measure Hardy's gradual and deliberate departure from the norm in those novels in which he did his greatest and most original work in fiction." *Madding Crowd* "centers on the life of Bathsheba Everdene, and her experience . . . is centered on marriage." The action is planned to allow the broadest possible scope for "the young lady's high-spirited, mannish tendencies; gradually to chasten, torment, and weaken her; and finally to make her manageable—in fact, to make her beg to be managed." Bathsheba's experience expands when she receives an unexpected legacy which causes her to assume complete management of a farm and precipitates her highly charged experience with Troy. When Bathsheba marries Troy, we are watching an "explosion (or expansion) in mid-career, and it will behoove us in our exploration of her experience as a form, to observe *when* Bathsheba's experience attains its greatest intensity, and to ascertain *whether*—and *in what sense*—the explosion of her experience is finally contained." After the death of Troy, "the rapid resolution of Bathsheba's intense distress . . . begins." The end of the novel and Bathsheba's marriage to Oak is "a kind of coda *da capa*, or rather a movement *al capo*, toward the beginning. It is a process which not only resolves tensions and . . . reduces them, but does all this by suggesting a movement *backwards* away from their fullest expansion in the climax." At the beginning of the novel Bathsheba had rescued Oak, and "he *succeeds* in rescuing her from farming disasters . . . and having repetitively *attempted* to rescue her from the disasters of love, he succeeds in doing *that*, both at once now, in the ending." The final pages of *Tess of the d'Urbervilles* also "constitute a patent and deliberate attempt at an *al capo* maneuver." To "appreciate the closing maneuver, or to deprecate it, it may be necessary to retrace the journey from innocence to experience." Tess's experience expands in a single direction: disintegration. "And in keeping with that paradox, the disintegration begins from somewhere near 'zero,' close to the bottom, and continues downhill from there"—her fall is from poverty to penury. In *Tess* there are movements toward solution and resolution, but these movements are "crippled by Hardy's deliberate reversal of the narrative order he has used in his early works; and by his juxtaposition of hints of decay in the midst of growth." H is "playing with a narrative pattern; toying with and within an already established form; building his irony by the frustration of the reader's expectations." For instance, "Tess's 'Rally' is converted into its opposite; the expanding disintegration of the first two 'phases' continues unchecked. . . ." The expansion of Tess's innocence into experience has been toward disintegration and death. Tess's elopement with Angel "is a ghastly parody of the classic ending of a novel, its traditional solution and consummation in marriage." Also, like her marriage to Angel, Tess's "death cannot and does not 'contain' or synthesize her disintegrated experience. Nor does it bring . . . relative relief, satisfaction, or ebbing after the floodtide of experience." When "Angel and Tess's sister walk hand and hand out of the book, that final event, that new and symbolic moral synthesis of Tess's experience is apparently . . . intended to suggest a containment of the experience: intended, that is, to reverse and control the expanding momentum of destruction and dissolution. . . . It is a compromise (with his audience, we can speculate), a formal constriction of events which, after the uncompromisingly explosive narrative form upon which Hardy has insisted until now, cannot persuade." The "unreversed disintegration of experience in *Tess* comes indeed close to the form of experience in *Jude the Obscure*." The "author's manipulation of the stream of conscience in *Jude the Obscure*—the enlarging and narrowing of 'views'—is a conscious attempt to give his fiction a double structure: to set the open form of experience directly and explicitly against the traditionally closed form, and thereby . . . convey his meaning through deliberate counterpoint." For example, at "the deaths of the children Hardy explicitly divides the novel's expanding stream of experience into two distinct branches: Sue's is diverted, redirected, and constricted: Jude's is allowed to continue and to widen." Sue's "explosively unconventional experience 'veers round' after the death of the children, 'goes back on itself,' and 'narrows'; . . . her experience undergoes a reversal and a contraction. . . ." Jude's experience "after the children's death undergoes no reversal (of his own moral experience) but on the contrary undergoes an inexorable 'enlarging.'" His history is a linear progress toward moral dissipation and disintegration. H is careful to deprive both the book's wedding (Sue's) and the book's funeral (Jude's) of their customary effectiveness for controlling the narrative expansion of experience. "He will provide no relief of emotional distress and no containing moral synthesis." All "three of the novels we have examined in this chapter come to rest in both weddings and funerals. But Hardy's use of these fictional conventions is conventional only in *Far From the Madding Crowd.* In *Tess* and still more vehemently in *Jude*, he undermines the conventionally closed form of the flux of conscience by so weakening its most traditional fictional techniques for securing a 'close'—marriage and death—that they cannot possibly resolve the dilemma, reduce the tensions, or contain the expanding moral and emotional force of the story."

2921 Fujita, Shigeru. "Symbolism in 'The Son's Veto,' " BULLETIN OF THE HARDY SOCIETY OF JAPAN, I (Nov 1966), 15–21.
Randolf is a symbol of urban sophistication, Sam of ruralism, and Sophy of a child of nature at the mercy of these two sets of values. [In Japanese.]

2922 Garrison, Chester Arthur. "Hardy's *Dynasts*," DISSERTATION ABSTRACTS, XXVI (1966), 4658. Unpublished dissertation, Columbia University, 1965.

2923 Gifford, Henry. "Thomas Hardy and Emma," ESSAYS AND STUDIES BY MEMBERS OF THE ENGLISH ASSOCIATION, ns XIX (1966), 106–21.
Emma Gifford thought of herself as a lady, since she came from a genteel family in which all her male relatives were professional men. While her snobbery and tactlessness cannot be denied, she had a lively side to her not usually remembered. She was a vital and sometimes humorous woman, with strong opinions. It was probably their childless marriage which H found so trying in their relationship. There are some resemblances between Elfride and Henry Knight in *A Pair of Blue Eyes* and Emma and H, but the fictional characters should not be taken as identical with H and his fiancée.

2924 Gregor, Ian. "What Kind of Fiction Did Hardy Write?" ESSAYS IN CRITICISM, XVI (1966), 290–308.
Simplistic critical views aside, we read H because, as D. H. Lawrence noted, he had a "sensuous understanding deeper perhaps than that of any other English novelist." *The Return of the Native* is faulty in structure because H could not sufficiently integrate character and environment; *The Mayor of Casterbridge*, by contrast, presents an integrated tragic structure. Eustacia is *not* integrated with the Heath; Henchard *is* integrated with the village of Casterbridge. Tess, likewise, is integrated with family but is more interiorized than Eustacia or Henchard. In *Tess of the d'Urbervilles*, also, H is able to make domestic details portentous. In *Jude the Obscure*, the psychic life of individuals is revealed through relationships: the nerve-ends have cosmic significance. Jude and Sue's relations should be at the novel's center, but H weakens it by adding Jude's relation with Arabella. It fails, as does *Native*, from overwriting.

2925 Hardy, Evelyn. "An Unpublished Poem," TIMES LITERARY SUPPLEMENT (Lond), 2 June 1966, p. 504.

"A Victorian Rehearsal," discovered among the Max Gate Papers, may reflect an actual rehearsal H observed from the wings, in the last month of 1866 or the opening ones of 1867. A finished draft in ink and pencil, the poem is in H's mature hand and may have been redrafted from old lines when he was preparing the publication of *Winter Words*. [Contains a reproduction of the poem.]

2926 Harper, George G., Jr. "An Unpublished Hardy Letter," ENGLISH LANGUAGE NOTES, III (March 1966), 207–8.

The letter is to James Rose, Esq., regarding H's ancestry. That much of the information in it is printed in Florence Hardy's THE EARLY LIFE OF THOMAS HARDY (1928) suggests that H had recourse to this letter in preparing the text of EARLY LIFE, thus substantiating Lionel Stevenson's claim that EARLY LIFE is H's work, not that of his wife.

2927 Heilman, Robert B. "Hardy's Sue Bridehead," NINETEENTH CENTURY FICTION, XX (March 1966), 307–23.

H's main success is that he creates Sue and lets her exist on her own terms without trying to explain her. Sue's inconsistency is a combination of the romantic notion of spirit and the "Victorian self-congratulatory spirituality." This split causes her to be at constant war both in her own soul and against society. She is the first fictional character honestly (albeit mistakenly) to feel that a convention is an unnecessary restraint and not realize that it is important to the welfare of both the individual and the society. In creating Sue, H presented, before it was commonly understood, the growing modern dilemma: "The threat of the intellect to the life of feelings and emotions."

2928 Heilman, Robert B. "Introduction," *Jude the Obscure*, ed with an introduction and notes by Robert B. Heilman (NY: Harper & Row, 1966), pp. 1–46.

H's intention in *Jude the Obscure* is to portray a wretched world in which "coarse, callous, and calculating individuals and insentient, complacent institutions flourish; [while] gifted individuals, who aspire to truth and integrity and who neglect customs and forms, are beaten down to suffering and early death." The basic method is contrast (Sue vs. Arabella, Jude vs. Sue); the basic instrument is irony; the basic "tonal effects" are the pathetic and the satirical. The satire is directed mainly at various social mechanisms: the law, the church, the university. However, these "apparently clear lines" of the novel are complicated by the novel's fluctuation "between two opposing views of 'nature,' between a romantic naturalism . . . and the pessimistic aftermath of scientific naturalism." H's satire of contemporary institutions is constantly moving into philosophical investigations. For example, the novel's treatment of the marriage theme involves both "social complaint" and "the very large problem of the relation between feelings and institutional forms." Furthermore, the characters (even secondary ones like Arabella and Phillotson) do not serve to merely advance a thesis but are "allowed to develop spontaneously and to grow from allegorical univalence . . . into novelistic fullness." In the case of Jude as well, we see "Hardy the artist triumphing over Hardy the allegorist and topical commentator." Sue is "a work of genius" which steals the book from Jude "because she is stronger, more complex, and more significant and because her contradictory impulses, creating a spontaneous air of the inexplicable and even the mysterious, are dramatized with extraordinary concreteness and fullness and with hardly a word of interpretation and admonishment by the author." [A balanced assessment.]

2929 Hellstrom, Ward. "*Jude the Obscure* as Pagan Self-Assertion," VICTORIAN NEWSLETTER, No. 29 (Spring 1966), 26–27.
Robert Fleissner's position in "The Name Jude," ibid, No. 27 (Spring 1965), 24–26, in which Fleissner asserts that *Jude the Obscure* is "pro-Christian," is wrong. Jude chooses active, stoic self-assertion, a pagan view, as opposed to passive, Christian self-denial. The novel "is certainly anti-Christian."

2930 Howe, Irving. "A Note on Hardy's Stories," HUDSON REVIEW, XIX (Summer 1966), 259–66.
The reputation of H's poetry has risen while that of his novels has fallen, but little has been said about his stories. Most of them are not very impressive, but seven or eight are "very fine," and one, "The Fiddler of the Reels" can be called "great." H's stories are "fragments chipped off his larger work." The crucial distinction between the stories and the novels is that the former have little of the " 'modern' " H. In atmosphere the stories "recall the pastoral fiction of George Eliot."

2931 Howe, Irving. "The Short Poems of Thomas Hardy," SOUTHERN REVIEW, ns II (Oct 1966), 878–905.
H's poems "range in quality from a mass of routine work to a small portion that is distinguished and occasionally great." There is no development in H's thought; he "wrested his ideas during his twenties and thirties . . . and he clung to them into deep old age, like a man still doting on a childhood sweetheart." The assaults upon untested conviction that we have come to expect from modern poetry are not found in H's poetry. He is one of "the few major English poets whose origins are plebian and values throughout his life also plebian." He writes about ordinary life and never "accepts a posture of superiority over any living creature or defenseless object." The best of H's poems brood "upon the most terrible facts of existence while refusing the sentimentalism of despair." His ballads are not complete successes because "he was trying to give a personal flavor to a form that

achieves its finest effects through impersonality." His dramatic vignettes "often decline into mere illustrations for a settled opinion." H's beliefs are "irritants, provocations, and stimulants for the release of his sensibility." The voice of H's finest poetry "is the voice of the mature Hardy, a poet supremely honest before his dilemmas and failures, no matter what the cost." His group of elegies "Veteris vestigia flammae" are probably the mature poet's finest achievement. In these poems the poet tries to recapture experiences of frustration and struggle that all men hold in common. They lack moralizing and because of this become moral examples of how man must "live through what it seems he cannot, and how he learns not to tamper with his grief and not even to seek forgiveness in his own eyes."

2932 Jennings, Carroll Wade. "Interconnected Love Relationships in the Novels of Thomas Hardy," DISSERTATION ABSTRACTS, XXVI (1966), 4660. Unpublished dissertation, Texas Technological College, 1965.

2933 Karl, Frederick R. "Introduction," *The Life and Death of the Mayor of Casterbridge*, ed with an introduction and notes by Frederick R. Karl (NY: Harper & Row, 1966), pp. vii–xxxvi.

In *The Mayor of Casterbridge*, H writes a parable for our times: "life itself destroys even when man is basically good."

2934 Kennedy, X. J. AN INTRODUCTION TO POETRY (Boston, Toronto: Little, Brown, 1966), pp. 30, 51, 113, 155–57, 311–13.

"The Workbox" is an example of irony; "The Ruined Maid" illustrates poetic diction; "Neutral Tones" illustrates symbol and allegory; "The Five Students" illustrates metrics. ["Channel Firing," "The Convergence of the Twain," and "During Wind and Rain" are included.]

2935 Kettle, Arnold. HARDY THE NOVELIST: A RECONSIDERATION (Singleton Park, Swansea: University College of Swansea, [1966]); given as the W. D. Thomas Memorial Lecture.

H and Dickens are a problem to critics because they are both "unsophisticated writers." We must learn to see H in a more popular and democratic tradition. A contradiction between conservative and radical "informs Hardy's art just as persistently as it divided his life." The tendency of *Under the Greenwood Tree* is to celebrate "the virtues of the older, rural culture of the Dewys at the expense of the newer liveliness and instability which Fancy touches off. . . . Yet Hardy knows very well that the issue isn't so simple. He cannot reject education for his heroines any more than he can reject the realities of Darwin and T. H. Huxley for himself." He is suspicious of "sophisticated attitudes" but recognizes the need for an "advanced culture." Guérard wonders why H continued to be pessimistic even when the standard of living of the peasants improved. H was not primarily concerned with the standard of living; "it was the destruction of the old rural culture that worried him and the replacement of the older relationships, grounded in centuries of custom and shared necessities, by the new relationships based on nothing kinder than the negotiation of a wage contract." It is also a mistake to see H as contra-town and pro-country. "Life in the Hintocks in . . . *The Woodlanders* is not idyllic. Giles and Marty are not 'pastoral figures.' Nor is there anything mystic about their close relationship with nature and its processes." Nature in the novels is "always linked with man and his history and his work and almost always used as a contrast with ideas." In dealing with "ideas" in the novels one must always emphasize "the negative role, in novel after novel, of any way of thinking that gives abstract ideas or principles a priority over the actual needs of specific situations." H evokes "a world of actions and values more truly 'natural' and therefore more fully human." He never questions the social nature of man, and "the natural and the social are never fully separable" in H's novels. H's social concern makes all of his novels—in a broad sense— "Historical Novels." For the most part, his novels are not "mechanistic" or "pessimistic." His characters are "free enough to recognize and make real choices . . . free enough to make irreparable mistakes or to struggle to make their lives whole and unified, at one with the external world; free enough, in short, to be human beings."

2936 Kettle, Arnold. "Introduction," *Tess of the d'Urbervilles*, ed with an introduction and notes by Arnold Kettle (NY: Harper & Row, 1966), pp. vii–xxiii.

Tess of the d'Urbervilles exhibits "a deeply sustained mistrust not merely of particular dogmaticisms but of all dogmaticism; all ways of thinking that give abstract ideas or principles—whether religious or social—a priority over the actual needs of specific human situations." Tess may be "a pure woman" as H says, but she is not a platonic conception of womanhood. Tess's fall is bound up with the social situation of the Durbeyfields and the d'Urbervilles. Illuminating approaches to *Tess* link H with the ballad tradition, Shakespeare (*Tess* might be compared with the fourth act of THE WINTER'S TALE), and a cosmology expressed through the narrators' voices in the novels far less pessimistic than the thought which his characters utter. [See Kettle's INTRODUCTION TO THE ENGLISH NOVEL, II (1953). "My assessment of Tess in that essay I now feel to be somewhat one-sided."]

2937 Kitamura, Chigako. "On *The Woodlanders*," BULLETIN OF THE HARDY SOCIETY OF JAPAN, I (Nov 1966), 32–39.
[Stresses the spirit of reconciliation and unmatchable beauty of the characters and the descriptions of the woodland.]

2938 Lagarde, Fernand. "A propos de la construction de *Jude the Obscure*" (Concerning the Construction of *Jude the Obscure*), CALIBAN, III [Special issue: "Hommage à Paul Dottin"] (Jan 1966), 185–214.

In several novels prior to *Jude the Obscure*, H uses several chapters as a base for the structure. In four novels he imposes on the chapter division a division into parts. In *Under the Greenwood Tree*, he adopts the rhythm of the seasons. In *The Return of the Native*, the most dramatic, the first five parts are exploited in a manner to underscore the cleanness of the grand line and to increase the tension. The very brief sixth part forms an epilogue and somewhat spoils the architecture of the whole. In *A Laodicean*, H justifies the construction, in six parts, in the midst of a skillful grouping of characters, bringing in one, then the others, and he possesses the expertise to alternate long and short sections. *The Well-Beloved* recounts three quests for beauty by a man at twenty, forty, and sixty years of age. Only in *Native* does the construction usefully serve the action. In the others the artifice is transparent, with the exception of *Well-Beloved*, a fantasy which was composed while H was thinking about *Jude*. Without doubt H was not satisfied with prior results because with *Tess of the d'Urbervilles* he returned to composition by chapters, but he does not reject out of hand an organization by action which gives the book its framework, as in *Jude* and which, for some, rates *Jude* over *Tess*. The failures and successive comebacks, the tests and provisory solutions which accompany the movement to the unhappiness of Jude, correspond to the acts of a tragedy, which H wished to show by the skillful hammering out of the book in six acts. The entr'actes do not represent pleasant interludes but serve to break the continuity of development to recall to the reader that time pursues its course between the two visions of Jude.

This was hardly noticed when *Jude* appeared. H was astonished that the geometric shape went unnoticed. The construction was rigid in six chapters of near equal length (fanning out to twelve others) but was relieved by each part being given the name of a village or town. The enlarging of the titles toward the end marks the acceleration of the rhythm. The citations placed as epigraphs announce the tone of the action and often permit insight into the content. To the attentive, the notations constitute "stations of the cross" to Jude's calvary. Each part generally begins with a notation of time and a description of a period in the hero's life. Each chapter depicts either a moment of action or a state of being. In each chapter is a paragraph that acts as its constitutive element; reflections succeed descriptions and descriptions carry the proof from the reflections. The art has effaced the geometry so that the geometry does not intrude on the progression. There is nothing banal. H adds art to artifice. The first and last parts are eleven chapters; the birth of aspirations and their annihilation are of equal importance to the author. The number of other chapters of other sections seem to proceed according to content or position in the book. The third part is divided into ten chapters, which is explained by the multiplication of interruptions the chronicler must relate. The three other parts are naturally very brief. The return of the past, the vengeance of the gods in Arabella, occurs at chap 27 of fifty-three chapters. The crisis of each part occurs at the middle and is dedicated to a moment of existence of the principals.

The interior movement of each part is identical: hope, theories put in practice or applied to decisions, and the defeat and final fall to a point of new hope and new life (e.g. the marriage to Arabella puts an end to Jude's intellectual aspirations but allows him to go to Christminster; Sue's marriage to Phillotson dashes his hopes and efforts but incites the redoubling of his efforts for reunion with his cousin). The disposition of the chapters makes evident the alteration of periods of hope and despair. This is done with such adroitness that there is no sense of the utilization of architecture. The first chapter of the two consecutive sections treat apparently identical subjects. In the second part Jude goes to Christminster to pursue his study and career in religion, but in reality to confront Sue. In the third part he decides to live at Melchester for the same reasons and unavowed motives.

Because of such alternation the curved pattern traced by the central characters should not be overlooked. The curve resembles a slow upward movement and then a decline. The first four parts bring the note of hope and nothing seems to dampen it in the hero, who is again and again sparked by Sue, the university, and Arabella. The failure of Jude is a social failure because the adventure with Arabella is not a sentimental adventure. On the contrary, the failure in the last three parts is sentimental only if the author sees it as society does. This double division proceeds out of the search for symmetry. The sentimental and social failures are mingled so that the book ends as it began, in isolation and despair. The opposition between the opening and final chapters, between the call of Christminster (consequent upon God and man) and the rejection of Jude by the university, was not totally necessary to H's artistic ends but rather to oblige the reader to note the division of the work. The geometric construction of actions and scenes in *Jude* is not due to the fact of serialized publication. The structure is organic, and all the moments of the tragedy are in mutual reaction not in isolation.

The dramatic chronicle is a tragedy in six acts. The first part is more than a prologue, since, with the second, it exposes the action and the birth of passions—it accumulates all the elements containing the tragedy in germ. The second part completes the exposition. Parts II and III constitute Act II. The question that has been in suspense all too long is raised: is Jude able to be happy? The tragedy of the individual becomes the tragedy of the couple: is Sue able to be happy? Part IV, given to exterior obstacles concluding in Sue's decision to join her cousin, and Part V, given to the obstacles the couple encounter concluding in the awakening of Jude's passion for knowledge, lead to the crisis. The crisis to this point had been avoided since Sue and Jude had lived at peace with themselves, but the problems posed by their reunion are pressing. This resembles the theater, where the characters try to run from their destiny but Destiny stops them and forces them to stand their ground. Part V is static and opposed to the dynamism of the first four parts. Jude and Sue are quickly at Aldbrickham, and the notion of happiness corresponds to a stopping. The denouement, interior and exterior, is achieved by the suicide of Father Time after killing the children, because it possesses simultaneously the quality of accident and psychological blow which provokes remorse in Sue and as a consequence, a fierce attitude in the face of Destiny and death. This is the habitual curve of tragedy: a movement to happiness in spite of periods of sorrow, in spite of traps, then the dizzy decline to nothingness. The last scenes contain the remarriages, the expiation of Sue, and the death of Jude, and they are only the transposition in tableaux of the failure and the annihilation of the characters. The curve is less simple than at first sight. The points of conflict multiply as the action progresses. The first part studies the conflicts of Sue; the second and third analyze the interior drama of Jude; the fourth and fifth, the interior drama of Sue, all of which are complicated by the intimate association of Sue and Jude. There is not intrigue. H adopts determinism and is content to explain the present. What little intrigue there is comes from Arabella and Cartlett and is taken care of briefly.

Division into acts constitutes a division into equal segments of affective time, although real duration in life is very different. The chronology is a thread: the mention of Jude's age at each stage, and in the end, Jude is old because of unhappiness not years. The work takes the rhythm of events. H used time to attain tragic grandeur and to preserve dramatic vigor. *Jude* is an alternation of periods of equilibrium and ruptured equilibrium, and in the quiet of equilibrium the characters want and wish permanence but find it provisory. The rhythm and its impression are reinforced by the use of geographic names. The titles of the six parts confirm the idea of a "round" and counterbalance the effect of the title. The destiny of the characters, especially of Jude, is that of a voyage. The return to the same situations and places attests to the relationship with tragedy. The geographic places are above all the dramatic places (Marygreen is the symbol of the experiences of old, the return to zero, nature, false peace). The village names which belong to the tragic failure also are the proof of *Jude* as the modern odyssey of a "small man." The symbolism of the place names must not be forgotten (the walks to the north would be meaningless). The names of villages occur as *leitmotivs*.

The secondary characters confirm the impression of a "round," as they come regularly to the same places (the parents of Arabella, Anny, and Vilbert). "Rounds" without sense incarnate the past in the repetition of human experiences. The immutable "round" is threaded throughout the route of the novel by place names around which situations and characters are organized. H recalls situations in silhouette which represent the anonymity of the order in which Jude lives. The decor in the story altogether unites Jude and Sue to their immediate ancestors and must, in the eyes of H, unite the principals to all men. Without doubt, H adds these geographic details to place an evolutive value ineluctably in Jude's life and, consequently, in the dramatic chronicle to show that vanity of the principals' and Man's existence in the universe. This justifies the use of place and time on the psychological level.

The term "quadrille" points to order and symmetry. The characters give the impression of dancing a "round." The four principals are introduced in the first part, and the book is remarkable for its quasi-absence of secondary characters. The atmosphere demands the presence of groups, but they live anonymously. In the quadrille two partners open the dance and close it after several changes of partners: section 1 (Jude/Arabella), section 2 (Sue/Jude), section 3 (Sue/Phillotson), section 4 (Jude/Sue), section 5 (Jude/Sue and Arabella/Phillotson, but they are grouped to Jude/Arabella and Sue/Phillotson). In the "quadrille" there are moments when a couple or a dancer, in the process of changing, finds himself in the position of observer, as does H (Sue's observance of Phillotson). The separations of the dancers are brief lest the harmony be endangered. In the "quadrille" there is a relationship of all the dancers, and thus all combinations of the four principals are valid. In the "quadrille" oppositions are easily permitted so that the dancers will know each other: Arabella, dark and sensual; Sue, pale and ethereal—the good and evil as understood by normal moral criteria; the men, the young and old, handsome and deformed, the sensual and little suited for marriage. The oppositions prepare for the figure to follow. H's vision of the novel as a "quadrille" constrains him to the simplification of extremes, not only in the tragedy of Jude but also in the characters, to permit temporary confrontations and contrasts. The grouping of characters in the design shows the perpetual recycling of human experiences, where one destiny prefigures that of another (Phillot-son's for Jude's). The contrasts take the mask off. The tragedy of Jude arises from his thirst for beauty and purity and his instincts, and the same is seen in the relation of Sue and Phillotson. The contrasts and parallels help to give *Jude* its rigidity (it must not be forgotten that H had constructed *Well-Beloved* on the repetition of situation). Not only must figures of the "quadrille" repeat but in such a manner that the onlooker will not grow tired. But H possesses other means to enhance the effect of a reprise. The architect is able to give proper place in his edifice to complimentary situations (the first part achieves it by Jude's prayers, the second by Jude's re-citation of the *Credo*, the last showing the child looking at the mines and the adolescent near the mines, having advanced somewhat in his quest for knowledge and wisdom).

All this seems to say that H had certain procedures at his disposal and that he repeats them unceasingly as if this economy or poverty coincides with the atmosphere of tragedy. Art consists in the economy which makes a detail necessary as a symbol and as a motif (the piano of Phillotson). The novel in its entirety is a subtle interlocking of correspondences. A subtle interlock is synonymous with rigidity and transparency. The construction serves the work and contributes to the force of tragedy. The method used risks lack of spontaneity. Others criticized *Jude* as an abuse of coincidence, chance, circumstance, and useless confessions. To H the rigidity of construction is justified by the existence of a Destiny. The coincidences become the mani-festation of the gods of the ancient theater, as in the tragedy of Seneca. With ancient tragedy and Renaissance tragedy, the novels of H explore repetitions, premonitions, strange relations of cause and effect. If man does not perceive the design of the universe, the gods, as well as the novelist and reader, see and project to the canvas the basis of ordinary suffering. The art consists in making the design appear. [A remarkably close study of structure.] [In French.]

2939 Laird, John. "The Manuscript of Hardy's *Tess of the d'Urbervilles* and what it tells us," JOURNAL OF THE AUSTRALASIAN UNIVERSITY LANGUAGE AND LITERATURE ASSOCIATION, No. 25 (May 1966), 68–82.

There is an Ur-text concealed in the MS of *Tess of the d'Urbervilles*. The main evidence for distinguishing it relates to the foliation and naming of characters. Hardy used three main systems of foliation (with traces of minor systems as well), thus identification and isolation of those folios is now pos-sible. If we follow Florence Hardy's THE EARLY LIFE OF THOMAS HARDY (1928), H, in preparing the First Edition of Nov 1891, merely restored the text to its earlier form; such an account, however, is little more than a travesty of the real history of the MS after Nov 1889. The truth is that, after the third rejection within two months, H undertook a major revision of his MS; it was far more than a bowdlerization and affected more than the serial text: it was a reconstruction of the novel which produced changes in the plot, characters, and themes and permanently affected the text. If we compare the Ur-text and the final text, we find that some incidents do not correspond and that there are important differences in detail, emphasis, and treatment of events. For example, the Ur-text heroine is described as "slender and flexible"; in the final text she possesses "a luxuriance of aspect, a fullness of growth, which made her appear more of a woman than she really was." The development of the character of the heroine throughout the MS and printed text was a process of refining, ennobling, and idealizing. The main qualities that H develops in his heroine are her moral courage, dignity, gracefulness and modesty, her womanly warmth, her purity of soul, her youthful freshness, and her heroic stoicism. As late as 1895, when a new edition was prepared, H introduced new amendments emphasizing the purity of the heroine. The immature and commonplace hoyden of the Ur-text had disappeared.

2940 Lodge, David. The Language of Fiction: Essays in Criticism and Verbal Analysis of the English Novel (Lond: Routledge & Kegan Paul; NY: Columbia UP, 1966), pp. 164–88. The intention in this chapter "is primarily to try and define as clearly as possible the sense in which the author of *Tess* may be said to 'write badly'; and to show that the consideration of this question, even when based on the close examination of short extracts, must inevitably involve us in the consideration of the meaning and artistic success of the novel as a whole." Vernon Lee's famous criticism of a passage from chap 16 is wrongheaded. The passage will be discussed "with an attempt to describe the function of the 'author's voice' in *Tess*, and proceed to discuss the attitudes of that author to Nature." *Tess of the d'Urbervilles* "reveals a fundamental uncertainty about the author's relation to his readers and to his characters, an uncertainty which is betrayed again and again in the language of the novel." There is the H who writes flawless dialect speech and the H who writes sentences of labored syntax and learned vocabulary; "the second Hardy . . . is responsible for the most spectacular stylistic lapses." Both H's are needed; however, "one aspect of the novelist's undertaking in *Tess* demands a quality of immediacy, of 'felt life' . . .—in other words the voice of the first Hardy—other aspects demand a quality of distance, both of Time and space, through which the characters can be seen in their cosmic, historical, and social settings—in other words, the voice of the second Hardy." H's intrusions are necessary and only "offend when they are crudely expressed." The author of *Tess* as local historian convinces us that her story "is already finished, that it took place in living memory, and is reported to us by someone who lived in the locality, second hand, and whose account is one of imaginative reconstruction." The voice of the local historian "is in a state of uneasy co-existence with the voice of the author as creator and maker, as one acquainted with the deepest interior processes of his character's mind." Many times the transition between the mode of literary paraphrasing of Tess's thoughts and "precisely rendering the verbal quality of Tess's consciousness" is abrupt and jars the reader. Tess is associated and identified with Nature on several different levels. She is a " 'daughter of the soil' " and a Nature-worshipping pagan. Also, this "schematic association of Tess with Nature is enforced by insistent allusion, literal and figurative, to flora and fauna," and "her behavior is often compared to that of animals." Although Tess is close to nature, "its moral neutrality [is] emphasized by the sceptical philosopher." The fly and billiard table image that bothered Vernon Lee is "designed to dissociate us from Tess at this point, to check any tendency to find reassurance in the identification of Tess's renewed hope with the fertile promise of the valley." H exhibits a conflict in "struggling to reconcile the view of Nature inherited from the Romantics with the discoveries of Darwinian biology." H's confusion about Nature "is not merely in the abstractable philosophical content on the novel, but inextricably woven into its verbal texture." Sometimes H's various voices "subtly make their points and modulate smoothly into one another; at other times they seem to be interrupting and quarreling between themselves."

2941 McCamus, Barbara Jean. "Patterns of Perception in Hardy's Novels," Dissertation Abstracts, XXVI (1966), 3926. Unpublished dissertation, University of Wisconsin, 1965.

2942 Madden, William A. "The Search for Forgiveness in Some Nineteenth-Century Novels," Comparative Literature Studies, III:2 (1966), 139–53.
In the course of the nineteenth century, the ideal of forgiveness lost the religious significance Scott had given it in The Heart of Midlothian. In H's later novels forgiveness is less important than the anguished search for a source of guilt. This search leads ultimately to despair, for the "President of the Immortals" who condemns Tess is beyond the compass of human forgiveness. To forgive may ameliorate human misery, but it no longer has a transcendent religious function.

2943 Madison, Charles A. "Gleanings from the Henry Holt Files," Princeton University Library Chronicle, XXVII (Winter 1966), 86–106.
Henry Holt was the first American publisher of H; there is a considerable correspondence between them.

2944 Marshall, George O., Jr. "Thomas Hardy's Eye Imagery," Colby Library Quarterly, VII (June 1966), 264–68.

Eye imagery recurs with unusual frequency in H's novels. Elfride (*A Pair of Blue Eyes*), Elizabeth-Jane (*The Mayor of Casterbridge*), Tess (*Tess of the d'Urbervilles*), and Eustacia (*The Return of the Native*) are all described in terms of their eyes, and Clym in *Native* goes blind. Non-human eyes are also important; the spectral eyes of the polar birds in *Jude the Obscure* broaden the purview of suffering in that novel. [Amasses a list of passages, but does little with it.]

2945 Miller, J. Hillis. "Some Implications of Form in Victorian Fiction," COMPARATIVE LITERATURE STUDIES, III:2 (1966), 109–18.

Recognition of the split between objective and subjective worlds led to a nihilism among the Victorian novelists, which, while it culminates in Conrad, may be traced in late Dickens, George Eliot, Trollope, Meredith, and H. The inability of man to comprehend or possess anything outside his own mind was realized fully by H, who shows again and again in his novels the painful hollowness of consciousness itself. Specifically, Michael Henchard in *The Mayor of Casterbridge* exemplifies the mental collapse which occurs to a character whose mind has turned in upon itself, cutting itself off from the objective world and living on its own emptiness.

2946 Nakamura, Shiro. "*The Mayor of Casterbridge* and LES MISERABLES," BULLETIN OF THE HARDY SOCIETY OF JAPAN, I (Nov 1966), 22–32.

Though there is close similarity between the two novels, Hugo's romantic social novel is an extraneous prototype from which H derived the genuine tragic novel. [In Japanese.]

2947 Orel, Harold. "Hardy and the Epic Tradition," ENGLISH LITERATURE IN TRANSITION, IX:4 (1966), 187–89.

We must infer H's opinion about epic poetry from his own self-labeled "epic-drama." [Raises a number of speculative questions relating to the genesis and development of *The Dynasts*.]

2948 Orel, Harold (ed). THOMAS HARDY'S PERSONAL WRITINGS: PREFACES, LITERARY OPINIONS, REMINISCENCES (Lawrence: University of Kansas P, 1966).

[Reprints all of the prefaces H wrote for his own novels and volumes of poetry and for eight volumes by other writers (five on Wessex; two selected editions of William Barnes's poetry; one by a friend's wife). Reprints seventeen pieces "On Literary Matters," including "Dialect in Novels," "The Profitable Reading of Fiction," "Candour in English Fiction," "The Science of Fiction," "Why I Don't Write Plays," and "A Plea for Pure English"; three statements on *The Dynasts*; biographical comments on Barnes, R. L. Stevenson, and George Meredith; "British Authors on French

Literature"; and three notes on poetry. Several of these are contributions to symposiums or letters to the editor. Reprints eleven pieces on "Reminiscences and Personal Views," including "How I Built Myself a House," "The Dorsetshire Labourer," "Some Romano-British Relics Found at Max Gate," "Shall Stonehenge Go?" "A Christmas Ghost-Story," "Memories of Church Restoration," "Dorset in London," "Maumbury Rings," "Which is the Finest View in Dorset?" "The Ancient Cottages of England," and "Dedication of the New Dorchester Grammar School." There is also an appendix made of paraphrases and brief quotations from sixty-nine items of various sorts Orel considers too limited in interest to be reprinted in full. Each piece reprinted has a bibliographical headnote and an explanatory afternote; there are also footnotes to explain allusions and minor matters in the pieces. Indispensable research tool; excellent commentary and notes by Orel.]

2949 Parker, W. M. "Thomas Hardy's Fighting Men," LITERARY REPOSITORY, No. 2 (1966), 4–5.

H "was always sympathetic to the courage and patriotic qualities of sailor and soldier." [Lists military characters found in H's works, relates their plot function, and quotes descriptions of them. Trivial.]

2950 Paterson, John. "Introduction," *The Return of the Native*, ed with an introduction and notes by John Paterson (NY: Harper & Row, 1966), pp. ix–xxviii.

The Return of the Native cannot be ranked with *The Mayor of Casterbridge, Tess of the d'Urbervilles* or *Jude the Obscure*. As an imitation of classical tragedy, it falls short of "the solemn burden of tragedy." While the action and characters barely qualify as tragic, the accumulating allusions to the geography, history and literature of antiquity enrich the novel. The Promethean theme and imagery is particularly outstanding. Nor as a symbolic romance does *Native* inspire the fullest confidence. One accepts the book because H himself did. Clym is in many respects H; his disillusionment with the city echoes the author's. Mrs. Yeobright resembles H's mother, and Eustacia suggests his cousin Tryphena Sparks. H was "a reluctant novelist to the bitter end." Serial publication and its repressive editing damaged his novels besides. *Native*, written expressly for serial publication, "records the results of an imagination operating under strained circumstances."

2951 Phelps, Kenneth. ANNOTATIONS BY THOMAS HARDY IN HIS BIBLES AND PRAYER-BOOK, PRESENTED AGAINST THE BACKGROUND OF HARDY'S LIFE, WORKS AND LOVES, WITH NEW LIGHT ON CERTAIN POEMS (Mount Durand, St. Peter Port, Guernsey: Toucan P, 1966).

H's notes, penciled in the margins of his Bibles and Prayer-Book, can be linked to persons and events. "At the Wicket-Gate" is probably a description of H's final parting with Tryphena Sparks in 1869. [Conflicts with dates given in Lois Deacon, TRYPHENA AND THOMAS HARDY (1962). Reprints "At the Wicket-Gate." Quotes H's marginal notes. Also see J. Stevens Cox (pub and general editor), Monographs on the Life of Thomas Hardy (1962).]

2952 Pinney, Lady Hester. THOMAS HARDY AND THE BIRDSMOOR-GATE MURDER 1856 (Beaminster, Dorset: Toucan P, 1966).

H was quite interested in the story of Martha Brown of Birdsmoorgate, whose execution for murder in 1856 H witnessed as a boy of sixteen. [Reprints a letter of 20 Jan 1926 from H, part of one from Mrs. H, and a photograph of H at age sixteen. Appendix: "Martha Brown, told by Jim Lane of Blackdown, June 13, 1926." Also see J. Stevens Cox (pub and general editor), Monographs on the Life of Thomas Hardy (1962).]

2953 Ross, Donald Harley. "The Fiction of Richard Jefferies," DISSERTATION ABSTRACTS, XXVI (1966), 5417. Unpublished dissertation, University of Colorado, 1964.

2954 Sakai, Yoshie. "On *Jude the Obscure*," BULLETIN OF THE HARDY SOCIETY OF JAPAN, I (Nov 1966), 39–46.

The fall of Jude and Sue is due to the indifferent "Immanent Will." [In Japanese.]

2955 Schweik, Robert C. "The 'Duplicate' Manuscript of Hardy's *Two on a Tower*: A Correction and a Comment," PAPERS OF THE BIBLIOGRAPHICAL SOCIETY OF AMERICA, LX (1966), 219–21.

Carl J. Weber's position ["The Manuscript of Hardy's *Two on a Tower*," ibid, XL (First Quarter 1946), 1–21, espec 7–9] that the Houghton Library manuscript of H's *Two on a Tower* consists partly of the original and partly of a "duplicate" copy H sent to America to insure against loss is essentially correct. But the slip of paper bearing the title of the novel and the author's name is from the original MS, not from the "duplicate," as Weber suggests.

2956 Schweik, Robert C. "An Error in the Text of Hardy's *Far From the Madding Crowd*," COLBY LIBRARY QUARTERLY, VII (June 1966), 269.

The 1895 Osgood-McIlvaine edition of *Far From the Madding Crowd* incorporated an error into the fortieth chapter of the novel, which was perpetuated by the 1912 Macmillan Wessex Edition and all later texts deriving from that standard edition. The sentence (which describes Fanny Robin's despair) reads: "Whilst she sorrowed in her heart she cheered with her

voice, and what was stranger than that the strong should need encouragement from the weak was that cheerfulness should be so well stimulated by
such utter dejection." As comparison with the CORNHILL serial shows,
"stimulated" should be "simulated."

2957 Taylor, Edmund Dennis. "The Rhetoric of Hardy's Poetry,"
DISSERTATION ABSTRACTS, XXVII (1966), 189A. Unpublished
dissertation, Yale University, 1966.

2958 Teets, Bruce. "Thomas Hardy's Reflective Poetry," ENGLISH
LITERATURE IN TRANSITION, IX:4 (1966), 183–85.
An over-emphasis on H as a "thinker" and "pessimist" and the necessity to
understand "his transitional place in the tradition of reflective poetry" are
three difficulties in recognizing H's solid achievement.

2959 Wain, John. "Introduction," SELECTED SHORTER POEMS OF
THOMAS HARDY, chosen and introduced by John Wain (Lond:
Macmillan, 1966), pp. ix–xix.
H was, "constitutionally and by inclination, primarily a poet" and as such
"not unmarkedly works over the same themes we find in his prose"—
generally, suffering; particularly, "the human sense of impotence in the face
of a ruthless destiny." Both H and Wordsworth aimed "to view everyday
experience from an unusual angle and give the unexpected insight," and
both "had the same knack of slipping in and out of autobiography. Hardy's
utter unselfconsciousness in this respect is one of the most interesting
features of his work." His poetry is remarkably consistent, both stylistically
and in theme. But beyond the steady consistency of diction ("texture and
movement"), there is "his incessant switching of metrical forms." When
compared with W. B. Yeats and A. E. Housman ("two other poets of the
tragic vision, working during the same years"), H is "very much his own
man." He has "the peasant's realism, his grim resignation to the fact that life
will be harsh, that the best part of it will be over soon and after that years
will bear heavily down. But he also has the dour humour, the relish for an
odd tale about his neighbour, and the slow endurance that carries on in spite
of all." The "times" severely limited public acceptance of his poetry.

2960 Wain, John. "Introduction," SELECTED STORIES OF THOMAS
HARDY, chosen and introduced by John Wain (Lond: Macmillan,
1966), pp. ix–xx.
In his stories, H's mind "delights to move in that region of the folk imagination which underlies and to some extent sustains the more refined products
of polite literature." His stories appealed not to the city dweller, whose
craving for realistic fiction attempts to make sense of his "milieu," but to the

countryman, who "prefers to be entertained with stories of the marvellous." Elements of the traditional country tale common to these stories are an old-fashioned interest in high-born folk and great families and the love of recalling bygone days. H "seems to have had no respect for the short story as a literary form." Unlike the best modern short stories, in which "we feel that the material has dictated its own natural length," H's stories "are (in his own words) 'minor novels'; they differ from his longer fictions not essentially, in their very nature, but merely by the fact of their shortness." If the "meditative and analytical strain in these stories recalls Hardy's lyrical poems, the narratives themselves, in their choice of character and incident, will often remind us of his narrative poems." H's achievement as a writer of stories is best viewed "in the perspective of this rural tradition, the countryman's love of an unlikely or eerie tale." His realistic detail and truthful background make his novels and short stories "more satisfying in their incidental qualities than in their overall impression." He excels not as a tragic artist but as "a writer of superb, evocative documentary." The selection of stories is designed "to illustrate Hardy's rough humor as well as his relentlessness."

2961 Wain, John. "The Poetry of Thomas Hardy," CRITICAL QUARTERLY, VIII (Summer 1966), 166–73; rptd as an introduction in SELECTED SHORTER POEMS OF THOMAS HARDY (Lond: Macmillan; NY: St. Martin's P, 1966).

H is primarily a poet who draws his strength from his tragic stoicism and owes most to Wordsworth, both poets recognizing that normality is not the simple thing it is supposed. H's poems are like the "work of a village craftsman," he builds plainly and to last, with a "certain stiff deliberation." He is as indifferent to nature as a peasant would be, although under his clumsy language there is a richness and cunning. He has had an unspectacular but persistent influence on later poets. "Afterwards" is one of his most beautiful poems. [A survey with one or two good points but flawed by the repetition of critical clichés debunked two years earlier in the same magazine, see Raymond Williams, "Thomas Hardy," ibid, VI (Winter 1964), 341–51.]

2962 Wright, Robert C. "Hardy's Heath and Cather's Prairie as Naturalistic Symbols," MANKATO STATE COLLEGE STUDIES, I (May 1966), 55–68.

Although Cather is not often spoken of as a naturalist, if one abstracts parallel passages from O PIONEERS! and *The Return of the Native*, it becomes clear that both H and Cather "see man at the mercy of his heredity and environment. To particularize this naturalistic view of life, they use heath and prairie to symbolize a universe that is harshly beautiful, permanent, indifferent, and pagan."

1967

2963 Anonymous, of Fordington. "A Fragment," HARDYANA: A COLLECTION OF SHORT MEMORABILIA AND OTHER MATTERS OF HARDY INTEREST, ed by J. Stevens Cox (Birling, Mount Durand, St. Peter Port, Guernsey: Toucan P, 1967), p. 29.

H "never did anything for Dorchester." [Also see J. Stevens Cox (pub and general editor), Monographs on the Life of Thomas Hardy (1962).]

2964 Bartlett, Lynn C., and William R. Sherwood (eds). THE ENGLISH NOVEL: BACKGROUND READINGS (Phila & NY: Lippincott, 1967).

Contents, abstracted under date of first publication: A. C. Swinburne, "A Letter to Thomas Hardy, November 5, 1895," from THE SWINBURNE LETTERS, ed by Cecil Y. Lang, 6 vols (1959–1962); Jeannette L. Gilder, "Thomas Hardy Makes a New Departure," WORLD (NY), 8 Dec 1895; M[argaret] O[liphant] W. O[liphant], "The Anti-Marriage League," BLACKWOOD'S EDINBURGH MAGAZINE, CLIX (Jan 1896), 137–42; Edmund Gosse, "Mr. Hardy's New Novel," COSMOPOLIS, I (Jan 1896), 60–69. By H and not abstracted: "Letters to Edmund Gosse," from THE LIFE OF THOMAS HARDY (1962; see THE LATER YEARS under 1930). [All items deal with *Jude the Obscure*.]

2965 Beatty, C. J. P. STINSFORD—A HARDY CHURCH (Mount Durand, St. Peter Port, Guernsey: Toucan P, 1967).

[A guide to the Stinsford Church which H attended and helped in plans for rebuilding. Also see J. Stevens Cox (pub and general editor), Monographs on the Life of Thomas Hardy (1962).]

2966 Brooks, Cleanth. "The Language of Poetry: Some Problem Cases," ARCHIV FÜR DAS STUDIUM DER NEUEREN SPRACHEN UND LITERATUREN, CCIII (April 1967), 401–14.

H's verse offers a good example of a poet whose combination of traditional and unusual dictions often verges on disaster, but at times rises to sublimity. He accepted Victorian poetic diction and was not a conscious rebel, yet his great lyrics usually mix Victorian diction with Dorset words or technical expressions. "The Convergence of the Twain" is a case in point: words like "stilly" (1. 3) seem impossible but actually work effectively in H's poem (in this case, by slowing the line down).

2967 [Cox, J. Stevens (ed)]. HARDYANA: A COLLECTION OF SHORT MEMORABILIA AND OTHER MATTERS OF HARDY INTEREST. With an introduction by Richard Curle (Birling, Mount Durand, St. Peter Port, Guernsey: Toucan P, 1967).

Contents, abstracted separately by author, all under 1967: Thomas Loveday, "Hardy Honoured by Bristol University"; Derek Neville, "Mrs. Hardy and the 'Tramp' "; Robert Harding, "Glimpses of Thomas Hardy"; Clive Sansom, "Hardy—An Anecdote"; H. E. A. Platt, "A Youthful Encounter With Thomas Hardy"; Millicent Wedmore, "A Childhood Meeting with Hardy"; Mrs. A. Stanley, "Cook to the Hardy Household—1916–1918"; Lorna Stephanie Heenan, "Random Memories of Hardy and Dorset Folk"; Mrs. M. Shepherd, "William Barnes and Thomas Hardy"; Dorothy Meggison, "Anecdote of Hardy's Heart Burial"; R. H. Tilley, "Hardy and the Safety Bicycle"; Charles William Groves, "My Grandfather Worked for Thomas Hardy"; Mary F. Walker, "Remembers An Encounter with Hardy"; Emma Mary Webber, "Daily Help at Max Gate"; Emily Mary Benita Weber, "The Social Hardy"; C. D. Day, "Hardy and the Bees"; H. R. Harraway, "A Note"; Margaret Male, "Cleaner at Max Gate"; and Anonymous, of Fordington, "A Fragment." Also see J. Stevens Cox (pub and general editor), Monographs on the Life of Thomas Hardy (1962).]

2968 [Cox, J. Stevens (pub)]. THOMAS HARDY'S WILL AND OTHER WILLS OF HIS FAMILY (Mount Durand, Guernsey: Toucan P, 1967).
[Contains the wills of H; Florence Emily H, his wife; Katherine H, his sister; and Henry H, his brother. Also see J. Stevens Cox (pub and general editor), Monographs on the Life of Thomas Hardy (1962).]

2969 Crane, John K. "The Psychological Experience of Time in the Novels of Thomas Hardy," DISSERTATION ABSTRACTS, XXVII (April–June 1967), 3834A–35A. Unpublished dissertation, Pennsylvania State University, 1966.

2970 Day, C. D. "Hardy and the Bees," HARDYANA: A COLLECTION OF SHORT MEMORABILIA AND OTHER MATTERS OF HARDY INTEREST, ed by J. Stevens Cox (Birling, Mount Durand, St. Peter Port, Guernsey: Toucan P, 1967), p. 28.
[Inconsequential. Also see J. Stevens Cox (pub and general editor), Monographs on the Life of Thomas Hardy (1962).]

2971 Deacon, Lois. HARDY'S SUMMER ROMANCE, 1867: AN INTERPRETATION AND A RECONSTRUCTION (Mount Durand, St. Peter Port, Guernsey: Toucan P, 1967); mainly absorbed earlier in PROVIDENCE AND MR. HARDY, by Lois Deacon and Terry Coleman (1966).
H's poem "The Revisitation" is an immortalization of Tryphena. Damon Wildeve and Clym, and Eustacia and Thomasin of The Return of the Native are H and Tryphena. In the summer of 1867, Tryphena was two months pregnant and H was planning marriage, but Tryphena was the child

of Rebecca, H's sister. The crucial episode of the "secret year" (1867) is reflected in such novels as *An Indiscretion in the Life of an Heiress, Under the Greenwood Tree, Desperate Remedies, Native,* and *Tess of the d'Urbervilles,* as well as in such poems as "The Revisitation," "Neutral Tones," "At Rushy-Pond," "A Poor Man and a Lady" [the poem], and many others [listed as sources on p. 50]. [Also see J. Stevens Cox (pub and general editor), Monographs on the Life of Thomas Hardy (1962).]

2972 Deacon, Lois. TRYPHENA'S PORTRAIT ALBUM AND OTHER PHOTOGRAPHS OF HARDY INTEREST (Mount Durand, St. Peter Port, Guernsey: Toucan P, 1967); absorbed earlier in PROVIDENCE AND MR. HARDY, by Lois Deacon and Terry Coleman (1966).

[Contains photos of Tryphena Sparks, H, Randy (identified as H's son), Eleanor Tryphena Gale, Rebecca Sparks. Notes refer to an engagement between H and Tryphena in 1867, identify Tryphena as the heroine of many H novels and Randy as the Little Father Time of *Jude the Obscure.* Also see J. Stevens Cox (pub and general editor), Monographs on the Life of Thomas Hardy (1962).]

2973 DeGroot, Elizabeth M. "Archetypes in the Major Novels of Thomas Hardy and Their Literary Application," DISSERTATION ABSTRACTS, XXVIII (1967), 1048A. Unpublished dissertation, New York University, 1967.

2974 De Laura, David J. " 'The Ache of Modernism' in Hardy's Later Novels," JOURNAL OF ENGLISH LITERARY HISTORY, XXXIV (Sept 1967), 380–99.

Three themes exist in H's three "modern" novels (*The Return of the Native, Tess of the d'Urbervilles,* and *Jude the Obscure*): an attempt to formulate a "Greek" or "hellenic" view of life, the theme of "modernism," and the attack on religion. The sources behind these themes are Arnold, Pater, and ROBERT ELSMERE. Eustacia is drawn from Pater's description of the Mona Lisa in STUDIES IN THE HISTORY OF THE RENAISSANCE. The creation of Clym is indebted to both Pater and Arnold, and specifically to CULTURE AND ANARCHY. Angel Clare is also quite Arnoldian, particularly in terms of his enthusiasm for Greek ideas, but Angel's character owes just as much to the publication of ROBERT ELSMERE and the controversy that it aroused, for the religious overtones in *Tess* are fashioned on this controversy. Further, Angel's wrong-headed religious views are very similar to Robert's and are directly responsible for Tess's tragedy. The exploration of this religious problem is continued in *Jude.* Each of the three men— Clym, Angel, and Jude—are "modern" in that they began life with a noble humanitarian ideal, which they are unable to achieve because of the division between his ideals and the nineteenth-century situation.

2975 Deutsch, Babette. "Thomas Hardy and Walter de la Mare —Who Used to Notice Such Things," Columbia University Forum, X (Summer 1967), 40–44.

In his poetry H presents "the black history of Nature's dealings with us and of our dealings with one another." But H did not despair; he is "candid about men's joys as well as . . . men's miseries." Evil may be stronger than good but that does not cancel the fact that nobility, truth, and beauty exist.

2976 "The Dorset Hardy," Times Literary Supplement (Lond), 15 June 1967, p. 531.

H is less interesting than his art. In the Wessex world H "was a profound artist," but "in Dorset, he was simply an old-fashioned, countrified eccentric." It is the Dorset H who wills the pages in Thomas Hardy's Personal Writings, ed by Harold Orel (1966), which is "superlatively well-edited." The non-fiction is uninteresting, revealing H as provincial; the prefaces contain "scarcely one literary idea in a page." [For comment, see Peter Levi, "Dorset Hardy," ibid, 22 June 1967, p. 559.]

2977 Dove, John Roland. "Thomas Hardy and the Dilemma of Naturalism (A Study of Hardy's Lyric Poetry)," Neueren Sprachen, ns XVI (June 1967), 253–68.

Many of H's poems are "poems of protest against the natural order in the name of the victimized individual." Yet H is "baffled and troubled by the source of this protest. How is it possible that nature should be condemned by a moral consciousness which emerges within nature herself?" On one hand H is "the poet of existential pathos," but on the other he "is forever trying to transcend pathos in an attempt to rescue individual life from the flux of time." Although H, Swinburne, and Meredith agreed "that the God of Revelation is an anthropomorphic myth that must simply be abandoned," this conclusion was a "tragic dilemma" for H since, "like Tennyson, [H] sees the supernatural as man's only guarantee against the jungle of nature." In H's love poems "love is defined by its absence": either it is located in the past as a not-to-be-recaptured experience or "on a distant horizon in an improbable future." Love, although stifled by habit, may burst into new life, "but in his poetry this is always too late." As in the poems on his first wife, H shows that death is at once "a loss and a recovery." Her "death is a sort of macabre epiphany: it subtracts the non-essential and reveals what was truly fundamental in her personality." Death is never "a beneficent point of natural exhaustion in an orderly life cycle; [but] a wanton frustration of personal destiny." Man is a child of nature, doomed to death, yet H was forever struggling "against the all-embracing nihilism of this world view."

2978 Efron, Arthur. "The Tale, The Teller and Sexuality in *Tess of the d'Urbervilles*," Paunch, No. 28 (Feb 1967), 55–82.

In the seduction scene in *Tess of the d'Urbervilles*, "Hardy has reached his subject . . . an exploration of sexual possibilities in a life. Despite every manner of wavering, that subject is never lost from the novel after this point. It remains demonstrably central even when Hardy and the characters themselves seem not to know it. And the novel illuminates the nature of their failure to know it."

2979 Fernando, Lloyd. "The Radical Ideology of the 'New Woman,' " SOUTHERN REVIEW (Adelaide), II (1967), 206–22.

The theme of the unhappy marriage in the works of H and other prominent novelists can be traced to the re-examination of the nature of marriage prompted by women's movements in the nineteenth century. *The Woodlanders* illustrates the unsolvable problems created by indissoluble marriages and the difficulty encountered by inhabitants of remote districts in attempting divorce. Unlike the typically idealized heroines of other novels who merely served as vehicles for advocating or rejecting emancipationist theories, H's Sue Bridehead in *Jude the Obscure* is a detailed portrait of a confused, neurotic, sexually-maladjusted idealist. Her desire for independence is expressed in sexual caprice governed only by impulse, and her complete dedication to her ideal leads to a general erosion of her personality. The marriage-divorce-remarriage confusion in the novel can be understood best if it is read in the context of the female emancipation controversy.

2980 Friedman, Alan Warren. " 'Beeny Cliff' and 'Under the Waterfall': An Approach to Hardy's Love Poetry," VICTORIAN POETRY, V (Autumn 1967), 224–28.

In "Under the Waterfall," there is "neither fatalism nor indifference, despair nor joy—for, unlike 'Beeny Cliff' and other less successful love poems, 'Under the Waterfall' is simply a beautiful poetic statement."

2981 Gordon, Walter K. "Father Time's Suicide Note in *Jude the Obscure*," NINETEENTH CENTURY FICTION, XXII (Dec 1967), 298–300.

Father Time's use of the word "menny" may be H's way of suggesting that "tragedy and grief are the lot of both children and men" (i.e. "menny": a macabre pun meaning "like men"), or "one of the several adumbrations of tragedy and despair" (i.e. "menny" recalls the biblical "Mene, mene, tekel, upharsin").

2982 Groves, Charles William. "My Grandfather Worked for Thomas Hardy," HARDYANA: A COLLECTION OF SHORT MEMORABILIA AND OTHER MATTERS OF HARDY INTEREST, ed by J. Stevens Cox (Birling, Mount Durand, St. Peter Port, Guernsey: Toucan P, 1967), pp. 23–24.

The men who worked for Watts, a masterbuilder who often made repairs at Max Gate, thought H a terror, for H was particular about the quality of the work and the industry of the men. But H was kind to young Groves, though one sensed hostility in H's presence. The Dorchester people didn't much like H, who was said not to be very "thoughtful for his wife." [Also see J. Stevens Cox (pub and general editor), Monographs on the Life of Thomas Hardy (1962).]

2983 Harding, Robert. "Glimpses of Thomas Hardy," HARDYANA: A COLLECTION OF SHORT MEMORABILIA AND OTHER MATTERS OF HARDY INTEREST, ed by J. Stevens Cox (Birling, Mount Durand, St. Peter Port, Guernsey: Toucan P, 1967), pp. 10–12.

[H wrote, 15 Dec 1906, declining to write an introduction for a book by Harding's father, later encouraged Harding in his own writing, preferred the accent on *Dy* (nasts) as in "diner." Also see J. Stevens Cox (pub and general editor), Monographs on the Life of Thomas Hardy (1962).]

2984 Harraway, H. R. "A Note," HARDYANA: A COLLECTION OF SHORT MEMORABILIA AND OTHER MATTERS OF HARDY INTEREST, ed by J. Stevens Cox (Birling, Mount Durand, St. Peter Port, Guernsey: Toucan P, 1967), p. 28.

"In 1907 or 1908 two or three scenes from *The Dynasts* were produced by Tilley or Evans in connection with a Merrie May Fair, and some of the members of the Dramatics Section of the Debating Society took part." Later some scenes were produced in London. In "Atkins [sic] time," the H household was "much more sociable and human than I experienced it." [Also see J. Stevens Cox (pub and general editor), Monographs on the Life of Thomas Hardy (1962).]

2985 Heenan, Lorna Stephanie [née Fisher]. "Random Memories of Hardy and Dorset Folk," HARDYANA: A COLLECTION OF SHORT MEMORABILIA AND OTHER MATTERS OF HARDY INTEREST, ed by J. Stevens Cox (Birling, Mount Durand, St. Peter Port, Guernsey: Toucan P, 1967), pp. 17–18.

[The author's father was H's medical adviser between 1880 and 1910, as well as doctoring other members of the H family; the author did not know how famous H was until he died; reports the presence of many London reporters at the performance of *Far From the Madding Crowd* at Dorchester; notes progressive deterioration of Emma Hardy's mental condition and H's embarrassment by her " 'heretical' outbursts in the local papers." Also see J. Stevens Cox (pub and general editor), Monographs on the Life of Thomas Hardy (1962).]

2986 Holmes, Theodore. "Thomas Hardy's City of the Mind," SEWANEE REVIEW, LXXV (Spring 1967), 285–300.

While the great "cities of the mind," such as those of Dante, Homer, Petrarch, had their vital being in a divine spirit (Beatrice, the gods, Laura), H's "has become one with the city of this earth, and the heavenly mediation of its tutelary goddess has disappeared, or returns in death." His novels portray this city's creation, his poems are an "elegiac celebration" of it. In his countless short lyrics "addressed to an anonymous lost love in the first person," H conveys "the soul's love for the ideal it once contained" but has irrevocably lost. The spiritual story that obsessed H is everywhere evident in the novels: "the new human and mechanical forces of modern society [were] subverting, perverting, and deranging the more settled order of the English countryside and his own rural background." In some of his poems "the allegorical technique almost wholly absorbs the narrative level into it" to become a portrayal of H's "bent of mind," as in "At a Seaside Town in 1869" with its lament for a vanished "my Love" which once "shone" in the poet's inner "temple." On one hand, H believed "the whole soft-minded faith of latter-day humanism in man's ability to find salvation on his own terms," while on the other "he knew that each step the world took in this direction carried it away from the good, the true and complete of his boyhood background."

2987 Howe, Irving. THOMAS HARDY (NY: Macmillan, 1967). The two strongest influences upon H's work were "the formative experience of Dorset and the pressure of 19th century thought." His fiction and poetry are the product of a regional consciousness invaded by innovative and iconoclastic thought. The novels were composed under "the pressures of an inescapable subject—the fate of Wessex—as it came welling up in memory." The poems are shaped by H's "plebeian . . . origins and values," i. e., by his "complete refusal to accept a posture of superiority toward any living creature or defenseless object." [Chap 1 treats background and influences; Chap 2 ("Entertainments and Digressions") examines the minor fiction of 1870–1880: *The Poor Man and the Lady, Desperate Remedies, A Pair of Blue Eyes, The Hand of Ethelberta, The Trumpet-Major*. Chap 3 ("The World of Wessex") treats the main line of H's fiction as it developed between 1870–1880: *Under the Greenwood Tree, Far From the Madding Crowd, The Return of the Native*. Chap 4 ("Comic Fiction, Middle Age, Short Stories") discusses the much ignored comic elements of *Greenwood Tree* and *Madding Crowd*, as well as *A Laodicean* and *Two on a Tower* as romantic comedies; also *Wessex Tales, A Group of Noble Dames*, and *Life's Little Ironies*. Chap 5 ("The Struggles of Men") treats *The Mayor of Casterbridge* and *The Woodlanders*; Chap 6 ("Let the Day Perish"), *Tess of the d'Urbervilles* and *Jude the Obscure*; Chap 7 ("An Iliad of Europe"), *The Dynasts*. At this point Mr. Howe seems to have tired of inventing titles; thus Chap 8 ("The Lyric Poems") and Chap 9 ("Last Years").]

2988 Huss, Roy. "Social Change and Moral Decay in the Novels of Thomas Hardy," DALHOUSIE REVIEW, XLVII (Spring 1967), 28–44.

In H's vision of the world, the creative force manifests itself unconsciously and indifferently, though not necessarily maliciously, through Nature. Man is, however, not only the victim of nature; he is also the victim of his own psychological development. The first cause, the Immanent Will, is imperfect, hence, Nature, man and finally Society, must also be imperfect and in conflict. This theme (man vs. society) is most characteristic of H's final work. H may have been impressed by the Parnell scandal of 1890 (cf. parallel between Parnell and Jude). The works of Ibsen may also have exerted some influence on H. One of H's most basic notions is the antithesis between town life (social evils) and a rural existence (natural goodness). In *The Return of the Native* the intrusion of the values of an urban culture (Paris) into the social and cultural values of a rural existence is part of the tragic situation. In *Under the Greenwood Tree*, an idealization of rustic culture is implicit in the notion of its stability; the tone is mock-tragic, humorous, but the book nevertheless carries H's conviction that change in the form of material progress is undesirable. For H, social convention, of which he speaks pejoratively, must be carefully distinguished from custom and tradition, of which he generally approves. Certain rural customs (in Freudian terms, libido finding expression in the superego) like rural dancing are sensual, though not immoral pleasures. But a "skimmity-ride" (*The Mayor of Casterbridge*) in a semi-rural town develops, with the urban spirit, into a cruel device of torture. It is not marriage *per se* that H attacks in the later novels but rather society's legal and sacerdotal sanction of its inflexibility. For H, any remnant of a convention or law which falsifies and distorts the human natural law will inevitably cause a psychological derangement (cf. Angel Clare's sleep-walking scene, Grace Melbury's schizophrenic personality and Sue Bridehead.) At best, H's concept of social amelioration remains stated only in negative terms, as in Jude's dying speech. For any further hope one must turn to *The Dynasts* with its suggestion of the possible development of consciousness in the Immanent Will.

2989 Hynes, Samuel. "Introduction," GREAT SHORT WORKS OF THOMAS HARDY, ed with an introduction by Samuel Hynes (NY: Harper & Row, 1967), pp. vii–xxvii.

Under the Greenwood Tree is H's most "amiable" novel. The genre of the work might be described as "Parish history," "the literary representation of the collective content of the rustic mind, as it exists in a traditional rural society." The Parish history form provides the basic structure of the work, i.e., seasonal.

2990 Kovacsi, Gabor, and Ross Pudaloff. "Either Rage or Submit: The Human Body in Casterbridge," PAUNCH, No. 30 (Dec 1967), 48–66.

Chap 29 of *The Mayor of Casterbridge* provides an opportunity for H to comment on man's own brutality and gives revealing insight into the lives of some of the principal characters. The bull with a ring through its nostril is an example of man's use of brutality to control the bull. "Although a symbol of sexual potency, the bull is subject to man's will." The bull may symbolize human passion without restraint. The bull also symbolizes Henchard: "manhood can only rage with blind force or submit completely, having a copper ring of conscience and false ideas welded around it." Henchard is controlled by consciousness and community morals. Susan used the weapons of "mildness and defenselessness which best controls Henchard." Henchard, like other characters, is troubled by a "conflict between flesh and spirit." Elizabeth and Farfrae are also caught up in the conflict. They are led around like the bull with "the nose-ring of the culture" and social morality which dictates and controls their actions. "But Henchard also shows that our involvement in the culture may be too deep to create new and better alternatives without violently destroying ourselves along with the culture."

2991 Kramer, Dale. "Two 'New' Texts of Thomas Hardy's *The Woodlanders*," STUDIES IN BIBLIOGRAPHY, XX (1967), 135–50.

To the five known distinct texts of this H novel are now added two "American" texts which "constitute separate stages of composition of that novel"; also, the manuscript seems now to be itself a separate version. In view of the number and types of differences among the four earliest versions of *The Woodlanders*, it is evident that H sent, in monthly installments, one set of advance proof sheets to America for use by HARPER'S BAZAR after he had made only a comparatively few revisions. These revisions were copied onto another set of proof sheets. This second set was sent to America after more revisions were made, and this set provided copy for the Harper book text. The absence of trends in the Harper book revisions indicates that this second set of proofs was also mailed in installments, probably within a few days after the installments of the first set; this indication is supported by noting that the main purpose of the second set was precautionary, against loss of the first. In revising still a third set of proofs, to be returned to MACMILLAN'S MAGAZINE, H altered or deleted some of the revisions made in the two sets of advance proofs sent to America, in addition to making many completely new revisions.

2992 Lawyer, W. R. "Thomas Hardy's *Jude the Obscure*," PAUNCH, No. 28 (Feb 1967), 6–54.

Jude the Obscure "perceived contextually is the most vivid and intense expression of sexual repression and frustration in the English novel." Jude Fawley's life is impoverished as a "direct result of his pursuance of a boy-embraced and socially reinforced image of himself as 'one of society's worthies.'" This image so dominates his experience that the natural man rarely achieves expression. "The body-life however, cannot be put down completely and it seeks expression in an austere life with Sue." But this life fails to give Jude the fulfillment that he needs. Once Jude's body-life has been activated by Arabella, it never gives in to the point that it will permit Jude to make socially acceptable advances in his mind-life. "Despite his [H's] damning portrait of Arabella, there is no doubt that it is she who brings Jude to life. . . . Sue is obviously a compromise between a life with Arabella, and a death in Academia . . . she is sexually 'fastidious' and so narcissistic that to live with her can only be damaging to the physical and psychic well-being of the male [Jude] who fails [sic] for her image without recognizing her limitations."

2993 Levi, Peter, S. J. "Dorset Hardy," TIMES LITERARY SUPPLEMENT (Lond), 22 June 1967, p. 559.
Visits to H were rewarding; the antiquarian aspect of his work "is fundamentally important to Hardy's mind." His prefaces were not intended to be about literary theory but to provide information. H had "personal profundity." [Letter to editor opposing reviewer of Orel's HARDY'S PERSONAL WRITINGS ("The Dorset Hardy," ibid, 15 June 1967, p. 531).]

2994 Litz, A. Walton. "Introduction," *The Return of the Native* (NY: Houghton Mifflin, 1967), pp. v–xv.
In *The Return of the Native*, "the dark workings of circumstance are lightened occasionally by a nobility of character which owes nothing to heredity or environment." In his later works, H sought "the perspective of philosophical understanding, but in *The Return of the Native* perspective and balance come most often from an almost theatrical sense of the past." Even if Egdon Heath itself is a timeless setting, H "as narrator is acutely aware of his own uneasy place in time." The tension of H's mind is reflected in both the structure and the characterization of the novel. In order to integrate the "old illusions" of the ballad-literature with the "new alignment of his own age," H needed a conventional form which would "give order to his experience and mediate between the extremes of ancient ritual and deterministic philosophy." He found it in the classical tragedies of Greece and the neoclassical tragedies of Continental literature. His use of the tragic conventions may be divided into three categories: "his observance of the neoclassical unities, his use of 'chorus' figures, and his adherence to a five-part pattern of rising and falling action." H was probably not entirely aware of his failure to give the same stature and dignity to the novel's two major characters. Clym Yeobright is "not a tragic but a

pathetic figure, a victim of outside events rather than those conflicting passions which mark the tragic hero." In sharp contrast, Eustacia Vye "stands forth as a compelling and fully realized character, the main source of the novels' extraordinary power over our imaginations."

2995 Loveday, Thomas. "Hardy Honoured by Bristol University," HARDYANA: A COLLECTION OF SHORT MEMORABILIA AND OTHER MATTERS OF HARDY INTEREST, ed by J. Stevens Cox (Birling, Mount Durand, St. Peter Port, Guernsey: Toucan P, 1967), pp. 7–9.

[An exchange of letters, March to July 1925, between H and Loveday to arrange the conferring of an honorary degree on H by the newly founded Bristol University; it was conferred at H's home 15 July 1925. Also see J. Stephens Cox (pub and general editor), Monographs on the Life of Thomas Hardy (1962).]

2996 Male, Margaret. "Cleaner at Max Gate," HARDYANA: A COLLECTION OF SHORT MEMORABILIA AND OTHER MATTERS OF HARDY INTEREST, ed by J. Stevens Cox (Birling, Mount Durand, St. Peter Port, Guernsey: Toucan P, 1967), pp. 28–29.

H "never would recognise people who worked for him if he passed them in the street." H was a very shy man. Mrs. H was nice, quiet, and reserved. [Memories of 1920. Also see J. Stevens Cox (pub and general editor), Monographs on the Life of Thomas Hardy (1962).]

2997 Marshall, William H. "The End of the Quest," THE WORLD OF THE VICTORIAN NOVEL (South Brunswick & NY: A. S. Barnes, 1967) pp. 34, 93, 99, 127–28, 404–24, 456, 466, 480–81.

The Return of the Native is a late use of the myth of identity. Although there are certain elements of irony in *Jude the Obscure*, the novel emphasizes absurdity, which by definition excludes irony. Unlike earlier writers, H uses chance and coincidence to show the lack of purpose and order in the universe. Jude's stubborn belief in and love of order indicates his failure to adapt and causes him to repeatedly misinterpret his own experience. Jude is unable to establish his identity because he tries to base it on an order he supposes exists outside the self rather than seeking order within the self. Jude and Sue Bridehead represent the ideal combination of Matthew Arnold's Hebraism and Hellenism which can exist only in art, never in reality.

2998 May, Charles E. "The Loss of God and the Search for Order; A Study of Thomas Hardy's Structure and Meaning in Three Genres," DISSERTATION ABSTRACTS, XXVII (Jan–March 1967), 2535A. Unpublished dissertation, Ohio University, 1966.

2999 Meggison, Dorothy. "Anecdote of Hardy's Heart Burial," Hardyana: A Collection of Short Memorabilia and Other Matters of Hardy Interest, ed by J. Stevens Cox (Birling, Mount Durand, St. Peter Port, Guernsey: Toucan P, 1967), p. 21.

Dorchester people resented the separate burial as sacrilegious. [Also see J. Stevens Cox (pub and general editor), Monographs on the Life of Thomas Hardy (1962).]

3000 Montgomery, Marion. "The Pursuit of the Worthy: Thomas Hardy's Greekness in *Jude the Obscure*," Denver Quarterly, I (Winter 1967), 29–43.

There has been an "overwhelming movement in fiction during this century away from the lively, elusive center of dramatic art, the mystery of the perversely heroic." H's great strength is not a sophisticated technique but "a huge and brooding sympathy with and love of worthy human desire, a desire inevitably thwarted by human frailty and the gin of the world." When Arthur Mizner ("*Jude the Obscure* as a Tragedy," Southern Review, VI (Summer 1940), 193–213) says H fails as a tragedian in *Jude the Obscure*, he "is putting too much trust in the autobiographical nature of Jude and not enough emphasis on Hardy's ironic view of Jude's failure." H presents "a complication of drama and not a failure of his philosophy." "Jude is *worthy*, but his sense of his true worth, his opinion of his capabilities, exceeds the reality of his possibilities."

3001 Neville, Derek. "Mrs. Hardy and the 'Tramp,' " Hardyana: A Collection of Short Memorabilia and Other Matters of Hardy Interest, ed by J. Stevens Cox (Birling, Mount Durand, St. Peter Port, Guernsey: Toucan P, 1967), pp. 9–10.

[Anecdote of peddling some poems to H's widow. Also see J. Stevens Cox (pub and general editor), Monograph on the Life of Thomas Hardy (1962).]

3002 O'Dea, Raymond. "The 'Haunting Shade' that Accompanies the Virtuous Elizabeth-Jane in *The Mayor of Casterbridge*," Victorian Newsletter, No. 31 (Spring 1967), 33–36.

Elizabeth-Jane, " 'that flower of nature' " as H calls her, has a dual role in the novel: she is at once associated with and symbolizes life, knowledge, love and death, ignorance, sin. On one hand she functions as the unwitting cause of much of the sorrow. From not knowing the truth of her parentage springs much of Henchard's sorrow; her " 'craving for correctness' " contributes to Lucetta's final agony. "The malignancy that accompanies this maiden is never really understood by her." On the other hand, Elizabeth-Jane embodies "the creative or life force." Unlike Henchard and Lucetta who "try to fulfill personal wishes and desires" and therefore lose the will to live, Elizabeth-Jane "cooperates with nature," has a minimum of personal wishes and so triumphantly survives. [Badly written.]

3003 Palmer, Leslie H. "The Ironic Mr. Hardy; Irony As a Technique in the Novels of Thomas Hardy," DISSERTATION ABSTRACTS, XXVII (April–June 1967), 4262A. Unpublished dissertation, University of Tennessee, 1966.

3004 Parsons, W. G. L. A "MELLSTOCK QUIRE" BOY'S RECOLLECTIONS OF THOMAS HARDY (Mount Durand, St. Peter Port, Guernsey: Toucan P, 1967).

[Reminiscences of the production of THE MELLSTOCK QUIRE, adapted from H's *Under the Greenwood Tree*, in 1918 at the Corn Exchange, Dorchester, by one of the two lead singers in the production and written about fifty years after the production. Also see J. Stevens Cox (pub and general editor), Monographs on the Life of Thomas Hardy (1962).]

3005 Peterson, Audrey C. "Point of View in Thomas Hardy's *The Mayor of Casterbridge* and *Tess of the d'Urbervilles*," DISSERTATION ABSTRACTS, XXVIII (1967), 240A–41A. Unpublished dissertation, University of Southern California, 1967.

3006 Pitts, Arthur W., Jr. "24. Hardy's 'Channel Firing,' 9," EXPLICATOR, XXVI (Nov 1967), Item 24.

At the beginning of stanza three, cows stop chewing and drool with fright: this realistic touch indicates, more vividly than any detail in stanza two, the effect of the continual loud "gunnery practice" mentioned later.

3007 Platt, H. E. A. "A Youthful Encounter With Thomas Hardy," HARDYANA: A COLLECTION OF SHORT MEMORABILIA AND OTHER MATTERS OF HARDY INTEREST, ed by J. Stevens Cox (Birling, Mount Durand, St. Peter Port, Guernsey: Toucan P, 1967), pp. 12–13.

On the one occasion of meeting H (1919) in the company of Miss Mansell, "who was understood to be a leading member of the Hardy Circle" and who seemed to be propagating a " 'Hardy Cult,' " H and his wife were kind and offered to provide introductions to various publishing firms. [Also see J. Stevens Cox (pub and general editor), Monographs on the Life of Thomas Hardy (1962).]

3008 Sampson, Edward C. "Telling Time by the Stars in *Far From the Madding Crowd*," NOTES AND QUERIES, XIV (Feb 1967), 63–64.

Since H's astronomical calculations are scientifically correct, it is possible to ascertain the chronology of the novel through H's descriptions of the stars.

3009 Sanders, Mary Kirven. "*Leaves of Grass* in the Prophetic Tradition: A Study of Walt Whitman's Poetic Method." Unpublished dissertation, University of North Carolina, 1967.
[Contains about forty pages comparing Whitman with H as a prophetic poet.]

3010 Sansom, Clive. "Hardy—An Anecdote," Hardyana: A Collection of Short Memorabilia and Other Matters of Hardy Interest, ed by J. Stevens Cox (Birling, Mount Durand, St. Peter Port, Guernsey: Toucan P, 1967), p. 12.
[Hearsay anecdote about fussiness of the first Mrs. H. Also see J. Stevens Cox (pub and general editor), Monographs on the Life of Thomas Hardy (1962).]

3011 Schweik, Robert C. "The Early Development of Hardy's *Far From the Madding Crowd*," Texas Studies in Literature and Language, IX (Autumn 1967), 415–28.
[Reconstructs from the early manuscript segment of *Far From the Madding Crowd*, which Hardy submitted to the Cornhill Magazine in 1873, the original nature of the novel which H later (probably in late 1873) revised extensively. In this revision, Hardy dramatizes Fanny Robin's story and develops Boldwood as another principle character, thus laying "the ground work for a broader treatment of human feeling than was possible within the conventional love triangle with which he had begun." His efforts to revise suggest also that he was seeking (in spite of his own disclaimers) to be something more than merely a skillful serial novelist.]

3012 Shepherd, Mrs. M. "William Barnes and Thomas Hardy," Hardyana: A Collection of Short Memorabilia and Other Matters of Hardy Interest, ed by J. Stevens Cox (Birling, Mount Durand, St. Peter Port, Guernsey: Toucan P, 1967), pp. 18–21.
John Shepherd, a farmer and a parishioner of William Barnes at Whitcombe, first met H "before 1890" but did not like H as he liked Barnes; he considered H "as a very unpleasant man" who "did not treat his wives kindly." [Also see J. Stevens Cox (pub and general editor), Monographs on the Life of Thomas Hardy (1962).]

3013 Siemens, Lloyd George. "The Contexts of Hardy's Poetry," Dissertation Abstracts, XXVIII (1967), 643A–44A. Unpublished dissertation, University of Wisconsin, 1967.

3014 Smith, Curtis C. "Natural Settings and Natural Characters in Hardy's *Desperate Remedies* and *A Pair of Blue Eyes*," Thoth, VIII (Spring 1967), 84–97.

Although setting in *Desperate Remedies* rarely "has its own independent life" as it has in H's greater novels, H "is already preoccupied with whether his characters fit into Nature." The three main characters in the novel are natural, but in vastly different ways. Cytherea is "vibrant, healthy, and normal"; Miss Aldclyffe is all "instinct and passion"; she resembles " 'Nature in the tropics.' " From these contrasting viewpoints we learn that H's view is that "although natural instinct can be good, it is dangerous unless controlled." In *A Pair of Blue Eyes* H associates Elfride Swancourt with unrestrained, intense Nature: "she is thoroughly its creature," wild, changeable, mortal. Stephen Smith seems unsuited to Elfride because he "has lost touch with Nature." Henry Knight is also unnatural in his ignorance of Nature's beings and ways. In both early novels, H "hesitates between youth and maturity, innocence and experience, passiveness and aggressiveness."

3015 Smith, Peter D. "William Cox and *The Trumpet-Major*," NOTES AND QUERIES, XIV (Feb 1967), 64–65.
[Quotes from a letter which appeared in TIMES (Lond), 2 Jan 1871, p. 12: a possible source for H's knowledge of Napoleonic Wars and for *The Trumpet-Major*.]

3016 Stanley, Mrs. A[dolphine]. "Cook to the Hardy Household —1916–1918," HARDYANA: A COLLECTION OF SHORT MEMORABILIA AND OTHER MATTERS OF HARDY INTEREST, ed by J. Stevens Cox (Birling, Mount Durand, St. Peter Port, Guernsey: Toucan P, 1967), pp. 14–17.
[Trained as a maid in the Dugdale household, before Florence became H's secretary and later his wife, Mrs. Stanley was hired as cook for the Hs in 1916. She found Florence Hardy kind and generous but H a very stingy man who hated children, dogs, and visitors.]

3017 Sweeney, Patricia R. "The Dangerous Journey: The Initiation Theme in Eight Victorian Novels," DISSERTATION ABSTRACTS, XXVIII (1967), 1451A. Unpublished dissertation, University of California (Berkeley), 1967.

3018 Taube, Myron. " 'The Atmosphere . . . from Cyprus': Hardy's Development of Theme in *Jude the Obscure*," VICTORIAN NEWSLETTER, No. 32 (Fall 1967), 16–18.
The scene in church in which Jude watches Sue is not proof that Jude is at heart a pagan but that his sexual attraction to Sue "is a rebound from the animal sexuality of Arabella . . . to a higher sexual attraction." The key is H's reference to Cyprus which, during the Hellenistic period, was "most intimately connected with Aphrodite." Hence, H here has substituted a higher sexual symbol—Cyprus—for a lower—the pig's penis—to show the

different, although still sexual, attraction Sue and Arabella exert on him. [Reply to Ward Hellstrom, "*Jude the Obscure* as Pagan Self-Assertion," ibid, No. 29 (Spring 1966), pp. 26–27.]

3019 Tilley, R. H. "Hardy and the Safety Bicycle," HARDYANA: A COLLECTION OF SHORT MEMORABILIA AND OTHER MATTERS OF HARDY INTEREST, ed by J. Stevens Cox (Birling, Mount Durand, St. Peter Port, Guernsey: Toucan P, 1967), p. 22.
[Ernest William Tilley taught H how to ride the new bicycle about 1890. He thought H was a very shy man. Also see J. Stevens Cox (pub and general editor), Monographs on the Life of Thomas Hardy (1962).]

3020 Walker, Mary F. "Remembers An Encounter with Hardy," HARDYANA: A COLLECTION OF SHORT MEMORABILIA AND OTHER MATTERS OF HARDY INTEREST, ed by J. Stevens Cox (Birling, Mount Durand, St. Peter Port, Guernsey: Toucan P, 1967), p. 25.
[Inconsequential anecdote by daughter of Lady Pinney, "a frequent visitor to Max Gate." Also see J. Stevens Cox (pub and general editor), Monographs on the Life of Thomas Hardy (1962).]

3021 Weatherby, Hal L. "Jude the Victorian," SOUTHERN HUMANITIES REVIEW, I (Summer 1967), 158–69.
In *Jude the Obscure*, more than other novels, H specifically designs characters to illustrate Victorian ideas. Jude is a Wordsworthian child, Tractarian youth, and freethinking "old" man at his death; Sue Bridehead is an enlightened woman/enthusiastic liberal (George Eliot), Paterian aesthete (sensation for its own sake), and Swinburnian pagan ("abstract and bloodless"); Arabella Dunn is Victorian crassness and *parvenu* (i.e., false hair, dimples, materialism). Jude's humanity partakes of Arabella's coarseness and Sue's spirituality (both are *femmes fatales* to him; both are forces in Victorian life). Jude's progress from "innocence to painful experience," a Victorian leitmotif, parallels Matthew Arnold's. Jude is also the Victorian Quentin Compson caught between Modernity and Traditionalism, " 'between two worlds, one dead, the other powerless to be born.' "

3022 Weatherby, H[al] L. "Old-Fashioned Gods: Eliot on Lawrence and Hardy," SEWANEE REVIEW, LXXV (Spring 1967), 301–16.
Although D. H. Lawrence and T. S. Eliot saw close similarities between H's and Lawrence's work, "both Eliot and Lawrence are mistaken in their estimate of Hardy." The view of Lawrence and Eliot that H is essentially a "Romantic primitivist" is unfortunate because it is only one strain in his writing. Moreover, in H's novels, radical individualism is "measured against the demands of a [thoroughly traditional] society." A major difference between Lawrence and H is that while Lawrence has confidence in the Life

Force, H does not. H's pessimistic philosophy is "based on the old view of the Will as original sin," while for Lawrence "redemption is *in* the Will." While H shares Lawrence's "belief in the power of the Will . . . he hated and feared that power." In H's novels, radical individualism may be tamed by subduing self to the traditional community; failing to achieve this harmony leads to tragedy. As in *The Return of the Native* Clym, Eustacia, Mrs. Yeobright and Wildeve "have separated themselves from these patterns of traditional life" and seem to "have literally lost the consciousness which can see above time and which would be necessary for their survival." Wessex, although in some novels in "a radical state of decay," is "a fertile, and . . . a primitive order" which offers hope of healing and restoration to deracinated, modern, urban men and women. Except for the absence of widely shared religious belief, Wessex meets Eliot's requirements for a "traditional order."

3023 Webber, Emma Mary. "Daily Help at Max Gate," HARDYANA: A COLLECTION OF SHORT MEMORABILIA AND OTHER MATTERS OF HARDY INTEREST, ed by J. Stevens Cox (Birling, Mount Durand, St. Peter Port, Guernsey: Toucan P, 1967), pp. 25–26.
[Anecdotes of T. E. Lawrence's visits (1924), H's quietness, H's dislike of American callers. Also see J. Stevens Cox (pub and general editor), Monographs on the Life of Thomas Hardy (1962).]

3024 Weber, Carl J. "Hardy's Debt to Sir Frederick Macmillan," ENGLISH LANGUAGE NOTES, V (Dec 1967), 120–29.
Frederick Macmillan, according to evidence in Harold Macmillan's WINDS OF CHANCE and evidence from an extant letter in the Dorchester museum, was responsible for Holt's publication of the 1873 edition of *Under the Greenwood Tree*, with H's name on the title page, and for the profitable publication, after 1902, of H's Wessex novels by Macmillan of London.

3025 Weber, Carl J. "Two Fires at Max Gate," ESSAYS IN AMERICAN AND ENGLISH LITERATURE PRESENTED TO BRUCE ROBERT MCELDERRY, JR., ed by Max F. Schulz, et al (Athens, Ohio: Ohio UP, 1967), pp. 306–26.
The two bonfires of letters and papers which H and his second wife made in 1919 and 1928 "have doubtless deprived the reader and the future biographer of much that would have been helpful." Even so, the cache of H letters, now in the Dorset County Museum, contains much valuable material.

3026 Weber, Carl J., and Frank B. Pinion. "*The Mayor of Casterbridge*: An Anglo-American Dialogue," LIBRARY CHRONICLE OF THE UNIVERSITY OF TEXAS, VIII (1967), 3–12.

[Spirited dialogue which touches on the time-setting of *The Mayor of Casterbridge*, H's alleged recklessness in crowding too much incident into the novel, and on the novel's relative position among H's other novels.]

3027 Weber, Emily Mary Benita. "The Social Hardy," Hardyana: A Collection of Short Memorabilia and Other Matters of Hardy Interest, ed by J. Stevens Cox (Birling, Mount Durand, St. Peter Port, Guernsey: Toucan P, 1967), pp. 26–27.

Visits to Max Gate in the 1890s revealed H and his wife to be hospitable, to enjoy the company of the young, and H's "wide general knowledge" to include "a remarkable knowledge of Spain and its history." "The local folk had little interest in Hardy." Among interesting people who visited Max Gate was Siegfried Sassoon. H thought his own poetry would live and was surprised to hear *Tess of the d'Urbervilles* and *Jude the Obscure* suggested instead. [Prints a letter of Oct 1902 from H to Miss Thornton (Mrs. Weber) accompanying a copy of *Under the Greenwood Tree*. Also see J. Stevens Cox (pub and general editor), Monographs on the Life of Thomas Hardy (1962).]

3028 Wedmore, Millicent. "A Childhood Meeting With Hardy," Hardyana: A Collection of Short Memorabilia and Other Matters of Hardy Interest, ed by J. Stevens Cox (Birling, Mount Durand, St. Peter Port, Guernsey: Toucan P, 1967), pp. 13–14.

Sir Frederick Wedmore, who visited H at Max Gate in the 1880s, greatly admired H. On the occasion of the production of a one-act play version of "The Three Strangers," H was "absolutely absorbed in his own characters and their sayings and doings." [Also see J. Stevens Cox (pub and general editor), Monographs on the Life of Thomas Hardy (1962).]

3029 Williams, Raymond. "Literature and Rural Society," Listener, LXXVIII (16 Nov 1967), 630–32.

New conditions after 1840 produced "a social crisis of a specifically modern kind" in rural England: low wages and high prices for the laborer, shortage of capital and increasing rents for the tenant farmer. "This is the real world of Hardy." It blinds us to H's real meaning if we impose a "pastoral convention" or "a vision of a prospering countryside destroyed by Corn Law repeal" on H's vision of rural England. H's characters are "subjected to pressures from within the system of living, not from outside it." Each of H's rural characters "has a dominant personal history, which in psychological terms bears a direct relation to the social character of the change" in rural life. The marriage choice becomes more difficult within a changing society, hence, H's concern with "false marriage" parallels a very real social problem.

3030 Wright, Walter F. THE SHAPING OF THE DYNASTS: A STUDY IN THOMAS HARDY (Lincoln: University of Nebraska P, 1967).
The philosophic framework which informs *The Dynasts* and much of H's other important work is traceable both to his very extensive reading in poets and philosophers, dating from the 1860s and ranging from the Bible to Hartmann, and to his own "philosophic impressions" as they are recorded in his autobiography, in the margins of his books, and in his notebooks. The philosophy thus derived is remarkably eclectic and is not a borrowing from any individual thinker. H's thinking and reading seem to have been consistently pointed toward an effort to reconcile determinism with man's capacity for significant moral choice. His attitude toward metrics and poetic technique in general is, similarly, the result of a careful, analytical study of the verse and the poetic theories of a host of earlier writers. In both cases, his notes and comments indicate that he sought to learn from others without implicitly denying the truth of his own thinking and feeling. When he came to write and later to revise *Dynasts*, he employed basically the same pattern of thought and procedure: that is, he studied extensively the history of the Napoleonic era but steadfastly refused to allow his respect for history to override his conviction that fact had to be interpreted imaginatively. The finished drama is, therefore, conspicuously faithful to historical fact and rich in historical detail, but it remains an individualized imaginative synthesis rather than a literal transcription of its sources. [An extremely valuable source of factual information and hitherto unpublished notes, comments, etc.]

3031 Yevish, Irving A. "The Attack on *Jude the Obscure*: A Reappraisal Some Seventy Years After," JOURNAL OF GENERAL EDUCATION, XVIII (Jan 1967), 239–48.
The chief cause of the uproar over *Jude the Obscure* was "Hardy's attack on Oxford (Christminster) and the whole of the caste system that Oxford implied." And so the press's attack on *Jude* was made when the novel, "at the moment of its appearance was most vulnerable"—the whole sex-marriage problem—"and the outcry all but obscured the university theme." It was Christminster, then, not sex that was Jude's ruling passion; "sex, for Jude, was merely a refuge from disappointment."

3032 Ziegler, Carl H. "Thomas Hardy's Critical and Popular Reception in Germany, 1873–1963," DISSERTATION ABSTRACTS, XXVII (April-June 1967), 4233A. Unpublished dissertation, Vanderbilt University, 1966.

3033 Zietlow, Paul. "The Tentative Mode of Hardy's Poems," VICTORIAN POETRY, V (Summer 1967), 113–26.
The hypothesis of earlier critics that H's poems "reveal traceable intellectual

growth" is questionable. Rather, a "tentative mode [a questioning, probing uncertainty] prevails throughout Hardy's career."

1968

3034 Alcorn, John M. "Hardy to Lawrence: A Study in Naturism," DISSERTATION ABSTRACTS, XXIX (1968), 251A–52A. Unpublished dissertation, New York University, 1966.

3035 Atkinson, F. G. "Hardy's *The Woodlanders* and A Stanza by Keats," NOTES AND QUERIES, XV (Nov 1968), 423.
H's ironic passage, near the end of chap 17 in *The Woodlanders*, concerning trees budding before their time, is similar to a passage in Keats's lines beginning "In drear-nighted December." H's lines are a definite echo of Keats's.

3036 Bailey, J. O. "Fact and Fiction in Hardy's Poetry," CEA CRITIC, XXX (March 1968), 10–11.
Most but not all of H's poems are factual. "After the Last Breath" talks of peaceful death after the infirmity of his mother; another fact—from observation years earlier—is "I Watched a Blackbird"; a fact from reading—"The Inscription"—is perhaps linked with investigation. "Squire Hooper," however, is based solely on reading, and "The War-Wife of Catknoll" is possibly based on registry-study but is mostly fiction. "Standing by the Mantelpiece" may be either.

3037 Ball, Reginald Lacy. RECOLLECTION OF A VISIT TO THOMAS HARDY (Mount Durand, St. Peter Port, Guernsey: Toucan P, 1968).
H's major novels, read in youth, revealed "a romantic, dramatic and suffering world." Army experience in Dorchester from May to Sept 1916 vivified scenes in H's *The Mayor of Casterbridge*. During a visit on 16 Sept 1915, recollections of scenes in *The Trumpet-Major* and *The Woodlanders* were discussed. [Reproduces a postcard from H and a photograph of H's grave.]

3038 Barber, D. F. (ed). CONCERNING THOMAS HARDY: A COMPOSITE PORTRAIT FROM MEMORY (Lond: Charles Skilton, 1968).
[Based on the first forty-two titles of Monographs on the Life of Thomas Hardy, published by J. Stevens Cox at the Toucan Press. These pamphlets are listed under 1962, and each pamphlet is abstracted under the date of first publication. Barber's volume organizes the material under the follow-

ing heads: Hardy's Ancestors, The Child and the Young Man, Love and Thomas Hardy, Man, Host and Employer, The Social Celebrity, Death and Burial. Appendix I lists the first forty-two titles in the monograph series, although not as fully or accurately as the listing in the present bibliography; Appendix II is essentially a reprinting of Monograph 39, IDENTIFICATION OF FICTITIOUS PLACE NAMES IN HARDY'S WORKS, ed by J. Stevens Cox (1968).]

3039 Benvenuto, Richard E. "The Romantic Tradition in Thomas Hardy's Major Novels," DISSERTATION ABSTRACTS, XXIX (1968), 1508A–9A. Unpublished dissertation, Ohio State University, 1968.

3040 Brinkley, Richard. THOMAS HARDY AS A REGIONAL NOVELIST. With special reference to *The Return of the Native* (Mount Durand, St. Peter Port, Guernsey: Toucan P, 1968).

"The regional novel describes a particular area so as to show the reader the peculiarities which distinguish life, landscape and settlement of that area from those of other districts." H is regional because of his background, his temperament, and the society he describes. H is attracted by the characteristic features that are preserved and unchanged, and paradoxically, the same society affected by change. *Far From the Madding Crowd*, *The Return of the Native*, and *The Woodlanders* describe communities not greatly changed. *Tess of the d'Urbervilles* and *The Mayor of Casterbridge* look to the customs being supplanted in town and country. H used the regional novel to express his own view on human life. H's regional character has peculiarities characteristic of his locality or characteristics integrated and associated with that locality, as exemplified in the characters of *Native* who illustrate both the static and the changing. Some are linked to the locale by occupation (the furze cutter) or temperament (Clym Yeobright), but this does not eliminate their likes and antagonisms. Nonetheless, the characters are universal. The local aspect of the characters increases the reality. Events in *Native* spring from Egdon Heath, such as the 5 November celebrations or the Christmas mumming play. They emphasize geography and the relations between the people who live there, as in the relationship between Eustacia Vye and Clym Yeobright. Other events are regional because they spring from the relationship of people to Egdon Heath. An event may also be regional because it becomes a topic of regional interest, i.e., when Thomasin Yeobright intends to marry Damon Wildeve. The regionality of the novel is also accomplished by the narrative style in description (by introduction of local words into "Standard English") and the conversational passages. Egdon Heath is passive but it is affected by the people who live there, and the character of Egdon Heath is the result of life upon it, the way its inhabitants move, act, and talk. H also considers Egdon Heath from geographical (detailed presentation of the landscape), historical (the past and the present), and social (the corporate life of the community) viewpoints. H attains the regional aspect by making the relationship between human beings and the Fate which controls them and their lives the theme which is mirrored in the relation of Egdon Heath and its inhabitants. [Contains two photographs of the region. Also see J. Stevens Cox (pub and general editor), Monographs on the Life of Thomas Hardy (1962).]

> **3041** Brunson, C. J. "Toward *Fin de Siècle* Emancipation: The Development of Independence in Thomas Hardy's Wessex Women," DISSERTATION ABSTRACTS, XXVIII (1968), 3138A. Unpublished dissertation, Texas Tech College, 1967.

> **3042** Casagrande, Peter J. "Conflict and Pattern in the Novels of Thomas Hardy," DISSERTATION ABSTRACTS, XXVIII (1968), 3664A. Unpublished dissertation, Indiana University, 1967.

> **3043** Chapman, Raymond. THE VICTORIAN DEBATE: ENGLISH LITERATURE AND SOCIETY, 1832–1901 (Lond: Weidenfeld & Nicholson, 1968), pp. 62, 68, 69, 122, 124, 152, 168, 243, 263, 291, 300, 321, 322, 327–31.

H taught himself German from Cassell's POPULAR EDUCATOR, and he contributed serial fiction to such "new" journals as CORNHILL MAGAZINE, GOOD WORDS, and MACMILLAN'S MAGAZINE, although his works were sometimes thought "unsuitable." Eliot's and H's "profounder creations" are not as memorable as some of Dickens's characters; H at his best depicted significant physical settings "magnificently," as did Emily Brontë. The "force of unfolding destiny" in Eliot's work is "not so stark and blind" as in H's. With his "Candour in English Fiction," H contributed to the attack on censorship. H and Meredith contributed to the "intellectual growth of the novel." H's early works were derivative, but *Far From the Madding Crowd* showed his characteristic powers for drama and characterization. *The Return of the Native* revealed his talent for using setting integrally. Later novels show his ability for absorbing the intellectual currents of his time. In *Jude the Obscure*, the gloom of H's fictional world "seemed to . . . envelop the reader's world." Greek classicism gave H his "skill in lyrical epigram" and helped form *The Dynasts*. Man's inhumanity to man plays a larger role in H's later novels. His view of the workings of an uncontrollable destiny is conditioned by his compassion for human beings. H and Meredith "gave imaginative voice to the extremes of optimism and pessimism which Darwinism engendered in its time."

> **3044** Cox, J. Stevens (ed). DORCHESTER IN 1851 (Mount Durand, St. Peter Port, Guernsey: Toucan P, 1968); rptd from Hunt and Co.'s DIRECTORY OF DORSETSHIRE, 1851.

[Also see J. Stevens Cox (pub and general editor), Monographs on the Life of Thomas Hardy (1962).]

3045 Cox, J. Stevens. IDENTIFICATION OF FICTITIOUS PLACE NAMES IN HARDY'S WORKS (Mount Durand, St. Peter Port, Guernsey: Toucan P, 1968); enlgd as HARDY'S WESSEX: IDENTIFICATION OF FICTITIOUS PLACE NAMES IN HARDY'S WORKS (Mount Durand, St. Peter Port, Guernsey: Toucan P, 1970).

[An alphabetical listing of fictitious names in H's works and their proper identification, derived, with thirteen exceptions, from Hermann Lea's THOMAS HARDY'S WESSEX (1913) and (J. Stevens Cox [ed]), THOMAS HARDY THROUGH THE CAMERA'S EYE (1964). Also see J. Stevens Cox (pub and general editor), Monographs on the Life of Thomas Hardy (1962).]

3046 [Cox, J. Stevens (ed)]. LETTERS FROM EDEN PHILLPOTTS TO MRS. F. E. HARDY (Mount Durand, St. Peter Port, Guernsey: Toucan P, 1968).

[Contains five letters written 1915 (2), 1936 (2), and 1937, mainly pleasant social exchanges. Also see J. Stevens Cox (pub and general editor), Monographs on the Life of Thomas Hardy (1962).]

3047 Cox, J. Stevens. "Preface," THOMAS HARDY: MATERIALS FOR A STUDY OF HIS LIFE, TIMES AND WORKS, ed by J. Stevens Cox (Mount Durand, St. Peter Port, Guernsey: Toucan P, 1968), pp. 5–8.

[A description of the genesis and aim of the series.]

3048 Cox, J. Stevens (ed). THOMAS HARDY: MATERIALS FOR A STUDY OF HIS LIFE, TIMES AND WORKS (Monographs 1–35) (Mount Durand, St. Peter Port, Guernsey: Toucan P, 1968).

"This preliminary section is for binding with Monographs 1 to 35 making Volume One of 'Materials for the Study of the Life, Times and Works of Thomas Hardy.'" Contents, abstracted separately under author, all 1968; J. Stevens Cox, "Preface"; Richard Curle, "Introduction"; H. S. L. Dewar, "A Contemplative View of Hardy"; also included but not abstracted: "Some Hardy Dates," being mainly dates of births, deaths and marriages in the H family; "Additional Notes and Corrections to Monographs 1 to 35," primarily relevant to Monographs 3, 4, 6, 8, 9, 12, 14, 19, 20, 21, 22, 24, 25, 32, 35; "Contents," a list of the first thirty-five titles, authors, dates, and prices. [Also see J. Stevens Cox (pub and general editor), Monographs on the Life of Thomas Hardy (1962).]

3049 Curle, Richard. "Introduction," THOMAS HARDY: MATERIALS FOR A STUDY OF HIS LIFE, TIMES AND WORKS, ed by J. Stevens Cox (Mount Durand, St. Peter Port, Guernsey: Toucan P, 1968), pp. 9–10.

[Essentially "an Introduction to the Introduction," this note gives a brief review of the material in the series. Curle provided separate introductions (not abstracted) to the first twenty titles. Also see J. Stevens Cox (pub and general editor), Monographs on the Life of Thomas Hardy (1962).]

3050 Dalton, R. F. "Thomas Hardy's Alleged Son," NOTES AND QUERIES, XV (July 1968), 265–66.
The mystery of H's alleged son Randolph [Randal] is still unsolved, due to lack of information about the person who photographed a boy alleged to be Randolph.

3051 Davies, Walford. "An Allusion to Hardy's 'A Broken Appointment' in Dylan Thomas's 'In Country Sleep,' " NOTES AND QUERIES, XV (Feb 1968), 61–62.
H, Thomas's favorite modern poet, influenced Thomas's later poems. In "In Country Sleep," the speaker seeks to persuade a child to recognize the danger that comes in the real and metaphorical night: "Time, Death, and the loss of innocence." By the end of the poem "she has accepted the inevitability of Time and maturity"—a conclusion that gains force by Thomas's allusion to H's "A Broken Appointment." Thomas echoed H's emphatic line "You did not come" with "to grieve he will not come." The persona of H's poem is "a time-torn man"—"and it is partly to such an epithet that Thomas sought to reconcile his young girl."

3052 Davis, W. Eugene. *"Tess of the d'Urbervilles*: Some Ambiguities About A Pure Woman," NINETEENTH CENTURY FICTION, XXII (March 1968), 397–401.
Contradictions exist between the Tess who lives in the novel as an independent entity and the Tess H tried to create through his narrative intervention. H tries to explain and qualify Tess's actions, but Tess's own dynamic character overshadows his attempts. Despite H's interference, the novel survives because the reader ignores H's editorial views and instead concentrates his attention on Tess herself.

3053 Deacon, Lois. HARDY'S GRANDMOTHER, BETSY, AND HER FAMILY (Mount Durand, St. Peter Port, Guernsey: Toucan P, 1968); absorbed earlier in PROVIDENCE AND MR. HARDY, by Lois Deacon and Terry Coleman (1966).
[Describes and gives evidence for various births, marriages, and deaths in the Hand and Sparks families and links several members to H's novels. Reprints H's "Family Portraits." One version of this title was published in error without covers and without illustrations. Also see J. Stevens Cox (pub and general editor), Monographs on the Life of Thomas Hardy (1962).]

3054 Deacon, Lois. THE MOULES AND THOMAS HARDY. With an introduction by Canon Edward B. Brooks (Mount Durand, St. Peter Port, Guernsey: Toucan P, 1968); originally given as a lecture during the Hardy Festival, 18 July 1968, in St. George Church, Fordington, Dorchester; absorbed earlier in PROVIDENCE AND MR. HARDY, by Lois Deacon and Terry Coleman (1966).

H lived his life in close connection with the members of the Moule family. Rev. Henry Moule's work in the cholera epidemic of 1854 is chronicled by H in *The Mayor of Casterbridge* and the short story "A Changed Man." Moule's influence on H's literature is immense. H was under the influence of the elder sons of Henry Moule, and he makes frequent references to the Moule family in F. E. Hardy's THE LIFE OF THOMAS HARDY (1928, 1930). The "Clare" family of *Tess of the d'Urbervilles* depicted the Moules. Horace Moule, like Angel, and H were the non-evangelicals. Horace was the teacher, the critic. Horace's advice turned H from the study of Greek at the University. Tryphena entered H's life in the summer-autumn of 1867. In 1869 Tryphena went to a teacher training college. Horace enters her life at this point. *Jude the Obscure* details this in Sue Bridehead's confession to Phillotson; *A Pair of Blue Eyes* in Henry Knight helping Elfride. *Jude* develops *Blue Eyes*. H was angered at Horace and Tryphena to 1870 (*Blue Eyes*) and sorrowful at the end (*Jude*). Horace continued to encourage H, and Horace is found as the winning tongue in *Blue Eyes* (originally titled "A Winning Tongue Had He"), as Maybold of *Under the Greenwood Tree*, and as Francis Troy of *Far From the Madding Crowd*. Horace, in reviews, likened H's *Greenwood Tree* to Goethe's HERMANN AND DOROTHEA, a perceptive comparison based on the parallels. H molded Horace and himself into a mix that went into two or more fictional characters in each book. In most of H's novels one male character "dazzles" the heroine, as Horace dazzled Tryphena. "Tryphena's" attraction is her indifference and her oscillations. Horace appears in some of H's poems. In "Her Dilemma," he appears with Tryphena. This is reinforced by a partial drawing of the church at Fordington by H to accompany the poem. H "prosed" the situation in *Desperate Remedies*. The heroines of H's novels define Tryphena. H's poem "Standing by the Mantlepiece," published posthumously, was subtitled with Horace's initials. H included it in *Winter Words* to show the truth. The poem is made clearer by the LIFE. Also, the poems "Before my Friend Arrived," "The Five Students," "Confession to a Friend in Trouble," and "The Mound" are revealing. [Contains a poem, "The Muffled Peel" by H. M. Moule, and two photographs and a reproduction. Also see J. Stevens Cox (pub and general editor), Monographs on the Life of Thomas Hardy (1962).]

3055 Dewar, H. S. L. "A Contemplative View of Hardy," THOMAS HARDY: MATERIALS FOR A STUDY OF HIS LIFE, TIMES and Works, ed by J. Stevens Cox (Mount Durand, St. Peter Port, Guernsey: Toucan P, 1968), pp. 11–19.

A survey of the monographs in the series to date suggests that the peasant background of H was very influential and that he came on the scene "at the right time, since change was starting to take place." He was much influenced by music and his father's work as stonemason; his capacity for "criticism and exactitude" he derived from his mother. His characters were all drawn from "individuals or relatives he had known." His first and most influential school was Nature, in which he witnessed the "battles of the seasons" and, in his immediate environment, "the undeclared war between the landed and the landless." Despite what nature had taught him of strife, in later life he believed that "wars were doomed to vanish." He disliked the United States because he was an introvert. He sought to add to the Dorset countryman's tongue by going out of his way to search out old dialect words. He was constantly "questing after more and more knowledge," he was a close observer of detail, and he had a "photographic mind." He regarded Tryphena Sparks's rejecting him as a trick of fate which resulted in his living " 'for 60 years in a multi-caverned hell.' " The steady advance of science and invention resulted in his loss of faith and interest in theology; after 1899, "he stopped making marginal notes in his Bible." London had an ill effect on his health; his dyspepsia "may well have been in part the cause of his two unhappy marriages." The end of his friendship with Horace Moule seems "obscurely connected with Hardy's love for Tryphena." The pamphlets suggest H "as the peasant lifted out of environment and resenting the fact, often perhaps unconsciously, that he had lost one world, but failed fully to win his way into the other." The peasant strain perhaps resulted in his "real stinginess." He probably married Florence "for the sake of propriety." [Also see J. Stevens Cox (pub and general editor), Monographs on the Life of Thomas Hardy (1962).]

3056 Dewar, Stephen. "Introduction," Paupers, Criminals and Cholera at Dorchester in 1854, by Henry Moule (Mount Durand, St. Peter Port, Guernsey: Toucan P, 1968), pp. 1–2.

H remembered vividly and described in *The Mayor of Casterbridge* the cholera epidemic of 1854 in Fordington. [Reprints two letters addressed to H. R. H. The Prince Consort, first published in the Dorset County Chronicle, 21 and 28 Sept 1854, and collected in Eight Letters to His Royal Highness Prince Albert (1855), which record the events from the view of the man who saved the area from worse disaster by fighting the epidemic. Letter 1: On the responsibility of the Prince Consort and the Council of the Duchy of Cornwall to alleviate the suffering, and on the probable cause of the epidemic. Letter 2: On the living conditions of the poor in the stricken areas and the responsibility of the Council to improve them. Appendix: "Short Title Catalogue of the Works of the Rev. Henry Moule, 1801–1880." Also see J. Stevens Cox (pub and general editor), Monographs on the Life of Thomas Hardy (1962).]

3057 Diakonova, Nina. "Notes on the Evolution of the *Bildungsroman* in England," ZEITSCHRIFT FÜR ANGLISTIK UND AMERIKANISTIK (Berlin), XVI: 4 (1968), 341–51.

Beginning as the story of a hero whose experience leads him through trials to a secure place within society, the *Bildungsroman* underwent many transformations throughout the nineteenth and twentieth centuries. Many Victorians stressed the need for the hero to save himself from the corrupting influences of his world, and by the end of the century the *Bildungsroman* became a novel of defeat. Heroes like Jude Fawley in *Jude the Obscure* possess an integrity that drives them into isolation. Twentieth-century novelists, stressing the theme of alienation, the collapse of social norms, and the subjectivity of experience have virtually destroyed the traditional idea of the *Bildungsroman*.

3058 Edwards, Duane Darrell. "The Impressions of an Artist: A Study of Hardy's Novels," DISSERTATION ABSTRACTS, XXIX (1968), 1892A–93A. Unpublished dissertation, University of Wisconsin, 1968.

3059 Evans, Evelyn L. THE HOMES OF THOMAS HARDY. With an introduction by Richard Curle (Mount Durand, St. Peter Port, Guernsey: Toucan P, 1968).

[The daughter of A. H. Evans, who produced the dramatic versions of many of H's novels, depicts life in the various houses where H and members of his family at various times lived before he settled permanently at Max Gate; many anecdotes about people and places are given; J. Stevens Cox supplied many photographs to illustrate the commentary. Also see J. Stevens Cox (pub and general editor), Monographs on the Life of Thomas Hardy (1962).]

3060 Evans, Robert. "The Other Eustacia," NOVEL, I (Spring 1968), 251–59.

The "crucial question" in assessing H's novels as tragedies is to what extent do his main characters possess "that measure of moral dignity and worth essential to their role as tragic protagonists?" While H persuades us rhetorically, through personal description and scene, to accept Eustacia as "a woman of genuinely tragic stature," we see another Eustacia in the novel, "a selfish and self-deceiving girl." This "other Eustacia" is "morally and aesthetically alien to that austere tragic eminence upon which Hardy, through a failure in sensibility, placed her." By "emphatically colored and manipulated language" H tries to persuade us that Eustacia is "a figure of such dimensions as would invite the tragic experience." The "other Eustacia," however, displays "many traits characteristic of adolescence," such as her erratic oscillations between lassitude and excitement, and her "tinsel romanticism." She "is incapable of confronting squarely any ethical problem." Because H "has failed technically to fuse [the two Eustacias] into one," "the very center of the book is violently displaced." Hence H's heroine is "a pseudo-tragic figure . . . [who cheats] the demanding reader of an experience he had been given every reason to anticipate."

3061 Faber [sic] M. D. [Farber?]. "*Tess* and THE RAPE OF LUCRECE," ENGLISH LANGUAGE NOTES, V (June 1968), 292–93.
In a passage shortly after Tess's rape, H writes "the serpent hisses where the sweet birds sing"; after Lucrece's rape, Shakespeare writes, "The adder hisses where the sweet birds sing." The two victims of rape are similar in several ways.

3062 Farris, Lillie May. MEMORIES OF THE HARDY AND HAND FAMILIES (Mount Durand, St. Peter Port, Guernsey: Toucan P, 1968).
[A short memoir by a member of the Hand family. Also see J. Stevens Cox (pub and general editor), Monographs on the Life of Thomas Hardy (1962).]

3063 Faurot, Ruth Marie. "The Halo Over Lucetta Templeman," ENGLISH LITERATURE IN TRANSITION, XI: 2 (1968), 81–85.
Several restored portions in the Mellstock edition of *The Mayor of Casterbridge* suggest ambiguities in Lucetta Templeman's character. The tea party scene in chap 26 invites comparison with that of Christ and the two disciples supping at Emmaus, with Elizabeth-Jane taking the part of the recording evangelist Luke. The "halo" over Lucetta's head seems to suggest that she plays three symbolic roles in the novel: the devil as disturbing element, man the victim, and a Christ figure. In her devil aspect she is an intruder, has a foreign name, and is associated with the color red. She represents the nature of a man in that she is both good and bad, consistent with H's monism. That she has redemptive power is illustrated in the result of the skimmity ride—it is fatal to her, but the effigy floating in the pond later saves Henchard's life.

3064 Gatlin, Hallie L., III. "Structure and Technique in the Poetry of Thomas Hardy," DISSERTATION ABSTRACTS, XXIX (1968) 1867A. Unpublished dissertation, University of Iowa, 1968.

3065 Giordano, Frank R., Jr. "Freedom and Self in Hardy's Novels." Unpublished dissertation, University of Florida (Gainesville), 1968.

[Listed in Lawrence F. McNamee, Dissertations in English and American Literature, Supp I (NY & Lond: Bowker, 1969).]

3066 Gregor, Ian. "*Jude the Obscure*," Imagined Worlds: Essays on Some English Novels and Novelists in Honour of John Butt, ed by Maynard Mack and Ian Gregor (Lond: Methuen, 1968), pp. 237–56.

The commonplace criticism of *Jude the Obscure* is that the novel succeeds in its parts but fails to cohere as a whole. Actually, H achieves a coexistence of views or emphases: the novel is pessimistic, but Jude is resilient; the novel is unequivocally tragic, but it questions the nature of tragedy; the novel has an inevitable tragic presence, but there is the contingency of particular circumstances; the novel demonstrates the cant and futility of conventional attitudes, but it is marked by great compassion; the novel presents Jude's total outlook, but it masses particulars in the presentation.

H uses his earlier method of presentation in *Jude*: the pattern and its parts (the figures) wherein the figure justifies the pattern. Rather than fusing man with the landscape, in *Jude* the method is to find an element in man that makes him part of the organic whole, that is, to confine the personal but never to forget its extra-personal nature. Man is an inseparable part of a vast continuing process, an inevitable cosmic process which is always balanced by the particular process, the only process the individual undergoes, and thus autonomous and also illustrative of the cosmic.

Jude deals in present and future time which shifts mood, themes, and structure. The set is one of wounding isolation, an occupation with awareness and definition of self, with the conflict interiorized, one temperament against another. The internal quest for the reality of the self is dominant, but reality is not grasped (marriage, job, etc.). This play of self against reality results in the contrapuntal structure of *Jude*, the "social moulds" versus "actual shapes." If one is stressed more than the other, the result is half-truth. The technique is to put the emphasis on the present and the contingent and then on the "great well of human doings."

Since H's landscape is man rather than Wessex, he employs Father Time as collective consciousness, the commentator; Sue as one so highly personalized she cannot fully form a human relationship; Jude as the tragic figure of the contingent. All of this is the result of H's multiple ways of regarding the theme, a series of seemings of great complexity. The totality of the novel lies in the acceptance of these disjunctions. Jude is obscure to society, education and its privileges; to himself and his development, his "actual shape" in "the social mould."

3067 Harris, Wendell V. "English Short Fiction in the 19th Century," STUDIES IN SHORT FICTION, VI (Fall 1968), 47–49, 60, 92.

H's tales of the Nineties are in "lax and careless form and are unsatisfying, lacking in central theme." In *A Group of Noble Dames*, the insulation of the past results in lack of tension. The plots are too complex. H's "finest short story, 'The Three Strangers,'" avoids these defects. "The Withered Arm" is "lightly supernatural" and has a contrived plot. What H and Moore did in *Jude the Obscure* and ESTHER WATERS to challenge Victorian taboos in the novel, the avant-garde periodicals were doing with situations and themes in the short story.

3068 Harris, Wendell V. "John Lane's Keynotes Series and the Fiction of the 1890's," PUBLICATIONS OF THE MODERN LANGUAGE ASSOCIATION, LXXXIII (Oct 1968), 1411.

[A brief treatment of the influence of H's dark view of village life on H. D. Lowry's WOMEN'S TRAGEDIES, J. S. Fletcher's GOD'S FAILURES, and Caldwell Lipsett's WHERE THE ATLANTIC MEETS THE LAND, and of H's plot construction on Florence Henniker's IN SCARLET AND GREY.]

3069 Hughes, Eugene E. "Hardy's Poetry: Unity in Dramatic Perspective," DISSERTATION ABSTRACTS, XXVIII (1968), 4600A–4601A. Unpublished dissertation, University of Missouri (Columbia), 1967.

3070 Hughes, Robert L. "The Process of Secularization in Thomas Hardy's Major Wessex Novels," DISSERTATION ABSTRACTS, XXVIII (1968), 2685A–86A. Unpublished dissertation, University of Missouri (Columbia), 1967.

3071 Hutchins, Patricia. "Ezra Pound and Thomas Hardy," SOUTHERN REVIEW, IV (1968), 90–104.

Pound read H's *Satires of Circumstance* in 1914. He asked H to contribute poems to DIAL in 1920 (H's "The Two Houses" appeared in DIAL, August 1921). Pound sent H inscribed copies of QUIA PAUPER AMAVI and HUGH SELWYN MOBERLY in 1921, begged for judicious criticism and apparently received some (though Pound discounted H's concern with content in two letters of 1922). In 1925, Pound offered to send H, upon request, a copy of XVI CANTOS. Pound periodically praised H's clarity in poetry and attributes it to his having written twenty novels first. Pound echoes H's strictures against critics in ABC of READING (1934) and refers to "apology" for *Late Lyrics and Earlier* in GUIDE TO KULCHUR (1938).

3072 Hynes, Samuel. THE EDWARDIAN TURN OF MIND (Princeton, NJ: Princeton UP, 1968), pp. 177, 181, 224, 270n, 275–78. Of the fourteen novelists consulted by John Lane in 1910 on the propriety of publishing Sudermann's SONG OF SONGS (DAS HOHE LIED), only H advised against it.

3073 Jackson, Arlene M. "Ideas and Realities in Victorian England. A Study of the Idealistic Quest Theme in the Novels of George Eliot and Thomas Hardy," DISSERTATION ABSTRACTS, XXIX (1968), 872A. Unpublished dissertation, University of Michigan, 1968.

3074 Keith, W. J. "Thomas Hardy and the Name 'Wessex,'" ENGLISH LANGUAGE NOTES, VI (Sept 1968), 42–44. H did not, as he claimed, " 'disinter' " the name "Wessex" while writing *Far From the Madding Crowd*; earlier, it had been used by William Barnes in a preface to his POEMS OF RURAL LIFE, IN COMMON ENGLISH (1868), and by Charles Kingsley in "Chalk-Stream Studies" (1858). Thus H could not, as Dr. Leavis claimed, have taken the term from George Eliot's DANIEL DERONDA, which was first published two years after H's initial employment of it in the serialization of *Madding Crowd*.

3075 Kiely, Robert. "Vision and Viewpoint in *The Mayor of Casterbridge*," NINETEENTH CENTURY FICTION, XXIII (Sept 1968), 198–200. While *The Mayor of Casterbridge* is "full of some of the most obvious and potentially ludicrous of narrative conventions," such as the concealed observer, H turns this awkwardness into a grace "because abrupt changes in viewpoint constitute an important aspect of Hardy's subject." What each character sees defines, to a great extent, what he is. One of Henchard's most basic desires is "to see without being seen": to appear good, powerful and to bury his past. Similarly, Lucetta masks her affairs with Henchard behind a façade of wealth and a marriage to Farfrae. But both Henchard and Lucetta are defeated by their inability to see their essential selves wholly and fairly. Lacking any "supernatural observer," H's characters "are left to watch and judge one another." They include "some of the busiest amateur spies in serious fiction." Despite their inquisitiveness, however, their vision is "tragically limited": no one really *sees* Henchard as he is, no one character's vision is a standard by which the less true vision of others may be tested. Because the chorus of townspeople openly disagree, they "come nearer than anyone else to an accurate description of Henchard."

3076 Knott, Olive. HARDY'S STURMINSTER HOME (Mount Durand, St. Peter Port, Guernsey: Toucan P, 1968).
[Some notes on Riverside Villa, H's first furnished home after marrying Emma. Contains a transcription in an appendix of Mrs. Mabel Penny's recollection of H's visits to Sturminster in later years. Also see J. Stevens Cox (pub and general editor), Monographs on the Life of Thomas Hardy (1962).]

3077 Landon, Philip J. "Themes of Conversion and Compromise in the Fiction of Thomas Hardy," DISSERTATION ABSTRACTS, XXVIII (April–June 1968), 4635A. Unpublished dissertation, University of Maryland, 1968.

3078 Lerner, Laurence, and John Holmstrom (eds). THOMAS HARDY AND HIS READERS: A SELECTION OF CONTEMPORARY REVIEWS (Lond: Bodley Head; NY: Barnes & Noble, 1968).
Reviews are organized under various titles by H, preceded by a bibliographical headnote, and linked with a commentary by the editors. Contents, abstracted under year of first publication: Laurence Lerner and John Holmstrom, "Preface," pp. 8–9, "Biographical Note," pp. 19–11, and headnotes and inter alia commentary [not abstracted]; "Novels of the Week," ATHENAEUM, No. 2266 (1 April 1871), 339; John Morley [Reader's Report for Macmillan on *Under the Greenwood Tree*], from THE HOUSE OF MACMILLAN, by Charles Morgan (1943); [Review of *Under the Greenwood Tree*], PALL MALL GAZETTE, 5 July 1872; [Horace Moule], "*Under the Greenwood Tree*," SATURDAY REVIEW (Lond), XXXIV (28 Sept 1872), 417–18; [R. H. Hutton], "Books: Some of the Magazines," SPECTATOR, XLVII (3 Jan 1874), 22; Leslie Stephen, [Selections from two letters to Thomas Hardy], in THOMAS HARDY: A BIBLIOGRAPHICAL STUDY, by Richard L. Purdy (1954); [Review of *Far From the Madding Crowd*], EXAMINER, 5 Dec 1874; [R. H. Hutton], "Books: *Far From the Madding Crowd*," SPECTATOR, XLVII (19 Dec 1874), 1597–99; Henry James, "Hardy's *Far from the Madding Crowd*," NATION (NY), XIX (24 Dec 1874), 423–24; [Review of *Far From the Madding Crowd*], OBSERVER, 3 Jan 1875; "*Far From the Madding Crowd*," SATURDAY REVIEW (Lond), XXIX (9 Jan 1875), 57–58; [Frederick Napier Broome], [Review of *Far From the Madding Crowd*], TIMES (Lond), 25 Jan 1875, [Review of *Far From the Madding Crowd*], MANCHESTER GUARDIAN, 24 Feb 1875; Leslie Stephen, [Selection from a letter to Thomas Hardy], in THOMAS HARDY: A BIBLIOGRAPHICAL STUDY, by Richard L. Purdy (1954); "Novels of the Week," ATHENAEUM, No.

2665 (23 Nov 1878), 654; W. E. H[enley], "New Novels," ACADEMY, XIV (30 Nov 1878), 517; [R. H. Hutton?], "Books: *The Return of the Native*," SPECTATOR, LII (8 Feb 1879), 181–82; "Three Novels," SATURDAY REVIEW (Lond), LXI (29 May 1886), 757; [R. H. Hutton], "Books: *The Mayor of Casterbridge*," SPECTATOR, LIX (5 June 1886), 752–53; [R. H. Hutton], "Books: *The Woodlanders*," SPECTATOR, LX (26 March 1887), 419–20; "Mr. Hardy's New Novel," SPEAKER, IV (26 Dec 1891), 770–71; [Review of *Tess of the d'Urbervilles*], DAILY CHRON- ICLE, 28 Dec 1891; Une Vieille Baderne, "The Editor of the DAILY CHRONICLE," DAILY CHRONICLE, 30 Dec 1891; [Review of *Tess of the d'Urbervilles*], PALL MALL GAZETTE, 31 Dec 1891; George Meredith, [Let- ter to Frederick Greenwood], from LETTERS OF GEORGE MEREDITH (1912); "Novels," SATURDAY REVIEW (Lond), LXXIII (16 Jan 1892), 73–74; [R. H. Hutton], "Books: Mr. Hardy's *Tess of the d'Urbervilles*," SPECTATOR, LXVIII (23 Jan 1892), 121–22; Andrew Lang, "Literature and the Drama," NEW REVIEW, VI (Feb 1892), 247–49; "New Books: *Tess of the d'Urbervilles*," BOOKMAN (Lond), I (Feb 1892), 179–80; "Mr. Hardy's *Tess of the d'Urbervilles*," REVIEW OF REVIEWS (NY), V (Feb 1892), 200; William Watson, "Literature," ACADEMY, XLI (6 Feb 1892), 125–26; The Baron de Book-Worms, "Our Booking-Office," PUNCH, CII (27 Feb 1892), 108; Henry James, [Letters to R. L. Steven- son], from THE LETTERS OF HENRY JAMES (1920); Mowbray Morris, "Culture and Anarchy," QUARTERLY REVIEW, CLXXIV (April 1892), 317–43; Francis Adams, "Some Recent Novels," FORTNIGHTLY REVIEW, LXVIII (1 July 1892), 19–22; "A Woman's View of Tess," from Harriet Preston, "Thomas Hardy," CENTURY, ns XXIV (July 1893), 352–59 [incorrectly cited in this volume]; Raymond Blathwayt, "A Chat with the Author of *Tess*," BLACK AND WHITE, IV (27 Aug 1892), 238–40; Edward Wright, "The Novels of Thomas Hardy," QUARTERLY REVIEW, CXCIX (April 1904), 499–523 [cited in three places]; [Henry M. Alden], "Thomas Hardy," HARPER'S WEEKLY, 8 Dec 1894; [Review of *Jude the Obscure*], DAILY TELEGRAPH, 1 Nov 1895; [Review of *Jude the Obscure*], MORNING POST, 7 Nov 1895; "Jude the Obscene," PALL MALL GAZETTE, 12 Nov 1895; [Review of *Jude the Obscure*], MANCHESTER GUARDIAN, 13 Nov 1895; Edward Arlington Robinson, "For a Book by Thomas Hardy," CRITIC (NY), 23 Nov 1895; [Review of *Jude the Obscure*], SUN (NY), 20 Nov 1895; W. D. Howells, "Life and Letters," HARPER'S WEEKLY, XXXIX (7 Dec 1895), 1156; Edmund Gosse, "Mr. Hardy's New Novel," COSMOPOLIS, I (Jan 1896), 60–69; [Review of *Jude the Obscure*], ILLUSTRATED LONDON NEWS, 11 Jan 1896; M. O. W. O[liphant], "The Anti-Marriage League," BLACKWOOD'S MAGAZINE, CLIX (Jan 1896), 137–42; A. M., "New Books: *Jude the Obscure*," BOOKMAN (Lond), IX (Jan 1896), 123–24; [Harry Thurston] P[eck?], "Chronicles and Comment," BOOKMAN (NY), II (Jan 1896), 374–75; "Two Novels: *Jude the Obscure*, THE EMANCIPATED," NATION (NY), LXII (6 Feb 1896), 123–24; [H. G. Wells], *"Jude the Obscure,"* SATURDAY REVIEW (Lond), LXXXI (8 Feb 1896), 153–54; Richard Le Gallienne, "Wanderings in Bookland," IDLER, IX (Feb 1896), 114–15; W. H. Howe, Bishop of Wakefield, "Thomas Hardy," YORKSHIRE POST, 8 June 1896, p. 4; Havelock Ellis, "Concerning *Jude the Obscure*," SAVOY, VI (Oct 1896), 35–49; *"The Return of the Native,"* SATURDAY REVIEW (Lond), XLVII (4 Jan 1879), 23–24; John A. Steuart, [Letter to Thomas Hardy], from LETTERS OF LIVING AUTHORS (1890); [Ernest Rhys?], " 'Hodge' As I Know Him. A Talk with Mr. Thomas Hardy," PALL MALL GAZETTE, LIV (2 Jan 1892), 1–2; Lionel Johnson, [General Appraisal], from THE ART OF THOMAS HARDY (1894); [W. H. Mallock], "The Popular Novel," QUARTERLY REVIEW, CXCIV (July 1901), 244–73.

3079 Maxfield, James F. "The Darkening Journey: A Study of the Major Novels of Thomas Hardy," DISSERTATION ABSTRACTS, XXVIII (1968), 3192A. Unpublished dissertation, University of Iowa, 1967.

3080 Maxwell, J. C. "The 'Sociological' Approach to *The Mayor of Casterbridge*," IMAGINED WORLDS: ESSAYS ON SOME ENGLISH NOVELS AND NOVELISTS IN HONOUR OF JOHN BUTT, ed by Maynard Mack and Ian Gregor (Lond: Methuen, 1968), pp. 225–36.
In Douglas Brown's THOMAS HARDY: THE MAYOR OF CASTERBRIDGE (1962), the interpretation of *The Mayor of Casterbridge* as "actual social history" is not convincing. He insists that Henchard is a type, the "agricultural man," in the sociological change from agrarian culture to industrial culture. However, Henchard is an exceptional character. The community in which he lives exists in a time of agricultural stability and prosperity. Henchard's loss is exceptional and impressive in the context of the community. Henchard, then, is not representative of "agricultural man" but clearly a man in the latest period at which price fluctuations dominated depending on the home harvest.

3081 Miller, J. Hillis. " 'Wessex Heights': The Persistence of the Past in Hardy's Poetry," CRITICAL QUARTERLY, X (Winter 1968), 339–59.
H's withdrawn watcher sees so intensely that geography becomes a collective present experience; the poet's mind is the world turned inside out and contains all time and space. Lyric poetry and mixed perspectives, as well as the abandonment of Tennysonian euphony, show the painful fluidity of present time, connected to the past and hovering between the physical and biographical. [Section by section explication of "Wessex Heights."]

3082 Morris, Jessie F. "Thomas Hardy's Style: A Syntactic Approach to the Poetry," DISSERTATION ABSTRACTS, XXIX (1968), 875A–76A. Unpublished dissertation, University of New Mexico, 1968.

3083 Perrine, Laurence. "Thomas Hardy's 'God-Forgotten,' " VICTORIAN POETRY, VI (Summer 1968), 187–88.
Although God's orders in the dream are usually taken to mean that "his messengers should eliminate suffering by correcting earth's evils," it is also possible that the messengers are "mercifully to put men out of their misery as one puts an animal out of its misery." The poem does not resolve this ambiguity.

3084 Pinion, F. B. A HARDY COMPANION: A GUIDE TO THE WORKS OF THOMAS HARDY AND THEIR BACKGROUND (Lond & Melbourne: Macmillan; NY: St. Martin's P, 1968).
[The first chapter summarizes the main events of H's life and career as a writer. Four chapters deal, respectively, with the novels, short stories, plays, and poems; each chapter providing information on the composition, publication, sources, and critical reception of individual works. Then follow five chapters on special problems in H's works: "The Wessex Tradition"; "Views on Art, Tragedy, and Fiction"; "Aspects of the Unusual and Irrational"; "Towards Symbolism"; and "Christianity, Scientific Philosophy, and Politics." One chapter deals with influences and recollections, with particular reference to architecture, music, painting, and literature. A long and useful section of some 300 pages is a "Dictionary of People and Places in Hardy's Works." The book concludes with a glossary of "dialect, literary (e.g. archaic and Shakespearian) and words of foreign derivation (chiefly French)," a manuscript location list, and a select bibliography. The book is well-illustrated with photographs and maps. Pinion has produced a thoroughly superior guide to H.]

3085 Pritchett, V. S. "The Anti-Soporific Art," NEW STATESMAN, LXXVI (6 Dec 1968), 793–94.
Some of H's short stories approach the instantaneous effect which short story writers now strive for, but this effect was blurred in *Desperate Remedies* by novelistic rambling.

3086 Raleigh, John Henry. TIME, PLACE, AND IDEA: ESSAYS ON THE NOVEL, with a preface by Harry T. Moore (Carbondale & Edwardsville: Southern Illinois UP; Lond & Amsterdam: Feffer & Simons, 1968), pp. 49–50, 51, 52, 140, 142, 145, 150–51, 153, 160.
With James and H, the "concept of time and history as a straight line,

leading upward, . . . begins to break down." H's "sense of the past is, partially anyway, a metaphorical expression of cosmic time, whose essence is the endless recurrence of things," as in *The Return of the Native*. H's universe "has only one certitude, the cyclic character of existence, and only one prop for humans, an allegiance to the past." The revolt against moral censorship reflected in the fiction of Butler, H, and Moore "was in a sense an upsurge from below." As Butler "embodies the comedy of this revolt against middle-class consciousness," H embodies "its antitype as pastoral" and "its antitype as tragedy" (*Far From the Madding Crowd* and *The Woodlanders; Tess of the d'Urbervilles* and *Jude the Obscure*).

3087 Rao, P. N. "The Minor Rustic Characters in Hardy's Novels; A Study of Their Presentation and Functions and of Their Relation Both to Literary Antecedents and to the Rural Life of the Time." Unpublished dissertation, University of London, 1968. [Listed in Lawrence F. McNamee, DISSERTATIONS IN ENGLISH AND AMERICAN LITERATURE, SUPP I (NY & Lond: Bowker, 1969).]

3088 Robillard, Douglas. "Landscape with Figures: The Early Fiction of John Cowper Powys," STUDIES IN THE LITERARY IMAGINATION, I (April 1968), 51–58. Powys's early novels reveal the influence of H. Powys not only shared a philosophical position close to that of his Dorset neighbor, but he also tended to "make the landscape a moving force in the fortunes of his characters."

3089 Smith, Curtis C. "The Concept of Nature in Thomas Hardy's Fiction," DISSERTATION ABSTRACTS, XXVIII (1968), 4647A–48A. Unpublished dissertation, Syracuse University, 1967.

3090 Southerington, F. R. THE EARLY HARDYS: AN INTRODUCTORY NOTE (Mount Durand, St. Peter Port, Guernsey: Toucan P, 1968); absorbed in HARDY'S VISION OF MAN (Lond: Chatto & Windus, 1971). It was natural for H to be deeply interested in the past. He saw the decline of his own once proud family, himself at the end of the family line. [Traces the probable career of Thomas Hardye, from whom the author believed himself to be descended, and the career of Sir Thomas Masterman Hardy. Reprints a tribute to Thomas Hardye by H which appeared in TIMES, 22 July 1927. Contains a simplified geneology in which the position of Rebecca Maria Sparks Payne, apparently the mother of Tryphena Sparks, seems confused. Appendix I: "Sources for the Hardy Pedigree," a bibliography. Appendix II: "The Hardye's School Foundation Deed," text taken from a 1631 copy, describing the property given by Hardye for the school and alloting authority for the governance of the school. Appendix III: "Additional Note," noting that H's relationship with Tryphena Sparks followed a pattern well established among H's ancestors which H must have regarded with "fear and bewilderment," and giving an account of hasty marriages, illegitimate children, and marriages between cousins in the Hardy family. Also see J. Stevens Cox (pub and general editor), Monographs on the Life of Thomas Hardy (1962).]

3091 Southerington, F. R. HARDY'S CHILD: FACT OR FICTION? (Birling, Mount Durand, St. Peter Port, Guernsey: Toucan P, 1968); absorbed in HARDY'S VISION OF MAN (Lond: Chatto & Windus, 1971).

Since the relationship of H and Tryphena strongly influenced the writing of H, and therefore is a critical problem, the question of whether or not they had a child begs a review of evidence. (1) H gave Tryphena a ring in 1871 and was probably engaged to her earlier; (2) Mrs. Eleanor Tryphena Bromell, the daughter of Tryphena, is a reliable witness when recalling the conversations of her mother; (3) when Mrs. Bromell was shown photographs of a boy, she stated several times on seeing the picture "that was Hardy's boy" [thorough discussion of the reliability of the witness is presented]; (4) there are persuasive parallels and biographical allusions in H's works, especially *Jude the Obscure* (the cousin relationship); (5) the change of Tryphena's teaching assignment in its timing and circumstance are supportive; (6) the direct question posed to Mrs. Bromell (Did H and Tryphena have a son?) is not answered with a yes but is given no denial on direct questioning. [Appendix I: An article in the DORSET EVENING ECHO, 18 March 1968, p. 5, states the paternity is a fiction which resulted from Miss Deacon's obsession with what she claims to have discovered. Appendix II: A letter to the DORSET EVENING ECHO, 8 April 1968, by Frank Southerington asserts that the article offers no proof but deals only with Miss Deacon's "obsession." The burden of proof then lies with the writer of the article. Contains two photographs of H's boy and one of H in 1862. Also see J. Stevens Cox (pub and general editor), Monographs on the Life of Thomas Hardy (1962).]

3092 Southerington, F. R. "Human Behaviour and Responsibility in Hardy's Novels." Unpublished dissertation, Oxford University, 1968.

[Listed in Lawrence F. McNamee, DISSERTATIONS IN ENGLISH AND AMERICAN LITERATURE, SUPP I (NY & Lond: Bowker, 1969).

3093 Steig, Michael. "Sue Bridehead," NOVEL, I (Spring 1968), 260–66.

Despite the obvious inconsistencies in Sue's character, she is "psychologically coherent." A vital "unresolved issue" in *Jude the Obscure* is whether Sue is sexless and if not, in what her sexuality consists. Although she is "an unbeliever and libertarian in her consciousness, she is unable to carry this over to the realm of feeling." While she "longs for the man . . . there is something in her that recoils from sex." Jude, too, is confused about Sue's sexuality vs. her obvious spirituality. His inconsistency of response is not just passivity or conscience typical of fictional Victorian heroes, but rather it is a projection of H's own uncertainty about Sue. William Reich's "hysterical character" combines " '*obvious sexual behavior*' " with " 'a more or less outspoken apprehensiveness,' " a contradiction evident in Sue, who is both coquettish and prudish. She needs to attract Jude sexually as "a defense against anxiety," as a means of testing how well grounded her basic sexual fears are. Sue, however, abandons typical hysterical behavior and "retreat[s] to religion"—perhaps because of the death of her children.

3094 Stickland, Dorothy. THOMAS HARDY AT CATTISTOCK (Mount Durand, St. Peter Port, Guernsey: Toucan P, 1968).
[A brief anecdotal reminiscence. Contains a letter from H to Mrs. Stickland and six photographs of the locale and the activities there. Also see J. Stevens Cox (pub and general editor), Monographs on the Life of Thomas Hardy (1962).]

3095 Sullivan, Thomas R. "A 'Way to the Better': Hardy's Two Views of Evolution," DISSERTATION ABSTRACTS, XXIX (1968), 276A. Unpublished dissertation, University of Iowa, 1968.

3096 Swanson, Roger M. "Guilt in Selected Victorian Novels: Hardy, Eliot, Dickens, and C. Brontë." Unpublished dissertation, University of Illinois, 1968.
[Listed in Lawrence F. McNamee, DISSERTATIONS IN ENGLISH AND AMERICAN LITERATURE, SUPP I (NY & Lond: Bowker, 1969).]

3097 Tanner, Tony. "Colour and Movement in Hardy's *Tess of the d'Urbervilles*," CRITICAL QUARTERLY, X (Autumn 1968), 219–39.
H selectively intensifies vocabulary so that visible omens define the rhythms of existence. The facts of sex and death center on blood—the moving spot across the white vacuity (where Tess is marked by blood, related to the death of the horse and her rape). Angel and Alec represent two forces—one roaming in thought and the other in lust—between which Tess is caught. The mystery of motion lies at the heart of H's vision here, while the "discontinuance of immobility" separates man from nature in *The Return of the Native*.

3098 Ure, Peter. "George Moore as Historian of Consciences," in IMAGINED WORLDS: ESSAYS ON SOME ENGLISH NOVELS AND NOVELISTS IN HONOUR OF JOHN BUTT, ed by Maynard Mack and Ian Gregor (Lond: Methuen, 1968), p. 265.

Alice Barton's marriage to Dr. Reed in Moore's A DRAMA IN MUSLIN is handled with satire similar to H's handling of Paula De Stancy's contemplation of marriage in *A Laodicean*.

3099 Weber, Carl. "Hardy and James," HARVARD LIBRARY BULLETIN, XVI (Jan 1968), 18–25.

Among the sixty H letters now in the Harvard Library, three deal with Henry James. The third letter (10 Jan 1916) was sent by H as President of the Society of Authors to James on the occasion of his appointment to the Order of Merit. But, in fact, H declined to draft the letter of congratulation. H had apparently got wind at an earlier date that in 1892 and 1893 Stevenson and James had discussed *Tess of the d'Urbervilles* behind H's back and had agreed that Tess was "vile." H was not one to forget or overlook such things. In THE LATER YEARS OF THOMAS HARDY, by Florence Hardy (1930), he referred to James and Stevenson as "the Polonius and the Osric of [English] novelists."

3100 Weber, Carl J. "Hardy's Mythical Visit to America," AMERICAN NOTES AND QUERIES, VII (Nov 1968), 39–40.

Although he received five specific requests to come to the United States, "Hardy never set foot on American soil."

3101 White, William. "Dreiser on Hardy, Henley, and Whitman: An Unpublished Letter," ENGLISH LANGUAGE NOTES, VI (Dec 1968), 122–24.

A Dreiser letter to Richard Duffy, dated 2 Feb 1902, says, "Hardys [sic] poems are rousingly beautiful to me," his most positive reference to H's poems. [Dreiser seems to have been attracted to H's brooding determinism.]

3102 Zaslove, J. "Counterfeit and the Uses of Literature," WEST COAST REVIEW, III (Winter 1968), 5–19.

Jude the Obscure takes its place among the many nineteenth- and twentieth-century works which seek to unmask the sort of counterfeit, socially acceptable experience encouraged by our culture.

3103 Ziegler, Carl. "Thomas Hardy's Correspondence with German Translators," ENGLISH LITERATURE IN TRANSITION, XI:2 (1968), 87–94.

H's works have met with only limited approval in Germany, for reasons not yet determined. The Dorset County Museum contains twenty-one letters from nineteen Germans requesting translation rights for at least one of H's novels. It may be determined from the marginalia that H answered and granted such rights to at least seven applicants. In spite of this, only two novels (*Tess of the d'Urbervilles* and *Jude the Obscure*), in addition to eight short stories, were translated and published during H's lifetime. Furthermore, since 1928, only three other novels, one short story, and fourteen poems have been presented to the German public. *Die Rückkehr* (*The Return of the Native*) is the only novel currently in print. H continues to be virtually unknown in Germany.

1969

3104 Asquith, Lady Cynthia. THOMAS HARDY AT MAX GATE (Mount Durand, St. Peter Port, Guernsey: Toucan P, 1969); first given as a talk on the Home Service of BBC, 1956.

H's dog Wessex was incredibly spoiled and was allowed to walk on the table at meals and to bite anyone. H always wanted to write a play, was disappointed in the dramatization of his novels. He had quite detailed plans for his own burial, which he was forever changing. [Also see J. Stevens Cox (pub and general editor), Monographs on the Life of Thomas Hardy (1962).]

3105 Beards, Richard D. "D. H. Lawrence and the Study of Thomas Hardy, His Victorian Predecessor," D. H. LAWRENCE REVIEW, II:3 (1969), 211–29.

H influenced Lawrence in three ways: Lettie Beardsall resembles Sue Bridehead and THE WHITE PEACOCK resembles the Wessex novels in style, tone, and atmosphere; he learned from H technical skills of integrating varied materials and introduction of characters; and the two shared such thematic and "sympathetic concerns as similar vision of the role of the individual life in the natural environment, a concern for the importance of sexual relationships in human development, and a sympathy for the hero, isolated by his nature and choice, from society." Lawrence's judgment in "A Study of Thomas Hardy," PHOENIX (1936) could serve as an effective summary of Lawrence's own works.

3106 Blythe, Mary A. "Hardy and Moule," TIMES LITERARY SUPPLEMENT (Lond), 13 March 1969, p. 272.

Contrary to Evelyn Hardy's claim, Horace Moule's fiancée was not a titled lady, nor was there any talk in the Moule family of her being the cause of his suicide. [See Evelyn Hardy, "Thomas Hardy and Horace Moule: Vindication of a Suicide," ibid, 23 Jan 1969, p. 89.]

3107 Cheney, Frederick William. "Lived Next to Jemima," HARDYANA II: A FURTHER COLLECTION OF SHORT MEMORABILIA AND OTHER MATTERS OF HARDY INTEREST, ed by J. Stevens Cox (Mount Durand, St. Peter Port, Guernsey: Toucan P, 1969), p. 227.

"The Hardys were very tight." H did not reply to friendly greetings. [Also see J. Stevens Cox (pub and general editor), Monographs on the Life of Thomas Hardy (1962).]

3108 Codd, Alfred Percy. LIFE IN BEAMINSTER (THE EMMINSTER OF HARDY'S NOVELS) 1864–1910 (Mount Durand, St. Peter Port, Guernsey: Toucan P, 1969).

H visited Rev. Codd at Beaminster before 1890. This essay is written to cover this small previously neglected area. It offers a detailed description of its woods, lanes, paths, and buildings; its people, their homes and customs, schools, and class distinctions; the work and the play of the inhabitants. [Contains forty-two photographs of inhabitants, buildings, and activities of Beaminster. Also see J. Stevens Cox (pub and general editor), Monographs on the Life of Thomas Hardy (1962).]

3109 Coleman, Terry. "Thomas Hardy and Horace Moule," TIMES LITERARY SUPPLEMENT (Lond), 30 Jan 1969, pp. 110–11.

Evelyn Hardy's claim that Horace Moule was engaged does not preclude a triangular affair between himself, H, and H's cousin Tryphena Sparks. Further, Evelyn Hardy erred in claiming that the conclusions in PROVIDENCE AND MR. HARDY by Lois Deacon and Terry Coleman (1966), depend upon the misreading of letters written by Moule to H. [See Evelyn Hardy, "Thomas Hardy and Horace Moule: Vindication of a Suicide," ibid, 23 Jan 1969, p. 89.]

3110 Cox, J. Stevens (ed). HARDYANA II: A FURTHER COLLECTION OF SHORT MEMORABILIA AND OTHER MATTERS OF HARDY INTEREST (Mount Durand, St. Peter Port, Guernsey: Toucan P, 1969).

Contents, abstracted separately under date of first publication: Julian Ennis, "Stinsford Churchyard: Thomas Hardy. January 16th, 1928" [an obit poem; not abstracted]; Hermann Lea, "Letter from Hermann Lea Referring to The Woodlanders" (1969); M. S. Creech, "Louisa Harding" (1969); "Marriage of the Greatest Living Author Mr. Thomas Hardy, O. M. and Miss Florence Dugdale," rptd from ENFIELD GAZETTE AND OBSERVER, 13 Feb 1914; E. L. Grasby, "A Note" (1969); F. Stemp, "Hardy at Kingston Maurward" (1969); F. W. Cheney, "Lived Next to Jemima"

(1969); Mrs. Gerald Williams, "An Interview with Mrs. Gerald Williams" (1969); Vera Wainwright, "She Knew Mrs. F. E. Hardy" (1969); Harold Voss, "Hardy's Playground," pp. 229–30 [trivial; not abstracted]; L. J. Medway, "Hardy Anecdotes" (1969); W. H. Weston, "He Worked at Max Gate" (1969); Sir James George Frazer, THE MAGIC ART (1911; not seen in this form) I, 136; rptd as "Sir James Frazer and Hardy," p. 231 [trivial; not abstracted]; "A Message from Mr. Thomas Hardy to Christ Church College Students," CHRIST CHURCH COLLEGE MAGAZINE (Cawnpore, India), XXII (Feb 1928), rptd as "Thomas Hardy's Message to Students in India," p. 232 [trivial; not abstracted.] [Also see J. Stevens Cox (pub and general editor), Monographs on the Life of Thomas Hardy (1962).]

3111 Cox, J. Stevens (ed). T. J. WISE, MRS. HARDY'S & HARDY'S MANUSCRIPTS (Guernsey: ptd for private circulation by Toucan P, 1969).

[The pamphlet contains three letters from T. J. Wise to Richard H. P. Curle. The letters throw light on the history of H's manuscripts. Curle is shocked at the revelation of Wise's indiscretions. 21 Oct 1929: Mrs. H is concerned over a letter by H on the affairs of John Middleton Murry, which she does not want to change hands. Wise has sold the letter and must now get it back to keep peace with Mrs. H. 3 Nov 1929: Wise calls the fuss of Mrs. H stupid, states that she is a foolish woman in some ways and is a most unreasonable person. Wise sold the manuscript of *The Woodlanders* for one thousand pounds. Mrs. H now wants back the manuscripts that she sold because they are now more valuable. 27 Nov 1929: Wise thanks Curle for the return of the "unhappy letter." He has had no word from Mrs. H about the letter, but he is not surprised because she is a most erratic person. Wise has obtained first editions from Clodd of H and others, inscribed by the authors to Clodd, and also a signed manuscript of a story by H.]

3112 Creech, M. S. "Louisa Harding," HARDYANA II: A FURTHER COLLECTION OF SHORT MEMORABILIA AND OTHER MATTERS OF HARDY INTEREST, ed by J. Stevens Cox (Mount Durand, St. Peter Port, Guernsey: Toucan P, 1969), pp. 219–20.

Louisa Harding did not speak to H because her family was his social superiors, but she thought of him "as a kind of sweetheart." H was "a mean man. Few in Dorchester cared for him." "My husband took part in the Hardy plays in Dorchester." [Also see J. Stevens Cox (pub and general editor), Monographs on the Life of Thomas Hardy (1962).]

3113 Deacon, Lois. HARDY'S TRYPHENA IN TOPSHAM, DEVON (Mount Durand, St. Peter Port, Guernsey: Toucan P, 1969);

first presented as a lecture to the Parochial History Section of the Devonshire Association on 6 April 1964; absorbed in PROVIDENCE AND MR. HARDY, by Lois Deacon and Terry Coleman (1966).
Both H's and Tryphena Sparks's marriages were expedients, when the two learned they could not marry each other. Tryphena was H's lifelong love and inspires all of his love poetry and the great novels. H's poem "My Cicely" records his shock at hearing of the death of Tryphena's mother-in-law and thinking it was Tryphena herself. "To a Motherless Child" records his feelings upon visiting Tryphena's grave and later visiting her daughter, a scene which also inspires a chapter in *Jude the Obscure* and the novel *The Well-Beloved*. [Much description of Topsham and Tryphena's life there after her marriage to Charles Gale. Also see J. Stevens Cox (pub and general editor), Monographs on the Life of Thomas Hardy (1962).]

3114 Emmett, V. J., Jr. "Marriage in Hardy's Later Novels," MIDWEST QUARTERLY, X (July 1969), 331–48.
Romantic triangles are important structural devices in H's later work. *The Return of the Native, The Mayor of Casterbridge, Tess of the d'Urbervilles*, and *Jude the Obscure* are "vehicles for metaphorical statements about the indifference or downright maleficence of the universe." H used Eustacia Vye's "sensuality, passion, vague longing, advanced thought, hostile relation to environment, and an inability to settle into a comfortable life with a compatible mate" in various combinations to create the major characters of his later books. In the end, through H's manipulation, the reader is made aware that the romantic triangle is as a device for dramatizing opposition to the metaphysical-theological view of marriage, that couplings sanctioned metaphysically insure human misery and violation of metaphysical sanction leads to "relative human happiness." The bonds that are correct in terms of Victorian piety are disastrous in real application. "Taken as an assault against both the theological view of the marriage bond and the use of marriage as a happy ending . . . *Jude* is doubly expressive of Hardy's hostility toward Victorian orthodoxy."

3115 Evans, Evelyn L. ROUND DORSET WITH HARDY (Mount Durand, St. Peter Port, Guernsey: Toucan P, 1969).
[A short description of four tours through the Dorset region. The tours are related to four different combinations of H's novels. Also see J. Stevens Cox (pub and general editor), Monographs on the Life of Thomas Hardy (1962).]

3116 [Gindin, James]. "Critical Essays," THOMAS HARDY: THE RETURN OF THE NATIVE: AN AUTHORITATIVE TEXT, BACKGROUND, CRITICISM, ed by James Gindin (NY: Norton, 1969 [Norton Critical Editions]), pp. 413–15.

[A bibliographical essay commenting on significant H criticism from his own lifetime to the present.]

3117 Gindin, James. "Hardy and Folklore," THOMAS HARDY: THE RETURN OF THE NATIVE: AN AUTHORITATIVE TEXT, BACK-GROUND, CRITICISM, ed by James Gindin (NY: Norton, 1969 [Norton Critical Editions]), pp. 396–401.

More than the other novels, *The Return of the Native* shows H's interest in folk culture. Folk festivals are an organizing element in the novel, combining Christian and pagan traditions. For the rustic characters, the Christian element is superficial, and it is always the pagan through which they interpret their experiences and on which their understanding of the world is based. The simplicity of Thomasin and Diggory enable them to live in harmony with pagan tradition, while the complexity of Clym and Eustacia illustrates a clash between the Christian and the pagan worlds. Eustacia in particular breaks with the old traditions, showing herself to be outside the folk culture. H allows folk beliefs to parallel his deeper examination of human nature in order to show that they involve real insights. Although H gives a truer, much less corrupted picture of folk customs than other modern writers, he never suggests that they are sufficient to explain human experience, and always probes beyond them.

3118 Gindin, James. "Preface," THOMAS HARDY: THE RETURN OF THE NATIVE: AN AUTHORITATIVE TEXT, BACKGROUND, CRITICISM, ed by James Gindin (NY: Norton, 1969 [Norton Critical Editions]), pp. vii–viii.

[Briefly traces publishing history of H's novel and justifies contents of the collection.]

3119 Gindin, James (ed). THOMAS HARDY: THE RETURN OF THE NATIVE: AN AUTHORITATIVE TEXT, BACKGROUND, CRITICISM (NY: Norton, 1969 [Norton Critical Editions]).

Contents, abstracted separately under date of first publication: James Gindin, "Preface" (1969); "[Publication of the Novel]," from Richard L. Purdy, THOMAS HARDY: A BIBLIOGRAPHICAL STUDY (1954); "[Composition and Revision of the Novel]," from John Paterson, THE MAKING OF THE RETURN OF THE NATIVE (1960); "[Scholarship on the Novel]," from Carl J. Weber, HARDY OF WESSEX (1940); "From Hardy's Autobiography," from Florence Emily Hardy, THE EARLY LIFE OF THOMAS HARDY, 1840–1891 (1928) and THE LATER YEARS OF THOMAS HARDY, 1892–1928 (1930); James Gindin, "Hardy and Folklore" (1969); from "Novels of the Week," ATHENAEUM, No. 2665 (23 Nov 1878), 654, including H's reply in ibid (30 Nov 1878); from "*The Return of the Native*," SATURDAY REVIEW (Lond), XLVII (4 Jan 1879), 23–24; from "Contemporary Literature: IV. Novelists," BLACKWOOD'S MAGAZINE, CXXV (March 1879),

338; from [H. M. Alden], "Editor's Literary Record," HARPER'S NEW MONTHLY MAGAZINE (NY), LVIII (March 1879), 627–28; [James Gindin], "Critical Essays" (1969); "[The Psychology of the Characters]," from D. H. Lawrence, chap 3 ("Containing Six Novels and the Real Tragedy") of "Study of Thomas Hardy," in PHOENIX: THE POSTHUMOUS PAPERS OF D. H. LAWRENCE, ed by Edward D. McDonald (1936); from D. H. Lawrence, "Why the Novel Matters," in PHOENIX: THE POSTHUMOUS PAPERS OF D. H. LAWRENCE, ed by Edward D. McDonald (1936) [not on H and not abstracted]; "[The Structure of *The Return of the Native*]," from Joseph Warren Beach, THE TECHNIQUE OF THOMAS HARDY (1922); "[Hardy's Faults as Novelist]," from Frank Chapman, "Hardy the Novelist," SCRUTINY, III (June 1934), 22–37; Allen Tate, "Hardy's Philosophic Metaphors," SOUTHERN REVIEW, VI (Summer 1940); "[Hardy and T. S. Eliot]," from Katherine Anne Porter, "Notes on a Criticism of Thomas Hardy," SOUTHERN REVIEW, VI (Summer 1940); Donald Davidson, "The Traditional Basis of Thomas Hardy's Fiction," SOUTHERN REVIEW, VI (Summer 1940); "[Hardy's Use of Literary Convention]," from Lord David Cecil, HARDY THE NOVELIST: AN ESSAY IN CRITICISM (1943); "[Pessimism in *The Return of the Native*]," from Harvey Curtis Webster, ON A DARKLING PLAIN: THE ART AND THOUGHT OF THOMAS HARDY (1947); R. W. Stallman, "Hardy's Hour-Glass Novel," SEWANEE REVIEW, LV (April–June 1947); "[Philosophy, Image, and Language in Hardy's Fiction]," from John Holloway, THE VICTORIAN SAGE: STUDIES IN ARGUMENT (1953); "[Clym Yeobright and Egdon Heath]," from George Wing, HARDY (1963); "[Action and Character in *The Return of the Native*]," from Charles Child Walcutt, "Character and Coincidence in *The Return of the Native*," TWELVE ORIGINAL ESSAYS ON GREAT ENGLISH NOVELS, ed by Charles Shapiro (1960). By H and not abstracted: *The Return of the Native*, passages from critical essays collected in LIFE AND ART, ed by Ernest Brennecke, Jr. (1925), twelve poems selected for relationships of various kinds to the novel.

3120 Goldknopf, David. "Coincidence in the Victorian Novel: The Trajectory of a Narrative Device," COLLEGE ENGLISH, XXXI (Oct 1969), 41–50.

H's use of coincidence exemplifies Victorian beliefs, in that character, rather than God, is responsible for coincidental occurrences; thus characters bring about their own doom. Examples of coincidence in *The Mayor of Casterbridge* make this especially clear.

3121 Grasby, E. L. "A Note," HARDYANA II: A FURTHER COLLECTION OF SHORT MEMORABILIA AND OTHER MATTERS OF HARDY INTEREST, ed by J. Stevens Cox (Mount Durand, St. Peter Port, Guernsey: Toucan P, 1969), p. 223.

H "was a mean man." [Also see J. Stevens Cox (pub and general editor), Monographs on the Life of Thomas Hardy (1962).]

3122 Grushow, Ira. "The 'Experience' of Poetry," COLLEGE ENGLISH, XXXI (Oct 1969), 25–29.

To each new poem that we encounter, we bring the experience that has accrued from our reading in the past. This experience will have a significant bearing on our comprehension of the "new" poem. Thus, when we encounter the word "darkling," in Johnson's "Vanity of Human Wishes," Arnold's "Dover Beach," and H's "The Darkling Thrush," we accumulate a sense of the word which increases our appreciation and understanding of each of the poems individually. "Johnson's almost existential leap of faith at the close of his classical and pessimistic catalogue of man's delusive hopes achieves a greater poignancy by association with Hardy's bird, whose assurance seems to derive only from the speaker's despair."

3123 Hardy, Evelyn. "Hardy and Moule," TIMES LITERARY SUPPLEMENT (Lond), 27 Feb 1969, p. 211.

Contrary to William Rutland's letter, the main points of "Thomas Hardy and Horace Moule: Vindication of a Suicide" are correct. Moule did not come between H and H's cousin Tryphena Sparks. [See Evelyn Hardy, "Thomas Hardy and Horace Moule: Vindication of a Suicide," ibid, 23 Jan 1969, p. 89; and William Rutland, "Hardy and Moule," ibid, 13 Feb 1969, pp. 158–59.]

3124 Hardy, Evelyn. "Thomas Hardy and Horace Moule," TIMES LITERARY SUPPLEMENT (Lond), 30 Jan 1969, p. 110.

The title of the article on Horace Moule and H was misleading and perhaps offensive to the Moule family. [See Evelyn Hardy, "Thomas Hardy and Horace Moule: Vindication of a Suicide," ibid, 23 Jan 1969, p. 89.]

3125 Hardy, Evelyn. "Thomas Hardy and Horace Moule: Vindication of a Suicide," TIMES LITERARY SUPPLEMENT (Lond), 23 Jan 1969, p. 89.

Contrary to the claims made by Lois Deacon and Terry Coleman in PROVIDENCE AND MR. HARDY (1966), Horace Moule was not involved in a triangular relationship with H and H's cousin Tryphena Sparks. At the time of this supposed relationship, Moule was engaged to an unknown lady. His suicide, as H's poem "Standing by a Mantlepiece" suggests, stems from the fact that this engagement was suddenly broken. [See Terry Coleman, "Thomas Hardy and Horace Moule," ibid, 30 Jan 1969, p. 110–11; Evelyn Hardy, "Thomas Hardy and Horace Moule," ibid, 30 Jan 1969, p. 110; William Rutland, "Hardy and Moule," ibid, 13 Feb 1969, pp.

158–59; Evelyn Hardy, "Hardy and Moule," ibid, 27 Feb 1969, p. 211; William Rutland, "Hardy and Moule," ibid, 6 March 1969, p. 242; Mary A. Blythe, "Hardy and Moule," ibid, 13 March 1969, p. 272.]

3126 Hazen, James. "The Tragedy of Tess Durbeyfield," TEXAS STUDIES IN LITERATURE AND LANGUAGE, XI (Spring 1969), 779–94.

The tragic quality of *Tess of the d'Urbervilles* rests in the value of Tess's life as a victim of society, a scapegoat, and a martyr. She is trapped between the laws of nature and social custom; however, her pride and recklessness also serve to increase her suffering. Angel Clare, the representative of moral progress, manages to learn and grow as a result of Tess's unjust suffering and death.

3127 Horsfall, Mary. LIFE IN BRIDPORT 1898–1918, PORT BREDY OF HARDY'S NOVELS (Mount Durand, St. Peter Port, Guernsey: Toucan P, 1969).

[A brief description of life and happenings at Bridport. Also see J. Stevens Cox (pub and general editor), Monographs on the Life of Thomas Hardy (1962).]

3128 Hyde, W. J. "Thomas Hardy: The Poor Man and the Deterioration of His Ladies," VICTORIAN NEWSLETTER, No. 36 (Fall 1969), 14–18.

The relationship between a poor man and a lady, a recurring theme in H's novels, was influenced by the social attitudes and ambitions of his mother and his first wife.

3129 Keith, W. J. "Thomas Hardy and the Literary Pilgrims," NINETEENTH CENTURY FICTION, XXIV (June 1969), 80–92.

In H's novels written during and after 1890, an obsession with topographical detail is evident in the prefaces. This is due largely to the influence of a late nineteenth-century group of zealots, the "literary pilgrims." They were preoccupied with associating the settings in H's fiction with actual locales in England. The movement began in Oct 1891, with the appearance of an anonymous article, "Thomas Hardy's Wessex," in the London BOOKMAN. The movement gained momentum, and H, who was initially disposed to ignore the correspondence between the fictional and real settings, was soon forced to bow to the weight of public opinion. Hesitantly, he acknowledged and finally encouraged the connection.

3130 Last, Edwin A. THOMAS HARDY'S NEIGHBOURS (Mount Durand, St. Peter Port, Guernsey: Toucan P, 1969).

[A brief note on the connections between H's neighbors in Stinsford Parish. Contains a map of part of Higher Bockhampton from a tithe map of 30 Nov 1838 and the 1851 Census of Parish of Stinsford, Village of Higher Bockampton [sic]. Appendix: 1851 Census. Also see J. Stevens Cox (pub and general editor), Monographs on the Life of Thomas Hardy (1962).]

3131 LaValley, Albert J. "Introduction," Twentieth Century Interpretations of Tess of the d'Urbervilles, ed by Albert J. LaValley (Englewood Cliffs, NJ: Prentice-Hall, 1969), pp. 1–13.

A review of H's life, the influences on him, his readings, and his work as a writer shows him to be simultaneously drawn to tradition and the emerging world of post-Darwinian science. While older critics concern themselves with the architectonics of H's novels, the newer critics "seek a more complex response to Hardy's plotting." [Conventional survey of life and work; survey of criticism of Tess of the d'Urbervilles based on essays printed in the collection.]

3132 LaValley, Albert J. (ed). Twentieth Century Interpretations of Tess of the d'Urbervilles (Englewood Cliffs, NJ: Prentice-Hall, 1969).

Contents, abstracted separately under date of first publication: Albert J. LaValley, "Introduction" (1969); Arnold Kettle, "Introduction," Tess of the d'Urbervilles (1966); Ian Gregor, "The Novel as Moral Protest: Tess of the d'Urbervilles," from The Moral and the Story (1962); Dorothy Van Ghent, "On Tess of the d'Urbervilles," from The English Novel: Form and Function (1953); Irving Howe, "Let the Day Perish," from Thomas Hardy (1967); D. H. Lawrence, ["Tess and Alec as Aristocrats"], from "A Study of Thomas Hardy," Phoenix (1936); David Lodge, "Tess, Nature, and the Voice of Hardy," from Language of Fiction (1966); David J. De Laura, " 'The Ache of Modernism' in Hardy's Later Novels," from English Literary History, XXXIV (Sept 1967); Douglas Brown, ["Hardy and the Art of the Ballad"], from Thomas Hardy (1961; see 1954); Irving Howe, ["Hardy's Use of Folk Material"], from Thomas Hardy (1967); Benjamin Sankey, ["Character Portrayal in Tess"], from The Major Novels of Thomas Hardy (1965); Ellen Moers, ["Tess as Cultural Stereotype"], from "Hardy Perennial," New Review of Books, 9 Nov 1967; Albert Guérard, ["The Originality of Tess"], from "Introduction," Tess of the d'Urbervilles (1955); Edmund Blunden, ["Hardy Talks About Tess"], from Thomas Hardy (1942); Florence Emily Hardy, from The Life of Thomas Hardy 1840–1928 (1962; see The Early Life of Thomas Hardy 1840–1891 [1928] and The Later Years of Thomas Hardy 1892–1928 [1930]).

3133 Lea, Hermann. "Letter from Hermann Lea Referring to *The Woodlanders*," HARDYANA II: A FURTHER COLLECTION OF SHORT MEMORABILIA AND OTHER MATTERS OF HARDY INTEREST, ed by J. Stevens Cox (Mount Durand, St. Peter Port, Guernsey: Toucan P, 1969), pp. 218–19.

Letter to Mrs. Dorothy White, 30 May 1928: The places alluded to in *The Woodlanders* had sometimes changed which made identification difficult. The places in *Jude the Obscure* could be readily identified. [Also see J. Stevens Cox (pub and general editor), Monographs on the Life of Thomas Hardy (1962).]

3134 Macleod, Alistair. "A Textual Study of Thomas Hardy's *A Group of Noble Dames*," DISSERTATION ABSTRACTS, XXIX (April–June 1969), 3977A. Unpublished dissertation, University of Notre Dame, 1968.

3135 Marsden, Kenneth. THE POEMS OF THOMAS HARDY: A CRITICAL INTRODUCTION (Lond: Athlone; NY: Oxford UP, 1969).

H's reputation as a poet is an anomaly because of the peculiar critical pressures and assumptions which accumulated during his early years as a published poet and because of the unevenness and eccentricity of the verse itself. These same difficulties have interfered with a complete and honest appreciation of his accomplishment as a poet. Because H's poetry is, however, "intensely personal," a little "sympathy" and "understanding" directed toward the persona which speaks in the poems and some cognizance of the "spiritual plight" from which the author writes goes far to remove the obstacles. Such an understanding explains, and in some cases justifies, many of the peculiarities of his poetry. H's habits of composition, for example, explain in large measure the unevenness of his verse. Like Wordsworth, H worked from remembered experience and usually wrote after the experience had remained more or less dormant for some time. Poems thus composed usually evidence conspicuous fidelity to the particular experiences which served as their inspirations. Those not based upon a precisely remembered inspiration—frequently the overtly philosophical ones—are in general his less successful efforts. Yet the habit of working from remembered experience sometimes did H a disservice: it caused him to see his "plentiful stock of trivia" as a uniformly serviceable source of subject matter. An ironic evidence of the "intensely personal" quality is to be found in his frequent claims to be writing personative or dramatic poems. These disclaimers appear to be principally an attempt to dodge responsibility for the views expressed in the poems. In truth, he rarely achieves anything of the dramatic, rarely creates a credible character other than his normal narrator—transparently himself. In his use of form and meter, his singularity arises principally from rhythmic variations within lines and from his unusual diction. The idea that he was an innovator in his use of poetic forms simply will not bear examination. By far the majority of his work is written in the traditional forms. His use of language, however, is strikingly personal. His dialectisms and neologisms comprise a mixture which is not a "possible language for any human being," but out of them he has created "a personal living language" for his persona. Like everything else about his verse, his development as a poet is peculiarly his own. It passed from relatively conventional early verse to an intensely personal and philosophic idiom in the early 1900s, to a still personal but more detached, more descriptive mode in his later verse. His textual revisions of the selections in *Wessex Poems* seem to be directed primarily at sharpening clarity. As he revised them later and later in his life, he tended to reduce the eccentricity of their language. Many influences on his verse are discoverable, but few are very important and none very strong. Traces of Shakespeare, Barnes, Browning, Wordsworth, Arnold, Housman and others are evident, but H has transformed his debt to each of them into his own personal idiom.

> **3136** Matthews, James H. "Particularity and Polarization: Realism in the Fiction of Hardy and Conrad," DISSERTATION ABSTRACTS, XXIX (Jan–March 1969), 3147A. Unpublished dissertation, Vanderbilt University, 1968.

> **3137** Medway, L. J. "Hardy Anecdotes," HARDYANA II: A FURTHER COLLECTION OF SHORT MEMORABILIA AND OTHER MATTERS OF HARDY INTEREST, ed by J. Stevens Cox (Mount Durand, St. Peter Port, Guernsey: Toucan P, 1969), p. 230.

" 'He put us in his books, he did, and then said all the worst about us and never anything that was good.' " H ignored polite greetings. [Also see J. Stevens Cox (pub and general editor), Monographs on the Life of Thomas Hardy (1962).]

> **3138** Mégroz, R. L. MODERN ENGLISH POETRY 1882–1932 (Lond: Ivor Nicholson & Watson, 1933); rptd (Folcroft, Pa: Folcroft P, 1969), pp. 69, 72–80, 126, 180.

H reaches forward to our own age with his pessimism and jibes at orthodox religion. H's poetry is more consistent than Meredith's and is unexcelled in its elemental vision. The interest of H's poetry comes from his gifts as a novelist. H speaks from an implicit mental attitude toward life, confirmed in what he sees. His perceptions take an internal structure of narrative. He is not musical but architectural, line to line in a determined pattern. The effect of *The Dynasts* is sheer mass. If H's command of verbal medium had been closer to Shakespeare in versatility *Dynasts* might have been successful, but the epic-drama is a failure. Nonetheless this failure is beyond the achievement of but a half dozen English poets. However, H's personal resources are not the basis of appreciation; *Dynasts* is a futile display of misdirected energy. Perhaps if H had stayed with the novel he could have made *Dynasts* a masterpiece. The fragments that are good owe their quality to excitement over situation and character, as in *Wessex Poems, Poems of the Past and the Present, Time's Laughingstocks, Satires of Circumstance, Moments of Vision*. There is inferior verse in these collections, but some of H's best lyric and elegiac poetry occurs in *Dynasts*. H's stature is due to a spiritual urgency in him, a powerful imagination which pushed him beyond a simple and sympathetic interpretation of life. H is likely to be remembered as a poet of human existence, in its simple and significant elements. H is better described as a poet of curious or dramatic thoughts than as metaphysical. His range is wider than Patmore's, Thompson's, or Meredith's. Sometimes H's reflections resemble Browning without sophistication or obscurity ("The Strange House," "The Ghost of the Past"). H is not deterred by fear of being hackneyed ("The Selfsame Song"). H's prolixity of ideas comes from his experience and skill as a novelist; his lapses can be traced to the "discursive" method of the story-teller. Walter de la Mare and Edward Thomas are akin to H in curious thought. Arthur Machen recognized H as a creator in words of the visionary reality that alone signifies anything to the essential self—H's true work is " 'shaping for us of ecstasy by means of symbols.' "

3139 Miyoshi, Masao. THE DIVIDED SELF: A PERSPECTIVE ON THE LITERATURE OF THE VICTORIANS (NY: New York UP; Lond: University of London P, 1969), pp. xv, 37, 40*n*, 96*n*, 261, 291, 301–9, 333, 336*n*, 337*n*.

The death on the gallows of the hero in Wordsworth's "Guilt and Sorrow" "bears striking resemblance" to *Tess of the d'Urbervilles*. In the literature of doubles, the "lie at the core of life" is exposed by the realization that art, though based on life, is nevertheless an illusion. H saw the lie as damnation, while Wilde saw it as salvation. In *Tess* and *Jude the Obscure*, H's protagonists recognize their doubles as true mirror images, and recoil in horror. There are strong thematic similarities between Charlotte Brontë's JANE EYRE and *Tess*. *Jude* may be read as a historical document. It treats a Shelleyan theme: Sue is Jude's intellectual beauty. But unlike ALASTOR, in *Jude* there is no glory. H believed that the illusion ultimately comes to nothing.

3140 Munro, John M. "Thomas Hardy and Arthur Symons: A Biographical Footnote," ENGLISH LITERATURE IN TRANSITION, XII:2 (1969), 93–95.

[This is the first publication of a letter from H to Mrs. Rhoda Symons, written after her husband's breakdown in 1908. It confirms that the two men were not close friends but did indeed maintain a desultory correspondence, exchanging common pleasantries and little else.]

3141 Paris, Bernard J. " 'A Confusion of Many Standards': Conflicting Value Systems in *Tess of the d'Urbervilles*," NINETEENTH CENTURY FICTION, XXIV (June 1969), 57–79.

As Lionel Johnson saw, *Tess of the d'Urbervilles*, "however powerful it is as a story, is thematically unintelligible." Part of the novel's "inner purpose or *telos* is the affirmation of Tess's purity; but the novel does not succeed in making this affirmation *even in its own terms*." The thematic inconsistencies in *Tess* result from H's "attempt to defend his 'doctrine of the moment'—Tess's purity or innocence—by as many arguments as he can find." These arguments often contradict each other "and can in no way be unified into a coherent moral vision." When H argues that Tess is pure "because she never meant to do wrong"; that "she is a worthwhile person despite her unfortunate sexual experience with Alec"; and that despite her fall she retains the capacity for regeneration and growth, he is accepting her experience with Alec as bad, but H also argues, using nature as a norm, that "there is nothing evil about her sexual relations with Alec." While H "uses nature as a moral norm . . . at the same time [he] regards nature as amoral." His stress in *Tess* on the need to be on guard, and his obvious mistrust of dreamy, intoxicated drifting "fits perfectly with his vision of the cosmos as amoral" but is "quite incompatible" with the doctrine of nature as a moral norm. The novel remains moving, however, "because despite her helplessness Tess has a stature that makes her suffering profoundly touching." H "was in love with Tess"; he sees "her and everything else in her terms."

3142 Pinck, Joan B. "The Reception of Thomas Hardy's *The Return of the Native*," HARVARD LIBRARY BULLETIN, XVII (July 1969), 291–308.

H's art is strikingly modern "in his acute psychological insights, in his frank treatment of sexuality, [and] in his symbolic use of coincidence." The "consensus of the reviews of *The Return* is unfavorable, despite the praise with which the criticism is larded." [Dreary rehash of reviews of *Native*.]

3143 Powys, Llewelyn. SOME MEMORIES OF THOMAS HARDY (Mount Durand, St. Peter Port, Guernsey: Toucan P, 1969).

[Typical personal reminiscences, including an account of an incident involving the writer's repeating some speculations of H regarding possible Dorset relatives of John Keats, and the questioning inflicted upon H by Amy Lowell as a result. See also J. Stevens Cox (pub and general editor), Monographs on the Life of Thomas Hardy (1962).]

3144 Rutland, William. "Hardy and Moule," TIMES LITERARY SUPPLEMENT (Lond), 13 Feb 1969, pp. 158–59.

There is no evidence to support Evelyn Hardy's explanation of Horace Moule's suicide. Her interpretation of H's "Standing by a Mantelpiece" is misleading. [See Evelyn Hardy, "Thomas Hardy and Horace Moule: Vindication of a Suicide," ibid, 23 Jan 1969, p. 89.]

3145 Rutland, William. "Hardy and Moule," TIMES LITERARY SUPPLEMENT (Lond), 6 March 1969, p. 242.

The idea that Horace Moule was involved with H's cousin Tryphena Sparks may be distasteful to Evelyn Hardy, but the evidence is difficult to refute. [See Evelyn Hardy, "Thomas Hardy and Horace Moule: Vindication of a Suicide," ibid, 23 Jan 1969, p. 89; William Rutland, "Hardy and Moule," ibid, 13 Feb 1969, pp. 158–59; and Evelyn Hardy, "Hardy and Moule," ibid, 27 Feb 1969, p. 211.]

3146 Spencer, Gloria B. "The Characterization and Use of the Rustics in Thomas Hardy's Works," DISSERTATION ABSTRACTS, XXIX (1969), 3621A. Unpublished dissertation, University of Texas at Austin, 1968.

3147 Stemp, F. "Hardy at Kingston Maurward," HARDYANA II: A FURTHER COLLECTION OF SHORT MEMORABILIA AND OTHER MATTERS OF HARDY INTEREST, ed by J. Stevens Cox (Mount Durand, St. Peter Port, Guernsey: Toucan P, 1969), p. 225.

H gave Lady Hanbury's daughter a poem in "a casket" upon her christening. He "was a very reserved man," but he liked visiting Kingston Maurward. *Desperate Remedies* was enjoyable because it dealt with Napwater House, his name for Kingston Maurward. The H house "never gave any sort of a meal worth eating." [Also see J. Stevens Cox (pub and general editor), Monographs on the Life of Thomas Hardy (1962).]

3148 Stevens, E. J. HARDY AS I KNEW HIM (Mount Durand, St. Peter Port, Guernsey: Toucan P, 1969); expanded from a talk given for the BBC on 16 Aug 1938.

The "Hardy Players" were established when H agreed that an Amateur Dramatic Society in Dorchester should adapt his novels for production as stage plays. As a young man H had wanted to write plays. He was a simple, unassuming, kindly man who enjoyed gardening and conversation. He often attended rehearsals of the plays and often had readings in his home. H said that all the characters in his novels represented people who had actually lived in the area around Dorchester. He said he gained his understanding of the nature of the "English country girl" when he, as a young man, wrote love letters for the village girls to send to their sweethearts in India. [Appendix: "The Trumpet Major," a synopsis of the scenes in the stage version. Also see J. Stevens Cox (pub and general editor), Monographs on the Life of Thomas Hardy (1962).]

3149 Titterington, Ellen E. AFTERTHOUGHTS OF MAX GATE (Mount Durand, St. Peter Port, Guernsey: Toucan P, 1969); expands THE DOMESTIC LIFE OF THOMAS HARDY (1921–1928) (1963).

In his old age, H was stubborn, ruled Mrs. H, and at times, displayed a sense of humor. He was fond of his dog, Wessex, who at times was difficult to control. Many things at Max Gate were difficult to keep clean. H was animated by the presence of younger women whom he looked upon as characters in his novels. Sir Sidney Cockerell was present at H's death and took care of many details. Cockerell's later assessment of Mrs. H was contemptible. Ruled as she was by H, she confided many thoughts on life at Max Gate. Mrs. H's attitude changed when she moved to London at the insistence of Cockerell. She became romantically inclined toward Sir James Barrie and would have liked to be Lady Barrie. Barrie was a frequent visitor to her flat. When the relationship failed, the "Max Gate" look returned and Mrs. H returned to Max Gate. [Contains a reproduction of the Hs' Christmas card of 1923 and seven recipes used at Max Gate. Also see J. Stevens Cox (pub and general editor), Monographs on the Life of Thomas Hardy (1962).]

3150 Tollers, Vincent L. "Thomas Hardy and the Professional Theatre, with Emphasis on *The Dynasts*," DISSERTATION ABSTRACTS, XXIX (1969), 3158A–59A. Unpublished dissertation, University of Colorado, 1968.

3151 Weber, Carl J. "Hardy, Thomas," ENCYCLOPEDIA AMERICANA (NY: Americana Corp, 1969), XIII, 701–6.

[Sketch of major events in H's literary life.]

3152 Williams, Mrs. Gerald. "An Interview with Mrs. Gerald Williams," HARDYANA II: A FURTHER COLLECTION OF SHORT MEMORABILIA AND OTHER MATTERS OF HARDY INTEREST, ed by J. Stevens Cox (Mount Durand, St. Peter Port, Guernsey: Toucan P, 1969), pp. 227–28.

H was a "gloomy man." Mother "did not approve of his books and I was forbidden to read them until I was a grown woman." The Hs "had a reputation of being the meanest people in the village." [Also see J. Stevens Cox (pub and general editor), Monographs on the Life of Thomas Hardy (1962).]

3153 Zietlow, Paul. "Thomas Hardy and William Barnes: Two Dorset Poets," PUBLICATIONS OF THE MODERN LANGUAGE ASSOCIATION, LXXXIV (March 1969), 291–303.

H's responses to Barnes appear in a series of pairings: Barnes's "The Motherless Child" vs. H's "To a Motherless Child," "Went Home" vs.

"Welcome Home," and "The Milk-Maid O' The Farm" vs. "The Milk-maid." Barnes's scenes and characters had both a negative and a positive influence on H. Negatively, Barnes failed to recognize the realistic possibilities in pastoral poems. Positively, Barnes and H had a shared affinity in their reverence for places and things. H is more emphatic in his treatment of the disparity between present and past, seeing conflict, discontinuity, and violence where Barnes saw edenic circumstances; but H admired and quoted such poems as "Woak Hill" and "Shaftesbury Feäir."

Index

AUTHORS

Included here are authors of articles and books on Hardy, editors and compilers of works in which criticism on Hardy appears. Editors and translators are identified parenthetically: (ed), (trans). Numbers after each name refer to the item(s) in the bibliography where the name occurs.

Rush, N. Orwin: 2000; (comp): 2152
Russell, Constance: 941
Russell, J. A.: 1375, 1482
Rutherford, Mildred Lewis: 136, 494
Rutland, William R.: 1621, 1622, 1843, 1886, 1887, 1888, 3144, 3145
Ryan, W. P.: 329
S., C. K.: 622
S., D.: 231
S., R.: 2405
Sackville-West, V.: 1376
Sadleir, Michael: 2070
Sagar, S.: 2094, 2130
St. Clair, George: 1572
St. George, George: 232
St. John-Stevas, Norman: 2729
Saintsbury, George Edward Bateman: 36, 58, 233, 649, 1377
Sakai, Yoshie: 2954
Salberg, Gerda: 1162
Salomon, Louis B.: 1573
Salviris, Jacob [See Sime, Jessie Georgina]
Sampson, Ashley: 2001
Sampson, Edward C.: 3008
Samson, George: 2071
Samuel, Viscount: 2002
Sanden, Gertrud von: 984
Sanders, E. N.: 2540
Sanders, Gerald DeWitt: (ed): 1483
Sanders, Mary Kirven: 3009
Sandison, Helen: 1921
Sankey, Benjamin: 2829, 2882, 2883, 2884, 2885, 2886
Sansom, Clive: 3010
Sassoon, Siegfried: 825, 1120, 2003, 2095, 2196, 2253
Saxelby, F. Outwin: 583
Schelling, Felix E.: 650
Scherr, Johannes: 1121
Schill, H.: 2773
Schirmer, Walter F.: 942, 1844, 2172
Schloesser, Anselm: 1755
Schlumberger, Jean: 1379
Schmidt, Adelbert: 2541
Schofield, Geoffrey: 2649
Schönfeld, Herbert: 1800
Schorer, Mark: (ed): 2412, 2636, 2688
Schröck, Margarethe: 2173
Schüdderkopf, A. W.: 624, 625, 626, 651
Schultheis, L. M.: 1163
Schulz, Max F.: (ed): 3025
Schumacher, Margot: 1801
Schwartz, Delmore: 2004
Schweik, Robert C.: 2730, 2731, 2955, 2956, 3011
Schweikert, H. C.: (ed): 1047
Scott, James Frazier: 2650, 2774, 2887

Scott, Nathan A., Jr.: 2651
Scott-James, Rolfe Arnold: 530, 652, 1380, 2342, 2343
Scripture, E. W.: 1528
Scudamore, Alfred T. D.: 2830
Scudamore, Joyce: 2831
Scudder, Harold L.: 2174
Seccombe, Thomas: 488, 507, 545
Sedgwick, Henry Dwight: 1708
Segrè, Carlo: 296
Selby, Thomas G.: 297
Selna, Barbara: 2732
Selver, P.: 943, 1484
Sencourt, Robert Esmonde: 1485
Shafer, Robert: 985, 1122
Shand, John: 1048, 1529
Shanks, Edward: 755, 1049, 1123, 1164, 1381, 1382, 1383
Sharp, Evelyn [Pseudonym of Mrs. H. W. Nevinson]: 1660
Sharp, William: 196
Shaw, C. G.: 711
Shaw, George Bernard: 1384
Shaw, William B.: 1530
Shawe-Taylor, Desmond: 2441
Shepherd, Mrs. M.: 3012
Sheppard, Alfred Tresidder: 1385, 1386
Sheppard, John T.: 2344
Sherman, Elna: 2005, 2006
Sherman, George Witter: 2197, 2218, 2254, 2280, 2345, 2375, 2376, 2406, 2407
Sherman, Stuart P[ratt]: 734, 986
Sherren, Wilkinson: 414, 584, 627
Sherwood, William R.: (ed): 2964
Shindler, Robert: 415
Shipp, Horace: 1124; (ed): 959
Shirreff, A. G.: 2542
Sholl, Anna McClure: 319, 1487
Short, Clarice: 2281, 2570
Shorter, Clement K.: 320, 430, 712, 713, 735, 736
Shuster, George N.: 1387
Siddhanta, N. K.: 1388
Siegel, Paul N.: 2377
Siemens, Lloyd George: 3013
Sime, A. H. Moncur: 1389, 2007
Sime, Jessie Georgina [Salviris, Jacob]: 623
Simon, Irène: 2282
Singh, G.: 2832
Sirimanne, A. M. G.: 2774
Sisson, Charles J.: 1709
Sixt, Erika: 2733
Skillington, S. H.: 585
Slack, Robert C.: 2378, 2442, 2543, 2607, 2888
Slaughter, Gertrude E. T.: 1488

Index

TITLES OF SECONDARY WORKS

Titles of articles in periodicals and chapters in books are in quotation marks; book titles are in upper case; translations of article titles originally appearing in a foreign language are in parentheses, without quotation marks and in lower case; translations of book titles originally appearing in a foreign language are in parentheses and in upper case. Numbers after each title refer to the item in the bibliography where the title appears.

PERIODICALS AND NEWSPAPERS

Included here are periodicals and newspapers for which entries occur in the bibliography. Numbers after each title refer to the number(s) of the item in the bibliography where the title appears.

Index

FOREIGN LANGUAGES

Included here are the languages in which articles and books listed in the bibliography originally appeared. Numbers under each language refer to items in the bibliography where the foreign-language title is given. English language items are not listed.

Danish: 1134

French: 21, 359, 363, 419, 438, 473, 493, 516, 570, 576, 621, 831, 840, 936, 956, 962, 1005, 1019, 1035, 1100, 1153, 1154, 1158, 1178, 1180, 1187, 1197, 1198, 1202, 1221, 1222, 1224, 1230, 1237, 1238, 1241, 1259, 1265, 1272, 1280, 1291, 1292, 1320, 1321, 1336, 1369, 1379, 1424, 1552, 1556, 1588, 1619, 1622, 1675, 1696, 1861, 2252, 2282, 2434, 2938

German: 90, 129, 131, 143, 157, 205, 221, 236, 262, 265, 266, 281, 307, 380, 388, 392, 395, 405, 406, 415, 437, 446, 453, 466, 486, 504, 509, 510, 514, 522, 534, 540, 558, 574, 599, 624, 625, 626, 630, 639, 651, 658, 678, 722, 748, 764, 775, 864, 881, 895, 900, 908, 910, 926, 942, 943, 984, 988, 1003, 1050, 1054, 1066, 1074, 1121, 1130, 1135, 1136, 1143, 1161, 1162, 1163, 1167, 1181, 1183, 1231, 1240, 1293, 1305, 1343, 1368, 1393, 1429, 1434, 1444, 1463, 1470, 1484, 1494, 1515, 1527, 1528, 1538, 1562, 1574, 1580, 1583, 1598, 1610, 1616, 1627, 1630, 1646, 1647, 1649, 1662, 1672, 1688, 1690, 1693, 1733, 1755, 1775, 1776, 1793, 1800, 1801, 1828, 1834, 1836, 1844, 1876, 1877, 1881, 1910, 1918, 1928, 1974, 1977, 1993, 2046, 2047, 2056, 2164, 2172, 2173, 2176, 2193, 2198, 2243, 2247, 2292, 2294, 2302, 2304, 2307, 2311, 2312, 2319, 2321, 2350, 2397, 2436, 2445, 2446, 2465, 2476, 2484, 2507, 2541, 2544, 2558, 2561, 2569, 2585, 2627, 2632, 2637, 2677, 2686, 2727, 2733, 2734, 2735, 2757, 2784, 2828, 2834, 2889

Italian: 296, 450, 896, 950, 1148, 1219, 1370, 1632, 1822

Japanese: 1744, 2551, 2725, 2921, 2946, 2954

Norwegian: 1169, 1449

Russian: 214

Spanish: 974

Swedish: 501, 717, 776, 836, 952, 968, 1146, 1281, 1442

Welsh: 2326

Index

PRIMARY TITLES

Included here are all titles by Hardy which occur in titles of articles or books or in the abstracts. Numbers after each title refer to the item in the bibliography where the title appears.